Dictionary of Literary Biography® • Volume Two Hundred Five

Russian Literature in the Age of Pushkin and Gogol: Poetry and Drama

Edited by
Christine A. Rydel
Grand Valley State University

A Bruccoli Clark Layman Book
The Gale Group
Detroit, Washington, D.C., London

Advisory Board for
DICTIONARY OF LITERARY BIOGRAPHY

John Baker
William Cagle
Patrick O'Connor
George Garrett
Trudier Harris

Matthew J. Bruccoli and Richard Layman, Editorial Directors
C. E. Frazer Clark Jr., Managing Editor
Karen Rood, Senior Editor

Printed in the United States of America

The paper used in this publication meets the minimum requirements
of American National Standard for Information Sciences–Permanence
Paper for Printed Library Materials, ANSI Z39.48-1984. ∞™

This publication is a creative work fully protected by all applicable copyright laws, as well as by misappropriation, trade secret, unfair competition, and other applicable laws. The authors and editors of this work have added value to the underlying factual material herein through one or more of the following: unique and original selection, coordination, expression, arrangement, and classification of the information.

All rights to this publication will be vigorously defended.

Copyright © 1999 by The Gale Group
27500 Drake Road
Farmington Hills, MI 48331

All rights reserved including the right of reproduction in
whole or in part in any form.

Library of Congress Cataloging-in-Publication Data

Russian literature in the age of Pushkin and Gogol: Poetry and Drama / edited by Christine A. Rydel.
  p. cm.–(Dictionary of literary biography; v. 205)
"A Bruccoli Clark Layman book."
Includes bibliographical references and index.
ISBN 0-7876-3099-3 (alk. paper)
1. Russian poetry–19th century–Bio-bibliography. 2. Poets, Russian–19th century–Biography. I. Rydel, Christine. II. Series.
Z2504.P7R87 1999
[PG2991.3]
016.89171'308–dc21   98-53956
                                                    CIP

---

10 9 8 7 6 5 4 3 2 1

Dictionary of Literary Biography

1. *The American Renaissance in New England*, edited by Joel Myerson (1978)
2. *American Novelists Since World War II*, edited by Jeffrey Helterman and Richard Layman (1978)
3. *Antebellum Writers in New York and the South*, edited by Joel Myerson (1979)
4. *American Writers in Paris, 1920-1939*, edited by Karen Lane Rood (1980)
5. *American Poets Since World War II*, 2 parts, edited by Donald J. Greiner (1980)
6. *American Novelists Since World War II, Second Series*, edited by James E. Kibler Jr. (1980)
7. *Twentieth-Century American Dramatists*, 2 parts, edited by John MacNicholas (1981)
8. *Twentieth-Century American Science-Fiction Writers*, 2 parts, edited by David Cowart and Thomas L. Wymer (1981)
9. *American Novelists, 1910-1945*, 3 parts, edited by James J. Martine (1981)
10. *Modern British Dramatists, 1900-1945*, 2 parts, edited by Stanley Weintraub (1982)
11. *American Humorists, 1800-1950*, 2 parts, edited by Stanley Trachtenberg (1982)
12. *American Realists and Naturalists*, edited by Donald Pizer and Earl N. Harbert (1982)
13. *British Dramatists Since World War II*, 2 parts, edited by Stanley Weintraub (1982)
14. *British Novelists Since 1960*, 2 parts, edited by Jay L. Halio (1983)
15. *British Novelists, 1930-1959*, 2 parts, edited by Bernard Oldsey (1983)
16. *The Beats: Literary Bohemians in Postwar America*, 2 parts, edited by Ann Charters (1983)
17. *Twentieth-Century American Historians*, edited by Clyde N. Wilson (1983)
18. *Victorian Novelists After 1885*, edited by Ira B. Nadel and William E. Fredeman (1983)
19. *British Poets, 1880-1914*, edited by Donald E. Stanford (1983)
20. *British Poets, 1914-1945*, edited by Donald E. Stanford (1983)
21. *Victorian Novelists Before 1885*, edited by Ira B. Nadel and William E. Fredeman (1983)
22. *American Writers for Children, 1900-1960*, edited by John Cech (1983)
23. *American Newspaper Journalists, 1873-1900*, edited by Perry J. Ashley (1983)
24. *American Colonial Writers, 1606-1734*, edited by Emory Elliott (1984)
25. *American Newspaper Journalists, 1901-1925*, edited by Perry J. Ashley (1984)
26. *American Screenwriters*, edited by Robert E. Morsberger, Stephen O. Lesser, and Randall Clark (1984)
27. *Poets of Great Britain and Ireland, 1945-1960*, edited by Vincent B. Sherry Jr. (1984)
28. *Twentieth-Century American-Jewish Fiction Writers*, edited by Daniel Walden (1984)
29. *American Newspaper Journalists, 1926-1950*, edited by Perry J. Ashley (1984)
30. *American Historians, 1607-1865*, edited by Clyde N. Wilson (1984)
31. *American Colonial Writers, 1735-1781*, edited by Emory Elliott (1984)
32. *Victorian Poets Before 1850*, edited by William E. Fredeman and Ira B. Nadel (1984)
33. *Afro-American Fiction Writers After 1955*, edited by Thadious M. Davis and Trudier Harris (1984)
34. *British Novelists, 1890-1929: Traditionalists*, edited by Thomas F. Staley (1985)
35. *Victorian Poets After 1850*, edited by William E. Fredeman and Ira B. Nadel (1985)
36. *British Novelists, 1890-1929: Modernists*, edited by Thomas F. Staley (1985)
37. *American Writers of the Early Republic*, edited by Emory Elliott (1985)
38. *Afro-American Writers After 1955: Dramatists and Prose Writers*, edited by Thadious M. Davis and Trudier Harris (1985)
39. *British Novelists, 1660-1800*, 2 parts, edited by Martin C. Battestin (1985)
40. *Poets of Great Britain and Ireland Since 1960*, 2 parts, edited by Vincent B. Sherry Jr. (1985)
41. *Afro-American Poets Since 1955*, edited by Trudier Harris and Thadious M. Davis (1985)
42. *American Writers for Children Before 1900*, edited by Glenn E. Estes (1985)
43. *American Newspaper Journalists, 1690-1872*, edited by Perry J. Ashley (1986)
44. *American Screenwriters, Second Series*, edited by Randall Clark, Robert E. Morsberger, and Stephen O. Lesser (1986)
45. *American Poets, 1880-1945, First Series*, edited by Peter Quartermain (1986)
46. *American Literary Publishing Houses, 1900-1980: Trade and Paperback*, edited by Peter Dzwonkoski (1986)
47. *American Historians, 1866-1912*, edited by Clyde N. Wilson (1986)
48. *American Poets, 1880-1945, Second Series*, edited by Peter Quartermain (1986)
49. *American Literary Publishing Houses, 1638-1899*, 2 parts, edited by Peter Dzwonkoski (1986)
50. *Afro-American Writers Before the Harlem Renaissance*, edited by Trudier Harris (1986)
51. *Afro-American Writers from the Harlem Renaissance to 1940*, edited by Trudier Harris (1987)
52. *American Writers for Children Since 1960: Fiction*, edited by Glenn E. Estes (1986)
53. *Canadian Writers Since 1960, First Series*, edited by W. H. New (1986)
54. *American Poets, 1880-1945, Third Series*, 2 parts, edited by Peter Quartermain (1987)
55. *Victorian Prose Writers Before 1867*, edited by William B. Thesing (1987)
56. *German Fiction Writers, 1914-1945*, edited by James Hardin (1987)
57. *Victorian Prose Writers After 1867*, edited by William B. Thesing (1987)
58. *Jacobean and Caroline Dramatists*, edited by Fredson Bowers (1987)
59. *American Literary Critics and Scholars, 1800-1850*, edited by John W. Rathbun and Monica M. Grecu (1987)
60. *Canadian Writers Since 1960, Second Series*, edited by W. H. New (1987)
61. *American Writers for Children Since 1960: Poets, Illustrators, and Nonfiction Authors*, edited by Glenn E. Estes (1987)
62. *Elizabethan Dramatists*, edited by Fredson Bowers (1987)
63. *Modern American Critics, 1920-1955*, edited by Gregory S. Jay (1988)
64. *American Literary Critics and Scholars, 1850-1880*, edited by John W. Rathbun and Monica M. Grecu (1988)
65. *French Novelists, 1900-1930*, edited by Catharine Savage Brosman (1988)
66. *German Fiction Writers, 1885-1913*, 2 parts, edited by James Hardin (1988)
67. *Modern American Critics Since 1955*, edited by Gregory S. Jay (1988)
68. *Canadian Writers, 1920-1959, First Series*, edited by W. H. New (1988)
69. *Contemporary German Fiction Writers, First Series*, edited by Wolfgang D. Elfe and James Hardin (1988)
70. *British Mystery Writers, 1860-1919*, edited by Bernard Benstock and Thomas F. Staley (1988)
71. *American Literary Critics and Scholars, 1880-1900*, edited by John W. Rathbun and Monica M. Grecu (1988)
72. *French Novelists, 1930-1960*, edited by Catharine Savage Brosman (1988)
73. *American Magazine Journalists, 1741-1850*, edited by Sam G. Riley (1988)
74. *American Short-Story Writers Before 1880*, edited by Bobby Ellen Kimbel, with the assistance of William E. Grant (1988)
75. *Contemporary German Fiction Writers, Second Series*, edited by Wolfgang D. Elfe and James Hardin (1988)
76. *Afro-American Writers, 1940-1955*, edited by Trudier Harris (1988)
77. *British Mystery Writers, 1920-1939*, edited by Bernard Benstock and Thomas F. Staley (1988)

78 *American Short-Story Writers, 1880-1910,* edited by Bobby Ellen Kimbel, with the assistance of William E. Grant (1988)

79 *American Magazine Journalists, 1850-1900,* edited by Sam G. Riley (1988)

80 *Restoration and Eighteenth-Century Dramatists, First Series,* edited by Paula R. Backscheider (1989)

81 *Austrian Fiction Writers, 1875-1913,* edited by James Hardin and Donald G. Daviau (1989)

82 *Chicano Writers, First Series,* edited by Francisco A. Lomelí and Carl R. Shirley (1989)

83 *French Novelists Since 1960,* edited by Catharine Savage Brosman (1989)

84 *Restoration and Eighteenth-Century Dramatists, Second Series,* edited by Paula R. Backscheider (1989)

85 *Austrian Fiction Writers After 1914,* edited by James Hardin and Donald G. Daviau (1989)

86 *American Short-Story Writers, 1910-1945, First Series,* edited by Bobby Ellen Kimbel (1989)

87 *British Mystery and Thriller Writers Since 1940, First Series,* edited by Bernard Benstock and Thomas F. Staley (1989)

88 *Canadian Writers, 1920-1959, Second Series,* edited by W. H. New (1989)

89 *Restoration and Eighteenth-Century Dramatists, Third Series,* edited by Paula R. Backscheider (1989)

90 *German Writers in the Age of Goethe, 1789-1832,* edited by James Hardin and Christoph E. Schweitzer (1989)

91 *American Magazine Journalists, 1900-1960, First Series,* edited by Sam G. Riley (1990)

92 *Canadian Writers, 1890-1920,* edited by W. H. New (1990)

93 *British Romantic Poets, 1789-1832, First Series,* edited by John R. Greenfield (1990)

94 *German Writers in the Age of Goethe: Sturm und Drang to Classicism,* edited by James Hardin and Christoph E. Schweitzer (1990)

95 *Eighteenth-Century British Poets, First Series,* edited by John Sitter (1990)

96 *British Romantic Poets, 1789-1832, Second Series,* edited by John R. Greenfield (1990)

97 *German Writers from the Enlightenment to Sturm und Drang, 1720-1764,* edited by James Hardin and Christoph E. Schweitzer (1990)

98 *Modern British Essayists, First Series,* edited by Robert Beum (1990)

99 *Canadian Writers Before 1890,* edited by W. H. New (1990)

100 *Modern British Essayists, Second Series,* edited by Robert Beum (1990)

101 *British Prose Writers, 1660-1800, First Series,* edited by Donald T. Siebert (1991)

102 *American Short-Story Writers, 1910-1945, Second Series,* edited by Bobby Ellen Kimbel (1991)

103 *American Literary Biographers, First Series,* edited by Steven Serafin (1991)

104 *British Prose Writers, 1660-1800, Second Series,* edited by Donald T. Siebert (1991)

105 *American Poets Since World War II, Second Series,* edited by R. S. Gwynn (1991)

106 *British Literary Publishing Houses, 1820-1880,* edited by Patricia J. Anderson and Jonathan Rose (1991)

107 *British Romantic Prose Writers, 1789-1832, First Series,* edited by John R. Greenfield (1991)

108 *Twentieth-Century Spanish Poets, First Series,* edited by Michael L. Perna (1991)

109 *Eighteenth-Century British Poets, Second Series,* edited by John Sitter (1991)

110 *British Romantic Prose Writers, 1789-1832, Second Series,* edited by John R. Greenfield (1991)

111 *American Literary Biographers, Second Series,* edited by Steven Serafin (1991)

112 *British Literary Publishing Houses, 1881-1965,* edited by Jonathan Rose and Patricia J. Anderson (1991)

113 *Modern Latin-American Fiction Writers, First Series,* edited by William Luis (1992)

114 *Twentieth-Century Italian Poets, First Series,* edited by Giovanna Wedel De Stasio, Glauco Cambon, and Antonio Illiano (1992)

115 *Medieval Philosophers,* edited by Jeremiah Hackett (1992)

116 *British Romantic Novelists, 1789-1832,* edited by Bradford K. Mudge (1992)

117 *Twentieth-Century Caribbean and Black African Writers, First Series,* edited by Bernth Lindfors and Reinhard Sander (1992)

118 *Twentieth-Century German Dramatists, 1889-1918,* edited by Wolfgang D. Elfe and James Hardin (1992)

119 *Nineteenth-Century French Fiction Writers: Romanticism and Realism, 1800-1860,* edited by Catharine Savage Brosman (1992)

120 *American Poets Since World War II, Third Series,* edited by R. S. Gwynn (1992)

121 *Seventeenth-Century British Nondramatic Poets, First Series,* edited by M. Thomas Hester (1992)

122 *Chicano Writers, Second Series,* edited by Francisco A. Lomelí and Carl R. Shirley (1992)

123 *Nineteenth-Century French Fiction Writers: Naturalism and Beyond, 1860-1900,* edited by Catharine Savage Brosman (1992)

124 *Twentieth-Century German Dramatists, 1919-1992,* edited by Wolfgang D. Elfe and James Hardin (1992)

125 *Twentieth-Century Caribbean and Black African Writers, Second Series,* edited by Bernth Lindfors and Reinhard Sander (1993)

126 *Seventeenth-Century British Nondramatic Poets, Second Series,* edited by M. Thomas Hester (1993)

127 *American Newspaper Publishers, 1950-1990,* edited by Perry J. Ashley (1993)

128 *Twentieth-Century Italian Poets, Second Series,* edited by Giovanna Wedel De Stasio, Glauco Cambon, and Antonio Illiano (1993)

129 *Nineteenth-Century German Writers, 1841-1900,* edited by James Hardin and Siegfried Mews (1993)

130 *American Short-Story Writers Since World War II,* edited by Patrick Meanor (1993)

131 *Seventeenth-Century British Nondramatic Poets, Third Series,* edited by M. Thomas Hester (1993)

132 *Sixteenth-Century British Nondramatic Writers, First Series,* edited by David A. Richardson (1993)

133 *Nineteenth-Century German Writers to 1840,* edited by James Hardin and Siegfried Mews (1993)

134 *Twentieth-Century Spanish Poets, Second Series,* edited by Jerry Phillips Winfield (1994)

135 *British Short-Fiction Writers, 1880-1914: The Realist Tradition,* edited by William B. Thesing (1994)

136 *Sixteenth-Century British Nondramatic Writers, Second Series,* edited by David A. Richardson (1994)

137 *American Magazine Journalists, 1900-1960, Second Series,* edited by Sam G. Riley (1994)

138 *German Writers and Works of the High Middle Ages: 1170-1280,* edited by James Hardin and Will Hasty (1994)

139 *British Short-Fiction Writers, 1945-1980,* edited by Dean Baldwin (1994)

140 *American Book-Collectors and Bibliographers, First Series,* edited by Joseph Rosenblum (1994)

141 *British Children's Writers, 1880-1914,* edited by Laura M. Zaidman (1994)

142 *Eighteenth-Century British Literary Biographers,* edited by Steven Serafin (1994)

143 *American Novelists Since World War II, Third Series,* edited by James R. Giles and Wanda H. Giles (1994)

144 *Nineteenth-Century British Literary Biographers,* edited by Steven Serafin (1994)

145 *Modern Latin-American Fiction Writers, Second Series,* edited by William Luis and Ann González (1994)

146 *Old and Middle English Literature,* edited by Jeffrey Helterman and Jerome Mitchell (1994)

147 *South Slavic Writers Before World War II,* edited by Vasa D. Mihailovich (1994)

148 *German Writers and Works of the Early Middle Ages: 800-1170,* edited by Will Hasty and James Hardin (1994)

149 *Late Nineteenth- and Early Twentieth-Century British Literary Biographers,* edited by Steven Serafin (1995)

150 *Early Modern Russian Writers, Late Seventeenth and Eighteenth Centuries,* edited by Marcus C. Levitt (1995)

151 *British Prose Writers of the Early Seventeenth Century,* edited by Clayton D. Lein (1995)

152 *American Novelists Since World War II, Fourth Series,* edited by James and Wanda Giles (1995)

153 *Late-Victorian and Edwardian British Novelists, First Series,* edited by George M. Johnson (1995)

154 *The British Literary Book Trade, 1700-1820,* edited by James K. Bracken and Joel Silver (1995)

155 *Twentieth-Century British Literary Biographers*, edited by Steven Serafin (1995)

156 *British Short-Fiction Writers, 1880-1914: The Romantic Tradition*, edited by William F. Naufftus (1995)

157 *Twentieth-Century Caribbean and Black African Writers, Third Series*, edited by Bernth Lindfors and Reinhard Sander (1995)

158 *British Reform Writers, 1789-1832*, edited by Gary Kelly and Edd Applegate (1995)

159 *British Short-Fiction Writers, 1800-1880*, edited by John R. Greenfield (1996)

160 *British Children's Writers, 1914-1960*, edited by Donald R. Hettinga and Gary D. Schmidt (1996)

161 *British Children's Writers Since 1960, First Series*, edited by Caroline Hunt (1996)

162 *British Short-Fiction Writers, 1915-1945*, edited by John H. Rogers (1996)

163 *British Children's Writers, 1800-1880*, edited by Meena Khorana (1996)

164 *German Baroque Writers, 1580-1660*, edited by James Hardin (1996)

165 *American Poets Since World War II, Fourth Series*, edited by Joseph Conte (1996)

166 *British Travel Writers, 1837-1875*, edited by Barbara Brothers and Julia Gergits (1996)

167 *Sixteenth-Century British Nondramatic Writers, Third Series*, edited by David A. Richardson (1996)

168 *German Baroque Writers, 1661-1730*, edited by James Hardin (1996)

169 *American Poets Since World War II, Fifth Series*, edited by Joseph Conte (1996)

170 *The British Literary Book Trade, 1475-1700*, edited by James K. Bracken and Joel Silver (1996)

171 *Twentieth-Century American Sportswriters*, edited by Richard Orodenker (1996)

172 *Sixteenth-Century British Nondramatic Writers, Fourth Series*, edited by David A. Richardson (1996)

173 *American Novelists Since World War II, Fifth Series*, edited by James R. Giles and Wanda H. Giles (1996)

174 *British Travel Writers, 1876-1909*, edited by Barbara Brothers and Julia Gergits (1997)

175 *Native American Writers of the United States*, edited by Kenneth M. Roemer (1997)

176 *Ancient Greek Authors*, edited by Ward W. Briggs (1997)

177 *Italian Novelists Since World War II, 1945-1965*, edited by Augustus Pallotta (1997)

178 *British Fantasy and Science-Fiction Writers Before World War I*, edited by Darren Harris-Fain (1997)

179 *German Writers of the Renaissance and Reformation, 1280-1580*, edited by James Hardin and Max Reinhart (1997)

180 *Japanese Fiction Writers, 1868-1945*, edited by Van C. Gessel (1997)

181 *South Slavic Writers Since World War II*, edited by Vasa D. Mihailovich (1997)

182 *Japanese Fiction Writers Since World War II*, edited by Van C. Gessel (1997)

183 *American Travel Writers, 1776-1864*, edited by James J. Schramer and Donald Ross (1997)

184 *Nineteenth-Century British Book-Collectors and Bibliographers*, edited by William Baker and Kenneth Womack (1997)

185 *American Literary Journalists, 1945-1995, First Series*, edited by Arthur J. Kaul (1998)

186 *Nineteenth-Century American Western Writers*, edited by Robert L. Gale (1998)

187 *American Book Collectors and Bibliographers, Second Series*, edited by Joseph Rosenblum (1998)

188 *American Book and Magazine Illustrators to 1920*, edited by Steven E. Smith, Catherine A. Hastedt, and Donald H. Dyal (1998)

189 *American Travel Writers, 1850-1915*, edited by Donald Ross and James J. Schramer (1998)

190 *British Reform Writers, 1832-1914*, edited by Gary Kelly and Edd Applegate (1998)

191 *British Novelists Between the Wars*, edited by George M. Johnson (1998)

192 *French Dramatists, 1789-1914*, edited by Barbara T. Cooper (1998)

193 *American Poets Since World War II, Sixth Series*, edited by Joseph Conte (1998)

194 *British Novelists Since 1960, Second Series*, edited by Merritt Moseley (1998)

195 *British Travel Writers, 1910-1939*, edited by Barbara Brothers and Julia Gergits (1998)

196 *Italian Novelists Since World War II, 1965-1995*, edited by Augustus Pallotta (1999)

197 *Late Victorian and Edwardian British Novelists, Second Series*, edited by George M. Johnson (1999)

198 *Russian Literature in the Age of Pushkin and Gogol: Prose*, edited by Christine A. Rydel (1999)

199 *Victorian Women Poets*, edited by William B. Thesing (1999)

200 *American Women Prose Writers to 1820*, edited by Carla J. Mulford, with Angela Vietto and Amy E. Winans (1999)

201 *Twentieth-Century British Book Collectors and Bibliographers*, edited by William Baker and Kenneth Womack (1999)

202 *Nineteenth-Century American Fiction Writers*, edited by Kent P. Ljungquist (1999)

203 *Medieval Japanese Writers*, edited by Steven D. Carter (1999)

204 *British Travel Writers, 1940–1997*, edited by Barbara Brothers and Julia M. Gergits (1999)

205 *Russian Literature in the Age of Pushkin and Gogol: Poetry and Drama*, edited by Christine A. Rydel (1999)

Documentary Series

1 *Sherwood Anderson, Willa Cather, John Dos Passos, Theodore Dreiser, F. Scott Fitzgerald, Ernest Hemingway, Sinclair Lewis*, edited by Margaret A. Van Antwerp (1982)

2 *James Gould Cozzens, James T. Farrell, William Faulkner, John O'Hara, John Steinbeck, Thomas Wolfe, Richard Wright*, edited by Margaret A. Van Antwerp (1982)

3 *Saul Bellow, Jack Kerouac, Norman Mailer, Vladimir Nabokov, John Updike, Kurt Vonnegut*, edited by Mary Bruccoli (1983)

4 *Tennessee Williams*, edited by Margaret A. Van Antwerp and Sally Johns (1984)

5 *American Transcendentalists*, edited by Joel Myerson (1988)

6 *Hardboiled Mystery Writers: Raymond Chandler, Dashiell Hammett, Ross Macdonald*, edited by Matthew J. Bruccoli and Richard Layman (1989)

7 *Modern American Poets: James Dickey, Robert Frost, Marianne Moore*, edited by Karen L. Rood (1989)

8 *The Black Aesthetic Movement*, edited by Jeffrey Louis Decker (1991)

9 *American Writers of the Vietnam War: W. D. Ehrhart, Larry Heinemann, Tim O'Brien, Walter McDonald, John M. Del Vecchio*, edited by Ronald Baughman (1991)

10 *The Bloomsbury Group*, edited by Edward L. Bishop (1992)

11 *American Proletarian Culture: The Twenties and The Thirties*, edited by Jon Christian Suggs (1993)

12 *Southern Women Writers: Flannery O'Connor, Katherine Anne Porter, Eudora Welty*, edited by Mary Ann Wimsatt and Karen L. Rood (1994)

13 *The House of Scribner, 1846-1904*, edited by John Delaney (1996)

14 *Four Women Writers for Children, 1868-1918*, edited by Caroline C. Hunt (1996)

15 *American Expatriate Writers: Paris in the Twenties*, edited by Matthew J. Bruccoli and Robert W. Trogdon (1997)

16 *The House of Scribner, 1905-1930*, edited by John Delaney (1997)

17 *The House of Scribner, 1931-1984*, edited by John Delaney (1998)

18 *British Poets of The Great War: Sassoon, Graves, Owen*, edited by Patrick Quinn (1999)

19 *James Dickey*, edited by Judith S. Baughman (1999)

Yearbooks

1980 edited by Karen L. Rood, Jean W. Ross, and Richard Ziegfeld (1981)

1981 edited by Karen L. Rood, Jean W. Ross, and Richard Ziegfeld (1982)

1982 edited by Richard Ziegfeld; associate editors: Jean W. Ross and Lynne C. Zeigler (1983)

1983 edited by Mary Bruccoli and Jean W. Ross; associate editor: Richard Ziegfeld (1984)

1985 edited by Jean W. Ross (1986)

1986 edited by J. M. Brook (1987)

1987 edited by J. M. Brook (1988)

1988 edited by J. M. Brook (1989)

1989 edited by J. M. Brook (1990)

1990 edited by James W. Hipp (1991)

1991 edited by James W. Hipp (1992)

1992 edited by James W. Hipp (1993)

1993 edited by James W. Hipp, contributing editor George Garrett (1994)

1994 edited by James W. Hipp, contributing editor George Garrett (1995)

1995 edited by James W. Hipp, contributing editor George Garrett (1996)

1996 edited by Samuel W. Bruce and L. Kay Webster, contributing editor George Garrett (1997)

1997 edited by Matthew J. Bruccoli and George Garrett, with the assistance of L. Kay Webster (1998)

Concise Series

Concise Dictionary of American Literary Biography, 6 volumes (1988-1989): *The New Consciousness, 1941-1968; Colonization to the American Renaissance, 1640-1865; Realism, Naturalism, and Local Color, 1865-1917; The Twenties, 1917-1929; The Age of Maturity, 1929-1941; Broadening Views, 1968-1988.*

Concise Dictionary of British Literary Biography, 8 volumes (1991-1992): *Writers of the Middle Ages and Renaissance Before 1660; Writers of the Restoration and Eighteenth Century, 1660-1789; Writers of the Romantic Period, 1789-1832; Victorian Writers, 1832-1890; Late-Victorian and Edwardian Writers, 1890-1914; Modern Writers, 1914-1945; Writers After World War II, 1945-1960; Contemporary Writers, 1960 to Present.*

Dictionary of Literary Biography® • Volume Two Hundred Five

Russian Literature in the Age of Pushkin and Gogol: Poetry and Drama

For Edward,
"na kholmakh Gruzii"．．．et in saecula saeculorum

Contents

Plan of the Series xiii
Introduction xv

Evgenii Abramovich Baratynsky (1800–1844) 3
  Luc J. Beaudoin

Konstantin Nikolaevich Batiushkov (1787–1855) 20
  Igor' A. Pil'shchikov and T. Henry Fitt

Vladimir Grigor'evich Benediktov (1807–1873) 38
  James West

Denis Vasil'evich Davydov (1784–1839) 45
  Sonia I. Ketchian

Anton Antonovich Del'vig (1798–1831) 58
  James West

Petr Pavlovich Ershov (1815–1869) 67
  Gary R. Jahn

Fedor Nikolaevich Glinka (1786–1880) 71
  Sofiya Yuzefpolskaya

Nikolai Ivanovich Gnedich (1784–1833) 77
  John A. Barnstead

Aleksandr Sergeevich Griboedov (1795?–1829) 84
  Marina Balina

Nikolai Mikhailovich Iazykov (1803–1846) 100
  Luc J. Beaudoin

Pavel Aleksandrovich Katenin (1792–1853) 107
  Vladimir Shatskov

Aleksei Stepanovich Khomiakov (1804–1860) 119
  Rosina Neginsky

Petr Vasil'evich Kireevsky (1808–1856) 131
  Rosina Neginsky

Vil'gel'm Karlovich Kiukhel'beker (1797–1846) 136
  Marina Kostalevsky

Aleksei Vasil'evich Kol'tsov (1809–1842) 147
  Veronica Shapovalov

Ivan Ivanovich Kozlov (1779–1840) 159
  James West

Nestor Vasil'evich Kukol'nik (1809–1868) 166
  Christine A. Rydel

Mikhail Iur'evich Lermontov (1814–1841) 179
  David Powelstock

Aleksandr Ivanovich Odoevsky (1802–1839) 206
  Evgeniia B. Sorokina

Karolina Karlovna Pavlova (1807–1893) 215
  Marina Balina

Petr Aleksandrovich Pletnev (1792–1865) 225
  Ruth Sobel

Aleksandr Ivanovich Polezhaev (1804–1838) 230
  Evgeniia B. Sorokina

Aleksandr Sergeevich Pushkin (1799–1837) 243
  George J. Gutsche

Vasilii L'vovich Pushkin (1766–1830) 281
  Irwin R. Titunik

Semen Egorovich Raich (1792–1855) 286
  Vera Proskurina

Evdokiia Petrovna Rostopchina (1811–1858) 292
  Sibelan Forrester

Kondratii Fedorovich Ryleev (1795–1826) 298
  James West

Stepan Petrovich Shevyrev (1806–1864) 308
  Richard Tempest

Viktor Grigor'evich Tepliakov (1804–1842) 319
  Richard Tempest

Fedor Ivanovich Tiutchev (1803–1873) 325
  Anatoly Liberman

Dmitrii Vladimirovich Venevitinov (1805–1827) . . 346
  Luc J. Beaudoin

Petr Andreevich Viazemsky (1792–1878) 353
  Luc J. Beaudoin

Vasilii Andreevich Zhukovsky (1783–1852) 361
  James West

Checklist of Further Readings 381
Contributors 385
Cumulative Index 389

Plan of the Series

... Almost the most prodigious asset of a country, and perhaps its most precious possession, is its native literary product—when that product is fine and noble and enduring.

Mark Twain*

The advisory board, the editors, and the publisher of the *Dictionary of Literary Biography* are joined in endorsing Mark Twain's declaration. The literature of a nation provides an inexhaustible resource of permanent worth. We intend to make literature and its creators better understood and more accessible to students and the reading public, while satisfying the standards of teachers and scholars.

To meet these requirements, *literary biography* has been construed in terms of the author's achievement. The most important thing about a writer is his writing. Accordingly, the entries in *DLB* are career biographies, tracing the development of the author's canon and the evolution of his reputation.

The purpose of *DLB* is not only to provide reliable information in a convenient format but also to place the figures in the larger perspective of literary history and to offer appraisals of their accomplishments by qualified scholars.

The publication plan for *DLB* resulted from two years of preparation. The project was proposed to Bruccoli Clark by Frederick C. Ruffner, president of the Gale Research Company, in November 1975. After specimen entries were prepared and typeset, an advisory board was formed to refine the entry format and develop the series rationale. In meetings held during 1976, the publisher, series editors, and advisory board approved the scheme for a comprehensive biographical dictionary of persons who contributed to North American literature. Editorial work on the first volume began in January 1977, and it was published in 1978. In order to make *DLB* more than a reference tool and to compile volumes that individually have claim to status as literary history, it was decided to organize volumes by topic, period, or genre. Each of these freestanding volumes provides a biographical-bibliographical guide and overview for a particular area of literature. We are convinced that this organization—as opposed to a single alphabet method—constitutes a valuable innovation in the presentation of reference material. The volume plan necessarily requires many decisions for the placement and treatment of authors who might properly be included in two or three volumes. In some instances a major figure will be included in separate volumes, but with different entries emphasizing the aspect of his career appropriate to each volume. Ernest Hemingway, for example, is represented in *American Writers in Paris, 1920-1939* by an entry focusing on his expatriate apprenticeship; he is also in *American Novelists, 1910-1945* with an entry surveying his entire career, as well as in *American Short-Story Writers, 1910-1945, Second Series* with an entry concentrating on his short stories. Each volume includes a cumulative index of the subject authors and articles. Comprehensive indexes to the entire series are planned.

Since 1981 the series has been further augmented by the *DLB Yearbooks,* which update published entries and add new entries to keep the *DLB* current with contemporary activity. There have also been *DLB Documentary Series* volumes which provide biographical and critical source materials for figures whose work is judged to have particular interest for students. One of these companion volumes is entirely devoted to Tennessee Williams.

We define literature as the *intellectual commerce of a nation:* not merely as belles lettres but as that ample and complex process by which ideas are generated, shaped, and transmitted. *DLB* entries are not limited to "creative writers" but extend to other figures who in their time and in their way influenced the mind of a people. Thus the series encompasses historians, journalists, publishers, book collectors, and screenwriters. By this means readers of *DLB* may be aided to perceive literature not as cult scripture in the keeping of intellectual high priests but firmly positioned at the center of a nation's life.

DLB includes the major writers appropriate to each volume and those standing in the ranks behind

*From an unpublished section of Mark Twain's autobiography, copyright by the Mark Twain Company

them. Scholarly and critical counsel has been sought in deciding which minor figures to include and how full their entries should be. Wherever possible, useful references are made to figures who do not warrant separate entries.

Each *DLB* volume has an expert volume editor responsible for planning the volume, selecting the figures for inclusion, and assigning the entries. Volume editors are also responsible for preparing, where appropriate, appendices surveying the major periodicals and literary and intellectual movements for their volumes, as well as lists of further readings. Work on the series as a whole is coordinated at the Bruccoli Clark Layman editorial center in Columbia, South Carolina, where the editorial staff is responsible for accuracy and utility of the published volumes.

One feature that distinguishes *DLB* is the illustration policy—its concern with the iconography of literature. Just as an author is influenced by his surroundings, so is the reader's understanding of the author enhanced by a knowledge of his environment. Therefore *DLB* volumes include not only drawings, paintings, and photographs of authors, often depicting them at various stages in their careers, but also illustrations of their families and places where they lived. Title pages are regularly reproduced in facsimile along with dust jackets for modern authors. The dust jackets are a special feature of *DLB* because they often document better than anything else the way in which an author's work was perceived in its own time. Specimens of the writers' manuscripts and letters are included when feasible.

Samuel Johnson rightly decreed that "The chief glory of every people arises from its authors." The purpose of the *Dictionary of Literary Biography* is to compile literary history in the surest way available to us—by accurate and comprehensive treatment of the lives and work of those who contributed to it.

The *DLB* Advisory Board

Introduction

Russian literature achieved greatness in the nineteenth century and retained its international renown mainly because of the prose works of its most famous writers—Nikolai Gogol, Ivan Sergeevich Turgenev, Fyodor Dostoyevsky, Leo Tolstoy, and Anton Pavlovich Chekhov. (For a brief survey of the rise of early nineteenth-century Russian prose, a description of the most important salons and circles, and a survey of the development of journalism in historical and social contexts, the reader should refer to *DLB 198: Russian Literature in the Age of Pushkin and Gogol: Prose,* the companion to this volume.) Russia's true Golden Age, however, begins and ends with its poets and roughly corresponds to the years when Romanticism gained ascendancy. Though later periods could boast of great poets, none could claim the poetic genius of writers such as Aleksandr Pushkin, Mikhail Iur'evich Lermontov, Evgenii Abramovich Baratynsky, and Fedor Ivanovich Tiutchev, who more than the prose writers acted as a bridge to Russia's Silver Age.

Beginning in the 1880s, the Silver Age spans approximately the thirty years that include Symbolism, Decadence, and Acmeism. Futurism followed on their heels. The poets who figured most prominently in this period include Aleksandr Aleksandrovich Blok, Andrei Bely (pseudonym of Boris Nikolaevich Bugaev), Nikolai Sergeevich Gumilev, Anna Andreevna Akhmatova, Sergei Aleksandrovich Esenin, Osip Emil'evich Mandel'shtam, Marina Ivanovna Tsvetaeva, Boris Leonidovich Pasternak, and Vladimir Vladimirovich Maiakovsky. The heritage of the nineteenth century lasted until Soviet repression cast it into a darkness far more profound than the one from which it evolved. Poets ushered in Russia's great age of literature, and poets escorted it out—almost like pallbearers.

To visualize nineteenth-century Russian literary life, one should imagine that it exists on a straight line with the sun, earth, and moon aligned. The first thirty years of the century—romantic, poetic, and idealistic—bask in the full glow of the sun; the next fifty years or so—realistic, prosaic, and utilitarian—come down to an earth that enjoys the diffused light of the sun until it fades into evening shadows; the last twenty years—symbolic, again poetic, and aesthetic—shimmer under the silver moon that receives only the light from the sun that the intervening earth cannot block. So, too, the Silver Age poets, tired of earthbound Realism and its dissolution into second-rate prose, looked back to Russia's Golden Age for inspiration. Not insignificantly, one of the Symbolist poets, Konstantin Dmitrievich Balmont, titled one of his collections *Budem kak solntse* (Let Us Be Like the Sun, 1903). The term "Golden Age" generally refers to any national literature at its apogee, a designation consistent with Russia's first thirty years of the nineteenth century. In Russia, however, the designation may be as historical as it is symbolic.

The common use of the term "Golden Age" to describe Russian literary culture in the period when it established "the accepted standard of excellence in its homeland and a model to be imitated by many writers in other countries," according to noted historian Nicholas V. Riasanovsky, suggests parallels with the phenomenon known as the Roman Golden Age, also known as the "Augustan Age." As a result of the eighteenth-century writers' fascination with the classical tradition, literary Russia at the dawn of the nineteenth century drew freely on this inheritance to the extent that Catherine the Great and the critics whom she silenced after the French Revolution (not to speak of Maximilien-François-Marie-Isidore de Robespierre himself) all considered themselves to be "republicans," at least in the sense of revering the upright virtues of the old Romans. This attitude partly explains the sense of cultural crisis that grew in the last decade of that century of the Enlightenment, when the guillotine became the symbol of a revolution gone wrong in Western Europe while the small cultural elite of Russia suffered under the bipolar repression of the aged Catherine and her son Paul I. Like patriots of the Golden Age of Cicero, Brutus, and Octavius, thoughtful Russians longed to reestablish their country on better principles, and they greeted the accession of Alexander I (reigned 1801–1825) in a spirit not dissimilar from that which the Romans lavished on the young Caesar Augustus, first emperor after the republic.

The ideas of Nikolai Mikhailovich Karamzin provide a striking and typical example of this mentality. An erstwhile "republican" who, it is said, wept upon hearing of Robespierre's death, Karamzin entered the new age ready to concede to the necessity of a "principate" (the euphemistic name of the Augustan monarchy), because Europeans, like the Romans of the late republic, had demonstrated an incapacity, or at least an insufficient maturity, for republican virtues. For his part, Karamzin, the highly influential figure whose language reforms helped create the medium for Pushkin's poetry and whose journalism has been credited with virtually creating the Russian reading public, retreated to his study to write a great history in part inspired by the Roman historian Livy. The idea that culture could provide an important impetus for reform was not new, of course; indeed, it explains why Catherine, and even her successor, were so attentive to cultural matters. The new ingredient was a sense of hope for the new regime. From the beginning of the nineteenth century, literary Russia obviously desired an "Augustan Age."

The Russian Golden Age had no Augustus, however, for the new ruler, Alexander I, repeatedly raised and dashed expectations, although these did not significantly dissipate until he entered his frankly reactionary period in the 1820s. Their Golden Age also lacked a Gaius Maecenas (Roman statesman and patron of literature), in the sense that one of the striking new characteristics of Russian literary culture in the nineteenth century was its rapidly growing independence from official patronage. These factors aside, a comparison of the two golden ages evokes some interesting parallels. For example, Nicholas I bears some distant resemblance to the Roman emperor Tiberius, especially in his conservatism and distrust of his elites. The Golden Age in Russia was also colored by the triumphalism (belief in the superiority of one religious creed) and imperial sense of destiny resulting from the victories over Napoleon Bonaparte. No doubt Russia, for a time the greatest military power in Europe, had a better claim than ever before to the title "Imperial." All these events and feelings had some noticeable effect on Russian drama and poetry. The aspect that most resembled that of the Roman age, however, was the poetic. In this age poetry outshone prose, perhaps partly for the same reason that writers and readers favored poetry during Rome's early principate: repressive rulers do not understand it as easily as prose.

Like the original Augustan Age, and also like the English period of the same name, the Russian literary flowering took place in the social context of a self-conscious agrarian aristocracy. The architectural setting included many of the Neoclassical estates so charmingly described in Priscilla Roosevelt's works as well as the great houses and salons of St. Petersburg, Moscow, and the provincial capitals. The education of the poets was markedly aristocratic even when it was acquired in the new universities and even when the poets themselves were not to the manor born. Many practiced their craft while serving the state in the traditions of their class, and others were motivated, especially in their politics, by a spirit that for better or worse may be called noblesse oblige. Another striking aspect of the period was the relatively small size of the reading public and the even smaller number of poets and dramatists. The beginning of the end of the Golden Age came in the 1830s and 1840s with the growth of the state and the less-educated talent pool this growth entailed. The Augustan Age could also be called the Golden Age of agrarian Russia, and this age, too, was doomed. These developments were reinforced by a general European turning away from Romanticism and idealism, when in the 1840s and 1850s Russian literature came down to earth with the growth of realism.

Another aspect of the Russian Golden Age is the spread of empire, most obviously concentrated in the military and political history of the country. Many of Russia's poets and dramatists saw active service with the Russian army, sometimes as an aspect of traditional aristocratic life and sometimes in consequence of punishments meted out by the tsar. From the standpoint of the dynasty and its chief servitors, the state was first and foremost a military enterprise. Military strength underlay all of its diplomatic prestige in Europe, and maintaining this importance became an obsession of the government. Of equal importance was defense of the imperial borders, which came up against many warlike states, including Persia, Turkey, Austria, Prussia, Sweden, and, in Central Asia, the lands approaching British India. The acquisition of the greater part of Poland had saddled the empire with the problem of a nationalistic Polish aristocracy that staged a significant revolt in 1830–1831. The assumption of responsibilities in Georgia introduced Russian power into the dangerous and mountainous Caucasus region. Finally, there loomed the great threat of Napoleonic France. Russian forces were always campaigning somewhere.

The first hostilities in the reign of Alexander I occurred as a result of the annexation of Georgia, a process that began in 1801 when a part of that ancient Orthodox land asked for Russian protection against Persia and Turkey. Two vexatious wars resulted: with Persia from 1804 to 1813 and with Turkey from 1806 to 1812. The next major action resulted from Russia's joining an Anglo-Austrian coalition against Napoleonic France in 1805; the war went badly for the allies, with Austria knocked out in the first year, with its replacement, Prussia, virtually annihilated in the second year, and with Russia humiliated early in 1807. Alexander signed the Treaty of Tilsit, making Russia a de facto ally of the Napoleonic Empire. Consequent upon this agreement, Russia fought Sweden in 1808 and 1809, acquiring Finland as a reward for its services to the French.

The unpopular Tilsit Peace collapsed in 1811; then in 1812, Napoleon, in the largest military operation in European history to date, invaded Russia. The Patriotic War of 1812 became an epic struggle for national survival, its centerpiece the great Battle of Borodino—which Tolstoy describes so masterfully in *Voina i mir* (War and Peace, 1863–1869)—some seventy-five miles west of Moscow. Napoleon's forces were driven out of Russia at the very end of the year, and from 1813 to 1814 Alexander and his army led the successful campaigns that liberated Europe and ultimately concluded in a Russian occupation of Paris. Alexander played a leading role at the Congress of Vienna and placed Russian power at the service of the congress system, which sought to guarantee the settlement in the years after Napoleon's defeat. For a few years a token force participated in the punitive occupation of France. Upon their return to Russia, many officers who had been stationed in France participated in Masonic and other movements; they made up a large portion of the Decembrists who in 1825 rebelled in the name of constitutionalism.

While supporting, as firmly as possible, the status quo in Europe, the Russian government continued to press into the Caucasus and Central Asia. Just as in the case of his brother and predecessor, the first hostilities in the reign of Nicholas I (reigned 1825–1855) developed into a two-year war (1826–1828) to defend Georgia from Persia. Russia ended up in possession of the city of Erevan and most of Armenia. A war with Turkey followed immediately, although this time the Russians supported Greek independence—the only revision to the 1815 map of Europe to which the Russian government reluctantly acquiesced. The Greeks, an Orthodox people, had strong supporters in St. Petersburg, and Russia had an obvious interest in the region. The tsar had to comfort himself with the hope that this operation would preserve the Turkish monarchy from further disintegration. The only actions of note were the spectacular naval victory of Navarino (1827) and the military campaign that ended in the Treaty of Adrianople (1829).

As a result of these victories, Russia made considerable gains, including the mouth of the Danube River (giving Russia another port on the Black Sea), a protectorate over the Danubian principalities (Moldavia and Wallachia), and much territory in the Caucasus. In this latter region many insurrections by Islamic mountaineers, the most famous of whom was called Shamil, kept Russian regiments busy for the rest of Nicholas I's reign. Total Russian domination did not become a reality until 1859.

The European powers restrained Nicholas I from taking action against the revolutions of 1830 in France and Belgium, and in any case the spread of revolution to the Russian puppet kingdom of Poland proved to be a major distraction. This insurrection was based in the Polish army, and while it enjoyed little support from the common people (Polish serfdom was reputed to be even harsher than the Russian institution), to put it down took a major military effort. As a consequence, the Russians treated Poland quite harshly indeed.

Humiliation of the Poles lowered the Russian regime in the eyes of Western governments; the British, in particular, became suspicious and fearful of Russian influence in Turkey and in Central Asia. Russian forces were rushed to Turkey in 1832–1833 to preserve the Sultan from an insurrection led by his powerful vassal Mohammed Ali of Egypt. The resulting Treaty of Unkiar Skelessi made Russia the virtual protector of Turkey and secretly closed the Straits (Dardanelles and Bosporus) to the warships of all other powers. When Egypt rebelled a second time, in 1839–1840, the Western governments moved to terminate Russia's monopoly of influence at the Sublime Porte (seat of government of the Ottoman Empire), and when in 1850 a dispute erupted between Orthodox Christians and Catholics over rights in the Holy Land, the brash and opportunistic Napoleon III of France weighed in, with British support, to encourage the Turks to stand up to the Russians. Rash Russian responses, including the military occupation of the Danubian principalities, set the stage for the Crimean War.

Russia was further alienated from the increasingly liberal governments of Western Europe by its bellicose attitude toward the revolutions of 1848 that engulfed France, Germany, and the Austrian Empire. At home, the government imposed severe restrictions on intellectual life, recalling students from abroad and arresting suspicious groups and individuals. Its only significant action in Europe came in 1849, when at the behest of the Austrians, the rebellious Hungarian army was defeated by Russian forces sent to restore stability to the region. In consequence of this action, Russia had every right to expect Austrian support in the Crimean crisis. For reasons of their own, however, Austrian statesmen not only held back, but even adopted a policy of malevolent neutrality.

Thus, when war came in 1854 to 1856, Russia fought alone against a coalition consisting of Turkey, France, Britain, and Piedmont-Sardinia. The major action occurred on Russian soil, consisted chiefly of the siege at Sevastopol, and exposed widespread corruption, weakness, and the folly of deliberately resisting various consequences of modernization, such as industrialization. Nicholas I is said to have died of heartbreak; his son and successor, Alexander II (reigned 1855–1881), hastened to make peace and to turn inward for purposes of enacting long-needed reforms. Such was the military and political backdrop of the age of Pushkin and Gogol.

The landmark event in this brief overview of Russia as empire was the Decembrist Revolt of 14 December 1825. Prior to this tragic episode, Russian literary culture was remarkably loyal to the tsars, even when critical of the regime, but afterward it became steadily and increasingly nationalistic, in keeping with the influences of Romanticism. From this time on the split between the government and literate society continued to widen, and serious misunderstandings grew out of the inability of the government to comprehend the new literary and artistic trends. Thus Romanticism itself became a significant historical force. It did not arrive suddenly or fully developed, however; it resulted from an evolution driven as much by the peculiarities of Russian culture as by strong European influences.

The Russians have always had a curious relationship with the West, a simultaneous fascination with and revulsion from its culture and traditions. The history of Romanticism in Russia exemplifies most profoundly this love/hate response to Western ideas and art forms. In the beginning of the century poets such as Konstantin Nikolaevich Batiushkov and Vasilii Andreevich Zhukovsky introduced the Russian reading public to popular European literature through their translations. Zhukovsky, more than anyone, is credited with importing Romanticism into Russia with his skillful translations, often closer to Russian adaptations, of the elegies of Thomas Gray, Jean de la Fontaine, and Charles-Hubert Millevoye as well as the lyrics, ballads, poetic tales, and various verse forms of Gottfried August Bürger, Friedrich von Schiller, Johann Wolfgang von Goethe, Friedrich Gottlieb Klopstock, Johann Ludwig Uhland, Sir Walter Scott, and Oliver Goldsmith. In addition he translated the *Iliad* as did Nikolai Ivanovich Gnedich, who also rendered into Russian the works of Schiller, Voltaire, and William Shakespeare, considered by Pushkin to be the first true Romantic. Batiushkov's interests lay more with Latin classics, Vicomte Evariste-Désiré de Parny, and Torquato Tasso. These translations were important not only for their sensibilities but also for providing Russian writers an opportunity to develop their own skills as poets and thus pave the way for the Golden Age of poetry in Russia.

Romantic sensibility also found its way into Russia through the writings of Western philosophers and literary theorists such as the brothers August Wilhelm and Karl Wilhelm Friedrich von Schlegel; Friedrich Wilhelm Joseph von Schelling; Anne-Louise-Germaine Necker, Madame de Staël; Jean Charles-Léonard Simonde de Sismondi; and Johann Peter Friedrich Ancillon. Their idealistic teachings and theories about national originality appealed to the budding Russian Romantics, who eventually acknowledged only one constant in the protean force that evolved into the Russian brand of Romanticism: the concept of *narodnost'*, or national identity. After much debate *narodnost'* became almost synonymous with Romanticism, thanks to Prince Petr Andreevich Viazemsky. Clearly the Russian cultural elite was well aware of the literary trends in Europe, especially Romanticism. When Romanticism finally stood firmly on Russian soil, however, debate about its definition and nature raged more furiously there than anywhere else, with the possible exception of France. The ultimate result of the initial debates over Romanticism was that the Russians realized that they had no true national literature of their own. They thus set out to remedy this situation, first by rejecting foreign models, then by creating their own.

Yet, before they could create their own Romanticism, they spent almost twenty years debating what it was on many levels: linguistic, literary, thematic, philosophical, political, and moral. In an extensive, informative essay in *"Romantic" and Its Cognates: The European History of a Word,* edited by Hans Eichner (1972), Sigrid McLaughlin traces the linguistic origins and evolution of the word *romantizm* (romanticism). She looks at its three adjectival forms, *romanicheskii, romanticheskii,* and *romanichnyi* (that is, romantic) from a first manifestation in 1791 in Karamzin's *Pis'ma russkogo puteshestvennika* (Letters of a Russian Traveler) as the word *romanicheskii* (derived from the word for novel, *roman*), which he used to mean "unnatural, exaggerated," to a use in another of his works, "Rytsar nashego vremeni" (A Knight of Our Time, 1802) to designate a feeling of the heart. She then discusses the complications that arose when in the 1810s the second variant, *romanticheskii,* gained popular usage not only as a synonym of the still undefined *romanicheskii,* but also as a description of a new type of poetry. McLaughlin follows the vagaries of the word *romantizm* up to the late 1960s and concludes that even then, no one could yet assign an exact meaning to it. What becomes clear is that the linguistic chaos continued for decades among the Romantics themselves, who added other variants and ever-changing meanings to the word. Apparently every "Romantic" or "anti-Romantic" believed in his own meaning(s) of the words. Perhaps the Romantics adopted August Schlegel's definition of *chaos* as "a fruitful abundance" for their platform rather than a mere explanation.

As late as 1824, only a few years before Romanticism wore itself out, Viazemsky wrote in a letter to Zhukovsky: "Romanticism is like a house spirit. Many people believe in it, convinced that it truly exists; but where are its distinctive features; how can one define it? How can one put his finger on it?" A year later Pushkin said in a letter of 25 May 1825 to Viazemsky and his own brother, Lev Sergeevich, "By the way, I have noticed that everybody (including you, too) has a most hazy understanding of romanticism." Almost twenty years later the critic Vissarion Grigor'evich Belinsky lamented in his "The Works of Pushkin. Second Article" (1843) that "the problem has not become clarified [from all these disputes] and romanticism, as before, has remained a mysterious and enigmatic subject." (McLaughlin cites these examples in her essay.)

Even a mere listing of the various meanings the words *romantic* and *romanticism* acquired over approximately thirty years hints at the enormity of the problem one faces in trying to understand the phenomenon. *Romanicheskii* could mean unnatural, exaggerated, emotional, novelistic, pertaining to the genre of "romance," fictitious, amorous, fabulous, fantastic, chimerical, musical, otherworldly, poetic, or marvelous. Not only a synonym for *romanicheskii*, *romanticheskii* could also mean new, unrealizable, beautifully fantastic, ideal, schismatic, depraved, treasonous, noxious, folkloric, incomprehensibly mysterious, postclassical, nonclassical, or contemporary. When the literati tentatively agreed that the basic characteristic of "Romantic" was that it was not "classical," the debates widened to include the true meaning of "classical." So, as McLaughlin says, "A definition of 'romantic' inevitably depended on how 'classical' was characterized."

When Viazemsky called for a definition of the word *romantic*, he first offered his view that to be Romantic, a work had to be based in nature; it also had to include local color, national history, and national spirit; in addition, it had to reject "classical, eternal, and universal norms of art." For Viazemsky any indigenous literature was Romantic. Of course, what ensued was not only disagreement but also discussions on the "nature of nature" and the nature of *narodnost'*. Others who joined the fray were Orest Mikhailovich Somov and Vil'gel'm Karlovich Kiukhel'beker, who tried to distinguish between true and false (fashionable) Romanticism. Since Kiukhel'beker saw true Romanticism as having originated in Provence, any attempt to import it into Russia was simply imitation and therefore could in no way be considered Romanticism. Kondratii Fedorovich Ryleev defined Romantic poetry as anything original; hence, any original, independent poet could be Romantic, even Homer, Aeschylus, or Pindar. Ryleev wanted to abolish the term altogether and to distinguish only between modern and ancient poetry, but the best path was to transcend the limitations of definitions and enter the realm of "true" poetry. Aleksandr Aleksandrovich Bestuzhev (Marlinsky) provided the broadest definition to date by concentrating on subject matter rather than form and insisting that it include national historical themes, freedom of the human spirit, and the Christian spirit of the Middle Ages. According to McLaughlin, Romanticism encompasses "spiritual longing, insatiability, preoccupation with ideals, with absolutes and abstractions, with the dissolution of the present for the sake of infinite goals.... Romanticism and idealism are interchangeable."

The most logical, rational, and ultimately ironic, attempt to define Romanticism came from the true genius of the age, Pushkin. He revealed the evolution in his own thinking about Romanticism over the years. He thought that Romanticism had to reject classical rules and strive for truth in descriptions of history or reality. Pushkin's ironic stance in his novel in verse, *Evgeny Onegin* (1823–1831, published in full in 1833) revealed the aberrations of Romanticism in the naive idealism of the character Lensky—a doomed, superficially Romantic poet—and in the Byronic stance of the main hero, a careless, world-weary youth. (For an excellent exposition of the poet's views, see John Mersereau Jr's "Pushkin's Concept of Romanticism.") Wearying of the debates, ultimately Pushkin turned instead to parody and Romantic irony as his way of dealing with Romanticism when it had, to his mind, run its course.

This brief survey skims only the surface of the controversy, in which several factions took part. The groupings, regroupings, intersection, merging, and opposition of various factions add to the confusion. Lauren Gray Leighton, one of the best critics of Russian Romanticism, traces the origins of the movement to the literary activity of two figures in the eighteenth century—Aleksandr Nikolaevich Radishchev and Karamzin. Leighton sees Radishchev as the source of Russia's tradition of "civic" or political Romanticism because in his *Puteshestvie iz Peterburga v Moskvu* (A Journey from Petersburg to Moscow, 1790) he was the first to discuss the central political question of modern Russia, albeit in a sentimental fashion—serfdom. On the other hand, Karamzin introduced a more "acquiescent, conservative," gentle sensibility to Russia with his travel notes and sentimental tales in the 1790s that inspired, according to Leighton, the "passive, escapist poetry of the early romantic poets, V. A. Zhukovsky and K. N. Batiushkov. The early romantic movement is even termed 'Karamzinian.'..." The repercussions of Karamzin's influence progressed in a steady stream all through the Romantic Age; however, Radishchev had to wait decades until his "political/literary" heirs came to the fore with their involvement in the momentous Decembrist Revolt of 1825.

The first true split centered on the question of what constituted proper literary language. Admiral Aleksandr Semenovich Shishkov tried to defend Russian, with its source in Church Slavonic roots, against the unnecessary "Europeanization" of the language, for which he blamed Karamzin. Shishkov wanted to preserve the eighteenth-century poet Mikhail Vasil'evich

Lomonosov's Neoclassical rubrics prescribing a set order of language levels and a stringent hierarchy of genre. His group, *Beseda liubitelei russkogo slova* (Colloquy of Lovers of the Russian Word), held sway until the 1820s. The writers who rallied around Karamzin propagated his language reforms, which tried to purify the Russian language of its awkwardness and reliance on Church Slavonic. Karamzin coined new words and expressions, often based on French calques; he also restructured the syntax to achieve a more logical, pleasant, though periphrastic, prose style. He created a versatile prose medium suitable for a variety of subjects.

The main vehicles for "Karamzinian" Romanticism and prose style were his almanac, *Aglaia* (2 volumes, 1794 and 1795) and his journal, *Vestnik Evropy* (Herald of Europe, 1802–1830). Karamzin's followers first met in a junior literary circle, *Druzheskoe literaturnoe obshchestvo* (The Literary Friendship Society), and later in the famous group known as "Arzamas," with twenty regular and seven honorary members. The most prominent of these were Batiushkov, Denis Vasil'evich Davydov, Pushkin, his uncle Vasilii L'vovich Pushkin, Aleksandr Ivanovich Turgenev, Count Sergei Semenovich Uvarov, Viazemsky, and Zhukovsky. Karamzin himself was an honorary member.

Some friends and schoolmates of Pushkin, however, aligned themselves with Shishkov, but were not necessarily anti-Romantic. For example, Kiukhel'beker thought of himself as a Romantic, though one who wrote mainly in a Neoclassical style; he opposed only Karamzin's language reforms. Pavel Aleksandrovich Katenin favored Shishkov's conservative approach to literature, but nevertheless criticized the highly Neoclassical French form of the play of his fellow *Beseda* member Aleksandr Sergeevich Griboedov, *Gore ot uma* (Woe from Wit, finished between 1823 and 1824). *Beseda* members Griboedov and Gnedich found themselves on opposite sides in the notorious "battle of the ballads" in which they debated the merits and defects of translations of Bürger's "Lenore" (1773) by Katenin and Zhukovsky. Despite their differences, however, neither group was unfriendly to Romanticism; each group simply defined Romanticism according to its own tastes. By the 1820s the "war against classicism" played itself out and left the field open to the Romantics to debate among themselves the true nature of Romanticism. They included Viazemsky, Bestuzhev (Marlinsky), Prince Vladimir Fedorovich Odoevsky, Ryleev, Baron Anton Antonovich Del'vig, Somov, Katenin, Kiukhel'beker, and their future "adversaries"–Faddei Venediktovich Bulgarin and Nikolai Ivanovich Grech.

By 1823 new groups of Romantics were forming: one based on politics, the other grounded in metaphysics. In its loosest grouping, Decembrist Romantics included not only those writers who believed that literature should express civic ideals as well as aesthetic ones but also ultimately anyone who had ever written works with political themes. Such a broad definition encompassed writers as disparate as Bestuzhev, Ryleev, Kiukhel'beker, Prince Aleksandr Ivanovich Odoevsky, Viazemsky, Griboedov, Pushkin, Grech, and Bulgarin. While the majority of the Decembrist Romantics were mainly sympathizers with the cause, Bestuzhev, Ryleev, Kiukhel'beker, and Aleksandr Odoevsky actually took part in the failed uprising. Ryleev was hanged for his role in the conspiracy while the others faced Siberian exile. The Decembrist writers mainly published in *Poliarnaia zvezda* (Polar Star, 1823–1825).

While the "political" Romantics met in the capital, St. Petersburg, in 1823 the "metaphysical" Romantics formed a Moscow salon around professor Semen Egorovich Raich, who had previously been a member of an early Decembrist society, *Soiuz Blagodentstviia* (The Union of Welfare). Other graduates of the university who worked in the Moscow Archives of the Ministry of Foreign Affairs and received the nickname *arkhivnye iunoshi* (archive youths) formed another group with affinities to Raich's. Disciples of German Romantic idealism, especially of Schelling's *Naturphilosophie* (philosophy of nature), this group came to be known as the *Liubomudry* (Lovers of Wisdom). Their native inspiration came from the erudite poet, critic, philosopher, artist, and musician Dmitrii Vladimirovich Venevitinov, who died when he was only twenty-two. They published their works in Vladimir Odoevsky and Kiukhel'beker's almanac *Mnemozina* (Mnemosyne, four volumes, 1824–1825). The main participants of this circle included the brothers Ivan Vasil'evich and Petr Vasil'evich Kireevsky, Aleksei Stepanovich Khomiakov, Aleksandr Ivanovich Koshelev, Nikolai Matveevich Rozhalin, and others who were sympathetic to German philosophy, especially two members of the Raich salon: the historian and journalist Mikhail Petrovich Pogodin and the literary historian and minor poet Stepan Petrovich Shevyrev. Baratynsky, Vladimir Odoevsky, and Kiukhel'beker also expressed their affinities with the young philosophers. The group disbanded after 14 December 1825 but later gathered again around Pogodin's journal, *Moskovskii vestnik* (Moscow Herald, 1827–1830). The importance of the *Liubomudry* cannot be stressed enough. As Riasanovsky says, "The Lovers of Wisdom reflected the Romantic temper of their generation in a certain kind of poetic spiritualism that pervaded their entire outlook, in their worship of art, in their pantheistic adoration of nature, and in their disregard for the 'crude' aspects of life, including politics."

After 1825 the "aristocrats" regrouped again, this time in opposition to the rise of the so-called "plebeians," partisans of the writers and journalists who came to be known as the "Unholy Triumvirate" of the viper press: Bulgarin, Osip Ivanovich Senkovsky, and Grech. The aristocrats, the last stronghold of the cultured elite, continued to champion the cause of poetry and published their works mainly in Del'vig's almanac, *Severnye tsvety* (Northern Flowers, 1825–1832), and his *Literaturnaia gazeta* (Literary Gazette, 1830–1831); later they published in Pushkin's *Sovremennik* (The Contemporary, 1836–1866). Known also as the "Pushkin Pleiad," this unofficial group consisted of Del'vig, Viazemsky, Somov, Zhukovsky, Davydov, the poet and translator Ivan Ivanovich Kozlov, the poet Nikolai Mikhailovich Iazykov, Baratynsky, and the poet, critic, and journalist Petr Aleksandrovich Pletnev, among many minor poets and writers. They fought to keep poetry alive, but the forces of the plebeians grew too strong for them to withstand. What also helped the plebeians was that the Unholy Triumvirate enjoyed the patronage of the highest court circles, including Tsar Nicholas I, and were rumored to be in league with the Third Section (the political police). These journalists, along with publisher and bookseller Aleksandr Filippovich Smirdin, wanted to turn reading from a leisure activity of the few into a commercial enterprise catering to the masses.

The plebeians' publishing activities really were a mixed blessing. They widened the scope of the Russian reading public, produced cheap editions, and provided a forum for prose writers. Indeed, Senkovsky and Grech's journal, *Biblioteka dlia chteniia* (Library for Reading, 1834–1865), with its encyclopedic table of contents, appealed to a wide reading public. Many good works of excellent writers appeared on its pages. However, the journal *Syn otechestva* (Son of the Fatherland, 1812–1852)–the literature section of which declined in quality in the 1830s and 1840s under the management of Smirdin, Bulgarin, Senkovsky, and Grech–and Bulgarin and Grech's newspaper, *Severnaia pchela* (The Northern Bee, 1825–1864), which enjoyed a wide circulation, pandered mainly to the low taste of the masses, who certainly did not want to read poetry.

No wonder, therefore, that the plebeians' greatest enemy was Pushkin, whom they tried to denounce at every possible opportunity. The prose writer Gogol also felt the full force of their venom on many occasions. Nevertheless, some of the great writers did publish with the plebeians, though generally writers of a lesser stamp most frequently found a place in the pages of their publications. Though not truly bad writers, Vasilii Trofimovich Narezhny, Aleksandr Fomich Vel'tman, Nikolai Filippovich Pavlov, and the poets Vladimir Grigor'evich Benediktov and Aleksandr Ivanovich Polezhaev might be called "the chorus and spear carriers" on the great stage, to use Mersereau's whimsical epithet.

The Polevoi brothers, Nikolai and Ksenofont Alekseevich, also joined the ranks of the plebeians after their brush with the monarchy. In an earlier incarnation the brothers championed the causes of liberalism and Romanticism in their journal, *Moskovskii telegraf* (Moscow Telegraph, 1825–1834). When *Moskovskii telegraf* harshly criticized the extravagantly patriotic play of the wildly popular playwright Nestor Vasil'evich Kukol'nik, *Ruka Vsevyshnego otechestvo spasla* (The Hand of the Almighty Saved the Fatherland, 1832, staged 1834), however, Kukol'nik's imperial patron ordered the closing of the journal. After hobnobbing with the gentry, the Polevois inevitably returned to the comfort of their merchant-class roots and found safe haven with their own kind. Betraying his "egalitarian" biases, Nikolai Polevoi earlier had written a polemical answer to Karamzin's *Istoriia gosudarstva Rossiiskogo* (History of the Russian State, 1816–1818; revised 1818–1829) called *Istoriia russkogo naroda* (History of the Russian People, 1829–1833), a controversial work that Pushkin parodied in his posthumously published "Istoriia sela Goriukhina" (History of the Manor of Goriukhino, 1830, published 1837).

In the 1830s two more opposing factions emerged–the Slavophiles (those who clung to old Russian traditions) and the Westernizers (those who advocated adoption of modern reforms). The former group bore some resemblance to the earlier *Liubomudry,* since its members found their initial inspiration in German Romantic philosophy, as did the original Westernizers. Ever since the seventeenth century some thoughtful Russians had championed the old ways, and some the new; but nineteenth-century idealism, organic historicism, and cultural nationalism, all imported from Europe, made possible the ideologies of the Slavophiles and Westernizers. Petr Iakovlevich Chaadaev raised the central issue of Russia's historical destiny in his "First Philosophical Letter," written and discussed years before its fateful publication in 1836; he proposed that because it had chosen the sterile path of Orthodoxy, Russia had gone nowhere while the Catholic nations marched progressively onward; thus, Russia had no past, no present, and no future. In a characteristic response, the state declared Chaadaev a "madman" and ordered him to stay home under a physician's care; it also closed the journal that published the letter, *Teleskop* (Telescope, 1831–1836), and sent its editor, Nikolai Ivanovich Nadezhdin, into exile. Slavophiles answered Chaadaev's claims by positing that Westernization had broken the "organic" development of Russia, to which the Westernizers replied that Russia should take the Western path as rapidly as possible. Although neither camp adhered to a rigid belief system, in general their attitudes toward Peter the Great summarized their positions: to most Slavophiles Peter was a villain while to Westernizers he was a hero.

Though many names spring to mind when the question of Westernization in Russia comes under discussion, the most influential of the liberal idealists were Belinsky, whose influence carried over even into the Soviet period, and Aleksandr Ivanovich Herzen, who left Russia to live in self-imposed exile until his death in 1870. Among the most prominent of the Slavophiles were the brothers Konstantin and Ivan Sergeevich Aksakov, Khomiakov, Iurii Fedorovich Samarin, Iazykov, Shevyrev, and Pogodin. All of these, in one way or another, sprang from Romantic roots.

Romanticism no longer figured as a major force in the 1830s; nevertheless, two of its greatest and most representative poets continued to write through Russia's poetic doldrums–Lermontov and Tiutchev. The latter was still writing long after the sun had set on Romanticism; Viazemsky, the only other living representative of the heyday of Romanticism, survived Tiutchev by five years. Although realistic prose now commanded first place in the Russian literary arena, Romanticism never completely died out. Vestiges of Romanticism remained in the "organic criticism," based on Schellingian ideas, of the poet and critic Apollon Aleksandrovich Grigor'ev, as well as in the works of the poets Afanasii Afanas'evich Fet (Shenshin), Apollon Nikolaevich Maikov, Lev Aleksandrovich Mei, and Aleksei Konstantinovich Tolstoi. The poet Karolina Karlovna Pavlova (née Janisch) also represented the age well. Recent critics have rediscovered Pavlova, unjustly ignored for decades.

From the earliest appearance of Romantic genres and sensibilities in Russia, poets followed Zhukovsky's lead and adapted the Western models to conform to their need to develop a national literature. While the Romanticism that emerged took on a decidedly Russian cast, it did not differ much from European Romanticism. The two poetic forms that gained the widest popularity in the early days of the century were the ballad and the *poema*, or long narrative poem. The former was most suited to the early Russian Romantic desire for *narodnost'*, mainly because its distinguishing characteristics as a genre stem from the origin of the ballad as a short folk song rooted in a nation's past. Ballads can have from thirty to eighty lines that tell a straightforward story without narrative comment or digression. The narrator relates his highly concentrated tale in a form that mimics oral narration with its necessary mnemonic devices such as repetitions, refrains, parallelisms, and stylized speech. Ballads generally tell of love in its infinite variety and of the ordinary citizens who fall prey to its attractions. These characters usually accept their fate without much quarrel, probably because the presence of supernatural forces in dreams, superstitions, premonitions, omens, incantations, and prognostications comprise a real and naturally accepted part of their lives. These traits of folk ballads appear in the literary versions that consciously imitate the originals. The ballad form enjoyed a strong revival in eighteenth-century Europe, particularly as a reaction against Neoclassical aesthetics.

The ballad first found its way into Russia mainly through the efforts of the eighteenth-century writers Karamzin, Mikhail Nikitich Murav'ev, and Ivan Ivanovich Dmitriev, who wrote the first original ballads in Russian. Primacy of place, though, goes to Zhukovsky, who wrote approximately forty ballads, some translated, others adapted, and still others original. His two most famous ballads are "Liudmila" (1808) and "Svetlana" (1813), both translations/adaptations of Bürger's "Lenore." In these works a young girl runs off with her lover, who has supposedly come back from the war; unfortunately, the lover is dead and only his phantom comes to claim his beloved. In "Liudmila" the young girl discovers too late that her lover is a corpse and his home a grave; "Svetlana" follows the same plot, but in this ballad, the young girl awakens early in the morning to discover her adventure was only a dream. The soft, abstract, decidedly literary language of the *poemy* and its stylized folk elements follow the dictates of the sweet, gentle, refined language of the Karamzin faction.

Katenin, who also translated much, wrote plays and poems in a more old-fashioned mold. A partisan of the Shishkov school, he attacked the sweetness of Zhukovsky's version of "Lenore" with his own translation, "Ol'ga" (1816). In spite of Katenin's Shishkovite loyalties, many considered him to be a Romantic, including Pushkin, who saw in Katenin's work national and folklore elements. Katenin denied that he was a Romantic; he insisted that no Russian could be one, since Romanticism in his view was a purely Western phenomenon and had absolutely no relation to Russian history and culture. Though he did not openly attack subject matter, he said that Russian writers should choose "national" topics to support the cause of *narodnost'* and hatred of tyranny. His ballads had a "rougher," more colloquial, quality that at times bordered on the prosaic. His "Ol'ga" is closer to the original; he restores the heroine's blasphemies and despair at the transformation of her lover into a corpse and also allows her to die. In contrast to Zhukovsky, Katenin locates the events in a definite time and locale. The emotional tone of Katenin's version is more violent and elemental than Zhukovsky's, especially when Ol'ga fulminates at her lover's failure to return to her. Ol'ga's desperate midnight ride with her dead bridegroom evokes strikingly forceful feelings of evil, terror, and ugliness.

Two critics, both members of the Shishkov faction, wrote reviews of both poets' translations in what has come to be known as the "battle of the ballads." The polemics first centered on language and morality. Gnedich attacked "Ol'ga" and defended Zhukovsky's "Liudmila." He mainly objected to Katenin's use of coarse language, illogical syntax and content, and incorrect grammar. Griboedov responded to Gnedich by defending "Ol'ga" as a more faithful translation of "Lenore." He could not find the illogic and incorrectness that so offended Gnedich, and he wittily used Gnedich's own arguments against him.

Pushkin's reaction to the controversy was much more fruitful—he produced his first long poetic narrative, *Ruslan i Liudmila* (1820), a lighthearted hybrid that includes lyric, ballad, mock heroic, fairy tale, folk motifs, and parodic forms. (In fact, chapter four parodies Zhukovsky's poem.) Such mixing of genres is a hallmark of Romanticism, and not just in Russia. The narrator's slightly ironic tone follows the hero on his quest to reclaim his bride, abducted on her wedding night. The Russian critic Iurii Vladimirovich Mann dates the beginning of real Romantic irony in Russia in 1820 with the appearance of this work, the main structural device of which is a confusing of its chronological plan by letting the present intrude upon the past. Five out of six cantos have "contemporary beginnings"—addresses to self and contemporaries, digressions on contemporary manners, and generalizations on life and human nature as a whole. Pushkin digresses thus while responding ironically to literary conventions. Within the tale the narrator engages in play between the subjective and objective worlds. Rhetorical questions or requests to leave or return to the story mark a point of conjunction of the two worlds. (Current critical thought is just beginning to study in greater depth the phenomenon of Romantic irony in Russia, which prose writers used more than poets did. Pushkin, however, turned to this device with some frequency, especially in his *Evgeny Onegin*.)

The popular Eastern tales (for example, *The Giaour* and *The Corsair*, both 1813) of George Gordon, Lord Byron, next appealed to Pushkin's fertile imagination, which led him to write his "Southern Poems"—*Kavkazskii plennik* (Prisoner of the Caucasus, 1820–1821), *Bakhchisaraiskii fontan* (The Fountain of Bakhchisarai, 1822), and *Tsygany* (Gypsies, 1824). These tales feature a typical Byronic hero, usually a naive youth who meets treachery, often at the hands of a woman. He does not believe in the moral worth of humanity and delights in voluptuous pleasures. Byron's heroes tend to be outcasts, criminals, or exiles. His women are either dark Eastern beauties or Christian blondes. The hero tries to overcome all obstacles to love, but through his actions dooms either himself or his beloved. Not uncommon in these tales by Byron are abductions, disguises, murders, acts of revenge, punishment of criminals, depictions of battle, robber scenes, and other adventurous escapades.

Pushkin's *poemy* are less hero-centered; other characters have lives of their own. In the first of the "Southern Poems," a Circassian beauty frees a nameless, disillusioned youth who finds himself a captive of a Caucasian tribe. No Byronic hero appears in *Bakhchisaraiskii fontan*; rather, two harem girls find themselves at odds with each other. Of the three Pushkin works, *Tsygany* offers the most complex and satisfying plot and structure, with the hero developing beyond the limits of his "Byronism." The critic Vasilii Zhirmunsky, in his book *Bairon i Pushkin* (Byron and Pushkin, 1924), exhaustively investigates the affinities between the poets. One of his better-known theories sets forth three basic distinguishing characteristics of the *poema* styled on the Byronic model: the narrator lends an air of mystery to the tales by withholding information, concentrating only on the "high point" of the story, and cultivating a "fragmentary" quality to his storytelling.

Pushkin directed his talents to other forms of verse narration as well and even returned to folk motifs in 1830 with his experiments in verse fairy tales, which in spite of their abundance of *narodnost'* came mainly from foreign sources. Yet, Pushkin's poetic genius elicited responses to these tales that almost seem extravagant. Victor Terras notes that "the tales are not only delightful but also unmistakably Russian. They were almost immediately absorbed by Russian folklore." The literary historian and critic D. S. Mirsky (Prince Dmitrii Petrovich Sviatopolk-Mirsky), known for his idiosyncratic judgments and keen insights into literature, waxes eloquent over the verse fairy tales, especially "Skazka o tsare Saltane" (The Tale of King Saltan, 1831), to which he devotes proportionately more commentary than he does to most works many times its length. He writes:

> The longer one lives, the more one is inclined to regard *King Saltan* as the masterpiece of Russian poetry. It is purest art, free from all irrelevancies of emotion and symbol, 'a thing of beauty' and 'a joy for ever.' It is also the most universal art. . . . It is light, exhilarating, bracing. It has high seriousness, for what can be more highly serious than the creation of a world of perfect beauty and freedom, open to all?

Mirsky recognizes that he may stand alone in ranking "Skazka o tsare Saltane" as the high point of Russian poetry and concedes that honor, as do most critics, to Pushkin's *Mednyi vsadnik* (The Bronze Horseman, 1833), the quintessential Petersburg tale, or novella, to use Pushkin's designation.

The 1820s and 1830s were the heyday of the *poema*. Baratynsky, Lermontov, and Kozlov, like Pushkin, wrote verse tales worthy of note. Not successful at adaptations of Byron, Baratynsky nevertheless tried to write verse tales, an experiment not at all suited to his more classicist taste and temperament. His *Eda* (1824), not well received by either the public or the critics, tells the conventional story of a naive young Finnish girl falling in love with a sophisticated soldier who predictably abandons her when he must leave to fight in a war. The characters fit the Romantic paradigm: she is an idealized heroine, and he is a bounder. Though Baratynsky relies heavily on the pathetic fallacy, in which nature reacts to the actions of the characters, and sentimental touches such as a description of Eda's grave at the end of the tale, the work is not without merit. Its beautiful descriptions of Finnish landscapes are stirring; they also offer a relief from the Eastern climes of the Byronic tales. All in all, *Eda* becomes important in Russian literary history mainly because it testifies to the all-pervasive spirit of Romanticism in Russia: even a poet of classical leanings such as Baratynsky felt compelled to write a Romantic *poema*.

Influenced by Zhukovsky, Karamzin, and various Western models, Kozlov's *poema*, *Chernets* (The Monk, 1825), reworks part two of Byron's *Giaour*. In this hackneyed tale set in a solitary monastery high upon a hill—with the required mists, moon glow, and clouds—a dying monk reveals the mystery of why he is ending his days in such a remote spot. His story holds no surprises: a complicated love triangle made up of stock characters from the Byronic repertory—an idealized beauty, a scurrilous villain, and a creature of nature (the monk himself, who has suffered beyond all endurance yet succumbs finally to the will of God)—lies at the source of his pain and grief. Unremarkable as a poem, *Chernets* nevertheless influenced the young Lermontov, and therein lies its importance.

Lermontov experimented with the verse narrative in works as diverse as *Boiarin Orsha* (The Boyar Orsha, 1835–1836), *Pesnia pro tsaria Ivana Vasil'evicha molodogo oprichnika i udalogo kuptsa Kalashnikova* (Song of the Tsar Ivan Vasil'evich, the Young Oprichnik, and the Valiant Merchant Kalashnikov, 1838), *Mtsyri* (1839), and *Demon*, on which he worked throughout the 1830s. In the first tale a young man of humble origins falls in love with a boyar's daughter, and in the second a merchant meets his death while defending the honor of his wife, disgraced by an *oprichnik* (a member of the tsar's personal guard). *Pesnia pro kuptsa Kalashnikova* (Song of the Merchant Kalashnikov, its common title) is a stylized version of the Russian folk genre, the *bylina* (either a mythical or historical song), another work brimming with *narodnost'*. *Mtsyri* (Georgian for novice), Lermontov's verse narrative masterpiece, is the lyric monologue of a young monk who has escaped from the monastery to enjoy the freedom, beauty, and glory of nature. His dying confession relates his adventures that have exhausted him to the point of death. The Georgian landscape forms the exotic backdrop to the tale, and Lermontov's expert descriptions of the lush surroundings raise this poem to great heights of artistic achievement. His last *poema*, *Demon*, more than any of the others, exemplifies full-blown Romanticism in its most unrestrained form: in this work an innocent maiden surrenders herself not just to a demon lover, but to the ultimate Romantic hero—a melancholy, alienated Demon whose burning kiss kills the woman he loves.

The Romantic revolt against the lofty, impersonal, heroic tone, language, and genres of the Neoclassical period manifested itself in other lyric genres that rivaled the popularity of ballads and *poemy*, chiefly elegies and songs. The poets of the Golden Age also wrote epistolary, personal, meditative, erotic, Anacreontic lyrics, epigrams, and light verse. Ryleev especially popularized a peculiarly Slavic genre, the *duma*, a type of seventeenth-century Ukrainian folk song, which he used mainly to incite patriotic feelings and revolutionary fervor in the spirit of 14 December 1825 as well as to provide a moral education. But whatever the genre, the heart dominated this age in which the prevailing mood combined sentimentality, pensiveness, melancholy, and dreaminess to produce an aura of intimacy between the poet and his reader.

The themes and concerns of Russian Romantic poets paralleled those of their Western counterparts. The world of contradictions and conflicts that dominated Sentimental and pre-Romantic poetry gave rise to the two fundamental motives of the Russian Romantic mind-set—individuality and *narodnost'*. These concepts in turn generated countless variations on man's perceptions of the basic oppositions of life—reason and feeling, the finite and the infinite, the real and the ideal; man's inner life in relation to the general concepts of existence, boredom with the mundane versus longing for another, transcendent reality; and an awareness of the basic disharmony of life coupled with an ineffable longing to discover the harmony of the universe. Other Romantic themes included the cult of friendship, tender feelings, love in all of its varieties, madness, disillusionment, inaccessible happiness, poetry, and the beauties of nature. The Romantics also pondered the problems of ethics, a tendency they inherited from Karamzin. They were interested in exploring man's capacity for a spiritual life and the possibilities for his relationship with God. They searched for divine correspondences in nature and contemplated the roles of the poet as creator and intermediary between mere mortals and God, with the poet's resultant disdain for the masses. The Romantics sought inspiration in Russian history, the Christian Middle Ages, German idealistic philosophy, and even the exotic, which they could find within the very borders of the Russian empire. The Romantics ultimately yearned for the unattainable: they longed for an ideal world, based on either moral or aesthetic perfection. All of these ideas found voice in the poetry whose richness of expression gave Russia its Golden Age.

Russian drama of the period did not fare as well. The plays of the first quarter of the century were classicist in style, derivative at best, and of no lasting value. French imports prevailed, though many of them were so heavily adapted for Russian audiences that they bore no discernible resemblance to the originals. In addition, the theater was not considered to be wholly respectable; consequently, actors could expect only scorn as their due, while actresses received financial support from "benefactors" with ulterior motives rather than from patrons of the arts. Any noblemen who became actors did so at the risk of losing all personal rights and privileges. Classical tragedy soon died out, but comedy survived, primarily in the plays and vaudevilles of Prince Aleksandr Aleksandrovich Shakhovskoi, which dominated the scene from about 1815 until 1825.

Griboedov emerged as the first great comic dramatist of the nineteenth century with his play *Gore ot uma*, which quickly became a classic of the Russian stage. Though written as rhymed verse of variable iambic lines, the dialogue most resembles natural speech, thanks to the poetic skill of Griboedov, whom Mirsky characterizes as "one of the cleverest men and greatest wits in Russia." The characters soon turned into national archetypes, and lines from the dialogue quickly became part of Russian lore, indistinguishable in many ways from native proverbs. A Shishkovite by inclination, Griboedov looked to French classical comedy as a model.

Pushkin, on the other hand, attempted to write a truly Romantic (by which he meant Shakespearean) historical play set in Russia's Time of Troubles (1598-1613): *Boris Godunov* (1825, published 1831). Not a completely successful experiment, the play survives mainly through Modest Petrovich Mussorgsky's opera based on it. The true gems of Pushkin's dramatic works are the closet dramas known as the *malen'kie tragedii* (little tragedies, 1830). Each of the plays considers one of the deadly sins—*Skupoi rytsar* (The Covetous Knight), avarice; *Kamennyi gost'* (The Stone Guest), a retelling of the Don Juan legend, lust; and *Mozart i Salieri*, envy. Lermontov's play *Maskarad* (Masquerade, 1835-1836) also looks at the dark side of man's soul. Arbenin, the main character of this Romantic melodrama, is a gambler who rashly kills his wife because he suspects her of being unfaithful, only to find out later that she was innocent.

The pinnacle of comic drama in Russia, Gogol's *Revizor* (The Inspector General, 1836) also hinges on a misperception—namely that an insignificant government clerk who arrives in town is really the inspector general the townsfolk are expecting because the postmaster learned of the upcoming visit when he read someone's mail. Though thoroughly Russian in execution, this truly hilarious play takes on universal meaning as it transcends time and place. Lacking even one positive character in this world of scoundrels, liars, opportunists, cheats, and rogues, the play satirizes the moral failures of all humanity rather than the social ills of the country. (See *DLB 198* for a discussion of Gogol's plays.)

After *Revizor* Russia had to wait decades for a worthy heir to Gogol. In the meantime the literary plebeians took control of the stage with their contrived historical dramas that catered to the tsar's ideological and educational program, Official Nationality (initiated in 1833). The tsar's minister of education, Uvarov, created its formula of "Orthodoxy, Autocracy, and Nationality" that championed repressive conservatism as a means of controlling the possible influence of Western liberal thought on Russian culture. As a result, excessively patriotic, often highly distorted historical melodramas that curried favor with the monarchy and appealed to the low tastes of the audience became the norm. The most popular, though certainly by no means the best of the playwrights of this time was Nestor Vasil'evich Kukol'nik. His plays exemplify the sorry state to which Russian literature was swiftly heading under the watchful eyes of the tsar, his political police, and the literary plebeians as its writers happily fulfilled the demands of the *chern'* (rabble), who now made up the bulk of the reading public. The Golden Age was rapidly losing its luster.

Yet, prose writers of genius were waiting to take up again the cause of good literature. Alongside them the poets Tiutchev, Fet, and Nikolai Alekseevich Nekrasov kept the spirit of the earlier age alive until genuine poetry could once more reassert itself at the beginning of a new century. Without a doubt Mandel'shtam, Akhmatova, Tsvetaeva, Maiakovsky, and Pasternak formed the poetic character of their time just as certainly as their predecessors had one hundred years before. At the dawn of the twentieth century the literary scene began to look bright again, though perhaps not quite as promising as it had at the onset of the nineteenth. Almost as if it had been commemorating the centenary of Official Nationality, in 1932 another repressive doctrine, Socialist Realism—with its tripartite formula of *tipichnost'* (typicality), *partiinost'* (party-mindedness), and *ideinost'* (ideological commitment)—plunged Russian culture into a darkness far deeper than one Nicholas I and his minions could ever have imagined. At the end of the twentieth century, the regime that squandered its artists is no more, and one hopes the renaissance of the spirit of the Golden Age is at hand.

—*Christine A. Rydel*

Note on Bibliography

The authors of the essays have provided the fullest bibliographical data available to them at the time of writing. For more detailed bibliographical information, the reader should refer to Kseniia Dmitrievna Muratova, ed., *Istoriia russkoi literatury XIX veka: Bib-

liograficheskii ukazatel' (Moscow-Leningrad: Akademiia Nauk SSSR, 1962). This work has been the main source for the bibliographies of individual authors. Other more modern sources provided information for some of the incomplete citations in Muratova's bibliography.

Note on Dates, Names, and Transliterations

All dates in this volume appear in Old Style, that is, according to the Julian calendar, which the Russians used until 1918. To convert to the Gregorian calendar (New Style), add twelve days.

Russian names appear in the text as they do in the Library of Congress transliteration system, with the following exceptions: Moscow appears in the bibliography instead of Moskva, and names that would end in *skii* generally appear as *sky* (for example, Viazemsky instead of Viazemskii). For a few well-known authors, such as Leo Tolstoy, the commonly accepted English spellings have been used. Also, the diacritical marks have been omitted over the letter *e* in names such as Fedor, Shevyrev, and Kishinev. Using *e* instead of *yo* in names gives the reader a more accurate means of conducting further research in library catalogues.

Acknowledgments

This book was produced by Bruccoli Clark Layman, Inc. Karen L. Rood is senior editor for the Dictionary of Literary Biography series. Penelope M. Hope and Tracy Simmons Bitonti were the in-house editors. Assistance with bibliographical research and translation was provided by Alexander A. Prokopenko.

Production manager is Philip B. Dematteis.

Administrative support was provided by Ann M. Cheschi, Tenesha S. Lee, and Angi Pleasant.

Accountant is Neil Senol.

Copyediting supervisor is Phyllis A. Avant. The copyediting staff includes Ronald D. Aiken II, Brenda Carol Blanton, Thom Harman, Melissa D. Hinton, Beth Peters, Raegan E. Quinn, and Audra Rouse. Freelance copyeditors are Brenda Cabra, Rebecca Mayo, Nicole M. Nichols, and Jennie Williamson.

Editorial associate is Jeff Miller.

Layout and graphics staff includes Janet E. Hill and Mark J. McEwan.

Office manager is Kathy Lawler Merlette.

Photography editors are Margo Dowling, Charles Mims, Scott Nemzek, Alison Smith, and Paul Talbot. Digital photographic copy work was performed by Joseph M. Bruccoli.

SGML supervisor is Cory McNair. The SGML staff includes Tim Bedford, Linda Drake, Frank Graham, Jennifer Harwell, Michelle Sabido, and Alex Snead.

Systems manager is Marie L. Parker.

Database manager is Javed Nurani. Kimberly Kelly performed data entry.

Typesetting supervisor is Kathleen M. Flanagan. The typesetting staff includes Karla Corley Brown, Pamela D. Norton, and Patricia Flanagan Salisbury. Freelance typesetters include Deidre Murphy and Delores Plastow.

Walter W. Ross and Steven Gross did library research. They were assisted by the following librarians at the Thomas Cooper Library of the University of South Carolina: Linda Holderfield and the interlibrary-loan staff; reference-department head Virginia Weathers; reference librarians Marilee Birchfield, Stefanie Buck, Stefanie DuBose, Rebecca Feind, Karen Joseph, Donna Lehman, Charlene Loope, Anthony McKissick, Jean Rhyne, and Kwamine Simpson; circulation-department head Caroline Taylor; and acquisitions-searching supervisor David Haggard.

The editor thanks Professor Harold Segel for inviting her to edit this volume and Professor Richard Tempest of the University of Illinois, Urbana-Champaign for most graciously coming to her aid on many occasions. The editor also thanks Professor David Powelstock of the University of Chicago for his great good humor, consummate professionalism, and willingness to take on–and complete–a difficult task on very short notice. Yet again, the editor thanks Lydia C. Thiersen. Gratitude is due to several people at Grand Valley State University, the library staff, in particular the Interlibrary Loan Department; and Associate Vice President for Academic Affairs, John Gracki, who funded student help for this project. The editor is especially grateful to Teresa Tickle, whose extraordinary skill at quickly locating obscure bibliographical data under extreme pressure exemplifies what we in Russian and East European Studies have come to expect from the excellent staff of the Slavic Reference Service of the library of the University of Illinois, Urbana-Champaign. Very special thanks are once more due to the in-house editors, Penelope M. Hope and Tracy Simmons Bitonti, the *sine qua non* of this volume, they are simply the best. However the editor reserves deepest appreciation for "service beyond the call of duty" to James Norris Class and Wayne Louis Robart for their technical assistance and tireless dedication to this project; and to Edward Alan Cole, who always generously gives intelligent help, sound advice, moral support, and much more.

Dictionary of Literary Biography® • Volume Two Hundred Five

Russian Literature in the Age of Pushkin and Gogol: Poetry and Drama

Dictionary of Literary Biography

Evgenii Abramovich Baratynsky
(19 February 1800 - 29 June 1844)

Luc J. Beaudoin
University of Denver

BOOKS: *Eda, Finliandskaia povest', i Piry, opisatel'naia poema* (St. Petersburg: Tip. Departamenta Narodnago Prosveshcheniia, 1826);

Stikhotvoreniia (Moscow: Tip. Avgusta Semena, pri Imperatorskoi Mediko-Khirurgicheskoi Akademii, 1827);

Nalozhnitsa (Moscow: Tip. Avgusta Semena, pri Imperatorskoi Mediko-Khirurgicheskoi Akademii, 1831);

Stikhotvoreniia (Moscow: Tip. Avgusta Semena, pri Imperatorskoi Mediko-Khirurgicheskoi Akademii, 1835);

Sumerki (Moscow: Tip. Avgusta Semena, pri Imperatorskoi Mediko-Khirurgicheskoi Akademii, 1842).

Editions and Collections: *Sochineniia* (Moscow, 1869);

Sochineniia, fourth edition (Kazan': Univ. Tipografiia, 1884);

Polnoe sobranie sochinenii (Kiev: F. A. Ioganson, 1894);

Polnoe sobranie sochinenii (St. Petersburg: E. Pavlova, 1894);

Polnoe sobranie sochinenii, edited by I. N. Bezherianov (St. Petersburg: M. K. Remezova, 1894);

Polnoe sobranie sochinenii, 2 volumes, edited by Modeste Liudvigorich Gofman (Petrograd: Imperatorskaia Akademiia Nauk, 1914–1915);

Polnoe sobranie stikhotvorenii, edited, with commentaries and biographical articles, by Elizaveta Nikolaevna Kupreianova and Irina Nikolaevna Medvedeva, introduction by Dmitrii Sviatopolk Mirsky, 2 volumes (Leningrad: Sovetskii pisatel', 1936);

Stikhotvoreniia, edited by Kupreianova (Leningrad: Sovetskii pisatel', 1937);

Stikhotvoreniia, edited by Medvedeva (Moscow: Goslitizdat, 1945);

Stikhotvoreniia, poemy, proza, pis'ma, edited by O. Muratova and Kirill Vasil'evich Pigarev (Moscow: Goslitizdat, 1951);

Polnoe sobranie stikhotvorenii, edited by Kupreianova (Leningrad: Sovetskii pisatel', 1957);

Stikhotvoreniia i poemy, edited by Lev Adol'fovich Ozerov (Leningrad: Sovetskii pisatel', 1958);

Lirika, compiled, with a preface, by Pigarev (Moscow: Khudozhestvennaia literatura, 1964);

Stikhotvoreniia i poemy, edited by Pigarev (Moscow: Detskaia literatura, 1974);

Stikhotvoreniia, proza, pis'ma, edited by V. A. Rasstrigin and A. E. Tarkhov (Moscow: Pravda, 1983);

Stikhotvoreniia, poemy (Kemerovo: Knizhnoe izdatel'stvo, 1984);

Stikhotvoreniia, pis'ma, vospominaniia sovremennikov (Moscow: Pravda, 1987);

Polnoe sobranie stikhotvorenii, edited by Iurii Andraevich Andreev (Leningrad: Sovetskii pisatel', 1989).

In Russia, when the name of Evgenii Baratynsky is spoken, it is usually accompanied by an almost obligatory reference to Aleksandr Pushkin, his contemporary, in comparison to whom Baratynsky is usually viewed by literary critics and historians as occupying second place on the scale of the literary ranking of Russian Romantic poets. There have been moments in literary history when the "poet-thinker," as Baratynsky is frequently called (thanks to Pushkin), is granted first place within this poetic pantheon. The most acclaimed of these moments occurred during the poet's rediscovery by the Russian neo-Romantic poets at the turn of the century. Initiated by Valerii Iakovlevich Briusov, the new generation of poets judged the intellectual power of Baratynsky superior to the lyric elegance of Pushkin. Certainly, it is this same poetic intellectual power that granted Baratynsky a lasting literary importance within the history of Russian letters. Appreciated mainly this century, his poetic career took him along exploratory paths that may have paralleled the adventures of other Russian Romantic poets but that nonetheless brought him to different conclusions about poetry and its role both in philosophy and in life itself. Though foreshadowing the issues that confronted the artists of the 1910s, 1920s, and 1930s, the questions asked by Baratynsky were answered or dealt with in a manner justifiable to a poet of the beginning of the nineteenth century–through the form, rhetoric, and philosophical power of poetry itself.

The first of seven children, Evgenii Abramovich Baratynsky was born in the village of Mara, Tambov Province, to Abram Andreevich Baratynsky and Agrafena Fedorovna Baratynskaia, née Cherepanova. Abram Andreevich descended from Polish nobility, whose Boratyn castle was located in Galicia. The family subsequently was called "de Boratyn" (analogous to medieval German practice), hence Baratynsky. (There is scholarly dispute about the proper spelling of the family name. Apparently, Baratynsky usually signed his name as "Baratynsky," though the historical evidence above indicates that the proper spelling should have been "Boratynsky.") Abram Andreevich himself was a military man, a general-lieutenant who inherited the wealth his father had acquired through marriage. All of his brothers were prominent in the civil and military services and thus were known to the imperial family. Through the intercession of a maid of honor to the empress, Abram Andreevich made the acquaintance of Aleksandra Fedorovna Cherepanova, herself an imperial maid of honor. At the end of January 1798 they married. Abram Andreevich, after falling into disfavor, retired from the service to the corner of the familial estate called Mara (part of a larger estate called Viazhla, which had been bequeathed by the emperor to the Baratynsky brothers in December 1796). There the retired general-lieutenant sought to maintain a cultured atmosphere. Thus, during the first ten years of Evgenii Baratynsky's life he was exposed to his father's sense of the artistic, as represented primarily by a garden later mentioned in an elegy of 1834, *Zapustenie* (Desolation). The young poet's father died at about age forty-three on 24 March 1810 in Moscow, leaving Baratynsky with his mother. The family had traveled to the city in a failed attempt to secure rehabilitation by the emperor. A pardon would have given the family a chance to move back to Moscow, thereby allowing Evgenii to develop in less isolated circumstances. With the death of the father, it was the mother who became the greatest single influence on Baratynsky's life, particularly as the young man was "almost ill with sensitivity," as Geir Kjetsaa has stated.

Baratynsky's education was typical of the gentry at the time: he studied mathematics and the French language and culture (which he assimilated as his own) from Giacinto Borghese, an Italian native who had become a tutor in rural Russia. Borghese remained dear to Baratynsky throughout his life. Yet the isolation of Mara convinced his mother to attempt again to send him somewhere else. With great effort she succeeded in enrolling "Bubinka," as Evgenii was known, into His Imperial Majesty's Pages Corps in St. Petersburg. His education at last seemed secure. In the boarding school Baratynsky became acquainted with seventeenth- and eighteenth-century French literature of the Classical period. He became so enamored of French literature that he overlooked studying his German, a language particularly important for the military nobility. Yet this neglect did not prevent him from forming a Schillerian secret society in February 1816. It was called *Obshchestvo mstitelei* (Society of Avengers), based on the German writer's (Friedrich von Schiller's) *Die Räuber* (The Robbers, 1781). The society's culminating trick was the theft of a gold snuff box with five hundred rubles in it. As a punishment the emperor not only expelled the young Baratynsky in April 1816 but also forbade him from ever serving in the military in any capacity other than a private. The shock and humiliation of this event was to stay with the poet until his death.

In May of that year Baratynsky returned to Mara, where he suffered a nervous breakdown but later recovered through the tender attentions of his mother.

He continued to read French Classical literature and in 1818 returned to St. Petersburg to prove and redeem himself by enlisting in the army. In 1819 he became a private in the Imperial Household Troops, with the right of residence in his own apartment in St. Petersburg. He chose to room with Anton Antonovich Del'vig. At this point began Baratynsky's exposure to the most influential poetic circles of the capital. He was introduced to poets such as Vasilii Andreevich Zhukovsky, Denis Vasil'evich Davydov, Nikolai Ivanovich Gnedich, Vil'gel'm Karlovich Kiukhel'beker, and Pushkin. In fact, it was Del'vig who published Pushkin's first poems.

Baratynsky's earliest lyrics reveal the influences of the poets whose acquaintance he had made after his arrival in St. Petersburg. Many of the poets he had come to know were members of the *Obshchestvo arzamasskikh bezvestnykh liudei* (Society of the Obscure People of Arzamas), or simply "Arzamas," a society that was officially founded in 1815 and lasted until 1818. This group, comprised of a core of "Older Innovators," as Tynianov has categorized them (mainly the literary circle of Nikolai Mikhailovich Karamzin, including Davydov, Zhukovsky, Konstantin Nikolaevich Batiushkov, Vasilii L'vovich Pushkin, Count Dmitrii Nikolaevich Bludov, and Aleksandr Ivanovich Turgenev) as well as some younger poets such as Pushkin. The primary goal of the Arzamas group was to defend the innovations Karamzin made on the Russian literary language against another group of writers. This rival group, centered on Aleksandr Semenovich Shishkov, was named the *Beseda liubitelei russkogo slova* (Society of Lovers of the Russian Word). It was formed in 1811 to prevent both what it viewed as the unnecessary Gallification of the Russian language and an alienating stylization of the literary genre itself (this alienation was certainly rooted in the French aristocratic heritage of the members of the Arzamas). The *Beseda* advocated a tripartite style of literary language based on the notions of Mikhailo Vasil'evich Lomonosov and offered the Russian folk language as an additional lexical source. The latter notion was to have a significant impact on Russian literature. The worry about literary genre had mainly to do with the frequent epithets and periphrasis used in Karamzinian style—often used to the point of incomprehension. The Arzamas group continued the distinctive eighteenth-century Karamzinian style of light, witty, and refined literature. Communication between the two rival groups was strident and was transmitted through virulent satirical verse and prose. From the start, however, Baratynsky showed himself reticent to participate in the literary polemics of the time, though his literary roots and intellectual interests evidently carried him to Arzamas.

Baratynsky at age twenty (lithograph by F. Chevalier)

Not surprisingly, then, Baratynsky's first published verses reveal the extent to which the young poet had imbibed the tenets of French Classicism. Even in these poems, though, the essential motifs of contradiction and paradox between particular and universal reveal themselves, already indicating how different Baratynsky would become from the other poets around him. It is, moreover, particularly difficult to examine Baratynsky's poetry chronologically, as he only rarely dated his verses. (The dates established in the 1989 edition of his works are observed in this article.) A quick reference to Baratynsky's letters will further reinforce the importance to his literary style of the French Classical tradition. Even while still at the boarding school in St. Petersburg, the young man's correspondence revealed the elegant stylization of the period. One example suffices: "*Serait il bien vrai? Je vais donc vous revoir, je vous embrasserai, je vous parlerai, je respirerai le même air que vous! Ma bonne maman, je n'ose espérer tant de bonheur. Cependant ce n'est pas un songe, je vous verrai, oui, mon cœur me le dit.*" (Could it really be true? I will see you again then, I will kiss you, I will speak with you, I will breathe the same air as you. My good mother, I do not dare wish for such happiness. Yet all the same it is not a dream; yes, my heart tells me—I will see you.)

Clearly the correspondence reveals the formalizing of expression already occurring within the young Baratynsky. The first poem (1818) chronologically reveals a similar affectedness:

Look: with the freshness of youth
And in autumn she takes the years captive,
And she has a greying stone,
Blushing roses she does not steal;
Himself defeated by her beauty,
He looks—and does not continue on his way!

At the same time, in this poem, as well as in the young Baratynsky's letters, can be discerned the beginning of his famed melancholy, which was to express itself in what Benjamin Dees has called the opposition of classical reason versus romantic spontaneity, or simply the conflict of rational thought versus happiness and emotional fulfillment. The element of melancholy remained in Baratynsky's poetry and writings in general throughout his career.

This early poetry reveals the immense influence of the members of Arzamas, including Batiushkov (who himself was influenced by the French Classicists), Zhukovsky, Del'vig, and Pushkin. The latter two poets in particular encouraged Baratynsky to continue his versification. In some respects, it was good fortune, at least artistically, for Baratynsky to have been made a noncommissioned officer and transferred in January 1820 to Finland (annexed to the Russian Empire after the end of the Russo-Swedish War in 1809). Poetically, his new situation permitted Baratynsky to acquire the mantle of exiled artist, much as Pushkin did during his banishment to the South. The location of Finland was suitably unusual, and Baratynsky alone was to conquer it artistically in the mind of the Russian reader. The surroundings were likewise sufficiently morose and dreary for Romantic poetry. Baratynsky learned to cultivate the Byronic pose well; his verses of the period suggest a far more Byronic stance than was actually the case. He was not in fact isolated in Finland: he resided in the house of the commander of the regiment, Georgii Alekseevich Lutkovsky, who likewise owned an estate near Mara in the Tambov province. The regiment moved about frequently and even performed tours of duty in St. Petersburg and Moscow. This movement, in addition to the frequent visits by his St. Petersburg friends to Finland, rendered Baratynsky's role as exiled writer somewhat artificial. During this period, however, Baratynsky achieved a rising popularity in Russian literary circles and a corresponding increase in public awareness. From 1820 to 1825, the years that coincided with his stay in Finland, Baratynsky's popularity crested.

This was also the time when Baratynsky became known as a writer of elegiac verse. Even though he conformed to the prevalent notions of the elegy—that his verse be suffused with melancholy and maintain a meditative and introspective aspect—he still managed to refine the expressions of melancholy, worn threadbare by epithetic overuse, into new forms—more abstract, more intellectual—revealing the intellectual tensions between thought and emotion and the ensuing intellectual isolation that Baratynsky always keenly felt. The elegies written in 1820 (though later revised) frequently dealt with the motif of parting, evidently as a result of Baratynsky's transfer. Exactly such a work is "Rasstalis' my; na mig ocharovan'em" (We have parted, charmed for a moment, 1820), a free adaptation of a translation by Batiushkov of a poem written by the French elegist Vicomte Evariste-Désiré de Parny. In this work Baratynsky explores the notion that the happiness he had felt was but a fleeting moment—a dream that when it ends, leaves the beholder dejected. Already in this work the tranquil introspective tone in Baratynsky's style is visible, despite the fact that the early verses still betrayed the external influence of other poets.

"Vesna (Elegiia)" (Spring [Elegy], 1820) continued the elegiac motif. The main current of the work is the futility of life and of lost dreams. Once again, the poet communes with the nature around him: "I'm fading,—everything is fading with me!" The poet observes the joy of renewed life in the spring but is paradoxically unable to partake in it, for he realizes that all is momentary. The joy passes him by, and he, the poet, while communing with the destroying force of nature, remains incapable of uniting with its force of perpetual rejuvenation.

Baratynsky's exposure to the rugged Finnish landscape first revealed itself in his elegy "Finliandiia" (Finland, written in 1820, published in 1826). It is quite a lengthy poem, and in it Baratynsky explores his new role as Romantic poet isolated in the desolate Ossianic wilderness of Finland. The speaker of the poem addresses the rocks and crags of his surroundings. The stones are the representatives of eternity. The poet is introduced in the third person, and the speaker begins to use the first person only in the second part of the work. In this introduction the poet himself is presented as equal in the framework of eternity to the rocks being addressed. In contrast to the silent presence of the surroundings, the heroes of past battles, who are evoked in the second part of the work, have disappeared. There is but one law, the poet disclaims: "For everyone there is but one law—the law of annihilation." He concludes with an introspective focus on his own situation: he lives but for the moment he has seized, and the moment lives for him. His verses, composed for no one but him, exist merely in their own right.

"Naprasno my, Del'vig, mechtaem naiti" (In vain, Del'vig, do we dream of finding, 1821) is the first of six poems by Baratynsky written in blank verse. As such, it immediately stands out from the other elegies of the period. It is also a striking example of Baratynsky's use of Classical allusion. The poem begins with an analogy of humankind's role as Promethean children denied access to the pleasures of the heavens, which they nonetheless can remember, the poet explains to the reader in the fifth stanza. Because of this cruel trick played upon it, humankind is condemned to live awaiting death, enslaved to fate. The work concludes with a description of Tantalus condemned to an everlasting death of thirst in a pool of cool water. The analogy is clear: humankind remembers that there is something greater to which it once belonged but no longer can reach. Humankind is therefore forced to experience continual longing for the unattainable. This quite Romantic notion of life became more and more frequent in Baratynsky's verse from this point on. It later developed into a fully Romantic philosophical schema of the role of art in the quest for understanding of this ultimate bliss that was understood to lie just beyond the realm of ordinary understanding. In this particular work, however, the poet is the incarnation of the knowledge of the paradox, for he creates the Classical references that explain it.

Classical allusions reappear in the elegy "Ty byl li, gordyi Rim, zemli samovlastitel'" (Was it you, O proud Rome, who was the ruler of the world, 1821), in which Baratynsky questions the paradoxes inherent to a powerful state that has fallen into ruin. The use of Church Slavonicisms, akin to a Russian Latin, adds to the solemnity of the poet's investigation. The role of Rome itself in history is questioned with an oblique mention of death in the third stanza: "Did the victories of a powerful genius betray you? / Is it you at the crossroads of the ages / Standing in the disgrace of the tribes, / Like a luxurious sarcophagus of perished generations?" This treatment of a city and its historical rise and inevitable decline foreshadowed later Russian writers such as Andrei Bely and his views on St. Petersburg.

"Shumi, shumi s krutoi vershiny" (Roar, roar from the steep peak, 1821)–more familiarly known as "Vodopad" (The Waterfall)–is a work that concentrates on sound and alliteration to represent the tension of the waterfall being described while at the same time developing the philosophical issues that always perplexed Baratynsky. The roar of the waterfall hides a battle of buried emotions, and the poet begins to question the angst lying within his own soul. He communicates to and understands the waterfall. Its discourse is silent, sufficing but for itself, just as his own poetry is silent and will exist for itself throughout the ravages of time. In this light the final stanza, in addition to encoding the basic issues of Friedrich Wilhelm Joseph von Schelling's *Naturphilosophie,* reveals the union of passion

Anastasiia L'vovna Baratynskaia, the poet's wife

with reason idealistically sought by the poet Baratynsky: "Shumi, shumi s krutoi vershiny / Ne umolkai, potok sedoi / Soediniai protiazhnyi voi / S protiazhnym otzyvom doliny!" (Roar, roar from the steep peak, / Do not fall silent, grey flow! / Unite your extended howl / With the extended response of the valley!). This poem reveals the beginnings of the Romantic notions of unification of the absolute–a philosophical solution to the Romantic paradoxes of existence questioned by Baratynsky within a Classical poetic structure.

One of the most frequently encountered and fundamental traits of Baratynsky's elegies, one that links him later to the thought of the German Romantic philosophers, is the frequent use of negatives in his poetry. An excellent example can be found in "Razuverenie" (Dissuasion, 1821). In this poem Baratynsky uses negatives nine times in sixteen lines. The poet focuses on an immovable inner peace that has replaced the feelings of the past: "I sleep; the lulling is sweet to me; / Forget former dreams: / In my soul is but one emotion, / And it is not love, which you will awaken."

This work is also interesting because of its concentrated detailing of the inner state of the speaker. The rhythm is unhurried and tranquil–a distinctive trademark of Baratynsky's elegies. In it Baratynsky rejects love outright, rather than simply bemoaning a lack of it: "Uzh ia ne veriu v liubov'" (Already I do not believe in love). In this poem are evident likewise the changes Baratynsky made on the epithets traditionally used in the *poésie légère* of the period. For instance, rather than the more common "drug bestsennyi," (priceless friend), Baratynsky chooses "drug zabotlivyi" (thoughtful friend) as a form of lyrical address, thereby adding a new psychological dimension to the elegiac genre and its fixed epithets. By this time most poets agreed that the epithets usually seen in elegiac verse had become monotonous. Because of innovations such as these, Pushkin later wrote that Baratynsky had triumphed in the elegiac genre.

The same notion of calculated withdrawal is present in Baratynsky's erotic elegies. The reader is not surprised to find that in his "Zachem, o Deliia! serdtsa mladye ty" (Why, O Deliia, do you young hearts, written in 1822, published in 1826), Baratynsky coldly delineates the course of bodily passions. For other elegists the same idea would be material for either inflamed discourse or at least a profound sense of emotional ennui. In Baratynsky's treatment, the inevitable physical decline is mapped out with the dispassionate view of a soothsayer: "With skill you will round out your withered breast, / Your gaunt cheeks you will color, / The winged Cupid you will want whatever the means required / To enchant once again . . . But you will not enchant!" The elegy has thus been transformed from the poet-centered expression of melancholy and longing to a philosophical commentary on the fate of beauty and youth. Baratynsky draws from the particular and expands it to a universal level. This broadening of focus within a lyric poem was one of the specific devices of his poetry that was later included in almost every instance of philosophical verse. Another trait revealing Baratynsky's philosophical inclinations is the juxtaposition of opposites within the verse structure. In the same elegy he writes: "And where for everyone tranquillity is possible, only turmoil awaits its victim." The poet ends his lyric in this manner, referring to the illusory nature of sleep: it provides rest and peace, but also nightmares and remorse. This virtually mathematical calculation of thesis and antithesis was quite unusual in the elegies of the 1820s in Russia.

In "Sei potselui, darovannyi toboi" (This kiss, bestowed by you, 1822) Baratynsky traces a circle of emotion centered on one kiss. Though the kiss may have been momentary, the pleasure derived from it is not. The joy of it is felt even in sleep and dreams; even when both these dreams and the face of the beloved have disappeared, the feeling of love and passion remains. Again one sees the parodoxes of life that continue to afflict Baratynsky–how to reconcile through the powers of reason and analysis the momentariness of pure passion with the inevitable void it permanently leaves in its wake.

"Dalo dve doli providenie" (Providence gave two fates, 1823) begins with a statement of its central thesis in Classical rhetorical style: "Providence gave two fates / To the choice of human wisdom: / Either hope and passion, / Or hopelessness and peace." The tone of the poem is likewise given with this opening stanza; the choices are preordained, so there is no escape. The fatality of the work is striking in both its theme and the vocabulary used in its expression and elaboration. The poet explores the two options logically: first he examines the uses of hope, then the quiet of those who realize that to indulge in passions by and for themselves is worthless. Those who still believe in hope will be condemned to relive their passions in an eternal cycle of despair.

"O schastii s mladenchestva toskuia" (Yearning for happiness since infancy, 1823) is striking in that the figure of Truth answers the question of how to attain happiness. In this elegy Baratynsky personifies his answer rather than leave it in a state of philosophical abstraction within the poet's mind. Thus, in the fifth stanza Truth appears with a lamp to illuminate the path to contentedness. She (truth is a feminine noun in Russian) reveals to him that a coldness of soul and an elevation of intellect and reason above all other concerns are the only ways to happiness. But the poet cannot accept her answer: he only wishes to accomplish her exhortations when he is about to be lowered in a grave. In doing so he renounces, albeit indecisively, what Baratynsky himself has been exploring in differing manners throughout the cycle of elegies.

"Pritvornoi nezhnosti ne trebui ot menia" (Do not demand feigned tenderness from me, written in 1823, published in 1832) is a departure from the previous elegiac poems discussed: it is a complete set of moods in itself, rather than a fragment of an isolated feeling, question, or observation. The work begins with a confession of the speaker's emotional state at the moment: "Do not demand feigned tenderness from me: / I do not hide the sad cold of my heart." The poem continues with an affirmation of the extent to which the poet is incapable of feeling love and emotion. The poet explains that perhaps only first love can burn brightly within the soul; subsequent love can only burn weakly and therefore quickly burns itself out for lack of emotional fodder. Having accepted this situation, the speaker continues to recount what could happen were he to find a "podrugu bez liubvi" (friend without love): he would marry her, but it would be without feeling. The addressee of the "confession," therefore, should not be jealous, for the married couple are but victims of their own union. The work concludes with a farewell, advising the addressee to choose a new path, just as the speaker has done. The conclusion, according to Dees, reveals, as do so many of Baratynsky's elegies, the same development of a universal generalization starting from the specific. The conflict between reason and emotion in this poem is won momentarily by reason.

"Cherep" (The Skull, written in 1824, published in 1826) is one of Baratynsky's best-known elegies, primarily because of a reference by Pushkin to the "Hamlet-Baratynsky" in a letter to Del'vig in 1827. The skull is a potent symbol of the thinking human after death. In fact, this skull still has some hair on it—thereby graphically reinforcing the motif of inevitable human decay. To emphasize the visual image—the decaying skull held in the hands of a poet commenting on the horror of death—the middle portion of the work uses sound. The combination of vowels and the consonant sound *m* repeats throughout the fourth stanza like a funeral dirge. Yet there is no answer from the skull—it keeps the secrets of eternity. The poet decides that he must accept life for what it is. This apparent resignation, however, proves to be short-lived.

In "Zavyla buria; khliab' morskaia" (The storm began to howl; the abyss of the sea, 1824) the connections between the forces of nature and human passions are made even more explicit than in the previous elegies. The poet identifies with the passions of nature in this poem as well, if only because of the power the storm has to overtake the quiet of daily life and destroy the world. In this way the storm is better than the promise of distant lands and better than the daily routines of existence. However, the poet is caught once again in a paradox of his own making. His mere presence belies the emotions he is expressing, and as before, the conflict inevitably centers on passion and reason. For the moment, the storm is victor, but the poet survives to return to his doubts and existential issues.

"Reshitel'no pechal'nykh strok moikh" (Decidedly my sad lines, written in 1824, published in 1826) deals with the poet's literary and emotional infidelities. The speaker apologizes to an unknown addressee for having praised other women, then expands the apology to include passionate statements he had previously disclaimed to yet other women. He ends the poem, however, on a different note: he was only a prankster, not a traitor, for the addressee herself is also guilty of infidelities. Since both are to blame, the end result is that neither can be burdened with guilt. The poet then departs forever.

The progression from emotional opening statement to philosophical conclusion is likewise reflected in "Ona pridet! K ee ustam" (She's coming! To her lips, 1825). This short elegy is a translation and adaptation of Parny's "Réflexion amoureuse." The beginning of

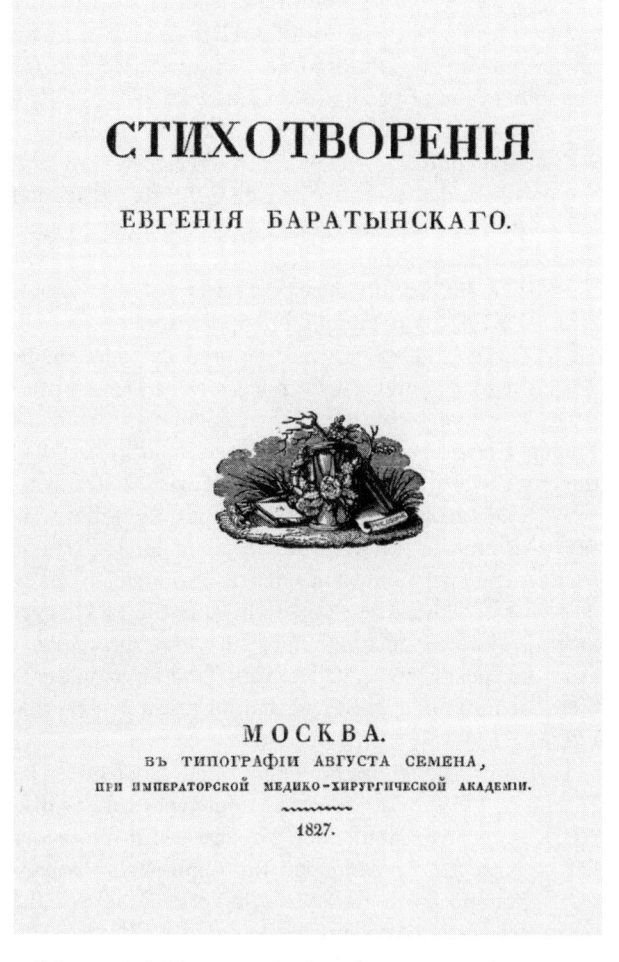

Title page for Stikhotvoreniia *(Poems), Baratynsky's first collection*

the poem is filled with passion, whereas the conclusion is modified into a questioning of this same emotion, thereby betraying the struggle between intellect and feeling:

> She's coming! To her lips
> I will press my own lips,
> Ours will be a secluded refuge
> Under these thick elm trees!
> I am tired of passionate emotion,
> But I am calmed by the proximity of my loved one,
> With the impatience of passionate desires:
> We damage happiness,
> And cut short pleasure.

The intellectual questioning of the basis for emotions is clearly an issue that Baratynsky continues to express throughout all of his elegies. A touching example of 1828, "Net, obmanula vas molva" (No, rumor has deceived you), returns to the theme of the deceit of passions, but this time on a more intimate level. Written to a married woman whom Baratynsky adored, this short work reiterates his love and respect for her. It ends, however, on a note of renunciation: he will turn to new ideas with the ardor of a religious convert. This newfound devotion, moreover, is rooted solely in the negation of the original passion itself.

In his elegies Baratynsky did not manage to resolve the conflicts he explored. Other genres, such as the epistle and the *poésie légère,* give the reader further clues with which to decipher the ever-changing tactics he used in his attempts to settle the issue, while at the same time setting the stage for Baratynsky's ultimate effort—his rarely understood long poems.

The epistle was a genre favored by those in the Arzamas group and by those poets who in general practiced the art of *poésie légère* as it was inherited from the French Classicists. Among the poets who adhered to this style were Pushkin, Petr Andreevich Viazemsky, Nikolai Mikhailovich Iazykov, Del'vig, and Baratynsky. Despite the tradition of the genre for expressing friendly and personal topics, it was modified by Baratynsky, just as was the elegy, in his quest to tackle ever more profound concerns. Therefore, not surprisingly, as in the epistolary elegy "Del'vigu," the topic matter is often far more of a universal than of a strictly personal interest.

Baratynsky's first epistle, "K Krenitsynu" (To Krenitsin, 1819), is a traditional, somewhat naïve work. As Dees correctly points out, however, in it the reader first sees poetically expressed the opposites so consistently juxtaposed in Baratynsky's verse. Many of the poet's epistles have epicurean themes as well, representing the sensual delights that must be overcome through reason in order to attain true happiness. The other frequent motif seen in Baratynsky's epistles is the appearance of a trusted friend as the solution to the quandaries of life, love, and intellect. This trusted friend is always above the torments of earthly passion. Though the first two epistles to Capt. Nikolai Mikhailovich Konshin (written in 1820, published in 1821) mention this particular solution, Baratynsky nonetheless does not continue any further with the idea in his later work.

One exception, which is entirely out of character when compared to the remainder of Baratynsky's output, is the second epistle to Gnedich, "G[nedich]u" (To G[nedich], written in 1823, published in 1826). This poem marks a rare occasion when Baratynsky addressed the literary debates raging at the time. Gnedich had called for poets to write socially edifying satires; in the poem the narrator chooses not to do so, mainly because of an ungrateful public. This theme, expressed in this poem in the traditional mode of French Classical epistolary works, is repeated with a twist in "Bogdanovichu" (To Bogdanovich, 1824). In this poem, however, Baratynsky rushes to the defense of elegiac poetry, criticized by Kiukhel'beker in that same year. Whereas Kiukhel'beker saw only languid melancholy, Baratynsky witnesses for and defends the talent of the new generation of poets in addition to himself: Batiushkov, Zhukovsky, and Pushkin.

The "smes'" (mixture), a section of poetry in Baratynsky's first published collection of 1827, was meant to be a grab bag of genres and ideas. The first collection of poems was divided into three formal parts: elegies, the "smes'," and the epistles. The poetry in the "smes'" ranges from verse written on the spur of the moment (occasional verse) to works virtually elegiac in their melancholy. Two of the most interesting lyrics are "Zhelan'e schastiia v menia vdokhnuli bogi" (The gods instilled in me the desire of happiness, 1823), and "V dorogu zhizni snariazhaia" (On the road of life equipped, 1825). The first work reiterates a theme discussed above: humankind (represented in the poem by the poet) is a Promethean caught between heaven and earth. He has the knowledge of bliss but must come to the same decision of acceptance as Prometheus. The second work again deals with the conflicts and contradictions of life itself. Finally, a third short poem, "Kak mnogo ty v nemnogo dnei" (How much you in few days, 1824–1825), addresses the specific enchantments of Agrafena Fedorovna Zakrevskaia, the wife of Gen. Arsenii Andreevich Zakrevsky. Baratynsky fell in love with her, and she became an embodiment of much of his questioning about the disparate roles of passion and reason. Baratynsky had met the general's wife after his transfer to Zakrevsky's headquarters in Helsinki. Baratynsky had been pointed out to Zakrevsky earlier. Through the supplication of his new friend, Nikolai Vasil'evich Putiata, Baratynsky secured the transfer in the spring of 1824. Zakrevskaia then became a source of infatuation for the poet. Just as he had written in his verse, however, the conflict between passion and reason was perpetual, never to be resolved. Only in 1825 did Baratynsky escape his dilemma. Primarily on account of Zhukovsky's intercession on his behalf at the Imperial Court in St. Petersburg, Baratynsky was promoted and permitted to leave Finland. Shortly thereafter he married Anastasiia L'vovna Engel'gardt and settled in Moscow.

In Moscow, Baratynsky came to know the members of the *Liubomudry* (Lovers of Wisdom). It was a circle of writers whose views were quite different from the French Classical leanings of the St. Petersburg poets. Instead of turning to the French tradition, these writers looked toward the philosophers of German Romanticism such as Schelling and Friedrich von Schlegel. This group later became increasingly Slavophile, opposing various Western European influences, primarily the commercial ones, on Russia's national character.

Within this circle was Ivan Vasil'evich Kireevsky, who personally tutored Baratynsky in German idealist thought. For Kireevsky, Johann Wolfgang von Goethe exemplified the striving of pure philosophical genius to which the Romantic philosophers who gathered under the banner of the *Liubomudry* were to seek inspiration. Goethe's influence in Russia was more ideological and philosophical than artistic. The change from Byronic inspiration to Faustian philosophical ruminations signaled a modification of Romantic aesthetics. Creation by inspiration alone, long the credo of pure Romanticism, became seen as futile if it were not coupled with a philosophical striving.

Baratynsky inherited this particular mandate from the poetical philosophies of German idealism. There is proof that Baratynsky had been exposed to German philosophy while still in the Pages Corps, probably from readings of Aleksandr Ivanovich Galich, who propagated distilled Schellingian notions for a Russian academic audience. One of the prime tenets of German Romantic philosophy was the equation of poetry to an all-encompassing absolute that embodied the ideal and the real. Poetry itself, at least in its purest essence, was the solution to the questions asked so consistently by Baratynsky—questions about life and death and the apparent futility of life. Both Pushkin and Baratynsky attempted to redefine poetry in that way through the comparatively new genre of the long poem, which had a primarily philosophical basis. In addition to being fundamentally Romantic in nature, this genre provided for a fusion of the ideal of verse and the reality of a narrative plotline. Pushkin's most famous effort in this vein has become his best-known work, *Evgeny Onegin* (Eugene Onegin, written in 1823, published in 1830). In the protagonist of the work, Onegin, Pushkin created a persona who took on a life of his own in Russian literature. As a result of this mythification of Onegin, Baratynsky was always at pains to explain that his own long poems were wholly different from his greater friend's creations. His attempts at finding a unique mode of expression within this new genre resulted in narrative poems considered failures by many critics: in fact, his popularity began to wane after the publication of *Bal* (The Ball, 1825-1828) and *Nalozhnitsa/Tsyganka* (The Concubine/The Gypsy Girl, written in 1829-1831, published in 1842), his final two verse tales. The publication of *Nalozhnitsa* prompted Baratynsky to reply in an essay titled "Antikritika" (Anticritique, 1831) to the critics who felt that the main protagonist of the poem was but an imitation of Onegin:

> It is impossible to reply to general judgments on a poem: everyone has his own taste, his own feelings, his own opinion. Only, finding similarities between

Title page for Baratynsky's Nalozhnitsa *(The Concubine), a verse tale*

Eletskoi and Onegin seems rather strange. Onegin is a disillusioned and satiated man; Eletskoi is passionate and romantic. Onegin has had his day; Eletskoi is only beginning to live. Onegin is lacking because of an emptiness of the heart; he believes that nothing will be able to interest it again. Eletskoi is lacking because of insufficient nourishment for it, and not because of an inability to feel. He is still full of hope; he still believes in happiness and seeks it out. Onegin is immobile; Eletskoi is moving forward.

Despite their apparent aesthetic failure, Baratynsky's verse tales were nonetheless conscious efforts at the creation of a new type of poetry. Though Baratynsky professed a lack of interest in German metaphysics, the reader should not conclude that Baratynsky did not deliberately apply Romantic philosophy to his works. The use of a feminine ideal—as represented in a desirable, pure woman—was a contemporary trope. The particular development of this same trope in Baratynsky's long poems was a continuous progression, which was reflected in narrative poems themselves resulting from the philosophical influences of the time. This was the period during Baratynsky's career when he received the personal tutelage of Kireevsky in German Romantic thought.

Not surprisingly, then, Baratynsky's long poems are among the most philosophical expressions, in a Romantic sense, of his body of works and carry his existential ruminations to the limits permitted by poetic structure. Certainly, his late poems continued to develop the main themes encountered in his elegies, for example, but these themes were never incorporated so fully into a poetic tapestry as in his long poems. Despite their philosophical inclinations, or perhaps as a result of these tendencies, they did not meet with success. Many of the most vocal and prominent critics, such as Vissarion Grigor'evich Belinsky, harshly censured them.

Long poems can be either narrative or simply longer lyric works. Among the latter, Baratynsky's first attempt was "Otryvki iz poemy 'Vospominaniia'" (Fragments from the Poem "Reminiscences," 1819). This work is a translation and adaptation of a poem by Gabriel-Marie-Jean-Baptiste Legouvé titled "Les souvenirs, ou les avantages de la mèmoire" (The Recollections, or The Advantages of Memory). In it the reader can discern Baratynsky's usual concerns: "the vanity and futility of life and its pleasures, as opposed to the quiet happiness of rural resignation."

Piry (Feasts, written in 1820, published in 1832) is really a paean to the poet's role in fusing the reality of the flesh with the desires of the mind and is reminiscent of Gavriil Romanovich Derzhavin's "Priglashenie k obedu" (Invitation to Dinner, 1795). *Telema i Makar* (Telema and Makar, 1826) is a free readaptation of Voltaire's *Télèma et Macare* (1764) in which Baratynsky abandons the moralistic ending. *Pereselenie dush* (The Transmigration of Souls, 1828) is a story of love set in ancient Egypt, spiced with references to Egyptian mythology. The first stanza of *Piry* sets out the poet's philosophy:

> My friends! I saw the world,
> Looked at everything with a true eye.
> My soul was full of vanity,
> And for a long time I swam with the general current . . .
> My debt to madness is paid,
> My gaze has cleared somewhat,
> But, like Solomon the Wise,
> I do not say everything in the world is a dream!

The poet concludes the stanza by stating that his stomach has never deceived him. This ending charts the dynamics of the poem as a whole. But the poet is speaking ironically: he speaks of his stomach because it was during feasts and meals that he enjoyed the acquaintanceship of his friends:

> We, those with a heart in a different age,
> Come together with a friendly crowd
> Under the peaceful roof of the home canopy:
> You, true to me, you my D[el'vi]g,
> My brother by muse and laziness;
> You, our P[ushki]n, to whom is given
> To sing of heroes and of wine,
> And of the passion of ardent youth,
> Is given with mischievous intellect
> To be a veritable expert of the heart
> And the best guest for a bottle.

Now, however, he can only reminisce about his gregarious past:

> And where is the traitress-love?
> O, in her both sadness and charm!
> I would like to feel anew
> Her known passion!
> And where are you, playful friends,
> You by whom lived my soul!

The feasts remain the poet's link to his youth and promise its return. Baratynsky's particular mixture of gaiety and melancholy earned him the name *poet pirov* (the poet of feasts) by Pushkin. On the surface the work appears to be a rejection of Romantic idealism in its basic form; yet, the poet still praises the genius of his writer friends. Although his stomach and the finite of food remain the connecting link, the poet misses the passions and energy present in his circle. He is confined instead to his finite, living an infinite created in his mind and in the text by reviving the spirit of his past feasts textually through active narration and poetic apostrophe, much like the expression that the lot of humankind is to be caught between heaven and earth.

The thematics of *Telema i Makar* are allegorical: Telema in a fit of anger loses Makar, whose departure she immediately regrets; hence, she searches the country for him. As a Romantic female protagonist she is completely objectified by the men who dominate her existence, as she lives entirely for Makar: "I'll find him, my father, / Don't worry about that. / No, I do not long / In vain for dear Makar; / I alone grant him life; / He cannot be in that world, / While I exist in this one!" She cannot find him, however, and returns home, where he is sitting, waiting for her. Telema had lost her love originally because she had attempted to assert herself. The result of the episode is Makar's formal empowering of his own position over Telema:

> "With me in peace and love,"
> He said, "from this time on live;
> Live, don't worry about the superfluous,
> And if you do not wish again
> To part from me, with a quiet temper
> I give you my friendship,

From my indulgence
Do not demand more
Than I give, than I can give you.

The work ends with a fully objectified woman living in a finite world (her reality controlled by Makar) with her love—*zhivi* (live!)! Happiness is only possible upon the denial of individuality and the related striving for knowledge.

Pereselenie dush is more complex than either *Piry* or *Telema i Makar*. The main vehicle for the expression of Romantic idealism in this work is the Princess Zoraida, who must choose and marry a suitor from guests present at a feast. She does not want any of them, whom she judges to be self-satisfied in their luxurious vulgarity: "Kak glupy eti dikari, / Raznoplemennye tsari!" (How stupid are these barbarians, / Tsars of different races!); rather she wants a musician who sang at the feast for the suitors. Not aware of how to proceed, the princess speaks with a renowned sage who knows the wisdom of the ages. He gives Zoraida a magical ring, which permits souls to change bodies. She switches souls with her maid, thereby permitting both to achieve what they desire; the maid wants to be royalty, and the princess, now perceived as a commoner, can marry the musician. The escape from the paradoxes of existence is present both in the symbolism of the ring as a token of marital union and in the knowledge/magic from the infinite that allows the souls to escape from their earthly confines into their desires. The poem, moreover, was inspired by a personal development in Baratynsky's life—his marriage. Thus, the artistic power of creation helps the narrator and the author achieve the absolute (access to ultimate knowledge and the resolution of life's contradictions) under the guise of love: "You appeared, my priceless friend, / And my life cleared up."

In *Pereselenie dush* the absolute is achievable. This is not the case, however, in the three major long poems that Baratynsky wrote. These poems can be categorized as Romantic narrative poems in all senses of the word *romantic*. In them Baratynsky strove to create a new mode of poetry that, through its mere existence, will provide the philosophical answers to the contradictions he expressed in his elegies and that were only resolved through denial in *Telema i Makar* and through magic in *Pereselenie dush*. These poems include *Eda* (Eda, written in 1824–1825, published in 1832), as well as *Bal* and *Tsyganka*.

Eda was Baratynsky's first attempt at what he labeled an "ultra-Romantic" poem. Set in the Finnish wilderness, where he was stationed at the time of its writing, it describes the story of a naïve young Finnish girl and her love for a Russian garrison soldier sta-

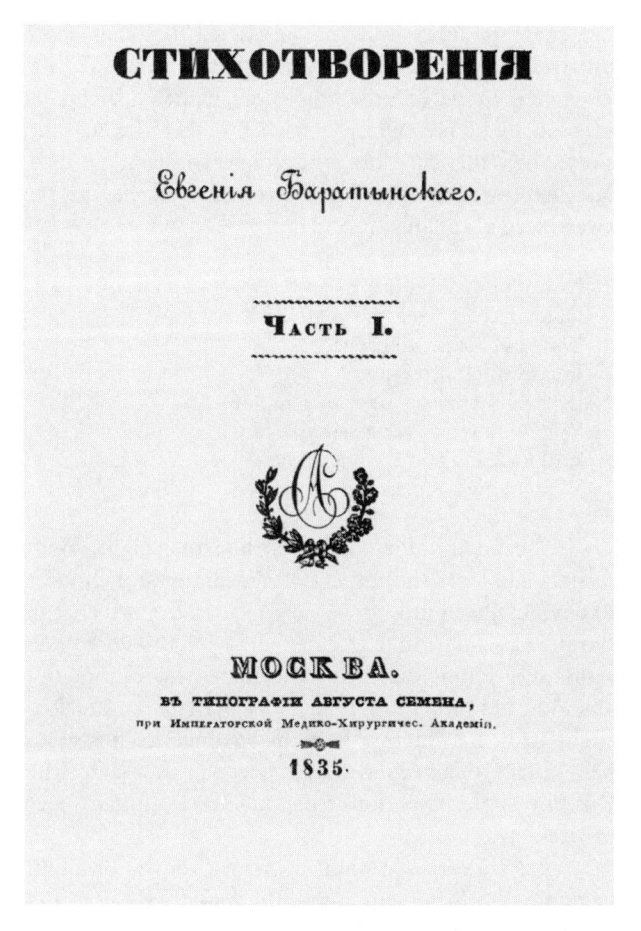

Title page for Baratynsky's second poetry collection, which was negatively received by critics

tioned in her vicinity. When the poem opens, she is described in Rousseauesque terms as at peace with herself and her Ossianic surroundings:

Up to now in this happy backwoods,
The simple daughter of a simple father,
With her beauty of face and with her beauty of soul,
Young Eda shone.
There was no one more beautiful in the mountains:
A tender flush on her cheeks,
A floating figure, golden hair
In careless curls upon her shoulders,
And pale-blue eyes,
Like the Finnish skies.

She is a "deva spokoina i iasna" (quiet and clear girl). Baratynsky re-creates a typical Romantic dream—the happy, simple peasant. This peasant is as much in communion with the ideal as the artist could ever be through his or her work of art. Foreboding is first expressed in the poem through nature—the "teplyi veterok" (warm breeze) will soon give way to the "khlad surovyi" and "mertviaschii" (bitter and deathly cold). She progressively loses her sense of unity with nature as she becomes more involved in her love affair with the soldier. Eventually she loses her connection to wholeness entirely, becoming plagued by desire, which robs her of her dreams and sleep. She is therefore losing her connection with the absolute, expressed so often in Baratynsky's elegies as the sweet sleep of resignation and death:

> Now, your soul is full
> Of anxiety for your vague desire,
> You won't close your eyes
> In refreshing drowsiness;
> Dreams previously unknown to you
> Will fly down to your bed of dreams,
> And for a long time your hot bed
> Will not give you sleep.

She finally gives herself to him one night. With this act she loses the respect of her family and chooses to devote herself fully to her lover—a recurrent theme in Baratynsky's narrative poems. The woman attempts to rediscover happiness through a man who cannot but abandon her; for though she was perhaps an ideal to begin with, his interest fades away once he possesses her. In fact, this sequence does occur in the poem; the Russian soldier abandons Eda, and she eventually dies of grief.

Bal addresses a similar theme from a different beginning. Critics assume that the main heroine in the work, Princess Nina, is modeled after Zakrevskaia. This assumption is accurate to a limited degree. The work, which has a circular plot, begins with the penultimate scene, when Princess Nina, a married woman, is seen fainting at a ball. An extended flashback then provides the reader with a picture of a woman, fatally attractive but with no soul behind her beauty:

> How in the close conversations of the heart
> She was captivating!
> How pleasingly tender!
> In her glances what affection
> Shone! But at times,
> Flaming in jealous anger,
> How evil in words and frightening to herself
> Was the new Medea!

Though typecast as lethal to men, she nonetheless attracts a young man named Arsenii. They carry on a fairly discreet affair behind the back of Nina's husband, who is portrayed as businesslike and cold-hearted in his dealings with his wife. His behavior makes it easier for the reader to accept that such a worldly woman as Nina should give herself so totally to a young Byronic man such as Arsenii. His Byronic aspect is true to the core: he carries the memory of a long-lost childhood love, Ol'ga. Ol'ga reappears, causing Arsenii to leave Nina and to write her a farewell letter that devastates her. In an attempt to exact revenge she withdraws entirely into her physical self. She looks at herself disembodied in a mirror, where she is reflected as but a parody of her true self and of her true physicality. The parody of physicality to which she has been reduced will avenge her lost love. Nina objectifies herself fully as a male object. She sees herself in comparison to Arsenii's new ideal of beauty, so that Ol'ga, fully possessed by her lover, will be able to mock her: "Really, I will quietly suffer / As, triumphing over me, / Her blooming beauty / With my withered beauty / She mockingly compares!" She faints, however, at the ball given in honor of Arsenii and Ol'ga. Then she rushes home and commits suicide. The moral of the story is provided by her nurse, who enters the room to find her body. In *Bal,* in contrast to *Eda,* Baratynsky provides a solution to the Romantic's quandary of how to attain the infinite in a finite existence. The nurse explains that Nina's error was that she forgot the real infinite—God, who would have protected her finite (her flesh) as well as her "dukh" (spirit): "You forgot God. . . . Yes / You never go to church: / Believe, whoever abandons God / Him God also abandons; / He governs over our soul / He guards our flesh!" The finitude of reality closes the poem with references to death and the gossip of the capital. The verses themselves end up on the pages of women's journals ("damskie zhurnaly"), again emphasizing the loss of any hope of transcending the limitations of earthly passions.

Tsyganka, originally published as *Nalozhnitsa* (Concubine—a title that many critics of the time found offensive), again grapples with similar themes. In this work is found the formal Romantic ideal of poetry—a combination of dramatic and novelistic features such as chapter divisions and direct dialogue. Thematically, the work reveals Baratynsky's ability to represent, as Kjetsaa says, the "light" and "dark" of reality. The poem was a fully conscious endeavor: Baratynsky felt that it was the culmination of his efforts at the creation of the new form of poetry demanded by Romantic philosophy. He added a lengthy foreword to the first edition of *Nalozhnitsa* in which he maintained that in order to create real art, the poet has the right, even the duty, to portray both the good and the bad in life. This foreword recalls the derivative philosophy of Jean Pierre Frederic Ancillon, an expounder of simplified Schellingian thought in the same vein as Galich's. Duality, central to the Romantic paradox of infinite and finite, inspired this new poem, and in it Baratynsky attempted to create a hero who strives, through love, to achieve an ideal state of awareness and bliss. In *Tsyganka* the main hero, Eletskoi, is in a relationship with a gypsy woman named Sara. He chose to live with her as much presumably because he loved her as because he wanted to shock the morals of proper society. Yet his relationship has become hollow to him. As in the paradigms of Baratynsky's elegiac lyrics, the vanities of sensual existence no longer mean anything. Eletskoi sees a woman in a crowd who appears to him to be his ideal. This woman, Vera, a woman of high society, seems unapproachable; but eventually, through some cunning, Eletskoi does meet her and convinces her to flee with him. She makes this decision in the peculiar state in which the poet of Baratynsky's elegies so often finds himself: between heaven and earth, "ni vo sne ni naiavu" (neither in a dream nor in reality). The promise of infinitude has been made, but it is the absolute within the finite of existence. Sara, the representation of Eletskoi's all-too-earthly reality, will not be shunted aside so easily. She is questing for answers to life's quandaries as well, and she feels that she had found those answers in the pleasures of life with Eletskoi. She calls upon an old gypsy woman for magical help. The old woman gives Sara a decanter that contains a potion intended to make Eletskoi love none but her. The potion is in fact poison (a deus ex machina that perplexed critics at the time) and is the semantic opposite of the magical transformations of *Pereselenie dush*. The magic does not attain the desired absolute. Rather, Eletskoi faces the inevitable end—death in Sara's arms. Sara's life is ruined (she goes insane), and Vera is left waiting in a snowstorm for the man who has become her reason for life.

Baratynsky's works progress chronologically in their philosophical complexity. In *Eda* the quest for Romantic ideals is located in the Finnish mountains and told in a toned-down Byronic manner. Eda's fate is tied to the Hussar who conquers her: having surrendered to male control and having been rendered sexual and finite, she dies. In *Bal* the level of complexity increases. Now it is Nina who represents the dangers of female sexuality and yet at the same time objectifies herself fully to her adulterer in the quest for true love. This love is her absolute, but it is not her lover's. He finds his absolute in Ol'ga and thereby destroys Nina. The dynamics of gender control are thus rendered more complex, for *Bal* is not the story of a fall from innocence; rather it is the story of a person who attempts to re-create it as a poet does a poem—through passion.

In *Tsyganka* Baratynsky reaches a level of philosophical complexity comparable to his better-known elegies. The male who quests for female completion is destroyed by the very finite woman with whom he has shared part of his life. Sara attempts to safeguard her passion. Vera is destroyed by having been abandoned in a state between heaven and earth—knowing of the

Evgenii Abramovich Baratynsky (after a portrait by Zh. Viv'en)

happiness she will feel but never attaining it. The ruin of all the protagonists is ensured. Baratynsky creates through his long poem living testimonies to Romantic philosophy. As Baratynsky himself explained in his forward to *Nalozhnitsa*:

> "That which is true, is moral," says the author of the foreword. "No," answers the critic, "that which is elegant is moral"; what is the point? The point is the following: in connection with morality, both formulae are synonymous—except that one embraces all of literature whereas the other only few literary works; except that the former goes straight to the heart of the matter, but the second demands explanation.

Baratynsky's narrative poems pushed the tenets of Romantic philosophy to their limits. The genre could only be developed further by transcending them, something that Baratynsky was not to do but that Pushkin accomplished in his *Evgeny Onegin*. Instead, Baratynsky chose to return to the genre of the shorter lyric verse. He did write one prose work, generally not discussed in scholarly literature. But his long poems had shattered his reputation, and by the publication of *Tsyganka,* the time for poetry in Russia had passed. Gogol, Dostoyevsky, and soon Tolstoy were already heralding the age of the Russian Realistic novel.

Baratynsky's renewed interest in shorter lyrical verse signaled a return, to some degree at least, to his pre-Schellingian notions of poetry. In some respects, it was a nostalgic reversion to his St. Petersburg literary connections and to the French Classical poetry on which his poetry had been based. Yet the exposure to German Romantic thought and to the literary circles of Moscow centered on Kireevsky had left their marks as well. Thus, Baratynsky's famous duality and his exploration of paradox took on new forms within his favored genre. There is a consistent exploration, even in his earliest work, of the relative value of passions and poetry as compared to the mundane and the prosaic. "Kogda, pechal'iu vdokhnovennyi" (When, inspired by sadness, 1826) reveals the early manifestations of this particular line of German Romantic thought. In it Baratynsky claims that those who are not inspired by sadness, for example, are reduced to being ridiculous with their "zhemannoe vyt'e" (affected howl). Only the true poet can express true feelings.

These feelings, however, are sometimes focused on the future fate of humankind. "Posledniaia smert'" (The Last Death, 1827) reveals the continuing influence of German philosophy at this stage in Baratynsky's creation. In this work the poet has access to that realm between being and non-being, between reality and unconsciousness—the same realm of viewing the absolute in which Vera Volkhovskaia makes her final decision to flee with Eletskoi in *Tsyganka*. In this state of exalted poetic vision, whose source he cannot discern, the poet witnesses the end of life: "And finally I saw, without a veil / The final fate of every living thing." In the future, he says, reason will overwhelm everything natural. Yet even further into the future, the poet witnesses a human populace receding into intellectuality, neglecting the physical, producing no offspring. The final vision is a horrific sight of starving animals and of humankind in its grave. In the end, however, nature regains control of the earth, replacing the void, both literally through fog and metaphorically through the sun. Yet there are no longer any humans left. Reason, in the Schellingian perception, can only lead to the death of the natural. Despite this outcome, the natural in itself will eventually win—hence the continuing paradox of Baratynsky's poetry. This poem is remarkable in its foreshadowing of later Romantic tales of apocalypse, notably of Vladimir Fedorovich Odoevsky's fantastic tales.

"Smert'" (Death, 1828) also attempts to deal with the issue of the finality of death. The work is written in an archaistic style, much of which is rather uncommon in literary Russian. In this poem death is not viewed as negative but rather as an inevitable condition of existence affecting all living things. The poet views death as a maiden who brings peace (*smert'*, or "death," is feminine in Russian). The maiden brings death to all, regardless of their station in life. The notion of the absolute, a fusion of peace and unity of all knowledge, is present in the final couplet: "You are the solution of all puzzles, / You are the deliverance from all chains." The same themes are also present in "Iz A. Shen'e" (From A. Chénier, 1828). In contrast to the earlier poem, although the poet sees death as inevitable, he confesses that the grave and its finality are frightening.

Baratynsky does not give up hope in the power of art to solve his existential crisis, however. Not surprisingly, the later "Ne podrazhai: svoeobrazen genii" (Do not imitate, genius is original, 1828) explains the importance of the artist. In it Baratynsky claims that Shakespeare has no double, that Byron and Mickiewicz are, as poets, gods. This primacy of the original artist (whose "genius," in German Romantic parlance, is unique and is the creator of art with its inspiration) is seen again in another short lyric of 1829, "Chudnyi grad poroi sol'etsia" (At times a wonderful city arises), in which a city emerges from the clouds and vanishes without a trace; this occurrence provides an analogy to the heights of poetic creation, which exist equally momentarily.

Yet Baratynsky was to return again to his existential questioning and to the role of death in existence. In "Otryvok" (Fragment, 1829) he turns toward religious belief as a solution. The poem is structured as a dialogue between *on* (he) and *ona* (she). The male (presumably the poet) turns to the heavens for answers to the problems he faces with existence. The solution is life after death, but the very concept of death is paralyzing. Death, or more precisely life after death, offers the solution of peace and tranquility. The work ends pessimistically: perhaps, she thinks, the whole exercise is only worthwhile to those who believe and have faith beforehand. Thus, the conclusion of the poem questions the solution religion provides.

Even in the realm of the fantastic, Baratynsky sees the human spirit as chained by its own consciousness. "Poroiu laskovuiu feiu" (At times an affectionate fairy, 1829) deals with the crossover of human fate into the realm of the dream, where the poet sees the fairy. Happiness is unachievable in the dream, as the fetters of human consciousness are transposed even there.

In "V dni bezgranichnykh uvlechenii" (In the days of limitless passions, 1831) Baratynsky constructs a lyric poem that is split into two parts. The first contrasts the passion of youth with the measured lyric beauty the poet carries within him. The second part ends the poem with a reiteration of the overall dominance of the Schellingian notion of eternal poetic beauty over the chaos of life. (Poetry in this notion embodies the absolute.)

Despite Baratynsky's belief in poetry, the final poem in his 1835 collection of verse (which had been negatively received and which Baratynsky thought was to be his final collection of poetry), "Byvalo, otrok, zvonkim klikom" (It was, as a youth, with a resounding call, 1831), ends on a pessimistic note: the poet will abandon poetry. Poetry is originally compared to nature (a Schellingian approach); yet in the final analysis, it loses its appeal: "But all passes by. I am getting cold / Both to the harmony of verse– / And as I don't call to oak groves, / So I do not seek harmonious words." Clearly Baratynsky was not able to resolve the conflict between reason and emotion through the catalyst of Romantic philosophy. It is curious to read Baratynsky's two epistles to Iazykov in this context– "N. M. Iazykovu" (To N. M. Iazykov, 1831) and "Iazykovu" (To Iazykov, 1831). Iazykov's most successful verse was Anacreontic, and Baratynsky is not able to accept that fact without adding that Iazykov will eventually turn to a more refined muse.

Del'vig's death in 1831 severed Baratynsky's last direct link to his beloved St. Petersburg group of poets. Though he sought new inspiration through the philosophical debates of the *Liubomudry,* the decline of his popularity only increased with his growing artistic isolation. In 1832 Baratynsky began to collaborate with Kireevsky on a new periodical named *Evropeets* (The European). This journal espoused the notion that Russia had to surpass Western Europe in spiritual growth through a rejection of West European materialism. The paper, however, was closed down almost immediately by the government. Baratynsky's work continued to reflect his growing involvement with Kireevsky nonetheless.

The German Romantic notion of all-embracing poetic creation returns in Baratynsky's "Kogda ischeznet omrachen'e" (When will the darkness disappear, 1832) and "Boliashchii dukh vrachuet pesnopen'e" (Poesy heals the ailing soul, 1832). In the first poem the return of philosophy is not without an element of transformation, for while the poet is aware that poetry will make the darkness vanish and illuminate the day, he is seized by a demon who will not allow him to create. The poet is buried alive, unable to resolve his conflict. In the second work, however, the poet's soul, through poetry, is able to ascend through poetic harmony to communion with the absolute. In "Na smert' Gete" (On the Death of Goethe, 1832), Baratynsky continues his exploration of poetic harmony. Of Baratynsky's poetry written during this period, this work was the best received. In the poem Goethe, who exemplified the quintessential German thinker to the *Liubomudry,* is seen as having explored every possibility in life. His only artistic limitation was the limitless, or so Baratynsky proclaims. Nonetheless, finality awaits him in the grave, even though his role in life has been fulfilled through his art.

In "K chemu nevol'niku mechtaniia svobody?" (To what end are dreams of freedom to a slave? 1832) limitation and its basis in life are progressively transposed from the slave of the first line to a river caught within its banks, and on to a fir tree existing on the spot where it was born, to heavenly bodies moving by laws imposed on them, and finally to the wind, itself governed by the laws of nature. In the final lines the poet returns to the human portion of the equation; yet he cannot reconcile the paradox. Life itself is caught within its own boundaries.

Death always returns in an untimely fashion. In "Zapustenie" (Desolation, 1832) Baratynsky wanders around the gardens of his home estate of Mara, now ill-kept and overgrown. The poem is at once a melancholy overview of the inevitable end and a celebration of life to come, for the poet compares autumn in the garden with its subsequent spring. The final section of the work is devoted to Baratynsky's father, whom the poet is not able to recall but who lives on in the garden in spirit. The elements of Romantic philosophy become apparent again: only after death are union and peace with nature and with existence itself achieved.

Baratynsky's final collection of poems, *Sumerki* (*Twilight*), named after a stream, the Sumer, which flowed through the estate of Muranovo, was published in 1842. It was hardly noticed at the time but included some of the poet's best and certainly most dejected verse. During the time in which these poems were written, Baratynsky helped the Kireevsky circle establish yet another journal, *Moskovskii nabliudatel'* (The Moscow Observer), which commenced publication in 1835. Shortly after this, however, Baratynsky ceased contributing. By this time, his association with the *Liubomudry* gathered about Kireevsky had waned, and Baratynsky lost all connections to literary life. His association with the Arzamas group of St. Petersburg had long since vanished, and his newer work with the philosophical group had fizzled away. Baratynsky retreated into his own world, and rumors of his alcoholism began to circulate. He was an embittered veteran of earlier literary trends, who along with Viazemsky had survived past his time. It comes as no surprise, then, that the first poem in this final collection was dedicated to the Prince himself. "Kniaziu Petru Andreevichu Viazemskomu" (To Prince Petr Andreevich Viazemsky, 1834) emphasizes Baratynsky's nostalgia for the traditions of the St.

Petersburg poetic circle. In it the poet falsely creates an air of acceptance and resignation; yet this is belied by the remainder of the cycle, particularly by the poem immediately following it.

"Poslednii poet" (The Last Poet, 1835) reflects once again the height of Baratynsky's interpretation of Romantic philosophy. The work was written at the peak of his involvement with the Kireevsky group. The poem portrays a society too preoccupied with material gain. Through its setting in Greece, the poem can explore the ramifications of pure practicality on the nature of poetry while implicitly endorsing the value of verse, for Greece, the cradle of the humanities, naturally provokes such an association in the reader's mind. Poetry is directly connected with nature, and humankind is abandoning nature. The last living poet declaims the virtues of Aphrodite and beauty to the masses who are imbued with science. They, however, scorn him, for his words lack rationality. The poet retires and meets the ghost of Sappho, whose appearance encourages him to drown himself and to drown with him his "bespoleznyi dar" (useless gift). Dees has noted that there is certainly an autobiographical element in this work. Baratynsky by this time had lost any popularity he had once had. The poet in the work, however, does not acquiesce to the new rule of reason but chooses death, where he can join eternally with others like him.

The following poem, "Nedonosok" (Stillborn, 1835), continues in an extremely cynical manner the themes that had occupied Baratynsky throughout his poetic career. In it, however, he extrapolates the pointlessness of earthly existence into a pointlessness of eternity—infinitely more terrifying. Written in the first person, the poem speaks from the point of view of a "krylatyi vzdokh" (winged sigh) caught for eternity between heaven and earth, though it can approach the heavens in good weather. The narrator in the final stanza reveals that it is the soul of a stillborn child, cheated out of its earthly life and thus unable to transcend it to a higher eternity.

Of all the poems in *Sumerki*, the most striking is certainly "Osen'" (Autumn, 1836–1837, 1841). Baratynsky in this poem compares the peasant who gathers his harvest in preparation for winter with the poet, who reaps only frustration and despair from his own labors. The desolation of winter allows no escape for the poet; in fact, the poem ends with the word "net" (no!). Once again, there is no escape for the poet or for his art; and as in "Poslednii poet," the material is destined to vanquish the poetic. The final poem in *Sumerki* is "Rifma" (Rhyme, 1840). Like "Poslednii poet," it is set in Greece. Yet in this work, poetry is seen as a source of solace. The poet is asked to decide for himself what importance his gift should have in modern society. It is rhyme, or in fact poetry, that is the answer.

After the publication of *Sumerki*, Baratynsky wrote relatively few poems. A few works deal with the poet's isolation and his distrust of his former literary companions. An example is the epigram "Kotterii" (To the Coterie, 1841), which was only published posthumously. In another poem, "Na posev lesa" (On the Planting of the Wood, 1842), also not published during the poet's lifetime, the poet views the bustle of a new spring with despair, feeling that his own gift can reap no harvest, as he had learned in "Poslednii poet." In the end he chooses to place the power of his poetry into the trees themselves, confident that in the future the gift will be appreciated. Thus, on much the same level of feeling as in "Zapustenie," Baratynsky places the notion of poetic spirit and knowledge with nature itself, avoiding the issues of broader existence by resorting to the quiet majesty of life itself in its undiluted essence.

In 1840 Baratynsky traveled to St. Petersburg, where he was able to meet old friends as well as make new acquaintances, including Mikhail Iur'evich Lermontov. The trip had a favorable effect on the disillusioned poet. He resolved to move back to the city after a planned trip to western Europe. That trip commenced in 1843, when he set out with his family for Paris, where they spent the winter of that year. He enjoyed great success in the Russian émigré community of the French capital. From France the family sailed to Naples in the spring of 1844. They had planned to return to Russia in the fall, but Baratynsky died in June. His death was little noticed in Russia.

Baratynsky's final poem, "Diadke-Ital'ianitsu" (To the Italian-Tutor, 1844), was written as an epistle to his Italian-born tutor, Borghese. The work provides a type of chronological unity in a loose amorphous sense to Baratynsky's life and the existential paradoxes he explored. It is suffused with a nostalgia for the past and a quest for *zabven'e* (oblivion). This is the oblivion that is reached by those heroes and heroines in the poet's long poems. In the end, it offers itself as the only peace.

Baratynsky's literary career is considered today to be one of the most important in the history of Russian literature. Had his work not been rediscovered by the Russian Symbolists, however, it might have remained half-forgotten, as it was at the time of his death. Prophetically, perhaps, the solution the poet proposed for the lack of appreciation of his work—to leave it to the future—was correct. Baratynsky was never able to reconcile the paradoxes of his own existence, preferring rather to raise these same puzzles to a universal level. He thus foreshadowed poetic developments that were to occur decades later and would in turn guarantee him a significant place in Russian poetry.

Letters:

Iurii Verkhovsky, *E. A. Baratynsky: materialy k ego biografii* (Petrograd: Tip. Imp. Akademii Nauk, 1916).

Biographies:

Mikhail Nikolaevich Longinov, "Baratynsky i ego sochineniia," *Russkii Arkhiv,* no. 2 (1867): 248–264;

Modest Liudvigovich Gofman, *E. A. Baratynsky: biograficheskii ocherk* (St. Petersburg, 1914);

Iurii Nikandrovich Verkhovsky, *E. A. Baratynsky: materialy k ego biografii* (Petrograd, 1916);

Pavel Antoninovich Stelliferovsky, *Evgenii Abramovich Baratynsky* (Moscow: Prosveshchenie, 1988);

Aleksei Mikhailovich Peskov, *Baratynsky: istinnaia povest', Pisateli o pisateliax* (Moscow: Kniga, 1990).

References:

L. Andreevskaia, "Poemy Baratynskogo," in *Russkaia poeziia XIX veka,* edited by Boris Mikhailovich Eikhenbaum and Iurii Nikolaevich Tynianov (Leningrad: Academia, 1929), pp. 74–102;

Sergei Arkad'evich Andreevsky, "E. A. Baratynsky," in *Filosofskie techeniia russkoi poezii,* compiled by P. Pertsov (Hildesheim: George Olms Verlag, 1978), pp. 89–98;

Glynn R. V. Barratt, *Selected Letters of Evgenij Baratynskij,* Slavistic Printings and Reprintings (The Hague: Mouton, 1973);

Luc Beaudoin, *Resetting the Margins: Russian Romantic Verse Tales and the Idealized Woman* (New York: Peter Lang, 1997);

Vissarion Grigor'evich Belinsky, *Vzgliad na russkuiu literaturu* (Moscow: Sovremennik, 1988);

Sergei Georgievich Bocharov, "Obrechen bor'be verkhovnoi . . . (liricheskii mir Baratynskogo)," *Kontekst: Literaturno-teoreticheskie issledovaniia* (1984): 96–143;

William Edward Brown, *A History of Russian Literature of the Romantic Period,* volume 3 (Ann Arbor, Mich.: Ardis, 1986);

Dora Burton, *Boratynskij: The Evolution of His Style and Poetic Themes* (Ann Arbor: University of Michigan Microfilms, 1975);

Benjamin Dees, *E. A. Baratynsky* (New York: Twayne, 1972);

Leonid Genriktovich Frizman, *Tvorcheskij put' Baratynskogo* (Moscow: Nauka, 1966);

Modest Liudvigovich Gofman, *Poeziia Boratynskogo* (Petrograd, 1915);

Geir Kjetsaa, *Evgenii Baratynsky: Zhizn' i tvorchestvo* (Oslo: Universitetsforlaget, 1973);

Vadim Liapunov, *Poet in the Middest: Studies in the Poetry of E. A. Baratynskij* (Ann Arbor: University of Michigan Microfilms, 1969);

Iurii Vladimirovich Mann, "Konflikt v romanticheskoj poeme Baratynskogo," *Izvestiia Akademii Nauk SSSR: Seriia literatury i iazyka* (Moscow, 1973), pp. 223–236;

Natalia Rostislavovna Mazepa, *E. A. Baratynsky: esteticheskie i literaturno-kriticheskie vzgliady* (Kiev: Izdatel'stvo Akademii Nauk Ukrainskoi SSR, 1960);

Nils Åke Nilsson, "Baratynskij's Elegiac Code," in *Russian Romanticism: Studies in the Poetic Codes,* edited by Nilsson, in *Stockholm Studies in Russian Literature,* 10 (Stockholm: Almqvist and Wiksell International, 1979), pp. 144–163;

Sarah Pratt, "Points of Contact: Two Russian Poets and Their Links to Schelling," *Germano-Slavica,* 4 (Spring 1982): 3–15;

Pratt, *Russian Metaphysical Romanticism: The Poetry of Tiutchev and Boratynskii* (Stanford, Cal.: Stanford University Press, 1984);

Andrea M. Sepich Rolich, "The Stanzaic Forms of K. N. Batjuškov and E. A. Baratynskij," dissertation, University of Wisconsin, 1981;

Irina Mikhailovna Semenko, "Baratynsky," in *Poety Pushkinskoi pory* (Moscow: Khudozhestvennaia literatura, 1970), pp. 221–291;

J. Thomas Shaw, *Baratynskii: A Dictionary of the Rhymes and a Concordance to the Poetry* (Madison: University of Wisconsin Press, 1975);

Iosif Markovich Toibin, "Poema Baratynskogo <Bal>," *Russkaia literatura,* no. 3 (1985): 118–132;

Toibin, "Poema Baratynskogo *Eda,*" *Russkaia literatura,* no. 2 (1963): 114–129;

Vadim Erazmovich Vatsuro, "Iz literaturnykh otnoshenii Baratynskogo," *Russkaia literatura,* no. 3 (1988): 153–163.

Papers:

Evgenii Baratynsky's papers are found in the Central State Archive of Literature and Art (TsGALI, fond 51), the Institute of Russian Literature of the Academy of Sciences of the Russian Federation, IRLI (Pushkin House), fond 33, and the Russian National Library, St. Petersburg (v. I, III, IV).

Konstantin Nikolaevich Batiushkov
(18 May 1787 – 7 July 1855)

Igor' A. Pil'shchikov
Moscow State University

and

T. Henry Fitt
Keele University

BOOKS: *Opyty v stikhakh i proze,* 2 volumes, edited by Nikolai Ivanovich Gnedich (St. Petersburg: N. Grech, 1817);

O grecheskoi antologii, by Batiushkov and Count Sergei Semenovich Uvarov, as A[khill] and St[arushka] (St. Petersburg: Tip. Dep. narodnogo prosveshcheniia, 1820);

Sochineniia v proze i stikhakh, second edition, 2 volumes (St. Petersburg: I. Glazunov, 1834);

Sochineniia Batiushkova, 2 volumes (St. Petersburg: A. Smirdin, 1850).

Editions and Collections: *Sochineniia K. N. Batiushkova,* 3 volumes, edited by Leonid Nikolaevich Maikov and Vladimir Ivanovich Saitov (St. Petersburg: V. S. Balashev, 1885–1887);

Sochineniia, fifth edition, edited by Maikov (St. Petersburg: [P. N. Batiushkov], 1887);

Stikhotvoreniia, edited by Aleksandr Nikolaevich Chudinov (St. Petersburg: I. Glazunov, 1906);

Sochineniia, edited by Dmitrii Dmitrievich Blagoi (Moscow-Leningrad: Academia, 1934);

Stikhotvoreniia, edited by Boris Viktorovich Tomashevsky and Irina Nikolaevna Medvedeva (Moscow: Sovetskii pisatel', 1936);

Stikhotvoreniia, edited by Boris Solomonovich Meilakh (Leningrad: Sovetskii pisatel', 1941);

Stikhotvoreniia, second edition, edited by Tomashevsky (Moscow-Leningrad: Sovetskii pisatel', 1948);

Stikhotvoreniia, edited by Nikolai Vladimirovich Fridman (Moscow: Goslitizdat, 1949);

Sochineniia, edited by Fridman (Moscow: Goslitizdat, 1955);

Stikhotvoreniia, third edition, edited by Georgii Panteleimonovich Makogonenko (Leningrad: Sovetskii pisatel', 1959);

Polnoe sobranie stikhotvorenii, edited by Fridman (Moscow-Leningrad: Sovetskii pisatel', 1964);

Opyty v stikhakh i proze, edited by Irina Mikhailovna Semenko (Moscow: Nauka, 1977);

Sochineniia, edited by Viktor Vasil'evich Gura and Viacheslav Anatol'evich Koshelev (Arkhangelsk: Severo-zapadnoe knizh. izd-vo, 1979);

Stikhotvoreniia, edited by D. P. Murav'ev (Moscow: Sovetskaia Rossiia, 1979);

Nechto o poete i poezii, edited by Koshelev (Moscow: Sovremennik, 1985);

Izbrannye sochineniia, edited by Andrei Leonidovich Zorin and others (Moscow: Pravda, 1986);

Izbrannaia proza, edited by Petr Georgievich Palamarchuk (Moscow: Sovetskaia Rossiia, 1987);

Opyty v stikhakh, edited by Nikita Glebovich Okhotin (Moscow: Kniga, 1987);

Stikhotvoreniia, edited by Igor' Olegovich Shaitanov (Moscow: Khudozhestvennaia literatura, 1987);

Sochineniia, 2 volumes, edited by Koshelev and Zorin (Moscow: Khudozhestvennaia literatura, 1989).

OTHER: Mikhail Nikitich Murav'ev, *Obitatel' predmestiia i Emilievy pis'ma. Sochinenie M. N. Murav'eva,* edited, with an introduction, by Batiushkov (St. Petersburg: Imperatorskaia Akademiia Nauk, 1815).

TRANSLATION: Platon Levshin, *Discours pour le couronnement de Sa Majesté l'Empereur de toutes les Russies Alexandre I. Prononce le 15 Septembre 1801 par Monseigneur Platon, Archevêque Metropolitaine de Moscou,* translated by Batiushkov (St. Petersburg: Platon Sokolov, 1801).

Konstantin Batiushkov–called the "Russian Tibullus" and the "Russian Parny" by his contemporaries–was a poet whose work largely determined the evolution of Russian poetry in the Golden Age. For contemporary as well as later critics, Batiushkov and Vasilii Andreevich Zhukovsky were the founders of a new school in Russian poetry that is usually defined as Romantic or pre-Romantic. Most of Batiushkov's poems, published during the mid 1800s and 1810s, were collected in the second volume of *Opyty v stikhakh i proze* (Experiments in Verse and Prose, 1817). General audiences were perhaps less impressed by Batiushkov's poetry than Zhukovsky's, but the former's influence on the younger generation of poets was extraordinary; in this sense Batiushkov could be called "a poet's poet."

Evgenii Abramovich Baratynsky, Kondratii Fedorovich Ryleev, and, to a large degree, Aleksandr Pushkin began their careers as imitators of Batiushkov. He not only created models of several important genres of the new poetry but also was the first to begin blurring genre boundaries in his lyrics (a tendency that was later an essential feature of Russian Romantic poetry). Although the formal "date of birth" of the Russian Romantic elegy is 1802 (with the work of Zhukovsky and Andrei Ivanovich Turgenev), Batiushkov's later elegies were what inspired the elegiac breakthrough in Russia in the mid 1810s. The most influential of his "friendly" epistles (as opposed to his "didactic" ones), "Moi Penaty" (My Penates, 1811), inspired a plethora of poetic replies and imitations. His free translations of Greek epigrams, published in *O grecheskoi antologii* (On the Greek Anthology, written with Count Sergei Semenovich Uvarov, 1820), showed a highly original approach to the classical heritage and established the Russian anthological genre. Unfortunately, Batiushkov's creative life was finished long before his death; he became mentally ill in the early 1820s and after 1822 was considered, to use critic Vissarion Grigor'evich Belinsky's words, "as if dead."

Konstantin Nikolaevich Batiushkov was the son of Nikolai L'vovich Batiushkov and Aleksandra Grigor'evna Batiushkova (née Berdiaeva); both parents belonged to the old nobility. Konstantin had three older sisters (Aleksandra, Elizaveta, and Anna) and one younger (Varvara). His father also had children by his second wife, Avdot'ia Tegleva, one of whom, Pompei Nikolaevich Batiushkov, later oversaw the publication of Konstantin's biography and collected works (1885–1887), edited by a leading academician, Leonid Nikolaevich Maikov. Family tradition spoke of Nikolai as a "nobleman out of imperial favour." His career difficulties could be explained by the unfavorable attitude of Catherine II, caused by his involvement in the affair of his uncle, who was exiled in 1770 for his opposition to the empress. From 1767 (or possibly 1764) to 1777 Nikolai was in the army. In 1781 he was appointed a procurator of the court in the civil service: at first in Velikii Ustiug, and later in Yaroslavl, Vologda (1786–1791), and Viatka. Konstantin was born in Vologda on 18 May 1787. The Batiushkov family's circumstances were complicated by financial difficulties and were made even worse when the poet's mother, Aleksandra, became mentally ill (apparently circa 1793, but not before, as a later family tradition supposed). Nikolai was obliged to take her to St. Petersburg, where she died on 21 March 1795.

The early years of Konstantin Batiushkov's life are difficult to reconstruct. He probably spent the first four years of his life in Vologda; the exact place he lived from 1792 to 1796 is unknown. Possibly he lived with his father (first in Viatka, and then in St. Petersburg) or possibly with his grandfather, Lev Andreevich Batiushkov, on their family estate, the village of Danilovskoe, Bezhetski district, Tver' province. However, Batiushkov's youth spent in St. Petersburg, however, played the most important part in his development as a poet.

Batiushkov's earliest extant letter from St. Petersburg is dated 6 July 1797. His first years there were spent in *pensionnats* (private boarding schools). Contact with his relatives was restricted to correspondence and rare meetings. From 1797 to 1800 he studied at the *pen-*

Self-portrait by Batiushkov, 1807 (from the 1977 edition of his Opyty v stikhakh i proze *[Experiments in Verse and Prose])*

sionnat directed by a Frenchman, Osip Petrovich Jacquinot; it was a rather expensive school for children of good families. Most subjects were taught in French, and the curriculum included French, Russian, German, divinity, geography, history, statistics, arithmetic, chemistry, botany, calligraphy, drawing, and dancing. In 1801 Batiushkov entered the *pensionnat* run by an Italian, Ivan Antonovich Tripoli; he graduated in 1802. Here Batiushkov began to study Italian. His first literary offering, however, was a translation into French of Moscow metropolitan Platon Levshin's address on the occasion of the coronation of Alexander I; in the fall of 1801 it was published as a separate pamphlet by Platon Sokolov, an acquaintance of the author's father.

Scholars conventionally consider 1802 as the beginning of Batiushkov's poetic career. He wrote in a letter to Nikolai Ivanovich Gnedich on 1 April 1810 that he had composed his first poem at the age of fifteen; he felt that its main idea—dissatisfaction with reality and a longing for "distant lands," both geographic and spiritual—anticipated his mature work. When he graduated from the *pensionnat,* he moved in with his father's cousin Mikhail Nikitich Murav'ev and his wife, Ekaterina Fedorovna Murav'eva. The friendship, patronage, and influence of Murav'ev, one of the most important writers of Russian Sentimentalism and the creator of Russian "light verse," were decisive in Batiushkov's spiritual biography. Batiushkov later confessed in "Rech' o vliianii legkoi poezii na iazyk" (A Discourse on the Influence of Light Verse on Language, 1816) that he was obliged to Murav'ev for his education. A passionate lover of antiquity, Murav'ev introduced Batiushkov to the Latin language and classical literature. In his house Batiushkov evidently became acquainted with poets he admired, Gavriil Romanovich Derzhavin and Vasilii Vasil'evich Kapnist; most likely he also formed there a friendship with Aleksei Nikolaevich Olenin, who was both a successful bureaucrat and a knowledgeable amateur of the arts. Olenin's circle, however varied the literary opinions of its members, was the aesthetic center of Russian Neoclassicism, or the Russian style empire, which combined the "cult of sentiment" with an interest in both classical and Northern antiquity. An appreciation of this circle's atmosphere contributes much to the understanding of Batiushkov's poetics.

On 20 December 1802 Batiushkov entered the newly formed Ministry of Public Education "without salary and self-supporting." Murav'ev became assistant minister of public education and also supervisor of educational institutions in Moscow. It is not surprising that with such a patron, Batiushkov served, in his own words, successfully but not assiduously. At first his service was wholly nominal; obviously, a fifteen-year-old would only take such a post to fulfill the prescribed number of years to obtain the first rank in the Petrine "Table of Ranks" (corresponding to the fourteenth, or lowest, class). He was granted this rank on 7 November 1803, and on 21 June 1804 he retired.

In early 1805 Batiushkov returned to the same ministry; this fact is the reason he later wrote that he had entered the civil service only in 1805 as a secretary of Murav'ev. This time the work was real, but Batiushkov's duties were clearly not too wearisome. In a letter to his good friend Gnedich (fall 1810) he tells an anecdote that fully reveals the character of his preoccupations. One of the higher clerks, annoyed that Batiushkov "did not want to do any office work," complained to Murav'ev; as proof of Batiushkov's idleness, the clerk produced verses by Vicomte Evariste-Désiré de Parny, copied in Batiushkov's hand, which served as an epigraph in an epistle to Gnedich and which celebrated *la paresse et l'insouciance* (idleness and the carefree life). Murav'ev merely smiled at Batiushkov's negligence. This anecdote, incidentally, testifies to Batiushkov's early interest in the French elegist Parny (in 1805, Batiushkov published his first translation from this poet).

He was already showing an interest in his other favorite French poet, Jean-Baptiste-Louis Gresset, whose *La Chartreuse* (The Charterhouse, 1735), imitated in an early piece, later became a model for "Moi Penaty."

Batiushkov began to write poetry seriously in 1804 (at least, the dating of his first works between 1802 and 1803 is not documented). Two poems are conventionally regarded as having been written before the earliest published one. The first of these, "Bog" (God, 1804), is a direct imitation of Derzhavin's spiritual odes. The other, "Mechta" (Dream, 1804–1806), he reworked for the rest of his literary life; thus it is possible to illustrate the evolution of Batiushkov's versification and verbal style using only examples from successive wordings of this piece. Written under the influence of Murav'ev's lyrics, and including both original and translated fragments, "Mechta" became a manifesto of Batiushkov's own aesthetics: "Mechtan'e est' dusha poetov i stikhov" (Dreaming is the soul of poets and of verse). This idea brings him close to Nikolai Mikhailovich Karamzin and the early Zhukovsky, but even in "Mechta" the literary pose of an escapist and hedonist is already evident. Most likely the programmatic nature of this rather weak poem accounted for the continued interest of its otherwise self-critical author.

The journals in which Batiushkov's first poems appeared are easy to link to his personal contacts. His first poetic offering was the satirical "Poslanie k stikham moim" (Epistle to My Verses); in January 1805 it was published in *Novosti russkoi literatury* (News of Russian Literature), the supplement to the periodical of Moscow University, where Murav'ev was the supervisor. Individual works of insignificant Sentimentalists and even Admiral Aleksandr Semenovich Shishkov's manifesto of "archaism" can be recognized in Batiushkov's descriptions, although this satire, as he pretended, was not "personal"; it mocks the stylistic extremes of contemporary literature. Three of the five poems Batiushkov published in 1805 appeared in *Severnyi vestnik* (The Northern Herald), edited by Ivan Ivanovich Martynov, a colleague of Batiushkov.

Batiushkov's relations with his colleagues in the Ministry form part of his literary biography. Many of them were, after all, poets, essayists, or publishers: for examples, Gnedich, a member of Olenin's circle and future translator of the *Iliad,* and Ivan Petrovich Pnin, a poet and publicist who served as the president (from July 1805 until his death in September 1805) of the *Vol'noe obshchestvo liubitelei slovesnosti, nauk i khudozhestv* (Free Society of Lovers of Letters, Sciences, and the Arts). Other colleagues were also members of the society, such as Nikolai Aleksandrovich Radishchev, son of the famous writer, and Dmitrii Ivanovich Iazykov, the secretary of the society (and its president from 1807 to 1811).

Batiushkov's stylistics and genre repertoire of that period were partly oriented to the tastes of this literary group. In 1804 and 1805 he wrote two more satirical pieces, one of which he presented to the society for his membership. It was read at a meeting on 22 April 1805 by Nikolai Petrovich Brusilov and reviewed by three "censors," among them one of Batiushkov's future fellow authors, Aleksandr Efimovich Izmailov. Batiushkov, however, was not formally accepted into the society. He was not present at the meetings dedicated to the late President Pnin, at which poems in memoriam were recited; nevertheless, Batiushkov published his own poem on the same subject. He was associated with this group for only a short time, but the friendship that he formed with Gnedich proved to be more lasting. In 1805 he wrote the first of many epistles to Gnedich, "Chto delaesh', moi drug, v Poltavskikh ty stepiakh . . ." (What do you do, my friend, on the Poltava steppe . . .), published in *Tsvetnik* (Flower Garden) in 1809.

In 1806 Batiushkov published the first version of "Mechta" and a new poem, "Sovet druz'iam" (Advice for Friends). The latter was soon completely rewritten, with a totally different metric scheme, and published in 1810 as "Veselyi chas" (A Happy Hour), which should be considered a different work. The subjectivist poetic formula found in the first and modified in the second– "Umru, i vse umret so mnoi!" (I'll die, and all will die with me!)–impressed his younger contemporaries so much that both Baratynsky and Pushkin repeated it. Also in 1806 Batiushkov wrote another epistle to Gnedich, published in 1807 in Aleksandr Petrovich Benitsky's almanac *Taliia* (Thalia): "Druzhba tol'ko obeshchaet / Mne bessmertiia venets" (It is friendship which can promise / An immortal crown for me). Although at this time Batiushkov was the author of only a dozen poems, Gnedich, in a non-extant epistle, predicts literary fame for his young friend. In his reply Batiushkov, glorifying friendship (this theme came to dominate their poetic correspondence), blithely denies his own literary merits. The concluding lines of the first wording of this epistle play upon Horace's "Non omnis moriar" (Not all of me will die): "Chut' ne ves' li i s stikhami / Vopreki tebe umru" (Almost all of me, with my verses, / Despite what you say, will die). Batiushkov's verses and personal letters reveal an abundance of echoes from Horace. "Sovet druz'iam," of his early works, is the most Horatian in character: it includes some half-dozen references to *carmina*. Incidentally, the opening line of the first epistle to Gnedich alludes to Horace's epistle to Albius Tibullus, with whose name Batiushkov soon became closely associated.

Contemporary depiction of the fires in Moscow after the invasion of Napoleon Bonaparte's forces in 1812, an event that influenced Batiushkov's poetry (after a drawing by English artist John Vedramini)

In the fall of 1806 Napoleon Bonaparte occupied Berlin and most of Prussia, Russia's ally; Alexander I declared a mass levy. On 13 January 1807 Batiushkov, with the civil rank corresponding to the twelfth class, was attached to General Nikolai Nikolaevich Tatishchev's staff under Olenin (the general was commander of the Petersburg Militia, a volunteer corps). On 22 February he enlisted in Colonel Nikolai Nikitich Verevkin's St. Petersburg battalion of the militia as *sotennyi* (a junior officer) and immediately set out for the West. When taking part in the Prussian campaign, he met Ivan Aleksandrovich Petin, an officer, who became another close friend. Batiushkov fought at the battle of Gutstadt (22–27 May); on 29 May he was seriously wounded at the battle of Heilsberg. (A year later, on 20 May 1808, he was awarded the Order of St. Anne, third class, for bravery.) After Heilsberg he was transported to a hospital and then to Riga, where he was convalescing during June and July 1807.

In Riga, Batiushkov was living at the house of a merchant, Müguel (Batiushkov's French spelling), with whose daughter (possibly named Emilie) he fell in love. This episode formed the background for two poems. The first, "Vyzdorovleniie" (Convalescence), not published until the appearance of *Opyty v stikhakh i proze* and considered by Pushkin one of Batiushkov's best elegies, is an exquisite twenty-line poem. Its lyric plot unfolds on the boundary between two abstract worlds: the bright world of life and a gloomy pseudoclassical Hades. The motif of "fading/withering" predominates. The first two quatrains describe the lyric "I" dying; the next two present "thou" as an incarnation of life: "No ty priblizhilas', o zhizn' dushi moei" (But thou hast come, o life of my soul). "Thou" is an active principle whose function is salvation; the first-person pronoun even grammatically acquires the function of object (*menia* [me]). The last quatrain binds together all the semantic and grammatic themes. In its first line, two pronouns appear in marked positions–"thou" and the feminine for "it," which refers to "life": "Ty snova zhizn' daesh'; ona tvoi dar blagoi" (Thou givest life anew; it is thy blessed gift). In the concluding line the "I" theme returns, and an unexpected point is introduced: the lyric persona, who has escaped the withering of death, predicts: "Ia ot liubvi teper' uvianu" (It is from love that I shall now wither).

The other elegy, "Vospominaniia 1807 goda" (Recollections of 1807), published in *Vestnik Evropy* (Herald of Europe) in 1809 and republished in *Opyty v stikhakh i proze* as "Vospominanie" (Recollection), is highly autobiographical: Heilsberg and Emilie are named. Although the love section of the poem is absent from *Opyty v stikhakh i proze,* the opposition of "war" and "love"–a polarity he also found in the works of Torquato Tasso and Tibullus–became a perennial theme for Batiushkov.

Batiushkov went through many difficulties in 1807. On leave, he went to Danilovskoe, where he learned that Murav'ev had died in late July. Moreover, instead of having a joyous homecoming, he quarreled with his father over the latter's second marriage. Batiushkov and his unmarried sisters, Aleksandra and Varvara, moved to their late mother's family estate, the village of Khantonovo, Cherepovetski district, Novgorod province. In the fall of 1807 Batiushkov (along with his friend Petin) obtained a transfer to the Guards Regiment of Jägers.

The following year, 1808, he was away from the capital: estate affairs kept him in Vologda and Khantonovo. He was not even able to be present at the funeral of his sister Anna, who died in St. Petersburg. In September he had to return to active service in Finland, in the war against Sweden, as a member of Colonel Andrei Petrovich Turchaninov's battalion of Jägers. Nevertheless, he became a generous contributor to *Dramaticheskii vestnik* (The Dramatic Messenger), the newly founded journal of Olenin's circle. Here Batiushkov published "Pastukh i solovei" (The Shepherd and the Nightingale, 1807), his fable in defense of Vladislav Aleksandrovich Ozerov, tragedian-playwright and the favorite of the Oleninites. Batiushkov compared the fate of Ozerov, who later became insane, with the similar fate of Tasso (ironically, he himself came to the same end). Tasso and his *Gerusalemme liberata* (Jerusalem Delivered, 1581)–the epic that Batiushkov always described as nothing less than "immortal"–became his main preoccupation in 1807 and 1808 as he worked on translating it into Russian. The idea of presenting the main works of world literature in the Russian language and making them part of Russian belles lettres is characteristic of the early nineteenth century. Batiushkov (also advised by Kapnist) might have come to similar ideas under the influence of Gnedich, who was already working on his translation of the *Iliad*.

Foremost in importance to the literati were heroic epopees. This estimation is why, in Batiushkov's correspondence with Gnedich, "your poet" and "my poet" are Homer and Tasso, although Batiushkov considered only two extracts from his incomplete verse translation of *Gerusalemme liberata* worth publishing. Tasso did, however, become a personage in Batiushkov's poems. The first such poem, "K Tassu" (To Tasso), appeared in 1808 in *Dramaticheskii vestnik* as a kind of introduction to Batiushkov's translation of a fragment from Canto I of *Gerusalemme liberata;* both were written during the Finnish campaign. Batiushkov's "introduction" is, in fact, a free adaptation of Jean-François de La Harpe's "Épître au Tasse" (Epistle to Tasso, 1775; La Harpe was also a translator of *Gerusalemme liberata*). Although Batiushkov's views sometimes differ from La Harpe's, they do come together at two points: an emphasis on the contrasting themes in Tasso's work (war and love) and an empathy with the poet's fate (misfortune and madness). Batiushkov ignored the metric and stanzaic form of the Italian original, ottava rima, and used the "classical" alexandrine (Gnedich was translating Homer into alexandrines). The extract from Tasso published in *Dramaticheskii vestnik* concludes with the promise "to be continued"; however, the journal was closed down, signaling a split in the circle. Another fragment from *Gerusalemme liberata* appeared the next year in *Tsvetnik,* the St. Petersburg journal edited by Batiushkov's old acquaintances Izmailov and Benitsky.

Another interesting work that had been published in *Dramaticheskii vestnik* was "Son Mogol'tsa" (The Mogul's Dream, 1808), a translation of one of Jean La Fontaine's fables previously translated by Zhukovsky. Batiushkov introduced a personal motif: "esli mne dana / Sposobnost' malaia i skudno darovan'e" (if I am given / A minor talent and a meager gift). A "minor talent" is, of course, "a gift for minor genres," but this motif also has an existential element (developed by Baratynsky). Although later Batiushkov came to dislike his own translation (republished by Zhukovsky in *Vestnik Evropy* in 1810), Gnedich included it in *Opyty v stikhakh i proze* against the author's wishes.

Batiushkov kept in contact with his St. Petersburg friends largely through correspondence. Actual meetings in the capital–in June and July 1809, on his return from Finland to his estate–were quite brief. For the first half of 1809 Batiushkov was still on active service: in March he took part in the campaign for the Åland Islands, and by the beginning of May he had achieved the rank of second lieutenant and submitted his application to resign (confirmed by June 1809). In July 1809 he went to Khantonovo, where he lived until December; there he wrote his famous "Videnie na beregakh Lety" (A Vision on the Shores of the Lethe). His first publishable prose pieces (including one on Finland) were also written in 1809.

A satirical poem that Batiushkov refused to have published (it finally appeared in *Russkaia beseda* [Russian

German engraving of victorious Russian, Prussian, and Austrian troops entering Paris after defeating Napoleon in 1814, a scene Batiushkov witnessed

Colloquy] in 1841), "Videnie" soon became widely known and brought the author a certain notoriety. In October 1809 the poem was sent to Gnedich, who allowed Olenin to make a copy, which rapidly multiplied. Batiushkov wrote the poem following the French satirical tradition, but its material was wholly Russian. It describes a dream in which all contemporary Russian poets have unexpectedly died and turned up in Elysium; their works are immersed in the waters of the Lethe, and those found wanting sink into oblivion. The Russian writers of the eighteenth century were not the main concern of satire. In the poem, not only the notorious Ivan Semenovich Barkov escapes oblivion but also Vasilii Kirillovich Trediakovsky, who was generally despised at that time; the latter's role, however, is reduced to that of defender of the Shishkovites, partisans of the archaist (Slavo-Russian) tendency in literature. Shishkov himself, like Trediakovsky, is saved for his diligent though ungifted work, but not other archaists, who had already been targets of Batiushkov's epigrams. As in Batiushkov's first satirical work, the Moscow "tearful" Sentimentalists (headed by Prince Petr Ivanovich Shalikov) are mocked. Batiushkov did not mention the leader of Russian Sentimentalism: he wrote to Gnedich in November 1809 that he "dare not drown" Karamzin because he respected him. Of contemporary writers, only Ivan Andreevich Krylov is saved. After the split in *Dramaticheskii vestnik*, Krylov published in *Tsvetnik;* the literary policy of the authors for that journal (including Batiushkov) was to distance themselves from both Slavophiles and pretentious Sentimentalists.

"Videnie" performs a balancing act between ridicule and obscenity; it is full of caustic allusions and offensively transformed or reinterpreted quotations. Pushkin, who otherwise did not like Batiushkov's poetic jokes, wrote in the margins of *Opyty v stikakh i proze* that he found this poem "clever and funny," and in "Gorodok" (The Town, 1815) he called the author "a daring mocker." With "Videnie," Batiushkov's reputation was established; he began to regard himself as a mature and original poet and started gathering material for a publication of his collected works.

In the same year, 1809, Batiushkov began his association with *Vestnik Evropy,* the Moscow journal founded by Karamzin; it was edited, at that time, by Zhukovsky and Mikhail Trofimovich Kachenovsky. Batiushkov came to know them personally a little later: he arrived in Moscow on 25 December 1809, invited there by Ekaterina Murav'eva, in whose house he stayed until the end of May 1810. He quickly entered Moscow literary circles, and not only Zhukovsky but also Prince Petr Andreevich Viazemsky, Vasilii L'vovich Pushkin, and Karamzin became his close friends. For the next three years he published almost exclusively in *Vestnik Evropy*. His first work to appear there was "Vospominaniia 1807 goda." The journal published many of his prose works (five in 1810), epigrams, and other miscellanea, but the most important were translations and "imitations" (free adaptations). Although he usually completed only two or three translations a year, from December 1809 until February 1811 he published more than ten (and composed even more): two from Tibullus, five from Parny, one from Giovanni Battista Casti, and two from Petrarch (some epigrams are also translations).

The translation-imitation of Lygdamus's elegy (III, 3), which was then considered authentic Tibullus, was composed at Khantonovo in the fall of 1809. As with his next two Tibullan imitations, Batiushkov used alexandrines. Unlike contemporary "hellenists," Batiushkov was neither interested in reforming Russian prosody nor in detailed antiquarianism. Significantly, his translation of Horace's Carmen I, 22, following the original stanzaic form, remained in draft form only. After Batiushkov's imitation, Tibullus III, 3, became popular: Mikhail Vasil'evich Milonov and Ryleev published versions, though the latter's translation is rather an imitation of Batiushkov than of the original. The presentation of Tibullus in Russia came to be closely linked with the name of Batiushkov, although Ivan Ivanovich Dmitriev had already imitated Tibullus I, 1. (Batiushkov came to Tibullus through "the French Tibullus," Parny; Dmitriev through La Harpe.) Dmitriev's influence is evident in Batiushkov's version of Tibullus I, 10 (published in 1810), echoes of which are frequent in Aleksandr Pushkin and Baratynsky. Later, Batiushkov translated Tibullus I, 3 (published in 1815). The choice of these elegies was clearly motivated by their theme: the contrast of war and love.

Translations from Parny, whom Batiushkov considered the greatest exponent of *poésie légère* (light verse), were also of exceptional importance for the Russian writer. The first to appear at that time was a free adaptation of "Le Revenant" (1778) titled "Prividenie" (The Ghost), composed in February 1810. Batiushkov was right when he wrote to Gnedich that month that he had not translated this piece but "conquered" it: filled with playful allusions to Karamzin's and Zhukovsky's poems, "Prividenie" fits perfectly into a Russian context, developing the theme of "apparition" initiated by Zhukovsky's Russified imitation of Gottfried August Bürger's ballad "Lenore" (1773). On the other hand Parny's works could, for Batiushkov, be associated with the Roman poets: Batiushkov acknowledged in letters to Zhukovsky on 26 July 1810 and to Gnedich on 13 March 1811 that he had introduced a Tibullan word theme in his verse translation of Parny's idyll in prose "Le Torrent" and Virgilian motifs in his extract from Parny's "Scandinavian" poem "Isnel et Asléga." Batiushkov's translations are highly original, while his own works are filled with classical reminiscences. In an elegant poem about Elysium (unpublished until 1834), Tibullan and Horatian motifs, having passed through the prism of Parny's and Antoine Bertin's poetics, are realized in pure Batiushkovian Russian stylistic formulae.

In summer 1810 Batiushkov spent three weeks on Viazemsky's estate, Ostaf'evo, in the company of his host, Karamzin and his wife, and Zhukovsky. Batiushkov left his friends suddenly and fled to Khantonovo, where in late July he wrote playfully apologetic letters to Zhukovsky and Viazemsky. He enclosed some pieces (including a new version of "Mechta") intended for *Vestnik Evropy* and for the five-volume *Sobranie russkikh stikhotvorenii* (Collected Russian Poems, 1810–1811) edited by Zhukovsky. Batiushkov stayed at Khantonovo until the end of the year. This pattern of living—half of the year spent in the "capitals," half in the countryside—became habitual for him. At Khantonovo he wrote a vast amount of prose (mostly non-extant), including "Predslava i Dobrynia," a tale of ancient Russia, published in Baron Anton Antonovich Del'vig and Aleksandr Pushkin's almanac *Severnye tsvety* (Northern Flowers) in 1832. In addition, Batiushkov, still unable to complete his translation of Tasso, made one more attempt at the grand genre: a verse variation of the Song of Songs. This non-extant poem was sent to Gnedich in St. Petersburg and to Viazemsky in Moscow; neither liked it. Its failure contrasted with his successful *poésies fugitives* (fugitive verses), which established the literary image of the "voluptuary" Batiushkov (of course, his friends knew his character was rather different). Nevertheless, his diversion into light verse displeased Gnedich, who considered the subjects he chose "unworthy" of his "excellent talent." Thus Batiushkov even had to defend his works from his closest friend.

In late February 1811 he went back to Moscow, but by the end of July he had run out of money and left for Khantonovo. He was often invited by his Moscow friends to visit, but in place of his company he presented them with "Moi Penaty," which he subtitled "an epistle to Zhukovsky and Viazemsky," one of the most original works of the 1810s. The literary background of the poem is heterogeneous: the title recalls Jean-François Ducis and Cardinal François-Joachim-Pierre de Bernis; the setting, Parny and Gresset; and the details, Gresset, Bertin, Tibullus, and Horace. There are also many allusions to Russian poets. The diversity of contrasting themes is extraordinary: imagination and reality, friendship and eroticism, country life and literature, and existence and death. All is merged in Batiushkov's unrepeatable intonation, in a "light" meter, iambic trimeter (in the eighteenth century this meter was used for Anacreontic and song genres). In reply Zhukovsky and Viazemsky composed similar epistles. With "Moi Penaty" several *topoi* (for example, the shades of poets' visits), original and borrowed details (such as Gresset's rickety table or the classical rusty sword), devices (chiefly the mixing of antiquity and modernity), and characters (such as the retired soldier) became fashionable. The trimeter epistle came to be recognized as a genre in its own right—an extremely popular one.

In January 1812 Batiushkov left his estate for St. Petersburg to find a post at the Imperial Public Library (the director was now Olenin). This move offended Viazemsky, who was waiting for him in Moscow, and who apparently feared the St. Petersburg influence on his friend. Batiushkov, however, arrived in the capital as a poet of the "Moscow" (i.e. Karamzinist) orientation. Somewhat avoiding his old literary acquaintances, he got to know future members of the "Arzamas" group: the future count Dmitrii Nikolaevich Bludov, Dmitrii Vasil'evich Dashkov, and Aleksandr Ivanovich Turgenev. While awaiting a position at the library, Batiushkov lived at Gnedich's house. His new friends became members of the *Vol'noe obshchestvo liubitelei slovesnosti, nauk i khudozhestv,* which had changed considerably in character (its president was now Izmailov). On 8 February 1812 Batiushkov was accepted into the society, but again his association with it was short-lived: on 14 March, Dashkov delivered his notorious speech, a tongue-in-cheek "eulogy" to the "graphomaniac" Count Dmitrii Ivanovich Khvostov, and was asked to withdraw from the society; Batiushkov, Bludov, and Dmitrii Petrovich Severin walked out in sympathy. Batiushkov became an assistant keeper of manuscripts at the library, under the palaeographist Aleksandr Ivanovich Ermolaev, on 22 April 1812. His colleagues included Gnedich, Krylov, and Uvarov. In June 1812 he bought an apartment nearby.

Napoleon invaded Russia on 12 June 1812; Batiushkov wrote to Viazemsky that had it not been for a fever, he would have immediately joined the army. Nevertheless, he left St. Petersburg: Ekaterina Murav'eva and her children were living, without any help, at her dacha near Moscow, and on 14 August, Olenin gave him leave to go to them. Two days after the Russian army had left Moscow, Batiushkov accompanied the Murav'evs to Nizhnii Novgorod, where most Muscovites had fled. It was probably here that he wrote a poem, "Razluka" (The Parting), which became a popular song (not to be confused with a later elegy of the same title). In October he accompanied Olenin—who had just arrived—to Tver', via the burned ruins of Moscow. The scenes of destruction deeply affected him and determined his attitude to the war; he wrote to Gnedich of the French: "Varvary! Vandaly! I etot narod izvergov osmelilsia govorit' o svobode, o filosofii, o chelovekoliubii!" (Barbarians! Vandals! And this nation of monsters even dares to speak of freedom, of philosophy, of philanthropy!). While in Nizhnii, Batiushkov became acquainted with General Aleksei Nikolaevich Bakhmetev, who promised to facilitate his joining the army and who sent the necessary papers to the capital. On 18 December he was released from the library, and in February 1813 he arrived, via Moscow, in St. Petersburg. Meanwhile the French army had been driven from Russia, and the foreign campaign began.

On 29 March 1813 Batiushkov again entered military service, with the rank of junior captain (tenth class), and was appointed Bakhmetev's adjutant. Because the general had been wounded, he was unable to take part in the campaign, and Batiushkov waited for him in St. Petersburg. The events of 1812 dictated the mood of an epistle-elegy, "K Dashkovu" (To Dashkov), a turning point in Batiushkov's poetics and weltanschauung. The poem echoes his personal letters and expresses his feelings on seeing Moscow in ruins: the apparently rhetorical "trikraty" (thrice) refers to three real visits. Together with a wounded hero (Bakhmetev), the speaker thirsts for revenge; hence the refusal to sing of love and joy. The war becomes an incarnation of evil: "Moi drug! ia videl more zla / I neba mstitel'nogo kary" (My friend! I saw a sea of evil / And wrath of the avenging heavens). The poem presents a strong contrast to Zhukovsky's hymn to the events of 1812: optimism was now alien to Batiushkov, and he was only able to use the form found in Zhukovsky as a pastiche.

One of two satires written with Izmailov, "Pevets v Besede liubitelei russkogo slova" (The Bard in the Colloquy of Lovers of the Russian Word, 1813, published in 1856 in *Sovremennik* [The Contemporary]), although not directed against Zhukovsky, parodies his title, composition, and meter. This satire on the colloquy, the Shishkovites' St. Petersburg nucleus after 1811, gave Batiushkov the reputation of a militant Karamzinist and became the precedent for the parodic and even obscene use of alternating lines of iambic tetrameter and trimeter by other poets from Aleksandr Pushkin to Vladimir Vladimirovich Maiakovsky. Probably at this time Batiushkov wrote an epistle to Aleksandr Turgenev (published in *Pamiatnik otechestvennykh Muz* [The Monument of Fatherland Muses] in 1827) describing Olenin's estate, Priiutino, and including portraits of its *habitués*: Gnedich, Krylov, and the painter Orest Adamovich Kiprensky. The presence of friends was not the only thing that attracted Batiushkov to Priiutino: in April or May 1813 he fell in love with Anna Furman, the Olenins' ward. He spent the rest of the war remembering and hiding his love.

In July 1813 Bakhmetev arrived in St. Petersburg and, still unable to take part in the campaign, gave Batiushkov permission to go on active service. Batiushkov set out for Count Petr Khristianovich Wittgenstein's headquarters near Dresden on 24 July. He was appointed adjutant to General Nikolai Nikolaevich Raevsky, commander of the Third Corps of Grenadiers, and took part in the battle of Teplitz on 15 August. Twice he met Petin; these, and earlier, meetings are described in his "Vospominanie o Petine" (Memoir on Petin), published in *Moskvitianin* (Muskovite) in 1851. Petin was killed at Leipzig in "The Battle of Nations" (4–6 October). Raevsky, whose corps was in the vanguard, was severely wounded, while Batiushkov (who on 27 January 1814 was awarded the Order of St. Anne, second class, for bravery) was not even scratched. Through October and November he stayed with Raevsky in Weimar, where his interest in German authors (Johann Wolfgang von Goethe, Christoph Martin Wieland, Friedrich Schiller, and Johann Heinrich Voss) grew. By mid December Raevsky and Batiushkov had caught up with the army. In January 1814 the Russians crossed the Rhine, entered France, and moved in on the capital. From the literary point of view the castle of Cirey, where the fugitive Voltaire had lived, was the most important place Batiushkov visited at that time; he describes the visit in a prose piece, "Puteshestvie v zamok Sirei" (Pis'mo iz Frantsii k g.D.) (A Visit to the Castle of Cirey: A Letter from France to Mr. D[ashkov]), published in 1816 in *Vestnik Evropy* and included in *Opyty v stikhakh i proze*. During the battle for Paris (17–18 March 1814) Raevsky's corps was held in reserve. The following day Alexander I, at the head of his armies, entered the city (a scene Batiushkov described in a 27 March 1814 letter to Gnedich).

The first month in Paris was an exciting time for Batiushkov. He even managed to attend a meeting of the French Academy (his favorite, Parny, was absent); he wrote to Dashkov that the age of glory for French literature had passed. This letter was also a literary work, and an abridged version was published as "Pis'mo k D. V. D. iz Parizha (25-go aprelia 1814-go)" (A Letter to D. V. D[ashkov] from Paris on 25 April 1814) by the poet's friends in *Pamiatnik otechestvennykh Muz* in 1827. In May, Batiushkov fell ill, grew depressed, and decided to return home. Severin suggested he go via England, following the emperor's retinue. Batiushkov arrived in London in mid May, spent two weeks in England, and from 30 May to 6 June sailed from Harwich to Gothenburg, Sweden. The crossing was described in a letter to Severin; Batiushkov later revised it as a traveler's sketch, "Pis'mo k S. iz Gotenburga. Iiunia 19, 1814 goda" (A Letter to S[everin] from Gothenburg, June 19, 1814) which appeared in *Severnye tsvety* in 1827, as did his letter to Dashkov. His sea trip also became the setting for his elegy "Ten' Druga" (The Shade of a Friend), in which the narrator is visited by the silent ghost of a fallen comrade-in-arms (meaning Petin). According to Viazemsky, this piece was actually composed during the voyage; however, it may have been written a year later, along with other works of reminiscence.

From Gothenburg, Batiushkov traveled to Stockholm and then set out for St. Petersburg via Finland, accompanied by Bludov. He arrived in early July and moved into Ekaterina Murav'eva's house. There he worked on "Stseny chetyrekh vozrastov" (Scenes of the Four Ages of Man), a libretto for the celebrations on the return of Alexander I, which took place in Pavlovsk on 27 July 1814. The Dowager Empress had entrusted the preparations to Iurii Aleksandrovich Neledinsky-Meletsky, a senator-poet, who passed on this task to Batiushkov, an acquaintance. Several others, including Derzhavin, had a hand in the composition of the libretto. The result was, according to Batiushkov, a "jumble," for which, nevertheless, the Dowager Empress presented him with a diamond ring; he sent it to his younger sister. At the same time he was editing, and writing an introduction to, an 1815 collection of Murav'ev's prose works. This introduction had also been published separately in *Syn otechestva* (Son of the Fatherland) in 1814 and appeared later in *Opyty v stikhakh i proze* and in Murav'ev's 1819 collected works. Batiushkov considered the returning of Murav'ev's works to society a moral and literary duty.

On his return to St. Petersburg, Batiushkov's matrimonial hopes collapsed. Although the Olenins, the Murav'evs, and his relatives all approved of the match, he realized that Anna Furman did not really love him, so he did not propose, using the excuse of a lack of money. Nevertheless, he continued to work. He wrote (consulting Olenin) an essay on Russian cultural history, "Progulka v Akademiiu khudozhestv" (A Stroll

Batiushkov in 1815 (copy by Il'ia Efimovich Repin of a portrait by Orest Adamovich Kiprensky; Rumiantsev Museum, Moscow)

through the Academy of Arts, published in 1814 in *Syn otechestva*) and composed several important poems. His works of this period are colored by his experiences of war, travels, and other cultures. Even an elegy, "Plennyi" (The Captive), is based on the real captivity in France of Lev Vasil'evich Davydov (Batiushkov's fellow officer and brother of the famous poet). Batiushkov had been wanting, at least since the end of Finnish campaign, to compose a long poem about the North; now he wrote "Na razvalinakh zamka v Shvetsii" (On the Ruins of a Castle in Sweden). This gloomy elegy, written in regular strophes combining six- and four-foot lines, was partly inspired by a poem of Friedrich von Matthisson and the work of the historian David Mallet. It was a marked departure from light verse. The theme of imagination acquired a historical dimension; this new modification of the meditative poem began developing in Russian poetry (for example, Aleksandr Pushkin's "Vospominaniia v Tsarskom sele" [Recollections at Tsarskoe Selo, 1815]) and essentially influenced the Russian elegiac vision of Scandinavia (as in "Finliandliia," Baratynsky's famous Finland elegy, written in 1820).

"Strannik i domosed" (The Wanderer and The Home-Lover, 1815), a tale conceived in London and completed in St. Petersburg, was also an attempt by Batiushkov, although of debatable success, to leave behind his intimate lyricism. At this time or a little later, however, he wrote one of his most beautiful love elegies, "Ia chuvstvuiu, moi dar v Poezii pogas . . ." (I feel my gift of Poetry has died . . .), an expression of his love and loss of Furman. Like Virgil's Tityrus (the character who personified Virgil in an epistle to Ivan Matveevich Murav'ev-Apostol, another of Batiushkov's works of the period), the poet teaches an echo to repeat his beloved's name, not in Arcady but in the heat of battle and during lonely wanderings through countries Batiushkov actually visited. The poet's existence is a far cry from the shepherd's innocent happiness: both love and poetic inspiration have left him in the desert of sad experience. An extract from this elegy appeared in *Opyty v stikhakh i proze* as "Vospominaniia" (Recollections), preceded by (and so paralleled with) the "Recollection" of his Riga love.

In early January 1815 a serious illness caused a nervous reaction that led to a temporary change in Batiushkov's opinion on his chosen poetic path. In February 1815 he wrote a dedication to Bludov in a manuscript collection. He claimed that his poetry was insufficiently crafted but that it comprised a true history of passions; he calls the collection "zhurnal . . . poeta" (a poet's diary). This piece, with the title "K druz'iam" (To Friends), became the dedicatory poem in the second volume of *Opyty v stikhakh i proze*. Tellingly, Batiushkov sought justifications for his "unworthy" poetry. In March he set off in search of spiritual healing, accompanied by Ekaterina Murav'eva; they spent the second week of Lent at a monastery in Tikhvin. Batiushkov apparently experienced a religious conversion, evidence of which may be found in a poem of this year, "Nadezhda" (Hope). Apparently in the same year he composed a poem combining the motifs of love and fatal illness: "Posledniaia vesna" (The Last Spring), a free adaptation of Charles-Hubert Millevoye's "La Chute des feuilles" (The Fall of Leaves, 1811), one of the most popular elegies among Russian translators of the 1810s and 1820s. Another translation from Parny, "Mshchenie" (Vengeance), was composed as both an addition to the earlier "Prividenie" (a "mirror image" of the same theme) and a possible sublimation of his disappointment in love, which was still eloquent in his poems.

In the first half of 1815 Batiushkov came to meet the young Aleksandr Pushkin at Tsarskoe Selo; in the eyes of later generations this meeting took on an historic or even symbolic meaning, but there is little available information about it. Pushkin's second epistle to Batiushkov may be a delayed response to some real remark. In mid April 1815, having at last obtained leave, Batiushkov went to Danilovskoe, where he spent six "torturous" days with his father (whose second wife had died in 1814), and then went on to Khantonovo. He was soon recalled to service and on 8 June set out for Kamenets-Podolsky in Bessarabia, where Bakhmetev had been made governor.

Batiushkov spent the rest of the year in this remote province occupying himself with Italian and writing prose and poetry. Essays on Ludovico Ariosto and Tasso, Petrarch, and Mikhail Vasil'evich Lomonosov, an article titled "Nechto o poete i poezii" (A Word on the Poet and Poetry), and two "allegories" all appeared the following year in *Vestnik Evropy* (republished in *Opyty v stikhakh i proze*); moral essays and memoir pieces were written and earlier drafts revised. On 11 August he sent a letter to Murav'eva, explaining his relationship with Furman; he enclosed "Moi Genii" (My Genius) and "Razluka" (The Parting), two elegies thematically close to "Ia chuvstvuiu. . . ." During a gloomy Moldavian autumn he wrote two masterpieces: the light, Neoclassical "Tavrida" (Tauris) and an epistle/elegy addressed to Viazemsky, "K drugu" (To a Friend). The latter synthesizes practically all the themes of his poetry, symbolically representing his life's path: epicurean motifs appear as the irretrievable past, while the loss of love and inspiration are the present; faith gives hope, but only for another world.

Meanwhile some humorous but significant events were taking place in St. Petersburg. In September, Aleksandr Aleksandrovich Shakhovskoi (a former member of Olenin's circle) attacked Zhukovsky in his comedy *Urok koketkam, ili Lipetskie vody* (A Lesson for Coquettes, or The Lipetsk Spa, 1815), which was considered by the Karamzinists as a declaration of war from the *Beseda liubitelei russkogo slova*. On 14 October 1815 a polemical, parodical, and oppositionist society, Arzamas, was founded; members were given nicknames borrowed from Zhukovsky's ballads. At the first meeting Batiushkov was accepted, in absentia, into the group as Achilles (a name contrasting to his appearance, and corresponding to his former merits as a satirist).

Provincial service was dissatisfactory to Batiushkov, and on 4 November he requested retirement. On 26 December he was given leave and departed for Moscow, where he obtained a transfer to the prestigious Izmailovsky Regiment but decided to end his military career. He stayed with the statesman and writer Murav'ev-Apostol, a relative and the addressee of Batiushkov's epistle on the role of poetry and of his letter/essay on Murav'ev. Batiushkov's poetic output was not high at that time, though he did write a version of Harald's Song, one of the most well-known ancient Scandinavian poems, previously translated into many languages, including Russian. On 26 February 1816 Batiushkov and Zhukovsky became, in absentia, members of the *Obshchestvo liubitelei rossiiskoi slovesnosti* (Society of Lovers of Russian Literature) at Moscow University. Although Batiushkov's attitude to this "Moscow Colloquy" was somewhat disdainful, his preliminary speech (delivered on 26 May by Fedor Fedorovich Kokoshkin) became his most famous critical work. It was modeled on Parny's address to the French Academy on *poésie fugitive*, and when it was published as the opening piece in the first volume of *Opyty v stikhakh i proze*, it was titled "Rech' o vliianii legkoi poezii na iazyk" (A Discourse on the Influence of Light Verse on Language). Batiushkov includes himself in a pan-European light-verse tradition, from the Greek idyllists and Roman elegists to Ippolit Fedorovich Bogdanovich, Murav'ev, and Dmitriev in Russia. He seems to have found a justification for the light verse: since it is "prelestnaia roskosh' slovestnosti" (a charming luxury of literature), it demands the utmost possible perfection and is thus fruitful for language and society. He also emphasized the unity of the poet's life and poetry; this connection became his principle. Half a year earlier, in "Nechto o poete i poezii," he had said: "zhivi, kak pishesh', i pishi, kak zhivesh'" (live as you write, and write as you live).

In early April, as a junior captain of the Household Guards' Izmailovsky Regiment (equal to major in ordinary regiments), Batiushkov retired. The rank corresponded to the eighth class, but Batiushkov was disappointed; many of his friends had been promoted to generals or colonels. An unexpected event distracted him from career problems: in August, Gnedich offered to publish his collected works at the publisher's own expense, with a 1,500-ruble honorarium for the author. Batiushkov replied with doubts about the enterprise. He also refused to include "Videnie" simply to boost the popularity of the collection: first, some of its "heroes" were actually in difficult straits; second, Batiushkov, although an Arzamas member, felt distant from literary polemics. The success of *Opyty v stikhakh i proze* exceeded all expectations. Gnedich finally paid the author 2,000 rubles (having made 15,000 in all–not unusual for the early nineteenth century). Gnedich actually broke all Batiushkov's desired publication conditions: the two volumes appeared with a five-month interval, not simultaneously; they were advertised in advance, and did not appear "suddenly"; moreover, a subscription for the second volume was announced. In the two "capitals" *Opyty v stikhakh i proze* had 183 subscribers (a number that, for its time, testifies to the author's fame).

The prose volume had been largely compiled by early October 1816. On 30 December 1816 a censor, Ivan Osipovich Timkovsky, permitted publication, and the volume appeared in early July 1817. The prose vol-

Title page for the first volume of Opyty v stikhakh i proze, *Batiushkov's financially successful first collection*

ume has a conceptual symmetrical design, partly developed by Gnedich. Two articles on poetry ("Rech' o vliianii legkoi poezii na iazyk" and "Nechto o poete i poezii") open the volume; two essays on moral philosophy conclude it. The former are followed by three essays on Russian poets (Lomonosov, Prince Antiokh Dmitrievich Kantemir, and Murav'ev), while the latter are preceded by three "Italian" pieces (an essay on Ariosto and Tasso, one on Petrarch, and a translation from Giovanni Boccaccio). Followed by two "military officer's sketches" and miscellanea, the cultural "Progulka v Akademiiu khudozhestv" forms the ideological center.

From late December 1816 until late July 1817 Batiushkov stayed at Khantonovo and worked on the verse volume of *Opyty v stikhakh i proze,* rewriting earlier pieces and composing new ones. The number of unfinished projects is tantalizing (tales, long poems, a collection of translations from Italian, even a history of Russian literature). Most of the poems written espe-

cially for *Opyty v stikhakh i proze* do not belong to the light-verse genre. Three of them, epic and lyric in character, were later called "historical (or epic) elegies," an expansion of an already accepted term used by Belinsky. The first, "Geziod i Omir–Soperniki" (Hesiod and Homer–Rivals), completed by mid January, is a translation from Millevoye, whom Batiushkov called, in a note, a rare true talent in contemporary France. The second, "Perekhod cherez Rein: 1814" (The Crossing of the Rhine: 1814), a military elegy with historical overtones describing a recent event of the Napoleonic Wars, was considered by Aleksandr Pushkin to be indisputably the strongest and best of Batiushkov's poems. The third, another famous elegy, "Umiraiushchii Tass" (The Dying Tass), was written in spring 1817. By that time Batiushkov had given up the idea of translating Tasso's work into verse; that same year he published (in *Vestnik Evropy,* along with a prose extract from Ariosto) a prose extract from *Gerusalemme liberata* intended for "Panteon Ital'ianskoi slovesnosti" (The Pantheon of Italian Literature), an unrealized 1817 collection. Kapnist, in an epistle, reproached Batiushkov for abandoning his verse translation efforts, but "Umiraiushchii Tass" eclipsed the translations. The younger generation, however, reevaluated the poem: despite its fame, Aleksandr Pushkin did not like it, preferring George Gordon, Lord Byron's version of the same subject. Both the work on the Hesiod-Homer competition and "Besedka Muz" (The Bower of Muses) testify to a renewal of Batiushkov's interest in classical antiquity; the latter poem, celebrating a real bower, elegantly resumes familiar Tibullan motifs.

In mid August 1817, having spent a few weeks at Danilovskoe, Batiushkov arrived in St. Petersburg. On 27 August he paid his first visit to Arzamas (at their twenty-sixth meeting), where he delivered his preliminary speech. At an earlier meeting on 6 January his essay "Vecher u Kantemira" (An Evening with Kantemir) had been read in his absence. The members of the group, however, began gradually to go their separate ways. In early September, in Tsarskoe Selo, Batiushkov, Zhukovsky, Aleksandr Pushkin, and Aleksandr Alekseevich Pleshcheev together composed an impromptu on Viazemsky's departure to Warsaw. On 18 September, Batiushkov attended an Arzamas meeting for the last time; on 5 October, with Aleksandr Pushkin, he saw off Zhukovsky (who left for Moscow).

The verse volume of *Opyty v stikhakh i proze* appeared in October 1817. It was divided into genre sections: "elegies" (opened by "Nadezhda" and concluded by a new version of "Mechta"); "epistles" (first, a "friendly" one, "Moi Penaty," and last, a "didactic" one to Murav'ev-Apostol); and "miscellanea" (a section with an undefined organizing principle, for some reason followed by three of Batiushkov's most recent works). The distribution, however, created a precedent for genre blurring: epistles to Gnedich, Dashkov, and "a Friend" (Viazemsky) turned up as "elegies." Public recognition immediately followed. On 17 October 1817 Batiushkov became an honorary member of the *Obshchestvo voennykh liudei* (Military Society); on 18 November he was made an honorary librarian at the public library; and in April 1818 he became an honorary member of the *Vol'noe obshchestvo liubitelei rossiiskoi slovesnosti* (Free Society of Lovers of Russian Literature). In late November 1817 his father died, and Batiushkov spent December at Danilovskoe and nearby. Meanwhile reviews of *Opyty v stikhakh i proze* began to appear; it was praised by Izmailov, Sergei Nikolaevich Glinka, and Vasilii Ivanovich Kozlov.

The most authoritative response came from Arzamas circles. Uvarov, in an unsigned French article, was the first to proclaim Zhukovsky and Batiushkov leaders of a "new school." He demonstrated both a unity and difference between the two poets; though representing the new poetics, in all else they followed different paths (for example, Anglo-German spirituality versus Franco-Italo-classical exquisiteness). This observation was to become a critical commonplace and was repeated during the 1820s and 1830s, with variations, by contemporaries such as Petr Aleksandrovich Pletnev, Aleksandr Aleksandrovich Bestuzhev (Marlinsky), and Aleksandr Pushkin. In "O napravlenii nashei poezii, osobenno liricheskoi, v poslednee desiatiletie" (On the Tendency of Our Poetry, Especially Lyric Poetry, in the Last Decade), Vil'gel'm Karlovich Kiukhel'beker's famous attack on the new elegists, published in *Mnemozina* (Mnemosyne) in 1824, the ephemeral coryphaei are again Batiushkov and Zhukovsky. This tradition was summarized by Belinsky, who, wanting to find a literary genealogy for Aleksandr Pushkin, created a triad, following the German Romantic philosophers' model. Since Pushkin represented the modern synthesis, Zhukovsky was to stand for the spiritual indefiniteness of the Middle Ages, and Batiushkov for the sculptural plasticity of classical antiquity.

In 1817 the desire in Arzamas was to give the society a more serious purpose. The idea of a journal was born, but it was not realized. As a potential contribution, in 1817 or 1818 Uvarov (possibly with Batiushkov) wrote a monograph article on the *Greek Anthology*, illustrated with imitations of epigrams by Batiushkov, who actually used Uvarov's French translations (also included) as a medium. In 1820 all this material was published by Dashkov as a separate pamphlet, *O grecheskoi antologii*. The work preserved evidence of its Arzamas origins: it was preceded by Dashkov's mystifying introduction, and the authors were revealed only by the initials of their Arzamas nicknames, Akhill (Achilles) and Starushka (The Old Lady). Along with another anthological (non-translational) cycle, written in 1821 under Johann Gottfried von Herder's influence, the "Greek epigrams" were to have been included in an unrealized, revised edition of *Opyty v stikhakh i proze*. When reviewing the pamphlet, Kiukhel'beker noted that, judging from their quality, the poems could belong only to Aleksandr Pushkin or Batiushkov; the style, he felt, was more likely to be Batiushkov's. This confusion was telling. Later Belinsky considered Batiushkov the creator of Russian anthological verse and traced not only Pushkin's but also Apollon Nikolaevich Maikov's and the young Afanasii Afanas'evich Fet's "anthologies" to him.

On 9 January 1818 Batiushkov returned to St. Petersburg and continued his attempts (begun in the fall) to enter the diplomatic service. The whole year was spent trying to get away from familiar places. He obtained leave from the library on 10 May to go to the South to research manuscripts and monuments. In late June, having spent some time in Moscow with Murav'ev's son, Nikita Mikhailovich (the future author of the Decembrists' constitution), he left for Odessa, accompanied by Murav'ev-Apostol's son, Sergei Ivanovich (who was later hanged with four other Decembrists). Before his departure, advised by Aleksandr Turgenev and helped by Zhukovsky, Batiushkov wrote a letter to Alexander I, describing his imperial service and asking for a post in Italy. On 16 July the emperor raised him to the seventh class and attached him to the consulate in Naples. After a month in Odessa, Batiushkov left for Moscow, arriving on 25 August. In September he sent the Karamzins an unsigned poem celebrating the publication of Karamzin's *Istoriia gosudarstva Rossiiskogo* (History of the Russian State, 1816–1818; revised, 1818–1829). On 11 September he wrote an epistle to Shalikov, which, ironically, turned out to be his farewell to Russia; Shalikov, a chance addressee, did not miss the opportunity to publish it in *Novosti russkoi literatury* in 1822 without the author's permission.

In mid October 1818 Batiushkov arrived in St. Petersburg, and on 19 November a farewell dinner in his honor was given at Tsarskoe Selo; among those present were Zhukovsky, Aleksandr Pushkin, Gnedich, Ekaterina and Nikita Murav'ev, and Aleksandr Turgenev. Batiushkov set off for Naples (arriving in late February 1819) via Vienna, Venice, and Rome. In January he met the Russian painters in Rome, among them Kiprensky. In spring he visited Pompeii and Baia, which he described in a short poem, "Ty probuzhdaesh'sia, o Baia, iz grobnitsy . . ." (Thou art awakening, o Baia, from thy grave . . .), that was published in *Sovremennik*

Page from a letter Batiushkov wrote from Naples to one of his sisters, 20 March 1819 (from the 1977 edition of his Opyty v stikhakh i proze) in 1857 and became well known. Among his extant "Italian" poems is a translation (from an Italian medium version) of a stanza from Byron's *Childe Harold's Pilgrimage* (1812–1818) that Aleksandr Pushkin added to his own copy of *Opyty v stikhakh i proze*. Later Batiushkov imitated an octave from Ariosto, reshaped as an "anthological" sixain.

During 1820 Batiushkov's depression grew. In August he applied for leave to go to Germany, confirmed only in April 1821. From December 1820 to May 1821 he lived in Rome, then went to Teplitz for convalescence; in November he moved to Dresden. The first signs of approaching insanity were a series of quarrels on relatively insignificant grounds. In 1820 an editor of *Syn otechestva*, Aleksandr Fedorovich Voeikov, permitted himself an unauthorized publication of an epitaph by Batiushkov. The author overreacted; Bludov came to his aid; and Voeikov bore a grudge. In February 1821 Voeikov published Pletnev's poem, "B-v iz Rima" (B[atiushko]v from Rome); Pletnev's name was (perhaps deliberately) missing, so the poem was taken as its "hero's" creation. Batiushkov, infuriated, sent Gnedich a letter intended for *Syn otechestva*, claiming he had abandoned his writing forever. Pletnev, a genuine admirer of Batiushkov, attempted to palliate his "guilt" by publishing a panegyrical "inscription" to Batiushkov–who took it as yet another insult. Batiushkov's mind became clouded, and in a fit of depression he destroyed his latest manuscripts.

On 18 September and 12 December 1821 Batiushkov applied for retirement. Instead, the emperor granted him indefinite leave. He came to St. Petersburg on 14 April 1822 and traveled to the Caucasus from May to July; in August he arrived in Simferopol, where, over the following months, symptoms of persecution mania became obvious. He burned his books and three times attempted suicide. On 4 April 1823 he was sent to St. Petersburg, supervised by a doctor. For a whole year his relatives and friends looked after him. In April 1824 he wrote a completely mad letter to the emperor with a request to enter a monastery. After a word with Zhukovsky, Alexander I decided to send the unfortunate writer for treatment at state expense. From 1824 to 1828 Batiushkov was at the "Maison de santé" (a psychiatric home) in Sonnenstein (Saxony); from 1828 to 1833 he stayed in Moscow; and from 1833 onward he lived in Vologda. On 9 December 1833 the incurable Batiushkov was at last released from service and granted a life pension.

In 1834 his works were republished, with additions. The same year, one of his pieces from the early or mid 1820s was published as "Izrechenie Mel'khisedeka" (The Apophthegm of Melchizedek) in *Biblioteka dlia chteniia* (Library for Reading), and fifty years later was republished in *Russkaia Starina* (Russian Antiquity) with a note stating that these verses had been found after Batiushkov's death, written on the wall. Actually, when "Izrechenie Mel'Khisedeka" appeared for the first time, he was still living, but refused to live within time. His obsessive devotion to "Eternity" was remembered, in the twentieth century, in "Net, ne luna, a svetlyi tsiferblat . . ." (No, not the moon, but a bright clock-face . . . , 1912), a poem by Osip Emil'evich Mandel'shtam. "Izrechenie Mel'khisedeka," a poem about the senselessness of human existence and suffering, is considered the last of Batiushkov's "normal" works. When ill, he wrote only a few incoherent texts. His final poem was written in Vologda on 14 May 1853; it is a quatrain that concludes as follows: "Ia prosypaius', chtob zasnut', / I spliu, chtob vechno prosypat'sia" (I only wake to fall asleep / And sleep, to awake without end). At 5:00 P.M. on 7 July 1855 Batiushkov died from typhus. Few noticed his passing–he was already living in history.

Biographies:

Leonid Nikolaevich Maikov, *Batiushkov, ego zhizn' i sochineniia*, second, revised edition (St. Petersburg: A. F. Marks, 1896);

Aleksandr Tikhonovich Sotnikov, *Batiushkov* (Vologda: Vologodskoe oblastnoe izd-vo, 1951);

Viktor Vasil'evich Afanas'ev, *Akhill, ili Zhizn' Batiushkova* (Moscow: Detskaia literatura, 1987);

Viacheslav Anatol'evich Koshelev, *Konstantin Batiushkov: Stranstviia i strasti* (Moscow: Sovremennik, 1987).

References:

Petr Ivanovich Bartenev, "Konstantin Nikolaevich Batiushkov: Ego pis'ma i ocherki ego zhizni," *Russkii Arkhiv*, 10 (1867): 1342–1360; 11 (1867): 1440–1536;

Vissarion Grigor'evich Belinsky, "Sochineniia v proze i v stikhakh, by Konstantin Nikolaevich Batiushkov, 2 volumes (St. Petersburg: I. Glazunov, 1834)," in his *Polnoe sobranie sochinenii*, volume 1 (Moscow: AN SSSR, 1953), pp. 164–174; "Rimskie elegii," volume 5 (Moscow: AN SSSR, 1954), pp. 229–263; "Sochineniia Aleksandra Pushkina. Stat'ia tret'ia," volume 7 (Moscow: AN SSSR, 1955), pp. 223–265;

Dmitrii Dmitrievich Blagoi, "Sud'ba Batiushkova," in his *Tri veka: Iz istorii russkoi poezii XVIII, XIX i XX vv.* (Moscow: Sovetskaia literatura, 1933), pp. 7–42;

William Edward Brown, "The Older Innovators: Konstantin Batyushkov," in his *A History of Russian Literature of the Romantic Period*, volume 1 (Ann Arbor, Mich.: Ardis, 1986), pp. 227–255;

Efim Grigor'evich Etkind, "Ostryi gall'skii smysl," in his *Russkie poety-perevodchiki ot Trediakovskogo do Pushkina* (Leningrad: Nauka, 1973), pp. 116–154;

Lazar' Solomonovich Fleishman, "Iz istorii elegii v pushkinskuiu epokhu," *Uchenye zapiski Latvüskogo gosudarstvennogo universiteta imeni P. Stuchki*, 106 (1968): 24–53;

Nikolai Vladimirovich Fridman, *Poeziia Batiushkova* (Moscow: Nauka, 1971);

Fridman, *Proza Batiushkova* (Moscow: Nauka, 1965);

Fridman, "Tvorchestvo Batiushkova v otsenke russkoi kritiki 1817–1820 gg.," *Uchenye zapiski MGU: Trudy kafedry russkoi literatury*, 3 (1948): 179–199;

Leonid Grigor'evich Frizman, "Evoliutsiia russkoi romanticheskoi elegii: (Zhukovsky, Batiushkov, Baratynsky)," in *K istorii russkogo romantizma*, edited by Iurii Vladimirovich Mann and others (Moscow: Nauka, 1973), pp. 73–106;

Maksim Isaakovich Gillel'son, *Molodoi Pushkin i arzamasskoe bratstvo* (Leningrad: Nauka, 1974), pp. 92–100, 153–155, 165–166;

Lidiia Iakovlevna Ginzburg, *O lirike* (Moscow-Leningrad: Sovetskii pisatel', 1964), pp. 22–43;

R. M. Gorokhova, "Iz istorii vospriiatiia Ariosto v Rossii (Batiushkov i Ariosto)," in *Epokha romantizma: Iz istorii mezhdunarodnykh sviazei russkoi literatury*, edited by Mikhail Pavlovich Alekseev (Leningrad: Nauka, 1975), pp. 236–272;

Grigorii Aleksandrovich Gukovsky, *Pushkin i russkie romantiki* (Moscow: Khudozhestvennaia literatura, 1965), pp. 99–108, 164–172;

I. V. Gura, ed., *K. N. Batiushkov, F. D. Batiushkov, A. I. Kuprin: Materialy Vserossüskoi nauchnoi konferentsii v Ustiuzhne* (Vologda, 1968);

Viktor Vasil'evich Gura, ed., *Venok poetu: Zhizn' i tvorchestvo K. N. Batiushkova* (Vologda: Vologodskoe obl. otdelenie Sovetskogo fonda kul'tury, 1989);

Doris V. Johnson, "The Simile in Batyushkov and Zhukovsky," *Russian Literature Triquarterly*, 7 (1973): 407–422;

Mara Kažoknieks, *Studien zur Rezeption der Antike bei russischen Dichtern zu beginn des XIX. Jahrhunderts* (Munich: Otto Sagner, 1968), pp. 77–153;

Sergei Akimovich Kibal'nik, "Ob istochnikakh poslednego stikhotvoreniia Batiushkova," *Izvestiia Akademii Nauk SSSR: Seriia literatury i iazyka*, 47, no. 4 (1988): 379–382;

Kibal'nik, *Russkaia antologicheskaia poeziia pervoi treti XIX veka* (Leningrad: Nauka, 1990);

Viacheslav Anatol'evich Koshelev, "K biografii K. N. Batiushkova," *Russkaia literatura*, 1 (1987): 69–179;

Koshelev, *Tvorcheskii put' K. N. Batiushkova: Uchebnoe posobie k spetskursu* (Leningrad: LGPI imeni A. I. Gertsena, 1986);

Koshelev, "Kratkaia letopis' zhizni i tvorchestva K. N. Batiushkova," in *Sochineniia*, by Batiushkov, volume 1 (Moscow: Khudozhestvennaia literatura, 1989), pp. 487–495;

Koshelev, *V predchuvstvii Pushkina: K. N. Batiushkov v russkoi slovesnosti nachala XIX veka* (Pskov & Nevel': Izd-vo Pskovskogo obl. in-ta usovershenstvovaniia uchitelei, 1995);

Koshelev, "K. N. Batiushkov i Murav'evy: K probleme formirovaniia 'dekabristskogo' soznaniia," in *Novye bezdelki: Sbornik statei k 60-letiiu V. E. Vatsuro*, edited by S. I. Panov (Moscow: Novoe literaturnoe obozrenie, 1995–1996), pp. 117–137;

Galina Aleksandrovna Kosmolinskaia, "Konstantin Batiushkov–redaktor 'Emilievykh pisem' M. N. Murav'eva," in *Rukopisi; Redkie izdaniia; Arkhivy: Iz fondov biblioteki Moskovskogo universiteta*, edited by Kosmolinskaia (Moscow: Arkheograficheskii tsentr, 1997), pp. 143–168;

R. M. Lazarchuk, "Novye arkhivnye materialy k biografii K. N. Batiushkova: (O printsipakh postroeniia nauchnoi biografii poeta)," *Russkaia Literatura*, 4 (1988): 148–164;

V. D. Levin, "Karamzin, Batiushkov, Zhukovsky-redaktory sochinenii M. N. Murav'eva," in *Problemy sovremennoi filologii: Sbornik statei k semidesiatiletiiu V. V. Vinogradova*, edited by Mikhail Borisovich Khrapchenko (Moscow: Nauka, 1965), pp. 182–191;

Svetlana Alekseevna Matiash, "Metrika i strofika K. N. Batiushkova," in *Russkoe stikhoslozhenie XIX v.: Materialy po metrike i strofike russkikh poetov*, edited by Mikhail Leonovich Gasparov (Moscow: Nauka, 1979), pp. 97–114;

Pavel Aleksandrovich Orlov, "Tvorchestvo K. N. Batiushkova i literaturnye napravleniia nachala XIX veka," *Filologicheskie nauki*, 138, no. 6 (1983): 10–16;

Igor' Alekseevich Pil'shchikov, "Batyushkov and French Critics of Tasso," *Essays in Poetics*, 19, no. 2 (1994): 114–125;

Pil'shchikov, "Literaturnye tsitaty i alliuzii v pis'makh Batiushkova: (Kommentarii k akademicheskomu kommentariiu. 1–4)," *Philologica*, 1, no. 1/2 (1994): 205–246, 2, no. 3/4 (1995): 219–262;

Pil'shchikov, "Batyushkov and La Harpe," *Essays in Poetics*, 19, no. 1 (1994): 110–112;

Pil'shchikov, "Iz istorii russko-ital'ianskikh literaturnykh svazei: (Batiushkov i Tasso)," *Philologica*, 4, no. 8/10 (1997): 7–84;

Oleg Anatol'evich Proskurin, "Batiushkov i poeticheskaia shkola Zhukovskogo: (Opyt pereosmysleniia problemy)," in *Novye bezdelki: Sbornik statei k 60-letiiu V. E. Vatsuro*, pp. 77–116;

Proskurin, "'Pobeditel' vsekh Gektorov khaldeiskikh': K. N. Batiushkov v literaturnoi bor'be nachala XIX veka," *Voprosy literatury*, 6 (1987): 60-93;

Aleksandr Sergeevich Pushkin, "Prichinami, zamedlivshimi khod nashei slovesnosti . . . " and "Kareliia, ili zatochenie Marfy Ioannovny Romanovoi," in his *Polnoe sobranie sochinenii*, volume 11 (Moscow-Leningrad: AN SSSR, 1949), pp. 21, 110; "Zametki na poliakh 2-j chasti 'Opytov v stikhakh i proze' K. N. Batiushkova," volume 12 (Moscow-Leningrad: AN SSSR, 1949), pp. 257-284;

Ivan Nikanorovich Rozanov, "K. Batiushkov," in his *Russkaia lirika* (Moscow: Zadruga, 1914), pp. 244-284;

V. B. Sandomirskaia, "Batiushkov, Konstantin Nikolaevich," in *Russkie pisateli 1800-1917: Biograficheskii slovar'*, edited by P. A. Nikolaev, volume 1 (Moscow: Sovetskaia Entsiklopediia, 1989), pp. 175-180;

Sandomirskaia, "K. N. Batiushkov," in *Istoriia russkoi poezii*, edited by Boris Pavlovich Gorodetsky, volume 1 (Leningrad: Nauka, 1968), pp. 266-281;

Irina Mikhailovna Semenko, "Batiushkov," in her *Poety pushkinskoi pory* (Moscow: Khudozhestvennaia literatura, 1970), pp. 11-57;

Semenko, "Batiushkov i ego *Opyty*," in *Opyty v stikhakh i proze*, by Batiushkov (Moscow: Nauka, 1977), pp. 433-492;

Ilya Zakharovich Serman, *Konstantin Batyushkov* (New York: Twayne, 1974);

Maksim Il'ich Shapir, "Iz istorii russkogo 'balladnogo stikha': Perom vladeet kak eldoi," *Russian Linguistics*, 17 (1993): 57-84;

Joseph Thomas Shaw, *Batiushkov: A Dictionary of the Rhymes & A Concordance to the Poetry* (Madison & London: University of Wisconsin Press, 1975);

Shaw, "Horizontal Enrichment and Rhyme Theory for Studying the Poetry of Puškin, Batjuškov and Baratynskij," in *Russian Verse Theory*, edited by B. P. Scherr and D. S. Worth (Columbus, Ohio: Slavica Publishers, 1989), pp. 351-376;

Tezisy dokladov k nauchnoi konferentsii, posviashchennoi 200-letiiu so dnia rozhdeniia Konstantina Nikolaevicha Batiushkova (Vologda, 1987);

Lev Valentinovich Timofeev, "Poslanie k A. I. T[urgenev]u K. N. Batiushkova," *Russkaia literatura*, 1 (1981): 136-138;

Boris Viktorovich Tomashevsky, "K. N. Batiushkov," in *Stikhotvoreniia*, by Batiushkov, second edition (Moscow-Leningrad: Sovetskii pisatel', 1948), pp. v-lix;

Vladimir Nikolaevich Toporov, "*Istochnik* Batiushkova v sviazi s *Le torrent* Parni: (1. K probleme perevoda. 2. Analiz struktury)," *Uchenye zapiski Tartuskogo gosudarstvennogo universiteta*, 326: *Trudy po znakovym sistemam*, 4 (1969): 306-334;

Marina Federica Varese, *Batjuškov: un poeta tra Russia e Italia* (Padova: Livania, 1970);

Varese, *Il Tasso nella poesia e nella critica di uno ecrittore russo dell' Ottocento: K. N. Batjuškov* (Bergamo, 1969);

N. P. Verkhovsky, "Batiushkov," in *Istoriia russkoi literatury*, volume 5, edited by Vasilii Vasil'evich Gippius (Moscow-Leningrad: AN SSSR, 1941), pp. 392-417;

Viktor Vladimirovich Vinogradov, *Stil' Pushkina* (Moscow: Goslitizdat, 1941), pp. 171-198;

Andrei Leonidovich Zorin, "K. N. Batiushkov v 1814-1815 gg.," *Izvestiia Akademii Nauk SSSR: Seriia literatury i iazyka*, 47, no. 4 (1988): 368-378;

Zorin, "Prochnaia slava poeta," *Russkaia rech'*, 3 (1987): 24-30;

Nikolai Nikolaevich Zubkov, "O sisteme elegii K. N. Batiushkova," *Filologicheskie nauki*, 125, no. 5 (1981): 24-28;

Zubkov, "Opyty na puti k slave," in *'Svoi podvig svershiv . . .'* by Zubkov, Zorin, and Andrei Semenovich Nemzer (Moscow: Kniga, 1987), pp. 265-350.

Papers:

Archives of Konstantin Nikolaevich Batiushkov's papers are located in Moscow at the Rossiiskii gosudarstvennyi arkhiv literatury i iskusstva (RGALI), fond 63 and fond 195, opis' 1, edinitsa khraneniia 1416; at the Gosudarstvennyi arkhiv Rossiiskoi Federatsii (GARF), fond 279, edinitsy khraneniia 323, 324, 1157; and at the Rossiiskaia gosudarstvennaia biblioteka, Otdel rukopisei, fond 211, karton 3619, edinitsy khraneniia I-1/1, I-1/2, I-1/3, I-1/4, I-1/5, I-1/6, I-8. Additional papers are in St. Petersburg at the Rossiiskaia natsional'naia biblioteka imeni M. E. Saltykova-Shchedrina, Otdel rukopisei i redkikh knig, fond 50 and fond 197, opis' 1, edinitsa khraneniia 38; and at the Institut russkoi literatury Rossiiskoi Akademii nauk (Pushkinskii dom), Rukopisnyi otdel, fond 19.

Vladimir Grigor'evich Benediktov

(5 November 1807 – 14 April 1873)

James West
University of Washington

BOOKS: *Stikhotvoreniia Benediktova* (St. Petersburg, 1835);
Stikhotvoreniia. Vtoraia Kniga (St. Petersburg: K. Neiman, 1838);
Stikhotvoreniia. Pervaia kniga (St. Petersburg: V tip. departamenta vneshnei torgovli, 1842);
Stikhotvoreniia, 3 volumes (St. Petersburg: Tip. Krylovskoi, 1856);
Novyia Stikhotvoreniia (St. Petersburg: A. Smirdin, 1857).

Editions and Collections: *Stikhotvoreniia*, 3 volumes, edited by Iakov Petrovich Polonsky (St. Petersburg: M. O. Vol'f, 1883–1884);
Sochineniia, edited by Polonsky, 2 volumes (St. Petersburg & Moscow: M. O. Vol'f, 1902);
Stikhotvoreniia, edited by Lidiia Iakovlevna Ginzburg (Leningrad: Sovetskii pisatel', 1939);
Stikhotvoreniia, edited by F. Ia. Priima (Leningrad: Sovetskii pisatel', 1983);
Stikhotvoreniia, edited by Vsevolod Ivanovich Sakharov (Moscow: Sovetskaia Rossiia, 1991);
Stikhotvoreniia (Moscow: Molodaia gvardiia, 1992).

TRANSLATIONS: Adam Mickiewicz, *Konrad "Vallenrod." Grazhina. Poemy A. Mitskevicha* (St. Petersburg, 1863);
Adam Mickiewicz, *Sobranie sochinenii Adama Mitskevicha v perevode russkikh pisatelei*, 5 volumes (St. Petersburg: M. O. Vol'f, 1882–1883).

Vladimir Benediktov, a slightly younger contemporary of Aleksandr Pushkin, whom he outlived by thirty-six years, left an ambivalent legacy in the history of Russian letters. Benediktov's reception has ranged at one time or another from fashionable enthusiasm to neglect, critical dismissal, and somewhat less-than-affectionate parody. A turn-of-the-century biographer found that he displayed "both a feeling for beauty and a lack of good taste, the sincerest patriotism and total ignorance of the Russian people," but his poetry, still read today, has an enduring quality best summed up by the late-nineteenth-century critic and poet Iakov Petrovich Polonsky: "For all his faults, Benediktov had a genuine lyrical quality that recalls Derzhavin, and that lyricism was his saving grace so often that even today some of his verses possess a striking ardor, freshness and beauty."

Vladimir Grigor'evich Benediktov was born in St. Petersburg on 5 November 1807. His father, Grigorii Stepanovich Benediktov, was a civil servant from the Smolensk region who rose successfully through the ranks and in 1814 was granted hereditary membership in the *dvorianstvo*, the landowning class in feudal Russia. Benediktov's mother, Pelageia Iakobovna Benediktova, née Vinokurova, was the daughter of a gentleman in the service of the tsar's court. Shortly after Benediktov was born, his father was transferred to a position in the provincial administration in Petrozavodsk, northeast of St. Petersburg on the shore of Lake Onega. Benediktov's earliest biographers suggested that the stern landscape and harsh climate of the region may have disposed the sensitive child to serious thoughts and somber emotions, a speculation that is perhaps borne out by such later poems as "Ozero" (The Lake, 1835), in which he reminisces about the "wild land" of his youth. In any event, he is reported to have shown no poetical gifts as a young child and indeed to have naively asked his father on several occasions: "How can people write poetry?"

After beginning his education at home with seminarians as tutors, Benediktov entered the Olonets provincial high school in 1817, where he first began to write verse. However, there are differing accounts of his earliest efforts. Some sources describe his talent as growing under the influence of one of his teachers, I. F. Iakonovsky, a minor poet of little consequence, a sample of whose work has survived in the unpublished notes of one of Benediktov's schoolmates. In this stilted poem, which displays none of the verbal exuberance that characterizes Benediktov's own verse, Iakonovsky urges the boy to be brave, stoic, and obedient to the needs of the tsar and the motherland. In other accounts, none of Benediktov's teachers are deemed capable of having had a beneficial influence on him, and his earliest poems are said to have been so bad that they became an object of derisive mirth among his schoolfellows. However, Lidiia Iakovlevna Ginzburg reports that Benediktov responded to his teacher's poems on political, philosophical, and artistic themes rather than to light verse of the type preserved by his friend.

Upon graduating from the Olonets high school in 1821, Benediktov moved to the capital to complete his education in the Second St. Petersburg Cadet Corps, where he revealed a strong interest and genuine ability in the military sciences and mathematics. He continued to study higher mathematics and astronomy beyond his school years, and these subjects are reflected in his later verses. His poetic endeavors, meanwhile, continued throughout his six years in the cadet corps, and he was a regular contributor to the cadet paper. He graduated in 1827 at the head of his class, and his academic excellence earned him an ensign's commission in the prestigious Izmailovsky guards regiment, an honor that his humble birth would normally have precluded. He participated in 1830–1831 in the campaign to subdue the insurrection in Poland, in which he performed his duties well enough to earn both the Order of St. Anne (fourth grade) for courage and a promotion to lieutenant. During and immediately following this campaign Benediktov wrote his first mature poetry, including "Prazdnik na bivake" (Celebration in the Bivouac), "Noch' bliz mestechka Iakats" (Night near the Village of Jakac), "Brannaia krasavitsa" (Martial Beauty), "K sosluzhivtsu" (To a Comrade-in-Arms), and "Proshchanie s sableiu" (Farewell to the Saber). These poems present a picture of war that is surprisingly romanticized, considering that their author had seen active duty. Even "Noch' bliz mestochka Iakats," in which a soldier on the eve of battle considers the possibility of death, forgoes any authentic details of Benediktov's own experience and deals only in epic stereotypes. The other poems praise the glories of war and the honors accorded to its heroes, and romance is not far behind: in "K sosluzhivtsu" Benediktov anticipates the bright-eyed maidens who await the heroes' return and envisions a meeting with his beloved, whose description resembles that of the "Brannaia krasavitsa," the personification of war.

Benediktov decided against continuing his military career, and in 1832 he resigned his commission to enter government service in the Ministry of Finance, where he was quite successful, becoming the head of his department in 1834 and in 1837 becoming the senior secretary of the General Chancellery. His aptitude and enthusiasm for mathematics contributed to his professional accomplishments, as did one social introduction in particular: through his membership in Vasilii Andreevich Zhukovsky's circle he made the acquaintance of the Minister of Finance, Count Yegor Frantsevich Kankrin, who invited Benediktov to be his personal secretary.

Benediktov's choice of profession was consistent with his temperament as well as his practical skills. Though some contemporaries tried to impute to him the characteristics of his lyrical protagonists, the majority knew him as a modest, rather shy civil servant who smiled amiably but spoke little and with lowered eyes. In his 1910 biography Iurii Ivanovich Aikhenval'd presents Benediktov sympathetically and imaginatively as a passionate and emotional poet who must have suffered greatly in the oppressive setting of his workplace and suggests that his flights of verbal fancy may have provided a much-needed outlet for his repressed poetic sensitivities. Aikhenval'd, however, considers that this divided life estranged the poet from his art as well as from his coworkers and finds Benediktov notably absent from his own verses.

In his biographical note on Benediktov, Polonsky writes that until 1836 the poet's closest friends were Petr Pavlovich Ershov, known today as the author of the story *Konek-Gorbunok* (The Humpback Horse, 1834), and a gentleman by the name of Konstantin Aleksandrovich Bakhturin, the author of a few unremarkable verses who was better known as a wit and a carouser. Ershov, to whom

Benediktov had been introduced in 1833, was probably not as close a friend as Polonsky suggests, but from 1835 his work shows Benediktov's influence. The three friends planned to publish their work in a literary miscellany titled "My vam" (From Us to You). The cover of the first publication was to show a sketch depicting an out-of-control troika and the caption: "Vot mchitsia troika, no kakaia? / Vdal' po doroge, no kakoi?!" ("There races a troika, but what kind? / Off down the road, but which one?!"). The young Benediktov also associated with Vladimir Sergeevich Filimonov, author of the poem "Duratskii kolpak" (The Dunce's Cap), and with several prominent members of the St. Petersburg theatrical circle. Although Benediktov did not take part in public theatrical productions, his early poetry shows a dramatic bent, with speechlike rhythms and the tendency for the protagonists to soliloquize; later in his life he revealed at literary soirées a certain talent for acting.

Benediktov's career as a published poet was launched in the early 1830s when he first read his work to a wider audience at the salon of Elizaveta Alekseevna Karlgof, the wife of a childhood friend who was now a guards officer, a dabbler in poetry, and a patron of the arts. Vil'gelm Ivanovich Karlgof was enchanted with his friend's verses and encouraged him to publish them, but Benediktov hesitated, partly for financial reasons but also because he was reluctant to submit his verses to the questionable judgment of the public. He was eventually persuaded by the Karlgofs' encouragement and financial backing, and *Stikhotvoreniia Benediktova* (The Verses of Benediktov) appeared in 1835 with an anonymous introduction by Karlgof. Only "K sosluzhivtsu" had been published earlier, in a literary periodical in 1832. The book was extremely well received, and a second edition was published in 1836.

The poems that won Benediktov his popularity deal for the most part either with nature or with society. His skill in depicting the life of Russia's growing bureaucratic class may have benefited him financially, and cynics attribute the bulk of his success to his fortunate choice of subject matter. Even today Benediktov is conventionally associated with the themes of his early work. In his play *Poslednie dni (Pushkin)* (Last Days, Pushkin; written 1935, published 1955) Mikhail Afanas'evich Bulgakov portrayed Benediktov as "the poet of curls," referring to the poem "Kudri" (Curls) from his first book of verse, which many modern reviewers single out as an illustration of his style during this period. Benediktov describes in this poem the curls that are the crowning beauty of a much-sought-after young socialite:

Kudri devy–charodeiki,
Kudri–blesk i aromat,
Kudri–kol'tsa, struiki, zmeiki,
Kudri–shelkovy: kaskad!
Veites', leites', syp'tes' druzhno,
Pyshno, iskristo, zhemchuzhno!

(Curls of a maid–of an enchantress,
Curls–luster and fragrance,
Curls–rings, wisps, snakelets,
Curls–a silky cascade!
Twine, pour, spill together,
Sumptuous, sparkling, gemlike!)

In another poem, "Val's" (The Waltz), he compares a social occasion to the stars and planets, introducing this unoriginal image with an unusually pedestrian phrase that shows off his technical knowledge of astronomy: "And the Copernican system / Rejoices in their eyes."

Love is an important theme in Benediktov's poetry, and his treatment of it has engendered some controversy, both critical and biographical. Many of his poems laud feminine beauty but at the same time show the lyric hero rejecting its temptations, and a piece titled "K poetu" (To the Poet), written in the 1840s, appears to make an explicit philosophy of this contradiction, urging the poet to resist the lure of romance and remain faithful to his true calling to serve God with his poetic talent. Benediktov took his own advice to the extent that he remained a bachelor, though one source suggests that he pursued a romance of long duration with a married Polish lady and engaged in shorter relationships with other admirers. T. Glagoleva, the author of a 1917 article, takes a less-guarded look at Benediktov's love poetry, remarking dryly that a large proportion of his verse was inspired by a whole succession of equally "unforgettable" passions and displays an unrefined, overly anatomical physical sensuality that often belies any idealized sentiments it may express. Indeed, the ideal is by no means always present in Benediktov's love lyrics. His poetical response to Classical sculpture was to describe a statue of Venus in erotic terms that deflate the symbol of ideal beauty, presenting the winged cherubs around her as "Pobochnye synki, / Preliubodeistva kroshki . . . " (Little scions of the love-bed, / Babes born of fornication) who rouse the envy of chaste Diana. Elsewhere he rejects in no uncertain terms the idea of mere friendship with a woman: "Net, merci! Ne nado– / Kholodnykh bliud ne em, boius' prostudy–vredno / Morozhennoe mne." (No, merci! I'll pass– / I shun cold cuts, for fear of catching one–chilled / Viands don't agree with me.) In three seldom-quoted lines that are uncharacteristically prosaic, Benediktov actually dismisses the conventional personification of beauty: "Krasavitsa! Zemnaia ty! / Tak chto-zh? Lish' v iunosti nachal'noi / My ishchem devy ideal'noi." (Fair one! So you're mortal! / So what? In youth alone we care / To seek an ideal maiden fair.) Aikhenval'd even admits the presence of implicit sadism in Benediktov's poetic attitude toward women.

In the 1830s the Russian public developed a preference for poetry in a more philosophical vein. The fashions that had dominated the first two decades of the nineteenth century were now deemed "vulgar romanticism," suited to the tastes of the bourgeoisie and civil servants. Although many modern critics accuse Benediktov of catering to exactly those vulgar tastes, his contemporaries greeted him as an innovator, both verbal and philosophical. This assessment of Benediktov was supported by Faddei Venediktovich Bulgarin's newspaper *Severnaia pchela* (The Northern Bee) and by Osip Ivanovich Senkovsky's *Biblioteka dlia chteniia* (Library for Reading), both of which published his poetry. Benediktov laced his poems with neologisms, unfamiliar words, and unexpected combinations. While this practice at the least saved his work from the clichés common in earlier Romantic verse and may be viewed more positively as extending the boundaries of the Romantic style, some critics found that he transgressed against the norms of logic and taste and even of the Russian language itself. Most contemporary readers were not prepared for his innovations. Polonsky, in an attempt to compensate for Benediktov's deliberate straining of the language and to make his poetry accessible to the general reader, provided in his edition of Benediktov's verse a glossary of more than 140 rare and irregularly spelled words. Benediktov's vocabulary, in fact, encompassed virtually the entire spectrum of the Russian language, from Old Church Slavic to contemporary urban slang, a characteristic that has been called "benediktovskii eklektizm" (Benediktovian eclecticism). Parodists such as Ivan Ivanovich Panaev and Dmitrii Dmitrievich Minaev found Benediktov's verbal extravagances an inviting target and his personality just as easy to lampoon. Koz'ma Petrovich Prutkov, the celebrated parody-poet created by Aleksei Konstantinovich Tolstoy and his friends Vladimir Mikhailovich and Aleksei Mikahilovich Zhemchuzhnikov, was at least partly based on Benediktov.

Benediktov's verbal daring has recently earned him more-serious attention, particularly from modernist critics. In his poetic language some think he was ahead of his time, and he has had some influence on the work of twentieth-century poets, including both Symbolists and Futurists. While Petr Nikolaevich Polevoi in 1900 considered Benediktov's poetic yearning for his muse's fiery embraces to be bizarre and in questionable taste, by 1910 Fedor Kuzmich Sologub (himself no stranger to bizarre embraces) proclaimed Benediktov a precursor of the Symbolist movement. Later still, Eduard Georgievich Bagritsky considered "Brannaia krasavitsa" to

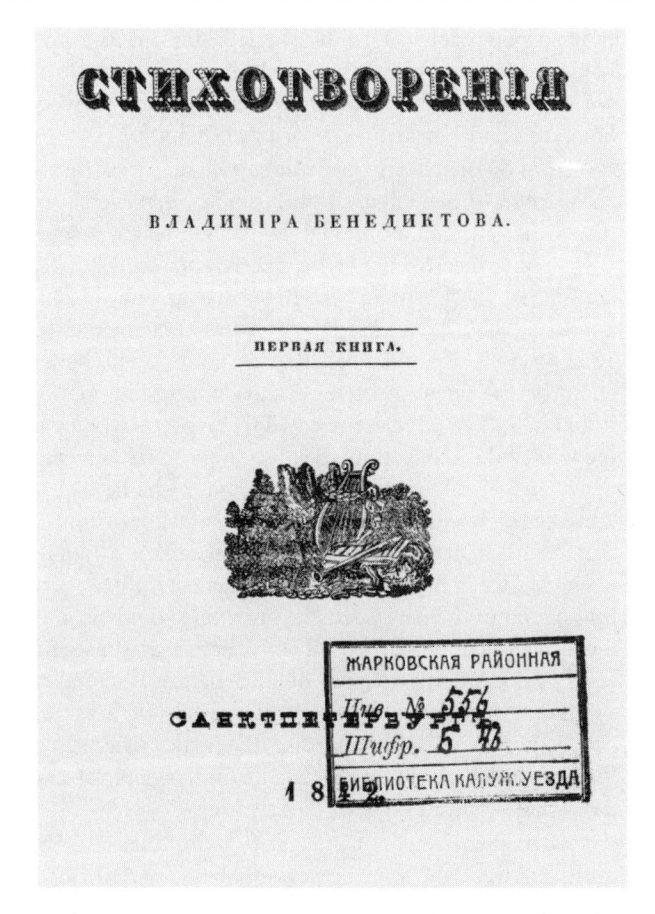

Title page for Benediktov's two-volume Stikhotvoreniia *(Poems), comprising the third edition of his well-received first book and a second edition of his second, which sold well but did not receive critical acclaim*

be an excellent example of an inverted metaphor and marveled at the poetic courage required to write a poem such as "Val's" in Benediktov's time, while Nikolai Nikolaevich Zabolotsky appreciated Benediktov's later poems, particularly "Bessonnitsa" (The Insomniac).

Contemporary readers prized Benediktov not so much for his language as for the thoughts he expressed and his original metaphors. Many indeed considered him a *poet mysli* (poet of ideas), a catchphrase of the Russian literary public of the 1830s. The influential critic Stepan Petrovich Shevyrev, who was a former member of the *Liubomudry* (the Lovers of Wisdom, a group of young, philosophically inclined poets, many of whom worked in the Moscow archive of the Ministry of Foreign Affairs) and was himself inclined to poetic experimentation, welcomed Benediktov enthusiastically as a poet of this stamp. In a review of Benediktov's 1835 verse collection Shevyrev included the poet among those who had outlived the period of "elegant materialism." Even without naming him, this remark hinted at a favorable comparison of Benediktov with Pushkin. Shevyrev's article made Benediktov an object of contention on two levels, as it both singled him out as a poet of a new type opposed to Pushkin's Classicism and placed him in the crossfire of a polemic between Shevyrev and Vissarion Grigor'evich Belinsky.

On the first score, many literary figures took up the comparison of Benediktov with Pushkin, and several predicted that Benediktov would enjoy the greater success. Benediktov, meanwhile, had a sincere and wholehearted admiration for Pushkin, whom he met at one of Zhukovsky's "Saturdays." He describes this encounter in his 1852 poem "Vospominanie" (Recollection), and his veneration of the great poet also finds expression in "31 dekabria 1837" (31 December 1837), a poem written in the year of Pushkin's death. Belinsky went so far as to suggest that Benediktov owed whatever strengths he had to imitation of Pushkin. Pushkin for his part knew how to damn with faint praise, and all of Benediktov's biographers cite the master's dry pronouncement, when asked his opinion of the new poet: "he has a fine comparison of the heavens to an upturned goblet." There is no consensus on Pushkin's real opinion of Benediktov, but taken together, his statements suggest that while he was not deeply impressed with Benediktov's work as a whole, Pushkin appreciated some of Benediktov's metaphors and the strong rhythmic qualities of his verse.

Benediktov was particularly unfortunate to be caught between the warring pens of Shevyrev and Belinsky, and it was in fact Belinsky who eventually brought about Benediktov's fall from public favor through his unexpectedly sharp criticism. In an 1835 article Belinsky drew attention to the rhetoric, allegorical diction, and lack of conceptual clarity in Benediktov's poetry. In later reviews Belinsky devoted most of his attention to what he perceived as Benediktov's lack of taste and popularized the term *benediktovshchina* (Benediktovitis) to describe the flaws he perceived. At best, Belinsky judged Benediktov to be a talented verse technician without real poetic gifts and his best poetry to be "endearing poetic trifles." Belinsky's remarks took root, and his critique of Benediktov was widely adopted by later detractors. Benediktov's literary career, in fact, peaked between 1835 and 1838, when for a brief while he enjoyed public favor, not just in St. Petersburg but throughout Russia. In this period he captured the attention of a variety of major literary figures, including Zhukovsky, Prince Petr Andreevich Viazemsky, Fedor Ivanovich Tiutchev, Ivan Petrovich Turgenev, Apollon Aleksandrovich Grigor'ev, Afanasii Afanas'evich Fet, Ivan Aleksandrovich Goncharov, and Nikolai Alekseevich Nekrasov. Zhukovsky learned of Benediktov through Shevyrev's laudatory article. Zhukovsky is said to have been so enthusiastic about the discovery that he could not put the article down for several days and could be seen on his walks in the royal park loudly declaiming Benediktov's verses to the trees. Fet's "Liricheskii panteon" (Lyric Pantheon) and Nekrasov's "Mechty i zvuki" (Dreams and Sounds), both published in 1840, reflect the influence of Benediktov.

At the height of its popularity Benediktov's work appeared in many of the leading literary periodicals and almanacs, including *Biblioteka dlia chteniia* and *Syn otechestva* (Son of the Fatherland). His published works of 1836 through 1837 were collected in a volume titled *Stikhotvoreniia. Vtoraia Kniga* (Verses. Second Book, 1838), which did not receive the critical or popular acclaim of his first book but sold three thousand copies more quickly, as Polevoi indignantly noted, than "the best works of Pushkin, Lermontov, and even Gogol." From 1838 to 1842 Benediktov published a two-volume collection titled *Stikhotvoreniia* (Poems), consisting of the third edition of his first volume and a second edition of his second volume.

After 1838 Benediktov's fame began to wane, although his reputation kept sales of his works at a high level for several more years. From 1845 to 1855 he published no verses of his own, but his poetry of the early 1840s began to progress beyond the society themes of his early work. A journey to Odessa and Crimea on offical business between May and September of 1839 inspired a "Crimean cycle," written over several years in the 1840s. His literary activity and his participation in periodicals were renewed after he published in 1854 the programmatic poem "K moei muze" (To My Muse), in which the poet bids farewell to the "boisterous immodesty" of the muse of his youth and welcomes her return to him in a new guise: "Dressed simply, buttoned up to her neck." However, this demure muse quickly revealed her reforming spirit, even if it was cloaked in respect for the tsar. During the 1850s, a period of enthusiasm for social change and inevitable disillusionment, Benediktov published an extensive collection of work devoted to civic themes, in which he displayed a predominantly liberal, though not revolutionary, bent. He wrote of "benevolent reforms" from above, legality, education, the struggle with bureaucratic corruption, and "reasonable" freedom of the press. With his civic poetry of the 1850s he made in fact a brief return to the limelight, and five poems that appeared in 1855 in *Biblioteka dlia chteniia* were considered by some critics to be better than the work to which he owed his original success.

Some of his unpublished poems include stronger statements than Benediktov dared to make in his published works. His translation of Auguste Barbier's revolutionary poem "La curée" (he gave it the title "Sobachii pir"–"A Dogs' Banquet") was circulated in Russia secretly and was published only in 1861 in Nikolai Platonovich Ogarev's *Russkaia potaennaia literatura XIX-go stoletiia* (The Underground Literature of Nineteenth-Century Russia). Despite its clandestine distribution, the poem became widely known and brought Barbier a fame that he had not hitherto enjoyed in Russia. In the poem "7 aprelia 1857" (7 April 1857), first published in 1939, Benediktov laments Russia's fate under Nicholas I, telling his homeland, "you were dead for thirty years." Petr Ivanovich Kapnist in *Ocherki napravleniia russkoi lirichnoi poezii c 1854 po 1864 god vkliuchitel'no* (Essays on the Trend of Russian Lyric Poetry from 1854 to 1864), written on the orders of the secret police, the so-called Third Department, even labeled the notoriously benign poet "a negator and exposer."

Through the literary soirées held at the home of her parents, Benediktov in 1853 met Elena Andreevna Shtakenshneider, whose journal, published in excerpted form in 1934, recorded the details of these occasions and the poets who attended them. This journal is a particularly valuable source of information on Benediktov, who quickly became a regular visitor and was eventually treated as a member of the family. At one of the Shtakenshneiders's evenings Benediktov met the populist critic, poet, and thinker Petr Lavrovich Lavrov, whose career was then at its outset. According to Elena Shtakenshneider, Lavrov "harbored a most sincere and deep respect" for Bendiktov "both as a man of learning and simply as a person." Lavrov's autobiographical poem "Chasovye" (Sentries), written around 1856 but not published until 1983, was dedicated to Benediktov.

In the second half of the 1850s Benediktov's work continued to appear in journals, and he also began to make appearances at public readings. In 1858 a young audience noisily welcomed the reading of the poem "K novomu pokoleniiu" (To a New Generation) with the subtitle "Ot starikov" (From the Old Men), in which Benediktov urged the younger generation to "step over us!" In January 1860 Benediktov appeared with Turgenev, Nekrasov, Polonsky, and Apollon Nikolaevich Maikov at a public benefit and read his appeals for the resurrection of poetry, "Bor'ba" (Struggle) and "I nyne" (Even Now), which had a similarly enthusiastic reception, and both of these poems were immediately printed by Nekrasov in *Sovremennik*. However, such successes were sporadic and proved to be of little consequence for Benediktov's reputation with the critics, as the leaders of democratic opinion, Nikolai Gavrilovich Chernyshevsky and Nikolai Aleksandrovich Dobroliubov, did not accept the new Benediktov. Like Belinsky before them, later reviewers felt that Benediktov's civic verse was little more than cold rhetoric. Chernyshevsky responded with a scathing review to the appearance in 1856 of a three-volume collection of Benediktov's work titled *Stikhovorenia* (Verses). The first volume consisted of poems selected from Benediktov's first collection—excluding some that he considered inferior—and previously unpublished poetry from the same period. The second volume included poetry written from 1835,

Title page for Benediktov's Novyia Stikhotvoreniia *(New Poems), which includes poems devoted to civic themes*

when the first collection appeared, to 1850 and translations of poetry from various languages made during the same period. The third volume included poetry and translations from 1850 to 1856. A collection of new poetry, published in 1857 with the title *Novyia Stikhotvoreniia*, prompted an equally deprecating review from Dobroliubov. In Dobroliubov's view Benediktov's poetry had always consisted of little more than elaborate devices and sound effects, for which the social questions of the day now often served as the background in replacement of the romantic dreams of the earlier period. He also condemned Benediktov's translations, finding in them essentially the same failings.

In his later works, as Dobroliubov correctly observed, Benediktov continued to make extensive use of metaphor and hyperbole, but these devices now came to serve other thematic and stylistic purposes. As he came under the influence of Nekrasov, the poets of *Iskra* (The Spark), and the later works of Viazemsky, Benediktov began to compose political couplets, poetic satires, and other forms that were unusual for him. He continued to combine disparate styles of speech in his verses, including conversational, official, and journalistic language, as for example in the poem "Sovremennyi genii" (Contemporary Genius), which was written in versified journalese. A few poems of this period make interesting use of folk elements, and Elena Shtakenshneider notes that in November of 1855 Benediktov was working on a play—yet another example of his desire to experiment with new literary techniques. While Benediktov's early work was remarkable only for its style and choice of themes, his later poems show much greater variety. Together with civic, realistic, and satirical verses, there are meditations on the problems of life, lyrics dominated by motifs of fatigue and loneliness, and both narrative and historical poems. However, in his later work Benediktov lacked the sharpness and energy that had once been a hallmark of his poetic manner.

Benediktov's successful civil service career ended with his retirement in 1860 (1858 according to some sources), and after 1862 he once again left the literary arena, not to appear in print again until near the end of his life. In the 1850s his social life had been confined to a narrow circle of friends who were sincerely fond of him; these included Maikov, Goncharov, Avdot'ia Pavlovna Baumgarten, and the Shtakenshneider family. Benediktov lived in increasing seclusion in his later years, relying on his sister to take care of his domestic needs, but true to his poetic convictions, he continued to write without an audience, alone and in obscurity. He translated Barbier; Johann Wolfgang von Goethe; Friedrich von Schiller; George Gordon, Lord Byron; William Shakespeare; André-Marie de Chénier; Victor Hugo; Théophile Gautier; and other poets; in 1863 his first translations of the renowned Polish poet Adam Mickiewicz's "Konrad Wallenrod" and "Grazyna" appeared to favorable reviews. Benediktov went on to translate a substantial number of Mickiewicz's works, and a surviving manuscript includes versions of Goethe's "Torquato Tasso" and Byron's "Cain."

When Benediktov died on 14 April 1873, few mourners conducted him to his final resting place, and Polonsky reports that even some of Benediktov's friends who wished to be at the funeral did not know where his apartment was. The summary words of one biographer provide a fitting epitaph: "He was an extraordinarily good-natured and mild-mannered man. He was gratified, of course, by praise for the promptings of his muse, but it did not make him proud or overbearing."

References:

Iurii Ivanovich Aikhenval'd, "Benediktov," in *Istoriia russkoi literatury XIX veka,* volume 2 (Moscow, 1910);

"Benediktov," in *Biografii russkikh pisatelei,* edited by A. P. Dobryv (St. Petersburg: Stolichnaia tipografiia, 1900);

"Benediktov," in *Istoriia russkoi literatury,* edited by E. N. Kupreianova, volume 2 (Leningrad, 1981);

"Benediktov," in *Istoriia russkoi literatury XIX veka,* edited by F. M. Golovenchenko and S. M. Petrov (Moscow: Uchpedgiz, 1960);

Thomas Stanley Berczinski, "V. G. Benediktov's Literary Debut: A Different Drum," *Russian Literature Triquarterly* (Ann Arbor, Mich.), 23 (1990): 287–301;

Lidiia Iakovlevna Ginzburg, "Benediktov," in *Russkie pisateli 1800–1917,* volume 1 (Moscow: Izd-vo Sov. Entsiklopediia, 1989);

Ginzburg, introduction to *Stikhotvoreniia,* by Benediktov, edited by M. Gor'kii (Leningrad, 1939);

Aleksandr Anatol'evich Iliushin, "Benediktov," in *Russkie pisateli. Bibliograficheskii slovar',* volume 1 (Moscow: Molodaia gvardiia, 1990);

E. A. Karlgof-Drashusova, "Zhizn' prozhit'—ne pole pereiti," *Russkii Vestnik,* no. 9 (1881): 141–143;

B. V. Mel'gunov, "Iz poeticheskogo naslediia Benediktova," *Russkaia literatura* (St. Petersburg), no. 3 (1982): 164–172;

Petr Nikolaevich Polevoi, "Benediktov," in *Istoriia russkoi slovesnosti,* volume 3 (St. Petersburg: A. F. Marks, 1900);

Iakov Petrovich Polonsky, "Biografiia V. G. Benediktova," in *Sochineniia,* by Benediktov (St. Petersburg & Moscow: M. O. Vol'f, 1902), pp. 1–27;

Fedor Iakovlevich Priima, introduction to *Stikhotvoreniia,* by Benediktov, edited by Priima (Leningrad: Sovetskii pisatel', 1983);

Stanislav Borisovich Rassadin, "Neudachnik Benediktov," *Voprosy literatury* (Moscow), no. 10 (1976): 152–183;

Vsevolod Ivanovich Sakharov, "V. G. Benediktov: Poeziia i sud'ba," in *Stikhotvoreniia,* by Benediktov, edited by V. I. Sakharov (Moscow: Sovetskaia Rossiia, 1991);

Barry Scherr, "The Verse Practice of Vladimir Benediktov," in *Russian Verse Theory,* edited by Barry Scherr and Dean Worth (Columbus, Ohio: Slavica, 1989), pp. 297–330;

Elena Andreevna Shtakenshneider, *Dnevnik i zapiski, 1854–1886* (Moscow: Academia, 1934);

Pavel Ioevich Veinberg, "Bezobraznyi postupok," *Veka,* 4, no. 5 (1900).

Papers:

Vladimir Grigor'evich Benediktov's papers are located in Rossiiskii gosudarstvennyi arkiv literatury i iskusstva (Moscow), f. 65; Rossiiskaia natsional'naia biblioteka (St. Petersburg), f. 62; IRLI (Pushkin House) in the archive of the Maikovs; and Rossiiskii gosudarstvennyi istoricheskii arkhive, f. 1349, op. 5, d. 3245 (from 1857).

Denis Vasil'evich Davydov
(16 July 1784 – 22 April 1839)

Sonia I. Ketchian
Davis Center for Russian Studies, Harvard University, and M.I.T.

BOOKS: *Opyt teorii partizanskago deistviia* (Moscow: S. Selivanovsky, 1821);

Razbor trekh statei pomeshchennykh v zapiskakh Napoleona (Moscow, 1825);

Stikhotvoreniia (Moscow: Tip. Avgusta Semena, pri Imperatorskoi Mediko-Khirurgich. Akademii, 1832);

Zamechaniia na nekrologiiu N. N. Raevskago (Moscow: A. Semen, 1832).

Editions and Collections: *Sochineniia v stikhakh i proze,* second edition, corrected and enlarged, 3 volumes (St. Petersburg: A. F. Smirdin, 1840);

Sochineniia (St. Petersburg: A. Smirdin, 1848);

Sochineniia Denisa Vasil'evicha Davydova, fourth edition, corrected and enlarged, 3 volumes (Moscow: Bakhmetev, 1860);

Zapiski Denisa Vasil'evicha Davydova, v Rossii tsenzuroiu ne propushchennye, edited by Prince Petr Vladimirovich Dolgorukov (London: S. Tchorzewski, 1863);

Stikhotvoreniia (St. Petersburg: A.S. Suvorin, 1889);

Sochineniia Denisa Vasil'evicha Davydova, 3 volumes, edited by Aleksandr Osipovich Kruglyi (St. Petersburg: E. Evdokimov, 1893);

Nekotorye vypiski iz bumag Denisa Vasil'evicha Davydova, ne propushchennye tsenzuroiu v Rossii, fourth edition (Leipzig: E. L. Kasprovich, 1906);

Polnoe sobranie stikhotvorenii, edited by Vladimir Nikolaevich Orlov (Leningrad: Izdatel'stvo pisateleiv Leningrade, 1933);

Stikhotvoreniia, edited by Orlov (Leningrad: Sovetskii pisatel', 1936);

Voennye zapiski, edited by Orlov (Moscow: Goslitizdat, 1940);

Dnevik partizanskikh deistvii 1812 goda (Moscow: Goslitizdat, 1941);

Stikhotvoreniia i stat'i, edited by S. V. Ivanov, Aleksandr Mikhailovich Egolin, E. N. Mikhailovna, and M. M. Essen (Moscow: Goslitizdat, 1942);

Polnoe sobranie sochinenii, edited by Orlov (Leningrad: Izd-vo pistelei, 1962);

Denis Vasil'evich Davydov

Sochineniia, edited by Orlov (Moscow: Khudozhestvennaia literatura, 1962);

Izbrannoe, edited by A. Il'in-Tomich (Moscow: Kniga, 1984);

Stikhotvoreniia, edited by Vadim Erazmovich Vatsuro, second edition (Leningrad: Sovetskii pisatel', 1984);

Zapiski partizana. Stikhi, edited by V. K. Osokina (Moscow: Molodaia gvardiia, 1984);

Gusarskaia tetrad', (Moscow: Voenizdat', 1992).

OTHER: "Wisdom," in *Specimens of the Russian Poets with Preliminary Remarks and Biographical Notices,* by John

Bowring, second edition (London: J. Bowring, 1821);

"The Song of an Old Hussar," "To a Pious Charmer," "Those Evening Bells," and "Dance," translated by Lauren G. Leighton, in *The Ardis Anthology of Russian Romanticism,* edited by Christine Rydel (Ann Arbor, Mich.: Ardis, 1984), pp. 56–57.

Poet, memoirist, and military theorist Denis Davydov was one of the most colorful and celebrated figures in Russian literature. He was a brilliant conversationalist, a legendary partisan hero of the Patriotic War against Napoleon Bonaparte in 1812, and a protégé of great Russian military figures General Aleksandr Vasil'evich Suvorov, Prince Petr Ivanovich Bagration, and Prince Mikhail Illarionovich Kutuzov. Leo Tolstoy depicted Davydov as Vas'ka Denisov in *Voina i mir* (War and Peace, 1863–1869) and Sir Walter Scott intended to portray him in a novel, to be titled "The Black Knight."

Denis Vasil'evich Davydov was born in Moscow on 16 July 1784. His old aristocratic family traced its roots to Genghis Khan, specifically to Murza Minchak in the fifteenth century, and was related to the Raevskys, Kakhovskys, Ermolovs, and Samoilovs. The military arena was a family tradition, and Davydov's father, Vasilii Denisovich Davydov, commanded the Poltava Light Cavalry Regiment near the Dniepr River. Davydov's mother, Elena Evdokimovna (née Shcherbina), was the daughter of a wealthy former vice-regent of Novorossiisk. The family owned the village of Borodino and an estate in Orlov.

Like most noblemen, Davydov and his brothers, Evdokim and Lev, received their education at home. Davydov's education seemed to be secondary to military preparation; indeed, from the age of seven Davydov and his brother Evdokim lived in a military tent with their father. The boy's military ideal was the Russian leader and hero Suvorov, who had never lost a battle and who crossed the Alps in 1799. All his life Davydov recalled with pride his first meeting, at age nine, with the Russian military genius who foresaw a military career for the boy, as recorded later in his reminiscences on Suvorov, "Vstrecha s velikim Suvorovym" (A Meeting with the Great Suvorov). Elsewhere, in his light-hearted, tongue-in-cheek record of his own life, "Nekotorye cherty iz zhizni Denisa Vasil'evicha Davydova: Avtobiografiia" (Some Traits from the Life of Denis Vasil'evich Davydov: An Autobiography, 1828), he confirms that Suvorov, in blessing this little "urchin" when reviewing the Poltava Light Cavalry Regiment, predicted: "You will win three battles." Upon hearing this, the young Davydov allegedly "gave up the Psalter, waved his sword, damaging his tutor's eye, piercing his nurse's train and chopping off the tail of a borzoi dog, convinced that he was thus fulfilling the great man's prophesy. The rod directed him toward peace and study."

Many of Davydov's later comments about himself must be understood as either humorous or bantering self-deprecation rather than the undue personal boasting that some writers perceive in him.

Davydov deplored the instruction received by young people in those years when the primary objective was to achieve social graces and polish for the pursuit of pleasure rather than service to society. Youngsters were taught to babble in French (actually Davydov's knowledge of French was superior), to dance, to draw, and to play music. All of these endeavors (so evocative of the inadequate education allegedly received by the contemporaries of Aleksandr Pushkin's Eugene Onegin) Davydov mastered in his adolescence, at which time he took to riding his horse and hunting. At the age of thirteen Davydov left for Moscow to study at the Moscow University Gentry Pension, which cultivated a literary bent. Here Davydov read the first Russian almanac, *Aonidy* (The Aonids), published between 1796 and 1799 by the Sentimental writer and historian Nikolai Mikhailovich Karamzin in collaboration with noted writers Gavriil Romanovich Derzhavin, Mikhail Matveevich Kheraskov, Vasilii Vasil'evich Kapnist, and Ivan Ivanovich Dmitriev. Davydov's first poem was "Pastushka Liza" (The Shepherdess Liza), in the vein of the Sentimental school of Karamzin. His subsequent poems of military conviviality, as well as the civic and satiric pieces, were eventually circulated in the highest social circles.

Davydov's military career was hampered from the beginning. Davydov's father was brought to trial in 1796 for alleged embezzlement of his regiment's funds. Some scholars believe the accusations were false and that the objective was Vasilii Davydov's removal from a prominent position because he was a high-ranking officer related to objectionable people. The result of the trial was the confiscation of the family estate, which plunged the family into poverty for many years. At times their only food was potatoes. Davydov's love for his father was in no way diminished, a fact that points to his conviction of his father's innocence. Yet, because Vasilii Davydov's gambling was cited as the reason for his alleged embezzlement and the family had to pay these debts until 1817, the poet refrained from gambling all his life.

The palace coup of 11 March 1801 ushering in Alexander I paved the way for military service in St. Petersburg for Davydov. With four hundred rubles in his pocket, the bold young man entered the Cavalry Guard Regiment, albeit with great difficulty supposedly because of his short stature. He was appointed a cadet. Chastised by his cousin Aleksandr Mikhailovich Kakhovsky for ignorance in matters of military science, Davydov extensively studied the subject both with a tutor and independently. He pursued his studies with such vigor that he

Engraving of the peace conference between Tsar Alexander I and Napoleon Bonaparte at Tilsit, 25 June 1807, which Davydov witnessed

became one of the top specialists of his time, as well as a proponent of Suvorov's humane treatment of soldiers.

The liberalizations of Alexander's reign rejuvenated political life and revitalized the periodical press to a certain extent. At this time Davydov met officers of the Preobrazhensky regiment, including participants in the palace coup such as Sergei Nikoforovich Marin and A. V. Argamakov. Boisterous, noisy merrymaking and its idealization became the order of the day among young officers, noblemen, and students. Buttressed by the freer sensibilities of the times and the development of young poets, the military ode of the eighteenth century soon turned into a less rigid military lyric or song that extolled camaraderie and conviviality rather than the battles and victories of the rulers. Apparently the friendly verse epistle that often praised fellowship and merriment was an important source in the evolution of this genre, along with the Anacreontic odes that had been translated into Russian by Nikolai Aleksandrovich L'vov in 1794 and works of the French writer Vicomte Evariste-Désiré de Parny. These trends influenced writers from Ippolit Fedorovich Bogdanovich to Derzhavin. While the Russian elite took part in the convivial drinking parties, some of the talented writers among them composed poems on their own interpretations and understanding of this philosophy of life, or on an aspect of it. Easily finding his own niche, Davydov made his acclaimed contributions to what came to be known as hussar drinking songs. His poetic output was, however, by no means limited to this genre; epigrams, civic fables, and sensitive elegies also figure prominently in his verse, although no more than ninety-five poems have survived.

The social milieu that shaped Davydov's thought and behavior included some of the wealthiest and most educated people of the time. In addition to his prominent relatives, he was friendly with the daring, educated duelist Fedor Ivanovich Tolstoy (a count known as Tolstoy the American and the uncle of Leo Tolstoy); Aleksandr Aleksandrovich Shakhovskoi, the dramatist who wrote high comedy in verse and was for a time the director of the Imperial Theaters; Konstantin Nikolaevich Batiushkov; Evgenii Abramovich Baratynsky; Baron Anton Antonovich Del'vig; Aleksandr Pushkin; Vasilii Andreevich Zhukovsky; and Prince Petr Andreevich Viazemsky. Critical and satirical pieces that in the time of Emperor Paul could only have been circulated furtively in manuscript among friends were now published with relative openness.

Davydov began his writing with satires, of which only the piece "Son" (Dream), written in 1802, has survived. This piece is in the form of a question with an answer, as the speaker recounts a dream of an ideally transformed St. Petersburg. He lists the improved former faults of acquaintances, such as the hospitable Aleksandr L'vovich Naryshkin's debts, Bagration's long nose, and his own short stature and unattractiveness: "And I myself who from birth / Bore with a stretch of the imagination the name of a human, / Look without recognizing myself, rejoicing: / Where did this attractiveness and height come from." Davydov's civic fables were widely acclaimed and circulated among his friends but brought him disfavor in administrative circles. In 1803 he wrote "Golova i nogi" (The Head and the Feet), which voices the complaint of the mistreated, tired feet against the head's tyranny because of its elevated position: "You exhausted us like exiled chain gang prisoners / And sitting on top merely bat your eyes." The lowly feet hint that if they were to stumble, the head could be hurt; the oblique criticism of the emperor was not appreciated. Vivid, dramatic, and imaginative, the work recalls Ivan Andreevich Krylov's acclaimed fables. It was not published until 1861, in *Russkaia potaennaia literatura XIX stoletiia* (Russian Secret Literature of the Nineteenth Century). Soon afterward Davydov wrote his second civic fable, "Byl' ili basnia, kak kto khochet nazovi" (A true story or a fable, name it as you will). He then reworked for Russian reality the French Comtesse Sophie de Ségur's fable "L'enfant, le miroir et la rivière" (The Child, the Mirror and the River). The Russian fable encloses the French fable as a quotation within its text. Because of strict censorship, it was published only posthumously in *Russkii vestnik* (The Russian Herald) in 1869 as "Reka i Zerkalo" (The River and the Mirror). Compounding the disquiet of the authorities who found its mention of a monarch and Siberia "rebellious," the poem prompted Davydov's demotion and transfer in 1804 to the Byelorussian Hussar Regiment near Kiev.

The only outlets for recreation there were cards (which Davydov avoided), discussions and drinking parties with fellow officers, and social dances. In his third-person autobiography "Ocherk zhizni Denisa Vasil'evicha Davydova" (A Sketch of the Life of Denis Vasil'evich Davydov, 1828) he recalls: "The young hussar captain of the cavalry twirled his moustache, set his shako at a rakish angle, tightened his belt, straightened up and began to dance the mazurka until he dropped." Davydov's romantic interest there was a Polish beauty whose name remains concealed. To her he wrote love poems (now presumed lost) that, according to the poet, she could not understand.

In the Byelorussian Hussar Regiment, Davydov served with Aleksei Petrovich Burtsov, a lieutenant who was a second cousin of S. N. Marin and was famous among the hussars as a great carouser and a desperate and reckless debaucher. Legends arose claiming that Burtsov died during a drunken escapade. In fact, wounded in the Patriotic War, Burtsov died in 1813 after a valiant struggle with the resulting illness. Such mundane facts are not the stuff of legend, so it was up to Davydov to immortalize the tough, fiery hussar in two poems of 1804 that bear his name in the titles: "Burtsovu: Prizyvanie na punsh" (To Burtsov: An Invitation to Punch) and "Burtsovu" (To Burtsov), included in the 1832 edition of Davydov's *Stikhotvoreniia* (Poems). The reason for the immense popularity of these poems lay in their sweeping bravado as well as the author's own expansive nature and love of carousing that made them authentic in the reader's mind. The innovation of the hussar songs with their high artistry commenced a new genre with sufficient tribute to tradition, particularly to the Anacreontic ode. "Burtsovu: Prizyvanie na punsh" represents a spirited invitation to drinking buddy Burtsov for punch ostensibly prepared with potent *arakh,* an Eastern form of vodka. Composed in an upbeat trochaic tetrameter, the poem manages to convey a celebration of life, youthful valor, and optimism in the face of danger during battle. It begins: "Burtsov, ladies man, brawler, / Dear drinking buddy! / For the love of God and . . . of arakh / Visit my hovel!" The location, a makeshift hussar's dwelling in which the only worthwhile decorations are the hussar's personal belongings—such as a leather pouch bearing the tsar's monogram, a sack of oats for a coach, his shining saber, and five inviting cups for punch—stands in stark contrast to the opulence of a highly placed court official's home. The poem concludes:

> And in lieu of beautiful vases
> Of white marble, large
> On the tables stand
> Five terrific punch cups!
> They are full, I assure you,
> In them is concealed heavenly fire.
> Come, I am waiting,
> Prove that you are a hussar.

In these songs hussar company, a strong drink, and a smoking pipe are more prized in the lull between battles than the wealth and influence of the courtier, a commonplace that arises even in the Anacreontic poems of ancient Greece. Burtsov must attend this gathering to prove his mettle.

The poem "Burtsovu" invites the addressee to a pre-battle celebration of fellowship and bravery in the ancient traditions of their forefathers, and in singling out his comrade's valor and boldness Davydov actually provides an example for all to follow : "Burtsov, you are a hussar among hussars! / You on your valiant steed / Are the cruelest of rowdies / And a rider in war!" The song turns into a battle cry invoking the men not to spare their lives for the glory of the homeland. As the officers drink and toast their past and future valor, the signals are given for battle, a symbolic feast, as it were: "God is giving us a different feast, / A more perky and daring feast, / Both more noisy and more cheerful . . ." Davydov's poem on the interim between battles differs in content from the earlier military ode that described battles and served as a panegyric to rulers or established leaders by treating officers as "ordinary" as the poetic speaker.

In the next poem of 1804, titled "Gusarskii pir" (A Hussar Feast), Burtsov is again addressed by name and enjoined in bracing trochees, as if after battle, to be merry in peaceful days and to convoke all the riders with twirling moustaches, an important recurrent symbol of valor and masculinity in Davydov. Most crucial for the officers is to enjoy to the fullest their brief days of rest: "Life is flying away: don't bring shame on yourself, / Don't sleep through its flight. / Drink, love and make merry! / That's my friendly advice." In fact, all this merrymaking and camaraderie is an important component in ensuring high morale and battle preparedness, for the men were forging "a fraternal friendship at the bloody feasts of the War of 1812."

On 4 June 1806, through the concerted efforts of his friends, particularly Prince Boris Antonovich Sviatopolk-Chetvertinsky, brother of Alexander's mistress Mariia Antonovz Naryshkina, Davydov was transferred as a lieutenant to the Imperial Life Guards in Pavlovsk near St. Petersburg, where Chetvertinsky served as squadron commander. Life in the squadron was pleasant, and Davydov shone with caustic epigrams and poems on members of society. On life in St. Petersburg, Davydov wrote in "Vstrecha s fel'dmarshalom grafom Kamenskim" (Meeting with Field Marshal Count Kamensky, written in 1806): "In our entire regiment there was more friendship than service, more stories than work, more gold on the purses than in them, more champagne (obviously on credit) than sadness . . . Always cheerful and always in one's cups." Efforts for a transfer to active duty were futile until the eager young officer resorted to ingenuity in obtaining an unorthodox meeting at 3:00 A.M. with Field Marshal Count Kamensky who knew both Davydov's father and grandfather.

Through Naryshkina's intervention Davydov was appointed aide to Bagration, commander of the field forces. Rejoicing at the prospects of impending battle, Davydov, who from childhood had lived only for military service, writes: "I knew where I was going: where there was fighting and not where there was kissing, and I was convinced, and remain so, that war is not soup made of sterlet broth."

As the Russian Army retreated to Preussisch-Eylau (now Bagrationovsk), Davydov burned with impatience to experience his first battle. His eagerness resulted in a hair-raising brush with captivity, thwarted by chance and the young officer's ability to seize the opportunity, as narrated humorously in the essay "Urok sorvantsu" (A Lesson to a Madcap, written in 1807). The battle at Preussisch-Eylau on 26–27 January 1807 provided Davydov with an opportunity to display his bravery, as he was to do on many occasions.

Field Marshal Mikhail Illarionovich Kutuzov, who authorized Davydov's partisan raids against the French army in 1812

As aide to the revered hero Bagration, Davydov benefited vastly from this great leader's knowledge and generosity. The young man received several citations for bravery, medals, and a gold saber with the inscription "For Valor." He suffered a severe contusion at the battle of Heilsberg on 29 May 1808. Davydov's bravery and audacity in battle were matched by his compassion away from the battlefield and a fierce loyalty to his family, as displayed when he discovered in Koenigsberg a captive French officer who a year earlier had saved the life of Davydov's seriously wounded brother at Austerlitz. Returning to the prisoner his personal belongings–the ring, hair, portrait, and letters of his beloved–Davydov provided care for the Frenchman, who did not survive.

The reasons Davydov began his prose writings were to set matters straight in the case of forgotten or maligned leaders, such as his first cousin General Aleksei Petrovich Ermolov; to describe what others had overlooked or were unaware of; or merely to add to existing accounts. Each one of his more than two dozen vivid prose reminiscences is impeccable from the standpoint of military accuracy without being like the crisp, dry entries of the nonliterary military leader. Humor, irony, proverbs, and literary tradition are generously sprinkled throughout his lively prose.

For all his bravery and dedication, Davydov encountered many obstacles to his advancement in military service. Contributing to the difficulties was the fact that his superior, Bagration, was not overly favored by Alexander, possibly faulted for not being ethnically Russian. Moreover, Davydov's family and relatives were in disfavor. Throughout his career he was called to battle only in time of dire need (which nevertheless put him in eight campaigns). Still, there were many happy moments as aide to Bagration, such as witnessing the meeting of Alexander and Napoleon at Tilsit and coming face to face with the latter. Following the peace treaty on 25 June 1807, Davydov accompanied his commander to Moscow, where his rank of staff platoon commander of the Imperial Life Guards and his gold decorations (two Orders of St. Anne and two Crosses) brought him much attention, admiration, and affection in society. Once again he showed true gallantry by not revealing the name of his current lady love.

At this time Davydov wrote the poem "Dogovory" (Agreements), published in *Vestnik Evropy* (The Herald of Europe) in 1808, a free translation of Louis Vigee's "Mes conventions" (My Agreements). When readers construed it as an elegy, Davydov made changes to facilitate comprehension of it as a satire on old bachelors who find young ingenues to marry and then try to seclude them from society under the pretense of love. The suitor attempts to persuade his fiancée to live without guests, the theater, and balls, opting for a life in the country removed from such temptations. The young lady's reply is not clear.

Davydov became close to his new commander, Iakov Petrovich Kul'nev. His long poem to Kul'nev is preserved only in the fragment quoted in his "Vospominaniia o Kul'neve" (Recollections on Kul'nev, 1833). It begins: "Tell me of the deeds of the mustachioed hero, / O Muse, recount how Kul'nev fought, / How he wandered among the snows in a shirt, / And in a Finnish cap appeared in the midst of battle. / Let the world hear / Of Kul'nev's vagaries and the thunder of his victories." Again Davydov was in love, and again the person is unknown. He translated Jacques Delille's fable "La Rose et l'Etourneau" (The Rose and the Starling) as "Chizh i roza" (The Siskin and the Rose) about a siskin that remains true to a rose even after its beauty fades; both are rewarded for such devotion. Once more he distinguished himself in battle. For valor in the Finnish War of 1808 Davydov received an Imperial Citation of Thanks.

In 1809 Davydov rejoined Bagration in Moldavia and Turkey where again he served bravely, but Bagration's recommendation for an award was not honored. Later, on Kul'nev's recommendation, Davydov was awarded the Order of St. Anne, second degree. At this time, having left behind his beloved in Russia, Davydov took frequent furloughs. Again no name has been documented, nor have any poems of dedication survived.

Davydov visited his tall, portly cousin Aleksandr L'vovich Davydov, who was famous for his hospitality and his attractive, aristocratic French wife, Aglaia, at their estate of Kamenka. While Aleksandr Pushkin is known to have had an affair with her, Davydov's infatuation received no reciprocation. The poem "Plemiannitse" (To My Niece, 1809–1811), written in the name of Aleksandr L'vovich's uncle Aleksandr Nikolaevich Samoilov, unfolds as a panegyric to Aglaia in which the closure may include a sly double entendre: "I wanted to treat you, / But you treated us to yourself! / My dear Aglaia, / I see an angel in you!"

When the war with Napoleon was announced in 1812, Davydov immediately transferred to the Akhtyr Hussar Regiment as a colonel in command of the first battalion. Patriotism became the order of the day; therefore, Russian replaced French as the language spoken among the nobility. At the village of Borodino, Davydov found his former family home turned into a bivouac. In the time-honored manner of representing battle as a symbolic feast, Davydov wrote to the amusement of some, "How can one leave a feast while cups are clinking?"

As the war progressed, Davydov became convinced of the benefit of partisan attacks in the rear of the enemy. Davydov decided to become a partisan leader who would sabotage the French. To this end he solicited Bagration's help in suggesting to Field Marshal Kutuzov this mode of warfare, which was rarely practiced. Approving the endeavor, yet unwilling to sacrifice many men to this dangerous but potentially rewarding undertaking, Kutuzov appointed fifty hussars and approximately one hundred cossacks to Davydov's command. Many highly placed people displayed outright amusement at the appointment of the bon vivant poet to this responsible and uncharted position. Davydov, however, brought to bear his considerable military expertise, his vast theoretical knowledge, his daring, and his intuition. Successful raids brought reinforcements. He wrote later in a letter of October 1829:

> I had the honor of proposing a partisan war to his late serene highness, Prince Kutuzov, on 22 August at the Kolotsky Monastery. A few days after my proposal I was sent by him from Borodino to the rear of the French army with 130 cossacks and hussars and carried out my first raid in the village of Tokarev on 1 September, and my second raid in the village of Tsarevo-Zaimitse on 2 September on the day the enemy entered Moscow.

Among Davydov's objectives were to show the peasants that the Russian Army would return and to urge them to defend themselves. Throughout his mission Davydov remained correctly humane toward captives (unlike his brutal, daredevil fellow officer in the partisans, Aleksandr Samoilovich Figner, who could shoot a few hundred captives in cold blood), opposed plunder, and at all times maintained impeccable honor. Traitors, few in number, were punished either by shooting or by flogging, but always after several priests gave them the last rites.

During the French occupation of Moscow, which was hurriedly but almost totally evacuated by the Russians, Davydov and his associates Figner and Aleksandr Nikitich Seslavin entered the city several times under disguise for reconnaissance. The city presented a gruesome sight, for the inhabitants had burned their houses rather than surrender them. Davydov soon adopted peasant garb and speech and grew a beard to gain greater acceptance by the local peasants, who were initially suspicious of his French-looking uniform, and to guarantee more effective protection and secrecy. His method of operation consisted of sabotage and lightning strikes by fighters constantly on the alert, proving, as he wrote, the correctness of the Russian saying "kill and leave." He was so effective that Kutuzov honored him, in his peasant dress, at dinner, where high-ranking officers in all their military regalia sat incredulous. Kutuzov promoted Davydov to colonel, simultaneously awarding him the Orders of St. Vladimir, third degree, and of St. George, fourth class. At this time Davydov's popularity in Russia rivaled that of Kutuzov, Bagration and the other hero, Ataman Count Matvei Ivanovich Platov. So notorious was he with the enemy that the French governor in Smolensk wanted Davydov dead or alive and even sent out a special detachment for his capture.

Davydov's immediate superior, General Lanskoi, permitted the Russian occupation of Dresden, and Davydov concluded a peace treaty after ten hours of battle. By that time his superiors had rescinded the order, and the envious and vindictive Gen. Baron Ferdinand Federovich Winzengerode immediately removed Davydov from his command (for his "unauthorized" occupation of Dresden). Further penalty was averted by the emperor, who spoke against punishing the victors. Davydov managed to return to the Akhtyr regiment, but his superior Gen. Count Mikhail Andreevich Miloradovich's many attempts at promoting Davydov to general remained futile. Davydov sent a strongly worded letter to Count Aleksei Andreevich Arakcheev in 1813 or 1814 to explain how he had been overlooked for promotion to the rank of major general. The vivid missive begins:

> From the first shot in fording the Neman to the Battle of Borodino, and then to the banks of the Rhine I never took my eyes off the enemy. Your highness is obviously aware that I had the most dangerous and hence the most flattering assignments, having conveyed the project to the late Prince Bagration on the peasants' actions and having myself proven in deed the advantages of my proposal. For a long time I enjoyed the appreciation of the Supreme Command; but malicious intrigues forced me to appear before the late Field Marshal to defend myself for occupying (following a ten-hour battle) the capital of Saxony at the same time that General Chernyshev was receiving the first Orders of St. Anne for the occupation of Berlin without a shot, and Colonel Tetenborg was promoted for his triumphal entry into Hamburg. Our defending tsar's fairness was the shield of this unprotected one! Due to the Emperor's command, I returned to my detachment, but its command had already been given to another, a fact that forced me, after various excuses presented to me,

Davydov in 1819 (portrait by V. P. Langer; from Viktor Vladimirovich Kunin, ed., Druz'ia Pushkina: Perepiska, vospominaniia, dneviki, *1984)*

> each more devious than the other, to depart for the Akhtyr Hussar Regiment, to which I belong.

Davydov closes by asking Arakcheev to review his military record and to promote him if it measures up.

While commanding a brigade in 1814 Davydov arrived in Paris. With him was Napoleon's fifteen-year-old drummer, whom the Russian returned safely to his father. Unlike the hero Platov, he did not go on to England, but his pictures and fame reached its shores. While studying in Edinburgh, his nephew, Vladimir Petrovich Davydov, made the acquaintance of one of the writers most venerated in Russia, Sir Walter Scott. Thus began Davydov's correspondence (in French) with Scott, which continued until 1827.

At this time Davydov was promoted to major general. In addition, the emperor forgave the Davydov family their father's alleged debt and lifted the sequester on the family estate. Returning to a Moscow bustling with the activity of recovering and rebuilding, Davydov regaled his friends with stories of his war experiences. He also fell in love with the beautiful, blue-eyed principal ballerina of the Moscow Theater, Tat'iana Ivanova. The first three of his "Elegies" are dedicated to his deep, unrequited love. "Elegiia I" (written in 1814), published in *Retsenzent* (Reviewer) in 1821, describes a warrior who is defeated by an ethereal beauty and who envies the fortunate youth who will love her. Mythology and military imagery augment his defeat: "Take my sword—I am unworthy of battle! / Tear the laurel from my brow—it has been darkened by passion! / O gods of Pathos! chain my mighty hands / And as a timid captive throw me into shameful captivity! / I am yours!—and who would not be inflamed!"

"Elegiia II" (written in 1814 or 1815), an imitation of the Roman Albius Tibullus published in *Amfion* in 1815, deplores the strict supervision of the speaker's beloved as he gazes at her window from Viazemsky's home, calling on the avenging god to free "young innocence" from her "hellish dungeon." The dramatic scenes dynamically unfold as in a ballet, as he exhorts her to escape at midnight: "Learn in the nocturnal darkness / How to steal between the guards, / How with your light foot barely to touch the floor / And groping make your way to the steep staircase; / Dare! I await you seething with impatience!" The poem concludes with an apparent victory for the lovers, pending the woman's decision. Obviously, the most important things in Davydov's life at this time were love and war. Comprising the very fabric of his being, they spurred him to craft poetry and to appreciate life. Later manifestations of the two turned into love for his family and enthusiasm for hunting; these passions did not generate poetry, only prose. The elegies tactfully withhold the ballerina's name. "Elegiia III" (written in 1815) notes, "Let them seek for whom I strummed my lyre."

Soon the promotions of "all Davydovs" were unprecedentedly rescinded. Davydov's frantic letter to the emperor remained unanswered. Settling for uneventful service in Warsaw was unpalatable to Davydov; he strove to leave the Polish capital. Only with his reinstatement as major general at the end of 1815 was he allowed to leave Warsaw. A letter of 2 September 1815 to Viazemsky from the capital reveals his still strong feelings for the alluring ballerina: "However, in a few days I am going to Paris, irrespective of oysters, patés de foie gras and the sirens of Paris—I must put an end to things and determine my fate! *A propos de Sirene,* what is my goddess doing? Is she as beautiful as ever? I swear to you by God that to this day I am in love with her like a fool. There are so many beautiful women here; honestly, not one can compare to her!"

Elected to membership in *Obshchestvo liubitelei rossiiskoi slovesnosti* (The Society of Lovers of Russian Literature), which was affiliated with Moscow University, Davydov received his hand-delivered diploma in Kiev from Fedor Tolstoy. He then joined the short-lived informal literary group Arzamas, named for the town near Karamzin's estate. The society was headed by Zhukovsky and Viazemsky, who strove for the Karamzin model of modernizing the Russian language and of promoting Western influences on Russian culture, and its fun-loving members, including Pushkin, were given nicknames. Davydov's was Armianin (The Armenian), taken from Zhukovsky's ballad "Alina i Al'sim" (Alina and Alsim, written in October 1814). In this group, Davydov's friendship with Pushkin began.

Cavalry officers were not allowed to have moustaches; not willing to shave off his moustache, a symbol of masculine prowess in his poems, Davydov took a boring position at headquarters in the south at Kremenchuk rather than command a cavalry chasseur brigade. There he met Elizaveta Antonovna Zlotnitskaia, the daughter of a lieutenant general, who accepted his proposal of marriage. Subsequently, the emperor assigned to him a service estate in the Podol'sk region with an annual income of six thousand rubles. In 1815 he wrote "Elegiia IV" for Elizaveta, a poem that reflects his new mood. In the poem he abandons his quest for glory and turns instead to his desire only to defend the homeland at all costs—even to the death:

> In the horrors of bloody war
> I sought danger,
> I burned with immortal glory,
> Breathed for destruction
> And eternally pursued by fate,
> "There's no happiness!" thought I . . .
> My dear friend, my sincere friend,
> I did not know you then!

On Davydov's return from a business trip he learned that Elizaveta had become engaged to a man much higher in society, General Prince Dmitrii Vladimirovich Golitsyn. Davydov poured out his grief in Elegies 5 through 7. In another poem, "Neuzhto dumaete vy" (Do you really think, written in 1817), he returns her lock of hair and once again turns to the comfort he finds in glory and wine.

Constantly on the move with the military, Davydov nevertheless composed "Elegiia VIII" (written in 1818) to an unknown addressee. His famous "Pesnia starogo gusara" (Song of an Old Hussar, written in 1817), published in *Blagonamerennyi* (The Well-Intended) in 1819, was translated into French by Emile Dupré de Saint-Maure in the *Anthologie russe* in 1823. While carrying out his military duties and still writing poetry, Davydov once again demonstrated his resiliency in his personal life. Not long after his rejection by Zlotnitskaia he found consolation with the woman who became his wife.

Davydov's proposal of marriage to Sof'ia Nikolaevna Chirkova, the daughter of a general under whom he served, was accepted over her mother's objections to the officer's "debauchery." The mother's judgment of her daughter's suitor was actually unjust, for Davydov was able to appreciate drinking and conviviality without overindulging. He was never known to be inebriated—this image was merely the pose of the time. Apparently, the young Sof'ia was an astute judge of character who seems to have seen beyond the man's reckless reputation. The couple married in February 1819 in Moscow and began their happy, peaceful life together, during which they had five sons and three daughters. They lived in Kremenchuk, where Davydov held the position of staff commander of the corps and read voraciously. Many of Davydov's famous attitudes as the bon vivant hussar who lived only for battle, wine, and women were a pose; they were the source and inspiration for his writing. Without the pose he could no longer write the poetry that made him famous. As he explained to his confidant, Viazemsky: "There is no poetry in a tranquil and blissful life." Davydov always maintained that he needed the danger and excitement of war or the emotions of courtship to write. To ensure that the memory of those glorious years and people did not fade, he began a series of reminiscences and portraits of the great military figures he had known.

The ruling circles who disliked the Davydov clan for their independence also resented Davydov's closeness to the imposing A. P. Ermolov, for whom some of the Decembrists had envisioned a high position in their new constitutional monarchy. Moreover, his fame of 1812 posed obstacles to Davydov's returning to active service under Ermolov, although he was twice recommended by the latter for the post of head of the Caucasian line in Stavropol'. The rejections of Alexander I made Davydov retire from the military in protest early in 1823. While basking in the love of his growing family he began to manage his estates, hunt with vigor, and write his memoirs to ensure the veracity of historical events. He wrote in a letter of 14 March 1824 that he was pleased to have removed "the shoulder chains of the general's office." Davydov wrote his autobiography "Ocherk zhizni Denisa Vasil'evicha Davydova" in the third person to mystify readers and to assuage resentment of his fame and his accounts of the facts. Wisely attributed to his deceased friend Gen. O. D. Ol'shevsky, the autobiography was well received.

Opposition to an unrestricted monarchy mounted among certain progressive noblemen who founded secret societies to promote a constitutional monarchy. In Davydov's southern region the group was known as the secret *Iuzhnoe obshchestvo* (Southern Society), whose members actively solicited his participation. Particularly adamant was his cousin Vasilii L'vovich Davydov, but Denis Davydov would have no part in the Decembrist movement that culminated in the coup attempt in Senate Square in St. Petersburg on the morning of 14 December 1825—a revolt that was brutally crushed by Nicholas I with the hanging of five leaders and long-term hard labor exile for many others.

Like other intellectuals of the time, Davydov carried on an active correspondence within the city and from his estates. His letters, many of which were published as volume three of the 1840 edition of his *Sochine-*

Title page for Stikhotvoreniia *(Poems), Davydov's first collection, which includes thirty-nine poems*

niia v stikhakh i proze (Works in Verse and Prose), are full of hard facts, wit, intellectual probing, and colorful imagery all couched in a multilayered language rich in nuances. Among Davydov's correspondents were Pushkin, Viazemsky, and Nikolai Mikhailovich Iazykov. Many of these forthright letters, which provide a vivid insight into the lives and art of these people, had to be sent through trusted friends because the ever-vigilant police read the letters sent by mail.

When in the city Davydov was a much-sought-after guest at the Moscow homes of friends and at the fashionable salons because of his entertaining stories and his wit. He attended the parties of the famous hostess Princess Zinaida Aleksandrovna Volkonskaia. Davydov became fascinated by the pianist Mariia Shimpanovskaia, who died of cholera in 1831 and whose daughter later married the Polish Romantic poet Adam Mickiewicz. The poem "Gusar" (The Hussar), published in *Moskovskii telegraf* (Moscow Telegraph) in 1827, refers to Shimpanovskaia. Davydov had a great love for the theater, and many of his friends were actors. He also defended the young Baratynsky, who had been expelled from the Corps of Pages, an exclusive military school, for involvement in a prankish theft. With Pushkin and Aleksandr Sergeevich Griboedov, Davydov collaborated in Prince Vladimir Fedorovich Odoevsky's journal *Mnemozina* (Mnemosyne, 1824–1825). Davydov completed his memoirs of his year as a partisan, "Zapiski partizana" (Notes of a Partisan), in 1831, but it was published only posthumously in 1872. He wrote the poems "Otvet" (The Answer, written in 1830) and "Vecher v iune" (An Evening in June, written in 1827), which the critic Vissarion Grigor'evich Belinsky considered his best. These years were quite busy for Davydov.

Nicholas I returned Davydov to the cavalry with an assignment as temporary commander of the troops on the borders of the Erivan (Yerevan) Khanate in the Caucasus. Davydov writes about this time in his unfinished "Vospominaniia o 1826 gode" (Recollections about the Year 1826), which he begins without recriminations but with a matter-of-fact statement: "From 19 November 1823 to 23 March 1826 I was in retirement. With the ascension to the throne of the sovereign emperor Nikolai Pavlovich, I again entered service and was assigned to the cavalry." Davydov was also favored as one of sixty high-ranking officers at an audience with the emperor. Despite the disarray of his estates, his large family, and his beloved wife's pregnancy, Davydov agreed to go to the Georgian theater of war to repel the Persian invasion. Here was an area "which had not yet resounded under the hooves of Davydov's horse," as he wrote in his autobiography. For all the wrenching pain in leaving his family, he admitted: "The word war to this day (to my misfortune!) has a magic sound for my soul." He then offered his evaluation of the situation: "Having served in two campaigns against the Turks, I knew that in a war with Asians the main thing was not the fight, because it is always easy to beat them, but in the skill to wage war, i.e. in the ability to make arrangements in such a way that our troops always have a full stomach, a bag with bullets, and the artillery, full depots, a task that is very difficult both in Turkey and in Persia." As part of his duties Davydov took some dispatches of the emperor to Ermolov.

In Moscow, Davydov learned that the heir to the Persian throne, Abbas-Mirza, had entered Karabakh with an army of one hundred thousand and had laid siege to the fortress of Shusha. The Sardar of the Erivan Fortress and Hassan Khan, having taken the provinces of Bambak and Shuragel, had moved fifty versts (roughly thirty-three miles) outside Tiflis (Tbilisi), where Khan and his men plundered a German colony and deported its inhabitants to Persia. The local Karabakhian hero of the Russian Army, Prince Valerian Grigor'evich Madatov, moved against Abbas-Mirza with three thousand troops. Davydov journeyed south in only ten days, marveling at the peak, Kazbek. Once in the Caucasus, Davydov obtained good results. He writes about himself:

> A few more days–and he is with his detachment beyond Bezobgal in pursuit of the enemy retreating from him along the Bambak Plain. Finally one more day–and he is near the cloud transcendent Alagez, striking the famous Hassan Khan's detachment of 4,000, forcing him to flee to the Erivan Fortress, where the Sardar of Erivan himself is hurrying with his troops from Lake Gorkchi. Here Ararat is revealed to Davydov's eyes in all its glory, in its snow mantle, with its blue sky and with all recollections of the cradle of mankind.

It must be recalled that Mount Ararat steadfastly remained hidden during the visit of Nicholas I, prompting the saying that it revealed itself only to the just. After this expedition, Davydov participated in the building of the fortress Jelal-Oglu until December.

Davydov had traveled part of the trip south with Griboedov, whose first cousin was Gen. Count Ivan Fedorovich Paskevich's wife. For the poorly educated Paskevich, Griboedov wrote dispatches and even private letters. Davydov credits Paskevich for bravery but decries his craftiness and treachery toward Ermolov, whom he ousted by maligning. Both Davydov and Ermolov found the amiable, intelligent amateur, Griboedov, a hindrance in military service. They bemoaned his desire to obtain glory greater than that which his drama, *Gore ot uma* (Woe from Wit, finished between 1823 and 1824), gave him. They were also uncomfortable with the fact that Griboedov's position of ambassador to Persia was obtained through Paskevich's strong protection. Demanding the freedom of Russian "servants" in Allaiar Khan's harem, Griboedov and most of his embassy staff were killed in 1829 by a mob obviously incited by the khan. Davydov separates his profound love for Griboedov as a person and for his talent from what he considers the man's immature, inexperienced behavior and vanity. Davydov relates this incident with the same unabashed honesty, sparkling wit, and arresting imagery that permeate all of his historical prose and memoirs.

Early in 1827 Davydov, ill with malaria, was granted a furlough by Ermolov, from which he returned sooner than intended because of his detractors' unwarranted criticism. Keeping company with the heroic General Madatov's lovely wife, with whom he long professed to be in love, lightened his mood, however. Rheumatism in his left leg sent him for treatment to the waters of the Caucasian resort Mineralnye Vody. There he regaled an admiring circle with his military tales. On 10 September 1827 he wrote an amusing description of the spa to his friend

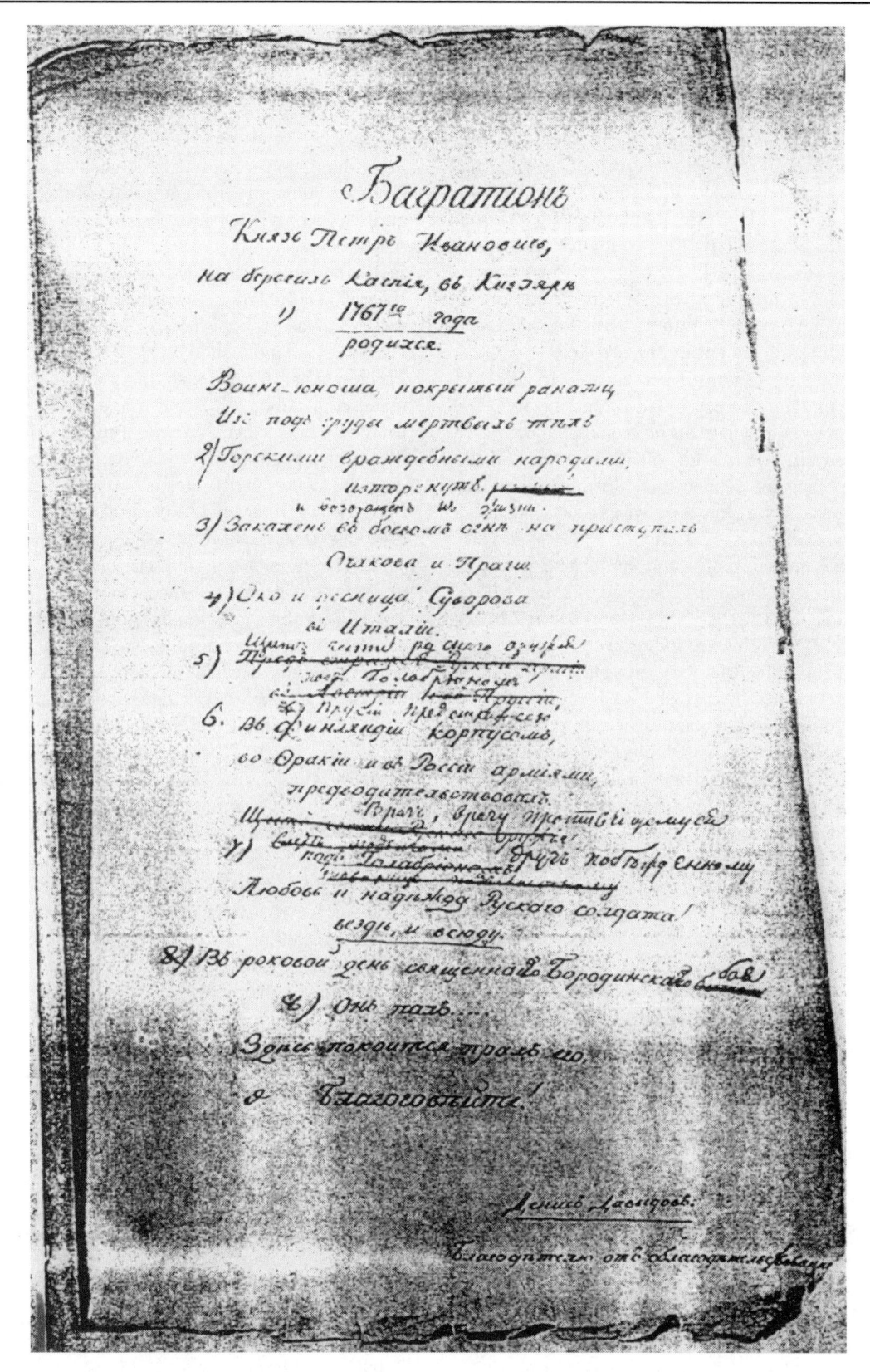

Draft for one of Davydov's last poetic endeavors, an inscription for a monument to one of his commanders, Prince Petr Ivanovich Bagration, 1839 (from the 1962 edition of Davydov's Sochineniia *[Works])*

Scott, who had hung a portrait of Davydov as the "Black Captain" on his library wall. Davydov found several Caucasian weapons for Scott's collection, but only a few reached him. Davydov's final letter to Scott was a long commentary by chapters on the Englishman's *Life of Napoleon Bonaparte: Emperor of the French* (1827). Never mailed because of Scott's death, it was published with a brief explanation as "Perepiska s Val'ter-Skottom" (Correspondence with Walter Scott, 1840). When Davydov was once again overlooked for promotion, this time to commander for a junior general, he resigned from the military, citing ill health and the decline of his estate.

Davydov liked to write in his letters to friends that he was tilling the land, hunting with dogs and hawks, reading the many books and journals he acquired, and writing his prose. His warm letters to his wife were written with an eye for instructing his sons as well. In their Orenburg estate, Verkhniaia Maza (part of his wife's dowry), he reorganized the wine distillery. In Saratov in 1829, he was fascinated by the landed gentry and the charm of Sof'ia Aleksandrovna Kushkina, the mayor's daughter, whose beauty he extolled in letters as "a wonder of nature." In his octet "S.A.K." ("Vy lichikom–Pafosskii bog," Your face reveals you as a Pathossian god), published in the 1832 *Stikhotvoreniia,* and in "Vy khoroshi! Kashtanovoi volnoi" (You are beautiful! With a chestnut wave), published in *Literaturnaia gazeta* (Literary Gazette) in 1830.

Davydov ranked as his best pieces the elegy to his heroes Bagration, Raevsky, and Ermolov, "Borodinskoe pole" (The Borodino Field, written in 1829), and a poem to Kushkina, "Dushen'ka" (Psyche, written in 1829), both of which appeared in *Literaturnaia gazeta* in 1830. Poetry continued to exhilarate Davydov, as he wrote to Viazemsky: "For me poetry is not a worm but intoxication." He so treasured all comments about his poetry—whether in verse or prose—that he copied them into a special notebook. Davydov was always humble about his literary talents; he reserved his bravado, that component of the pose which induced the warrior in him to fight heroically, for his military exploits. He also worked tirelessly in the civilian sector.

When the cholera epidemic of 1830 broke out, Davydov volunteered to supervise the Twentieth Cholera District in Moscow. The general governor of Moscow, Golitsyn, praised his vastly superior management; yet his immediate superiors greeted his accomplishments with silence. In Moscow during the winter season, Davydov often met Pushkin, and their friendship deepened. He referred to Pushkin as "my Parnassian father and commander." Together Davydov and Pushkin composed the poem "Geroiu bitv" (To the Hero of Battles), included in the 1832 *Stikhotvoreniia.* Viazemsky joined them in frequenting gypsy establishments famous for their music and good times. On 12 March 1831 Davydov was once more called to active duty against Poland. His participation was acknowledged with a promotion to lieutenant general and a Ribbon of St. Anne.

Friends urged Davydov to collect his poems for publication in book form, and the publisher offered attractive conditions. *Stikhotvoreniia* (Poems) appeared in 1832 with thirty-nine poems. Although Davydov's name appeared on this volume, the true authorship of the autobiography attributed to Ol'shevsky continued to be shrouded in secrecy. *Stikhotvoreniia* was warmly received, and Viazemsky even wrote a poem on this occasion, "Staromu gusaru" (To the Old Hussar, 1833). Davydov himself saw mostly limitations in his poetry; he compared his poems to Pushkin's as "moonshine next to champagne." Still, like Pushkin, who affirmed that "Inspiration is not sold, but a manuscript can be sold," and who appreciated his income from his writings, Davydov was astute in selling his works. More than once he wrote in letters: "Thank God that nowadays one can sell ravings just like suet and tar; one must take advantage of this particularly in a lean year." He saved his royalties for his sons' education.

The years of rugged military life had taken their toll on Davydov's health; he suffered from back and chest pains as well as asthma. He sought cures from homeopathy, a popular philosophy of treatment at that time. In their letters, he and Iazykov exchanged information on homeopathic treatments and discussed various books on the subject.

While at his Orenburg estate Davydov often visited the nearby town of Penza, where he met the beautiful Evgeniia Dmitrievne Zolotareva, a young, unmarried woman who seems to have encouraged the acclaimed hero's attentions with no intention of reciprocation. Davydov sent her the poem "Val's" (Waltz), which appeared in *Severnaia pchela* (The Northern Bee) in 1834 and which compares her to an airy dance. His infatuation with Zolotareva was causing problems even with his understanding wife, Sof'ia. Although the young woman seems to have encouraged Davydov, there was no mention of a divorce on his part or of love on hers. In 1834 he wrote the poem "O, kto–skazhite mne–kto ty" (Oh, who–tell me–who are you) to this eighteen-year-old woman, who appears to have merely wanted a close, friendly, literary correspondence with the renowned fifty-year-old general. Davydov, on the other hand, poured out the last vestiges of his passionate and romantic nature in poems to her, references to which appear often in letters to his friends.

Davydov's love for Zolotareva seems to have awakened his poetic muse; poems to her (written from 1834 to 1836) include "Na golos russkoi pesni" (In the Voice of a Russian Song), "Posle razluki" (After a Separation), "I moia zvezdochka" (And My Star), "Rechka" (The Brook), "Uneslis' nevozvratimye" (Passed are the Unreturnable), and "Zhestokii drug,–za chto muchen'e?" (Cruel friend,–why the torment?). Pressing the young woman for some kind of commitment, Davydov may have heard some reluctant (if not coquettish) acquiescence, to which the poem "Ia ne ropshchu. Ia voznesen sud'boiu" (I don't complain. I have been elevated by fate) is dedicated. Her subsequent behavior, however, made clear to Davydov the futility of his love, as shown in "Ia pomniu–gluboko" (I Remember–Deeply). When Zolotareva married in 1836, she refused to return Davydov's fifty-seven letters in French or his portraits. This act bespeaks her deliberateness in collecting them after having encouraged him merely to satisfy her vanity. On her marriage he wrote "Vyzdorovlenie" (Recovery), in which he finally seems to be free of her: "The struggle of my passions has passed, / The illness of my rebellious soul."

The engaging image of the carousing hussar of Davydov's early days plagued him all his life, and his detractors used it as an excuse not to take him seriously. Only his friends could separate fact from fiction. In spite of the poet's distinguished military service and his seminal prose memoirs, Nicholas I mentioned to Ermolov that "previously Davydov wrote indecorous poems." To this day Davydov is known only as the hussar poet of conviviality and military songs, while his elegies, civic fables, sentient epitaphs, and caustic epigrams are mainly ignored. Even in his own day, this misapprehension of his poetry, memoirs (some banned), and military career prompted Davydov to write his own biographical account and self-assessment. Indeed, in a letter he asks his friends half in jest to jointly prepare his obituary, which would depict him as "one of the most poetic persons in the Russian Army."

In 1836, while in St. Petersburg to place his two elder sons in college, Davydov had a triumphal reunion with friends–Pushkin, Viazemsky, and Zhukovsky. A confirmed monarchist and Russian patriot, he was displeased with the growing liberalization of Moscow. His intolerance of the liberal Petr Iakovlevich Chaadaev and the Westernizers found an outlet in the severe, allusion-laden "Sovremennaia pesn'" (A Contemporary Song). His friends were displeased with the attack on Chaadaev, who had already found himself in bad repute with the authorities.

As his last act of loyalty Davydov spent more than two years trying to have the government transfer the remains of his beloved commander Bagration to the Borodino field and to erect a monument there. His efforts resulted in the authorities' finally approving the transfer on 6 April 1839 and choosing Davydov to lead the honor guard at the ceremony, which gave him cause for great rejoicing. Though he did manage to write the epitaph for the monument, a stroke on 22 April ended his life before he could see the realization of his fervent wish. The respect and adulation denied to him in life became his only years after his death. Nevertheless, Davydov's place in Russian literature and history as poet, bon vivant, hero of eight campaigns, and author of seminal memoirs and military accounts remains secure.

Biographies:

Vladimir Nikolaevich Orlov, *Denis Davydov* (Moscow, 1940);

A. Gvozdarev, *Denis Vasil'evich Davydov, poet: geroi partizan Otechestvenno voiny 1812 goda* (Iaroslavl'-Ogiz: Iaroslavskoe oblastnoe izdatel'stvo, 1943);

Aleksandr Shik, *Denis Davydov: "Liubovnik brani" i poet* (Paris: Vozrozhdenie, 1951);

Mikhail Iakovlevich Popov, *Denis Davydov* (Moscow: Prosveshchenie, 1971);

Gennadii Viktorovich Serebriakov, *Denis Davydov* (Moscow: Molodaia gvardiia, 1985);

V. Gribanov, *Denis Davydov v Peterburge* (Leningrad: Lenizdat, 1991).

References:

Sonia I. Ketchian, "Drinks and Their Vessels in Early Nineteenth-Century Russian Poetry: Davydov, Puškin, Jazykov," *Russian Literature,* 40 (October 1996): 363–384;

Lauren G. Leighton, "The Anecdote in Russia: Puškin, Vjazemskij, and Davydov," *Slavic and East European Journal,* 10 (1966): 156–163;

Leighton, "Denis Davydov and *War and Peace*," in *Studies in Honor of Xenia Gasiorowska,* edited by Leighton (Columbus, Ohio: Slavica, 1983);

Leighton, "Denis Davydov's Hussar Style," *Slavic and East European Journal,* 7 (1963): 349–360;

V. V. Pugachev, "Denis Davydov i dekabristy," in *Dekabristy v Moskve,* edited by Iullian Grigor'evich Okaman (Moscow: Moskovskii rabochii, 1963);

Zoja Rozov, "Denis Davydov and Walter Scott," *Slavic and East European Journal,* 19 (1940): 349–360;

Nikolai Alekseevich Zadonsky, *Denis Davydov: Istoricheskaia khronika* (Moscow: Molodaia gvardiia, 1953; expanded edition, 1958);

V. V. Zherve, *Partizan-poet Denis Vasil'evich Davydov: Ocherk ego zhizni i deiatel'nosti, 1784–1839: po materialam semeinago arhkiva drugim istochnikam* (St. Petersburg: M. O. Vol'f, 1913).

Papers:

Some of Denis Vasil'evich Davydov's papers are housed in Moscow at the Central State Military History Archive (TsGVIA), f. 194; the Central State Archive of Literature and Art (TsGALI), f. 66, d.107, 108 (letters to Arsenii Andreevich Zakrevsky); and the Russian National Library, f. 232, St. Petersburg.

Anton Antonovich Del'vig

(6 August 1798 – 14 January 1831)

James West
University of Washington

BOOK: *Stikhotvoreniia barona Del'viga* (St. Petersburg: Tip. Departamenta narodnogo prosveshcheniia, 1829).

Editions and Collections: *Sochineniia* (St. Petersburg: A. Smirdin, 1850);

Polnoe sobranie stikhotvorenii (St. Petersburg: A. S. Suvorin, 1887);

Sochineniia, s prilozheniem biograficheskago ocherka (St. Petersburg: Evgeny Evdokimov, 1893);

Neizdannye stikhotvoreniia, edited by M. L. Gofman, Works of Pushkin House of the Russian Academy of Sciences (St. Petersburg: Kartonnyi Domik, 1922);

Polnoe sobranie stikhotvorenii, edited by B. V. Tomashevsky (Leningrad: Izd-vo pisatelei v Leningrade, 1934);

Stikhotvoreniia, edited by L. Plotkin (Leningrad: Sovetskii pisatel', 1951);

Polnoe sobranie stikhotvorenii, edited by Boris Viktorovich Tomashevsky (Leningrad: Sovetskii pisatel', 1959);

Stikhtovoreniia, edited by I. V. Isakovich (Leningrad: Sovetskii pisatel', 1963);

Stikhotvoreniia (Moscow: Sovremennik, 1983);

Sochineniia, edited by Vadim Erazmovich Vatsuro (Leningrad: Khudozhestvennaia literatura, 1986).

The poet Anton Antonovich Del'vig lived fewer than thirty-three years but left a mark on Russian literature that is out of proportion to the length of his career. He spent his short life in the intimate company of the leaders of Russian literary culture, and his repute is owing in considerable measure to the esteem in which they held him.

As his name would suggest, Baron Anton Antonovich Del'vig's family was of German origin. They were not, however, among the relatively recent German immigrants who sought their fortune in Russia in the seventeenth and eighteenth centuries as the need for their technical skills grew. The poet's ancestors had moved to the Baltic provinces in the late Middle Ages and were ennobled by the king of Sweden only in 1723.

Anton Antonovich Del'vig

At some point in the eighteenth century a branch of the family moved to Russia, where they became thoroughly Russified in the service of their adoptive country. Del'vig's father was an army staff officer and a notable Russophile. As a result, unlike many of his Russian schoolmates of similar social background, when the future poet began his serious education at the age of thirteen, he did not know a word of German.

Del'vig's mother was a Russian, the daughter of an astronomer employed by the Russian Academy of Sciences, with lofty ambitions for her children. The future poet was a sickly child and a late talker but was endowed with both a vivid imagination and the urge to give it expression, as when, at the age of five, he terrified his whole family with the story of a ghost he claimed to have seen. In most accounts his education began with tutors at home, though one biographer claims that he also attended a private boarding school in Moscow. He is reported to have had an early passion for mythology, fueled by a book on the subject in which he buried himself at every opportunity. This detail may be apocryphal, since it is used to account for what many saw as a weakness in Del'vig's poetry–his frequent use of mythological names and images. In any event, his early schooling does not appear to have been substantial. Through the determination of his mother, the future poet was enrolled in the renowned lycée at Tsarskoe Selo, an elite school instituted by Alexander I to provide a chosen handful of the sons of the nobility with an education that would fit them for the highest ranks of public service. The lycée is best known as the place where Aleksandr Pushkin was educated, but the list of its alumni includes many of the most notable figures in Russian public life of the first half of the nineteenth century, several of them men of letters. Indeed, the study of literature was a substantial part of the curriculum, and the pupils' own literary efforts were strongly encouraged. Del'vig took the entrance examination on the same day as Pushkin, and though Del'vig was successful, the results confirmed his ignorance of German, revealed that he was weak in French, and showed Russian grammar to be the only subject in which he excelled.

Del'vig was apparently not a good pupil at the lycée, placing as a rule twenty-eighth or twenty-ninth out of thirty in the class lists. He was described by one of the professors as insolent and disobedient as well as lazy and uninterested. He overslept habitually and was notorious for his frequent absences from the first class. As Pushkin remembers Del'vig, he never took part in games of skill and strength, preferring to take walks in the magnificent park at Tsarskoe Selo and engage in conversation with friends. His strong point was a vivid imagination. Pushkin tells how Del'vig held his schoolmates spellbound with tales of the campaign of 1807, of which he claimed to be a firsthand witness. When word of these unlikely experiences reached the director of the lycée, at that time Vasilii Fedorovich Malinovsky, he summoned Del'vig to retell his tales to a more intimidating audience, assuming that he would not dare to. Even under these circumstances Del'vig maintained his story for a while, to the amusement of all.

Where Del'vig's special interests were engaged, he showed himself to be exceptionally gifted. Literature, both Russian and European, formed a substantial part of the lycée curriculum, and the literary activities of its pupils far exceeded what was required of them. Those with literary interests found time to read voraciously in several languages, and even Del'vig, despite his initial weakness in foreign languages, became familiar with European literature through conversations with his more linguistically gifted and energetic companions. When Egor Antonovich Engelhardt became director of the lycée in 1816, Del'vig was encouraged to study German more seriously. As a result, he developed quite a strong interest in German literature, reinforced by the enthusiasm of his schoolmate Vil'gel'm Karlovich Kiukhel'beker, another scion of a Russian-German family, who was to attain both distinction as a poet and notoriety as a Decembrist conspirator. Del'vig, however, reserved his strongest enthusiasm for Russian poetry. According to Pushkin, Del'vig knew by heart everything in Vasilii Andreevich Zhukovsky's anthology of Russian verse, and he had throughout his life a particular admiration for the work of Gavriil Romanovich Derzhavin.

Encouraged in particular by the professor of Latin literature, Natan Fedorovich Koshansky, the pupils of the lycée also wrote poetry. They shared their compositions with each other and with their mentors and produced four manuscript literary journals, until the school banned the activity in 1813 because it was distracting the boys from their regular studies. This prohibition probably prompted Pushkin, Del'vig, and some others to submit their best pieces for publication. Del'vig became one of the most active members of this precocious literary coterie, although none of its leading lights initially thought of him as destined for fame and some in fact mocked him openly. A puerile couplet has been preserved as a reminder that the young gentlemen of the tsar's lycée, when they were not being precocious young men of letters, were indistinguishable from the common herd of schoolboys: "Kha, kha, kha, khi, khi, khi, / D–pishet stikhi" (Ha, ha, ha, hee, hee, hee, / D[el'vig's] writing poetry). Del'vig surprised them all, however, by becoming at the age of fifteen the first to have his poems appear in the leading periodical *Vestnik Evropy* (Herald of Europe), although under a pseudonym.

This early success does not, of course, mean that Del'vig's adolescent efforts were of a consistently high quality. Influenced like all his peers by Koshansky, he composed imitations of Classical verse, particularly in the Horatian vein, but also wrote Romantic ballads and many verses reflecting the mood of triumphant patriotism that swept over the country following Russia's participation in the concluding phase of the Napoleonic Wars. A surviving example, "Na vziatie Parizha" (On the Taking of Paris), is written as a Pindaric ode and even refers to Derzhavin as a "Russian Pindar." Among the energetic young poets of Tsarskoe Selo, Del'vig was acknowledged to be the most conversant with metrical forms and techniques, to the point, occasionally, of boring his companions with his insistence on metrical correctness. He was also admired for his poetic skills and judgment and was often asked to critique the efforts of others.

After six years at the lycée, Del'vig graduated in June of 1817 and was given the honor of writing the words for the celebratory anthem that was performed at this solemn occasion in a setting composed by the music teacher. Pushkin was the director's first choice for the honor, but he procrastinated until the task was reassigned to Del'vig, who procrastinated in his turn until Engelhardt pointedly handed him an outline. Nonetheless, the resulting piece was so successful that it was used for many years thereafter. Del'vig's graduation certificate provides an interesting summary of the kind of education that he and his fellow students received. It describes his knowledge as "good" in Divinity, Logic, and Moral Philosophy; Latin, Russian, German, and French Literature; Private, Public, and Natural Law; Economics and Finance; and Civil and Criminal Law. In history, both General and Russian, Geography, and Statistics his results were "fair," and the certificate notes that he "also studied" Physics and both Pure and Applied Mathematics. As the founder of the school intended, most graduates entered public service or the military, many of them to achieve considerable distinction. Del'vig, not noted for his energy and ambition, placed third from last in the public graduation examinations, immediately below Pushkin, and was therefore assigned to civil rather than the more prestigious military service.

Within a month of his graduation Del'vig began work at the Department of Mining and Salt Industry at a salary of seven hundred rubles a year. After eighteen months of this uncongenial service he resigned, and a month later, lacking an independent means of support, he entered the Chancellery of the Ministry of Finance, where he served for another eighteen months before resigning for a second time in October 1821. From September 1820 Del'vig had been working at the St. Petersburg Public Library as a voluntary assistant librarian, unpaid until a special order placed him on the payroll in 1821. This was not as demeaning a form of employment as it might sound, since the St. Petersburg Public Library was a prestigious institution, and several distinguished Russian literary figures worked there at one time or another. His colleagues included other poets, and in fact his immediate superior, the head of the Russian Section, was the celebrated author of fables, Ivan Andreevich Krylov. Contemporaries were quick to observe that Del'vig could not have found a more congenial position, since Krylov was himself notoriously indolent, and friction on the professional front was unlikely. The library was the perfect place, in fact, for Del'vig to complete his literary education. Krylov for his part viewed the situation from a slightly different perspective, since Del'vig replaced a highly energetic bibliographer on whom Krylov had come to rely. One of Krylov's biographers notes, however, that the two poets respected each other and conspired to get the work done somehow.

Partly through his library service, Del'vig quickly became a regular participant in the literary circles of the capital, making the acquaintance of many established writers. His reputation as a fine judge of verse preceded him, and he was hardly out of school before he was elected in 1818 to membership in the prestigious *Vol'noe obshchestvo liubitelei slovesnosti, nauk i khudozhestv* (Free Society of Lovers of Letters, Sciences, and the Arts) in St. Petersburg, which published two of the most significant periodicals of the time. Del'vig was quickly entrusted with the task of evaluating poetry submissions, became himself a frequent contributor, and was in due course elected to the Moscow branch of the society.

Like Pushkin, Del'vig formed lasting friendships during his school days, and after his graduation he missed both the general atmosphere of companionship in which his ideals and aspirations had been nurtured and the company of his closest friends: Aleksei Dem'ianovich Illichevsky left to pursue a service career in Siberia, and Pushkin's indiscretions obliged him to leave the capital in 1820. Just as in Pushkin's case, nostalgia for his lycée days found expression from time to time in Del'vig's poetry, as in "19 oktiabr' 1824" (19 October 1824), written impromptu on that date at an anniversary celebration, in which he extols the bonds of friendship and the school that nurtured them. Up to 1825 he visited Tsarskoe Selo fairly frequently, sometimes staying for several days and repeating his childhood walks in the park.

Del'vig found some compensation for the loss of Illichevsky's and Pushkin's company in a new and lasting friendship with Evgenii Abramovich Baratynsky, who had not been a *lycéen* and was younger by almost two years. In fact, Del'vig discovered and fostered the talent of Baratynsky, a poet who for many is second among his generation only to Pushkin. The two met in St. Petersburg in 1818 when Baratynsky was obliged to serve as a private in a guards regiment. After Baratynsky was posted to Finland, Del'vig visited him there, prompted no doubt in part by the Romantic enthusiasm that young Russians of his generation had for the "wild and untamed" beauty of Finland's forests, lakes, and rivers. The younger poet was forever grateful for the encouragement, both literary and personal, that he received from Del'vig at this difficult time in his life.

Between 1817 and 1825 Del'vig affected a deliberately Bohemian lifestyle, always short of money, often taking his meals at the most unlikely lower-class establishments and even entertaining his friends there. There is a contemporary account of a "dinner party" to which Del'vig's guests received flowery handwritten invitations, only to be led through the slums of St. Petersburg to dine at a tavern where the forks were attached by chains to the communal table to prevent their theft. When Baratynsky returned from Finland to St. Petersburg with his regiment, the two roomed together, with almost no furniture and little cash but with more than enough poetry and merriment to compensate. The domestic arrangements were left to Del'vig's servant Nikita, whose laziness was said to rival that of his master, and was compounded with frequent inebriation, misuse of Del'vig's money, and unreliability in the delivery of his letters. The character of Del'vig and Baratynsky's simple and carefree household is described with delightful wit and realism in a poem written jointly by the two of them, dating from 1819.

At the same time Del'vig and Baratynsky enjoyed excursions into a more respectable social life, frequenting the drawing rooms of several of the literary hosts and hostesses of the capital. Always attracted by the prospect of good conversation, Del'vig was a regular guest at the salon of Princess Zinaida Aleksandrovna Volkonskaia and was also frequently to be found in the company of Zhukovsky and other leading poets at the gatherings hosted by Aleksandr Fedorovich Voeikov, who was married to Zhukovsky's niece. Del'vig was a particularly assiduous visitor at the salon of Sofiia Dmitrievna Ponomareva, the sister of one of his former schoolmates, Ivan Dmitrievich Pozniak. She was a clever and gifted woman and a talented hostess, whose guests included many figures of note. Her literary tastes were close to those of the young Romantics, and she is said to have had a favorite dog named "Malvina" after a heroine in Ossian's epics.

Outside the literary salons Del'vig's preference was for a small but close group of like-minded friends. His circle drew satirical comment from some contemporaries, who saw only an ostentatious clique of young neo-Romantics writing poetry that often amounted to little more than a tiresome exchange of laudatory verse epistles. Del'vig was regularly lampooned in literary periodicals as "Surkov," a reference to the strong resemblance of his habits to those of a *surok* (marmot), and one particularly spiteful attack suggested that half of his poetry was written by Pushkin, the other half by Baratynsky. Del'vig for his part was not above responding in kind and made his own contribution to the popular genre of literary parody.

Title page for Stikhotvoreniia barona Del'viga *(Poems of Baron Del'vig), the only collection of Del'vig's works published during his lifetime*

Posterity has done the real Del'vig no service by consigning him to the stereotype of the indolent, unworldly but sociable, and brilliantly articulate Romantic poet. He certainly possessed most of the qualities, good and bad, that have been ascribed to him, but his character was more complex than is allowed for in the legend that has been generated around him. One of Del'vig's friends, recalling in his memoirs his first impressions of the poet, wrote of the inexplicable contrast between the warmth of his poetry and the coldness of his manner. On closer acquaintance Del'vig's engaging personality manifested itself, and those who knew him remembered him well as good-natured and careful not to offend. Unlike Pushkin, he was not given to exercising his sharp wit in personally directed epigrams. Baron Modest Andreevich Korff, who knew Del'vig at the lycée and went on to a distinguished career as a civil servant, described in his personal journal in later life the careers of some of his former classmates. Of Del'vig he wrote: "At the lycée a pleasant, good-natured and universally liked lazy-bones, later—a pleasing poet, counted in his day among our leading men of letters. Now, however, almost totally forgotten. Del'vig never learned anything, was never of any real service, and never did anything, but lived in fine style with a loving nature and a kindly, genuinely noble character...." Other contemporaries note his amiability and sense of humor, but few fail to mention his penchant for idleness, which is borne out by many accounts, including his own. Del'vig even composed a cheerful verse epistle to his friend Illichevsky with the title "Lentiai" (Lazybones):

> Hard work's reward, my friend, I've not
> Yet fathomed! Laziness, they say,
> Brings ruin, and it is my lot
> To laze my ruined life away.
> The cares that I had yesterday,
> On waking I have quite forgot.

There is obviously more to this characteristic than simple idleness. One near-contemporary biographer has suggested that Del'vig, finding that a certain degree of laziness drew embarrassing attention to him, responded by exaggerating the weakness as an affectation. After about 1817 such French Romantics as André-Marie de Chénier and Evariste Désiré de Forges, Vicomte de Parny, began to exert on Russian poets a strong influence that blended with the fashion for the Classical poets Horace and Anacreon, whose hallmark was a conventional tribute to the physical pleasures of life peacefully enjoyed. The resulting intellectual climate encouraged a posture of cultivated indolence, and Del'vig was not the only exponent of the genre, literary or behavioral: others, too, including Pushkin, made noteworthy contributions. A good example is Del'vig's "Tikhaia zhizn'" (A Quiet Life, 1816), a paraphrase of Horace's celebrated Second Epode that twists the Roman poet's serious message about the dangers of public life into a personal plea to be left in peace, free from demands and pressures.

It has also been suggested that Del'vig's apparent laziness was in reality a high degree of independence and indifference to the pressures and expectations of society and friends alike. On the one hand, he appears to have held to the view, unusual in his time and place, that literature and politics do not go well together. On the other hand, he had a reputation for voicing liberal ideas freely, sometimes even a little recklessly. Though he was never a member of their secret societies, he is said to have watched the execution of the five leading Decembrist conspirators; that he was able to find out the time and place is significant, since the authorities had kept both a closely guarded secret. In Del'vig's Russia avoidance of overt political activity was, of course, no guarantee of freedom from the attentions of the arbiters of law and order. Testimony to Del'vig's experiences is the scathing piece "Peterburgskim tsenzoram" (To the Petersburg Censors), written in 1823-1824 as a parody of a well-known hymn, in which he not only characterizes the censors as scoundrels and cowardly flunkies but also dares to name names. That it was not published until the 1870s is hardly surprising.

Del'vig was generous toward his friends and fellow poets, professionally as well as personally. He helped and encouraged Nikolai Mikhailovich Iazykov and did everything he could to support Pushkin, whose superior talent he had been one of the first to recognize. Del'vig maintained until his death a slightly risky friendship with Pushkin, who spent most of his short life in some degree of disfavor with the tsar and his political watchdogs. Pushkin in his years of exile wrote quite often to Del'vig but had few responses: Del'vig, in keeping with other aspects of his character, was a bad letter writer. In 1825, however, he visited Pushkin at Mikhailovskoe, his family's country estate, where he was languishing under house arrest during the clandestine activities in St. Petersburg that led to the Decembrist Uprising. Del'vig had, in fact, been refused permission to visit Pushkin and was even warned that to do so could be damaging to him, but he took a short leave of absence from the library "for family reasons" and made his way to Mikhailovskoe just the same, after a token visit to his parents in Vitebsk. He overstayed his leave by two months, and his resignation from his library post is linked by some to the unpleasant recriminations that ensued on his return to St. Petersburg. His most lasting tribute to Pushkin was the portrait that Del'vig commissioned (with his journal in mind) from Orest Adamovich Kiprensky in 1827. This is perhaps the finest, and certainly the most celebrated, likeness of Russia's greatest poet. An engraving from the portrait appeared in the first issue of *Servernye tsvety* (Northern Flowers) in 1828 and contributed to Pushkin's fame as he reached the peak of his literary powers. Del'vig's good judgment in matters of art was the determining factor in this commission. He was a sophisticated admirer of the fine arts and cultivated the acquaintance of artists, art critics, and musicians. His idyllic verse "Izobretenie vaianiia" (The Invention of Sculpture, written between 1825 and 1829) was in fact written for the *Zhurnal iziashchnykh iskusstv* (Journal of Fine Arts).

Del'vig's poetry shows an interesting variety, inventiveness, and willingness to experiment both with metrical forms and with the Russian language, archaic and folkloric as well as contemporary. He wrote songs, elegies, idylls, verse epistles, imitations of Russian folk poetry, and poems in a variety of more strictly classical genres, as well as comic and parodic verses. The subject of his poetry is as varied as its form, embracing historical themes, the inevitable Romantic themes of love, lost innocence, and memories of golden youth, and philosophical reflections on everything from the role of the poet to the blessed release that death brings from the turmoils of this world. He also reacted in verse to the trivia of everyday life and indeed to almost anything that he found striking. In the summer of 1827, for example, Del'vig made a visit to the Baltic port of Revel'. There he watched the Russian naval maneuvers and was so impressed by the sight that he recorded the experience in a sonnet.

In July of 1825, having resigned from the Public Library, Del'vig joined the Interior Ministry, which in the summer of 1828 sent him to southern Russia and the Ukraine on an investigative mission. That November he transferred to the State Properties Administration and a year later to the government department that regulated religions other than Orthodoxy in Russia. There he was promoted to senior rank and continued to serve until his death. An early biographer claimed to have talked to many of those who worked with Del'vig and reported that all found him a pleasant colleague and a brilliant raconteur but an extremely negligent civil servant.

In May 1825 Del'vig was introduced at his aunt's house to Sofiia Mikhailovna Saltykova, the daughter of Mikhail Evgrafovich Saltykov, a former gentleman-in-waiting to Alexander I, who cultivated his literary interests in the seclusion of his country residence. Sofiia Mikhailovna was well educated and shared Del'vig's passion for both poetry and music. Del'vig was immediately captivated by her, and their courtship proceeded quickly: by early June the salutation in his letters to her had changed from the formal first name and patronymic to an affectionate diminutive and the sentimental appellation "my friend." Corresponding with her between visits over the summer months, he plied her with the books that he felt most important to her continued education, ranging from the novels of Comtesse Stéphanie Félicité de Genlis to the life of Benjamin Franklin in Russian translation. Del'vig declared himself an admirer of Franklin "from earliest childhood," and indeed Franklin's life had become by the end of the eighteenth century in Russia a popular item in the library of self-improvement. "Sonin'ka" was an independent and strong-willed young woman who resented the strictness and possessiveness of her widowed father (her mother had died in 1814 when she was only eight). Her father, Mikhail Saltykov, tested her strength of character when he selfishly resisted her efforts to marry, placing every obstacle in the way of the young couple's plans, despite his initial liking for Del'vig. Karamzin interceded to obtain Saltykov's consent, and the couple married at the end of October.

Their daughter Elizaveta was born 9 May 1830, only eight months before Del'vig's death; she lived to be eighty-three.

After his marriage Del'vig's home became his own rather selective salon, the scene of Wednesday and Saturday soirées that were as much musical as literary. He wrote many songs that were set to music by his friend Mikhail Luk'ianovich Iakovlev and sung at these gatherings to Iakovlev's accompaniment by Del'vig himself, who was an accomplished amateur vocalist. Del'vig's romances in a folk vein proved popular with the public and have a secure place in the history of the Russian art song. In the summer of 1828 the noteworthy composer Mikhail Ivanovich Glinka was a guest and set several of Del'vig's poems to music. One of these melodies later found its way into Glinka's opera *Zhizn' za tsaria* (A Life for the Tsar, 1836). Del'vig's literary visitors included Zhukovsky, Krylov, Prince Petr Andreevich Viazemsky, Nikolai Ivanovich Gnedich, many of his former schoolmates, and eventually Pushkin, when he was allowed to return to St. Petersburg.

Besides poetry, Del'vig's surviving work includes some fragments of verse drama and a small body of prose writing, consisting of seven *Songs of the Young Baian* (a folkloric fantasy in a style faintly reminiscent of the famous medieval epic *Slovo o polku Igoreve* [The Tale of Igor's Campaign, circa 1187]), his review articles published in the journals he was associated with (of varying lengths, but for the most part short), and open letters to the editors of other literary periodicals on a variety of subjects. As was quite usual in his day, Del'vig injected his own thoughts and opinions into his reviews. Some of them yield interesting glimpses of his own literary standards and the ideals to which he held his literary art, especially toward the end of his life. A good example is his review, written in the year before his death, of a Russian translation of Friedrich von Schlegel's history of world literature:

> "We are not experiencing a shortage of young poets, but they are unfortunately sorely lacking in knowledge, and waste their efforts on the stringing together of fine-sounding words containing thoughts and feelings that have been expressed many times over by the best of our writers. This book will demonstrate to them that those whose works have achieved lasting fame have been representatives of their age and their people, and that their moral superiority has been the fruit of universally human progress." These thoughts, with their sober focus on the lessons to be learned from the greatest writers of the past, have their counterparts in Del'vig's contributions to the characteristically Romantic theme of the poet's role. In the allegorical "Udel poeta" (The Poet's Lot, 1829) an idealistic youth asks the Genius of Poetry to tell him beside what babbling brook the poet may find his inspiration; the Genius of

Drawing of Del'vig by Aleksandr Pushkin, a close friend (from Robin Edmonds, Pushkin, the Man and His Age, *1995)*

Poetry responds curtly that the poet is to be found "on a bed of sickness, more beggarly than old Homer, and more sorrowful than Tasso, martyr to the pangs of love!" In "Poet" (The Poet, 1830) the poet "harbors long in his heart deep feelings and thoughts" and brings "happiness, and life, and love" to ordinary mortals when he breaks into song.

It has become conventional to describe Del'vig as a Neoclassical poet writing in the age of Romanticism, a judgment fueled in part by the critical observations of his contemporaries, who even before his early death began to discern in his work a vein of archaism that contrasted with the newest poetic fashions. Ivan Vasil'evich Kireevsky summed up the opinion of many when he wrote that Del'vig's muse "dwelled in Greece." This view of Del'vig is inaccurate and in fact a symptom of a more widespread misunderstanding of the manifestation of European period styles in Russia. Neoclassicism, Sentimentalism, and Romanticism may be thought of as consecutive in Europe, though not without some overlap and occasional stylistic anachronism.

In Russia, Sentimentalism made its appearance later than in Europe, almost contemporaneously with the first stirrings of Romanticism, and both coexisted with a flourishing Neoclassicism that had not yet reached the point of decline. The language and form of Russian poetry in Del'vig's time was inevitably forged from actively competing strains of Neoclassicism and Romanticism, with a strong admixture of both lingering Sentimentalism and native traditions, and Del'vig was by no means the only Russian poet of this period to elude easy classification within the not-always-relevant framework of European literary history.

At least as significant as his poetry was Del'vig's contribution as an editor. In 1824 he founded his own literary journal, *Severnye tsvety,* which grew over the ensuing eight years into a leading force in the literary life of Russia, mainly by dint of its editor's ability to attract contributions from writers who had something out of the ordinary to offer. The last issue, which appeared in 1832, the year after Del'vig's death, was completed by Pushkin as a tribute to his deceased friend.

At a later stage, in 1829 and 1830, Del'vig edited the *Literaturnaia gazeta* (Literary Gazette), which was a conscious alternative to the conservative *Severnaia pchela* (The Northern Bee). Though its subscribers numbered barely a hundred to the four thousand of *Severnaia pchela*, the *Literaturnaia gazeta* fulfilled an important role: Del'vig was responsible for publishing work by writers who were shut out of the established periodicals, including the exiled Decembrists Kiukhel'beker, Mikhail Pavlovish Bestuzhev-Riumin, and Aleksandr Ivanovich Odoevsky, and, anonymously, posthumous work by Kondratii Fedorovich Ryleev, who had been executed for his role in the uprising.

The *Literaturnaia gazeta* was closed in November 1830 following the appearance in its pages of four lines from a work by the French poet Jean-François-Casimir Delavigne, dedicated to the victims of the revolution that had shaken France in July of that year. This publication occasioned an interview with Count Aleksandr Khristoforovich Benckendorff, the notorious head of Nicholas I's secret police. Benckendorff lumped Del'vig, Pushkin, and Viazemsky together as a trio of miscreants whom he would, he assured Del'vig in the most uncouth terms, sooner or later dispatch to Siberia. The account of the interview given in his memoirs by Baron Andrei Ivanovich Del'vig, a cousin of the poet, is most interesting for the details it provides of Benckendorff's source in this case. When pressed by Del'vig, who claimed that nothing other than literature was ever discussed at his gatherings and denied the charge that they were a meeting place for young malcontents, Benckendorff named as his informant the author Faddei Venediktovich Bulgarin, editor of *Severnaia pchela*, who was a notoriously self-serving propagandist of government policy. Rivals as editors and bitter ideological opponents, Del'vig and Bulgarin had clashed before. In 1825 Del'vig had even challenged Bulgarin to a duel, which Bulgarin had declined with a sarcastic reference to Del'vig's callow youth. With remarkable courage, Del'vig complained of Benckendorff's treatment of him and demanded an apology. Somewhat surprisingly, the apology was forthcoming, and *Literaturnaia gazeta* resumed publication in December of 1831.

Though outwardly serene, Del'vig's marriage suffered from problems beneath its surface. There was jealousy, even rumors of a love triangle, involving perhaps Sofiia Ponomareva, for whom Del'vig certainly had a great affection and whose early death distressed him greatly. She appears to have had an equal affection for him and is known to have cared for him during an illness before his marriage, but there is no clear evidence of a more intimate relationship. In any case, the lyrical expression of love to be found in Del'vig's poetry is generally assumed to be autobiographical. In the last two or three years of his life, discouraged by endless literary polemics and perhaps by personal turmoil that he kept to himself, Del'vig sank increasingly into apathy and indifference.

Del'vig died on 14 January 1831, in some accounts of a chill, in others of a heart ailment that had apparently afflicted him from childhood, though contemporaries speculated that the fatal attack was hastened either by his famously unpleasant interview with Count Benckendorff or by his marital problems. He was buried on 17 January at the Volkovo Cemetery in St. Petersburg. Characteristically for a Romantic poet, he had already composed two verse epitaphs for himself. They are in fact among his earlier works, and the contrast between them reflects the range of the rhetorical attitudes toward life that were fashionable in his day. The first is a variation, in a tragic minor key and with dramatically irregular line lengths, on the hoary cliché that "life is but a dream." It was inscribed in a friend's album when Del'vig was only nineteen:

Chto zhizn'ego byla Tiazhelyi son
Chto smert'–ot grez uzhasnykh probuzhdenie
Vproson'iakh ulybnulsia on–
I snova mozhet byt' tam nachal snovidenie

(What was his life? A sleep that gave no peace;
His death? An end to dreams with horrors teeming:
He smiled in his half-waking state
And once again, perhaps, began his life of dreaming.)

The second epitaph, somewhat cryptic but bursting with youthful insouciance, was written when Del'vig was twenty-three:

Zaviduite moei sud'be!
Menia schastlivtsy ne iskali,
Ia vek ne dumal o sebe,
I ne vidal v glaza pechali.

(Envy me! They sought me not
Who were the favored sons of fortune,
I paid no heed to my own lot,
And never had to face misfortune.)

Del'vig's death at the young age of thirty-two prompted a small flood of tributary verse and articles, suggesting that his popularity was greater than the literary polemics of the day had given reason to suppose. Some felt that Del'vig's relatively uneventful life gave rise to a serious flaw in his poetry, a theatrical alternation of joyous and plaintive notes that betrayed little in the way of real feeling and experience. Pushkin, on the other hand, summed up Del'vig with the suggestion that, even if true greatness as a poet eluded him, he represented for his contemporaries the ideals of his generation: "His life was rich not in romantic adventures, but in exalted feelings, the light of pure reason, and hopes." The conclusion of a short, popular biography from the beginning of the twentieth century shows that Del'vig's place in Russian letters had remained much as Pushkin defined it: his poetry shows neither depth of thought nor perfection of form, but his small poetic output reveals an attempt to introduce into Russian poetry both new content and new form. His personal qualities, however, outshone his literary gifts.

Letters:

Viktor Vladimirovich Kunin, *Druz'ia Pushkina: perepiska, vospominaniia, dnevniki* (Moscow: Izd-vo "Pravda," 1984);

Pis'ma, in Del'vig's *Sochineniia,* edited by Vadim Erazmovich Vatsuro (Leningrad: Khudozhestvennaia literatura, 1986), pp. 278-348.

Biography:

Iurii Nikandrovich Verkhovsky, *Baron Delvig; materialy biograficheskie i literaturnye* (St. Petersburg: A. S. Kagan, 1922).

References:

Andrei Ivanovich Del'vig, *Polveka russkoi zhizni: Vospominaniia A. I. Del'viga, 1820-1870,* edited by Solomon Iakovlevich Shtraikh, 2 volumes (Moscow-Leningrad: Academia, 1930), pp. 51-86, 92-112, 122-136, 158-196;

V. P. Gaevsky, "Del'vig," *Sovremennik,* 37, no. 2, section 3 (1853): 45-88; 39, no. 5, section 3 (1853): 1-66; 43, no. 1, section 3 (1854): 1-52; 47, no. 9, section 3 (1854): 1-64;

Tatiana Galushko, "Sud'ba i legenda. Etiudy k portretu Del'viga," in *"Raevskie moi—"* (Leningrad: Lenizdat, 1991);

S. Kibal'nik, "Zagadka 'Bronzovogo sfinksa': k 190-letiiu so dnia rozhdeniia A. A. Del'viga," *Neva* (St. Petersburg), no. 8 (1988), 195-198;

Ludmila Koehler, *Anton Antonovic Delvig: A Classicist in the Time of Romanticism* (The Hague: Mouton, 1970);

Viktor Vladimirovich Kunin, "Anton Antonovich Del'vig. Biograficheskii ocherk," in B. K. Kiukhel'beker's *Izbrannoe* (Moscow: Izdatel'stvo "Pravda," 1987);

Vladimir Vladimirovich Maikov, in Anton Antonovich Del'vig's *Sochineniia, s prilozheniem biograficheskago ocherka* (St. Petersburg: Evgeny Evdokimov, 1893);

John Mersereau Jr., *Baron Del'vig's "Northern Flowers," 1825-1832: Literary Almanac of the Pushkin Pleiad* (Carbondale: Southern Illinois University Press, 1967);

Stanislav Borisovich Rassadin, "Tsena garmonii (O poezii Antona Del'viga)," *Voprosy literatury* no. 4 (1972): pp. 98-122;

Vadim Erazmovich Vatsuro, "Anton Del'vig–literator," in Anton Antonovich Del'vig's *Sochineniia* (Leningrad: Khudozhestvennaia literatura, 1986), pp. 3-20.

Papers:

Anton Antonovich Del'vig's papers are in the Rossiiskii gosudarstvennyi arkhiv literatury i iskusstva, Moscow; the Rossiiskaia natsional'naia biblioteka, St. Petersburg; and IRLI (Pushkin House).

Petr Pavlovich Ershov

(22 February 1815 – 18 August 1869)

Gary R. Jahn
University of Minnesota

BOOKS: *Konek-Gorbunok. Russkaia skazka* (St. Petersburg: Kh. Gintse, 1834);
Suvorov i stantsionnyi smotritel'. Dramaticheskii anekdot (St. Petersburg: V Guttenbergovoi tipografii, 1836).

Editions and Collections: *Stikhotvoreniia*, edited by Mark Konstantinovich Azadovsky (Leningrad: Sovetskii pisatel', 1936);
Sochineniia, edited by Viktor G. Utkov (Omsk: Oblizdat, 1950);
Konek-Gorbunok. Stikhotvoreniia, edited by I. P. Lupanova (Leningrad: Sovetskii pisatel', 1976);
Stikhotvoreniia, edited by V. P. Zverev (Moscow, 1989).

Editions in English: *Humpy*, translated by William C. White (New York & London: Harper, 1931);
Little Magic Horse: A Russian Tale by Peter Ershoff, translated by Tatiana Balkoff Drowne (New York: Macmillan, 1942);
The Little Humpbacked Horse, translated by Louis Zellikof (Moscow: Foreign Languages Publishing House, 1960).

What D. S. Mirsky said of Aleksandr Sergeevich Griboedov—that he was *homo unius libri* (a one-book man)—is even more true of Petr Pavlovich Ershov, whose claim to literary remembrance is based entirely on his *Konek-Gorbunok. Russkaia skazka* (The Humpback Horse: A Russian Tale). This work, written in 1834 when Ershov was not yet twenty years old, never came close to being surpassed by any of its author's later efforts. *Konek-Gorbunok,* however, has been regarded since at least the middle of the nineteenth century as a Russian classic, a fact attested by the many times that the book has been reprinted. The poem served as the inspiration for a popular and still-performed nineteenth-century ballet and a prizewinning animated film from Soiuzmul'tfil'm Studios in 1947. *Konek-Gorbunok* is always mentioned prominently in any account of the history of folklore stylization in Russia; its proper literary context includes Aleksandr Pushkin's fairy tales in verse, Sergei Timofeevich Aksakov's *Alen'kii tsvetochek* (The Little Crimson Flower, 1858), Mikhail Iur'evich

Petr Pavlovich Ershov

Lermontov's *Pesnia pro tsaria Ivana Vasil'evicha, molodogo oprichnika i udalogo kuptsa Kalashnikova* (Song of the Tsar Ivan Vasil'evich, the Young Oprichnik and the Valiant Merchant Kalashnikov, 1838), Nikolai Alekseevich Nekrasov's *Komu na Rusi zhit' khorosho?* (Who Lives Well in Russia, written 1863–1878), and Leo Tolstoy's series of "Stories for the People" (written in the 1880s). I. P. Lupanova has made the claim that it would be proper to compare Ershov's literary gifts with those of his contemporary Hans Christian Andersen; Lupanova accounts for the enormous difference in the quantity of the output of these supposedly comparable writers by remarking that Ershov, unlike Andersen, never came to understand the true nature of his literary gifts and consequently did not devote himself to the creation of fairy tales, as did Andersen.

Petr Pavlovich Ershov was born on 22 February 1815 into the family of a civil servant. His father, Pavel Alekseevich Ershov, a police official, was stationed in the village of Bezrukovo (fifteen miles from the town of Ishima) in Tobol'sk province (western Siberia) at the time of Ershov's birth. Later assignments took the family to other locations, including Omsk, and finally to St. Petersburg. Ershov graduated from the Gymnasium in Tobol'sk at the head of his class. In 1830 he was accepted for higher study in the department of philosophy and law at St. Petersburg University. Throughout his student years he was inordinately fond of folklore and committed many fairy tales to memory. While at the university he became familiar with Pushkin's recently published fairy tales in verse; these works impressed Ershov greatly and were certainly the inspiration for his own *Konek-Gorbunok,* which he wrote before he finished college.

After the death of his father in 1833, it became difficult for Ershov to continue as a student at the university. He persevered, however, and sought to supplement his income by writing poems. He published some of them in the journal *Biblioteka dlia chteniia* (Library for Reading), which was then edited by Osip Ivanovich Senkovsky, better known under his pen name, Baron Brambeus. Ershov studied literature at the university with professor Petr Aleksandrovich Pletnev, to whom he submitted the draft version of *Konek-Gorbunok* to satisfy the requirement for an annual project. Pletnev was much impressed with the work, as was the audience to whom he read the first part of the poem at one of his public lectures on literature. The first part was published early in 1834 in *Biblioteka dlia chteniia.* The work was an immediate success and brought its author considerable celebrity for a nineteen-year-old. Later in 1834 the entire poem was published as a separate book, although with several excisions at the insistence of government censors. Pushkin, the acknowledged master of folklore stylization, declared that Ershov's work was so good that Pushkin might abandon this field of literary endeavor.

Ershov's poem is remarkable because it remains original while finding inspiration both in traditional folktales and in stylized versions such as Pushkin's *skazki* (tales). The poem, 2,510 trochaic tetrameter lines with paired rhymes, consists of three parts, each one relating three events in the life of Ivan the Fool and his little humpbacked horse. In typical Russian folk fashion, Ivan, the youngest son of three, solves a problem that baffles his two older, "wiser" brothers. In the process Ivan acquires a tiny double-humpbacked horse only six inches high but with ears twenty-eight inches long. The little horse helps Ivan in his first adventure, which eventually leads him to the position of the King's groom.

While in the King's employ Ivan finds a magnificent feather dropped by the wondrous Fire-Bird. Against the advice of the little humpbacked horse, Ivan cannot leave the brilliant, light-producing feather behind, so he puts it in his cap. This trophy incites the envy of the King's chamberlain, who sees in Ivan a rival. He tells the King about Ivan's prize, an act that results in the King's demand that Ivan capture the Fire-Bird itself. Though Ivan paid no heed to his horse's advice, the gracious animal helps him catch the magic creature. Foiled but not beaten, the chamberlain plots to have the King order Ivan to bring the beautiful Tsar-Maiden, "daughter of the Moon and sister of the Sun," to be the King's wife. The little horse again helps Ivan fulfill his tasks; however, another soon falls his way. The Tsar-Maiden, whom Ivan succeeds in delivering to the King, demands that someone find her ring, which is lying at the bottom of the ocean. Part two ends with Ivan going off in search of the ring.

Part three relates the details of his quest, including his meetings with the Moon and a "stranded monster—*'chudo-iudo-ryba-kit'*" (Wonder-Monster-Whale-Fish) who help the horse find the ring. Of course, more troubles postpone the resolution of the tale. Faced with marrying an old man, the Tsar-Maiden balks. In order to regain his youth the King must bathe in a cauldron of boiling water. Certainly this prospect does not appeal to the King, so he orders Ivan to "test the waters" first. Yet again the horse comes to Ivan's aid with an "antidote to the water." When Ivan emerges younger and handsomer, the King follows suit and is boiled to death. In true fairy-tale fashion the Tsar-Maiden marries Ivan and, with the little humpbacked horse, lives happily ever after. The source of the poem is probably the fairy tale "The Fire-Bird and the Princess Vasilissa." Humor, skillful blending of the real and fantastic, and masterful use of the Russian language have transformed a folk genre into a timeless work of art.

The publication of *Konek-Gorbunok* was the making of Ershov's literary reputation. Getting his work published in the then-popular journals became easier, and he tried his hand at a variety of forms: one-act plays, vaudeville sketches, and opera libretti, in addition to further poems. He also became acquainted with the literary society of St. Petersburg; he began to be seen with such writers as Senkovsky, Pletnev, and Vasilii Andreevich Zhukovsky. He became a member of the intellectual circle gathered around the figure of

Timofei Nikolaevich Granovsky, historian and professor.

Ershov's work was reviewed as a matter of course by Vissarion Grigor'evich Belinsky, who in the 1830s had not yet become the dominating force in Russian literary discussion that he was by the middle of the 1840s. Thus, Belinsky's unfriendly reaction to *Konek-Gorbunok* did not prove fatal to the popularity of the work. Belinsky's attitude toward Ershov's tale–that it "had no artistic worth whatever"–was similar to the one he adopted toward Pushkin's stylizations of popular lore, which he disregarded as "the fruit of a quite mistaken tendency toward the folkish." Ershov's other works of the 1830s suffered a variety of misfortunes. His libretto for the opera *Strashnyi mech* (The Terrible Sword), with music by his friend Iosif Karlovich Gunke, never reached the stage for want of a producer. His play *Suvorov i stantsionnyi smotritel'* (Suvorov and the Station Master, 1836) was not initially passed by the censorship for public performance. These literary reverses, combined with personal difficulties, moved Ershov to apply for a position as a teacher in his native Siberia. His application was successful, and he departed for his assignment to the Tobol'sk Gymnasium in 1836 after graduating from the university.

Ershov was acquainted with some of the exiled Decembrists as well as several Poles who had been sent to Siberia for their role in the Polish uprising of 1831. He and they played an active part in the provincial literary scene. He continued to write while living in Siberia. These works, published in periodicals, are his "mature" literary output, and they include a long narrative poem, *Suzge* (1838); several stories collected as *Osennie vechera* (Autumn Evenings) and published in *Zhivopisnyi sbornik* (Pictorial Collection) in 1857; the play *Kuznets Bazim* (The Smithy Bazim), included in volume 3 of *Sbornik literaturnykh statei posviashchenykh russkimi pisateliami pamiati . . . A. F. Smirdina* (Collection of Literary Articles Dedicated by Russian Writers to the Memory of A. F. Smirdin, 1858); and several lyric poems in the Romantic vein. None of these works raised Ershov's literary reputation above the level it had reached with the popularity of *Konek-Gorbunok*. With respect to that success, Ershov modestly declared, "My [book] exemplifies the Russian proverb: 'Don't be born clever or handsome, be born lucky.' The only merit that my book has is that I managed to strike the vein of the genuinely popular in it."

Ershov was evidently an exceptional teacher. If scholars are to judge by the unpublished favorable memoir left by his most famous student, the chemist Dmitrii Ivanovich Mendeleev, Ershov tried to instill in his pupils independence of thought, a love for their native language and literature, and an interest in and respect for the history of their nation.

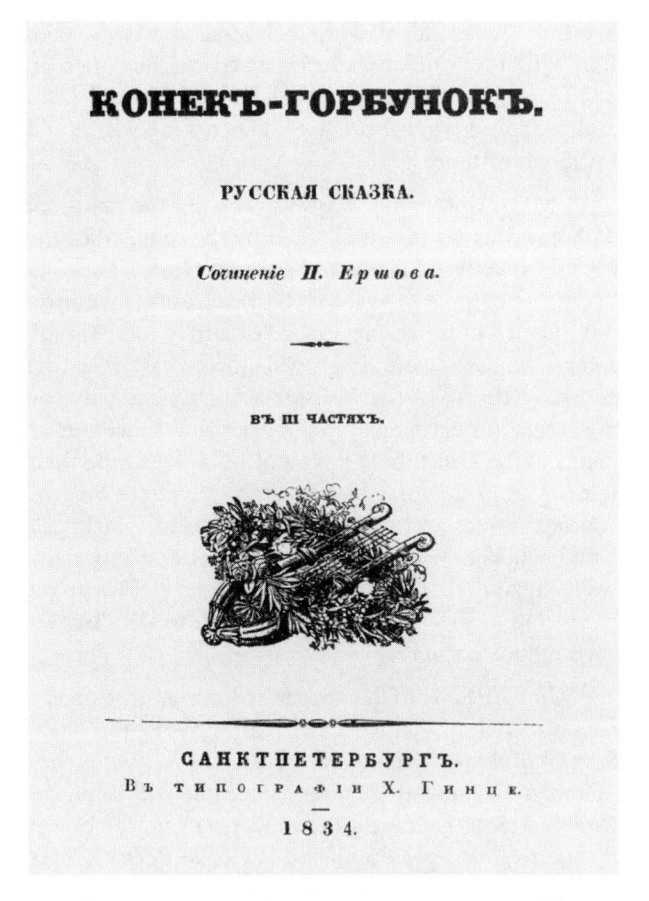

Title page for Konek-Gorbunok. Russkaia skazka *(The Humpback Horse. A Russian Tale), the fairy tale on which Ershov's literary reputation rests*

His first assignment was as teacher of beginning Latin in the younger grades, but he was soon made a teacher of philosophy and literature for the older pupils in the school. Ershov did much to enliven, with personal recollections and his awareness of the contemporary scene in the capital, the normally stodgy approach to these subjects. One of his innovative projects, a series of outings with the older pupils in the environs of Tobol'sk, resulted in the collection of local stories about the celebrated second wife of the legendary Tatar Khan Kuchum, which he later wove together into the poem *Suzge*. These promising new beginnings soon changed to disappointment, however; his superior at the high school forbade any further departure from the set curriculum (this crackdown included the closing of the student theater that Ershov had organized), and the St. Petersburg critics Faddei Venediktovich Bulgarin and Senkovsky dealt most unkindly with his *Suzge*. The poem was, in the end, published by *Sovremennik* (The Contemporary) in 1839 and received a sympathetic reading from Belinsky.

The late 1830s and the 1840s represented a period of transition in Ershov's life. In 1838 he married

Serafima Aleksandrovna Leshchevaia, a widow with four children from an earlier marriage. She died in 1845. A second marriage lasted from 1846 until 1853 and produced two offspring. Still later, Ershov married for the third time.

Meanwhile, the significance of the city of Tobol'sk was greatly diminished by the removal of the capital of western Siberia to the city of Omsk. Tobol'sk had never compared well with St. Petersburg, of course, but after 1839 it became a place of purely local significance. Matters were improved somewhat over the course of the 1840s, at least for Ershov personally, by the arrival (as permanent residents) of still-exiled participants of the Decembrist Revolt of 1825, following their releases from the forced labor camps of eastern Siberia. Among these were the poet Vil'gel'm Karlovich Kiukhel'beker, with whom Ershov became especially well acquainted. These educated new arrivals brought friendship, respect, and new inspiration to the discouraged school teacher.

In the 1850s Ershov began writing short stories, a new direction of literary activity for the longtime poet. Several of these stories were collected as *Sibirskie vechera* (Siberian Evenings); later the collection was renamed *Osennie vechera*. Following the model set long before in Pushkin's *Povesti pokoinogo Ivana Petrovicha Belkina* (Tales of the Late Ivan Petrovich Belkin, 1830) and Gogol's *Vechera na khutore bliz Dikan'ki* (Evenings on a Farm near Dikanka, 1831–1832), Ershov supplies a preface from the putative editor of seven tales told by various persons. The stories display a broad spectrum of the social and ethnic variety of Siberia: merchants, peasants, Tatars, gentry, and laborers are all presented in realistic linguistic detail, somewhat in the manner of the "physiological sketches" of the middle 1840s. The stories evoke the diversity of life in Tobol'sk: "Dedushkin kolpak" (Grandfather's Cap) explores the norms and traditions of the Siberian merchant class; "Panin bugor" (Panin Bluff) describes the life of government bureaucrats; "Rasskaz o tom, kakim obrazom dedushka moi, byvshi u tsaria Kuchuma pervym muftiem, byl pozhalovan v takoi chin" (The Story of How My Grandfather, Who Was First Councilor to Tsar Kuchum, Was Promoted to Such a Rank) is a retelling of Tatar legends of the region.

The sympathetic reception of at least some of the stories in *Osennie vechera* was accompanied, in 1857, by Ershov's appointment to the post of school director, which meant a significant improvement in his style of life. These improvements, however, were short-lived. By 1862 changes in town and regional administration cooperated to force Ershov into early retirement. His situation grew steadily worse; he became ill and fell into dire poverty. If not for the assistance of friends and former pupils, who gave tangible form to their fond memories of their former teacher, Ershov would doubtless not have survived as long as he did. He died on 18 August 1869 at the age of fifty-four. Only a single five-kopeck coin was found in his tiny apartment after his death.

Ershov's claim on the attention of modern readers consists exclusively of the single celebrated work of his youth, *Konek-Gorbunok*. This one work, however, both in and of itself as well as in its indubitable familiarity to all Russian writers since the middle of the nineteenth century, is an inheritance of which its author may be proud.

Biographies:

A. K. Iaroslavtsev, *Avtor skazki "Konek-Gorbunok": Biograficheskiia vospominaniia universitetskago tovarishcha ego* (St. Petersburg: V. Demakov, 1872);

Viktor G. Utkov, *Grazhdanin Tobol'ska* (Sverdlovsk: Sredno-Ural'skoe knizhnoe izd-vo, 1972).

References:

L. N. Mikheeva, "O *Konek-Gorbunok* i ego avtore," *Russkaia rech'*, 2 (1990): 16–24;

D. S. Mirsky, *A History of Russian Literature*, edited and abridged by Francis J. Whitfield (New York: Knopf, 1949);

Irina Z. Surat, "Slovesnyi mir skazki," *Russkaia rech'*, 4 (1984): 3–8;

Viktor G. Utkov, *Dorogi Kon'ka-Gorbunka* (Moscow: Kniga, 1970);

Utkov, *Rozhdennyi v nedrakh nepogody* (Novosibirsk: Zapadno-Sibirskoe Knizhnoe izdatel'stvo, 1966);

Utkov, *Skazochnik P. P. Ershov* (Omsk: Omskoe oblastnoe gosudarstvennoe izdatel'stvo, 1950);

Vladimir Nikolaevich Vakurov, "O slovakh i vyrazheniiakh skazki P. P. Ershova *Konek-Gorbunok*," *Russkaia rech'*, 2 (1990): 25–30.

Papers:

Some of Petr Pavlovich Ershov's papers are at the Tobol'skii gosudarstvennyi istorichesko-arkhitekturnyi muzei-zapovednik; the Muzei-arkhiv D. I. Mendeleeva at St. Petersburg University; the Rossiiskii gosudarstvennyi arkhiv, St. Petersburg, f. 1349, op. 5, d. 2284 and f. 733, op. 83, d. 121; the Rossiiski gosudarstvennyi arkhiv literatury i isskustva (RGALI), Moscow, f. 214; the Rossiiskaia natsional'naia biblioteka, St. Petersburg, ff. 438, 359, and 1,000. Illustrations and portraits can be found at the Institut russkoi literatury i isskustva (Pushkinskii dom), St. Petersburg.

Fedor Nikolaevich Glinka
(8 June 1786 – 11 February 1880)

Sofiya Yuzefpolskaya
University of Washington

BOOKS: *Vel'zen, ili Osvobozhdennaia Gollandiia* (Smolensk, 1810);

Podvigi Grafa Mikhaila Andreevicha Mileradovicha v otechestvennuiu voinu 1812 goda, s prisovokupleniem nekotorykh pisem ot raznykh osob. Iz zapisok F. G. (Moscow, 1814);

Cherty iz zhizni T. Kostiushki plenennago Rossiiskim Generalom Ferzenom (St. Petersburg, 1815);

Pis'ma russkogo ofitsera o Pol'she, Avstriiskikh vladeniiakh, Prussii i Frantsii, s podobnym opisaniem pokhoda rossiian protivu frantsuzov, v 1805 i 1806 gg, takzhe otechestvennoi i zagranichnoi voiny s 1812 po 1815 g., s prisovokupleniem zamechanii, myslei i rassuzhdenii vo vremia poezdki v nekotorye otechestvennye gubernii, 8 volumes (Moscow, 1815–1816);

Pis'ma k drugu, soderzhashchie v sebe zamechaniia, mysli i rassuzhdeniia o raznykh predmetakh, s prisovokupleniem istoricheskogo povestvovaniia: Zinobei Bogdan Khmel'nitskii, ili Osvobozhdennaia Malorossiia, 3 volumes (St. Petersburg, 1816);

Kratkoe obozrenie voennoi zhizni podvigov Grafa Mileradovicha (St. Petersburg, 1818);

Podarok russkomu soldatu (St. Petersburg, 1818);

Razsuzhdenie o neobkhodimosti deiatel'noi zhizni, uchenykh uprazhnenii i chteniia knig; takzhe o pol'ze i nastoiashchem polozhenii uchrezhdennago pri Gvardeiskom Shtabe, dlia voennykh chitatelei, Knigokhranilishcha (St. Petersburg: Tip. Gvardeiskago Shtaba, 1818);

Opyty allegorii ili inoskazatel'nykh opisanii, v stikhakh i v proze (St. Petersburg: Tip. Glavnago Shtaba Ego Imperatorskago Velichestva, 1826);

Opyty sviashchennoi poezii (St. Petersburg: Tip. Departamenta Narodnago Prosveshcheniia, 1826);

Kareliia, ili zatochenie Marfy Ioannovny Romanovoi. Opisatel'noe stikhotvorenie (St. Petersburg: Nepeitsyn, 1830);

Vospominanie o piiticheskoi zhizni Pushkina. Posviashena ottsu poeta (Moscow: A. Semen, 1837);

Ocherki Borodinskago srazheniia (Vospominaniia o 1812 gode), 2 parts (Moscow, 1839);

Ura! (St. Petersburg: Tip. Imp. Akademii Nauk, 1854);

Fedor Nikolaevich Glinka

Iov. Svobodnoe podrazhanie sviashchennoi knige Iova F. Glinki (St. Petersburg, 1859);

Sochineniia, 3 volumes (Moscow: Tip. gazety "Russkii," 1869–1872);

Tainstvennaia kaplia. Narodnoe predanie (Moscow: Tip. M. P. Pogodina, 1871);

Deva karel'skikh lesov. Povest' v stikhakh, edited by Vasilii Grigor'evich Bazanov (Petrozavodsk: Karel'skoe gosudarstvennoe izdatel'stvo, 1939).

Editions and Collections: *Izbrannoe,* edited by Bazanov (Petrozavodsk, 1949);

Stikhotvoreniia, edited by Bazanov, second edition (Leningrad: Sovetskii pisatel', 1951);

Izbrannye proizvedeniia, edited by Bazanov (Leningrad: Sovetskii pisatel', 1957);

Kareliia: Opisatel'noe stikhotvorenie v chetyrekh chastiakh (Petrozavodsk: Kareliia, 1980);

Pis'ma russkogo ofitsera, edited by S. Serkov and Iu. Uderevsky (Moscow: Moskovskii rabochii, 1985);

Sochineniia, edited by Vladimir I. Karpets (Moscow: Sovetskaia Rossiia, 1986);

Pis'ma russkogo ofitsera, edited by Georgii Aleksandrovich Galin (Moscow: Pravda, 1990);

Pis'ma k drugu, edited by V. P. Zverev (Moscow: Sovremennik, 1990);

Pis'ma russkogo cheloveka: Zinovii Bogdan Khmel'nitskii ili Osvobozhennaia Malorossiia, sbornik (Kiev: Dnipro, 1991).

Fedor Glinka left behind a small but remarkable body of work that encompasses poetry, historical prose, memoirs of the Napoleonic Wars, ballads, and plays. Though he took an active part in the literary and political life of the Golden Age of Russian literature, he remained one of its marginal figures. His poetry is original and imaginative, and he was a meticulous craftsman. Glinka's Romanticism, though, found its greatest expression in metaphysical realms rather than in formal perfection. His most important contribution to Russian literature is his religious poetry, which he wrote in his later years. Although he was a devout adherent of Russian Orthodoxy, his poetry is mystical and philosophically profound. Glinka has been neglected by posterity, a fate he does not deserve, especially since he may be one of the greatest religious poets Russia ever produced.

Although accounts differ on the date of Fedor Nikolaevich Glinka's birth, the most reliable source, the memoir of his friend and biographer Avgust Kazimirovich Zhiznevsky, indicates that he was born on 8 June 1786 in the village of Sutoki, near Dukhovnotsy, in the Smolensk province. A cousin of the famous composer Mikhail Ivanovich Glinka, Fedor Glinka came from a Russian noble family of ancient lineage. At the time of his birth, however, his parents (Nikolai Il'ich Glinka, a retired captain, and Mariia Iakovlevna Glinka, née Shakhovskaia) were comparatively poor landowners living on their small estate at Sutoki. Describing his early childhood in his "Avtobiografiia" (Autobiography, included in the 1949 edition of his works), Glinka recalled the quiet life of their sleepy provincial neighborhood, where intellectual activities were rather few and reading was limited exclusively to books of religious content. The appearance of Karamzin's first volume of selected works, *Moi bezdelki* (My Trifles, 1794), in the Glinka household made such a strong impression on the eight-year-old Fedor that he read and reread Karamzin's tales and verses until he knew them all by heart. Later, during the long and heated debates that accompanied the development of Russian literary style, Glinka (along with Pavel Aleksandrovich Katenin, Vil'gel'm Karlovich Kiukhel'beker, and Aleksandr Sergeevich Griboedov) associated himself with the "archaists" in opposition to the advocates of Karamzin's "Europeanized" style, which reflected the language of society salons. In his own literary works, however, Glinka constantly strove, for the most part successfully, to synthesize the solemn sounds of Church Slavonic, which had captured his heart in his early religious readings, with the language of tender feelings tinged with Sentimental philosophy, which he had found so appealing in the works of Karamzin.

Glinka was sent at the age of nine to St. Petersburg to enter a military school—the First Cadet Corps—following in the steps of his older brother, Sergei. In his school years Glinka soon became more interested in literature and poetry than in military matters, which was nothing unusual; at this time, poetry flourished in educational institutions for the children of the Russian nobility, and military schools were no exception. A characteristic trait of young Russians of Glinka's generation, besides their inclination to literary endeavors, was their striving for moral perfection, and the oath of complete honesty that Glinka took while in the Cadet Corps was just one example of such ethical idealism. A curious event that took place three years after Glinka's graduation from the Cadet Corps in 1802 demonstrates how serious he was about putting his moral ideals into practice. When Glinka, by then a young ensign of the Apsheronsky regiment, was asked by a famous general, Count Mikhail Andreevich Miloradovich, to become his adjutant, he only accepted this flattering invitation on the condition that he would never be forced to break his oath of honesty.

As Miloradovich's adjutant, Glinka took part in the campaign of 1805–1806 and fought in the Battle of Austerlitz. At the conclusion of the campaign he retired for medical reasons, settling on the family estate and devoting himself to literary work. In the serene solitude of the country, the triumphal sounds of the recently experienced battles continued to resound for him. Glinka aspired to give poetic form to the intense patriotic sentiments fostered by his military service and wrote his first poems in a lofty declamatory style modeled after the odes of Mikhail Vasil'evich Lomonosov and Gavriil Romanovich Derzhavin. These poems, along with *Pis'ma russkogo ofitsera* (Letters of a Russian Officer), consisting of excerpts from the diary that Glinka had kept during his military service, first appeared in *Russkii vestnik* (The Russian Herald) in 1807–1808 and were favorably received by the public. Also in 1808 Glinka published his historical tragedy, *Vel'zen, ili Osvobozhdennaia Gollandiia* (Vilzen, or Holland Liberated), in which, anticipating one of the favorite themes of the Decembrists, he explored the contrast between the tyrant and the "lawful" monarch, the liberator of his people.

In 1810–1811 Glinka undertook a journey around central Russia, visiting Kiev, Smolensk, the estuary of the Dnieper, the upper reaches of the Volga, Rzhev, Tver', Klin, and Moscow. Traveling on foot and on horseback, by coach and by boat, he stopped in villages and small towns where he had an opportunity to learn about life in rural Russia and to compare it with that of the other countries he had visited during the European campaigns. In the travel notes Glinka made during this grand tour, which were published in 1816 as a part of his *Pis'ma k drugu* (Letters to a Friend), he portrayed the barbarous feudal system of his country as the cause of the people's misery and contrasted the virtues of the old way of life that still existed in provincial Russia with what he regarded as the luxurious, materialistic, and morally corrupt spirit of European cities.

When Napoleon Bonaparte invaded Russia in 1812, Glinka was at home on his estate. In response to a personal invitation from Miloradovich, Glinka joined the retreating cavalry of Gen. Fedor Karlovich Korf, and, without his officer's badge of rank, which he could not retrieve from Sutoki as it had burned, he fought as a common soldier until he could rejoin the Apsheronsky regiment at Tarutino after the Battle of Borodino. There he resumed his duty as Miloradovich's adjutant and was soon promoted to the rank of lieutenant and eventually to colonel. While in Vilno on a special mission, he learned of the fall of Paris, and soon he set off with his regiment for the cultural capital of the world. As a war hero he was decorated by the king of Prussia and was awarded by the tsar a golden sword engraved with the words "For Valor."

The war did not interrupt Glinka's literary work; he continued to write between battles, recording his new experiences and reflections in his diary and working them into his poems. Most of his subsequent literary works celebrate the war against Napoleon, which he saw as a turning point in Russian history. In his cycle of poems *Podarok russkomu soldatu* (Gift to a Russian Soldier, 1818), Glinka paid tribute to the common people, whom he praised as the real heroes of the war. Although many of the poems were titled "soldiers' songs," stylistically they are a sometimes awkward blend of folk elements with civic rhetoric in the spirit of eighteenth-century classicism. They are in reality neither deeply rooted in popular songs, as their titles

Title page for Opyty sviashchennoi poezii *(Experiments in Sacred Poetry), which includes some of Glinka's elegies inspired by the Old Testament*

would suggest, nor destined to become popular, even though two of Glinka's later poems, "Troika" and "Uznik" (The Prisoner), which are less didactic and more personal, are still loved and sung in Russia.

The prose that Glinka devoted to the war was much more successful than his poetry. In his new and expanded version of *Pis'ma russkogo ofitsera* (1815–1816), despite the overwhelmingly patriotic spirit of the book, Glinka gave quite realistic descriptions of battle scenes, interspersing them with colorful portrayals of peaceful events, extremely interesting reflections of a connoisseur on European art and culture, and a shrewd analysis of the causes and moral implications of the Napoleonic Wars. Published shortly after the end of hostilities, the new version of *Pis'ma russkogo ofitsera* immediately won the hearts of the reading public all over Russia and later served as a source for Mikhail Iur'evich Lermontov's famous "Borodino" (1837) and Leo Tolstoy's *Voina i mir* (War and Peace, 1863–1869).

Though the public expected Glinka to continue to write about the war, as the 1820s approached, he was drawn into the vortex of political events, which both gave him literary inspiration and imparted a new direction to his activities. In 1816 Glinka, who was already a member of the "Izbrannyi Mikhail" Masonic lodge, joined the first of the Decembrist secret societies, the *Soiuz Spaseniia* (Union of Salvation). The initial aims of the union—the establishment of a constitutional monarchy, the achievement of social reform through education, and the gradual molding of public opinion—corresponded to Glinka's personal convictions and were generally reminiscent of Masonic ideas. Soon Glinka became one of the most active members of the union and used his position as president of the *Vol'noe obshchestvo liubitelei rossiiskoi slovesnosti* (Free Society of Lovers of Russian Literature), an influential literary circle, to disseminate the political views of the Decembrists. Glinka made similar use of his position as personal assistant to Miloradovich, who was now governor-general of St. Petersburg, to uncover instances of abuse of power by the government, reporting them to the union and giving assistance to the victims.

Resisting along with the other moderates the radically minded and vocal minority led by Pavel Ivanovich Pestel', Glinka reformed the *Soiuz Spaseniia* in 1818 into the *Soiuz Blagodenstviia* (Union of Welfare), a more publicly visible and inclusive organization. By 1820, however, the Decembrist movement again showed signs of drifting toward the left. In January 1820, during a meeting of the *Korennaia Duma* (Supreme Council) of the union, which took place at Glinka's St. Petersburg apartment, all of the delegates except the host were converted to republicanism by Pestel'. Glinka remained alone in defending constitutional monarchy as a form of government more suitable to the geographic and ethnographic conditions of Russia. A year later he represented the St. Petersburg branch at the Moscow Congress of both the Northern and the Southern wings of *Soiuz Blagodenstviia,* where the sharp division between moderates and radicals led to its final dissolution.

When the *Severnoe obshchestvo* (Northern Society), which later started the insurrection of 1825, was formed in St. Petersburg, Glinka did not join it. His poetry, however, which blossomed in the early 1820s, shows his faithfulness to the civic and ethical ideals of the Decembrists. To this period belong his elegies, most of which are free paraphrases of psalms written in an exhortatory spirit evocative of the Old Testament prophets and punctuated with ardent appeals to God to avenge the crimes of the tyrant and to free the slaves, referring respectively to the tsar and the people of Russia. Yet, there appears even among these solemn and strongly didactic verses a quieter vein suggestive of an intimate religious feeling, sometimes revealing the poet's fascination with the ultimate mystery of life, the theme that dominated the remainder of his poetry.

When Glinka's elegies were published in 1826 under the titles *Opyty sviashchennoi poezii* (Experiments in Sacred Poetry) and *Opyty allegorii ili inoskazatel'nykh opisanii, v stikhakh i v proze* (Experiments in Allegories or Circumlocutional Descriptions in Verse and Prose), the author was arrested, though he had not participated in the actual uprising of the Decembrists. He spent three months in the Peter-Paul Fortress, an infamous St. Petersburg prison that stands ominously over the gloomy waters of the river Neva. At the end of the investigation he was expelled from the Guards, reduced in rank to a "collegiate counselor," and exiled to Petrozavodsk, a city on the Karelian peninsula not far from the Finnish border. Compared to the fate of the other Decembrists (five of whom were hanged and thirty-one sentenced to hard labor in Siberian exile), Glinka's punishment was rather mild, but it was quite painful to the poet, who insisted on his complete innocence.

In his attempt to make sense out of the suffering of the innocent, one of the poems Glinka wrote while exiled in Karelia was devoted to the biblical Job, whose story he called "the saddest and the most sublime song of mankind in all the places of exile on earth." At the same time he wrote two other long narrative poems, *Deva karel'skikh lesov* (The Maiden of the Karelian Forests, written in 1828 but not published in full until 1939), and *Kareliia, ili zatochenie Marfy Ioannovny Romanovoi* (Karelia, or the Imprisonment of Marfa Ioannovna Romanova, 1830), the second of which brought him the greatest fame of his literary career. Though resembling in many ways Kondratii Fedorovich Ryleev's poem *Voinarovskii* (1825), it borrows one of its subjects from Karamzin's *Istoriia gosudarstva Rossiiskogo* (History of the Russian State, 1816–1818; revised, 1818–1829). Thematically and stylistically somewhat reminiscent of the Romantic movement, *Kareliia* was justly regarded by Aleksandr Pushkin and others as among the most original verse in Russian literature.

In *Kareliia* Glinka's lifelong preoccupation with the historical and political fate of Russia, his philosophical and religious searchings, and his ethnographic interests find their fullest expression. With the folk tales told by a peasant girl, the poem combines the stories of Marfa, the mother of the first tsar of the Romanov dynasty, exiled to Karelia by Boris Fedorovich Godunov in the early seventeenth century, and of a hermit, a seeker of a mystical vision, whose life story resembles that of a Byronic hero. Into these stories are woven the poet's reflections on the cultural treasures of human civilization and magnificent, almost scientifically precise, descriptions of the stern natural beauty of Karelia. Despite the somewhat fragmentary composition and the underdeveloped presentation of its several narratives, the poem succeeds in creating a unified vision in which individual human fates and aspirations merge with the eternal cycles of historical and cosmic time, returning forever to their divine cradle.

Despite his status as a political exile, Glinka's works continued to appear in the literary journals of both capitals, and in 1830, thanks to the entreaties of Pushkin, Vasilii Andreevich Zhukovsky, and Nikolai Ivanovich Gnedich, he was transferred to the city of Tver'. While there, Glinka had a chance to put to use the archaeological talents he had acquired studying ethnography in his exile: he conducted excavations of burial mounds. The results of his research were presented in his article "O drevnostiakh Tverskoi Karelii" (On the Antiquities of the Tver' Region of Karelia) for which he received a prize from the Geographical Society. About the same time he met Avdot'ia Golinishcheva-Kutuzova, also a writer, who soon became his wife and his dearest and most faithful friend.

In 1832 Glinka was again transferred, this time to Orel. Three years later he was released from government service, and the Glinkas moved to Moscow, where they settled for the next twenty-five years. Every Monday they opened the doors of their small house on the Sadovaya-Spasskaya street to welcome the elite of Moscow intellectual and artistic society for enthusiastic discussions over tea about the burning literary, philosophical, and religious questions of the time. The guests at Glinka's "Mondays" included Fedor Ivanovich Tiutchev, Aleksei Stepanovich Khomiakov, and the Kireevsky and Aksakov brothers, talented and famous poets, philosophers, and literary critics, as well as the leading figures of the Slavophile movement with which Glinka now associated himself.

Glinka gave expression in his works to the Slavophiles' assertion of the superiority of ancestral tradition and of moral and religious laws inscribed in the heart over those prescribed by reason or enacted by the state. In the 1840s and 1850s Glinka collaborated with the Slavophile journal *Moskvitianin* (Muscovite), became a permanent contributor to the *Moscow Gazette,* and devoted several poems to the glorification of Moscow, this "ancient city, the city of the heart," which Slavophiles saw as the sacred center of Holy Russia. Some of his other poems of this time were propelled by the patriotic and martial spirit that the events of the Crimean War awakened once again in this veteran of the campaign against Napoleon. Most of his poetry of this period, however, was devoted to mystical contemplation and philosophical reflections. In its striving to capture the flight of the poet's thought through the "boundless abyss of existence," to capture

Title page for Opyty allegorii ili inoskazatel'nykh opisanii, v stikhakh i v proze *(Experiments in Allegories or Circumlocutional Descriptions in Verse and Prose), which includes elegies that reveal Glinka's sympathies with the Decembrists*

the underlying "mystery of immortality," Glinka's verse converges with that of his great contemporary Tiutchev and foreshadows the Russian Symbolist school. Although Glinka's vision of the foundations of life was, unlike Tiutchev's, generally radiant and optimistic, his poetry was not totally without tragic and disquieting notes, which are definitely expressed in at least one of his poems, "Dve dorogi" (Two Roads, published 1849), which foretells the appearance of god-men who soar above the earth but are ultimately headed for self-destruction.

At the end of the 1850s the Glinkas left Moscow and moved back to Tver', where, after the death of his wife in 1860, the poet spent the last twenty years of his life. Though Glinka's collected works were published in three volumes from 1869 to 1872, his current work no longer appeared in print, partly because at that time he became the favorite target for the ridicule of the younger critics of the Nihilists' generation. He continued to write, as he said, "for himself and his friends," but unfortunately many of his last poems were lost. Glinka died on 11 February 1880 and was buried with military honors, as a hero of the Patriotic War, in the city that prized him so highly. He was remembered with gratitude by the citizens of Tver' for his benevolent activities and his contributions to its education system.

A soldier and a scholar, a mystical poet and a leader of the Decembrists, Glinka lived for almost a century. In his works he left readers a valuable and thoughtful testimony to the most important events and cultural movements of the century, in most of which he had actively participated in one way or another. Glinka's contribution to Russian literature is also significant. His characteristic combination of a grand, archaic, declamatory style with realistic detail, philosophical insights, and mystical visions makes him a quite original poet who deserves to be read and studied. Yet, Glinka's poetry has been largely forgotten by the general reading public in Russia and is hardly known at all in the West. Its true value remains to be rediscovered and appreciated.

Bibliography:
A. Toporov, "Spiski trudov russkikh pisateli," *Knigovedenie*, 2 (1895): 9–10.

Biographies:
Avgust Kazimirovich Zhiznevsky, *Biografiia F. N. Glinki* (Tver': Tip. Pravleniia, 1890);

Vasilii Sergeevich Orlov and V. G. Verzhbitsky, "F. N. Glinka," in their *Dekabristy-Smoliane* (Smolensk: Smolenskoe oblastnoe izd-vo, 1951);

Vladimir Karpets, *Fedor Glinka: Istoriko-literaturnyi ocherk* (Moscow: Molodaia gvardiia, 1983).

References:
Vasilii Grigor'evich Bazanov, *Karel'skie poemy Fedora Glinki* (Petrozavodsk: Karelo-Finskoi SSR, 1945);

Bazanov, *Poeticheskoe nasledie Fedora Glinki* (Petrozavodsk: Karelo-Finskoi SSR, 1950);

Vladimir Fedorovich Shubin, "Fedor Glinka and His Petersburg Salon in the 1850s," *Russkaia literatura*, 2 (1980);

Shubin, "Fedor Nikolaevich Glinka," in his *Poety Pushkinskogo Peterburga* (Leningrad: Lenizdat, 1985), pp. 118–130;

Natalia Mikhailovna Zharkevich, *Tvorchestvo F. N. Glinki v istorii russko-ukrainskikh literaturnykh sviazei* (Kiev: Nauka Dumka, 1981).

Papers:
Some of Fedor Nikolaevich Glinka's papers are housed at the Rossiiskii gosudarstvennyi arkhiv literatury i isskustva (formerly TsGALI), f. 141, and at the Rossiiskaia natsional'naia biblioteka, f. 192, St. Peterburg.

Nikolai Ivanovich Gnedich

(2 February 1784 – 3 February 1833)

John A. Barnstead
Dalhousie University

BOOKS: *Plody uedineniia,* with "A." (Moscow, 1802);
Morits, ili Zhertva mshcheniia (Moscow, 1802);
Don Korrado de Gerrera, ili dukh mshcheniia i varvarstva gishpantsev (Moscow, 1803);
Rozhdenie Omera (St. Petersburg: Tip. Imperatorskago teatra, 1817);
Prostonarodnye pesni nyneshnikh Grekov (St. Petersburg: N. Grech, 1825);
Stikhotvoreniia (St. Petersburg: Tip. Imp. Akademii nauk, 1832).

Editions and Collections: *Sochineniia Gnedicha* (St. Petersburg: A. Smirdin, 1854);
Sochineniia (St. Petersburg: M. O. Wol'f, 1884); republished as *Sobranie sochinenii N. I. Gnedicha,* 6 volumes (St. Petersburg: M. O. Wol'f, 1903);
Polnoe sobranie poeticheskikh sochinenii i perevodov (St. Petersburg: N. F. Mertts, 1905);
Stikhotvoreniia, edited by I. N. Medvedeva (Leningrad: Sovetskii pisatel', 1936);
Stikhotvoreniia. Poemy (Moscow, 1984).

TRANSLATIONS: Jean François Ducis, *Abufar,* translated as *Abiufar, ili Arabskaia sem'ia. Tragediia* (Moscow: Univ. tip. u Liubi, Gariia, i Popova, 1802);
Friedrich Schiller, *Die Verschwörung des Fiesko zu Genua,* translated as *Zagovor Fiesko v Genue* (Moscow, 1803);
William Shakespeare *Lear: tragediia v piati deistviiakh* (St. Petersburg: Tip. Imperatorskago teatra, 1808);
Homer, *The Iliad,* translated as *Iliada Gomera,* 2 volumes (St. Petersburg: Tip. Imp. Rossiskoi Akademii, 1829).

Though a poet, dramatist, novelist, librarian, and publisher, Nikolai Gnedich is best known as the translator of Homer's *Iliad.* He entered Russian literature as both an advocate of *Sturm und Drang* and an elegiac poet but soon yielded to the lure of the epic, hoping to create a new style for it that would avoid didacticism. He found his models not in the French Neoclassicism of Nicolas Boileau-Despréaux, so influential in Russia dur-

Nikolai Ivanovich Gnedich

ing the eighteenth century, but in the heroic grandeur, simplicity, and even crudeness of Homer and Theocritus. His metrical innovations, in particular his creation of a true logaoedic (dactylo-trochaic) Russian hexameter to replace the iambic hexameter customarily used to translate ancient Greek poetry up until his time, his use of combinations of trinary meters to translate contemporary Greek folk poetry, his naturalization of unrhymed verse, his mixture of lofty and colloquial vocabulary in his translation of the *Iliad*—all these left a lasting impression on the poets of the younger generation: Vil'gel'm Karlovich Kiukhel'beker, Kondratii Fedorovich Ryleev, Baron Anton Antonovich Del'vig,

Evgenii Abramovich Baratynsky, and Aleksandr Pushkin. Like Vasilii Andreevich Zhukovsky, translator of the *Odyssey,* he served as both their teacher and their judge.

Nikolai Ivanovich Gnedich, born 2 February 1784 in Poltava, was the scion of a Cossack clan, the Gnedenoks. His grandfather had earned the right to change the family name to Gnedich when elevated to the nobility, although little other advantage accrued to the family with the title. He exhausted his fortune in attempts to consolidate his estate; Gnedich's father was left impoverished and unable to provide for his only son. Gnedich's mother died in giving birth to him; in 1805 he commemorated her in the touching poem "Na grobe materi" (On Mother's Grave). In childhood he was stricken with smallpox, not only leaving his face pockmarked and covered with disfiguring seams but also depriving him of his right eye, a misfortune that may have drawn him to the blind poets Homer and Milton. Gnedich's first surviving literary works are a Christmas oration and poems, charmingly illustrated by their almost fourteen-year-old author, dating from 1795 and 1798.

Gnedich received his early education at the Poltava seminary and the Kharkov collegium. In this period of his life he became friends with Aleksei Petrovich Iushnevsky, who subsequently participated in the abortive Decembrist uprising of 1825. Together they enrolled in the pension for nobles of Moscow University and in 1800 became students at the university itself. During these years Gnedich devoted himself to the theater and to the study of classical Greek and Latin. Although he learned to read French, his abominable pronunciation remained an irritation to his friends.

Gnedich left the university at the end of 1802, perhaps to join Iushnevsky in obtaining a position in St. Petersburg, perhaps simply for lack of funds. Despite his difficulties, Gnedich retained his attachment to all things elegant and a rare, childlike simplicity of spirit that, according to poet Konstantin Nikolaevich Batiushkov, who was later to become a close friend and whose poetry Gnedich published, enabled him to seek out beauty in whatever he read. Some indication of the tenacity of his search may be gleaned from the fact (reported by another of his friends, Stepan Petrovich Zhikharev) that he went through Vasilii Kirillovich Trediakovsky's *Telemakhida* (a verse adaptation of Fenelon's *Telemaque*) three times from cover to cover "and even found incomparable verses in it," one of the few nineteenth-century readers of that interminable poem to do so.

His published career began in Moscow in 1802 with a verse translation of Jean François Ducis's 1795 tragedy *Abufar* as *Abiufar, ili Arabskaia sem'ia* (Abiufar, or an Arab family) and, perhaps with the assistance of Mikhail Ivanovich Dmitrevsky, a collection of articles, poems, and theater pieces (mainly imitations of Friedrich von Schiller) titled *Plody uedineniia* (Fruits of Solitude). A portion of this latter book was published separately as the tale *Morits, ili Zhertva mshcheniia* (Moritz, or the Victim of Vengeance). In 1803 his successful translation of Schiller's 1783 "republican tragedy" *Die Verschwörung des Fiesko zu Genua* as *Zagovor Fiesko v Genue* came out, as well as an original Gothic novel *Don Korrado de Gerrera, ili dukh mshcheniia i varvarstva gishpantsev* (Don Corrado de Herrera, or the Spaniards' Spirit of Vengeance and Barbarism), which depicts among other things the suppression of a popular uprising and cruelties perpetrated by direction of King Philip of Spain.

At the beginning of 1803 Gnedich moved to St. Petersburg, where he was granted a minor post in the Department of Public Education. He served there until 1817. The playwright and poet Vasilii Vasil'evich Kapnist introduced Gnedich to the Stroganov household, which was to serve as a setting for his poem "Rybaki" (The Fishermen, 1822). At work he found himself in the company of Batiushkov, Ivan Petrovich Pnin, Aleksandr Nikolaevich Radishchev, and Dmitrii Ivanovich Iazykov. He began to take an active part in the journals associated with that group of writers: *Severnyj vestnik* (The Northern Messenger), *Liubitel' slovesnosti* (Lover of Literature), *Tsvetnik* (Flower Garden), and *Dramaticheskii vestnik* (The Dramatic Messenger). A philosophical elegy in the liberal vein, "Obshchezhitie" (The Common Life, 1804—actually a free translation of an ode by the French poet Antoine Léonard Thomas), and the powerful 1805 poem "Peruanets k ispantsu" (From a Peruvian to a Spaniard), drawing, perhaps, on a novel by Jean-François Marmontel, established Gnedich's reputation in progressive circles. "Peruanets k ispantsu" was cited as a subversive influence during interrogation of some of the Decembrists after the suppression of their revolt, for Vladimir Fedoseevich Raevsky had distributed it as revolutionary propaganda within the army, and officers had read it to soldiers in the "schools of mutual education" that were organized before the rebellion. It was easy to see Russia beneath the one or two superficially Incan details of the poem:

> Destroyer of the land so dear to me and freedom,
> O thou who, laughing at all nature's holy rights,
> gave models to the world of matchless evil deeds,
> depriving me of all that's sacred evermore!
> Until what time wilt thou, barbaric without end,
> continue to devise new cruelties for me?
> O tyrant, ruler of my lamentable days!
> Who gave to thee the right to legislate my life?
> The law? what law? For has not Nature with one hand

made thee and me, and all the nations of the earth?
Thou art the stronger one; but though I am so weak,
although I am uncouth, must I then be thy slave?
Then let this planet end, on which so endlessly
innocence is trampled, evil-doing crowned;
Where weakness is a sin, and force has every right!
Where, grown all gray in evil deeds, a head
puts down the weak, defeats all innocence
and hides their blood upon it in porphyry!

In addition to such civic poetry, Gnedich wrote many elegies, poetic epistles, and romances during his first years in St. Petersburg. These remained largely in manuscript or, if published in the periodical press, were excluded by him from his collected works. He also undertook at this time his first attempts to combine the lyric and the epic, adaptations of James Macpherson's "Posledniaia pesn' Ossiana" (Ossian's Last Song, 1804) and "Krasoty Ossiana" (The Beauties of Ossian, 1805).

Gnedich continued to be heavily involved in the theater, which had interested him from childhood. At the university he had translated some medieval plays. Now he undertook a Russian version of Ducis's French paraphrase of *King Lear*. His translation of Voltaire's 1760 work *Tancred* had a long run. Later he published a prose fragment from William Shakespeare's *Troilus and Cressida* (1609) and a poetic adaptation of excerpts from Racine's *Andromaque* (1667). There exist unpublished original dramatic scenes from everyday life that he wrote in Ukrainian as well as two dramatic works that remained unpublished during his lifetime: the comedy *Stikhotvorets v khlopotakh* (The Versifier's Troubles), produced on Aleksei Nikolaevich Olenin's estate in 1815 but published only in 1914, in which Gnedich himself played the leading role of the poet Stikhopletkin, and fabulist Ivan Andreevich Krylov also acted; and the dramatic tableau "Vol'f, ili Prestupnik ot prezreniia" (Wolf, or the Criminal from Contempt), apparently written under the impression of Schiller's *Die Räuber* (The Robbers, 1781). Gnedich even worked as a drama coach, arranging secret training sessions at which he imparted his own ideas of elocution (chantlike and emphatically emotional), a system that he had developed especially for the actress Ekaterina Semenova. Zhikharev gives a vivid picture of Gnedich's style of declamation: "Seizing Shakespeare's works in French translation from the cupboard, he began to declaim a scene from *Hamlet* of Hamlet with the ghost, playing the parts in alternation, now one, now the other, with such strange body movements and such a wildly strained voice that his dog Mal'vina, who had come up to me to be petted, ran under the couch and began to howl most piteously." In later years Gnedich was to blame his respiratory illness on the strain that teaching his method placed on his lungs and throat.

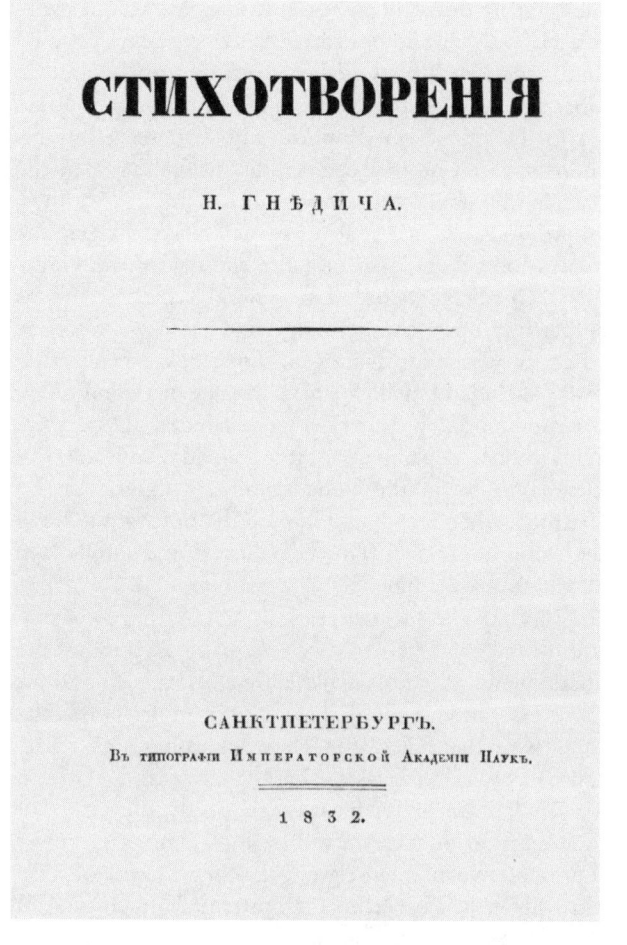

Title page for Gnedich's Stikhotvoreniia *(Poems), a collection published shortly before his death*

As an advocate of the high heroic mode of poetry, at the beginning of 1807 Gnedich drew close to the circle of Gavriil Romanovich Derzhavin, and when the publication *Beseda liubitelei russkogo slova* (Colloquy of Lovers of the Russian Word) was being organized at the end of 1810, he was invited by Derzhavin himself to join. Gnedich declined. When Derzhavin wrote to insist, Gnedich wrote a sharp reply, for he had noticed that he had been named to a rank lower than other participants: "From the note I see that all the gentlemen taking part are called Members, but on the envelope I am simply termed a Colleague. Every Member of a Society is a Colleague, but not every colleague may be honored with the title Member.... Since your excellency has allowed me the honor of being designated your Colleague, I, knowing the value of this honor, would ask permission to view myself both in the list of gentlemen Members and on all other occasions in the papers of the Atheneum as 'Member-Colleague of His Excellency Derzhavin'.... If the gentlemen members will not give their agreement to this, or if I do not have the right by rank, then in both cases there will be nothing left for me to do but earn a better opinion of myself and a higher rank." Gnedich made fun of the archaic language adopted by members of the colloquy in a letter to the playwright Kapnist, who had served as his sponsor when he first came to St. Petersburg: "In the hall of the Colloquy there will be public readings, where *notable persons of both sexes will copulate*—a genuine expression of one article of the statutes of the Colloquy" (Gnedich's italics). The venerable Derzhavin was sufficiently upset by such impertinence to write a rude letter to Aleksandr Ivanovich Turgenev when Zhukovsky included Gnedich and Turgenev in an anthology of contemporary poetry that excluded Derzhavin. Zhukovsky explained, "How could an ode by Derzhavin be in the same volume with an ode by Gnedich, when Derzhavin himself did not want to be in the same house with Gnedich: 'tome' and 'home' are almost the same thing."

Whatever his reservations about the conservatism of the *Beseda*, Gnedich was equally skeptical of the liberal views of Nikolai Mikhailovich Karamzin and his followers; and although he maintained friendly relations with their literary society "Arzamas," as represented by Zhukovsky, Batiushkov, and Dmitrii Vasil'evich Dashkov, he was frequently the target of their satirical attacks since they took him as the chief representative of the reigning aesthetic tastes of Olenin's circle, which occupied an intermediate position in the literary disputes of the day.

Gnedich began work on his translation of the *Iliad* in 1807, thinking at first merely to complete the work begun by Ermil Ivanovich Kostrov, who had published the first six chapters of his version in 1787 and an additional three in 1811. In 1808 Gnedich published excerpts from chapter 7, translated using Russian alexandrines (iambic hexameter with a caesura after the third foot). The results were sufficiently impressive to prompt Grand Princess Ekaterina Pavlovna to give him a pension to assist him in completing the work. He, however, became increasingly dissatisfied with the monotony of the alexandrine and eventually abandoned this initial attempt.

In 1810 Gnedich was invited to catalogue books and manuscripts in the St. Petersburg Public Library. In 1811 he was elected to the Russian Academy and on 12 April of that year was appointed assistant librarian in the public library. He soon settled at the library, establishing a friendship with the fabulist Krylov, who had a sinecure there. Gnedich was charged with organizing the division of Greek books and also compiled a catalogue for it. Although since his arrival in St. Petersburg he had been acquainted with the director of the library, Olenin, through the gatherings at the Stroganov home, at this time Gnedich formed a close friendship with Olenin. Olenin helped Gnedich during his translation of the *Iliad* with information about details of everyday life in ancient Greece. Gradually Gnedich became one of the central figures of the Olenin circle.

By 1813 a discussion of the Russian hexameter had begun in the journal *Chtenie v besede liubitelei russkago slova* (Readers in the Collegium of Lovers of the Russian Word) in which Kapnist, Sergei Semenovich Uvarov, and other literary figures took part. In a reply to Uvarov, Gnedich defended his own formulation of the Russian hexameter as the best and truest means of translating Homeric verse. Gnedich published his first hexametric excerpts from the *Iliad* in *Chtenie v besede liubitelei russkago slova* in 1813; excerpts continued to appear in the periodic press, primarily in *Syn otechestva* (Son of the Fatherland), until work on the translation was finished in 1826. The process of revision then began; Gnedich's *Iliad* eventually was published in book form in 1829.

Gnedich was constantly concerned with the state of the Russian literary language. On the occasion of the opening of the St. Petersburg Public Library at the beginning of 1814, Gnedich delivered an address titled "Rassuzhdeniia o prichinakh, zamedliaiushchikh uspekhi nashei slovesnosti" (Reflections on the Reasons Delaying the Successes of Our Literature), a kind of neoclassical manifesto. Rejecting the rules of French Classicism, he challenged authors to rival the Greeks and praised the advantages of Russian, which he felt owed much to the ancient Greek language.

Gnedich's own work now began to reflect the lessons he was learning from translating Homer. In 1815 he wrote the poem "Setovanie Fetidy na grobe Akhillesa" (Thetis's Lament on the Grave of Achilles) and in 1816 the long poem "Rozhdenie Gomera" (The Birth of Homer), both on themes drawn from his translation work. Gnedich's liberal views and his role as a poet engaged "in single combat with Homer" gave him great authority during the first two decades of the nineteenth century, for many saw Gnedich's labors at translation as not only a literary but also a civic achievement of the highest order. He enjoyed this authority in the eyes of the younger generation of poets as well. Many of them wrote to him—Ryleev, Pushkin, Del'vig, Baratynsky, and Petr Aleksandrovich Pletnev. All corresponded with him and praised his work. Both Pushkin and Ryleev dedicated poems to him. Gnedich himself could be a severe critic, particularly if a work was published before being shown to him, but he had a discerning eye and did not hesitate to offer advice even in poetic form:

> Pushkin, Proteus
> With your agile tongue and the wizardry of your singing!
> Close your ears to the praise and comparisons
> Of Good friends!
> Sing as you sing, dear nightingale!
> The genius of Byron or Goethe or Shakespeare
> Is the Genius of their sky and customs and countries—
> But you, who've attained the mystery of Russian soul and world,
> Sing to us in your own way, Russian bayan!
> Inspired by your native sky,
> Be in Russia a singer *beyond compare*.

The problem of determining the proper mixture of colloquial and literary elements in the Russian literary language, which Gnedich had touched upon when he spoke at the library opening in 1814, continued to preoccupy him. In 1816 he spoke on "Rassuzhdeniia o vkuse, ego svoistvakh i vliianii na nravy i iazyk naroda" (Reflections on taste, its properties and influence on the customs and language of the people), and he treated the question again in a review of Pavel Aleksandrovich Katenin's version of Gottfried August Bürger's ballad "Lenore" (1773). Gnedich was quite critical of Katenin's identification of *narodnost'* (national character) with *prostonarodnost'* (rusticity) and expressed a preference for Zhukovsky's translation of the ballad as "Liudmila" (1808). The playwright Griboedov came to Katenin's defense, calling Gnedich the implacable enemy of simplicity. Gnedich based his views on his work with the *Iliad*, in which he had developed a special language that combined elements of Church Slavonic with vulgarisms, colloquialisms, and dialect words under the theory that it would accurately reflect Homer's simplicity.

As portions of the *Iliad* began to appear, the magnitude of Gnedich's effort and accomplishment began to be clear, and he was honored in many ways. At the end of 1818 he was elected an honorary member of the *Vol'noe obshchestvo liubitelei russkogo slova* (Free Society of Lovers of the Russian Word). In 1819 he was invited to read at meetings of the literary society *Zelenaia lampa* (Green Lamp). When he was elected to full membership in the *Vol'noe obshchestvo liubitelei russkogo slova*, he delivered a speech on the poet's calling that subsequently played a significant role in the formation of the aesthetics of civil literature. Elaborating a concept of literature as lofty service, Gnedich proclaimed: "Let the servant of the muses not betray himself in any circumstances of life; let him not abase himself before fortune or fear poverty!" This speech not only became policy for the society when Gnedich later became its vice president but also served as a forerunner to the philosophy of Russian civic poetry of the mid nineteenth century.

Gnedich continually tried to adapt the lessons of classical Greek poetry to the needs of Russian literature. In the preface to his translation of Theocritus's fifteenth idyll, "Syracusan Women," Gnedich expressed a desire to create a native Russian context for this genre. He took issue with the conventional view of the form, which by this time was seen simply as a kind of pastoral or country verse with imaginary shepherds in a fictitious Arcadia. This was the definition implicit in the affected pastorals of such poets as Vladimir Ivanovich Panaev and Boris Mikhailovich Fedorov. Gnedich preferred to emphasize the vivid pictorial qualities and lifelike language of the idyll. In his translation he succeeded in re-creating the sharp contrast between the racy vocabulary of the women and the solemn words of the hymn that they are on the way to the palace to hear. Later he composed an original example of the idyll in amphibrachic pentameter, "Rybaki" (Fishermen, 1821), in which he depicts Russian everyday life as a classical ideal, combining Homeric stylistics with Russian folklore. This idyll, however, was not able to approach his translation of Theocritus in its use of contrasting styles of language. The poem, though, is the source of the well-known description of the white nights in St. Petersburg that Pushkin calls "delightful" in a note to *Evgeny Onegin* (1823–1831):

> It's night, but the gold bands of clouds do not dim,
> No stars and no moon but all distance aglow.
> On faraway shores there gleam silvery sails
> Of ships barely seen: through blue heaven they swim.
> The night heavens shine with a shadowless sheen,
> The purple of dusk meets the gold of the dawn:
> As if blushing morn after evening were drawn
> By the sun.

By the beginning of the 1820s Gnedich had also started to create his first plans and sketches for original compositions to be based on themes drawn from Russian history—a plan for a long poem to be titled "Sviatoslav" and the plan and drafts for the first act of a dramatic work on the spread of Christianity in Russia, as well as sketches for a poem on the martyred Prince Vasil'ko Konstantinovich Terebovl'sky. None of these plans were realized, however, and it remained for Pushkin to create a genuine national epic.

In 1821 when the Greeks rose up against the Turks, Gnedich translated Konstantinos Rigas's "War Hymn of the Greeks." The Greek struggle for independence was one factor prompting Gnedich to write "Prostonarodnye pesni nyneshnikh grekov" (Folksongs of the Modern Greeks), which he translated from Claude Charles Fauriel's French collection *Chants populaires de la Grèce moderne* (1824). These songs influenced Pushkin's thinking about popular poetry when he came

Title page for the second edition of Gnedich's translation Iliada Gomera *(The Iliad of Homer), based on the copy of the first edition revised by Gnedich*

to produce his own "Pesni zapadnykh slavian" (Songs of the Western Slavs), drawing on the French versions of Prosper Mérimée.

Gnedich remained unmarried and throughout his life, despite his enjoyment of the social life of St. Petersburg, lived a lonely existence. In 1825 he lost his niece, who was his "last tie to the world" since the death of his sister in 1819. He was stricken that same year with a severe respiratory illness. From 1 May until 1 September 1825 he was in the Caucasus to take the waters. At the end of the year he was stunned by the events of the Decembrist rebellion; among those hanged or exiled as a result of their activities were people close to him: Nikita Mikhailovich Murav'ev, Fedor Nikolaevich Glinka, Ryleev, and Iushnevsky. His work had had a formative influence on Decembrist poetry, even though he himself never participated in the political movement.

Despite his bad health, the poet continued to work on his translation of the *Iliad* and finished it on 15 December 1826. Honors began to pour in: he was elected corresponding member of the Petersburg Academy of Sciences in the division of literature and history of the Slavic peoples; he was confirmed as librarian of the Imperial Public Library; and he was made a civil councillor. Illness, however continued to plague him. On 17 June 1827 it forced him to retire from the state chancellery. For much of the following year he was confined by his illness to southern Russia. The complete translation of the *Iliad* with the poet's preface was published in 1829. It was greeted with fulsome congratulations. Vissarion Grigor'evich Belinsky considered it the foundation for future aesthetic education. Pushkin printed an epigram upon its appearance and a note in *Literaturnaia gazeta* (Literary Gazette). Despite the public praise Pushkin bestowed, however, he may have considered the translation to be faulty, perhaps because of its overly lofty language, for a carefully crossed-out epigram was found after his death among his papers: "Gnedich the poet was lame, the translator of sightless old Homer, / And his translation as well looks like its dam on one side."

On 4 November 1830 Gnedich left his work at the St. Petersburg Library. His last poems–"Na smert' barona A. A. Del'viga" (On the Death of Baron A. A. Del'vig), "K nemu zhe pri pogrebenii" (To Him as Well at his Burial), "Lastochka" (A Swallow), and two meditations–are filled with gloom and loneliness. One of the meditations is particularly moving:

> My lot is a sad one, my portion is cruel!
>   Caressed by nobody's hand,
> From childhood I grew up alone and an orphan,
>   And entered life's path all alone;
> I walked it alone, that unkempt, scraggy field,
> On which, as within sultry Libya's valley,
> My gaze was not met by a shadow or flower;
>   My lonely path draws to an end,
>   I'm met by decrepit old age
>   Alone in my everyday life:
>   My lot is a sad one, my portion is cruel!

Gnedich died of influenza on 3 February 1833, shortly after publishing his collected poetry. On his gravestone his friends inscribed "To Gnedich, who enriched Russian letters with his translation of Homer" and followed it with a line from the *Iliad*: "Rechi iz ust ego veshchikh sladchaishie meda lilisia" (And from his prophetic lips poured speeches much sweeter than honey–*Iliad,* song 1, line 249).

Letters:

Glynn R. Barratt, "A View of Petersburg: New Correspondence of M. E. Lobanov and N. I. Gnedich, 1827–1828," *Russian Literature,* 9 (1975): 25–36;

O. N. Oven, "Neizvestnye pis'ma N. I. Gnedicha I. M. Murav'evu-Apostolu," *Russkaia literatura,* 21, no. 2 (1978): 115–121.

Bibliographies:

Mikhail Nikolaevich Longinov, "Materialy dlia polnogo sobraniia sochinenii N. I. Gnedicha," *Russkii arkhiv,* nos. 10–11 (1863): 845–850;

Stepan Ivanovich Ponomarev, "N. I. Gnedich. Materialy dlia biografii i otsenki," *Russkaia starina,* no. 7 (1884): 115–122;

Semen Afanas'evich Vengerov, *Istochniki slovaria russkikh pisatelei,* 1 (1900): 780–782.

Biography:

Pavel Tikhanov, *Nikolai Ivanovich Gnedich (1784–1833). Neskol'ko dannykh dlia ego biografii po neizdannym istochnikam,* Sbornik Otdeleniia russkogo iazyka i slovesnosti, 33, no. 3 (St. Petersburg: Tip. Imp. Akademii Nauk, 1884), pp. 1–98.

References:

Richard Burgi, *A History of the Russian Hexameter* (Hamden, Conn.: Shoe String Press, 1954);

A. N. Edunov, *Gomer v russkikh perevodakh XVIII–XIX vv* (Moscow-Leningrad, 1964);

Haim Gamburg, "Gnedich, Nikolai Ivanovich," in *Encyclopedia of Russian Literature,* pp. 198–201;

Grigorii Petrovich Georgievsky, "Gnedich," in *Russkii biograficheskii slovar',* volume 5 (1896–1918), pp. 410–427;

Georgievsky, "A. N. Olenin i N. I. Gnedich. Novye materialy iz oleninskogo arkhiva," *Sbornik Otdeleniia russkogo iazyka i slovesnosti,* 91, no. 1 (1914): 1–137;

M. A. Khavamova, "K tvorcheskoi istorii odnogo neizvestnogo zamysla N. I. Gnedicha," *Russkaia literatura,* 29, no. 1 (1986): 156–163;

Sergei Akimovich Kibal'nik, "Gnedich," in *Russkie pisateli 1800–1917: Biograficheskii slovar',* edited by P. A. Nikolaev, volume 1 (Moscow: Prosveshchenie, 1989), pp. 585–588;

Irina Nikolaevne Medvedeva, "N. I. Gnedich i dekabristy," in *Dekabristy i ikh vremia. Materialy i soobshcheniia* (Moscow-Leningrad: AN SSR, 1951), pp. 101–154;

Medvedeva, "N. I. Gnedich," in *Stikhotvoreniia,* by Gnedich (Leningrad: Sovetskii pisatel', 1956), pp. 5–55;

Stepan Ivanovich Ponomarev, "K izdaniiu Iliady v perevode Gnedicha," *Sbornik Otdeleniia russkogo iazyka i slovesnosti,* 38, no. 7 (1886): 1–144.

Papers:

Nikolai Ivanovich Gnedich's manuscript for "Vol'f, ili Prestupnik ot prezreniia," a play, is held in St. Petersburg at the Rossiiskaia natsional'naia biblioteka, fond 550, Q. XIV, no. 119. Other Gnedich papers can be found at Rossiiskii gosudarstvennogo arkhiv literatury i iskusstva, Moscow fond 1225; IRLI (Pushkin House), St. Petersburg, nos. 80–108, no. 13812, no. 28006, nos. 9642, 10089, 10102, 14370; Rossiiskii gosudarstvennyi istoricheskii arkhiv, fond 1162, op. 7, d. 242.

Aleksandr Sergeevich Griboedov
(4 January 1795? – 30 January 1829)

Marina Balina
Illinois Wesleyan University

BOOKS: *Molodye suprugi: Komediia v odnom deistvii, v stikhakh* (St. Petersburg: Tip. Imp. Teatra, 1815);

Svoia sem'ia, ili Zamuzhniaia nevesta: Komediia v trekh deistviiakh v stikhakh, by Griboedov, Aleksandr Aleksandrovich Shakhovskoi, and Nikolai Ivanovich Khmel'nitsky (St. Petersburg: Tip. Imp. Teatra, 1818);

Gore ot uma. Komediia v chetyrekh deistviiakh, v stikhakh (expurgated edition, Moscow: Tip. Avgusta Semena, pri Imperatorskoi Mediko-Khirurgich. Akademii, 1833; complete edition, St. Petersburg: Izd. N. Tiblena, 1862; second, corrected edition, 1862);

Putevye zapiski. Kavkaz-Persiia, edited by I. K. Enikolopov (Tiflis: Zakkniga, 1932).

Editions and Collections: *Gore ot uma. Komediia v chetyrekh deistviiakh, v stikhakh,* second edition, introduction by Ksenofont Alekseevich Polevoi (St. Petersburg: Voennaia tip., 1839);

A. S. Griboedov i ego sochineniia (St. Petersburg: E. Serchevsky, 1858);

Komediia "Gore ot uma." Lubochnyi teatr. Svoia sem'ia. Gruzinskaia noch'. Khishchniki na Chegeme. Perepiska (St. Petersburg: M. Stasiulevich, 1875);

Sochineniia (Moscow: K. K. Shamov, 1886);

Polnoe sobranie sochinenii, 2 volumes, edited by Il'ia Aleksandrovich Shliapkin (St. Petersburg: I. P. Vargunin, 1889);

Polnoe sobranie sochinenii, edited by Arsenii I. Vvedensky (St. Petersburg, A. F. Marks, 1892);

Polnoe sobranie sochinenii, 3 volumes, edited by Piksanov and Shliapkin (St. Petersburg: Razriad iziashnoi slovesnosti Imp. Akademii Nauk, 1911–1917);

Gore ot uma. Komediia, edited by Andrei Andreevich Zhandr and Piksanov (Moscow: L. E. Bukhgeim, 1912);

Kto brat, kto sestra, ili Obman za obmanom. Opera-vodevil' v odnom deistvii, by Griboedov and Prince Petr Andreevich Viazemsky, music by Aleksei Nikolaevich Verstovsky, edited by Nikolai Kiriiakovich Piksanov (Moscow-Leningrad: Gos. muz. izd-vo, 1949);

Sochineniia v stikhakh, edited by Vladimir Nikolaevich Orlov (Leningrad, 1951);

Izbrannye proizvedeniia, edited by Orlov (Leningrad: Sovetskii pisatel', 1952);

Sochineniia, edited by Orlov (Moscow: Goslitizdat, 1953);

Izbrannye sochineniia, edited by Ia. S. Bilinkis (Leningrad, 1961);

Sochineniia v stikhakh, edited by Irina Nikolaevna Medvedeva (Leningrad: Sovetskii pisatel', 1967);

Sochineniia, 2 volumes, edited by Mikhail Pavlovich Eremin (Moscow: Biblioteka "Ogonek"–Izdatel'stvo "Pravda," 1971);

Gore ot uma: komedia v 4 d., v stikhakh (Moscow: Kniga, 1991);

A. S. Griboedov: litso i genii, edited by Viacheslav Trofimovich Kabanov (Moscow: Knizhnaia palata, 1997).

Editions in English: *Gore ot Ouma. A Comedy,* translated by Nicholas Bernardaky (London, 1857);

The Mischief of Being Clever, translated by Sir Bernard Pares (London: School of Slavonic Studies in the University of London, King's College, 1925).

PLAY PRODUCTIONS: *Molodye suprugi,* St. Petersburg, Malyi Theater, 29 September 1815;

Svoi sem'ia, St. Petersburg, 24 January 1818;

Pritvornaia nevernost', St. Petersburg, Bolshoi Theater, 11 February 1818; Moscow, 3 September 1818;

Proba intermedii, St. Petersburg, Bolshoi Theater, 10 November 1819;

Kto brat, kto sestra, ili Obman za obmanom, Moscow, January 1823; St. Petersburg, September 1824;

Gore ot uma, St. Petersburg, Bolshoi Theater, 2 December 1829.

TRANSLATION: Nicolas Thomas Barthé, *Pritvornaia nevernost': komediia v odnom deistvii v stikhakh,* translated by Griboedov and Andrei Andreevich Zhandr (St. Petersburg: N. Grech, 1818).

Shortly before Aleksandr Griboedov's death, Aleksandr Pushkin said, "He is one of the smartest people in Russia." When the news of Griboedov's death reached him, Pushkin added that Griboedov had truly "accomplished something. After all, he wrote *Gore ot uma*" (Woe from Wit, finished between 1823 and 1824). In his *Puteshestvie v Arzrum* (Journey to Arzrum, 1836)–with his visit to Griboedov's grave in the summer of 1829 on the road from Tiflis (Tbilisi) to Kars fresh in his mind–Pushkin summed up his thoughts on the fate of his friend:

> His abilities as a statesman remained unutilized; his talent as a poet remained unrecognized; even his cool and brilliant courage for a time remained suspect. Several friends knew his worth and saw his skeptical smile–that silly, unbearable smile–when they happened to speak of him as an extraordinary person.

Indeed, Pushkin's judgment of Griboedov conveys the most essential elements of Griboedov's life and character.

Everything in the literature about Aleksandr Sergeevich Griboedov is full of contradictions. Even the exact date of his birth is subject to dispute. According to some sources he was born on 4 January 1795, but other sources say earlier, in 1794. In his *Vospominaniia o nezabvennom Aleksandre Sergeeviche Griboedove* (Recollections of the Unforgettable Aleksandr Sergeevich Griboedov, 1830), the journalist and critic Faddei Venediktovich Bulgarin, who was normally quite accurate with names and dates, resorts to writing that "Griboedov was born sometime around 1793." The chief source of this confusion is the fact that Griboedov's birth certificate has never been found.

There are, of course, many other documents that refer to his age, but they too are so full of contradictions that they shed no light on the subject. For example, Griboedov's military records (he was in a regiment of hussars in Irkutsk) list him as being twenty years old in 1813 and twenty-one years old in 1814, which would establish his year of birth as 1793. But two years later, in 1816, Griboedov was issued a passport upon his discharge from the army in which he is listed as being twenty-two years old, which points to 1794 as the year of his birth. There are also documents that establish Griboedov's year of birth as early as 1790. In a document pertaining to the investigation of the Decembrists, he himself wrote: "My name is Griboedov, Aleksandr Sergeevich . . . I was born in 1790."

After his death Griboedov's friends who were compiling the literature about him must have been concerned with establishing the date of his birth, but no matter how close they had been to him or how much they respected his memory, they all avoided this topic for some reason. In fact, he may even have been born before his mother got married, and his acknowledged father, Sergei Ivanovich Griboedov, may not have been his natural father. In any case, Sergei Ivanovich was not at all interested in the boy and lived in the country far from his family.

Griboedov did enjoy a close, warm relationship with his mother, Nastas'ia Fedorovna Griboedova, an intelligent–although strong-willed and despotic–woman who spared no expense in the education of her son. In 1803 Griboedov entered the *Moskovskii universitetskii blagorodnyi pansion* (Moscow University Preparatory School for Nobles), and three years later he became the youngest student of literature and philosophy at the university. Receiving his degree in literature in 1808, he immediately enrolled in the political ethics (law) division of the philosophy department. He earned a law degree in 1810, and with an unquenchable thirst for knowledge, he remained at the university to study natural science and mathematics.

During his student years Griboedov made his first attempts at writing. In 1809 he first sent some poems to the Moscow journal *Vestnik Evropy* (Herald of Europe). Vasilii Andreevich Zhukovsky, who was then editor of the journal, selected one of Griboedov's poems for publication: "Oda na poedinki" (Ode to Duels). Since Griboedov at that time signed his works with only the first and last letters of his surname ("G–v"),

Gen. Aleksei Petrovich Ermolov, with whom Griboedov served as a secretary of foreign affairs in Tiflis (State Pushkin Museum, Moscow)

some scholars doubt his authorship of these poems. In 1810 Griboedov wrote "Dmitrii Drianskoi" (Dmitrii the Trashy One), a parody of Vladislav Aleksandrovich Ozerov's much-lauded tragedy *Dmitrii Donskoi* (Dmitrii of the Don, 1806); Griboedov humorously described the enmity between the Russian and German professors at the university in terms of a great battle. Unfortunately, there are no extant copies of this parody, and knowledge of it comes only through the memoirs of Griboedov's contemporaries. Griboedov's plans were fundamentally changed in 1812 with the escalation of the Napoleonic Wars. He left the university in order to enlist as a volunteer in the army, where he served until 1816. For two years he served as aide to Gen. Andrei Semenovich Kologrivov in Brest-Litovsk, but he never had any actual combat duty. During this period he continued his literary experimentation, examples of which have survived.

In 1814 Griboedov had two pieces of war correspondence published in *Vestnik Evropy:* "Pis'mo iz Brest-Litovska" (A Letter from Brest-Litovsk), and "O kavaleriiskikh rezervakh" (On the Cavalry Reserves). The genre of journal "letters" was quite popular at this time. They were used for descriptions of sentimental journeys, for polemics, and also in place of critical reviews. Half of each "letter" consists of asides written in verse. Each one of these pieces stands almost independently and is almost serious; that is, it borders on parody. The first letter describes the celebration in Brest-Litovsk when Kologrivov received the Order of Vladimir, first degree. It includes many earnest observations but is also filled with "hussar" comments on the joys of drinking wine and constant celebrating, almost as if Griboedov were afraid of being completely serious.

In "O kavaleriiskikh rezervakh" Griboedov writes dryly and sincerely about the economic factors in organizing an army. His detailed analyses of battles and his descriptions of successfully organized rear guards hint at his future activities as a statesman and as someone capable of thinking on a large scale. This article is accompanied by a message to the editor: "I don't think your readers will reproach me for my dryness. In the *Vestnik* they find news about the incomes, expenses, and debts of France and other nations; surely the economy of their own homeland deserves attention as well." This article is no less forthright on another theme: Griboedov's glorification of Tsar Alexander I, whom he sees as the conqueror of Napoleon Bonaparte and the savior of Europe.

In 1816 Griboedov left the military and went to St. Petersburg, where a year later he entered the service of the Office of Foreign Affairs. At this time he made his first attempts at writing theatrical pieces. Actually, his first play, *Molodye suprugi* (Young Wives, 1815), had been written during his years in the army, and in 1817 Griboedov, in collaboration with Pavel Aleksandrovich Katenin, wrote a prose comedy, "Student," and five scenes for the comedy *Svoia sem'ia, ili Zamuzhniaia nevesta* (All in the Family, or the Married Fiancée), whose chief author was Aleksandr Aleksandrovich Shakhovskoi. These scenes were first published in *Syn otechestva* (Son of the Fatherland) in 1817. In 1818 he and Andrei Andreevich Zhandr translated the French comedy *Les fausses infidélités* (Sham Infidelities, 1768), by Nicolas Thomas Barthe, as *Pritvornaia nevernost'*. With the exception of "Student," which was not published or performed, these various works were staged with considerable success. Both *Molodye suprugi* and *Pritvornaia nevernost'* revolve around the ideas of the Enlightenment: they make a strong statement against the prejudices and stale conventions of society. Both plays are quite original, although they appear on the surface to be either free adaptations or loose translations of French comedies. Griboedov's comedies were natural and uncontrived in their plot development, and the verse was unforced. William Edward Brown quotes one critic who commented: "Reading *Pritvornaia nevernost'*, one forgets that it is a translation."

Just as he valued inner freedom in his own life, Griboedov also created characters who act in accordance with their wishes and desires, and he did not judge them. His sympathies clearly lay with those who felt free in their emotions and actions, unrestrained by traditions and conventions and showing resourcefulness, energy, and initiative in conducting their personal affairs, no matter how seemingly trivial those might be. In *Molodye suprugi,* Elmira—acting not according to tradition, but rather of her own volition and at her own risk—gains the attention of her husband, Arist, who had earlier ignored her affections. Griboedov's own propensity for freedom appears in an 1825 response to Katenin's criticism that *Gore ot uma* displayed "more talent, than art":

> He, who has by sweat and much sitting learned through enough art to please the theoreticians, that is, to mouth stupidities; he, I, say, who has more ability to satisfy the requirements of school, convention, habit, and the superstitions of old women than his own creative energy—if he is an artist, then break his palette and his brush, or throw his chisel or pen out the window.... Just as I live freely, so I also write freely.

In "Student" Griboedov and Katenin poke fun at protagonist Benevolsky, who lives in a sentimental world of distracted dreams and flights of fancy. This parody is also aimed at the literary style of Nikolai Mikhailovich Karamzin and his followers, who cultivated a "sensitivity" in all their work, and at all the sentimental sighings of youth that were so prevalent in the literature of that period. The work is right on the mark as it reiterates a statement made by Griboedov somewhat earlier in his article "O razbore vol'nogo perevoda Biurgerovoi ballady *Lenora*" (On the Critique of the Free Translation of Bürger's Ballad *Lenore*), published in *Syn otechestva* in 1816: "Forget about them, those dreams; nowadays, whatever book you glance in, whatever you might read, a play or a message [*poslanie*], there are dreams everywhere, but not a trace of the natural."

The only "natural" characters in the play, however, who stand in contrast to Benevolsky, are the extremely successful state councilor Poliubin and the officer Sablin, who are far removed from the ideological battles of the time. Poliubin, in particular, is Benevolsky's lucky rival in love. No other representatives of "natural" behavior appear in the play. There is reason to believe that the name of the main character alludes directly to Mikhail Nikolaevich Zagoskin, who signed his journal articles "Juvenal Benevolsky."

Griboedov's acquaintanceship with Shakhovskoi opened doors not only into the world of St. Petersburg theater but also into one of the literary societies, the *Beseda liubitelei russkogo slova* (Colloquy of Lovers of the Russian Word), which was founded in 1811 and headed by the writer and statesman Admiral Aleksandr Semenovich Shishkov. Griboedov thus also became involved in the literary debates of the period.

The literary fight of the 1820s is most often characterized as the battle between classicism and Romanticism. As Iurii Nikolaevich Tynianov rightly notes, however, both of these concepts were brought in from outside and only applied to particular literary phenomena. To begin with, the terms themselves were not always clearly defined, and in one polemic by Prince Petr Andreevich Viazemsky there appeared the term "classical romanticism." In 1825, in the journal *Mnemozina* (Mnemosyne), which was edited by Vil'gel'm Karlovich Kiukhel'beker and Prince Vladimir Fedorovich Odoevsky, there appeared an article on the "struggle against the Slavs" of the archaist school in literature, which was a group united around Katenin that opposed genres connected with the new Karamzinian literature and proposed other genres in their place. In his notes for the article, Kiukhel'beker pointed out that the Slavs had "their own classicists and romantics.... Among the former are Shishkov and Shakhmatov, while Katenin, Griboedov, Shakhovskoi, and Kiukhel'beker are representatives of the latter." Tynianov called Griboedov a "young archaist."

The polemic surrounding the translations by Zhukovsky and Katenin of Gottfried August Bürger's 1773 ballad "Lenore" gives a clearer view of Griboedov's position. As early as 1808, Zhukovsky, the founder of Russian Romanticism, had published his translation/adaptation, which he called "Liudmila." Zhukovsky purposely avoided the colloquial style of the original, adapting it to "Russian rules" and elevating the style. Katenin called his 1816 translation "Ol'ga." He too moved the events of the ballad to Russian soil, but unlike Zhukovsky, he made every attempt to preserve the original style. This attempt at competition with Zhukovsky was perceived as sacrilege by Zhukovsky's admirers. The well-known poet and translator Nikolai Ivanovich Gnedich came out in defense of "Liudmila." In his 1816 *Syn otechestva* article "O vol'nom perevode Biurgerovoi ballady *Lenora*" (On the Free Translation of Bürger's ballad *Lenore*) he harshly criticizes Katenin's translation and is surprised and indignant at the impudence of Zhukovsky's "rivals and enviers." Griboedov, in "O razbore vol'nogo perevoda Biurgerovoi ballady *Lenora*," attacks Gnedich for his criticism of the stylistic simplicity in Katenin's translation, writing that "he is in general an implacable foe of simplicity." Griboedov pointed out the harmoniousness and aestheticism in the style of "Liudmila," and he objected to the demand for "propriety," referring to the

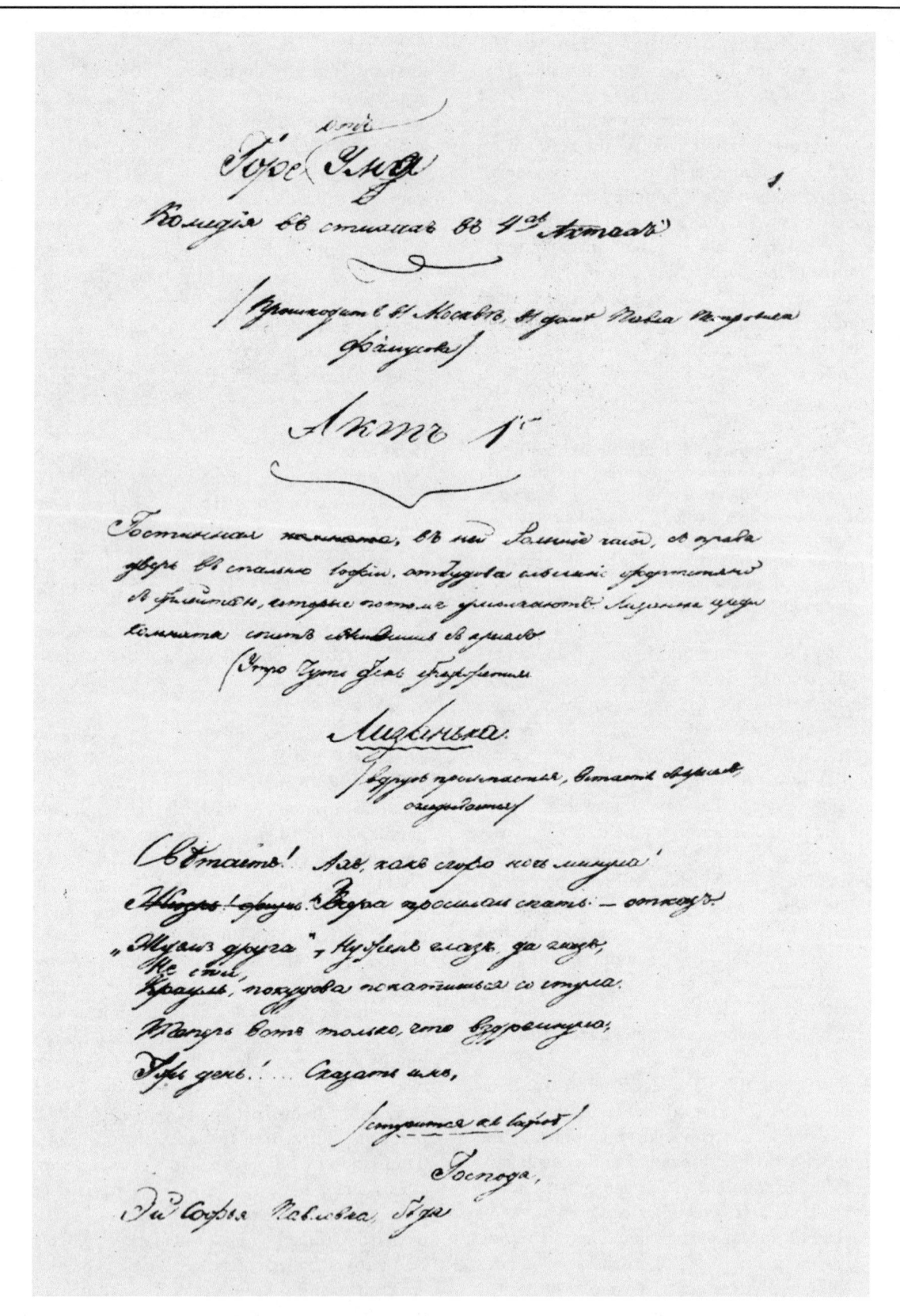

First page of the earliest surviving manuscript for Gore ot uma *(Woe from Wit, completed by 1824), Griboedov's comedy about a young man who is rumored to be insane after he criticizes Moscow society (Moscow Historical Museum)*

fact that Katenin's heroine is prepared to share her bed with her deceased lover. While Zhukovsky poses a rhetorical question in this scene, Katenin depicts carnal desire vividly and naturally, and this handling is precisely what Gnedich attacked. Griboedov responded: "What was she supposed to do? Give herself over to empty dreams of ideal love?" Thus Griboedov, like Katenin, holds to the principle that "truth, nature, and common sense are the chief criteria of contemporary literature." With his defense of Katenin, Griboedov established his reputation as a critic whose opinions were to be reckoned with.

Griboedov's literary activities were interrupted in 1818 when he was appointed to a Russian diplomatic mission in Persia. On a brief visit to Tiflis before departing for Persia, Griboedov formed a friendship with Gen. Aleksei Petrovich Ermolov, who played an important role in later events in Griboedov's life. During his years in Persia, Griboedov managed to learn the Persian language, and from the Persian shah he received the Order of the Lion and the Sun for his service. In 1818 Griboedov participated in a duel with Aleksandr Ivanovich Iakubovich, a future Decembrist. Earlier, on 12 November 1817, the two had stood as seconds in a duel between Count A. P. Zavodosky and Vasilii Vasil'evich Sheremet'ev who was killed. Zavodosky and Sheremet'ev were fighting over the famous ballerina and actress Evdokiia Il'inichna Istomina. The duel between the seconds was delayed and took place in Tiflis on 23 October 1818. Rumor had it that Griboedov's role, though clouded in silence, was not particularly honorable.

Griboedov remained in Persia as secretary to chargé d'affaires Semen Ivanovich Mazarovich until November 1821, when Ermolov sent a letter to Karl Robert von Nesselrode, the minister of foreign affairs, successfully requesting that Griboedov be assigned to Tiflis under his command as secretary for foreign affairs. During this time Griboedov became well acquainted with the family of his future wife, Nina Aleksandrovna Chavchavadze. Kiukhel'beker came to Tiflis on business, and he became the first and only spectator of an early version of *Gore ot uma,* which at that time was called "Gore umu" (Woe to Wit).

Apparently, Griboedov first came up with the idea for *Gore ot uma* in 1816, but he did not get around to working directly on this comedy until later. He wrote two acts while in the Caucasus in 1821–1822. E. P. Sokovnina, the niece of Griboedov's close friend Stepan Nikitich Begichev, recalled in an article in *Istoricheskii vestnik* in 1889 that while Griboedov was on vacation in Moscow from the Caucasus he "continued to put the finishing touches on the comedy *Gore ot uma,* and, in order to grasp all nuances of Moscow society more accurately, he went to dinners and balls, which he never really enjoyed, and then would shut himself up for days in his study." The work was finished in St. Petersburg by the fall of 1824, but he continued to make corrections right up to his departure for the Caucasus in 1825.

The protagonist of *Gore ot uma,* Chatsky, is a typical character for the period after 1812. The reader learns the previous details of his life through Famusov, the father of the girl Chatsky loves. Chatsky had lived for a time in St. Petersburg and was interested in literature. Rumors that Chatsky "wrote and translated wonderfully" reached Famusov all the way in Moscow. Along with literature, Chatsky was also concerned with social problems. He had "connections with ministers," which, however, ended up being "broken off." This split is a clear allusion to Griboedov's disagreement with the policies of the government and his differing ideas about how to serve one's country. Chatsky explains that he wanted to serve, but to serve the affairs of state and not specific individuals: "To serve I would be glad, but to be subservient is nauseating."

Chatsky then went to the country, where, according to Famusov, he "indulged in his whims." Just what these whims were, it is hard to say, but one may assume they are connected with an effort to run his affairs in a different, nontraditional manner. After this unsuccessful attempt to live in the country, Chatsky went abroad, which hints at Griboedov's familiarity with the European liberal tradition.

Finally Chatsky returns to Moscow, disenchanted but convinced of the love of Sofia, the girl whom he has not seen in three years. He is so convinced of the steadfastness of Sofia's feelings that he is oblivious to her love for her father's secretary, Molchalin. Trying to understand the reason for the change in Sofia, Chatsky comes face to face with Moscow society, which itself is, of course, horrified at Chatsky's unorthodox ideas and quickly decides he is insane. In fact, Sofia declares his insanity to get revenge for all his critical comments; then she acquiesces as the rumor spreads. In a long January 1825 letter to Aleksandr Aleksandrovich Bestuzhev (Marlinsky), Pushkin wrote: "Everything he [Chatsky] says is very clever. But to whom does he say all this? To Famusov? To Skalozub? To the old ladies of Moscow at the ball? To Molchalin? This is inexcusable!" This situation, however, is precisely "woe from wit": that the intelligent Chatsky is surrounded by idiots, and he must serve as the herald of this bitter truth.

Among those who read it, *Gore ot uma* was a rousing success. In a letter to Begichev, after a reading of the play, Griboedov wrote: "There is no end to the uproar, noise, delight, and curiosity. Shakhovskoi has confessed that he was completely taken by it." Then the trouble

Nina Aleksandrovna Chavchavadze, whom Griboedov married in 1828 (portrait by an unknown artist; from M. V. and T. G. Muratov, Aleksandr Sergeevich Griboedov, 1965)

with the censors began, primarily because of the many allusions in the play to contemporary political and social situations. Attempts to publish the play were in vain, as were attempts to have the play staged in a theater. Even an effort to perform the play in the St. Petersburg Theater School in May 1825 was unsuccessful. Griboedov only managed to publish heavily censored versions of the third act and some scenes from the first act in Bulgarin's almanac *Russkaia Taliia* (Russian Thalia).

Despite all the critical praise, however, there were also some dissenting voices. For example, Mikhail Aleksandrovich Dmitriev and Aleksandr Ivanovich Pisarev objected in *Vestnik Evropy* that the play was not a true reflection of Russian life. Instead, they claimed, it was nothing more than an imitation of foreign comedies. Dmitriev mocked the contentious patriotism of Chatsky, who was said to be "a caricature of a Molièrean misanthrope." The language was criticized for being harsh, uneven, and incorrect; in other words, the characters spoke like *Lezghins* (a Caucasian people).

Pushkin, however, shared the positive reaction to *Gore ot uma*. In his letter to Bestuzhev, he notes Griboedov's independence and theatrical innovations. In Pushkin's opinion the point of this comedy lay in its depiction of the characters and its sharp critique of social mores. In many characters Pushkin saw evidence of "true comic genius."

The originality and distinctness of the genre of *Gore ot uma* was also noted by critic Vissarion Grigor'evich Belinsky. As he wrote in *Otechestvennye zapiski* (Notes of the Fatherland) in 1840, he saw the play as a comedy-drama:

> Comedy, in my opinion, is exactly the same sort of drama as that which one would normally call a tragedy. Its theme is the depiction of life in contrast with the idea of life; its element is not that innocent wit that good-naturedly pokes fun at everything purely for the sake of scoffing. No, its element is that bilious humor, that terrible indignation that does not smile jokingly, but laughs furiously; that punishes pettiness and egoism not with epigrams, but with sarcasm.

In an article titled "Mil'on terzanii" (A Million Lacerations), published in *Vestnik Evropy* in 1872, Ivan Aleksandrovich Goncharov also pointed out the uniqueness of the genre of *Gore ot uma*. He saw it as the depiction of social mores, a gallery of living types, and an eternally burning satire—as well as a brilliant comedy.

Everything in *Gore ot uma,* as indicated by the name, revolves around the theme of, and the problems caused by, the intellect (*um*). Intellect appears as an active, dynamic factor in the play, and this aspect is what sets *Gore ot uma* apart. The very appearance of Chatsky in the Famusov circle ties together the plot. In 1833 Kiukhel'beker noted in his diary:

> In *Gore ot uma* the whole plot consists of the contrast between Chatsky and the other characters; there are not, to be sure, any particular schemes on the part of some characters that are opposed by the others, there is no fight for advantage, there are no—as they are called in dramaturgy—intrigues. Chatsky is presented, other characters are presented, they are brought together, and we are shown what must happen when these opposite poles meet—and that's that. It's very simple, but in this simplicity lies the new, the daring, the sublimity . . . of poetic expression.

Griboedov himself, in explaining the plot of *Gore ot uma,* clearly tried to emphasize that the decisive meaning of the play lies in how those who possess intellect stand in contrast to those who do not and how the two groups interrelate in life. Speaking of the "plan" of *Gore ot uma,* he wrote to Katenin in the spring of 1825:

It seems to me that it is simple and clear in its goal and in its performance; the girl, herself no fool, prefers the fool to the intelligent man (not because intelligence is so common among us poor sinners, no! In my comedy there are 25 idiots for every person with common sense); and this person, needless to say, stands in contrast to the society surrounding him; nobody understands him, no one wants to forgive him for being slightly above the others. At first he is happy, and this is a vice: "Go ahead and joke! Joke all you want!" He lightly runs through the peculiarities of his former acquaintances, and what can he do if there are no particularly noble traits to be found? His laughter is not mean-spirited as long as they don't anger him, but all the same: "He's not a man! He's a snake! . . . He likes to humiliate and poke fun at people, he is envious! He's arrogant and wicked . . . My God, he's a carbonari!" Someone dreams up the idea that he's insane; no one believes it but everyone repeats it; the voice of general ill will reaches him, including the disdain for him of the young woman who was the only reason he came to Moscow. Everything becomes perfectly clear to him and he leaves Moscow.

At the time Griboedov was finishing *Gore ot uma*, his attitude toward flights of fancy and idle dreams had not changed at all since the days of *Student* and his polemic over the translations of "Lenore." In *Gore ot uma* Sofia's sentimental romanticizing renders her incapable of seeing Molchalin for the scoundrel he really is. Instead she creates her own Molchalin, as she wishes him to be. For Chatsky (which means for Griboedov), the distinction between Sofia's romanticizing and the genuinely lofty aspirations of the intellect and the soul is perfectly clear. In Sofia's maid Liza's characterization of Chatsky, Griboedov changed the final text from "Who then is as cheerful and clever, and adroit, and witty, as Aleksandr Andreich Chatsky?" to "Who is as sensitive, and cheerful, and witty, as Aleksandr Andreich Chatsky!" He emphasizes that "sensitivity" in itself is no vice, and that the forms it takes can vary; in particular, it can point to a sincere openness to the experiences of life and to one's own noble motives, to a natural and positive trustfulness and a freedom and ease in associating with people.

Feeling and intellect, however, do not stand in direct contrast in *Gore ot uma*. Something entirely different comes up: it is revealed that both the ability to experience genuine feelings and the "lofty intellect" are equally unsuited for Famusov's way of life, for common sense triumphs over everything. Chatsky is the only one among all the characters in the play who is both a deeply feeling and an intelligent person. In Famusov's circle there can be only false sensitivity and vulgar common sense, but there can be no feeling and intellect in the proper meaning of these words. The "sensitive" Sofia easily forgets Chatsky, and the soberly rational Molchalin has reason to state: "She once loved Chatsky; she'll stop loving me, just as she stopped loving him."

Neither Famusov, nor Molchalin, nor even Skalozub (Famusov's favored suitor for Sofia) is stupid. But they have no real intellect, just the vulgar common sense into which the possibilities granted them by nature have degenerated. Famusov can succeed wonderfully in his own circle, but he is incapable of perceiving that Sofia would not be the least bit taken with Skalozub, or that she would dream up her own idealized image of Molchalin. The secretary, in turn, can endlessly concoct schemes for climbing the career ladder, but he is by nature incapable of analyzing Chatsky's life in any terms other than "he's unsuccessful"; this conclusion is the absolute limit of his reasoning powers. Finally, it is no coincidence that upon encountering Sofia, who is somewhat unusual in terms of the old established norms of Famusov's circle, Molchalin can no longer calculate everything so accurately. The power of vulgar common sense is valid only where it originated. Griboedov, without wavering, even gave a certain degree of wit to Skalozub, the hapless object of merciless mockery, but this fact does not lessen the intensity of the mockery: wit that is born of the barracks, and not of the bold and easy play of the free intellect, only underscores the limitations of the one who, even in joking, is incapable of exceeding his established limits.

The first two acts of *Gore ot uma* reveal not only to what degree the demands of the intellect do not correspond to the concrete reality of Famusov's way of life but also how deeply and firmly entrenched the principles that oppose intellect are. Chatsky has the opportunity to encounter many different examples of the products of this way of life, such as Molchalin and Skalozub. He is forced, after much tormented doubting, to recognize that Sofia prefers Molchalin over him. The possessor of intellect stands alone among those he has met, and his aloneness cannot be overcome. The more Chatsky learns of the strength of the principles that oppose the intellect, the more insistently he challenges them.

In the third act, at the ball, Chatsky's aloneness becomes especially sharp. The people at the ball stop listening to him; everyone shrinks from him. In response, Chatsky fights even harder. His accusations become more and more infused with anger, extending further and further in scope; and he leaves absolutely nothing unsaid. Famusov's world goes on the offensive and declares him a madman. Chatsky is devoid of any of the common sense so lauded in the comedies of Shakhovskoi and Zagoskin. In scorning everyone, Chatsky

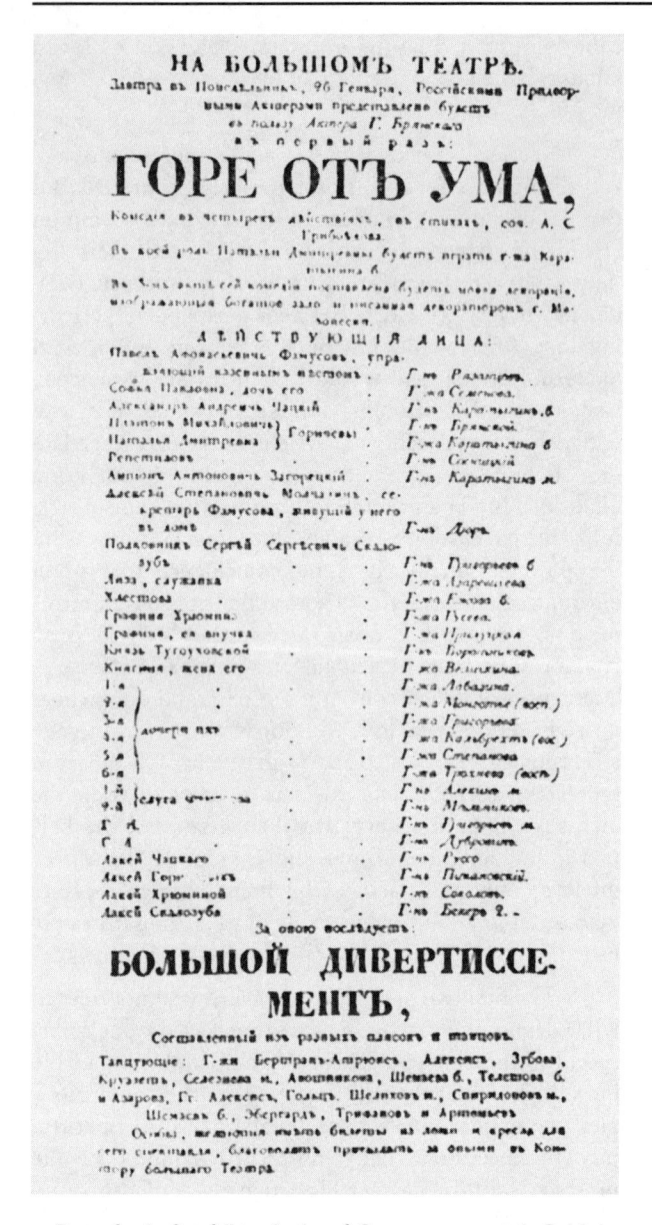

Poster for the first full production of Gore ot uma, *at the Bolshoi Theater in 1831*

violates the rules of common sense. He neither submits to tradition nor fears appearing ridiculous.

Another example of the tragedy of "woe from wit" is represented by Sofia. Challenging society, tradition, and her upbringing, she invents a hero (for want of a real one), all the while believing in her feelings and standing ready to fight for them. In this fight, any means justify the end, including starting rumors that Chatsky is mad. While Pushkin stated that Sofia was "drawn vaguely," Goncharov wrote:

> She is a mixture of good instincts with deceit, of a lively intellect with the absence of any trace of ideas or convictions, a confusion of thoughts, intellectual and moral blindness—and these are not her own personal vices, but rather are characteristic of her entire circle. In her own personal physiognomy there is hidden a trace of something that is hers alone, something warm, tender, and even pensive. All the rest is a product of her upbringing.

Sofia experiences woe from a false "intellect," that is, from purely bookish ideas and thoughts, planted by the reading of romantic novels. Just like Chatsky, Sofia resists prevailing common sense. She wants genuine feeling in a society of marriages of convenience. She looks for honesty and sincerity amid deceit and pretense; and just like Chatsky, she is punished with lack of love and understanding.

In *Gore ot uma* intellect provides the basis for all courageous, worthy, and noble behavior, as well as for the purity of motives, sincerity, and the depth of feeling. Griboedov makes clear that when clashing with prevailing common sense, the truly intelligent person is always correct and irreproachable. In fact, the degree of deviation from triumphant common sense indicates the degree of originality of intellect. For example, Molchalin, according to Griboedov, cannot be called truly intelligent first and foremost because he takes the idea of Famusov's circle seriously and believes that he has no choice but to adhere to their principles. After Sofia, when listing all of Molchalin's good points, names only qualities that happen to coincide with the Famusov circle's version of what is admirable, Chatsky is convinced that she could not possibly love or respect Molchalin. Finally, when Molchalin himself lays out his life's credo for Chatsky, which turns out to be perfectly in line with the laws of existence of Famusov's society, Chatsky is put completely at ease concerning the relationship between Sofia and Molchalin. For Griboedov, the intellect, the ability to feel deeply and sincerely and to elicit the serious feelings of others, stands diametrically opposed to the prevailing common sense.

Several Soviet scholars have noted the special significance of the problem of the intellect in Griboedov's comedy. For example, Vladimir Nikolaevich Orlov writes:

> The very concept of the intellect in this work becomes both very broad and historically concrete in that it appears essentially as a synonym for concepts such as freedom of thought. The presence of intellect in and of itself turns out to be characteristic of the political convictions of the person and his attitude toward the existing political system.

One of Griboedov's contemporaries, Osip Ivanovich Senkovsky (Baron Brambeus), maintained that the real value of *Gore ot uma* was the fact that it was the first Russian "political comedy."

Gore ot uma deals with many features of the everyday life of that time. Invariably these aspects are directly and emphatically brought into the play in the clash between the intellect and the forces opposed to the intellect that so occupies Griboedov. There are not really any descriptions of everyday life in the proper sense of the term; precisely for this reason, the "picture of morals" combines naturally with the central position of the protagonist, who is shown outside of the flow of daily existence. His entire life gains meaning because it exists exclusively in the realm of the intellect and has no connection with ordinary events.

Griboedov uses mundane details to develop the characters who function in the closed world of Famusov's Moscow, a society hostile to Chatsky and furthermore, to intellect in general. Amid the rules of this "charmed" circle, the details and symptoms of this way of life, the characters comprising Famusov's world appear. *Gore ot uma* was the first Russian play to confront the problem of the ensemble cast: none of the roles could be cut without fundamentally affecting the play. At first glance it would appear that Maksim and Kuzma Petrovich, who are introduced only in Famusov's speech, are not essential, nor are the Goriches, Zagoretsky, Khlyostova, or even Repetilov, all of whom actually appear on stage. Yet, they are indeed all needed in order to represent Famusov's Moscow and his way of life as an integrated whole. Thus all of them are involved in a manner that was not typical before *Gore ot uma;* they are involved in a new way, just as the dramatic conflict that provides the foundation for the play was itself essentially new. As Viazemsky rightly noted in *Sovremennik* (The Contemporary) in 1837: "In expanding the stage and filling it with a world of characters, he undoubtedly also expanded the borders of art." The special nature of the participation of many characters in the plot—as those who unfold and express the ideological content of their everyday mode of life—is revealed by the fact that some of them do not even have a last name (Mr. N, Mr. D); others never appear on stage; and still others can only be distinguished by their names, since their appearances and behavior are virtually identical (Kuzma and Maksim Petrovich, Tat'iana Iur'evna and Princess Mariia Alekseevna).

For Griboedov, the important thing about the characters in Famusov's circle is that they do not want to deviate from tradition, convention, and habit, and they absolutely cannot be intelligent. When Griboedov gives one of them a "meaningful" surname—such as Molchalin (from *molchat',* to be silent), or Repetilov (from the French *répéter,* to repeat)—then this name indicates exactly which trait this person possesses that counteracts the intellect. Griboedov uses the principle of "name-masks," borrowed from classicism, in his own way and for his own ends. For Griboedov the classical "unities" of time, place, and action were not in the least burdensome and perhaps even worked to his advantage. Adherence to these unities underlines the main, essentially rationalistic unity that is created in this play by the all-encompassing and decisive role of the intellect.

At the same time these aspects of the plot and composition offer the reader a chance to see the connection of the play with classical Russian comedies of the eighteenth and nineteenth centuries. Even though *Gore ot uma* observes the classical unities of time, place, and action, it still does not lose its innovative aspects. As Belinsky pointed out, Griboedov rejected the "artificial love, philosophizers, home-wreckers, and the entire vulgar, worn-out mechanism of the ancient drama." Unlike classical comedy, in which good is always rewarded and vice always punished, Griboedov did not leave the reader facing the expected "moral of the story."

Griboedov's contemporaries praised the folk origins of the style and the quality of the language of *Gore ot uma*. Meshcherikov quotes Odoevsky:

> Before Griboedov the strained, smoothed-out phrases set in six-foot verses, adorned with the names Milonov and Malen, make one consider even original comedies to be translations. . . . Only in Griboedov do we find unforced, easy language; the exact language in which we actually converse in society. In his style we find Russian coloring.

Griboedov, in fact, enriched the colloquial language of Russian society. According to Odoevsky, one could often hear "whole conversations that consisted largely of verses from *Gore ot uma*." In the letter to Bestuzhev, Pushkin remarked: "I am not speaking of verses, half of them should become proverbs."

In *Gore ot uma* Griboedov achieved an amazing lightness of verse that is almost imperceptible in the dialogue; at the same time it is unusually measured and expressive. Such style set the play sharply apart from the heavy verse of most comedies of that time. Comedies of the eighteenth and early nineteenth centuries were generally written in iambic hexameter. *Gore ot uma,* as well as almost half of the verse, is also written in iambic feet; however, the number of syllables in a line varies between one and thirteen, a technique that breaks up the monotony and the heaviness of the verse. The poetry of the comedy, as the language itself, struck Griboedov's contemporaries as unforced and natural.

Scene from act 3 of a 1906 production of Gore ot uma *at the Art Theatre in Moscow*

One of Griboedov's major accomplishments in *Gore ot uma* was his ability to combine colloquial speech with the literary forms of the verse. He managed this feat by various means: not only by using folk lexicon and phraseology but also by transforming the structure of the dramatic monologues and dialogues by deviating from traditional comedic forms. To begin with, the themes of several monologues are instantly apprehended by other characters present during the monologue; their reactions are immediately reflected in the subsequent course of the monologue. Thus, in the first act, Chatsky's discourse on the people in Famusov's Moscow, which is essentially a monologue, is repeatedly interrupted by his own questions to Sofia and her answers and comments, which Chatsky then promptly incorporates into his monologue. In this way even lengthy monologues do not appear to interrupt the natural flow of conversation among the characters. The lines in the dialogues in *Gore ot uma* are almost exclusively directed at the interlocutor and elicit a direct response, which then provides further material for continuing the conversation. The spacing out of a poetic line over two, three, or even four rejoinders often gives it a particular pithiness and evocative force.

Thus the rumor of Chatsky's madness is at first met with bewilderment and disbelief. Mr. D even objects, to Mr. N. Their rejoinders, momentarily replacing each other, enter into a single poetic line and continue each other within the composition of the line. Doubting and objecting, not having had time to stop and think, they are already caught up in the whirlwind of a rumor turned loose; they have surrendered to its rhythm, so to speak, and they now take part in its further propagation.

While *Gore ot uma* was an extraordinary work in terms of its stylistic innovations, it was no less extraordinary in terms of the reception it received among the widest possible circles of readers. Goncharov wrote: "Immediately grasping its beauty, and not finding any faults in it, the literate masses wore the manuscript down to tatters, to verses, to hemistiches; they distributed all its pith and wisdom into colloquial speech; they turned a million into kopecks." The popularity of *Gore ot uma* made its official censorship useless and ridiculous, and the imperial government was forced to lift the ban. The play was performed in its entirety on the stage for the first time in 1831. The first Russian-language edition of the play appeared in print in 1833, but it was thoroughly bowdlerized: anything critical of the status quo in Russia was cut. According to Aleksandr Ivanovich Herzen, Tsar Nicholas I approved the play in order to "eliminate all the attractiveness of forbidden fruit" and to stop the spread of manuscript copies. *Gore ot uma* was not published in its original uncensored form until 1862.

Griboedov spent 1824 and the first half of 1825 in Moscow and St. Petersburg. He again became involved in the theater and wrote a comedy with Viazemsky and Aleksei Nikolaevich Verstovsky called *Kto brat, kto sestra, ili Obman za obmanom* (Who is the Brother, Who is the Sister, or Deception upon Deception), which, although staged in Moscow, did not meet with success. Griboedov extended his leave for another year and spent part of that time in St. Petersburg. Among Griboedov's acquaintances were the Bestuzhev brothers, Kondratii Fedorovich Ryleev, Petr Grigor'evich Kakhovsky, and many others who were actively involved in Decembrist circles. Griboedov himself was not a member of their secret societies; however, to him was attributed the slogan: "A hundred ensigns want to change the entire form of government of Russia." When questioned by the authorities, Griboedov said: "In conversation with them [the Decembrists], I heard many a bold discussion concerning the government, in which I also took part; I condemned what seemed harmful and wished for something better."

Militsa Vasil'evna Nechkina, a Soviet scholar of the Decembrist movement, wrote in *A. S. Griboedov i dekabristy* (A. S. Griboedov and the Decembrists, 1947): "One can be quite sure that Griboedov knew of the plans of the Decembrists and of their impending revolt." There is no doubt that he was connected with the group, but Ryleev had purposely not recorded his membership because he did not want to "expose such a talent to danger." During the investigation following the revolt, Ryleev said: "I had several general conversations with Griboedov about the state of affairs in Russia and I hinted at the existence of our society, which was dedicated to changing the form of government in Russia and introducing a constitutional monarchy."

It is difficult to draw a firm conclusion concerning the extent of Griboedov's involvement with the Decembrists. Many of the conspirators had been in the military with him, and others he knew from the university. One thing is certain: Griboedov was not present with the Decembrists during the revolt in Senate Square on 14 December 1825.

In late January 1826, several weeks after the suppression of the revolt, General Ermolov received an order to arrest Griboedov. He carried out this order, but not before warning Griboedov, thus giving him the opportunity to destroy compromising correspondence. Upon his arrival in St. Petersburg, Griboedov was taken into custody and held in the guardhouse of the Winter Palace, where he made his first statements denying any involvement in the revolt: "I have engaged in no activities that might serve to cast suspicion upon me, and why suspicion has fallen upon me all the same, I cannot fathom." After four months in custody Griboedov petitioned Nicholas I, and as a result he was released in June with a full pardon. In compensation for his detainment he was granted an annual salary and was promoted to court councillor.

This series of events was reflected in Griboedov's draft of a tragedy called "Rodamist i Zenobiia." The play was set in Georgia and Armenia during the first century A.D., an historical period Griboedov used to draw parallels with contemporary events. The protagonist is a reflection of Griboedov: he is "dangerous to the government and a burden to himself, for he is a citizen of another age." Griboedov attempts to describe the course of a political plot, and the impending revolt is viewed as the affair of a small group of revolutionaries. Also represented in this play is the tsar. Having been warned of an assassination attempt, he leads the investigation himself, in which he "feigns sympathy, lures out ... the secret, and then turns brutal." Griboedov never finished this tragedy; the draft was published in *Russkoe slovo* (Russian Word) in 1859.

Griboedov again returned to the Caucasus in the service of Ermolov. The general was soon relieved of his duties, however, as he had been unable to halt the advance of Persian troops. Persia had taken advantage of the political instability in Russia and attacked border regions in the Trans-Caucasus, which also served to fuel an uprising among many Caucasian peoples who hoped to gain independence from the Russian empire. In the summer of 1826, Persian troops advanced into the Trans-Caucasus without warning. Their advance troops almost reached Tiflis, in the process destroying a German colony near the city and taking many prisoners. Ermolov was forced to retreat, and Nicholas I sent General Ivan Fedorovich Paskevich to his aid. Paskevich later took over complete command of the army, leaving Ermolov no choice but to retire.

Griboedov had also decided to retire along with Ermolov, but he was not allowed to do so. He was one of few people with diplomatic experience and knowledge of the Persian language and customs, and he had earlier worked with the Persian shah. Furthermore, he was related to Paskevich, who had helped him when he was in custody after the Decembrist revolt. Griboedov saw continued service as the chance to put his plans for the government into practice. Many of his contemporaries condemned him for this decision and accused him of being ungrateful to Ermolov.

Griboedov took an active part in negotiations with local princes and khans, and given his knowledge of local customs, he was quite successful. The Russian army went on the offensive, and the Persian shah began peace negotiations. Paskevich assigned Griboedov to conduct the negotiations on the Russian side. He succeeded in getting the shah to agree to a cease-fire, but this agreement was soon broken by the Persians. The Russian army responded by storming Yerevan and several other cities. Russia was forced to make peace with Persia, however, since there was also the threat of war with Turkey at that time. Griboedov was assigned to write a protocol of the peace negotiations and the text of the agreement itself. This treaty is known as the Peace of Turkmanchai. A special point of the contract was the return of all prisoners of war and other Russian subjects who had fallen under Persian rule. The agreement was signed on 10 April 1828, largely through the efforts of Griboedov. For this accomplishment he received a promotion, 4,000 rubles in gold, and an extended leave in St. Petersburg.

Griboedov left for the capital with the hope that he would never again have to return to Persia. On 15 April 1828, however, he was given a new assignment from Foreign Minister Nesselrode—he was selected to lead the Russian mission to Persia. Griboedov tried to persuade Nesselrode that it was necessary to send a fully empowered ambassador and that his own rank was not sufficient

Model of a monument honoring Griboedov, sculpted by V. Beklemishev and erected in 1900 at the Russian embassy in Tehran

for such a lofty post. This evasion, however, was not to be; Nicholas I conveniently forgot about Griboedov's indiscretions with the Decembrists and appointed him as a fully empowered ambassador. Maksim Iakovlevich von Fok, head of the Third Section (the secret police that played a leading role in the main censorship committee), reported to his superiors in April 1828:

> promotion of Griboedov to the post of ambassador has caused a commotion in the city [St. Petersburg] the likes of which has never been seen before for any previous appointment. The entire younger generation is ecstatic. Griboedov's appointment has bought thousands of votes in favor of the government. The literati, young and capable civil servants, and all intelligent people are celebrating . . . I must add that Griboedov has a special gift for drawing people to him with his intellect, his open and noble manner, and his pure spirit, in which there burns an enthusiasm for all that is great and noble. He has legions of admirers everywhere he has been, and many people are united by their mutual acquaintanceship with him. Getting such a man in government service is of extreme political importance.

Even someone as openly hostile to Griboedov as Nikolai Nikolaevich Murav'ev-Karsky, one of Griboedov's supervisors at the Office of Foreign Affairs who had expressed his reservations about "Griboedov's much-lauded virtues and habits, which . . . I have never found all that enticing," confessed that: "I am sure that in Persia Griboedov had found his niche, that he single-handedly took the place of a 20,000-man army, and that one could not, perhaps, find a more capable man for this post in all of Russia."

Griboedov himself, however, looked upon this matter quite differently. His friend Zhandr wrote in his memoirs (quoted in Meshcheriakov) that Griboedov arrived at Zhandr's home late one night and said that he had come to say good-bye and that they would never see each other again–Griboedov was sure of it. Many of Griboedov's friends recalled his fateful premonitions and anguish at this time. In his *Zapiska ob A. S. Griboedove* (Note on A. S. Griboedov), quoted by Meshcheriakov, Begichev wrote:

> During his entire visit he was extremely gloomy. I mentioned this to him, and he took my hand and said with deep sadness: "Farewell, my dear friend Stepan, it is most unlikely that we shall see each other again!!!" "What can you be thinking, why are you so depressed?" I objected. "You have been in battles, and God has spared you." He answered: "I know the Persians. Allaiard Khan is my personal enemy, and he will kill me! He will not give me the peace we concluded with the Persians."

Little is known of Griboedov's literary activities during this period. Many of his works perished with him in Tehran. Only a few rough drafts survived, and other remnants of his work were reconstructed through the memoirs of his contemporaries.

In the mid 1820s Griboedov had an interesting idea for a drama based on the Patriotic War. A draft of the plot, part of the epilogue, and one act survived and were first published in *Russkoe slovo* in 1859 with the title "1812-i god." He wanted to analyze recent historical events in which he had participated. The protagonist of this drama was quite unusual: he was a serf, called only M. In the epilogue Griboedov had noted that "all poetry of great feasts disappears," and serf M., who had proven to be a hero in battle, was now "scorned by the military command. He is sent home with patriotic admonitions about submission and obedience. . . . The same old cruel treatment. Right back to the whip."

Griboedov's treatment of the enemy is also interesting. The French are portrayed in a variety of ways. In the French camp there appears a "gray-haired soldier," who, during the period of Napoleon's victorious offensives, "with the bitter premonitions of experience warns of future misfortunes." Napoleon strives to understand the distinctiveness of the Russian people–"youthful, prototypical." Napoleon's invasion meets with disaster, and extreme suffering befalls both the gray-haired soldier and another Frenchman, both of whom act courageously and "die heroes." The Russian victory does nothing to alter M.'s situation, however. In this work Griboedov tries to understand the complexity of the historical process and to grasp its internal mechanisms; he no longer attempts to reduce everything to the battle between the intellect and its opposing forces.

The content of Griboedov's tragedy "Gruzinskaia noch'" (Georgian Night) is known through Bulgarin's retelling. A Georgian prince has traded his slave for a horse, even though this slave is his childhood companion, whose own mother was the prince's wet nurse. She in turn reproaches the prince and demands the return of her son. At first the prince promises to get him back, but soon becomes distracted by other affairs and forgets. In desperation the wet nurse turns for help to the evil spirit Ali. By black magic, she makes the prince's daughter fall in love with a Russian officer, who kidnaps the girl from home. The prince goes in pursuit. He sees the couple on the crest of a hill and takes aim at the kidnapper, but Ali directs his bullet at the daughter's heart. The wet nurse then grabs the rifle from the prince in order to strike him with it; but again Ali interferes with black magic, and as a result, the mother ends up killing her own beloved son. Both the prince and the wet nurse perish in despair. A reading of excerpts from this tragedy took place at the home of Pavel Petrovich Svin'in in the spring of 1828. Also present was Pushkin, who praised the originality of Griboedov's verses and the subtle interweaving of aspects of Georgian culture.

In early June 1828 Griboedov left for the Caucasus en route to Persia. Zhandr recalled:

> We accompanied Griboedov sadly. . . . Only two of us accompanied him as far as Tsarskoe Selo: Aleksandr Vsevolozhsky and I. This is what kind of a mood we were in: We had a farewell breakfast at my place, we started smoking and made a terrible cloud of smoke, and when the crowd dispersed, we were alone. We left. It was a dreary, rainy day. We went all the way to Tsarskoe Selo without saying a single word. In Tsarskoe Selo, as evening was approaching, Griboedov told us to get a bottle of Burgundy, which he loved, and a bottle of Champagne and to have a bite to eat. Nobody touched a thing. Finally we said farewell. Griboedov got in the carriage, and we watched it disappear around the corner. Vsevolozhsky and I returned to St. Petersburg, and again we didn't say a word for the whole trip. Not a single word.

On the way to Persia Griboedov stopped to visit his friend Begichev, who wrote in his *Zapiska ob A. S. Griboedove*:

> On the way to his post Griboedov spent three days at my place. During the course of our conversations I asked him if he had written any more comedies or other works. He replied: "I already told you the last time I saw you that I no longer write comedies. I have lost my sense of humor, and without humor it's difficult to write a good comedy. But I have written a tragedy." And right there he described the story to me and recited scenes from memory the scenes that he had read in St. Petersburg. . . . But he would not agree to read the whole thing for me. "I am still too attached to it," he said. "I have promised myself not to read it for five years, and then, when I have distanced myself from it, I will be able to read it as if it were someone else's work, and if I like it, I'll have it published."

Upon arriving in Tiflis, Griboedov visited the home of his old friend Praskovia Nikolaevna Akheverdova, where, after many years, he once again met Nina

Chavchavadze. She was the daughter of poet and social activist Prince Aleksandr Gersevanovich Chavchavadze, a friend from Griboedov's first stay in Georgia under the command of Ermolov, and he had known her as a young girl. To his own surprise, as well as the surprise of his friends (as can be seen from his letter of 24 June 1828 to Bulgarin), he proposed to her, and they were married on 22 August.

Almost nothing is known of Griboedov's married life. Only one of his letters to his young wife has survived, from 24 December 1828:

> My precious friend, I miss you terribly and couldn't possibly be sadder. Now I truly feel what it means to love. I have parted with many others to whom I was very close, but after a day or two, a week, my sadness passed. Now, the longer I am without you, the worse it gets. Let us endure a little longer, my angel, and we will pray to God that after this he will never part us.

On 27 February 1829 the news reached the Caucasus that Russian Ambassador Griboedov and almost his entire retinue had been murdered by a mob in Persia on 30 January. His pregnant wife lost their child when she learned what had happened. Griboedov was probably killed for his persistence in trying to obtain the release of Russian prisoners of war, which was one of the stipulations of the Peace of Turkmanchai. Griboedov insisted upon observing all the conditions of this treaty to the letter, which aroused the anger of the Persian shah. Anti-Russian sentiments were running high in Persia, where the Peace of Turkmanchai was viewed as a disgrace. Griboedov, as the author and executor of this treaty, became one of the first victims of mob violence. In April 1829 a Persian delegation arrived in Russia to atone for the murder of Griboedov. This delegation was headed by one of the shah's sons, who gave Tsar Nicholas I the eighty-eight-karat Shah Diamond as the "price of Griboedov's blood."

In his *Puteshestvie v Arzrum* Pushkin described his visit to Griboedov's grave, which is located atop a mountain in Tiflis at the Monastery of St. David:

> I had never imagined that I would ever meet our Griboedov again! I had parted with him the year before in St. Petersburg before his departure for Persia. He was sad and had strange premonitions. I was about to comfort him, and he said to me: "Vous ne connaissez pas ces gens-lá: vous verrez gu'il faudra jouer des couteaux." [You do not know these people: you will see that it will come to knives.] He assumed that the cause of bloodshed would be the death of the Shah and the internecine strife among his seventy sons. But the ancient Shah is still alive, and Griboedov's prophetic words have come true. He died by the knives of the Persians, the victim of ignorance and treachery....

> His perfect knowledge of the region where the war began opened up new horizons for him: he was appointed ambassador. Upon arriving in Georgia, he married the woman he loved . . . I can think of nothing more enviable in the last years of his stormy life. Death itself, overtaking him in the heat of a valiant, one-sided battle, did not frighten him. It was quick and wonderful.

> How unfortunate that Griboedov did not leave behind his notes! His biography ought to be written by his friends; but our noteworthy people disappear without a trace.

Though Griboedov is known for only one work, *Gore ot uma*, that play alone suffices to guarantee him a high place among the talents of Russian literature. His stylistic and metrical innovations, witty language, mordant satire, and memorable characters contributed to the status of the play as a classic of world literature. Many lines and aphorisms have become part of Russian popular culture; Russians frequently quote the play, sometimes not even knowing the source of the adage. Griboedov's truly groundbreaking work in drama set an example later Russian playwrights tried to emulate but seldom surpassed. The inscription on his tombstone aptly summarizes Griboedov's place in Russia: "Um i dela tvoi bessmertnyi v pamiati russkoi. . . ." (Your mind and deeds are immortal in Russian memory. . . .).

Letters:

Griboedov Kollezhskii Assesor, sluzhashchii sekretarem po diplomaticheskoi chasti pri glavnoupravliaiushchem v Gruzii (St. Petersburg, 1905);

Ol'ga Ivanovna Popova, ed., *A. S. Griboedov v Persii 1818–1923 g.g.: Po novym dokumentam* (Moscow: Kooperativnoe izd-vo "Zhizn' i Znanie," 1929).

Bibliography:

Nikolai Kir'iakovich Piksanov, *Materialy dlia bibliograficheskago ukazatelia proizvedenii A. S. Griboedova i literatury o nem* (Iur'ev, 1903).

Biographies:

Nikolai Kir'iakovich Piksanov and Il'ia Samoilovich Zil'bershtein, eds., *A. S. Griboedov v vospominaniiakh sovremennikov* (Moscow: Federatsiia, 1929);

Vladimir Nikolaevich Orlov, *A. S. Griboedov: ocherk zhizni i tvorchestva* (Leningrad: 1954);

Sergei Mitrofanovich Petrov, *A. S. Griboedov. Kritiko-biograficheskii ocherk,* second edition (Moscow: Goslitizdat, 1954);

A. S. Griboedov: Tvorchestvo, biografija, iradicii. Sbornik statei (Leningrad: Nauka, 1977);

Sergei Aleksandrovich Fomichev, ed., *A. S. Griboedov: zhizn' i tvorchestvo* (Moscow: Russkaia Kniga, 1994).

References:

L. M. Arinshtein, "Novye dannye ob obstoiatel'stvakh gibeli Grivoedova po angliiskim istochnikam," *Russkaia literatura*, 2 (1981): 225–233;

A. P. Arkhipova, "Proza Griboedova," *Russkaia literatura*, 1 (1992): 87–94;

Vissarion Grigor'evich Belinsky, "Gore ot uma. Komediia v 4-h deistviiakh," in his *Stat'i i retsenzii: 1834–1841*, volume 1 (Moscow: OGTZ, 1948), pp. 453–518;

Iurii Nikolaevich Borisov, *Gore ot uma i russkaia stikhotvornaia komediia: U istokov zhanra* (Saratov: Izd. Saratovskogo universiteta, 1978);

William Edward Brown, "Alexander Griboedov and Woe from Wit," in his *A History of Russian Literature of the Romantic Period*, volume 1 (Ann Arbor, Mich.: Ardis, 1986), pp. 93–99, 105–115, 311–313;

Faddei Venediktovich Bulgarin, *Vospominaniia o nezabvennom Aleksandre Sergeeviche Griboedove* (St. Petersburg: N. Grech, 1830);

J. Douglas Clayton, "'Tis Folly to Be Wise: The Semantics of *um-* in Griboedov's *Gore ot uma*," in *Text and Content: Essays to Honor Nils Ake Nilsson*, edited by P. A. Jensen and others (Stockholm: Almqvist & Wilksell, 1987);

Zinovii Davydov, ed., *A. S. Griboedov: Ego zhizn' i gibel' v memuarakh sovremennikov* (Leningrad: Krasnaia gazeta, 1929);

M. D. El'zon, "'Chad' ili 'chaiat'? O smysle familii 'Chatskii,'" *Russkaia literatura*, 2 (1981): 182–183;

I. K. Eniklopov, *Griboedov i Vostok*, second edition (Ereven: Ajastan, 1974);

M. Giergielewicz, "Structural Footnotes to Griboedov's *Woe from Wit*," *Polish Review*, 1, no. 24 (1979): 3–21;

I. A. Gladys, *Gore ot uma: Stranitsy istorii* (Moscow: Kniga, 1971);

Ivan Aleksandrovich Goncharov, "Mil'on Terzanii," in his *Sobranie sochinenii*, volume 8 (Moscow: "Pravda," 1952), pp. 250–255;

Arkady Moiseevich Gordin, ed., *A. S. Griboedov v russkoi kritike. Sbornik statei* (Moscow: Goslitizdat, 1958);

Evelyn J. Harden, "Griboedov in Persia: December 1828," *Slavic and East European Review*, 57 (1979): 255–267;

Harden, *The Murder of Griboedov: New Materials* (Birmingham, U.K.: University of Birmingham, 1979);

Viacheslav Trofimovich Kabanov, ed., *A. S. Griboedov: litso i genii* (Moscow: Knizhnaia Palata, 1997);

George Kalbouss, "Rhyming Patterns in Griboedov's *Gore ot uma*," *Slavic and East European Journal*, 39 (Spring 1995): 1–13;

Wolfgang Kasack, "Die Struktur von Grivoedovs Gore ot uma in der Geschicte des russischen Dramas," in *VII Miedzynarodowy Kongres Slawistów w Warszawie 1973* (Warsaw: PAN, 1973);

Svetlana Alekseevna Matiash, "Basennyi i dramaticheskii vol'nyi iamb: K probleme genezisa stikha komedii A. S. Griboedova *Gore ot uma*," *Russkaia literatura*, 1 (1984): 182–188;

Viktor Petrovich Meshcheriakov, *A. S. Griboedov. Literaturnoe okruzhenie i vospriiatie* (Leningrad: Nauka, 1983);

Meshcheriakov, "Byl li A. S. Griboedov chlenom obshchestva dekabristov?" *Voprosy Russkoi literatury*, 1, no. 57 (1990): 94–102;

Meshcheriakov, "Zagadka Griboedova," *Novyi Mir*, 12 (December 1984): 209–219;

A. V. Motorin, "The Evolution of A. S. Griboedov's Artistic *Weltanschauung*," *Russkaia literatura*, 1 (1993): 21–36;

M. V. and T. G. Muratov, *Aleksandr Sergeevich Griboedov* (Moscow: Detskaia literatura, 1965);

Militsa Vasil'evna Nechkina, *A. S. Griboedov i dekabristy*, second edition (Moscow: AN SSSR, 1951);

Vladimir Ivanovich Nemirovich-Danchenko, *Gore ot uma v postanovke Moskovskogo Khudozhestvennogo teatra* (Moscow: Gos. izd-vo, 1923);

Anna Isaakovna Ostrovskaia, *Aleksandr Sergeevich Griboedov* (Moscow: Ladia, 1994);

P. Ovcharova, "Lichnost' Griboedova," *Voprosy literatury*, 3 (March 1982): 230–240;

Nikolai Kir'iakovich Piksanov, *Tvorcheskaia istoriia Goria ot uma* (Moscow: Nauka, 1971);

Ol'ga Ivanovna Popova, *Griboedov-diplomat* (Moscow: Mezhdunarodnye otnosheniia, 1964);

L. S. Semenov, "Piat' pisem A. S. Griboedova i materialy, otnosiashchiesia k ego gibeli," *Russkaia literatura*, 2 (1986): 151–156;

Iurii Nikolaevich Tynianov, *Arkhaisty i novatory* (Leningrad: Priboi, 1929);

Tynianov, *Death and Diplomacy in Persia 1894–1943*, translated by Alec Brown (London: Boriswood, 1938).

Papers:

Some of Aleksandr Segreevich Griboedov's papers are located at the Institute of Russian Literature (Pushkin House); the Russian National Library, f. 178 (including the authorized "Bulgarin manuscript" of *Gore ot uma*); and the St. Petersburg State Theater Library, all in St. Petersburg; and in the Central State Archive of Literature and Art (TsGALI), f. 136; the Russian State Library, f. 221; and the Russian Central Theater Museum, all in Moscow. The initial manuscript for *Gore ot uma* (known as the "museum manuscript") is in the Moscow Historical Museum.

Nikolai Mikhailovich Iazykov
(4 March 1803 – 26 December 1846)

Luc J. Beaudoin
University of Denver

BOOKS: *Stikhotvoreniia* (St. Petersburg: Tip. vdovy Pliushar s synom, 1833);

Piat'desiat shest' stikhotvorenii (Moscow: A. Semen, 1844);

Novye stikhotvoreniia (Moscow: V universitetskoi tipografii, 1845).

Editions and Collections: *Stikhotvoreniia N. M. Iazykova,* 2 volumes (St. Petersburg: Tip-iia Imperatorskoi akademii nauk, 1858);

Stikhotvoveniia, edited by Aleksei Sergeevich Surovin (St. Petersburg: Deshevaia biblioteka, 1898);

Liricheskiia stikhotvoreniia N. M. Iazykov, edited by Vadim Shershenevich (Moscow: Aksionernoe Obshchestvo Universal'naia Biblioteka, 1916);

Polnoe sobranie stikhotvorenii, edited, with an introduction, by Mark Konstantinovich Azadovsky (Moscow: Academia, 1934);

Stikhotvoreniia, edited, with an introduction, by Azadovsky (Moscow-Leningrad: Sovetskii pisatel', 1936);

Sobranie stikhotvorenii, edited, with an introduction, by Azadovsky (Moscow: Sovetskii pisatel', 1948);

Stikhotvoreniia i poemy, edited, with an introduction, by K. K. Bukhmeier (Leningrad: Sovetskii pisatel', 1958);

Stikhotvoreniia, skazki, poemy, dramaticheskie stseny, pis'ma, edited, with an introduction, by I. D. Glikman (Moscow-Leningrad: Goslitizdat, 1959);

Polnoe sobranie stikhotvorenii, edited, with an introduction, by Bukhmeier (Moscow-Leningrad: Sovetskii pisatel', 1964);

Sochineniia, edited by A. A. Karpov (Leningrad: Khudozhestvennaia literatura, 1982).

Nikolai Iazykov would most likely have perceived his role in the development of Russian Romantic literature quite differently than did either his contemporaries or the subsequent generations of critics. He would have placed a greater value upon the works written during the latter stage of his career, whereas both his contemporaries and later critics extolled, and continue to extol, the virtuosity of his early lyric verse. These same critics and colleagues, who had earlier been dazzled by Iazykov's speedy rhythms, unusual rhymes, and daring innuendos, began around 1828 to view the poet's work as derivative and repetitious. Fellow poets who had appreciated the friendly Anacreontic verses of student life quickly found fault with the ponderous moralistic posing of Iazykov's late works. By then, however, his genius had already secured him a position in the Russian poetic pantheon, and any shortcomings accredited to the Muses of later years were overshadowed by the lyric brilliance of his youthful work. As the influential critic of the mid nineteenth century Vissarion Grigor'evich Belinsky stated, Iazykov was "a poet-student—carefree and overflowing with an excess of youthful feelings—who sang of the amusements of youth, celebrating the festival of life, the crimson lips, the dark eyes, the lily-white bosoms and marvelous brows of earthly beauties, the passionate nights and unforgettable lands."

Nikolai Mikhailovich Iazykov was born to a family of the gentry in the Simbirsk district on 4 March 1803. The family fortune supported him throughout his life. His father gave his children a desire for the various forms of independence that would come about with a good education. Iazykov's two older brothers, Petr Mikhailovich and Aleksandr Mikhailovich, were sent to the Mining Military School in St. Petersburg, where the young poet was himself sent in 1814 at the tender age of eleven. The heavily regimented school did not suit him, however, and he transferred to the Engineering Corps Institute five years later, never having completed his program. He spent one year in his new environment but was expelled because of a miserable attendance record. Despite his initial academic failure, Iazykov had already begun to sense his calling. Although the severity of the academic regimen in its concentration on the mathematical sciences certainly oppressed the young Iazykov, he began to test his poetic talents in the Military Mining School. The school boasted a classical curriculum, introducing pupils to literary and dramatic interests, including music, drawing, and dance. Few of these early works have survived, however. The earliest known are the "Poslanie k Kulibinu" (Epistle to Kulibin) and "A. I. Kulibinu" (To A. I. Kulibin)–both written to Aleksandr Ivanovich Kulibin, a schoolmate and devotee of poetry–published in the *Sorevnovatel' prosveshcheniia i blagotvoreniia* (Champion of Enlightenment and Beneficence) of 1819, which simultaneously included poems by Kulibin. Though Iazykov's works of the time were fairly derivative and revealed the influence of Mikhail Vasil'evich Lomonosov and Gavriil Romanovich Derzhavin, they did draw the attention of Amplii Nikolaevich Ochkin, a minor author. Indeed, Iazykov wrote a poem to Ochkin in 1822 and continued to send his works to Ochkin even after leaving St. Petersburg, giving his mentor a *liberum veto* as to the quality of the poetry. Ochkin directed Iazykov's early poetry to various journals in the capital.

When the young poet left St. Petersburg, he transferred to Dorpat University, located in present-day Tartu, Estonia, but only after a short sojourn in Simbirsk and an attempt at a university education at St. Petersburg University. The more liberal atmosphere of the heavily German town of Dorpat permitted the young poet to better develop his talents and provided an education that gave him liberties greater than could be attained in the capital itself.

The traditions of German student life, transplanted as they were onto the soil of the Russian Empire in the town of Dorpat, consisted of drinking, flirting, and carousing. Under these conditions, Iazykov's Muse flourished, and the poet began to produce his renowned Anacreontic verse. Yet, it was this early in his literary career that the young poet wrote what many perceive as his best work. Critics agree, moreover, that Iazykov's poetry of this period is not to be read as a personal autobiography, but rather that the reader must keep in mind that invocations of Bacchus and Venus and the tales spun around them were a standard feature of Romanticism, a movement that opposed the formality of Classicism and turned instead to the headiness of pure emotion when creating works of art. Iazykov created through his lyrics a new Romantic biography of the ideal Romantic student-poet, who sings the rapturous praises of life and of its attendant emotions. The Iazykov who has come to be known as a literary figure undoubtedly took part in student licentiousness but also concentrated on his education, studying such subjects as history, philosophy, aesthetics, and economics. In Dorpat he also attained competence in German and French, while also studying English, Greek, and Latin. He developed a fondness for William Shakespeare, Friedrich von Schiller, Johann Wolfgang von Goethe, and George Gordon, Lord Byron, in Western literature. In particular, he read works by the German writers of the Romantic school. These interests perhaps served later to reinforce motifs that developed into consistent themes–love of personal freedom and love of the Motherland–as witnessed in his early poem "Moia rodina" (My Native Land, 1822). In his early verse, however, those motifs remain buried in the mass of invocations to the pleasures of youth. "Pesni" (Songs, 1823), a collection of nine songs with a tenth concluding "Hymn," permits a view into the Anacreontic Iazykov. Song VIII admirably summarizes the tone of these works:

> Freedom, song and wine–
> That's the joy that's given to us,
>   That's our Holy Trinity!
> Love?–Well, what is love? She's
> Without Bacchus quite cold,
>   But with Bacchus quite daring.
> Yesterday I knew Paradise with Lileta,
> Today it's this and that–goodbye:
>   She has fallen in love with another,
> But I'm not a slave of love,
> Pour me a glass that's full!
>   Not to your health, Lila!

This cycle not only introduces the themes of drink and lust but also that of irreverence. Part of the cult of youth is a disrespect for authority, a trait that Iazykov carried with him for the remainder of his life. Song VII portrays to what degree he dares to be bold (keeping in mind the autocratic nature of the Russian Empire of the time):

> He is happy to whom fate has given
> A glass that never empties:
> He asks God for nothing,

> He bows not to rumor,
> And carries no heavy thoughts
> In his unsober head.
> From morning till night he
> Is not bored—even when alone,
> Not occupied with the newspaper's tedium,
> Sitting with his wine, he does not know,
> Like the Tsar, that short-sighted politician,
> That he is mocked or laughable.
> Let the Holy Triumvirate judge Europe
> As it likes,
> Let them battle in Spain for the rights
> Of proud freedom—
> His innocent words don't criticize
> The guilty.
> With wine he is cheerful and happy—
> He lives for raptures alone,
> And between his and the Tsar's lot
> We don't find any great difference:
> The Tsar sleeps on his throne,
> And he—oblivious—under the table.

Despite the daring references to the tsar, this poem is an invocation to drunken bliss. That these poems are artistically re-created drinking songs is clear from the periodic structure Iazykov uses. In the majority of stanzas, the first two lines return as the final fifth and sixth. The final stanza of Song VI exemplifies this structure:

> Da budut nashi bozhestva
> Vino, svoboda i vesel'e
> Im nashi mysli i slova!
> Im i zaniat'e i bezdel'e!
> Da budut nashi bozhestva
> Vino, svoboda i vesel'e!
>
> Let our gods be
> Wine, freedom and merriment!
> Of them our thoughts and words!
> To them our work and leisure!
> Let our gods be
> Wine, freedom and merriment!

Certainly, another of Iazykov's gods was Venus, an entity who occupies much of his poetic output. Song VIII mentions a woman named Lileta, presumably an invented name for a woman with whom Iazykov associated. The young poet dedicated a cycle of elegies (1823–1825) to this woman, and in his typical irreverent style he appropriated the genre in a fashion both provocative and conservative, returning to the thematics of the classical Latin erotic elegy but changing the verse structure to a style of his own by employing short lines previously never used in the genre. The result was an elegy by name but with a style more suited to songs. He begins with a poem in which he sees his beloved in a dream and ends with a work expressing his dismay that his beloved has left him for a priest. Even this cycle concludes with a characteristic defiance of authority: "O God, O God! With your priest, on Saturday, on a bed of sin, young Lila sinned! Who would not be hesitant to go pray before a priest who in the daytime prepares himself for Paradise, and at night enjoys someone else's girl? No! Let them ring—they won't entice me to Mass!" Between the initial mystical experience and its perversion in the final elegy are works so risqué in their sexual allusions that they were never published in their full form in Soviet editions of Iazykov's works.

Iazykov also wrote political elegies that confronted what he saw as the injustices inherent in the Russian political system. In his political elegies, the poet rails against the submissiveness of the Russian people toward the tsarist yoke that oppresses them. One particularly striking instance can be seen in the final stanza of his "Elegiia" (Elegy, 1824): "I saw slavish Russia: / Before the sanctuary of the altar, / Rattling her chains, having bowed down her neck, / She was praying for the Tsar." This type of striking and direct imagery was as much a hallmark of Iazykov's political poetry as of his love poetry and his exhortations of student life.

Romantic liaisons and love for the young poet, however, became less earthy and more Romantic (in the spirit of Romantic love and its inherent idealization of an ideal woman) in quite a few poems dating between 1825 and 1830. These works are dedicated to Aleksandra Andreevna Voeikova, the niece of Vasilii Andreevich Zhukovsky and wife of Aleksandr Fedorovich Voeikov, a well-known journalist, who provided Iazykov with contacts upon his arrival in Dorpat. Aleksandra Voeikova was a model not only for Iazykov but also for other poets of the time, who named her Svetlana, after the heroine of Zhukovsky's ballad of the same title. Zhukovsky modeled his ballad after Gottfried August Bürger's "Lenore" (1773), a popular German Romantic poem of that period, but he modeled the heroine after Aleksandra herself. She was considered a beautiful and charming woman—in every respect the epitome of feminine grace that Romantic poets had come to idealize.

This ideal of feminine beauty was seen by Iazykov, in the traditional Romantic manner, as something that could purify his body and soul, raising him to a higher state of awareness. In one of the first poems addressed to her, "A. A. Voeikovoi" (To A. A. Voeikova, 1825), he wrote:

> I swear by my divinities!
> I call you genuinely!
> Already for a long while with sinful verses
> I have busied my speech,
> You are able to give fire and life
> To the singer who idolizes you,
> And nobility and modesty to his mind, to his dreams.
> With a smile I accept your bonds,
> I shall not sing of my tricks,
> Seeing you I am the favorite of the Muses,
> I am only a troubadour without you.

Dorpat University, which Iazykov attended and where he wrote some of his best poetry

Iazykov's passion for his idol waned and grew, but she nonetheless fulfilled a Romantic love for him: she remained unapproachable. Indeed, Iazykov would apparently spend entire evenings simply watching his ideal, not exchanging a word, then writing inflamed verses proclaiming his love. This practice reveals how his emotion was different from that felt during the liaison with Lileta. With the latter Iazykov experienced earthly love; yet with Voeikova he was to rediscover a new type of passion, a new manifestation of his poetic gifts. The poet summarized her role in his artistic and personal life upon her death in 1829. In the final stanza of "Vospominanie ob A. A. Voeikovoi" (Remembrance of A. A. Voeikova, 1831), Iazykov writes: "She understood each poet– / And, proud, quiet, trembling, the poet / Would bring to her his gift of worship; / And joyfully in the name of the deity, / Would gather into the choir harmonious words: / Like incense would burn inspiration." The motif of his ideal's becoming his artistic religion begins with the very opening of the work: "Already she is no more, but a paradise of holy memories she has left me."

Romantic poets extolled the artistic ideal for which they strove not only through the idealized feminine but also through an idealized historical past. Begun primarily by German Romantic writers such as Schiller and subsequently transplanted to Russia, this quest for a nationalistic Arcadia took on varied forms, from the recovery of fairy tales to long narrative poems and dramas on historical themes. Iazykov attempted both in verse. The former he attempted only in the later stages of his literary career. He wrote the latter while still a student in Dorpat. Influenced by the *Slovo o polku Igoreve* (The Lay of Igor's Campaign, approximately 1187) and by the later *Zadonshchina* (approximately 1393), the central character in Iazykov's stylizations is the *baian* (bard or singer), a proper name in *Slovo o polku Igoreve,* but one used by the Russian Romantics as an equivalent to the term *bard*. The conception of the historical bard was popularized in West European Romantic works such as the tales of Ossian, imitated from Gaelic by James MacPherson. In 1823 Iazykov composed "Pesn' Baiana" (Song of Baian), a love song supposedly written by the figure of *Slovo o polku Igoreve*. In this poem, as in his later historical works, the dominant theme is the worship of art as a true freedom that can overcome all earthly oppression. Thus Iazykov writes in his "Baian k russkomu voinu" (The Bard to the Russian Warrior, 1823)–dedicated, incidentally, to Aleksandra Voeikova: "The arm of a free man is stronger than the arm burdened by yoke.... So is the song of victory louder than the deaf clatter of chains!" Iazykov's attempts at historical ballads continued with "Uslad" (1823), "Ala" (1824), and "Evpaty" (1824). The first two works were to have been full-length narrative poems but remained fragments.

The issues of freedom are seen in the context of Anacreontic works, love poems, and historical ballads. The various generations of Soviet critics felt particularly drawn to Iazykov's so-called revolutionary poems. Certainly, the poet felt a lack of respect for the centralized authority upon which the Russian Empire was founded. Evidence suggests he also felt the same disregard for the Russian Orthodox Church, one of the pillars on which imperial rule was based. Iazykov, however, had the good fortune of studying in Dorpat, farther from the throne than he would have been otherwise. This distance worked particularly to his advantage during the Decembrist uprising of 14 December 1825, when a handful of the nobility, excited by the political situation of Western Europe they had witnessed during the War of 1812 with Napoleon (Russian soldiers had marched through the streets of Paris), attempted to overthrow the government in an abortive coup. Those poets and nobles who were more closely associated with the uprising were dealt a quick and decisive punishment: Kondratii Fedorovich Ryleev, for example, was executed in 1826. His execution prompted this short lyric from Iazykov, "Ne vy l' ubranstvo nashikh dnei" (Were You All Not the Attire of Our Days, 1826):

> Were you all not the attire of our days,
> The burning sparks of freedom?
> Ryleev died, like a criminal!
> Remember him, O Russia,
> When you arise from your chains
> And strike with thunderous might
> At the despotism of the Tsars!

This work was most likely inspired by Iazykov's brief sojourn with Aleksandr Pushkin in Trigorskoe during the summer of 1826. The estate was owned by the mother of one of Iazykov's Dorpat friends, Aleksei Nikolaevich Vul'f, to whom the young poet dedicated many lyrics. The estate was also located close to Pushkin's own estate of Mikhailovskoe. Iazykov quickly became the great poet's unabashed admirer, even though originally Iazykov had been skeptical of Pushkin's lyrics and had criticized the first chapters of *Evgeny Onegin* (Eugene Onegin, 1823–1831, published in full in 1833) as well as *Ruslan and Liudmila* (1821). However, he had a less problematic relationship with the lyrics of his other great contemporary, Evgenii Abramovich Baratynsky, who likewise took issue with some of Pushkin's works. Iazykov criticized Pushkin, as did many of the Decembrist poets, for not writing scathing critiques of the reality in which they found themselves, for having abrogated his "political" duty. In fact, after his student years, Iazykov himself concentrated on political verses, usually of a Slavophile nature and concerning Slavophile polemics.

At Trigorskoe, Iazykov began a cycle of works now known as the "Pushkin Cycle," incorporating poems written between 1826 and 1830. The most renowned of these is the pastoral lyric "Trigorskoe" (1826), dedicated to Praskoviia Aleksandrovna Osipova. The work begins with an evocation of the area's history as viewed by a freedom-loving Romantic, calling out its inherited tradition of republicanism (the German Hansa and the city of Pskov), and its role as residence of Pushkin—the "refuge of the free poet." References both to the joys of life at the estate and to Pushkin follow. Then come what William Edward Brown has called "two of the most successful of Yazykov's landscapes." Nikolai Gogol and generations of subsequent critics have commented on the motion inherent in Iazykov's landscapes—the shade trembles; the valley grows empty; the breeze whispers in the darkening wood; and the moon has been enveloped. Brown notes that the style is atypical of Iazykov's body of work and most likely reveals the influence and help of Pushkin.

Iazykov later does not hesitate to praise his new friendship with the greater poet. In his epistle "A. S. Pushkinu" (To A. S. Pushkin, 1826) he declaims their union as poets: "Two sons of Orthodox Rus', / Two firstborn of the northern muses, / Willfully established / Our poetic union." The poetic union with Pushkin and the stay at Trigorskoe brought about the most mature period in Iazykov's verse. His praise of freedom had continued to develop; yet, upon his return to Dorpat this concept becomes less private and personalized and more conventional and abstract—in line with the Romantic philosophers he undoubtedly studied. After the tragedy of 1825 he turned inward, as did many of his contemporaries. In "K muze" (To the Muse, 1827) his poetic inspiration appears to him "v tishine" (in the stillness) and reveals to him the "velikii mir uedinen'ia" (great world of solitude). It is not surprising, then, that his inevitable departure from his seven-year life at Dorpat brought about great changes.

Iazykov left Dorpat for Moscow in the spring of 1829. His impatience with the bustle of existence in Moscow made itself clear poetically. He pined for his lost student life, which he realized would never return. In his "Proshchal'naia pesn'" (Parting Song, 1829), the fifth portion of a cycle called "Pesni" (Songs), he writes: "And to me, my friends, a sacred joy / Will remain the happy dream / Of you and Dorpat, of the dear places / Where I strolled, young and inspired, / Where I sang with you: everything is but a momentary vanity!"

His new Moscow circle, however, was comprised of Slavophile poets and thinkers, including the Kireevsky brothers (Ivan and Petr Vasil'evich) and the poet Karolina Karlovna Pavlova. This circle proved to be a natural, though literarily unfortunate continuation of Iazykov's interests in the themes of history and freedom. The Slavophile movement emerged concurrently with Russian

Romanticism; it had at its core the notion that Russia would rediscover its existence by itself and through itself. Poetically speaking, this meant a return to Russian genres and motifs, as well as an abandonment of light "occasional" verse. Politically, it implied a return to the perceived values of the peasantry, who were hopelessly idealized. The movement is pure Romanticism. Iazykov quickly furthered his beliefs in the sanctity of the Russian Orthodox Church and the role of Russia throughout Europe. As he explains in his poem "A. N. Vul'fu" (To A. N. Vul'f, 1833), he has abandoned his antics of the past and turned his poetic gifts to the service of Holy Russia. The end result is the obliteration of his literary stature.

During the period from 1833 to 1846 Iazykov produced little verse of worth. He did, however, attempt the second method of reclaiming the national fictionalized past, as mentioned earlier—the fairy tale. These re-created fairy tales and the historical ballads that frequently go with them are attempts at projecting an Arcadia into a future utopia. As much as they idealize a past, they implicitly project that same ideal past into a newly created ideal future. For someone with political persuasions as strong as Iazykov's, this idea is of major importance. Iazykov probably first attempted the genre of the artistic fairy tale as a result of Pushkin's success with his *Skazki* (Fairy Tales, 1828–1834) and made his first foray into the genre with *Skazka o pastukhe i dikom vepre* (Tale of the Shepherd and the Wild Boar, 1835). His second attempt was *Zhar-Ptitsa* (The Firebird, 1836), a work of twenty-two cantos. Both of these poems attempt to create a new form of lyric fairy tale, but both have the shortcoming that the characterization is not sufficient—the personalities lack depth and development. Iazykov uses anachronistic detailing and vocabulary to convey a new genre, but these devices merely impede the naturalness of the language itself. After these works, the poet attempted yet again a new twist on the genre—a tale from daily life: *Serzhant Surmin (byl')* (Sergeant Surmin—A Real-life Tale, 1839). In it Iazykov addresses the issue of compulsive gambling in a colloquial style that largely vanished from his later verse.

A solitary incursion into verse drama might be mentioned as well. Iazykov's work of 1844 *Otrok Viachko* (The Page Viachko) is perhaps a reaction to, or influenced by, Pushkin's *Boris Godunov* (1825) in that it also takes an historical account—here from *Povest' vremennykh let* (Tale of Bygone Years, also known as the Primary Chronicle, compiled and revised by Nestor circa 1113) and develops a Romantic narrative around it. Yet, the most striking of Iazykov's narrative poems is the last. *Lipy* (The Lindens, 1846)—though refused for publication by the Moscow censors—deals with the corruption of government and its disregard for the individuals who give it its right to govern. A prince in Moscow has ordered that a boulevard be lined with linden trees within eight days. The bureaucrats commandeer the trees that adorn two citizens' gardens. There is no question of their authority:

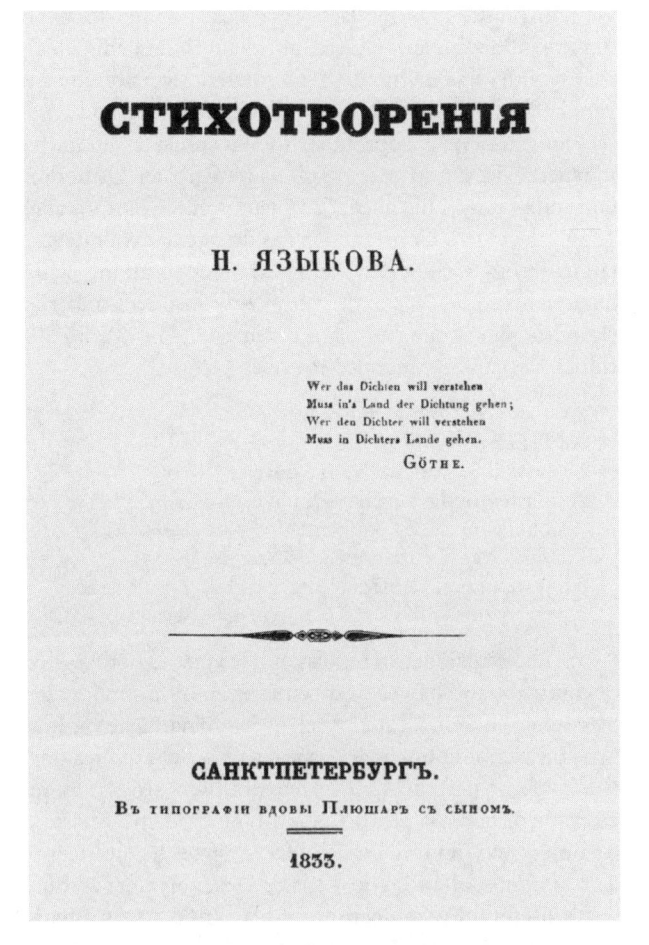

Title page for Stikhotvoreniia (Poems), Iazykov's first collection, which includes the so-called Pushkin Cycle, written at Trigorskoe, Pushkin's estate, where Iazykov was a guest in summer 1826

"Papa, papa, go right away to the garden,
Maman is sick—thieves came to the garden
And took our linden trees." He runs.
And what does he see: collapsed in a dead heap lies
His Alina. At that moment they bled
her—the blood hardly flowed.
Unhappy husband! Alina has died!

The innocent pay the price for the whims of those in power—a theme that is demonstrated throughout Iazykov's poetry.

These attempts at fairy tales and narrative verse are nestled within a copious quantity of the xenophobic Slavophile verse that formed the predominant quantity of Iazykov's efforts during his later periods. After a four-year retreat to Simbirsk (1832–1836), his developing spinal disease forced him to travel to Western Europe in search of treatment. Though not rabidly xenophobic during his stays abroad (during 1837 to 1842 he traveled through

Germany and France), Iazykov quickly seems to have developed a dislike for Germans, even though his idealized youth was spent at a German university in the Empire. He divided the world between Russians and *nenashi* (not ours). As is appropriate to Slavophile tradition, he pursued a firm and true belief in the Russian Orthodox Church. Thus in his poem "Zemletriasen'e" (Earthquake, 1844), the city of Constantinople is threatened with devastation by an earthquake, despite the supplications of its inhabitants. Then a youth is heavenly inspired, and the churches join in the chorus of his prayer. The work concludes with an invocation to the poet:

> So you, poet, in the time of terror
> And shaking of the earth
> Be carried in spirit above the dust,
> And listen to the angelic assemblies,
> And bring to the quaking men
> Prayers from the mountainous heights,
> That we may take them to heart and be
> Saved by our faith.

The remainder of his Slavophile verse is not worthy of comment and has been criticized even by his moderate Slavophile contemporaries, such as Karolina Pavlova. It is generally ignored by Soviet critics, and Brown quotes one work ("K ne nashim" [To Those Not Ours, 1844]) as an example of Iazykov at his worst. In these poems, Iazykov becomes petty and vindictive. Yet, despite the shortcomings of almost all of Iazykov's later verse, his uneven output is useful for a comparison of his early successes with the occasional spark toward the end of his career. They permit the reader to confirm the lyric brilliance of much of his early work. There are a few poems that deserve specific mention, however. One outstanding example of Iazykov's later political verse is "D. V. Davydovu" (To D. V. Davydov, 1835). Dedicated and addressed to Denis Vasil'evich Davydov (a fighter of the War of 1812 and member of the Arzamas group, primarily noted for his rousing and earthy soldier poems), the work is striking if only because of Iazykov's obvious enthusiasm for a work dedicated to a man he was too young to have met.

Iazykov's early Anacreontic verse solidified his reputation as a Russian Romantic poet. During his Dorpat years he created verse that glittered in technical and linguistic brilliance. He expanded the definition of poetic genres, to which his erotic elegies can attest. He also wrote other elegies, on political and personal themes. His poetry was best when it concentrated on the personal. Iazykov was not able to translate abstract political beliefs into verse without becoming didactic. Despite this drawback, his reputation as an innovator in Russian Romantic poetry remains assured.

Letters:

Pisma N. M. Iazykova k rodnym za derptskii period ego zhizni (1822–1829), edited by Evgenii Viacheslavovich Pietukhov (St. Petersburg: Izd. Otd-niia russkago iazyka i slovesnosti Imp. Akademii nauk, 1913);

Pisma P. V. Kireevskogo-k N. M. Iazykovu, edited by Mark Konstantinovich Azadovsky (Moscow: Izd-vo Akademii nauk SSSR, 1935).

Biography:

D. Iazykov, *N. M. Iazykov, biograficheskii ocherk* (Moscow, 1903).

References:

Mark Konstantinovich Azadovsky, "Sud'ba literaturnogo nasledstva N. M. Iazykova," *Literaturnoe nasledstvo,* 19–21 (1935): 341–370;

Vissarion Grigor'evich Belinsky, *Vzgliad na russkuiu literaturu* (Moscow: Sovremennik, 1988);

William Edward Brown, *A History of Russian Literature of the Romantic Period,* volume 3 (Ann Arbor, Mich.: Ardis, 1986);

Benjamin Dees, "Yazykov's Lyric Poetry," *Russian Literature Triquarterly,* 10 (1974): 316–329;

E. I. Khan, "K Voprosu o zhanrakh liriki N. M. Iazykova," *Vestnik Moskovskogo Universiteta. Seriia VII, Filologiia, Zhurnalistika,* no. 5 (1979): 31–38;

Ian K. Lilly, "N. M. Iazykov as a Slavophile Poet," *Slavic Review,* 31 (1972): 797–804;

Iurii Vladimirovich Mann, *Poetika russkogo romantizma* (Moscow: Nauka, 1976);

Sergei Mitrotanovich Petrov, ed., *Istoriia russkoi literatury XIX veka* (Moscow: Prosveshchenie, 1970);

Aleksandr Sergeevich Pushkin, *Mysli o literature* (Moscow: Sovremennik, 1988);

Stanislav Borisovich Rassadin, "Drama Nikolaia Iazykova," *Voprosy Literatury,* no. 8 (1979): 158–195;

Rassadin, *Sputniki: Del'vig, Iazykov, Davydov, Benediktov, Viazemsky* (Moscow: Sovetskii pisatel', 1983);

Irina Mikhailovna Semenko, *Poety pushkinskoi pory* (Moscow-Leningrad: Khudozhestvennaia literatura, 1970);

Victor Terras, ed., *Handbook of Russian Literature* (New Haven, Conn.: Yale University Press, 1985);

Iurii Nikolaevich Tynianov, *Arkhaisty i novatory* (Leningrad: Priboi, 1929);

Petr Andreevich Viazemsky, "Iazykov–Gogol'," in *Estetika i literaturnaia kritika* (Moscow: Iskusstvo, 1984), pp. 162–187;

"Yazykov's Unpublished Erotica," *Russian Literature Triquarterly,* 10 (1974): 408–413.

Papers:

Nikolai Mikhailovich Iazykov's papers are located in the Institute of Russian Literature (Pushkinskii dom) and the Russian National Library in St. Petersburg. Some papers are also located in the Russian State Library in Moscow.

Pavel Aleksandrovich Katenin
(11 December 1792 - 23 May 1853)

Vladimir Shatskov
St. Petersburg University of Civil Engineering and Architecture

BOOKS: *Esfir'. Tragediia iz sviashchennogo pisaniia. Sochineniie Rasina* (St. Petersburg: F. Drekhsler, 1816);

Spletni. Komediia v trekh deistviiakh, v stikhakh. Podrazhanie Gressetovoi komedii "Le Mechant" (St. Petersburg: N. Grech, 1821);

Sid. Tragediia v piati deistviiakh Sochinenie P. Kornelia (St. Petersburg, 1822);

Govorit' pravdu—poteriat' druzhbu, Podrazhenie komedii Marivo "Les sinceres" (St. Petersburg, 1826);

Obman v pol'zu liobvi. Komediia v trekh deistviiakh Marivo "Les fausses confidences" (St. Petersburg, 1827);

Andromakha. Tragediia v 5-ti deistviiakh (St. Petersburg: N. Grech, 1827);

Sochineniia i perevody v stikhakh s priobshcheniem neskol'kikh stikhotvorenii kniazia Nikolaia Golitsina, 2 parts (St. Petersburg: vdova Pliushara, 1832);

Kniazhna Milusha. Skazka (St. Petersburg: Kh. Gintse, 1834).

Editions and Collections: *Stikhotvoreniia*, edited by Vladimir Nikolaevich Orlov (Leningrad: Sovetskii pisatel', 1937; second edition, 1954);

Izbrannye proizvedeniia, edited by G. V. Ermakova-Bitner (Leningrad: Sovetskii pisatel', 1965);

Razmyshleniia i razbory, edited by Leonid Genrikhovich Frizman (Moscow: Iskusstvo, 1981);

Izbrannoe, edited by Aleksandr I. Kazintsev (Moscow: Sovetskaia Rossiia, 1989).

PLAY PRODUCTIONS: *Ariadna*, translation of Thomas Corneille's *Ariane*, St. Petersburg, 3 February 1811;

Esfir'. Tragediia iz sviashchennogo pisaniia. Sochineniie Rasina, St. Petersburg, Bolshoi Theater, 3 May 1816;

Goratsii, translation of Pierre Corneille's *Horace*, Petersburg Theater, 29 October 1817;

Medeia, St. Petersburg, Bolshoi Theater, 15 May 1819;

Spletni. Komediia v trekh deistviiakh, v Stikhakh. Podrazhanie Gressetovoi komedii "Le Mechant," St. Petersburg, Bolshoi Theater, 31 December 1820;

Sid. Tragediia v piati deistviiakh Sochinenie P. Kornelia, St. Petersburg, Bolshoi Theater, 4 December 1822;

Pavel Aleksandrovich Katenin

Andromakha. Tragediia v 5-ti deistviiakh, St. Petersburg, Bolshoi Theater, 3 February 1827.

SELECTED PERIODICAL PUBLICATIONS—
UNCOLLECTED: "Vospominaniia o Pushkine," edited by Iurii Oksman, *Literaturnoe nasledstvo*, 16-18 (1934): 619-656;

"Epigrammy iz antologii–Epigrammy svoi–Novokreshchennomu," *Uchebnik Leningradskogo universiteta*, no. 33 (1939): 292-303;

Topor. Basnia, edited by Vladimir Nikolaevich Orlov, *Literaturnoe nasledie*, 60 (1956): 583-586.

In the history of Russian culture it would be difficult to find a figure more enigmatic than Pavel Katenin. A member of a secret revolutionary society, the *Soiuz Spaseniia* (Union of Salvation), he remained a "Decembrist without December," for on the day of the 1825 uprising he was far from the scene of the action. A man of broad education and a sharp mind, he nevertheless seemed to many of his contemporaries to be a literary retrograde. His artistic views frequently provoked heated polemics in literary circles. Late in the 1820s, under the general rubric of *Razmyshleniia i razbory* (Considerations and Critiques) his aesthetic articles were published in the *Literaturnaia gazeta* (Literary Gazette). These articles reflected the contradictions of the epoch in which Romanticism lost its leading role, yielding to Realism. Katenin was an innovative writer and experimenter who, from his first steps into Russian literature, devoted himself to the quest for distinctive national development. More than any of Aleksandr Pushkin's other contemporaries, Katenin approached closest to the great poet in the understanding of reality, its transformation, its movement, and the necessity of reflecting this movement in concrete national and historical forms. Historicism, which characterized Katenin's philosophy, found theoretical and artistic/stylistic expression in his oeuvre. As a writer he belonged to Russian revolutionary Romanticism, in the bosom of which the principles of the classical realistic method, including historicism, were nurtured.

On 11 December 1792, at the estate of Shaevo in Kostroma province, Pavel Aleksandrovich Katenin was born into a family belonging to an ancient noble clan. Little is known about his childhood, but as a fourteen-year-old youth he arrived in St. Petersburg and entered the service of the Ministry of Public Education. In 1810 he gave this job up in favor of a military career, becoming an ensign in the Preobrazhensky Life Guard Regiment. While serving as a soldier he also involved himself in the literary life of the capital: he visited the salons, in particular the society that met at the home of Aleksei Nikolaevich Olenin, the well-known connoisseur and lover of antiquities who published the first of Katenin's poems in the journal *Tsvetnik* (Flower Garden).

There were then many literati among the Preobrazhensky officers: Sergei Nikiforovich Marin, the poet-satirist and author of lyric songs in the folk spirit; Sergei Pavlovich Potemkin, the translator from the French of Jean Racine's tragedy *Athalie* (1691), which had been successfully performed on the St. Petersburg stage; and P. F. Shaposhnikov, Katenin's closest friend. They were frequent visitors at Gavriil Romanovich Derzhavin's literary evenings, and connections with such well-known figures were of great significance for Katenin's literary development. On 3 February 1811 *Ariadna,* Katenin's translation of Thomas Corneille's tragedy *Ariane* (Ariadne, 1672) premiered in St. Petersburg. The piece was a success; its leading role became the favorite of the famous actress Ekaterina Semenova, and the public regarded the young translator as a promising poet-dramatist.

In 1812 Katenin and his regiment fought at Borodino, Lutzen, Bautzen, and Kulm and at Leipzig, "the battle of the nations." At Borodino the Preobrazhensky Guards were in the center, under the enemy artillery crossfire. At Kulm, for ten hours, they repulsed attacks by the enemy's best forces; for the rest of his life, Katenin was proud of his part in this battle. In 1814 Katenin's regiment entered Paris and spent two months there. He employed this time familiarizing himself with the French stage, meeting such famous actors as François Joseph Talma and Mars (the stage name of Anne François Hyppolyte Boutet), and seriously interesting himself in the problems of their craft. These activities had a great effect on the formation of Katenin's own views concerning the nature of dramatic art. Upon returning home to St. Petersburg, he coached the rising young actor Vasilii Andreevich Karatygin, who successfully made a debut on 3 May 1820 in the main role of Vladislav Aleksandrovich Ozerov's 1805 tragedy *Fingal*. Karatygin went on to become one of the leading Russian actors of the times, and Katenin became known as "the tsar of the Russian stage."

For Katenin, as for any man of Decembrist views, the theater was a powerful means of social enlightenment, a platform that had to be used to introduce the leading ideas into social consciousness. The Decembrists, and Katenin in particular, regarded the stage as one of the means of political agitation. The times in which Katenin lived, times of social shocks, revolutions, and national liberation movements, aroused interest in the history of Russia and other nations, and on the whole, historical questions gained significance in association with the acute problems of the day. The majority of plays that were close to the Decembrists' dramaturgic principles were the Romantic historical tragedies in which the fundamental clash was a collision between freedom-loving individuals and an unjust social system. Exactly such a piece was Racine's *Athalie,* which Katenin translated in 1815. So much of it was devoted to struggle against cruel and unjust power that it attracted the censor and was neither published nor preserved in the archives.

Katenin critically valued the Romantic works of Friedrich Schiller and George Gordon, Lord Byron, and he considered that a dramatic work could not reflect the personal form of the author's thought alone. Above all, Katenin required of a dramatist that he observe the historical coloration of the time and place. Actually, exact local color is why he valued so highly Racine's *Britannicus* (1669), *Bajazet* (1672), and *Esther* (1689). Katenin's second most important task for the dramatist was the creation of historically true characters. A similarity of views concerning historical drama was what led to the friendship between Katenin and Pushkin.

Like many other participants in the Russian army's foreign campaigns, Katenin returned home a convinced opponent of both autocracy and serfdom. He was one of several advocates of impatient and radical action who banded together in the *Soiuz Spaseniia* or the *Obshchestvo istinnykh i vernykh synov otechestva* (Society of the True and Faithful Sons of the Fatherland). The Decembrists Ivan Dmitrievich Iakushkin, Aleksandr Nikolaevich Murav'ev, and Ivan Grigor'evich Burtsov attested to Katenin's participation in this radical group, and Pavel Ivanovich Pestel', one of the leaders of the Decembrist movement, pointed out the important role played by Katenin in the *Voennoe obshchestvo,* (Military Society), formed in 1817 at Moscow as an intermediary organization between the *Soiuz Spaseniia* and the *Soiuz Blagodenstviia* (Union of Welfare). It is obvious from Murav'ev's deposition to the authorities after the 1825 revolt that in Moscow, in 1817, an attempt on the life of Alexander I was proposed. The brothers Nikita Mikhailovich and Artemon Mikhailovich Murav'ev volunteered to kill the tsar; Nikita was then Katenin's closest friend. Political radicalism was reflected in Katenin's literary activity: *Tsinna,* his 1817 translation of an excerpt from Pierre Corneille's *Cinna* (1641), published in *Syn otechestva* (Son of the Fatherland) in 1818, includes a covert political signal asserting the right to destroy a tsar-tyrant. In 1817 Katenin also published in *Syn otechestva* his "Ugolini," a fragment from Dante's *Inferno* in which the government is censured. In light of the fact that in 1817 members of the secret societies were considering regicide, the theme of treason in Katenin's works acquires an important political significance.

There are no documents proving that Katenin was a member of the *Soiuz Blagodenstviia,* the successor to the *Soiuz Spaseniia*. It is possible that he did not agree with its tactic of "gradual action on opinion." There is, however, Evgenii Petrovich Obolensky's testimony in his memoirs that in 1819 Katenin joined the *Soiuz dobra i pravdy* (Union of the Good and the True), a political society that, according to its statutes, prepared new decrees, projects, and laws concerning serf emancipation and constitutionalism. In essence the creed of the *Soiuz dobra i pravdy* differed little from that of the *Soiuz Blagodenstviia;* the former assisted in the greatest extension of the influence of the latter and functioned as the herald of its ideas. The *Soiuz dobra i pravdy* did not last

Vasilii Andreevich Karatygin, for whom Katenin was a mentor, in the role of Hamlet

long, but Katenin's participation in it demonstrated that he had not abandoned his radical views, even after 1817.

In those years (1815–1820) there was in St. Petersburg a famous and popular literary salon called "Shakhovskoi's Attic" after its host, Aleksandr Aleksandrovich Shakhovskoi, to whom Katenin had the honor of introducing Pushkin in 1818. In "Shakhovskoi's Attic" the critical relationship to Schiller's Romantic theater was formed, and an interest in the classic French drama of Racine and Pierre Corneille was begun. The dramatist and diplomat Aleksandr Sergeevich Griboedov also visited this salon, and in 1817, in collaboration with Griboedov, Katenin wrote the comedic prose pamphlet "Student" (The Student), which was not published or performed. It is impossible to establish the degree of his contribution, but it was probably not inconsiderable.

In general, Russian comedy of the first two decades of the nineteenth century rarely rose above the genre of the dramatic sketch. Katenin's successfully staged 1820 comedy *Spletni* (The Gossip), a free imitation of Jean-Baptiste-Louis Gresset's *Le Méchant* (The

Wicked One, 1747), is interesting as an attempt to create a satiric work that would carry on the tradition of Denis Ivanovich Fonvizin. Katenin even underscores a connection with Fonvizin by introducing a direct reference to the central character of Fonvizin's well-known comedy *Nedorosl'* (The Minor, 1783). There is also a parallel between Katenin's hero, Zel'sky, and Chatsky, the hero of Griboedov's comedy *Gore ot uma* (Woe from Wit, finished between 1823 and 1824), although it goes no farther than the fact that they are both intelligent and critical of Moscow society. In distinction from Chatsky, Katenin depicts Zel'sky as a sated and empty man who amuses others only out of boredom. This personage is an early prototype of the charming skeptics frequently met in Russian literature who were, according to Katenin, fatally "demonic" heroes.

The governmental harassment that Katenin underwent beginning in 1820 obviously restricted his participation in the activities of the secret societies after that date. He became a colonel in 1818, but in September 1820 the upward curve of his military career was broken, and he was unexpectedly retired from service. Clearly, the real reason for this dismissal was his political radicalism. In an unpublished article by Petr Andreevich Karatygin, however, there is an interesting story about the ostensible cause seized upon by the establishment to justify Katenin's early retirement:

> As a commander, Katenin's humane manner toward the lower ranks made him a pleasant exception to the military practices of those times; as a comrade he was sincerely loved by his peers, and because of this, as a subordinate he was unable to get along with his superiors, especially on those occasions when their reprimands were unjust. The grand prince Mikhail Pavlovich conducted an unannounced review of Katenin's battalion. Inspecting the soldiers' uniforms with his characteristic attentiveness, his Highness was unexpectedly astounded by a patch on the sleeve of one of the soldiers or non-commissioned officers. Having beckoned to Katenin, the grand prince pointed out this flaw in the uniform, and harshly inquired: "What's this? A hole?" "Nothing of the sort," Katenin responded. "It is a patch, so there won't be a hole." For this retort, Katenin was sent into retirement.

Katenin's quarrel with a representative of the ruling family was a daring action, an insubordination that one would not normally make to a senior in rank, let alone to a grand prince. But in this matter Katenin acted like a typical Decembrist, insofar as one of the tasks that proceeded from his Decembrist activism was the creation of social opinion. In particular, members of the secret societies considered it important to influence their younger peers. As a reporter for the Third Section (the secret police) later recorded: "Colonel Katenin was the oracle of the Preobrazhensky Regiment and the governor of the young officers' opinions and actions." Furthermore, by intervening for a simple soldier Katenin strove to protect him, because a "lower rank" was liable to severe punishment for any infraction, even the tiniest imaginable.

Following his retirement, Katenin continued to devote himself to the theater. In 1822 he wrote *Sid,* a translation of Corneille's *Le Cid* (1637). It was a free translation, and Katenin introduced much bravery and will to victory into the character of the heroes while weakening and shortening the love scenes. His revolutionary and antimonarchic inclinations are revealed, for example, in the fact that when Corneille's Cid, conforming to courtly etiquette in telling of a battle, speaks first of the king and not of the fatherland, Katenin's translation of this strophe reverses the order and assigns the king to last place. Another, similar, transposition is also not accidental: the contrast between the characters of the pitiful and defeated king and that of the Cid, the savior of the fatherland who strikes the telling final blow for freedom, would, of course, have been met with understanding on the part of the young Decembrists. Katenin's rendition greatly pleased Pushkin, but nonetheless, the critics reproached the translator because he departed from the "elevated style" of tragedy by having his heroes speak in the style of simple and ordinary people.

On 4 December 1822 *Sid* premiered at the St. Petersburg Bolshoi Theater, but the translator's chair was empty, for he had been exiled. This banishment may have been provoked by the antimonarchic elements in the play; but as in the case of his military retirement, there is only anecdotal evidence concerning the reason. The story goes that Katenin was indicted for "chicanery in a theater." On 17 September 1822 there was a performance of Ozerov's *Poliksena* (Polyxena), with Vasilii Karatygin superb in the role of Pirros, and Polyxena played by the untalented but comely M. A. Azarevicheva, the protégée of St. Petersburg governor-general Mikhail Andreevich Miloradovich. Katenin applauded the talented Karatygin but hissed at the mediocre actress, an action that was seen as politically nuanced. The government seized upon this incident to rid the capital of the free-thinking Katenin, but his contemporaries considered the real reasons to have been his membership in a secret society and his attempts to create a certain social opinion.

The imperial *ukaz* (order) of exile that Katenin received on the morning of 7 November banned him from residence in either of the capital cities, and by early December he was at his estate of Shaevo in Kostroma province, where he spent three long years in the backwoods under police surveillance. Even in these circumstances, however, he remained faithful to his political views. There were instances in which he granted freedom to his peasants and endeavored to assist them in lean years. In October 1824, upon learning that Tsar Alexander was to visit the province, Katenin sought to absent himself so as to avoid a meeting. Meanwhile the tsar became interested in the case of his disgraced, retired colonel, and yielding to the persuasive arguments of Vasilii Karatygin and Griboedov, Katenin submitted a request for leniency. It was granted in August 1825, and Katenin then returned to the capital.

He was in St. Petersburg on the fateful day of 14 December 1825 but did not take part in the uprising. Katenin was subsequently interrogated by the investigatory commission, but there was no evidence of his participation in the *Severnoe obshchestvo* (Northern Society), and the government was not much interested in earlier revolutionary associations. After the inquiry Katenin's name was entered in a "List of members of former evil-intentioned secret societies" with the notation: "highly recommend no further attention." The times consequent upon 14 December, when on one side there were the investigations and judgments of the Decembrists, and on the other, the solemnities leading to the coronation of Tsar Nicholas, were "black days" for Katenin. When five of the Decembrist leaders were executed in the outworks of the Peter-Paul Fortress, fear and despair possessed the core of the gentry intelligentsia.

For his part, Katenin returned to the drama. His greatest dramatic work, that which occupied the whole period from 1810 to 1822, was his original tragedy *Andromakha* (Andromache). He began it in 1809, completed the first version in 1818, but did not publish the piece until 1827. The first notable thing about the play is its connection to a certain historical period: that of the Decembrists. Although the tragedy includes no exact contemporary parallels or any open appeals to struggle against tyranny, in spirit it has to be classified as Decembrist because all of the heroine's thoughts, feelings, and actions are organically defined by her inherent free thinking and refusal to submit to force. As in his other works, Katenin remains faithful to the principle of historicism. Historical tonality is strictly maintained: the style of *Andromakha* is close to that of antique tragedy, and the exploits of the heroes are conditioned by the morals, customs, and prejudices of those times. Having renounced any kind of external effects, undertakings, and intrigues, Katenin concentrates all his attention on the behavior and psychology of the characters. The piece depicts a solitary, strong, and suffering woman in opposition to a cruel society.

Katenin chose for *Andromakha* those limitations of Racine's classical tragedy that he considered most appropriate to his two main tasks: the psychological disclosure of the heroes' characters and an adequate depiction of the ancient times in which the action was set. Nevertheless, in his psychological depictions Katenin far overstepped the bounds of classicism. It was impossible for him to provide his many-sided hero with a monosemantic characteristic. A warrior trained for combat, brave and daring, Katenin's Pyrrhus steps forward as his father's avenger, but from another angle he is seen as almost tender and, in the depths of his soul, neither ill-willed nor vengeful. Pyrrhus loves Andromache and on her account makes enemies of his former friends. But she, by force of character, does not give in to him. She might well have been charmed by such a gifted and many-sided hero, but for her he was, above all, an enslaver. Happy love between a conqueror and his captive would have contradicted the author's freedom-loving ideas. Civic duty and the pathos of love for the fatherland: these were the main stuff of tragedy. Born into Russian literature in the early years, the idea of citizenship is a thread through all the literature of the nineteenth century.

According to Katenin, part of the historical environment was the intervention of the gods. Indeed, according to the ancients, life and death depended upon an implacable, superhuman, divine power. Here Romanticism opposed the oversimplified and abstract treatment of humanity characteristic of classicism. There are also strong Romantic elements in *Andromakha*. When speaking of the interweaving of classical and Romantic methods in tragedy, one must recall the general situation in literature during the first decades of the nineteenth century: the collision of Romanticism (and the Sentimentalism of Karamzin and his followers) and emergent Realism. Katenin's significance consists of the fact that he was one of the first to open up this transitional period. Perhaps his concept of the tasks of literature was still too narrow and did not decisively break with the Romantic method, and perhaps Katenin lacked the broad view of historical conflict; but nonetheless, he made the first steps in this direction. It is no accident that Pushkin considered tragedy as one model for the depiction of the individual character, although he also noted that tragedy speaks too much of the fate of heroes and too little about that of the people.

Andromakha finally premiered at the St. Petersburg Bolshoi Theater on 3 February 1827, but it failed to find favor among the public and was withdrawn from the repertory after three or four performances. Katenin was profoundly shaken by the event and bore the marks of it for the rest of his life. *Andromakha* was his "pride and joy," and he considered it to be his real contribution to literature.

Title page for Kniazhna Milusha. Skazka *(Princess Milusha. A Tale), one of Katenin's narrative poems*

Katenin had also made some contributions in the field of poetry. In 1810 he had begun publishing a few of his poems in *Tsvetnik*. (In those days Vasilii Andreevich Zhukovsky, Konstanin Nikolaevich Batiushkov, and Prince Petr Andreevich Viazemsky, all followers of Nikolai Mikhailovich Karamzin's literary school, ruled the Olympian heights of poetry. Hypertrophic sensitivity and a dreamy divorce from reality were characteristic of the "Karamzinists." (The actual term "writer-Karamzinists" was introduced in the 1966 book *Pushkin i ego sovremenniki* [Pushkin and his Contemporaries] by the Soviet scholar Iurii Nikolaevich Tynianov.) The social, and even more so, the political, aspects of life generally did not interest the poets and writers of Sentimentalist inclination. Extreme individualism was inherent in all Karamzinists, so that, according to Zhukovsky, the world presents itself only as a stage on which the human soul reveals its secrets. Similarly characteristic were the stylistics and the lexicon of the poet-Karamzinists. There was not a single poem of theirs in which a reader would not encounter "languorous sighs," "gentle dreams," or "downcast gazes."

Along with his friends from the Preobrazhensky Regiment, Marin and Shaposhnikov, Katenin immediately came out against the Karamzinists, against their social indifference and their immersion in personal experience. Civic pathos could already be heard in Katenin's poetry. In "Pevets uslad" (The Singer of Delights, 1810–1812), published in *Vestnik Evropy* (The Herald of Europe) in 1818, the form of the fatherland appears as the *Sviataia Rus'* (Holy Rus') that the lyric hero will defend from enemies and that he will long for when he finds himself in alien lands. An aesthetic strictness in Katenin's style was almost determined by a feeling of protest against the sweetness and mannerism typical of many Sentimentalists. In his selection of a means of expression, he inclined to the laconic, not suffering any adornment. One of his first poems, "Idiliia" (Idyll, 1809), published in *Tsvetnik* in 1810, serves as an example.

In the romance "Pevets uslad" and the elegy "Grust' na korable" (Shipboard Grief), included in Katenin's first collection, popular speech forms appear. Katenin even employs nonliterary, common words. Interestingly, while polemicizing against the Karamzinists, Katenin used their own characteristically "diminutive" forms, the elegy and the romance, which took on a new tone and direction under his control. The ballad, however, is the form with which Katenin really engaged the Karamzinists in battle. In his body of work Katenin set himself the task of the utmost precision in depicting Russian culture and in depicting the details of landscape and everyday life, of striving to communicate the ways of the people. Katenin's simple, popular ballads were among his most successful attempts to convey the uniqueness of Russian national culture. They may be classified as works of a Decembrist inclination since they were perceived as forms of the native and popular literature for which the members of the secret societies struggled.

Clarity in moral and ethical values, expressed in aphorisms similar to popular proverbs and sayings, is a common characteristic of these ballads. Such an approach was also used by Vil'gel'm Karlovich Kiukhel'beker, the poet-Decembrist and friend of Pushkin. Utmost simplicity and even naïveté was the subject of Katenin's first ballad, "Natasha" (1814), which was shot through with patriotic ideas. In this ballad, published in *Syn otechestva* in 1815, Katenin sought to depict the most essential side of the Russian national character. He thought that the principle feature of his heroine was her willingness to act for the sake of saving the fatherland. An ordinary girl who lives only to love her fiancé, she sends him to death in battle, having resolved on a self-sacrificing deed.

In his ballad "Leshii" (The Wood-Goblin), which also appeared in *Syn otechestva* in 1815, Katenin describes a fantastic world born of the popular tale. Despite its fairy-tale content, this poem is saturated with concrete detail from the life of the people. There is nothing in it of the strictly fantastic and horrible with mystical overtones such as in Zhukovsky's ballads. The only aspect of "Leshii" that elicits any feeling of watchfulness and fear is the haughty and malicious appearance of the main character. In opposition to the lyric subjectivism of Zhukovsky and his circle, Katenin proposes the objective depiction of actuality.

"Ol'ga" (1816), one of Katenin's programmatic works, a translation of the 1773 ballad "Lenore" by Gottfried August Bürger, touched off a literary dispute on the pages of the journal *Syn otechestva,* where it was first published. This translation was a direct challenge to Zhukovsky, who in 1808 had published his own imitation of "Lenore": the ballad "Liudmila." The leading literati of the day took part in the resulting dispute concerning Katenin's version. The question he raised in this and other ballads was the question of genuine nationalism in literature, and he provoked the critic and publisher Nikolai Ivanovich Gnedich, the famous diplomat and writer Griboedov, and the Karamzinists Ivan Ivanovich Dmitriev, Batiushkov, and Viazemsky. Later Pushkin wrote, concerning Katenin's "Ol'ga," that he actually regarded this ballad as a model of folk art. Even Zhukovsky eventually vindicated Katenin when in 1831 he returned to Bürger's "Lenore" and created a new version of his translation that differed significantly from the one of 1808.

Like all the poet-Decembrists, Katenin recognized folklore as one of the most important sources of national literature. In his narrative poem *Mstislav Mstislavich,* published in *Syn otechestva* in 1820, he quotes the Russian epic *Slovo o polku Igoreve* (The Lay of Igor's Campaign) which, dating from the twelfth century and miraculously preserved, serves as the model for national creative motifs and popular turns of speech. *Mstislav Mstislavich* also may serve as a general example of Katenin's innovative quest for metric forms. If the Karamzinists mainly developed the iambic pentameter in Russian poetry, then Katenin created the forms of the octave and hexameter, and in his verses readers also encounter the trochee, the amphibrachic tetrameter, and the dactyl. Striving for rhythmic and intellectual expression, in *Mstislav Mstislavich* Katenin employs thirteen different poetic meters. In his work *Arkhaisty i novatory* (Archaists and Innovators, 1929) Tynianov notes that Katenin's poetry foreshadows that of Mikhail Iur'evich Lermontov, Aleksei Vasil'evich Kol'tsov, and Nikolai Alekseevich Nekrasov.

Katenin also used Church Slavonic speech in his verses. Subjected to the attacks of literary critics for this element, the poet all the same considered that literary form should correspond to content and that the use of Church Slavonic was justified and necessary when it was a question of lending historical coloration to the description of time and place. Thus, for example, Katenin's *Esfir',* an 1816 translation of Racine's *Esther,* is abundantly adorned with Church Slavonic turns of phrase justified by the fact that the action of the tragedy is set in biblical times.

Katenin's quest, his nontraditional approach to poetry, drew sharp attacks on the pages of the literary journals throughout the years 1810 to 1820. Each of his new publications provoked a squall of criticism, for his contemporaries found his verses heavy and intentionally labored. Many considered that he had been born too late. Later, in the 1830s, they called him "the poet forgotten in his own lifetime." He never obtained the glory of being a major poet. Nevertheless Katenin's contribution to the development of Russian poetic language is beyond dispute. Pushkin, Griboedov, and Kiukhel'beker all recognized Katenin's original poetic gifts. Pushkin borrowed much from Katenin, and Kiukhel'beker considered him to have been in some sense his mentor.

Katenin's poetic destiny was paradoxical. He was perceived by his contemporaries as a man of the past, as one in some degree literarily retrograde, even in the very time when his entire oeuvre was directed toward the creation of new forms in poetry. With his first poems he renounced the ruling ideology of Sentimentalism and sought to introduce new themes and forms into Russian poetry. For this effort he was much criticized by the poet-Karamzinists. After a few years, however, Karamzin and later even Zhukovsky became disappointed in the aesthetic principles of their schools, and they themselves introduced into their work themes of historicism and nationality. Karamzin wrote *Istoriia gosudarstva Rossiiskogo* (The History of the Russian State, 1816–1818; revised, 1818–1829), one of the best historical studies. Zhukovsky completed a translation of Ossian that has not yet been rendered obsolete. In these works there is much less individualism and more of the epic, the history of the people, for which they had previously criticized Katenin.

After the failure of *Andromakha* in 1827, Katenin fled to his estate in Kostroma, where he lived until 1832. During these five years he immersed himself in literature and in the history of drama. Having lost the battle on the stage, he sought to take revenge on the field of artistic theory. Perhaps in this realm he succeeded most of all, insofar as his series of critical articles published by Baron Anton Antonovich Del'vig and

Pushkin in *Literaturnaia gazeta* under the title *Razmyshleniia i razbory* may be called a landmark in the history of Russian aesthetic thought.

Katenin's involvement in the aesthetics and theoretics of literature and art had begun in 1820, when he took part in a polemic about the Russian and French theaters that broke out on the pages of the "fat" journals. At that time there formed a group of like-minded people who considered historicism, healthy thought, and nationality to be the main values of any dramatic production. Later, in 1833, the critic Ksenofont Alekseevich Polevoi wrote of them that they were literati who accepted Romanticism only under Slavonic banners. Katenin's true friend and publisher of his works, Nikolai Ivanovich Bakhtin, came to adhere to this group, along with the literary critics Dmitrii Petrovich Zykov and S. F. Iakovlev, the latter a translator of Sophocles. The unity of the group was strengthened by their proximity to Decembrism. In the literary arguments occasioned by the 1820 St. Petersburg performances of Ozerov's tragedy *Fingal,* the critic Vasilii Ivanovich Sots and the poet Viazemsky opposed Katenin's circle. They demonstrated that from the position of Romantic individualism the only elements of consequence were the experiences of the hero, whereas all the rest, including the historical place of action and the language spoken by the hero, were secondary.

In 1822 Katenin entered a polemic surrounding Nikolai Ivanovich Grech's *Opyt kratkoi istorii russkoi literatury* (An Attempt at a Short History of Russian Literature, 1822). Grech was a figure well-known in literary circles and the publisher of *Syn otechestva,* which was begun in 1812 for the purpose of stimulating patriotic sentiment. Grech's book was the first history of Russian literature, so naturally it provoked great interest among his contemporaries. Disputes flared up around the questions it raised: disputes between Katenin and Grech, between Katenin and the writer-Decembrist Aleksandr Aleksandrovich Bestuzhev (Marlinsky), and between Katenin and the critic Sosnov. In these quarrels, conducted in various journals, Katenin formulates the problems of nationality, national distinctiveness, and local color, and he attaches great importance to these so that a work will be original and not a translation. At that same time he was working on his ballads and *Andromakha*. Katenin devotes great attention to the problem of style, connecting it to that of artistic content. He wrote that every type of work demands a special style that corresponds to content, and therefore one should refuse an enticing, deliberately beautiful, facile, and easy style.

Yet, another of Katenin's undertakings was an attempt at bringing together the Russian language of his day with Slavonic and Church Slavonic. On account of this effort he was called a Slavophile, although, faithful to the idea of historicism, Katenin simply considered that the only language to employ in an historical work was the one that was close to Church Slavonic. In a series of letters to Mikhail Petrovich Pogodin and Pushkin in 1834 and 1835, Katenin emphasized that form is not something arbitrary that can change in the course of a work; that the connection between form and content is inseparable; and that the alteration of one means the alteration of the other. In this series of letters Katenin proposes that the octave is the form of strophe most suitable to the epic. A century later Tynianov wrote:

> Katenin's octave answers Pushkin's *Domik v Kolomne* (A Little House in Kolomna) although a year after Katenin's article Pushkin undertook the epic-scale novel in verse *Evgenii Onegin* (Eugene Onegin). And though Pushkin's strophe is not identical to Katenin's octave, the idea is the same: namely that a conversion in a poetic epic in and of itself entails the necessity in the strophe as a poetic means of expression of a diverse content, surmounting, and uniqueness: this very idea found embodiment in Pushkin's creativity.

The position that was established in Katenin's assertions was not appreciated for its worth. Opponents avoided discussion of those issues that Katenin considered to be the most important. Katenin presented three issues: the harm to Russian letters done by the so-called schools of literature; the preservation of the purity of the language over the course of several centuries by means of studying Church books; and the superficial success of some works, which would soon be forgotten. In these few points is the whole program of the literary struggle that Katenin developed. These questions were the subject of his attention over the course of many later years, especially in the period when he created *Razmyshleniia i razbory*.

In 1822, however, discussion was interrupted by Katenin's exile. Naturally Grech and Bestuzhev refrained from replying to the fallen literatus, although in the course of more than seven years he entrusted all of his secret thoughts and reflections concerning literature and art to the mails. Katenin's extant correspondence, most of which was written from 1822 to 1829, can be used to reconstruct to some extent the evolution of his views on literature. It is possible to ascertain how and why Katenin's relationship to Romanticism changed.

Katenin does not speak about a changed opinion of Romanticism so much as of the alteration in content, which he took to be a controlling factor. In the period from 1820 to 1822 he recognized the most important signs of Romanticism to be national distinctiveness, local color, and the inclusion of folk subjects. Time passed, however, and the evolution of Romantic literature took a turn that he could not follow because it generated forms that contradicted his notions of truth and beauty. He frequently came to use the term "Romantic" to describe artistic phenomena that were alien to him, and even distasteful. In particular, Katenin saw in Pushkin's *Bakhchisaraiskii fontan* (The Fountain of Bakhchiserai, 1822) an example of the Romantic work of which he disapproved. He also gave a severe reception to Pushkin's poem *Tsygany* (The Gypsies, 1824), Kondratii Fedorovich Ryleev's *Voinarovskii* (Voinarovsky, 1825), and Nikolai Mikhailovich Iazykov's "Razboiniki" (The Brigands, 1825). In letters to his friend Bakhtin, Katenin expresses a negative evaluation of the poems of Adam Mickiewicz and Byron. He manifests the most interest in Pushkin's work on the drama *Boris Godunov* (published in 1831), asking of the author on 14 March 1826: "How is your Godunov? How have you worked him over? In strict historical taste or in Romantic conceits?"

As a literary critic Katenin was sagacious. He was one of a few who valued and approved of the changes in Karamzin's works and views. Karamzin's name was a banner representing what Katenin had bitterly opposed for many years, but this disagreement did not hinder him from an understanding of Karamzin's role in the history of Russian culture. Katenin dared to see Karamzin in motion and development as few did, and he did not posit an equality between the later Karamzin and all that he himself had previously designated under the term "Karamzinist." Katenin notes that Karamzin's style purified itself in both poetry and prose in accordance with the spirit of the times. In a letter to Bakhtin dated 12 August 1829 the critic gave a final and reflective evaluation of Karamzin's *Istoriia gosudarstva Rossiiskogo*, praising both the massive undertaking and the undoubted social utility that would result from its publication. A person of such radical convictions as Katenin would of course have found much in Karamzin that was unacceptable, but nevertheless he emphasized that such a work had to be considered valuable and that Karamzin could be criticized only with the greatest respect.

The relationship between Pushkin and Katenin is interesting. Pushkin saw in Katenin an attentive and honest critic, paid attention to his opinion, and considered that Katenin's undoubted poetic talent certainly did not prevent him from being a subtle evaluator of literature. For example, there is the well-known critical observation that Katenin made concerning Pushkin's novel in verse, *Evgeny Onegin* (1823–1831, published in full in 1833): in one of his letters to Pushkin, Katenin observed the unjustifiable inexplicability of the transformation of Tatiana, a provincial girl, into Tatiana, the worldly lady. The poet replied that the instantaneous

Aleksei Feofilaktovich Pisemsky, a friend and protégé during the last years of Katenin's life

change in his heroine was due to the necessity of eliminating an entire chapter for other reasons.

Katenin's creative inquiries were close to Pushkin's and of much interest to the poet, especially where they touched on historicism and dramaturgy. Katenin's and Pushkin's artistic-historical conceptions coincided in the resolution of the basic problems of the representation of historical reality and of dramatic production. Both writers were of one mind concerning the determination of fundamental criteria: for both, the main goal was a truthful depiction of the historical spirit of an epoch; both came out against external imitation of its historic signs and superficial penetration into its particulars; and both advanced to the task of depiction of historical existence, historical means, and the use of the folkish lexicon and popular turns of speech.

Katenin's historicism outgrew the framework of the Romantic; including in itself elements of the realistic approach, it might be characterized as transitional between Romanticism and Realism, although it is worth noting that on a whole series of questions, Katenin's approach to Realism never reached Pushkin's level. Such was the case, for example, with Pushkin's *Boris Godunov*. Katenin did not or could not recognize the integrity of a work that, in accordance with Pushkin's innovative design, arose from "scraps" of scenes. Although Katenin even valued the style of *Boris Godunov* as the best thing about it, an understanding of the deeply authentic role of style in Pushkin's work remained obscured from him. Katenin never recognized the true unity of style in the tragedy, although Pushkin remarked that for the realization of his design it would actually be necessary to employ a mixed style, for on a single page the reader might meet vulgar expressions and elevated style, depending on the way a hero pronounces this or that word. This general correspondence of a word's style to a character was the core of the whole tragedy. Katenin did not recognize any of these points, and he reproached Pushkin for the flaccid and fragmentary depiction of the hero. Having become accustomed to the vivid representation of one or two facets of a hero in Romantic tragedy, Katenin was not able to comprehend the whole realistic complexity and many-sidedness of Pushkin's characters. Katenin's declarations about historical truth coincided with Pushkin's only when it was a question of national color or historical context, but Pushkin's objective of breadth and many-sidedness in the depiction of human character remained alien to Katenin. He did not even comprehend the importance of Pushkin's attempts to reveal historic reality by means of his characters.

Razmyshleniia i razbory is the central part of Katenin's literary legacy and is the most complete and multifaceted embodiment of his views concerning art. The seven articles that had appeared in *Literaturnaia gazeta* can give only a partial notion of the grandiose design of Katenin's tract. The idea of creating a cycle of critical and aesthetic articles occurred to him after his *Andromakha* was withdrawn from the stage and he had retreated from St. Petersburg to his Kostroma estate.

The general plan was to lop off all of antique literature from a general historical survey and to turn to the particulars of Italian, Spanish, and French literature, tracing, for instance, the development of world literature by means of the appearance in various languages of new poetic forms. If the subject of the *razbory* (critiques) was literature ancient and medieval, the *razmyshlenniia* (considerations) provoked by these critiques would bear contemporary literature in mind. The attempt to understand the past for the purpose of putting its lessons at the disposal of the present, characteristic of Decembrist thought in general, found its vivid manifestation in Katenin's aesthetic works. Much of what was written–for example, the section on French literature–was not published and was destroyed (it is not known by whom). The part of *Razmyshleniia i razbory* that did appear, however, and that was republished in 1981, is one of the most remarkable aesthetic studies from the 1820s and 1830s.

Most of Katenin's contemporaries could not appreciate the worth of his aesthetic views. Vasilii L'vovich Pushkin, the great poet's uncle and a member of the literary society "Arzamas," found Katenin's articles to be boring attempts to return to archaic views. His nephew was of a different opinion and considered Katenin to have been, from the first, one of the apostles of Russian Romanticism, the first to introduce into the exalted circle of poetry the simple expressions of the people, only then turning back to the "classic idols."

The complexity and inconsistency of Katenin's aesthetic system, which had been formed in a transitional epoch, reflected complexity and diversity in the quest for new paths of art and the study of art. A thread running through all of this super-polemical tract leads the argument out from one of the most significant Romantic aesthetic manifestos of that age: August Wilhelm Schlegel's book *Über dramatische Kunst und Litteratur: Vorlesungen* (On Dramatic Art and Literature: Lectures, 1809–1811). This book was the "gospel" of the new direction in literature. Disputing with Schlegel, however, Katenin concentrated his attention not so much on Romanticism itself as on "Romanticism á la mode," or the readiness to sacrifice elements of original and undoubted artistic value for the sake of vain attempts at conformity. Katenin frequently joined Schlegel against his followers and epigones. An almost satiric image of a Romantic-literary liberal rises from the pages of *Razmyshleniia i razbory:* one scornful of classic French theater and bored with antique art. Similar sharp opinions give Katenin the reputation of an "archaist." It must be taken into account, however, that Katenin was always an intransigent opponent of imitation and bowing to authority.

While sensing the impending decline of Romanticism, Katenin did not then comprehend the forces that would come to take its place. His view was drawn to the past, there to find models for imitation and creative material. While labeling him an "archaist," Tynianov took note of the nonmonosemanticity and inconsistency of Katenin's creative work.

After five years of writing literary criticism on his estate in Kostroma, Katenin was obliged by straitened material circumstances again to seek service. He arrived once more in St. Petersburg on 18 June 1832. He was enrolled in the Yerevan Cavalry Regiment on 8 August 1833, and on 13 March 1834 he departed for the Caucasus. Caucasian service entailed great difficulties and hardships for Katenin. There he collided with the unlimited autocracy of high-ranking persons. He discharged his military duties with honor, and in 1836

Katenin was given the command of the fortress at Kizliar and the rank of major-general. Nevertheless, he was displeasing to the leadership, and in 1838 he was let go "on orders from on high" and was retired without cause or reproach.

Going once more into retirement, Katenin headed for Shaevo, and there he spent the remaining fifteen years of his life. Alone and almost forgotten, he knew need and deprivation. In the early 1850s he carried on an active correspondence with Pavel Vasil'evich Annenkov, Pushkin's biographer, and at the request of Annenkov he wrote his "Vospominaniia o Pushkine" (Recollections of Pushkin), included in Annenkov's 1873 collection of biographical sources. Also in the 1850s he, the veteran of the Patriotic War of 1812, became the friend of the middle-class student Aleksei Feofilaktovich Pisemsky. Thanks to this friendship, scholars know something of Katenin in his last years, as he appears in Pisemsky's novel *Liudi sorokovykh godov* (Men of the 1840s, 1869) as the character Archpriest Koptin. On 9 May 1853 the aged writer suffered an accident: he was struck by horses. He lingered for two weeks, but on 23 May 1853 he died.

Katenin was a man of a difficult character: suspicious, quarrelsome, exasperating, and impatient. These qualities may explain why Katenin's influence on the minds of his contemporaries seems less than his critical talent might have commanded. Living on his estate as a recluse in his last years, he nonetheless had a great influence on his neighbor, Pisemsky, who became an outstanding figure of mid-century literary life and who considered Pavel Katenin to have been his mentor.

Letters:
"N. I. Grechu. (4) 1817–1822," *Syn otechestva*, 55, no. 33, part 76, no. 13 (1822): 334;

"N. I. Grechu i F. V. Bulgarinu. 23 dekabria 1824 g.," *Syn otechestva*, part 99, no. 3 (1825): 333–335;

"P. N. Sokolovu. 1 maia 1833 g.," edited by Mikhail Ivanovich Sukhomlinov, in his *Istoriia rossiiskoi Akademii*, volume 8 (St. Petersburg: Imperatorskaia Akademiia nauk, 1875), pp. 89–91;

"A. S. Pushkinu (14) 1825–1836," with notes by P. Bartenev, *Russkii arkhiv*, no. 1 (1881): 144–161;

"Neizvestnomu. 1 fevralia. 1831," edited by A. Stankevich, *Pomoshch' golodaiushchim* (Moscow: Russkie vedomosti, 1892), pp. 252–258;

Pis'ma P. A. Katenina k A. M. Kolosovskoi. 1822–1826 (St. Petersburg, 1892);

"A. M. Kolosovskoi. (25) 1822–1826," edited by V. F. Botsianovsky, *Russkaia starina*, no. 3 (1893): 625–656; no. 4 (1893): 179–212;

"N. I. Grechu. 18 Iulia 1924," *Russkaia starina*, no. 4 (1905): 209–210;

Pis'ma P. A. Katenin k N. I. Bakhtinu.(Materialiy dlia istorii russkoi literatury 20-kh i 30-kh godov 19 veka), edited by A. Chebyshev (St. Petersburg: t-vo "Elektrotip. N. Ia. Stoikovoi," 1911);

"M. P. Pogodinu. 28 marta 1828 g.," *Literaturnoe nasledstvo*, 16–18 (1934): 699;

"Pis'ma V. P. Annenkovu. 24 aprelia 1853 goda," *Literaturnaia kritika*, no. 7–8 (1940): 231;

"Neizvestnomu. Konets ianvaria-nachalo fevralia 1831 g.," edited by E. N. Konshinoi, *Literaturnoe nasledie*, 58 (1952): 101–102.

Biographies:
Petr Aleksandrovich Pletnev, "P. A. Katenin. Nekrolog," *Zhurnal Ministersva narodnogo prosveshcheniia*, part 81, sect. 3 (1854): 53–56;

E. V. Petukhov, "P. A. Katenin (Biograficheskii i istoriko-literaturnyi ocherk)," *Istoricheskii vestnik*, no. 9 (1888): 553–575.

References:
Mikhail Pavlovich Alekseev, "Etiudy po istorii ispano-russkikh literaturnykh otnoshenii," in *Kul'tura Ispanii* (Moscow-Leningrad: Akademiia nauk SSSR, 1940), pp. 417–423;

Pavel Vasil'evich Annenkov, *A. S. Pushkin: Materialy dlia biografii i otsenki proizvedenii* (St. Petersburg: Obshchestvennaia pol'za, 1873), pp. 50–56;

Nikolai Ivanovich Bakhtin, as G., "O zamechaniiakh g. Z na komedii *Shkola zhenshchin* i *Spletni*," *Syn otechestva*, part 68, no. 12 (1821): 218–227;

G. Bitner, "Dramaturgiia Katenina," *Uchebnik zapadnogo Leningradskogo universiteta*, no. 33, part 2 (1939): 71–93;

Bitner, "Pozdnii Katenin. Stikhotvoreniia Katenina 30-kh godov," *Uchebnik zapadnogo Leningradskogo universiteta*, no. 33, part 2 (1939): 285–292;

Faddei Venediktovich Bulgarin, as F. V., "Sochineniia i perevody v stikhakh Pavla Katenina s priobshcheniem neskol'likh stikhotvorenii kniazia Nikolaia Golitsyna, 2 chast, (St Petersburg, 1832). Pis'mo k dame v Kostromu," *Severnaia pchela*, no. 97 (3 May 1833): 385–388; no. 98 (4 May 1833): 389–391;

Leonid Genrikhovich Frizman, "Paradoks Katenina," *Izvestiia Akademii Nauk SSSR*, 39 (1980): 22–32;

Nikolai Ivanovich Gnedich, "O vol'nom perevode Biurgerovoi ballady *Lenora*," *Syn otechestva*, part 31, no. 27 (1816): 4–22;

Aleksandr Sergeevich Griboedov, "O razbore vol'nogo pervoda Biurgerovoi ballady *Lenora*," *Syn otechestva*, part 31, no. 30 (1816): 150–160;

Nikolai Vasil'evich Izmailov, "Iz istorii russkoi otkavy," in *Poetika i stilistika russkoi literatury: Pamiati aka-*

demika Viktora Vladimirovicha Vinogradova, edited by Alekseev (Leningrad: Nauka, 1971);

E. N. Kireeva, "Neizvestnye proizvedeniia P. A. Katenina," *Russkaia literatura,* 3, no. 20 (1977): 86–89;

Vil'gel'm Karlovich Kiukhel'beker, "Vzgliad na tekushchuiu slovesnost' (Pesn' o pervom srazhenii russkikh s tatarami na reke Kalke . . .)," *Nevskii zritel',* no. 2 (1820): pp. 107–113;

Ivan Andreevich Kubasov, "Teatral'nye intrigi v 1822 g. (V. A. Karatygin i P. A. Katenin)," *Russkaia starina,* no. 11 (1901): 293–304;

V. L–v, "*Andromakha,* Tragediia v 5-ti deistviiakh v stikhakh," *Syn otechestva,* part 114, no. 13 (1827): 78–88; no. 14 (1827): 164–173;

Dmitrii Letopisets [D. D. Iazykov], "Bibliograficheskie svedeniia o M. V. Malonove, S. E. Raiche (Amfiteatrove) i P. A. Katenine," *Bibliograficheskie zapiski,* no. 12 (1892): 879–880;

Irina Petrovna Lupanova, *Russkaia narodnaia skazka v tvorchestve pisatelei pervoi poloviny XIX veka* (Petrozavodsk: GIZ K.-F. SSR, 1959), pp. 450–458;

S. I. Maslov, "K istorii russkogo teatra 1820-kh godov (Pis'mo V. A. Karatygina k P. A. Kateninu)," *Russkaia bibliografiia,* no. 4 (1915): 68–73;

Vsevolod Fedorovich Miller, "Katenin i Pushkin," in *Pushkinskii sbornik, Stat'ia studentov imperatorskogo Moskovskogo universiteta,* edited by Aleksandr Ivanovich Kirpichnikov (Moscow: Universitetskaia tip., 1900), pp. 17–40;

Vladimir Nikolaevich Orlov, "Katenin," in *Istoriia russkoi literatury,* volume 7 (Moscow-Leningrad: Akademiia nauk SSSR, 1953), pp. 52–61;

"O stikhotvoreniiakh Katenina," *Vestnik Evropy,* no. 3–4 (1823): 193–214;

P. K. (Ksenofont Alekseevich Polevoi), "O napravleniiakh i partiiakh v literature (otvet k g-nu Kateninu)," *Moskovskii telegraf,* no. 12 (1833): 594–611;

Nikolai Kiriakovich Piksanov, "Zametki o Katenine. S. Bertenson, P. A. Katenin. Literaturnye materialy. St. Petersburg, 1909," in *Pushkin i ego sovremenniki,* part 12 (St. Petersburg: Peterburgskaia akademiia nauk, 1909), pp. 60–74;

Ksenofont Alekseevich Polevoi, "Sochineniia i perevody v stikhakh P. Katenina s priobshcheniem neskol'kikh stikhotvorenii kniazia N. Golitsyna. 2 chasti. St. Petersburg, 1832," *Moskovskii telegraf,* no. 8 (1833): 562–572;

A. V. Popov, "Katenin na Kavkaze," *Materialy po izucheniiu Stavropol'skogo kraia,* part 5 (1953), pp. 113–129;

V. A. Popov, "Novye materialy o zhizni i tvorchestve A. S. Pushkina," *Literaturnyi kritik,* no. 7–8 (1940): 230–245;

Aleksandr Sergeevich Pushkin, "Sochineniia i perevody v stikhakh Pavla Katenina. Literaturnoe prilozhenia," *Russkii invalid,* no. 26 (1833): 206–207;

Hans Rothe, "Kateninstudien II: Vers, Strophe, and Gattung in Katenins Balladendichtung," *Zeitschrift fur Slavische Philologie,* 37 (1973): 117–138;

Rothe, "Neue Kateninstudien: Auf der Suche nach der verstummten Deklamation," *Zeitschrift fur Slavische Philologie,* 38 (1975): 128–150;

Rothe, "Philologische Ausgrabungen oder Katenin und die Nachwelt," *Zeitschrift fur Slavische Philologie,* 36 (1972): 237–265;

I. N. Rozanov, *Pushkinskaia pleiada. Starshee pokolenie* (Moscow: Zadruga, 1923), pp. 93–183;

Sinel'nikov, "Obozrenie tragedii *Esfir',* perevedennoi s frantsuzkogo P. Kateninym," *Nevskii zritel',* no. 2 (1821): 164–172;

Irina Z. Surat, "Skazka P. A. Katenina *Kniazhna Milusha*: K probleme Katenin i Pushkin," *Filologicheskie Nauki,* 1, no. 145 (1985): 68–72;

Boris Viktorovich Tomashevsky, "Master perevoda," *Iskusstvo i zhizn'* (1940), pp. 10–13;

Iurii Nikolaevich Tynianov, *Arkhaisty i novatory* (Leningrad: Priboi, 1929), pp. 103–177;

Viktor Vladimirovich Vinogradov, *Stil' Pushkina* (Moscow: Khudozhestvennaia literatura, 1941), pp. 422–426;

R. M. Volkov, "Russkaia ballada pervoi chetverti XIX stoletiia i ee nemetskie paralleli. Ballady P. Katenina," *Uchebnik zapadnogo Leningraskogo universiteta,* volume 37 (1957): 3–48;

Z., "Shkola zhenshchin i Spletni," *Syn otechestva,* part 58, no. 2 (1821): 218–227.

Papers:

A few Pavel Aleksandrovich Katenin items can be found at the Rossiiskii gosudarstvennyi arkhiv literatury i isskustva (formerly TsGALI), f. 1833, and at the Gosudarstvennyi literaturnyi muzei, f. 95. Moscow.

Aleksei Stepanovich Khomiakov
(1 May 1804 – 23 September 1860)

Rosina Neginsky
University of Illinois

BOOKS: *Ermak, tragediia v piati deistviiakh, v stikhakh* (Moscow: Selivanovsky, 1832);

Dmitrii Samozvanets: Tragediia v piati deistviiakh (Moscow: Tip. Lazarevykh Instituta Vostochnykh Iazykov, 1833);

Quelques mots sur les communions occidentales, à l'occasion d'une brochure de M. Laurentie, as Ignotus (Paris: Printed by Ch. Meyrueis for A. Franck, 1853);

Sravnenie russkikh slov s sanskritskimi (1856);

Stikhotvoreniia (Moscow: Bakhmetev, 1861).

Editions and Collections: *Stikhotvoreniia A. S. Khomiakova* (Moscow: Tip. Bakhmeteva, 1861);

Sochinenia, 4 volumes; volume 1, edited by Ivan Sergeevich Aksakov (Moscow & Prague, 1861); volume 2, edited by Iurii Samarin (Moscow & Prague, 1867); volumes 3 and 4 (Moscow, 1872);

Polnoe sobranie sochinenii, edited by Dimitrii A. Khomiakov and G. F. Samarin, 8 volumes (Moscow: Russkii Arkhiv, 1900–1911);

Stikhotvoreniia (Moscow: Russkii Arkhiv, 1910);

Sochineniia (Prague, 1915);

Stikhotvoreniia, edited by Vladimir Andreevich Frantsev (Prague: Orbis, 1934);

D. Venevitinov, S. Shevyrev, A. Khomiakov: Stikhotvoreniia, edited by M. Aronson and I. V. Sergievsky (Leningrad: Sovetskii pisatel', 1937);

Izbrannye sochineniia, edited by N. S. Arsen'ev (New York: Izd-vo imeni Chekhova, 1955);

Stikhotvoreniia i dramy, edited by B. F. Egorov (Leningrad: Sovetskii pisatel', 1969);

Sochineniia v dvukh tomakh, edited by Viacheslav Anatol'evich Koshelev (Moscow: Moskovskii filosofskii fond Izd.–vo "Medium," 1994).

SELECTED PERIODICAL PUBLICATIONS– UNCOLLECTED:
POETRY
"Bessmertie vozhdia," *Poliarnaia zvezda* (1824);

"Elegia na V. K.," *Moskovskii vestnik*, part 1, no. 8 (1827);

"K. V. K.," *Moskovskii vestnik*, part 6, no. 23 (1827);

"Molodost'," and "Starost'," *Moskovskii vestnik*, part 2, no. 5 (1827);

"Poet," *Moskovskii vestnik*, part 4, no. 15 (1827);

"Zaria," *Moskovskii vestnik* (1827);

"V Al'bom sestre," *Moskovskii vestnik*, part 1, no. 4 (1827);

"Ekspromt k N. A. M.," *Moskovskii vestnik* (1828); part 1 (1829): 210;

"Na novy 1828 god," *Moskovskii vestnik*, part 8, no. 5 (1828);

"Otzyv odnoi dame," *Moskovskii vestnik*, part 11, no. 21 (1828);

"Son," *Moskovskii vestnik*, part 11, no. 27 (1828);

"Stepi," *Moskovskii vestnik* (1828); part 1 (1829): 47;

"Tri p'esy pri proshchan'iakh," *Moskovskii vestnik,* part 10, no. 13 (1828);

"Vadim," *Moskovskii vestnik,* part 11, no. 17 (1828): 107; part 1 (1829): 147;

"Vdokhnovenie," *Moskovskii vestnik,* part 7, no. 3 (1828);

"Ermak," *Moskovskii vestnik,* part 7, no. 4 (1828): 397–402; part 1 (1829): 113–130, 208–209;

"Iz Saadii," *Moskovskii vestnik,* no. 5 (1830);

"Klinok," *Moskovskii vestnik,* part 12 (1830);

"Priznanie," *Moskovskii vestnik,* part 9 (1830);

"Proshchanie s Adrianopolem," *Severnye tsvety* (1830);

"Poslanie k Venevitinovym," *Moskovskii vestnik,* part 6, no. 21 (1830);

"Izola Bela," *Teleskop,* part 1, no. 3 (1831): 326;

"Dumy," *Teleskop,* part 3, no. 10 (1831): 187–188;

"Na son griadushchii," *Teleskop,* part 2, no. 7 (1831): 311–313;

"Pros'ba," *Teleskop,* part 2, no. 6 (1831): 166–168;

"Inostranke," *Evropeets,* book 2 (1832);

"K ney zhe," *Evropeets,* book 2 (1832);

"Kliuch," *Moskovskii nabliudatel',* part 3 (1835): 340;

"Ostrov," *Moskovskii nabliudatel',* part 6 (1836): 16;

"Rossii," *Otechestvennye zapiski,* 6 (1839): 143;

"Videnie," *Moskvitianin,* no. 1 (1841);

"7 noiabria," *Moskvitianin* (1841);

"Eshche o nem," *Moskvitianin* (1841);

"Ritterspruch-Ritterspruch," *Moskvitianin* (1841);

"David," *Moskvitianin, Biblioteka dlia Vospitaniia* (1844);

"Kremlevskaia zautrenia na Paskhu," *Moskvitianin,* no. 9 (1850);

"My rod izbrannii," *Moskovskii sbornik* (1852);

"Ne gordis' pered Belgradom," *Russkaia beseda* (1856);

"26 avgusta 1856 g.," *Russkaia beseda,* 3 (1856);

"Vecherniaia pesnia," *Russkaia beseda* (1856);

"Kak chasto vo mne probuzhdalas'," *Russkaia beseda* (1856);

"Noch'," *Russkaia beseda* (1856);

"Zvezdy," *Russkaia beseda* (1856);

"Serbskaia pesnia," *Russkaia beseda,* book 4 (1857);

"Po prochtenii psalma (49-ogo)," *Russkaia beseda,* book 1 (1857);

"Zhal' mne vas, liudei bessonnykh," *Russkaia beseda,* book 4 (1857);

"Shiroka, neobozrima," *Russkaia beseda,* book 1 (1858);

"Truzhenik," *Russkaia beseda,* book 2 (1858);

"Po povodu kartiny Ivanova," *Russkaia beseda,* book 3 (1858);

"Blagochestivomu metsenatu," *Almanakh Utro* (1859);

"Parus podniat," *Parus,* no. 1 (1859);

"Sud Bozhii," *Russkaia beseda,* book 1 (1859);

"Podvig est' i v srazhen'i," *Russkaia beseda,* book 2 (1859);

"Po mertvym kostiam," *Russkaia beseda,* book 3 (1859);

"Spi," *Russkaia beseda,* book 5 (1859);

"Pomnish', po steze nagornoi," *Russkaia beseda,* book 6 (1859);

"Rossii," *Russkaia beseda* (1860).

PROSE

"Zamechaniia na stat'iu o cherezpolosnom vladenii," *Moskovskii nabliudatel',* book 2 (April 1835);

"O sel'skikh usloviiakh," *Moskvitianin* (1842);

"Eshche o sel'skikh usloviiakh," *Moskvitianin* (1842);

"Pis'mo v Peterburg o vystavke," *Moskvitianin,* book 7 (1843);

"Pis'mo v Peterburg po povodu zheleznoi dorogi," *Moskvitianin,* book 2 (1845);

"Sport, okhota," *Moskvitianin,* book 2 (1845);

"Mnenie inostrantsev o Rossii," *Moskvitianin,* book 4 (1845);

"Tridtsat' let tsarstvovaniia Ivana Vasilevicha," *Biblioteka dlia vospitaniia,* 2, part 1 (1845);

"Mnenie russkikh o inostrantsakh," *Moskovskii sbornik* (1846);

"O vozmozhnosti russkoi khudozhestvennoi shkoly," *Moskovskii sbornik* (1847);

"Vozrazhenie na stat'iu Granovskogo," *Moskovskii gorodskoy listok,* no. 86 (1847);

"Pis'mo ob Anglii," *Moskvitianin,* book 7 (1848);

"Predislovie k russkim pesniam," *Moskovskii sbornik* (1852);

"Predislovie k russkoi besede," *Russkaia beseda,* book 1 (1856);

"Ivan Vasilevich Kireevsky," *Russkaia beseda,* book 2 (1856);

"Predislovie i posleslovie k biographii lorda Metkal'fa," *Russkaia beseda,* book 2 (1856);

"Razgovor v podmoskovnoi," *Russkaia beseda,* book 2 (1856);

"Pis'mo k T. I. Filippovu," *Russkaia beseda,* book 4 (1856);

"Pis'mo k izdateliu *Russkoi Besedy,*" *Russkaia beseda,* book 1 (1857);

"Po povody otryvkov, naydennykh v bumagakh I. V. Kireevskogo," *Russkaia beseda,* book 1 (1857);

"Primechanie k stat'e Ivanisheva: O drevnei sel'skoi obshchine," *Russkaia beseda,* book 3 (1857);

"Po povodu malorossiiskikh propovedei (sviashchennika Grachulevicha)," *Russkaia beseda,* book 3 (1857);

"Sovremennyi vopros," *Molva,* no. 28 (1857);

"O stat'e Checherina v *Russkom Vestnike,*" *Molva,* no. 29 (1857);

"O iuridicheskikh voprosakh," *Russkaia beseda,* book 2 (1858);

"Kartina Ivanova. Pis'mo k Redaktoru *Russkoi Besedy,*" *Russkaia beseda,* book 3 (1858);

"Encore Quelques mots d'un chretien orthodoxe sur les confessions occidentales a l'occasion de plusieurs publications religiouses, latines et protestantes" (Leipzig, 1858);

"Primechanie k stat'e: 'Golos greka v zashchitu Vizantii,'" *Russkaia beseda,* book 1 (1859);

"Sergey Timofeevich Aksakov," *Russkaia beseda,* book 3 (1859);

"K stat'e: O Vizantiiskoi zhivopisi," *Russkaia beseda,* book 1 (1859);

"O sovremennykh iavleniiakh v oblasti filosofii," *Russkaia beseda,* book 1 (1859);

"Deviat' rechei, proiznesennykh v Obshchestve liubitelei Rossiiskoi Slovesnotsi," *Russkaia beseda,* book 1, nos. 1-6 (1860);

"O bibleyskikh trudakh Bunzena," *L'Union Chrétienne,* nos. 30, 33, 36, 41, 42 (1860);

"Pis'mo k redaktoru *L'Union Chrétienne* o znachenii slov 'katolicheskii' i 'sobornii.' Po povodu rechi Iezuita Gagarina." *L'Union Chrétienne,* no. 45 (1860);

"Primechaniia k pesniam, pomeshchennym v stat'e G-zhi Kokhanovskoi," *Russkaia beseda,* book 1 (1860);

"Vtoroe pis'mo o filosofii k Iuriiu Fedorovichu Samarinu," *Russkaia beseda,* book 2 (1860);

"Neskol'ko slov pravoslavnogo khristianina o Zapadnykh veroispovedaniiakh," *Pravoslavnoe obozrenie,* no. 10 (1863): 75-100;

"Neskol'ko slov Pravoslavnogo khristianina o Zapadnykh veroispovedaniiakh. Po povodu odnogo okruzhnogo poslaniia Parizhskogo arkhiepiskopa," *Pravoslavnoe obozrenie,* no. 1 (1864): 7-38; no. 2 (1864): no. 2 (1864): 105-144;

"Eshche neskol'ko slov Pravoslavnogo khristianina o Zapadnykh veroispovedaniiakh," *Pravoslavnoe obozrenie* (1875): 6-57;

"Ob otmene krepostnogo prava v Rossii. Pis'mo Ia. I. Rostovtsevu," *Russkii arkhiv,* book 1 (1876);

"Poslanie k serbam iz Moskvy," *Russkii arkhiv,* book 3 (1876): 104-127;

"Zametka ob Anglii i angliiskom vospitanii," *Russkii arkhiv,* book 2 (1881): 38-40;

"O sel'skoi obshchine," *Russkii arkhiv,* book 2 (1884): 261-269;

"Stat'ia o zodchestve," *Russkii arkhiv,* book 2 (1893): 106-109.

Aleksei Khomiakov—poet, playwright, literary critic, theologian, and journal publisher—was one of the founders of the Slavophile movement in Russia. He believed in the fundamental role of the Russian Orthodox Church in bringing authenticity to Russian culture; he also believed in the distinctive nature of Russian history that, in his view, would lead Russians toward an understanding of themselves and their destiny. He believed that the Russian Orthodox Church and its historical evolution make Russians and Russia a divine nation whose mission is to extend its own salvation to the rest of the world, delivering other nations from their sins. He expressed these ideas throughout his works, regardless of genre—poetry, essays, or religious writing.

Aleksei Stepanovich Khomiakov was born on 1 May 1804 in Moscow at Ordynka to Stepan Aleksandrovich Khomiakov, a landowner. The Khomiakov name is first recorded in the court book of Basil III (1505-1533). The family had been historically wealthy, amassing estates in the Tula, Riazan', and Smolensk provinces. A family legend reports that the great grandfather of Stepan Fedor Stepanovich, who was not rich, was elected to the ownership of the enormous Khomiakov estate by the peasants. According to the legend, in the middle of the eighteenth century Kirill Ivanovich Khomiakov, an extremely wealthy landowner who possessed an estate called Bogucharovo and many villages in the Tula region, an estate in the Riazan' region, and a house in St. Petersburg decided, on the death of his wife and only daughter, to find a son and heir among the Khomiakov clan. He asked his peasants to elect their new master. They found and elected Stepan Aleksandrovich Khomiakov, a man of modest means, to become the new owner of the huge estate. He was known as an excellent master and a practical man who enriched and embellished his property.

His son, Aleksandr, did not inherit his father's pragmatism. He did not value what he had and, like many young men from wealthy Russian families, unwisely used the resources of the estate. Aleksandr loved to feast, hunt, and gamble. He married Nastasiia Ivanovna Griboedova, for whom Lipitsy, an estate in the province of Smolensk, was given as a dowry. By the end of their lives, however, Aleksandr's style of living had greatly depleted their wealth. Their son, Stepan, the father of Aleksei Khomiakov, was well read, spoke several languages, enjoyed studying mathematics, and at his estate in Bogucharovo built an excellent French library. Like his father, however, he liked to gamble; instead of rebuilding the estate, he further jeopardized it by gaming away more than one million rubles at the English Club in Moscow. The family fortune was saved only through the intervention of Maria Alekseevna Kireevskaia, his wife, a woman of iron will and tenacity who took over management of the family wealth and successfully rebuilt the estate. This incident largely contributed to the separation of Aleksei's parents. Stepan moved to Lipitsy, while his wife and their three children (Fedor, Aleksei, and Anna) lived in their Moscow house and on the Bogucharovo estate.

Maria Alekseevna—a woman of strong convictions, Orthodox religious views, and great patriotism—

Khomiakov as a young man

deeply influenced her children, especially Aleksei. The spirit of the Khomiakov home was set by Maria Alekseevna: Russian culture was valued over European culture, and great importance was given to traditional religious practices. Of his mother Khomiakov wrote: "she had strong spiritual and religious, political and social interests.... She was generous of spirit and had strong spiritual convictions.... She had great love for and confidence in Russia. For her, the question of national wealth was also a question of private wealth. She suffered, got angry and delighted over Russia much more than over herself and her family."

Though the Russian spirit was quite important in the Khomiakov family, Aleksei's parents considered it important to give their children a good, basic, universal education. Like all children of Russian aristocratic families, Aleksei was educated at home by private tutors. His first tutor was the French abbé Boivin. He taught Aleksei Latin so effectively that at the age of fourteen Aleksei was able to translate Tacitus's *Germania,* which he published two years later in *Trudy obshchestva liubitelei russkoi slovesnosti* (Works of the Society of Lovers of Russian Literature); Horace's odes; and parts of Virgil. He twice translated Virgil's ode "Pareus deorum," using two different meters. Arbe, Aleksei's native tutor of Greek, was an agent of the Philhellenic Society working for Greek independence from the Ottoman Empire. Aleksei also studied modern foreign languages and was fluent in French, German, and English. Later he learned Sanskrit and wrote a Sanskrit dictionary. In his education, great stress was put on the study of Russian language and literature. When Aleksei was eleven and his family moved to St. Petersburg, he was tutored by a Russian dramatist, Andrei Andreevich Zhandr, (Gendre) a friend of Aleksandr Sergeevich Griboedov, a famous Russian dramatist and author of the play *Gore ot uma* (Woe from Wit, finished by 1824, published in full, 1861).

Aleksei's first strong nationalistic experience came in 1812 at the time of Napoleon's invasion of Russia. The family's Moscow home on Petrovka, near *Kuznetskii most* (Kusnetsky Bridge), was destroyed in the fire. The family, however, had already left for their Riazan' estate, Krugloe, located near that of their friend Praskov'ia Mikhailovna Tolstaia, the daughter of Field Marshal Prince Mikhail Illarionovich Kutuzov. Aleksei was concerned about the war and together with his older brother, Fedor, wished to fight against Napoleon and the French. When the news of Napoleon's defeat at the battle of Waterloo reached the Khomiakov family, Fedor is said to have asked Aleksei: "Whom shall we fight now?" Aleksei answered: "We shall stir up revolt among the Slavs."

Aleksei's next strong impressions were urban, since his family moved from Moscow to St. Petersburg early in 1815. Aleksei saw St. Petersburg as "a sort of pagan city where he expected to be forced to change his faith; however, he firmly resolved to endure torture but not to accept a foreign law." In 1817 Aleksei was delighted when the family decided to go back to Moscow. In Moscow the Khomiakov boys continued their education and, under their private tutors, studied in the company of the Venevitinov brothers. The younger of the two, Aleksei Vladimirovich, remained Aleksei's lifelong friend. The older and quite gifted brother, Dmitrii Vladimirovich, acclaimed to be one of the most promising poets of Russia, died at the age of twenty-two. Their major teacher at that time was the philosopher Andrei Gavrilovich Glagolev. During these years Aleksei began to write a tragedy, "Idomenei," but he stopped at the second act. The youths also studied mathematics under Professor Pavel Stepanovich Shchepkin from Moscow University. Aleksei enjoyed mathematics and passed his final examination at Moscow University with a major in that subject. The rich library of Stepan Aleksandrovich Khomiakov also contributed a great deal to Aleksei's education, providing him with a source for extensive literary and philosophical reading.

In 1821, when Aleksei was only seventeen, the Greeks revolted against the Turks. Both the Khomiakov brothers (especially Aleksei) were greatly concerned by the revolt. Aleksei decided that to be a silent sympathizer was not enough, that to be an active participant in the Greeks' fight for freedom was more important. With the help of his tutor Arbe, Aleksei obtained a false passport and left home; his *diad'ka* (servant), however, discovered Aleksei's plan and reported it to his father, who retrieved his idealistic son. Aleksei remembered that event in the poem "Poslanie k Venevitinovym" (A Message to the Venevitinovs), written in 1821 and published in 1830 in *Moskovskii vestnik* (Moscow Herald).

In the spring of 1822, with the permission of his parents, Aleksei Khomiakov enlisted in the army. His father took him to Kherson Province in southern Russia, where he served in Count Osten Saken's *Cuirassier* regiment. His service there did not last long. In October of the same year he was transferred to the Horse Guard Regiment in St. Petersburg. In 1823, while on leave in Moscow, at the Venevitinovs' home, Khomiakov met Aleksandr Ivanovich Koshelev, who later became one of his closest friends. Through his relative Nikolai Alekseevich Mukhanov, Khomiakov met many of the future Decembrists in St. Petersburg. He had passionate discussions with Kondratii Fedorovich Ryleev, Prince Aleksandr Ivanovich Odoevsky, and many others. His views, however, differed from the views of future Decembrists and from those of the contemporary aristocracy. He claimed, for instance, that Odoevsky was "not at all a liberal, but only preferred the tyranny of an armed minority to autocracy." The poem "Zhelanie pokoia" (The Desire for Tranquillity), written in 1824, reflects the state of Khomiakov's soul and mind. According to his first biographer, Valerii Nikolaevich Liaskovsky, this is the first work by Khomiakov that "has an independent artistic meaning."

In early 1825 Khomiakov decided to visit France; his brother, Fedor, worked at that time in the Russian embassy in Paris and was constantly urging him to come. When Khomiakov asked his parents whether he might be allowed to resign from the army, his father immediately agreed. His mother, who was at that time in Wurzburg for her daughter's health, objected at first but then was persuaded to relent on the urging of her beloved older son, Fedor. In early 1825 Khomiakov left for Paris and spent one and one-half years there. He studied painting and also wrote his important dramatic verse work, a long poem titled *Ermak, tragediia v piati deistviiakh, v stikhakh*. It was presented on the stage of the Maly Theater in Moscow and published in 1832. Written in a lush style with the structure of a tragedy, the play generally lacks originality, though the excessive patriotic feeling and the exaggerated pride of Russian people were novel for that time. The characters are two-dimensional, and some, such as the figures of Ermak's father, Timofei, and of his fiancée, Olga, are highly artificial. The conspiracy against Ermak is predictable, except for the death of the hero, who prefers suicide to capture. Khomiakov artificially introduces this heroism to stoke the pride of the Russian people. The author's notion of dreams and death provides a double life for Ermak: a life of reality and a life of dreams; in his putative glory both realms unite. In death, Ermak escapes not only his enemies but also the eternal dissatisfaction with a reality that constantly intrudes into his dream life.

In Paris, Khomiakov remained a faithful and Orthodox believer and strictly observed Church rules and fast days. At one point he had financial problems and was commissioned to paint a Catholic church. At first he accepted, but he soon realized that because of his religious convictions, he would not be able to complete the work, so he abandoned the job. At the end of 1826, when Khomiakov was returning to Moscow, he visited northern Italy, Switzerland, and the Slavic countries of Austro-Hungary, where he was impressed by the reception given him; he mentions it later in his writing.

On his return from Paris, Khomiakov first went to the family estate at Lipitsy to visit his father and subsequently to Bogucharovo, with the intention of staying with his mother and helping her in the management of that estate; however, he was soon drawn to Moscow and then to St. Petersburg, where he visited with his brother, Fedor. In Moscow, on 12 September 1826 at a meeting for an informal celebration of the appearance of the *Moskovskii vestnik*, Khomiakov met for the first time the brothers Ivan and Petr Vasil'evich Kireevsky, future fellow Slavophiles. In St. Petersburg Khomiakov spent time writing poetry, painting in the Ermitage, and visiting his friends with whom he had an intense intellectual exchange. He was close to the Mukhanovs and often visited Ekaterina Andreevna Karamzina and Prince Vladimir Fedorovich Odoevsky, who after the disintegration of *Obshchestvo liubomudry* (Society of Lovers of Wisdom) and the Decembrist revolt, moved from Moscow to St. Petersburg. Khomiakov's stay in St. Petersburg was interrupted in April of 1828, when war between Russia and the Ottoman Empire broke out.

Khomiakov volunteered for the army to fight against the Turks and was posted to northeastern Bulgaria, as far away as Adrianople. In the camp near Bazardzhik, he wrote the poem "Son" (Dream), and then in early 1829 while Russia was still at war, he wrote the poems "Sonnet" (Sonnet), "Proshchanie s Adrianopolem" (Farewell to Adrian), and "Klinok" (Blade). As verse, "Son" is not impressive, but its content is interesting. The poem shares its central idea, creativity, with Aleksandr Pushkin's "Ia pamiatnik sebe vozdvig nerukotvorny" (I erected to myself a monument not made by human hands, 1836). Khomiakov believes that the role of creativity is to awaken human hearts, move them, and incite joy and suffering. He believes that artists who have this ability are not only inspired by the divine but also speak with a divine voice; thus, their words, their voices, and their art are eternal and forever speak to human hearts. Their words then become a "monument not made by human hands."

"Sonnet" also veers toward the philosophical as it explores the mutability of everything earthly and the necessity for finding in mortal life something that rises above the pleasures and worries of momentary existence. "Proshchanie s Adrianopolem," a patriotic poem, glorifies the victory of Russia over the Turks. Artistically it is more successful than the other two. Its rhythm and imagery convey the enthusiasm and passion of war and Khomiakov's belief in the victory and glory of Russia. The poem "Klinok" is stylistically more successful than Khomiakov's philosophical poems but less picturesque than "Proshchanie s Adrianopolem." Patriotism is encapsulated in the image of the blade, the protector of Mother Russia.

At the end of the war, in September 1829, Khomiakov returned to Moscow, where he resumed his exploration of poetry. One of his most eminent poems of that period was "Oda" (Ode), written in 1830 and inspired by the Polish revolt of that year. This poem asks all Slavs to live in peace with each other and curses those who incite conflict among them. In "Orel" (Eagle), written in 1832, he compares the Slav nations to young eagles who he believes will become strong and powerful with time. In March and April of 1831 he went to St. Petersburg and began work on his new historical tragedy, *Dmitrii Samozvanets* (Dmitrii, the Pretender), published in Moscow in 1833. Interestingly, this tragedy was written at about the same time as Pushkin's *Boris Godunov* (1831) and deals with approximately the same period in Russian history. The dialogue is well written, and its structure builds dramatic tension. The play focuses on the relationship between Russia and the West, on relationships between Slavic nations and regions, and on Russian historical development. Khomiakov depicts Muscovite Russia as a perfidious and vile place where, under the cover of love for Russia, characters struggle to consolidate personal power. He portrays the aristocracy of Moscow as rotten, ambitious, vile, and devoid of any moral qualities. Khomiakov is sympathetic to Dmitrii and describes him as a beautiful and noble person. Even though Dmitrii cannot legitimately inherit the crown since he is a Pole, Khomiakov supports his coronation. For Khomiakov a patriotic feeling for Russia, a pure heart, and a noble soul are more important than Russian blood to insure the renewal of Russia.

Khomiakov supports the idea of a union among Slavic nations but remains intolerant of the Roman Church. The character Dmitrii fails because he is too easily manipulated—first by the Catholic Church, which brought him to power hoping that he would, in turn, bring the Catholic cross to Russia; and then by the woman he loves, whom the Catholic Church uses to influence him. Dmitrii's tragic weakness is set against the hostility of a Russia foreign to him; his naive and kind nature prevents him from recognizing the animosity directed against him. Khomiakov casts the Roman Church as the agent of Dmitrii's downfall. If Dmitrii had remained true to his convictions and intuition and had gone to war with Lithuania instead of being swayed by warnings from the Roman Church delivered by Marina Mnishek, his wife, he would have retained his crown and, in the view of the play, probably the whole of Russian history would have taken a more positive direction. The play suggests that the Catholic Church caused the divisiveness between Russians and Poles by fueling their mutual hatred; but for the intrigues of the Roman Church, Russia would have been more tolerant and brotherly toward Poland.

In June of the same year Khomiakov went to the Crimea but was recalled almost immediately because of the health problems of his uncle, Stepan Alekseevich Kireevsky. In July 1832 Khomiakov returned to the Crimea, but again only for a short time; soon after his arrival he received news of his father's stroke and subsequent paralysis. Maria Alekseevna took Stepan Aleksandrovich to Bogucharovo to rest; he died two years later.

The early 1830s were also a period in which Khomiakov was inspired to write several poems that reflect his views and feelings about love. He and his brother, Fedor, had promised their mother to remain virgins until their marriage, and apparently they kept their promises. In the poem "Priznanie" (Recognition), written in 1830, Khomiakov describes his feeling about women. The poem shows him as a passionate person but restrained and pure. He begins and ends the poem with the same words: "Dosele bezvestna mne liubov'" (Up to now I did not know anything about love). His first romantic interest was Aleksandra Osipovna Rosset, but for a variety of reasons the relationship did not last a long time, though long enough to inspire the poem "Inostranke" (To a Foreigner). In 1834 he was much in love with Zinaida Nikolaevna Poltavtseva, who rejected his offer of marriage; she became the subject of three poems: "Kogda gliazhu, kak chisto i zerkal'no tvoe chelo" (When I see how pure and smooth your brow), "Elegiia" (Elegy), and "Blagodariu tebia" (I thank you). The latter three poems have a confessional character and describe the states of his soul in the period of his love for Poltavtseva. On 5 July 1836 Khomiakov married eighteen-year-old Katerina Mikhailovna Iazykova, the sister of the Russian poet Nikolai Mikhailovich Iazykov. Khomiakov was quite happy in his marriage and describes the state of his soul in the poem "Lampada pozdniaia gorela" (The late light was burning), written two years after his marriage. The couple had nine children. When the first two children, Stepan and Fedor, died in 1838, Khomiakov dedicated to them a poem, "K detiam" (To my Children). The Khomiakovs subsequently had seven more children, five daughters and two sons.

In the early 1830s Khomiakov had begun his visits to the salon of the Elagins at Red Gates, where Khomiakov started to formulate his Slavophile views. In discussions with Petr Iakovlevich Chaadaev, Aleksandr Ivanovich Herzen, Nikolai Platonovich Ogarev, and Timofei Nikolaevich Granovsky, Khomiakov always expressed a view opposite from theirs because he saw Russia's destiny as separate from that of Western Europe. At the Elagins' home he also became close to Ivan and Petrasil'evich Kireevsky and to the Aksakovs (Sergei Timofeevich and his sons Ivan and Konstantin Sergeevich). Until the late 1830s Khomiakov wrote only poetry that expressed his feelings. His social and political views and ideas he expressed only orally in arguments and intellectual discussions. In 1838, at the insistence and under the influence of his friend and relative Dmitrii Aleksandrovich Valuev, Khomiakov began to express his ideas in prose. He promised his friend to spend an hour each day writing; he kept his promise until the last day of his life. For almost twenty years he spent one hour per day recording his ideas about world history. This unfinished manuscript has the strange title "I.i.i.i.," while Khomiakov's friends called it "Seramida" (Seramides). In this manuscript, Khomiakov recorded in a systematic way his thoughts and conclusions about the history of mankind. The manuscript was published after Khomiakov's death, in part in 1860 in *Russkaia beseda* (Russian Colloquy) and then in the third and fourth volumes of his *Sochinenia* (Works) in 1872.

The winter of 1839 is generally considered the "official" birth date of the Slavophile movement. At one of the weekly soirees at the Elagins' home, Khomiakov read his essay "O starom i novom" (On the Old and the New). This essay stands as the first public work to formulate his Slavophile ideas, and together with Ivan Kireevsky's "Otvet Khomiakovu" (An Answer to Khomiakov), it became the foundation of the Slavophile movement. In his essay Khomiakov describes the social and spiritual beauty of Old Russia, which he believes existed long before Muscovite Russia. He describes Russia's special destiny and stresses its independence from that of Western Europe; he bases his belief on Russia's different historical and religious evolutions. He attempts, moreover, to predict the path that Russia will take in its future development. He cautions against overweening Russian pride, however, and prescribes Russian humility as necessary for growth.

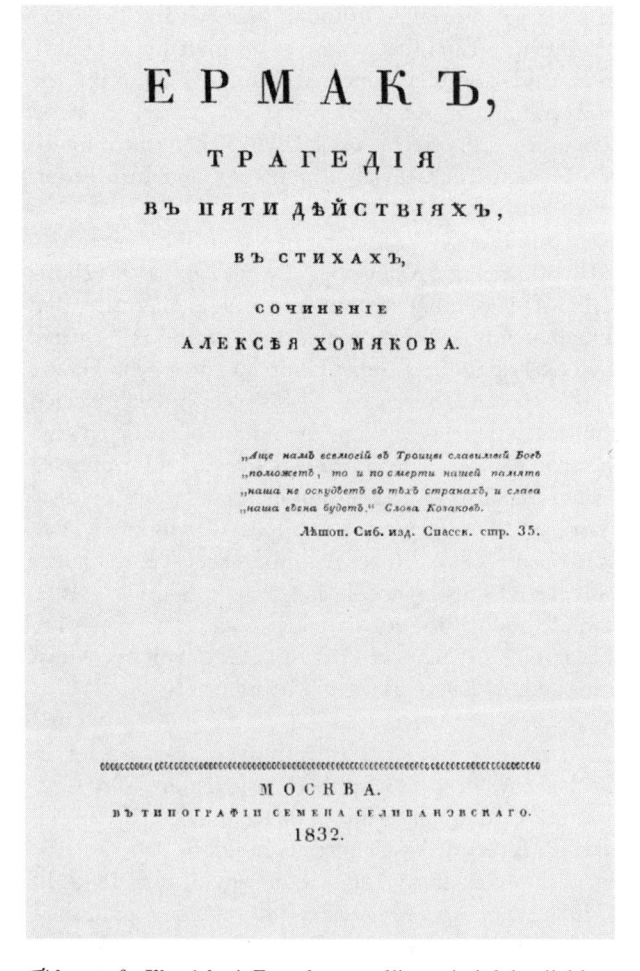

Title page for Khomiakov's Ermak, tragediia v piati deistviiakh, v stikhakh *(Ermak, a Tragedy in Five Acts, in Verse), a patriotic play performed at the Maly Theater in Moscow in 1832*

The same idea is expressed in his poem "Rossii" (To Russia), published in November 1839 in *Otechestvennye zapiski* (Notes of the Fatherland). At about the same time, Khomiakov began an essay, "O Tserkvi" (On the Church), which he finished in the early 1840s. Khomiakov considered making a Greek translation and publishing it in Athens, but he never completed this project. He originally gave this essay the title "Tserkov' odna" (There Is Only One Church), but it was changed at the first publication of the essay in

Pravoslavnoe obozrenie (Orthodox Survey) in 1864, after his death. In 1864 this work was translated into English in Brussels and then appeared again in 1867 in the second volume of Khomiakov's *Polnoe sobranie sochinenii* (Complete Collected Works, 1900–1911), edited by his son Dimitrii Alekseevich Khomiakov and Iurii Fedorovich Samarin.

"O Tserkvi" is the first of Khomiakov's theological works; in it he develops the idea of *sobornost'*, the unity of all members within the Church. He insists that the only Christian church is the Orthodox Church, thus excluding the Roman Church. Those who belong to the Roman Church he calls *otverzhennye deti* (rejected children); he later develops the notion of "rejected children" in "Kiev." This poem was scheduled for publication in *Kievlianin* (The Kievian) in 1840, but for political reasons it was not printed; it appeared only in 1841 in *Moskvitianin* (The Muscovite). In "Kiev" Khomiakov calls for all those who did not remain faithful to Russian Orthodoxy to return to their home. The symbol of that home, the heart of Orthodox faith, is Kiev, which according to Khomiakov will be reborn, with all of its beauty and power restored.

In 1842 Khomiakov published two articles in *Moskvitianin,* titled "O sel'skikh usloviiakh" (On Agricultural Conditions) and "Eshche o sel'skikh usloviiakh" (More on Agricultural Conditions), to describe his position on the agricultural reform of April 1842. In 1843, also in the *Moskvitianin,* Khomiakov published another article, "Pis'mo v Petersburg o vystavke" (A Letter to St. Petersburg about the Exhibition). In this epistolary article the author not only recognizes his own subjectivity but also clearly establishes and takes pride in his point of view. He severely criticizes contemporary, and especially Western European, art.

In 1844 Khomiakov published an article dedicated to the Russian composer Mikhail Ivanovich Glinka in which he celebrates the birth of Russian music, the beginning of a truly Russian art. Later in 1844 he published a collection of his poems that provoked several negative reactions, including that of Vissarion Grigor'evich Belinsky, who was quite critical of Khomiakov's style. One poem from that collection was translated into English by Khomiakov's English friend William Palmer, who had a great interest in Russian Orthodoxy and had traveled in Russia twice to learn more about the country, its people, and its religion. Palmer met Khomiakov in 1844 during his second trip to Russia and thereafter corresponded with him for ten years. The correspondence came to an end in 1855 when Palmer, instead of converting to Orthodoxy, became a Catholic.

In 1845 Khomiakov wrote an introduction to Valuev's book *Sbornik istoricheskikh i staticheskikh svedenii o Rossii i o narodakh ee edinovernykh i edinoplemennykh* (A Collection of Historical and Statistical Descriptions about Russia and about Nations of the Same Religion and of the Same Origins). This book is the first to express the ideas of the future Slavophile movement. In his introduction, which surveys the history of the Slavs, Khomiakov concludes that the renewal of the world will come by means of the Slavic nations, through whose suffering a new level of spiritual nobility has been achieved. This article caused a great commotion at the Elagins' soirees, particularly among the Westernizers, Granovsky, and Khomiakov. The first public objection to the ideas expressed in Khomiakov's article appeared in *Otechestvennye zapiski*. Khomiakov responded to them in a sarcastic manner. Then Granovsky backed the view of the journal and defended its position. These public arguments lasted for two years and were more a public display of intellectual prowess than a lucid definition of the principles of the movement.

In 1845 Khomiakov also published three more articles. The most interesting among them is "Mnenie inostrantsev o Rossii" (The Opinions of Foreigners about Russia). This well-written, accessible article—filled with passion, conviction, and persuasion—focuses on the essential ideas of Khomiakov's Slavophile teaching. According to him, Russia does not really need Western enlightenment and education; rather, Russia should look to its cultural roots (to its unique history) as a basis for future development. Only after Russia has established a firm foundation on these Slavic underpinnings will it gain the respect of Western Europe and eliminate the condescension that outsiders have traditionally felt for Russia. The Western Enlightenment visited on Russian culture in the eighteenth and nineteenth centuries represents its most superficial layer, its "pozolochenye kupola" (gilded domes). As a complement to this article, an essay titled "Mnenie russkikh ob inostrantsakh" (The Opinion of Russians about Foreigners) appeared in 1846 in *Moskovskii sbornik* (Moscow Miscellany). In it Khomiakov continues to develop the idea that he began in the previous article—that the Western cultural patina that overlies essential Slavic elements has had a negative effect on Russian society because it has masked important Russian cultural values. Rediscovering these Slavic strengths to produce a real Russian enlightenment is possible but will require much effort and some pain. He does not describe the path that should be taken for this rediscovery; he only prescribes the process.

The article "Mnenie russkikh ob inostrantsakh" is addressed to Valuev, Khomiakov's friend who gave him the idea for its publication, but Valuev died before it was published. Khomiakov, who was deeply attached to Valuev, was quite affected by his death. Valuev had always supported Khomiakov: the two friends shared spiritual beliefs in addition to their emotional ties.

In 1847, in the second book of *Moskovskii sbornik*, Khomiakov published the article "O vozmozhnosti russkoi khudozhestvennoi shkoly" (On the Possibility of a Russian School of Art), in which he explains that such a school would be popular because it would express the essential nature of the nation. People would appreciate authentic Russian art because it originated in the distinctive character of the people, untainted by a Western European education.

That same year, 1847, Khomiakov, together with his wife and two older children, traveled to Europe and visited England, France, Germany, and Czechoslovakia. Khomiakov was quite impressed by England and recorded his views in a piece for an 1848 issue of *Moskvitianin*. This article presents a description of English life (written with admiration and warmth) and shows a thorough understanding of English history. Khomiakov was especially sensitive to issues of partisan politics in England because they reminded him of the conflicts between the Slavophiles and the pro-Western faction in Russia. Positive aspects of English life find similarities in those essential Slavic strengths identified in the earlier articles. Khomiakov expresses his feelings on his trip to Prague in the poem "Bezzvezdnaia polnoch' dyshala prokhladoi" (The starless night breathes the chill). Khomiakov was interested in the question of peasants and, in his letters to his friend Koshelev, wrote about the importance of *obshchina* (community). He believed *obshchina* was the only remaining vestige of Old Russia and should be supported and preserved, not only because of its being a characteristic of Russian culture but also because of its social usefulness. In his article "Po povodu Gumbol'ta" (On Humboldt), written in 1849, Khomiakov criticizes Georg Wilhelm Friedrich Hegel's philosophy, expresses his happiness that basic Russian nature was not affected by these theories, and then contrasts Russia to Western Europe.

In 1851 Khomiakov wrote an article, "Aristotel' i vsemirnaia vystavka" (Aristotle and the World Exhibit), in which he describes what he perceives as the destructive influence of Aristotle on Western European culture. In 1852 he provided the introduction to Petr Vasil'evich Kireevsky's songs published in *Moskovskii sbornik*. His article of that year, titled "Po povodu stat'i I. V. Kireevskogo o kharaktere prosveshcheniia Evropy i ego otnoshenie k prosveshcheniiu voobshche" (On I. V. Kireevsky's Article about the Character of Western European Enlightenment and Its Attitude toward Education in General) failed to appear in the next issue of *Moskovskii sbornik* because the government closed the journal; it was only published posthumously in his collected works. In this polemical but well-reasoned article Khomiakov agrees with all Kirevesky's statements except one. Kireevsky claims that Christian teaching is deeply rooted in the daily social life of old Russian society, a view that he inherited through his study of the writings of the Church fathers rather than from a more direct source–the reality of everyday Russian life. Khomiakov's study of secular history leads him to a different view of Russian cultural development not consistent with Kireevsky's conclusions. Khomiakov cites as evidence the dark moments of Russian history that he perceives as necessary for the construction of the state.

In 1852 Khomiakov's wife died from cholera. He suffered greatly from his loss. In a letter to Palmer he says that the sun went down and the only thing that remains for him is the obligation to fulfill his spiritual and social vocation. At that time he felt himself to be devoted to the Russian Orthodox Church and wrote three articles with the same title: "Neskol'ko slov pravoslavnogo khristianina o zapadnykh veroispovedaniiakh" (A Few Words of a Russian Orthodox Christian on Western Confessions). Signed with Khomiakov's pseudonym, Ignotus, they were all written in French and published abroad in 1853, 1855, and 1858. Typically well-conceived, well-argued, and eminently convincing, the first article alternately responds to an essay written by Pierre-Sebastian Laurentie, answers an article by Fedor Ivanovich Tiutchev, and takes the opportunity to explain to the Western reader the meaning of the Russian Orthodox Church and its view of the Western Church.

He first establishes criteria for judging "the true Church." The Christian Church cannot replace the figure of Christ with a pope. Khomiakov refutes Laurentie's assertion that the Russian Church has its own papal persons in the tsar and patriarch by arguing that they do not replace Christ, but rather serve him, without pretensions and with humility. While the pope speaks to humanity for God, the patriarch only speaks to God on humanity's behalf–for Khomiakov and the Orthodox Church an essential and critical difference.

He secondly addresses Laurentie's accusation that the Russian Church and Russians have followed the path of Protestantism. Khomiakov responds to this assertion by explaining the tenets of Protestantism and its history and then comparing them to his criteria for the real Church. He chides the Roman Church for its own protest, which he equates with Protestant reformation; Khomiakov sees both Roman Catholicism and Protestantism as a revolt against divine dogma, which only Russian Orthodoxy follows.

Finally Khomiakov explores how the Russian Church feels about its own relationship with the Western churches and how it feels about the relationship

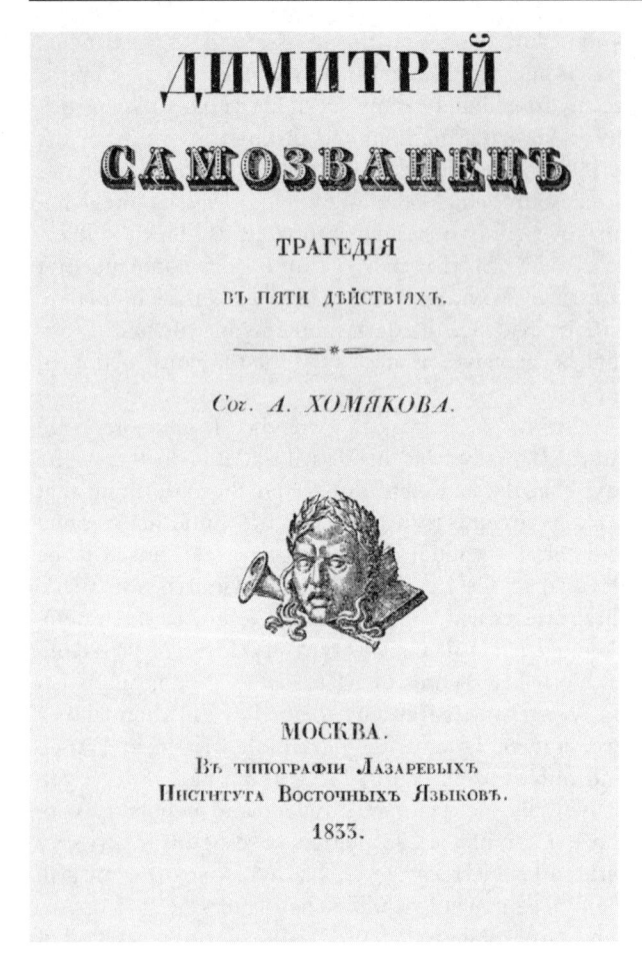

Title page for Khomiakov's Dmitrii Samozvanets: Tragediia v piati deistviiakh *(Dmitry the Pretender: A Tragedy in Five Acts), an historical play focusing on the development of Russia*

between the two Western confessions. He explains why *sobor,* a union encompassing the entire Christian world, is not possible in the view of the Russian Orthodox Church. He believes that such a union will be possible only when the entire Christian world recognizes the legitimacy of and becomes part of the true Church—that is, Russian Orthodoxy. He does not believe that a meeting between Western religions and Orthodoxy would constitute an assembly of the universal Church because the Western churches are not part of the true Church. The Western churches remain outside the true Church because they base their teaching not on the word of God and divine dogma but on human opinion and human views. Khomiakov accuses the West of pretensions based on the rationalizing of faith; he believes that *sobornost'* (unification within the Church of Christ) is possible only with those who can come to the world of mysticism where the Word of God is more important than the word of humanity. Khomiakov explains that both the Roman and the Protestant churches grew from the same root and that the disagreement between them revolves around a competition for power rather than a quest for faith.

The second article responds to a letter written by the archbishop of Paris; in it Khomiakov expands the views he put forth in the first article about the Roman Church and Protestantism. He claims that both have failed in two inseparable foundations of Christian faith: *sobornost'* and freedom. Catholicism proclaims freedom, but without unity within the Church. Protestantism calls for *sobornost'* but does not recognize the notion of freedom. According to Khomiakov, the Roman Church is not a church of freedom that comes from Christ. He argues that when the power of the pope replaces the power of Christ, the pope's mission will be diabolic rather than divine. According to Khomiakov, a pope seeks secular, worldly power and therefore seeks to unite people only so that he can control them, thus depriving them of their freedom. This has nothing in common with real *sobornost'* in Christ's name.

In the third article, subtitled "Po povodu raznykh sochinenii Latinskikh i Protestanskikh o predmetakh very" (On Different Latin and Protestant Writings on the Subject of Faith), Khomiakov endeavors to present yet again the views he expressed in the first two. In this final argument of the "trilogy," however, Khomiakov cites Roman and Protestant theology to support his views.

Khomiakov followed closely the events of the Russian war with the Ottoman Empire. Principally he expressed his feelings about the war in his poetry, especially in "Rossiia" (Russia) and in "Raskaiavshaiasia Rossiia" (Repentant Russia), both written in 1854. Both poems are nationalistic and written in an expansive style. In "Rossiia" Khomiakov expresses his belief in Russia's divine mission on the world stage. One of its responsibilities is to save other Slavic nations. In the second poem he avows his faith in Russia's great future. He calls Russia the angel of God with the radiant forehead. He does not describe this great future in detail, but he is entirely convinced that it will develop.

The death of Nicholas I and the ensuing relaxation in surveillance came as a relief for Slavophiles and other intellectuals. In this more liberated environment Slavophiles were able to start the publication of their own journal, *Russkaia beseda* (Russian Colloquy). Khomiakov's final literary activity was largely related to his collaboration on this journal. His friend Koshelev held an editorial position with *Russkaia beseda* and invited Khomiakov to contribute articles. Khomiakov was active not only in fulfilling his literary responsibility but also in doing administrative work for the journal. He contributed many short, rather insignificant, articles to *Russkaia beseda,* such as "Predislovie k *Russkoi Besede*"

(Introduction to the *Russian Colloquy*), "Razgovor v podmoskovnoi" (A Conversation Near Moscow), an introduction to the biography of Metcalfe, an article about Ivan Kireevsky, and a letter to Tertii Ivanovich Filippov about Aleksandr Nikolaevich Ostrovsky's comedy, *Ne tak zhivi, kak khochetsia* (Do Not Live the Way that You Want, 1854).

Khomiakov's last year of life was quite productive. He was active in chairing the *Obshchestvo liubitelei rossiiskoi slovesnosti* (Society of Lovers of Russian Literature). He began to organize the publication of a dictionary by Vladimir Ivanovich Dal', the letters of Karamzin and Griboedov, and a selection of songs from P. V. Kireevsky's collection. At the same time Khomiakov continued to be interested in theology and submitted three articles to the Paris journal *Union Chrétienne,* two of which were accepted: "O bibleiskikh trudakh Bunzena" (On Bounzen's Biblical Works) and "O znachenii slov 'katolicheskii' i 'sobornii' v slavianskom perevode simvola very" (On the Meaning of the Words *Catholic* and *Sobornii* in the Slavic Translation of the Symbol of Faith). The first article is a critical review of Bounzen's translation of the Bible, which he challenges on the grounds that it is based on the teaching of the Western Church and, as a consequence, does not reflect true Christian principles.

The article "About the Meaning of the Words . . ." is written with considerable insolence and shows a contempt and intolerance toward the Roman Catholic Church, especially toward Jesuits. Khomiakov is responding to a talk given by the Russian Jesuit Ivan Sergeevich Gagarin on the same subject. The main thrust of the article hinges on the meaning of the word *catholic,* which in Greek means "universal." Khomiakov says that the Catholic Church has not adopted the idea of universality; rather, only the Greek Orthodox Church remains true to the concept. The French journal did not accept the article "Pis'mo k Utrekhtskomu episkopu" (A Letter to the Bishop of Utrecht). Though it is written with passion, conviction, and powers of persuasion, the article is replete with its profound intolerance of the Roman Catholic Church. Khomiakov addresses this article to an archbishop who was a Jansenist rejected by the Roman Church. Khomiakov endeavors to show that the religious philosophy of the Jansenists, though the right one, is inconsistent with the historical status of their order. In his opinion, their philosophy can become consistent only if they, and in particular the bishop to whom the letter is addressed, become part of the true Church–the Russian Orthodox Church. The journal also did not publish Khomiakov's letter to the editor protesting the idea of the Uniate Church. For him, the idea of such a church is intolerable, because by borrowing parts from Russian Orthodoxy and parts from Catholicism it determined itself to be a sect and not a part of the Church. That such an attack would not be acceptable to a journal that was essentially the voice of the Uniates is understandable. Khomiakov then abandoned writing articles and turned to literary translations of the Epistles to the Galatians and to the Ephesians from the New Testament.

Khomiakov died unexpectedly on 23 September 1860. He contracted cholera in the village of Ivanovskoe in the region of Riazan', where he was visiting, and died almost immediately. He was interred in the Danilov Monastery, the burial site of several friends and relatives. On 2 October a special funeral service (*panikhida*) was dedicated to him at the University of Moscow, and on 5 October the *Obshchestvo liubitelei rossiiskoi slovesnosti* held a special meeting at which members read speeches and other works about Khomiakov.

Aleksei Stepanovich Khomiakov was a gifted person who was successful in realizing the major part of his potential. He practiced medicine, and ironically he invented a medication for the cholera, but it did not save him. He was interested in technology and invented a machine, a *vapeur,* that he sent to an exhibition in London, where it received patents. He was most active in literature and philosophy. Though his poetry is not particularly lyrical, his polemical writings and articles on subjects that interested him were elegant and persuasive. He succeeded in transmitting to the reader the passion and the clarity of his oral arguments.

He shared with Ivan Kireevsky the formulation of Slavophile thinking, though he approached Slavophile ideas from a less tortuous path than Kireevsky took. Khomiakov's main merit lies in writing lucidly about the Russian Orthodox Church as the basis of the Russian character. He can be viewed as Russia's first modern theologian. Though his works exhibit relentless intolerance toward the West, he bases his views on his sincere religious beliefs. His views and writings had a great impact on the future development of Russian religious philosophy.

Biographies:

Valerii Nikolaevich Liaskovsky, *Aleksei Stepanovich Khomiakov: ego zhizn' i sochineniia* (Moscow, 1897);

Vladimir Zenonovich Zavitnevich, *Aleksei Stepanovich Khomiakov* (Kiev: I. I. Gorbunova, 1902–1913);

Nikolai Aleksandrevich Berdiaev, *A. S. Khomiakov* (Moscow: Put', 1912);

Albert Gratieux, *A. S. Khomiakov et le mouvement slavophile*, 2 volumes (Paris: Editions du cerf, 1939);

Peter K. Christoff, *An Introduction to Nineteenth-Century Russian Slavophilism: A. S. Khomiakov*, volume 1 (s-Gravenhage: Mouton, 1961).

References:

Mark I. Aronson and Solomon Reiser, *Literaturnye kruzhki i salony* (Leningrad: Priboi, 1929);

Nikolai Arsen'ev, "A. S. Khomiakov. Ego lichnost' i mirovozzrenie," in *Izbrannye sochineniia* (New York: Izd-vo imeni Chekhova, 1955);

Pierre Baron, *Un theologien laic orthodoxe russe au XIXe siecle: Alekxis Stepanovich Khomiakov (1804-1860). Son ecclesiologie expose et critique* (Rome: Pont. Institutum Orientalium Studiorum, 1940);

Serge Bolshakoff, *The Doctrine of the Unity of the Church in the Works of Khomiakov and Moehler* (London: Society for Promoting Christian Knowledge, 1946);

Boris Nikolaevich Chicherin, *Vospominaniia. Moskva sorokovykh godov* (Moscow: M. i S. Sabashnikovy, 1929);

Astolphe Louis Léonor de Custine, *La Russie en 1839*, 4 volumes (Paris: Amyot, 1843);

Boris Fedorovich Egorov, "Poeziia A. S. Khomiakov" in *Stikhotvoreniia i dramy* (Leningrad: Sovetskii pisatel', 1969);

Mikhail Osipovich Gershenzon, *Epokha Nikolaia I* (Moscow: Obrazovanie, 1911);

Gershenzon, *Istoricheskie zapiski* (Moscow, 1910);

Gershenzon, *Istoriia molodoi Rossii* (Moscow: I. Sytin, 1908);

Abbott Gleason, *European and Muscovite: Ivan Kireevsky and the Origins of Slavophilism* (Cambridge, Mass.: Harvard University Press, 1972);

Aleksandr Ivanovich Herzen, *Polnoe sobranie sochinenii i pisem*, 22 volumes (Petrograd, 1919-1925);

Aleksandr Ivanovich Koshelev, "Moi vospominaniia ob A.S. Khomiakove," *Russkii arkhiv,* no. 11 (1879): 265-272;

Raymond McNally, "Chaadaev vs. Khomiakov in the late 1830s and the 1840s," *Journal of the History of Ideas,* 27 (January-March 1966): 73-91;

A. A. Polovtsev, ed., "Khomiakov Aleksei Stepanovich," in *Russkii biograficheskii slovar'* (St. Petersburg: Tip. Imp. Russkago istoricheskago obshchestva, 1901);

Nicholas Riasanovsky, "Khomiakov on *Sobornost'*," in *Continuity and Change in Russian and Soviet Thought,* edited by Ernest Simmons (Cambridge, Mass.: Harvard University Press, 1955), pp. 183-196;

Riasanovsky, *Russia and West in the Teaching of the Slavophiles* (Cambridge, Mass.: Harvard University Press, 1952);

Afanasy Vasilev, *Aleksei Stepanovich Khomiakov. K stoletiiu so dnia ego rozhdeniia, 1 maia 1804* (St. Petersburg, 1904);

Leonid Evstaf'evich Vladimirov, *Aleksei Stepanovich Khomiakov i ego etiko-sotsial'noe uchenie* (Moscow: T-vo Skoropech. A. A. Levenson, 1904);

Andrzej Walicki, "The Paris Lectures of Mickiewicz and Russian Slavophilism," *Slavonic and East European Review,* 46 (January 1968): 155-175;

Nicholas Zernov, *The Church of the Eastern Christians* (London: Society for Promoting Christian Knowledge / New York: Macmillian, 1942);

Zernov, *The Russians and Their Church* (London: Society for Promoting Christian Knowledge, 1945);

Zernov, *Three Russian Prophets. Khomiakov, Dostoevsky, Soloviev* (London: S. C. M. Press, 1944).

Petr Vasil'evich Kireevsky

(11 February 1808 – 25 October 1856)

Rosina Neginsky
University of Illinois

TRANSLATIONS: Excerpt from Pedro Calderón de la Barca's "Trudno sterech dom o dvukh dveriakh," *Moskovkii vestnik,* nos. 19-20 (1828): 234-271;

"Sovremennoe sostoianie Ispanii" (from the English review *The Foreign Quarterly Review) Evropeets,* no. 2 (1832): 221-257;

Samuel Collins, "Nyneshnee sostoianie Rossii, izlozhennoe v pis'me k drugu, zhivushchenu v Londone," *Chteniia v Obshchestve istorii i drevsnostei Rossiyskikh,* no. 1 (1846);

Washington Irving, *Zhizn' Magometa* (Moscow, 1904).

OTHER: "Russkie pesni," collected by Kireevsky, *Dennitsa almanakh* (1834): 153-167;

"Russkie narodnye pesni," collected by Kireevsky, *Chteniia v Obshchestve istorii i drevnostei Rossiiskikh,* no. 9 (1848): 145-226;

"Russkie pesni," collected by Kireevsky, *Moskovskii sbornik,* no. 1 (1852);

"Russkie pesni," collected by Kireevsky, *Russkaia beseda,* no. 1 (1856): 44-64;

Pesni, sobrannye P. V. Kireevskim, collected by Kireevsky, edited by Petr Alekseevich Bessonov, 10 volumes (Moscow: Ob-vo liubitelei rossiiskoi slovesnosti, 1860-1874); *Novaia seriia,* collected by Kireevsky, edited by Mikhail Nestorovich Speransky and Vsevolod Fedorovich Miller, 2 volumes (Moscow Ob-vo liubitelei rossiiskoi slovesnosti, 1911-1929);

Collection: *Pesni, sobrannye pisateliami. Novye materialy iz arkhiva P. V. Kireevskogo,* edited by S. A. Makashin and others (Moscow, 1968);

Sobranie narodnykh pesen P. V. Kireevskago, edited by V. I. Kalygin (Tula: Proikskoe knizhnoe izdatel' stvo, 1986).

SELECTED PERIODICAL PUBLICATIONS–UNCOLLECTED: "Kurs novogrecheskoi literatury Iakovaki Rizo Nerulosa," *Moskovskii vestnik,* no. 13 (1827): 85-103; no. 15 (1827): 284-304;

Petr Vasil'evich Kireevsky

"O drevnei russkoi istorii. Pis'mo k Pogodinu," *Moskvitianin,* no. 3 (1845): 11-46;

Excerpts from "Filosofskie zametki ili Filosofskii dvenik," *Literaturnoe nasledstvo,* 79 (1968): 26-29;

"A. Saint Simon," *Literaturnoe nasledstvo,* 79 (1968): 33-38.

Petr Kireevsky is known as an ethnographer, a collector of Russian songs, and an historian and shares with his brother, Ivan Vasil'evich, a vivid interest in articulating Slavophile thought, though not his brother's interest in articulating its theory. His ethnographic interest was related to his aspirations to discover the roots of Russian culture and to present them as proof of the originality and distinctiveness of Russia's history and people. His introductions and commentaries on collections of his songs reflect his deep interest in the history of Slavic nations and particularly of Russia. Though he did not leave any theoretical writings on Slavophile thought, his only article–"O drevney russkoi istorii. Pis'mo k Pogodinu" (On the Old Russian History. A letter to Pogodin, 1845), a description of the structure of the old Slav society–attempts to prove that an independent nature and highly democratic principles governed all Slavic nations. His works reveal his ardent Slavophile belief in the distinctiveness of the historical destiny of his people.

Petr Vasil'evich Kireevsky was born on 11 February 1808 in the village of Dolbino, the Kireevsky estate located in the Belev-Kozel'sk area. His father, Vasilii Ivanovich Kireevsky, was a nobleman of Belev and the owner of Dolbino; he was a cultured man with interests in medical sciences. On 13 January 1805 Vasilii Ivanovich married Avdot'ia Petrovna Iushkova, a well-educated young woman from old Russian nobility and a relative and friend of the Russian poet Vasilii Andreevich Zhukovsky. The marriage lasted until 1812 when Vasilii Ivanovich died from typhoid, contracted at the hospital he had established during the Napoleonic war.

Petr spent his childhood in Dolbino. Both Zhukovsky and Avdot'ia Petrovna's second husband, Aleksei Andreevich Elagin, guided the education of Petr and his brother Ivan. Elagin enjoyed a modest reputation as a translator of Wilhelm Joseph von Schelling. In 1822 the Elagin-Kireevsky family moved to Moscow, where both Petr and Ivan became students of Professors Aleksei Fedorovich Merzliakov and Ivan Mikhailovich Snegirev. In 1823 Petr met the Polish ethnographer and folklorist Zoryjan Dolega-Chodakowski, whom he helped with his folklore collection, gathered in the Russian north. Twice Petr attempted to enter military service but was never able to overcome his mother's opposition. In 1824 Petr met Ivan's friends from the *Obshchestvo liubomudriia* (Society of the Lovers of Wisdom) and became friends with Dmitrii Vladimirovich Venevitinov and Mikhail Aleksandrovich Maksimovich. At the same time, he also met with Aleksei Stepanovich Khomiakov, Sergei Aleksandrovich Sobolevsky, Stepan Petrovich Shevyrev, and Adam Mickiewicz. In 1827 Petr published his first article, a review of Rizo Nerulo's book *Kurs grecheskoi noveishei literatury* (A Course of the New Greek Literature), in *Moskovskii vestnik* (Moscow Herald), a journal originally conceived to be the *porte-parole* (mouthpiece) of what was left of the *Liubomudry*.

Petr Kireevsky knew seven languages and was quite interested in translation. In 1828 he published in *Moskovskii vestnik* an excerpt from Pedro Calderón de la Barca's comedy, "Trudno sterech dom o dvukh dveriakh. Den' pervyi." (It is difficult to watch over a house that has two doors. Day number one.), translated from Spanish. In the introduction to the translation, the editorial board mentioned Kireevsky's intention to translate the best of Calderón's works and to publish them in forthcoming issues of *Moskovskii vestnik,* but these translations never appeared in the journal. (However, after Kireevsky's death many unfinished translations of works by Calderón and William Shakespeare were found in Kireevsky's papers.) In 1828 Kireevsky published a separate book of his translation of George Gordon, Lord Byron's *Vampire*. The story is based on a legend about werewolves, which the British poet had heard in Greece. Kireevsky included in this edition commentaries about the popular traditions of the region where the legend was born, an early sign of his interest in and considerable knowledge of folklore.

In July 1829 Kireevsky went to Germany to continue his education. He settled in Munich and enrolled as a student at Munich University, where he was exposed to works of Joseph von Gorres, Lorenz Oken, and Schelling. He knew Schelling and Oken personally and visited them on their reception days. In Munich he also met Fedor Ivanovich Tiutchev, who worked at the Russian Embassy. Together they read works of French philosopher Victor Cousin. From that period Kireevsky left notes related to his philosophical studies, "Filosofskie zametki ili Filosofskii dvenik" (Philosophical Notes or Philosophical Diary, 1968). At that time he also began to write an article dedicated to another French philosopher, Claude-Henri de Rouvroy, Comte de Saint-Simon, but never finished it. His philosophical views of that period mirror his faith in the predetermined destiny of humanity and in the importance of understanding one's own fate.

In Germany, in addition to philosophy, Kireevsky studied history and Latin. In the fall of 1830 he spent a month in Vienna, and at the end of November he decided to return to Moscow to be close to his family because of the reappearance of cholera. On the way back to Russia he was detained in Kiev by the governor, Boris Iakovlevich Kniazhin. Kireevsky's retention was related to political disorders in Poland. His Polish-sounding name coupled with the speed with which he was returning to Russia caused Kniazhin to suspect Kireevsky of being involved in the troubles in Poland. Eventually, Kireevsky was cleared and allowed to return to Moscow.

Kireevsky knew from his childhood that his life was inseparable from Russia and its popular and historical roots, but he only began to pursue his vocation actively in Germany. There he started to collect Russian songs and to study their history. He preserved songs for his "Sobranie russkikh pesen" (Collection of Russian Songs), which Aleksandr Pushkin and Sobolevsky had planned to publish. This first collection included 150 songs that he transcribed as his serf Rodion sang them. Unfortunately, these songs were all lost when Kireevsky entrusted them to his friend Nikolai Matveevich Rozhalin, who died before delivering them to Sobolevsky.

Kireevsky's interest in Russia's past, especially folklore, continued to grow throughout the 1830s. After his return to Russia, he dedicated himself entirely to the transcription of Russian popular songs and to the study of Russian history. In 1831, with Zhukovsky's help, he entered state service at the same archives of the Foreign Ministry where his brother had served earlier, and there Kireevsky stayed until 1835. During this period he remained faithful to his vocation as a collector and discoverer of Russia's roots. In 1833 he received collections of popular songs from Pushkin, Sobolevsky, and Shevyrev, who saw him as a good custodian of Russian folk songs. Kireevsky did not disappoint them. In 1834 he traveled to the regions of Novgorod, Valdai, and Ostashkov in order to enrich his collection. The songs from these regions especially appealed to him because of the richness of their dialects. The same year he published five songs from his collection in the almanac *Dennitsa* (Dawn). The first song concerns how unhappy life is away from home. Two other songs are ballads, one of which describes a soldier who returns home from war only to be rejected by his wife and children. The fourth song belongs to the ceremonial genre, while the fifth has an historical theme. Kireevsky wrote extensive commentaries about the fifth work, describing historical events in the song, the character of its text, the time of its creation, and the area where it was recorded. Kireevsky also explained the general folkloric context of the song and the background of folk song development. His publication evoked a great interest in Russian literary society; Nikolai Vladimirovich Stankevich mentioned it in his letter to Nikolai Iakovlevich Neverov, and Nikolai Alekseevich Polevoi wrote about it in *Moskovskii telegraf* (Moscow Telegraph). In November of the same year Kireevsky was accepted as a member of the *Obshchestvo liubitelei rossiiskoi slovesnosti* (Society of Lovers of Russian Literature).

As early as 1833 Kireevsky established a social group eventually known as the Slavophiles. In that year he clearly stated his views in a letter to his friend Nikolai Mikhailovich Iazykov as well as to the gatherings of the literary salon of his mother, Avdot'ia Petrovna Elagina. In the letter to Iazykov, Kireevsky argued against the views of Petr Iakovlevich Chaadaev, one of the first Westernizers. In the spring of 1835 Kireevsky went abroad with his mother and her children from her second marriage. He stayed in Europe for a year, again visiting Germany, and returned to Russia only in the spring of 1836 for the division of the family estate. He received the village Slobodka near Orel. His brother, Ivan, became the owner of Dolbino.

Kireevsky never married. He treated Ivan's children as if they were his own. Of his brother's second child, Petr wrote in 1838: "He is a son for me no less than for you. You know that I do not want to have other children, except yours, and I will not have any." Thereafter, Petr spent a considerable amount of time in the management of his estate. This arrangement left considerable time for reading. Kireevsky was interested at that time in the works of Ignacy Krasitskii, the Polish bishop who participated in the preparation of the Constitution of 1791. Krasitskii, known for his sharp tongue, wrote many satires on Polish monastic life that Kireevsky especially enjoyed. He spent some time in Moscow, in his house located near the Church of the Ascension; financial problems forced him to sell this house in 1846. He continued after that to travel around Russia in order to enrich his song collection.

In 1845 Kireevsky published "O drevnei russkoi istorii. Pis'mo k Pogodinu" (On Old Russian History) in *Moskvitianin* (Muscovite), a response to Mikhail Petrovich Pogodin's article "Parallel' russkoi istorii s istoriei zapadno-evropeyskikh gosudarstv, otnositel'no nachala" (Parallels of Russian History with the History of Western European States at Their Beginnings). In the article Kireevsky refutes Pogodin's allegation that Slavic nations were passive tribes waiting to be dominated. Through his historical study of the social structure of the Slavic tribes and their culture, Kireevsky endeavored to show that Slavic society operated on the principles of democracy and tranquillity, unlike the tribes of Western European states. He defined all political choices and events in Slavic societies as natural results of social and cultural evolution. He emphasized that Slavic culture developed independently, without military domination. He also stressed that Slavic leaders did not come to power by force but were almost always democratically chosen. According to Kireevsky's idealistic views, the old Slavic societies were based on the highly developed sense of responsibility and inner nobility of their citizens. His scholarly articles present a well-defended, if arguable point of view.

In 1846 Kireevsky published in the first volume of *Chteniia v Obshchestve istorii i drevsnostey Rossiyskikh* (Readings in the Society of History and Russian Antiquities) a translation from Samuel Collins's work "Nyneshnee sostoianie Rossii, izlozhennoe v pis'me k drugu, zhivushchenu v Londone" (The Modern Condition of Russia, Described in a Letter to a Friend Living in London), which first appeared in London in 1671. Kireevsky prefaced his translation with biographical details of Collins's life and explained the importance of this book for Russian historiographic studies.

One of Kireevsky's main goals in life was to publish his song collection. His first attempt was a set of *dukhovnye pesni* (popular religious songs). Unexpectedly, he encountered many difficulties in publishing them, not the least of which was official censorship. The Censorship Committee felt that the songs did not represent Russians in a way that corresponded to the officially established picture of the people. Kireevsky's friend Iazykov, also a song collector, provided enormous help and support in the struggle to obtain official authorization for the publication of Kireevsky's songs. Iazykov conducted virtually all of the correspondence with the Censorship Committee and with the minister of education, Komorovsky, to obtain official permission. The struggle lasted until Iazykov's death in December 1846.

Ultimately, Kireevsky did not receive the authorization to publish his collection. The entire abortive attempt left Kireevsky psychologically debilitated; nevertheless, he remained resolute in his determination to publish his collection. Help finally came from the editor of the journal *Chteniia v Obshchestve istorii i drevnostei rossiiskikh* (Reading in the Society of History and Russian Antiquities), Osip Maksimovich Bodiansky, who used the right of the society for *svobodnaia tsenzura* (independent censorship). Independent censorship consisted of the free choice of at least one work for publication that did not have to go through the official Censorship Committee. In 1848 the journal of the *Obshchestvo istorii i drevnostei rossiiskikh* (Society of History and Russian Antiquities) published fifty-five religious songs from Kireevsky's collection.

Though Kireevsky prepared commentaries for these songs, the songs were not published. Kireevsky's scholarly introduction to the songs did appear, however, and significantly added to the value of the collection. He detailed the methods he employed in collecting the songs and acknowledged the people who had contributed to the volume. He stressed that his collection included only original Russian songs reflecting the ancient Russian cultural tradition. He also revealed a curious feature of the volume: blind beggars were a source for the majority of the songs.

The journal *Chteniia v Obshchestve istorii i drevnostei rossiiskikh* planned to continue the publication of Kireevsky's collection. The editors hoped to publish in the following issue *raznochteniia* (various readings) that would include all possible commentaries. They also planned to publish *byliny* (epic folk songs), historical songs, ballads, and lyrical songs from Kireevsky's collection in future volumes. Because of the political situation in Europe and the resulting reactionary politics of the Russian government, the journal was closed. In spite of this desperate situation, Kireevsky continued to work on commentaries for his songs. His sister, Maria Vasil'evna, who visited him regularly at his estate, helped him in the organization and copying of his collection.

In 1852 Kireevsky published four more of his collected songs in *Moskovskii sbornik* (Moscow Miscellany). In his commentaries he divided the development of Russian epos into two parts: the old Russian epos before Peter the Great and the subsequent epos that became less creative and more imitative. In Kireevsky's opinion, the decline in the composition of songs resulted from the effect that Peter the Great's Westernizing policies had on Russian popular culture. He also noted decreases in the numbers of songs originating in the most devastating periods of Russian history, such as the period of Mongol yoke. *Moskovskii sbornik* planned to continue the publication of Kireevsky's collection in its future issues, but after the appearance of the first issue the government, because of its fear of backlash from the intellectuals, closed the journal. Kireevsky's last collection of songs to appear during his lifetime came out in 1856 after the death of Russian Tsar Nicholas I, at the beginning of the period of Russia's great reforms under Alexander II. Kireevsky also published twelve more songs in the first issue of a newly established Slavophile review, *Russkaia beseda* (Russian Colloquy). These songs were those originally prepared for the second issue of the defunct *Moskovskii sbornik*.

Kireevsky's health had never been good. In his youth, he had suffered from a chronic, incurable liver disease that became increasingly serious as he grew older. During most of 1854 he was an invalid. The death of his beloved brother, Ivan, in June 1856 completely devastated him, and on 25 October 1856 Petr died of physical and spiritual exhaustion. He was buried with his brother at Optina Pustyn' Monastery. Kireevsky spent his last days with his half brother, Vasilii Alekseevich Elagin, who kept a diary of this period. Until the moment of his death, Kireevsky's main preoccupation was his collection of 15,000 songs. He expressed many times the hope that Elagin and the family, together with his friend Pavel Ivanovich Iakushkin, would continue the publication of the collection. The publication of Kireevsky's collection did continue after his death, and even today new editions occasionally appear. The first publisher of Kireevsky's collection after his death was *Obshchestvo liubitelei rossiiskoi slovesnosti*.

The society did not respect Kireevsky's wish that his friend Iakushkin edit the songs, and they were prepared for publication by Petr Alekseevich Bessonov.

Petr Vasil'evich Kireevsky's role in the history of Russian culture is quite unusual. His single-mindedness and powers of persuasion were responsible for creating an interest in Russian folk songs. His views on the distinctiveness of Russian culture influenced his friends and especially his brother, Ivan, who became one of the principal theoreticians of the Slavophile movement. Kireevsky's work represents a major contribution to Russian folklore, establishing its place in world culture.

Letters:

Mark Konstantinovich Azadovsky, ed., *Pis'ma P. V. Kireevskogo k N. M. Iazykovu* (Moscow: AN SSSR, 1935).

Biographies:

Valerii Nikolaevich Liaskovsky, *Bratiia Kireevskie, zhizn' i trudy ikh* (St. Petersburg: Obshchestvo revnitelei russkago istoricheskago prosveshcheniia v pamiati imp. Alex III, 1899);

Aleksei Dmitrievich Soimonov, *P. V. Kireevsky i ego sobranie narodnykh pesen* (Leningrad: Nauka, 1958).

References:

Mark Konstantinovich Azadovsky, *K istorii russkoi fol'kloristiki* (Moscow: Gos.uchebno-pedagog. izd-vo, 1958);

Petr Alekseevich Bessonov, *Kaliki perekhozhie* (Moscow: A. Semen, 1861–1864);

Mikhail Osipovich Gershenzon, *Obrazy proshlogo* (Moscow: Izd-vo OKTO, 1912);

Abbott Gleason, *European and Muscovite: Ivan Kireevsky and the Origins of Slavophilism* (Cambridge, Mass.: Harvard University Press, 1972);

A. Markovich, "Vospominaniia o Kireevskom," *Russkaia beseda,* no. 6 (1857);

A. A. Polovtsev, ed., "Kireevsky, Petr Vasil'evich," in *Russkii biographichesky slovar',* volume 9 (St. Petersburg: Imp. Russkago istoricheskago obshchestva, 1901);

S. M. Sergeiv, "Kireevsky, Petr Vasilevich," in *Russkie pisateli 1800–1917: Biograficheskii slovar',* volume 2 (Moscow: Sov. Entsiklopediia, 1992): 538–540;

Aleksei Dmitrievich Soimonov, "K istorii sobraniia P. V. Kireevskogo. (Rol' brat'ev Iazykhovykh v ego sozdanii)," *Ocherki istorii russkoi etnografii, fol'kloristiki I antropologii,* no. 3 (1965);

Soimonov, "Novye materialy o Pushkine I Kireevskom," *Izvestiia Akademii Nauk. Otedelenie literatury i iazyka,* 20 (1961): 143–153;

Soimonov, "Pesennaia proklamatsiia P. V. Kireevskogo," *Sovetskaia etnografiia,* no. 4 (1960);

Soimonov, *Pesni, sobrannye pisateliami: Novye materialy iz arkhiva P. V. Kireevskogo, Literaturnoe nasledstvo,* 70 (1968);

Soimonov, *P. V. Kireevskii i ego sobranie narodnykh pesen* (Leningrad: Izdatel'stvo Nauka, 1971).

Papers:

Petr Vasil'evich Kireevsky's papers are located in "Filosofskie zametki ili filosofskii dnevnik," Rossiiskaia gosudarstvennaia biblioteka, Moscow, fond 99, carton 11, no. 19; Rossiiskii gosudarstvennyi arkhiv literatury i iskusstva (Moscow), fond 236; Rossiiskaia natisional'naia biblioteka (St. Petersburg) fond 850, no. 291 (letters to Stepan Petrovich Shevyrev); Gosuldarstvennyi istoricheskii muzei (Moscow), fond 56, nos. 178–183, 188, 407, 523, 508; Gosudarstvennyi arkhiv rossiiskoi federatsii (Moscow), fond 109.

Vil'gel'm Karlovich Kiukhel'beker
(10 June 1797 – 11 August 1846)

Marina Kostalevsky
Bard College

BOOKS: *Shekspirovy dukhi* (St. Petersburg: N. Grech, 1825);

Izhorskii, misteriia, anonymous, parts 1 and 2, edited by Aleksandr Pushkin (St. Petersburg: Tip. III Otdeleniia Sobstvennoi E. I. V. Kantseliarii, 1835);

Russkii Dekameron 1831 goda, anonymous, edited by Pushkin (St. Petersburg: I. Ivanov, 1836);

Nashla kosa na kamen (St. Petersburg: A. Semen, 1839);

Izbrannyia stikhotvoreniia Vil'gel'ma Karlovicha Kiukhel'bekera (La Chaux-de-Fonds: F. I. Buturlin, 1880);

Dnevnik V. K. Kiukhel'bekera; materialy k istorii russkoi literaturnoi i obshchestvennoi zhizni 10-40 godov XIX veka, edited by Vladimir Nikolaevich Orlov and S. I. Khmelnitsky (Leningrad: Priboi, 1929);

Poslednii Kolonna. Roman v dvukh chastiakh 1832 i 1843 g., edited by Orlov (Leningrad: Khudozhestvennaia literatura, 1937);

Prokofii Liapunov. Tragediia V. Kiukhel'bekera, 1834, edited by Iurii Nikolaevich Tynianov (Leningrad: Sovetskii pisatel', 1938);

Puteshestvie; Dnevnik; Stat'i, edited by N. V. Koroleva and V. D. Rak (Leningrad: Nauka, 1979).

Editions and Collections: *Polnoe sobranie stikhotvorenii V. Kiukhel'bekera* (Moscow, 1908);

Lirika i poemy. Dramaticheskie proizvedeniia, 2 volumes, edited by Tynianov (Leningrad: Sovetskii pisatel', 1939);

Izbrannye proizvedeniia, 2 volumes, edited by N. V. Koroleva (Leningrad: Sovetskii pisatel', 1967);

Sochineniia, edited by Rak and N. M. Romanov (Leningrad: Khudozhestvennaia literatura, 1989).

OTHER: *Mnemozina,* nos. 1-4, edited by Kiukhel'beker and Prince Vladimir Fedorovich Odoevsky (Moscow, 1824-1825).

SELECTED PERIODICAL PUBLICATION– UNCOLLECTED: "Liubov' do groba, ili Grenadskie mavry," *Russkaia literatura,* 4 (1989): 69-87.

Vil'gel'm Karlovich Kiukhel'beker

Of all the brilliant literary figures of the "Pushkin pleiad," Vil'gel'm Kiukhel'beker has probably suffered the most: both his life and his literary fate are marked by great drama and, at the same time, bad luck. He was a remarkable poet who should be ranked just after Aleksandr Pushkin and Evgenii Abramovich Baratynsky; a writer who worked in widely varying genres from travelogue to heroic tragedy (including lyric and epic poetry, opera libretto, short tales, novels, essays, epistles and diaries); and a polymath noted for his learning even among his most cultivated contemporaries. Yet, he was for many long years excluded from the literary process: because of his participation in the uprising at Senate Square on 14 December 1825, Kiukhel'beker spent ten years in solitary confinement and the rest of his life in Siberian exile. His legacy has still not been published in its entirety: the unpublished material includes his grandiose epic poem *David* (1829), available fragments of which attest to its broad scope and masterful execution.

As a result of Kiukhel'beker's Decembrist activity his name remained half-forgotten before the Russian Revolution of 1917: the few of his works that were ever published usually appeared in abbreviated form. Under Soviet rule, through the efforts of scholar Iurii Nikolaevich Tynianov, Kiukhel'beker was rescued from oblivion; yet, the editions and studies of his writings never really reached a wide audience. Moreover, at that time the Soviet censors made it impossible for Tynianov or subsequent editors to include the poetry of his later years—which is his best, permeated with religious meditations—as well as, it seems, the complete text of *David*. In the end the bulk of Kiukhel'beker's archive, which Tynianov then had in his possession, perished during World War II.

Vil'gel'm Karlovich Kiukhel'beker was born in St. Petersburg on 10 June 1797 into the family of a German immigrant. His father, the Saxon nobleman Karl Heinrich von Küchelbecker, studied at the University of Leipzig at the same time as Johann Wolfgang von Goethe, Friedrich Gottlieb Klopstock, and Aleksandr Nikolaevich Radishchev and attempted to write poetry in his youth. He received an education in law, mining, and agriculture before moving to Russia in the 1770s. The poet's mother, Iustina Iakovlevna, née von Lohmen, was a person of strict morality, but at the same time she shared her husband's and her son's interest in literature. Vil'gel'm's elder sister Iustina played a major role in his life: she married one of the Glinkas, a family that included several poets, scholars, and in the following generation, the great composer Mikhail Ivanovich Glinka (who, incidentally, became one of Kiukhel'beker's pupils). Two of the Glinkas participated in the Decembrist movement.

In Russia, Karl von Küchelbecker embarked on a career at the court, culminating in his appointment first as a steward of Kamennyi Ostrov (Stone Island), which belonged to the future emperor Paul I, and then as director of the latter's summer residence in the St. Petersburg suburb of Pavlovsk. For his services he was awarded the land estate Avinorm in Estonia, where he and his family lived upon his retirement. The surviving documentation attests that von Küchelbecker was an enlightened landowner concerned with the welfare of his serfs. With the accession of Alexander I, Karl von Küchelbecker's fortunes changed for the worse: the new emperor resented von Küchelbecker's proximity to Paul I and was prepared to terminate his proprietorship of the Avinorm estate. Consequently, the death of the poet's father in 1809 from tuberculosis left the family in straitened circumstances.

At the age of ten Vil'gel'm barely recovered from a grave illness that partially impaired his hearing. After three years at a boarding school in the town of Verro, in 1811 he was enrolled, thanks to the intercession of his distant relative the war minister Barclay de Tolly, in the Imperial Lyceum at Tsarskoe Selo. The school later became famous, but at this time it had only recently been founded by Alexander I for the purpose of educating the future cultural and governmental elite. At the Lyceum the young man fully devoted himself to the study of many diverse subjects, including philosophy, folklore, and Eastern languages; he became close friends with Aleksandr Pushkin and Baron Anton Antonovich Del'vig and began to write poetry, with his first work published as early as 1815.

Kiukhel'beker's natural talent was evident from the beginning, as were his personal idiosyncrasies. In the official report on him, the inspector of the Lyceum noted: "Capable and most industrious; is incessantly preoccupied with reading and writing; is indifferent to all the rest which accounts for his lack of ordered and tidy habits. On the other hand, is kind-hearted, sincere..., speaks smoothly and behaves strangely." Kiukhel'beker's eccentric personality, odd appearance (he was tall, thin, and extremely awkward), slight deafness, archaic tastes, and standoffish manner all had an unfortunate effect on his personal and literary reputation—often those around him refused to take him seriously. Already by his school years an entire anecdotal lore had grown up around Kiukhel'beker to which he sometimes responded irascibly, sometimes good-naturedly, but always without holding a grudge. At the same time Kiukhel'beker possessed an exceptional charm, which earned him a great many loyal friends who, whatever their own political and cultural views, did everything they could to help him at every stage of his arduous path through life.

Friendship is the main theme of his lyric verse, and among poets of male friendship Kiukhel'beker stands out even against the background of the literary group "Arzamas" and Decembrist literature with its cultivation of both the bonds of solidarity and the genre of the friendly epistle. Among his closest friends were Pushkin and, in later years, dramatist and diplomat Aleksandr Sergeevich Griboedov, the latter being perhaps the most powerful emotional attachment of his life. Kiukhel'beker kept sacred the memory of these two friendships to the end of his days.

The first decade in the history of the Imperial Lyceum is renowned for its exceptionally liberal style of education under the leadership of its first reform-minded director, Vasilii Fedorovich Malinovsky. At the opening ceremony on 19 October 1811, professor of moral sciences Aleksandr Petrovich Kunitsyn declared: "The time will arrive when the fatherland will bestow upon you the sacred duty of preserving the welfare of the society." This language is emphatically that of the Enlightenment. Remarkably, the teaching staff included a professor of French, David Boudry, who was the brother of Jean-Paul Marat. The ambience was conducive to the growth of social awareness among the students of the Lyceum and to their interchange with the dissident officers stationed at Tsarskoe Selo (who formed a proto-Decembrist circle, *Sviashchennaia Artel'* (The Sacred Artel), of which, as the evidence suggests, Kiukhel'beker was a member). This environment affected the development of Kiukhel'beker's political views, centering on the idea of enlightened statehood and tending toward Republicanism.

Upon graduating from the Lyceum with a silver medal, Kiukhel'beker repeatedly attempted to secure a post in civil service (applying, for example, together with Pushkin and Griboedov, to the Central Archive of the Foreign College), but with little success. Instead, he distinguished himself as a pedagogue by lecturing on Russian literature at the St. Petersburg Gentry Pension, offering private lessons and becoming secretary to the Society for the Propagation of the Lancaster Method of Education.

These activities occurred parallel to Kiukhel'beker's fervent literary activities. He took part in the proceedings of two major literary associations, the *Vol'noe obshchestvo liubitelei slovesnosti, nauk i khudozhestv* (Free Society of Lovers of Letters, Sciences and the Arts) and the *Vol'noe obshchestvo liubitelei rossiiskoi slovesnosti* (Free Society of Lovers of Russian Literature), led by Aleksandr Efimovich Izmailov and Fedor Nikolaevich Glinka, and regularly wrote for their journals; he even considered starting a journal of his own. Finally, it appears that he secretly entered a branch of the proto-Decembrist *Soiuz Blagodenstviia* (Union of Welfare) in addition to the Masonic Lodge of Michael the Chosen. All these pursuits coincided with an increase in government pressure on liberal circles. In 1820 Pushkin was banished from St. Petersburg, an act followed by political scandals surrounding Del'vig's and Kiukhel'beker's public recitations of their poetry. The authorities became suspicious, and to stay clear of trouble Kiukhel'beker took advantage of an opportunity to travel to Europe as a companion and secretary to a Russian nobleman. He described this journey, which lasted about a year, in an unfinished travelogue or *puteshestvie* (published in full only in 1979), modeled on Nikolai Mikhailovich Karamzin's *Pis'ma russkogo puteshestvennika* (Letters of a Russian Traveler, 1797–1801). As he passed through Germany, France, and Italy, Kiukhel'beker, like his illustrious predecessor, felt himself to be a representative and propagandist of Russian culture in the West. He met Goethe, Ludwig Tieck, and Benjamin Constant. His foreign travels ended abruptly, however, when his lecture on Russian literature at the liberal club "Athenée" in Paris caused a stir because of his political radicalism. Banned by the French police from making further public appearances, Kiukhel'beker was ordered to return home.

His friends helped him to obtain service in the Caucasus under the noted general Aleksei Petrovich Ermolov, but this position also ended on a sour note when Kiukhel'beker got himself into a duel with one of the general's relatives. Subsequently, he was forced to give up his post under the pretext of "morbid fits."

Kiukhel'beker's most successful venture in the period before his imprisonment was the publication, together with Prince Vladimir Fedorovich Odoevsky, of four numbers of *Mnemozina* (Mnemosyne, 1824–1825), an almanac that brought together notable writers of various leanings. In this almanac he published several of his own critical articles, which provoked lively debate. Of these the most important is "O napravlenii nashei poezii, osobenno liricheskoi, v poslednee desiatiletie" (On the Direction Taken by Our Poetry, Especially Lyrical, in the Last Decade, 1824). A characteristic trait of Kiukhel'beker was the unconventionality of his literary judgments, which often went against not only the current fashion but also the trend that eventually prevailed in Russian letters. As a literary theorist, he was a kind of radical conservative who produced his own idiosyncratic brand of Romanticist aesthetics and constantly sought to embody it in his own creative work. Kiukhel'beker defines Romanticism as "svoboda, izobretenie i novost'" (freedom, invention, and novelty) and postulates its origin in ancient Greece.

His opposition to the influence of the French tradition promoting light rococo poetry in the manner of Vicomte Evariste-Désiré de Parny and Charles-Hubert Millevoye (evident in Konstantin Nikolaevich Batiushkov's and in Pushkin's early lyrics) started when he was still in the Lyceum. At the same time, he refused to recognize the generic superiority of the elegy, imported from Germany by the followers of Karamzin and members of Arzamas who advocated a poetry of nuanced psychological insight. In "O napravlenii nashei poezii" he wrote: "Let us be grateful to Zhukovsky [Vasilii Andreevich Zhukhovsky was the leading figure of Arzamas] that he liberated us from the yoke of French letters . . . , but we should not allow either him, or anyone else, even if possessing ten times greater talent than he, to put on us the chains of German or English domination." In agreement with the Romantics, Kiukhel'beker

St. Peter's Gate to the Peter-Paul Fortress in St. Petersburg, where Kiukhel'beker was imprisoned after taking part in the Decembrist Revolt of 1825

never ceased to emphasize the importance of *narodnost'* (native roots or national spirit–the Russian equivalent of the German *Volkstum*) as the source and inspiration of any creativity. In contrast to them he rejected both the cult of the hero-outcast and the metaphysics of weltschmerz, as well as the particular concentration on the individual self. He championed an art of a lofty, dithyrambic style, seeing in the ode a universal principle applicable to every literary endeavor:

> The ode, engaged with sublime matters, transmitting heroic exploits and patriotic glory from age to age, floating to the throne of the Ineffable, and prophesizing before an awe-inspired nation, soars, roars, glistens, enslaves both the hearing and the soul of the reader. Furthermore, the author of an ode is unselfish; he neither rejoices in nor deplores insignificant events of his own life; but rather utters the truth and the judgment of Providence, he celebrates the majesty of his native land, he throws bolts of lightning against a foe, bestows blessings on a righteous one, and curses on a fiend.

Kiukhel'beker's attitude comes close to the pre-Romantic Sturm und Drang literature (in the spirit of Friedrich Maximilian Klinger, whom he knew personally). In sum, although he shared Romanticist sensibilities–among them, particularly, an interest in folklore and a penchant for emotional exultation–he tended to appropriate the poetics of Pindar, Dante, John Milton, Klopstock, André-Marie Chénier, and Gavriil Romanovich Derzhavin more than that of popular contemporaries such as Alphonse de Lamartine or George Gordon, Lord Byron, whom he viewed with skepticism. These affinities account for the solemn, even bombastic tone of most of Kiukhel'beker's writings, both in poetry and prose, which often impedes their full appreciation by the modern reader. Kiukhel'beker's language is for the most part highly rhetorical, even though, following the Romanticist doctrine of "mixed style," he admits the occasional use of the prosaic.

Kiukhel'beker's vocabulary abounds in biblicisms, archaisms, and Slavicisms (he repeatedly called for the Russian language to be cleansed of all foreign words). One must bear in mind, however, that rhetoric does not necessarily imply insincerity. For all his ecstatic qualities, Kiukhel'beker's poetic voice is genuine and natural; he wrote as he thought, and thought as he wrote:

> Blazhen, kto pal, kak iunosha Akhill,
> Prekrasnyi, moshchnyi, smelyi, velichavyi,
> V sredine poprishcha pobed i slavy,
> Ispolnennyi nesokrushimykh sil!
> Blazhen! Litso ego, vsegda mladoe,
> Siianiem bessmertiia goria,
> Blestit, kak solntse vechno zolotoe,
> Kak pervaia edemskaia zaria.
>
> (Blessed is he who, like the youth Achilles,
> Beautiful, strong, courageous, majestic,
> Has fallen amidst a field of victory and fame,
> Full of invincible force!
> Blessed! His face, forever young,
> Shines with the radiance of immortality,
> Like a sun eternally golden,
> Like the first dawn of Eden.)

The seemingly unpolished texture of Kiukhel'beker's poetry can often be explained by his reliance on the spontaneity of inspiration. Yet, this quality stems not from any lack of ability, but rather from a conscious repudiation of the refined technique of Pushkin and his epigones. Despite his admiration and even worship of Pushkin, Kiukhel'beker set his approach to poetry in opposition to Pushkin's from the beginning and never abandoned this posture. Thus, in prison he wrote in his diary on 17 January 1833: "I love and respect Pushkin's splendid talent, but, to tell the truth, I should never wish to become one of his imitators.... After 1820 we seem to have followed entirely different roads." In his turn, Pushkin, while also respecting his friend's talent, viewed much of his work with often considerable irony (which, incidentally, is discernible in the character of Lensky, in part modeled on Kiukhel'beker, in Pushkin's *Evgeny Onegin,* written 1823–1831, published in 1833). This conflict had a devastating effect on any valuation of Kiukhel'beker's literary activity and on the fate of his writings. Pushkin's views and predilections, later simplified by critic Vissarion Grigor'evich Belinsky, served for the next century and a half as the principle of canonical selection in Russian criticism, according to which Kiukhel'beker was relegated to the remote literary outskirts, alongside Vladimir Grigor'evich Benediktov and Count Dmitrii Ivanovich Khvostov. Even Tynianov's brilliant attempt to rehabilitate him critically and artistically achieved less than its desired result: Tynianov's scholarly work *Arkhaisty i novatory* (Archaists and Innovators, 1929) attracted scant notice, while the success of his 1925 novel about Kiukhel'beker, *Kiukhlia,* left the average reader with an impression that its protagonist was a fictional personage rather than a real historical figure.

Kiukhel'beker's first published prose fiction, "Ado" (1824), set in a stylized medieval Estonia, is a typical example of Romantic Decembrist prose with the theme of a national liberation struggle (led by the protagonist) against a foreign invader, in this case, the German feudal barons. It appeared in *Mnemozina.* This remarkably sympathetic treatment of the small Baltic nation must have been inspired by the author's memories of the Estonian environment of his childhood. This work is encumbered, however, by a convoluted language fraught with Slavicisms and archaisms in accordance with Kiukhel'beker's literary theories of the time. Later he produced another version of the tale (1840–1844), yet unpublished, in which most of those defects were presumably corrected.

It is not surprising that Kiukhel'beker, under the influence of his friends Pavel Aleksandrovich Katenin and, especially, Griboedov, came to ally himself with *Druzhina slavian* (Brigade of Slavs), a successor group to Admiral Aleksander Semenovich Shishkov's archaizing and classicizing *Beseda liubitelei russkogo slova* (Colloquy of the Lovers of the Russian Word). He proclaimed his favorite poet to be Prince Sergei Aleksandrovich Shirinsky-Shikhmatov, the author of portentous, though powerful, epic poems on subjects culled from Russian history, whom the Arzamasians would ridicule relentlessly. Kiukhel'beker's conservative literary tastes, however, did not affect his political inklings: all this time he strove to enhance his ties to such Decembrist figures as Fedor Glinka, Aleksandr Ivanovich Odoevsky, and Kondratii Fedorovich Ryleev, becoming a member of *Severnoe obshchestvo* (Northern Society) a month before the demonstration in Senate Square.

Besides his essays and criticism, Kiukhel'beker published little at this point: a few minor pieces, mainly in periodicals; an unsuccessful comedy, *Shekspirovy dukhi* (Shakespearean Spirits, 1825), with many allusions to the literary debates of his time; and some excerpts, in periodicals, from a tragedy on the classical theme of tyrannicide, "Argiviane" (The Argives, written 1823–1825), which he later reworked and which, as Pushkin pointed out, for the first time utilized the iambic pentameter in Russian verse drama. During this period, however, he was working on a variety of projects, which included his first long poem; an opera libretto, "Liubov' do groba, ili Grenadskie mavry" (Love until the Grave, or The Moors of Granada, written 1823; first published 1989), based on the work of Pedro Calderón de la Barca; and an ambitious plan for a "Russkii Dekameron" (Russian Decameron). This latter project he conceived as a series of poems set within the framework of critical discussions involving several characters; some features of this composition are reminiscent of both Pushkin's unfinished "Egipetskie nochi" (Egyptian Nights) and the later philosophical work *Russkie nochi* (Russian Nights, 1844) by Vladimir Odoevsky. The poet succeeded in realizing only part of this project.

During the events of 14 December 1825 Kiukhel'beker, no doubt owing to his passionate and eccentric temperament, played an extremely active, although somewhat awkward role: a thoroughly civil person, he visited several regiments to rally the soldiers to the cause. Addressing them in French, he sought for a substitute to replace the Decembrist "dictator" Prince Sergei Petrovich Trubetskoi, who failed to show up at the decisive moment. Kiukhel'beker even made a vain attempt to shoot the Grand Duke Mikhail Pavlovich and General Aleksandr L'vovich Voinov. Finally, when the insurgents started to disperse, he tried to talk them into launching an offensive against the vastly superior government force, which was equipped with cannons. Alone of all the members of *Severnoe obshchestvo*, he managed to flee St. Petersburg and make his way to Warsaw, where he was arrested a month later and jailed in Peter-Paul Fortress. On 12 July 1826, after a series of interrogations conducted both by Nicholas I personally and by members of the investigative commission, Kiukhel'beker was sentenced to death by beheading, which was soon commuted to twenty years of hard labor and deportation to Siberia for life. Still later his sentence was mitigated to ten years of solitary confinement and subsequent exile.

During his years in prison, between 1826 and 1835, Kiukhel'beker composed all his major works, though few were published, either anonymously or under a pseudonym (mainly because of Pushkin's intercessions), during his lifetime. In their quality and range, these prison writings represent a creative feat almost without parallel in Russian literature. This achievement is made even more remarkable by the fact that the texts written by Kiukhel'beker in prison are replete with cultural and historical references bridging space and time from West to East and from antiquity to the present, although he had limited access to any literature and was forced to rely, by and large, on his obviously prodigious memory. In addition to his own creative work (he often pursued several projects at once), he occupied himself with reading and memorizing the classical literature he could obtain, such as Homer's *Iliad* in the original, and with rendering Shakespeare into Russian. He completed translations of several of the tragedies, most of which remain unpublished.

Kiukhel'beker never stopped writing lyrics, including some exceptional examples of civic poetry, most often addressed to friends; but his main attention now focused on larger forms, epic and dramatic. His earliest long poem, "Kassandra" (written 1823; first published 1939), which portrays the woman prophet's vision of her fate at the hands of Agamemnon after the fall of Troy, still bears the heavy influence of Friedrich von Schiller, Byron, and Zhukovsky. One written while he was in jail, however—*Sirota* (The Orphan, written 1833; first published 1939)—is a considerably more original work, even though its appearance coincided in time with its author's interest in the melodramatic poetry of George Crabbe. Kiukhel'beker's poem was written on a theme from contemporary provincial suburban life. Its proem offers a moving tribute to Pushkin, followed by five "conversations" between the characters, thus allowing the protagonist—a retired hussar—to tell the tale of the misery he suffered in childhood and adolescence to an audience that includes his wife, the family of a local pharmacist, and a priest. By using this structural device the author provides a perspective not only on the personages participating in the story, but also on the environment in which they lived. *Sirota* appears to be Kiukhel'beker's sole consistent attempt at realistic writing in response to the quest for realism that became gradually manifest in the literature of the time. The poem is not devoid of literary merit, although in contrast to Pushkin it exhibits neither the carnivalesque humor of *Domik v Kolomne* (The Little House in Kolomna, 1830) nor the somber poignancy of *Mednyi vsadnik* (The Bronze Horseman, 1833).

Almost simultaneously with *Sirota*, Kiukhel'beker worked on yet another long poem, "Iurii i Kseniia" (written 1833, first published 1939), this time based on an old Russian legend. Dealing with the relationship of passion, power, and faith, and set against a romanticized background of Kievan Rus, the poem tells of a triangle consisting of a prince, his squire, and a young daughter of a country priest. The amorous contest between two men is portrayed as a noble one (*'chest'* [honor] was a key concept in Kiukhel'beker's worldview); it finds resolution when the maiden chooses the prince. The squire becomes a hermit, and his death leads to the foundation of a monastery. The poem ends with the author's evocation of his stay in the Caucasus and a tribute to his friendship with Griboedov, an inclusion that reveals Kiukhel'beker's tendency to infuse epic material with lyrical and subjective elements. In the quest for *narodnost'* Kiukhel'beker experimented with folk prosody; he wrote in his diary on 3 December 1832: "The most difficult task for me is that I must maintain not only the spirit, but also the meter of our simple folk poetry." Although he eventually chose iam-

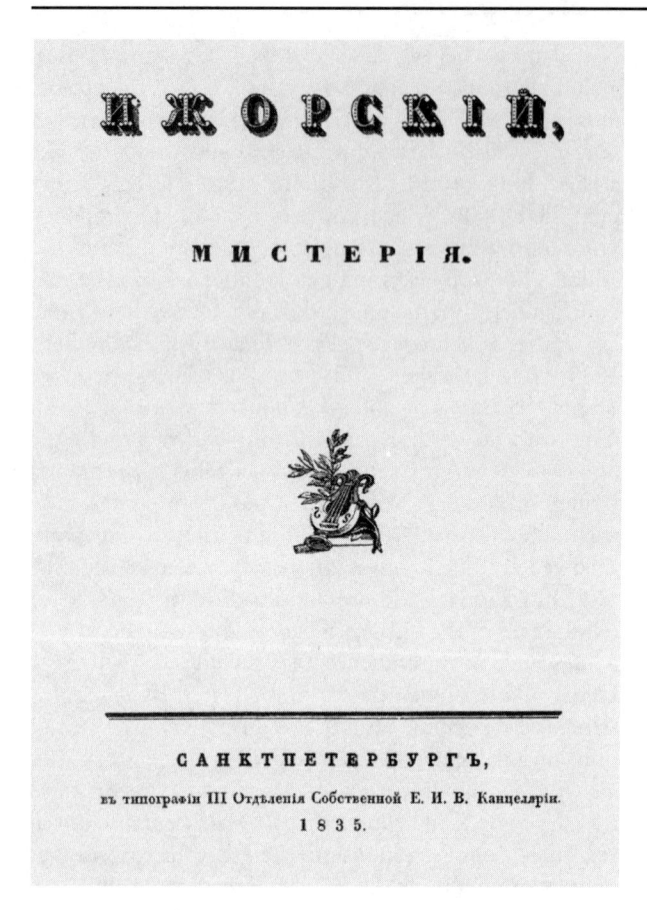

Title page for Izhorskii, misteriia *(Izhorsky, A Mystery Play), Kiukhel'beker's drama with a Faustian protagonist*

bic tetrameter, which made his verse resemble that of Pushkin's *Ruslan i Liudmila* (1820), the resulting product is by no means imitative; it is distinguished by a peculiar pathos (in the Greek sense), entirely absent from Pushkin's heroic and comic masterpiece.

Kiukhel'beker's massive epic *David,* insofar as can be judged from the published fragments (in the 1939 and 1967 editions of his collected works), is in many respects a staggering achievement. Perhaps inspired by Griboedov's programmatic short poem of the same title, this work consists of ten cantos and presents the amalgamation of a detailed account of the exploits performed by the biblical psalmist-king with many lyrical digressions (occupying one third of the text), authorial monologues, and addresses to friends, both living and dead—as though the compositional principle of Pushkin's *Evgeny Onegin* had been superimposed to Voltaire's *Henriade* (1723 and 1728). The result is a sui generis subjective-objective epic equally opposed to the classicist tradition of Mikhail Vasil'evich Lomonosov and the frivolous ruminations of Byron's *Don Juan* (1819-1824). The conception of the epic indicates Kiukhel'beker's moral and political interests as well as the views of some other moderate Decembrists; it focuses on the figure of a heroic and benevolent monarch who succeeds, despite overwhelming odds, in building up harmonious relations with his people. The narrative proceeds at a slow pace, offering a rich and picturesque panorama—as the poet envisaged it—of life in ancient Judaea, including military, religious, and domestic scenes. Although *David* depicts a large cast of characters who lace the stream of narrative with their stories, experiences, and recollections, Kiukhel'beker's chief concern is with his own and his reader's *sokrovishche serdtsa* (sanctuary of heart): at every turn of David's fate, the poet indulges in introspections that justify his claim that what he wrote is not only a reinterpretation of biblical material but also, as he described it in a 20 October 1830 letter to Pushkin, "a private, personal confession of everything that disturbed, consoled, tormented, deceived, antagonized and reconciled" him with himself during the first five years of imprisonment.

Throughout all this time Kiukhel'beker continued to work on *Russkii Dekameron,* the first chapter of which was published anonymously in 1836. It comprises a prose frame and the poem "Zorovavel" (Zorobabel, 1831) attributed to one of the characters, a young poet. In the poem itself the Old Testament tale about the return of the Jews from Babylonian captivity is placed in the mouth of a Muslim storyteller entertaining his comrades at the time of the Russian conquest of the Caucasus. The poet embroiders the traditional story by portraying an artistic contest at the court of the Persian king Darius. It is won by the young Jew Zorobabel who, as a prize, requests that his people be allowed to return home from exile.

Under the influence of Griboedov, Kiukhel'beker became increasingly interested in Oriental literature. Much of the poetry he wrote during his incarceration is permeated with Islamic lore; and characteristically, it is not the Greek Muse but the Koranic angel Isphragil whom he repeatedly invokes as a source of poetic inspiration. Kiukhel'beker intended another poem, "Sem' spiashchikh otrokov" (Seven Sleeping Youths, written 1835; first published 1939), to be the second installment of the same project. It retells the early Christian legend preserved in the Koran of the group of faithful Christians who, persecuted by the Roman emperor Diocletian, fell asleep in a cave, to be awakened only several centuries later. The contexts of the two poems described—liberation of the Jews and persecution of the Christians—clearly allude to the vicissitudes of the Decembrists and issue a disguised appeal for clemency. The third installment in *Russkii Dekameron* was to be *Nashla kosa na kamen'* (The Mower's Blade Hits the Stone, written 1831; anonymously published 1839), an adaptation of William Shakespeare's *The Taming of the Shrew*.

The unfinished poem "Agasver" (Ahasuerus, 1835–1836; first censored publication in *Russkaia starina* [Russian Antiquities], written 1878; published in full 1967) was originally conceived as a part of *Russkii Dekameron* but soon developed into an independent enterprise, comparable to *David* in scale and ambition. In contrast to the latter, however, its chief intent was philosophical and satirical: an attack, as Kiukhel'beker called it in a 9 December 1835 letter to his nephew Nikolai Grigor'evich Glinka, "at almost everything that wisdom, in repudiating faith, is accustomed to pass off to us as glory, virtue and the sublime." He continued to work on this epic in Siberian exile until his death. Its seven lengthy fragments present a panorama of mass follies committed by nations in various historical periods, seen through the cynical eyes of the Wandering Jew. In these fragments the action takes place against the background of the Crucifixion, the fall of Jerusalem to Titus, the persecution of Christians under Trajan, the confrontation of Pope Gregory VII with the German emperor, the Reformation, and the French Revolution. The last extant scene of the poem depicts the collapse and the despair of the last representatives of humankind on the threshold of the Day of Judgment. In one respect Kiukhel'beker's pessimism is akin to the Romantic existentialism of Byron, Mary Wollstonecraft Shelley (*The Last Man,* 1826), and in particular, Baratynsky ("Posledniaia smert'," The Last Death, 1827). In another respect it anticipates the novels of catastrophe that became popular in the twentieth century. Finally, it is eschatological, like the subject of the poem: the belief in the impending Apocalypse is a fundamental constituent of the Russian religious consciousness.

In Kiukhel'beker's literary oeuvre, drama in verse has as important a role as the long, or epic, poem. His first effort in that genre, "Argiviane" (first draft 1823, published 1967; second, incomplete draft, 1825, published 1939), even formally imitates the structure of Greek tragedy, including the role of the chorus. Its message is civic and political, consonant with Decembrist sensibilities and bearing an affinity to French revolutionary drama (such as that of Marie-Joseph Chénier). Kiukhel'beker's main source was Plutarch's biography of Timoleon, a fourth-century B.C. Corinthian politician who committed tyrannicide by assassinating his own brother, Timophanes, after the latter seized power in their native city. The comparison of the earlier and later drafts reveals a tendency toward radicalization: if the author's original emphasis was on his protagonist's torment arisen from the conflicting family and public loyalties, it subsequently shifted to an unequivocal commitment to the latter. Nonetheless, even the minor characters of the drama remain sufficiently complex to suggest many dimensions of the human psyche. As a work of art, "Argiviane" is by no means inferior to another successful attempt to re-create a Greek tragedy in Russian literature–Katenin's *Andromakha* (1827). Not surprisingly, Pushkin was interested in and approved of both of these works. With no sympathy for classicist aesthetics for its own sake, he did value, however, a creative reinterpretation of a classical theme, even if it was done along strictly formal lines, provided that it reflected contemporary problematics. Kiukhel'beker's ambition was to become a national Russian poet. His dream, as he once expressed it, was "to leave something that will in this land make my German name sound supremely Russian."

This desire is the chief concern of Kiukhel'beker's patriotic drama *Prokofii Liapunov* (written 1834, first published 1938) on which he worked at the same time he was preparing a translation into Russian of Schiller's unfinished and unpublished 1805 play, *Demetrius*. Both works deal with the so-called Time of Troubles (1598–1613) when Russia, upon the death of Tsar Boris Godunov, dissolved into chaos and suffered occupation by Poland. Prokofii Petrovich Liapunov, the protagonist of the play, was an historical figure who presided over the liberation movement consisting of cossack militia and mobilized gentry; after his murder by his own subordinates, the movement collapsed, to be revived a few years later under the leadership of Koz'ma Zakhar'ich Minin and Prince Dmitrii Mikhailovich Pozharsky, who finally succeeded in expelling the Poles from Russian lands. If the earlier tragedy revolved around the struggle against tyranny, this one centered on the opposite issue, the control of anarchy, possibly a result of Kiukhel'beker's meditations on what could have happened had the Decembrists won. Although the poet does not idealize his dramatic hero, described by him in a 13 February 1834 letter to his mother as "the man who committed many blunders, but was full of strength and inner dignity," he portrays him as an exemplary champion of law and order. The tension of the plot is built through the relationship of a leader possessing a vision with popular demagogues, motivated exclusively by self-interest but supported by an unruly and bloodthirsty mob. Because of his moral worth and inability to compromise, Kiukhel'beker's Liapunov meets his death, lamented only by an *iurodivyi,* a holy fool. This resolution of the conflict suggests the author's eventual disappointment with Romanticist revolutionary ideology and his change of priorities from public to personal ethics. In artistic terms this work arguably constitutes Kiukhel'beker's best creation, and as an authentic historical drama written on the Russian theme, it appears second only to Pushkin's great *Boris Godunov* (1831).

Kiukhel'beker's new emphasis on an individual moral being is central in his most ambitious and peculiar endeavor–a dramatic trilogy, *Izhorskii, misteriia* (Izhorsky, A Mystery Play, 1826–1841; parts 1 and 2 published anonymously in 1835, part 3 first published in 1939). He worked on this project for a more than a decade, during the entire period of his incarceration and later during his Siberian exile.

He conceived it as a satirical mystery play. The major influence on the play–although Kiukhel'beker himself tried to obscure it, citing instead Aristophanes, German *Minnesang* (courtly love lyrics), and Spanish *autos sacramentales* (short allegorical verse plays about the Eucharist)–was apparently that of Goethe, and its thrust is directed against Byron and Byronism, toward the ultimate discrediting of the Romantic hero. In fact, *Izhorskii* is the first serious attempt to create a Russian Faust, an effort later repeated in Count Aleksei Konstantinovich Tolstoi's *Don Zhuan* (1862), in Leonid Nikolaevich Andreev's *Anatema* (1909), and finally in Mikhail Afanas'evich Bulgakov's *Master i Margarita* (1928–1940; first expurgated edition 1966–1967, first unexpurgated edition 1973).

In keeping with his own view of *narodnost'* and ethnic folk culture, Kiukhel'beker replaces Goethe's demonic personages, from Mephistopheles to the Walpurgis Night witches, with the Russian wood goblins, such as Kikimora and Buka, with mermaids, and other creatures who tempt, taunt, and ultimately drive the hero toward the brink of moral ruin. At the same time, *Izhorskii* provides a sober diagnosis of the spiritual malaise that plagued the generation of the 1830s. Even the water-oriented name of the protagonist (named for the Izhora River) is no accident: a displaced individualist, he logically develops, as it were, the personality of Onegin (named for the Onega River) and anticipates that of Pechorin (named for the Pechora River) in Mikhail Iur'evich Lermontov's *Geroi nashego vremeni* (A Hero of Our Time, 1840).

In the first part of the trilogy, Izhorskii is, in Kiukhel'beker's words, "a natural man," that is to say, "as every natural man, he is self-confident, haughty and proud." Similar to Byron's Manfred, he declares that he has experienced everything and become incapable of loving. To Kiukhel'beker, early disappointment in life is not a commendable expression of weltschmerz but a symptom of self-indulgence that may easily turn into noxious nihilism, a development on which he commented in a 15 November 1832 letter to Nikolai Glinka: "I am convinced, that a youth who at the age of twenty became indeed already an old man, that is to say, is already good-for-nothing, that at the age of thirty he may grow into a rascal, and at the age of forty he must inevitably become and inevitably will become a fiend." Consequently, in the course of the trilogy Izhorskii progresses from the seduction of women to their ruin and from treachery to the murder of his best friend. Izhorskii manages to extricate himself from the tenets of evil imagination only at the very last moment and is allowed to achieve a religious insight before perishing, like Byron, in the struggle for Greek independence. Notwithstanding the abundance of the fantastic, this "mystery play" exhibits enough psychological truth and lively detail to claim a degree of realism lacking in most Decembrist literature.

Despite the depth of its conception, many striking episodes or images, and the concentrated effort Kiukhel'beker invested in its completion, however, *Izhorskii* cannot be considered a success. Many structural links between individual episodes are weak, and the whole composition suffers from verbosity–an inadmissible (albeit all too common) fault in Romantic drama. Some of the dramatic effects in the trilogy are inadvertently comic: irrespective of his own claims to the contrary, Kiukhel'beker seems to have been deficient in his sense of humor, as his intentional satire is sarcastic rather than ironic and is never funny. One is not surprised that *Izhorskii* was met with critical disapproval, notably by Belinsky, who saw in it an outdated and barely comprehensible hodgepodge.

The dramatic fairy tale "Ivan, kupetskii syn" (Ivan, the Merchant's Son, written 1839–1842, first published 1939), which Kiukhel'beker created while still in jail and completed in exile, serves as a kind of appendage to *Izhorskii* (with which it shares a supernatural framework and demonic personages, such as Kikimora, thereby reminding one of the Greek practice when a tripartite tragedy was followed by a satyr play). If the hero of the early work is, like Faust, ultimately saved by means of religious conversion in spite of all his early villainy, the new protagonist was designed by the poet to reveal, as he put it (in a 7 July 1834 diary entry), only "the base and mean half of human nature." Ivan possesses not a single redeeming feature and is irremediably vitiated with greed, cowardice, and hypocrisy.

Not unlike Izhorskii, but differently motivated (by greed instead of resentment), Ivan comes to destroy both the woman who loves him and his best friend, experiencing no remorse in the process. The overall plot is complicated and fraught with sorcery and gore (including infanticide). The author seems to have entertained doubts regarding this performance: "Is it indeed possible," he inquires rhetorically in the preface to the play, "to solder together satire and elegy, narrative and drama, comedy and tragedy, lyrical poetry and fairy tale, the ideal and the grotesque, laughter and horror, enthusiasm and the prose of routine–and expect out of all this to create a harmony?" Predictably, the result barely coheres: thus, placed in a stylized Orient populated by surreal creatures, the action also boasts an historical character, Thomas Bruce, seventh Lord Elgin (the plunderer of the Athenian Acropolis), to whom Ivan sells, as a sculpture, the (literally) petrified body of his benefactor, who had been turned into a stone by an exercise of black arts. The grim outcome of the play, with evil triumphant and all favorably portrayed characters dead, reflects the deep pessimism about the human condition (evident also in "Agasver") that had begun to dominate Kiukhel'beker's outlook late in his life.

In contrast, in his last dramatic project, the unfinished "Arkhilokh" (Archilochus, written 1845–1846; first published 1939), Kiukhel'beker returns not only to a classical Greek theme but also in a large measure to his earlier style of "dithyrambic ecstasy." Along with some other contemporary authors (notably, in Russia, Aleksandr Aleksandrovich Shakhovskoi), he anticipated the later genre of "heroic comedy" with a story of a sharp-tongued, socially and politically sensitive poet, unjustly exiled from his native land, who wins the Olympian artistic contest only to die from exhaustion. This depiction could not but offer a poignant commentary on Kiukhel'beker's own fate, along with a dose of wishful thinking. It was his private testament and, at the same time, a nostalgic recapitulation of imagery that by then had become virtually obsolete, although it earlier had been prominent in the literature of the Decembrists (including, of course, Kiukhel'beker's lyrics of the 1820s) as they celebrated the commitment to the public good pursued by the Romantic figure of the poet-citizen, "warrior bard."

It took Kiukhel'beker many years to complete his only novel, *Poslednii Kolonna* (The Last of the Colonnas, written 1832–1845; first published 1937), an outstanding literary achievement. Written in epistolary form, interspersed with diary entries, the narrative consists of an intricate plot with elements of Gothic suspense in the manner of E. T. A. Hoffmann and Washington Irving but without either the subtle irony of the former or the healthy humor of the latter. Despite the fact that the author often resorts to artifices characteristic of Romanticism, the aim of the novel, like that of *Izhorskii*, was the demystification of the Romantic hero. (Here one may suspect the inverse influence of Lermontov, in whom Kiukhel'beker, to judge from his diary, took a great interest.)

The story is centered on an artist of genius, Giovanni Colonna, and his involvement with a Russian couple staying in Italy. An enthusiastic friendship with the young Iurii does not impede the Italian's growing passion for Iurii's fiancée, Nadezhda, which ultimately leads him to a fit of insanity in which he murders them both. This tragic denouement—"so horrible that I myself got frightened," as Kiukhel'beker wrote to his niece Natal'ia Grigor'evna Glinka on 8 December 1843—was designed to underscore the anti-Romantic message: the cult of a solitary "superior" individual (a precursor of the Nietzschean *Übermensch,* the superman) is never justifiable, and even worse, it is both destructive and self-destructive. The world is not necessarily hostile to the genius: often the genius is hostile to the world. In other words, the conflict in *Poslednii Kolonna* is akin to the problematics of "genius and malefaction" explored by Pushkin. Yet this work, rich with moral and psychological insights, was not published until one hundred years after its composition.

Kiukhel'beker's *dnevnik* (diary), which he started in prison in April 1831 and continued to write with varying regularity until the end of his life, though only part of it survived (the fullest version published in 1979), is a major literary and historical document. Despite the virtual vacuum of his solitary confinement, the impossibility of meaningful communication with his friends and colleagues, and the perforce random character of his reading and correspondence, the poet succeeded in providing a fascinating account of his inner life and his aesthetic and philosophical meditations. Hundreds of entries, a treasure trove filled with names, titles, and opinions, demonstrate how closely the political prisoner managed to follow contemporary intellectual life and respond, in his thorough and original manner, to the phenomena of Nikolai Gogol, Lermontov, and Belinsky.

Kiukhel'beker was released from jail at the end of 1835 and subsequently deported to Siberia, where he was reunited with the family of his younger brother, Mikhail, also an exiled Decembrist. There he married a simple, illiterate woman and tried his hand, rather unsuccessfully, at farming in an effort to feed his family. The marriage was not a happy one; his health was beginning to decline noticeably; his sight was failing; and his own requests to be published, as well as similar petitions by his friends in the capital, proved futile. Nonetheless, he stubbornly continued to work on the projects he had begun in prison, striving to complete them all. Despite all adverse circumstances, Kiukhel'beker's total commitment to literature and worship of poetry were unabated. "I hope I will remain the poet to the very moment of death," he stated in a letter to Nikolai Glinka, "and I confess that if, renouncing poetry I could by the price of such abdication purchase freedom, high standing, wealth . . . I would not hesitate: I would prefer grief, bondage, poverty, illness of the body and the soul, all that together with poetry, to the happiness without it." In this final decade of his life the poet compiled his sole, and superlative, verse collection,

"Pesni otshel'nika" (Songs of a Hermit), which has yet to be published in full. In comparison with his earlier lyrics, Kiukhel'beker's mature poetry is contemplative rather than enthusiastic, and it movingly communicates (as, for instance, in a cycle of Easter sonnets) an authentic religious experience.

In June 1846, after many moves, the poet was in Tobolsk for treatment of his tuberculosis when he took a sudden turn for the worse and dictated a literary testament to a friend from the Lyceum years, Ivan Ivanovich Pushchin, also a political exile. On 11 August 1846 Vil'gel'm Kiukhel'beker died. Exactly two months earlier he had sent Zhukovsky a last desperate appeal for help in which he wrote:

> I am speaking to a poet, and what is more, a half-dying man has the right to speak with little ceremony:*I feel and I know, I am utterly convinced as I am convinced of my own existence,* that Russia has hardly a dozen writers to set against the Europeans who are my equals in imagination, in creative power, in erudition and diversity of work. Forgive me, my dear mentor and first guide in the field of poetry, this proud outburst! But in truth, it makes my heart bleed to think that everything, everything I have created, will perish with me like an empty sound, like an insignificant echo!

One may say that Kiukhel'beker's parting words perfectly sum up both the place in Russian literature that is his by right and the dramatic fate that for so long denied him appropriate recognition.

References:

Vasilii G. Bazanov, *Poety-dekabristy: K. F. Ryleev, V. K. Kiukhel'beker, A. I. Odoevskii* (Moscow: Akademiia Nauk SSSR, 1950);

Simon Karlinsky, "Trilogiia Kiukhel'bekera *Izhorskii* kak primer romanticheskogo vozrozhdeniia srednevekovoi misterii," in *American Contributions to the Seventh International Congress of Slavists, Warsaw, 1973,* volume 2 (The Hague: Mouton, 1973), pp. 307–320;

N. N. Kholmukhamedova, "Vostok v russkoi poezii 30-kh godov XIX v.: V. K. Kiukhel'beker i M. Iu. Lermontov," *Izvestiia Akademii nauk SSSR, seriia literatury i iazyka,* 44, no. 1 (1985): 57–67;

M. G. Mazia, "Fol'klor i problemy samobytnosti i narodnosti v proizvedeniiakh V. K. Kiukhel'bekera 1830-kh godov," *Russkaia literatura,* 4 (1986): 121–128;

Mazia, "Rannee perevodnoe stikhotvorenie V. K. Kiukhel'bekera 'Pesn' laplandtsa,'" *Russkaia literatura,* 3 (1982): 160–163;

Mazia, "V. K. Kiukhel'beker i literaturnyi iazyk 20-kh godov XIX v.," *Russkaia rech',* 4, (1986): 27–32;

Viktor Petrovich Meshcheriakov, "A. S. Griboedov i V. K. Kiukhel'beker," *Russkaia literatura,* 3 (1981): 49–68;

R. G. Nazarian and M. G. Salupere, "Estonskie stranitsy biografii V. Kiukhel'bekera," *Russkaia literatura,* 1 (1990): 156–163;

L. D. Pashkina, "Odin fakt iz biografii V. K. Kiukhel'bekera: V. K. Kiukhel'beker–uznik Keksgolmskoi kreposti," *Russkaia literatura,* 2 (1984): 187–188;

V. K. Rezhko and Leonid Genrikhovich Frizman, "V. K. Kiukhel'beker i V. A. Zhukovskii," *Voprosy russkoi literatury,* 1, no. 51 (1988): 11–16.

Aleksei Vasil'evich Kol'tsov
(3 October 1809 – 29 October 1842)

Veronica Shapovalov
San Diego State University

BOOK: *Stikhotvoreniia* (Moscow: N. Stepanov, 1835).

Editions and Collections: *Stikhotvoreniia Kol'tsova,* with article by Vissarion Grigor'evich Belinsky (St. Petersburg: N. Nekrasov & P. Prokopovich, tip. Voenno-uchebnykh zavedenii, 1846);

Stikhotvoreniia A. V. Kol'tsova. Pervoe polnoe sobranie, edited by P. V. Bykov (St. Petersburg: Kn-vo G. Goppe, 1892);

Stikhotvoreniia A. V. Kol'tsova. Polnoe sobranie, edited by Arsenii Ivanovich Vvedensky (St. Petersburg: A. F. Marks, 1892);

Pesni A. V. Kol'tsova (Moscow: t-vo I. D. Sytina, 1893);

Stikhotvoreniia i pis'ma, edited by A. I. Liashchenko (St. Petersburg, 1895);

Dumy (Kiev: Gil'zovaia fabrika S. M. Karakoza, 1896);

Polnoe sobranie stikhotvorenii i pisem, edited by Vvedensky (St. Petersburg: Prosveshchenie, 1896);

Zhenskaia dolia. Stikhi i pesni A. V. Kol'tsova (Moscow: t-vo I. D. Sytina, 1902);

Stikhotvoreniia: 87 stikhotvorenii, with articles by Belinsky and Valerian Nikolaevich Maikov (St. Petersburg: I. Glazunov, 1905);

Polnoe sobranie sochinenii A. V. Kol'tsova, edited by Liashchenko (St. Petersburg: Razriad iziashnoi slovesnosti Imp. Akademii nauk, 1909);

Sobranie stikhotvorenii i pisem (Moscow-Leningrad: Khudozhestvennaia literatura, 1933);

Stikhotvoreniia, edited by A. V. Desnitsky (Moscow-Leningrad: Sovetskii pisatel', 1937);

Polnoe sobranie stikhotvorenii, edited by Lev Abramovich Plotkin (Leningrad: Sovetskii pisatel', 1939);

Sochineniia, edited by Viacheslav Alekseevich Tonkov (Voronezh: Kn. Izd-vo, 1950);

Sochineniia, edited by Iurii L'vovich Akimov (Moscow: Khudozhestvennaia literatura, 1955);

Sochineniia, 2 volumes, edited by Tonkov (Moscow: Sovetskaia Rossiia, 1958);

Pesnia pakharia, edited by Tonkov (Moscow: Gos. izd-vo detskoi literatury, 1962);

Sochineniia, edited by Vladimir Prokop'evich Anikin (Moscow: Khudozhestvennaia literatura, 1966);

Stikhotvoreniia, edited by Tonkov (Moscow: Sovetskaia Rossiia, 1973);

Stikhotvoreniia 1827–1842, illustrated by F. Domogatsky (Moscow: Khudozhestvennaia literatura, 1986).

Edition in English: *The Complete Poems of Aleksey Vasil'evich Kol'tsov,* translated by C. P. L. Dennis (London, 1922).

OTHER: "Russkie poslovitsy, pogovorki, prirechia i prislovia," in *Voronezhskaia beseda na 1861 god* (St. Petersburg, 1861), pp. 1–20;

"A. V. Kol'tsov," edited by I. M. Kolesnitskaia and A. D. Soimonov, *Literaturnoe nasledstvo,* 79 (1968): 281–338.

Aleksei Kol'tsov occupies a distinctive place in Russian literature because of his craftsmanship in the genre of the Russian song. There is no other poet whose songs have been more popular in all strata of Russian society. More than three hundred composers–among them Petr Il'ich Tchaikovsky, Nikolai Andreevich Rimsky-Korsakov, Modest Petrovich Mussorgsky, and Anton Grigor'evich Rubinstein–have written music for his songs, which were circulated orally, often without even mention of the poet's name.

Aleksei Vasil'evich Kol'tsov was born on 3 October 1809 in the provincial town of Voronezh. His father, Vasilii Petrovich Kol'tsov, a wealthy livestock dealer and member of a merchant guild, was well known in the area for his honesty and strict adherence to old traditions. Vasilii Kol'tsov was also involved in other business ventures such as subletting arable and timber land. Aleksei Kol'tsov's mother, Praskovia Ivanovna (née Pereslavtseva), was a kind, mild, and industrious woman who did not play a dominant role in the household. According to his letters, in his childhood Kol'tsov had a special affection for his nanny, Fedos'ia Pavlovna, whom he cherished until his death.

At the age of nine Kol'tsov commenced his education with a private tutor, a student of a theological school. He showed such aptitude that in 1820 he was able to enter a two-year district school, bypassing parochial school altogether. He continued his studies for sixteen months, at which time his father interrupted his schooling and made him work in the family business. The environment in which he grew up did not place a high value on education and art. From his shortened school attendance, however, Kol'tsov retained a passion for reading and a thirst for education. Initially he read fairy tales and picture books that he bought from street vendors, and then he moved on to a classmate's library of seventy books. He read *Arabian Nights* and works by eighteenth-century Russian authors. He especially liked the novel *Kadm i Garmoniia drevnee povestvovanie* (Cadmus and Harmony, 1789) by the Russian classicist Mikhail Matveevich Kheraskov.

In 1825 Kol'tsov bought a collection of poems by Ivan Ivanovich Dmitriev, one of the founders of the Russian Sentimentalist school, who wrote highly acclaimed verses in forms favored by Sentimentalists–songs and epistles. Kol'tsov was profoundly moved by Dmitriev's poetry, especially by his Russian songs "Stonet sizyi golubochek" (The blue-grey dove is moaning, 1792) and "Akh, kogda b ia prezhde znala" (If I Only Knew Before, 1792). According to his reminiscences, Kol'tsov hid in the garden and began singing Dmitriev's poems, convinced that all poems are songs to be sung and not read. Thus began a desire to write poetry. His first poem was a friend's story of a dream, which Kol'tsov turned into rhymes. He titled it "Tri videniia" (Three Visions), but he later destroyed it.

Since Kol'tsov's family did not appreciate his passion for reading and learning it took great strength of will to continue educating himself. Kol'tsov's father wanted his only son (of five surviving children) to participate in the family business, to become his close assistant and manager. Consequently, Kol'tsov assumed many responsibilities. His father's business brought him into contact with a wide variety of people and taught Kol'tsov to interact with representatives of all walks of life. This closeness to the common people played an important role in the development of Kol'tsov's talent. As a cattle rancher he had to spend much of his time outdoors at primitive campsites, often in the saddle for days on end. He was rewarded, however, by the beauty of nature. The vast, scenic steppe, for which he had a boundless love, became his school of life. Later this love provided inexhaustible material for his works.

Kol'tsov soon became acquainted with a book dealer, Dmitrii Antonovich Kashkin. Although Kashkin did not have any formal education, he passionately loved Russian and West European literature and was well versed in it; he had also learned French in order to read Jean Racine and Molière in the original. Kashkin possessed a substantial library, which he was constantly enlarging. A typical Russian educator, he devoted his life to the dissemination of books and knowledge. Local intellectuals–teachers, actors, theological students–often gathered in Kashkin's bookstore to discuss the latest literary works. Kashkin inspired Kol'tsov to continue his education, and he also encouraged him to write poetry. Kashkin gave Kol'tsov a copy of *Russkaia prosodiia ili pravila kak pisat' Russkie stikhi* (Manual of Russian Prosody or the Rules on How to Write Russian Verses), a boarding-school textbook. He was Kol'tsov's first reader, adviser, editor, and critic. Kol'tsov valued Kashkin's permission to use his library as much as he valued his literary advice, and he availed himself of the opportunity for more than five years. In Kashkin's bookstore Kol'tsov was introduced to the poetry of the Russian classicists Mikhail Vasil'evich Lomonosov, Gavriil Romanovich Derzhavin, and Ippolit Fedorovich Bogdanovich and to the works of his contemporaries Aleksei Fedorovich Merzliakov, Baron Anton Antonovich Del'vig, and Aleksandr Pushkin. From Kashkin's bookstore Kol'tsov began building his own personal library. With his allowance Kol'tsov bought those books he liked most of all and, a few years later, he inherited his classmate's collection of seventy books. This love for collecting books remained with Kol'tsov for the rest of his life.

Under the guidance of his new friend, Kol'tsov devoted himself with great passion to writing poetry.

Classical literary influences are strong in Kol'tsov's early works and his epistles and in his lyrical elegies of the period–for example, "Pesn' utru" (Song to the Morning, 1826), "Pridi ko mne" (Come to me, 1829), and "Prekrasnoi poselianke" (To a Beautiful Peasant Girl, 1828)–are literary imitations of popular Romantic and Sentimental poetry. His distinctive talent, however, becomes obvious in such poems as "Putnik" (Traveler, 1828), "Nochleg chumakov" (The Camp of Ukrainian Carters, 1828), and "Sirota" (Orphan, 1828).

In "Putnik" Kol'tsov recalls his own experience during his journeys across the steppe and captures the romance of travel. The image of a campfire as a bright guiding star, which appeared for the first time in "Putnik," recurred in Kol'tsov's later poems. Although the influence of Pushkin's *Tsygany* (The Gypsies, 1824) is obvious in the intonation, rhythm, and iambic meter of "Nochleg chumakov," the poem relates to Kol'tsov's personal impressions of his meeting with a group of Ukrainian peasants, their songs, and their tales of the past. "Sirota" is simultaneously a lament and a meditation on the hard lot of an orphaned peasant girl. In his early poems Kol'tsov deals primarily with the description of his own experiences, his milieu. Yet, in these poems, naive and imitative as they are, he does more than just describe; he focuses on those aspects of humanity from which he formulated his worldview regarding the human condition.

By the beginning of 1829 Kol'tsov had become well known in Voronezh intellectual circles as his poems were passed among friends. In the early nineteenth century cultural and intellectual life in Russian provincial towns was an interesting and little-known phenomenon. At the turn of the eighteenth century the old town of Voronezh had been one of the most rapidly growing trade and cultural centers of the country. Historical-ethnographical societies were founded in Voronezh at the end of the eighteenth century, and in 1798 an anthology of Russian poetry was published there in the newly opened print shop. The Voronezh theater, which was opened in 1787, staged the plays of William Shakespeare, Friedrich Schiller, and the Russian dramatists Aleksandr Petrovich Sumarokov and Vladislav Aleksandrovich Ozerov. In the 1830s and 1840s the famous Russian actors Pavel Stepanovich Mochalov, Mikhail Semenovich Shchepkin, and Vasilii Ignat'evich Zhivokini came on tour to Voronezh. There were many musical salons and several literary societies in the town. Literary societies included not only the nobility but also children of merchants, state officials, and petty bourgeoisie. Kol'tsov joined one of these literary circles headed by Andrei Porfirievich Serebriansky, a poet, critic, and talented performer of both his own and other poets' works. Serebriansky was the author of a popular student song, "Bystry kak volny dni nashei zhizni" (Fast as the Waves are the Days of Our Lives, 1830s). At the time of his first meeting with Kol'tsov, Serebriansky was a student in the Voronezh theological school. He introduced Kol'tsov to friends who shared his interests in literature, the majority of whom were students and professors of the theological school. Their interests were quite diverse: they discussed the problems of classicism and Romanticism in literature, German philosophy, and aesthetics. The seminarists wrote poems and songs and compiled several manuscript anthologies of Russian poems.

Kol'tsov's talent and thirst for education were noticed by two professors of the theological school, Aleksandr Dmitrievich Vel'iaminov and Petr Ivanovich Stavrov. Vel'iaminov, who taught philosophy, physics, and mathematics, took an active interest in Kol'tsov from the time of their first meeting. He undertook to broaden Kol'tsov's intellectual horizons: he brought Kol'tsov books from the school library, urging him to quit his father's business and to engage in serious and systematic studies. Kol'tsov, who grasped every available opportunity to learn, often brought his notebooks of poems to Vel'iaminov, requesting his advice and instructions.

Serebriansky's circle helped Kol'tsov to realize and refine his talent. This group was his first audience. Since most of the seminarists were Kol'tsov's peers and had a similar family background, he was not intimidated by their criticism. Their arguments concerning poetry did not preclude serious disagreements, but however they disagreed, all of them assumed that poetry mattered deeply. Together with Serebriansky, Kol'tsov worked at both the form and style of his poems, trying to get rid of Sentimentalist clichés and elevated style. Later Kol'tsov wrote that he and Serebriansky "were maturing up together, shared a passion for Shakespeare, meditated, and argued."

Serebriansky stimulated Kol'tsov to develop an interest in philosophy. Kol'tsov's philosophical poems of the 1830s–"Velikaia taina" (The Great Mystery, 1833), "Bozhii mir" (God's World, 1837), and "Molitva" (The Prayer, 1836)–reflect Serebriansky's interest in universal things and natural philosophy. Like most Russian Romantics, Kol'tsov strove to present opposite categories as absolutes. Good and evil, beauty and ugliness, the elevated and the low were represented in his works as imminent categories. In his poems he often contrasted absolutes: spirit and matter, truth and mystery, eternal and temporary.

"Velikaia taina" is Kol'tsov's meditation on the mystery of being. Kol'tsov sees a marvelous unity not only on earth but also in the universe. He sees the universe as endless in space and time: "Bezdna zvezd na nebe / Bezdna zhizni v mire / . . . Idut nevozvratno veki za vekami" (The multitude of stars in the sky, / The multitude of life in the world / . . . Century follows century without return). The mysterious universe is governed by God, who pervades all things on earth and in the depth of the heavens. The poet describes his own restless striving and the heavens' reply. The poet is present as an earthling to whom the eternal universe is accessible only through special circumstances. The mystery of the future cannot be comprehended by reason; only faith brings the sweetness of consolation: "O gori lampada iarche pred raspiat'em / Tiazhely mne dumy / Sladostna molitva" (Burn brighter, O lamp in front of the crucifix / My thoughts are heavy / My prayer is sweet). He achieves communion with eternity through prayer.

"Molitva" is the poet's meditation on life and death and is enormously powerful in its fervent religious feeling. In his religious poems Kol'tsov comes close to Russian folk religious poetry–spiritual verses. Like many Romantics, however, he adapted Christian modes of thought to render his own spiritual experience.

Serebriansky recognized Kol'tsov's distinctive talent and promoted his poetry. In 1834 he wrote an article, "Voronezhskaia novost'" (Novelty in Voronezh), praising Kol'tsov's literary works; it was published in *Otechestvennye zapiski* (Notes of the Fatherland) in 1867. Their friendship continued after Serebriansky left for Moscow, where he became a student at the Medical-Surgical Academy. Kol'tsov grieved deeply over Serebriansky's early death in 1838.

In 1827 Kol'tsov experienced a love affair that profoundly influenced his life and poetic works. Since the Kol'tsovs did not belong to the nobility, they could not officially own serfs; thus it was a common practice to acquire serfs under someone else's name. Kol'tsov's father bought a serf girl, Duniasha, who became a servant in the house. Kol'tsov fell in love with the young girl and was ready to marry her. His family, however, was against this marriage, and while Kol'tsov was out of town on business, his father sold the girl to a landowner from the Don region. Although Kol'tsov looked for the girl, he could not find her, and according to Kol'tsov's letters, Duniasha soon died from grief and from the cruelty of her new owner. Their tragic love story became the subject of local folklore. One of these stories (which was recorded by a folklore expedition in Voronezh) reports that Kol'tsov found Duniasha at her deathbed. According to other sources, Duniasha's fate was not so dramatic: she married and, after Kol'tsov's death, even came to Voronezh to visit his sister. The loss of Duniasha caused Kol'tsov acute and haunting distress, and he could not forgive his family for their cruel interference. To his last day he carried in his heart the captivating image of his first love, and the serf girl Duniasha became the heroine of Kol'tsov's romantic legend.

The motif of death of a loved one and the lasting sorrow of love appears in Kol'tsov's works not only in the late 1820s to early 1830s but also through many of his later works. In the poems "Esli vstrechus' s toboi" (If I meet you, 1827), "Pervaia liubov'" (First Love, 1830), "Nichto, nichto na svete" (Nothing, nothing in the world, 1829), "Posledniaia bor'ba" (The Last Struggle, 1838) and "Razluka" (Separation, 1840) he repeatedly returns to Duniasha's image. In his love poems Kol'tsov expresses feelings and emotions he could not discuss even with his friends. He dramatizes the lyrical theme, reflecting shades and nuances of his personal feelings.

By 1830 Kol'tsov's poems had appeared in print. The novice poet Vasilii Ivanovich Sukhachev included four of Kol'tsov's poems–"Ne mne vnimat'" (Not for me to listen), "Razuverenie" (Dissuasion), "Pridi ko mne" (Come to me), and "Mshchenie" (Revenge)–in his collection of poems *Listki iz zapisnoi knizhki Vasiliia Sukhacheva* (Pages from the Notebook by Vasilii Sukhachev, 1830). All four of the poems are imitative, replete with Romantic and Sentimental clichés. Since Kol'tsov gave these poems to Sukhachev for publication, however, it is likely that he considered them his most important ones. Because Sukhachev published the poems without mentioning Kol'tsov's name, Kol'tsov's biographers often refer to Sukhachev's publication as an instance of plagiarism. However, the tradition of anonymous anthologies of poems and songs was still alive, especially in the provinces. It is quite possible that Sukhachev, who was from the provinces, was following tradition and published his collection as an anthology, signing his name as the compiler.

In 1830 Kol'tsov met Nikolai Vladimirovich Stankevich, a philosopher and poet whose family estate was not far from Voronezh. The friendship with Stankevich profoundly changed Kol'tsov's worldview and literary career. In 1831, while attending to his father's business in Moscow, Kol'tsov stayed with Stankevich. There Kol'tsov became acquainted with the members of Stankevich's philosophical circle, all students at Moscow University. The members of Stankevich's circle later became prominent in literature, journalism, publishing, and politics.

During this stay in Moscow, Kol'tsov met Vissarion Grigor'evich Belinsky, who became his friend and literary mentor. At this time Belinsky was at the beginning of his prominent literary career, but by the late 1830s he was one of the leading Russian literary critics and journalists, as well as a leader of the Westernizing movement. He not only contributed much to Kol'tsov's intellectual development but also helped the young poet to find his way into the mainstream of Russian literature. Throughout the years of their friendship Belinsky exerted great influence upon Kol'tsov.

At the beginning of 1831 Kol'tsov's poems "Vzdokh na mogile Venevitinova" (A Sigh at Venevitinov's Grave), "Poslanie K." (Epistle to K.), and "Poslanie Ogarkovoi" (Epistle to Ogarkova) were published in the Moscow journal *Listok* (The Flier). "Vzdokh na mogile Venevitinova" is a most remarkable poem that demonstrates Kol'tsov's literary taste and orientations. He admired Dmitrii Vladimirovich Venevitinov's poetry and understood the profound loneliness of the poet, whose untimely death he mourned.

There is little documentary data on Kol'tsov's literary connections at the beginning of the 1830s or on his first stay in Moscow. However, it is possible that he was acquainted with the poets who contributed to *Listok*. Among them was Vasilii Stepanovich Mezhevich, poet, journalist, author of the book *O narodnosti v zhizni i poezii* (On National Traits in Life and Poetry, 1835), and a contributor to the journals *Teleskop* (Telescope), *Molva* (Rumor), *Otechestvennye zapiski,* and *Severnaia pchela* (The Northern Bee). Mezhevich, like Kol'tsov, wrote songs, some of which became quite popular. Stankevich recommended Kol'tsov's poem "Russkaia pesnia" (Russian Song) for publication in *Literaturnaia gazeta* (Literary Gazette) in 1831. The publications in *Listok* and in *Literaturnaia gazeta* brought Kol'tsov's name to the reading public.

Although Kol'tsov had to devote most of his time to his father's business, he was still able to continue his education. The burden of his work as a cattle dealer did not prevent him from writing. Upon his return to Voronezh he kept in touch with his Moscow friends and contributed to *Molva* and *Teleskop*. He even considered the publication of a Voronezh literary almanac. When Stankevich suggested to Kol'tsov that he publish a collection of his poems, Kol'tsov already had many works from which to make a selection. Stankevich asked his friends to pledge money for the publication, and the first volume of Kol'tsov's poetry, *Stikhotvoreniia* (Poems), came out in 1835. The book was successful beyond Kol'tsov's wildest expectations. In an article for *Molva* Belinsky praised Kol'tsov's works as "a remarkable event in our literature, a real surprise of our time." In his journal, *Sovremennik* (The Contemporary), Pushkin also expressed considerable enthusiasm about Kol'tsov's works.

The secret of Kol'tsov's immediate success lay in his songs, especially the Russian ones. The literary genre of the Russian song dates back to the eighteenth century. Only in the 1820s, however, did the Russian

Vissarion Grigor'evich Belinsky, friend and literary mentor to Kol'tsov

song become popular, with the genre truly flourishing in the 1830s. This genre falls at the crossroads of bookish poetry and oral folk poetry. According to Ivan Nikanorovich Rozanov, in order to understand the origin of the Russian song as a genre one must look at the authors who contributed to it. Like the masterpieces of oral folk poetry that were created by talented anonymous authors, the works in the genre of the Russian song were also created by people who did not belong to the educated minority. There were noblemen among the authors, such as Del'vig, Prince Aleksandr Aleksandrovich Shakhovskoi, Prince Petr Ivanovich Shalikov, and Count Aleksei Konstantinovich Tolstoi, or statesmen close to court, such as Iurii Aleksandrovich Neledinsky-Meletsky and Chamberlain Ivan Petrovich Miatlev. Yet, there were also many poets who did not belong to the nobility: from the merchant families, along with Kol'tsov, came Merzliakov and Ivan Ivanovich Lazhechnikov; from the clergy, Serebriansky and Vasilii Ivanovich Krasov; from peasants, Nikolai Grigor'evich Tsyganov, Mikhail Dmitrievich Sukhanov, and Ivan Zakharovich Surikov. Thus, the Russian song resulted from two separate tendencies: that of the educated nobility toward oral folk poetry and a much stronger tendency of the unprivileged classes toward literature.

It should be borne in mind that the genres of the song, and particularly the Russian song, were literary genres for both poets and the reading public. Often composers wrote music to these literary texts, thus turning them into musical romances. The majority of songs, however, remained only for reading. The characteristics of the genre can be traced to its origin. Words and expressions used only in intellectual circles are not acceptable in the Russian song. Also not permitted are complex syntactical constructions and sentences. The tropes that are characteristic of Russian folklore—negative comparisons, tautology, constant epithets—are widely used in the Russian song. Unlike folk songs, the genre of the Russian song permits for neither rude folk expressions nor the abundance of everyday details. While the folk song is always realistic and does not avoid the prosaic detail of life, the Russian song, under the influence of Sentimental poetry, does not re-create real life; rather, it focuses mostly on sad and tender feelings. Favorite nature images in the Russian song are flowers and birds. Although these images also often occur in folk songs, they do not predominate there.

Kol'tsov's superiority over his forerunners, and even his followers and successors, lies in the fact that he could come closer not only to the form but also to the spirit and mood of the folk song. Even in his Russian songs there is an environment of realistic everyday life. Kol'tsov's favorite meter—the double amphibrach—is common in folk songs, in which the lines flow freely and musically. The melodiousness of Kol'tsov's songs, as well as the use of vowel harmony, attracted many composers. Often several composers wrote music for the same song. Thus, his "Ty ne poi solovei" (Nightingale, do not sing, 1832) has six musical versions.

In his songwriting Kol'tsov certainly drew upon traditional models for content, form, and style. Sometimes he took a line from a folk song and built a new song around it. Since Kol'tsov acquired much of the material orally he often used themes and commonplaces native to folk material. In his first collection of poems Kol'tsov included such songs as "Ty ne poi solovei" and "Ne shumi ty, rozh'" (Do not rustle, rye, 1834). In these songs Kol'tsov's relationship with poetry and the folk song manifests itself in an obvious way. He uses themes and images inherent to both genres: in "Ty ne poi, solovei" Kol'tsov turns to the theme of unshared love, while in "Ne shumi ty, rozh'" he writes about the death of the beloved one. In both songs Kol'tsov uses stylistic devices, tropes, and tonality characteristic of the folk song. The profoundness and intensity of feelings and emotions, however, as well as the dramatic conflict, come from poetry. In "Ty ne poi, solovei" the images are not symbolic, but at the same time neither are they merely ordinary objects. The song "Ne shumi ty, rozh'" ends on a dramatic note: "Spit mogil'nym snom / Krasnaia devitsa / Tiazhelei gori / Temnei polnochi / Legla na serdtse / Duma chernaia" (The beautiful girl / Sleeps a deadly sleep / Heavier than a mountain / Darker than midnight / A dark thought / Lies upon the heart). In these songs the literary word supplants the traditional and oral word that formed the basis for the songs.

The genre of the Russian song made Kol'tsov famous among his contemporaries. Usually Kol'tsov's contemporaries did not go beyond a fine stylization of Russian folk songs. Literary poetry in the songs by Del'vig, Dmitriev, Merzliakov, and Fedor Nikolaevich Glinka stylizes the images and plots of folk songs. Kol'tsov came to the Russian song from folk poetry, which was inherent with him since he had grown up with and lived among the people. Belinsky was not mistaken when he explained Kol'tsov's excellence in the genre of the Russian song as deriving from his origin, upbringing, and way of life. Indeed, Kol'tsov knew the life of Russian peasants not from the books but from firsthand experience.

In his first collection Kol'tsov also included poems about peasant life. One of the most important is "Krest'ianskaia pirushka" (The Peasants' Feast, 1830). In this poem Kol'tsov gives an original picture of the life of the common people, artistically conveyed. He describes the traditions: "Molodaia zhena / Obkhodila podrug s potseluiami / Raznosila gostiam chashu gor'kogo" (Young wife / Went around friends kissing each one / Offered a goblet of wine to the guests). Everything in this poem is in the folk-song tradition, especially fixed epithets and repetitions of prepositions. As in folk songs, the lines are not rhymed, but they have regular alternation of stressed and unstressed syllables. Although the language of "Krest'ianskaia pirushka" is that of popular speech, there is no use of dialect.

Kol'tsov continued the theme of peasant life in his works of the 1830s and turned to what he considered one of the most important motifs—that of the working peasant. In "Pesnia pakharia" (Song of a Plowman, 1831) Kol'tsov's plowman is close to Mother Earth: he will be fed by her ("Ego vspoit, vskormit mat' syra zemlia"). Mother Earth is perceived as a living being; through the eyes of a peasant poet the work is perceived as a creative process. He is not only a plowman; he does all peasant work. While plowing the field he knows that he will also be sowing, gathering the crop, and threshing. Thus, the poem is not merely an idyllic picture of pastoral labor. While walking along the field in spring, the plowman sees in his mind the threshing floor and stacks. He works and thinks about rest at the end of all the seasonal field work: "Sladok budet otdykh na snopakh tiazhelykh" (Sweet will be rest on the heavy sheaves). Peasant work, according to Kol'tsov's poem, bears almost cosmic overtones: symbolically, the poem begins with the plowman's addressing his horse and ends with his address to God. There is a definite ascent in the hierarchy of feelings. He poeticizes those aspects of the peasants' everyday life and work that give their life a special force, staunchness, and a power of endurance: "Veselo ia lozhu boronu i sokhy / Telegu gotovliu zerna zasypaiu / Veselo gliazhu ia na gumno i skirdy / Molochu i seiu . . . " (Joyfully I work with harrow and plow / Get the cart ready, pour in seeds, / Joyfully I look at threshing floor and sheaves / I thresh and sow . . .). For Kol'tsov's peasant, work brings joy and bears spiritual meaning.

In his Russian songs Kol'tsov captured the very essence of the national spirit—the poetry of agricultural labor. In Kol'tsov's poetry a peasant who preserves ties with Mother Earth is a wholesome person. Agricultural labor satisfies his spiritual needs. In the poem "Urozhai" (The Harvest, 1835) Kol'tsov again depicts not only harvesttime but also the sowing, reaping, and gathering of the harvest. Work is a joy and a festival—the sound of laden carts is music to the peasants. "Urozhai," like "Pesnia pakharia," ends with a prayer to the Mother of God. Kol'tsov's peasant believes that everything on earth was created by God for the good of the people. In Russian folk conscience the idea of Mother Earth was close to that of the Mother of God; both were bearers of life and consolation. In his peasant poems Kol'tsov captured the unity of peasant work with the cycles of nature. For him a peasant's household and village make up the fundamental unit of society. Since his works reflect the way of life of such a community, they acquire universality. He moves from the immediate surroundings toward the nation. The poet thereby enfolds not just a specific village and field but rather the whole earth. Kol'tsov's plowman possesses the cosmic perception of the earth and the sun, thus making the peasant approach epic characterization. In his songs about peasant work Kol'tsov preserves the national heritage. "Dobry molodtsy"—fine young men, fair maidens, plowmen—are all characters of the national Russian scale.

Kol'tsov's acquaintance with Stankevich and Belinsky opened the doors to the literary salons of Moscow and St. Petersburg for him. By 1836 his friendship with Belinsky had grown stronger. In January 1836 Kol'tsov left for St. Petersburg. It is hard to overestimate the influence of the Moscow and St. Petersburg intellectual circles on Kol'tsov. In St. Petersburg he became close to Petr Aleksandrovich Pletnev, a prominent literary critic, poet, and journalist. There he also met Andrei Aleksandrovich Kraevsky, a journalist and the

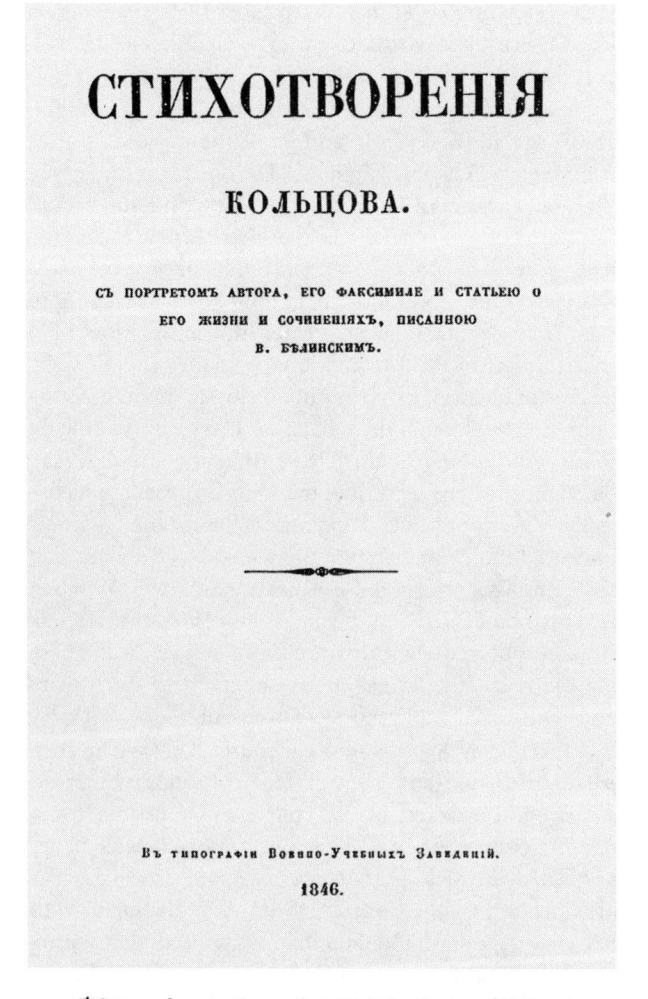

Title page for a posthumously published collection of Kol'tsov's Stikhotvoreniia *(Poems), with an essay by Belinsky about the poet's life and works*

publisher of *Otechestvennye zapiski;* Prince Vladimir Fedorovich Odoevsky; Prince Petr Andreevich Viazemsky; and many other prominent poets, writers, and intellectuals. He attended the literary gatherings held by Vasilii Andreevich Zhukovsky.

Kol'tsov valued his friendships and dedicated his poems to his friends. "Voennaia pesnia" (The Military Song, 1840) is dedicated to Viazemsky, whom Kol'tsov considered to be an influential statesman. Viazemsky had connections at the tsar's court and helped Kol'tsov in his many business lawsuits over property disputes and risky transactions. "Voennaia pesnia" is written in the tradition of the Russian military epic. Though the second half of the eighteenth century—the times of Gen. Aleksandr Vasil'evich Suvorov's victories—is referred to as the distant past, the song is recent. Nevertheless, Kol'tsov uses speech forms characteristic to old Russian *byliny* (heroic poems): "Gei sestra gei sablia ostraia / Popiruem my u nedruga . . . Vyp'em bragi busurmanskoi" (Hey, my sister, my sharp saber / We shall have a feast at our enemy's place . . . We shall drink the infidels' beer).

Kol'tsov dedicated the poem "Noch'" (Night, 1840) to Odoevsky, the author of the cycle of stories *Russkie nochi* (Russian Nights, 1844). To a certain degree the poem reflects Odoevsky's fantastic and supernatural world of art, music, and madness. Music forms the background of Kol'tsov's poem: "Ne smotria v litso / Ona pela mne" (Not looking at me / She was singing to me). The second stanza creates the impression of a musical stream: "A v okno luna / Tikho svet lila / Sladostrastnykh snov / Byla noch'" (And the moon quietly / Poured light through the window / The night was filled / With voluptuous dreams). The dramatic story of jealousy, murder, mystery, and madness is presented laconically. Although the Romantic plot of the poem is universal the characters are unmistakably Russian, and all the images are rooted in Russian soil. In 1840 when Kol'tsov dedicated this poem to him, Odoevsky's stories had not yet been organized into a cycle. It is possible that the title *Russkie nochi* was given to the stories after Odoevsky had read Kol'tsov's poem.

While living in St. Petersburg Kol'tsov participated in discussions, contributed to the journal *Sovremennik*, and worked at his collection of poems for a revised edition of his 1835 collection that was never published. Most important for Kol'tsov, however, was his meeting with Pushkin, who was familiar with Kol'tsov's poems and had highly praised the young poet's first book. He learned about Kol'tsov's arrival in St. Petersburg from Zhukovsky and Viazemsky and invited the young poet to his house. Since Kol'tsov was too shy to accept the invitation of the poet he admired so greatly, Pushkin had to send a second invitation to him. Kol'tsov met with Pushkin several times, and he treasured these meetings so much that he never shared the content of their conversations with anyone. Pushkin's attention to Kol'tsov's works was profound and serious. He recognized Kol'tsov's distinctive talent and described him as a person who possessed a wide range of interests. Yet, Pushkin did not overestimate the young poet's abilities and noted Kol'tsov's insufficient education and lack of systematic knowledge. In the third volume of *Sovremennik* Pushkin commented favorably on his friend's works, noting the "kind attention of the reading public to the poetic works by Kol'tsov."

Kol'tsov, who considered Pushkin to be the greatest poet of the time, was devastated by Pushkin's untimely death. In the poem "Les" (The Forest, 1837) he mourns the poet. Kol'tsov creates the image of a forest and of the legendary knight Bova, defeated in unequal struggle: "Ne osilili / Tebia sil'nye / Tak dorezala / Osen' chernaia / Znat' vo vremia sna / K bezoruzhnomu / Sily vrazhnye ponakhlynuli" (You could not be / Defeated by the strong ones / But dark autumn finished you / Probably while you were asleep / Unarmed, / The enemy forces attacked you).

Kol'tsov was interested in the theoretical problems that were being discussed in Stankevich's circle. In the 1830s Kol'tsov continued to work at his *dumy* (meditations). Kol'tsov was well acquainted with Ukrainian folk poetry, and in genre his meditations are, to a certain degree, related to Ukrainian folk ballads (also called *dumy*). Kol'tsov's *dumy*, however, are philosophical meditations on life and death, on the mysteries of the universe, and on the fate of his generation. A striving for the absolute Truth, inherent to the Russian religious mind, found its reflections in Kol'tsov's meditations, and they bear heavy traces of mysticism. Kol'tsov's *dumy* are not rooted in folk poetry. Rather, their origin is literary. In his *dumy* of the 1830s—such as "Molitva," "Velikoe slovo" (Great Word, 1835), and "Mogila" (The Grave, 1836)—Kol'tsov juxtaposes spiritual striving with human bondage.

The impossibility of reconciliation between the eternal truths of the universe and the earthly thoughts of a human being became the dominant idea of many of Kol'tsov's works. The themes of unhappy, tragic love and the impossibility of finding happiness are characteristic of Kol'tsov's lyrical poetry. In the poem "Razluka" (The Parting, 1840) the intensity of feelings reaches the highest point and ends tragically and abruptly as the woman pleads: "Ne khodi, postoi, dai vremia mne / Zadushit' grust', pechal' vyplakat' / Na tebia, na iasna sokola . . . / Zanialsia dukh, slovo zamerlo" (Do not go away. Give me time / To subdue my sadness, to cry out my grief, / About you, bright falcon . . . / The breath stopped, the word died). In this poem he shows the hopelessness of human life when faced with the malevolence of inscrutable fate.

In Moscow Belinsky introduced Kol'tsov to the prominent literary critic and ethnographer Nikolai Ivanovich Nadezhdin and to the poet Glinka, the author of Karelian poems that were based on his study of the ethnography and folklore of Karelia, a region along the eastern border of Finland. The friendship with Glinka continued after Kol'tsov's departure for Voronezh, where Glinka and his wife, Avdot'ia Nikolaevna, visited him. Vasilii Kol'tsov, the poet's father, was flattered by his son's prominent friends. A practical man, Vasilii Kol'tsov urged his son to use those literary connections for the advancement of their family's business. With the help of Viazemsky, Zhukovsky, and Odoevsky, Kol'tsov's business and legal problems were solved quickly and invariably to Kol'tsov's satisfaction.

In the summer of 1837 Grand Prince Aleksandr Nikolaevich arrived in Voronezh. Zhukovsky, who was

Manuscript for Kol'tsov's "Russkaia pesnia" (Russian Song) (from the 1846 edition of Stikhotvoreniia)

Prince Aleksandr's tutor, came with him; Zhukovsky met Kol'tsov's family and spent all of his free time with him. It is possible that Kol'tsov was introduced to the grand prince. This visit made Kol'tsov even more important in his father's eyes. Vasilii Kol'tsov had never appreciated his son's literary works and considered them to be harmful and destructive for the business. In his view, the connections in high society were the only "excuse" for his son to write and publish. In 1837 Kol'tsov's reputation in Voronezh reached its zenith. He was recognized as a famous poet and a well-connected person.

In 1838 Kol'tsov returned to Moscow and St. Petersburg. During his stay in St. Petersburg he spent most of his time with his friends discussing literature, art, and philosophy. He also visited the Hermitage, admired the works of Karl Briullov, went to the theaters, and became acquainted with Mochalov and

Shchepkin. Kol'tsov became popular in artistic and intellectual circles of the Russian capital. He acquired the reputation of a "peasant self-taught poet." Almost every day he was invited to literary readings and discussions, and he even hosted Monday literary evenings at his residence. He made plans to stay in St. Petersburg and devote his entire life to literary work, though circumstances did not permit him to adhere to this goal.

During this time he became quite close to Belinsky, who had contributed much to Kol'tsov's education and intellectual development. Belinsky, however, underestimated Kol'tsov's lack of formal education. In spite of Kol'tsov's attempts to master philosophy and aesthetics, many of the philosophical concepts were too abstract for the poet. In a 15 June 1838 letter to Belinsky, Kol'tsov wrote that he could not understand the idea of an absolute in philosophy, poetry, or history: "I still don't understand the endless play of life . . . and there is nothing in the world that would set my mind at peace so much as a complete understanding of these ideas." He was frustrated and dissatisfied with himself. Although he considered himself to be an inseparable part of the literary circles of St. Petersburg and Moscow, he felt insecure among the intellectuals. The result of his emotional crisis was obvious in his poetical works.

When Kol'tsov returned to Voronezh he did not find peace within himself in quiet, provincial life. Although he was welcomed back as a distinguished person, he could not overcome his discontent. He missed not only his intellectual friends but also the cultural life of St. Petersburg. He could not find inspiration anywhere; even in his favorite steppe he became bored. He wrote that the steppe "was beautiful only for a minute, but not for me." His father's business was in disarray, but Kol'tsov was not interested in putting things in order. He wanted to sever contacts with this milieu. In his letters to Belinsky he describes his Voronezh environment as a small and suffocating world where the poet's life was bitter. Because he had returned to Voronezh as a poet well-known in the state capital, Kol'tsov felt superior to many of his former friends and acquaintances. He wrote to Belinsky that on his arrival in Voronezh he "wanted to convince them that they have a distorted view of everything, that they are mistaken, I tried to explain in this or that way. They laugh at me, think that I speak rubbish." As a result Kol'tsov alienated many of his former friends as well as his family.

In spite of his bitterness and dissatisfaction Kol'tsov still actively participated in the cultural life of Voronezh. He treasured all his acquaintances who reminded him of Moscow or St. Petersburg. He surrounded himself with a circle of friends with whom he discussed the works of Pushkin, Mikhail Iur'evich Lermontov, Johann Wolfgang von Goethe, and George Gordon, Lord Byron. Among Kol'tsov's acquaintances there were several talented poets whom he tried to help. He gave advice on their works, which he sent to his friends in St. Petersburg in an attempt to have them published.

Kol'tsov also continued to expand his own library. From 1838 to 1840 he received journals and books from St. Petersburg and often copied newly published poems for his friends. He managed to obtain and read all the important Russian literary journals of the time. In 1839 he wrote his famous song "Khutorok" (The Farm), which he called a drama or Russian ballad; it was published in *Otechestvennye zapiski* that year. The plot of the song includes love, death, murder, and mystery. The characters are from the world of folklore–a young widow, a merchant, a fisherman, a fine young man. Music accompanies action in "Khutorok" and remains alive after the death of all the characters: "I s tekh por v khutorke / Uzh nikto ne zhivet / Lish' odin solovei / gromko pesni poet" (And since then nobody / Lives on the farm / Only the nightingale / Sings loudly alone.) "Khutorok" is saturated with passion and emotions. Fyodor Dostoyevsky included this song in *Prestuplenie i nakazanie* (Crime and Punishment, 1866).

During the years 1837 through 1842 Kol'tsov continued to collect Russian folk proverbs, sayings, and songs. He read almost everything that had been previously published on the subject. With great interest he read the ethnographical works by Ivan Petrovich Sakharov and Ivan Mikhailovich Snegirev. Kol'tsov accumulated 438 proverbs and sayings; his collection was one of the largest of the time. Since his business kept him in touch with various people, it seemed natural for him to record folklore material that he heard during his travels. Unlike many ethnographers who took their material from historical manuscripts and books, Kol'tsov included in his collection only those proverbs and sayings that he had personally heard from peasants. He recorded folklore material primarily from villages. In his records Kol'tsov preserved not only the variants of every proverb or saying but also the phonetic peculiarities of the local dialect. Kol'tsov painstakingly compared his records with the already published collections by other ethnographers. His collection was a serious attempt at a scientific recording and classification of folklore. Besides proverbs and sayings, Kol'tsov collected folk songs in both Russian and Ukrainian; some of these were published in *Literaturnoe nasledstvo* (Literary Heritage) in 1968.

Kol'tsov's friends in St. Petersburg were aware of his discontent and his wish to leave Voronezh forever. In 1839 he was offered positions as a manager of a cooperative bookstore or in the office of the journal *Otechestvennye zapiski*. As a practical and experienced businessman Kol'tsov immediately saw the financial groundlessness of these projects and stayed in Voronezh.

In September 1840 Kol'tsov made his last trips to St. Petersburg, to conclude two pending court cases, and to Moscow, to sell cattle. His father hoped to receive more than 12,000 rubles for the latter transaction. Kol'tsov spent more than three months in St. Petersburg. He welcomed the new year of 1841 with a circle of close friends, including Belinsky, Shchepkin, and Timofei Nikolaevich Granovsky. While staying in St. Petersburg he lived with Belinsky, who made another attempt to publish a new collection of Kol'tsov's poems. The years 1840–1841 were the last of Kol'tsov's and Belinsky's close friendship. After Kol'tsov's departure for Voronezh, their association became more and more distant.

Kol'tsov was no longer interested in his family business. He lost an important court case and sold the cattle at a loss. He spent all the money in St. Petersburg and Moscow and did not want to return home. He asked his father for money to start his own business in one of the capitals, but received an adamant refusal.

He returned to Voronezh in March 1841 penniless. His family blamed him for all their business losses. Family conflicts were inevitable since Kol'tsov had failed to fulfill his father's expectations. The discord became even more serious after Kol'tsov fell passionately in love with Varvara Grigor'evna Lebedeva (née Ogarkova), who was an outcast in Voronezh society because she had the reputation of a kept woman. In his letters to Belinsky, Kol'tsov portrayed her as a beautiful, clever, and educated woman. For a brief time he was happy. Their affair, however, was a short one; Lebedeva left Kol'tsov for a young officer. Kol'tsov suffered from this breakup profoundly, and Lebedeva's betrayal evoked the memory of his first loss–the peasant girl Duniasha. In his poems he mourned his losses. He recollected the hours spent with Duniasha, and thoughts of her fate did not leave him. He often returned to her in his songs of the 1840s.

Kol'tsov was already ill with tuberculosis, and his condition was aggravated by his unhappiness about the ending of the affair with Lebedeva. In 1842 his illness was progressing rapidly. It was obvious that Kol'tsov was not going to continue his family business; he still wanted to obtain money and return to St. Petersburg. The conflict in his family became bitter when Kol'tsov's beloved younger sister Anisia, who used to inspire her brother and often performed his songs, became involved in the conflict and received his share of their inheritance as her dowry. His family no longer needed him. Kol'tsov wrote his friends about his sufferings and misery, and in his poems and songs of 1842 he foresaw his approaching death. His only consolation was his friends' letters and books; by March 1842, however, he had become too weak to read. Aleksei Kol'tsov died on 29 October 1842 in Voronezh.

Letters:

Pis'ma A. V. Kol'tsova, preface by P. Smirnovsky (Moscow, 1901).

Biographies:

Mikhail F. De-Pule, *A. V. Kol'tsov v ego zhiteiskikh i literaturnykh delakh, i v semeinoi obstanovke* (St. Petersburg, 1878);

Vasilii Vasil'evich Ogarkov, *A. V. Kol'tsov, ego zhizn' i literaturnaia deiatel'nost'* (St. Petersburg, 1891);

Natal'ia Alekseevna Maksheeva, *A. V. Kol'tsov, ego zhizn' i pesni* (St. Petersburg, 1905);

Antonina Andreevna Moiseeva, *A. V. Kol'tsov. Kritiko-biograficheskii ocherk* (Moscow: Khudozhestvennaia literatura, 1956);

Viacheslav Alekseevich Tonkov, *A. V. Kol'tsov. Zhizn' i tvorchestvo* (Voronezh: Voronezhskoe knizhnoe izd-vo, 1958);

Tonkov, ed., *Sovremenniki o Kol'tsove* (Voronezh: Voronezhskoe knizhnoe izd-vo, 1959);

Nikolai Nikolaevich Skatov, *Kol'tsov* (Moscow: Molodaia gvardiia, 1983).

References:

A. V. Kol'tsov i N. S. Nikitin (Moscow: Nikitinskie subbotniki, 1929);

A. V. Kol'tsov. Stat'i i materialy (Voronezh, 1960);

Vissarion Grigor'evich Belinsky, "O zhizni i sochineniiakh Kol'tsova," in his *Polnoe sobranie sochinenii*, volume 9 (Moscow: AN SSSR, 1955), pp. 497–542;

N. F. Bunakov, "Kol'tsov kak chelovek i kak poet," *Filologicheskie zapiski*, 5 (1892): 1–55;

E. Caffrey, "Kol'tsov: A Study in Rhythm and Meter," dissertation, Harvard University, 1968;

Nikolai Aleksandrovich Dobroliubov, "A. V. Kol'tsov," in his *Polnoe sobranie sochinenii v shesti tomakh*, volume 1, edited by Iulian Grigor'evich Oksman (Leningrad, 1934), pp. 119–161;

N. A. Ianchuk, "Literaturnye zametki (Pushkin i Kol'tsov. Etnograficheskie zaniatiia Kol'tsova)," *Izvestiia otdela russkogo iazyka i slovesnosti*, 12, book 4 (1907): 199–255;

Vladimir Avvakumovich Istomin, "Osnovnye motivy poezii Kol'tsova," *Russkii filologicheskii vestnik*, 4, section 2 (1892): 37–77;

S. M. Kliuev, "K voprosu o dumakh A. V. Kol'tsova," *Uchenye zapiski Moskovskogo gorodskogo pedagogicheskogo instituta*, 48, no. 5 (1955): 241–265;

S. A. Kudriashov, "Dialektizmy v stikhotvoreniiakh Kol'tsova," *Izvestiia Voronezhskogo pedagogicheskogo instituta,* 20 (1956): 87–102;

Viktor Ivanovich Kuznetsov, *Netlennye stroki: Etiudy ob Aleksee Koltsove i Ivane Nikitine* (Voronezh: Tsentr.-Chernozemnoe knizhnoe izd-vo, 1984);

Vladimir Vladimirovich Litvinov "Novoe o poete A. V. Kol'tsove," *Literaturnyi Voronezh,* 2 (1938): 420–422;

Valerian Nikolaevich Maikov, "Stikhotvoreniia Kol'tsova," in his *Kriticheskie opyty (1845–1847)* (St. Petersburg: "Panteon literatury," 1889), pp. 1–116;

Ia. Neverov, "Poet-prasol," *Syn otechestva,* 2, section 1 (1836): 259–272, 309–324;

Iulian Grigor'evich Oksman, "A. V. Kol'tsov i tainoe 'Obshchestvo nezavisimykh,'" in his *Ot "Kapitanskoi dochki" k "Zapiskam okhotnika." Pushkin, Ryleev, Kol'tsov, Belinskii, Turgenev; issledovaniia i materialy* (Saratov: Saratovskoe knizhnoe izd-vo, 1959), pp. 50–91;

Nikolai Vasil'evich Os'makov, ed., *A. V. Kol'tsov i russkaia literatura* (Moscow: Nauka, 1988);

Viktor Ostrogorsky, *Khudozhnik russkoi pesni A. V. Kol'tsov* (Moscow: D. I. Tikhomirov, 1893);

Nikolai Kiriakovich Piksanov, "Kol'tsov," in *Istoriia russkoi literatury,* volume 7 (Moscow-Leningrad, 1955), pp. 381–406;

Vasilii Ivanovich Pokrovsky, ed., *Aleksei Vasilievich Kol'tsov. Ego zhizn' i sochineniia. Sbornik istoriko-literaturnykh statei* (Moscow: Sklad v knizhnom magazine V. Spiridonova i A. Mikhailova, 1905);

A. M. Putintsev, "Kol'tsov kak sobiratel' russkikh narodnykh poslovits," *Trudy Voronezhskogo universiteta,* 3 (1926): 75–94;

Aleksandr Nikolaevich Pypin, "Lermontov i Kol'tsov," *Vestnik Evropy,* 1 (1896): 291–341;

Ivan Nikanorovich Rozanov, *Russkie pesni XIX veka* (Moscow: Khudozhestvennaia literatura, 1944);

Mikhail Evgrafovich Saltykov-Shchedrin, "Stikhotvoreniia A.V. Kol'tsova," in his *Polnoe sobranie sochinenii,* volume 5 (Moscow: Goslitizdat, 1952), pp. 31–52;

A. A. Seliverstov, "K voprosu o khudozhestvennom metode A.V. Kol'tsova," in *Iz istorii russkogo romantizma. Sbornik statei,* edited by A. M. Mikeshin (Kemerovo, 1971), pp. 118–130;

Nikolai Nikolaevich Skatov, *Poeziia Alekseia Kol'tsova* (Leningrad: Khudozhestvennaia literatura, 1977);

E. Stalinsky, *Kol'tsov i Serebriansky* (Voronezh, 1868);

Viacheslav Alekseevich Tonkov, *A. V. Kol'tsov i fol'klor* (Voronezh, 1940);

B. T. Udodov, ed., *A. V. Kol'tsov: stranitsy zhizni i tvorchestva* (Voronezh: Izd-vo Voronezhskogo universiteta, 1984);

L. K. Veinberg, "K biografii Kol'tsova," *Istoricheskii vestnik,* 1 (1893): 188–197;

A. Volynsky (Akim L'vovich Flekser), "A. V. Kol'tsov," in his *Bor'ba za idealizm. Kriticheskie stat'i* (St. Petersburg: M. Merkushev, 1900), pp. 149–180;

Ivan Ivanovich Zamotin, "A. V. Kol'tsov i russkie modernisty," *Russkii filologicheskii vestnik,* 3–4 (1909): 312–334.

Papers:

Some of Aleksei Vasil'evich Kol'tsov's papers are at the Institute of Russian Literature (Pushkin House), f. 93 and f. 586, and the Russian National Library, f. 361, both in St. Petersburg; and at the Central State Archive of Literature and Art (TsGALI), f. 263, Moscow.

Ivan Ivanovich Kozlov

(11 April 1779 - 30 January 1840)

James West
University of Washington

BOOKS: *Chernets, kievskaia povest'* (St. Petersburg: Tip. Departamenta narodnago prosveshcheniia, 1825);
Stikhotvoreniia (St. Petersburg: Tip. Departamenta narodnago prosviescheniia, 1828);
Bezumnaia (St. Petersburg: A. F. Smirdin, 1830);
Sobranie stikhotvorenii, 2 volumes (St. Petersburg: Tip. Inspektorskago Departamenta Voennago Ministerstva, 1833);
Tri poemy I. I. Kozlova, s biografiei i portretom avtora (St. Petersburg, 1889);
Stikhotvoreniia, edited by Aleksandr Ivanovich Vvedensky (St. Petersburg: A. F. Marks, 1892);
Dnevniki Kozlova, edited by Konstantin Iakovlevich Grot, *Starina i novizna*, volume 11 (St. Petersburg: M. Stasiulevicha, 1906).

Editions and Collections: *Stikhotvoreniia*, edited by Ts. Vol'pe (Leningrad: Sovetskii pisatel', 1936);
Stikhotvoreniia, edited by E. N. Kupreianova (Moscow: Sovetskii pisatel', 1948);
Stikhotvoreniia, edited by Isaak Davidovich Glikman (Leningrad: Sovetskii pisatel', 1956);
Polnoe sobranie stikhotvorenii, edited by Glikman (Leningrad: Sovetskii pisatel', 1960);
Stikhotvoreniia, edited by Vserolod Ivanovich Sakharov (Moscow: Sovetskaia Rossiia, 1979).

TRANSLATIONS: George Gordon, Lord Byron, *Nevesta abidosskaia, turetskaia povest'* (St. Petersburg: A. Smirdin, 1826);
Robert Burns, *Sel'skii subbotnii vecher v Shotlandii. Svobodnoe podrazhanie R. Bornsu* (St. Petersburg, 1829);
Adam Mickiewicz, *Krymskie sonety Adama Mitskevicha. Perevody i podrazhaniia Ivana Kozlova* (St. Petersburg: Nepeitsyn, 1829).

There is not a great deal of information available about the life of Ivan Kozlov, and during the twenty years of his literary career there is little to tell beyond the "inward biography" of a blind and paralyzed invalid. The gap has been filled by an impression of his life that is more hagiographic than realistic, generated by his courageous struggle with his afflictions and by the autobiographical nature of much of his poetry. During his lifetime the result of his well-publicized disability was a sometimes patronizing appreciation on the part of contemporary critics and poets. The most blatant example is the Polish poet Adam Mickiewicz's praise for Kozlov's translation of his Crimean sonnets (*Krymskie sonety Adama Mitskevicha. Perevody i podrazhaniia Ivana Kozlova*, 1829): Mickiewicz confided to friends that he found the translation extremely poor and had spoken well of it only because its author was blind. Vasilii Andreevich Zhukovsky's obituary on Kozlov, which transformed him into a typically Romantic noble sufferer, has tended to set the tone for subsequent estimation of his place in the history of Russian poetry. Kozlov did, however, enjoy in the 1820s and 1830s a reputation that cannot be explained simply by a sympathetic response to his misfortunes.

Ivan Ivanovich Kozlov was born on 11 April 1779 in Moscow. His father had been a senior official in the administration of Catherine the Great and was sufficiently wealthy to have his sons educated privately. Under the supervision of his mother (Anna Apollonovna, née Khomutova) Kozlov was schooled at home, for the most part by European rather than Russian tutors. He completed his education by voracious reading in several languages.

Following a practice that was common among Russian families of his class and that is familiar to readers of Aleksandr Pushkin's *Kapitanskaia dochka* (The Captain's Daughter, 1836), Kozlov was enrolled at the age of five as a sergeant in the Izmailovsky Guards regiment. At sixteen he was promoted to ensign, but, unlike Pushkin's Grinev, a military career in a fashionable regiment was not his fondest dream. Even to young men whose family traditions expected it of them, army service was particularly unappealing during the brief reign of Paul I, whose militarism took the form of an almost pathological obsession with discipline and drill parades, making him hated by all classes of Russians and eventually the victim of a palace coup in 1801. In September of 1798 the nineteen-year-old Kozlov found it preferable to obtain a transfer to the civil service at an appropriate rank, and in December he was assigned to a position in the chief prosecutor's office in Moscow. There he served until 1807, when he was transferred to the office of the army chief of staff in Moscow and promoted to senior rank.

Kozlov had a lively and convivial personality, and in the early 1800s he was a frequent and welcome guest at social occasions in Moscow, as might be expected of a well-educated and cultivated young man of his class. Too much has been made of his reputation during this period as a socialite whose talents found their outlet on the dance floor, by contrast with his later renown as a literary figure. Kozlov obviously had literary and intellectual interests from his early twenties that attracted the attention of Russian writers of stature, and it was in 1808, rather than on the appearance of his first verses more than a decade later, that he made the acquaintance of the poet Zhukovsky. Zhukovsky, who became in that year the editor of the literary journal *Vestnik Evropy* (Herald of Europe), was to prove a great deal more to Kozlov than an influential social contact.

In 1809 Kozlov married Sofiia Andreevna Davydova, the daughter of an army brigadier. A son, Pavel, was born in 1810 and a daughter, Aleksandra, in 1812. Kozlov's close and happy family life more than anything else sustained him through his later incapacitation and made possible his self-discovery as a poet. He was particularly fond of his daughter, to whom he gave an excellent education despite the circumstances of his later life. She became his principal reader and amanuensis after he went blind, and at least one visitor recalled her father's impatient and irritable treatment of her in this role. After her father's death, Zhukovsky petitioned the tsar for a pension to support her.

When Napoleon launched his invasion of Russia in 1812, Kozlov was appointed to a commission to recruit defense forces in the Moscow region but was shortly dismissed from this post and lived for the next few months with relatives of his mother in Rybinsk, in the Yaroslav Province. At the end of the war against Napoleon, Kozlov reentered government service, this time in St. Petersburg, and in July of 1813 received a senior post in the State Property Administration. In 1816 Kozlov was stricken with the illness that was to change his life profoundly. A form of progressive paralysis left him without the use of his legs, and he began to suffer a loss of eyesight that led over the next five years to total blindness. It was, however, only in 1823 that he was finally placed on the retired list and awarded a disability pension of 836 rubles a year. His health worsened during the 1830s, adding to his problems both difficulty in using his hands and deterioration of his hearing and speech.

Kozlov's first published poem was "K Svetlane" (To Svetlana), which appeared in *Syn otechestva* (Son of the Fatherland) in 1821, closely followed by "K drugu V. A. Zh." (To My Friend V. A. Zh.). The initials are those of his friend and mentor Zhukovsky, and Svetlana was the heroine of Zhukovsky's celebrated ballad, as well as his name for the favorite niece to whom it was dedicated. From the outset Kozlov's was a tributary muse, and his work abounds in poems to or about poets—George Gordon, Lord Byron; Robert Burns; Sir Walter Scott; William Wordsworth; Ludovico Ariosto; Petrarch; Alphonse-Marie-Louis de Prat de Lamartine; André Chénier; and Mickiewicz, who lived in Russia and was championed by many Russian poets of the time. A relatively large proportion of Kozlov's work, in fact, consists of translations or "imitations" of the poets he most admired. In the context of his time this interest does not necessarily equate with a lack of originality, since throughout Romantic Europe the poetic "imitation" became almost a genre in its own right. In any event, Kozlov's emergence onto the Russian literary scene as a publishing poet took place in circumstances that ensured him an indulgent reception.

In the conventional view, Kozlov's affliction drove him to explore his inner resources and to discover life anew as a poet. "Misfortune made him a poet," wrote Zhukovsky, and Vissarion Grigor'evich Belinsky elaborated: "Without the loss of his sight, Kozlov would have lived out his life without ever suspecting that he was a poet." Another critic of the time opined more bluntly: "Now he will be known to posterity as a fine and sensitive poet, whereas, while he could see and dance, his contemporaries said of him that his whole mind was in his legs." Pushkin, who was not given to empty praise of fellow poets, expressed the same thought in loftier form in a poem he wrote to Kozlov on receiving a copy of his poem *Chernets* (The Monk, 1825):

> When the eternal shroud of night
> The mortal world cloaked from your sight,
> Then woke your genius, and with longing
> Did gaze on every once seen thing,
> And stood with radiant visions thronging,
> And wondrously began to sing.

Pushkin's lines betray the motivation of Kozlov's literary contemporaries to misstate the connection between his illness and the beginning of his poetic creativity. Given Kozlov's education, reading, and earlier literary acquaintanceships, the connection is certainly not as simple as Zhukovsky, Belinsky, and others have suggested. Clearly, Kozlov's circumstances had an almost metaphysical appeal to his contemporaries. A paradoxical image dear to Romantic poets throughout Europe was of the darkness of night banishing the trivial reality of day and setting free the vision of a higher world, while the poetic inspiration of misfortune is a commonplace that can be found in virtually every age of European literature. Both Kozlov's works and the responses of his contemporaries suggest that there was a programmatic dimension to his refuge from blindness in poetry. He wrote in "K drugu V. A. Zh." that poetry was, of course, a source of strength and comfort for all, but that ". . . dlia menia lish' v nei odnoi / tsvetet prekrasnaia priroda / V nei mir raznoobraznyi moi / V nei vesel'e i svoboda" (. . . in poetry alone for me / Does nature's beauty bloom; / Therein my world's variety, / My merriment, my room!)

Kozlov found comfort in religion, and this characteristic also endeared him to Zhukovsky, whose response to the soul-wrenching disappointments of his own life was a similarly heightened religiosity. Zhukovsky noted Kozlov's astonishing patience and fortitude and described his poetic world as "illuminated by

Ivan Ivanovich Kozlov (portrait by A. Bryzgalov; Rumiantsev Museum, Moscow)

faith and purged by suffering." Resignation to the unfathomable will of God is certainly a constant motif in Kozlov's poetry, and one of his biographers has even suggested that he regarded his misfortune as "a kind of redemptory sacrifice" that might eventually bring happiness to his children. The devotion of his family was a powerful factor in enabling Kozlov to remain productive in his infirmity, and in this respect, too, his circumstances were attuned to the climate of an age that was more inclined to see love as an almost miraculous sustaining power than as a simple and universal domestic virtue, as had an earlier age. Kozlov himself, when the theme of family love appears in his poetry, gives it a strongly personal treatment, more characteristic of sentimentalism. The 1836 poem "Zhnetsy" (The Reapers) is a tribute to a young peasant family whose love helps them to bear their lot. The description is sentimental but down to earth and more characteristic of the eighteenth century than of the Romantic age. In the last few lines Kozlov declares that their memory is an inspiration to him in his blindness and immobility, a vision to which his thoughts, his heart, and his imagination reach out. The verse preface to his celebrated narrative poem *Chernets* dedicates the work to his wife as "Prekrasnyi drug minuvshikh svetlykh dnei" (Fair friend of bygone days of brightness), a form of address that is as archetypically sentimental as the elegiac tone.

Kozlov's literary activity through two decades of blindness was made possible by an extraordinary memory, which he turned to good advantage in many ways. Most importantly, his memory fueled his imagination: he dwelt in his mind's eye on sights remembered from his past, especially from his richest and happiest years in Moscow. When his sight began to fail, he garnered these memories deliberately. In "K drugu V. A. Zh." he describes the poet, as blindness overtakes him, directing his fading gaze to his wife and children in order to retain their image when his sight is gone. Nikolai Alekseevich Polevoi recalled his amazement at Kozlov's knowledge and interests, the range of his conversation, and his ability to recite from memory even the recent poetry of his contemporaries. Zhukovsky wrote to Kozlov in 1838 that, like Tsar Berendei of legend, Kozlov seemed to know everything that happened in the world without having seen it. He is reported to have known by heart the poetry from which he drew most inspiration, including, according to Zhukovsky, all of Jean Racine's poetic dramas, all of Byron and Torquato Tasso, the verse tales of Scott, extensive passages from William Shakespeare and Dante, the whole of the New Testament, and all of the standard prayers of the Russian Orthodox Church. His capacity for memorization even enabled the blind Kozlov to extend his knowledge of languages. He had been since childhood fluent in French and conversant with Italian, but he managed to add English, German, and Polish without the benefit of being able to read. For the Romantics memory itself had a metaphysical dimension, so the particular way in which Kozlov coped with his disability found a fortuitous echo in the philosophy of his age and could not fail to enhance his reception.

While his contemporaries saw his poetic awakening as a triumph of the spirit, the reader should remember that after 1823 Kozlov was obliged by circumstances to make a profession of his literary endeavors. Indeed, he took considerable pride in his new professional calling, and his early success gave him a robust opinion of his own talents. According to contemporary records, in the years of his greatest renown, when poetry almanacs approached him for a contribution, he would observe that both he and Pushkin charged five rubles a line for their verse and that he was unable to take less. His financial hardships were real and embarrassing. Il'ia Vasil'evich Selivanov recounts that the Kozlovs sometimes expended their last resources on offering hospitality to Zhukovsky, whom they regarded as a patron as well as a friend.

Kozlov's earlier conviviality stood him in good stead in his later years. His enforced immobility did not leave him isolated from the world, for he continued to receive visitors, who included many of the leaders in Russian culture of the 1820s and 1830s: Zhukovsky, Ivan Andreevich Krylov, Pushkin, most of the poets of the "Pushkin pleiade," (Aleksandr Sergeevich Griboedov, the Decembrist Kondratii Fedorovich Ryleev, Fedor Ivanovich Tiutchev, and later Mikhail Iur'evich Lermontov), and such figures as the composer Aleksandr Sergeevich Dargomyzhsky. As Polevoi observed, this was not a cavalcade of dutiful well-wishers, for Kozlov had a gift for lively conversation and for sharp observations on the characteristics of guests he could hear but not see; his drawing room was by no means the least lively of the literary gathering places of the capital. His literary biography is little more than a chronicle of visitors and publications, a fact that should not obscure his position as a characteristic representative of Russian cultural life.

Kozlov is of particular interest to the English-speaking reader as a translator of English poets, particularly of Byron and Burns. He was, in fact, probably the first to acquaint the Russian reader with the work of Burns, but he gives a somewhat distorted impression of the Scottish poet. Kozlov misconstrued Burns's reason for the use of dialect English, seeing the Scotsman through Russian eyes as a "peasant poet." Kozlov rendered Burns accordingly, as a simple soul singing of country pleasures and hardships rather than as the passionate voice of a proud Scotland. His best-known translation of Burns is the version of "The Cotter's Saturday Night" that appeared in 1829 under the title *Sel'skii subbotnii vecher v Shotlandii* (A Rural Saturday Night in Scotland). Kozlov described this piece as a "free imitation of Burns," and it is interesting more as a "transposition" of Burns into another key than a translation in the normal sense.

Kozlov is perhaps best known even within Russia as one of the earliest translators of Byron. Lermontov and his contemporaries at Moscow University probably became acquainted with Byron's poetry in Kozlov's translations, and someone has suggested that Pushkin's first experience of the influential English poet was through a poem (it has not survived) that Kozlov translated into French in 1819. The most ambitious of Kozlov's translations of Byron's works is *Nevesta abidosskaia* (The Bride of Abydos), which appeared in 1826 with an epigraph that does not appear in later editions, taken, a little unexpectedly for the English-speaking reader, from Burns's "Ae Fond Kiss." However, Kozlov's greatest success as a translator was probably with poets of lesser prominence, and his version of Thomas Moore's "Those Evening Bells" (*Vechernii zvon*) has been convincingly argued to exceed the somewhat trite original in every respect.

The legacy of Byron is often discernible in Kozlov's own poetry, and *Chernets* in particular is an outright imitation of Byron's *Giaour* (1813). The critic Aleksandr Vasil'evich Druzhinin wrote even in 1855 that Kozlov's development as a poet in his own right was arrested by his infatuation with Byron. This is certainly an overstatement. Kozlov's modest contribution to what must be regarded as a European-wide epidemic of imitation, translation, and tributary verse to Byron should be seen in perspective. In Russia even more than in Europe, Byron was lauded as the Romantic champion of national movements. The monk who is the hero of *Chernets* tells a somber tale that is as much Gothic as Byronic. Set in Kiev, it is replete with local and historical detail. Long a mysterious outsider in the monastic community, the monk tells the abbot on his deathbed the story of his life. After a difficult and loveless childhood, as a young man he was betrothed to the object of his passionate affections, the daughter of a Russian officer who had retired to Kiev. The marriage was prevented by a villainous rival, a Polish officer (this detail alone makes clear that the work has an underlying theme of Russian nationalism) who had had designs on her in the past and poisons her father's mind with compromising innuendos. The narrator responds by abducting the young lady and marrying her in secret. For a while they live happily, but the news, falsely propagated by the villain, that her father has cursed and disowned her, causes her to die while expecting their child. Mindless with grief, the narrator wanders in foreign lands for seven years until, in a moment of grace that comes to him one night on a starlit riverbank, he finally makes his peace with God. He returns to his native Kiev and is at first soothed by the sight of familiar places, but a chance glimpse of a happy young couple with their child restores his memory of the wrong he has suffered. When he encounters the villain, the monk kills him in a fit of rekindled rage; he then takes refuge in the monastery. There he lives in a state of inner turmoil, unable to discern a higher meaning in the loss of his love; he finds peace again only at his death.

The narrative of *Chernets* and its setting are reminiscent of the Gothic tales of Nikolai Mikhailovich Karamzin, who had introduced the genre to Russia some forty years previously. Though the psychology of the uprooted hero in this work is more clearly Byronic and is of the type that would shortly become celebrated in Lermontov's *Geroi nashego bremeni* (A Hero of Our Time, 1840), the religious attitude that is implied throughout is distinctly Russian. As is true of many important works of Russian literature in this period, the poem is a complex hybrid in which several strands of

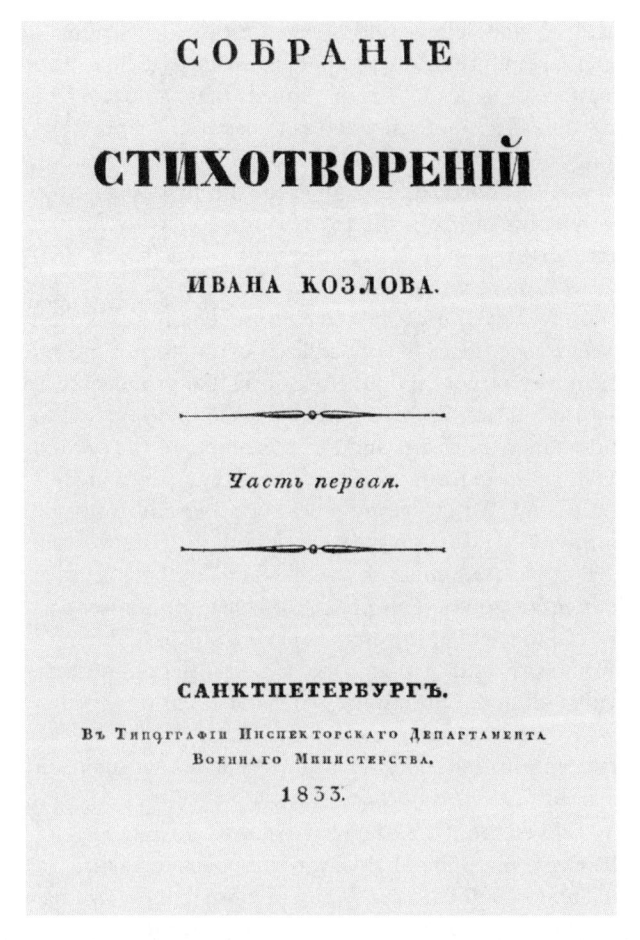

Title page for Kozlov's Sobranie stikhotvorenii *(Collected Poems), many of which he wrote after he became blind*

European influence are synthesized with a post-Napoleonic pride in Russian culture. Clearly, to Kozlov's European contemporaries, *Chernets* had something more to offer than another imitation of Byron; it even brought Kozlov some renown outside Russia. In the twenty-five years following its first publication, the poem appeared three times in French, three times in German, and once in Italian.

Chernets was the first of Kozlov's works that brought him literary fame rather than polite recognition. Not surprisingly, he followed it with other more or less Byronic narrative poems on Russian themes—*Kniaginia Dolgorukaia* (Princess Dolgoruky) in 1827 and *Bezumnaiia* (The Madwoman) in 1830. Both works were well received, though they appeared at a time when the Russian historical novel was coming into its own as the vehicle for a relatively newfound pride in the distinctiveness of Russian culture.

Kozlov's lyric verse is of uneven quality but includes some gems that caught the attention of critics, readers, and fellow poets, sometimes even eliciting a poetic response. He was appreciated in particular as a creator of climactic lines or couplets that capture a feeling with special intensity and as a master of "romances," songs in which he voiced his feelings for his addressees. A widely appreciated example of the first type, from early in his career, is the 1823 "Romance" with the first line "Est' tikhaia roshcha u bystrykh kliuchei; . . ." (I know a quiet grove beside fast-rushing streams; . . .). Loosely based on a passage from Thomas Moore's *Lalla Rookh,* it extols with stylized orientalism the fond memories of youthful love. A substantial proportion of Kozlov's lyrics, however, are dedicated or addressed to individuals by name, and a late example of the second type—closer in form to a verse epistle than a romance—is the wistful "Drugu vesny moei" (To a Friend from the Spring of My Life), written in 1838 to his cousin Anna Grigor'evna Khomutova, with whom he had been in love in his youth. This poem, to which Lermontov was moved to respond in verse, displays some psychological complexity and tempers the familiar elegiac posture with a glimpse of the spirit that carried Kozlov through twenty years of adversity, a declaration that he is content with his lot and grateful for the love that makes it bearable.

Even though Kozlov lived and wrote in the age of the elegy, disappointingly few of his poems break out of that all-too-popular vein. Many of those that do are, significantly, of Italian or Classical inspiration or reflect such inspiration in others. For example, "K Italii" (To Italy), written in 1825, is based on canto 4 of *Childe Harold's Pilgrimage,* in which Byron abandons the convention of the hero and addresses the reader directly. "Gimn Orfeia" (Orphic Hymn), written the year before the poet's death, transmutes the conventions of the classical elegy into a tribute to the immortal inspiration of art and music. A handful of poems about music and musicians are among the best that Kozlov wrote and reflect an intense love of music that is understandable in a poet deprived of his eyesight. Lastly, Kozlov produced a small number of poems that are overtly political in nature. Most do not go beyond a conventionally Romantic advocacy of freedom, and those that do, understandably, have European rather than Russian subjects.

Kozlov's poetic talent bears comparison with that of Zhukovsky in the sense that an unusually high proportion of his poetry, including some of his best, consists of translations or imitations. Though he lacked Zhukovsky's literary stature, Kozlov had similar strengths: both poets translated what answered to their own inward feelings and the spirit of the Russia of their time, and both imparted something of their own to their translations. In Kozlov's case, however, the personal note could sometimes be a distortion, since the tone of all he wrote reflected to some extent the peculiar hardship of his circumstances. His translations were sometimes unjustifiably colored by the mood that predominates in his work, an elegiac celebration of the inconstancy of human happiness. Here and there a direct influence of Zhukovsky on Kozlov is apparent, as in the closing lines of *Chernets,* which are a recognizable imitation of a poem by Zhukovsky.

Kozlov's predilection for translation from European poetry should not be misconstrued as a distaste for things Russian. In the early decades of the nineteenth century some European writers inspired Russians to a greater appreciation of their own national identity and fostered, paradoxically, Russian nationalism. The historical vision and patriotism of both Scott and Burns activated Kozlov's feelings for his own country and prompted him to turn to Russia's historical past. Like so many Russian writers of his generation, he drew both his knowledge of Russia's past and his sense of its importance from the work of a historian who was no less influential as a poet: the monumental *Istoriia gosudarstva Rossiiskogo* of Karamzin, written in the first decade of the nineteenth century. The French poet Prosper Mérimée was another European who unexpectedly activated the national awareness of Russian poets of this period; Kozlov, like Pushkin, was inspired by Mérimée's romantic imitations of the folk songs of the Southern Slavs to compose some verse in the spirit of Russian folk poetry.

Aside from the biographical component, Kozlov's brief but considerable popularity is owing to some additional factors. In Belinsky's rather scathing assessment, Kozlov's poetry suffers from a monotonous repertoire of motifs of suffering, endurance, and pious hope, mitigated only by the appeal of his melodious verses; he ascribed Kozlov's popularity almost entirely to his poem *Chernets*. In Belinsky's view, moreover, the critical acclaim of *Chernets* was not based purely on the merits of the poem. Many reviewers did refer to Kozlov's circumstances and indeed saw the poet in the image of his monk, not without some prompting from Kozlov himself in the introduction to the poem. Despite Belinsky's reservations, however, Kozlov owed some of his enthusiastic reception to a genuine gift for expressing the thoughts and feelings of his contemporaries.

Kozlov died on 30 January 1840 shortly after hinting to Zhukovsky during a visit that his end was near. Kozlov was buried in the Alexander Nevsky Monastery in St. Petersburg, where Zhukovsky was eventually laid to rest beside him. Afanasii Afanas'evich Fet (real name, Shenshin) provided a fitting poetic epitaph in his "Vechernii zvon. Pamiati Kozlova." (Evening Bells. To the Memory of Kozlov.): "Singer of earthly woes, / You will not die in people's hearts!" Readers who would like to explore further should take note that the sketchy accounts of Kozlov's life that have accumulated since his death have included an unusual number of factual errors, many of them propagated by borrowing from each other. His birth date has been given as variously as 1774 and 1789, and the date of his death has been given as 1838; moreover, he has been described as completing several years of military service. The onset of his illness has been set at 1818 and even the improbable date of 1802, and the first publication of *Chernets* has been given as 1827. The most reliable dates are found in the biographical sketch written by K. Trush in 1899, which is meticulously researched, includes references to sources, and corrects many of the erroneous dates given by others.

Letters:

Pis'ma I. I. Kozlova, in *Zven'ia,* volume 9 (Moscow: Goskul'tprosvetizdat, 1951).

Biographies:

Il'ia Vasil'evich Selivanov, "Moe znakomstvo s Kozlovym," *Russkii arkhiv,* 12 (1893);

K. Trush, *Ocherk literaturnoi deiatel'nosti I. I. Kozlova* (Moscow: I. Kushnerev, 1899);

Konstantin Iakovlevich Grot, *K biografii I. I. Kozlova* (St. Petersburg: Akademii nauk, 1904);

V. Afanas'ev, *Zhizn' i lira: Khudozhestvenno-dokumental'naia kniga o poete Ivane Kozlove* (Moscow, 1977).

References:

Glynn R. V. Barratt, *Ivan Kozlov: A Study and a Setting* (Toronto: Hakkert, 1972);

Barratt, *I. I. Kozlov: The Translations from Byron* (Bern & Frankfurt am Main: Herbert Lang, 1972);

Barratt, "Somov, Kozlov and Byron's Russian Triumph," *Canadian Review of Comparative Literature,* 1 (1974): 104–122;

Kenneth H. Ober and Warren U. Ober, "Kozlov's Translations of Two English Romantic Poems," *Germano-Slavica,* 9 (1989): 209–217.

Papers:

Ivan Ivanovich Kozlov's papers are in Rossiiskii gosudarstvennyi arkhiv literatury i iskusstva, Mosco, fond 250; and Rossiiskaia natsional'naia biblioteka, St. Petersburg, fond 357.

Nestor Vasil'evich Kukol'nik

(8 September 1809 – 8 December 1868)

Christine A. Rydel
Grand Valley State University

BOOKS: *Prakticheskii kurs russkoi grammatiki* (Vil'na, 1830);

Torkvato Tasso. Bol'shaia dramaticheskaia fantaziia v stikhakh. Sochinenie N. K. (St. Petersburg: N. Grech, 1833);

Ruka Vsevyshnago otechestvo spasla. Drama v piati aktakh, v stikhakh. Sochinenie N. Kukol'nika (St. Petersburg: Ghintse, 1834);

Dzhakobo Sannazar. Dramaticheskaia fantaziia v chetyrekh aktakh, v stikhakh. Sochinenie N. Kukol'nika (St. Petersburg: Pliushar, 1834);

Kniaz' Mikhail Vasil'evich Skopin-Shuisky. Drama v piati aktakh, v stikhakh. Sochinenie N. Kukol'nika (St. Petersburg: Pliushar, 1835);

Roksolana. Drama v piati aktakh, v stikhakh. Sochinenie N. Kukol'nika (St. Petersburg: Pliushar, 1835);

Dzhulio Mosti. Dramaticheskaia fantaziia v chetyrekh chastiakh, s intermediei, v stikhakh. Sochinenie N. Kukol'nika (St. Petersburg: E. Prats, 1836);

28 ianvaria 1725 goda. Dramaticheskaia kartina v dvukh iavleniiakh, v stikhakh. Sochinenie N. Kukol'nika (St. Petersburg: E. Prats, 1837);

Ioann Anton Leizevitz. Dramaticheskaia fantaziia v piati aktakh, s prologom, v proze, in series, *Sto Russkikh Literatorov*, volume 1 (St. Petersburg, 1839);

Kniaz' Daniil Dmitrievich Kholmsky. Istoricheskaia drama v piati aktakh, v stikhakh i proze (St. Petersburg: Tip. K. Kraiia, 1840);

Evalina de Val'erol. Roman. Sochinenie N. Kukol'nika, 4 parts (St. Petersburg: I. Glazunov, 1841);

Al'f i Al'dona. Istoricheskii roman. Sochinenie N. Kukol'nika (St. Petersburg: I. Glazunov, 1842);

Dva Ivana, dva Stepanycha, dva Kostyl'kova. Roman. Sochinenie N. Kukol'nika, 4 parts (St. Petersburg: K. Zhernakov, 1846);

General-poruchik Patkul'. Tragediia v piati aktakh, v stikhakh. Sochinenie N. Kukol'nika (St. Petersburg: K. Zhernakov, 1846);

Baron Fanfaron i markiz Petimetr. Byl' vremen Petra Velikago. Sochinenie N. Kukol'nika (St. Petersburg: I. Fishon, 1847);

Nestor Vasil'evich Kukol'nik (after a portrait by K. P. Briullov)

Denshchik. Istoricheskaia drama v piati aktakh, v stikhakh (St. Petersburg: I. Fishon, 1852);

Morskoi prazdnik v Sevastopole. Dramaticheskoe predstavlenie v piati kartinakh. Sochinenie N. Kukol'nika (St. Petersburg: I. Fishon, 1854);

Markitantka. Drama. Sochinenie N. Kukol'nika (St. Petersburg: I. Fishon, 1854);

Azovskoe siden'e. Istoricheskoe skazanie v litsakh, v piati aktakh i deviati kartinakh. Sochinenie Nestora Kukol'nika (St. Petersburg: I. Fishon, 1855);

Boiarin Fedor Vasil'evich Basenok. Istoricheskaia drama v piati aktakh, v stikhakh (St. Petersburg, 1860);

Domenikino. Dramaticheskaia fantaziia v stikhakh. Sochinenie N. V. Kukol'nika (St. Petersburg, 1860);

Tri perioda. Roman N. V. Kukol'nika (St. Petersburg, 1860);

Maksim Sozontovich Berezovsky. Istoricheskii razskaz N. V. Kukol'nika (St. Petersburg, 1860);

Dve sestry. Epizod iz poslednei pol'skoi smuty. Sochinenie N. Kukol'nika (St. Petersburg: Tip. Dep. udelov, 1865);

Ioann III, sobiratel' Zemli Russkoi. Istoricheskii roman N. Kukol'nika (St. Petersburg, 1874).

Collections: *Povesti i razskazy Nestora Kukol'nika*, 2 parts (St. Petersburg: I. P. Bocharov, 1843);

Polnoe sobranie sochinenii russkikh avtorov. Sochineniia Nestora Kukol'nika, 10 volumes in 3 parts: Novels, Dramatic Works, Novellas and Stories (St. Petersburg: I. Fishon, 1851–1853);

Povesti razskazy, books 1–6 (St. Petersburg: Tip. Tva obshchestvennaia pol'za, 1871);

Povesty i razskazy N. V. Kukol'nika, 2 series in 5 volumes (St. Petersburg, 1874);

Istoricheskie povesti, books 1–6 (St. Petersburg: A. S. Suvorin, 1884).

SELECTED PERIODICAL PUBLICATIONS–UNCOLLECTED:

PROSE

Tortini. Intermediia-fantaziia v trekh chastiakh. Al'tsiona, section 2 (1833): 1;

"'Severnoe siian'e,' Kartina," *Syn otechestva*, 41 (1834): 379;

"Zagadka," *Syn otechestva*, 41 (1834): 466;

"Zamechanie na slovo g. professora Nadezhdina," *Syn otechestva*, 41 (1834): 41;

"Villa," *Entsiklopedicheskii leksikon*, 10 (1837): 196;

"Vo, Le-Vo, znamenityi frantsuzskii arkhitektor," *Entsiklopedicheskii leksikon*, 11 (1838): 110;

"Vorota," *Entsiklopedicheskii leksikon*, 11 (1838): 53;

"Vortmann, graver," *Entsiklopedicheskii leksikon*, 11 (1838): 78;

"Gabii," *Entsiklopedicheskii leksikon*, 13 (1838): 10;

Ivan Riabov, rybak arkhangelogorodskii. Dramaticheskii anekdot v dvukh aktakh, Biblioteka dlia chteniia, 32, no. 12, section 1 (1839): 131;

"Antonio," *Urenniaia zaria*, part 1 (1840): 3;

"Pervaia stsena iz bol'shoi dramaticheskoi fantazii: *Avrora i Rikardo*," *Maiak*, part 1 (1840): 3;

"Monolog iz dramaticheskoi fantazii: *Ernest Minnezinger*," *Biblioteka dlia chteniia*, 38, no. 1, section 1 (1840): 5;

Statuia Kristofa v Rige, ili–budet voina. Istoricheskaia drama v shesti aktakh, v proze, Biblioteka dlia chtenia, 38, no. 1, section 5 (1840): 101;

"Avdot'ia Petrovna Likhonchikha," *Biblioteka dlia chteniia*, 41, no. 7, section 1 (1840): 9;

"Novyi god," *Biblioteka dlia chteniia*, 43, no. 12, section 1 (1840): 69;

"Muzyka v Peterburge," *Khudozhestvennaia gazeta*, no. 8 (1840): 15;

"Kontserty Dreishoka," *Khudozhestvennaia gazeta*, no. 9 (1840): 19;

"Muzyka," *Khudozhestvennaia gazeta*, no. 11 (1840): 1;

"G-zha Bishop i serdtse v banke. Vtoraia novella doktora Sil'vio Testa" and "G-za Bishop i G-n Bokso," *Khudozhestvennaia gazeta*, no. 12 (1840): 22;

"Torzhestvo Evangelii," *Khudozhestvennaia gazeta*, no. 14 (1840): 19;

"Proshchanie s Peterburgom" *Khudozhestvennaia gazeta*, no. 17 (1840): 8;

"Kontsert g-zhi Pasty," *Khudozhestvennaia gazeta*, no. 22 (1840): 16;

"Sabina Geinefetter," *Khudozhestvennaia gazeta*, no. 23 (1840): 23;

"Psikheia. Pervaia novella doktora Sil'vio Testa," *Utrenniaia Zaria* (1841): 311;

"Kniaz' Marger Pilonsky," *Russkaia beseda*, 1, section 6 (1841): 1;

"Dzhiordzio Fenoroli, ili serdtse v banke. Vtoraia novella doktora Sil'vio Testa," *Utrenniaia Zaria* (1842): 65;

"Blagodetel'nyi Andronik, ili romanticheskie kharaktery starago vremeni. Povest' s emblemami," *Biblioteka dlia chteniia*, no. 4, section 1 (1842): 139;

Durochka Luiza, Biblioteka dlia chteniia, 53, nos. 7–8, section 1 (1842): 9, 123; 54, no. 9, section 1 (1842): 9;

"Nadin'ka. Sluchai," *Utrenniaia Zaria* (1843): 79;

"Istoricheskiia zametki o kartinakh pomeshchennykh v al'manakhe: *Utrenniaia Zaria na 1843 god*," *Utrenniaia Zaria* (1843): 552;

"Preferans, ili + I –. Razskaz," *Kartinki Russkikh Nravov*, book 6 (1843): 1;

"Sovremennyia khudozhestva v Rossii," *Biblioteka dlia chteniia*, 56, nos. 1–2, section 3 (1843): 45, 57; no. 3, section 3 (1843): 31, 67;

Istoricheskaia krasavitsa, Biblioteka dlia chteniia, 57, no. 4, section 1 (1843): 133, 58; nos. 5–6, section 1 (1843): 13;

"Monument. Istoricheskii anekdot, v stikhakh i proze," *Biblioteka dlia chteniia*, 61, section 1 (1843): 5;

"Kvit. Sluchai," *Repetuar i Panteon*, 1, no. 2 (1843): 155;

"Klikusha," *Syn otechestva*, no. 1 (1844): 9; no. 2 (1844): 41; no. 3 (1844): 71;

"Egor Ivanovich Sil'vanovsky, ili pokorenie Finliandii pri Petre Velikom," *Finskii Vestnik*, 1, section 1 (1845): 5;

Tri perioda, Biblioteka dlia chteniia, 72–73, nos. 9–12, section 1 (1845): 65, 178;

"Staryi khlam. Predanie," *Novosel'e*, part 3 (1846): 21;

Kartiny russkoi zhivopisi, 3 volumes (St. Petersburg: Kantseliarii, 1846);

"Deviatoe marta. Byl'," *Biblioteka dlia chteniia,* 90, no. 10, section 1 (1848): 141;

"Tretii ponedel'nik. Byl'," *Sovremennik,* 30, no. 11, section 1 (1851): 5;

"Registrator. Epizod iz romana: *Abrikosovoe derevo,*" *Biblioteka dlia chteniia,* 3, section 1 (1852): 55;

Ermil' Ivanovich Kostrov. Drama v piati aktakh v stikhakh, Biblioteka dlia chteniia, 117, section 1 (1853): 1;

Tonni, ili Revel' pri Petre Velikom, Biblioteka dlia chteniia, 122–124, section 1 (1853–1854): 99, 100, 101, 151;

"Listki iz zapisnoi knizhki russkago," *Biblioteka dlia chteniia,* 126, section 1 (1854): 91;

"Azovskie pis'ma," *Severnaia pchela,* no. 157 (1854);

"Neskol'ko slov o pedagogicheskom dvizhenii v Germanii," *Syn otechestva,* no. 18 (1857): 420;

"Stat'i bez zaglaviia. Iz pamiatnoi knizhki. Tri stat'i," *Syn otechestva,* no. 46 (1857): 124; no. 1 (1858): 18; no. 6 (1858): 169;

"Martyn Lukich D'iakonov. Istoricheskii razskaz iz vremen Petra Velikago," *Sbornik Literaturnykh Statei,* 2 (1858): 1;

"Azovskiia pis'ma. 4 pis'ma," *Sanktpeterburgskiia Vedomosti,* nos. 29, 76 (1859); nos. 28, 148 (1860);

David Garrik. Drama v piati aktakh, Russkoe Slovo, no. 3, section 1 (1861): 1;

"Azovskie pis'ma. Pis'mo XII," *Sanktpeterburgskiia Vedomosti,* no. 20 (1862);

"Muzykal'nyi vopros. Dve stat'i," *Sanktpeterburgskiia Vedomosti,* nos. 50, 68 (1862);

"Po muzykal'nomu voprosu. Stat'ia posledniaia," *Sanktpeterburgskiia Vedomosti,* 116 (1862);

"Zametka," *Golos,* no. 33 (1863);

"M. S. Shchepkin," *Golos,* nos. 77–78 (1864);

"Zheleznyia dorogi v Rossii," *Severnaia Pochta,* nos. 246–247 (1865);

"Korrespondentsiia iz Odessy," *Sanktpeterburgskiia Vedomosti,* nos. 124, 151, 161, 172, 180, 223, 246, 256, 269 (1865);

"Po voprosu o sredstvakh dlia sooruzheniia zheleznykh dorog v Rossii," *Birzhevyia Vedomosti,* nos. 278, 282 (1865);

"Azovskaia zheleznaia doroga," *Golos,* no. 158 (1866);

"Ob iskazhenii faktov kasatel'no postroiki dorogi ot Kurska cherez Khar'kov," *Sodeistvie Russkoi Torgovli i Promyshlennosti,* no. 60 (1868);

"Otryvki iz dnevnika, 1834–1842," in *Baian,* nos. 9–16 (1888);

"Iz vospominanii N. B. Kukol'nika," edited by P. A. Puzyrevsky, *Istoricheskii Vestnik,* 45 (July 1891): 79–99.

POETRY

"K Lenore," *Syn otechestva,* part 183, section 1 (1837): 3;

"Zakon," *Biblioteka dlia chteniia,* 25, no. 11, section 1 (1837): 5;

"Iz zapisok vliublennago," *Biblioteka dlia chteniia,* 25, no. 11, section 1 (1837): 57;

"K. P. . . . ," *Literaturnyia pribavleniia k Russkomu invalidu,* no. 3 (1837): 289;

"Shkola," *Utrenniaia zaria* (1838): 3;

"Demon somneniia," *Utrenniaia zaria* (1838): 184;

"Itallu-pesnopevtsu," *Utrenniaia zaria* (1838): 305;

"Vstrecha parokhodov," *Biblioteka dlia chteniia,* 27, no. 3, part 1 (1838): 5;

"Pros'ba poèta," *Biblioteka dlia chteniia,* 27, no. 3, part 1 (1838): 168;

"Stikhi, napisannye pri perepiske dramaticheskoi fantazii: *Domenikino,*" *Biblioteka dlia chteniia,* 28, no. 5, part 1 (1838): 135;

"Lenora," *Sbornik na 1838 god* (1838): 214;

"Okhlazhdenie," *Sbornik na 1838 god* (1838): 214;

"Rasput'e," *Utrenniaia zaria* (1839): 162;

"*Exordium* iz bol'shoi romanticheskoi poèmy: *Mariia Stiuart,*" *Utrenniaia zaria* (1839): 367;

"Elegiia," *Odesskii Al'manakh* (1839): 111;

"Iz al'boma Ritstsio," *Biblioteka dlia chteniia,* 38, no. 1, section 1 (1840): 10;

"Lenore," *Biblioteka dlia chteniia,* 38, no. 1, section 1 (1840): 13;

"Proshchal'naia pesnia," *Biblioteka dlia chteniia,* 42, no. 9, section 1 (1840): 5;

"Zhavoronok," *Biblioteka dlia chteniia,* 42, no. 9, section 1 (1840): 7;

"Imperiia," *Biblioteka dlia chteniia,* 51, no. 3, section 1 (1842): 5;

"Romans Davida Ritstsio," *Molodik* (1843): 110;

"Angliiskii romans," *Molodik* (1843): 297;

"K Bugu," *Biblioteka dlia chteniia,* 57, no. 3, section 1 (1843): 13;

"Est' obraz u menia zhivoi," *Molodik* (1844): 105;

"Improvizator," *Biblioteka dlia chtenia,* 67, section 1 (1844): 5;

"Russkaia shkola zhivopisi," *Severnaia pchela,* no. 92 (1848): 365;

"Sila Rossii," *Zhurnal Ministerstva Narodnago Prosveshcheniia,* part 60, section 6 (1848): 208.

From the 1830s through the 1840s Nestor Kukol'nik dominated the Russian literary scene. A prolific writer of plays, stories, novels, and poetry, he also became active in the world of publishing. Though critical reactions to Kukol'nik's literary works run the gamut from highest praise to lowest contempt, commentators generally agree that he was not without talent and was even a gifted musician and connoisseur of the arts. He became a favorite of the court, the reactionary press, and the government bureaucrats who made up the dominant theatergoing and reading public of the time. In fact, Kukol'nik emerged as the champion of the "plebeian" faction of Russian literature, the sworn enemies of the "aristocrats," whose chief representative was Aleksandr Pushkin. Kukol'nik's popularity grew as Pushkin's waned, thanks mainly to the changing tastes of the reading public, whose indifference Kukol'nik also felt by the beginning of the 1850s.

By the time of his death Kukol'nik had long outlived his popularity, though he occasionally tried to revive it with new forays into writing literature. Instead, in his capacity as a local bureaucrat, he was reduced to writing articles about bringing railroads to Taganrog, quite a progressive idea for the man who a quarter of a century earlier had epitomized Sergei Semenovich Uvarov's reactionary, conservative doctrine of Official Nationality. Kukol'nik, in fact, built his fame mostly by courting favor with Tsar Nicholas I and the government officials who sympathized with the sentiments found in his bombastic, pseudo-Romantic, patriotic plays and stories.

Always a controversial figure, Kukol'nik through his life and works elicited conflicting views from his contemporaries, though their opinions were most often negative. Such reactions persist to this day, that is when critics mention him at all. In his book on Russian drama Simon Karlinsky refers to Kukol'nik only in passing while discussing the work of another playwright. The eminent historian Nicholas V. Riasanovsky calls Kukol'nik a "popular, if not distinguished writer," who wrote "feeble plays." Elsewhere Riasanovsky calls Kukol'nik a "pretentious but feeble dramatist" and shows him in an almost buffoonish light as the founder of Russia's "Bohemia." On the other hand, a scholar as distinguished as Vadim Erazmovich Vatsuro finds some merit in Kukol'nik's abilities, not necessarily as a writer but as a compiler of historical anecdotes. Art critics John E. Bowlt and Elizabeth Kridl Valkenier regard Kukol'nik as an established authority on Russian art. Memoir accounts range from vitriolically hostile to uncritically ecstatic, though the general opinion of him that ultimately emerges is a highly unflattering composite of a character so two-dimensional that it would be worthy of one of his own plays—according to most of the critics. Supposedly Fyodor Dostoyevsky used Kukol'nik as the model for his odious character Foma Fomich Opiskin in *Selo Stepanchikovo* (The Village of Stepanchikovo, 1859) while Mikhail Afanas'evich Bulgakov showed Kukol'nik's negative side in his play *Poslednie dni. (Pushkin)* (Last Days. Pushkin; written 1935, premiered 1943, published 1955).

Nestor Vasil'evich Kukol'nik was born on 8 September 1809 in St. Petersburg, the seventh child, "the fifth and penultimate son," as he describes himself in his posthumously published memoirs, of Vasilii Grigor'evich and Sofiia Nikolaevna (née Piliankevich or Pilankiewicz) Kukol'nik. The Kukol'niks were descended from a Carpatho-Russian noble family living in Hungary; at one time they even had held the title of prince, which they supposedly lost during a time of persecution of Uniate Christians under the Jesuits. Vasilii Grigor'evich was an educator whose wide background in many areas, especially languages, agriculture, physics, chemistry, and law allowed him to teach in various institutions of higher learning in Austria, Poland, Russia, and Ukraine. Under the patronage of Nikolai Nikolaevich Novosil'tsev, Vasilii Grigor'evich was invited to St. Petersburg, where his pedagogical career flourished in various institutions such as the Main Pedagogical Institute, the Upper School of Law, and even the newly founded University of St. Petersburg, where he declined the position of rector in order to move to Nezhin as the director of a new gymnasium. He also moved south because of the precarious health of family members, especially of his daughter, Mariia. The high point of Vasilii Grigor'evich's teaching career was his position as official tutor to the Grand Princes Nikolai Pavlovich (later Tsar Nicholas I) and Mikhail Pavlovich, to whom from 1813 until 1817 he taught Roman and Russian civil law.

Vasilii Grigor'evich went to Nezhin at the invitation of Count Aleksandr Grigor'evich Kushelev-Bezborodko, whose father, Prince Il'ia Andreevich Bezborodko, stipulated that a gymnasium in his honor be founded in the town. Vasilii Grigor'evich went enthusiastically to the south with great hopes of running a first-class school. The reality of the situation did not live up to his high expectations. Overwork and a sense of hopelessness led him to become despondent, melancholic, and hypochondriacal. In a fit of despair he threw himself from a third-story window of the school and plunged to his death on 6 February 1821. His wife died soon after.

Of the eight children born to the Kukol'niks, five survived to adulthood, three with some measure of success. The children, in order of birth, were Nikolai, Pavel, Aleksandr, Platon, Mariia, an unnamed child who probably died in infancy, Nestor, and Vladimir, who died in childhood. Nestor describes in his *Vospominaniia* (Recollections, 1891) a fun-loving household in which he and his brothers engaged in pranks and amateur theatricals. He speaks with great affection and admiration of his father but describes his mother, a Pole, as a "passionate, proud, touchy woman, but one of outer beauty." He avows that his mother hated him and treated him with disdain. He enjoyed warm relations, however, with his older brothers Pavel, Aleksandr, and Platon (with whom he later shared living

Title page for Torkvato Tasso, *Kukol'nik's first and best-known dramatic fantasy*

quarters in St. Petersburg). Nestor tells nothing about the oldest brother, who presumably died young. Pavel was an accomplished writer of plays, poetry, and prose; but his main accomplishment lay in his teaching of general history as a professor at the University of Vil'no (now Vil'nius) in Lithuania. Platon held jobs in academic circles in Nezhin and Vil'no but then moved to St. Petersburg to work in government offices dealing with matters concerning Poland. He retired in 1838 and lived only ten years more.

Nestor describes his brother Aleksandr as the most talented of the lot. An accomplished artist, he also liked to play practical jokes with a group of his friends who fancied themselves as great pranksters. Aleksandr's love of sport and fun, however, ultimately led to his early demise: he made a bet that he could eat one hundred Polish meat dumplings instead of an hors d'oeuvre before dinner. His gluttony resulted in a severe case of gastroenteritis, of which he died three days later.

Young Nestor's association with the court began when he was an infant. At the urging of his mother, Nestor's father asked that Tsar Aleksandr I act as Nestor's godfather. The tsar agreed, and the minister of education, Petr Vasil'evich Zavadovsky, acted as the tsar's proxy at the baptism on 31 October 1809. In his memoir Kukol'nik laments that protocol prevented his having a godmother to dote on him, because his "godfather never succeeded in doing anything" for him. Nestor fared much better in his later relations with the next tsar, his father's former pupil, Nikolai Pavlovich.

In Nezhin, Nestor attended his father's school. After the death of Vasilii Grigor'evich, Sofiia Nikolaevna took Nestor with her to live on a small estate in the Vil'no region, according to the will of her late husband. The new director of the gymnasium, Ivan Semenovich Orlai, a friend of the elder Kukol'nik, however, persuaded Sofiia Nikolaevna to return with Nestor to Nezhin so that her son could attend the gymnasium. There Kukol'nik worked hard and every year was the top student. He wrote poems in French but also knew German, Latin, and Polish while still at school. Later he mastered Italian. He took an active part in every activity dealing with literature and the theater; he also edited the school paper, *Zvezda* (Star), in which he published his own works.

Already at that early age Kukol'nik exhibited a fondness for the theater and even acted as the young, spoiled ignoramus Mitrofan in a school production of Denis Ivanovich Fonvizin's *Nedorosl'* (The Adolescent, 1782). The future great writer Nikolai Gogol played the boy's mother, Madame Prostakova, in the same production. Nestor carried on a rivalry with Gogol, who was not the least bit impressed with young Kukol'nik. In fact, the hatred that the two later felt for each other had its roots at the gymnasium. Kukol'nik also excelled in literature, music, and Russian history—all subjects that lay at the basis of his future career as a writer of historical drama and fiction. Another future characteristic manifested itself during Nestor's school years—a proclivity for riotous drinking bouts and excessive gambling.

After receiving the title of *kandidat* (candidate, first level of higher degrees) in 1829, Kukol'nik became a teacher of Russian language and literature at two gymnasiums in Vil'no, where he worked for almost two years. He was quite successful at his jobs, applying to them his characteristic diligence and zeal. While in Vil'no he wrote a textbook, *Prakticheskii kurs russkoi grammatiki* (A Practical Course of Russian Grammar, 1830), which was used in the northwest regions of the Russian Empire until long after. He moved to St. Petersburg in the summer of 1831 to take a position as a bureaucrat dealing with literary matters. Later in the year he returned for a short while to Vil'no, where he served as a secretary of a commission set up to establish a medical-surgical academy. At that time Novosil'tsev managed to have Kukol'nik receive the rank of collegiate assessor. In April of 1833 he began his career in the office of the Ministry of Finance and settled in the capital. His government work from 1834 to 1836 was nominal; he served as a *stolonachal'nik* (head of a desk in the civil service) in the Second Section of the Imperial Chancellery. From 1837 to 1839 he acted as a translator from Polish in another government office, the *Kapitul rossiiskikh ordenov* (the chapter of Russian ecclesiastical or canonical orders). Government service, however, was not Kukol'nik's goal in moving to the capital; he wanted a career in literature and the theater.

In 1833 Kukol'nik published his first, practically unnoticed, play, *Tartini,* in the almanac *Al'tsion* (Halcyon); the same year he published his first and, according to most critics, his best play, the "dramatic fantasy" (a play devoted to the Romantic theme of the unrecognized artist unappreciated by the masses who realizes he will be vindicated only sometime in the distant future) in verse *Torkvato Tasso* (Torquato Tasso). It was staged at the Aleksandrinsky Theater in 1835 and had such a successful reception that Kukol'nik turned to a literary career as a playwright despite a recent promotion at the ministry. In this play about an artist unappreciated in his own time Kukol'nik inserted an autobiographical note. He included among the characters a poet of genius from the future, an heir to the great Tasso, undoubtedly Kukol'nik himself.

In 1834 he published another dramatic fantasy, *Dzhakobo Sannazar* (Jacobo Sanazar), and had his famous historical play *Ruka Vsevyshnago otechestvo spasla* (The Hand of the Almighty Saved the Fatherland) performed at the Aleksandrinsky Theatre under the sponsorship of the head of the Third Section (the political police), Count Aleksandr Khristoforovich Benckendorff, who provided government funding for the lavish production of this play about Russia in the *Smuta* (Time of Troubles) during the early seventeenth century. The play was wildly successful, and all of the reviews, save one, were laudatory. Unaware of the patronage of the tsar and his enthusiasm for the play, Nikolai Alekseevich Polevoi printed a negative review of *Ruka Vsevyshnago otechestvo spasla* in his journal *Moskovskii telegraf* (Moscow Telegraph), which as a result was soon forced to close. Consequently, an anonymous, now quite notorious, epigram made the rounds of the two capitals.

> *Ruka Vsevyshnego tri chuda sovershila:*
>   Otechestvo spasla,
>   Poetu khod dala
> I Polevogo utopila.

(*Almighty's Hand three miracles has wrought;*
  The fatherland was saved and liberated,
  Its author with a cross was decorated,
  And Polevoi–reduced to naught.)

From that time on Kukol'nik's fame was assured–at least until the taste of the Russian reading public changed.

For many years to come–until 1847–Kukol'nik's works appeared in quick succession. He alternated his highly patriotic plays–often distorted by factual errors in history (all in the name of giving glory to the tsar)– with his dramatic fantasies. The plays about the unjustly ignored artists include *Dzhakobo Sannazar, Dzhulio Mosti* (Giulio Mosti, 1836), *Ioann Anton Leizevitz* (Johann Anton Leisewitz, 1839), *Meister Mind* (Master Mind, 1839), *Domenikino* (Domenicino, 1838), *Improvizator* (Improviser, 1844), *Ermil' Ivanovich Kostrov* (1853), *David Garrik* (David Garrick, 1861), and the fragments *Prolog iz bol'shoi fantazii Pietro Aretino* (The prologue from the fantasy Pietro Aretino, 1842) and *David Ritstsio* (1839). Kukol'nik's historical plays include *Kniaz' Mikhail Vasil'evich Skopin-Shuisky* (Prince Mikhail Vasil'evich Skopin Shuisky, 1835), *Ivan Riabov, rybak arkhangelogorodskii* (Ivan Riabov, an Archangel Fisherman, 1839), *Statuia Kristofa v Rige, ili–budet voina* (The Statue of St. Christopher in Riga, or–There Will be War, 1840), *Kniaz' Daniil Dmitrievich Kholmsky* (Prince Daniil Dmitrievich Kholmsky, 1840), *General-poruchik Patkul'* (Lieutenant General Patkul, 1846), *Denshchik* (The Orderly, 1852), and *Markitantka* (A Female Sutler, 1854).

Kukol'nik also wrote many historical novels and stories, some based on anecdotes of Peter the Great's life, still others concerned with artists in conflict with their less-talented rivals. In the 1840s Kukol'nik went through what could be called his "Petrine Period" (for want of a better term) in which he wrote many stories and a novel set in the time of Peter the Great. These include "Serzhant Ivan Ivanovich Ivanov, ili Vse zaodno" (Sergeant Ivan Ivanovich Ivanov, or Everything in Agreement, 1841), "Avdot'ia Petrovna Likhonchikha" (1840), "Prokuror" (Public Prosecutor, 1841), "Kapustin, moskovskii kupets" (Kapustin, a Moscow Merchant, 1842), "Novyi god" (New Year, 1840), "Pozumenty" (Galloons, 1842), "Skazan'e o sinem i zelenom sukne" (A Tale about Blue and Green Cloth, 1844), "Chasovoi" (The Sentinel, 1843), and a novel in four parts, *Dva Ivana, dva Stepanycha, dva Kostyl'kova* (Two Ivans, Two Stepanyches, Two Kostylkovs, 1846). The stories about Peter the Great make up some of Kukol'nik's best prose fiction; Xenia Gasiorowska calls them "literary animations of anecdotal material." Of Kukol'nik's tales about the plight of the artist, "Psikheia" (Psyche, 1841) stands above the rest.

In 1836 Kukol'nik became acquainted with the artist Karl Pavlovich Briullov and the composer Mikhail Ivanovich Glinka; the three formed a close

The Aleksandrinsky Theater, where Kukol'nik's Torkvato Tasso *was performed in 1835 (engraving by E. E. Bernadsky)*

friendship, according to most accounts. Kukol'nik saw the triumvirate as a union of the best representatives of Romanticism in art, music, and literature. His aspirations were as unrealistic as the exquisite portrait Briullov painted of him as a tormented, handsome Romantic poet, dressed all in black, staring out from brooding, thoughtful eyes. Kukol'nik was not without poetic talent, however; in fact, some of Glinka's best romances are based on his friend's verses. The most popular of Kukol'nik's poems that Glinka set to verse is "Somnenie" (Doubt, text and music, 1838). Glinka also composed a cycle of songs, "Proshchanie s Peterburgom" (Farewell to Petersburg; text and music, 1840) from Kukol'nik's poems; especially noteworthy are "Zhavoronok" (The Lark), "Kolybel'naia pesnia" (Lullaby), and "Proshchal'naia pesn'" (Farewell Song). In addition Kukol'nik collaborated with Glinka on his operas *Ruslan i Liudmila* (Ruslan and Liudmila, 1817–1820), based on Pushkin's narrative poem, and *Zhizn' za tsaria* (Life for the Tsar, 1836).

A gifted dilettante, Kukol'nik also became a credible art critic and a fairly accomplished pianist-improviser. His close association with the world of art and music prompted him in 1836 to publish *Khudozhestvennaia gazeta* (Art Gazette), devoted to acquainting the Russian public with their own Russian art and music. Even though (or because) *Khudozhestvennaia gazeta* was an ambitiously full and competently edited newspaper, it found little favor with the public. Nevertheless, publication of the journal continued until 1842 and merited for Kukol'nik the title of honorary member of the Imperial Academy of Arts and induction into the *Obshchestvo Pooshchreniia Khudozhnikov* (Society for Encouragement of Artists).

Heavy involvement in editing the newspaper did not deter Kukol'nik from publishing extensively: between 1838 and 1845 he produced nine plays, five novels in seventeen volumes, and twenty-six novellas and short stories. In addition, he engaged heavily in editing and publishing. He edited *Russkii vestnik* (Russian Herald, 1841); the collections *Novogodnik* (Journal for the New Year, 1839) and *Skazka za skazkoi* (Fable after Fable, 4 volumes, 1841–1844); and his own journal, *Dagerotip* (Daguerrotype, 12 issues in 1842). He also contributed to the *Entsiklopedicheskii leksikon* (Encyclopedic Lexicon, 1837–1838). In 1845 Kukol'nik began publication of *Illiustratsiia* (Illustration, 4 volumes in three years), a periodical devoted to Russian art and all aspects of Russian life. This journal also failed, mainly because of the expenses connected with publishing it. Concurrently he continued to contribute articles and stories to other journals and in 1846 even edited a lavishly (for the time) illustrated book, *Kartiny russkoi zhivopisi* (Pictures from Russian Painting), in which appeared his own article, "Russkaia zhivopisnaia shkola" (The Russian School of Painting).

In 1847 Kukol'nik took a five-year break from literary activity while on business trips all over the empire for his ministry, though his *Polnoe sobranie sochinenii* (Complete Collected Works) in ten volumes came out in 1851 to 1853. From 1853 until 1856 he worked in Rostov and Voronezh in government service. For his devotion to his job he was awarded the rank of Full Councillor of State. After a short rest in St. Petersburg he realized his need for radical medical treatment and went to "take the waters" in Germany. At his request he retired to Taganrog in the south of Russia "to devote the rest of his days to learning and literature." He outlived his time; he spent his last years in Taganrog, almost a forgotten man–a real contrast to the days when he was the toast of St. Petersburg.

The accounts of Nestor Kukol'nik on the pages of memoirs, diaries, and reminiscences of his contemporaries provide some understanding of his popularity; they also furnish clues to unraveling the mystery of why most literary scholars, especially in the twentieth century, have treated him with a fair amount of disdain. The most uncritical and charming description of him appears in Maria Fedorovna Kamenskaia's *Vospominaniia* (Recollections, 1894; separate edition, 1991), in which she describes Kukol'nik in terms most appropriate to a Romantic hero–not unlike Briullov's portrait. She recounts the course of their friendship from the time they first met to the time they parted, concentrating mainly on her feelings for him, the intense emotions of her first love. In all probability the feelings were "mutual, but they could not bless their union in marriage: Kukol'nik was married, although he did not advertise this condition overly much. He married before he ever arrived in St. Petersburg in 1831 but met Mashen'ka Tolstaia [Kamenskaia's maiden name] at the end of 1833. Kamenskaia probably did not even know Kukol'nik was married, though the misty vagueness of her descriptions of their relationship still leaves unanswered questions," according to V. M. Bokova, who wrote the introduction to the memoirs.

Facts concerning Kukol'nik's marital state continue to elude confirmation. One wonders whether the Amalia Ivanovna, to whom Glinka refers as Kukol'nik's wife, is this pre–St. Petersburg bride, or the Finnish housekeeper whom he married in the 1840s after a disappointing love affair, or the woman known as Mumusha, with whom he lived while his Wednesday night "salons" went on during the late 1830s and early 1840s. In his archives one can also find a letter signed by his widow, Sofiia Kukol'nik. Kukol'nik apparently enjoyed quite a reputation as a ladies' man, a fact difficult to understand in light of several descriptions of his appearance.

Pavel Mikhailovich Kovalevsky tells of Kukol'nik's corpulent, flabby body, quite unlike the Schilleresque youth of Briullov's portrait. He says that Kukol'nik spoke "in a greasy voice, overly stressing o's; when he laughed, his entire huge trunk swayed, while his small eyes watered and his lips formed a funnel, the way children's do when they cry." Vladimir Petrovich Burnashev describes him as "clumsy, crudely fashioned, angular (awkward), forcefully inhaling snuff." Nevertheless, people liked him and found him to be attractive in other ways. He was a witty conversationalist, a good oral storyteller, a generous friend, and a gracious host; most people, however, felt reservations about accepting him at face value.

In a perceptive description of Kukol'nik's reading of his story that she calls "The Death of Peter," Elizaveta Alekseevna Drashusova-Karlhof offers this view of him:

> Our anticipation to hear something extraordinary was not warranted, as is often the case. We heard many words, meant to touch us, but they never reached their goal, because in them one could find no warmth, only artificiality. Only the impressions and feelings of the Russians at the death of Peter were well done. Kukol'nik had many good thoughts, was very well-read, but something was lacking in him. Excessive self-esteem and arrogance damaged him. In his ardent love for the arts there was something poetic, but his reticence and cunning were anti-poetic. He was gracious in an original way: I have listened to very few people with such pleasure as I did him; I always found out from him something new, especially about the arts. But one could not unconditionally enjoy his conversation, because in it there was always a feeling of its being inflated.

Drashusova-Karlhof recognized Kukol'nik's good qualities in spite of his flaws:

> Whatever you say, Kukol'nik was a gifted person. His numerous works, although hastily done, nevertheless all carried the stamp of talent; and when often he would for hours on end improvise at the piano with feeling and passion, then one could not but be convinced, that in his very self there was much poetry.

Drashusova-Karlhof was not alone in being drawn to Kukol'nik. Perhaps the most complete account of his literary evenings and Wednesday salons can be found in Ivan Ivanovich Panaev's *Literaturnye vospominaniia* (Literary Reminiscences, 1860-1861) in *Sovremennik* (first separate edition, 1950). In them Panaev recounts the tales of the jolly, convivial company that gathered to hear Kukol'nik read his works

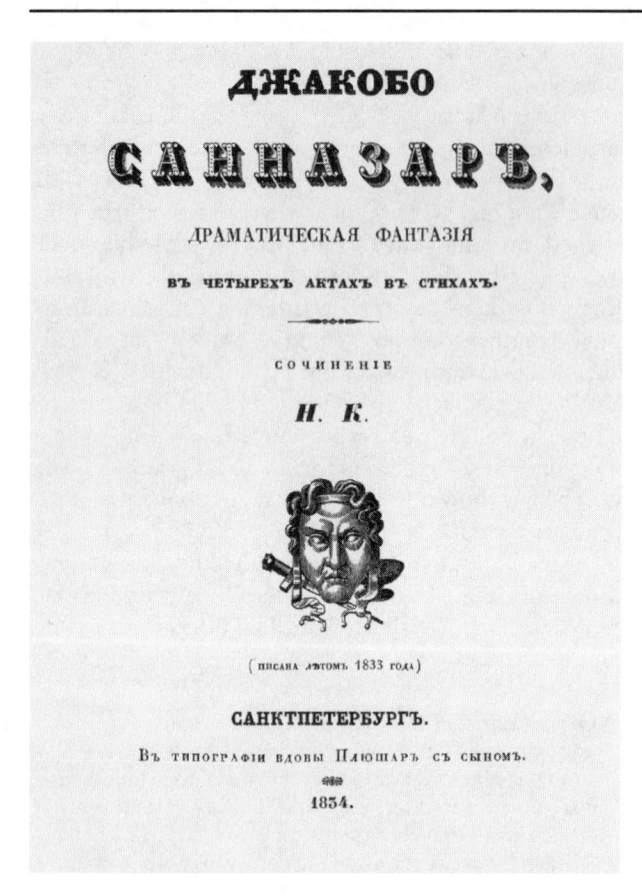

Title page for Dzhakobo Sannazar *(Jacobo Sanazar), Kukol'nik's second dramatic fantasy, about an unjustly neglected artist*

aloud and discuss art while eating much food and drinking even more. Panaev also tells of his ability to make one feel like a special, privileged friend. Therefore, not surprisingly, many young men fell under his spell. At the same time, Panaev's candid description of a now notorious incident perhaps reveals more than he intended:

> "Should I tell you, gentlemen, what troubles me?"–Kukol'nik said in conclusion–"I shall be candid with you: I am disturbed by the thought that the Russian public has not yet grown up to an understanding of serious creations. Does it contain many like you? I think that I shall cease writing in Russian, I shall write in Italian or in French."
>
> These words had a shattering effect on all of us. "Oh! oh! Just look at him!"–we thought, exchanging glances with one another, and we gazed at Kukol'nik with a certain fear, as at a being completely out of the ordinary, superior. . . . Next it seemed to me a little suspicious that one could command foreign languages as well as one's native tongue, but I immediately became ashamed of my doubt.
>
> "This is painful, bitter for me"–continued the poet, and in his eyes, at least so it seemed to us, there were tears–"I love Russia ardently, but there is nothing to be done! still, I think, it will be necessary to abandon the Russian language. . . . "
>
> We began to beg the poet not to do this and not to deprive Russian literature and our dear fatherland of glory; we entreated him that in Russia too he will find many true adherents and admirers. . . . As for ourselves, we almost swore him an oath of fidelity for life.
>
> Kukol'nik was silent for a long time. The bottle was empty. He leaned against the back of the sofa and closed his eyes.
>
> After several minutes had passed he raised his eyelids and slowly examined all of us with his eyes.
>
> That gaze seemed to me to be so pregnant with meaning that I shuddered.
>
> "I thank you, I thank you sincerely and from the bottom of my heart"–Kukol'nik pronounced the words in a deeply moved voice–"Not for myself I thank you, but for art, for the great cause of art which you make so passionately your own. . . . Yes, I shall write in Russian, I must write in Russian, for the simple reason that I can find such friends as you!"

Following the lead of Mark I. Aronson and Solomon Abramovich Reiser, whom he quotes, Riasanovsky sees this atmosphere as the beginning of Russian Bohemianism:

> This is a cult of high, pure art, a cult of the powerful individual talent, and at the same time a burning of life in drinking bouts and other pleasures with a marked philistine aroma. . . . The characteristic thing [of this cult] is the close link between creativity and Bohemianism, creation in the poisonous, intoxicated atmosphere of Bohemia, of "Nestor's stock exchange" which knew no proprieties of the *salon*. . . .

Riasanovsky describes the new types of salons as having "a more plebeian, commercial, professional, and at the same time a more personal, subjective, emotional, and even wild character." In his memoirs about Glinka and Iurii Karlovich Arnol'd–a composer, music critic, theorist, and pedagogue–Riasanovsky shows the Kukol'nik "fraternity" at its most sordid and accuses Kukol'nik, his brother Platon, and the whole "brotherhood" of ruining Glinka's life through their pernicious influence on him and their depraved carousing whenever they gathered. Even Panaev eventually saw through the facade and revised his thoughts about Kukol'nik in his essay/memoir *Literaturnye Kumiry, Diletanty i proch* (Literary Idols, Dilettantes, and Others) in *Sovremennik,* no. 12 (1855).

Contemporary critics of Kukol'nik's literary output were also divided in their opinions on the merit of his work. Unlike the memoirists, however, the critics rarely tempered their criticism because Kukol'nik improvised well on the piano or acted as a congenial host. They left out the personal and responded to the works themselves, especially those writers known as the aristocrats (that is, the Pushkin coterie). His advocates, the so-called dreaded unholy triumvirate of the viper press (Nikolai Ivanovich Grech, Faddei Venediktovich Bulgarin, and Osip Ivanovich Senkovsky), on the other hand, usually lavished him with fulsome praise, although Senkovksy (as Baron Brambeus) did at times gently take him to task.

An anonymous review of Kukol'nik's collected works of 1851 and 1852 in *Biblioteka dlia chteniia* (Library for Reading) admits to the ticklish situation of assessing the works of an author that appeared mainly on the pages of that very journal. The reviewer, however, overcomes his scruples. After discussing the merits of reviewing multivolume sets, he states that he will try to explain Kukol'nik's place in and meaning for Russian literature. The reviewer regrets that because of circumstances, Kukol'nik–like many other deserving and ignored writers of genius–was not fated to be a "representative of his age, of a certain school," or to have an entire epoch named for him. He was not able to begin a new period of literature because a contemporary poet, another writer of genius (Pushkin), was the culminating, final representative of the "Age of Karamzin." In other words, Kukol'nik was a victim of bad timing and Pushkin's privileged education and training. If not for Pushkin, the early nineteenth century might have been known as the Age of Kukol'nik. No wonder, says the reviewer, that Pushkin himself once envied Kukol'nik's success. Granting Pushkin grudging praise, the reviewer actually compares the two writers and has Kukol'nik emerge the winner of the contest. "As a poet in the narrow sense of the word, Pushkin stands higher than Kukol'nik; Pushkin's works are more delicate, more elegant, more intelligible, more polished than the works of Kukol'nik. But Kukol'nik is more intelligent, more learned, more solid than Pushkin, and looks at things more sensibly than he." And if that were not enough the reviewer says that as a fiction writer Gogol is on a much lower level than Kukol'nik. This reviewer concludes by urging the new generation to read the works of Kukol'nik, which he says will give them great pleasure. Such comments are not surprising from the pages of a journal whose editor (Senkovsky) called Kukol'nik a "Russian Goethe."

Statements such as these prompted Belinsky to proclaim in his *Literaturnoe Mechtanie* (Literary Reverie) in 1834 that Russia had no literature. He cannot believe that Senkovsky actually said, "Kukol'nik is the great Kukol'nik; Kukol'nik is a Byron; Kukol'nik is a courageous rival of Shakespeare; on your knees before Kukol'nik!" Belinsky does not stand alone in his disbelief. His comparison of Pushkin and Kukol'nik stands on the opposite side of the critical spectrum from previous reviewers. "By no means thinking to insult the fine talent of Mr. Kukol'nik, we, nevertheless, without hesitating, can say decisively that between Pushkin and him, Mr. Kukol'nik, the gulf is infinite, that for him, Mr. Kukol'nik, the distance to Pushkin is 'as far away as a star in the heavens.'" On several occasions, however, Belinsky wrote fair and good reviews of some of Kukol'nik's works and acknowledged that he was not without talent.

Perhaps the most famous review of Kukol'nik is Polevoi's negative reaction to *Ruka Vsevyshnago otechestvo spasla,* which gave the authorities a chance to close *Moskovskii telegraf.* First acknowledging that earlier works of Kukol'nik showed talent and promise, Polevoi then says that the play under review completely saddens him. He continues: "We in no way ever expected that the poet who in 1830 could write *Tasso,* in 1832 could allow himself to write–but if that were not enough: in 1834 to *publish* such a play, as the new play of Mr. Kukol'nik, *The Hand of the Almighty Saved the Fatherland!* How could he show so little mercy on himself, how could he think so little about his very own worth! It is only one step from the sublime to the ridiculous. This is what one man, completely experienced in glory [Napoleon] once said."

In order to try to explain his view of the play, Polevoi first says that, objectively speaking, the roles the heroes of the play, Koz'ma Zakhar'ich Minin and Prince Dmitrii Mikhailovich Pozharsky, played in history are hardly worthy of drama–either in a play by Kukol'nik or in a work by anyone else who tried to make them dramatically interesting characters. The main point for criticism, however, is that Kukol'nik "took advantage of romantic freedom to make such frightful changes of history." Polevoi finds nothing resembling history in the play–neither the events nor the characters. He also says that Kukol'nik should not write just to please the crowds. Twenty years later Ivan Sergeevich Turgenev echoed the same sentiments in his review of Kukol'nik's play, *General-poruchik Patkul'.*

By far the most scathing criticism of Kukol'nik came from his putative archenemy, Pushkin. It probably cut the deepest simply because it was so offhand and dismissive. As Aleksandr Vasil'evich Nikitenko relates in his memoirs: "It is interesting how Pushkin judges Kukol'nik. Once at Pletnev's the conversation turned to the latter; I was there, too. Pushkin, chewing, as was his wont, on his nails or on an apple, I don't remember which, said: 'So, what, does Kukol'nik really have any good poems? They say that he even has thoughts.' This was said with a tone doubly aristocratic: The aristocracy of nature and of position in the world. Pushkin sometimes takes on that tone and

Caricature of Kukol'nik by K. P. Briullov (Tret'iakov Gallery, Moscow)

then becomes extremely unpleasant." At another time Pushkin supposedly said that in Kukol'nik burns "the fire not of poetry but of fever."

Kukol'nik was no less caustic about Pushkin, and according to his own accounts, he shed no tears at the slain poet's funeral. That Kukol'nik saw in Pushkin a rival was no secret. In his diary entry for 26 January 1837 he wrote: "They say that some military man challenged Pushkin to a duel for some kind of insulting gibe. A man who does not know how to control his tongue can always expect such a turn of events." On 29 January he records his reaction to Pushkin's death: "Pushkin died.... I should really be rejoicing—he was my most vicious enemy: how many offenses, how many unwarranted insults did he pile up against me and for what? I never gave him even the slightest cause. On the contrary I avoided him, the way I generally avoid all of the aristocracy; but he relentlessly tormented me. I always respected his great talent, his poetic genius, although I found his learning to be superficial, aristocratic; but at this minute I forget everything and, like a Russian, I grieve to my soul over the loss of such a remarkable talent." Kukol'nik's death certainly was not as dramatic as Pushkin's.

On 9 December 1868 the newspaper *Birzhevye Vedomosti* (Stock Exchange News) ran a dispatch by its Taganrog correspondent, who reported that on the previous day the once-famous playwright, poet, and prose writer, Nestor Vasil'evich Kukol'nik, had died. Unprepared for death, though syphilis supposedly caused it, he

> had not shown even the slightest sign of such a sad end, and according to his established routine, he took a walk along the main street after dinner; when he returned home he gave instructions about his forthcoming outing to the Italian opera that very evening; after that he settled down in an armchair and began to converse with his doctor about the art of the stage and its celebrities—at which point—because he had been sitting for quite a while in a sideways, bent position, he wanted to shift to his other side, away from his doctor; instead he collapsed on the floor and there breathed his last.

Such was the dramatic, but somewhat farcical, end to the life and career of one of Russia's once enormously popular literary "superstars." The man who on many occasions had proclaimed about himself, albeit in a drunken state, "Kukol'nik is great! Posterity will appreciate Kukol'nik" would hardly have wanted death to visit him in such an unseemly fashion. He was buried at his own *dacha* (summer home), *Dubki* (Little Oaks) near Taganrog.

Except for *Torquato Tasso,* Kukol'nik's plays—both historical and artistic—share the same pattern; they follow the paradigm of a bland hero besieged by uninteresting villains enemies who find themselves in plotless dramas, forced to deliver long, boring, bombastic speeches about vindication in the future. The novels generally ramble, though some not as much as others. And as Dmitrij Čiževsky says, "the novellas are more substantial." In fact, some of the stories and novellas are no worse than those of most respectable prose writers contemporary to Kukol'nik. Some of his poems are quite good, especially those Glinka set to music. Excerpts from Kukol'nik's *Vospominaniia,* particularly those about his father and brothers, are touchingly, lovingly narrated. On the other hand, diary entries can be self-serving and pompously rhetorical. Lines worse than these from his play *Denshchik,* which refer to Peter the Great, are hard to imagine:

> I saw how the Great Anatomist
> Split open the decrepit body of Russia.
> Changed her rotten insides,
> Put together her cleansed members,
> Skillfully bandaged her all properly,
> Lifted her by her shoulders, and put her on her feet. . .[.]
>
> (translation by Riasanovsky)

In spite of such horrid poetry, Kukol'nik was a man of talent. His need to be popular dominated his writing. That Kukol'nik had talent is clear; that he prostituted it to gain the approbation of the tsar and the adulation of influential critics is less clear, but probably accurate. That he chose to waste his talent is tragic. Even if he had used his gifts wisely, he might never have been able to surpass the geniuses who gave their names to their age and his: Pushkin and Gogol. Most likely the Age of Kukol'nik was never even a remote possibility. Nestor Vasil'evich Kukol'nik chose easy fame over the earned respect he so desperately craved from posterity.

Letters:
Ivan Kubasov, ed., "Nestor Kukol'nik i ego pis'ma," *Russkaia starina,* no. 3 (1901): 685–710.

Bibliography:
Gimnaziia Vysshikh nauk i litsei kniazia Bezborodko, second edition (St. Petersburg, 1881).

Biography:
A. I. Sherubovich, *Brat'ia Kukol'niki* (Vil'no: Tip. gubernskago pravleniia, 1885).

References:
Moisei Semenovich Al'tman, "Iz arsenala imen i prototipov literaturnykh geroev Dostoevskogo," in *Dostoevskii i ego vremia,* edited by B. G. Bazanov and G. M. Fridlender (Leningrad: AN SSSR, 1971), pp. 204–209;

Mark I. Aronson and Solomon Abramovich Reiser, *Literaturnye salony i kruzhki* (Leningrad: Priboi, 1929);

Vissarion Grigor'evich Belinsky, *Polnoe sobranie sochinenii* (Moscow: AN SSSR, 1953–1959), volume 1, pp. 21–25, 534–536; volume 2, pp. 3, 130, 204–205; volume 3, pp. 125, 136–138; volume 5, pp. 474–477, 491–499, 510–511; volume 6, pp. 52–55, 176–181, 187, 226–228, 261–263, 550–556; volume 10, pp. 123–135;

John E. Bowlt, "Russian Painting in the Nineteenth Century," in *Art and Culture in Nineteenth Century Russia,* edited by Theophanis George Stavrou (Bloomington: Indiana University Press, 1983), pp. 113–139;

Nikolai Leont'evich Brodsky, *Literaturnye salony i kruzhki* (Moscow-Leningrad: Academia, 1930);

Dmitrij Čiževsky, *History of Nineteenth-Century Russian Literature,* volume 1, *The Romantic Period,* translated by Richard Noel Porter, edited by Serge A. Zenkovsky (Nashville, Tenn.: Vanderbilt University Press, 1974);

Igor' Vital'evich Chernyi, *Dramaturgiia N. V. Kukol'nika* (Khar'kov: Maidan, 1997);

Chernyi and Z. E. Kudzaeva, *N. V. Kukol'nik. Metodicheskie rekomendatsii k spetskursu po russkoi literature* (Khar'kov: MP "V.V.V.," 1992);

M. F. Filin, "Skvoz' peterburgskie ochki," *Russkaia rech',* 4 (1994): 15–19;

Xenia Gasiorowska, *The Image of Peter the Great in Russian Fiction* (Madison: University of Wisconsin Press, 1979);

Nikolai Vasil'evich Gerbel', *Russkie poety v biografiiakh i obraztsakh* (St. Petersburg, 1873), pp. 403–414;

Maksim Isakovich Gillel'son, "Problema 'Rossiia i zapad' v otzyvakh pisatelei pushkinskogo kruga," *Russkaia literatura,* 17, no. 2 (1974): 121–130;

Gleb Gridin, "Nestor Vasil'evich Kukol'nik (1809–1868)," in *Ioann III, Sobiratel' Zemli Russkoi,* by Kukol'nik (Moscow: Sovremennik, 1995), pp. 423–426;

Mariia Fedorovna Kamenskaia, *Vospominania*, edited by V. M. Bokova (Moscow: Khudozhestvennaia literatura, 1991), pp. 189, 208–214, 217–219, 221–224, 226–228;

Simon Karlinsky, *Russian Drama. From its Beginnings to the Age of Pushkin* (Berkeley: University of California Press, 1985), p. 258;

Pavel Mikhailovich Kovalevsky, *Vstrechi na zhiznennom puti*, in Dmitrii Vasil'evich Grigorovich's *Literaturnye Vospominaniia*, edited by Kovalevsky (Leningrad: Academia, 1928), pp. 286–452;

Lidia Mikhailovna Lotman, "Dramaturgiia tridtsatykh-sorokovykh godov," in *Istoriia russkoi literatury*, volume 7 (Moscow: AN SSSR, 1955), pp. 629–638;

Aleksandr Vasil'evich Nikitenko, *Zapiski i dnevnik (1826–1877)* (St. Petersburg: Tip. A. S. Suvorina, 1893);

Ivan Ivanovich Panaev, *Literaturnye Vospominania*, edited by N. L. Brodsky (Leningrad: Khudozhestvennaia literatura, 1950);

Avdot'ia Iakovlevna Panaeva, *Vospominaniia, 1824–1870* (Leningrad: Academia, 1928);

Nikolai Alekseevich Polevoi, "Ruka Vsevyshnago otechestvo spasla, v 5-ti aktakh, v stikhakh," *Moskovskii telegraf*, part 55, no. 3 (1834): 498–506;

Nicholas V. Riasanovsky, *Nicholas I and Official Nationality in Russia, 1825–1855* (Berkeley: University of California Press, 1959), pp. 112–113;

Riasanovsky, *A Parting of Ways* (Oxford: Clarendon Press, 1976), pp. 160–163;

Valerii N. Sazhin, "Iz biografi pisatelia N. V. Kukol'nika," in *Issledovanie pamiatnikov pis'mennoi kul'tury v sobraniiakh i arkhivakh otdela rukopisei i redkikh knig*. (Leningrad: Gos. publichnaia im. M. E. Saltykova-Shchedrina, 1985), pp. 105–112;

Sazhin, "N. V. Kukol'nik: k 175-letiiu so dnia rozhdeniia," in *Pamiatnye knizhnyo daty: 1984* (Moscow: Kniga, 1984);

Vladimir Fedorovich Shubin, *Poety Pushkinskogo Peterburga* (Leningrad: Lenizdat, 1985), pp. 293–311;

Ivan Sergeevich Turgenev, "General-poruchik Patkul'. Tragediia v 5-ti deistviiakh, v stikhakh. Sochineniia N. Kukol'nika," *Sovremennik*, 1, no. 1, section 3 (1847): 59–81;

Elizabeth Kridl Valkenier, "The Intelligentsia and Art," in *Art and Culture in Nineteenth Century Russia*, edited by Theofanis George Stavrou (Bloomington: Indiana University Press, 1983), pp. 153–171;

Boris Vasil'evich Varneke, *History of the Russian Theatre*, translated by Boris Brasol, revised and edited by Belle Martin (New York: Macmillan, 1951), pp. 239, 241–243, 248–249, 251, 256, 267, 297;

Vadim Erazmovich Vatsuro, "Mezhdu fol'klorom i literaturoi" and "Nestor Kukol'nik: Anekdoty," 1 (1991): 66–75;

Vikentii Vikent'evich Veresaev, *Sputniki Pushkina*, 2 volumes (Moscow: Sovetskii sport, 1993);

Vladimir Rafailovich Zotov, "Peterburg v sorokovykh godakh," *Istoricheskii vestnik*, 39, no. 2 (1890): 324–343.

Papers:

Nestor Vasil'evich Kukol'nik's papers are located in the Rossiiskii gosudarstvenny i arkhiv literatury i isskustva (Moscow), fond 254; IRLI (Pushkin House), St. Petersburg, fond 371; and the Rossiiskaia natsional'naia biblioteka (St. Petersburg), fond 402.

Mikhail Iur'evich Lermontov
(3 October 1814 – 15 July 1841)

David Powelstock
University of Chicago

BOOKS: *Geroi nashego vremeni* (St. Petersburg: I. Glazunov, 1840; second edition, corrected, with preface by Lermontov, 1841);

Stikhotvoreniia M. Lermontova (St. Petersburg: I. Glazunov, 1840);

Demon. Vostochnaia povest' (Karlsruhe: V Pridvornoi tipografii V. Gaspera, 1856; corrected and augmented, 1857);

Iunosheskiia dramy, edited by Petr Aleksandrovich Efremov (St. Petersburg: Izdanie Knizhnago Magazina "Novago Vremeni," 1880);

Sashka. Poema (Moscow: I. N. Kushnerev, 1882);

Maskarad, drama v 4-kh deistviiakh, v stikhakh i Maskarad, drama v 5-ti deistviiakh, v stikhakh (St. Petersburg: A. S. Suvorin, 1891);

Lermontov. Kartiny, akvareli, risunki, curated by E. A. Kovalevskaia (Moscow: Izobrazitel'noe iskusstvo, 1980).

Editions and Collections: *Stikhotvoreniia M. Lermontova,* 4 volumes, edited by A. A. Kraevsky (St. Petersburg: I. Glazunov, 1842–1844);

Sochineniia Lermontova, 2 volumes (St. Petersburg: Izd. A. Smirdina, V tip. Imperatorskoi Akademii Nauk, 1847);

Sochineniia M. Iu. Lermontova, 6 volumes, edited by Pavel Aleksandrovich Viskovatov (Moscow: V. F. Rikhter, 1889–1891);

Poemy "Mtysri" i "Demon" (St. Petersburg: A. S. Suvorin, 1891);

Polnoe sobranie sochinenii M. Iu. Lermontova, 4 volumes, edited by Arsenii I. Vvedensky (St. Petersburg: A. F. Marks, 1891);

Sochineniia M. Iu. Lermontova, 5 volumes, edited by I. M. Boldakov (Moscow: E. Gerbek, 1891);

Sochineniia M. Iu. Lermontova, 8 volumes, edited by Petr Vasil'evich Bykov (St. Petersburg: S. Dobrodeev, 1891);

Illiustrirovannoe polnoe sobranie sochinenii M. Iu. Lermontova, 6 volumes, edited by Vladimir Vladimirovich Kallash (Moscow: Pechatnik, 1914–1915);

Polnoe sobranie sochinenii, 5 volumes, edited by Boris Mikhailovich Eikhenbaum (Moscow-Leningrad: Academia, 1935–1937);

Sochineniia, 6 volumes, edited by Nikolai Fedorovich Bel'chikov, B. P. Gorodetsky, and Boris Viktorovich Tomashevsky (Moscow-Leningrad: AN SSSR, 1954–1957);

Geroi nashego vremeni, edited by Eikhenbaum and Erik Ezrovich Naidich (Moscow: AN SSSR, 1962);

Sobranie sochinenii, 4 volumes, edited by Viktor Andronikovich Manuilov and others, corrected and augmented edition (Leningrad: Nauka, 1979–1981);

Polnoe sobranie stikhotvorenii, 2 volumes, edited by Iurii Andreevich Andreev and others (Leningrad: Sovetskii pisatel', 1989).

Editions in English: *A Hero of Our Own Times* (London: D. Bogue, 1854);

The Demon: A Poem, translated by Sir Alexander Condie Stephen (London: Trübner, 1875);

The Demon . . . A Literal Translation in the Metre of the Original, translated by Ellen Richter (London: David Nutt, 1910);

A Hero of Our Time, translated by Vladimir Nabokov in collaboration with Dmitri Nabokov (New York: Doubleday Anchor, 1958);

Selected Works, translated by Avril Pyman and others (Moscow: Progress Publishers, 1976);

Major Poetical Works, translated by Anatoly Liberman (Minneapolis: University of Minnesota Press, 1983);

Vadim, translated and edited by Helena Goscilo (Ann Arbor, Mich.: Ardis, 1984).

Mikhail Lermontov is considered by many to be the greatest poet of Russia's Golden Age after Aleksandr Pushkin. Although he died at the age of twenty-six, his legacy in poetry and prose gained him a firm place in Russian literary history. The handful of mature lyrics upon which his reputation as a poet rests are characterized by a direct intimacy and personal pathos that distinguish him from his virtuosic predecessor. These poems bear the imprint of a strong Romantic individualism: the hero battles for the poet's right to self-expression against the background of a society viewed as antagonistic to poetry and poets. Indeed, the 1830s, when Lermontov wrote, was a period marked by the "turn to prose" in Russian literature. Critics began to react against the gentry-dominated school of Pushkin's age, branding poetry "a golden plaything." They demanded a new literature to deal with current cultural concerns (such as national identity, serfdom, and the moral emptiness of high society) and to address broader readerships. Marked by Nikolai Gogol's satires and Pushkin's increasing interest in prose, the literature of this decade is usually viewed as a transition from Romanticism to realism. Lermontov's work comprises both the residue of Romantic elegiac lyricism and the urge to look upon the world "realistically," that is, without flinching. Thus, Lermontov, whose literary career precisely spanned this decade, has a curious double role as both the last great lyric poet in the Age of Pushkin and the author of the first Russian psychological novel, *Geroi nashego vremeni* (A Hero of Our Time, 1840). Lermontov was acutely conscious of this changing cultural landscape. His efforts to respond to the situation by redefining literature and recasting the role of the poet account in large part for his successful inscription into the Russian literary memory.

To characterize Lermontov's life and art definitively is difficult. Biographical sources are sparse and contradictory. Lermontov left few letters and almost no direct evidence of his aesthetic views. Moreover, because Lermontov died just as several of the great nineteenth-century Russian debates were getting started, his image and art became fodder for these arguments, but he could no longer speak for himself. Orthodox Soviet scholarship worsened the distortions by bolting the iron halo of Bolshevism to the poet's head and ignoring certain issues, such as Romantic individualism, that are critical to understanding Lermontov but anathema to the party line. As part of the general post-Soviet reexamination of the Russian literary and cultural past, interest in Russian Romanticism and Lermontov has increased, promising a better understanding of the enigmatic poet and his time.

Mikhail Iur'evich Lermontov was born in Moscow on 3 October 1814. His mother, Mariia Mikhailovna Lermontova, née Arsen'eva, came from a wealthy and distinguished gentry family. The family of his father, Iurii Petrovich Lermontov, can be traced to a Scotsman, George Learmont, who entered the tsar's service after being captured by Russian troops in Poland in the early seventeenth century. Family legend asserted that Learmont descended from the legendary thirteenth-century Scottish bard, Thomas the Rhymer. At the time of Iurii's marriage to Mariia Arsen'eva, however, the Lermontov family was neither famous nor particularly wealthy. The young family moved to the Arsen'ev estate of Tarkhany (near Penza) shortly after Mikhail's birth. His mother died in early 1817, when Mikhail was not yet three years old. The boy's maternal grandmother, Elizaveta Alekseevna Arsen'eva, who had never approved of Iurii Lermontov as a match for her daughter, subsequently banished him from Tarkhany, letting it be known that she alone would be responsible for the upbringing of her grandson. Iurii Lermontov, perhaps aware that Arsen'eva could offer the boy much more than he in the way of money and social connections, put up little resistance. He saw his son only rarely until his own death from tuberculosis in 1831. Having lost both her husband (who poisoned himself in 1810 after a series of domestic troubles) and her only daughter, Arsen'eva treasured her grandson, perhaps to a fault. Throughout his childhood in Tarkhany, young Mikhail wanted for nothing.

The single-minded attentions of his grandmother imbued Lermontov with a strong sense of self-worth. At the same time, the early death of his mother, who remained a faint memory throughout the poet's life, marked him with a sense of loss that never faded. His father's absence, too, left a strong, although more ambiguous, mark. As a child Mikhail alternately longed for reconciliation and condemned the estranged father for abandonment. Arsen'eva foresaw a brilliant career for her grandson and spared no expense in providing him with the best tutors available. Memoirs of those close to the family depict the boy as strong-willed, sensitive, and especially precocious in music and drawing.

Two family trips to the Caucasus in 1820 and 1825 left particularly lasting impressions. The lush and dramatic mountainscapes of the region took root in young Lermontov's imagination. During the early nineteenth century the Russian empire was continuously engaged in the process of conquering territories and subduing native populations in the Caucasus. In Russian literature of the time, the region played a role analogous to that of the Orient in the English cultural consciousness and later provided Lermontov with a stage for presenting violent confrontations between "native" (that is, "natural," from the Rousseauist perspective) and "European" ethical and cultural systems. The Caucasus served as a fertile incubator for an entire gamut of Romantic themes such as national, social, and personal identity; freedom; the original innocence and social corruption of the soul; and vengeance.

Lermontov also identified with the Caucasus in a deeply personal way. It served as a "lost paradise," the object of his strongest spiritual longings. In one early poem the Caucasian landscape speaks to him in his dead mother's voice:

V mladencheskikh letakh ia mat' poterial
No mnilos' chto v rozovyi vechera chas
Ta step' povtoriala mne pamiatnyi glas.
Za eto liubliu ia vershiny tekh skal,
    Liubliu ia Kavkaz.

(In my childhood years I lost my mother,
But it seemed, in the rosy hour of evening,
That the steppe repeated that memorable voice.
For this I love the summits of those cliffs,
    I love the Caucasus.)

In his "Avtobiograficheskie zametki" (Autobiographical Comments), written in 1830 and published in *Otechestvennye zapiski* (Notes of the Fatherland) in 1859, he recalls the mountain region as the site of his first experience of love, for a little girl whose name he could not remember. This association of love and loss with the Caucasus persisted into Lermontov's later work; the Caucasus played a central role in the poet's later biography as

Lermontov as a child, circa 1820–1822 (portrait by an unknown artist; Institute of Russian Literature [Pushkin House], St. Petersburg)

well. His poetic voice was both shaped and ultimately silenced there.

In the fall of 1827 Arsen'eva brought her grandson to Moscow with the intention of securing an education for him. After a year of private tutoring, the thirteen-year-old Lermontov was enrolled in the elite Moscow University Gentry Pension, where he studied for two years. The Pension, which shared faculty with the venerable university, had a tradition not only of academic excellence but also of political "freethinking." Several of the officers who staged the Decembrist Revolt of 1825 had been products of the Pension. Mindful of this tradition, Tsar Nicholas I effectively closed the Pension in the spring of 1830 by converting it to an ordinary gymnasium (high school). Lermontov withdrew and in the fall entered Moscow University, where he studied until 1832. Although many subjects were taught at both the Pension and the university, literature was the favorite among the students, who "published" several hand-copied literary journals and almanacs.

Lermontov wrote furiously during his Moscow years, from 1827 to 1832. The early works, more notable for quantity than quality, nevertheless helped him to assimilate a variety of literary models and to develop his own tastes. Moreover, Lermontov later returned frequently to rummage through his early lyrics, where he found nuggets he could polish and transform into superb lyrics. Strikingly, many early Lermontovian themes carry over into the late period, making study of the early works indispensable to understanding the late. The earliest lyrics (1828–1829) are rather uninspired exercises in the anthological forms of an earlier period, old-fashioned enough to suggest their origin in class assignments: epigrams, fables, alexandrine idylls, and Anacreontics. By 1830, however, Lermontov already showed a preference for the Romantic lyric genres of elegy, literary song, and ballad, frequently blurring the boundaries between them in emphasizing the lyric hero's emotional state.

The summer of 1830 marked the beginning of Lermontov's obsession with George Gordon, Lord Byron, whose influence seems to have encouraged the young poet's growing desire to express his own personality in verse. For Lermontov, the rebellious Englishman represented a fully poetic personality, that is, a poet whose public persona closely resembled a complete biography. In several places Lermontov measures his own past and future against those of Byron. That summer Lermontov was rarely seen without the recently published first volume of Byron's letters and diaries, and many of his own lyrics began to resemble diary entries in verse, bearing dates in lieu of titles.

Lermontov shared the Romantic titanism typical of his time. He was convinced—or at least tried to convince himself—that he was a man of fate, destined for *slava* (glory or fame), a role epitomized by the heroic figure of Napoleon Bonaparte, who appears in several of these early lyrics. It was not unusual for a young man of Lermontov's class, whether Russian or European, to seek a "brilliant career" in government or military service, but Lermontov's case is remarkable for its extreme fervor and literary orientation. Lermontov projected a great future for himself specifically as a poet, which helps to explain his attraction to Byron's artistic manipulation of his public persona. As he wrote in an 1832 poem published in *Biblioteka dlia chteniia* (Library for Reading) in 1843: "Net, ia ne Bairon, ia drugoi, / Eshche ne vedomyi izbrannik, / Kak on, gonimyi mirom strannik, / No tol'ko s russkoiu dushoi" (No, I am not Byron, I am another, / As yet unknown chosen one, / Like he, a wanderer, persecuted by the world, / But with a Russian soul).

During the summer of 1830 Lermontov became infatuated with a young woman two years his elder, Ekaterina Aleksandrovna Sushkova, and addressed a series of love lyrics to her. Although for the most part these poems are typically Romantic appeals, they are marked by a peculiar insistence that switches to contempt when the poet's love goes unrequited. Sushkova treated Lermontov like a child, to which the poet responded with more bitterness than regret. The most notable feature of the Sushkova cycle is the self-referential focus of the poems. Their tone is strikingly unaffectionate. The poet's desire for glory takes the form of a need to live on in the woman's memory. Instead of praising the love object, the poet self-absorbedly threatens her with the "dagger of remorse" she will feel later when recalling the lover she so casually spurned. Similar lyrics from 1830 through 1832 are devoted to Natal'ia Fedorovna Ivanova; many of these works were later destroyed by her jealous husband. While Lermontov's "love" poetry magnifies the female love object into an indispensable ideal, it simultaneously reduces her to a function of the poet's mythology of self. This phenomenon is especially clear in the case of Varvara Aleksandrovna Lopukhina, the most lasting of Lermontov's loves, whom he immortalized as Tamara in the narrative poem he worked on throughout the 1830s, *Demon*, in which the heroine plays the passive angel to Lermontov's restless demon.

Lermontov's lyric hero exhibits a double nature. At times he is the reflective, passive hero of the elegy: disillusioned, world-weary, incapable of action. This side of the hero is most evident in Lermontov's earliest works. At other times the hero appears as an active, willful rebel, vengeful instead of defeated, whose energies are directed against the perpetrators of his suffering: society, unrequited loves, or even God. This double hero's experience is frequently accorded cosmic significance. His suffering is emblematic of the suffering of all mankind; his creative and destructive powers are compared with those of God and Satan. Astral motifs (heaven, stars, and angels) represent the target of the hero's ideal striving, as well as his purity of soul, dramatically juxtaposed to the imperfection of the earthly rabble. The hero's active aspect takes the form of a poetic individualism (Romantic "demonism") that renounces its attachment to creation and revels in vengeful destruction. Like other Lermontovian heroes, the demon figure stands far above the world of moral distinctions: the greatness of his deeds and passions, the assertion of his "rights" as an individual, transcend the boundary between good and evil.

Lermontov's preference for fateful heroes and his fascination with the Caucasus are evident in his early *poemy* (verse narratives). Under the influence of Byron's Eastern tales of the 1810s and Pushkin's Caucasian verse narratives of the early 1820s, the *poema* became an intensely popular genre in Russian Romantic literature. Lermontov began at least eighteen of them between the years 1828 and 1832. He experimented with different situations, trying out the full range of heroic types from the Byronic-Pushkinian tradition: brigands, noble savages, the world-weary wanderer, and legendary and pseudohistorical figures. In some cases, names of characters and even titles of works are taken directly from Pushkin and Byron. Scholars have also long noted that sizable portions of these poems are adapted from Vasilii Andreevich Zhukovsky, Ivan Ivanovich Kozlov, Friedrich Schiller, and Decembrist writers, in addition to Byron and Pushkin.

Despite their heavy reliance on others' works, the subjugation of plot and setting to the portrayal of the hero's inner life sets Lermontov's *poemy* apart. Events are arranged to expose most dramatically the hero's psyche and the Romantic conflicts raging therein. Because of his essential sympathy with his heroes, Lermontov favors the confessional mode over objective narration. Several of the earliest *poemy* are constructed wholly as confessions, in which the hero tells his own story as a monologue: for example, in "Prestupnik" (The Outlaw), written in 1829 and published in *Otechestvennye zapiski* in 1859, a brigand leader tells his men the story of how he arrived at his present state of criminal alienation after being cast out from human society while young. Most of these tales include at least one moment in which the hero discloses the "history of his soul." Although much of this characterization could also apply to the heroes of Byron's own verse tales, Lermontov's heroes soon distinguish themselves as more active and strident in their rebellion rather than passively world-weary. They actively resist societal conventions and justify their actions with the cruelty they have suffered. It is typical of Romanticism and Lermontov that these heroes do not "choose" their actions in any modern moral sense. Rather, they act in accordance with their personalities, which are in turn shaped by their experiences and "fates." The plots of these *poemy* revolve around correspondingly extreme and irrational antisocial deeds: adultery, incest, fratricide, patricide, and blood vengeance.

The three plays (one in verse, two in prose) Lermontov completed during this active period betray a deep interest in the dramaturgy of Schiller, particularly the early Schiller of the Sturm und Drang period. This influence is most obvious in the first of the three, *Ispantsy* (The Spaniards, 1830), the setting of which–Spain during the Inquisition–is borrowed from Schiller's *Don Carlos* (1787). Unsurprisingly, Lermontov seems to have been more interested in the turbulent passions of the first part of Schiller's transitional work than in its second part, which already foreshadows the more classical, universalistic direction the German writer's works took. The bloody denouement of the play (the hero fails to kill the lustful villain, but murders the heroine, presumably in order to preserve her virtue) and its verse form (blank iambic pentameter) also suggest the influence of William Shakespeare's *Hamlet* (1602). The hero's hesitation between nonviolence and revenge is what necessitates the heroine's death, and in a perverse twist wholly characteristic of the Lermontovian imagination the hero himself is forced to carry out her execution.

The two other plays Lermontov completed during this time frame, *Menschen und Leidenschaften* (Men and Passions, 1830; Lermontov's German title evokes Schiller's *Kabale und Liebe,* Intrigues and Loves, 1784) and *Strannyi chelovek* (A Strange Man, 1831), eschew exotic historical locations for contemporary Russia. Unlike *Ispantsy*, both of these plays are written in prose. Their plots, heroes, and secondary characters have clearly autobiographical roots, although they have been transformed to heighten dramatic conflict. The plays amplify Lermontov's own troubled family situation to paranoiac heights of manipulation and intrigue. For example, in *Menschen und Leidenschaften* the protective grandmother plots to divide father and son; the misinformed father curses his son; and the son, thinking he is betrayed, commits suicide. Only when he is nearly dead does he discover that his father has been deceived. Yet, despite the melodramatic and unbelievable plots, the plays reveal an important component of Lermontov's dawning artistic consciousness: the Romantic focus on the conflict between the feeling hero and the cruel otherness of his surroundings. The poet's morbid sensitivity to injury is perceived as a virtue in an otherwise insensitive world.

The years 1829 through 1832 were a time of feverish literary experimentation for Lermontov. He tried his hand at almost all the current literary genres, with the notable exception of prose works. Of the approximately four hundred surviving Lermontov lyrics, more than three-quarters were written in this period. Almost two-thirds of the narrative poems he began were undertaken in these years. In 1830 and 1831 he wrote three of his four completed plays. Although all this activity produced little of the work for which Lermontov is known today, its products are critical to an understanding of the better-known works. The early poems and plays can be seen as a laboratory, in which Lermontov, borrowing and imitating a broad range of poets–foreign and domestic, traditional and contemporary–searched for the means to convey his strongly felt vision of the individual human consciousness. At the same time, he sought to carve a place for himself in Russian literary history, for he possessed from an early age a driving ambition to be recognized as a person and as a writer.

In the spring of 1832 Lermontov requested a transfer from Moscow University to St. Petersburg University, citing "domestic circumstances" as the reason

Ekaterina Aleksandrovna Sushkova, to whom Lermontov devoted a cycle of poems in the early 1830s

for his request. Exactly what prompted this move remains unclear, although previously overlooked sources—and Lermontov's averred dislike for St. Petersburg—suggest that it was not entirely voluntary. It appears that relations between the sometimes imperious Lermontov and those around him had deteriorated to the point of becoming disruptive. Two of Lermontov's professors complained that although he displayed an impressive knowledge of extracurricular readings at his exams in 1831, he did not know the course material. He had also been censured for his role in a scandal in the spring of 1831, when a group of students rebelled against a particular professor whom they considered stupid and rude, driving him from the classroom. By all reports, Lermontov's peers and teachers found him extremely intelligent, but often unbearably arrogant. In any case, Lermontov's "request" to leave the university was granted in June.

When Lermontov was informed that St. Petersburg University would not accept his course credits from Moscow University, the possibility of completing a university education was effectively eliminated. Career options for young men at that time in Russia were rather limited. A civil servant's desk job was hardly an attractive option for a young man of Romantic sensibilities. All that remained was the military. Lermontov decided to enroll in the School of Ensigns of the Guard and Cavalry Hussars (the Junker School), also in St. Petersburg.

Lermontov was frequently depressed during his first months in St. Petersburg. For one thing, the move from the richly literary milieu of Moscow University to the decidedly more pragmatic program of a military school reinforced Lermontov's sense that embarking on a military career precluded the possibility of a literary life. For another, the dull, flat landscape of St. Petersburg could not please a young man accustomed to the hills and cupolas of Moscow and who, in fact, yearned for the soaring peaks and plunging gorges of the Caucasus. Writing from St. Petersburg to friends, Lermontov complained that his life lacked "impressions," that "the poetry of my soul has been extinguished." Finally, Lermontov, who did not have the kind of social connections in St. Petersburg that he had enjoyed in Moscow, felt rather like an outsider. His letters condemn St. Petersburg society as cold and superficial; yet, at the same time, he was hatching plans to gain entry into it. This alienated, deeply ambivalent attitude toward "high society" remained an important theme in the poet's later works. Disappointed by his loss of social status and discouraged by what seemed to be an abrupt end to his literary prospects, Lermontov still burned with the desire to win glory. If anything, these frustrations charged his pursuit of that goal with frenzied desperation.

The curriculum at the Junker School was not restricted to military affairs. Nevertheless, although it also covered a fairly broad range of general disciplines (such as Russian and European history, philology, and French), it must have been quite a departure from the literary orientation of Moscow University. Although he initially feared that his military career would supplant his old dreams of literary greatness, it seems he devoted himself to this new life with a certain enthusiasm. Given his limited options and Romantic inclinations, it is not surprising that he resigned himself to his new fate, preferring "a bullet in my heart" to "the slow death agony of an old man," as he wrote in one letter.

During his two-year stint at the Junker School, the discouraged Lermontov wrote considerably less than in the previous two years. At the same time, his military training, which focused his attention on less solitary activities, seems to have decreased his interest in the passive, elegiac mode of poetic expression. Lermontov produced few lyric poems during this time, preferring instead to concentrate on genres more explicitly oriented on action: two verse narratives and one unfinished adventure novel.

The two narrative poems written during this period continue the line of bloody tales of vengeance set in the Caucasus, but they show clear progress in narrative pacing. There is much less authorial sermonizing, and actions and motivating passions are brought into sharper focus. The first of these poems, *Aul Bestundzhi* (1832), first published in full in *Russkaia mysl'* (Russian Thought) in 1883, breaks from Lermontov's earlier confessional *poemy* by placing the heroic monologue before the hero's main action (which is to spitefully murder his brother's wife, whom he covets), thus contributing fullness and resonance to the action rather than indulging in retrospective mediation.

Khadzhi Abrek (Hadji the Blood Outcast, 1833) is told with even greater narrative economy than *Aul Bestundzhi*. The story (another innocent woman killed out of revenge) unfolds through monologue, dialogue, and concise poetic description, maximizing the effects of its dramatic collisions of fate. The piece has the distinction of being Lermontov's earliest substantial publication. One of Lermontov's schoolmates, without the poet's knowledge, gave the manuscript of *Khadzhi Abrek* to Osip Ivanovich Senkovsky, the editor of a popular literary journal, *Biblioteka dlia chteniia,* where it was published in 1835. Senkovsky was ecstatic over the piece and asked Lermontov's friend for more. When Lermontov, who did not yet feel confident enough in his work to seek publication, heard that the poem was to be published, however, he was enraged. When no criticism of the poem appeared, he was greatly relieved.

While Lermontov had made great strides in his verse narratives, his first substantive attempt at prose did not fare so well. The novel in question, first published in *Vestnik Evropy* (Herald of Europe) in 1873, is conventionally referred to as *Vadim,* after the name of its hero. Lermontov's own title for the novel, which he worked on between 1832 and 1834 but never finished, remains unknown. The story is set in the 1770s against the backdrop of the peasant rebellion led by Emilian Ivanovich Pugachev. Unlike Pushkin's novella on the subject, *Kapitanskaia dochka* (The Captain's Daughter, 1836), which made careful use of historical sources, Lermontov's piece makes little effort to depict the historical moment. Rather, the choice of period seems motivated by its potential for bloody conflict. The social and historical facts of the rebellion retreat to the background and only reemerge in the form of gratuitous and gory bloodbaths perpetrated by and upon frequently nameless characters. As in all of Lermontov's *poemy,* the focus is on the irrational and hypertrophied personal motivations of the protagonists, whose passions are here particularly lustful. The eroticism, violent passions, and gore of *Vadim* frustrate any reader's expectation of redemptive value. Romantic maximalism reaches its inevitable conclusion in the metaphysical paradox of the coexistence of good and evil, as symbolized in the revelation of the common parentage of the disfigured Vadim and the beautiful Ol'ga, who is also the object of his incestuous desire. As the narrator asks rhetorically, "Did not the angel and the demon come from the same source?"

Although Lermontov was unhappy from the outset of his Junker School period, by the second year he appears to have joined in the drinking and wenching for which the hussars were legendary. Several verse narratives, the so-called *Iunkerskie poemy* (Junker Poems), testify to his effort to fit into this tradition, as perhaps does the wanton sensationalism of *Vadim*. These poems, however, lack the apparently serious literary intent of the unfinished novel. Published in early 1834 in the underground cadet journal *Shkol'naia zaria* (School Dawn), the *Iunkerskie poemy* resemble modern-day locker-room humor, featuring the sexual escapades of several of Lermontov's fellow cadets, who are identified by nicknames. Interestingly, the primary participants in the journal were Lermontov and Nikolai Solomonovich Martynov, who was the poet's opponent in a fatal duel seven years later. The poems feature genitally explicit language, but are far from erotic. Sex is depicted as the jocular fulfillment of the male urge for conquest. One poem describes, with casual frivolity, a gang-rape scene.

Lermontov's poems of this type are far from unique: there are many known examples written by cadets at the St. Petersburg Junker School and its Moscow equivalent. The poems have been left out of all editions of Lermontov's work except for the "Academia" edition, published in the Soviet Union from 1935 to 1937, where they are relegated to an appendix and objectionable words are replaced by ellipses. While some Soviet scholars have tried to ignore the existence of these verses, others, perhaps stretching the point, have incorporated them into their accounts of Lermontov's literary evolution by seeing them as crucial to the development of "naturalistic" narrative style. It is probably best to view these poems as attempts to gain acceptance in a rowdy, all-male environment. At the same time, they reflect the darker side of the ethos of military heroism.

Upon graduating from the Junker School in November 1834, Lermontov was commissioned as an officer with the Life Guard Hussar Regiment, stationed in Tsarskoe Selo, a few miles outside of St. Petersburg and the location of the Imperial Summer Palace. This post was a prestigious and comfortable one, utterly without danger, a circumstance that greatly pleased the poet's doting grandmother. The hussar's responsibilities were largely limited to guard duty in the palace and participation in parades. Otherwise, the hussars were free to spend their time in the capital, attending balls and the theater, and organizing their famed drinking fests.

Lermontov wasted little time in exercising his new freedom and status. Within days of receiving his commission he appeared, in the splendor of his new uniform, at a ball where he knew his old love, Ekaterina Sushkova, would be present. Although Sushkova had been living in St. Petersburg all along, she and the poet had not seen one another since their tearful (for Lermontov) parting in Moscow in the summer of 1830. Lermontov had not forgotten what he considered to be her humiliation of him four years earlier, and he wasted no time in exacting revenge. Having grown and donned a hussar uniform, Lermontov calculated that Sushkova might now take his attentions more seriously. He decided to present himself as a suitor for her hand.

At the time, Sushkova was being seriously courted by Aleksei Aleksandrovich Lopukhin, a friend of Lermontov from Moscow University, but Lermontov succeeded in winning Sushkova's favor. Lopukhin, incidentally, was also the brother of Varvara Lopukhina, the object of Lermontov's affections since 1831. Whether Lermontov's motivation was to impress Varvara or to save his friend Aleksei from a dangerous coquette, as he himself claimed, he managed to play his game, without Lopukhin's knowledge, until the latter finally despaired of Sushkova's indecision. At this point Lermontov changed tactics: while continuing to behave warmly toward Sushkova in private, he began to treat her with mild disdain in public. The social effect was to make it seem as if Sushkova worshipped Lermontov, while he himself remained indifferent. Once this impression had been made, Lermontov needed a way out. This goal he achieved by means of a letter, anonymously addressed to Sushkova, which condemned "that young man M. L." as a dangerous scoundrel. Lermontov further made sure that the letter would be intercepted by Sushkova's parents, with predictable results: Sushkova was mildly disgraced, and Lermontov was banned from her parents' residence.

Lermontov describes the entire premeditated intrigue in a chillingly triumphant tone in a letter to his friend and relative Aleksandra Mikhailovna Vereshchagina, who had been Sushkova's close companion in the summer of 1830. Most significantly, the letter reveals the poet's primary motivation in staging this piece of theater: by casting himself as the object of unreciprocated desire, he became the object of the curiosity and desire of others. In this way the episode served to elevate the poet's status in St. Petersburg society, providing him with what he called in his letter a "pedestal."

This anecdote makes clear Lermontov's focus on public success, the other side of his urge to express his innermost feelings and the impulse that drove his authorial as well as social ambitions. At the same time, Lermontov consciously used the plot of this real-life intrigue—and its themes of Romantic love, cynical manipulation, and revenge—as material for his writing. Thus, social behavior (real-life action) and literary activity merge in Lermontov's biography. The poet's own biography is transformed into literature, and his written word (such as his anonymous letter to Sushkova) becomes a relevant action in the world, an action with willed results. The poet becomes the author of his life. As Lermontov commented in his letter to Vereshchagina, "I no longer merely write novels, I make them happen."

The clearest evidence of Lermontov's attempts during this period actively to promote himself through literature is his play *Maskarad* (The Masquerade, 1835–1836). Although Lermontov had not attempted to publish any other writings during this period, he tried three times to have the play approved for performance in St. Petersburg. It was rejected each time by the censor. It was published, with the censor's changes, only after Lermontov's death, in the 1842–1844 edition of his works, and the complete play was performed on the stage for the first time only in 1862. Lermontov's efforts suggest his concentration during this period on making an impression in high society, not merely in literary circles. To have a play succeed on the St. Petersburg stage would have afforded him much wider exposure than a work published in a literary journal.

The full first version of the play, as originally submitted to the censor, has not survived, but existing fragments suggest its content. Its hero, Evgenii Arbenin, is a grown man, probably in his thirties, who has married and settled down after a youth of carousing, womanizing, and card playing. Through unhappy coincidence, he becomes convinced his wife, Nina, is having an affair with Prince Zvezdich. The true adulterer is in fact the rich Baroness Strahl, who, fearing for her own reputation, does not reveal her role. Everyone is taken in, including Arbenin, who plots revenge. He embarrasses Zvezdich by accusing him of cheating at cards and refuses to allow him the "honorable" satisfaction of a duel. Then he poisons Nina, whose death scene is chilling: as she insists on her faithfulness and resists death, Arbenin rails against the futility of life and the treachery of society in general, and of women in particular.

Evidence suggests that the version of the play Lermontov first submitted to the censor in the fall of 1835 ended with Nina's death. The censors rejected it on the grounds that it was insulting to St. Petersburg society and that Arbenin, a murderer, goes unpunished. Lermontov revised the play by adding a fourth act, in which Arbenin repents of the murder, then goes insane from grief. This reversal is achieved by the introduction of a character called the "Stranger." The Stranger reveals that he was fleeced at cards by Arbenin some years earlier and since returning to St. Petersburg has been watching him constantly. The Stranger tells Arbenin that he has known of Nina's innocence all along, and that he watched Arbenin poison her, but said nothing. Zvezdich is also on hand to tell his story, thus emphasizing Nina's innocence. These revelations drive Arbenin to madness. Although introduced in response to the censor's demands, these changes hardly serve to condemn the vice of murder. Moreover, neither Zvezdich nor the Stranger is a noble character fit to represent the voice of virtue. Rather, the changes merely reaffirm and amplify the depiction of Arbenin as a disillusioned victim of the real villain: treacherous society. Unsurprisingly, this version, submitted to the censors in December 1835, was also rejected by the censor.

A third version, titled *Arbenin*, which had five acts, was submitted in early 1836. This time, in what seems like a desperate attempt to satisfy the censor, Lermontov deprived the play of all its bite. The social satire is defanged, and the perfidious Baroness disappears entirely. The action is changed so that Arbenin's wife actually does commit adultery and Arbenin merely pretends to poison her in order to extract a confession. Afterward, Arbenin leaves her for foreign lands. This last attempt at accommodation stripped the play of any dramatic value. Without the motivated venom of the original plot, Arbenin is reduced to the type of victimized hero Lermontov had long since abandoned. Even with these changes, which the censor acknowledged in his report, the play was ultimately rejected for obscure reasons.

Despite its fate at the hands of the censors, the original version of *Maskarad* must be considered one of Lermontov's early literary successes. Arbenin's character is intriguingly and convincingly sketched through dialogue, and the unfolding of the action is compelling. Abandoning the prose of his previous two plays, Lermontov opted for the "free iamb" (iambic lines of varying lengths, with no fixed rhyme scheme) earlier made famous by Aleksandr Sergeevich Griboedov's underground classic, *Gore ot uma* (Woe from Wit, finished between 1823 and 1824). Lermontov's verses read well, even if they lack the pyrotechnic prowess exhibited in Griboedov's play. The author's condemnation of the St. Petersburg society for whom the play was written surely would have made *Maskarad* a scandalous success on the stage. These same reasons explain why it could not be performed. Much of the passionate indictment of society in this play reappeared in Lermontov's later

Aquarelle by Lermontov (circa 1835–1838) of Varvara Aleksandrovna Lopukhina, with whom he was in love (Institute of Russian Literature [Pushkin House], St. Petersburg)

poems and in the novel *Geroi nashego vremeni*, but using the more subtle weapon of irony.

Like *Maskarad*, Lermontov's two narrative poems written between 1834 and 1836 are set in Russia rather than the exotic Caucasus. Whereas his earlier *poemy* had borrowed freely from other poets, he now began to scavenge from his own material, salvaging the best lines from poems that had failed as wholes. Later, he cannibalized one of these two poems, *Boiarin Orsha* (The Boyar Orsha, 1835–1836), published in *Otechestvennye zapiski* in 1842, in writing his most perfect narrative poem, *Mtsyri* (The Novice, 1839), and in revising his most famous one, *Demon*. Although an historical setting is specified in *Boiarin Orsha*, there is less specific detail than ever. The conflicts and themes are treated as timeless and universally indicative of the human condition. The title character of the poem is released from Tsar Ivan's service and returns to his castle near the Lithuanian border. His treasure in life is his daughter, of whom he is insanely protective. When he hears rumors of her involvement in a love affair, he locks her in a room and throws away the key. The illicit suitor, the foundling Arsenii, is captured but escapes. Later, during a battle between the Lithuanians and Russians, Arsenii finds Orsha wounded and dying on the battlefield. Orsha bemoans his inability to exact revenge on Arsenii, but with his tyranny humbled by imminent death, he tells Arsenii where to find his incarcerated daughter. Arsenii gallops off to rescue her, but when he arrives, he finds only her skeleton. In an anticlimactic ending, Arsenii briefly announces his intention to become an aimless wanderer. Although the plot of *Boiarin Orsha* disappoints, in Arsenii's confession can be seen the development of a major Lermontovian motif: the passionate orphaned hero who symbolizes the condition of the human individual–loving, abandoned by God, doomed to mortality, and persecuted by earthly forces. This theme was fully realized in *Mtsyri.*

In 1835 Lermontov began work on another narrative poem. He may have continued reworking it until as late as 1839, but the majority of its lines seem to have been written in 1835 and 1836. Called *Sashka* (the hero's name), the poem is considered by many to be fundamentally different from anything the poet had attempted earlier. It was published in *Russkaia mysl'* in 1882, but readers should consult the 1954–1957 edition of Lermontov's collected works for its thorough textological research. Like *Maskarad,* the poem is satirical in intent, although it abandons the frenzied passion and venomous attacks of the play for the lighter, playful irony of Pushkin's novel in verse, *Evgeny Onegin,* the first full edition of which had been published in 1833. Other likely models for the tone of the poem are Byron's *Beppo* (1818) and *Don Juan* (1819–1824), and Pushkin's *Graf Nulin* (Count Nulin, 1825) and *Domik v Kolomne* (A Little House in Kolomna, 1830). Each of these works marks its author's transition away from his well-established style. Similarly, the unexceptional hero of *Sashka* marks a departure from the titanic personalities of Lermontov's early "men of destiny." Indeed, from the opening stanza the poem reveals for the first time the mind of the artist reflecting openly and critically on the value of his earlier works. Poems about "executions, chains and exiles," he writes, are fine for "those who sleep little, who love to think, who waste their days in reminiscence." Lermontov confesses that he was once such a person but claims that he has changed.

The ostensible kernel of the plot is a prank Sashka considers playing on society. After an amorous encounter with his lower-class mistress, Tirza, the latter suggests that Sashka dress her up and take her to a fashionable ball. The sleepy hero answers indifferently, "perhaps." While the lovers are sleeping, the narrator takes the opportunity to fill the reader in, at great length, on Sashka's youth, misadventures in love, and conflict with his tyrannical father. At the end of the existing manuscript Sashka has left his lover's apartment and is considering the merits of this prank as a means of "punishing" society for it vapidity. Some scholars consider the work finished as is, while others believe an additional fragment, written in the same stanzaic form but without any other evident connection to the manuscript, to be the beginning of a second chapter. The latter scenario seems more likely. It is hard to believe that Lermontov did not plan eventually to bring the plot to a head. All of his finished works depict in some form a confrontation between the hero and the world at large. It is quite conceivable that the author intended to continue the story, perhaps stretching it to the length of *Evgeny Onegin,* but lacked the patience to carry the project through.

In any case, despite its rejection of melodrama, the poem does not depart entirely from the poet's early pattern of depicting the hero's disenchantment and antisocial actions (here, as yet merely contemplated by Sashka) as the consequence of past suffering. The main difference is that Lermontov, represented by a first-person narrator who is Sashka's friend, no longer throws the full weight of his passionate support behind the hero. Lermontov's own spiritual longings, however, are far from absent. They are simply expressed apostrophically by the narrator. At the same time, it is worth noting that some, but not all, of Sashka's background and attitudes reflect Lermontov's own. This partial distancing of the author from the hero presages the complex, ambivalent authorial stance Lermontov took in his later narratives, including his novel *Geroi nashego vremeni.*

Of the few lyrics Lermontov wrote during 1835 and 1836, about half are loose translations or interpretations of Byron. The others are occasional pieces, prompted by personal encounters or political news. A common thread of nostalgia for a lost age of heroism runs through most of these lyrics, framing the potentially great man against a contemporary age condemned as banal, superficial, and unheroic. Lermontov's sense of the wasting of his own potential in a society tightly regulated by constrictive conventions also clearly resonates.

Lermontov's unfinished prose novel, *Kniaginia Ligovskaia* (Princess Ligovskaia), deserves mention in this context. The poet apparently worked on the piece during 1836 and the beginning of 1837, in collaboration with his friend and fellow officer Sviatoslav Afanas'evich Raevsky. Based on autobiographical material (the poet's love for Lopukhina, by now married, as well as the Sushkova intrigue), *Ligovskaia* is told rather clumsily by a jocular third-person narrator, apparently in an uninspired attempt to imitate the tone, but not the social profile, of Gogol's narrators. Another tale of social revenge, the novel is most notable as a transitional moment on the way to the creation of *Geroi nashego vremeni.* While the latter novel recycles many of the characters of *Ligovskaia,* it also marks Lermontov's discovery of his own organic narrative forms and style. Work on *Ligovskaia* was interrupted in early 1837 by more compelling events. It was eventually published in *Russkii vestnik* (Russian Herald) in 1882.

During the post-Junker-School period spent in St. Petersburg (November 1834 through February 1837), Lermontov remained fairly disheartened about his prospects for a prominent public career. This depression was no doubt deepened by the triple rejection of *Maskarad* by the censors. Even immediately upon his graduation from the Junker School, Lermontov was wracked by doubts about his future. He wrote to his good friend Mariia Aleksandrovna Lopukhina (Varvara and Aleksei's sister):

> my future, although brilliant to the eye, is in fact empty and insipid . . . with each day I perceive more and more that I will never be good for anything: with all my beautiful dreams and unsuccessful efforts along life's path . . . for I lack either opportunity or nerve! . . . I am told that one day the opportunity will arrive! Experience and time will give you the nerve! . . . And who knows, when all of that comes, whether I will still have something of that burning young soul which God has most inappropriately given me.

As it turned out, Lermontov did not have to wait long for his opportunity, nor did he lack the nerve to seize it when it arose. In January 1837, outside of St. Petersburg, Pushkin was fatally shot at the age of thirty-seven in a duel with a Frenchman who had insinuated that the great poet had been a victim of cuckoldry. There had already been talk in St. Petersburg to the effect that Pushkin had been provoked into the duel as part of a conspiracy by the tsar's court. Pushkin, after all, represented one of the last holdovers from the politically freethinking gentry of the 1810s and 1820s. There is also evidence, however, to suggest alternative interpretations of the duel. Pushkin's own depression and paranoia may have contributed as much to the denouement as any rumored overtures made to the poet's wife. Be that as it may, Lermontov gave this event the mythological spin that determined its cultural trajectory for generations of Russian intellectuals to come. Moreover, in Pushkin's death Lermontov attained his destiny as a poet-hero.

Lermontov responded immediately to the duel with the first fifty-six lines of his angry elegiac ode, "Smert' poeta" (Death of the Poet, 1837). The poem framed Pushkin as the archetypal poet of the title and as the victim of a mercenary and reactionary court composed in large part of European imports who were hostile not only to Pushkin in particular but also to poetry as a whole. This first version of the poem was widely circulated in handwritten copies throughout St. Petersburg society, where liberal circles received it with great enthusiasm. This reception is hardly surprising, since the old Russian aristocracy was sensitive to its displacement by foreigners and other parvenus at court. Almost literally overnight, Lermontov became the heroic voice of the educated gentry. In the meantime, however, loyalists at court were circulating versions of the duel defending Pushkin's opponent, saying that Pushkin had behaved improperly and that his killer could not have acted otherwise. When Lermontov's cousin Nikolai Arkad'evich Stolypin visited the ailing poet in the days after Pushkin's death, he voiced just such views. Lermontov and Stolypin became engaged in a heated argument, resulting in the poet's addition to the poem of sixteen rage-filled lines, directly addressing Nicholas's court and condemning it to eternal cultural damnation. The new version of the poem was circulated in the same manner as the first, to even greater acclaim.

The addition of these lines had two consequences. First, by directly addressing the cultural enemies of poetry as if from the first person, the lines explicitly framed Lermontov as the avenger of poetry. While the first part of the poem had emphatically declared the death of Pushkin as archetypal poet, its conclusion pushed Lermontov's own voice into the vacated space. Second, and even more significantly, the vituperative concluding lines brought the poem to the attention of the authorities. Lermontov's punishment, decided by the tsar himself, was transfer from the capital to active duty in the Caucasus, where the empire was engaged in the continuous process of subduing the native populations, foremost among them the Chechens. He was sentenced on 25 February 1837 and departed for the Caucasus on 19 March.

Lermontov's exile magnified the frame of poet-hero established by the heroic act of "Smert' poeta." Moreover, exile broadened the appeal of Lermontov's heroic image beyond liberal gentry circles. To be exiled to this dangerous, exotic locale, especially as a potentially active combatant, brought Lermontov's public image into consonance with the heroic type familiar to the Romantic imagination from works of fiction popular in Russia at the time. Lermontov was thus born into the cultural consciousness of his day as a literary hero come to life.

Lermontov's response to his newfound fame extended beyond the recognition of his own personal success as a poet. Rather than merely enjoying his new cultural status as a potential aid in selling books, Lermontov developed an entire mythology of the poet's place in culture. Lermontov fused his ever-present dual desires to be both a great lyric poet and a Romantic hero by interweaving his two careers as writer and warrior in such a way that each framed the other. As he resumed writing lyric poetry, his lyric voice acquired the pathos of the sensitive poet confronting mortal fate in perilous battle. His thoughts and feelings as an individual were framed by his status as an eyewitness to the death and savagery of war. Conversely, he cast the act of lyric utterance as the heroic defense of the poetic values of individual feeling and sincerity against the hostile onslaughts of an increasingly commercial, superficial society, indifferent to individual fate. By framing poetry as an act of war, Lermontov raised its stakes: culture was a battlefield, and the poet was a warrior. The sentimental poet had turned militant as a means of reestablishing his role in Russian culture.

Lermontov was aware of the cultural value attached to his exile. In a letter to his friend Raevsky just prior to his departure for the Caucasus, he strikes a stoic pose, consoling himself with the words of Napoleon: "the great names are made in the Orient." Where some would see misfortune, Lermontov found confirmation of his own youthful conviction that his destiny lay in the Caucasus. What is more, his predicament reawakened his voice as a lyric poet. While in prison prior to his exile, Lermontov wrote four lyrics (one of them a reworking of an earlier poem), reportedly with a matchstick on the scraps of gray paper in which his bread rations were wrapped. Two of the poems treat the theme of imprisonment directly: "Uznik" (The Prisoner), published in the *Odesskii al'manakh* (Odessa Almanac) for 1840, and "Sosed" (The Neighbor), included in the 1840 edition of his collected poems. Each in its way strikes a hopeful tone—the first through an image of escape into wide-open spaces, the second through wordless spiritual communion with the inhabitant of the neighboring cell. A third, "Molitva" (Prayer), published in *Otechestvennye zapiski* in 1840, prays to the Mother of God to intercede not in the poet's own interests but on behalf of a woman the poet loves. It is as if Lermontov's arrest and separation from the frenzied life of high society suddenly jarred loose the part of him that longed for human love. The fourth of these poems, "Kogda volnuetsia zhelteiushchaia niva" (When the yellowing cornfield ripples), included in his 1840 collection, is one of the best nature lyrics in Russian poetry. As the poem progresses, natural phenomena become gradually more personified, growing increasingly more intelligible to the poet until, prompted by a spring whispering the "secret saga" of its origins, the poet's troubled soul is eased by a sudden ability to envision happiness on earth and a God in the heavens. The subtle and carefully paced unfolding of the imagery in the poem and its atmosphere of intimate self-revelation mark it as Lermontov's first truly outstanding lyric.

Despite Lermontov's Romantic visions of grandeur, his first months in the Caucasus were less than glorious. He fell ill during the first leg of his journey southward and detoured to take the mineral waters near Piatigorsk, where he spent all of June, July, and August. During this period his grandmother lobbied unceasingly to have the poet reassigned to a guard regiment near St. Petersburg. By the middle of September, Lermontov finally headed for his assigned regiment. For unknown reasons, he was repeatedly delayed along the way, and before he could reach his unit his grandmother's efforts proved successful. He was transferred to the Grodnensky Hussar Guards, stationed near Novgorod, some eighty miles southeast of St. Petersburg, effective in late November. By the end of January 1838 Lermontov was back in St. Petersburg. Since he never reached his active unit, Lermontov's first exile amounted to little more than an extended vacation through the southern regions of the empire, although he participated in a few minor skirmishes on the way back to St. Petersburg. More importantly from a literary standpoint, during the course of 1837 Lermontov managed to meet several of the most prominent Russian men of letters, including some of the exiled Decembrist rebels and the influential critic Vissarion Grigor'evich Belinsky, who later played a decisive role in shaping the poet's literary reputation.

Upon returning to St. Petersburg, Lermontov was pleased to find himself feted by some new acquaintances, as well as old friends, although he also complained of being "persecuted" by his relatives, especially the female ones. From this point on, the Caucasus and St. Petersburg appear in Lermontov's correspondence and literary works as counterposed worlds, modeling the conflict between freedom and social constraint that informs the mature poet's worldview. One of Lermontov's most important new acquaintances was Zhukovsky, the elder statesman of Russian Romanticism, who arranged to have Lermontov's *Tambovskaia kaznacheisha* (The Tambov Treasurer's Wife), a satirical *poema,* published in the fashionable literary journal *Sovremennik* (The Contemporary) in late 1838.

Lermontov reported to his new regiment in Novgorod in late February 1838, but by late March, again as a result of his grandmother's pleas to the authorities, he was granted a full pardon and transferred back to his original unit, the Life Guard Hussars stationed in Tsarskoe Selo. This reassignment gave Lermontov the opportunity to participate fully once again in the salon society of the capital. Lermontov constantly professed boredom with this society, but he also seemed to derive a certain perverse satisfaction from his role as its literary enfant terrible. Lermontov became a regular at the fashionable St. Petersburg salon hosted by the widow, daughter, and sons of Nikolai Mikhailovich Karamzin, who died in 1826. Karamzin had been the foremost Russian man of letters, and the salon, known for its literary tenor, strove to continue his legacy. The greatest Russian writers, painters, and composers appeared regularly there. The opportunity to read his works at these prestigious gatherings greatly enhanced Lermontov's growing reputation.

Lermontov's reputation was not merely literary. He continued to be known for his scathing remarks at others' expense and was not beyond juvenile pranks. One such stunt was the wearing of an undersized saber during review, which cost him fifteen days in the guardhouse. Meanwhile, some of his fellow alumni of the Junker School remembered the poet's scandalous student poems. Unable to imagine Lermontov capable of writing anything else, they were incredulous that others spoke of him as talented and alarmed to find copies of his manuscripts in the hands of their wives and sisters. At this time Lermontov was part of a group of young officers known as the *Kruzhok shestnadtsati* (Circle of Sixteen). The members met at each others' apartments, where they apparently discussed contemporary issues with complete frankness. Little else is known about the group, although some Soviet scholars have attributed to it radical political and philosophical ideas. However that may be, the circle did arouse the suspicions of Grand Prince Mikhail Pavlovich, who promised to "destroy this nest."

Although only two of Lermontov's poems appeared in print in 1838, his literary reputation and connections were growing. The first of the poems to appear, the verse narrative *Pesnia pro tsaria Ivana Vasil'evicha, molodogo oprichnika i udalogo kuptsa Kalashnikova* (Song of the Tsar Ivan Vasil'evich, the Young Oprichnik and the Valiant Merchant Kalashnikov), published in *Literaturnye pribavleniia k Russkomu invalidu* (Supplement to the Russian Invalid), even earned a positive response in print from Belinsky—the poet's first review. In *Pesnia* Lermontov approaches popular Russian tradition, adopting the rhythm and narrative voice of the *bylina* (Russian historical folk song). Its narrator poses as a folk singer of old and tells a tale set in the time of Ivan the Terrible. The plot revolves around one of the tsar's *oprichniki* (Ivan's elite and repressive political police), named Kiribeevich, who has fallen in love with a young woman of the merchant class. Unaware that she is married to the merchant Kalashnikov, Ivan encourages Kiribeevich to court her. Kiribeevich proceeds to accost her and force a kiss upon her. Kalashnikov exacts revenge by killing Kiribeevich, a renowned fighter, at the tsar's regular boxing match. Kalashnikov protects the honor of his wife by refusing to reveal to the angry tsar his true reason for killing the *oprichnik*. Ivan sentences Kalashnikov to death, but out of respect for Kalashnikov's "conscience," the tsar grants the merchant's family special trading rights and promises a quick and painless execution. The merchant is in turn grateful for Ivan's mercy. Thus the men part with mutual honor and respect. *Pesnia* moves rapidly and simply, with little lyric digression or narrative complication. The reader is spared lengthy emotional outpourings by any of the main actors. Lack of Romantic ornamentation, however, hardly signifies a complete departure from Lermontov's heroic aesthetic, as some have claimed. If anything, the simplicity of the story line and Kalashnikov's stoicism serve to accentuate the merchant's tragic heroism. The national-historical content of the poem, with its implied comparison to contemporary Russia, helped the poem to become one of Lermontov's first public successes.

Lermontov's other *poema* published in 1838, *Tambovskaia kaznacheisha,* also features a corrupt official. This time, however, the narrative tone is satirical rather than heroic, with clear indebtedness to Pushkin's *Evgeny Onegin* (also adopting the complex fourteen-line stanza of that work) and Gogol's provincial satires. The town of Tambov, a manifestly dingy backwater, is ironically described as a "glorious little city." The treasurer of the title, Bobkovsky, is an embezzler and card-cheat. He also neglects his attractive younger wife, Avdot'ia. This mistreatment is the worst of his sins from the perspective of the officer, Garin, who rides into town one day with his regiment. Garin courts Avdot'ia. When Bobkovsky catches him at it, instead of challenging him to a duel, he invites him to his name-day party. During a card game, Bobkovsky loses everything: house, horses, furniture, and his wife's jewelry. Finally, he stakes his wife on one card against his whole estate. The tone of narration then shifts awkwardly to deadly seriousness, as Avdot'ia's grief and shame are described. When Bobkovsky loses, she rises, throws her wedding ring in his face, then faints. Garin catches his prize in his arms and carries her home. The poem ends with a description of the ensuing provincial rumors and the narrator's mock apology for ending his story so abruptly.

The narrator's stance in this poem is awkwardly ambivalent: is this a serious moral fable or an erotic farce in the manner of the *Iunkerskie poemy* and *Sashka?* Most of the poem points to the latter, although the final fainting scene seems meant to be taken quite seriously. It is possible that the answer lies in censorial changes in the poem, the original manuscript for which has not survived. Lermontov was furious when he saw the printed version, but it is not clear precisely why. In any case, the version of the poem that has endured does not represent Lermontov's best work, despite its often lively verse and some Soviet critics' praise of its "realistic" treatment of provincial morality.

The growth of Lermontov's reputation during 1838 was greatly fueled by the narrative poem *Demon,* which in many respects represents the polar opposite of

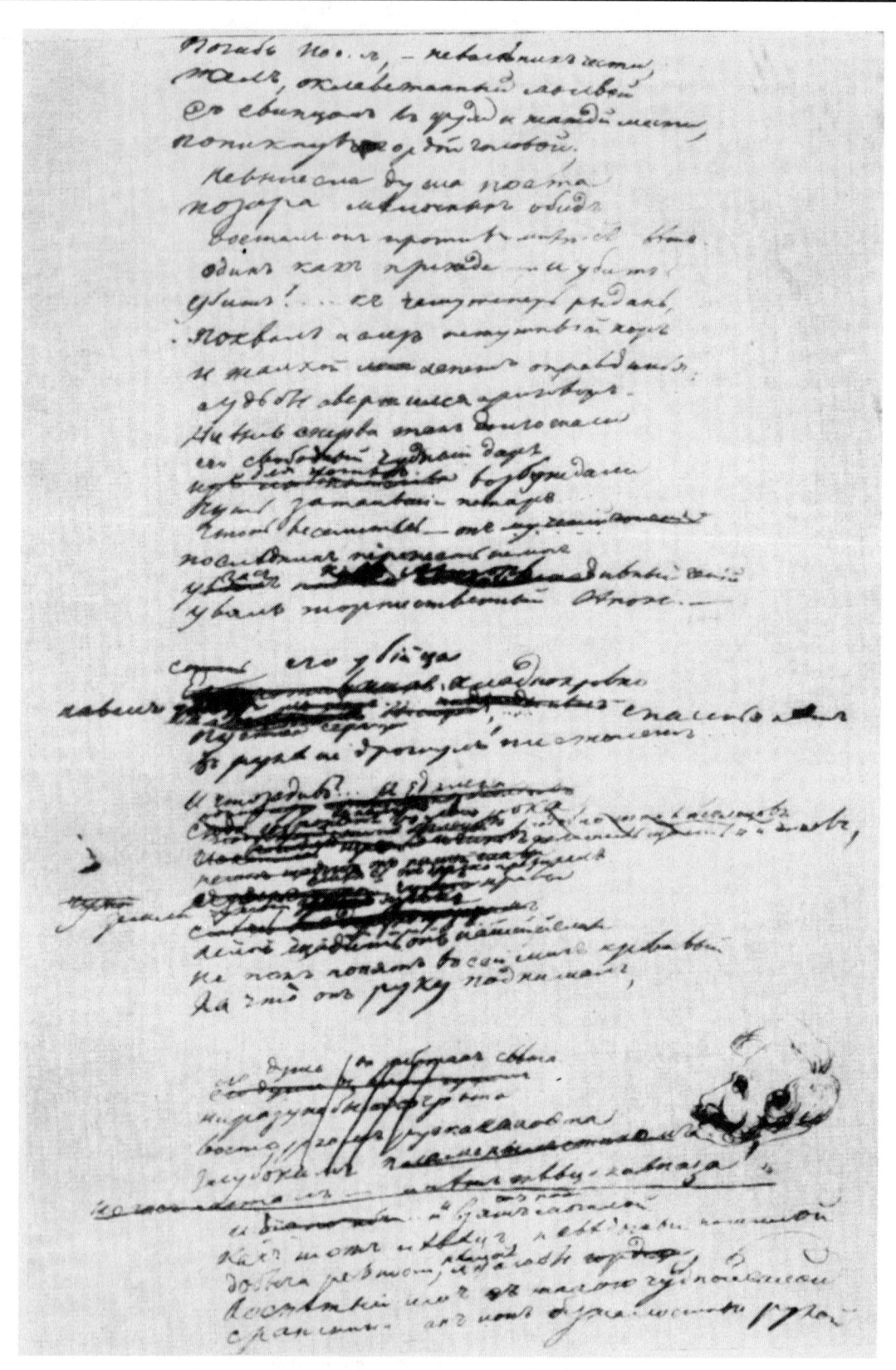

Page from a draft for "Smert' poeta" (Death of the Poet, 1837), Lermontov's denunciation of the tsar's court after the death of Aleksandr Pushkin; the sketch is of Gen. Leontii Vasil'evich Dubel't, a chief of the gendarmes (Central State Archive of Literature and Art, TsGALI fond 427, Moscow)

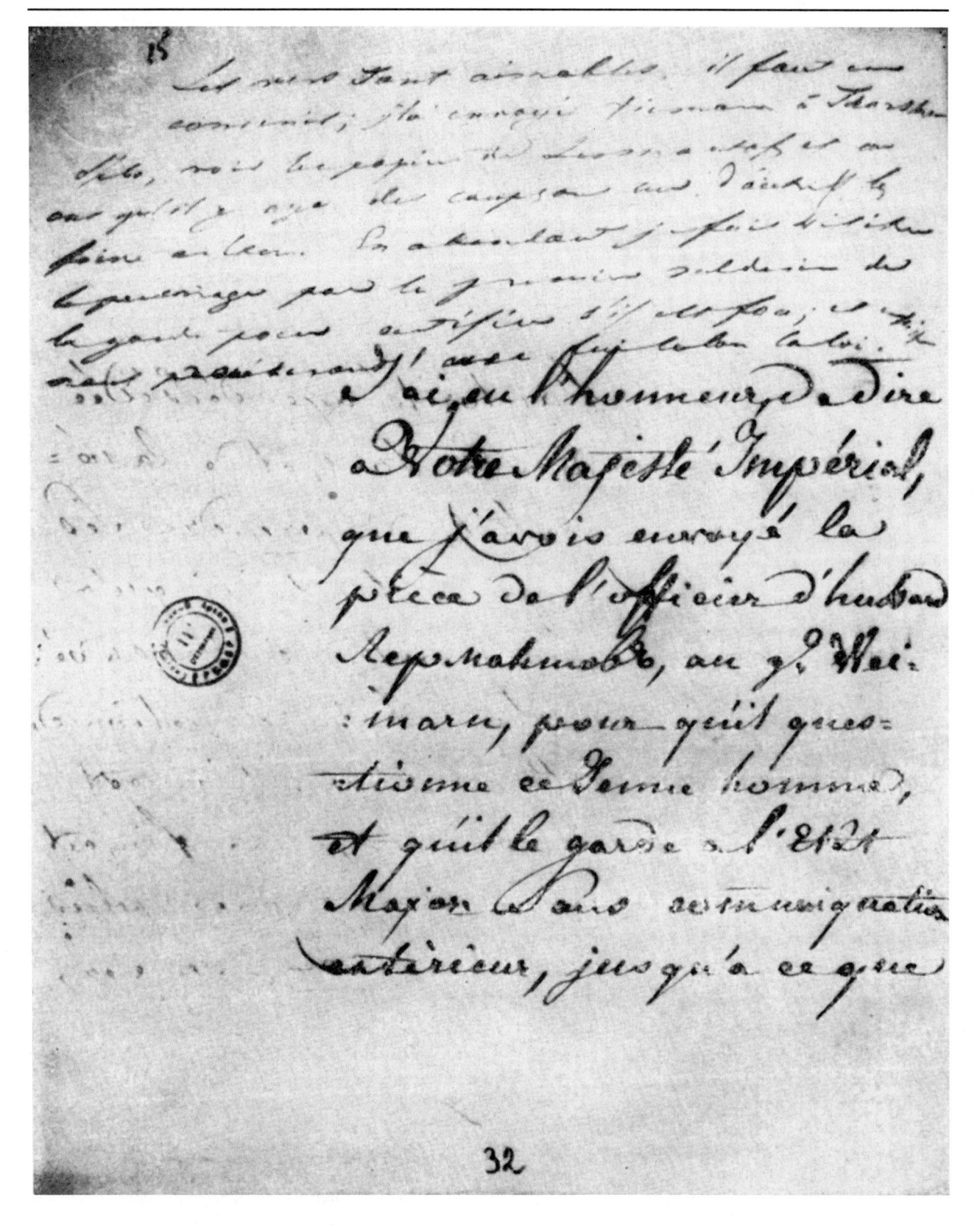

Page from the report of Count Aleksandr Khristoforovich Benckendorff to Tsar Nicholas I about Lermontov's "Smert' poeta," with the tsar's response (State Archive of the Russian Federation, TsGAOR fond 728)

Tambovskaia kaznacheisha in Lermontov's aesthetic system. The plot of *Demon* presents Lermontov at his most mythological and allegorical. Its eponymous hero is the archetypal fallen angel, doomed to fly eternally across the face of the earth doing evil, trapped in a limbo between heavenly peace and the vanity and passions of earthly life.

At the outset, the poem depicts the Demon flying across the landscape, utterly indifferent to its beauty. Later redactions, beginning in 1838 after the poet's return from his first exile, set the action concretely in the Caucasus, depicted in lush symbolic verses that include some of the best descriptions of nature ever written in Russian poetry. The Demon's gaze, however, responds to the soaring and plunging landscape with a scorn and hatred born of his resentment of a creation from which he has been excluded. Suddenly, in an operatic moment, the Demon's soul is awakened by the sight and sound of the beautiful princess Tamara, who is about to be married into an "unknown family" at the behest of her father. The Demon intercedes to arrange the groom's death, then engages in supernatural courtship of the princess, visiting her dreams. Tamara, disturbed by these visitations, begs her father to send her to a convent. The Savior's protection, however, fails to curtail the Demon's efforts to possess her. Tamara is torn between prayers to the saints and her heart, which "prays to *him*." In Tamara, Lermontov continues the treatment, developed in his early lyrics, of feminine erotic desire as the product of the male's insinuation into her consciousness through words and behavior.

The centerpiece of the poem is the Demon's long and passionate confession of love, replete with the story of his downfall and his hope for redemption through earthly love. Tamara is seduced by this speech, but the Demon's burning kiss, accompanied by her climactic cry of pleasure mixed with agony, kills her instantly. While Tamara's body is buried, the battle for her soul continues. In a scene added to the penultimate version, perhaps intended to appease the censors, an angel bearing her soul heavenward succeeds in frustrating the Demon, who has appeared to claim it. The Demon flies off, the spark of love extinguished, his futile dream of redemption crushed. The poem ends with a Gothic description of Tamara's father's castle and the church where she and her family are buried, both now utterly abandoned, visited only by the clouds, but still haunted by the tragic story that unfolded there.

In the mythic plot of the poem, Lermontov emphasizes the Romantic theme of alienation from God, creation, and humanity. The Demon's all-too-human striving is thwarted, transformed into bitterness by his preordained fate as an outcast. In this respect the Demon represents the culmination of Lermontov's line of Romantic outlaw-heroes. One of Lermontov's most enigmatic and controversial works, *Demon* was never published in his lifetime. Excerpts from it were published posthumously, with great censorial difficulties, in *Otechestvennye zapiski* in 1842. The first complete publication did not occur until 1856 in Germany. Only in 1860, under the reformist reign of Alexander II, could the complete text be published in Russia. Nevertheless, Lermontov circulated the manuscript in handwritten form and read it at salons. His readings earned high praise from several prominent salon figures. Word of it even reached the Empress Aleksandra Fedorovna, who requested a copy in early 1839 and responded with favor. The empress's approval, however, did not help get *Demon* past the censors. As in the case of *Maskarad*, no changes Lermontov made sufficed to erase the fundamentally unacceptable eroticism and suspicious religious deviance in the poem. There are eight known redactions of the *poema*, dating from 1829 to 1839. Spanning nearly the entirety of Lermontov's creative career, *Demon* serves as a palimpsest of the poet's artistic development, presenting special interest and problems for Lermontov scholars. It is also one of Lermontov's most popular works, having continued to capture the imagination of generations of readers, notably the Symbolist painter Mikhail Aleksandrovich Vrubel', who at the turn of the twentieth century executed a cycle of haunting evocations of the characters and events of the poem.

Despite Lermontov's increasing social and literary successes, by the end of 1838 he felt bored and constrained by life in St. Petersburg. Having been conscious of the disdain of aristocratic society earlier in his life, he was now deeply skeptical of its approbation. He fully expected that at any moment the praise would turn to calumny. As shown by the case of Sushkova, a once-bitten Lermontov was unlikely to forget the slight. Instead of enjoying his newfound fame, Lermontov requested a transfer to duty in the Caucasus. His comment in a letter to Mariia Lopukhina when he was denied: "They don't even wish me to be killed." In the same letter he credits his St. Petersburg salon experience with having prepared him with "arms against society" to use as "the means of revenge" should society ever begin to "persecute" him with its "slander." The combination of victimhood and militant vengeance, apparent in Lermontov's early confessional *poemy* (the renegade's actions justified by his past sufferings) and in the simultaneous pathos and aggressiveness of the Demon, persists here in the poet's approach to life itself.

The few lyrics Lermontov wrote in 1838 testify to his dissatisfaction with society. In one of these, "Kinzhal" (The Dagger), the poet addresses his weapon, tempered by the tears of the young woman who gave it to him, vowing to be "hard of soul, like you, like you, my iron friend." In a thematically related poem, "Poet," an inscribed dagger stands for poetry itself, whose now-forgotten mission Lermontov connects to its historical roles in both religion and warfare:

> Byvalo, mernyi zvuk tvoikh moguchikh slov
>   Vosplamenial boitsa dlia bitvy,
> On nuzhen byl tolpe, kak chasha dlia pirov,
>   Kak fimiam v chasy molitvy.
>
> Tvoi stikh, kak Bozhii dukh, nosilsia nad tolpoi. . . .
>
> (In days gone by, the measured sound of your mighty words
>   Inflamed the warrior for battle,
> It was as needed by the crowd as the chalice for feasts,
>   As incense in the hour of prayer.
>
> Your verse, like the Spirit of the Lord, drifted above the crowd. . . .)

Poetry has come to represent for Lermontov the lost, sacred values of sincerity, fidelity, and passion and, at the same time, the means of revenge against a society seen as the enemy of these values. Lermontov's indictment of society is openly displayed in the famous lyric "Duma" (Meditation), which condemns his generation as timid, passionless, and indifferent to the "reveries of poetry." Future generations, the poet declaims, will "deride our remains . . . with scornful verse, the swindled son's bitter mockery of his dissipated father."

Beginning with "Smert' poeta," Lermontov's adversarial stance vis-à-vis his society increasingly defined his image as a poet. His exile to the Caucasus helped fuel the evolving image of poet as both political exile and military officer. By depicting his lyric persona as a righteous social rebel, Lermontov sought to justify the poet's role at a time when poetry was under attack for failing to address "serious" social and national issues.

Lermontov's fame began to spread into print in January 1839 with the revival of the important monthly journal *Otechestvennye zapiski,* which became the poet's main venue until his death. "Duma" appeared in the first issue, "Poet" in the second. All told, the journal published eleven lyrics and two stories by Lermontov in its twelve issues for the year. (The stories were later included in *Geroi nashego vremeni.*) In addition to lyrics of the rebellious sort, *Otechestvennye zapiski* published two poems of a new type: "Tri pal'my" (Three Palms) and "Dary Tereka" (The Gifts of the Terek), both written in 1839. These lyrics translate the pathos of the traditional elegy into a new symbolic language, that of folkloric animism. In each the usual Romantic lyric hero is displaced by personified nature. "Tri pal'my," subtitled

Self-portrait of Lermontov in the uniform of the Nizhegorodtskii Dragoon Regiment, 1837 (State Literary Museum, Moscow)

"An Eastern Legend," tells the tale of three palm trees clustered around an oasis in "an Arab land." Though they flourish in harmonious symbiosis, the palms and spring complain to God that no travelers have ever visited. Soon their prayers are answered. When a caravan visits the oasis, the trees and spring are delighted to offer shade and water to the visitors. But when night falls, the visitors chop down the palms for firewood. Unshaded, the oasis soon fills with sand. The poem allegorically extends Lermontov's skepticism about human society, contrasting the exploitative motives of men and the innocence of their victims.

In "Dary Tereka," another allegory, the Terek, a Caucasian river, speaks to the Caspian Sea, into which it flows, offering precious gifts in exchange for "refuge" in its waters. The only humans in the poem are the gifts: the corpses of a Kabardinian warrior and a young cossack woman. Indifferent to the first gift, the sea rears up "full of joy" to embrace the second. The power of the poem resides in the indirect, distant evocation of the suffering of its human victims against the background of an all-powerful, animated nature. Desire and beauty take the form of mighty natural forces, reflecting their dominion over humanity. Simple in imagery, yet rich in music and allusion, these lyrics brought an unprecedented freshness into Russian nature poetry. Moreover, in these two poems the limited perspective of Lermontov's formerly omnipresent lyric "I" gives way to an external world with an independent life of its own, no longer serving as mere background for the subject. This embracing of extrapersonal perspective drove much of Lermontov's poetic evolution in the last two years of his life.

Toward the end of 1839, Lermontov's disgust for society was reaching a peak. Around this time a sequence of events began that led to his first duel and second exile. The French ambassador, having heard suggestions that Lermontov's poem on the death of Pushkin expressed anti-French sentiments (Pushkin's slayer was French), had asked a mutual acquaintance to provide him with the stanza in question. Yet, before even receiving the lines, the ambassador seems to have been satisfied, for he invited Lermontov to a ball. Nevertheless, among French diplomats, notably the ambassador's son, Ernest de Barante, the suspicion remained that Lermontov had slandered France. At the same time, de Barante and Lermontov were competing for the affections of the young widowed Princess Mariia Alekseevna Shcherbatova. According to one report, this rivalry served as the initial cause of de Barante's challenge to Lermontov at a ball on 16 February 1840 when Shcherbatova showed apparent favor toward Lermontov. Reportedly, de Barante said to Lermontov, "You profit too greatly, sir, from the fact that we are in a country where dueling is forbidden!" The poet responded, "That is no matter, I am entirely at your service." The duel was set for 18 February. Clearly there is something missing from this story: no doubt Lermontov had done or said something to provoke the challenge. In any case, de Barante's antagonism was doubtless augmented by the suggestion of Lermontov's anti-French feelings.

Other possible contributing causes of the duel should be mentioned. At a New Year's Eve masked ball Lermontov had apparently said something insulting (exactly what, is not known) to the daughters of the tsar (although some claim it was the empress herself, at a different ball). Furthermore, Lermontov wrote a lyric, "1-go ianvaria" (January 1), published in the January issue of *Otechestvennye zapiski* and apparently set at the same ball, that expressed his contempt for society in the baldest terms yet. "Kak chasto, pestroiu tolpoiu okruzhen . . . " (How often, surrounded by the motley crowd . . .) begins the poet's internal monologue, as he observes the insincerity and spiritual corruption of society from its midst. Person after person is introduced to the now-famous poet, each one taking his hand and complimenting him:

Kogda kasaiutsia kholodnykh ruk moikh
S nebrezhnoi smelost'iu krasavits gorodskikh
    Davno bestrepetnye ruki,–

Naruzhno pogruzhas' v ikh blesk i suetu,
Laskaiu ia v dushe starinnuiu mechtu,
    Pogibshikh let sviatye zvuki.

(When with careless audacity the city beauties'
Long no longer trembling hands
    Touch my hands,–
Externally absorbed in their glitter and vanity,
I caress in my heart an ancient reverie,
    The sacred sounds of years long past.)

This lyric, the distillation of Lermontov's view of society as the antithesis of poetic integrity, could not help antagonizing those who had met him at the New Year's Eve ball, especially the tsar's daughters, whom he had insulted to their faces. For this reason, it has been suggested by Lermontov's biographer Pavel Aleksandrovich Viskovatov that those close to the tsar's daughters helped provoke the duel. However that may be, it is quite clear that Lermontov's already tenuous relationship with the authorities was worsening.

The duel proved not to be fatal. The two first fought with rapiers, and Lermontov was slightly wounded in the forearm before his rapier broke. The duelists then switched to pistols. According to Lermontov's own testimony to his commanding officer, de Barante shot first and missed. Then Lermontov intentionally missed, ending the duel. After the duel the poet was reportedly "unusually merry and talkative," showing off his wound to his friends. Lermontov was arrested on 11 March. His case dragged on, and witnesses to the duel were also questioned, facts suggesting that at least some representatives of the authorities were determined to punish him. A month after Lermontov's arrest, the tsar himself felt it necessary to order that the case be concluded before Easter. In the meantime, Lermontov's duel was the talk of St. Petersburg; his poems continued to be published in journals; and he continued to write new ones, which were praised, albeit grudgingly, by the very people who condemned his actions. The poet's grandmother, who was gravely ill, was quite upset. Lermontov, probably caught up in the Romantic narrative of his imprisonment, gave little thought to her suffering. After some confusion, and nearly two months of imprisonment, Lermontov was transferred to the Tenginsky Infantry Regiment, at that time involved in some of the most dangerous army operations in the Caucasus. After being feted by his friends the Karamzins, Lermontov left St. Petersburg in early May, stopping in Moscow on the way. Most of the members of the *Kruzhok shestnadtsati* left St. Petersburg and passed through Moscow on the way to the Caucasus at the same time, leading to speculation that they had been secretly ordered to leave the capital.

Pencil drawing by Lermontov of Taman', a Black Sea port that he visited in 1837 and later used as a setting for part of his novel Geroi nashego vremeni *(A Hero of Our Time, 1840) (Institute of Russian Literature [Pushkin House], St. Petersburg)*

In April 1840, while Lermontov was still in the guardhouse, his novel *Geroi nashego vremeni* appeared in print. All the stories that comprise the novel feature the same hero, Grigory Pechorin, but their order in the book does not correspond to the chronology of events in Pechorin's biography. (This arrangement has led some to question its classification as a novel.) The first two stories, "Bela" and "Maksim Maksimych," form a unit and recount the most recent events of Pechorin's life. The last three stories–"Taman'," "Kniazhna Meri" (Princess Mary), and "Fatalist"–are presented as Pechorin's own journal. These stories trace the arc of Pechorin's life prior to the events in the first two. This composite structure echoes many of the early *poemy,* in which the hero's actions, seen from without, are followed by his own "confession." Like Lermontov's lyric poetry, the novel assembles a variety of views of a single hero, whose persona is stable, partially autobiographical, and never fully exhausted in the literary text. In emphasizing the ineffability of the human soul, Lermontov remains true to his Byronic roots despite an increasingly critical presentation of the hero.

Geroi nashego vremeni begins with the story "Bela" (the title is the name of the heroine). The story is narrated by an unnamed traveling military officer who later turns out to be the "editor" of the entire collection. While crossing a mountain pass, this narrator encounters a Russian officer, Maksim Maksimych, who has been serving in the region for many years. The two travel together for a while, and Maksim recounts for the narrator the story that serves as the body of the chapter. This tale concerns the officer Pechorin, with whom Maksim has served about five years earlier. Pechorin arranges to kidnap the Circassian princess, Bela. Pechorin keeps Bela imprisoned in the fort until she finally falls in love with him. As soon as she does, however, he seems to grow bored with her, spending increasing amounts of time hunting. In the end, Bela is killed by a fiery Circassian whose horse Pechorin has stolen.

This account is the reader's first glimpse of Pechorin, and it is not a flattering one. Nevertheless, readers are given this view through the eyes of Maksim, who seems fascinated by Pechorin's derring-do. Part of the psychological complexity of the story resides in this double vision. Maksim has sentimental ideas of love and friendship. While as an officer he cannot condone such behavior, at least part of him sees the kidnapping of Bela as a heroic overcoming of love's obstacles. Pechorin, on the other hand, seems to be acting out a different script, that of the Romantic, larger-than-life Napoleonic hero, who must incessantly test his will against the fateful forces arrayed around him. Maksim gets an inkling of Pechorin's "true" character when he laughs in response to Maksim's efforts to console him after Bela's death. Maksim, however, is unable to fathom the inner motives of this demonic character. In this respect, "Bela" successfully exploits an early Lermontovian theme: the rift between the inner world of the hero and others' perceptions of him.

The inadequacy of Maksim's sentimentalist view of Pechorin is made painfully clear in the next, much shorter story, "Maksim Maksimych," narrated by the traveling editor. The editor and Maksim meet again at a way station. By chance, Pechorin is staying in the same place with a colonel, on his way to Persia for undisclosed reasons. Maksim is thrilled at the prospect of a reunion with his old companion. Pechorin, however, greets him coldly, resisting the older man's emotional overtures and insisting that he must depart. This rejection leaves Maksim crushed. He mutters a criticism of the current age, with its dandyism and flightiness. The traveling editor, however, seizes the opportunity to acquire Pechorin's notes, which Maksim has been holding for his friend. The editor realizes that contemporary readers will be interested in a hero such as Pechorin.

The last three stories are presented as Pechorin's personal journal. The editor provides an ironic foreword that seems to make fun of the contemporary fashion of moral tales as well as publishing in general. He announces that he has heard word that Pechorin has died on the way back from Persia. The news greatly "gladdens" him since it gives him the opportunity to "place my own name over someone else's work." In declaring his reason for publishing Pechorin's notes, the editor wavers between public service ("the history of a human soul, even the most petty" is "interesting and useful") and vindication of Pechorin's actions ("we almost always forgive what we can understand").

The first chapter of Pechorin's journal is titled "Taman'," after a small Black Sea port town where Lermontov spent a few days in 1837. No doubt the fact that Lermontov's belongings were stolen while he was in Taman' lie behind the opening words of the story: "Taman' is the most wretched burg of all the seaside towns in Russia." In search of housing, Pechorin is finally quartered in a ramshackle hut owned by an absent mistress, a young blind boy, and a girl initially described as an undine. As events unfold, Pechorin at first sees them through the lens of supernatural fiction. Before long, though, it becomes clear that the family business is actually smuggling. A rather gullible Pechorin is seduced by the girl, who tries to drown him, afraid that he will report their activities to the authorities. The deflation of literary expectations in the story is capped by the revelation of the smuggler Yanko as cruel and mercenary.

The second entry, the longest in the book, is "Kniazhna Meri." It is both representative and critical of the genre of society tales popular at the time. The plot is eerily reminiscent of Lermontov's real-life intrigue with Sushkova. Once again, two heroes compete for precedence. One is Pechorin; the other is Grushnitsky, an ineffectual poseur whom Pechorin sets out to teach a lesson by interfering with the latter's budding romance with Princess Mary. He is successful in gaining the affections of the beautiful young woman, although he does not love her. Grushnitsky is incited by a group of other malcontents to plot revenge against Pechorin. Against Grushnitsky's feeble protests, his cohorts convince him to rig the duel by loading only Grushnitsky's pistol, but Pechorin finds out about the plot. Grushnitsky shoots first, aiming to kill, but succeeds only in grazing Pechorin's knee. Pechorin then fires, killing Grushnitsky, who plunges over the edge of a cliff. The subplot of the story, involving the renewal of Pechorin's youthful affair with a married woman, Vera, shows a softer side of the hero. After the duel, when Vera's husband finds out about the affair, she is forced to depart in a hurry. Pechorin gallops off to see her before she leaves, but rides his horse to death and is left sobbing by the road. As punishment for the duel Pechorin is sent to serve at a remote fort, where the events of "Bela" take place.

While serving with Maksim, probably before the events of "Bela," Pechorin experiences the adventure recounted in the last tale, "Fatalist." This short and dramatic story ends the book and points to its philosophical center. One night, while away from the fort at a cossack station, Pechorin bets against a Serb officer, Vulich, who wagers that man's fate is predestined. To prove that man cannot choose the moment of his death, he puts a loaded gun to his head and pulls the trigger. Pechorin, sure that he can read imminent death on Vulich's face, bets that he will die. The gun does not fire. Vulich wins, but later that evening he is killed by a drunken, rampaging cossack. Pechorin was right. Deciding to test his own fate, Pechorin heroically storms the hut where the cossack is holed up, taking him alive. Pechorin's subsequent musings echo Lermontov's own ethical skepticism: "Who knows for sure whether or not he is convinced of anything? . . . How often we mistake feeling's deceit or a lapse of reason for conviction! . . . I love to doubt everything: this disposition of mind does not interfere with decisiveness of character–on the contrary; as for me, I always go forward more boldly not knowing what awaits me. After

The Demon Seated *(1890), one of the paintings by Mikhail Aleksandrovich Vrubel' inspired by Lermontov's narrative poem* Demon, *which was published in full in 1856 (Tret'iakov Gallery, Moscow)*

all, nothing worse than death can happen to you—and you can't escape death!"

Much of the debate about the novel has focused on the character of Pechorin. Are readers to see him as a twisted egoist, pursuing his own needs at the expense of others' happiness, or as an exceptional individual (the Romantic "man of destiny"), misunderstood and provoked by an ignorant society? Both sides have been argued at length. Probably both are true, given Lermontov's characteristic ambivalence about the human soul. It is important, however, to keep in mind Lermontov's literary goals in creating Pechorin. He sought, as he did in earlier works, to create a full-blooded hero who would capture the imagination (rather than the good will) of his readers. His technique in doing so in *Geroi nashego vremeni* is typically Romantic: Pechorin is a charismatic hero who both attracts and repels, much like the Gothic and Romantic heroes Dracula, Frankenstein, and Melmoth. Readers should also be aware that Pechorin's personality embodies many of the contradictions of Lermontov's own. Therefore, it is apparent that the novel (like Pechorin's own journal entries) is ruthlessly self-examining. Lermontov does not necessarily like everything that he finds in himself, but he nevertheless attempts to make it understood and to show it as emblematic of human nature in general. The Lermontovian hero embodies the same characteristics of pride, willfulness, pathos, and pain as any human being, only magnified to Romantic proportions. The plausibility of this interpretation is supported by the fact that the minor characters in the novel evince the same qualities, only on a more banal level. These two ideas—that the "unusual man" best mirrored the contradictions of his time, and that microscopic examination of such a man's psyche helped to understand all men—dominated the era in which Lermontov wrote.

The controversy surrounding the novel propelled Lermontov to the center of critical attention. Critics of a nationalist bent complained that Pechorin, with his Europeanized dandyism, was not a truly Russian character. Others, including the tsar, were outraged that such an immoral hero should be held up as a model. Nicholas raged that "such novels destroy morals and embitter the character." He expressed disappointment that Pechorin, and not the mild-mannered and obedient Maksim, turned out to be the "hero" of the title. The great critic Belinsky, however, was thrilled by the depth of characterization in the book. After it appeared, he visited Lermontov in the guardhouse and waxed ecstatic at the writer's talent and passion. From this point on Belinsky proved to be Lermontov's most loyal and influential advocate. Partially fueled by the controversy, the book sold well, and a second edition appeared a year after the first. For this edition Lermontov wrote an author's foreword in which he rather sarcastically answers his critics. Lermontov takes aim at his readers' inability to recognize irony and to understand a work that does not put forth a clear moral. The foreword seeks to liberate the novel from the old-fashioned notion of literature as morally uplifting. Lermontov had never seen his role as morally didactic in a simplistic way. If *Geroi nashego vremeni* has a moral message, it is at least as condemnatory of the society in which Pechorin operates as of Pechorin himself.

Lermontov reported for duty in Stavropol' at the headquarters for Caucasian operations in early June 1840. He then reported to the left-flank base in the Chechen capital of Grozny. He participated in five separate military excursions against the Chechens between July and November. Lermontov's experiences on the front lines left a deep impression. In particular, a bloody battle at the river Valerik (the name means "river of death" in Chechen), in which the Russians were outnumbered three to one, served as the inspiration for a well-known lyric, "Ia k vam pishu sluchaino . . . " (I write to you by chance . . . , 1840), first published in *Utrenniaia zaria* (Morning Dawn) in 1843. The poem takes the form of a letter to an object of the poet's earlier, unrequited love. After confessing the torments associated with this love, the lyric hero announces his reconciliation with his fate. Most of the narrative is occupied by the description of the battle at Valerik, including a pathos-filled description of the death of an officer with his soldiers looking on. After recounting the battle, the poet ironically declaims that he is afraid he will "bore" the addressee, who is seen as absorbed in the "amusements of society," with the "savage horrors of war":

Svoi um vy ne privykli muchit'
Tiazheloi dumoi o kontse.
. . . i vy edva li
Vblizi kogda-nibud' vidali,
Kak umiraiut. . . .

(You are not accustomed to tormenting your mind
With weighty meditations on the end.
. . . you can scarcely have ever
Seen at close range
How men die. . . .)

The thrust of the poem is to expose the superficiality of St. Petersburg society by contrasting its carefree activities with the firsthand experience of cruelty and death. At the same time, the poem privileges the poet's view of the world by revealing that it encompasses the full range of experience from love to death. This image of the poet comes to stand at the center of Lermontov's literary self-presentation.

A variety of sources report that Lermontov repeatedly displayed remarkable bravery in battles, bordering on suicidal recklessness. The poet was recommended at least twice by his superiors for decoration and put in command of a brigade of volunteers in October. When a list of recommended decorations for the battle of Valerik was submitted, Nicholas himself crossed Lermontov's name off of it. When Lermontov's name was later submitted for the Order of St. Vladimir, the tsar again exercised his veto. These actions suggest an interesting dynamic between the empress, who loved Lermontov's poetry, and the tsar, who despised the poet.

In October 1840, while Lermontov was on the front, the first collection of his poetry came out, the only one published during his life. The volume includes only twenty-eight poems, selected by Lermontov. Realizing how greatly his art had matured since the "Smert' poeta" affair, he chose only three poems written prior to 1837: two short lyrics from 1836 (adapted from Byron and previously published in *Otechestvennye zapiski*) and a ballad written in 1832. The most significant new piece to appear in the collection was *Mtsyri,* written in 1839. The last narrative poem Lermontov completed, it represents a distillation of the confessional device of his earlier *poemy*. After a concise introduction the hero's confession comprises the majority of the poem. The hero has been captured as a child by a Russian general on the march and separated from his native Caucasian tribe. When he falls ill, he is left in the care of the monks at a monastery in Georgia, where he is brought up as a monastic novice. Raised by foreigners, the young novice has made a failed attempt to escape to his homeland. He is brought back, wounded and dying, to the monastery. His confession, which begins at this point, recounts his homesickness and failed escape. The hero's separation from his homeland symbolizes the soul's alienation from earthly creation, which Lermontov sees as the archetypal state of the human soul.

By December his grandmother's latest flurry of intercessions brought Lermontov a two-month furlough in St. Petersburg on the condition that he remain "diligent in duty and congenial in morals." He was allowed to leave for St. Petersburg on 14 January 1841. For perhaps the first time, Lermontov seemed genuinely happy to arrive in St. Petersburg. With the help of his grandmother, he petitioned for a discharge from the army. Lermontov began to take the possibility of a literary career more seriously, and he discussed with several associates the possibility of starting a journal. As the end of his leave approached, and the discharge failed to materialize, he asked for an extension of his furlough. Thanks to great efforts on the part of his friends and admirers, this request was granted.

The extension proved to be merely a reprieve, however. On 11 April, Lermontov was ordered to leave St. Petersburg for his unit within forty-eight hours. He stopped in Moscow on the way to the Caucasus. Lermontov spent a pleasant week in Moscow but disturbed his friends with prophetic visions of his own death. It is characteristic of Lermontov's Romantic mindset that he could look upon his own death not just calmly, but with a sense of inevitability and spiritual relief. Lermontov's rare bouts of optimism were often connected with artistic productivity. He had had little time to write while on active duty, and he relished the opportunity to do so while on furlough. He wrote a dozen or so good lyrics during this time. Meanwhile, *Geroi nashego vremeni* and his verse collection were being widely reviewed. If some reviews of the novel were not wholly positive, the ever-contentious Lermontov welcomed the controversy. Clearly Lermontov was pleased to be at the center of attention.

En route to operational headquarters in Stavropol', Lermontov fell ill, probably with scurvy. As in 1837, the poet was given medical leave to convalesce at the fashionable mineral spas of the region, where he spent the last two months of his life. Lermontov rented a house with his relative and old friend Aleksei Arkad'evich Stolypin in Piatigorsk, where the two settled into the relaxed social life of the resort. Here, too, Lermontov attracted attention as well as a retinue of admirers among the young officers. Together with this cohort, Lermontov organized several outings and social events.

Less than a week after putting on an enormously successful ball, Lermontov and assorted friends were enjoying an impromptu evening of music and dance at the home of Maj. Gen. Petr Semenovich Verzilin. Lermontov was exchanging barbed witticisms with Lev Sergeevich Pushkin, brother of the poet Aleksandr, while another friend played the piano. One of those present, the retired army major Nikolai Martynov, had been Lermontov's schoolmate and fellow editor of the handwritten journal in which Lermontov's scabrous *Iunkerskie poemy* had appeared. The two men's relationship has been the subject of much speculation. It is possible that Martynov, who also had literary and social aspirations, may have been envious of Lermontov's successes on both counts, as well as annoyed by the poet's barbed wit, of which he was frequently the target. Contemporaries and subsequent scholars have surmised, not without reason, that Grushnitsky, the literary poseur of *Geroi nashego vremeni,* was modeled on Martynov. There is also some evidence of a longer-standing antagonism. In the spring of 1837 Lermontov had visited Martynov's sisters at their residence in Moscow. Martynov's mother subsequently wrote to her son, making clear her dislike for Lermontov. Perhaps Lermontov courted one of the women. In any case, later rumors claimed that one of the sisters was the model for Princess Mary in *Geroi nashego vremeni.* As Lermontov left for the Caucasus in 1837, the Martynovs gave him letters and money for Nikolai, who was serving

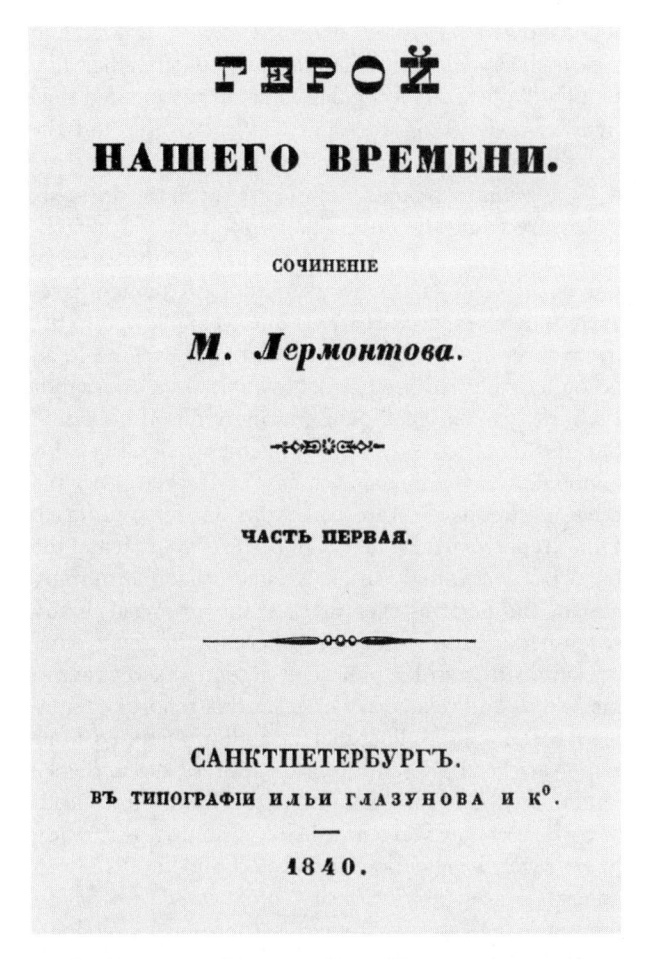

Title page for Geroi nashego vremeni, *a novel whose flawed, Romantic protagonist, Grigory Pechorin, became controversial among Russian readers*

there. The letters were lost, apparently when Lermontov's baggage was stolen, but Martynov's mother suspected that Lermontov had opened and read them himself (even though he repaid the money), adding to the friction between the poet and Martynov's family.

Martynov was a tremendous flirt and a particular kind of fop: at Verlizin's, Martynov was dressed up in native Circassian garb and sporting an extremely long dagger as he chatted with a young woman. According to contemporary sources, whether by intention or bad luck, just after the pianist suddenly struck the last chord, Lermontov's words resounded throughout the parlor in the ensuing silence: "le montagnard au grand poignard" (the highlander with the big dagger). In a pique, Martynov strode over to Lermontov and said, "I have told you many times to cease your jokes in front of the ladies." He then marched away before Lermontov could reply. Lermontov dismissed the episode, saying that the two would be good friends again the next day; however, Lermontov underestimated Martynov, who showed up at his door the next morning and repeated his comment. Lermontov replied rather flippantly: "What, are you going to challenge me to a duel over it?" Martynov responded affirmatively, and the two set the duel for the next day, 15 July 1841.

Lemontov seemed almost carefree in the thirty-six hours preceding the duel. The two fought with pistols, from barriers placed fifteen paces apart. At the signal of one of the seconds, the two were to approach ten paces each to their respective barriers and were allowed to fire up to three shots at will. At the signal, according to an account published by Lermontov's second, Aleksandr Illarionovich Vasil'chikov, Lermontov raised his pistol, but did not take a step. Vasil'chikov describes his expression as "calm, almost gay." Martynov, on the other hand, strode rapidly to the barrier and fired. Other reports suggest that both duelists approached the barriers. Witnesses variously state that Lermontov aimed, and perhaps even fired, in the air. Vasil'chikov recounted the duel somewhat differently in private conversations than in his published accounts, according to his friends and relatives. These sources report Lermontov's second as recalling that Lermontov taunted Martynov at the barrier, turning to address the audience with the words: "I will not fire on this fool!" This narrative suggests that Martynov, like Lermontov, was ready to be reconciled without bloodshed and fired only in angry response to the poet's provocative words. In omitting this detail from his published versions, Vasil'chikov was ostensibly motivated by a desire to spare Lermontov's reputation. Whatever the case may be, Martynov's bullet punctured both the poet's lungs, killing him instantly. Lermontov fell to the ground without so much as taking a step or putting his hand to the wound, dead before his twenty-seventh birthday.

After an investigation, a military tribunal recommended that Martynov be stripped of his rank and "rights of position," but Nicholas reduced the sentence to three months in the guardhouse and fifteen years of Church penance, which was later reduced to five years. The tsar's mercy is not surprising, given his reported response to the poet's demise: "A dog's death for a dog." Lermontov's death was a shock for his friends, but hardly a surprise, given his impetuous nature and taste for confrontation. The poet's grandmother seemed least surprised of all and took the news with near equanimity, perhaps because her doctors took the precaution of bleeding her beforehand. The poet's death by dueling coincided perfectly with both his way of life and the Romantic mythology of self he and his culture had conspired to create. This coincidence of life and art have long served as the background against which Lermontov's works are read, so much so that scholarship and memoiristic accounts about the poet's life often blur together with the content of his poetry and prose, making objective biography nearly impossible.

In his last days Lermontov wrote several of his best lyrics. These poems, filled with premonitions of death, add to the mythology of the poet fated to die young. "Son" (The Dream), published in *Otechestvennye zapiski* in 1843, begins with a striking image of the poet-speaker lying wounded in a Caucasian ravine: "V poldnevnyi zhar v doline Dagestana / S svintsom v grudi lezhal nedvizhim ia, / Glubokaia eshche dymilas' rana, / Po kaple krov' sochilasia moia" (In the noon heat, in a Dagestan valley, / With a bullet in my chest, I lay unmoving, / The deep wound still steamed, / Drop by drop my blood oozed out). The picture is all the more haunting given its nearly precise fulfillment by reality. In the remaining four stanzas the poet dreams of a joyous feast in his native land, where one woman, Cassandra-like, sits gloomily apart from the others, immersed in a vision of the poet's corpse lying in a Dagestan valley, the blood growing cold as it flows, steaming, from his chest. The poem completes a circle in which the supernatural visions of hero and heroine connect them spiritually, forcefully evoking the themes typical of Lermontov's early lyrics: pathos, the hero's death, immortality in memory, and longing. The mark of the poet's maturity, however, is in the restrained language and symmetry of the poem. It begins and ends with a refrain—the vision of the poet's dying body—that is rhetorically stoic and almost naturalistic in imagery.

The poet as prophet lies at the center of "Prorok" (The Prophet), probably written after "Son." Lermontov's vision characteristically emphasizes the poet-prophet's isolation and rejection from society rather than the divinity of poetic inspiration stressed by Pushkin's lyric of the same name. Another poem, "Vykhozhu odin ia na dorogu . . ." (Alone, I go out on the road . . .), concentrates on the lyric hero's contemplation of his own desires and fate. Its power resides in its recognition and rejection of the elegiac themes of lost paradise and uncertain future. Lermontov's persona replaces these stock lamentations with an image of a state of immortal repose, neither death nor life, serenaded by a song of love, the peaceful rustling of a "dark oak, eternally greening."

For one whose life was so short, Lermontov's achievements were remarkable. From the time of his earliest Romantic imitations, his art developed rapidly toward originality. In keeping with the individualistic tendency of Romanticism, Lermontov sought to imbue his poetry with the irreducible essence of his own personality. At a time when Russian literature was thought to have stagnated, Lermontov stepped forward, fighting off the ghost of his great predecessor, Pushkin, in an attempt to forge for himself a place in culture. To a large degree Lermontov's sense of alienation from contempo-

Monument on the site of Lermontov's fatal duel in Piatigorsk (sculpture by B. M. Mikeshin, 1915)

rary literature and society fueled his evolution. The theme of the "great man," distinctive and elevated in his feelings and thoughts, misunderstood by his contemporaries, remained central to his art throughout his life. As Lermontov grew as a writer, he repeatedly asserted this heroic type both in his fictional heroes and in his elaboration of the role of the poet as a cultural figure. The major themes of his work emerge out of the conflict between this individual, who stands for what is most human, for better or worse, and a surrounding world that seeks to reduce him to an imitation of others or a merely functional part of a greater entity. This urgent emphasis on the rights of the individual, a notion with a tenuous foothold in Russia at any time, was tremendously sharpened by the reactionary and repressive atmosphere of Nicholas's reign.

Lermontov's importance for Russian literature is twofold. His contribution in the area of the novel is his hero, Grigory Pechorin, who stands together with Pushkin's Evgeny Onegin at the beginning of a line of Russian characters known as "superfluous men." Some of these (such as Onegin) are so taken in by the surface of society that they fail to grasp the reality of their own lives in time to achieve fulfillment. Others (such as Ivan Aleksandrovich Goncharov's Oblomov in the 1859 novel of that title) are simply so inactive and disconnected from society life that they are unable to participate in any meaningful activity. Pechorin represents yet another type, the talented but disaffected loner whose demonic misbehavior is a form of active rebellion against society and the universe. Like a long line of ensuing heroes in the works of Fyodor Dostoyevsky, Leo Tolstoy, Ivan Sergeevich Turgenev, Boris Nikolaevich Bugaev (Andrei Bely), and beyond, Pechorin feels the need to test his will against external forces. While Dostoyevsky and Tolstoy view this desire as fatal hubris, however, Lermontov remains essentially ambivalent: his Pechorin has no answer for the question of what to do; he can only ask the question of free will. Pechorin's progeny are also evident in the line of "revolutionary" heroes that culminated in the Romantic type of the ruthless real-life Bolshevik. When read as a positive figure, Pechorin appears as the *übermensch* (superior man), whose unmediated experience of the world promises a liberation from the shackles of convention and mediocrity. The ambivalence of Lermontov's hero has helped to keep him alive as a paradoxical and controversial paradigm in Russian culture.

Lermontov's second major contribution has been in lyric poetry. He can be considered the last great poet of the Golden Age of Russian poetry. When, after the age of realism, poetry was revived as the dominant medium, interest in Lermontov surged. Although as yet little studied, the influence of Lermontov's intimately autobiographical lyric persona on such writers as the early Symbolists and the Futurists was enormous. For the Russian poetic mind of the early twentieth century, Lermontov's deeply personal, stormy relationship with the world of language and culture stood in polar opposition to the perfect artistic poise of Pushkin. Coming as he did after Pushkin, Lermontov has always been considered Russia's second-best poet, a fact of which he was painfully aware. While many Silver Age poets wanted to identify with Pushkin, the very impossibility of this desire at times brought them closer to Lermontov, who struggled with his predecessor's legacy at closer range. Whereas Pushkin's lyric persona feels completely at home in the world of poetry, independent of the poet's biography, Lermontov's hero constantly directs the reader to the author's personal search for poetic identity and spiritual sanctuary. The resulting lyrics achieve an unprecedented emotional intimacy, the influence of which can be traced through a range of twentieth-century poets from Vladimir Vladimirovich Maiakovsky and Aleksandr Aleksandrovich Blok to Boris Leonidovich Pasternak, Anna Andreevna Akhmatova, and Marina Ivanovna Tsvetaeva.

Bibliographies:

O. V. Miller, *Bibliografiia literatury o M. Iu. Lermontove: 1917–1977 gg.* (Leningrad: Nauka, 1980);

Miller, comp., *Literatura o zhizni i tvorchestve M. Iu. Lermontova. Bibliograficheskii ukazatel', 1825–1916*, edited by G. V. Bakhareva and Vadim Erazmovich Vatsuro (Leningrad: Biblioteka AN SSSR, 1990).

Biographies:

Pavel Aleksandrovich Viskovatov, *Mikhail Iur'evich Lermontov. Zhizn' i tvorchestvo*, volume 6 of *Sochineniia M. Iu. Lermontova,* edited by Viskovatov (Moscow: V. F. Rikhter, 1889–1891);

Viktor Andronikovich Manuilov, *Letopis' zhizni i tvorchestva M. Iu. Lermontova* (Moscow-Leningrad: Nauka, 1964);

Laurence Kelly, *Lermontov: Tragedy in the Caucasus* (London: Constable, 1977);

Jessie Davies, *The Fey Hussar: The Life of the Russian Poet, Michael Yur'evich Lermontov, 1814–41, to Commemorate the 175th Anniversary of the Poet's Birth* (Liverpool: Lincoln Davies, 1989).

References:

Mikhail Pavlovich Alekseev, Antonia Glasse, and Vadim Erazmovich Vatsuro, eds., *M. Iu. Lermontov. Issledovaniia i materialy* (Leningrad: Nauka, 1979);

Iraklii Luarsabovich Andronikov, *Lermontov. Issledovaniia i nakhodki* (Moscow: Khudozhestvennaia literatura, 1977);

Andrew Barratt and A. D. P. Briggs, *A Wicked Irony: The Rhetoric of Lermontov's A Hero of Our Time* (Bristol: Bristol Classical, 1989);

Vissarion Grigor'evich Belinsky, *M. Iu. Lermontov. Stat'i i retsenzii,* edited by N. I. Mordovchenko (Leningrad, 1940);

A. D. P. Briggs, ed., *Mikhail Lermontov: Commemorative Essays (1991)* (Birmingham, U.K.: University of Birmingham, 1992);

I. S. Chistova and others, eds., *Lermontovskii sbornik* (Leningrad: Nauka, 1985);

Sergei Nikolaevich Durylin, *"Geroi nashego vremeni" M. Iu. Lermontova* (Moscow: Gosudarstvennoe uchebno-pedagogicheskoe izdatel'stvo, 1940);

Boris Mikhailovich Eikhenbaum, *Lermontov: Opyt istoriko-literaturnoi otsenki* (Leningrad: Gosudarstvennoe izdatel'stvo, 1924);

Eikhenbaum, *Melodika russkogo liricheskogo stikha* (St. Petersburg: Opoiaz, 1922);

Eikhenbaum, *O proze, o poezii. Sbornik statei* (Leningrad: Khudozhestvennaia literatura, 1986);

Vladimir Fisher, "Poetika Lermontova," in *Venok M. Iu. Lermontovu. Iubileinyi sbornik* (Moscow-Petrograd: V. V. Dumnov, Nasledniki Br. Salaevykh, 1914), pp. 196–236;

John Garrard, *Mikhail Lermontov* (Boston: Twayne, 1982);

Emma Gershtein, *Sud'ba Lermontova* (Moscow: Sovetskii pisatel', 1964);

Maksim Isaakovich Gillel'son and O. V. Miller, eds., *M. Iu. Lermontov v vospominaniiakh sovremennikov* (Moscow: Khudozhestvennaia literatura, 1989);

Marie Gilroy, *The Ironic Vision in Lermontov's A Hero of Our Time* (Birmingham, U.K.: University of Birmingham, 1989);

Lidiia Iakovlevna Ginzburg, *O lirike* (Leningrad: Sovetskii pisatel', 1974);

Ginzburg, *O psikhologicheskoi proze* (Leningrad: Sovetskii pisatel', 1971);

Ginzburg, *Tvorcheskii put' Lermontova* (Leningrad: Khudozhestvennaia literatura, 1940);

Vladimir Golstein, "Heroes of Their Time: A Study of Lermontov's Major Fiction," dissertation, Yale University, 1994;

Kamsar Nersesovich Grigor'ian, *Lermontov i romantizm* (Leningrad: Nauka, 1964);

Katya Elizabeth Hokanson, "Empire of the Imagination: Orientalism and the Construction of Russian National Identity in Pushkin, Lermontov, and Tolstoi," dissertation, Stanford University, 1994;

E. A. Kovalevskaia and Viktor Andronikovich Manuilov, eds., *M. Iu. Lermontov v portretakh, illiustratsiiakh, dokumentakh. Posobie dlia uchitelei* (Leningrad, 1959);

Janko Lavrin, *Lermontov* (New York: Hillary House, 1959);

Sergei Lominadze, *Poeticheskii mir Lermontova* (Moscow: Sovremennik, 1985);

Georgii Pantaleimonovich Makogonenko, *Lermontov i Puskhin. Problemy preemstvennogo razvitiia literatury* (Moscow-Leningrad: Sovetskii pisatel', 1987);

Dmitrii Evgen'evich Maksimov, *Poeziia Lermontova* (Moscow: Nauka, 1964);

Iurii Vladimirovich Mann, *Poetika russkogo romantizma* (Moscow: Nauka, 1976);

Viktor Andronikovich Manuilov, *Roman M. Iu. Lermontova "Geroi nashego vremeni." Kommentarii* (Moscow-Leningrad: Prosveshchenie, 1966);

Manuilov, ed., *Lermontovskaia entsiklopediia* (Moscow: Sovetskaia entsiklopediia, 1981);

Dmitrii Sergeevich Merezhkovsky, *Lermontov. Poet sverkhchelovechestva* (St. Petersburg: Panteon, 1909);

John Mersereau Jr., *Mikhail Lermontov* (Carbondale: Southern Illinois University Press, 1962);

Helen Michailoff, "The Vereshchagina Albums," *Russian Literature Triquarterly,* 10 (Fall 1974): 363-407;

I. I. Podolskaia, *Mikhail Iur'evich Lermontov* (Moscow: Laida, 1993);

David Powelstock, "Living into Language: Mikhail Lermontov and the Manufacturing of Intimacy," in *The Subject's Space: New Approaches to Russia's Golden Age,* edited by Monika Greenleaf and Stephen Moeller-Sally (Evanston, Ill.: Northwestern University Press, 1998), pp. 297-324;

Powelstock, "Poet as Officer and Oracle: Mikhail Lermontov's Aesthetic Mythology," dissertation, University of California, Berkeley, 1994;

Natasha Alexandrovna Reed, "Reading Lermontov's *Geroj nashego vremeni:* Problems of Poetics and Reception," dissertation, Harvard University, 1994;

Robert Reid, *Lermontov's "A Hero of Our Time"* (London: Bristol Classical Press, 1997);

Vladimir Sergeevich Solov'ev, "Lermontov," in his *Literaturnaia kritika* (Moscow: Sovremennik, 1990), pp. 274-291;

William Mills Todd III, *Fiction and Society in the Age of Pushkin* (Cambridge, Mass.: Harvard University Press, 1986);

Viktor Vladimirovich Vinogradov, *Stil' prozy Lermontova* (Ann Arbor, Mich.: Ardis, 1986);

D. Zonova, ed., *M. Iu. Lermontov v russkoi kritike. Sbornik statei* (Moscow, 1951).

Papers:

Most of Mikhail Iur'evich Lermontov's manuscript archive is housed at the Institute of Russian Literature (Pushkin House), f. 524, and the Russian National Library, f. 429, both in St. Petersburg. There are also some papers at the Central State Archive of Literature and Art (TsGALI), f. 276, the Russian State Library, f. 178; and the State Historical Museum, f. 445, all in Moscow. The majority of his drawings and paintings are located at the Russian Museum and the Institute of Russian Literature, both in St. Petersburg, and at the State Literary Museum in Moscow. There are also some albums with his drawings at Columbia University, New York.

Aleksandr Ivanovich Odoevsky

(26 November 1802 – 15 August 1839)

Evgeniia B. Sorokina
St. Petersburg House of Culture

BOOKS: *Polnoe sobranie stikhotvorenii kniazia Aleksandra Ivanovicha Odoevskago, dekabrista,* compiled by Andrei Evgen'evich Rozen (St. Petersburg: Tip. A. A. Kraevskago, 1883);

Sochineniia, edited by M. N. Mazaev (St. Petersburg: E. Evocikimov, 1893).

Editions and Collections: *Polnoe sobranie stikhotvorenii i pisem,* edited by D. D. Blagoi (Moscow-Leningrad: Academia, 1934);

Stikhotvoreniia (Leningrad: Sovetskii pisatel', 1936);

Stikhotvoreniia. Biblioteka poeta, malaia seriia, izdanie, edited by Vasilii Grigor'evich Bazanov (Leningrad: Sovetskii pisatel', 1954);

Polnoe sobranie sochinenii (Leningrad: Sovetskii pisatel', 1958);

Stikhotvoreniia (Stavropol, 1981);

Stikhotvoreniia (Moscow: Sovetskaia Rossiia, 1982).

Prince Aleksandr Ivanovich Odoevsky, a descendant of the ancient clan of the Rurikids, was born on 26 November 1802 in St. Petersburg. An illustrious ancestor, Prince Ivan Vasil'evich, had served as president of the Votchinaiia Kollegiia, the department in charge of landed estates, established in 1721 by Peter the Great. Odoevsky's father, Prince Ivan Sergeevich Odoevsky, served in his youth as adjutant to Prince Grigory Aleksandrovich Potemkin, fought in Poland and Turkey, attained the rank of general-major, which was fourth from the top in the Table of Ranks, and married his cousin, Princess Praskov'ia Aleksandrovna Odoevskaia, receiving as a wedding gift the substantial estate of Nikolaevskoe in Iaroslavl' Province, including a thousand serfs. Soon after the birth of his son, Prince Ivan went into retirement.

Aleksandr's youth and adolescence were passed in St. Petersburg, but the Odoevskys customarily spent summers in Nikolaevskoe. Devoted to their son, the parents expended all their energy on his education and upbringing. To be sure, Aleksandr received his instruction at home, but in the manner of those times, his education was sufficiently thorough and well-rounded.

Aleksandr Ivanovich Odoevsky

Literature, French, other languages, and history were the young Aleksandr's favorite subjects. Petr Ivanovich Sokolov, the permanent secretary of the Academy of Sciences, taught him Russian language and literature. The young prince, called Sasha as a child, was especially drawn to translations of ancient authors. Konstantin Ivanovich Arsen'ev, a young teacher who considered serfdom the main question that Russia must answer, taught Sasha history and statistics. Although the tutor did not share his views with Aleksandr's parents, he did not conceal them from the boy. Jean-Marie Chopin, the French instructor—librarian and secretary to Chancellor Prince Aleksandr Borisovich Kurakin–completely agreed with Arsen'ev about serfdom. Chopin and French literature were great influences on Aleksandr, whose favorite French authors were Jean-Jacques Rousseau, Charles-Louis de Secondat Montesquieu, and Voltaire. Aleksandr was also impressed by the English writers William Shakespeare and George Gordon, Lord Byron. The German poet and dramatist Friedrich von Schiller, with his exalted passions and heroism, likewise attracted the youth. Of Russian authors, Aleksandr studied Prince Antiokh Dmitrievich Kantemir, Mikhail Vasil'evich Lomonosov, Aleksandr Petrovich Sumarokov, Mikhail Matveevich Kheraskov, Vasilii Vasil'evich Kapnist, and Gavriil Romanovich Derzhavin, but to their heavily-laden styles he secretly preferred those of Nikolai Mikhailovich Karamzin and Konstantin Nikolaevich Batiushkov. Odoevsky also studied mathematics and fortifications, and sometimes he was taken to hear fashionable lectures by the imperial physical mechanic Anton Rospini.

Upon the outbreak of the Patriotic War of 1812, Odoevsky's father became chief of the Moscow militia and commander of a Cossack regiment. In 1815, according to the customs of the old gentry families, Aleksandr entered service under the Chancellor of the Imperial Cabinet, where he began to accrue rank even though, owing to his youth, he could not actually serve. Since he was only thirteen years old, he was still, as before, in the service of his tutors.

At that time he met his cousin, Aleksandr Sergeevich Griboedov, then a clever youth interested in literature and conversant with all the news of the capital. Griboedov heard and approved Odoevsky's first poetic attempts. Aleksandr also met another of his cousins, Vladimir Fedorovich Odoevsky, who was captivated by music and western-European literature and philosophy. Contacts with both of these relatives gave a strong impetus to Aleksandr's poetic creativity and spiritual growth. He read Aleksandr Nikolaevich Radishchev, Kondratii Fedorovich Ryleev, Pavel Aleksandrovich Katenin, Vil'gel'm Karlovich Kiukhel'beker, and, of course, Aleksandr Pushkin, whom he greatly esteemed. The youth dreamed of the arts and sciences and of devoting himself to the service of the fatherland.

In October 1820 Odoevsky's mother died. His father went gray with grief, and Aleksandr also found it difficult to survive his mother's death. He wrote, "This cruel loss bore off with itself the best part of my feelings and thoughts. The finest and best string snapped in my heart. . . ." He also wrote a poem about his mother's death: "Tebia uzh net–no ia toboiu / Eshche dyshu; / Tuda v lazur' ia za toboiu / speshu, speshu . . . !)" (You are no longer here–but I still sigh for you– / I hurry, hurry there / after you into the azure heights . . . !).

The 1812 war revealed not only the patriotism and greatness of the Russian people but also all the defects of the autocratic order. Impoverished, the peasants began to rebel. In the words of Vladimir Odoevsky, "the representatives of all that was talented, educated, knowledgeable, well-born and brilliant in Russia" could not remain indifferent to what was going on. In 1816 the *Soiuz spaseniia* (Union of Salvation), the first secret society, sprang up; then came the *Soiuz Blagodenstviia* (Union of Welfare). In St. Petersburg the Semenovsky Guards regiment rose up against the cruelty of its commander. As a result, the entire unit was confined to the Peter-Paul Fortress.

This uprising made a great impression on Odoevsky because he had many acquaintances among the officers of the guards. In 1821 Odoevsky was enlisted "from among the retired governmental secretaries by right of volunteer assignment as a noncommissioned officer in the Life-Guards Cavalry Regiment" and immediately took part in military maneuvers at Vilizh. In the regiment Odoevsky was loved for his sociable disposition, merriment, and readiness to help his comrades. In his free time he read a great deal and composed verses–about which, in truth, he had a casual attitude.

In May 1822 the regiment departed Vilizh and returned to St. Petersburg. There Odoevsky led a carefree social life, once again met with an old friend, Konstantin Stepanovich Serbinovich, and also grew close to Griboedov, who by then had just completed his celebrated comedy *Gore ot uma* (Woe from Wit, 1833; full text, 1861). Odoevsky tells how he spent his time in St. Petersburg: "I occupied myself with literature and the service, passed my time among my relatives, and my life blossomed. . . ."

St. Petersburg's greatest flood occurred in 1824. Griboedov lived on the second floor, but the waters mounted and inundated the house. Greatly concerned for his cousin and having barely succeeded in getting off duty, Odoevsky rushed to the dwelling. The water had already risen to his waist when at last he spotted his relative. Odoevsky swam toward Griboedov in order to help him escape the flood.

At that time of his life Odoevsky became acquainted with Aleksandr Aleksandrovich Bestuzhev, who in turn introduced him to a circle of people close to the poet in spirit and weltanschauung. These were collaborators on the almanac *Poliarnaia zvezda* (Polar Star), to which many of the leading writers and poets of the day contributed–for example, Evgenii Abramovich Baratynsky, Baron Anton Antonovich Del'vig, Pushkin, and Ryleev. Soon, attracted by its revolutionary spirit and hopes of liberating the Russian people from tyranny and serfdom, Odoevsky entered the *Severnoe*

Odoevsky in the uniform of the Nizhnegorodsky Dragoon Regiment

obshchestvo (Northern Society), consisting mainly of revolutionary-minded officers.

Odoevsky then began to write poems that included freedom-loving ideas but, unfortunately, these poems have not survived. Some of them, printed under the pseudonym "Zagorsky," were burned later. The poet frequently shredded and burned those of his own works that he considered insufficiently serious and that, in his own words, "disdained a printed existence." However, just then he published the critical article "On the tragedy *Venceslas* by Rotrou, translated by Zhandr [Gendre]" in *Otechestvennye zapiski* (Notes of the Fatherland). Kiukhel'beker, in whose apartment the future Decembrists gathered and with whom Odoevsky formed a close friendship, later spoke of this article with approval. In a letter to his cousin Vladimir Odoevsky, Aleksandr wrote that in this period he created "some tens of poems, and an ode, epistles, elegies, and the beginnings of two poems...."

Odoevsky's new circle gathered at his apartment, where Griboedov lived for some time. Here they reworked the latter's comedy *Gore ot uma,* never hoping for its publication; and here they considered the affairs of the secret society. At a later date, ill and in need of a dry room, Kiukhel'beker moved in with Odoevsky. They lived together in friendship, since they were close not only in literary interests and political views but also by sharing the same circle of friends.

Odoevsky's father then summoned him home to the estate, but Odoevsky's departure from St. Petersburg was delayed on account of a love affair that had to be concealed because the lady in question was married and had children. Odoevsky opened his heart only to Griboedov, who persuaded his comrade "not to get carried away by this friendship" since "it will become dangerous." Receiving a leave of absence, Odoevsky at length departed the capital in November and went to his father, who was highly dissatisfied with both his son's way of life and his disposition. Odoevsky's father reproached his son and asked him not to disgrace their ancient clan, but despite pity for his father, Aleksandr could not alter his own convictions. Then, upon learning of the unexpected death of Alexander I at Taganrog on 19 October 1825, Odoevsky hastily returned to St. Petersburg.

Using the death of the tsar as a catalyst, the members of the *Severnoe obshchestvo* decided on an armed uprising on 14 December, the day on which the military were to take the oath of allegiance to the new emperor, Nicholas I. The Decembrists made Ryleev's apartment their headquarters and named the Colonel and Prince Sergei Petrovich Trubetskoi the leader of the insurrection. On the designated day the revolutionary-minded forces were to enter the Senate Square, block the senators from swearing the oath, proclaim the government to be deposed, and issue to the Russian people a manifesto by which autocracy would be destroyed and a provisional government established. Troops under the command of Aleksandr Ivanovich Iakubovich would take the Winter Palace, while Petr Grigor'evich Kakhovsky intended to kill Nicholas I. However, at the last moment both Iakubovich and Kakhovsky declined to act on their plans.

On the eve of 14 December, Odoevsky found himself in the twenty-four-hour honor guard of the Winter Palace. Upon going off duty that morning, he hastened in the company of Kiukhel'beker to the Senate Square, where the insurrectionary troops had already assembled. There Odoevsky was placed in charge of a platoon of pickets. On the square stood the Moskovsky Regiment and a few other formations whose members refused to pledge allegiance to the new emperor. They awaited Trubetskoi, but he did not appear.

Gen. Count Mikhail Andreevich Miloradovich, the governor-general of St. Petersburg, next attempted to talk the mutineers into giving up, but he was mortally wounded by a shot from Kakhovsky's pistol. Nicholas I had already been apprised of the uprising by means of reports, mainly the one from Iakov Ivanovich Rostovtsev. Having learned of the preparations for the revolt, the tsar had arranged for the Senate to administer the oath earlier than the planned time; he had also arranged for artillery to be deployed to the square and for the insurrectionists to be surrounded. The uprising was overwhelmed; the arrests began; and then came the consequences.

Along with other Decembrists, Odoevsky was conveyed to the Peter-Paul Fortress and lodged in the Alekseevsky ravelin. He perceived everything that had happened as a catastrophe: he had just been a glittering Horse Guards officer, and now here he was, a prisoner. In the first months of confinement, unable to accept this thought, he was close to madness, a condition to which his half-religious verses written in the Alekseevsky ravelin bear witness, as does his behavior under interrogation.

Arrest, confinement in the fortress, and the subsequent interrogations affected many of the Decembrists in just this way. They were not shaken so much by the suppression of the uprising and the ruin of all their hopes as by the mockery and insults to which they were subjected in the Winter Palace, whither they were taken for questioning. Subsequently, Aleksandrovich Bestuzhev reminisced about those times: "I was witness to such disgraceful scenes that I unwillingly asked myself: are these really men? A glittering band of Guards transformed themselves into the insolent menial servants of a rowdy straw-boss . . . and at his pleasure they heaped desecrations on those bound to them as brothers-in-uniform. . . ."

In despair, Odoevsky tried to justify himself to the tsar—explaining his participation in the mutiny as merely fortuitous and as a youthful adventure; he repented and wrote of his delusions. The proceedings oppressed him, and the future frightened him even more. Many of his comrades conducted themselves in the same manner. For the most part, this behavior derived not so much from cowardice as from his isolation from people of his own circle and his own sympathies. His condition was horrible: he fell into depression and sat motionless for hours, then was seized by a feverish mood and ran about the cell, wildly singing romances or beating his head on the door. During this period he wrote strange, sickly, and half-religious verses; one such verse he wrote on the night before Easter in April 1826. The poem "Utro" (Morning), written at the beginning of the same year, is permeated with the melancholy and despair of a prisoner who has lost all hope of freedom. But melancholy and madness gradually dissipated, and the poet's spirit revived, as is demonstrated by a poem of 1826, "Son poeta" (A Poet's Dream). In this poem, written by Odoevsky soon after his judgment, he speaks of a poet sacrificed for freedom who, in his soul, preserves his former feelings.

On 12 June 1826 the high court pronounced sentence on the prisoners. Those convicted were divided into eleven classes according to their degree of guilt. Five of the Decembrists–Ryleev, Kakhovsky, Pavel Ivanovich Pestel', Sergei Ivanovich Murav'ev-Apostol', and Mikhail Pavlovich Bestuzhev-Riumin–were declared "outside the categories" and were sentenced to death by hanging. Odoevsky was assigned to the fourth class and sentenced to fifteen years of penal exile, subsequently reduced to twelve upon confirmation by the emperor. In February 1827 Odoevsky was dispatched to Chitinsky Stockade in Siberia along with other Decembrists. Taken by night from the Peter-Paul Fortress, they were driven in sleds through the streets of St. Petersburg, right past the palace of the Interior Ministry where a ball was in progress. Verses that Odoevsky had written back in 1825 under the title "Bal" (The Ball) came back to him, but with a new and different meaning. In this poem worldly society now seemed to be an assemblage of the dead: "The light has faded . . . the entire enormous hall / Was full of skeletons . . . in couples / Entwined, thronging together and rushing about / Their yellow bones embracing, / Whirling about, knocking on the floor, / They quickly flew about the ball."

In March 1827 the Decembrists were taken to Chita and lodged in a building consisting of five rooms housing fifty-five "state criminals." Field work occupied the prisoners in summer and autumn, and in winter they ground meal in hand mills. Evenings were spent conversing on various themes with their fellows, reading, and playing musical instruments. Here it was possible to live without their spirits failing, because they lived together and also because the wives of many of them arrived to share the fates of their husbands. Concerning this new, more hopeful feeling Mikhail Bestuzhev wrote: "The building unified us, provided us mutual support, and, finally, through our protecting angels, was to reconnect us with that world from which we were forever isolated by political death . . . it gave us the desire to live . . . it furnished us with the moral nourishment of our spiritual iife."

Many of the exiles had had a splendid classical education, and they gave evening lectures to their comrades. Thus, the "prison academy" came into being. Odoevsky informed his fellow Decembrists about Russian literature, and they spent considerable time on literary occupations–all who were able read their own works, translations, and poems to their friends. Odoevsky recited poems that he composed on the spot and seldom wrote down. His comrades recorded them for him. He was quite demanding of literature and for that reason perceived his own works as insufficiently serious. In letters to his cousin Vladimir Odoevsky, which

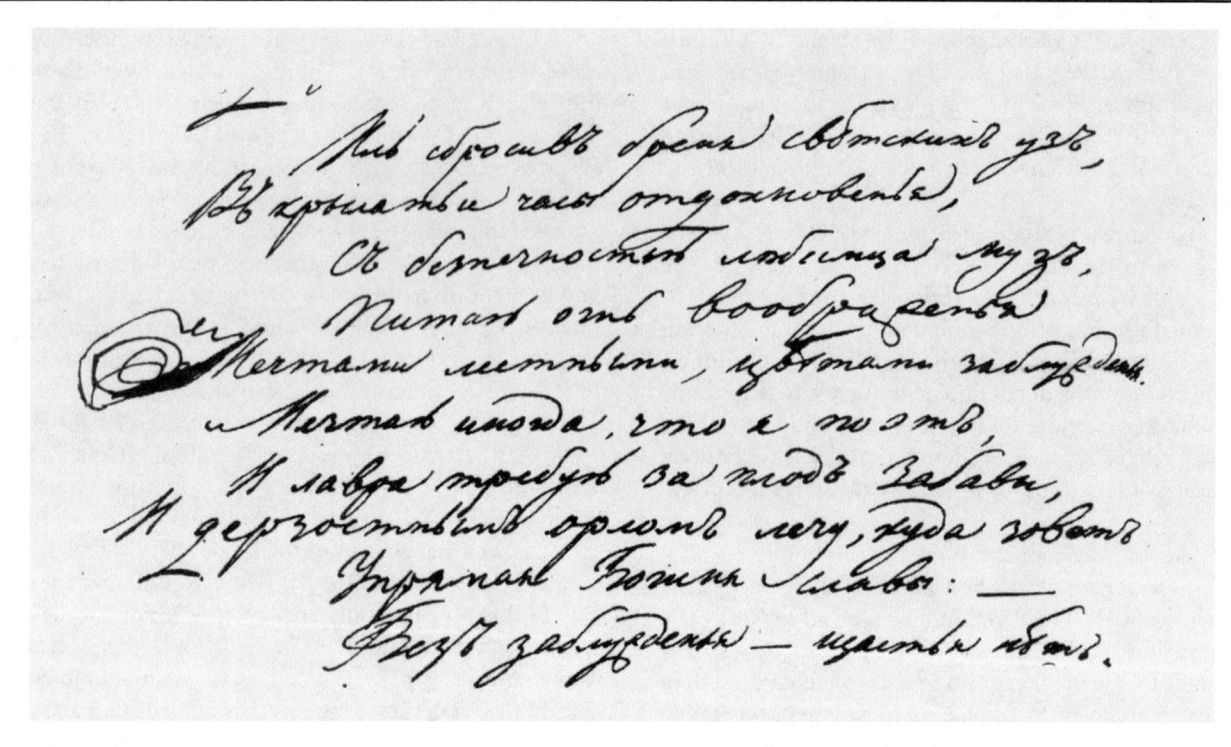

Manuscript for a poem written by Odoevsky in 1821 and published in 1883 by his prison comrade Baron Andrei Evgen'evich Rozen in Polnoe sobranie stikhotvorenii kniazia Aleksandra Ivanovicha Odoevskago, dekabrista *(Complete Collected Poems of Prince Aleksandr Ivanovich Odoevsky, Decembrist)*

were published in the almanac *Mnemozina* (Mnemosyne), he wrote: "I compose verses and spoil very much paper not only in the course of a year, but even in that of a week.... But unwillingly: I love to recite verses, but not to commit them to print.... If it should be necessary to increase the quantity, but not the quality–then so be it! Not from journalistic ambition, but out of friendship for you, I might send you ten odes, the same number of epistles, five or six elegies, and the beginnings of two poems that lie, as usual, under my table, half-torn and half-burned."

For the most part Odoevsky's poems that have survived are those written in exile, and they only survived thanks to his comrades–Petr Aleksandrovich Mukhanov, Nikolai Ivanovich Lorer, Mikhail Aleksandrovich Nazimov, and, especially, Odoevsky's close friend and the publisher of his works, Baron Andrei Evgen'evich Rozen. Odoevsky's creativity reached its prime in exile. On 30 August 1828, on the occasion of the celebration of the name day of the sixteen Aleksandrs among the Decembrists, he extemporaneously declaimed the poem "Trizna" (The Funereal Feast), in which he tells of how the spirits of the Decembrists did not fail or let prison destroy them.

Odoevsky's favorite poetic theme was patriotic history, and he wrote that "the history of Russia serves as the wellspring of my inspiration." From a projected poem titled "Vasilii Shuisky" there is an extract called "Deva 1610 goda" (A Virgin of 1610), in which he created an exalted allegorical image of the Virgin of Liberty calling for a struggle to liberate the fatherland. Such 1829 poems as "Zosima," "Nevedomaia strannitsa" (Mysterious Wanderer), "Staritsa-prorochitsa" (The Old Prophetess), and others were also dedicated to Russian history. But Odoevsky's historical subjects always applied to his own times, for he spoke allegorically of the Decembrists and the ruin of their hopes.

In the 1829 poem "Elegiia" (Elegy) Odoevsky tries to think through the fatal drama of Decembrism in a philosophical manner; he writes of the successive revolutionary tragedies, censures those who have lost heart and "do not prepare for future struggles," and tells of the movement toward a better future and those who fight for it: "No v nas poryvy est' sviatye . . ." (But among us there are holy enthusiasms . . .).

On 19 October 1829 in St. Petersburg, the fellows of the Lyceum gathered as they always did for Lyceum Day. That year many were missing, and when the gathering broke up, Pushkin, thinking of his exiled friends, wrote his celebrated poem "Poslanie v Sibir'" ("Vo glubine sibirskikh rud . . .") (Epistle to Siberia [Deep in the Siberian mines . . .]), in which he encouraged the Decembrists, reminding them that those yet at liberty had not forgotten them. And in their name, Odoevsky made poetic reply in the most famous of his verses: "Strun veshchikh plamennye zvuki . . .":

The ardent sounds of the seer's strings
Reached our ears.
Our hands rushed to our swords,
But they found only fetters.

But be calm, bard: we are proud
Of our chains, of our fate,
And behind the locks of our prison
We laugh in our soul at the tsars.

Our sorrowful work will not be lost:
The spark will kindle a flame–
And our enlightened people
Will gather under a holy banner.

We will forge swords from our chains
And will again light the flame of freedom,
It will appear unexpectedly to the tsars–
And nations will breathe joyfully again.

Odoevsky was recognized as the poet of the Siberian imprisonment, the one who inspired his comrades with courage and manliness, belief in their own strength, and faithfulness to their ideals. His friends set many of his verses to music, and the exiles frequently performed them. The poet also wrote romances in which folkloric motifs feature prominently, having borrowed them from popular songs and legends. These figure most clearly in "Po doroge stolbovoi . . ." (Along the High Road), a romance popular among the Decembrists, which tells of the arrival of their fiancées.

The longest of Odoevsky's poems still extant is "Vasil'ko" (1829–1830). Unfortunately only two songs from it remain, the third having been lost by one of the Decembrists during his many transfers. The basic theme of the poem is taken from the primary chronicle account of Prince Vasil'ko Rostoslavich, who fell victim to an internecine power struggle among his eleventh-century peers. The work was never completed, and Odoevsky was dissatisfied with it. Also, two other historical poems have survived only as sketches: the aforementioned "Vasilii Shuisky" and "Posly Pskova" (The Ambassadors of Pskov). While in Siberia, Odoevsky also wrote "Elegiia na smert' A. S. Griboedova" (Elegy on the Death of A. S. Griboedov, 1829), "Slavianskie Devy" (Slavonic Maids, 1830), and other poems.

Friends strove to publish as much as possible of the poet's works; with the assistance of the Decembrist Pavel Aleksandrovich Mukhanov, ten poems were anonymously published by Prince Petr Andreevich Viazemsky and Baron Anton Antonovich Del'vig in *Literaturnaia gazeta* (Literary Gazette) and in *Severnye tsvety* (Northern Flowers) throughout 1830. These poems constituted Odoevsky's first published creations from the period of exile.

In August 1830 the Chita Decembrists were transferred to Petrovskii Zavod, where Odoevsky spent more than two years. Here, as everywhere, he was the soul of society, and all his friends loved him. They frequently declaimed his poems in chorus. Even the agent-provocateur Roman Mikhailovich Medoks gave the following sketch of him: "A bard and a scholar. . . . In spite of his wealth, he is always in need, for he shares it all to the last." In December 1832 Odoevsky's place of exile was changed to the Tel'minskoi Fabric Works, but the tsar considered the work to be too exhausting for Odoevsky and communicated this rare expression of dissatisfaction to the autonomous governor-general of eastern Siberia. Owing to the tsar's intercession, in June 1833 Odoevsky was transferred to the village of Elan, not far from Irkutsk, and here the poet spent three years. In Elan he lacked any society whatever and had none of his friends around him. A man of moods, he frequently fell into gloom and despair.

In Elan he rarely wrote poems, for he had no one to whom to write. At his request, his family sent him many books and journals that he read attentively, reflecting upon his own fate and that of Russia. Upon earnest requests from his family, in 1836 the authorities transferred Odoevsky to the city of Ishim in Tobolsk Province, and there life was somewhat easier, the climate less severe, and Europe not so far away. There, in verses extolling poetry and its charms, he remembered his comrades from the years of prison and exile: "Ty znaesh' ikh, Kogo ia tak liubil, / S kem chernuiu godinu ia delil . . ." (You know those whom I loved so / with whom I shared a black time–, 1836).

In May 1837 to Count Aleksandr Khristoforovich Benckendorff, commander of the Third Section, Odoevsky sent a request for transfer into the ranks of the Caucasian Corps; to this Tsar Nicholas responded: "into the ranks of the Caucasian Corps with him." On the way to Stavropol, Odoevsky met with his father, who had journeyed to Kazan especially to see his son. Throughout his entire stay in the city Ivan Sergeevich was never separated from Aleksandr, and the son was greatly comforted by his father's understanding and forgiveness for his participation in the uprising. On 28 August they bade one another farewell for the last time, and Aleksandr departed for Tbilisi.

A close friendship between Odoevsky and Mikhail Iur'evich Lermontov began in Stavropol. Aleksandr served in the Nizhnegorodsky Dragoon Regiment, stationed near Tbilisi; there he met other demoted Decembrist friends and also the poet and translator Prince Aleksandr Gersevanovich Chavchavadze, the father-in-law of his murdered cousin, Griboedov, whose grave Odoevsky repeatedly visited.

Manuscript for Odoevsky's 1829 elegy for his cousin and friend Aleksandr Sergeevich Griboedov, who had encouraged Odoevsky's first poetic attempts (from Polnoe sobranie stikhotvorenii, 1958)

There he wrote his last verses, filled with grief for those nearest to him.

In general, Odoevsky wrote little during his time in the Caucasus, but not from any decline in his spirit; according to the recollections of contemporaries, he was as merry and joyous as he was sad and reflective. The Decembrist Aleksandr Petrovich Beliaev remembered that "to the end, Odoevsky remained just the same as he had been, according to those of his friends who had known him in prison: as ever, either serious, thoughtful and somewhat depressed, or lively, merry, and laughing to a frenzy." In June 1839 Odoevsky's father died unexpectedly; the son wrote of him: "I don't know how I bore this blow which seems to be the last–anything else of any kind would be feeble in comparison."

The poet's happiest time in the Caucasus was that of his friendship with Lermontov. The two quickly became close comrades. Lermontov esteemed Odoevsky's exalted morality and noble aspirations. Bestuzhev recorded that Odoevsky and Lermontov became "good friends . . . in the Caucasus, unwillingly attracted by the general force of poetry, drawing them in the same direction." Odoevsky also became acquainted with Aleksandr Ivanovich Herzen's friend Nikolai Platonovich Ogarev, who, considering Odoevsky his mentor, showed him his own first verses. The poet was also frequently in the home of Chavchavadze, with whom he enjoyed a warm friendship. There he also became close with Chavchavadze's daughter Nina, Griboedov's widow.

On 6 August 1839 Odoevsky fell ill with a fever and took to his bed. He well knew the danger inherent in his condition, but he remained cheerful, joked, improvised verses, and read old ones. On 15 August he died in the arms of his friends and was buried beyond the fort on the cliffs of the Black Sea.

In profound grief Lermontov experienced the death of a friend who had not even reached his thirty-seventh year. Upon this loss Lermontov wrote the following lines: "V mogilu on unes letuchii roi / Eshche nezrelykh, temnykh v dokhnovenii, / Obmanutykh nadezhd; gor'kikh sozhalenii . . ." (Into the grave he carried away a flying swan / Of still unripe, dark inspirations, / Of deceived hopes and bitter regrets . . .).

Seventeen poems of the young Decembrist were published in Leipzig, Germany, in 1862, and in 1883 Baron Rozen, Odoevsky's prison comrade, published a complete collection of Odoevsky's poems, *Polnoe sobranie stikhotvorenii kniazia Aleksandra Ivanovicha Odoevskago, dekabrista,* based upon all the poems that Rozen had collected in the days of their acquaintanceship. What has been preserved of Odoevsky's works is only a small part of all that he had created. What remains, however, constitutes an important page from the history of Russian literature.

Letters:
"Pis'ma I. D. Iakushkinu. 27 fevralia 1834–6 fevralia 1836," in *Literaturnoe nasledstvo,* 60, book 1 (1956): 262–264.

Bibliographies:
S. A. Pereselenkov, "A. I. Odoevsky," in *Russkii biograficheskii slovar'* (St. Petersburg, 1905), pp. 18–122;

I. A. Kubasov, "Iz literatury ob A. I. Odoevskom," in Odoevsky's *Polnoe sobranie stikhotvorenii i pisem* (Moscow-Leningrad: Akademiia, 1934), pp. 464–470.

Biographies:
Vasilii Grigor'evich Bazanov, *Poety-dekabristy. K. F. Ryleev, V. K. Kiukhel'beker, A. I. Odoevsky* (Moscow-Leningrad: AN SSSR, 1950);

S. N. Golubov, *Iz iskry - plamia* (Moscow-Leningrad: Detskaia literatura, 1950);

V. P. Iagunin, *Aleksandr Odoevskii. (Zhizn' zamechatel'nykh liudei)* (Moscow: Molodaia gvardiia, 1980);

I. V. Dedusenko, *Pevtsa nesuetnaia lira. Povest' ob A. I. Odoevskoi* (Stavropol, 1985).

References:
Iulii Isaevich Aikhenval'd, "Kniaz' A. I. Odoevskii," in *Istoriia russkoi literatury XIX veka,* volume 1, edited by D. N. Ousianiko-Kulikovsky (Moscow: Mir, 1908), pp. 163–169;

Mark Konstantinovich Azadovsky, *Vospominaniia Bestuzhevykh,* Redaktsiia, stat'ia i kommentarii M. A. Azadovskogo (Moscow-Leningrad: Akademiia nauk SSSR, 1951);

Azadovsky, "Zateriannye i utrachennye proizvedeniia dekabristov (Poeticheskie proizvedeniia dekabristov)," *Literaturnoe nasledstvo,* 59 (1954): 702–705;

Vasilii Grigor'evich Bazanov, "A. I. Odoevskii," in *Poety-dekabristy* (Moscow-Leningrad: Akademiia nauk SSSR, 1950), pp. 170–216;

Aleksandr Petrovich Beliaev, "Vospominaniia o perezhitom i perechuvstvovannom," *Russkaia starina,* no. 3 (1881): 498–501; no. 4 (1881): 799–838;

M. A. Briksman, "Mnimye stikhotvoreniia A. I. Odoevskogo," in *Dekabristy i ikh vremia* (Moscow-Leningrad: Akademiia nauk SSSR, 1951), pp. 204–213;

Briksman, "'Slavianskie devy' (Muzyka dekabrista F. F. Vadkovskogo na stikhi Odoevskogo)," *Literaturnoe nasledstvo,* 60, 1 (1956): 264–270;

V. A. Gnedin, "A. I. Odoevskii," in *Ocherki po istorii russkoi literatury pervoi poloviny XIX veka,* volume 1 (Baku: Azerbaizhanskii zaochnyi pedagogicheskii institut, 1941), pp. 12-22;

Nestor Aleksandrovich Kotliarevsky, "A. I. Odoevskogo," in *N. Kotliarevskii, Dekabristy. Kniaz' A. I. Odoevskii i A. A. Bestuzhev-Marlinskii (ikh zhizn' i literaturnaia deiatel'nost')* (St. Petersburg: M. M. Stasiulevich, 1907), pp. 1-104;

Ivan Andreevich Kubasov, *Dekabrist A. I. Odoevskii i vnov' naidennye ego stikhotvoreniia* (Petrograd: Rossiskaia gos. akademicheskaia tip., 1922);

S. Liubimov, "Neizdannoe stikhotvorenie kniazia A. I. Odoevskogo (Kolybel'naia pesnia)," in *Literaturnaia mysl', Almanakh,* volume 2 (Petrograd: Mysl', 1923), pp. 235-237;

N. I. Mordovchenko, "Poety-dekabristy v tiur'me i na katorge (A. I. Odoevskii)," in *Istoriia russkoi literatury,* volume 6 (Moscow-Leningrad: Akademiia nauk SSSR, 1953), pp. 105-112;

Nikolai Platonovich Ogarev, *Izbrannye proizvedeniia,* volume 2 (Moscow: Goslitizdat, 1956), pp. 382-391;

Ogarev, "Kavkazskie vody. (Otryvok iz moei ispovedi)," in *Poliarnaia zvezda na 1861 god,* volume 6 (London, 1861), pp. 346-358;

G. Pokhvisnev, "Lermontov i Odoevskii," in *Zemlia rodnaia,* volume 9 (Penza: Oblizdat, 1952);

A. V. Popov, "A. I. Odoevskii na Kavkaze," *Materialy po izucheniiu Stavropol'skogo kraia kraevogo muzeia,* 4 (1952): 219-238;

T. Posse, "Zhizn' i tvorchestvo Ryleeva i Odoevskogo s sviazi s obshestvennymi i literaturnymi techeniiami nachalo XIX veka–Zhizn' Odoevskogo–Proizvedeniia Odoevskogo," in K. F. Ryleev's *Odoevskii A. I., Sochineniia* (St. Petersburg: Zhizn' dlia vsekh, 1913), pp. 3-31, 71-90;

P. N. Sakulin, "Odoevskii v neizdannykh pis'makh," in *Dekabristy na katorge i v ssylke* (Moscow: Obshchestvo politkatorzhan, 1925), pp. 125-137;

A. I. Sirotinin, "Kniaz' A. I. Odoevskii (Biograficheskii ocherk)," *Istoricheskii vestnik,* no. 5 (1883): 398-414;

M. A. Tseitlin, "Tvorchestvo A. I. Odoevskogo," *Uchenye zapiski Moskovskogo oblastnogo pedinstituta,* 11, 2 (1956): 87-112.

Karolina Karlovna Pavlova

(10 July 1807 – 2 December 1893)

Marina Balina
Illinois Wesleyan University

BOOKS: *Das Nordlicht: Proben der neuen russischen Literatur, Erste Lieferung* (Dresden & Leipzig, 1833);

Les préludes, edited by A. Tourguenieff and L. de Ronchaud (Paris: Didot, 1839);

Dvoinaia zhizn' (Moscow, 1848);

Razgovor v Kremle; stikhotvorenie (St. Petersburg: Ia. Trei, 1854);

Stikhotvoreniia (Moscow: L. I. Stepanova, 1863).

Editions and Collections: *Sobranie sochinenii,* edited by Valerii Iakovlevich Briusov, 2 volumes (Moscow: K. F. Neskrasov, 1915)—includes *Dvoinaia zhizn',* translated by Barbara Heldt Monter as *A Double Life* (Ann Arbor, Mich.: Ardis, 1978)—also includes *Razgovor Trianone;*

Polnoe sobranie stikhotvorenii, edited by E. P. Kazanovich (Leningrad: Sovetskii pisatel', 1939);

Karolina Pavlova. Polnoe sobranie stikhotvorenii, edited by N. M. Gaidenkov (Moscow: Sovetskii pisatel', 1964);

Stikhotvoreniia (Moscow: Sovetskaia Rossiia, 1985).

SELECTED PERIODICAL PUBLICATION—UNCOLLECTED: "Moi vospominaniia," *Russkii arkhiv,* 3 (1875): 222–240.

In his introduction to the two-volume edition of the works of Karolina Karlovna Pavlova that he edited in 1915 Valerii Iakovlevich Briusov wrote: "I hope that our edition will at least partially satisfy all true lovers of poetry, who until recently had been deprived of the opportunity to acquaint themselves with the works of one of our best poets. We see our work as a first step in the study of Karolina Pavlova's poetry and the publication of her works." Pavlova has periodically attracted the attention of literary scholars. Her life vividly demonstrates the fate of one of the few woman poets in nineteenth-century Russia, the discord present in the literary era of that century, and the fate of a gifted individual who was misunderstood and underappreciated by her contemporaries, as well as almost forgotten by posterity.

Karolina Karlovna Pavlova

Karolina Karlovna Janisch was born on 10 July 1807 in Yaroslavl. She was German on her father's side, French and English on her mother's. Her father, Karl Andreevich Janisch, was a well-educated man. He considered himself a bit of an artist; he was well read and had great love for literature. Although he had trained to be a doctor, he did not practice medicine, since, according to his daughter's memoirs, he did not want to "be responsible for the deaths of people." Shortly after Karolina's birth he was appointed professor of physics and chemistry at a medical-surgical academy in Moscow. The Janisches were quite prosperous until the Patriotic War of 1812 ruined them. Their estate in the Smolensk district was destroyed, and their home in Moscow burned down. For several years the family was forced to rely on the hospitality and generosity of wealthy friends and relatives. This state of affairs could not have failed to leave its mark on Karolina Janisch. Proud and gifted as she was by nature, to reconcile herself to being the "poor relation," living in others' homes "on charity," was difficult.

As a child Janisch began to reveal her rare and multifaceted talents, which all her contemporaries noted. She was educated by her father. According to the memoirs of family friends, she could already speak four languages at the age of five, and she early developed an interest in both drawing and poetry. In her own memoirs she depicts herself as a child whose unusual love of nature revealed a delicate and sensitive soul with a deep poetic vision.

Raised in the patriotic fervor of 1812, Janisch responded keenly to the events happening around her. The uprising of the Greeks in 1821 and their fight for freedom deeply interested her, and George Gordon, Lord Byron, became one of her favorite poets. To this period also belongs one of the most difficult and yet at the same time, according to Pavlova herself, one of the happiest periods in her personal and creative life: her love for the Polish poet Adam Mickiewicz.

Janisch met Mickiewicz at one of the most brilliant cultural centers of Russia in the 1820s, the artistic and literary salon of Princess Zinaida Aleksandrovna Volkonskaia. Regular visitors to the salon included Aleksandr Pushkin, Dmitrii Vladimirovich Venevitinov, Aleksandr Ivanovich Odoevsky, Baron Anton Antonovich Del'vig, and Prince Petr Andreevich Viazemsky. Janisch was invited by the Elagin-Kireevsky family, who were later to become well-known Slavophiles. She was immediately drawn to Mickiewicz, who seemed to many to be a sort of living Byronic hero—a poet and an exile. Knowing that it would be difficult for a nineteen-year-old girl to attract Mickiewicz's attention at the salon, she asked her father for permission to study the Polish language. Her father invited Mickiewicz to be her teacher. Mickiewicz was so taken by the rapturous and profound love of his young pupil that, against his better judgment, he declared his love to Janisch and proposed marriage. Later she considered this the happiest day of her life.

This happiness, however, did not last long. There are two versions of what subsequently happened. According to the first, which is supported by Pavlova herself, a rich and childless uncle on whom the material well-being of the Janisch family depended was adamantly opposed to the marriage and threatened to disinherit her. Her parents were also alarmed at the prospect of their daughter's marrying a poor exile who was in disfavor with the government, but they were prepared to make this sacrifice for her. In a letter to Mickiewicz's son Wladislaw in April 1890 Pavlova wrote, "I could not accept. I felt bound by duty."

The second version of the breakup is that Mickiewicz had second thoughts about his true feelings for Janisch. He went to St. Petersburg, and she heard nothing from him for ten months. Finally, she wrote to ask him to come to Moscow. This letter, written when she was twenty years old, demonstrates not only the depth of her love but also the nobility of her character:

> I can no longer bear such endless uncertainty, this tiresome waiting and eternal worry. You must decide my fate one way or the other. It would give me peace knowing that I have nothing more to lose. I have thought much during these ten months of your absence. I am convinced that I cannot live without thinking of you, I am convinced that my life will always be a chain of memories of you, Mickiewicz. Whatever might happen, my heart belongs to you alone. If I am destined not to live for you, then my life is over, but I will bear this without complaint.

Mickiewicz was planning to leave for the West, but the sincerity of Janisch's feelings obliged him to go to Moscow to explain himself. There he offered Janisch friendship rather than love. On 5 April 1829, the night after their final meeting, she wrote him a parting letter:

> Hello, my dear. Once again I thank you for everything. For your friendship and for your love. I took a vow that I would try to be worthy of this love. Don't ever think that I could break that vow—this is the only thing I ask of you. If I can be certain that your opinion of me will never change, then I will be content, satisfied, and happy. I am happy now as well, parting with you, perhaps forever; and even if we are destined not to see each other again, I will always be convinced that this is best for both of us, for such is the will of God. Whatever may happen in the future, my life will be pleasant; I will often reach deep into my heart for the precious memories of you, thinking of them with joy, because all of them for me are like the purest diamonds. Farewell, my friend! It is very hard for me to close this letter with the thought that we may never again have the chance to exchange even words. . . . But it must be so—farewell, my friend! I know all the same that you love me!

Mickiewicz answered with a message in verse in which he raised Janisch's hopes by promising: "I shall rush from the south back to the north on the wings of joy, back to you again."

Thirty years later, reflecting on her first love, Pavlova wrote: "Who has not stood terrified and dumb-struck before his dethroned idol?" The story might have been merely banal, if it did not illustrate the future poet's nobility and delicate sensibilities.

In 1829 two major events occurred in Janisch's life. The great German scientist Alexander von Humboldt came to Moscow, met her, and was greatly impressed by her. At the same time she started to exchange letters in verse with the poets Evgenii Abramovich Baratynsky and Nikolai Mikhailovich Iazykov, a traditional form of "reflections" or "messages" that was a genre canonical for the age. In one such message from 1831 Iazykov thanks Janisch for her translations of his poems into German. This is the first mention of her professional translating activities, for which she was to become quite well known in 1833.

Janisch's translating secured her a place in the prevailing literary circles. During the first half of the 1830s she was primarily occupied with translating. Her outstanding education, her knowledge of several foreign languages, and her deep understanding of Russian poetry made her one of the best interpreters not only of the words but also of the underlying emotions conveyed by the original works.

Manuscripts of Janisch's German translations of Russian poems came into the hands of Johann Wolfgang von Goethe, who approved of them and sent her an affectionate letter. These translations were published abroad separately under the title *Das Nordlicht: Proben der neuen russischen Literatur. Erste Lieferung* (The Northern Light: Samples of New Russian Literature. First Printing); it was published in Dresden and Leipzig in 1833. Most of these poems were translations of Pushkin, but several of Janisch's original works were included at the end. The collection was arranged this way by design: putting her original poetry at the end reflects the literary biography of a woman poet who must enter the literary world through someone else's poetry, representing herself as merely the interpreter of someone else's thoughts in order to spare her own feelings and protect herself from direct attack.

One of the most important events in Janisch's life was her marriage in 1837 to the famous literary figure Nikolai Filippovich Pavlov. After the death of the rich uncle who had been so opposed to her marrying Mickiewicz, she suddenly became a wealthy marriage prospect. Contemporaries considered Pavlov to be motivated by material concerns, since whenever he met her in literary salons, he always treated her rather derisively. At the time of their marriage he was a successful author, and a collection of his stories had been suppressed by the censors because of their provocative political content. Pushkin commented that "Pavlov is the first among us to write truly engaging stories," and "his success is fully deserved."

As a young man Pavlov had been quite poor. Before becoming a writer he had been an actor and a petty official. This history made quite an impression on

Pavlova as a young girl (from Polnoe sobranie stikhotvorenii, *1964)*

Janisch, as Pavlov seemed to represent, according to her, a valiant champion of the downtrodden and oppressed. Another significant fact was that in 1837 she was approaching thirty and was facing the prospects of life alone, without family and children. In his letter to Venevitinov of January 1837 the poet Khomiakov wrote: "Pavlov is marrying Karolina Janisch. They say she has received a large inheritance.... Whatever the case may be, he's doing the smart thing, and no matter what they say, I think that he is marrying, as he writes (in his own words), not for money but also certainly not without money."

In her next collection of translations, *Les préludes* (The Preludes), published in Paris in 1839, Pavlova included–along with Russian–German, English, Italian, and Polish poets translated into French. This collection also included several original works in French by Pavlova. The history of this collection is extremely confused. Some scholars (Briusov, for example) believe that the collection–which was published anonymously in Paris–should not be attributed to Pavlova. Archival evidence and a direct analysis of the poetic style, however, support her authorship.

In evaluating Pavlova's first published poems, critics ignored her original works and considered only her translations. The first reaction to *Das Nordlicht* came from Ivan Vasil'evich Kireevsky: "These translations were done by a young woman of the most diverse and unusual talents. As far as I am able to judge, these translations are superior to all other known translations from Russian into any other language." Three years after the publication of *Das Nordlicht,* Mikhail Nikiforovich Katkov wrote about this collection in his article "Otsyv inostrantsa o Pushkine" (A Foreigner's Comments on Pushkin): "These translations can be considered models for translation: the artistic coloring is combined with amazing accuracy and faithfulness to the original. The talent of the translator enabled her to convey all the melodiousness, all the harmonious luster of Pushkin's brilliant poetry. Not one of his images is distorted, not one nuance has lost its original freshness and purity." In his 1839 article "Russkie zhurnaly" (Russian Journals) Vissarion Grigor'evich Belinsky notes that her "amazing talent" in "translating poetry from and into all languages known to her is finally beginning to get universal recognition." He goes on to say that one should not be surprised that she was able to convey in French the "noble simplicity, strength, conciseness, and poetic charm of 'Polkovodets'" [Geneva], which Belinsky considers to be one of Pushkin's best poems. He considers her translations into Russian "even better," referring to "this conciseness, this manly energy, the noble simplicity of these brilliant poems, brilliant in their strength and in their poetic artistry."

Belinsky critiqued Pavlova's translations on more than one occasion. In his well-known letter to Vasilii Petrovich Botkin of 16 April 1880, for example, he comments ironically: "Wonderful poems, wonderful translations—I just don't have the strength to read them all through." This comment, however, characterizes neither the good points nor bad points of her work. Belinsky's vacillations in evaluating her translations are connected with her social status and her place in the literary battles of the age. At this time Belinsky was waging a fierce battle with the Slavophile tendencies in literature, and her predilection for the Slavophile poets Iazykov and Aleksei Stepanovich Khomiakov and her translations of them alongside Pushkin elicited comments from Belinsky such as, "Even with all her talent as a translator, she does not know how to choose her material for translation." In other words, Belinsky is not criticizing her skill as a translator but rather the objects of her translation.

In 1843 Belinsky commented on her rare translation skills in a more measured tone. He writes that she "possesses an unusual gift for translating poetry from one language into another." Although in Belinsky's eyes she was not a literary figure in her own right, he held her talent as a translator in high regard.

Pavlova continued to translate throughout her life. She acquainted the European reader with the poems of Aleksei Konstantinovich Tolstoi, and she translated his dramas *Don Juan, Smert' Ivana Groznogo* (The Death of Ivan the Terrible), and *Tsar Feodor Ivanovich*. To the Russian reader she brought Friedrich von Schiller's "The Death of Wallenstein" and the poetry of Byron, Ferdinand Freiligrath, Sir Walter Scott, and Victor Hugo.

Pavlova's original poetry can be divided into two periods. The first period lasts from the 1830s, when she first began writing original works, to the late 1840s and early 1850s. The second period encompasses the 1850s and 1860s and is connected with her voluntary exile and her life far from Russia.

In the 1840s Moscow had become a hotbed of literary activity. A battle was raging between the Westernizers and the Slavophiles; Pavlova, who organized her own literary salon, did not take sides but reacted quite negatively to Iazykov's poems "K Konstantinu Aksakovu" (To Konstantin Aksakov), "K nenashim" (To Our Opponents), and "K Chaadaevu" (To Chaadaev), in which he substitutes literary differences for political differences. The friendship between Pavlova and Iazykov fell apart, and in reply to his message in verse to her she said in verse that it was "embarrassing" and "painful" for her when, in her eyes, the ideas of others were infringed upon and insulted. Pavlova may have felt the embarrassment personally, however, since she was widely published in the Slavophile press at this time, and her works were highly touted by proponents of this position.

The period of Pavlova's life with Pavlov comprises the most productive stage in her literary career. She considered a day lost when "thoughts of happiness and sadness, flashing by, did not shine with the golden riza [icon frame] of poetry." The lyric themes of her poetry during this period are found mainly in her "messages" and "reflections." The function of the lyric "I" in these poems is given to the figure of the "poet," who stands in a special, usually dramatic, relation to the surrounding world. The lyric hero-poet is typically conversing with the person to whom the poem is addressed, at times anonymously. Sometimes the poet reflects on the same themes in a monologue or "thought." The lyric speech in the name of the poetic "I," whom the reader usually identifies with the author, gives way to reflections in the person of some "poet" character. This type of structure gives Pavlova the chance to address universal issues and avoid criticism for strictly feminine themes in her poetry. One of these themes is the place of the poet in society, a theme that permeates all of her work. Again and again it appears in various incarnations in her "messages" and "reflections."

In her "messages" to Mickiewicz and in poems describing her relationship with her husband Pavlova combines the theme of love–so typical of lyric poetry–with reflections on the lives of ordinary people and the poet's place among them. In the poem "Est' liubimtsy vdokhnovenii" (There are Those Favored by Inspiration, written in 1839, published in 1863) she deals with this theme in her own way. According to her, the tragedy of the poet does not lie in the failure of society or the masses to acknowledge his genius. The original poet deals with major themes and "elevated labors," so sooner or later such poets are understood and esteemed. The theme with which Pavlova deals is more difficult to understand and resolve. She contrasts the "poet favored by inspiration" with the "mute poet," one of "fruitless dreams, with reticent eyes, with a hidden soul." She sees such a person as a poetic individual with a particular poetic perception of the world. The theme itself is transformed into a conflict between the individual and society, the "soul" of the individual person and the generally accepted norms of human relations. The drama of society's lack of understanding of the individual with a poetic relationship to the world–a relationship based not on "practicality" or "profit" but on immediate experience that is silent and invisible to others, on the perception of beauty and poetry existing in the world–leads Pavlova to a particular conception of the individual, to her own definition of personhood.

Of particular significance in Pavlova's works of this period are poems that, given their form, could be called "stories in verse." In 1841 Khomiakov wrote to one of his correspondents: "Recently Pavlova read one of her wonderful ballads, 'Starukha'" (Old Woman, 1840). Pieces such as "Starukha," "Doch' zhida" (The Jew's Daughter, 1840), "Monakh" (The Monk, 1840), "Rudokop" (The Miner, 1841), "Donna Inezilla" (1842), and "Tri Dushi" (Three Souls, 1845), however, are difficult to place in any poetic genre. In fact, one of these works is actually called "Rasskaz" (Story). These are not lyric poems. Each has a protagonist and a plot, but they are not ballads, either, since neither the plot nor the characteristic features of the protagonist's fate are the main subject of the narration. These works are also too lyrical to be ballads, but both the protagonist and the plot carry the theme that typically develops in the genre of lyric poetry. Characteristic of this genre is not merely the story of a particular protagonist with a particular fate but also the lyric tension in the psychology of the protagonist and the penetration of this lyricism into the plot itself. This "story in verse" represents a special modification of lyric poetry in Pavlova's hands and is undoubtedly an innovation on her part.

Karolina Karlovna Pavlova, frontispiece to Barbara Heldt Monter's 1978 English translation of Pavlova's 1848 novel, Dvoinaia zhizn' *(A Double Life)*

The protagonists of Pavlova's stories in verse are obsessed with some particular passion that has taken hold of them and possesses them, like a reverie, shutting out all the joy and sorrow from their lives. Among these works the poem "Monakh" stands out. To determine the gist of this reverie is difficult: it involves both a morbid isolation in the realm of personal experience and the inaccessibility of this isolated world to anyone else. The power of the past, the power of real-life experience, stands in contrast to monastic solitude, which does not allow the protagonist out of the world of reminiscences. These verses reveal the "conception of the individual" as formulated by Pavlova–the inability of the poetic nature to adapt to life and enter into a dialogue with society. Pavlova sees the futility of such an existence.

In "Rudokop" the protagonist sees and knows nothing in life outside of his work–the search for metal ores. He knows no earthly pleasures; life passes him by; and his eternal labor deadens his soul. The protagonist is doomed the moment he prepares to break with his passion–there is no longer any reason to live.

In this series of poems one can see the connection between Pavlova's work and the German Romantics. In the poetry of such German writers as Novalis (pseudonym of Friedrich von Hardenberg), Ludwig Tieck, and Achim von Arnim, the protagonist ruined by his unconquerable passion reflects the author. In Pavlova's works, however, the subjectivity in the depiction of the protagonist is removed: he or she is depicted not from the inside but from the outside. The protagonist is an object of the author's observations, and so she can remove the autobiographical touches from these works, although parallels with her own life are undoubtedly present. At the same time, the plot of the "story in verse" grows beyond the framework of personal experience and becomes a general observation, touching on universal themes and transporting these works into a category dealing with the general conditions of life.

Themes treating the human condition become the basis of one of her best works–the novel *Dvoinaia zhizn'* (translated as *A Double Life*, 1978). Published in six-page abstract in a Moscow literary journal in 1847, and in full in the 1915 edition of her collected works, the novel has an epigram from Byron ("Our life is twofold . . .") and a dedication "to my mute sisters of the soul," or "Psyches deprived of their wings." It is written in a combination of verse and prose. According to Konstantin Aksakov, "Related in prose is the external, empty, wordy life surrounding the heroine of the novel. Expressed in verse is the inner voice of her soul–unconsciously, unknown to her, but always accompanying this external world, which cannot extinguish it." According to the author herself, *Dvoinaia zhizn'* is an *ocherk* (sketch). Pavlova's choice of this particular genre may be connected with the trends of the time–the development of the "natural school" in prose and the so-called *del'naia* poetry (poetry dealing with real-life experience and everyday themes). In the 1840s the genre of the essay was also popular for exploring hitherto unexamined sides of Russian life. By calling her work a sketch, Pavlova in all likelihood was stating that the life of her heroine, the tragedy of the sensitive soul, was not an isolated case but rather an everyday occurrence, a typical story.

Dvoinaia zhizn' relates the story of Cecily von Lindenborn, a young woman in Moscow who is to be married. The mothers of Cecily and her friend Olga Valitskaia get involved in a fierce battle over the highly eligible bachelor, Prince Viktor. No one is concerned with feelings; emotions are subordinated to practical and material considerations, thereby creating a situation that destroys everything. Friendship proves to be ephemeral: to remove Cecily from the competition for Viktor, Valitskaia's mother comes up with a grand scheme to marry Cecily to Dmitrii Ivachinsky, who is seeking a rich bride, but her plan fails. The intrigues are written in prose: the narration of the course of events is extremely dynamic. Pavlova's goal, though, is not to depict the "worldly" buying and selling of brides but the inner life of the heroine Cecily, the poetry in the novel. The theme is the same one Pavlova dealt with in "Est' liubimtsy vdokhnovenii," a poem crucial to understanding her works of the 1840s.

Cecily belongs to those "people without an occupation," the "mute poets," namely the ordinary people of contemporary society of whom Pavlova speaks in "Est' liubimtsy vdokhnovenii." In Pavlova's work a person exists in accordance with his or her place in society but at the same time outside of it. The deepest secrets of his or her soul are inaccessible to others and to society in general. In the depths of his or her soul, a person is far removed from sociability; the reality of social life certainly has an impact on the person, but it is completely unspiritual. This dualism constitutes the "double life."

The relationship between poetry and prose in this novel is extremely interesting. Prose plays the role of "real life," the objective world. The paradox is that the prose part is able to exist independently of the poetry. If all the poetry were removed, there would remain a sort of "physiological sketch" (which is rather socially provocative, as well), a "worldly life" whose plot revolves around marriage for money. The poetry, however, cannot exist independently of its parallel associations with the prose, for it is precisely in these parallels that the depth of the tragedy of the sensitive poetic soul is revealed.

Critical reaction to *Dvoinaia zhizn'* was varied. Since Pavlova was interested in Slavophile ideas and published in the Slavophile press, and since Slavophiles widely praised her work, the novel was attacked for its Slavophile bent. For example, in the journal *Syn otechestva* (Son of the Fatherland) Pavlova was accused, like all Slavophiles, of "waging a personal battle with individuality in contemporary society." This accusation is unconvincing, inasmuch as Pavlova in this work is only concerned with the personality of her heroine. Moreover, the Slavophile journal *Moskvitianin* (Muscovite) carried a negative critique by Stepan Petrovich Shevyrev. His main criticism was that the "prose half of the essay is a skeletal version of life, but not life." In other words, the weakness of the novel lies in its social critique, and this weakness comes "from the German way of thinking." Thus, both Westernizers and Slavophiles criticized the novel for something that was not there in the first place. Many contemporaries saw direct parallels between the life of the heroine, Cecily, and the life of Pavlova herself; but to Pavlova's credit, she was able to transform her personal experience into a discussion of universal themes.

Pavlova's last major work in the first stage of her writing was *Razgovor v Trianone* (A Conversation at Trianon), written in 1848 and published in the 1915 collection; she was inclined to consider it her best work. She attempted in this work–in the form of a "story in verse"–to make sense out of history. The events of 1848 had to have had an impact on Pavlova. The memoirist Sergei Aleksandrovich Rachinsky, who met her in the early 1850s, wrote: "At that time her artistic interests . . . were already being significantly overshadowed by her political and social interests. There were vague hopes floating around in her mind that had been awakened by the storm of 1848. But the old writer was skeptical about these hopes."

Having always presented her position as that of a "poet" rising above social contradictions and social battles, Pavlova had a difficult time turning her attention to everyday themes. *Razgovor v Trianone* attempts historical-philosophical analysis of contemporary events. The story takes place during one of the many festive occasions at the king's court in the time immediately preceding the French Revolution. A conversation takes place between Honoré-Gabriel Riqueti, Comte de Mirabeau and Count Alessandro di Cagliostro. Mirabeau speaks of the necessity for revolution, while Cagliostro's responses express the thoughts of the author. Cagliostro has seen much, and he knows that the conduct of people is governed more by "wild tyranny" than by "rational thought." People are "either ferocious tigers or peaceful oxen," and "their love is fruitless." The course of history determined by fate and reality is sorrowful, void of spirituality. These are the conclusions to which Pavlova comes in her attempt to see reflections of the present in the past.

It was not only her social life that brought discord into Pavlova's soul. Her personal life fell apart, and the well-being of her family was threatened, as well. Pavlova had taken into her home a poor relation, Evgeniia Alexandrovna Tannenberg, with whom she spent days on end in conversation about art. Her husband formed a more intimate relationship with Tannenberg, with whom he eventually had three children and established a second household. Other strains in their relationship developed. Pavlov was a compulsive gambler, and his huge losses at cards drained his wife's financial resources. The final break came in 1852. Pavlova's father complained to Governor-General Arseni Andreevich Zakrevsky that Pavlov had secretly mortgaged Pavlova's estate. Already antagonistic toward Pavlov because of his epigrams, Zakrevsky ordered a raid on Pavlov's house, where a card game was always in progress, under the pretext that the game might be fixed. The officials did not find any marked cards, but they found that Pavlov's library was filled with banned

Pavlova after her marriage to writer Nikolai Filippovich Pavlov (from Polnoe sobranie stikhotvorenii, *[Complete Collection of Poems] 1964)*

books. The compulsive gambler and unfaithful husband was exiled to Perm.

The liberals hailed Pavlov as a martyr to their cause and made life difficult for his wife, whom they blamed for sending her husband into exile. Life in Moscow became unbearable for Pavlova, who moved to St. Petersburg with her only son, Ippolit, who had been born in 1839. Shortly after Pavlova's arrival in St. Petersburg, her father died of cholera. When she did not attend his funeral, supposedly because she feared infection, society judged this act as disrespectful. As a result she decided to leave Russia for Derpt (Tartu, Estonia) and took her mother and son along.

Thus began the second period in Pavlova's creative life. Her poetry of the 1850s has a decidedly unhappy ring to it. The act of creation, so necessary for Pavlova, underwent fundamental changes. In her poem "Molchala duma rokovaia" (The Fateful Thought was Silent, written in 1852, published in 1863) she describes life without poetry, without art, as a "half-life." Random occasions awaken a transitory creative impulse, but Pavlova no longer has faith in the continuity and essentiality of this awakening of poetic energy.

The most noteworthy work of this period is the poem *Kadril'* (Quadrille), which she had begun in the 1840s but did not complete until 1859. *Kadril'* includes

Manuscript for "Eto bylo blestiashchee more..." (That was a glistening sea) (from Polnoe sobranie stikhotvorenii, *1964)* direct references to the era of Pushkin. It opens with a dedication to Baratynsky, and the poetic formulation of its basic theme—a woman's fate in contemporary society—is given in a special digression on Tatiana Larina and on the impudence of the attempt at poetic competition with her creator. The theme of this poem is clearly related to the essential questions Pavlova wrote of in *Dvoinaia zhizn'*. *Kadril'* depicts a woman entering into independent life and the disparities between a young woman's conceptions of people and society and their true nature. In *Dvoinaia zhizn'* Cecily does not know what the future has in store for her, whereas in *Kadril'* the four women telling each other their life stories have already crossed that decisive threshold. Marriage, the first bitterness at discovering the inevitable discord in life, and the problems associated with a woman's fate in society form the focus of these women's attention. The basic question is who is more to blame for the misfortunes of a woman's fate—society or the woman herself? The poem answers this question, and the answer is complex and multifaceted. The poem flows out of the interrelations, the cohesion among these four different fates. Pavlova's typical "story in verse" is multiplied here into a series of related stories united by plot and theme into a single work.

The critics attacked the poem. Ivan Ivanovich Panaev in the journal *Sovremennik* (Contemporary) did not attack Pavlova's poetic talent but rather her "uncertain position," her attempt to "be neutral" in the battle over social questions, but the result was the same: "Journalists, perhaps, were expecting the poetic talent of Mrs. Pavlova, traces of which they saw in her resonant and vivid verse, to express itself more clearly. And meanwhile time passed. . . . " There were no further publications of *Kadril'*.

Pavlova explained her move to Derpt by pointing out the need to see to the education of her son and the low cost of living there; the depletion of her financial resources would not allow her to live in typical Moscow style. In Derpt, Pavlova became acquainted with a law student named Boris Isaakovich Utin, and they became close in spite of the twenty-five-year difference in their ages. Serious feelings developed on Pavlova's part: according to her poetry, not only was this the greatest love of her life, but it also largely determined her subsequent fate.

In the spring of 1854 Utin graduated from the university and left for St. Petersburg. Pavlova followed him and apparently tried to reenter the social and literary life there by getting involved with moderately liberal journals. Her attempt to carve out a serious niche for herself in literature was doomed by the lack of success of her *Razgovor v Kremle; Stikhotvorenie* (Conversation at the Kremlin, Poems, 1854).

By the end of the year her relationship with Utin had soured; they parted soon thereafter.

Pavlova's lyric poetry of the 1850s reveals an "Utin theme"—the image of a poet who does not rise above the level of the everyday but rather exhausts his inspiration through the torment and pain that life heaps upon him. The person tormented by life, by a "wretched heart," perceives the reawakening of creative abilities as a potential means of overcoming the "ashes" of his burdens and grief. While earlier the very possibility of a poetic relationship to the world separated the "mute poet" from everyday reality, now the specific occupation of poetry provides a connection to the world. Instead of leading him away from life, poetry has the opposite effect; it leads him into life by instilling a renewed ability to live and feel. The poems of the "Utin cycle" are connected by their unified theme, their unified pain, and a special psychological truthfulness. The resulting collection, published in 1863, caps off Pavlova's creative life. The mingling of personal, creative, and social contradictions leads her to a dual decision: geographically she leaves Russian life, and creatively she leaves Russian poetry.

Pavlova settled in Dresden. She continued to do translations, primarily of Aleksei Konstantinovich Tolstoi, whom she had met in 1860. He became her last true literary friend and ally. In 1868 she came back to Russia to read her translation of Schiller's "The Death of Wallenstein" at a meeting of the *Obshchestvo liubitelei rossiiskoi slovesnosti* (Society of Lovers of Russian Literature). According to the memoirs of contemporaries, she read badly, with pompous declamations, behavior that made her the subject of epigrams. She returned to Dresden, and Russia forgot about her. In fact, many thought that she was dead. In 1890, however, she wrote a letter to Mickiewicz's son, Wladislaw, in which she said that "time, rather than weakening my love, has only made it stronger." On 2 December 1893 Pavlova died, alone and forgotten.

The Symbolist poets reevaluated her work. Briusov brought out the two-volume edition of her works in 1915. Andrei Bely ranked her as high as Baratynsky (whom she considered her master) and Zhukovsky in her mastery of versification. Interest in women's writing has led critics to reevaluate her work once again. A century after her death Karolina Karlovna Pavlova is finally beginning to claim her rightful place in the history of Russian literature.

Letters:

B. Rapgof, *K. Pavlova, Materialy dlia izucheniia zhizni i tvorchestva* (Prague: Trirema, 1916), pp. 68–77.

References:

Petr Ivanovich Bartenev, "K. K. Pavlova," *Russkii arkhiv,* 12 (1984): 961–970;

Aleksandr Ivanovich Beletskii, "Novoe izdanie sochinenii K. Pavlovoi," 22, book 2, *Izv. AN* (1917): 200–220;

Valerii Iakovlevich Briusov, "Materialy dlia biografii Karoliny Pavlovoi" in Pavlova's *Sochineniia* (Moscow: K. F. Nekrasov, 1915), pp. ix–xlix;

Sergei Ernst, "Karolina Pavlova i grafinia Evdokiia Rostopchina," *Russkii bibliofil,* 6 (1916): 7–35;

B. Griftsov, "K. Pavlova," *Russkaia mysl',* 11 (1915): 11–16;

Leonid Petrovich Grossman, *Vtornik u Karoliny Pavlovoi: Stseny iz zhizni moskovskikh salonov 40-kh godov* (Odessa: Omfalos, 1919);

Nikolai Pavlovich Kashin, "Eshche. 'O sochineniakh' Karolinoi Pavlovoi," *Kniga i revolutsiia,* 3–4 (1921): 8–9;

Vladislav Felitsianovich Khodasevich, *Odna iz zabytykh, Almanakh "Novaya zhizn,"* volume 3 (Moscow, 1916), p. 198;

K. Khranevich, "Mickiewicz i Karolina Pavlova," *Istoricheskii vestnik,* 3 (1897): 1080–1086;

Anatolii Fedrorovich Koni, "Karolina Pavlova," *Evropa,* 4–5 (1918): 24–28;

Barbara Lettmann-Sadony, "Karolina Karlovna Pavlova. Eine Dichterin russisch-deutscher Wechselseitigkeit," *Slavische Beiträge,* Band 50 (Munich, 1971);

Ivan Ivanovich Panaev, "Razgovor v kremle. *Stikhotvoreniia K. Pavlovoi.* (St. Petersburg, 1854)," *Sovremennik,* 47, no. 9 (1854), IV: 34–38;

Boris Sadovskoi, "Karolina Pavlova," in his *Ledokhod. Stat'i i zametki* (St. Petersburg: B. Sadovskoi, 1916);

Mikhail Evgrafovich Saltykov-Shchedrin, *Stikhotvoreniia K. Pavlovoi* (Moscow, 1863);

Munir Sendich, "The Life and Works of Karolina Pavlovna," dissertation, New York University, 1968;

Sendich, "Moscow Literary Salons: Thursdays at Karolina Pavlova's," *Welt der Slaven,* 17 (1972): 341–357;

Sendich, "Ot Moskvy do Drezdena: Pavlova's Unpublished Memoirs," *Russian Language Journal,* 102 (1975): 57–78;

B. Smirenksii, "Zabytyi romans Lista," *Smena,* 13 (1957): 24;

O. G. Zolotareva, "K voprosu o 'Nesobrannykh stikhotvornykh tsiklakh 40-60khgg.: Utinskii tsikl' K. K. Pavlovloi," *Problemy metoda i zhanra,* volume 9 (Tomsk, 1983);

V. K. Zontikov, "'Pishu ne smelo ia, ne chasto . . .' (Stikhotvorenie Karoliny Pavlovnoi)," *Vstrechi s proshlym. Sbornik materialov TsGALI* (Moscow, 1982), pp. 35–39.

Papers:

Karolina Karlovna Pavlova's papers are in the State Archive of Literature and Art (TsGALI) and the State Literary Museum, Moscow, and the Institute of Russian Literature (Pushkin House), St. Petersburg.

Petr Aleksandrovich Pletnev

(10 August 1792 – 29 December 1865)

Ruth Sobel
Defence School of Languages

BOOKS: *Khronologicheskii spisok russkikh sochinitelei i bibliograficheskie zamechaniia o ikh proizvedeniiakh* (St. Petersburg: Ekspeditsiia zagotovleniia gos. bumag, 1836);

O stikhotvoreniiakh Vasiliia Andreevicha Zhukovskago (St. Petersburg: Tip. Imp. Akademii nauk, 1852);

O zhizhni i sochineniiakh Vasiliia Andreevicha Zhukovskago (St. Petersburg: Tip. Imp. Akademii nauk, 1853);

Pamiati Grafa Sergeia Semenovicha Uvarova, prezidenta Imperatorskoi Akademii nauk (St. Petersburg: Tip. Imperatorskoi Akademii nauk, 1855).

Editions and Collections: *Sochineniia i perepiska P. A. Pletneva*, 3 volumes, edited by Iakov Karlovich Grot (St. Petersburg: Tip. Imp. Akademii nauk, 1885);

Poety 1820–1830-kh godov, volume 1, edited by Vadim Erazmovich Vatsuro and V. S. Kiselev-Sergenin (Leningrad, 1972);

Stat'i, stikhotvoreniia pis'ma, edited by A. A. Shelaeva (Moscow: Sovetskaia Rossiia, 1988);

K moei rodine: sobranie stikhotvorenii, edited by Mikhail Viktorovich Stroganov (Tver': Tverskoi gos. universitet, 1992).

OTHER: *Sovremennik,* edited by Pletnev (1837–1846).

Petr Aleksandrovich Pletnev

Petr Pletnev lived a long life and was fortunate to have known most of the great men of nineteenth-century Russian literature, including the most famous, Aleksandr Pushkin and Nikolai Gogol. His own contribution to Russian belles lettres, both as a poet and as a critic, is fairly modest. Indeed, he himself had few illusions about his poetic talent and believed that his immortality would instead be assured through his friendships with his more talented contemporaries. Pletnev did publish many poems in various early-nineteenth-century periodicals; some of them were included by Iakov Karlovich Grot in his three-volume edition of Pletnev's work. His other works, which appeared in several periodicals between 1820 and 1860, have been mostly forgotten. A complete edition of his works has never been published. As a critic he likewise failed to leave his mark on the genre, which was just beginning to take root in Russia. After Pushkin's death in 1837 Pletnev took over the editorship of Pushkin's journal, *Sovremennik* (The Contemporary), but despite all his efforts it was steadily losing subscribers and falling into decline. Finally, in 1846 Pletnev was forced, largely for financial reasons, to lease the journal to Nikolai Alekseevich Nekrasov and Ivan Ivanovich Panaev. Besides writing poetry and criticism Pletnev also taught from 1814 until 1861. Though his contribution is minor, he nevertheless deserves mention in the history of Russian literature.

Petr Aleksandrovich Pletnev was born on 10 August 1792 in Tver', or in the Bezhetsk district of the

Tver' province. He came from a family of priests; his parents were poor and could not afford to give him a good education. He first attended the religious seminary in Tver', then moved on to St. Petersburg. For four years, from 1810 to 1814, he studied at the Central Pedagogical Institute, where the director at that time was Egor Antonovich Engel'gardt (later the headmaster of the Lyceum in Tsarskoe Selo), who noticed Pletnev's talents. After graduation Pletnev was asked to stay on and teach at his alma mater. As was customary in those days, Pletnev held more than one teaching post; thus in 1815 he was appointed to teach history in a *voenno-sirotskii dom* (military educational establishment). Soon afterward, having proven his talents as an educator, he was invited to teach at two prestigious institutes: the Ekaterininsky and the Patriotic. On Vasilii Andreevich Zhukovsky's recommendation he was also appointed as private tutor in Russian to some members of the tsar's family.

His career developed successfully, and in 1828 he began teaching Russian literature to the heir to the throne, Alexander II, and the grand-princesses. In 1832 he was appointed a professor at St. Petersburg University, where for seventeen years he taught Russian literature; he also continued to lecture at the Central Pedagogical Institute. During his time as professor he held the post of chancellor (rector) of the university and became a member of the Academy of Sciences. In the course of his university career he taught several young men who later made significant contributions to Russian literature, among them Nekrasov, Ivan Sergeevich Turgenev, and Petr Pavlovich Ershov. According to a memoir left by Turgenev, Pletnev was by no means an "academic" type, but more of a tutor of the old school, though wise in his way.

As a professor of Russian literature Pletnev introduced into his discussions of literary works the notion of historicism, explaining the work through the period— an approach that had begun to take root during the 1830s. As a teacher Pletnev was always interested in new works and young authors, closely following current developments in literature. His good friend Gogol once remarked that in his lectures Pletnev "trained students' literary taste."

In about 1817, when Pletnev first started to teach at the Central Pedagogical Institute, he made the acquaintance of Vil'gel'm Karlovich Kiukhel'beker, who introduced him to an old schoolmate, Baron Anton Antonovich Del'vig. Pletnev later met Pushkin and Zhukovsky, to whom he became quite close. He was one of the first to welcome Gogol when the latter arrived in the capital, and Gogol remained his lifelong friend. In later years, when working on Del'vig's journal *Severnye tsvety* (Northern Flowers) and then on Pushkin's *Sovremennik,* Pletnev offered help and encouragement to many young talents, notably Turgenev, whose early poem "Parasha" was published in *Sovremennik* in 1843. In her memoirs on Pletnev, children's writer Aleksandra Osipova Ishimova wrote that after she had shown him her own work Pletnev became her most caring guardian and the best advisor on all matters pertaining to literature and publishing.

Pletnev's own poems had begun to appear in 1818. "K Gonorskomu" (To Gonorsky) and "Zagorodnaia Roshcha" (The Country Grove) are both somewhat archaic in the sentimental tone the young poet adopted. This Sentimental vein, undoubtedly introduced under the influence of Nikolai Mikhailovich Karamzin, blended with the Romantic influence of Zhukovsky and Konstantin Nikolaevich Batiushkov in Pletnev's initial efforts at poetry. In the early 1820s Pletnev also produced some civic verse, again influenced by one of the dominant poetic currents of the times. In 1823 he wrote an ode titled "Dolg grazhdanina" (A Citizen's Duty), dedicated to Admiral Nikolai Semenovich Mordvinov, who had been considered a liberal advisor to the reigning tsar, Alexander I.

The mood that pervades many of Pletnev's poems has often been described as elegiac: a mood of regret and quiet resignation. One of his best poems, "K A. S. Pushkinu" (To A. S. Pushkin, 1822), strongly expresses this mood when the speaker admits his failure to achieve anything of note in poetry: ". . . na poprishche moem / Ia ne svershil dostoinoe poeta" (. . . in my chosen field I / Haven't achieved anything worthy of a poet). This poem, probably one of Pletnev's most moving and most personally revealing, does end on a hopeful note: "Mne v slave ikh uchastie dano / Ia budu zhit' bessmertiem mne milykh" (I can partake in their glory / I will live through the immortality of those dear to my heart). In a way this early work both predicts and summarizes the extent of Pletnev's poetic achievement.

One of his early elegies, "Grobnitsa Derzhavina" (Derzhavin's Tomb, 1819), paints in a Romantic vein a gloomy landscape, strewn with graves, through which the desolate poet wanders until he reaches the urn with Gavriil Romanovich Derzhavin's ashes. In another elegiac poem, "K moei rodine" (To my Fatherland, 1820), the speaker confesses his desire to leave St. Petersburg and flee to his native haunts. Pletnev patently favored this genre; elegies predominate in his poetic output. He seems especially fond of their *unylyi* (gloomy) tone. Many of his poems dedicated to his comrades Del'vig, Zhukovsky, Nikolai Ivanovich Gnedich, and Pushkin belong to the genre of the epistle and deal with a theme that was central to that age, especially in Pushkin's circle: friendship. Pletnev also turned to another popular nineteenth-century theme with several poems that look to nature for their inspiration. In addition, he wrote some pieces that can be classified as anthology verse. Except for his last two poems, written in 1832 and 1842, Pletnev effectively gave up writing poetry at the end of the 1820s. The realization of his rather modest talents as a poet, along with the corroboration of the literary critics, most likely led him to turn his attention to another area of literary life–criticism.

Pletnev's career as a literary critic began around 1819 when he joined two organizations: *Obshchestvo liubitelei slovesnosti, nauk i khudozhestv* (Free Society of Lovers of Letters, Science and Arts) and *Obshchestvo liubitelei rossiiskoi slovesnosti* (Society of Lovers of Russian Literature). Pletnev was quite active in the latter and regularly published his critical assessments in the proceedings of the society.

In an 1822 article, "Zametka o sochineniiakh Zhukovskogo i Batiushkova" (A Note on the Works of Zhukovsky and Batiushkov), Pletnev made his first attempt to provide an outline of Russian poetry, a topic that preoccupied him in later years as well. He begins his article by saying that poetry has long existed in Russia, at least since the twelfth century. With the appearance of such eighteenth-century poets as Mikhail Vasil'evich Lomonosov and Derzhavin, he says, the process of shaping and changing Russian poetic language began in earnest, while its first successes came with the appearance of Batiushkov and Zhukovsky, who initiated a new and distinguished period in its history. Pletnev identifies the main flaw of Russian poetry up to that time as careless language, that is, one in which mistakes abound. These two poets, he argues, purified the language and endowed it with harmony. Pletnev discusses their individual contributions, defining Zhukovsky as the founder of the Russian Romantic school and Batiushkov as the exponent of the latest manifestation of the neoclassical school. The evaluation of Russian literature was one of the most important concerns at that time, and many writers and journalists posed the question of whether Russia could indeed be said to possess a national literature. Pletnev, unlike many of his contemporaries–Aleksandr Aleksandrovich Bestuzhev (Marlinsky), Ivan Vasil'evich Kireevsky, Dmitrii Vladimirovich Venevitinov, and especially Vissarion Grigor'evich Belinsky, to name but a few–answered the question in the affirmative.

In the 1820s Pletnev published several critical pieces, first in *Sorevnovatel' prosveshcheniia i blagotvoreniia* (The Champion of Enlightenment and Beneficence) and in the journal of the *Obshchestvo liubitelei rossiiskoi slovesnosti* and later, from 1824 on, in *Severnye tsvety*. Pletnev was a close collaborator on *Severnye tsvety* as well as an important contributor. Later in 1825 he joined Del'vig as the editor of the journal, and there he published his

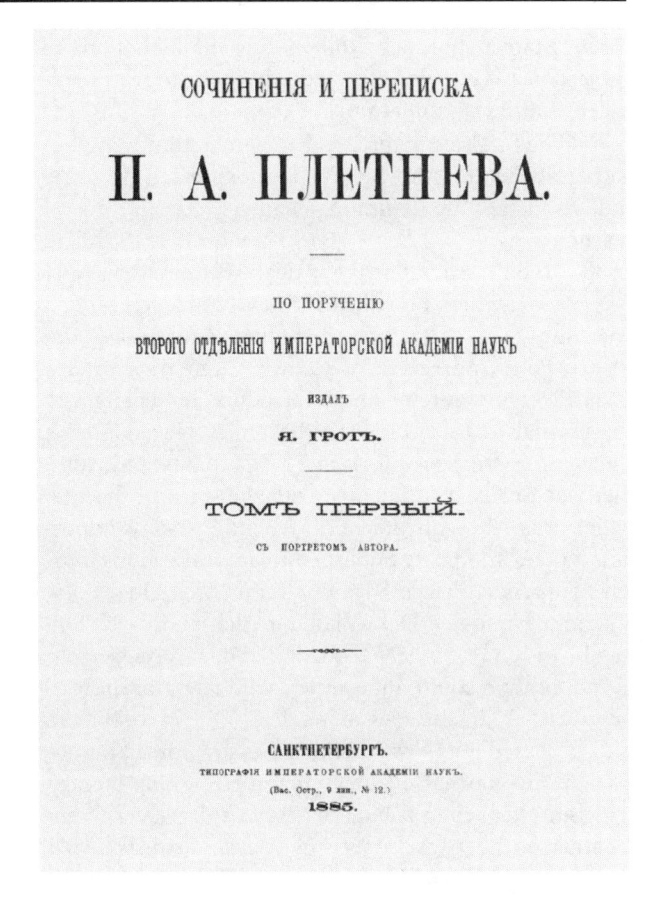

Title page for the first volume of Sochineniia i perepiska P. A. Pletneva *(Works and Correspondence of P. A. Pletnev)*

"Pis'mo grafine S. I. S." (Letter to the Countess S. I. S.), another attempt to present a panoramic view of Russian poetry in the form of a letter to Countess Sofiia Ivanovna Sollogub, a society lady who greatly admired French poetry and Alphonse de Lamartine in particular. Pletnev maintains that for all its faults, such as lack of conversational language, Russian poetry nevertheless could boast of great achievements. To prove his point he discusses the major poets from the second half of the eighteenth century to the early years of the nineteenth. In his overview Pletnev also includes Pushkin. As a critic of poetry Pletnev took his cue from Karamzin, who preached that one must avoid the condemnation of what is bad and instead encourage praise of what is good.

In this period Pletnev became one of the more important critics in the Pushkin circle. In addition to developing the genre of Karamzinian "kind critiques," Pletnev also formulated his views on Romanticism in articles for *Sovremennik,* juxtaposing Friedrich Schiller and George Gordon, Lord Byron, on the one hand and William Shakespeare on the other. In Pletnev's opinion the first two represent the subjective approach, while Shakespeare is the model of objectivity. Pletnev extols

Shakespeare's approach while noting the limitations of subjectivity as an aesthetic method; he describes subjectivity as artificial, unnatural.

The brightest figures in Russian literature used to gather at Pletnev's house. Pushkin expressed his gratitude to Pletnev by dedicating chapters four and five of his novel in verse, *Evgeny Onegin* (published in full in 1833), to him. After Pushkin's death Pletnev took over *Sovremennik,* which he edited for nearly nine years, first with the help of friends, including Zhukovsky and Prince Petr Andreevich Viazemsky, and then on his own. Pletnev was reluctant to introduce any changes to the journal or to move with the times. He adopted a stance of *bespristrastie i spokoistvie* (impartiality and calm) that was totally incompatible with the spirit of the age, which was rife with polemics. Although many important writers and poets published their works in his journal (Turgenev, Prince Vladimir Fedorovich Odoevsky, Vladimir Ivanovich Dal', Vladimir Aleksandrovich Sollogub, Fedor Ivanovich Tiutchev, and, rarely, Gogol), his publication could not compete with its more successful rivals. A drastic loss of readers (233 in 1846, the year he leased it to Nekrasov and Panaev) forced him to give up this journal. Pletnev continued writing literary criticism after relinquishing *Sovremennik,* however, commenting on new works such as Aleksei Feofilaktovich Pisemsky's play *Gor'kaia Sud'bina* (Bitter Fate, 1859) and Aleksandr Nikolaevich Ostrovsky's play *Groza* (The Storm, 1860).

In the late 1830s Pletnev began to develop a genre that proved to be one of his best endeavors, namely the literary essay/biography, which he was the first to attempt in Russia. Pletnev decided to write only about those authors with whom he had been personally acquainted (Pushkin, Ivan Andreevich Krylov, Evgenii Abramovich Baratynsky, and Zhukovsky). This knowledge gives his essays an additional dimension of being memoirs as well; Pletnev often quoted in them the letters he received from the subjects. His first such essay/biography, which deals with Pushkin, was published in *Sovremennik* in 1838. In an article on Krylov that was published in the 1847 edition of Krylov's *Polnoe sobranie sochinenii* (Complete Collected Works), Pletnev emphasizes the fabulist's Russianness: "in the person of Ivan Andreevich Krylov we see the Russian character with all its positive qualities and with all its weaknesses."

During the period of his editorship of *Sovremennik* Pletnev's best critical work was undoubtedly the essay "Chichikov ili Mertvye dushi Gogola" (1842), devoted to Gogol's epic poem in prose *Mertvye dushi* (Dead Souls, 1842). Pletnev was also instrumental in helping to pass this great novel through the censorship committee. When the novel appeared in 1842, it aroused one of the fiercest polemics in the Russian press of the period. Its publication coincided with the emergence of what later became known as Slavophilism. The novel was interpreted by the representatives of the nascent Slavophile movement as a new epic, a genre that had flourished in ancient Greece but had been forgotten in Western Europe and was now resurrected by Gogol. Pletnev was one of the first critics to review *Mertvye dushi,* and his assessment was much more balanced than that of many other participants in the polemic. He admired Gogol's art precisely for its objectivity, for the skill of an author who leaves no trace of his own personality in his work. He also put forward the idea, undoubtedly inspired by Gogol himself, that this novel was just an introduction to a much greater work in which Gogol would present a man governed by petty passions. This "prognosis" is also interesting because Pletnev saw Gogol as an author capable of tackling a serious subject, whereas most contemporaries regarded Gogol almost exclusively as a comic writer.

Pletnev describes Gogol as an objective painter of reality because nowhere in his work does he attempt to put forward his aims: he does not lead readers toward his favorite ideas; he does not seek to amuse them by presenting a funny scene; nor does he try to move them by painting an unrealistic picture of someone's misery. Gogol follows the rule of the aesthetic independence of his creation, presenting a model for an art-life relationship.

This praise does not mean that Pletnev was blind to his friend's faults as a writer. Pletnev, interestingly enough, identifies the flaw of the novel as the lack of what he terms *ser'eznyi obshchestvennyi interes* (serious society interest, the social element). Yet, this lack, admits the critic, is hardly Gogol's fault; the society he lives in has failed to provide him with such an interest. Pletnev's article was well received by Belinsky, who presumably agreed with Pletnev's view on the main flaw of the novel and the source of that flaw. He believed Pletnev's article was the only good piece to be written on Gogol's novel.

In 1846, when Gogol began working on his notorious *Vybrannye mesta iz perepiski s druz'iami* (Selected Passages from Correspondence with Friends, 1847), he chose Pletnev to supervise its publication. Pletnev also partly managed Gogol's complicated financial affairs; he was instrumental in procuring loans and paying the author's debts. His connections at the imperial court were important, and he used these several times to help his friend.

In 1859 Pletnev became chairman of the second section of the Academy of Sciences, and in 1861 he retired from his post as chancellor of St. Petersburg University. The last five years of his life were spent in Paris. By that time he was already seriously ill. He never wrote his memoirs, but his voluminous correspondence presents an interesting and illuminating picture of his times. He was married twice: his first wife was Stepanida Aleksandrovna Raevskaia, and after her death he married Countess Aleksandra Vasil'evna Shchetinina. He died in Paris at the age of seventy-three and was buried in St. Petersburg.

If Pletnev's contribution to Russian letters is modest, his generosity toward his friends, who made incomparably greater contributions to the field, made possible the publication of some of their masterpieces. For that alone he deserves a niche in the pantheon of Russian literature.

Letters:

Perepiska Ia. K. Grota s Pletnevym, 3 volumes, edited by Konstantin Iakovlevich Grot (St. Petersburg: Tipografiia Ministerstva Putei Soobshcheniia, 1896);

Pis'ma A. S. Pushkina, bar. A. A. Del'viga, E. A. Baratynskogo, P. A. Pletneva k kniaziu P. A. Viazemskomu, 1824–1843, edited by Nikolai Barsukov (St. Petersburg: M. Stasiulevich, 1902).

Biography:

Dmitrii Dmitrievich Iazykov, *Petr Aleksandrovich Pletnev* (Moscow: Univ. tip., 1896).

References:

Evgeniia Pavlovna Gorbenko, *P. A. Pletnev–literaturnyi deiatel' pushkinskoi epokhi* (Krasnodar: Kubanskii gos. univ., 1992);

Iakov Karlovich Grot, "K istoriia zhurnalistiki v 40-e rody proshlogo beka. 'Sovremennik' Pletneva i satira," in *Sbornik stat'ei no istorii i statistike russkoi periodicheskoi pechati. 1703–1903* (St. Petersburg: Russkoe bibliograficheskoe obshchestvo, 1903), pp. 84–98;

Dmitrii Dmitrievich Iazykov, "Zhizn' i trudy P. A. Pletneva v russkoi literature," *Bibliograficheskie zapiski,* 7 (1892): 485–488;

V. A. Kaminsky, "Pletnev kak kritik i publitsist," *Russkaia starina,* 11 (1906): 245–286;

V. N., "Zhizn' i literaturnaia deiatel'nost' P. A. Pletneva," *Russkaia starina,* no. 6 (1908): 633–658; no. 7 (1908): 89–119; no. 8 (1908): 265–316;

B. N. Orlov, "Drugie poety dvadtsatykh-tridtsatykh godov," in *Istoriia russkoi literatury,* volume 6 (Moscow-Leningrad: In-t rus. Lit-ry., 1953);

Vera Julievna Proskurina, "Esteticheskaia pozitsia P. A. Pletneva–izdatelia Sovremennika," *Vestnik MGU, seriia Filologia,* 6 (1984);

Proskurina, "P. A. Pletnev–literaturnyi kritik," *Nauchnye doklady vysshei shkoly, filologicheskie nauki,* 5 (1985);

Ivan Nikanorovich Rozanov, "Pletnev, P. A.," in his *Pushkinskaia pleiada* (Moscow: Zadruga, 1923), pp. 47–90;

Ivan Sergeevich Turgenev, "Literaturnyi vecher v. P. A. Pletneva," in his *Sochineniia,* volume 14 (Moscow, 1967), pp. 11–21.

Aleksandr Ivanovich Polezhaev
(30 August 1804 – 16 January 1838)

Evgeniia B. Sorokina
St. Petersburg House of Culture

BOOKS: *Erpeli i Chir-Iurt. Dve poemy* (Moscow: Tip. Lazarevykh Instituta vostochnykh iazykov, 1832);

Stikhotvoreniia A. Polezhaeva (Moscow: Tip. Lazarevykh Instituta vostochnykh iazykov, 1832);

Kal'ian. Stikhotvoreniia (Moscow: Tip. Lazarevykh Instituta vostochnykh iazykov, 1833);

Arfa. Stikhotvoreniia Aleksandra Polezhaeva (Moscow: Izd. Sergeia Andreeva Kharitonova, Tip. V. Kirilova, 1838);

Chasy vyzdorovleniia. Stikhotvoreniia (Moscow: Tip. Alekseia Evreinova, 1842).

Editions and Collections: *Stikhotvoreniia A. Polezhaeva,* with an article by Vissarion Grigor'evich Belinsky (Moscow: Izd. K. Soldatenkova and N. Shchepkina, Tip. Katkova, 1857);

Sobranie sochinenii, s biografiei, portretom i faksimile, edited by Petr Aleksandrovich Efrimov (Moscow: Izd. V. N. Ulitina, 1888);

Stikhotvoreniia A. I. Polezhaeva. S biograficheskim ocherkom, portretami i snimkami s rukopisei, edited by Efremov (St. Petersburg: A. S. Suvorin, 1889);

Stikhotvoreniia A. I. Polezhaeva, edited by Arsenii I. Vvedensky (St. Petersburg: A. F. Marks, 1892);

Sobranie sochinenii s biografiei (Moscow: Tip. Elizavety Gerbek, 1894);

Stikhotvoreniia, edited by V. V. Baranov (Moscow: Academia, 1933);

Stikhotvoreniia, edited by Nikolai Fedorovich Bel'chikov (Leningrad: Sovetskii pisatel', 1937);

Izbrannye proizvedeniia. Stikhi 1826–1838 (Saransk: Mordovskoe gosudarstvennoe izdatel'stvo, 1938);

Polnoe sobranie stikhotvorenii, edited by Bel'chikov (Leningrad: Sovetskii pisatel', 1939);

Sochineniia, edited by V. I. Bez'iazychnyi (Moscow: Goslitizdat, 1955);

Stikhotvoreniia i poemy, edited by Baranov, second edition (Leningrad: Sovetskii pisatel', 1957);

Stikhotvoreniia (Saransk: Mordovskoe knizhnoe izdatel'stvo, 1977);

Stikhotvoreniia i poemy, edited by V. L. Skuratovsky (Moscow: Sovetskaia Rossiia, 1981);

Stikhotvoreniia i poemy, edited by V. A. Gadaev (Saransk: Mordovskoe knizhnoe izdatel'stvo, 1981);

Stikhotvoreniia i poemy, edited by V. S. Kiselev-Sergenin (Leningrad: Sovetskii pisatel', 1987);

Sochineniia, edited by V. N. Abrosimova (Moscow: Khudozhestvennaia literatura, 1988);

Stikhotvoreniia. Poemy i povesti v stikhakh. Perevody. Vospominaniia sovremennikov i kritika, edited by A. N. Versovin (Moscow: Pravda, 1990).

Aleksandr Polezhaev was one of the poets of the Pushkin school, and in his day his name was not the least among them. His writing career began shortly before the 1825 Decembrist uprising, and for his entire life he remained faithful to its memory. Polezhaev was a follower and successor of the Decembrist tradition; even during his lifetime his name was connected to the revolutionary circles of the post-Decembrist period, with his politically conscious work continuing from 1825 to 1838.

The poet wrote in the fearful years of Nicolaevian reaction following the Decembrist revolt, under conditions of constant oppression from the autocracy at a time when, according to Nikolai Platonovich Ogarev, society consisted of "an educated minority and an incorrigible manoriality . . . Pushkin grew up among the former, and among the latter: Polezhaev." This environment figured prominently in his life and work, promoting and supporting what Ogarev called "habits of indiscipline which did not allow him to develop his talent to a sufficient degree." Nevertheless, in contrast to the verses of many of his contemporaries, Polezhaev's work presents one of the sharpest and most talented reflections of the life and mood of Russia in the 1820s and 1830s.

Polezhaev continued the traditions of Aleksandr Pushkin and the Decembrists, but he also proved to be one of the earliest representatives of the revolutionary democratic poetry that flourished in the 1860s. He wrote many verses and songs that reveal him to have been an innovator in the realm of poetic forms.

The illegitimate son of Leontii Nikolaevich Struisky and the domestic serf girl Agrafena Ivanovna Fedorovaia, Aleksandr Ivanovich Polezhaev was born on 30 August 1804 at the main country seat of the Struisky family, in the village of Ruzaevka Insarskoe in Penza province. Struisky was a typical serf-owning gentleman of the age, born in 1783 and educated at home. In 1801 he had entered the Semenovsky Life Guard Regiment as a noncommissioned officer, mustering out in 1803 to settle in Ruzaevka. Soon after Aleksandr's birth, Agrafena was married to Ivan Ivanovich Polezhaev, the son of a merchant of Saransk; he adopted Aleksandr, giving the boy his patronymic and family name.

The Struiskys provided Agrafena a dowry so that Ivan Polezhaev would marry her, but soon they also found themselves purchasing a house for him in Saransk. In 1803 he left the mercantile industry and began to live on his wife's dowry and on the proceeds of a lease for part of the house, frequently showing up at the Struisky estate to demand support money for Aleksandr. In 1808 he vanished without a trace. His disappearance occasioned various rumors, but the circumstances of it remained obscure.

Agrafena and her children continued on at Saransk, but then she had only the lease monies, which proved insufficient for the support of the family. Aleksandr's father renewed his visits to Agrafena, and in 1810 he brought her and her family to the village of Pokryshkino. There she saw again what she had earlier realized: Struisky was a drunkard who seduced and beat his peasants. All this stress undermined her health, and on 16 July 1810 she died. Ivan Polezhaev's father, Ivan Fedorovich Polezhaev, wanted to bring Aleksandr home, but Struisky did not want to surrender either Agrafena's boy or her estate, and he engaged the old man in a lawsuit. As a result Aleksandr was placed under the wardship of Agrafena's sister, Anna, a cowherd.

In 1812 Aleksandr was reclassified up from the merchantry into the lower middle class, but his childhood was spent among the offspring of domestic serfs. He was educated alongside his brother Konstantin, another of Struisky and Agrafena's progeny. Struisky never engaged any tutors for his sons: their first teacher was a cobbler, Iakov Andreianov, who taught the boys to read, write, and cipher. Aleksandr's life at Pokryshkino was filled with painful impressions: he witnessed his father's orgies and the punishments meted out to the serfs; he also saw the peasants' heavy, involuntary labors.

In 1816 Struisky took Polezhaev to Moscow and settled at Vizar's private pension near the Moscow State Gymnasium. In 1819 Struisky was sent to Siberia because, in a fit of rage, he had beaten his bailiff, Vol'nov, to death. Thus left behind at the pension, Polezhaev lost the support of his father. An irregular expenditure for his studies was supplied by his relatives, including an uncle, his father's brother, Col. Aleksandr Nikolaevich Struisky.

In 1820, without having completed his course at the gymnasium, Polezhaev entered the literature program at Moscow University as a simple auditor because, not belonging to the gentry class, he was not allowed to be an official student. The institution played a decisive role in the education and formation of this poet, who had grown up in the depths of the provinces. Then the center of Russian education, Moscow University was where the best scholars of the day taught, and Polezhaev immediately plunged into its atmosphere. His pronounced character and tempestuous nature enabled him quickly to dominate in disputes with his fellow students, who were much given to idleness, amusement, and debauchery. These were strange times: on one hand the authorities suppressed the slightest sign of freethinking, and on the other they permitted complete moral dissipation. Polezhaev's social life developed in the context of his studies alongside students of middling income—for the most part, untitled men of various ranks who, because their fortunes were improved by education, might be called a "middle class." Even among these men, however, he secretly suffered on account of his illegitimate birth.

Following the news of his father's death in Siberia in 1823 Polezhaev went to St. Petersburg, where for several months he visited his uncle, the colonel. In 1825 Polezhaev was about to finish the university, but he failed to show up for the final examination, so his uncle terminated the already scanty support he was furnishing. In the spring of that year Polezhaev wrote the poem *Sashka,* in which he vividly, and possibly with some exaggeration, depicted his university escapades. The plan of the poem came to him in connection with the appearance in print of the beginning of Pushkin's novel in verse, *Evgeny Onegin* (1823–1831, published in full in 1833). Polezhaev's work describes the exploits of the students, but in addition much of the material incorporates political themes, eventually giving Nicholas I cause to see in the work "traces and last remnants" of Decembrism.

A great success that circulated widely in manuscript, *Sashka* touched upon many problems of the day: Polezhaev expressed criticisms of autocracy and the necessity of struggle with it; he also was concerned with questions of education in the conditions of a monarchic regime. Polezhaev depicted a new hero just beginning to appear as an actuality in society: the energetic commoner. The poem features a student who emerged from the merchantry, the prototype of whom was the author himself. Polezhaev describes the character of the hero: "His character traits: / Freedom in thought and deed, / No one can judge him / Either for cowardly subordination / Or for bigoted hypocrisy / But [he has] a thirst for obstinate liberty / And a lack of restraint of his passions." In general the entire poem bears an obviously autobiographical character. The author's name even appears in the text. In addition, Polezhaev did not think to keep it a secret, and many handwritten copies of the notebook with the poem were circulated among the young people. An incomplete version was published in *Russkaia potaennaia literatura XIX stoletiia* (Russian Secret Literature of the Nineteenth Century) in 1861, and the first definitive version appeared in the 1955 edition of his collected works.

In between student drinking bouts Polezhaev wrote more poems, and along with manuscripts of forbidden works of Kondratii Fedorovich Ryleev, he circulated his own. Some of these were published in journals, and his reputation began to grow. While still a student, he published a whole series of verses, both translated and original, in *Vestnik Evropy* (Herald of Europe), and in 1826 his translation of Alphonse de Lamartine's *L'homme* appeared in Mikhail Petrovich Pogodin's almanac, *Uraniia*. In Polezhaev's first works Sentimental and Romantic motifs predominate, with signs of imitation of Nikolai Mikhailovich Karamzin, Vasilii Andreevich Zhukovsky, and Konstantin Nikolaevich Batiushkov.

Polezhaev frequently appeared with his verses at public gatherings at the university, and on 18 February 1826, on the recommendation of the rector, Anton Antonovich Prokopovich-Antonsky, he was accepted into the *Obshchestvo liubitelei rossiiskoi slovesnosti* (Society of Lovers of Russian Literature) at Moscow University. There he read his translation of George Gordon, Lord Byron's 1807 poem "Oscar of Alva" and an extract from Lamartine's *La Mort de Socrate* (1823). At the rector's request Polezhaev wrote "Stikhi, proiznesennye pri vospominanii dnia osnovaniia Moskovskogo universiteta, 12 ianvaria 1826 g." (Verses, Declaimed on the Anniversary of the Founding of Moscow University, 12 January 1826) and "Genii" (Genius).

Soon after the execution of the Decembrists, Tsar Nicholas I arrived in Moscow in 1826 for his coronation. The tsar had been badly frightened by the revolt, and everywhere he sought out "the sedition," the source of which he considered to be Moscow University. The local colonel of the gendarmerie, Ivan Petrovich Bibikov, seeking to demonstrate his loyalty to the tsar, made a report on the university, and he gave Polezhaev's poem *Sashka* as one example of sedition at the institution. As a result, on the night of 28 July 1826 Polezhaev, who had at last completed his final examination, was taken from his bed and conducted to the Kremlin, where he was brought before the tsar.

This meeting was fateful for the poet—in essence, it determined his furthest destiny. Moreover, the conversation between Polezhaev and Tsar Nicholas demonstrated the poet's distinctiveness and the strength of his talent. It was described by Aleksandr Ivanovich Herzen in his memoir, *Byloe i dumy* (My Past and Thoughts, 1861–1867):

> One night, at three a.m., the Rector himself woke Polezhaev and ordered him to put on his uniform and present himself at the university, where the director of the pedagogical district was expected. He took him along without any explanation. The two went to the Minister of Education, who, in his turn, led Polezhaev into the tsar's palace. Notebook in hand, the tsar entered into conversation with the minister. Upon seeing Polezhaev he threw a nasty, searching look.
>
> "Did you," he asked, "really write these verses?"
>
> "It was I," answered Polezhaev.
>
> "Here," continued the sovereign, "here I give you a specimen of university education. I will show you what it is that young people study. Read this poem aloud," he added, turning to Polezhaev.

"I cannot," said Polezhaev.

"Read!" commanded the sovereign, raising his voice.

At first it was difficult for Polezhaev to read, but then, growing more and more inspired, he finished off loudly. During the especially harsh passages the tsar made signs to the minister, who covered his eyes in horror.

"What do you have to say?" Nicholas inquired upon the conclusion of the reading. "I intend to set a limit to this depravity and, all these, the traces and last remnants, I shall eradicate. How has he comported himself?"

Upon reflection, the minister did not know Polezhaev's record, but some sort of humanity awoke within him, and he answered: "Excellently, your highness."

"This report has saved you, but it is necessary that you be punished as an example to the others. Do you want to enter military service?"

Polezhaev stood mute.

"I offer you military service as a means of redeeming yourself. Is that what you want?"

"I must obey," Polezhaev replied.

The tsar approached Polezhaev and laid a hand on his shoulder, saying: "your fate depends upon you yourself, and should I forget you, you may write me," and with that *he kissed the poet on the forehead*. . . . Polezhaev was then conducted to a camp and enlisted in the ranks.

Nicholas thought that army service, which at that time was quite heavy (twenty-five years), would destroy the young man, but it happened that by his sentence he confirmed that Russia had a new poet in Polezhaev.

Polezhaev was made a noncommissioned officer in the Butyrskii Infantry Regiment, which was then stationed near Moscow but later moved to Tver' province. Polezhaev was also under strict surveillance. Thus began his almost twelve-year punishment of service in the army, which turned out to be the remainder of his life.

The army could not silence the poet, although it was uncommonly difficult for him to write. His relatives, including the uncle who had supported him at the university, completely turned away from him. Former friends also feared to maintain a relationship with him. Thus he felt himself to be alone and orphaned. According to Nikolai Aleksandrovich Dobroliubov, "From the young, debauched circle of his student comrades, Polezhaev fell into one which was yet more crude, more vicious and more ignorant, where they regarded him as a criminal and a scoundrel. He neither wanted to, nor was he able, to submit to that to which others submitted so easily; but they compelled him to submit, and so Polezhaev became embittered toward people, and toward fate."

Polezhaev's first work composed in the army was the 1826 verse "Vecherniaia zaria" (Sunset), published in *Galateia* in 1829, of which Belinsky wrote: "'Sunset,' one of the best pieces by Polezhaev . . . is a dirge for the whole life of the poet, but in it despair is dissolved into a quiet melancholy which, under the pressure and powerful strength of expression, of the usual qualities of his poetry, is especially striking." Yet, despite the motifs of "quiet melancholy," there are also those of "sweet revenge" on a cruel tsar.

Next Polezhaev wrote "Tsepi" (Fetters), published in *Severnoe siianie* (Northern Lights) in 1831, a poem in which the motifs of the struggle against absolutism and of vengeance on the tsar are even stronger than in the previous work. Polezhaev could not see the way to accomplish this vengeance, however, and the motifs of doom, fate, and fatal destiny that appeared to him are also present in the 1826 poem "Rok" (Fate).

In 1827 Polezhaev wrote the biting pamphlet *Chetyre natsii* (Four Nations), in which, depicting the tsar flogging his subjects with the knout while his accomplices, the priests, hold crosses in their hands, the poet waxes indignant that the peoples of Russia still endure this knout, and he speaks of the necessity of combating autocracy. This pamphlet is the earliest evidence of his transition from the idea of Decembrism to that of democratism. Polezhaev first read through *Chetyre natsii* as an improvisation at a dinner party at the home of his grandmother, Aleksandra Petrovna Struiskaia, in Ruzaevka. She was the only one of his relatives not alienated from the poet. After the death of her son, Leontii, she invited Polezhaev to Ruzaevka during his furloughs. There he encountered Leontii's servants, then just back from Siberia, and they told him of his father's life in the settlement there.

The first regimental performance report on Polezhaev sent to the general staff stressed his "good deportment," but it was not long before a second, dated 16 July 1827, informed headquarters that "noncommissioned officer Polezhaev, detailed to the staff training command, having departed quarters on 14 July for training, has vanished." Led to despair by unbearable regimentation, the poet had decided to flee from his unit to St. Petersburg, there to beg the tsar for mitigation of his sentence. While on the road, however, he realized the hopelessness of this action, and on the seventh day of his absence he returned to his regiment, where he reported on his intentions and his repentance. In accordance with "the imperial will," Polezhaev was bound over to a military court. During his absence without leave the authorities searched his billet and seized all his remaining manuscripts and letters, from

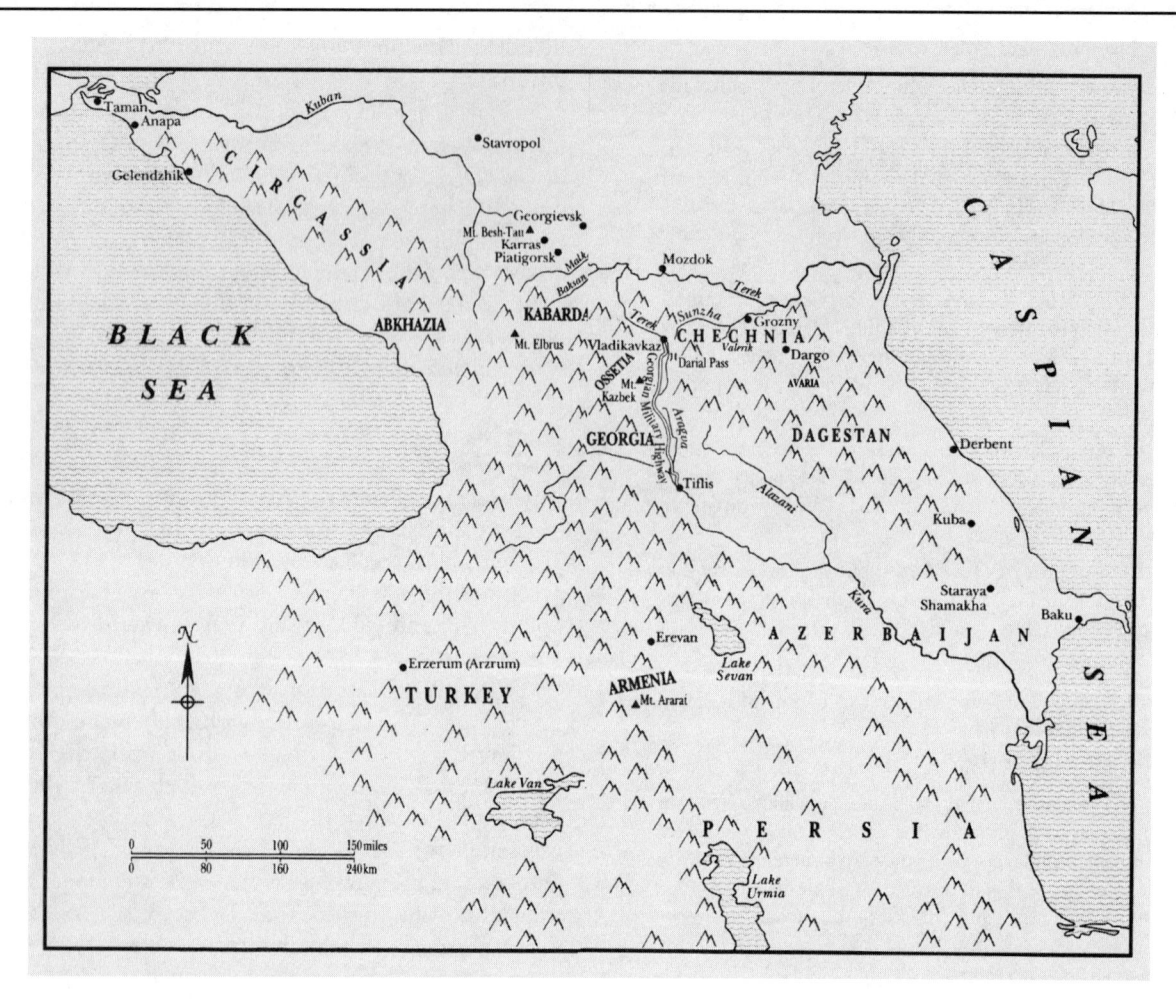

Map of the Caucasus, where Polezhaev spent his punitive military service (from Susan Layton, Russian Literature and Empire, *1994)*

which they learned of his family connection to the Struiskys. Of all the poems written before 1827, only the pamphlet *Chetyre natsii* has survived in manuscript. Friends and acquaintances made and circulated copies, and it was first published in *Bibliograficheskie zapiski* (Bibliographical Notes) in 1859.

The military court demanded that Polezhaev confess his "illegal" activities, and it sentenced him to deprivation of the noncommissioned rank that was his by virtue of the personal nobility earned at the university. Nicholas I considered even this punishment to be inadequate, however, and added: "the emperor confirms the loss of personal nobility without tour of duty," which meant that Polezhaev would lose all rights and any hope of attaining officer's rank or of ever getting out of the army.

Now a private, Polezhaev was subject to corporal discipline, and all might mock him. There was another unpropitious circumstance: within two months of his trial the authorities uncovered the secret society of the Kritsky brothers (Vasilii, Mikhail, and Petr Ivanovich), a group of students who actively hated the tsar. There was evidence that in 1826 Polezhaev had handed to one of the members of this group some propagandistic verses written by the Decembrists Ryleev and Aleksandr Aleksandrovich Bestuzhev (Marlinsky). It was well known that, like the suppressed verses of the Decembrists, his own also circulated from hand to hand.

The authorities did not forgive Polezhaev for participation in the secret society. Early in 1828 there were new accusations. A sergeant-major's constant carping made Polezhaev turn to drinking and to hurling obscenities at his superior. There was a new trial, and on the strength of the charges, Polezhaev was confined in Spassky Prison in Moscow, where he sat for a year in irons and contracted tuberculosis.

In prison in 1828 he wrote the poem "Arestant" (The Prisoner), dedicated to his friend Aleksandr Petrovich Lozovsky and published as "Aleksandrovna Petrovichu Lozovskomu" in *Galateia* the next year. This poem was the central work of Polezhaev's second creative period. In it he expressed the despair that haunted him in prison, where for an entire year he awaited sentence, fearing the terrible punishment of the gauntlet. He even thought of suicide. At that time his only comfort was his friendship with Lozovsky, a bureaucrat in the Moscow Charitable Section. As the many poems written to Lozovsky testify, this friendship remained sincere and lasting. Lozovsky gave Polezhaev moral support, insisting that he continue to write.

Little is yet known about Lozovsky. There are only a few details, such as the fact that in the 1830s he was a collegiate secretary in the service of the Moscow Department of the Senate. Polezhaev's friendship with Lozovsky lasted to the end of the poet's life. In a note on "Arestant" Polezhaev provided a warm characterization of his friend:

> . . . under the sun illuminating the immeasurable dark abyss . . . we sometimes meet something with the noble, comforting, ineradicable stamp of absurdity and insignificance . . . on my thorny road of life I met this nobility, this comfort, in the person of my true friend A. P. Lozovsky.
>
> He frequently laid the balsam of consolation upon my lips, which had been poisoned by the gall of life: he never abandoned me in the moment of sorrow. Perhaps someone will ask: who was this Lozovsky? Was he not a well-known patron? Oh no! He was more: he was a *mensch*.

Dreams of freedom tear through the mood of despair in "Arestant." In the poem one also glimpses a critical attitude toward the clergy. Moreover, the poet doubts the existence of God as creator of the universe; such an outlook was the result of Polezhaev's acquaintance with the philosophies of Russian and French materialists. The representatives of the protesting people also appear in the poem: the soldiers, with whom the poet feels solidarity. Also, there is an accurate description of prison. "Arestant" was the first realistic Russian work of a certain type: a terrifying and candid confession that reflects the poet's nerves stretched to the limit. The prison life depicted in the poem is in itself a symbol of the reaction under Nicholas.

While in prison in 1828, Polezhaev wrote works that will endure forever in Russian literature, including "Pesn' plennogo irokeza" (The Song of the Captive Iroquois), "Pesn' pogibaiushchego plovtsa" (The Song of the Lost Swimmer), "Osuzhdennyi" (The Convict), "Ozhestochennyi" (The Bitter One), and "Zhivoi mertvets" (The Living Corpse). As was the case with so many of Polezhaev's verses, these circulated among his friends in manuscript, and copies of some were picked up and published by journalists as early as 1829.

For his offenses the military court sentenced Polezhaev to run the gauntlet at the discretion of the tsar. Polezhaev later told Herzen of his despair: not counting on leniency, the poet decided upon suicide, which resolve he communicated to one old soldier whom he had befriended. Understanding the prisoner's despair, his friend brought him a bayonet, and handing it over, said through his tears: "I sharpened it myself." The sufferer was saved, however: the tsar altered the sentence, and Polezhaev was transferred into the Moscow Infantry Regiment. The poet was discharged from prison in December 1828, upon which occasion he wrote his superb poem "Providenie" (Providence): "I perished without consolation / My wicked genius / triumphed."

In the verses of this year, composed in prison, Polezhaev created the allegorical forms of the warrior: the "captive" and the one "destroyed" by "the enemy." It is clear that "the enemy" is the tsar. These verses reveal the "uncommon strength of feeling which testifies to the uncommon strength of his nature and his spirit," which Belinsky considered the distinctive feature of Polezhaev's character and poetry. The poems of this period include the 1828 "Eshche nechto" (Something More), in which Polezhaev depicts the oppressor of his freedom as a "monster" with "the black heart of a villain."

In the works of Polezhaev's second period appear features that are characteristic for him as well as for all of the "middle class": he looks on life with the eyes of one who has lost all social privileges. These features appear also in the poet's democratizing style. He thinks of the "happiness of millions" in "Kremlevskii sad" (The Kremlin Garden), written in 1828. Great intensity and passion characterize the rhythmic structure of the verses of this period. His lyric hero is a fighter against autocracy who identifies with the Decembrists, passionately longs to see freedom, and is persecuted by the powers-that-be but does not give in to them. The allegorical or Aesopian language that gave the poet the opportunity to write about his own time and place is an important innovation. The poem "Tabak" (Tobacco) might serve as an example. Among the circles of the leading activists of the 1820s, "tobacco" and "smoking tobacco" were terms signifying revolutionary activity. Three of Polezhaev's 1828 poems stand out above the others: "Na smert' Temiry" (On Temira's Death), "Renegat" (The Renegade), and "Sultan" (The Sultan). The first of these, a remembrance of the premature death of a beautiful woman, compares her to a wilted rose; the second and third include erotic motifs and recall his early verses.

Polezhaev was transferred to the Moscow Infantry Regiment on 2 January 1829, and later that month the unit was dispatched to the Caucasus, where war had broken out. Religious fanatics led by Kazi-Mulla (Gazi-Mukhamed) and Shamil and supported by England sought to join the Caucasus to Turkey; and in order to strengthen the Russian forces in the region, the government decided to send a few military detachments from the central provinces.

For about six months, weakened from his confinement in prison, Polezhaev marched to the front carrying heavy weapons and ammunition. He continued to write verses during halts, but conditions were extremely difficult. For the second half of 1829 the regiment was based at Goriachevodsk (Piatigorsk) and at the little village of Aleksandrovo. Among the poems Polezhaev wrote to convey his impressions of the campaign and of the Caucasian environment are "Zvezda" (The Star), "Kol'tso" (The Ring), "Buket" (The Bouquet), and "Naden'ke" (To Nadenka).

From 1829 through 1833 Polezhaev's life proceeded in the campaigns, expeditions, and battles of the war in the Caucasus. The fighting was frequently bitter; Polezhaev fulfilled his duty as much as anyone, and he even tried to distinguish himself, for he passionately desired to lighten his situation by rising from the lowest ranks. Service was entirely foreign to his nature, however; he was not cut out for the military life about which he wrote in his poems *Erpeli* and *Chir-Iurt,* both named for places where there was fighting. The monotony of soldiering, and especially the consciousness of his compulsory situation in the lowest ranks, depressed him—particularly because for the foreseeable future there was no prospect of escape. A sad and depressed mood permeates all his poems from this period. The natural beauty of the Caucasus, which served as inspiration for many poets, failed to excite Polezhaev, who could not forget for a moment the woes that had befallen him.

According to the testimony of eyewitnesses, Polezhaev was completely indifferent to danger but was constantly tormented by alienation from his comrades, which he probably exaggerated because his prolonged unhappiness resulted in a sickly, suspicious, and mistrustful character. In fact, he had no basis for reproaching himself for even one dishonorable act. As critic D. D. Riabinin wrote, he was "like many, simply sinful; like few, very unfortunate; but he was not morally a criminal." Not having the strength to wrestle with melancholia and spiritual solitude, Polezhaev's morale declined, and he turned to drink in order to forget and to stifle his despondency. Of his tour of duty in the Caucasus, Riabinin wrote: "He never came to know, in his whole lifetime, either the semblance of warm family relations or the true, sincere love of a woman . . . and all his eroticisms never went beyond the base incentive to which he had uncontrollably given way since his youth and which, early on, ruined his healthy powers." Belinsky also wrote that "The abundant power of a flaming nature drove him to adore a terrible idol: sensuality." Only friendship with Lozovsky provided some consolation for Polezhaev. All the verses dedicated to his friend display an unusual warmth, revealing the considerable significance this relationship had for Polezhaev. Lozovsky lived far away in Moscow, however, and the poet's own family was of no comfort at all.

In 1830 Russia was swept by a cholera epidemic that infected even the Moscow Regiment. Ensign S. A. Karpov, Polezhaev's brother-in-arms, wrote that "One of the first to fall ill was Polezhaev. Like the others, he was rubbed down with vinegar and spirits. When the masseur departed, Polezhaev drank the remaining spirits, and after a day or two he came to me in complete health and, with a laugh, described his illness and the means of curing it."

Because of the epidemic, the regiment spent almost the entire second half of 1830 in quarantine at the Groznyi fortress, and there Polezhaev wrote the poem *Erpeli*. Completely without romanticization, he described Caucasian military action. He considered that joining the peoples of the Caucasus to Russia was more progressive than uniting them with Turkey. The followers of Kazi-Mulla were smashed near the village of Erpeli, and Polezhaev took part in the fight. In the concluding part of the poem, Polezhaev writes of the fate of his works. As though predicting his own tragic end, the poet writes of the difficulties through which his works will have to pass in order to break through to posterity, but he does not believe that they will be lost without trace. Liubavsky, the regimental commander, was sympathetic to Polezhaev and presented him to Gen. Roman Fedorovich Rosen, who rewarded the poet with a prize of five rubles.

In December 1830 a new campaign and war began, and the Moscow Regiment joined an expedition against Kazi-Mulla under the command of Gen. Aleksei Aleksandrovich Vel'iaminov. Vel'iaminov was also sympathetic to Polezhaev and even defended him to the high command. As always, the poet took part in the expeditionary operations, and at the end of 1831 he was made a noncommissioned officer once again. In recommending this promotion Vel'iaminov wrote that "in the battles with the Chechens . . . [Polezhaev] was constantly in the exposed positions and he fought with remarkable bravery and presence of mind . . . I most humbly request the restoration of his noncommissioned officer rank and noble dignity." The return of his rank eased things somewhat for Polezhaev but did not free him from military service.

Kazi-Mulla undertook a new offensive in the autumn of 1831, capturing a few *auls* (mountain villages in the Caucasus) and taking up position in the settlement of Chir-Iurt, but this place was seized by Russian troops on 19 October. Polezhaev participated in these battles and to these events he dedicated his new poem, *Chir-Iurt*. He wrote to Lozovsky concerning its creation: "among the daily skirmishes and battles, . . . in the noise of the camp, under the roof of a lonely tent, in 12 and 15 degrees of frost, in the snow, I inflamed my imagination with the exploits of battles past, and in eleven days I wrote Chir-Iurt, which I am sending to you."

Chir-Iurt is a chronicle of the most prominent events in the Caucasus in the 1830s; in it, with greater force than in *Erpeli*, Polezhaev depicts the circumstances of the war in the Caucasus and describes the fantastic character of Kazi-Mulla, the "defiant falcon." The poet depicts the Russian soldier and his hard life with great sympathy, which the author also feels for the Chechens, and he dreams of a future in which wars will cease and all peoples may live in peace. Polezhaev curses the perpetrators of the war and writes about the fact that often simple soldiers understand the essence and meaning of events more profoundly and truly than representatives of high society. In Polezhaev's Caucasian poems the influences of Pushkin, especially his *Poltava* (1828), are noticeable. The poet not only recalls Pushkin's name several times but also underscores this connection by parallelisms of phraseology.

For almost three years after Polezhaev was sent to be a soldier none of his poetry was published. Then in 1829 his works began to appear under various pseudonyms and in several journals, for example, in Semen Egorovich Raich's *Galateia,* Nikolai Ivanovich Nadezhdin's *Teleskop* (Telescope), and Nikolai Alekseevich Polevoi's *Moskovskii telegraf* (Moscow Telegraph). The poet, however, scarcely received any money from the publishers for his printed verses. The censorship mechanism at that time was both severe and capricious; some of Polezhaev's poems were approved, and some were suppressed.

In Belinsky's words, "Polezhaev's verses circulated in notebooks, and journalists printed them without the permission of the author, who was far away; finally they even published them, without either his knowledge or his consent, on cheap paper, messily and crudely, indiscriminately and unselectively, the good with the mediocre, the beautiful with the ugly." The first collection came out in 1832, in Moscow, and in the same year appeared *Erpeli i Chir-Iurt. Dve poemy,* the writer Sergei Timofeevich Aksakov having been the censor who approved them for publication.

In spite of the difficulties of life in the Caucasus, the climate improved Polezhaev's health so much that his tuberculosis became less active. The influence of the south can also be clearly felt in the verses of this period, such as "Raskaianie" (Repentance), written in 1833.

For Polezhaev, however, opportunities for study and educated discourse were extremely limited, and he was tormented because it was all but impossible to obtain essential books and journals. Nevertheless, he did all that he could for his own education: he read everything that came his way, tried to approach cultivated people, and established connections with the exiled Decembrists of whom he was the heir and successor.

Descriptions of nature, which had not been included at all in earlier works, now appeared in Polezhaev's Caucasian creations. He accompanied the contemplation of the environment with philosophic musings in poems such as "More" (The Sea, 1832), "Vodopad" (The Waterfall, 1832), and "Raskaianie," poems that appeared not only in journals but also in his collections. He developed an interest in songs and romances that had occurred to him even in his youth in Saransk and Pokryshino. In the Caucasus he created many beautiful examples of musical lyrics in which he depicted laboring people of various nationalities and sang of their liberty and their thoughts of freedom. The influence of the verbal folk tradition is clearly discernible in these works, and along with it that of Pushkin, especially his poems "Uznik" (The Prisoner, 1822) and "Ne poi, krasavitsa, pri mne . . ." (Don't sing, beauty, in my presence . . . , 1828).

Polezhaev also wrote satire in these years: in both *Den' v Moskve* (A Day in Moscow) and *Kreditory* (The Creditors), which were included in his 1832 collection, he ridicules representatives of high society and the merchantry. The democratic inclinations of this period were most clearly reflected in his "Videnie Bruta" (Brutus's Vision), a poem of 1832–1833 in which he creates the figure of the intransigent republican. There are parallels in this work with that of Aleksandr Nikolaevich Radishchev, who was also an exile, although in Siberia, not in the Caucasus. Polezhaev sings of the patriotism of Brutus, who fought against the Roman dictators, and he also declares that rulers should represent the interests of the people.

In October 1832 Russian troops took the village of Gimry, which had been occupied by Shamil and Kazi-Mulla; the latter was killed in the attack, but Shamil managed to escape. This fight was Polezhaev's last Caucasian battle, for in the spring the Moscow Regiment returned to central Russia. Shortly before this move, Polezhaev was recommended for promotion to ensign, but "His Majesty's Pleasure" was not forthcoming, and he remained at noncommissioned rank.

The Moscow Regiment was quartered on the city of Kovrov in Vladimir province, and there the nongentry youth were fairly active politically. Their leader, Nikolai Iseevich Shaganov, a merchant's son, was a cultivated person for the times, and there were rumors

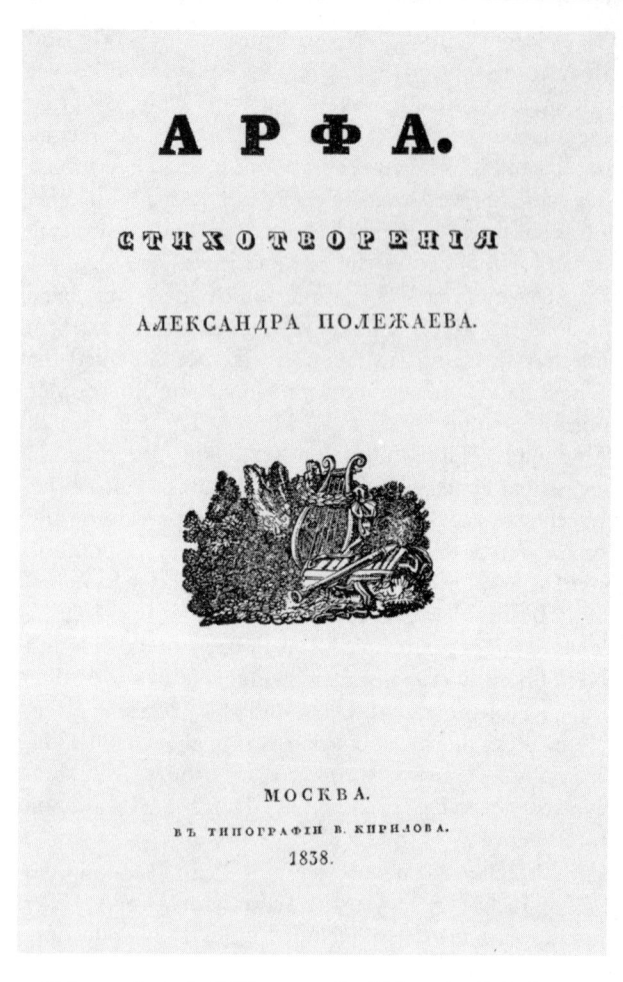

Title page for Arfa. Stikhotvoreniia Aleksandra Polezhaeva *(The Harp. Poems of Aleksandr Polezhaev), a posthumously published collection*

that he tried to organize a secret society in Kovrov. During his sojourn there, Polezhaev met with Shaganov and gave him several notebooks of his verses.

In the summer of 1833 Polezhaev returned with his regiment to Moscow, where he already enjoyed some popularity and where his suppressed poetry had circulated in manuscripts. There he met Herzen and Ogarev, the leaders of the revolutionary-minded youth, and these acquaintances soon turned to friendships. He read them his verses and described for them the war in the Caucasus and the soldier's life. Their closeness is revealed in Herzen's statement that he "had heard, several times, from the poet himself, the story of poor Polezhaev." Contact with Herzen, in its turn, must have had an eventual effect on Polezhaev's own political consciousness, evident in the poems of his last creative period.

In 1833 Polezhaev became acquainted with Vladimir Ignat'evich Sokolovsky, whose antigovernmental verses were recited in Herzen's and Ogarev's circle. Sokolovsky was also close to Polezhaev in his social and material circumstances. Another friendship dating from the Caucasus was with the poet Luk'ian Andreevich Iakubovich, one of the first to promote Polezhaev's verses, having published a critical article in *Severnaia pchela* (The Northern Bee) in 1832 welcoming the appearance of the first collected poems. Polezhaev also renewed his friendship with Fedor Alekseevich Koni, then serving as the last editor of the journal *Repertuar i Panteon* (Repertoire and Pantheon).

The military leadership was disturbed by Polezhaev's popularity and decided to send him out of Moscow. Therefore, on 1 September 1833 he was transferred to the Tarutinskii Jaeger Regiment, then stationed at Zaraisk in Riazan' province. Before his departure he visited Lozovsky, and he inscribed in his friend's album the poem "Imeninniku" (To One Whose Name-Day It Is). He also wrote "Ivan Velikii" (Ivan the Great) while in Moscow, dedicating it to the capital; and he prepared for publication *Kal'ian* (The Hookah), his second collection of poems.

"Gal'vanizm, ili poslanie k Zevesu" (Galvanism, or a Missive to Zeus), another poem written during his two-month stay in Moscow, was not published until 1933 in the journal *Zvezda* (Star). From this poem readers learn of yet another misfortune that had overtaken Polezhaev. In a note published with the poem he explains: "I wrote this humorous poem extemporaneously when I first felt the beneficial power of electricity, because a famous and experienced physician decided to try galvanic force on me, and by this means, after my long and relentless suffering, restored my hearing, which I had lost in consequence of a severe head-cold. I had been completely deaf for a year and a half and had given up hope of a cure, but within two months, galvanism . . . had restored my hearing." Polezhaev had fallen ill in the Caucasus, where there had been a severe frost in January and February 1832. This poem constitutes a hymn to science.

In Zaraisk, Polezhaev met up with Colonel Bibikov, who, seven years before, had written the report on sedition at Moscow University. Bibikov probably had not intended that the tsar would deal so cruelly with Polezhaev; he had simply wanted to excel at his duties. Therefore, accidentally meeting the author of three critically acclaimed volumes of poetry, Bibikov decided to redeem himself and somehow relieve the poet's situation. He obtained the permission of the regimental command to take Polezhaev along on a family visit to the village of Il'inskoe, near Moscow. In truth, Polezhaev did not suspect that he was the guest of the author of all his unhappiness.

In Il'inskoe, for the first time in many years, Polezhaev tasted something of freedom, happiness, and love. He managed to meet a girl, to love her passionately, and to experience a period of "ideal feeling." This girl's identity remained a matter of speculation for half a century, and the secret was not revealed until 1882, when the editors of the journal *Russkii arkhiv* received a letter written by the colonel's daughter, Ekaterina Ivanovna Bibikova. With profound sincerity, the letter describes the love story of Bibikova and Polezhaev. She writes:

> In 1834 we spent the summer in the village of Il'inskoe ... I was then very young, having just turned sixteen. ... My father departed to his estate in the steppes. ... At length he notified us that he would be home in a matter of days, bringing with him a noncommissioned officer for the purpose of training my younger brothers in the manual of arms preparatory to their entrance into the junker school. ... On the next day we gathered for tea. My brothers and their teachers arrived, and among these, the non-com. ... Suddenly I noticed something out of the ordinary. Father arose and assumed a rather solemn expression.
>
> "My heart," said father, turning to mother, "... children! I have deceived you all! May I introduce Aleksandr Ivanovich Polezhaev ..." Everyone immediately arose. ... All of us were brimming with tears. My gaze met that of Polezhaev, and it seemed to me that he was touched by our reception of him.

Polezhaev spent fifteen days in Il'inskoe, where he translated Victor Hugo and read verses, among them his "Koriolan" (Coriolanus). Bibikova's brothers, in her words, "all but idolized the poet." She was learning to draw, and she did a watercolor portrait of him that was later copied and widely used to illustrate his published works. Of his appearance, she writes: "Aleksandr Ivanovich was not good-looking as such. He was short and his features were irregular; but his whole unsightly appearance could brighten up in an instant, transformed by a single glance of his magical, flashing, big dark eyes."

Although Bibikov repeatedly inquired about Polezhaev's parents, the latter declined to answer, and so the Bibikovs learned nothing of his origins. At Il'inskoe, Polezhaev rested both physically and morally, as Bibikova describes:

> From dinner to midnight we, as a family, and Aleksandr Ivanovich with us, walked in the garden and among the charms of Il'inskoe's surroundings. ... We avidly listened to his tales. ... He told them simply, without boasting, without bombast ... and every word breathed truth and wit, and between the lines was to be heard so much inexpressible suffering, loss, and woe.

Polezhaev and Bibikova's love was mutual, but there could be no thought of marriage, because he was a soldier under surveillance and she was the daughter of a wealthy gentleman.

Perhaps to clear his own conscience, Bibikov decided to intercede for the poet and wrote a plea to Count Aleksandr Khristoforovich Benckendorff, the chief of the gendarmes, begging that Polezhaev be made an officer so that he might "return to his society and his literature." To this request Bibikov appended a poem, "Tainyi golos" (The Secret Voice), which he had elicited from Polezhaev, and to which Bibikov added a conclusion asking for clemency, since the poet, because he did not consider himself guilty of anything, categorically refused to ask forgiveness from the tsar. Having sent off his plea, however, Bibikov still forbade his daughter to consort with the suspect officer. She writes:

> The idyll continued for two weeks: the only fifteen pure, clear days in the whole life of the long-suffering poet! Father ... was implacable. ... Upon departure, [Polezhaev] gave me that book of Hugo from which he was always making translations. ... On a sheet tucked into it was written the poem 'Zachem khotite vy lishit'...' (Why do you want to deprive me. ..).

The poem was included in *Russkii arkhiv* in 1882.

Knowing of Polezhaev's poverty, Bibikov's children collected some money, and Bibikov completed the sum; he persuaded the poet to accept the gift only after great difficulty, for Polezhaev was proud and scrupulous. Polezhaev and Bibikova never met again. In her words, their love had been "the brief but total harmony of two souls. ... One's inner sufferings and torments remain forever buried with him, but in the awakened soul this harmony generates an aspiration to all that is really beautiful and also an insuperable defense against everything from the past." Out of his love for Bibikova, Polezhaev created the poems "Zachem khotite vy lishit'...," "Talanty vashi otsenit'" (To Value Your Talents, also published as "K E.....I.....B......i" in his 1838 collection), and "Grust'" (Melancholy). Belinsky called the last of these "a beautiful piece of music."

Soon a new woe befell Polezhaev: his friends Herzen and Ogarev were arrested on the charge of being "persons who in Moscow have sung satiric verses of an anti-governmental content." These two were sent into the provinces under police surveillance, but Sokolovsky, as well as Polezhaev's friend the artist Aleksei Vasil'evich Utkin, were incarcerated in the Schluesselburg Fortress. Utkin died in prison after two years, and Sokolovsky was sent to the Caucasus, where he also died. Polezhaev was gravely concerned over the fate of his friends. His mood following their arrest is reflected in the 1834 poem "Negodovanie" (Indignation).

His own life also did not improve. Although Bibikov's intercession in favor of Polezhaev's promotion was supported by Benckendorff, the tsar did not approve it, because the authorities still kept an 1829 secret dossier, titled "Concerning Moscow University and verses composed by the student Polezhaev," including the Bibikov report and Polezhaev's student poems.

There was one more event of 1834 that made a strong impression on Polezhaev: the Ruzaevka peasants settled scores with his uncle, Aleksandr Struisky, a gentleman known as "the terrifying master" owing to his cruel treatment of his serfs. There was in that year a great famine at Ruzaevka. The people demanded bread, but instead "they were punished with birch rods and placed under guard." Then Semen Kuratov, who had been Polezhaev's father's cook in Siberia, undertook vengeance on the master, and on 2 July 1834, upon meeting him in the fields, struck off his head with an axe, for which crime Kuratov was tortured and sent into Siberian exile.

In the autumn of that year the Tarutinsky Regiment was transferred to the Zhizdrinskii district of Kaluga province, and there Polezhaev wrote his verses "Selo Pechki" (The Village of Pechki) and "Nechto o dvukh brat'iakh kniaz'iakh L'vovykh" (Concerning the Two Brothers, the Princes L'vov). Life there was difficult, with frequent moves and hard labor. In 1835 Polezhaev wrote the poem "Opiat' nechto" (Something Again), which reflects the discontents of a soldier's life. In this poem he developed the tradition of the propaganda songs of the poet-Decembrists, coming forward in the name of the people. In these years the censorship continued to harass him: in 1835 his next collection of verses, *Razbitaia arfa* (The Broken Harp), was suppressed and later appeared with omissions, as *Arfa* (1838). Many individual poems were also suppressed as well as, in 1837, his collection *Chasy vyzdorovleniia* (Convalescent Hours), which eventually appeared in 1849. Lozovsky, to whom Polezhaev had entrusted some of his verses, waited until the poet's name did not elicit such a negative response from the authorities in order to get them published.

Polezhaev's tuberculosis flared up with new force, and his health began to fail. In November 1835 he wrote the poem "Proshchanie s zhizn'iu" (Farewell to Life), dedicated to Iakubovich, in which he says that he does not fear death and "can live and die without regret or fear." Of his life in these years Herzen writes: "Years and years went by; the inescapable, boring circumstances broke him. He could not become a police-poet and sing the praises of Nicholas, although this was the only way to be free of the rucksack. There was, however, another way which he preferred: he drank in order to forget. There is a frightening poem of his: 'K sivukhe' (To Spirits)."

Polezhaev's acquaintance, the officer V. I. Lents, recorded that "from 1836 on the poet became terribly ill. . . . Lively conversation provoked in him a strong, liquid coughing. The consumption had done its work." According to the testimony of witnesses, Polezhaev was incommunicative with persons he did not know well, but with friends he was quite talkative, read his own and others' works, and told interesting tales of his life in the Caucasus. In Lents's words, Polezhaev frequently said: "Why mope and go around with a gloomy countenance? This woefulness will not help." Similarly, he was too proud to put his mental grief on display. Despite his extreme poverty Polezhaev had no regard for money, and according to Lents, "money he either gave to those as poor as himself, or simply drank away."

Pushkin was killed in a duel in 1837, and on 2 March of that year Polezhaev wrote "Venok na grobe Pushkina" (A Wreath on Pushkin's Grave), which among those poems dedicated to Pushkin's memory ranks second in forcefulness only to Mikhail Iur'evich Lermontov's "Smert' poeta" (The Death of a Poet, 1837). In general, Polezhaev's and Lermontov's poetry have much in common: descriptions of the Caucasian wars, political inclinations, motifs of longing and pessimism, and similar poetic techniques. Lermontov even wrote a poem, *Sashka* (begun in 1835 but not finished), with the same title as one of Polezhaev's. Although Lermontov surpassed Polezhaev in many ways, the influence of the latter is indisputable.

In the spring of 1836 Polezhaev's health improved slightly. He received a short furlough, which he spent with his university comrade Vasilii Alekseevich Burtsev in the vicinity of Murom. Burtsev was a passionate hunter, and Polezhaev described the adventures of the local hunt club in his poem "Tsar' okhoty" (Tsar of the Hunt). He depicted himself in the poem as a rival to the "tsar of the hunt." Polezhaev's nickname among his friends was Dolgios (from *dolgii nos,* long nose), and he gave this name to his character. At first glance it might seem that the poem describes a conventional gentry hunt, but there are also political ideas expressed allegorically; in fact, the entire poem is filled with allegory. The image of the "tsar of the hunt" symbolizes the autocratic gentry structure of Russia. As a dying hunter observes in the poem, the Russian peasant, "a terrible giant," must throw off his oppression. "Tsar' okhoty" is one of the most profound and mature poems of Polezhaev's entire body of work. Generally, the deepest considerations of the role of the people in the fate of Russia are incorporated in the works of his last period. Similar musings are to be found in the 1834 poems "Koriolan" and "Negodovanie."

Following his return from Murom, Polezhaev's health sharply declined. In the fall of 1837, despairing of liberation from his unbearable military service, he willfully deserted the regiment and squandered all his ammunition on drink. When he was captured and returned to the regiment, his fellow soldiers beat him with birch rods. In the words of M. P. Perfil'ev, an eyewitness, "for a long time after the punishment they were pulling shards out of his back." On 26 September, following this ordeal, he was taken in serious condition to the Moscow military hospital. Only his closest friends called upon the dying poet. Not long before his death, Polezhaev wrote the poem "Chakhotka" (Consumption), addressed to Lozovsky. There is nothing sentimental about this poem; on the contrary, it treats death as something almost humorous. Polezhaev died on 16 January 1838. Shortly before the end he was promoted to the rank of ensign–the rank he had been denied so many times in his life.

According to Herzen, Polezhaev's friends had difficulty finding his body in order to inter it. Finally they located the poet's corpse in a cellar where "he had been rolled under others, and the rats had eaten off one of his feet." They dressed him in the officer's uniform that he had never worn in life; an unknown artist painted his portrait; and then they buried him in the Semenovsky cemetery. His friend Iakubovich took great but futile pains to obtain a monument for the grave. A year later Iakubovich was also dead. The grave remained without a marker, and in consequence, its location has been forgotten.

In the last years of his creative life Polezhaev was much occupied with translation. Nineteen of his translations have now been identified and published: sixteen from the French language, and three from the English. He translated the French poets Charles-François Panard, Lamartine, Jean-François-Casimir Delavigne, and Hugo; from the English he translated Ossian (James Macpherson) and Byron. In these translations he frequently departed from the originals, blotted out whole lines, or substituted ones of his own. The last translations, done in 1837, were devoted to Napoleon Bonaparte. Belinsky greatly valued Polezhaev's translations, calling them beautiful.

In all of Polezhaev's works the lyric confession of the poet is there, because his verses offer themselves as a genuinely human document. Devoid of refinement, Polezhaev's style is the simple and sincerely agitated poetic speech that found a response in the circles of the democratically minded youth. He was an innovator in the realm of poetic technique.

During the life of the poet, his verses were seldom published; nevertheless, the influence of his poetry on the culture of the nineteenth century was significant. For example, many Russian composers wrote romances based on his verses. On the text of "Sarafanchik" (Tunic Dress) alone there are romances composed by Aleksandr Nikolaevich Aliab'ev, Aleksandr L'vovich Gurilev, and Iurii Karlovich Arnold'. Polezhaev's influence has been felt even in the twentieth century. Valerii Iakovlevich Briusov was especially interested in his poetry, and Maksim Gorky quotes Polezhaev's verses in his own works. Polezhaev's name is even well known abroad. Thomas Mann remembers *Chetyre natsii* in his *Betrachtungen eines Unpolitischen* (1918; translated as *Reflections of a Nonpolitical Man*, 1983). The circumstances of his life prevented the poet from developing his talent to the utmost. Nevertheless, Polezhaev's body of work is greatly esteemed by historians of literature, and his verses are of interest even for the contemporary reader.

Letters:

"Pis'ma A. I. Polezhaeva k L. Ia. Iakubovichu. Fevral'– 8 Oktiabria 1836," edited by T. G. Dinesman, *Literaturnoe nasledstvo*, 60, book 1 (1934): 608–614.

Bibliographies:

V. V. Baranov, "Sud'ba literaturnogo nasledstva A. I. Polezhaeva (Obzor)," *Literaturnoe nasledstvo*, 15 (1934): 251–257;

Nikolai Leonidovich Vasil'ev, *A. I. Polezhaev: Bibliograficheskii ukazatel'* (Saransk: Mordovskii Gosudarstyennyi Universitet N. P. Ogareva, 1988).

Biographies:

D. D. Riabinin, "Aleksandr Polezhaev. (1807–1838). Biograficheskii ocherk," *Russkii arkhiv*, 1 (1881): 314–365;

P. Ustimovich, *A. I. Polezhaev. (Biograficheskii ocherk)* (Warsaw, 1888);

Ivan Dmitrievich Voronin, *Novye dannye o Polezhaeve*, edited by A. Bikhter (Saransk: MNIIIali, 1940);

Voronin, *A. I. Polezhaev: Zhizn' i tvorchestvo* (Saransk: Mordovskoe gosudarstvennoe izdatel'stvo, 1941; revised edition, 1954);

Voronin, *A. Polezhaev: Kritiko-biograficheskii ocherk* (Moscow: Goslitizdat, 1954);

A. M. Borshchagovsky, *Vosstan' iz t'my: Povest' o Polezhaeve* (Moscow: Politizdat, 1988).

References:

Nikolai Fedorovich Bel'chikov, "A. I. Polezhaev," *Literaturnaia ucheba*, no. 12 (1936): 52–70;

Vissarion Grigor'evich Belinsky, *Polnoe sobranie sochinenii*, volumes 3, 6 (Moscow: Akademiia nauk SSSR, 1953–1955), pp. 24–33, pp. 119–160;

Belinsky, *Izbrannye sochineniia*, volume 2 (Moscow, 1936);

V. I. Bez'iazychnyi, "Kavkaz v zhizni i tvorchestve A. I. Polezhaeva. (1829–1833)," *Izvestiia Groznenskogo instituta i muzeia kraevedeniia,* no. 2-3 (1950): 76-111;

Bez'iazychnyi, "A. I. Polezhaev. (1804–1838)," *Lektsii po istorii russkoi literatury XIX veka,* no. 1 (Moscow: Moskovskii universitet, 1951), pp. 244–263;

Ekaterina Ivanovna Bibikova, "Starushka iz stepi: Vstrecha s Polezhaevym (Pis'mo k izdateliu)," *Russkii arkhiv,* no. 6 (1882): 233–243;

E. A. Bobrov, "A. I. Polezhaev ka perevodchik," *Russkii filologicheskii vestnik,* 49, no. 1-2 (1903): 336–355;

Bobrov, "Etiudy o Polezhaeve," *Varshavskie universitetskie izvestiia,* nos. 4, 5 (1909); nos. 1, 2 (1913);

Bobrov, "Iz zhizni i poezii A. I. Polezhaeva," *Varshavskie universitetskie izvestiia,* no. 2 (1904): 1–40;

Bobrov, "O baironizme A. I. Polezhaeva," *Russkii filologicheskii vestnik,* no. 4 (1905): 294–309;

Bobrov, "Polezhaev ob A. S. Pushkine," *Pushkin i ego sovremenniki,* no. 5 (St. Petersburg: Akademiia nauk, 1907): 84–109;

V. A. D'iakov, "Pod sermiazhnoi bronei: Novye materialy o voennoi sluzhbe A. I. Polezaeva," *Russkaia literatura: Istoriko-Literaturnyi Zhurnal,* 2, no. 18: 158–168;

Nikolai Aleksandrovich Dobroliubov, *Polnoe sobranie sochinenii,* volumes 1, 4 (Leningrad: Khudozhestvennaia literatura, 1934–1941), pp. 277–281, 435–436, 542–544;

Efim Grigor'evich Etkind, *Stikhi i liudi* (Tenafly, N. J.: Hermitage, 1987);

A. I. Grushkin, "Polezhaev," *Istoriia russkoi literatury,* volume 6 (Moscow-Leningrad: Akademiia nauk SSSR, 1953), pp. 460–471;

Aleksandr Ivanovich Herzen, *Byloe i dumy* (Leningrad: Khudozhestvennaia literatura, 1946);

Herzen, *Sobranie sochinenii,* volume 8 (Moscow: AN SSSR, 1956), pp. 165–168;

Viacheslav Evgen'evich Iakushkin, "A. I. Polezhaev, ego zhizn' i poeziia," *Vestnik Evropy,* no. 6 (1897): 716–729;

Aleksandr Anatol'evich Iliushin, "Poeziia A. I. Polezhaeva: K 150-letiiu so dnia smerti," *Vestnik Moskovskogo Universiteta,* Seriia 9, Filologiia, no. 2 (March–April 1988): 21–27;

S. A. Karpov, "Vospominaniia," *Russkii arkhiv,* volume 6 (1881): 459–460;

Iurii Mikhailovich Lotman, "Neizvestnyi tekst stikhotvoreniia A. I. Polezhaeva 'Genii,'" *Voprosy literatury,* no. 2 (1957): 165–172;

K. Makarov, "Vospominaniia o poete A. I. Polezhaeve," *Istoricheskii vestnik,* nos. 4, 6 (1891): 110–115, 776;

Nikolai Platonovich Ogarev, *Stikhotvoreniia i poemy* (Leningrad: Sovetskii pisatel', 1937), pp. 327–329;

N. Popov, "Novye svideniia o Polezhave," *Russkii arkhiv,* 4 (1881): 471–474;

V. Potto, "Kuisubulinskaia ekspeditsiia," in his *Kavkazskaia voina v otdel'nykh ocherkakh, epizodakh, legendakh i biografiiakh,* volume 5, no. 2 (Tiflis, 1890), pp. 177–192;

Aleksandr Nikolaevich Pypin, "Zabytyi poet," *Vestnik Evropy,* no. 3 (1889): 153–197;

B. Sadovsky, *Russkaia kameia* (Moscow: Musaget, 1910), pp. 71–86;

D. Samoilov, "Razdaisia, vechnost', predo mnoi!" *Literaturnaia gazeta,* 5, 6;

N. M. Shanskii, "Stikhotvorenie 'K svoemu portretu' A. I. Polezhaeva," *Russii Iazyk v Shkole: Metodicheskii Zhurnal,* 1 (January–February 1988): 56–61;

Nikolai Leonidovich Vasil'ev, *A. I. Polezhaev i russkaia literatura* (Saransk: Izd-vo Mordovskogo universiteta, 1992);

Vasil'ev, *A. I. Polezhaev: Problemy mirovozzreniia, estetika, stilia i iazyka* (Saransk: Mordovskoe knizhnoe izdatel'stvo, 1987).

Papers:

Some of Aleksandr Ivanovich Polezhaev's papers are located at the Central State Archive of Literature and Art (RGALI), Moscow, and at the Institute of Russian Literature (Pushkin House) in St. Petersburg, particularly in the archives of Fedor Alekseevich Koni.

Aleksandr Sergeevich Pushkin
(26 May 1799 – 29 January 1837)

George J. Gutsche
University of Arizona

BOOKS: *Ruslan i Liudmila* (St. Petersburg, 1820);

Kavkazskii plennik, povest' (St. Petersburg: N. Grech, 1822); revised as *Kavkazskii plennik. Povest' Aleksandra Pushkina. Vtoroe ispravlennoe izdanie* (St. Petersburg: Tip. Departmenta Narodnogo Prosveshcheniia, 1828);

Bakhchisaraiskii fontan (Moscow: A. Semen, 1824);

Evgenii Onegin, roman v stikhakh, chapter 1 (St. Petersburg: Tip. Departmenta Narodnogo Prosveshcheniia, 1825); second, corrected edition (St. Petersburg, 1829); chapter 2 (Moscow, 1826); chapter 3 (St. Petersburg, 1827); chapters 4 and 5 (St. Petersburg, 1828); chapter 6 (St. Petersburg, 1828); chapter 7 (St. Petersburg, 1830); chapter 8 (St. Petersburg, 1832); first separate edition, *Evgenii Onegin, roman v stikhakh. Sochinenie Aleksandra Pushkina,* with "Otryvki iz puteshestviia Onegina" added (St. Petersburg: A. Smirdin, 1833);

Stikhotvorenii Aleksandra Pushkina (St. Petersburg: Tip. Departamenta Narodnogo Prosveshcheniia, 1826);

Tsygany (Pisano v 1824 godu) (Moscow: A. Semen, 1827);

Brat'ia razboiniki. A Pushkina (Pisano v 1822 godu) (Moscow: A. Semen, 1827);

Graf Nulin. Sochinenie Aleksandra Pushkina (St. Petersburg: Tip. Departamenta Narodnogo Prosveshcheniia, 1827);

Dve povesti v stikhakh (St. Petersburg, 1828); includes "Bal. Povest', sochinenie Evgeniia Baratynskogo" and "Graf Nulin. Sochinenie Aleksandra Pushkina";

Poltava, poema Aleksandra Pushkina (St. Petersburg: Tip. Departamenta Narodnogo Prosveshcheniia, 1829);

Stikhotvoreniia Aleksandra Pushkina, 4 volumes (St. Petersburg: Tip. Departamenta Narodnogo Prosveshcheniia, volumes 1–2, 1829; volume 3, 1832; volume 4, 1835);

Boris Godunov (St. Petersburg: Tip. Departamenta Narodnogo Prosveshcheniia, 1831);

Na vziatie Varshavy. Tri stikhotvoreniia V. Zhukovskogo i A. Pushkina (St. Petersburg: Voen. Tip., 1831); includes "Klevetnikam Rossii" and "Borodinskaia godovshchina";

Povesti pokoinogo Ivana Petrovicha Belkina, izdannye A. P. (St. Petersburg: Tip. Pliushra, 1831);

Stikhotvoreniia A. S. Pushkina. (Iz Severnykh tsvetov 1832 goda) (St. Petersburg, 1832); includes "Motsart i Sal'eri," "Delibash," "Anfologicheskie epigrammy," "Dorozhnye zhaloby," "Ekho," "Anchar, drevo iada," and "Besy";

Povesti, izdannye Aleksandrom Pushkinym (St. Petersburg: Kh. Gintse, 1834);

Istoriia pugachevskogo bunta. Chast' pervaia (St. Petersburg: Tip. II Otdeleniia sobstvennoi E. I. V. Kantseliariia, 1834);

Poemy i povesti Aleksandra Pushkina, 2 volumes (St. Petersburg: Voen. Tip., 1835).

Editions and Collections: *Romany i povesti Aleksandra Pushkina,* 2 volumes (St. Petersburg, 1837);

Sochineniia Aleksandra Pushkina, edited by Vasilii Andreevich Zhukovsky and others, 11 volumes (St. Petersburg: Tip. Ekspeditsii zagotovleniia gos. bumag, volumes 1–8, 1838; volumes 9–11, 1841);

Sochineniia Aleksandra Pushkina, 7 volumes (St. Petersburg: Pavel Vasil'evich Annenkov, 1855–1857);

Sochineniia (St. Petersburg, Petrograd & Leningrad: AN SSSR, 1899–1916, 1928–1929), volumes 1–4, 9, 11;

Pushkin [Sochineniia], edited by Semen Afanas'evich Vengerov, 6 volumes (St. Petersburg & Petrograd: Brockhaus-Efron, 1907–1915);

Dnevnik Pushkina, 1833–35, edited by Boris L'vovich Modzalevsky (Moscow & Petrograd: GIZ, 1923);

Dnevnik Pushkina, 1833–35, edited by Vladimir Fedorovich Savodnik and Mikhail Nestorovich Speransky (Moscow & Petrograd: GIZ, 1923);

Polnoe sobranie sochinenii, edited by Marislav Aleksandrovich Tsiavlovsky and Iulian Grigor'evich Oksman, 6 volumes (Moscow-Leningrad: Academia-Goslitizdat, 1936–1938);

Polnoe sobranie sochinenii, edited by Vladimir Dmitrievich Bonch-Bruevich and others, 17 volumes in 21 (Moscow: AN SSSR, 1937–1959);

Polnoe sobranie sochinenii, edited by Boris Viktorovich Tomashevsky, 10 volumes (Moscow-Leningrad: AN SSSR, 1949);

Sobranie sochinenii, edited by Dmitrii Dmitrievich Blagoi and others, 10 volumes (Moscow, 1959–1962);

Dnevniki. Avtobiograficheskaia proza (Moscow: Sovetskaia Rossiia, 1989);

Stikhotvoreniia litseiskikh let 1813–1817, edited by Vadim Erazmovich Vatsuro (St. Petersburg: Nauka, 1994);

Polnoe sobranie sochinenii, edited by Vatsuro and others, 11 volumes (St. Petersburg: Voskresen'e, 1994–).

Editions in English: *The Bakhchesarian Fountain,* translated by William D. Lewis (Philadelphia: C. Sherman, 1849);

Eugene Onéguine, translated by Henry Spalding (London: Macmillan, 1881);

A Collection of Short Lyrics by Pushkin, translated by Mary Kramer Grey (Boston, 1888);

Poems by Alexander Pushkin, translated by Ivan Panin (Boston: Cupples & Hurd, 1888);

The Prose Tales of A. Poushkin, translated by T. Keane (London: G. Bell, 1915);

Boris Godunov, translated by Alfred Hayes (New York & London: Dutton / Kegan Paul, Trench, Trübner, 1918);

Gabriliad, translated by Max Eastman (Paris, 1927); republished as *Gabriel, a Poem in One Song* (New York: Covici-Friede, 1929);

"The Captain's Daughter" and Other Tales, translated by Natalie Duddington (London & New York: Dent/Dutton, 1933);

"The Captain's Daughter" and Other Stories, translated by Duddington and T. Keane (New York: Dutton, 1935);

Verse from Pushkin and Others, translated by Oliver Elton (London: E. Arnold, 1935);

The Russian Wonderland, translated by Boris Brasol (New York & London: Williams & Norgate, 1936);

The Poems, Prose and Plays of Pushkin, translated by Avrahm Yarmolinsky (New York: Random House, 1936);

Eugene Onegin, translated by Dorothy Prall Radin and George Z. Patrick (Berkeley: University of California Press, 1937);

Evgeny Onegin, translated by Oliver Elton (London: Pushkin Press, 1939);

The Golden Cockerel, translated by Edmund Dulac (New York: Limited Editions Club, 1950);

Boris Godunov, translated by Philip L. Barbour (New York: Columbia Slavic Studies, 1953);

Evgenij Onegin, a Novel in Verse, translated by Dmitri Čiževsky (Cambridge, Mass.: Harvard University Press, 1953);

Dubrovsky, translated by Ivy Litvinova (Moscow: Foreign Languages Publishing House, 1954);

The Queen of Spades; The Negro of Peter the Great; Dubrovsky; The Captain's Daughter, translated by Rosemary Edmonds (London: Neville Spearman, 1958);

"The Queen of Spades" and Other Tales, translated by Ivy and Tatiana Litvinov (New York: New American Library, 1961);

Pushkin: A Laurel Reader, translated by Ernest J. Simmons (New York, 1961);

Eugene Onegin, translated by Walter Arndt (Ann Arbor, Mich.: Ardis, 1963; revised, 1992);

Pushkin, translated by John Fennell (Baltimore: Penguin, 1964);

Eugene Onegin, translated by Eugene Kayden (Yellow Springs, Ohio: Antioch, 1964);

Eugene Onegin, revised and edited by Vladimir Nabokov, 4 volumes (Princeton, N.J.: Princeton University Press, 1964);

The Little Tragedies, translated by Kayden (Yellow Springs, Ohio: Antioch, 1965);

The Complete Prose Tales of Aleksander Sergeyevitch Pushkin, translated by Gillon R. Aitken (New York: Norton, 1966);

The Critical Prose of Aleksander Pushkin with Critical Essays by Four Russian Romantic Poets, translated by Carl R. Proffer (Bloomington: Indiana University Press, 1969);

The Golden Cockerel and Other Stories, translated by James Reeve (London & New York, 1969);

The Queen of Spades, The Captain's Daughter, translated by Aitken (London, 1970);

Pushkin on Literature, translated by Tatiana Wolff (New York: Barnes & Noble, 1971);

Pushkin Threefold, translated by Walter Arndt (New York: Dutton, 1972);

Ruslan and Liudmila, translated by Arndt (Ann Arbor, Mich.: Ardis, 1974);

A Journey to Arzrum, translated by Birgitta Ingemanson (Ann Arbor, Mich.: Ardis, 1974);

Pushkin: Three Comic Poems, translated by William E. Harkins (Ann Arbor, Mich.: Ardis, 1977); includes *Gavriiliada, Count Nulin, Little House in Kolomna;*

Eugene Onegin, translated by Charles Johnston (New York: Viking, 1978);

Pushkin's Fairy Tales, translated by Janet Dalley (London: Barrie & Jenkins, 1978);

The Bronze Horseman; Selected Poems of Aleksander Pushkin, translated by D. M. Thomas (New York: Viking, 1982);

Mozart and Salieri: The Little Tragedies, translated by Antony Wood (London: Angel Books, 1983);

The Complete Prose Fiction of Aleksander Pushkin, translated by Paul Debreczeny (Stanford, Cal.: Stanford University Press, 1983);

The History of Pugachev, translated by Earl Sampson (Ann Arbor, Mich.: Ardis, 1983);

Aleksander Pushkin: Collected Narrative and Lyrical Poetry, translated by Walter Arndt (Ann Arbor, Mich.: Ardis, 1984);

Epigrams and Satirical Verse, translated by Cynthia Whittaker (Ann Arbor, Mich.: Ardis, 1984);

Eugene Onegin, translated by James E. Falen (Carbondale: Southern Illinois University Press, 1990);

The Tale of Tsar Saltan, translated by Pauline Hejl (New York: Dial, 1996);

Tales of the Late Ivan Petrovich Belkin; The Queen of Spades; The Captain's Daughter; Peter the Great's Blackamoor, translated by Alan Myers and Andrew Kahn (Oxford & New York: Oxford University Press, 1997).

OTHER: *Severnye tsvety na 1832 god,* edited by Pushkin (St. Petersburg: Tip. Departamenta vneshnei torgovli, 1831);

Pushkin in 1822 (engraving by E. I. Geitman)

Vil'gel'm Karlovich Kiukhel'beker, *Izhorskii, misteriia,* edited by Pushkin and published anonymously (St. Petersburg: Tip. III Otdeleniia sobstvennoi E. I. V. Kantseliarii, 1835);

Sovremennik, literaturnyi zhurnal, izdavaemyi Aleksandrom Pushkinym, volumes 1–4, edited by Pushkin (St. Petersburg, 1836);

Vastola, ili zhelaniia. Povest' v stikhakh, sochinenie Vilanda. V trekh chastiakh, translated by Efim Petrovich Liutsenko (St. Petersburg: Tip. Departamenta vneshnei torgovli, 1836);

Kiukhel'beker, *Russkii Dekameron 1831 goda,* edited by Pushkin and published anonymously (St. Petersburg, 1836);

Sovremennik, literaturnyi zhurnal A. S. Pushkina. Izdannyi po smerti ego Kn. P. A. Viazemskim, V. A. Zhukovskim, A. A. Kraevskim, Kn. V. F. Odoevskim i P. A. Pletnevym, volume 5 (St. Petersburg, 1837).

Aleksandr Pushkin continues to exert an enormous influence on Russian culture and literature more than a century and a half after his death. The impact he has made bears witness to the enormous scope of his talent as well as its continuing appeal to succeeding generations. His importance is not to literature alone.

Almost every Russian composer of note and several European ones have some work based on one of Pushkin's writings. Even Pushkin's unfinished works (such as "Dubrovsky," which was made into a play; *Motsart i Sal'eri,* which was made into the motion picture *Amadeus*) have found expression in other forms. Long genres and short ones all illustrate his genius—lyrics of all kinds (odes, elegies, poetic epistles, epigrams, songs), narrative forms in verse and prose (novels, verse tales, short stories, dramas), and even his literary criticism and letters—have earned high praise. His writings and the mythology that they and his persona have engendered hold a seminal and intrinsic significance.

As a recognized literary genius with major writings over a period spanning the 1820s and 1830s (until his death in a duel in early 1837), Pushkin has had a profound influence on the nature and content of Russian Romanticism. Nonetheless, assessing his contribution and relationship to Romanticism remains problematic, entailing the usual considerations of definition and emphasis. Even though his writings relate to all of the major themes of European Romantic writers—highlighting the role of the poet; exalting freedom from social and cultural restrictions; showing a new understanding of emotion; exhibiting irony, generic diversity, and an interest in folk literature and history; and urging political activism and opposition to the state—Pushkin remained dedicated to such Neoclassical virtues as clarity, reasonableness, common sense, and moderation, rarely yielding to the extremes in emotion or self-indulgence often associated with Romantic poetry.

Pushkin's literary reputation was late in establishing itself in the West, although shortly after his death some European writers recognized his value. Even today, though his place at the head of the Russian literary pantheon remains unchallenged, not all are convinced that he has the universal stature of a Johann Wolfgang von Goethe or a William Shakespeare. His stylistic qualities are muted in English translation: the conciseness, terseness, and economy of expression used in presenting plot and suggesting psychology work against him when compared to the more explicit and deliberate psychological and dramatic narratives of a Fyodor Dostoyevsky or a Leo Tolstoy. That seemingly deliberate lack of flashiness of his narratives in verse and in prose (many of which were adapted from Western models but shaped unusually), the subtlety, delicacy, and even humor of his evocation of a wide range of human feelings and presentation of human dilemmas, and the suggestive and spare characterization—all these can affect readers as rather flat and unexceptional. There is no striking imagery, no obvious passion borne in moral commitment that has come to be associated with the great Russian novelists of the second half of the nineteenth century.

Much, in fact, has been made of Pushkin's negative capability: his refusal to present in dramatic fashion the "eternal" questions and answers to them. This generalization perhaps deserves refinement and more discussion, for really Pushkin presents no simple solutions to moral dilemmas, mysterious happenings, or historical and political controversies. To say, however, that he accepted the world in all of its multiplicity (his works superficially give that impression) is overstatement. At the same time the dilemma pays tribute to the subtlety and power of his pen to evoke and suggest. The same evocativeness and subtlety account for why his works (as those of any great writer) leave themselves open to a wide variety of approaches and temperaments: everyone has his or her own Pushkin, as indeed the critics Valerii Iakovlevich Briusov, Marina Tsvetaeva, and Anna Andreevna Akhmatova have made clear.

Aleksandr Sergeevich Pushkin was born on 26 May 1799 into a noble family with a pedigree extending for more than six hundred years. Various relatives had played roles in major historical events of Russia. His black heritage extended from his mother's side: she was a granddaughter of Hannibal, an Abyssinian prince who became a favorite of Peter I. At the time of Pushkin's birth, however, his family no longer enjoyed the power or prestige it had once held. His frequent references to his relatives in his letters and his spirited defense of his heritage in several polemical poems of the 1830s reveal that Pushkin was all too well aware of the contrast between the lack of status and influence of the Pushkins in the early nineteenth century and their earlier leading role in historical events.

Pushkin's education came by way of tutors and his father's extensive collection of books (mostly French), to which the boy had relatively free access. Building on this foundation, Pushkin at the age of twelve began his formal schooling at Alexander I's new school for children of the nobility, the Tsarskoe Selo Lyceum, not far from St. Petersburg. His application accepted, Pushkin became part of the first class of the Lyceum in 1811. Designed as a selective and prestigious institution for the sons of the privileged, the Lyceum was intended to turn young males into government officials and to provide them with opportunities for serving the state and creating brilliant futures for themselves. Pushkin accomplished the latter, but hardly in the expected way.

The Lyceum itself was situated in a wing of the palace at Tsarskoe Selo (renamed as the city Pushkin). At the Lyceum, Pushkin achieved his first successes as a poet: participation in student literary "publications"; a moving reading (in 1815) of one of his poems, "Vospominaniia v Tsarskom sele" (Recollections at Tsarskoe Selo) in the presence (and to the delight) of the leading poet of the Russian Neoclassical age, Gavriil Romanovich Derzhavin; publication of his first verses; and participation in the literary society Arzamas, whose members—established and much older literary figures—welcomed him with enthusiasm. Through Arzamas, Pushkin developed personal and later professional alliances with older, influential poets who would nourish his talent and protect him throughout his life. From this network, three were particularly close: the aristocratic writers Vasilii Andreevich Zhukovsky, Konstantin Nikolaevich Batiushkov, and Prince Petr Andreevich Viazemsky.

They were mentors and, in the case of Zhukovsky and Viazemsky, lifelong friends. Of course, they all were products of the salon tradition that inspired and sustained the young Pushkin, providing for him the same sort of stimulating milieu in which they themselves had flourished. Pushkin's early years were spent at the center of a confluence of forces extending from eighteenth-century (and earlier) French poetry and Russian Neoclassical and pre-Romantic poetry. All these forces combined and left their mark in subtle and not-so-subtle ways during his formative years on a wide variety of poems—mostly shorter, generically diverse, and light ones. Elegies, poetic songs, and poetic epistles occupied a prominent place. In this highly favorable atmosphere of camaraderie, books, literary and personal experiences, and occasional (but significant) contacts with leading literary figures of the day, Pushkin produced much of value; in fact, he returned to many of his earlier poems and reworked them for publication in his first collection of poetry in 1826.

After his graduation in 1817 Pushkin passionately immersed himself in the social life of St. Petersburg, succumbing to all of the delights in the capital: attending the opera and the theater, gambling, drinking, and pursuing women. These enticements were irresistible to the eighteen-year-old Pushkin, who after virtually monastic confinement in the Lyceum could now live a carefree life. Now he could associate with well-traveled military men, many of whom had taken part in the Napoleonic campaigns of 1805 to 1812. These young officers were fond of discussing political systems and their suitability for conditions in contemporary Russia. Pushkin adopted quite easily the fashionable liberalism of these circles. He did so, however, with an imprudent passion and outspokenness, expressing his views in poetry that he could not publish. What he gained in liberal credentials he lost in official standing. Such widely circulated poems (and unpublished, except with major changes) as his odic "Vol'nost'" (Liberty), written in 1817, and "Kinzhal" (The Dagger), written in 1821; the generically

Abraham Petrovich Hannibal, Pushkin's maternal grandfather, 1790 (portrait by an unknown artist; from Henri Troyat, Pushkin, *1970)*

anomalous—elegiac and odic—"Derevnia" (The Village), written in 1819 and published in 1825 under the title "Odinochestvo" (Solitude); and "Skazki. Noel" (Fairy Tales. A Noel), written in 1818, made bold statements about the rule of law and the limits of autocracy. "Vol'nost'," for example, is quite presumptuous in its concluding advice to "tsars":

I dnes' uchites', o tsari:
Ni nakazan'ia ni nagrady
Ni krov temnits, ni altari
Ne vernye dlia vas ogrady.
Sklonites' pervye glavoi
Pod sen' nadezhnuiu zakona,
I stanut vechnoi strazhei trona
Narodov vol'nost' i pokoi.

(And from now on learn, oh, tsars:
That neither punishment nor rewards,
Nor the covers of dungeons, nor altars
Are true protection for you.
Bow your heads first
Under the reliable shade of the Law
And liberty and peace will become
The eternal guard of the throne.)

Pushkin also wrote biting epigrams directed at highly placed government officials of the day, including Alexander I and advisers such as Count Aleksei Andreevich Arakcheev. In general, Pushkin earned the reputation of a talented but intemperate youth and a political hothead.

But political poetry was not his only interest. In this same turbulent time period, from 1817 to 1820, he was writing his first major verse narrative, *Ruslan i Liudmila* (1820), a mock epic in iambic tetrameter verse with fairy-tale elements and a story line loosely linked with Kievan Rus's times. Woven among many improbable events (told with a delightful verve and lightness) is a tale of a bride magically taken from her spouse on their wedding night and transported to a magic realm by a wizard who holds her captive. Her husband, Ruslan, and his rivals seek her, eventually find her, and return her to her father, Vladimir; ultimately Ruslan, whom one of the rivals had slain earlier in the narrative, magically is restored to life and reclaims her. The poem made a strong impression on the reading public upon its publication and generated several literary controversies over its genre, language, tone, and obvious literary brilliance. Many critics noted its buoyancy, surprising twists, and mixed generic heritage of elements so different they just barely hung together. Although critics found fault with its lack of seriousness—its bizarre characters and devices, including a magic sword and hat, and a talking giant head and its sibling, the bald and bearded villain Chernomor—the surface is deceptive. The bouncy lines of the narrative somehow mute the disturbing themes of kidnapping, betrayal, disappointment, defeat, violence, sex, and death—death overcome and lovers reunited only with the help of magical resurrecting waters.

Some have pointed to this poem as one of the crucial Romantic episodes in Russian cultural history. With its bending of genres and its innovative language, the poem can easily be seen as disrupting literary expectations of the Neoclassical and pre-Romantic age. On the other hand, the mock epic is not a Romantic genre, and the defenders of the poem were quick to point to the distinguished heritage of this genre.

Pushkin was not in St. Petersburg long enough to experience the popular success of his poem, for his all-too-vocal expression of his political views had drawn officials' attention. The governor general interrogated him and saw to it that he was transferred, or "exiled" in an administrative sense. Alexander I apparently had a more serious exile in mind—Solovki or Siberia—but Pushkin's influential protectors persuaded Alexander to settle on the milder punishment. When graduated from the Lyceum, Pushkin had almost automatically acquired official employment in the Collegium of Foreign Affairs, and it was through the collegium that he received his transfer-exile. His "sentence" was to serve in the southern reaches of the empire under the supervision of General-Lieutenant Ivan Nikitich Inzov, administrative head of the Committee on Foreign Residents/Migrants of the southern region of Russia.

The first part of Pushkin's exile consisted of the time under Inzov in Bessarabia (1820–1823), primarily in the city of Kishinev (capital of contemporary Moldova). Inzov has become known as benevolent with respect to his charge, tolerating excesses as normal expressions of youth and giving the poet permission to travel relatively freely, as long as he was properly chaperoned. Within this period Pushkin made several excursions, most important among them a trip with the family of Gen. Nikolai Nikolaevich Raevsky to the Caucasus and Crimea. Members of that family played an important and complex role in Pushkin's life and works. The older son, Aleksandr Nikolaevich, though never a close friend, exerted a strong political and philosophical influence on Pushkin with his worldly cynicism and political liberalism. Such poems as "Demon" and "Angel" (1824), have been associated with Aleksandr Raevsky. Aleksandr's younger brother, Nikolai, became a close friend to whom Pushkin dedicated several important literary works, such as the narrative verse tale *Kavkazskii plennik, povest'* (Prisoner of the Caucasus, written in 1820 and published in 1822) and the historical elegy "Andrei Shen'e" (André Chénier, written in 1825 and published in a censored version in 1826). The Raevskys's daughters also provided stimulation for the young poet. He befriended and discreetly dedicated verses to most of them—Ekaterina, Elena, Maria, and Sof'ia. A major part of Pushkiniana, in fact, consists of speculation and argumentation relating to Pushkin's amatory history and the biographical links between his loves and his love poetry. Maria Raevskaia has often been the focus of such speculation.

Pushkin first met the Raevsky family in May 1820 in Ekaterinoslav, the first city of his exile. In June he went with them to Caucasus mineral waters and then in August and September made with them a brief excursion to the Crimea. In November he saw members of the family again at Kamenka (the estate of Raevsky family relatives, the Davydovs), and early in 1821 he saw them in Kiev and in Kishinev.

The short but stimulating trips to the Caucasus and Crimea ended with Pushkin's return to Kishinev, where he spent the next three years, with many sojourns to the nearby Kamenka estate. He visited there not just for social reasons—attractive women, champagne, cards, and conversation—but also for the intense political discussions. He came into contact with political liberals, including the Davydov brothers Aleksandr and

Pushkin's drawing of the Lycée at Tsarskoe Selo, where he and many other young nobles attended school, in the manuscript for the eighth canto of Evgeny Onegin *(from David Magarshack,* Pushkin: A Biography, *1967)*

Vasilii L'vovich, who were active in the *Iuzhnoe Obshchestvo* (Southern Society), a branch of the Decembrists (a loosely organized group of aristocrats who planned and unsuccessfully carried out a revolt against the autocracy in December 1825).

Pushkin's creative output for his three years or so in exile to this point consisted of many lyrics, much less derivative of his French and Russian mentors than those of the Lyceum period, and several narrative poems. Many of the lyric poems relate to his amatory experiences and feelings. These include "Redeet oblakov letuchaia griada" (The fleeting bank of clouds scatter, written in 1820), "Tavrida" (Tauris, written in 1822), "Nenastnyi den' potukh" (The gloomy day has passed away, written in 1824), and "Buria" (The Storm, written in 1825)–all linked by some commentators with Mariia Nikolaevna Raevskaia, who later married the Decembrist Sergei Grigor'evich Volkonsky and went with him to Siberia, where he was exiled following the ill-fated Decembrist revolt. She also came to be associated with post-exile lyrics such as "Ne poi, krasavitsa, pri mne . . . " (Don't sing, my beauty, in my presence . . . , written in 1828) and "Na kholmax Gruzii" (On the Georgian Hills, written in 1829) and the tales *Bakhchisaraiskii fontan* (Fountain of Bakhchisarai, written in 1821–1823 and published in 1824) and *Poltava* (written in 1828 and published in 1829).

The narrative poems of the exile period have been called Byronic verse tales because of their indebtedness to the poetry of George Gordon, Lord Byron, whose works (in French translation) Pushkin had become acquainted with in his travels with the Raevskys in the summer of 1820. The early tales *Kavkazskii plennik* and *Bakhchisaraiskii fontan,* published separately in St. Petersburg and in Moscow, became critical and financial successes. A third Byronic verse tale, *Razboiniki* (The Robbers, written in 1821–1822) was unfinished, although part of it was published with popular success.

The tales of these years represent Pushkin at his most Byronic and, in at least one important sense, Romantic, although his tales differ in many ways from Byron's Oriental verse tales. First of all, Pushkin usually includes different perspectives in his verse tales, typically in the epilogue. These perspectives often contrast with the tone of the narrative and thereby raise questions regarding the artistic unity of the whole. In *Kavkazskii plennik* a Russian soldier, captured by a Caucasian mountain tribe, befriends a native woman who falls in love with him. Willingly accepting her help in escaping, he swims across a river to freedom; disconsolate because he could not love her, she throws herself into the river and drowns. Pushkin barely hints at motivation, and the hero's past life remains mysterious. The epilogue, seemingly at odds with the preceding narrative, offers praise to Russian military prowess that has resulted in the conquest of the Caucasus.

In *Bakhchisaraiskii fontan* a Crimean khan has captured a Polish beauty, but her presence represents a threat to his previous beloved, a Georgian woman. Yielding to jealousy, the Georgian woman kills the new captive, and in revenge, the khan has the Georgian killed by dropping her into the sea in a sack of stones. Various Romantic devices and themes cluster in this tale: exotic settings, strong emotions, a suggestive atmosphere, violence, nocturnal scenes, and brooding Byronic heroes. In addition, as narrator Pushkin speaks of his own visit to Bakhchisarai and draws parallels with his own love life; a subsequent edition includes a letter about his visit and various other notes illuminating the story on which the poem is based. Literary conservatives were outraged by the elliptical descriptions and the morally questionable thematics of the poem. Many of the younger generation, however, welcomed the new "romanticism," the breaking of conventional genre categories and stylistic norms. One of the most enthusiastic defenders of Pushkin's tales was his friend Viazemsky, whose articles in the mid 1820s about *Kavkazskii plennik* and *Bakhchisaraiskii fontan* promoted the notion of the poet's "true romanticism."

Publishing his poetry in absentia was no easy task. Pushkin relied on the assistance of his brother and friends for editing, publishing, and distribution. He also wrote works at this time that were unpublishable. Another narrative poem, *Gavriiliada* (The Gabrieliad), written in 1821, because of its impious and blasphemous treatment of Christian thematics—the Annunciation and the Virgin birth (Mary is depicted as having sex with Satan, Gabriel, and God in the form of a dove on the same day)—could only be circulated in manuscript. Though not published until 1861, this tale was well known apparently throughout the 1820s, creating problems for Pushkin with Nicholas I that he eventually resolved (probably by admitting authorship and apologizing) in a private meeting with the emperor in 1828.

In the several months before leaving Kishinev in 1823 Pushkin began work on his novel in verse and magnum opus, *Evgeny Onegin* (Eugene Onegin, written 1823–1831), which he would publish serially in chapters, beginning in 1825 and continuing over the next seven years (published in full, 1833). After convincing authorities that he was languishing in Kishinev, Pushkin was able to obtain a transfer in the summer of 1823 to Odessa, where he served under the governor general, Count Mikhail Semenovich Vorontsov. For reasons both personal and professional Pushkin's relationship with Vorontsov developed poorly after a promising beginning. Vorontsov, some seventeen years Pushkin's senior, had a long and distinguished military and civil service record and had little understanding of or appreciation for poetry. Pushkin, moreover, imprudently pursued Vorontsov's wife, Elizaveta, for whom Pushkin wrote a whole cycle of lyric poems and of whom he made many drawings during the 1820s. Indeed, Elizaveta, who apparently returned Pushkin's affection, remained one of the principal loves of his life, although not many details of their post-Odessa relationship are known. The Vorontsova cycle (written primarily during 1824–1825) includes "Vse koncheno, mezh nami sviazi net" (All is finished, there's no link between us), "Priiut liubvi" (Love's shelter), "Khrani menia, moi talisman" (Preserve me, my talisman), "Puskai uvenchannyi liubov'iu krasoty" (Let him be crowned with the love of beauty), "Sozhzhennoe pis'mo" (The Burnt Letter), "Vse v zhertvu pamiati tvoei" (All is in sacrifice to your memory), "V peshchere tainoi, v den' gonen'ia" (In the secret cave, on a day of persecution), and possibly others. "Sozhzhennoe pis'mo" includes in its final lines a remarkably effective image closely associated with the feelings of separation evoked in the poem:

Svershilos'! Temnye svernulisia listy;
Na legkom peple ikh zavetnye cherty
Beleiut.... Grud' moia stesnilas'. Pepel milyi,
Otrada bednaia v sud'be moei unyloi,
Ostan'sia vek so mnoi na gorestnoi grudi... [.]

(It's done! The dark pages have curled;
On the light ashes their cherished writing
Turns white.... My breast constricts. Dear ashes,
Poor consolation in my sad fate,
Remain forever with me on my mournful breast... [.])

Presumably annoyed by the poet's attention to his wife and also by the differences in their personalities, Vorontsov by early 1824 grew more insistent about Pushkin's fulfilling the responsibilities of his official position. By convention Pushkin expected his job to be only nominal. Embroiled in controversy engendered not just by personal friction with Vorontsov (which found expression in a number of rather pointed and unflattering epigrams) but also by an intemperate letter (intercepted) expressing a fondness for atheism, Pushkin found himself in the summer of 1824 dismissed from the service and exiled to his mother's family estate at Mikhailovskoe near Pskov. There he continued to write as well as visit neighbors at the nearby estate in the village of Trigorskoe. These neighbors included the young officer Aleksei Nikolaevich Vul'f, whom Pushkin came to know well during the latter's several visits in

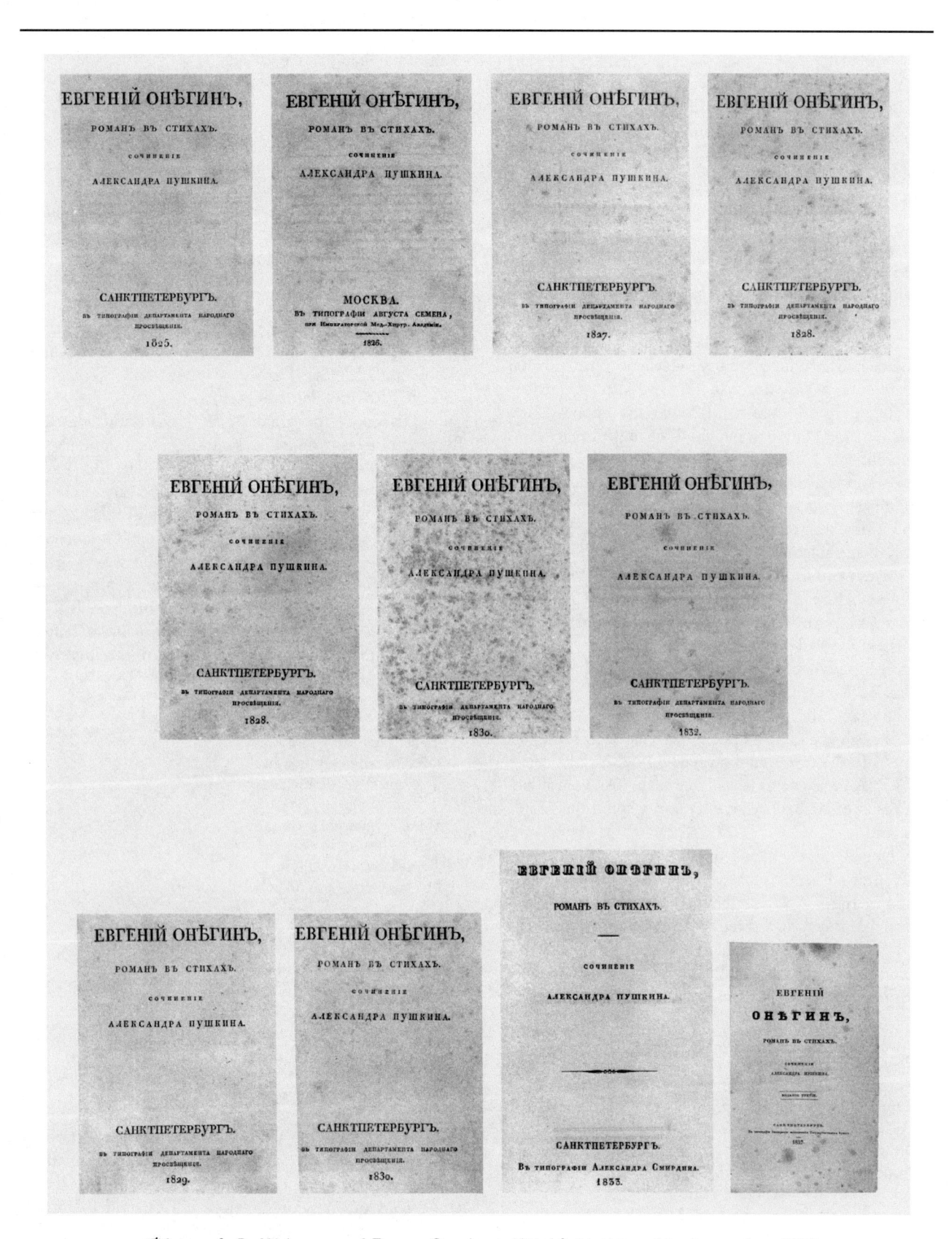

Title pages for Pushkin's verse novel Evgeny Onegin, *published first in parts and then in one volume, 1833*

1824 and 1825 (and in post-exile years), Aleksei's brother Mikhail, and also a lively and well-read group of women in or associated with the Vul'f household: Ekaterina, Mariia, and Aleksandra Osipova and Valeriana, Anna, and Evpraksiia Vul'f. Aleksandr Ivanovich Turgenev recorded that Pushkin "spent the best years of his poetic life" in Trigorskoe. The matriarch of the family was Praskoviia Aleksandrovna Osipova, who, widowed twice (her first husband was Nikolai Vul'f), raised a large family that many commentators believe provided Pushkin with a more positive model for family life than he found in his own family.

Up to the time of his exile to Mikhailovskoe, Pushkin had produced many excellent lyric poems, some relating to experiences connected with love at various stages. In addition to his other love poems, one stands out: "K*** (Ia pomniu chudnoe mgnoven'e . . .)" (I remember a wondrous moment, written in 1825), a poem about a meeting recollected. It is considered one of the finest lyric poems in Russian; the first quatrain is "Ia pomnia chudnoe mgnoven'e: / Peredo mnoi iavilas' ty, / Kak mimoletnoe viden'e, / Kak genii chistoi krasoty" (I remember the wondrous moment / When you appeared before me; / Like a fleeting vision / Like a Genius of pure beauty). The poem marvelously expresses recalled feelings associated with an earlier relationship with a frequent Trigorskoe visitor (a niece of Praskoviia Osipovna), Anna Petrovna Kern. The final quatrain reflects the poet's response to his recollection: "I serdtse b'etsia v upoen'e / I dlia nego voskresli vnov' / I bozhestvo, i vdokhnoven'e / I zhizn', i slezy, i liubov'" (And my heart beats in ecstasy, / And for it has been resurrected again / Divinity and inspiration, / Life, tears, and love).

Not all of Pushkin's lyrics have clear referents: highly praised lyrics such as "Nereida" (The Nereid, written in 1820), "Noch'" (Night, written in 1823), and "Vinograd" (Grapes, written in 1824), sometimes associated with the influence of André Chénier's laconic style, are characteristically Pushkinian with their concrete images, clarity, conciseness, and musicality:

Ne stanu ia zhalet' o rozakh,
Uviadshikh s legkoiu vesnoi;
Mne mil i vinograd na lozakh,
V kistiakh sozrevshii pod goroi,
Krasa moei doliny zlachnoi,
Otrada oseni zlatoi
Prodolgovatyi i prozrachnyi,
Kak persty devy molodoi.

(I won't regret the roses
That withered with the light spring;
For me the grapes on the vines are also dear,
Ripened, in clusters, on the hillside,
A beauty in my fertile valley,
A solace of golden autumn,
Oblong and translucent
Like the fingers of a young maiden.)

Pushkin wrote more-general "philosophical" poems as well, such as one of 1823, "Telega zhizni" (Wagon of Life), which outlines the stages of human life. He also experimented with folk themes, writing "Pesnia o veshchem Olege" (The Song of Oleg the Wise) in 1822 and poems relating to other cultures such as "Podrazhaniia Koranu" (Imitations of the Koran) in 1824. Later he wrote a folktale ballad "Zhenikh" (The Bridegroom) in 1825, followed in 1828 by two more ballads—"Utoplennik" (The Drowned Man) and "Voron k voronu" (Raven Flies to Raven).

His more personal "exile" lyrics include the Byronic "Pogaslo dnevnoe svetilo" (The Luminary of the Day Has Gone Out) written in 1820; the poetic epistle to Ovid, "K Ovidiiu" (also written in 1821), in which he compares his lot to Ovid's; and in 1824 his so-called farewell to Byronism, "K moriu" (To the Sea), which, while echoing the crashing of the waves in its refrains, expresses a complex attitude of praise and regret for the passing of Byron and Napoleon I. The poem muses on the nature of government, personal freedom, and happiness while marking in the final two stanzas the passing of a stage in his own life:

Proshchai zhe, more! Ne zabudu
Tvoei torzhestvennoi krasy
I dolgo, dolgo slyshat' budu
Tvoi gul v vechernie chasy.

V lesa, v pustyni molchalivy
Perenesu, toboiu poln,
Tvoi skaly, tvoi zalivy,
I blesk, i ten', i govor voln.

(Farewell, then, sea! I shall not forget
Your solemn beauty,
And long, long shall I hear
Your roar in the evening hours.

Into forests, silent wildernesses
I'll carry, full of you,
Your cliffs, your bays,
And the glitter, shadow, and murmur of your waves.)

In the 1820s, in exile, Pushkin began a cycle of poems about the poet and inspiration; the first in the series was "Razgovor mezhdu poetom i knigoprodavtsom" (A Conversation Between a Poet and a Bookseller), written in 1824. This poem, which served as a foreword to early editions of chapters of *Evgeny Onegin*, consists of a dialogue proposing that a poet should write poetry out of inspiration but sell manuscripts for

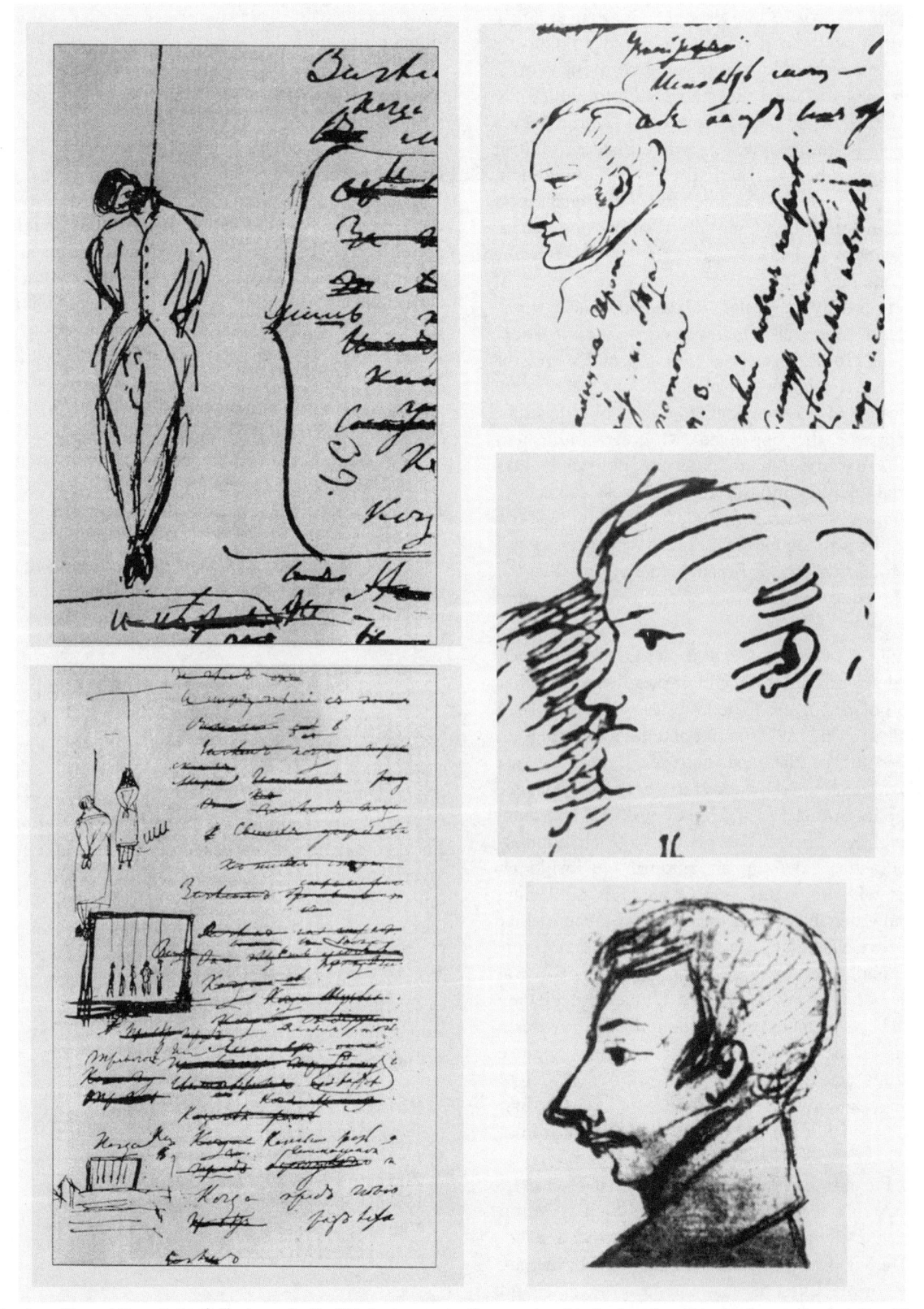

Two sketches of hanged Decembrists (left), drawn by Pushkin in the margin of manuscripts; his sketches of two friends who were hanged, Pavel Ivanovich Pestel' and Kondratii Fedorovich Ryleev (right top and center); and his sketch of his friend and fellow poet Vil'gel'm Karlovich Kiukhel'beker (right, bottom), who was exiled (The Taylor Institution Library, Oxford; right, bottom: from Ronald Hingley, Russian Writers and Society, 1825–1904, *1967)*

publication. "Prorok" (The Prophet), written in 1826, suggests that poetry is divinely inspired and politically charged (the poet should "burn" people with his Word). Other lyrics of the late 1820s and 1830s continued the cycle: in "Poet" (The Poet), written in 1827, the poet is shown as quite ordinary except when inspired; and in "Poet i tolpa"(The Poet and the Crowd), written in 1828, the poet defends the freedom of his inspiration from demands that he be morally uplifting and useful. "Ekho," written in 1831, suggests that the poet is like an echo and need have no effect on events to be of value. The last in the cycle, "Ia pamiatnik sebe vozdvig" (I raised to myself a monument), written in 1836, is based on Horace's *Exegi monumentum* and expresses the notion that the poet's name will long be remembered because of his thematics—freedom, kind feelings, and mercy for the oppressed: "I dolgo budu tem liubezen ia narody, / Chto chuvstva dobrye ia liroi probuzhdal, / Chto v moi zhestokii vek vosslavil ia Svobody / I milost' k padshim prizyval" (And long will my name be dear to people, / Because with my lyre I evoked good feelings, / Because in my cruel age I praised Freedom / And mercy for the fallen summoned).

While in Odessa, Pushkin wrote many lyrics, completed several poems begun earlier, began another narrative poem, *Tsygany* (The Gypsies, written in 1824 and published in 1827), and continued working on *Evgeny Onegin*. For the next two years, until August 1826, Pushkin lived and worked under the surveillance of local police and clerics at Mikhailovskoe. He continued to publish and republish his works—their popularity undoubtedly aided by an aura of the forbidden associated with his status as an exile. His publishing activity now benefited from the able assistance of Petr Aleksandrovich Pletnev, a minor poet and literary critic who eventually became a professor of Russian literature and rector of St. Petersburg University. Pletnev proved to be an excellent editor and publisher for Pushkin, taking on the responsibilities (at some risk, because of Pushkin's status with the authorities) in 1825 of supervising the printing and distribution of the first chapter of *Evgeny Onegin* and Pushkin's first collection of poetry, *Stikhotvorenii Aleksandra Pushkina* (1826). Up to this time, Pushkin had relied on the editorial services of his brother, Lev Sergeevich, and friends such as Anton Antonovich Del'vig and Sergei Aleksandrovich Sobolevsky. Del'vig was one of Pushkin's closest lifelong friends—a former Lyceum classmate, a poet, critic, and editor whose untimely death after a brief illness in 1831 had a strong and disturbing effect on Pushkin. Del'vig was one of only a few friends to visit Pushkin at Mikhailovskoe (April 1825). Sobolevsky remained a close friend who more than once saved Pushkin from difficult situations involving duels.

Pushkin's stay at Mikhailovskoe, especially in the beginning when the rest of the family was also there, was emotionally unsettling. He quarreled with his father, who, according to some accounts, had been charged by the government with monitoring his son's behavior. The atmosphere improved significantly when the family left in November and Pushkin could move about freely. He spent his time visiting friends at neighboring estates (Trigorskoe) and writing at home in the company of his peasant nursemaid, Arina Rodionovna. After Pushkin's death, and particularly in Soviet times, Arina Rodionovna achieved no little fame as a kind of "people's" muse. Literary works of this period of relative isolation include the verse tale *Tsygany*, *Boris Godunov* (an historical drama, 1825, published in 1831), *Graf Nulin* (Count Nulin, a humorous narrative poem written in 1825 and published in 1827), and chapter two of *Evgeny Onegin,* which was published separately as a book in 1826.

Tsygany, which Pushkin began in Odessa and finished in Mikhailovskoe, was the last and, in the eyes of many, the best of his southern Romantic tales. Pushkin's modification of the characteristic features of the genre is easily visible in the presence of many dramatic exchanges and an increased objectivity on the part of the narrator. Like the other southern tales, the poem develops themes of violence, betrayal, freedom, and contrasting social norms. The hero, Aleko, has fled civilized society (where he is sought by the authorities) and taken up with Zemfira, a woman in a band of gypsies. But she, having grown weary of him, has taken a new lover. The character of the Old Gypsy, her father, represents gypsy social norms that include tolerance and, in particular, acceptance of female infidelity. Finding Zemfira with her lover, Aleko is deaf to the Old Gypsy's wisdom and kills both Zemfira and her lover. For this he is ejected from the band. After Aleko is abandoned and alone, the narrator reminisces on his own experience with gypsies:

No schast'ia net i mezhdu vami,
Prirody bednye syny! . . .
I pod izdrannymi shatrami
Zhivut muchitel'nye sny,
I vashi seni kochevye
V pustyniakh ne spaslis' ot bed,
I vsiudy strasti rokovye,
I ot sudeb zashchity net.

(But there is no happiness with you as well,
Poor sons of nature! . . .
And under tattered tents
Tormenting dreams reside.

Pushkin's caricatures of Gen.-Lt. Ivan Nikitich Inzov and Prince and Princess Viazemsky (from Henri Troyat, Pushkin, 1970)

And your nomads' shelters
Have not been spared misfortunes in the wilderness,
And everywhere there are portentous passions,
And against the fates there's no defense.)

Interpretations of the tale have focused on the character and plight of Aleko and the implied view of civilization in the tale. Dostoyevsky in his famous Pushkin speech, generalized about the rootlessness of Russian intellectuals on the basis of the Old Gypsy's words about the alienation of the "European wanderer." Biographical interpretations center on the identity of character and author (taking Aleko as a thinly disguised version of Pushkin's own name, Aleksandr). The topics of revenge, civilized man versus natural man, and freedom (for whom? from what? for what?) have evoked much scholarship and criticism.

Fortunately for Pushkin, he was at the Mikhailovskoe estate when the Decembrist Revolt took place in 1825. Even though he was never invited to join the revolutionary societies implicated, he likely would have been involved in the revolt had he been in St. Petersburg. Since copies of his poetry—his early political verse—were in the hands of virtually all of the Decembrists, there was no hope that he would entirely escape the consequences of the revolt. This indirect participation in revolutionary activity caused anxiety for Pushkin and his friends Zhukovsky and Viazemsky. Fearing arrest, Pushkin burned anything he thought might be incriminating, including his diaries, and waited to see what would follow.

Although most of his political verse was written early, he had continued to express political sentiments, though with a more muted and ambiguous message, throughout the 1820s. His liberalism and hopes for reform had faded by the mid 1820s. He defended freedom in "K Chaadaevu" (To Chaadaev), written in 1818, and "Napoleon," written in 1821, in which he presents Napoleon as pointing the way to world freedom (and also giving an opportunity to Russia for world fame). In "Kinzhal" (Dagger) Pushkin suggests that the dagger is an ultimate arbiter in redress of grievances when the law will not help, but in "Svobodnyi seiatel' v pustyne" (Freedom's Sower in the Wilderness), written in 1823, he expresses disillusionment, skepticism, and pessimistic resignation to the status quo. *Kavkuzkii Plennik* (The Prisoner) and "Ptichka" (The Little Bird, 1823), though not political lyrics, exult in the virtues of freedom. His historical elegy "Andrei Shen'e," which represents a blend of genres combining political and personal themes, eloquently promotes liberation from tyranny. Post 1826 poems relating to the Decembrist Revolt include two poems written in 1827, his poetic epistle to the exiled Decembrists, "Vo glubine sibirskikh rud" (In the depths of Siberian mines), and his allegorical poem "Arion," which refers indirectly to the Decembrists, suggesting that he, the poet of the Decembrists, was miraculously saved from death: "Lish' ia, tainstvennyi pevets, / Na bereg vybroshen grozoiu, / Ia gimny prezhnie poiu / I rizu vlazhnuiu moiu / Sushu na solntse pod skaloiu" (Only I, the mysterious singer, / Swept ashore by the storm, / I sing the former hymns / And my damp garments / Dry in the sun under the cliff).

With the execution of five of the Decembrists and the exile of several hundred the next spring, Pushkin may have concluded that he was at least temporarily safe from serious consequences. Indeed, he had waited almost a year for repercussions of the revolt to reach him. Instead of maintaining a humble profile, however, he petitioned Nicholas for release from exile late in the spring of 1826. His motivation was perhaps to bring matters to a head, to clarify his position with respect to the new monarch. Interpreted this way, his request achieved the results he aimed for. In September, Nicholas sent a courier to Mikhailovskoe and ordered Pushkin to appear before him in Moscow. The unusual and dramatic qualities of this summons probably unnerved Pushkin. He was anxious enough as it was, still suspecting that his personal ties with the Decembrists and their possession of his political poetry might bring further difficulties with the government.

The meaning of the summons and the subsequent audience with Tsar Nicholas I still pose tantalizing questions for Pushkin scholars. Although what was said is not altogether clear, the outcome seemed an enormous improvement: Pushkin gained release from exile, permission to live wherever he pleased, Moscow or St. Petersburg, and "relief" from the censorship. From then on Nicholas himself (but more probably, his aide Aleksandr Khristoforovich Benkendorff) would act as censor for Pushkin's works. On his part, or to gain such sovereign favor, Pushkin is generally understood to have admitted his complicity as author of "incendiary" verses and his potential role as a Decembrist participant and to have promised to behave as a loyal subject in the future. Allowing Pushkin to return from exile, to travel with some degree of (but not total) freedom, and to publish with Tsar Nicholas as his personal censor—all these concessions in exchange for some expression of fidelity to the crown—made the situation a winning one for both parties.

With the end of exile and his return to urban society came the beginning of a new stage in Pushkin's life. His productivity in exile, however, had been noteworthy. One of the first major works to pass through his new "censor" was his historical tragedy, *Boris Godunov*, which he had been working on for about a year in

Pushkin's home at his estate, Mikhailovskoe (drawing by Edward Alan Cole; private collection)

Mikhailovskoe (he finished it in November of 1825). Only part of it was allowed publication in 1831: Nicholas and Benkendorff proved to be exacting critics with little taste for what was innovative. In addition, they were excessively suspicious of any reference to the political or the religious—even in a clearly historical work. The play has a complicated story, at least from the point of view of audience reception. Pronounced a failure by Vissarion Grigor'evich Belinsky, it nonetheless captured the praise of other critics and continues to attract critical and scholarly attention (for example, that of Stephanie Sandler and Caryl Emerson). Related most closely to Shakespeare's *Richard III*, *Boris Godunov* nevertheless differs a great deal from tragedies of character.

The story centers on the reign of Boris, chosen tsar after the death of Dmitrii. As Pushkin's contemporary Ivan Vasil'evich Kireevsky noted, the play does not present a tragic hero or conflict but a tragic mood; indeed, the mood that envelops all of the action (and in fact unifies the twenty-three scenes better than the personality of the hero or the consequences of the characters' actions) underscores the futility of ambition, the fragility of power, the vanity of temporal pursuits, and the insignificance of human striving in the face of forces beyond human control (for example, fate or destiny). A gloomy pall overwhelms all in the play, despite the comic interludes, the machinations of the many characters surrounding Boris, and several quite moving, and sometimes turbulent, personal scenes (for example, Boris giving advice to his sons, Pimen talking to Grigorii, Grigorii-Dmitrii talking to Marina, and Grigorii-Dmitrii talking to his horse). The play is amazingly suggestive in its thematics and in its formal properties and has generated many and varied interpretations and structural studies. In its freedom from restraints of genre, its innovations, and its sincerity, it is a paradigm of Romanticism according to Pushkin's understanding of the term.

Another work Pushkin labored over, though hardly as long as he worked on *Boris Godunov*, was the comic narrative poem *Graf Nulin*. Pushkin's turn to lighter verse tales in some respects parallels Byron's turn from his more serious Oriental verse tales to the less serious *Beppo* (1818). Set in the countryside, Pushkin's poem, in freely rhymed iambic tetrameter, tells of a landowner's wife who entertains with dinner and conversation a stranded stranger, retires to bed, and is surprised when the stranger comes into her room to press his amorous intentions. Rebuffed with a hardy slap, the stranger is amazed the next morning when nothing is said about the incident. With his carriage repaired and her husband returned, he leaves, still in love. She tells her husband what happened; he is enraged, but their neighbor, a young man of twenty-three, is amused. The literary roots of the poem are Italian, French, and British, with Byron's *Beppo* and Shakespeare's *Rape of Lucrece* (1594) the most obvious sources. But, clearly, all is trivialized in Pushkin's poem—an anecdote set in the mundane world of provincial Russian society with figures who are far from heroic. Pushkin makes fun of the shallowness of his characters: Nulin's Gallomania and pretense (his name is derived from the Russian word for *zero*), the husband's blindness to what is really going on, and the heroine's superficiality and total dependence on the care of her servants. Beneath the humorous veneer lie the more serious themes of infidelity, betrayal, and honor. The lightness, good humor, and urbane wittiness of the narrative, however, keep the dark side at a comfortable distance. Pushkin continued in this lighter vein with another verse tale in 1830, *Domik v Kolomne* (The Little House in Kolomna).

Even though his prospects looked good in the beginning, Pushkin did not adjust well to his new freedom. Lionized in Moscow after his meeting with Tsar Nicholas, Pushkin took advantage of his prestige. Society found him a relatively safe "hero" in these cautious post–Decembrist times. He had managed to walk the thin line between political liberalism—just barely implicated with the Decembrists—and state favor. His audience with Tsar Nicholas was well known (although what was actually said in the conversation between tsar and poet was far from clear), and the fact that he was freed from exile and personally pardoned by the monarch enhanced his position in high society. From a personal standpoint, he must have felt that he expressed himself honorably with Tsar Nicholas and that the tsar understood and respected his position. Pushkin's poem "Stansy" (Stanzas), written in 1826 and published in 1828, expresses his hope (with a certain amount of flattery for the emperor) that Tsar Nicholas will rule with an enlightened and forgiving spirit:

> V nadezhde slavy i dobra
> Gliazhu vpered ia bez boiazni:
> Nachalo slavnykh dnei Petra
> Mrachili miatezhi i kazni.
>
> No pravdoi on privlek serdtsa,
> No nravy ukrotil naukoi,
> I byl ot buinogo strel'tsa
> Pred nim otlichen Dolgorukoi.
>
> Samoderzhavnoiu rukoi
> On smelo seial prosveshchen'e,
> Ne preziral strany rodnoi:
> On znal ee prednaznachen'e.
>
> To akademik, to geroi,
> To moreplavatel', to plotnik,
> On veseobĕemliushei dushoi
> Na trone vechnyi byl rabotnik.
>
> Semeinym skhodstvem bud' zhe gord;
> Vo vsem bud' prastiuru podoben:
> Kak on, neutomin i tverd,
> I pamiat'iu kak on, nezloben.

(With hope for glory and good deeds
I look ahead without misgiving:
Rebellions and executions also shrouded
The start of Peter's glorious days.

But he attracted hearts with justice,
But he used learning to tame customs.
For him a Dolgorukii was distinguished
From the ungovernable *strelets*.

With autocratic hand
He boldly sowed enlightenment;
He did not hate his native land:
He knew its predestination.

Now academic, now hero,
Now navigator, now carpenter,
With all-encompassing soul, he was
Eternal worker on the throne.

Be proud of your family likeness;
Be like your ancestor in everything:
Untiring and firm like him,
And of past wrongs forgiving.)

Praise and high hopes for the tsar, however, did not guarantee Pushkin's financial security or happiness. His Southern poems continued to be popular, providing him with badly needed financial support. Living in inns or with friends and taking part in the social whirl of high society made constant demands on his resources. Now, pressed by financial need and a desire to augment his earnings from his poetry, he took an active role in the publishing business, working closely with Pletnev, who had helped so much with Pushkin's business affairs while he was in exile, and his long-term Lyceum comrade, Del'vig. Pushkin acquainted himself or renewed acquaintance with leading publishers of the day–Pavel Petrovich Svin'in and Aleksandr Filippovich Smirdin–and influential editors–including Nikolai Ivanovich Grech, who published Pushkin's first verses in *Syn otechestva* (Son of the Fatherland) in 1815; Faddei Venediktovich Bulgarin (with whom Pushkin had a spirited journalistic polemic from 1830 to 1831); and Osip Ivanovich Senkovsky, editor of the popular *Biblioteka dlia chteniia* (Library for Reading) from 1834 through 1856. In the immediate postexile years Pushkin collaborated with Del'vig as editor, contributor, and assistant on issues of the almanacs *Severnye tsvety* (Northern Flowers, 1825-1831) and *Podsnezhnik* (Snowdrop,

1829), and the newspaper *Literaturnaia gazeta* (Literary Gazette, 1830).

Pushkin soon learned that the conditions of his freedom were more onerous than he had anticipated. Benkendorff watched his movements carefully, patronizingly admonishing him for any infractions, lecturing him on proprieties at every occasion and for every request, and censoring Pushkin's works for Nicholas. Several memoir accounts from these years indicate that Pushkin alternated between bouts of social revelry and lonely despair, exhilaration and desperation. Exacerbating all of these problems was the embarrassing return of *Gavriiliada*, brought to official attention in 1828 and requiring another series of "explanations" with the authorities. Although Pushkin initially denied he was the author, he presumably admitted he wrote it (and asked for forgiveness) in a sealed letter to Tsar Nicholas, who then called off the official government investigation. Also threatening Pushkin's fragile position with regard to the authorities was the widespread dissemination of politically suggestive lines from his pre-Decembrist historical elegy "André Chénier." He gave explanations, but the situation was far from settled.

Despite personal difficulties, Pushkin continued to write. Increasingly he turned to history for literary and narrative material. He devoted three weeks of October 1828 to his new verse tale, *Poltava* (1829). Written in freely rhymed iambic tetrameters, the three cantos and sixteen-line dedication (to Maria Raevsky or Anna Olenina, whom Pushkin was courting) represent a mixture of styles and genres (ode, drama, ballad, folk poetry, Romantic narrative poem, and epic) totally consistent with Pushkin's new attitude toward conventional genres. He virtually eliminated distinctions of genre in the format of his 1829 collection of verse, whereas he had used conventional labels in his 1826 collection.

The historical focal point of *Poltava* is an important battle in 1709 in the Great Northern War between Peter's Russia and Charles XII's Sweden. All the characters in the tale are historical personages, although the heroine's name was altered from Matriona to Maria. Pushkin himself thought highly of the work, believing it to be "almost totally original"—one of the principal positive qualities of poetry, in his aesthetic view—and of a much higher quality than the quite popular and financially rewarding *Kavkazskii plennik*.

The plot centers on Maria's love for and elopement with Mazepa, a military leader in Ukraine, and her eventual recognition that she had hopelessly idealized him. Her parents had forbidden the union, thinking Mazepa too old, and her father, Kochubei, vowed vengeance on Mazepa for the dishonor of marrying without his permission. Meanwhile, Mazepa plots against Peter, intending for Ukraine to join forces with

Pushkin's study at Mikhailovskoe, where he wrote part of Evgeny Onegin, Boris Godunov, *and many poems*

Sweden. Kochubei attempts to warn Peter, but Peter does not believe his charges and sentences Kochubei to torture and execution. The intrigue mounts as Maria finds out too late what has happened to her father. Psychologically devastated by all that has happened, she leaves Mazepa. He soon realizes transferring his allegiance to Charles was a mistake. Nonetheless, he stays with his plan, admitting to his friend Orlik that he can never go back to Peter, who had humiliated him many years before. The battle develops as Mazepa anticipated, with Russia victorious and Charles and his forces retreating to Sweden. Mazepa, too, flees but is visited late at night by a crazed Maria, who raves disjointedly before running away. Mazepa, filled with remorse, abandons the empire. An epilogue then provides historical closure, referring in nationalistic terms to strong personages such as Peter who make their mark on history. The epilogue, along with other patriotic references to the monarchy and empire, have been understood, perhaps simplistically, as Pushkin's paying his respects to Tsar Nicholas at a time when Pushkin needed government support.

Poltava occasioned a great deal of critical controversy, beginning with Pushkin's contemporaries, who tended to be highly negative for historical or literary reasons when the work was first published in 1829. Some critics found the presentation of Mazepa's motivation unsatisfying, insisting that Ukrainian nationalism overrode all considerations of personal honor. Moreover, Charles was in real life a much more impressive figure than Pushkin had made him. Those who faulted *Poltava* for literary reasons also focused on Pushkin's characterization, critical of his presenting Mazepa as a stereotypical melodramatic Gothic villain. In addition, the scene in which Mazepa makes Maria choose him over her father evoked negative commentary. Critics also faulted the description of the battle, with its hyperbolic imagery and exaggeratedly positive picture of Peter; the silly picture of Charles and Mazepa plunged in thought during the battle; and finally the lack of a convincing unity of the personal and the historical. From Belinsky on, critics returned to the issue of "unity" when discussing *Poltava*. Pushkin's use of multiple perspectives (including the patriotic sentiments of the epilogue), as in his earlier verse tales, challenges critical sensibilities seeking unity and resolution to perceived paradoxes and ambiguities.

Frustrated and disappointed by his soured relations with the authorities, increasingly put under financial pressure (made more acute by his gambling), wearied by the social scene in Moscow and St. Petersburg, and hopeful that travel might again afford him opportunities for revitalization and inspiration, Pushkin sought permission to go abroad with various Russian missions. The travels in his early twenties with the Raevskys had led to the writing of his popular verse tales, which continued to be profitable. Turned down in his request, he nonetheless went off without authorization (but not secretly) to join the Army of the Caucasus in 1829, ostensibly to visit his brother and friends. Because he did not receive official permission, the trip occasioned official displeasure toward him when he returned. Nevertheless, this temporary escape freed him from pressures associated with his urban life, which made strong demands on his financial and psychological resources. In creative terms, his journey accounted directly for many fine lyric poems and for his *Puteshestvie v Arzrum* (Journey to Arzrum), a fascinating travel journal. Pushkin's lyrics associated with his return to the south in 1829 are far more subdued and down-to-earth than his earlier poems set in the mountain regions of the empire. Examples are "Obval" (The Avalanche), "Monastyr' na Kazbeke" (Monastery on Mount Kazbek), and "Na kholmakh Gruzii lezhit nochnaia mgla" (On the Georgian hills lies the night mist):

    Na kholmakh Gruzii lezhit nochnaia mgla;
        Shumit Aragva predo mnoiu,
    Mne grustno i legko; pechal' moia svetla;
        Pechal' moia polna toboiu,
    Toboi, odnoi toboi. . . . Unyn'ia moego
        Nichto ne muchit, ne trevozhit',
    I serdtse vnov' gorit i liubit–ottogo,
        Chto ne liubit' ono ne mozhet.

(On the Georgian hills lies the night mist;
    Before me the Aragva river roars.
I am both sad and light at heart; my sorrow is luminous;
    My sorrow is full of you,
Of you, of you alone . . . Nothing torments,
    Nothing troubles, my despondency,
And once again my heart burns and loves–because
    It cannot not love.)

Returning to St. Petersburg, Pushkin took steps to change the course of his life. There is little doubt that marriage represented a last opportunity for Pushkin, a chance to escape overwhelming feelings that his life was over and that only the past remained as a source of joy. Pushkin had failed in an earlier courtship with Anna Olenina, a young woman nearly twenty whom he had known from childhood and for whom he developed a strong infatuation in the summer of 1828. Rejected probably for political reasons (Anna's father was part of the official investigation in the "André Chénier affair") Pushkin, after returning from his trip to Arzrum, turned now to Natalia Nikolaevna Goncharova, who was just making her entrance into Moscow society. Her beauty was matched only by her poverty and the general undesirability of the match. Pushkin also was no great catch, barely respectable, socially unstable, with a long history of profligacy and intemperate living. Nonetheless, Pushkin secured Benkendorff's help to assure his future wife's parents of his acceptability as a spouse, and the marriage took place in February 1831, though not before Pushkin had disposed of many practical problems. Natalia was nineteen and he was thirty-one at the time of their marriage.

The months preceding his marriage turned out to be quite productive for Pushkin–perhaps because he viewed his imminent betrothal as a summing up of a stage in his life. A more concrete reason relates his burst of creativity to the beneficial consequences of confinement on his father's Boldino estate, where he had gone on prewedding business and where he was quarantined by the cholera epidemic of late 1830. A creatively fruitful tension was occasioned by anticipation and hope for the future and regret, recollection, and despair over the past. The seriousness of the epidemic (which had to give rise to thoughts of mortality and the fragility of life) gave his stay an additional sense of urgency.

Two of Pushkin's most productive periods have been associated with the time he spent at Boldino. This particular stay, in the autumn of 1830, led to the creation of three of the four short dramas most often referred to as the "little" or "miniature" tragedies. The three written in Boldino (though conceived earlier) were *Skupoi rytsar'* (The Covetous Knight); *Motsart i Sal'eri* (Mozart and Salieri), a play based on the supposed rivalry of composers Wolfgang Amadeus Mozart and Antonio Salieri; and *Kamennyi gost'* (Stone Guest). The fourth, *Pir vo vremia chumy* (Feast During the Plague—a translation of part of an English play), was written after he left. All the plays share some formal properties: they are in unrhymed iambic pentameter with no regular caesura after the fourth syllable and with some thematic affinities. They are also commonly referred to as psychological studies, reflecting Pushkin's interest in the complexity and well-roundedness of Shakespeare's characters. Serving as a genre model for these little tragedies, ranging from 231 to 542 lines, were the short dramatic scenes of Barry Cornwall, a now little-read English writer. The reader should not be misled, however, by normal genre expectations; these works are not conventional dramas or tragedies. Indeed, Pushkin at one time thought of calling them "dramatic investigations." Their drama inheres not in the action but in what the scholar Walter N. Vickery calls their lyric highlights: what they "say about life, a specific problem, or an emotional attitude." Their style is quintessentially Pushkinian: extremely concise yet filled with associative power.

Skupoi rytsar' deals with generational conflict, father and son arguing about money and by extension over patrimony. To avoid unwanted biographical speculation, or to sidestep such charges in a convenient way, Pushkin subtitled it "Scenes from Shenstone's Tragicomedy." There is no evidence William Shenstone ever wrote such scenes. At odds because he can borrow no more money without security and blaming his miserly father, the baron, for his poverty, the son listens attentively to the moneylender's suggestion that poison may help him escape his poor circumstances. The second scene, dominated by a long soliloquy, shows the baron's motivation for his perceived miserliness: money for him represents power over all. But at the same time he is gravely disturbed by concerns over his heir, his son's gullibility and misplaced values, and the likelihood that he will squander all the riches gained through his father's enormous sacrifices. At the end of the baron's impressive monologue he specifies the one thing he can have no dominion over—death: "Could I but from the grave / Come hither as a ghostly sentinel, / Stand watch upon my chests, and from the living / Preserve my treasures as I can today . . . !" Consulting with the duke in the final scene, the son pleads his case against his miserly father. The duke then talks to the baron, asking why his son is never at the court. After several excuses, the baron blames his son for wanting to kill him and for trying to steal from him, whereupon the outraged son

Dust jacket for Pushkin's historical tragedy Boris Godunov, *based on the reign of Boris, chosen tsar after the death of Dmitrii*

rushes in, calling his father a liar. In a highly charged scene, the baron throws down his glove and the son picks it up: the father has given a challenge and the son has accepted it with the view that it is his father's "first gift" to him. The baron then falls and dies uttering "Where are my keys, my keys!"

Critics have explored the biographical dimension, knowing well the sensitive relations between the author and his father; they have also sought to determine the dramatic center, whether in the baron's monologue, which is a masterpiece of psychological depth, or in the conclusion, which traces out in disturbing and suggestive ways the themes of parricide, patrimony, and displaced sexual rivalry. These were issues Dostoyevsky subsequently dealt with so effectively in his novels.

A profound problem also occupies the center of *Motsart i Sal'eri,* a problem effectively handled in modern times by Peter Shaffer's play (and the subsequent motion picture version) *Amadeus.* Envy of the hardworking and merely talented for the easy success of genius is raised to metaphysical levels by Salieri, who

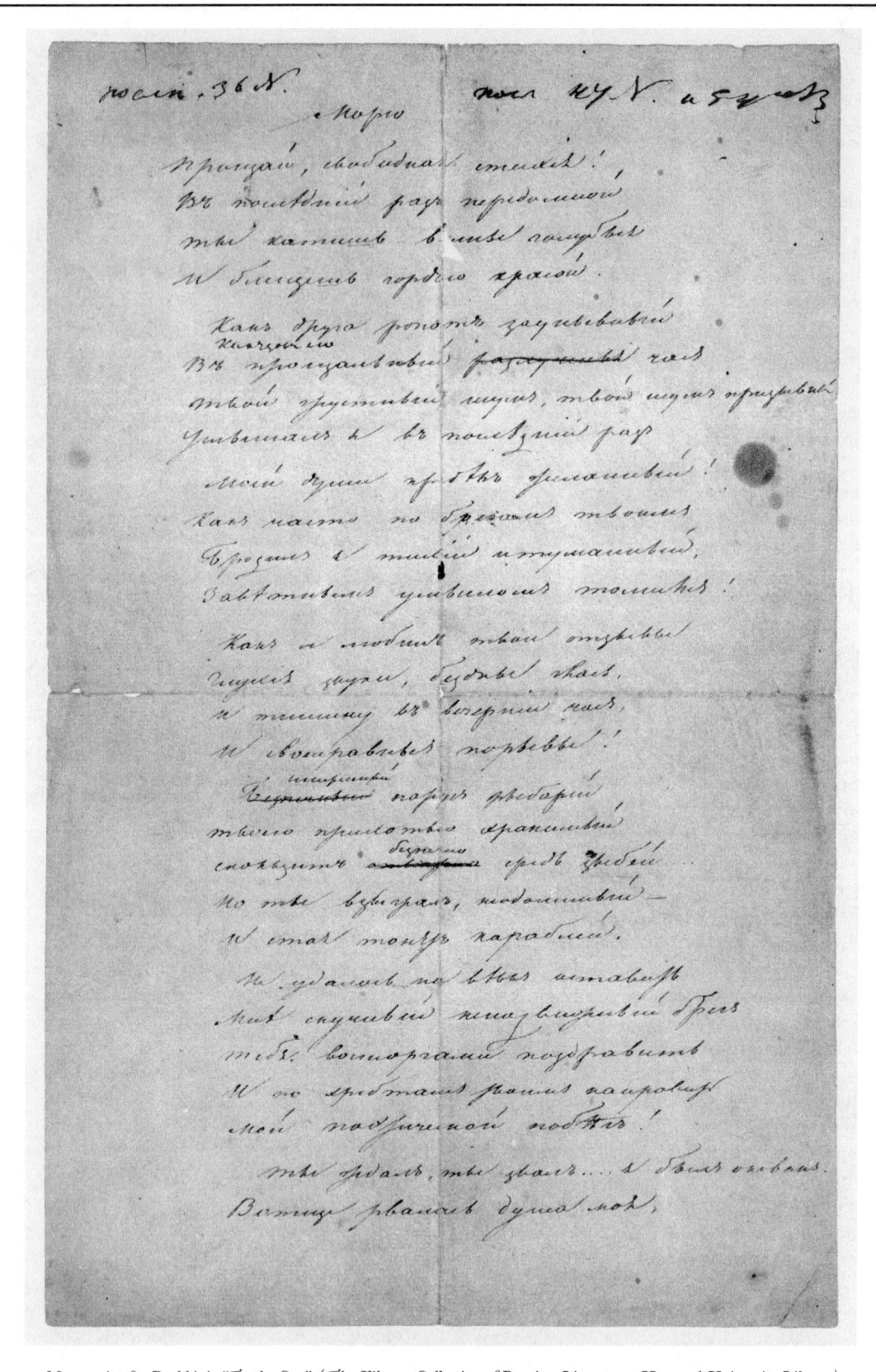

Manuscript for Pushkin's "To the Sea" (The Kilgour Collection of Russian Literature, Harvard University Library)

questions whether justice exists in the universe. The tragedy presents deep matters concisely and maximally compressed. Unhappy in his life, now racked with envy for the easy and unself-conscious genius of Mozart, Salieri poisons him, but not before a final scene that invokes the theme of whether genius and evil are compatible. Indeed, in the end Salieri is left with doubts. The central theme of the work, however, concerns justice and truth. Reiterated in this second miniature tragedy is the essential injustice of life, represented in Salieri's resentment that something valuable can be acquired without effort or even without consciousness of value. Part of Pushkin's brilliance in characterization is that he shows Mozart at the end somehow conscious of his own imminent death while playing his own *Requiem* to Salieri.

Kammenyi gost' is longer and more eventful than the other dramas. Its four scenes, set in or near Madrid, follow key incidents in Don Juan's life after his return, incognito, from exile. The theme of remorse finds expression in Don Juan's regret over past loves who apparently perished as a result of his attentions. He encounters Dona Anna, draped in a cloak and in mourning, making her daily visit to the monument she built in memory of her husband (whom Don Juan had slain in a duel). In the second scene he comes to see another woman, Laura, and slays another rival, Don Carlos. Don Juan and Laura make love in the presence of the corpse. In the third scene Don Juan, dressed as a monk, meets Anna by the statue, declares his love (pretending to be someone else), and persuades her to meet him later at her home. Confident of his abilities, he invites the statue to come and stand guard during the visit. The statue, much to Don Juan's horror, mysteriously nods its agreement. In the final scene, though she professes that she must remain faithful to her dead husband (chosen for her in an arranged marriage), she listens to Don Juan, hears him admit his identity, worries for his safety, agrees to see him again the next day, and kisses him farewell. The statue knocks, enters, reaches out to Don Juan, and disappears with him. Don Juan mutters Dona Anna's name until the end, suggesting that she may have been his true love.

Obviously Pushkin built on a long tradition (represented by Tirso de Molina, Molière, Mozart, and Lorenzo Da Ponte), but, as was his custom, he modified tradition to suit his purposes. One notable difference is that the Commander is presented as Dona Anna's husband, not her father. As scholars have noted, Pushkin's Don Juan differs from his predecessors in his appreciation for women as more than simply prizes, as individuals. A love for the spirit of the chase, a knowledge of the devices of seduction, and considerable patience while in pursuit, however, are also part of his psychological makeup. His beloveds in the drama represent a variety of types–characters whose individual beauties or strengths he appreciates and values. He is also capable of remorse, though hardly without bravado. He proves by his willingness to admit his identity that he is capable of risks and also opposed to presenting himself in the end as someone other than himself. He wants to be loved "as himself and for himself." He is also a poet.

Many have noted the self-referential dimension: the character traits, the exile, and the return from exile. Pushkin too had contemplated an illegal return to St. Petersburg in 1825. Intensely possessive on the eve of marriage, he apparently harbored morbid thoughts about being replaced by another man. Natalia Goncharova, like Dona Anna, was marrying a man her mother (not without hesitation) designated. Shifts from father to husband, of course, can also be explained within psychoanalytical frames. And finally, the question running through the final scene–whether love can bring happiness to the hero and whether it can turn his life around and give it new value–was quite plausibly Pushkin's question.

Critics have focused on the sincerity of Don Juan's declaration of love and the ambiguity or indefiniteness of his motivation as crucial issues. Ambiguity is characteristic of much of Pushkin's creation: some readers form conclusions that depend on their own views of human nature and psychology (and their view of Pushkin's sincerity at this important juncture in his life), while others withhold judgment, assuming that motivation in life and art is difficult to assess. The ambiguity in the tragedy, though productive of interpretations, may also affect the reader's sympathy for the hero and the reader's sense of tragedy. Don Juan, if he is understood as sincere, seemingly finds redemption–in a purely secular sense–at the very moment of his destruction by Nemesis in the form of a statue.

The fourth and final miniature tragedy is somewhat anomalous. It is a translation of John Wilson's "The City of the Plague" (1816), set in London in 1665. The biographical impetus was the analogous cholera epidemic in Russia confining Pushkin to his Boldino estate. At the center of the play is a group of young people celebrating in defiance of the ubiquitous threat of death, reveling in "living on the edge." The message is that those moments when life is intensified, because it is so seriously threatened, are particularly valuable. Pushkin introduced two songs that were not in the original–one by Mary, who sings an elegy filled with references to death, fidelity to loved ones, regret, and lost innocence, and another by the Master of Revels, the Chairman or Presider, who sings in honor of the plague, praising those who live boldly while threatened with death. A priest darkens the mood by reminding

Pushkin's wife, Natalia, whom he married in February 1831 (from Henri Troyat, Pushkin, *1970)*

the revelers of their personal losses. The Presider, recalling his wife's death, then leaves the group. In offering a fascinating study of psychology in a life-threatening situation, the play shows its affinities with the other Don Juan works. Most scholarship has endeavored to identify features Pushkin's play shares with the others as well as its literary models and biographical dimensions.

Another project Pushkin brought to completion in the early 1830s was his novel, *Evgeny Onegin,* arguably his most important literary accomplishment. Work on *Evgeny Onegin* spanned some eight years of his creative life. Generally recognized as a masterpiece of world literature, it was begun in May 1823 while Pushkin was in Kishinev. Publishing chapters throughout the 1820s (as he completed them), he finished the work, adding one last passage (part of Onegin's letter to Tat'iana) in October 1831. The novel was published as a book in 1833 and 1837. Serving as a focus of Pushkin's creative energy for so many years, the novel reflects various life stages the poet passed through, from young manhood to mature adulthood. The final work consists of eight chapters, or cantos, though Pushkin worked on (but did not publish) additional cantos describing Onegin's journey and Onegin's further adventures as a Decembrist. The latter Pushkin burned in 1830 because of its political content, although some fragments have survived in coded form.

One critical problem the novel poses relates to its completeness. The reader's knowledge of the existence of plans for a continuation easily engenders speculation on what would have and should have happened to the main characters. Indeed, a good part of the Pushkin critical tradition is devoted to his projected continuation and to other works he did not complete, especially prose works, such as "Arap Petra Velikogo" (The Moor of Peter the Great), "Dubrovsky," "Egipitskie nochi" (Egyptian Nights), and "Istoriia sela Goriukhina" (Story of the Village of Goriukhino). By publishing fragments from Onegin's journey in the separate editions of the novel, Pushkin did not discourage speculation.

Chapter lengths in *Evgeny Onegin* run from forty to fifty-four fourteen-line stanzas with a regular (with some exceptions) rhyme scheme. The stanzas themselves represent something new in Russian literature. They are iambic tetrameter with alternating masculine and feminine rhymes (ababeecciddiff)–a form vaguely like the sonnet but closer to the eight-line stanza or ottava rima of Byron's *Beppo* and *Don Juan* (1819-1824). The language of Pushkin's poem has a remarkable lightness and spontaneity, a freshness and aptness that cannot be captured easily in translation and that have been highlighted as Pushkin's contribution to the development of the Russian literary language. (Pushkin is often given credit for his pioneering efforts in nurturing the growth of the Russian language in suppleness and potentialities for greater expressiveness.)

The very form of the novel indicates Pushkin's early discomfort with conventional genres, his striving to make his own mark in an original way. First of all he called his work not simply a novel but (he emphasized this) a "novel in verse" and termed sections "chapters" rather than cantos. While clearly seeking to be innovative, he also showed an awareness of European models. The novel can be viewed quite productively within the tradition of prose novels by Jean-Jacques Rousseau and Benjamin Constant and of Byron's novel in verse, *Don Juan,* as well as the whole picaresque tradition, French and Italian contes, and comic epics of Voltaire and Ludovico Ariosto. As far as its major provenance is concerned, however, the novel in verse combines the sentimental novel and the comic epic. The narrative aura is casual; the verses flow one after another almost unpoetically, not calling attention to themselves, deceptive in their apparent superficiality. Nonetheless, running deeply through the text are serious themes that have stimulated generations of critics and readers.

The novel follows the young Evgeny Onegin, a superficially educated and somewhat shallow dandy, through a social whirl that no longer thrills him and into a country milieu (his recently deceased uncle left him an estate) that quickly loses its charm for him. There he has one friend, an idealistic poet named Lensky, schooled in German philosophy and given to elegiac lyricizing. Lensky confides his love for Olga, one of two sisters living on a neighboring estate, to Onegin. Onegin, who clearly views himself as far beyond the stage in which he can lose himself in love, tolerates Lensky. Olga's older sister, Tat'iana–a dreamer, a loner, not at all as sociable as Olga–is smitten with Onegin, though the narrator (a poet much like Pushkin), who is a friend of Onegin, shows concern for such a liaison. In her naïveté Tat'iana (Tania) writes a letter to him declaring her love. Onegin, in turn, feels the need to be brutally honest with her; finding her in the garden of her parents' estate, he tells her that if he could settle down it would be with her, but, alas, he cannot. He then lectures her on the importance of restraint and the worldly dangers that threaten inexperienced women.

In subsequent developments, Onegin and Lensky arrive late to Tania's name-day party, with Onegin in a bad mood that he blames on Lensky. Determined to seek vengeance, Onegin begins to court Olga, who responds to his attentiveness. Lensky is outraged by this behavior, thoroughly disenchanted with Olga (and women in general), and challenges Onegin to a duel. Onegin kills Lensky in the duel, leaving only the narrator to mourn him and speculate on what might have happened to him had he lived. Olga eventually marries an officer and leaves Tania alone on the estate with her parents. Time goes by, and Tania wanders to Onegin's estate, long abandoned by him; she examines his study and his books, which suggest to her that he may be a parody of Byron or Childe Harold. Her family eventually takes her to Moscow and finds a husband for her. Onegin only finds her again in the final chapter; she is with her husband and is now a striking high-society hostess. After seeing her, Onegin writes her one letter after another declaring his love. Receiving no response, he impetuously rushes to her house and falls at her feet, putting himself at her mercy. She questions his sincerity, admits she still loves him, but says she will be faithful to her husband and leaves the room.

A schast'e bylo tak vozmozhno,
Tak blizko! . . . No sud'ba moia
Uzh reshena. Neostorozhno,
Byt' mozhet, postupila ia:
Menia s slezami zaklinanii
Molila mat'; dlia bednoi Tani
Vse byli zhrebii ravny . . .
Ia vyshla zamuzh. Vy dolzhny,
Ia vas proshu, menia ostavit';
Ia znaiu: v vashem serdtse est'
I gordost', i priamaia chest'.

Ia vas liubliu (k chemu lukavit'?),
No ia drugomu otdana;
Ia budu vek emu verna.–

(But happiness had been so possible,
So near! . . . But my fate is already
Settled. Impetuously,
Perhaps, I acted.
With tears of incantations
My mother begged me; for poor Tania
All lots were equal.
I married. You must,
I implore you, leave me;
I know in your heart are
Both pride and genuine honor.
I love you [why dissimulate?],
But to another I have been given;
I shall be faithful to him all my life.–)

Her husband enters the room, and the story ends. The bare outline of the plot development does little justice to the spirit of the work, the frequent and playful digressions and ironic commentary of the narrator. Indeed, the narrator's presence and his observations temper, refract, and determine in significant ways the reader's perceptions of the characters, relationships, and events.

The varied reception of *Evgeny Onegin* has been noted by such scholars as Sona Stephan Hoisington. Critics have often cited the work's fundamental symmetries (rejected loves, ironic reversals, parallels in plot, and behavior of the characters). Some have focused on motivation of the major characters, while others have examined the meaning of particular significant events, such as Tania's disturbing dream after being rejected by Onegin. Many interpretations have centered on the character of Onegin, with the goal of assessing his culpability and potential for love. Belinsky showed more interest in revealing Pushkin as a critic of the age and in condemning Onegin's society than the man. Subsequently, the nineteenth-century critic Dmitrii Ivanovich Pisarev saw the novel as a defense of Nikolaevan society. Dostoyevsky in his famous Pushkin speech (1880) focused on Onegin as an alienated soul, divorced from his people and native Russian soil. The Russian novelist Dmitrii Sergeevich Merezhkovsky saw this alienated hero as a universal and fundamentally positive type, the self-willed individualist. Various interpretational strands involve the presentation of character and society in the work and implied criticism of each. These strands, even tendencies, became more rigid in the twentieth century. Soviet critics, exploiting the perceived critique of Russian social conditions and various textual clues to this effect, assessed Onegin's character in terms of his potential as a Decembrist. In addition, critics have pointed to Onegin as an early manifestation of the

The November 1836 letter that led to the duel in which Pushkin was mortally wounded (The Taylor Institute Library, Oxford)

social type known as "superfluous man"—a man alienated from but also a natural byproduct of Russian society, stifled by social conditions and prevented by them from doing anything worthwhile. Superfluous men such as Onegin populate Russian novels and heroes' roles from this point on through Mikhail Iur'evich Lermontov and Ivan Sergeevich Turgenev, though the type owes much to European literary figures such as Adolphe (hero of an 1816 novel by Benjamin Constant) and Childe Harold (hero of Byron's *Childe Harold's Pilgrimage,* the first two cantos published in 1812 and 1818). Extending the social into the metaphysical, interpretations also have given a major role to destiny, which rules over and determines the fate of (and limits the responsibility of) individuals such as Onegin.

In psychological terms the two lead characters, Onegin and Tat'iana, are both under the spell of Western literary and social models. That they live an illusory life (or one characterized by self-delusion) is suggested in their reading and their tastes. On character, interpretations present a variety of views of Onegin, the narrator, Tat'iana, Lensky, and Olga. Onegin's culpability in provoking Lensky is often mitigated by reference to social determinism and Onegin's frustrated idealism (a point of view that is even supported by the narrator). The question of motivation has prompted questions about Tat'iana's attraction to Onegin, his toward her (at the end), and his provocation of Lensky. Answers to these questions are entwined in issues of environment, education, fate, and biological inevitability.

All the characters have been subjected to interpretations emphasizing their qualities on scales from the prosaic to the sublime and mysterious. There is a good enough case for condemning Onegin as a Childe Harold type: self-centered, good at nothing in particular, killer of Lensky in a duel that he could have easily prevented or even stopped, and pursuer of married women. Pushkin, in this novel as elsewhere, however, indicates an understanding of and even sympathy for the type. He may be quite aware of the hard edges and pitfalls of Onegin's lifestyle and aware of its affinities with his own but also conscious that abandoning them was not easy. Olga, more often than not reviled by critics for her shallowness, nonetheless has the virtue of being able to forget. She is seemingly unaware of the problems and burdens of life, for they appear simply to flow over her. She loses a beloved and then simply moves on, unburdened by sentimental notions of true love lost. Since she easily finds another mate, the novel can accordingly be read as a commentary on Romantic love and various approaches to it.

Many questions have arisen about the ending and Tat'iana's rationale for remaining faithful. Pushkin, as Prince D. S. Mirsky speculates, may well have intended Tat'iana's reaction to serve as a model for his own young wife, who, he must have thought, would be dealing with similar challenges to her fidelity. Other critical issues center on the authenticity and sincerity of Onegin's "love" for Tat'iana, questioning whether this love could save Onegin from his negative, ironic, and detached approach to life. Pushkin, with the assistance of his ironic and sympathetic narrator, offers two sides, two angles, two approaches to every interpretation.

Early on, critics noted the overall impact of the novel, underlining the metaphor of seasonal change and the overwhelming feeling of time passing. The movement of time evokes different perspectives and leaves its imprint on the narrator's personality. The narrator indeed is a unifying presence, underlining the importance of the flow of time in his digressions, sympathies, irony, personal experiences, and attitudes toward life in general. In the end *Evgeny Onegin* is much more than an unhappy love story or analysis of Romantic ailments. The critic Semen Frank, in characterizing Pushkin's works as expressing a "luminous sadness" (the expression from "Na kholmakh Gruzii lezhit nochnaia mgla . . .") offers a satisfying approach to defining this quality of the novel. Something positive and life-affirming remains, counteracting the increasingly somber mood that derived largely from the growing awareness that there was no return and what lay ahead would be worse than what lay behind. Part of what is positive lies in the unexpected (as Tat'iana's husband comes in unexpectedly at the end), the promise of sudden changes in fortune or twists of fate. Whatever the source, the brightness remains, for surely both positive and negative emotions are left with readers of this wonderfully evocative novel. In this work as elsewhere Pushkin leaves a rich, but suggestive, picture, one capable of several almost contradictory interpretations. This richness is surely a reflection of the long creative history of the work, spanning eight quite turbulent years of the poet's life.

Pushkin's productivity of the 1830s included other narrative poems, notably *Domik v Kolomne* (forty stanzas of ottava rima, comparable in this respect to Byron's *Beppo* and *Don Juan*), another 1830 product of Boldino. The poem is extremely digressive, even more casual in its tone than *Evgeny Onegin,* and its iambic pentameter lines are completely free of the obligatory caesura after the fourth syllable. *Domik v Kolomne* is a veritable poetics in verse, discussing rhyme (comparing rhymes to soldiers in martial imagery) and other poetic matters, with a flimsy plot. A widow and her daughter hire a cook found by the daughter (their regular cook has just died). The new cook, presumably a woman, does not demand a fixed wage, cooks poorly, and constantly breaks dishes. One Sunday the mother discovers "her" shaving. Caught in this masculine behavior, the cook runs away; when the daughter learns what has happened, she is properly outraged. Pushkin offers a double moral: first, do not hire a cook for little pay, and second, men should not put on women's clothes because in the end they will have to shave.

Beneath its seemingly frivolous surface, critics have discovered (and speculated on) serious issues. A Freudian subtext has been found, as well as a treatise on poetics. Certainly the story, no matter how flimsy, can be related to Pushkin's concerns (as expressed in many other works) with people presenting themselves as something they are not (pretenders), using deceptive behavior for sexual purposes (Don Juan), and eventually disclosing their true natures.

Andzhelo (Angelo, written in 1833), another "Shakespearean" narrative poem (based on *Measure for Measure*) with dialogue (like the little tragedies and *Poltava*), is Pushkin's only verse tale written in iambic hexameter. Pushkin removed much in his adaptation of the original, giving particular attention to the character of Angelo. Critics of Pushkin's time did not think highly of this work, but later critics and scholars have come to quite different conclusions. It is not a bright and sunny work but one that implies a rather cynical view of human nature. The plot involves a duke who has been somewhat lax in law enforcement; he temporarily yields the reigns of power to Angelo. He hopes that Angelo will reinstate law and order. Angelo is up to the task and quickly enforces laws against fornication, bringing charges against a patrician named Claudio. Claudio asks his sister Isabella to intercede on his behalf; she agrees and intercedes, but Angelo propositions her. She tells her brother, who is willing to trade her virtue for his life. The duke overhears all this and replaces Isabella with Angelo's wife for a late evening rendezvous. (Angelo and she had separated because he believed false rumors about her behavior.) Although the plan is carried out, Angelo still orders the death of Claudio. The plot is foiled when the duke confronts

Baron Georges d'Anthes-Heeckeren, whose duel with Pushkin resulted in the poet's death (The Taylor Institution Library, Oxford)

Angelo, and he asks to be executed. The duke forgives him, as Isabella has forgiven her brother.

What troubles some critics (for example, Vickery) is the implication that principles do not stand for much: Claudio measures his own life against his sister's virtue, and Angelo clearly is willing to go against his word. The tone is also somewhat jarring: the poem begins in a jocular spirit but quickly turns to more sordid matters. One cannot help but think of the biographical affinities: the play of power and principles and sexual desire that had to reflect matters in Pushkin's personal life—his relationship with Nicholas and his attitude toward his wife and her involvement in court society.

Indeed, Pushkin's marriage did not bring that idyllic peace he had dreamed of. Although not totally insensitive to literature, Natalia was unsophisticated in her approach and understanding of it and resentful when her husband discussed his literary projects with other women. Her interests were largely social, and her mode in social life was largely (by training) based on flirtation. Pushkin himself showed ambivalence on this score, on the one hand proud of his wife's status in court society (achieved early, in the first summer of their marriage while they stayed in Tsarskoe Selo) but on the other hand inevitably jealous and warily concerned about the attention of young men she attracted. These concerns became more obvious and explicit in his correspondence to her as the years went by. In the beginning, however, all seemed well.

Pushkin married in February 1831, finished *Evgeny Onegin* in October, and in May of 1832 had his first child, Maria. Nicholas—evidently pleased with Pushkin's marriage, apparent stability, and dedication to the state (which Pushkin expressed in jingoistic poems supporting Russia's quashing of the Polish rebellion of 1831)—reinstated Pushkin in state service as a historiographer with a salary and access to state archives. The situation changed gradually as Pushkin grew more dependent on Nicholas's favors, as his debts increased, and as more children came. Yet his presence (and that of his wife) at society functions was made obligatory by Pushkin's unflattering appointment at the end of 1833 to the rank of Kammerjunker (gentleman of the emperor's bedchamber), usually given to much younger men. Matters came to a head when he found out Tsar Nicholas had been reading letters Pushkin had written to Natalia, and Pushkin's indignant attempt to resign to save face was met with threats of access to archives denied and the monarch's disfavor. Indeed, Pushkin requested permission twice, in 1834 and again in 1835, with a persuasive rationale based on financial need. Each attempt met with refusal.

Throughout these difficult years Pushkin continued writing lyrics, narrative tales, and then prose. Among the more interesting works of his early married years are his *skazki* (fairy tales in verse), "Skazka o tsare Saltane" (The Tale of Tsar Saltan, written in 1831), "Skazka o rybake i rybke" (The Tale of the Fisherman and the Fish, written in 1833), "Skazka o mertvoi tsarevne i semi bogatyriakh" (Tale of the Dead Princess and the Seven Heroes, written in 1833), and "Skazka o zolotoi petushke" (The Tale of the Golden Cockerel, written in 1834). Scholars usually point to Pushkin's growing interest in authentic folk poetry as the motivation for his turn to this genre. At the same time they refer to his exile at Mikhailovskoe and the beneficial presence of his nurse, Arina Rodionova, who could recite many tales and poems, some of which Pushkin wrote down. Rather than literally transcribing what he heard, Pushkin created new poems of hybrid sources, incorporating sophisticated literary and folk themes and devices in unusually original narratives.

The poems have little plot and apparently little in the way of ideology; their claim to fame is their formal excellence, manifested in the structures of their rhythms and rhymes. All were written in trochees with verse paragraphs of uneven lengths and rhyming couplets; some critics say that because of these qualities, the *skazki* are "better read than discussed." Another view holds, however, that an author's choice of material is never fortuitous and that indeed much of importance can be detected beneath the magical surface. Thus, any poem that talks of deceiving the tsar, expresses concerns about patrimony, and includes transformations, things that are not what they seem to be, untruthful advisors, and truth winning out in the end could easily have application to Pushkin's life.

Pushkin wrote fewer lyrics in the 1830s than in earlier periods, but what he wrote was of high quality. His "Èlegiia" (Elegy, 1830), unusual because of its genre used as title at a time when Pushkin tended to avoid such labels, suggests that the meaning of life lay in thought and suffering:

> Bezumnykh let ugasshee vesel'e
> Mne tiazhelo, kak smutnoe pokhmel'e.
> No, kak vino–pechal' minuvshikh dnei
> V moei dushe chem stare, tem sil'nei.
> Moi put' unyl. Sulit mne trud i gore
> Griadushchego volnuemoe more.
>
> No ne khochu, o drugi, umirat';
> Ia zhit' khochu, chtob myslit' i stradat';
> Ia vedaiu, mne budut naslazhden'ia
> Mezh gorestei, zabot i trevolnen'ia
> Poroi opiat' garmoniei up'ius',
> Nad vymyslom slezami obol'ius',
> I mozhet byt'–na moi zakat pechal'nyi
> Blesnet liubov' ulybkoiu proshchal'noi.

(The extinguished merriment of madcap years
Weighs on me like a hangover's dull ache.
But–as with wine–the sadness of past days
With age its strength increases in the soul.
My path is dark. The future's troubled sea
Holds little for me, mostly sorrow, toil.

But no, my friends, I do not wish to die;
I wish to live that I may think and suffer;
And I know too that pleasures will be mine
Amid my troubles and my tribulation:
At times again the Muses will delight,
Creation's work will cause my tears to flow;
Perhaps once more my waning star will shine
Beneath the fleeting, farewell smile of Love.)

"Besy" (Devils, written in 1830) is a ballad-like lyric, powerful in its sound instrumentation and personal and political symbolism relating to pernicious forces in the world. Pushkin wrote a sonnet, "Madonna" (Madonna), to his fiancée in 1830 and many poems suggestive of Greek and Roman models. He also continued with "imitations," writing "Pesni o zapadnykh slavianakh" (Songs of the Western Slavs) in 1834, based to some degree on Mérimée's "Illyrian translations" (or inventions) of 1827. Some of the more important lyrics of the last years include "Ne dai Bog soiti s uma" (God grant that I don't go mad), written in 1833 or later; the fragment "Osen'" (Autumn), written in 1833; "Pora, moi drug, pora . . . " (It's time, my friend, it's time . . .), written in 1834; and "Kogda za gorodom, zadumchiv, ia brozhu. . . . " (When outside the city pensive I wander. . . .), written in 1836.

Pushkin had yet another productive fall at the Boldino estate, where he completed *Mednyi vsadnik* (The Bronze Horseman) in the fall of 1833. He stopped at Boldino after researching in the Urals the history of the revolt led by Emilian Pugachev in the years 1773 to 1775. His research led to the historical study *Istoriia pugachevskogo bunta* (History of the Pugachev Revolt, written in 1833, published in 1834). *Mednyi vsadnik*, not published in its entirety until 1837 after Pushkin's death, easily deserves status as a masterpiece among his narrative poems. It has had an extraordinary life in the hands of critics, generating untold numbers of studies from a variety of perspectives. The principal critical question concerns the central emphasis of the poem.

There are three major characters–the narrator, who provides a commentary and panegyrical introduction; the civil servant Evgeny; and Peter I, who first appears as an historical figure and then is represented by an equestrian statue (the Falconet statue commissioned by Catherine II) in St. Petersburg. One dimension of the poem is historical: the narrative is set in the time of the flood of November 1824, although the introduction goes back in time to picture Peter surveying the Baltic and the surrounding forests and marshes and deciding to build his city "to open a window to Europe." When the narrative begins a century later, the city is thriving.

The narrator's views figure prominently in his seeming praise of Peter and of St. Petersburg and in his sympathetic portrayal of Evgeny. Part 1 focuses on Evgeny's dreams of success, independence, and marriage to Parasha. She and her mother unfortunately live on one of the islands, whose access to the city an impending storm threatens. The storm leads to a flood that brings massive destruction. Evgeny, distraught by what is happening around him, finds shelter sitting on a marble lion near Peter's statue. He fears his beloved may have perished. In the next part of the poem–as the flood begins to subside–Evgeny travels to the island where Parasha lived, finds only destruction, and begins to lose his mind. He eventually becomes a homeless wanderer, living through the winter and into the next autumn, one day finding himself again by the lion and the statue of Peter. In a moment of clarity he accuses the statue, defies it, and the statue seems to respond angrily and turn toward him. Cowed by this display of regal anger at his insolence, Evgeny loses his spirit, runs (with the statue in pursuit), eventually dies and is found

Pushkin's coffin being taken to Mikhailovskoe for burial (painting by A. A. Naumov; from Historiia russkoi literatury, *volume 18 [1908])*

lying on the threshold of what is left of his fiancée's house.

The poem utilizes a variety of styles, depending on the section and its focus: odic in the introduction, abrupt and disjointed in describing the actions of Evgeny, and filled with rhetorical devices and imagery that enhance the emotional effect. Although the poem can be interpreted as a conflict between the rights of the individual and the claims of historical necessity, there is far too much complexity to make this abstract formulation satisfying. Scholars and critics have tried to determine where the narrator's sympathies truly lie, with Peter or Evgeny. One answer has been that the author is essentially neutral in his artistic expression, endeavoring to keep both sides in balance throughout. Although such a solution may be satisfying to some, there are many subtexts that show quite definite partisanship: the poem as a response to Adam Mickiewicz in its defense of Russian imperialism (which Pushkin would call historical destiny), the poem as an expression of sympathy for the sacrifices that went into the building of St. Petersburg, and the poem as showing sympathy for the impoverished nobility and those living in the oppressive atmosphere of the capital. In a broader sense, the poem suggests the indifference of the state and the paranoia of the citizenry, highlighting their persecution, irrational anger, defiance, and repression. Moreover, the view that sees Evgeny's feelings of being persecuted and powerless, that sees him going mad in the face of the government or emperor's demands, certainly gives basis for an identification of Pushkin with Evgeny. Indeed, Evgeny's misery, because it is so powerfully evoked, cannot help but play a central role in the poem and its interpretations. To say that Pushkin was merely being neutral does a gross disservice to the strength of conviction the poem communicates. In the end, even Peter's "victory" is ambiguous, for nature (as the elements) appears to be the all-powerful force, not Peter or his creations.

Probably Pushkin's most significant creative development in the 1830s was his turn to prose. He tended to formulate broad theories of genre before actually implementing them concretely; accordingly, he approached the problem of drama in Russian by delineating what was appropriate and what was not, using Shakespeare's dramas as his models. Similarly, he considered prose carefully, looking not only for identifying principles but also for what Russia's literature required in this genre. Thus, he showed considerable interest in Voltaire's precise style and Viazemsky's translation of Constant's *Adolphe*. He also evidenced a desire to keep prose clearly separated from poetry, which in his mind had quite different values. Pushkin had always been a master of the prose of epistolary writing, and in later years he showed increased interest in literary criticism.

His attempts at fiction in the 1820s were marked by many false starts and incomplete projects. "Arap Petra Velikogo" (The Moor of Peter the Great), for example, which he started in 1827, remained unfinished. He really did not complete a prose work until he was in Boldino in 1830; from that time on he devoted more and more of his time to prose, completing the fictional works *Povesti pokoinogo Ivana Petrovicha Belkina, izdannye A. P.* (Tales of the Late Ivan Petrovich Belkin, edited by A. P., written in 1830, published in 1831), "Pikovaia dama" (The Queen of Spades, written in 1834), and *Kapitanskaia dochka* (The Captain's Daughter, written in 1836). His nonfiction belletristic writings before 1830 included some journalistic criticism and the travel journal *Puteshestvie v Arzrum*. After 1830 his historical study *Istoriia pugachevskogo bunta* is noteworthy.

Povesti Belkina is a collection of five tales, told to and then recast in prose by the fictitious Ivan Petrovich Belkin. The Belkin frame represents a literary obfuscation that was enhanced by additional removes: different authors and different narrators play roles in the tales. All five stories and the introduction (which also has been viewed as a tale) were written in Boldino during the fall of 1830. The stories are "Vystrel" (The Shot), "Metel'" (The Snowstorm), "Stantsionnyi smotritel'" (The Stationmaster), "Grobovshchik" (The Undertaker), and "Baryshnia-krest'ianka" (Lady to Peasant). All are masterpieces of precision, with nothing ornamental or superfluous. Narration and explicit psychologizing, though not entirely absent, are minimal. The apparent simplicity, however, belies a depth and suggestive power—even mystery—awaiting solution by the serious reader. At a minimum they represent parodies or ironic commentaries on popular fiction of Pushkin's time.

"Vystrel" deals with problems of honor and the nature of bravery in the face of death. An officer, Silvio, patiently waits years to take his shot in a postponed duel; not until his opponent is married and has a different perspective on and new respect for the value of life does Silvio resume the duel. "Metel'" deals with a couple mistakenly married because of a storm and confused identities. A series of fortuitous events reveals that they indeed were destined for each other, and what had been a mistake ends as good fortune. "Stantsionnyi smotritel'" offers a twist on the prodigal son story by having the "prodigal" daughter actually end up with a seemingly good life while the father, who had predicted his daughter's ruin, dies unhappily, an alcoholic until the end. "Grobovshchik" treats the hero of the title to a visit (at least in his nightmare) from his former customers, who come serving Nemesis. And finally, "Baryshnia-krest'ianka" plays with identity and class issues as well as disputes between families. The poem has a happy resolution, although along the way important issues relating to death, honor, pretense, fate, justice, and pride are raised.

Some readers see the stories as relatively innocent parodies of existing prose models, twists on ordinary plots, a building and defeating of expectations. On this level the stories parody works of such writers as Nikolai Mikhailovich Karamzin and Byron. On another level the stories are far more serious, treating (at a comfortable distance) problems of honor, deception of parents, marital fidelity, revenge, and the values of life. Some critics have given the tales a prominent place in affecting the development of Russian prose while others have given them much less credit, characterizing them as skillfully told anecdotes.

"Pikovaia dama" is another matter, however, even though some critics warn of exaggerating the virtues of the work. With a plot revolving around the quest of the hero Hermann to discover the secret of winning at cards—and thus to assure his wealth, patrimony, and happiness—the tale presents a picture of obsession degenerating into madness. Along the way a wealth of suggestive details provides ample material for a variety of literary and psychological approaches. The story is paradoxically simple yet dense with tantalizing and mysterious hints. It even yields fascinating insights to those seeking codes in the text, according to Lauren Leighton. The troubled hero, in his quest for the secret, uses one woman to advance his plans and unintentionally is responsible for the death of another, the old Countess, whom he frightens to death. Once he has learned the secret from her (in a dream or in her post-death appearance before him), he makes a mistake utilizing it, loses everything, and goes mad. With elements from fiction of the age—dreams, secrets, Napoleonic ambitions, mysterious life histories, references to fate, unresolved oedipal issues, numerological puzzles, and eventually madness for the hapless hero—the work presents an extremely engaging story with formidable material for critical analysis.

Pushkin's last major completed prose work, *Kapitanskaia dochka,* is a novel of notable scope and merit. The literary provenance is not E. T. A. Hoffman, who had a discernable relationship to some of Pushkin's earlier fiction, but Sir Walter Scott, whose historical novels were quite popular in the late 1820s and early 1830s. The stage was already set for novels in Russia, which had quickly warmed to prose novels of, for example, Bulgarin, whose works enjoyed an extremely good reception. In fact, Bulgarin's work represented some of the first Russian novels published abroad in English translation. Choosing the time of the Pugachev rebellion (the early 1770s) as his setting, Pushkin tells of the separation and reunion of his hero and heroine, with

Catherine II and Pugachev playing cameo roles. As usual, interpretational questions concerning genre and central theme loom large. The narrative, though thoroughly enjoyable on its own, leaves much room for speculation on profound issues associated with the best prose fiction. A list of the various themes—violence, revolt, the threat of death, honor, relations with parents, the beneficence of sovereigns, and finally the sovereign's involvement in marital happiness—makes difficult maintaining that the work is simply an engaging Romantic novel. Though short for a novel, it can easily stand as one of the first and best historical novels in Russian literature, fascinatingly suggestive in its psychology and thematics.

For Pushkin to find time and the proper circumstances for writing became increasingly difficult in the mid 1830s. His personal anxieties—not just the "official" pressures of attendance at court social events but matters far more serious—made enormous demands on him. In the fall of 1834 Natalia's two sisters came to live with the Pushkins, adding another financial burden to the onerous responsibilities Pushkin had already assumed when he agreed to pay his brother's debts and manage the Boldino estate. Desperate for additional means, Pushkin sought opportunities in journalism. He had long been familiar with the journalistic scene in Russia (and to a certain degree in France and in England), having personally negotiated with editors for more than ten years and having edited *Literaturnaia gazeta* with his friend Del'vig in 1830. Believing he could make a financial and popular success out of his own journal, *Sovremennik* (The Contemporary), Pushkin sought and was granted publication permission from the government in 1835. The first issues appeared in 1836, but hardly with the success he had hoped for. In no way could he compete with leading periodicals of the day, *Biblioteka dlia chteniia* (edited by Senkovsky) and *Severnaia pchela* (The Northern Bee, edited by Bulgarin). Pushkin saw four issues to press and prepared a fifth, which was published posthumously.

Beyond his anxiety relating to finances, the most serious life complication for Pushkin in his last years was dealing with his wife's apparent flirtation with Baron Georges d'Anthès-Heeckeren, a French émigré who worked in the Russian service and who played a prominent role in court society. By 1834, when d'Anthès first met Natalia, the Pushkins had two children, Maria and Aleksandr. Natalia had a third child, Grigory, in May of 1835, and a fourth, Natalia, in May of 1836. He openly pursued Natalia after their first meeting, and apparently not sufficiently discouraged by her behavior toward him (or her almost constant state of pregnancy), rumors of an affair emerged. Indeed, in the fall of 1836 Pushkin received notice that he had been nominated as the "coadjutor of the Society of Cuckolds and Historiographer of the Order." For one so sensitive to his own and his family's honor, a challenge was required. The details make morbidly fascinating reading, for the personages involved are striking in their individuality. D'Anthès had been adopted by the Dutch Ambassador, Louis van Heeckeren (rumored to be homosexual), and it was through Heeckeren that Pushkin passed his provocations to a duel. Efforts were made, at first successfully, to postpone and even avoid the duel when d'Anthès indicated it was Natalia's sister Ekaterina he loved; in fact, in January 1837 he married her, although Pushkin refused to attend the ceremony. This event, if anything, made Natalia even more accessible to d'Anthès, and he continued the pursuit. Finally, Pushkin learned that Natalia and d'Anthès had been discovered alone together by one of his children. He promptly wrote an insulting letter to Heeckeren, blaming him for the "nomination" and accusing him of being the panderer for his bastard son. At the now inevitable duel, on 27 January 1837, Pushkin suffered mortal wounds, dying two days later on 29 January. D'Anthès was also wounded (though not seriously), and the opinion of high society tended to be sympathetic toward him. To avoid large crowds at Pushkin's funeral, the authorities limited the audience to those with tickets (largely, the d'Anthès sympathizers). The body was removed to Mikhailovskoe in a cart at midnight to avoid difficulties with crowds, and Pushkin was buried 6 Februrary 1837 next to his mother at *Sviatye gory*, a monastery not far from the estate.

The place of Pushkin in Russian letters is secure, although his relationship to Romanticism, whether conceived in a Russian or European sense, is problematic. By chronology, his rejection of the "archaizers" and Neoclassical writers of his age, his outspoken defense of freedom from rules (whether those of style or those of genre), and his embrace of characteristic themes and attitudes toward literature, he is clearly a Romantic. But critics always have had problems reconciling all these characteristics with the stylistic qualities of his writing—its conciseness and precision, its spareness, and its moderateness. Also difficult to resolve is Pushkin's refusal to adopt and express a universal worldview (he is usually termed a protean genius) that can be linked with Romantic philosophy, since his distaste for German metaphysics is well known. The fact remains that he was influenced by Romantic writers, particularly Byron and Goethe, and by Shakespeare, recognized by Romantics as their spiritual and artistic father. Although Pushkin, according to some of his pronouncements, conceived of Romanticism largely in formal terms—as a rejection of Classical genres—he also gave special importance to artistic sincerity (suggestive of an organic view of art) and freedom from rules–paradigmatic Romantic qualities. When his propensity for irony and many other affinities with the Romantics are added, his status as a Romantic writer cannot be challenged.

Letters:

Perepiska Pushkina, 3 volumes, edited by Vladimir Ivanovich Saitov (St. Petersburg: AN SSSR, 1906–1911);

Pis'ma Pushkina i k Pushkinu, ne voshedshie v izdanie Rossiiskoi akademii nauk "Perepisku Pushkina," edited by Mstislav Aleksandrovich Tsiavlovsky (Moscow: GAKhN, 1925);

Pis'ma Pushkina k Elizavete Mikhailovne Khitrovo, 1827–32, edited by Sergei Fedorovich Platonov (Leningrad: AN SSSR, 1927);

Pis'ma, volumes 1 and 2, edited by Boris L'vovich Modzalevsky (Moscow-Leningrad: GIZ-Akademia, 1926, 1928); volume 3, edited by Modzalevsky (Moscow: GIZ, 1935);

Pis'ma Pushkina k N. N. Goncharovoi, edited by Modeste L. Gofman and Sergei Lifar' (Paris: Cooperative Etoile, 1936);

The Letters of Alexander Pushkin, translated and edited by J. Thomas Shaw, 3 volumes (Philadelphia: University of Pennsylvania Press / Bloomington: Indiana University Press, 1963);

Pis'ma poslednikh let, 1834–37, edited by Nikolai Vasil'evich Izmailov (Leningrad: Nauka, 1969);

Perepiska A. S. Pushkina, edited by Vadim Erazmovich Vatsuro and others, 2 volumes (Moscow: Kudozh. lit-ra., 1982);

Tainye zapiski 1836–1837 godov (Minneapolis: MIP, 1986) (Attribution to Pushkin doubtful);

Pis'ma k zhene, edited by Ia. L. Levkovich (Leningrad: Nauka, 1986).

Bibliographies:

Vladimir Izmailovich Mezhov, *Puschkiniana: Bibliograficheskii ukazatel' statei o zhizni Pushkina, ego sochinenii i vyzvannyx im proizavodenii literatury i iskusstva* (St. Petersburg: V. Bezobrazov, 1886);

Nikolai Kir'iakovich Piksanov, *Pushkinskaia studiia* (Petrograd: Atenei, 1922);

A. G. Fomin, *Puschkiniana, 1900–1910* (Moscow-Leningrad: AN SSSR, 1929);

Samuel H. Cross, "Pouchkine en Angleterre," *Revue de litterature comparee,* 17 (1937): 163–181;

Puschkiniana, 1911–1917 (Moscow-Leningrad: AN SSSR, 1937); *Bibliografiia proizvedenii A. S. Pushkina i literatury o nem: 1918–1936;* Chast' 1, edited by L. M. Dobrovol'sky and N. I. Mordovchenko (Moscow-Leningrad: AN SSSR, 1952); Chast' 2, edited by Ia. L. Levkovich (Leningrad, 1973); *1937–1948,* edited by Ia. L. Levkovich (Moscow-Leningrad, 1963); *1949, iubileinyi god.,* edited by L. G. Grinberg (Moscow-Leningrad, 1951); *1950,* edited by Grinberg (Moscow-Leningrad, 1952); *1951,* edited by Levkovich (Moscow-Leningrad, 1954); *1952–1953,* edited by Levkovich and A. S. Morshchikina (Moscow-Leningrad, 1959); *1954–1957,* edited by Levkovich and N. N. Petrunina (Moscow-Leningrad, 1960);

Avrahm Yarmolinsky, *Pushkin in English: A List of Works by and about Pushkin* (New York: New York Public Library, 1937);

N. Siniavsky and Mstislav Aleksandrovich Tsiavlovsky, *Pushkin v pechati, 1814–1837,* revised edition (Moscow: Sotsekgiz, 1938);

Pavel Naumovich Berkov and V. M. Lavrov, *Bibliografiia proizvedenii A. S. Pushkina i literatury o nem: 1886–1899* (Moscow-Leningrad: AN SSSR, 1939);

Nikolai Leont'evich Brodsky, *A. S. Pushkin, 1799–1837: Rekomendatel'nyi ukazatel' literatury* (Moscow, 1949);

L. M. Dobrovol'sky and Lavrov, *Bibliografia Pushkinskoi bibliografii, 1846–1950,* (Moscow-Leningrad: AN SSSR, 1951);

B. S. Meilakh and N. S. Gornitskaia, *A. S. Pushkin: Seminarii* (Leningrad: Uchpedgiz, 1959);

V. V. Zaitseva, "Knigi o Pushkine," *Vremennik Pushkinskoi komissii* (1962–1970) (books published 1961–1970);

J. Thomas Shaw, "Recent Soviet Scholarly Books on Pushkin: A Review Article," *Slavic and East European Journal,* 10 (1966): 66–84;

B. P. Gorodetsky and others, *Pushkin: Itogi i problemy izucheniia* (Moscow-Leningrad: Nauka, 1966);

Zaitseva, "Pushkiniana," *Vremennik Pushkinskoi komissii* (1970–);

Patrick J. and April I. Wreath, "Alexander Pushkin: A Bibliography of Criticism in English, 1920–1975," *Canadian-American Slavic Studies,* 10 (1976): 279–304;

Sergei Aleksandrovich Fomichev, "Soviet Pushkin Scholarship of the Last Decade," *Canadian-American Slavic Studies,* 11 (1977): 141–154;

Garth M. Terry, "Pushkin, Alexander Sergeevich," in *East European Languages and Literatures: A Subject and Name Index to Articles in English-Language Journals, 1900–1977* (Santa Barbara, Cal.: Clio Press, 1978), pp. 127–133;

June Pachuta, "A Bibliography of Pushkin Bibliographies," *Russian Language Journal,* 35, no. 120 (1981): 187–194;

Munir Sendich, "Pushkin's *Malen'kie tragedii:* A Bibliography of Literary Criticism in English, 1882–

1978," *Russian Language Journal,* 35, no. 120 (1981): 175–186;

E. M. Sakharova and V. I. Petrovskaia, "Aleksandr Sergeevich Pushkin," in *Ekho russkogo naroda: Poeziia dorevoliutsionnoi Rossii: Rekomendatel'nyi bibliograficheskii ukazatel'* (Moscow: Kniga, 1985), pp. 122–137;

M. P. Alekseev, "Pushkin na Zapade," in his *Pushkin i mirovaia literatura* (Leningrad: Nauka, 1987);

Carl R. Proffer and Ronald Meyer, comps., *Nineteenth-Century Russian Literature in English: A Bibliography of Criticism and Translations* (Ann Arbor, Mich.: Ardis, 1990), pp. 122–138;

Beatrice van Sambeek-Weideli, *"Evgenii Onegin A. S. Pushkina: Bibliografiia: Eine Bibliographie zu Pushkins Evgenii Onegin." Slavica Helvetica,* 35 (1990);

Leslie O'Bell, "American Pushkin Scholarship since 1945: A Review Article and Selected Bibliography," *Pushkin Journal,* 1 (1993): 121–146.

Biographies:

Pavel Vasil'evich Annenkov, ed., *A. S. Pushkin: Materialy dlia ego biografii i otsenki proizvedenii,* volume 1 of Pushkin's *Polnoe sobranie sochinenii* (1855); facsimile reprint, together with *Kommentarii,* edited by Aleksandr L. Ospovat and N. G. Okhotin, 2 volumes (Moscow: Kniga, 1985);

Petr Ivanovich Bartenev, *Pushkin v iuzhnoi Rossii* (Moscow: Tip. Gracheva, 1862);

Annenkov, *Pushkin v Aleksandrovskuiu epokhu* (St. Petersburg: M. Stasiulevich, 1874);

Iakov Karlovich Grot, *Pushkin: Ego litseiskie tovarishchi i nastavniki* (St. Petersburg: Akademii nauk, 1887);

Leonid Nikolaevich Maikov, *Pushkin: Biograficheskie materialy i istoriko-literaturnye orcherki* (St. Petersburg: Panteleev, 1899);

Nikolai Osipovich Lerner, comp., *Trudy i dni Pushkina* (St. Petersburg: Tip. Imp. Akademii nauk, 1903);

Pavel Eliseevich Shchegolev, *Pushkin i ego sovremenniki* (1916); reprinted as *Duel i smert' Pushkina* (Moscow-Leningrad: Federatsiia, 1928); reprinted and edited by Ia. L Levkovich (Moscow, 1987);

Boris L'vovich Modzalevskii, *Byloe* (1918); reprinted as *Pushkin pod tainym nadzorom* (Petrograd, 1922);

Petr Konstantinovich Guber, *Don-Zhuanskii spisok A. S. Pushkina* (St. Petersburg: Petrograd, 1923);

Petr Ivanovich Bartenev, *Rasskazy o Pushkine, zapisannye so slov ego druzei P. I. Bartenevym v 1851–1860 godakh,* edited by Mstislav Aleksandrovich Tsiavlovsky (Moscow: M. i S. Sabashikov, 1925);

Vikentii Vikent'evich Veresaev, *Pushkin v zhizni* (Moscow: Sovetskii pisatel', 1926–1927);

A. Tyrkova-Vilyams, *Zhizn' Pushkina* (Paris: YMCA Press, 1929);

Sergei Iakovlevich Gessen and Modzalevskii, *Razgovory Pushkina* (Moscow: Federatsiia, 1929);

Gessen, *Knigoizdatel' Pushkina: liteaturnye dokhody Pushkina* (Leningrad: Akademiia, 1930);

Shchegolev, *Iz zhizni i tvorchestva Pushkina* (Moscow: GIKhL, 1931);

Tsiavlovsky and others, eds., *Rukoiu Pushkina* (Moscow & Leningrad: Akademiia, 1935);

Nikolai Leont'evich Brodsky, *Pushkin: Biografiia* (Moscow: GIKhL, 1937);

Ernest J. Simmons, *Pushkin* (Cambridge, Mass.: Harvard University Press, 1937);

Veresaev, *Sputniki Pushkina,* 2 volumes (Moscow: Sovetskii pisatel', 1937);

Leonid Petrovich Grossman, *Pushkin* (Moscow: Mol. Gvardiia, 1939);

Henri Troyat, *Pouchkine: Biographie,* 2 volumes (Paris: A. Michel, 1946); translated by Nancy Amphoux as *Pushkin: A Biography* (Garden City, N.Y., 1970);

Vladislav Mikhailovich Glinka, *Pushkin i voennaia galereiia Zimnego dvortsa* (Leningrad: Lenizdat, 1949);

Tsiavlovskii, comp., *Letopis' zhizni i tvorchestva A. S. Pushkina, 1799–1826* (Leningrad: AN SSSR, 1951);

Ettore Lo Gatto, *Pushkin: Storia di un poeta e del suo eroe* (Milano: U. Mursia, 1959);

Nikolai Vasil'evich Izmailov, ed., *Pushkin v pis'makh Karamzinykh, 1836–1837 godov* (Leningrad: AN SSSR, 1960);

Nikolai Pavlovich Smirnov-Sokol'skii, *Rasskazy o prizhiznennykh izdaniiakh Pushkina* (Moscow: Izd-vo Vsesoiuznoi knizhnoi palaty, 1962);

Andre Meyneiux, *Pouchkine: Homme de lettres et al litterature professionnelle en Russie* (Paris: Librairie des Cinq Continents, 1966);

David Magarshack, *Pushkin: A Biography* (London: Chapman & Hall, 1967);

Walter N. Vickery, *Pushkin: Death of a Poet* (Bloomington: Indiana University Press, 1968);

Boris Solomonovich Meilakh, *Zhizn' Aleksandra Pushkina* (Leningrad: Khudozh. lit-ra, 1974);

Vadim Erazmovich Vatsuro and others, eds., *A. S. Pushkin v vospominaniiakh sovremennikov,* 2 volumes (Moscow: Khudozh. lit-ra, 1974);

Lazar' Chereiskii, *Pushkin i ego okruzhenie,* second edition, revised (Leningrad: Nauka, 1975);

Natan Iakovlevich Eidel'man, *Pushkin i dekabristy: Iz istorii vzaimootnoshenii* (Moscow: Khudozh. lit-ra, 1979);

Irina Mikhailovna Obodovskaia and Mikhail Alekseevich Dement'ev, *Posle smerti Pushkina. Neizvestnye pis'ma* (Moscow: Sovetskaia Rossiia, 1980);

Evgenii Aleksandrovich Maimin, *Pushkin: Zhizn' i tvorchestvo* (Moscow: Nauka, 1981);

Iurii Mikhailovich Lotman, *Aleksandr Sergeevich Pushkin: Biografia pisatelia: Posobie dlia uchashchikhsia,* second edition (Moscow-Leningrad, 1981);

Vladimir Vladimirovich Kunina, ed., *Druz'ia Pushkina: Perepiska, vospominaniia, dnevniki,* 2 volumes (Moscow: Pravda, 1984);

Eidel'man, *Pushkin: Istoriia i sovremennost' v khudozhestvennom soznanii poeta* (Moscow: Sovetskii pisatel', 1984);

Svetlana Tikhonovna Ovchinnikova, *Pushkin v Moskve* (Moscow: Sovetskaia Rossiia, 1984);

Vadim Erazmovich Vatsuro, *Pushkin v vospominaniiakh sovremennikov* (Moscow: Khudozh. lit-ra, 1985);

Eidel'man, *Pushkin: Iz biografii i tvorchestva, 1826–1837* (Moscow: Khudozh. lit-ra, 1987);

Vladimir Mikhailovich Fridkin, *Propavshii dnevnik Pushkina* (Moscow: Znanie, 1987);

Vladimir Ustinovich Kuleshov, *Zhizn' i tvorchestvo A. S. Pushkina* (Moscow: Khudozh. lit-ra, 1987);

Kunina, ed., *Zhizn' Pushkina: Perepiska, vospominaniia, dnevniki,* 2 volumes (Moscow: Pravda, 1987);

Ia. L. Levkovich, *Avtobiograficheskaia proza i pis'ma Pushkina* (Leningrad: Nauka, 1988);

Gevrikh Markovich Deich, *Vse li my zhaem o Pushkine?* (Moscow: Sovetskaia Rossiia, 1989);

Semen Dmitrievich Abramovich, *Pushkin. Poslednii god* (Moscow: Sovetskii pisatel', 1991);

Iurii Druzhnikov, *Uznik Rossii: Po sledam niezvestnogo Pushkina* (Orange, Conn.: Antiquary, 1992);

Druzhnikov, *Dos'e begletsa: Po sledam neizvestnogo Pushkina* (Tenafly, N. J.: Izd-vo Ermitazh, 1993);

Semen Laskin, *Vokrug dueli* (St. Petersburg: Prosveshchenie, 1993);

Lidiia Slonimskaia, *Mir Pushkina,* volume 1 (Dnevniki pis'ma N. O. i S. L. Pushkinykh, 1828–1835); (St. Petersburg: Pushkinskii fond, 1993);

Robin Edmonds, *Pushkin: The Man and His Age* (London: Macmillan, 1994).

References:

Iurii Aleksandrovich Aikhenval'd, *Pushkin,* second edition (Moscow: Nauch. slovo, 1916);

Anna Andreevna Akhmatova, *O Pushkine: Stat'i i zametki* (Leningrad: Sovetskii pisatel', 1977);

Mikhail Pavlovich Alekseev, *Pushkin i mirovaia literatura* (Leningrad: Nauka, 1987);

Alekseev, *Pushkin: Sravnitel'no-istoricheskie issledovaniia* (Leningrad: Nauka, 1972);

Alekseev, *Stikhotvorenie Pushkina "Ia pamiatnik sebe vozdvig": Problemy ego izucheniia* (Leningrad: Nauka, 1967);

Alekseev, ed., *Pushkin: Issledovaniia i materialy: Trudy tret'ei Vsesoiuznoi pushkinskoi konferentsii* (Moscow-Leningrad: AN SSSR, 1953);

Alekseev, ed., *Pushkin: Stat'i materialy,* 3 volumes (Odessa: Odespoligry, 1925–1926);

Alekseev and others, eds., *Pushkin v stranakh zarubezhnogo Vostoka: Sbornik statei* (Moscow: Nauka, 1979);

Alekseev, ed., *Shekspir i russkaia kul'tura* (Moscow-Leningrad: Nauka, 1965), pp. 165–200;

Alexandre Pouchkine 1799–1837 (Paris: Paris-Musées, 1997);

Evgenii Vasil'evich Anichkov, ed., *Belgradskii Pushkinskii sbornik* (Belgrad: Izd. Russkogo Pushkinskogo komiteta v Iugoslavii, 1937);

Arion: Jahrbuch der Deutschen Puschkin-Gesellschaft, volume 1 (Bonn: Bouvier, 1988);

Victor Arminjon, *Pouchkine et Pierre le Grand* (Paris: Libraire des Cinq Continents, 1971);

A. S. Pushkin. Problemy tvorchestva (Kalinin: Gos. in-t, 1987);

Mark Konstantinovich Azadovsky, *Literatura i fol'klor: Ocherki i etiudy* (Leningrad: Goslitizdat, 1938), pp. 5–292;

Gabib B. Babaev, *Tvorchestvo A. S. Pushkina* (Moscow: Izd-vo Moskovskogo universiteta, 1988);

Vadim Baevsky, *Skvoz' magicheskii kristall: Poètika "Evgeniia Onegina" romana v stikhakh A. Pushkina* (Moscow: Prometei, 1990);

Petr I. Barta and Ulrich Goebel, eds., *The Contexts of Aleksandr Sergeevich Pushkin* (Lewiston, N.Y.: Edwin Mellen Press, 1988);

John Bayley, *Pushkin: A Comparative Commentary* (Cambridge: Cambridge University Press, 1971);

Vissarion Grigor'evich Belinsky, *Polnao sobranie sochinenii,* 13 volumes (Moscow: AN SSSR, 1953–1959);

Andrei Belyi, *Ritm kak dialektika i "Mednyi vsadnik": Issledovanie* (Moscow: Federatsiia, 1929);

Al'fred Liudvigovich L. Bem, *O Pushkine: Stat'i* (Uzhgorod: Pis'mena, 1937);

David M. Bethea, ed., *Pushkin Today* (Bloomington: Indiana University Press, 1993);

Petr Mikhailovich Bitsilli, "Poezii Pushkina," in his *Etiudy o russkoi poèzii* (Prague: Plamia, 1926), pp. 65–224;

Dmitrii Dmitrievich Blagoi, *Dusha v zavetnoi lire: Ocherki zhizni i tvorchestva Pushkina* (Moscow: Sovetskii pisatel', 1977);

Blagoi, *Ot Kantemira do nashikh dnei,* 2 volumes, second edition (Moscow: Khudozh. lit-ra, 1979);

Blagoi, *The Sacred Lyre: Essays on the Life and Work of Aleksandr Pushkin,* translated by Alex Miller (Moscow: Raduga, 1982);

Blagoi, *Sotsiologiia tvorchestva Pushkina: Ètiudy,* second edition (Moscow: Mir, 1931);

Blagoi, *Tvorcheskii put' Pushkina (1813–1826)* (Moscow-Leningrad: AN SSSR, 1950);

Blagoi, *Tvorcheskii put' Pushkina (1826–1830)* (Moscow: Sovetskii pisatel', 1967);

Blagoi and V. Ia. Kirpotin, eds., *Pushkin: Rodonachal'nik novoi russkoi literatury: Sbornik nauchno-issledovatel'skikh rabot* (Moscow-Leningrad: AN SSSR, 1941);

Elizaveta Maksimovna Blinova, *Literaturnaia gazeta A. A. Del'viga i A. S. Pushkina, 1830–1831: Ukazatel' soderzhaniia* (Moscow: Kniga, 1966);

G. P. Blok, *Pushkin v rabote nad istoricheskimi istochnikami* (Moscow-Leningrad: AN SSSR, 1949);

Harold Bloom, ed., *Aleksandr Pushkin* (New York: Chelsea Home Publishers, 1987);

Sergei Georg'evich Bocharov, *Poetika Pushkina: Ocherki* (Moscow: Nauka, 1974);

Boldinskie chteniia, volumes 1– (Gor'kii: Volgo-Viatskoe knizhnoe izd-vo, 1976–);

Sergei M. Bondi, *Chernoviki Pushkina: Stat'i 1930–1970 gg.* (Moscow: Prosveshchenie, 1971);

Bondi, *Novye stranitsy Pushkina: Stikhi proza, pis'ma* (Moscow: Mir, 1931);

Bondi, *O Pushkine: Stat'i i issledovaniia,* second edition (Moscow: Khudozh. lit-ra, 1983);

A. D. P. Briggs, *Aleksandr Pushkin: A Critical Study* (London: Croom Helm, 1983; Totowa, N. J.: Barnes & Noble, 1983);

Briggs, *Aleksandr Pushkin: Eugene Onegin* (New York: Cambridge University Press, 1993);

Briggs, *A Comparative Study of Pushkin's "The Bronze Horseman," Nekrasov's "Red-Nosed Frost," and Blok's "The Twelve"* (Lewiston, N.Y.: Edwin Mellen Press, 1990);

Valerii Iakovlevich Briusov, *Moi Pushkin: Stat'i, issledovaniia, nabliudeniia* (Munich: W. Fink, 1970);

William Edward Brown, *History of Russian Literature of the Romantic Period,* 4 volumes (Ann Arbor, Mich.: Ardis, 1986), volume 3, pp. 1–239;

Boris Ivanovich Bursov, ed., *Pushkin: Issledovaniia i materialy: Trudy pervoi i vtoroi Vsesoiuznykh pushkinskikh konferentsii* (Moscow-Leningrad: AN SSSR, 1952);

Canadian-American Slavic Studies, special Pushkin issues, 10, no. 4 (1976); 11, no. 1 (1977);

Canadian Slavonic Papers, special Pushkin issues, 29, nos. 2–3 (1987);

Nikolai Ivanovich Cherniaev, *Kriticheskie stat'i i zametki o Pushkine* (Kharkov: Iuzhnogo kraia, 1900);

J. Douglas Clayton, *Ice and Flame: Aleksandr Pushkin's "Eugene Onegin"* (Toronto: University of Toronto Press, 1985);

Colloquio italo-sovietico: Pushkin poeta e la sua arte: Roma 3–4 giugno 1977 (Rome: Accademia nazionale, 1978);

Neil Cornwall, *Pushkin's "The Queen of Spades"* (London: Bristol Classical Press, 1993);

Samuel H. Cross and Ernest J. Simmons, eds., *Centennial Essays for Pushkin* (Cambridge, Mass.: Harvard University Press, 1937);

A. M. Deborin, ed., *Sto let so dnia smerti A. S. Pushkina: Trudy Pushkinskoi sessii Akademii nauk SSSR* (Moscow-Leningrad: AN SSSR, 1938);

Paul Debreczeny, *The Other Pushkin: A Study of Pushkin's Prose Fiction* (Stanford, Cal.: Stanford University Press, 1983);

K. N. Derzhavin, ed., *"Boris Godunov" A. S. Pushkina: Sbornik statei* (Leningrad: Tip. Tranzheldorizdala NKPS, 1936);

Aleksandr Dolinin, *Istoriia, odetaia v roman: Val'ter Skott i ego chitateli* (Moscow: Kniga, 1988);

Sam Driver, *Pushkin: Literature and Social Ideas* (New York: Columbia University Press, 1989);

Sergei Nikolaevich Durylin, *Pushkin na stsene* (Moscow: AN SSSR, 1951);

Abram Markovich Efros, *Risunki poeta,* second edition (Moscow: Akademia, 1933);

Natan Iakovlevich Eidel'man, *Pushkin i dekabristy* (Moscow: Khudozh. lit-ra, 1979);

Iosif Eiges, *Muzyka o zhizni i tvorchestve Pushkina* (Moscow: Muzgiz, 1937);

Nikolai El'iash, *Pushkin i baletnyi teatr* (Moscow: Iskusstvo, 1970);

Caryl Emerson, *Boris Godunov: Transpositions on a Russian Theme* (Bloomington: Indiana University Press, 1986);

Mikhail Pavlovich Eremin, *Pushkin-publitsist,* second edition (Moscow: Khudozhestvennaia literatura, 1976);

Ivan Dmitrievich Ermakov, *Ètiudy po psikhologii tvorchestva A. S. Pushkina* (Moscow & Petrograd: GIZ, 1923);

Efim Grigor'evich Ètkind, *Simmetricheskie kompozitsii u Pushkina* (Paris: Institut d'Etudes Slavs, 1988);

Il'ia L'vovich Feinberg, *Abram Petrovich Gannibal, praded Pushkina: Razyskaniia i materialy* (Moscow: Nauka, 1983);

Feinberg, *Chitaia tetradi Pushkina* (Moscow: Sovetskii pisatel', 1976);

Feinberg, *Nezavershennye raboty Pushkina,* sixth edition (Moscow: Sovremennik, 1976);

O. M. Fel'dman, *Sud'ba dramaturgii Pushkina: "Boris Godunov"; "Malen'kie tragedii"* (Moscow: Iskusstvo, 1975);

John Fennell, "Pushkin," in *Nineteenth-Century Russian Literature: Studies of Ten Russian Writers,* edited by John Fennell (London: Faber, 1973), pp. 13–68;

Nina Fedorovna Filippova, *Narodnaia drama A. S. Pushkina "Boris Godunov"* (Moscow: Kniga, 1972);

Sergei Aleksandrovich Fomichev, *Poeziia Pushkina: Tvorcheskaia evoliutsiia* (Leningrad: Nauka, 1986);

Semen Liudvigovich Frank, *Étiudy o Pushkine* (Munich, 1957);

Nikolai Vladimirovich Fridman, *Romantizm v tvorshestve A. S. Pushkina* (Moscow: Prosveshchenie, 1980);

Boris Gasparov and others, eds., *Cultural Mythologies of Russian Modernism: From the Golden Age to the Silver Age* (Berkeley: University of California Press, 1992);

Nikolai Konstantinovich Gei, *Proza Pushkina: Poetika povestvovaniia* (Moscow: Nauka, 1989);

Mikhail Osipovich Gershenzon, *Mudrost' Pushkina* (Moscow: Kn.-vo pisatelei v M., 1919);

M. Gershenzon, *Mudrost' Pushkina* (Moscow: Ki-vo pisatelei v M., 1919);

Gershenzon, *Stat'i o Pushkine* (Moscow: Gos. akad. khudozh. nauk., 1926);

Arnol'd Il'ich Gessen, *Vse volnovalo nezhhnyi um . . . : Pushkin sredi knig i druzei* (Moscow: Nauka, 1965);

Aleksandr Nikolaevich Glumov, *Muzikal'nyi mir Pushkina* (Moscow-Leningrad: Muzgiz, 1950);

Modeste L. Gofman, *Pervaia glava nauki o Pushkine* (Petrograd: Atenei, 1922);

Gofman, *Pushkin: Psikhologiia tvorchestva* (Paris, 1928);

Boris Pavlovich Gorodetsky, *Dramaturgiia Pushkina* (Moscow-Leningrad: AN SSSR, 1953);

Gorodetsky, *Lirika Pushkina* (Moscow-Leningrad: AN SSSR, 1962);

Gorodetsky, *Lirika Pushkina: Posobie dlia uchitelia* (Leningrad, 1970);

Gorodetsky, *Tragediia A. S. Pushkina "Boris Godunov"* (Leningrad: Prosveshchenie, 1969);

Monika Greenleaf, *Pushkin and Romantic Fashion: Fragment, Elegy, Orient, Irony* (Stanford, Cal.: Stanford University Press, 1994);

Leonid Petrovich Grossman, *Étiudy o Pushkine; Pushkin v teatral'nykh kreslakh* (Moscow: Sovr. problemy, 1928);

Arusiak Georg'evna Gukasova, *Boldinskii period v tvorchestve A. S. Pushkina* (Moscow: Prosveshchenie, 1973);

Grigorii Aleksandrovich Gukovsky, *Pushkin i problemy realistichekogo stilia* (Moscow: Goslitizdat, 1957);

Gukovsky, *Pushkin i russkie romantiki* (Moscow: Khudozh. lit-ra, 1965);

George Gutsche, "Pushkin's *The Bronze Horseman*," in his *Moral Apostasy in Russian Literature* (DeKalb: North Illinois University Press, 1986), pp. 16–42;

Gutsche and Lauren Leighton, eds., *New Perspectives on Nineteenth-Century Russian Prose* (Columbus, Ohio: Slavica, 1982);

Karla Hielscher, *A. S. Pushkins Versepik: Autoren-Ich und Erzalstruktur* (Munich: Signer, 1966);

Sona Stephan Hoisington, *Russian Views of Pushkin's "Eugene Onegin"* (Bloomington: Indiana University Press, 1988);

Viacheslav Evgen'evich Iakushkin, *O Pushkine: Stat'i i zametki* (Moscow: M. & S. Sabashinikovy, 1899);

Irina Sergeevna Il'inskaia, *Leksika stikhotvornoi rechi Pushkina: "Vysokie" i poeticheskie slavianizmy* (Moscow: Nauka, 1970);

Razumnik Vasil'evich Ivanov, *Pushkin i Belinskii: Stat'i istoriko-literaturnye* (Petrograd: M. M. Stasiulevich, 1916);

Nikolai Vasilevich Izmailov, *Ocherki tvorchestva Pushkina* (Leningrad: Nauka, 1975);

Izmailov, ed., *Stikhotvoreniia Pushkina 1820–1830-kh godov: Istoriia sozdaniia i ideino-khudozhestvennaia problematika* (Leningrad: Nauka, 1974);

Roman Jakobson, *Pushkin and His Sculptural Myth*, translated by John Burbank (The Hague: Mouton, 1975);

Matvei Matveevich Kalaushin, ed., *Pushkin i ego vremia: Issledovaniia i materialy* (Leningrad: Izd-vo Gos. Ermitazha, 1962);

Michael R. Katz, "Pushkin's Literary Ballads," in his *The Literary Ballad in Early Nineteenth-Century Russian Literature* (London: Oxford University Press, 1976), pp. 139–165;

Vladislav Felitsianovich Khodasevich, *O Pushkine*. (Berlin: Petropolis, 1937);

Sergei Akimovich Kibal'nik, *Khudozhestvennaia filosofiia Pushkina: Uchebnoe posobie po spetskursu* (St. Petersburg: Rossiiskaia akademiia nauk, 1993);

Kibal'nik, *Russkaia antologicheskaia poeziia: Pervoi treti XIX v.* (Leningrad: Nauka, 1990);

Zoia Ivanova Kirnoze, ed., *Merime-Pushkin: Sbornik* (Moscow: Raduga, 1987);

Andrej Kodjak, *Pushkin's I. P. Belkin* (Columbus, Ohio: Slavica, 1979);

Kodjak and Kiril Taranovsky, eds., *Aleksandr Pushkin: A Symposium* (New York: New York University Press, 1976);

Kodjak and others, eds., *Aleksandr Pushkin: Symposium II* (Columbus, Ohio: Slavica, 1980);

Vasilii Ivanovich Kuleshov, ed., *Zamysel, trud, voploshchenie* (Moscow, 1977);

Galina Alekseevna Lapkina, *Na afishe-Pushkin* (Moscow-Leningrad: Iskusstvo, 1975);

Nadezhda Vasil'evna Lapshina and others, *Metricheskii spravochnik k stikotvoreniiam A. S. Pushkina* (Moscow-Leningrad: Academia, 1934);

Janko Lavrin, *Pushkin and Russian Literature* (London: Hodder & Stoughton, 1947);

Waclaw Lednicki, *Aleksandr Pushkin: Studja* (Krakow, 1926);

Lednicki, *Bits of Table Talk on Pushkin, Mickiewicz, Goethe, Turgenev, and Sienkiewicz* (The Hague: Martinus Nijhoff, 1956);

Lednicki, *Pushkin's "Bronze Horseman": The Story of a Masterpiece* (Westwood, Conn.: Greenwood, 1978);

Lednicki, ed., *Pushkin, 1837–1939,* 2 volumes (Krakow: Drukania W. L. Anczycz i spolki, 1939);

Lauren Leighton, *The Esoteric Tradition in Russian Romantic Literature: Decembrism and Freemasonry* (University Park: Penn State University Press, 1994);

Nikolai Osipovich Lerner, *Proza Pushkina,* second edition, revised (Moscow & Petrograd: Kniga, 1923);

Lerner, *Rasskazy o Pushkine* (Leningrad: Priboi, 1929);

Vladimir Lazarevich Levin, ed., *Poeticheskaia frazeologiia Pushkina* (Moscow: Nauka, 1969);

Marcus Levitt, *Russian Literary Politics and the Pushkin Celebration of 1980* (Ithaca, N.Y.: Cornell University Press, 1989);

Abram Lezhnev, *Proza Pushkina: Opyt stilevogo issledovaniia,* second edition (Moscow, 1966);

Lezhnev, *Pushkin's Prose,* translated by Roberta Reeder (Ann Arbor, Mich.: Ardis, 1983);

Literaturnoe nasledstvo, volumes 16–18 (Moscow, 1934); 58 (Moscow, 1952);

Natalia Georgievna Litvinenko, *Pushkin i teatr: Formirovanie teatral'nykh vozzrenii* (Moscow: Iskusstvo, 1974);

Ettore Lo Gatto, ed., *Alessandro Pushkin: Nel primo centarios della morte* (Rome: Instituto per l'Europa orientale, 1937);

Iurii Mikhailovich Lotman, *Roman A. S. Pushkina "Evgenii Onegin": Kommentarii; Posobie dlia uchitelia,* second edition (Leningrad: Prosveshchenie, 1983); reprinted in *Pushkin: Biografiia pisatelia, Stat'i i zametki. 1960–1990, "Evgenii Onegin." Kommentarii* (St. Petersburg: Iskusstvo SPB, 1995);

Arthur Luther, ed., *Solange Dichter Leben: Puschkin Studien* (Krefeld, Germany: Scherpe-Verlag, 1949);

Georgii Panteleimonovich Makogonenko, *"Evgenii Onegin" A. S. Pushkina* (Moscow: Khudozh. lit-ra, 1963);

Makogonenko, *Gogol' i Pushkin* (Leningrad: Sovetskii pisatel', 1985);

Makogonenko, *Izbrannye raboty: O Pushkine, ego predshestvennikakh i naslednikakh* (Leningrad: Khudozh. lit-ra, 1987);

Makogonenko, *"Kapitanskaia dochka" A. S. Pushkina* (Leningrad: Khudozh. lit-ra, 1977);

Makogonenko, *Lermontov i Pushkin: Problemy preemstvennogo razvitiia literatury* (Leningrad: Sovetskii pisatel', 1987);

Makogonenko, *Tvorchestvo A. S. Pushkina v 1830-e gody (1830–1833)* (Leningrad: Khudozh. lit-ra, 1974);

John Malmstad, ed., *Pushkin and His Friends: The Making of a Myth: An Exhibition of the Kilgour Collection* (Cambridge: Houghton Library, 1987);

Semen Iosifovich Mashinsky, ed., *V mire Pushkin: Sbornik statei* (Moscow: Sovetskii pisatel', 1974);

Boris Solomonovich Meilakh, *A. S. Pushkin: Ocherk zhizni i tvorchestva* (Moscow-Leningrad: AN SSSR, 1949);

Meilakh, *Khudozhestvennoe myshlenie Pushkina kak tvorcheskii protsess* (Moscow-Leningrad: AN SSSR, 1962);

Meilakh, *Pushkin i ego epokha* (Moscow: AN SSSR, 1958);

Meilakh, *Pushkin i russkii romantizm* (Moscow-Leningrad: AN SSSR, 1937);

Meilakh, *Talisman: Kniga o Pushkine* (Moscow: Sovremennik, 1975);

Meilakh, *Tvorchestvo A. S. Pushkina: Razvitie khudozhestvennoi sistemy* (Moscow: Prosveshchenie, 1984);

John J. Mersereau Jr., *Baron Del'vig's "Northern Flowers" 1825–1832: Literary Almanac of the Pushkin Period* (Carbondale: Southern Illinois University Press, 1967);

Dmitrii Sviatopolk Mirsky, *Pushkin* (New York: Haskell House, 1974);

Mirsky, "A. S. Pushkin: Iz biografii," in *Literaturno-kriticheskie stat'i* (Moscow: Sovetskii pisatel', 1978), pp. 21–186;

Mark Mitnik, *Pushkin bez legend* (New York: Russkii Iazyk, 1994);

Boris L'vovich Modzalevsky, *Biblioteka A. S. Pushkina: Prilozhenie k reprintomy izdaniiu,* edited by Lev Sergeevich Sidiakov (Moscow: Kniga, 1988);

Modzalevsky, *Pushkin* (Leningrad: Priboi, 1929);

Valentin Semenovich Nepomniashchy, *Poeziia i sud'ba* (Moscow: Sovetskii pisatel', 1983);

Isaak Markovich Nusinov, *Pushkin i mirovaia literatura* (Moscow: Sovetskii pisatel', 1941);

Leslie O'Bell, *Pushkin's "Egyptian Nights": The Biography of a Work* (Ann Arbor, Mich.: Ardis, 1984);

Iulian Grigor'evich Oksman, *Ot "Kapitanskoi dochki" k "Zapiskam okhotnika"* (Saratov: Saratovskoe knizhnoe izd-vo, 1959);

Evgenii Ivanovich Osetrov, ed., *Venok Pushkinu (1837–1987),* Al'manakh bibliofila, part 23 (Moscow: Sovetskaia Rossiia, 1987);

Aleksandr L'vovich Ospovat and Roman Davidovich Timenchik, *Pechal'nu povest' sokhranit'* (Moscow: Kniga, 1987);

Redzhinal'd Vasil'evich Ovchinnikov, *Pushkin v rabote nad arkhivnymi dokumentami ("Istoriia Pugacheva")* (Leningrad: Nauka, 1969);

Dmitrii Nikolaevich Ovsianiko-Kulikovsky, *Pushkin,* volume 4 of Pushkin's *Sobranie sochinenii* (Petrograd: Oschch. Nol'za–Prometei, 1909);

John P. Pauls, *Pushkin's "Poltava"* (New York: Shevchenko Scientific Society, 1962);

Sergei Mikhailovich Petrov, *Istoricheskii roman A. S. Pushkina* (Moscow: AN SSSR, 1953);

Nina Nikolaevna Petrunina, *Proza Pushkina: Puti evoliutsii* (Leningrad: Nauka, 1987);

Delbert Phillips, *Spook or Spoof? The Structure of the Supernatural in Russian Romantic Tales* (Washington, D.C.: University Press of America, 1982);

Nikolai Kir'iakovich Piksanov, ed., *Pushkin: Sbornik*, 2 volumes (Moscow: Gos. izd-vo, 1924, 1930);

Rostislav V. Pletnev, *O lirike Pushkina* (Montreal, 1963);

Nikolai Semenovich Pospelov, *Sintaksicheskii stroi stikhotvornykh proizvedenii Pushkina* (Moscow: AN SSSR, 1960);

A. Pozov, *Metafizika Pushkina* (Madrid, 1967);

Problemy sovremennogo pushkinovedeniia: Mezhvuzovskii sbornik nauchnykh trudov (Leningrad: Herzen Institute, 1986);

Pushkin i ego sovremenniki, parts 1-39 (St. Petersburg & Leningrad: AN SSSR, 1903-1930);

Pushkin: Issledovaniia i materialy, volumes 1-[15]- (Leningrad: Nauka, 1956-[1995]-);

Pushkin na iuge: Trudy Pushkinskoi konferentcii Odessy i Kishineva, 2 volumes (Kishinev: Gos. izd-vo MSSR, volume 1, 1958; volume 2, 1961);

Pushkin v mirovoi literature: Sbornik statei (Leningrad: GIZ, 1926);

Pushkin: Poeta e la sua arte (Rome, 1978);

Pushkin i russkaia literatura (Riga: Latviiskii gos. universitet im P. Stuckhi, 1986);

Pushkin: Vremennik Pushkinskoi komissii, volumes 1-6 (Moscow-Leningrad: AN SSSR, 1936-1941);

Pushkinist: Istoriko-literaturnyi sbornik, volumes 1-3, edited by Semen Afanas'evich Vengerov (Petrograd: A. F. Dressler, 1914); volume 4 published as *Sbornik v pamiati S. A. Vengerovym* (Moscow-Leningrad: GIZ, 1922);

Pushkinskie chteniia: Sbornik statei (Tallinn: Eesti raamat, 1990);

Pushkinskii sbornik, part 1 (Riga: Redaktsionno-izdatel'skii otdel LGU, 1968); part 2 (Riga, 1974);

Pushkinskii sbornik (Prague: Politika, 1929);

Pushkinskii sbornik, 3 volumes (Pskov: Pskovskii gos. pedagog. in-t im. S. M. Kirova, 1962, 1968, 1972); volume 4 published as *Pushkin i ego sovremenniki* (Pskov, 1970);

Putevoditil' po Pushkinu, volume 6 of *Polnoe sobranie sochinenii,* 6 volumes (Moscow-Leningrad, 1930-1931);

Stanislaw Borisovich Rassadin, *Dramaturg Pushkin: Poetika, idei, evoliutsiia* (Moscow: Iskusstvo, 1977);

Robert Reid, *Pushkin's "Mozart and Salieri": Themes, Character, Sociology* (Amsterdam & Atlanta: Rodopi, 1995);

Revue des études slaves, special Pushkin issues, 59, 1-2 (1987);

Rossiia i Pushkin: Sbornik statei (Kharbin, 1937);

Beatrice van Sambeek-Weideli, "Wege eines Meisterwerks: Die russische Rezeption von Pushkins Evgennii Onegin," *Slavica Helvetica,* 34 (1990);

Stephanie Sandler, *Distant Pleasures: Aleksandr Pushkin and the Writing of Exile* (Stanford, Cal.: Stanford University Press, 1989);

L. Scheffler, *Das erotische Sujet in Pushkins Dichtung* (Munich: W. Fink, 1968);

Wolf Schmid, *Pushkins Prosa in poetischer Lekture: "Die Erzahlungen Belkins"* (Munich: W. Fink, 1991);

Savelii Senderovich, *Aleteiia: Elegiia Pushkina "Vospominanie: i problemy ego poetiki,* Wiener slawistischen almanach, 8, special Pushkin volume (Vienna, 1982);

Munir Sendich and Savely Senderovich, eds., *Russian Language Journal,* special Pushkin issues, 27, no. 101 (1974); 35, no. 120 (1981); 43, no. 145 (1989);

Vsvolod Setchkareff, *Aleksandr Pushkin: Sein Leben und sein Werk* (Wiesbaden, 1963);

J. Thomas Shaw, comp., *Pushkin: A Concordance to the Poetry,* 2 volumes (Columbus, Ohio: Slavica, 1985);

Shaw, *Pushkin: Poet and Man of Letters and His Prose,* 2 volumes (Los Angeles: Charles Schlacks Jr., 1995);

Shaw, *Pushkin's Poetics of the Unexpected: The Nonrhymed Lines in the Rhymed Poetry and the Rhymed Lines in the Nonrhymed Poetry* (Columbus, Ohio: Slavica, 1994);

Shaw, comp., *Pushkin's Rhymes: A Dictionary* (Madison: University of Wisconsin Press, 1974);

Viktor Borisovich Shklovsky, *Zametki o proze Pushkina* (Moscow: Sovetskii pisatel', 1937);

Vol'f Shmid (Wolf Schmid), *Proza kak poeziia: Stat'i o povestvovanii v russkoi literautre* (St. Petersburg: Izd-vo Gumanitarnoe agentsvo "Akademicheskii prospekt," 1994);

S. Shvartsband (Schwarzband), *Logika khudozhestvennogo poiska A. S. Pushkina ot "Ezerskogo" do "Pikovoi damy"* (Jerusalem: Magnes Press, 1988);

L. S. Sidiakov, *Khudozhestvennaia proza A. S. Pushkina* (Riga, 1973);

Vasilii Vasil'evich Sipovsky, *Pushkin: Zhizn' i tvorchestvo* (St. Petersburg: Trud, 1901);

Vitalii D. Skvoznikov, *Lirika Pushkina* (Moscow: Khudozh. lit-ra, 1975);

Skvoznikov, *Proza Pushkina* (Moscow, 1962);

Aleksandr Leonidovich Slonimsky, *Masterstvo Pushkina* (Moscow: GIKhL, 1963);

Slovar' iazyka Pushkina, edited by V. V. Vinogradov and others, 4 volumes and *Prilozheniia* (Moscow: Gos. izd-vo inostrannykh i natsional'nykh slovarei, 1956-1961); supplemented by *Novye Materialy k*

"Slovariu A. S. Pushkina," compiled by V. V. Pchelkina and E. P. Khodakova (Moscow, 1982);

Nikolai Fedorovich Sumtsov, *A. S. Pushkin: Issledovaniia* (Khar'kov: Pechatnoe delo, 1900);

Abram Terts (Andre i Donat'evich Siniavsky), *Progulki s Pushkinyn* (London: Collins, 1975);

Terts, *Strolls with Pushkin,* translated by Catharine Theimer Nepomnyashchy and Slava I. Yastremski (New Haven, Conn., 1994);

William M. Todd III, *The Familiar Letter as a Literary Genre in the Age of Pushkin* (Princeton, N.J.: Princeton University Press, 1976);

Todd, *Fiction and Society in the Age of Pushkin* (Cambridge, Mass.: Harvard University Press, 1986);

Boris Viktorovich Tomashevsky, *Pushkin,* 2 volumes (Moscow-Leningrad: AN SSSR, 1961);

Tomashevsky, *Pushkin i Frantsiia* (Leningrad: Sovetskii pisatel', 1960);

Vladimir Nikolaevich Toporov, *Pushkin i Goldsmit . . . , Wiener Slawistischer Almanach,* 29 (Vienna, 1992);

Transactions of the Association of Russian-American Scholars in the USA. (Zapiski russkoi akademicheskoi gruppy v SSHA), special Pushkin issue, 20 (1987);

Josef Tretiak, *Mickiewicz i Pushkin: Studja i szkice* (Warsaw: Nakl. Ksiegarni E. Wende, 1906);

Tat'iana Grigor'evna Tsiavlovskaia, ed., *Prometei,* 10 (Moscow, 1974);

Tsiavlovskaia, *Risunki Pushkina* (Moscow: Iskusstvo, 1980);

Mstislav Aleksandrovich Tsiavlovsky, ed., *Letopisi gosudarstvennogo literaturnogo muzeia: Kniga pervaia: Pushkin* (Moscow: Zhurn.-gaz. ob'ed., 1936);

Tsiavlovsky, ed., *Moskovskii pushkinist,* 2 volumes (Moscow, volume 1, 1924; volume 2, 1930); volume 2 (Moscow, 1930);

Tsiavlovsky, *Stat'i o Pushkine* (Moscow: AN SSSR, 1962);

Marina Ivanova Tsvetaeva, *Moi Pushkin* (Moscow: Sovetskii pisatel', 1981);

Tsvetaeva, "My Pushkin" and "Pushkin and Pugachev," in her *A Captive Spirit: Selected Prose,* edited and translated by J. Marin King (Ann Arbor, Mich.: Ardis, 1980), pp. 319–362;

Iurii Niklolaevich Tynianov, *Pushkin i ego sovremenniki* (Moscow: Nauka, 1968);

Jan Van der Eng, ed., *Russian Literature,* special Pushkin issues, 24, no. 3 (1988); vol. 26, no. 4 (1989); vol. 28, no. 4 (1990);

Van der Eng and others, eds., *"The Tales of Belkin" by A. S. Pushkin: Essays* (The Hague, 1968);

Vadim Erazmovich Vatsuro, *"Severnye tsvety": Istoriia al'manakha Del'viga-Pushkina* (Moscow: Kniga, 1976);

Vatsuro, *Zapiski kommentatora* (St. Petersburg: Akademicheskii prospekt, 1994);

Walter N. Vickery, *Aleksandr Pushkin,* second edition, revised (New York: Twayne, 1992);

Viktor Vladimirovich Vinogradov, *Iazyk Pushkina: Pushkin i istoriia russkogo literaturnogo iazyka* (Moscow-Leningrad: Academia, 1935);

Vinogradov, *Stil' Pushkina* (Moscow: Goslitizdat, 1941);

L. I. Vol'pert, *Pushkin i psikhologicheskaia traditsiia vo frantsuzskoi literature* (Tallinn: Eesti ramaat, 1980);

Vremennik Pushkinskoi komissii, annual 1962– (Leningrad: AN SSSR, 1963–);

Viktor Maksimovich Zhirmunsky, *Izbrannye trudy: Bairon i Pushkin; Pushkin i zapadnye literatury* (Leningrad: Academia, 1978).

Papers:

Aleksandr Pushkin's papers are found at the Institute of Russian Literature (Pushkin House) in St. Petersburg.

Vasilii L'vovich Pushkin
(27 April 1766 – 20 August 1830)

Irwin R. Titunik
University of Michigan

BOOKS: *Dva poslaniia* (St. Petersburg: Shnor, 1811);

Stikhotvoreniia (St. Petersburg: Departamenta narodnago prosveshcheniia, 1822);

Zapiski v stikhakh, edited by Petr Ivanovich Shalikov (Moscow: Universitetskaia tip., 1834);

Opasnyi sosed. Stikhotvorenie, edited by S. D. Poltoratsky (Leipzig: F. A. Brockhaus, 1855).

Editions and Collections: *Sochineniia Pushkina (Vasiliia L'vovicha)* (St. Petersburg: A. Smirdin, 1855);

Sochineniia, edited by Vladimir Ivanovich Saitov (St. Peterburg: Evdokimov, 1893);

Sochineniia V. L. Puskina (St. Petersburg: Izd. Ia. Sokolova, 1895);

Opasnyi sosed, edited by V. I. Chernyshev (St. Petersburg: Atenei, 1922);

Stikhi, proza, pis'ma, edited by Natalia Ivanovna Mikhailova (Moscow: Sovetskaia Rossia, 1989).

OTHER: *Iroi-komicheskaia poema,* edited by Boris Viktorovich Tomashevsky (Leningrad: Izd-vo pisatelei, 1933), pp. 649–652, 733–738;

Karamzin i poety ego vremeni, edited by Tomashevsky (Leningrad: Sovetskii pisatel', 1936), pp. 337–433;

Russkie poety–sovremenniki Pushkina (Leningrad: Khudozhestvennaia literatura, 1937), pp. 117–126, 586–591;

Russkaia basnia XVIII I nachala XIX veka, edited by N. L. Stepanov (Leningrad: Sovetskii pisatel', 1949), pp. 243–252;

Poety satiriki kontsa XVIII-nachala XIX veka, edited by G. V. Ermakova-Bitner (Leningrad: Sovetskii pisatel', 1959), pp. 261–292;

Poety 1790–1810-kh godov, edited by Iurii Mikhailovich Lotman and M. G. Al'tshuller (Leningrad: Sovetskii pisatel', 1971), pp. 654–702, 863–871.

Vasilii L'vovich Pushkin

The popular notion is that Vasilii Pushkin is remembered in the annals of Russian literature only because he was the paternal uncle of Russia's supreme poetic genius, Aleksandr Pushkin. The fact is, however, that Vasilii Pushkin had entirely on his own earned a literary reputation among his contemporaries and has received attention in the history of Russian literature ever since. The nature of that reputation is peculiar; Vasilii Pushkin achieved fame, indeed legendary status, above all as a figure of fun—benevolent fun on the part of his friends and associates, malicious on the part of his opponents. At the core of that image stood the lifelong versifier extraordinaire who, in the final verse of a poem titled "K liubimstam muz" (To the Beloved of the Muses) exclaimed: "O radost', o vostorg! I ia . . . I ia piit" (O joy, o rapture! I too . . . I too am a poet), a line much repeated in satires against him. He was also an audacious, if somewhat simplistic, partisan polemicist for the Karamzinian (pro-European) orientation in the literary controversies of early-nineteenth-century Russia.

Also integrally a part of his legend were certain characteristics of Vasilii Pushkin's appearance, manners, and behavior. He is reported to have been a funny-looking man (hook-nosed, prematurely balding, and toothless, with a pudgy torso and pendulant belly on skinny legs) but at the same time was a devotee of fashion, often appearing in society extravagantly dressed and coiffed in the latest French style. Exceedingly cheerful, good-natured, and sociable, he was also notoriously gullible and naive, drolly jealous of his fame, and ingenuously proud of his comradeship with three generations of eminent Russian literary men. Few people, whether friend or foe, were able to take him seriously, but no one failed to take notice of him. Virtually all commentators in the nineteenth and twentieth centuries have judged his poetic body of work to be mediocre, with the important exception of one work and the qualified exception of one or two others. Yet, Vasilii Pushkin is a Russian literary figure of undoubtable interest in his own right.

On 27 April 1766 (some sources say 1767 or 1770) Vasilii L'vovich Pushkin was born in Moscow, the eldest of four children of a second marriage. The noble Pushkin family fell out of favor with the accession of Catherine II to the throne but continued to be sufficiently affluent, so Vasilii's generation was able to enjoy a privileged childhood and a lifetime of leisure. He and his brother Sergei (the father of Aleksandr Pushkin) received what was, by all accounts, a brilliant education at home in the French manner. Vasilii thoroughly mastered French and acquired a working knowledge of German, Italian, Latin, and English. He became, at the same time, well-schooled in the social graces, thanks in part to the lavish entertainments his father, Lev Aleksandrovich Pushkin, was fond of giving for Moscow high society and distinguished visitors. As a young man Vasilii Pushkin was welcomed into the Moscow salons, where he won a reputation not only as a dandy and wit but also as a declaimer of poetry (a talent much employed throughout his life), an amateur actor, and above all, an improviser of verses in French (such as album poetry, epigrams, and *bouts-rimés*, or rhymed ends, a literary game).

Having been enrolled as a child in an army regiment (such was the custom among Russian aristocratic families in the eighteenth century), Vasilii Pushkin moved to St. Petersburg in 1791 to begin his military service. It would be a gross exaggeration to speak of this activity as his "profession" or "career" since his performance of military duties was casual at best and lasted only some six years. In 1797, with the modest rank of *poruchik* (lieutenant), he retired from service. His life in the capital had in fact been largely devoted to the social whirl just as it had been in Moscow. Also during this time, however, his literary ambitions had begun to take definite shape and to produce results.

In 1793 he formed one of the first, and the firmest, of his many lifelong literary friendships when he met the poet Ivan Ivanovich Dmitriev, at the time also an army officer serving in the capital. Dmitriev is supposed to have encouraged Vasilii Pushkin (some say facetiously) to begin writing Russian verse. In any case, that same year the latter published his first poem, an idyll/satire titled "K kaminu" (To My Hearth), in the journal *Sankt-Peterburgskii Merkurii* (St. Petersburg Mercury); it was soon followed by publication in various journals of more idylls and satires as well as epigrams, songs, fables, elegies, verse epistles, and *èksprompty* (improvisations)—all genres of the so-called *poésie légère* (light verse) cultivated by Dmitriev and also Nikolai Mikhailovich Karamzin, whom Vasilii Pushkin revered. Later, Konstantin Nikolaevich Batiushkov and Vasilii Andreevich Zhukovsky, two more of his eminent literary friends, complimented the poet on these and similar verses for their fluency and for his excellent command of Russian grammar.

Upon retirement from army service Vasilii Pushkin returned to his former life of leisure in Moscow and there entered into marriage with a famous beauty of Moscow high society, Kapitolina Mikhailovna Vysheslavtseva. This bizarre marriage soon faltered. In 1802 his wife initiated divorce proceedings, alleging as grounds her husband's flagrant unfaithfulness. Four years later the ecclesiastical court decided in the wife's favor, granting her a full divorce and imposing on Vasilii Pushkin a penance prohibiting him from remarrying. He had, in the meantime, acquired another permanent female companion, Anna Nikolaevna Vorozheikin, a merchant's daughter, marriage to whom was now impossible. The two children he had by her, Margarita and Lev, were given the family name of Vasil'ev.

Meanwhile, during the period of the divorce proceedings, Vasilii Pushkin left Russia for a one-year sojourn (1803–1804) in Europe, visiting Germany, France, and England. The major portion of his time abroad was spent in Paris, where he made the acquaintance and enjoyed the company of various learned and literary celebrities and was even presented to Napoleon Bonaparte, then first consul. He frequented the Parisian theaters; took a lively interest in matters of the latest fashions, refurbishing himself and his wardrobe accordingly; and collected a substantial library. Two enthusiastic (but rather banal) letters to Karamzin describing his experiences in Berlin and Paris were printed in the latter's journal *Vestnik Evropy* (Herald of Europe) in 1803. Dmitriev, for his part, composed a waggish farce in verse, "Puteshestvie N. N. v Parizh i London, pisannoe za tri dnia do puteshestviia" (The Journey of Mr. X to Paris and London, Written Three Days before the Journey), in which, speaking in the persona of Vasilii Pushkin, he deftly depicted the naively enthusiastic traveler. The work was published in a limited edition for private circulation in 1806, and it is reported that Vasilii Pushkin quite enjoyed the joke.

The period from his return to Russia in 1804 to September 1812 was spent mainly in Moscow, with several trips to St. Petersburg, the most memorable of which was his accompaniment of his twelve-year-old nephew Aleksandr to the capital for the purpose of enrolling him at the newly established preparatory school, the *Litsei* (Lyceum). In Vasilii Pushkin's own literary life this period was an especially important and productive one. He continued producing verses of the same kind as before, but he also wrote on behalf of the Karamzinians. This party of Russian literary men, following Karamzin but without Karamzin's actual participation, advocated rapprochement of the development of Russian language and literature with the culture of Western Europe. Their opponents were the Shishkovites, or Slavics (later Slavophiles), the party headed by Admiral Aleksandr Semenovich Shishkov that opposed foreign influence and argued for a development of Russian language and literature derived from indigenous sources and values. This dispute, dating back to 1803, was carried on both in serious disquisitions and in epigrams, stage lampoons, and satires. In 1810 a significant new phase in this dispute ensued when in the December issue of the journal *Tsetvnik* (Flower Garden) appeared Vasilii Pushkin's "Poslanie k V. A. Zhukovskomu" (Epistle to V. A. Zhukovsky), in which the author sang the praises of what he understood as the Russian "enlightenment" initiated by Peter the Great and championed by Dmitriev and Karamzin, while satirically charging the Slavic party with the desire to overthrow that enlightenment and return to pre-Petrine xenophobia and obscurantism. The following year a similar, somewhat more brazen, "Poslanie k D. V. Dashkovu" (Epistle to D. V. Dashkov) was published in a brochure together with a preface and the reprint of the first *poslanie*. These polemical epistles in verse, composed in a surprisingly vigorous conversational style, were received with applause by fellow Karamzinians and have been reputed, along with the essays of Dmitrii Vasil'evich Dashkov, to be the first major counterattacks against the Slavic party. The latter, of course, duly attacked Vasilii Pushkin in turn, with Shishkov himself even resorting to innuendos about the poet's dubious moral and religious qualifications. It should be noted,

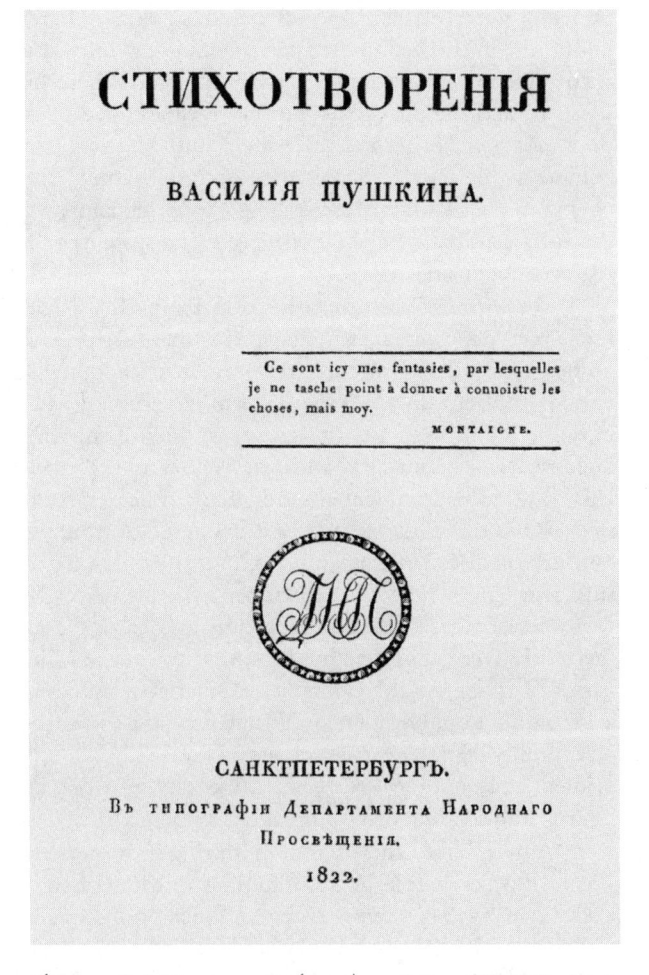

Title page for Stikhotvoreniia *(Poems), a collection of Vasilii Pushkin's light verses*

incidentally, that Vasilii Pushkin's detractors were not limited to members of the conservative Shishkovite party but also included the Western-oriented poet Mikhail Vasil'evich Milonov in the 1810s and the left-wing, younger generation "Slav" and future Decembrist Vil'gel'm Karlovich Kiukhel'beker in the 1820s.

If Vasilii Pushkin's polemical epistles had surprised and pleased his friends and riled his enemies, another work of the same period, *Opasnyi sosed* (The Dangerous Neighbor), written in 1810, positively astonished and delighted almost everybody. This work was a short narrative poem of the mock-epic variety composed in alexandrine couplets and that piquant combination of vernacular and lofty Russian typical for the Russian mock-epic tradition from the 1770s (as in the works of Vasilii Ivanovich Maikov). The poem relates a racy anecdote about how the narrator is persuaded to visit a local bordello by his rogue of a neighbor, Buianov (who later made a guest appearance in Aleksandr Pushkin's *Evgeny Onegin,* published in full in 1833). At the bordello the narrator succumbs to temptation and goes off with one of the "hostesses." Thereupon, however, Buianov creates a rumpus by brawling with some other clients of the establishment. When the noise attracts the police, the narrator escapes out a back door, leaving his purse, his watch, and his overcoat behind in his haste. Such is the anecdotal plot of the poem. In the course of describing those shenanigans, the author added a bit of literary-polemical spice by taking occasional sideswipes at the Shishkovites.

Opasnyi sosed was not printed in the author's lifetime but was widely circulated in manuscript. Its immense popularity is attested to by an exceptionally curious incident. In 1815 the Russian government was in desperate need of a swift and secure way of copying documents in connection with the victory over Napoleon. The recently invented lithographic process promised a solution. The diplomat put in charge of trying it out wished to use a Russian poem, but the only one of sufficient length he could remember by heart perfectly was *Opasnyi sosed*. The experiment was carried out, and the results were approved by the authorities at the Ministry of Foreign Affairs. Thus, its popularity resulted in a lithographic publication of Vasilii Pushkin's masterpiece in his lifetime, unbeknownst to himself. The first printed edition of *Opasnyi sosed* came out in 1855 in Leipzig and the first edition in Russia only in 1913.

Among his other activities during this period, Vasilii Pushkin's role in the founding of the Moscow *Obshchestvo liubitelei rossiiskoi slovesnosti* (Society of Lovers of Russian Literature) in 1811 should be noted. In September 1812, when Napoleon briefly occupied Moscow, Vasilii Pushkin escaped the city at the last possible moment, but his house and all his property, including the priceless library he had brought back from abroad, perished in the Great Moscow Fire. As did many other Muscovites, he made his way to Nizhnii-Novgorod, where he managed to survive under trying conditions and even, to some extent, continue his former way of life. In early 1813 he left Nizhnii-Novgorod, going first to St. Petersburg and then back to permanent residence in Moscow.

In 1816 he made a trip to St. Petersburg in the company of Karamzin and Prince Petr Andreevich Viazemsky, one of his closest acquaintances from the younger generation of Russian literary men. This visit had a special purpose: he was to be inducted into the *Arzamasskoe obshchestvo bezvestnykh liudei* (Arzamas Society of Obscure Persons). This society had been established in 1815 as a sort of joke—a mock literary-society counterpart to the *Beseda liubitelei russkogo slova* (Colloquy of Lovers of the Russian Word) founded by the Shishkovites in 1811. Arzamas included Zhukovsky, Batiushkov, Viazemsky, and later (1817) Aleksandr Pushkin among its members. Vasilii Pushkin was by far the oldest inductee and, thanks to his already well-established reputation as a figure of fun, he was subjected to a hilarious initiation ritual that farcically imitated the Masonic ritual (he had become a mason in 1810) and was designed specifically and solely for him (no other inductee was ever "initiated"). The gullible and good-natured Vasilii Pushkin took it all quite seriously and heroically endured a series of "trials," all of them playing on events in his literary-polemical encounters with the Slavic party. At its conclusion he was given the Arzamasian nickname *Vot* (Take that!), which, when he was appointed *starosta* (dean) of the society soon afterward, was expanded to *Vot ia vas* (Take that you!).

On returning to Moscow the same year, Vasilii Pushkin was inspired to compose a few poems for the delectation of his new fellow Arzamasians. The membership, however, subjected these offerings to mock-critical derision, depriving him of his office and changing his nickname to *Votrushka* (punning on *vatrushki*, a word that means a cheese-filled pastry). Genuinely aggrieved at this turn of events, he immediately sent off a verse epistle to the Arzamasians in which he good-humoredly apologized for his defective verses but also chided his colleagues for offending the first of their champions against the "numbskulls" and "ignoramuses" of the Slavic party. His new epistle met with approval; the office of *starosta* was returned to him; and his nickname was restored and further expanded to *Vot ia vas opiat'* (Take that you again!), all of which elated him enormously. These events undoubtedly were the quintessential episode in Vasilii Pushkin's entire literary life and legend.

In 1822, after much difficulty and delay, Vasilii Pushkin succeeded in bringing out a collection of his poetry, *Stikhotvoreniia* (Poems). The volume consisted mainly of previously published poems of the *poésie légère* type. The majority of these were acknowledged translations, adaptations, or imitations of other poets. Among the ancients, Horace and the Anacreontics were the author's favorites. Not surprisingly, the largest share of these poems represented or reflected French poetry—either that of Neoclassicism (such as Jean La Fontaine and Voltaire) or, and especially, the late- or post-classicist period (such as Jean-Pierre Claris de Florian, Vicomte Evariste-Désiré de Parny, and Charles-Hubert Millevoye). Some translation of English poetry appeared: excerpts from James Macpherson's Ossianic poems (1760–1763) and James Thomson's *The Seasons* (1726–1730). Vasilii Pushkin, it should be noted, also did some translations from Russian into French: Russian folk songs for *Mercure de France* (Mercury of France) in 1803 and his nephew's "Chernaia shal'" (Black Shawl, written in 1820) for *Bulletin du nord* (Northern Bulletin) in 1828.

The 1820s were also the period of greatest contact between Vasilii Pushkin and Aleksandr Pushkin since the latter's childhood. Vasilii Pushkin was extremely devoted to his nephew, eagerly and proudly followed his literary career, and was ever jealous for his reputation. Aleksandr Pushkin owed his introduction to the world of poets and poetry to his uncle, whom he called his "Parnassian father." He addressed several of his own poems to his uncle, as did many other eminent Russian poets, and he greatly admired *Opasnyi sosed*, which he remarked in a 2 January 1822 letter to Petr Andreevich Viazemsky was "worth all the rest of his poetry combined." Although Aleksandr Pushkin seems to have been genuinely fond of his uncle, he did not hesitate to join in making light of him and even indicted the latter's occasional sly parodies.

The new trend in Russian poetry to which Aleksandr Pushkin's name was linked–Romanticism–did not meet with his uncle's sympathy, however. An 1826 "imitation" of the two opening stanzas of George Gordon, Lord Byron's 1816 verse tale *Parisina* indicated, perhaps, a momentary attraction, but Vasilii Pushkin soon began expressing a distaste for Romantic poetry. The most ambitious of such expressions was a parodic narrative poem titled *Kapitan Khrabrov* (Captain Khrabrov), the direct target of which was the Byronic poems of Ivan Ivanovich Kozlov. Doubtless, his nephew's *Evgeny Onegin* also played an inspiring role: Vasilii Pushkin returned a compliment by introducing the heroine of that work, Tat'iana Larina, into his poem. *Kapitan Khrabrov* was not a success, for it was too contrived and too blatant in its anti-Romantic parodies. Although four chapters were published in 1829 and 1830, the work remained unfinished at the author's death.

In the last decade of his life Vasilii Pushkin experienced increasing ill health (gout and associated diseases) and a depletion of his fortune. The closest of his friends at this time was Petr Ivanovich Shalikov, a fellow Muscovite poet and a person of similarly bizarre character and appearance. Shalikov was also a publisher; many of Vasilii Pushkin's poems appeared on the pages of his *Damskii zhurnal* (Ladies Journal). The two engaged in an exchange of impromptu notes in verse, the majority of Vasilii Pushkin's apologizing for delaying or canceling a get-together because of illness or inviting his friend to come and visit "the invalid." His complaints about his miseries are conveyed in remarkably mild and good-humored terms. These notes were never intended for publication, but Shalikov decided to do just that, producing *Zapiski v stikakh* (Notes in Verse) in 1834. The poems in question add nothing to Vasilii Pushkin's stature as a poet, but they considerably enhance his image as a doughty and admirable human being.

Vasilii Pushkin died on 20 August 1830. His funeral was attended by a host of Russian literary celebrities, including his nephew, of course, who paid all of the expenses. Vasilii Pushkin's death did not fail to enter into his legend. His nephew reported in a 9 September 1830 letter to Petr Aleksandrovich Pletnev that his uncle died historically, "*le cri de guerre a la bouche*" (a war cry on his lips), since his last words were: "How boring Katenin's essays are!" (Pavel Aleksandrovich Katenin was one of the younger generation of Slavophiles). On the first anniversary of his death, his friends gathered together and commemorated the old Arzamasian by feasting at his grave on those pastries called *vatrushki*.

Letters:

"Pis'ma V. L. Pushkina P. A. Viazemskomu," introduction and commentary by Natalia Ivanovna Mikhailova, in *Pushkin, Issledovaniia i materialy*, volume 11 (Leningrad, 1983), pp. 213-249.

Biography:

Natalia Ivanovna Mikhailova, *Parnasskii moi otets* (Moscow: Sovetskaia Rossiia, 1983).

References:

Mikhail Aleksandrovich Dmitriev, *Melochi iz zapasa moei pamiati* (Moscow, 1869), pp. 88-93;

Viktor Vladimirovich Kunin, "Vasilii L'vovich Pushkin," in *Druz'ia Pushkina: Perepiska, vospominaniia, dnevniki* (Moscow: Pravda, 1986), pp. 9-39;

Iurii Mikhailovich Lotman, "V. L. Pushkin: biograficheskaia spravka," in *Poety 1790–1819-kh godov*, edited by Lotman and M. G. Al'tshuller (Leningrad: Sovetskii pisatel', 1971), pp. 651-653;

Nikolai Kiriakovich Piksanov, "Pushkin V. L.," in *Russkii biograficheskii slovar'*, volume "Pritivis-Reis" (St. Petersburg, 1911), pp. 302-307;

Vladimir I. Saitov, "Vasilii L'vovich Pushkin (Istoriko-literaturnyi ocherk)," in *Sochineniia V. L. Pushkina*, edited by Saitov (St. Petersburg: A. Smirdin, 1895), pp. viii-xxi;

Boris Viktorovich Tomashevsky, "V. L. Pushkin," in *Iroi-komicheskaia poèma*, edited by Tomashevsky (Leningrad: Sovetskii pisatel', 1933), pp. 639-645.

Semen Egorovich Raich

(September 1792 – 28 October 1855)

Vera Proskurina
Cornell University

BOOKS: *Razsuzhdenie o didakticheskoi poezii* (Moscow: Universitetskaia tip., 1822);
Areta; skazanie iz vremen Marka Avreliia, 2 volumes (Moscow: V. Got'e, 1849).

OTHER: *Novye Aonidy,* edited by Raich (Moscow: V Tip. A. Semena, Pri Imp. Mediko-Khirurgicheskoi akademii, 1823);
Severnaia lira, edited by Raich and Dmitrii Petrovich Oznobishin (Moscow: S. Selivanovsky, 1827);
Galateia, edited by Raich (Moscow: N. Stepanov, 1829-1830, 1839-1840);
Poety 1820–1830 kh godov, volume 2, edited by V. S. Kiselev-Sergenin (Leningrad: Sovetskii pisatel', 1972), pp. 10-30.

TRANSLATIONS: Virgil, *Georgiki* (Moscow: A. Semen, 1821);
Torquato Tasso, *Osvobozhdennyi Ierusalim,* 4 volumes (Moscow: A. Semen, 1828);
Ludovico Ariosto, *Neistovyi Orland,* 3 volumes (Moscow: Tip. Lazarevykh Instituta vostochnykh iazykov, 1831-1837).

SELECTED PERIODICAL PUBLICATION– UNCOLLECTED: "Avtobiografia," edited by B. Modzalevsky, *Russky Bibliofil,* 8 (1913): 5-33.

Semen Egorovich Raich

Semen Raich—poet, translator, and journalist—was a significant figure in the Russian literary scene of the 1820s and 1830s. His experiments in the transplantation of Italian poetry on Russian soil played a large role in the development of the so-called Golden Age of Russian poetry. An expert in Italian and Russian aesthetic culture, Raich became a teacher of a whole school of Russian poets, to whom he imparted a sense of the elevating role of poetry.

Semen Egorovich Amfiteatrov was born in September 1792 in the little village of Rai-Vysokoe, in Orel province. His father, Egor Nikitich Amfiteatrov, was a clergyman; his mother, Anastasia Amfiteatrova, died when Semen was seven years old. Father and son apparently had no affection for each other. The large family, in which there were nine children, kept patriarchal customs in their everyday life, a course typical for the Russian country clergy. All of Semen's brothers graduated from the seminary. At the age of ten Semen was placed in Sevsk seminary, where his elder brother, Fedor Egorovich Amfiteatrov, was rector. Afterward Fedor Amfiteatrov came to be known as Filaret, metropolitan of Kiev and Galich from 1837 to 1857. According to seminary tradition, when he turned to literary pursuits Semen discarded his family name and took a nom de plume, Raich, the maiden name of his mother.

According to another story, his name comes from the word *rai,* which means "paradise."

The rather high level of seminary education, and the system of studying classical languages (Latin and ancient Greek), gave Raich the chance to read classical literature in the original, which stimulated his great interest in translation. Impressed by Russian poetry, he began to write his first verses while still in the seminary. The Russian poets Gavriil Romanovich Derzhavin and Ivan Ivanovich Dmitriev were his models; as Raich wrote in his "Avtobiografia" (Autobiography, 1913), "Derzhavin and Dmitriev were my guides to Parnassus."

Raich became a student at the Orel seminary, where he worked hard and lived an ascetic life. Although the seminary teachers treated him like a future monk, young Raich dreamed of abandoning his clerical career and enrolling in the university. After completing the course of study in the Orel seminary, Raich underwent a medical examination and, under pretense of illness, received authorization for civil service.

In 1810 Raich worked as a clerk in the *zemstvo* (rural council) of the court of Ruza. Soon afterward he started his career as a tutor to various children of aristocratic families. First, he served as a tutor in the household of Anastasiia Nikolaevna Nadarzhinskaia (née Tiutcheva), who then recommended him to her sister, Nadezhda Nikolaevna Sheremeteva. Raich went to live at her country estate, Pokrovskoe, near Moscow. In 1812 during the Napoleonic invasion, after a half-hearted attempt to enter the *opolchenie* (civil guard), Raich left Moscow with Sheremeteva and lived in Uglich, Yaroslavl', and Bryansk.

After the deliverance of Moscow in 1813, Sheremeteva recommended Raich to young Fedor Ivanovich Tiutchev, her nephew. As tutor of the future poet, Raich lived in Tiutchev's household for seven years. During this time teacher and pupil attended private lectures of the well-known professor of literature and rhetoric, Aleksei Fedorovich Merzliakov. Raich played an important role in the aesthetic and literary orientation of young Tiutchev's poetry, especially by cultivating Tiutchev's interest in classical literature and anthological poetry. Later, Tiutchev's first poems appeared in Raich's almanac *Severnaia lira* (The Northern Lyre, 1827). Tiutchev certainly surpassed his mentor in poetic talent; nevertheless, he always held Raich in high regard. The two had soon become companions, rather than simply teacher and student. Tiutchev devoted several poems to his tutor and friend.

From 1815 to 1818 Raich attended Moscow University, where he studied Russian literature and Italian language with particular zeal. From 1819 to 1820 Raich took part in the meetings of an unofficial literary group, *Obshchestvo gromkogo smekha* (The Society of Loud Laughter), organized by several of his university friends: Mikhail Aleksandrovich Dmitriev, M. A. Volkov, and Aleksandr Dmitrievich Kurbatov. At their meetings the members usually discussed literary problems, especially problems of translation; sometimes they criticized their professors. In February 1818 Raich received the degree of candidate in the department of ethics and politics. At the same time, he began his literary career with a translation in rhymed iambic pentameter of one of the most difficult of Latin cycles of poems, Virgil's *Georgics* (circa 37–30 B.C.). In 1821 he published this translation prefaced by an extensive study titled *Razsuzhdenie o didakticheskoi poezii* (A Discourse on Didactic Poetry), one of the first declarations of linguistic purism in Russian poetics.

Raich intended to search for a "middle" didactic poetic language different from the Old Slavonic language proposed by the conservative literary group of "archaists." Unlike them, Raich tended to prefer the French tradition (the style of Jacques Delille especially) in his translations. He tried to free his language of any Old Slavonic words and expressions and to prove that it was possible to translate Virgil's bucolic and descriptive poetry into modern Russian. Raich argued for the harmony of that which is both "useful" and "pleasant" in literature. His translation and his theoretical preface were highly appreciated by Ivan Dmitriev. After the publication of the translation, Raich (recommended by Dmitriev) was awarded a silver medal by the Russian Academy.

From 1820 to 1822 Raich lived in the house of the liberal gentleman Nikolai Nikolaevich Murav'ev (mathematician and founder of the School of Minor Officers) as a tutor to his son, Andrei Nikolaevich Murav'ev, the future religious writer. Aleksandr Murav'ev (a brother of Andrei) or his friend Fedor Petrovich Shakhovskoi possibly involved Raich in the early Decembrist society *Soiuz Blagodenstviia* (Union of Welfare). In all likelihood Raich took no active part in the Decembrist movement, though he clearly had pro-Decembrist sympathies.

In October 1822 Raich defended his thesis, *Razsuzhdenie o didakticheskoi poezii,* for a master's degree in literature, and it was published separately. On 28 October 1822 Raich became a member of the *Obshchestvo liubitelei rossiiskoi slovesnosti* (Society of Lovers of Russian Literature) at Moscow University; later, from 1830 to 1837, he became the secretary of this society. Previously, in 1818, Raich had become a member of the *Vol'noe obshchestvo liubitelei rossiiskoi slovesnosti* (Free Society of Lovers of Russian Literature) in St. Petersburg.

Title page for Razsuzhdenie o didakticheskoi poezii *(A Discourse on Didactic Poetry), Raich's thesis for his master's degree at Moscow University*

In 1823 Raich hosted his own literary circle, *Obshchestvo druzei* (The Society of Friends), which was aimed at the study of literary theory, aesthetics, and translation. Among the members of the society were the future writers and poets Mikhail Aleksandrovich Dmitriev and Dmitrii Petrovich Oznobishin (both were close friends of Raich) as well as Aleksandr Ivanovich Pisarev, Mikhail Petrovich Pogodin, Vladimir Pavlovich Titov, Stepan Petrovich Shevyrev, Prince Vladimir Fedorovich Odoevsky, Tiutchev, Avraam Sergeevich Norov, Mikhail Aleksandrovich Maksimovich, Andrei Murav'ev, and Sergei Dmitrievich Poltoratsky. They met every Thursday at Raich's house to read and discuss their own works and translations. Because translation was their special subject, they practiced translating from different languages: ancient Greek, Latin, Arabic, Persian, English, Italian, German, and French. This circle was close to the philosophical society *Liubomudry* (Wisdom Lovers), though Raich himself was not interested in specific philosophical problems as much as clearly aesthetic ones. Raich published works of the participants of the circle in his almanac *Novye Aonidy* (The New Aonids, 1823) and later in his almanac *Severnaia lira*.

From 1 January 1827 until 1831 Raich served as a master of Russian literature at the Moscow University Gentry Pension, where one of his students was Mikhail Iur'evich Lermontov. The future writer Elizaveta Vasil'evna Sukhova-Kobylina (Evgeniia Tur) also took Raich's courses. During this time Raich lived in the library building of the Pension, and every Saturday he hosted a literary circle for his students. There they discussed their works and translations. Among the participants of Raich's circle were the novice poets Semen Ivanovich Stromilov, Nikolai Nikolaevich Kolachevsky, Luk'ian Andreevich Iakubovich, Nikolai Aleksandrovich Stepanov, Vladimir Mikhailovich Stroev, and Lermontov. "Raich's school" influenced Lermontov's early works, some of which appeared in the literary almanac *Tsefei* (Cepheus), which Raich's senior students edited. Lermontov mentions Raich in his pension diary and in special notes to his short poem "Russkaia Melodiia" (Russian Melody, 1829). The circle existed until the end of April 1825, when Raich went to Ukraine as a tutor to the Grigorii Nikolaevich Rakhmanov family. He returned to Moscow in August 1826.

Raich wrote the majority of his poems in the 1820s and 1830s. Unfortunately, he never published a collection of his short poems, though they did appear in journals and almanacs such as Pogodin's *Uraniia* (Urania), which was close to the *Liubomudry* circle in its orientation; Baron Anton Antonovich Del'vig's *Severnye tsvety* (Northern Flowers); and his own *Severnaia lira*. His pieces in the classic anthological genre appeared in the most popular magazines of the day, such as *Moskovskii telegraf* (Moscow Telegraph), *Moskovskii vestnik* (Moscow Herald), and *Teleskop* (Telescope).

Raich's poetry follows a closed and narrow system based on his aesthetic and theoretical ideas. A staunch supporter of Italian poetry, he followed the model of the poetry he translated. His contemporaries even associated his works with Petrarch. As a result, his works, as well as those of his close friends, were called the "Italian school" by Russian critics. Raich attempted to re-create Russian poetic language to give to Russian verses "the sweetness" and "the harmony" of the Italian. He cultivated Anacreontic genres and motifs in poems such as "K Lide" (To Lida, 1826) and "Solov'iu" (To a Nightingale, 1826). In addition, he experimented with rhythms and meter, trying to imitate the complicated melodiousness of Italian patterns, especially in "Perekati-pole" (The Tumble-weed, 1825) and "Druz'iam"

(To Friends, 1826). The latter was set to music and achieved considerable popularity.

In his poetic experiments Raich tried to combine new, harmonic sound play; gallant, accurately chosen vocabulary; sweet melodies; aesthetic formulas; and optimistic, hedonistic motifs. "Proschal'naia pesn' v krugu druzei" (A Farewell Song among Friends, 1825), "Pesn' solov'ia" (Song of the Nightingale, 1827), and "Vecher" (Evening, 1827) exemplify these experiments. In his poems "Poetu" (To the Poet, 1826) and "Zhaloby Salvatora Rozy" (The Complaints of Salvator Rosa, 1831) Raich developed his theory of the "high destiny" of poetry as a "sacred fire" opposed to "low," real life. Raich's escape to the world of Italian artists and poets of the seventeenth century, however, was the obvious sublimation of the author's own feelings, and the reflection of the real complexes of a lonely "little man" in a "cold" and "cruel" aristocratic world. The initial impulse of Raich's poetic searches and his Neoclassic orientation came from Konstantin Nikolaevich Batiushkov, to whom Raich later devoted one of his final poems, "Tsvetok na mogilu Batiushkova" (A Flower on the Grave of Batiushkov, 1855).

In 1829 Raich married Tereza Andreevna Olivier. At the same time, he began to edit the literary journal *Galateia* (Galatea) mainly out of financial necessity. The life of this journal was short: publication ceased in 1830. In 1839 Raich tried to restore *Galateia,* but conflicts with his fellow editor P. I. Artemov prevented it from coming out as planned. In addition, *Galateia* elicited scorn and contempt from writers such as Prince Petr Andreevich Viazemsky and Aleksandr Pushkin for its attempt to lure subscribers by publishing pictures of the latest Paris fashions.

The narrow aesthetic position of Raich as editor complicated his relationships with different literary groups and journals. Soon after beginning the publication of *Galateia,* Raich found himself in almost complete literary isolation. On the one hand, he published in *Galateia* magnificent poems of Russian poets such as Aleksandr Pushkin, Viazemsky, Tiutchev, Evgenii Abramovich Baratynsky, Fedor Nikolaevich Glinka, and Aleksandr Ivanovich Polezhaev. He was also interested in young Russian poets such as Dmitrii Vladimirovich Venevitinov, Dmitrii Iur'evich Struisky (Trilunny), Luk'ian Andreevich Yakubovich, and Vladimir Ignat'evich Sokolovsky. On the other hand, Raich entered into violent polemics with the editors and contributors of various literary journals and almanacs. His debates with Pushkin and his literary circle proved to be the most heated.

Raich met Pushkin in Odessa in 1823. At first he admired Pushkin's early works, especially his poem *Ruslan i Liudmila* (1820), inspired, as Raich believed, by Ludovico Ariosto's heroic poem *Orlando furioso* (Mad Orlando, 1516). Then, writing in *Galateia* in 1830, Raich argued against Pushkin's "realistic" descriptions of "low society" and reproached him with "insufficiency of thought" in his works. In 1839 Raich wrote in *Galateia* that Pushkin had strayed away from his "velikoe prednaznachenie" (genuine destiny) and "svel poeziu s nebes na zemlyu" (led poetry down from heaven to earth). Of course Pushkin sharply disagreed with Raich's critical articles and had nothing good to say about Raich's poetry. In his epigram "Sobranie nasekomykh" (An Insect Collection, 1829) Pushkin venomously ridicules Raich's works.

In 1828 Raich finished and published his translation of Torquato Tasso's *Gerusalemme liberata* (Jerusalem Delivered, 1581), which he had begun in 1823. He described the principles of this translation in a separate article, "O perevode epicheskikh poem Iuzhnoi Evropy i v osobennosti italianskikh" (On the Translation of Epic Poems of Southern Europe, Especially Italian Ones), published in the journal *Sochineniia v proze i stikhakh* (Works in Prose and Poetry) in 1823. Raich refused to retain the Italian octave form in Russian translation, replacing it instead with a peculiar stanza: twelve iambic verses and symmetric interchange of tetrameter and trimeter strophes. This rhythmic structure, however, had been earlier associated with fantastic and mystic ballads by Vasilii Andreevich Zhukovsky, who used this rhythm for his musical and stylistic attempts to imitate the gloomy atmosphere of the Middle Ages.

Raich's work was subject to further criticism in Russian periodicals. The monotonic rhythm, good for a ballad, but too heavy for a huge heroic poem, became the most popular subject of reproach. Del'vig wrote in *Syn otechestva i Severnyi arkhiv* (Son of the Fatherland and Northern Archive) in 1829 that Raich "prevratil v balladu bessmertnuiu poemu Tassa" (turned Tasso's immortal poem into a ballad).

Raich refused to admit to error, and as he considered his translation of Tasso to be his great mission, he continued his work with persistence. In 1831 Raich started his translation of *Orlando furioso,* using the rhythmic structure of his previous experiment with *Gerusalemme liberata.* After work on the first fifteen (of the original forty-six) cantos, Raich began their publication in three installments: in 1831, 1833, and 1837. Nevertheless, the cold reception of the press forced him to stop publication. After some unavailing efforts to find new publishers, Raich gave up his translation. He had ceased work at the twenty-seventh canto.

In 1832 when the Gentry Pension where he worked was reorganized as a gymnasium (high school), Raich could not accept the new rules and left after a conflict with Nikolai Fedorovich Koshansky, professor of Russian literature. On 29 February 1832 he began his tenure as a professor of Russian in the Aleksandr Military Institute and on 1 March 1832 began a concurrent appointment in the Lazarev Institute of Oriental Languages.

Raich lived in a small house near the Sukharev Tower in Moscow, purchased for him by his brother Filaret. His large family included his son, Vadim (born in 1836), and four daughters to whom (except for Nadezhda, born in 1841) he gave Greek names: Lidia (born in 1833), Polyksena (born in 1839), and Sophia (born in 1846). The financial situation of the family was hard. They lived an exceedingly modest life. One of the Raichs' close friends, poet and memoirist Mikhail Dmitriev, described their life in his "Vospominanie o Semene Egoroviche Raiche" (Recollection of Semen Egorovich Raich, 1855): "Ne mnogo nuzhno bylo emu pri ego umerennykh zhelaniiakh, khotia on zhil i ne bez nuzhdy. Edinstvennoe izlishestvo, kotoroe on pozvolil v svoem priiute,– eto ustanovlennaia na okne Eolova arfa, k unylym zvukam kotoroi liubil on prislushivat'sya" (He needed not many things to fulfill his moderate wishes, although he lived not without need. He ventured himself only one luxury in his refuge–he installed in his window an Aeolian Harp, whose doleful sounds he liked to hear). During the last years of his life Raich served as a professor of Russian literature and inspector of classes in the Moscow Nabilkov Institute.

For approximately ten years (from the end of the 1830s) Raich worked on the long original poem *Areta; skazanie iz vremen Marka Avreliia* (Areta; A Tale of the Time of Marcus Aurelius), which grew into his spiritual biography. The poem was named after its protagonist, the Roman Areta, whose life story it depicts. Areta, a young epicurean, leaves his pagan country and becomes a true Christian. In the preface to the book Raich confesses that he took the plot from the 1827 novel *The Epicurean* by Thomas Moore. The adventures of the hero, however, were not the main point of the poem. The poem consists of several lyrical digressions with obvious autobiographical motifs. Raich developed the ideological oppositions typical for the end of the 1830s and the beginning of the 1840s: Russia versus Europe, Christianity versus paganism, the past (by which he meant the Golden Age of the 1820s) versus the present. For Raich, Russia, Christianity, and the past symbolized the lost paradise of patriarchal life and the happy kingdom of poetry. On the other hand, paganism and the present made way for the coming of the devil, the fall of poetry, and the reign of materialism. Raich's descriptions of the present offer a picture of the moral and spiritual collapse of Russian society in 1840 in contrast to the world of writers of the previous generation, such as Viazemsky, Ivan Dmitriev, and Petr Aleksandrovich Pletnev. To emphasize his main points, Raich compared Russia to the Roman Empire in its decline.

Areta was published as a book in 1849. Earlier the poem had appeared in fragments in several journals. Allegorical form, religious ideas, ancient style, and the structure of the verse seemed archaic for the literary atmosphere of the middle of the century. Only the journal *Moskvitianin* (Muscovite) appreciated the work. Critics for other journals, including *Sovremennik* (The Contemporary), *Otechestvennye zapiski* (Notes of the Fatherland), and *Biblioteka dlia chteniia* (Library for Reading) treated *Areta* as a literary anachronism. Raich's last, mystical poem, "Raiskaia ptichka" (The Bird of Paradise) has survived in manuscript form only.

On the surface it would be easy to dismiss Raich as a member of the "ranks . . . of humble, talentless but industrious literary figures, the memory of whom either disappears or evokes . . . a smile" of mockery, as the entry in the *Entsiklopedicheskii slovar'* (Encyclopedic Dictionary, 1890–1904) characterizes him. After all, few remember his poetry, and even fewer read his translations. Yet, at the same time, it is difficult to find fault with someone who could see value not only in traditional poets such as the eighteenth-century Mikhail Vasil'evich Lomonosov but also in his more "innovative" contemporaries. Raich's ability to discern the subtleties and complexities of literatures as diverse as Latin, Greek, Persian, Italian, and German not only reveals his tastes for antiquity and oriental cultures but also hints at a mind more complex and sophisticated than the dismissive *Entsiklopedicheskii slovar'* summary of his talents might indicate. In spite of some lapses in judgment while editing *Galateia,* he somehow managed to gain a reputation as "the only knowledgeable journalist in Moscow." The empress even rewarded him with two diamond rings in the late 1820s for his literary activities, especially the work on *Severnaia lira*. Finally, one cannot ignore the zeal and dedication Raich exhibited as a true teacher, especially in taking the risk of meeting secretly with his students to teach them Romantic philosophy and aesthetics. An enthusiastic and erudite mentor to a generation of poets, he helped form the poetic outlook of two poets of genius: Lermontov and Tiutchev. Even if he had not accomplished anything else, his beneficent influence on two of Russia's greatest poets assures him a modest, though important, place in the history of Russian culture.

References:

Mark I. Aronson and Soloman Abramovich Reiser, *Literaturnye kruzhki i salony* (Leningrad: Priboi, 1929), pp. 123–128;

Nikolai Liont'evich Brodsky, ed., *Literaturnye salony i kruzhki. Pervaia polovina XIX veka* (Moscow-Leningrad: Academia, 1930), pp. 139–140;

Mikhail Dmitriev, "Vospominanie o Semene Egoroviche Raiche," *Moskovskie vedomosti,* 24 (November 1855): 577;

Efim Grigor'evich Etkind, *Russkie poety-perevodchiki ot Tred'iakovskogo do Pushkina* (Leningrad: Nauka, 1973), pp. 171–175;

Teodor Levit, "Literaturnaia sreda Lermontova v Moskovskom blagorodnom pansione," *Literaturnoe nasledstvo,* 45–46 (1948): 225–254;

V. D. Morozov, "Iz istorii zhurnal'noi kritiki 20–30-kh godov XIX veka (Zhurnal Raicha *Galatea*)," in *Khudozhestvennoe tvorchestvo i literaturnyi protsess,* volume 3 (Tomsk, 1982), pp. 101–114;

Kseniia Dmitrievna Muratova, A. G. Grum-Grzhimailo, and V. V. Sorokin, "*Obshchestvo gromkogo smekha,*" in *Dekabristy v Moskve: Sbornik statei,* edited by Iulian Grigor'evich Oksman (Moscow: Moskovskii rabochii, 1963), pp. 146–149;

Andrei Nikolaevich Murav'ev, *Znakomstvo s russkimi poetami* (Kiev, 1871), pp. 5–6;

A. A. Nikolaev, "Sud'ba poeticheskogo naslediia Tiutcheva 1822–1836 godov i tekstologicheskie problemy ego izucheniia," *Russkaia literatura,* 1 (1979): 130–135, 140–143;

Kiriel Vasil'evich Pigarev, *Tiutchev i ego vremya* (Moscow: Sovremennik, 1978), pp. 10–12;

Nikolai Alekseevich Polevoi, *Materialy iz istorii russkoi literatury i zhurnalistiki tridtsatykh godov* (Leningrad, 1934), pp. 155, 387–389;

K. Iu. Rogov, "K Istorii 'Moskovskogo Romantizma': Kruzhok i obshchestvo S. E. Raicha," in *Lotmanovskii sbornik,* volume 2 (Moscow: O.G.I., Izd-vo RGGU, 1997), pp. 523–576;

Iurii Nikolaevich Tynianov, *Poetika. Istoria literatury. Kino* (Moscow: Nauka, 1977), pp. 40, 42, 51, 410–411;

M. Vasil'ev, "Iz perepiski literatorov 20–30-kh gg. XIX veka: D. P. Oznobishin–S. E. Raich–E. P. Pertsov," *Izvestiia Obshchestva arkheologii, istorii i etnografii pri Kazanskom Universitete,* 34 (1929): 3–4;

Vadim Erazmovich Vatsuro, "Literaturnaia shkola Lermontova," in *Lermontovskii sbornik,* edited by I. S. Chistova and others (Leningrad: Nauka, 1985), pp. 49–90.

Papers:

Some of Semen Egorovich Raich's manuscripts are located in fonds 1634 and 505 (Tiutchev archive) of the Central State Archive of Literature and Art (TsGALI), Moscow.

Evdokiia Petrovna Rostopchina
(23 December 1811 – 3 December 1858)

Sibelan Forrester
Swarthmore College

BOOKS: *Ocherki bol'shago sveta. Sochinenie Iasnovidiashchei* (St. Petersburg: K. Neiman, 1839);

Stikhotvoreniia grafini E. Rostopchinoi (St. Petersburg: Izd-e Kontory privil. tip. Fishera, 1841);

Donna Mariia Kolonna-Manchini (St. Petersburg, 1848);

Neliudimka. Drama v piati deistviakh (Moscow: Universitetskaia tip., 1850);

Compte rendu de la derniére représentation de M-lle Fanny Elssler, insére dans la Garelte de Police, du 23 février, 1851 (Moscow, 1851);

Iziashchnaia slovesnost'. Domashnee Ulozhenie. Komediia v odnom deistvii (St. Petersburg, 1852);

Iziashchnaia slovesnost'. Kto kogo prouchil? Komediia v odnom deistvii (St. Petersburg, 1853);

Stikhotvoreniia, 4 volumes (St. Petersburg: A. Smirdin, 1856–1859);

U pristani. Roman v pis'makh, 9 volumes (St. Petersburg: Tip. Imp. Akademii nauk, 1857);

Schastlivaia zhenshchina (St. Petersburg: A. Smirdin, 1858);

Vozvrat Chatskago v Moskvu, ili Vstrecha znakomykh lits posle dvadtsatipiatiletnei razluki. Prodolzhenie komedii Griboedova "Gore ot uma" (St. Petersburg: Izd. N. K. Flige, Tip. tovarishchestva Obshchestvennaia pol'za, 1865);

Dnevnik devushki. Roman (St. Petersburg: V. Golovin, 1866).

Editions and Collections: *Poemy, povesti, razskazy i noveshiia melkiia stikhotvoreniia grafini E. P. Rostopchinoi* (St. Petersburg: V. Golovin, 1866);

Sochineniia grafini E. P. Rostopchinoi, 2 volumes, edited by Sergei Petrovich Sushkov (St. Petersburg: I. N. Skorokhodov, 1890);

Stikhotvoreniia (St. Petersburg: A. A. Kaspari, 1910);

Stikhotvoreniia, proza, pis'ma, edited by Boris Romanov (Moscow: Sovetskaia Rossiia, 1986);

Talisman, edited by Viktor Afanas'ev (Moscow: Moskovskii rabochii, 1987)—include *Izbrannaia lirika, Neliudimka. Drama,* and *Dokumenty, pis'ma, vospominaniia;*

Schastlivaia zhenshchina. Literaturnye sochineniia, edited by Andrei Mikhailovich Ranchin (Moscow: Pravda, 1991);

Palatstso Forli, edited by Elena M. Gribkova (Moscow: Moskovskii rabochii, 1993).

OTHER: "Rank and Money," translated by Helena Goscilo, in *Russian and Polish Women's Fiction,* edited by Goscilo (Knoxville: University of Tennessee Press, 1985), pp. 44–49.

Countess Evdokiia Rostopchina, who sometimes used the pseudonyms Iasnovidiashchaia (Clairvoyant) and Russkaia zhenshchina (A Russian Woman), was one of the most popular female poets of nineteenth-century Russia. Undoubtedly talented, she used her wealth, beauty, and prominent position to advance her literary career. She ran a stylish salon and knew Aleksandr Pushkin, Mikhail Iur'evich Lermontov, and other leading writers and publishers. She was an insider in a period when serious literature was dominated by the nobility, when rich and beautiful women could exploit Romantic conventions to enjoy considerable influence. Like many of the poets who outlived Pushkin and Lermontov, Rostopchina found herself out of date in the 1850s, when leading utilitarian critics saw her, at best, as the author of a few unpublished poems about the exiled participants in the failed Decembrist uprising of 1825. Rostopchina's many prose and dramatic works, uncompromisingly Romantic in the age of emerging realism, never enjoyed the popularity of the early "salon" poems that formed her reputation. Perhaps because of its "feminine" character, however, her work remained widely accessible until the Soviet period, and her influence on later generations of women poets has yet to be studied.

Evdokiia Petrovna Sushkova was born in Moscow on 23 December 1811 in the house of her grandfather, Ivan Aleksandrovich Pashkov; she was a baby when her family fled before the march of Napoleon Bonaparte's army. She had two younger brothers, Sergei (born in January 1816) and Dmitrii (born in March 1817). Her mother, née Dar'ia Ivanovna Pashkova, died of tuberculosis at twenty-eight, in May 1817, and her father, Petr Vasil'evich Sushkov, turned the children over to his late wife's parents. Educated unsystematically by governesses and tutors, Evdokiia—known by the childhood nickname Dodó—had a brilliant memory and a marked gift for languages, managing to acquire a good command of French and German, to which she later added reading knowledge of English and Italian. Her writing often refers to a childhood of tears and suffering in which books were the primary comfort. She read voraciously and maintained a lifetime interest in Western European women writers, from Madame Anne-Louise-Germaine de Staël and Marceline Desbordes-Valmore to the Brontës.

Evdokiia began writing poetry in French at about seven, and by fourteen she was also secretly writing poems in Russian. Well-known literary figures frequented the Pashkov house, and literary interest ran in the family: her paternal grandmother, Mar'ia Vasil'evna Sushkova (née Khrapovitskaia), and uncle Nikolai Vasil'evich Sushkov were minor writers. Evdokiia Sushkova first met Pushkin at a ball in 1829, where he is said to have spent most of the evening enjoying her whispered verses. She recalled the encounter in the 1838–1839 poem "Dve vstrechi" (Two Meetings). Without her knowledge, Prince Petr Andreevich Viazemsky published her poem "Talisman" in 1830 in the St. Petersburg almanac *Severnye tsvety na 1831 god* (Northern Flowers for 1831), over the pseudonym "D...S...a." Sushkova's family condemned this publication, considering it—and poetic activity in general—improper for a decent unmarried girl. She was compelled to promise not to publish until after her marriage, and indeed published nothing else until 1834.

"Talisman" is a charming and musical love poem; dozens of Rostopchina's poems have been set to music, some by more than one composer. Many of her poems, explicitly titled "Slova dlia muzyki" (Words for Music), should be read as song lyrics. Composers such as Mikhail Ivanovich Glinka, Aleksandr Sergeevich Dargomyzhsky, Anton Grigor'evich Rubinstein, and Petr Il'ich Tchaikovsky ensured Rostopchina's lasting presence in the libretti of *romansy* (art songs). Singing was a drawing-room accomplishment for noble girls, and writing for the *romansy* was more acceptable for women than the literary publishing world, which was dominated by men. Several of Rostopchina's song-poems are adaptations or imitations of folk songs, a sign of Romantic nationalism, which idealized the peasant class as a linguistic source. Other youthful poems remained unpublished under tsarist censorship throughout Rostopchina's life: her passionate poems to the Decembrists circulated widely in manuscript but were first published in the Soviet period.

Like Lermontov, Rostopchina in many ways represents Romanticism more purely than earlier Russian Romantics. She presents her poetry as a kind of "lyrical diary," carefully including the date and place of composition for most poems, as if these were needed to understand the emotional geography of the text. Her fluent and musical verse fits the Romantic conceit that true poets write with inspired effortlessness, and some of her works read like improvisations. Although it suited the mood of the late 1830s, her poetry quickly became old-fashioned. The topics of love and religion were easy targets for critics of the next generation, and their eventual mockery and persecution provided her with another beloved Romantic trope: the sensitive individual's isolation amid the misunderstanding of the vulgar crowd.

Once she came of age to attend balls and other society events, Sushkova's beauty led to great success and eventually to a proposal of marriage from Count Andrei Fedorovich Rostopchin, which she refused. Under family pressure she changed her mind and in May 1833 married Rostopchin, who was two years younger than she, though his premature baldness made him appear older. Her family considered this match advantageous; Rostopchin's father, Fedor Vasil'evich, was the Moscow military commander who supposedly started the famous fire that led to Napoleon's retreat in 1812. After the wedding Rostopchina immediately moved to her husband's village, Anna, where the couple lived until 1836. Rostopchina and her husband had little in common since his interests ran mainly to drinking bouts, cards, and horses. In their memoirs, relatives delicately but significantly skirt the question of why the couple had no children for several years.

Rostopchina was supposedly in love with another man, and the plot of a young woman forced by family and society to marry against her inclinations became a staple in her prose and poetry. She wrote the *povest'* or long story "Chiny i den'gi" (Rank and Money) in 1835; first published in *Syn otechestva i Severnyi arkhiv* (Son of the Fatherland and Northern Archive) in 1838 over the pseudonym Iasnovidiashchaia, it is available in a good English translation by Helena Goscilo (1985). The long story "Poedinok" (The Duel), also published in *Syn otechestva i Severnyi arkhiv* in 1838, depicts a young woman who finds true spiritual love outside her marriage to a much older man and who mourns her beloved's death in a duel without revealing her sorrow to the vindictive society around her. Rostopchina acquired a reputation for "George-Sandism" because of her insistence on a woman's right to follow her heart. Her society tales resembled other examples of this important genre of the 1830s and 1840s: an obligatory central love plot involving exceptional individuals and criticizing the pettiness and inhumanity of society.

Like many poets, Rostopchina never fully adapted to prose, and her first *povesti* went unremarked. Her language is somewhat archaic and her style often long-winded, with little development between early stories and those written nearly twenty years later. At its best, though, her prose is psychologically subtle and sometimes quite gripping in plot. Her heroines are distinguished by intelligence, education, and high moral character, but by beauty above all. As in her poems, woman's fate revolves around love, and the rest of the story depends on whether that love goes happily. Rostopchina's heroes motivate the heroines' emotions and development and symbolize the women's happy or unhappy fates; the last name of the hero of *Palatstso Forli* (The Forli Palazzo, 1854), indicatively, sounds just like "Mon roi" (my king) in Cyrillic transliteration. Realistic elements in Rostopchina's Romantic *povesti* include her descriptions of upper-class life and of a kind of "problem that has no name" in the privileged but circumscribed lives of upper-class Russian women.

In autumn 1836 Rostopchina and her husband moved to St. Petersburg, where she was well received. Pushkin, Viazemsky, Vasilii Andreevich Zhukovsky, Petr Aleksandrovich Pletnev, and Prince Vladimir Fedorovich Odoevsky visited her Saturday salon, along with the most famous Russian and Western European musicians. Memoirists of the period stress Rostopchina's beauty, scintillating wit, and delightful conversation, which made her a pleasant interlocutor even when the talk strayed from literature. Given her social position in the era of gentry poets, she easily used her salon for contact with important publishers. Rostopchina soon returned to her husband's isolated estate, but by this time she was publishing widely in Moscow and St. Petersburg journals. Between 1837 and 1839 Rostopchina gave birth to two daughters, Ol'ga and Lidiia, and one son, Viktor. One daughter, Countess Lidiia Andreevna Rostopchina, also later wrote and published poetry in French and Russian.

Rostopchina's reputation peaked in the late 1830s when Pletnev, editor of the journal *Sovremennik* (The Contemporary) after Pushkin's death, wrote that she was undoubtedly the foremost poet in Russia. Zhukovsky sent her a notebook Pushkin had prepared for rough drafts before his death and said that she must fill its pages now that the book had found its true purpose. Her poem on that occasion, "Chernovaia kniga Pushkina" (Pushkin's Notebook, 1838), published in *Sovremennik* in 1839, has been beautifully analyzed by Stephanie Sandler. Rostopchina briefly renewed her youthful acquaintance with Lermontov, her younger brother's former schoolmate, and he dedicated to her his 1841 poem "Ia znaiu, pod odnoi zvezdoiu . . ." (I know, under one star . . .). Lermontov dined at Rostopchina's house the evening before his last departure from St. Petersburg in the spring of 1841, and she wrote the poem "Na dorogu" (For the Road) to calm his forebodings. It was published in *Russkaia beseda* (Russian Talk) that year. After his death in a duel that July, she wrote "Nashim budushchim poetam" (To Our Future Poets), also published in *Russkaia beseda* in 1841, about the seeming doom of Russian poets. She had already, in "Chernovaia kniga Pushkina," expressed her hope that she, the woman who now took the next place in the chain linking Pushkin and Lermontov, would bring an end to the deadly cycle of duels and death.

Rostopchina's first book of verse, *Stikhotvoreniia* (Poems), included ninety-one poems written between 1829 and 1839 and met with high praise upon its publication in 1841. The most influential critic of the day, Vissarion Grigor'evich Belinsky, tellingly muted his compliments, however, by remarking that the poet's talent might find a broader and more dignified sphere than the salon. That reproach indicates the double bind of women writing in the period: topics and places that women knew well enough to write about were considered limited and unimportant.

In the spring of 1845 Rostopchina left with her husband and three children for a two-year sojourn in

Rostopchina in the early 1840s (portrait by P. F. Sokolov; from M. I. Gillel'son and V. A. Maniulov, eds., M. Iu. Lermontov v vospominaniiakh sovremennikov, 1972)

France, Italy, Germany, and Austria. In Italy she read her poem "Nasil'nyi brak" (The Forced Marriage) to Nikolai Gogol, who persuaded her that the Russian censors were too stupid to catch the allegorical depiction in the poem of Poland oppressed by Russia. Removing the dedication of the poem—"in thought, to Adam Mickiewicz"—and other clues to its meaning, Rostopchina sent it to Faddei Venediktovich Bulgarin's newspaper *Severnaia pchela* (The Northern Bee), in which she had never published before. The poem was indeed taken as a bold depiction of the author's own marital unhappiness and published anonymously in December 1846. Once the allegory was noted, Tsar Nicholas I was enraged, and quite a scandal ensued; the journal issue was confiscated from subscribers. Bulgarin, widely known as an informer, no doubt revealed the author's identity. Rostopchina returned to Russia in 1847 newly notorious and is said to have been summoned by the chief of gendarmes before being banished from St. Petersburg. Her relatives insisted that the poem had been misunderstood. Rostopchina and her family moved to Moscow, living first with the poet's difficult mother-in-law but later buying a house of their own. Rostopchina was humiliated to lose the imperial favor she had previously valued and enjoyed. Since her literary and social connections were mostly in St. Petersburg, where she had lived for many years, Rostopchina found Moscow uncultured and full of conflicting and petty literary circles. She lived reluctantly there and on the family estate of Voronovo until the death of Nicholas I in 1855.

By the late 1840s fashions were changing in Russian literature: prose increasingly predominated over poetry, and the Romantic *povest'* Rostopchina favored was in decline. Her political opinions, which resemble those of Pushkin or other gentry poets, began to seem reactionary in the new context. Rostopchina resumed her Saturday salon in Moscow, but she had little sympathy with the younger generations of Slavophiles and Westernizers, who were replacing the older gentlemen poets as arbiters of literary importance and of access to prestigious journals. In return, the men who attended her salon complained about being forced to listen to their hostess reading her own lengthy works.

It would be untrue to say that Rostopchina did not relish the battles of insider literary politics; she sent one poem mocking Karolina Karlovna Pavlova's polyglot literary production to Pletnev for anonymous publication. Indeed, in the several poems these two Muscovite poets wrote to or about one another, Rostopchina appears less charitable than Pavlova. At the same time, Rostopchina was touchy about criticism and tended to take critics' praise for any other woman writer–Pavlova, Elena Andreevna Gan (Zeneida R-va), Nadezhda Dmitrievna Khvoshchinskaia (V. Krestovsky), or Elizaveta Vasil'evna Sukhovo-Kobylina (Evgeniia Tur)–as a personal affront. In part, this sensitivity reflected the common critical tendency to lump women writers together under that rubric alone and then to rank them according to a philosophy in which only one, perhaps, would be granted the status of male writers. In a 27 May 1854 letter to Aleksandr Vasil'evich Druzhinin, Rostopchina complained of the tone of the criticism to which she was exposed:

> I still cannot equip myself with the triple armor of indifference, and any kind of unfairness, any kind of slander, even from persons whom I do not respect at all, can still wound me painfully; and if it does not offend my self-esteem, does not arouse my feminine dignity, then once and for all I permit them and anyone at all to scold me as a writer, to deny that I have any talent, to laugh and criticize me literarily; but it is unbearably annoying and painful to me that people here are still so savage and crude that they always mix one's person into literary questions; I stand only *for my public character and my womanly respectability.*

In Moscow, Rostopchina produced several dramatic works in blank verse, including *Neliudimka* (The Unsociable Woman, 1850); *Semeinaia taina* (The Family Secret), first published in *Biblioteka dlia chteniia* (Library for Reading) in 1851; and *Doch' Don-Zhuana* (Don Juan's Daughter), published in *Panteon* in 1856, and prose *povesti* such as *Schastlivaia zhenshchina* (A Happy Woman, written in 1851–1852, published in 1858), *Palatstso Forli,* and *U pristani. Roman v pis'makh* (At the Pier. A Novel in Letters, 1857). *Palatstso Forli,* first published in *Biblioteka dlia chteniia* in 1854, is rife with prejudicial generalizations about foreigners and Jews, but the perspicacious though minor character of Dzhuditta draws attention to a range of interesting secondary female characters in the *povesti*. Rostopchina also occupied herself writing light dramatic works for benefit matinees. Her mostly unrhymed novel in verse, *Dnevnik devushki* (A Young Woman's Diary, written 1842–1850), is largely autobiographical. Originally published in multiple journal installments in 1866, it has been republished in the 1991 edition of *Schastlivaia zhenshchina. Literaturnye sochineniia,* though extensively abridged.

Rostopchina's dramatic "conversation in verses," *Vozvrat Chatskago v Moskvu, ili Vstrecha znakomykh lits posle dvadtsatipiatiletnei razluki* (Chatsky's Return to Moscow, or A Meeting of Acquaintances after Twenty-Five Years Apart, written in 1856, published in 1865), and her satiric poem "Dom sumasshedshikh v Moskve v 1858 godu" (Madhouse in Moscow in the Year 1858), published in *Russkaia starina* (Russian Antiquities) in 1885, both "continue" famous literary works from the previous generation–Aleksandr Sergeevich Griboedov's *Gore ot uma* (Woe from Wit, completed by 1824) and Aleksandr Fedorovich Voeikov's "Dom sumasshedshikh" (The Madhouse, circulated in manuscript during the author's lifetime). Rostopchina may have seen "continuing," responding or adding to works by famous men, as the best guarantee for a woman's participation in the literary process of the time. Readers in the nineteenth and twentieth centuries have been offended by the energetic and witty treatment in these works of hallowed Russian cultural figures; the mock-Slavophile verses of Eleikin in *Vozvrat Chatskago* are particularly funny and also neatly illustrate the potential slip of Slavophilism into Great Russian political expansionism. The inventive wit that often emerges in Rostopchina's letters, published only in small selections, complements her more ethereal poetic persona.

Rostopchina's poetry was out of fashion by the mid 1850s, and the first two volumes of her four-volume collected poems, published in 1856, were harshly attacked by the new critics. Nikolai Gavrilovich Chernyshevsky and Nikolai Aleksandrovich Dobroliubov treated Rostopchina as an amusing relic, though the intensity of their attacks belies their depiction of her as a "forgotten poetess." Her 1856 poem "Moim kritikam" (To My Critics), published in the four-volume collection, declares her allegiance to the values of the Russian Golden Age of poetry, which she (like many other contemporaries of Pushkin) had the misfortune to outlive:

> I have parted from the new generation,
> My path leads away from it,
> In concepts, soul and conviction
> I belong to another world.
> I honor and call upon other gods,
> And I speak another language;
> I am alien to them, laughable–I know that,
> But I am not embarrassed before their judgment.
> . . . .
> The throng of my brothers and friends is far away–
> It has passed to its rest, completing its life.
> No wonder that, as a solitary priestess,
> I stand at an empty altar!

Vladislav Felitsianovich Khodasevich, in a well-known article first published in 1908, cites this poem as the only moment in Rostopchina's later life when she answered her enemies with the dignity befitting a poet. Aside from Khodasevich's condescending tone and his ignorance of the pro-Decembrist verses that were then still unpublished, his article includes a surprising number of misquotations and misattributions. Like the mistaken or misleading quotations that abounded in the Soviet period, these make Rostopchina appear more foolish or reactionary than she was. In reclaiming the Romantic poetry of the Golden Age from its epigones, Khodasevich also perhaps strove to reclaim it for the serious men of the Russian Silver Age.

"Moim kritikam" underplays Rostopchina's continuing engagement in the literary life of the period—and in the Russian writer's traditional difficulties with censorship. She was one of the Moscow literary set who "discovered" Aleksandr Nikolaevich Ostrovsky and presented him to the publishers of St. Petersburg, and she had the pleasure of introducing him to Leo Tolstoy, then the young and promising author of *Detstvo* (Childhood, 1852). It may be coincidental that elements of Rostopchina's *povest'* "Schastlivaia zhenshchina," briefly detained by the censor for its quasi-adulterous immorality, foreshadow the plot of *Anna Karenina* (1873–1877). The satirical *Vozvrat Chatskogo*, like the Griboedov play it "continued," was banned from performance or publication by the censor until after the author's death.

Rostopchina continued her literary activity until her death, though she was often in great pain. She died of stomach cancer in Moscow on 3 December 1858 and was buried in Piatnitskii cemetery.

After her death, Rostopchina's reputation plummeted further among the "radical" critics of the 1860s. As Diana Greene has pointed out, she could be safely attacked as a woman in order to attack her covertly as an aristocrat. On the other hand, the "womanly" limitations of her poetry made many readers prefer her to the more "manly" and less self-indulgent Pavlova. After all, Rostopchina's poem "Kak dolzhny pisat' zhenshchiny" (How Women Should Write, 1840), published in the 1845 anthology *Vchera i segodnia* (Yesterday and Today), advises women poets to remain in the shadows and glow there peacefully. The idea that "woman" and "writer" were contradictory terms also shaped Nikolai Platonovich Ogarev's often-quoted poetic scolding of Rostopchina, "Otstupnitse" (To the Apostate, 1857). The poem describes her long-ago poetic enthusiasm for the Decembrists almost exclusively in terms of her youthful physical beauty; and since, according to Ogarev, a woman in her forties can never regain the fresh and impressionable appearance of her youth, no matter what her politics, the only real option he leaves to Rostopchina is silence.

With such blurring of enthusiasm for her writing and for her looks, she may have received little useful criticism of her work until she had become accustomed to paeans. Her works, however, remained in print in one form or another until the Soviet period. The form was generally not as prestigious as other editions—for example, in the 1910s Rostopchina's collected works were published as a free multivolume literary supplement to the St. Petersburg journal *Vsemirnaia nov'* (Universal Novelty). For decades after the Russian Revolution of 1917 her poems appeared in small selections in anthologies of works by minor writers. Several substantial editions of her works have come out in Russia beginning in 1986, hinting that her obscurity in the Soviet period was as politically motivated as the attacks of the 1850s. Perhaps Rostopchina's gentry origins and society themes are no longer obstacles to appreciation of her work and may even be attractions to it.

References:

Vissarion Grigor'evich Belinsky, "Stikhotvoreniia grafini E. Rostopchinoi," in his *Polnoe sobranie sochinenii,* volume 5 (Moscow: AN SSSR, 1953–1959), pp. 456–461;

Nikolai Aleksandrovich Dobroliubov, "U pristani: Roman v pis'makh grafini Evdokii Rostopchinoi," in his *Sobranie sochinenii,* volume 2 (Moscow: Khudozhestvennaia literatura, 1961–1964), pp. 70–87;

F. Gobler, "A Russian Woman Poet, Evdokiia Rostopchina, and Modern Literary Criticism," *Welt der slaven-halbjahresschrift fur Slavistik,* 39, no. 2 (1994): 369–386;

Diana Greene, "Nineteenth-Century Women Poets: Critical Perception vs. Self-Definition," in *Women Writers in Russian Literature,* edited by Greene and Toby Clyman (Westport, Conn.: Greenwood Press, 1994), pp. 95–109;

Vladislav Felitsianovich Khodasevich, "Grafinia E. P. Rostopchina. Ee zhizn' i lirika," in his *Stat'i o russkoi poèzii* (Letchworth, U.K.: Prideaux Press, 1971), pp. 7–42;

Vladimir S. Kiselev-Sergenin, "Po storomii sledu: o ballade E. Rostopchinoi 'Nasilnyi brak,'" *Russkaia literatura,* no. 3 (1995): 137–152;

Stephanie Sandler, "The Law, the Body, and the Book: Three Poems on the Death of Pushkin," *Canadian-American Slavic Studies,* 23 (Fall 1989): 281–311.

Kondratii Fedorovich Ryleev

(18 September 1795 – 13 July 1826)

James West
University of Washington

BOOKS: *Dumy, stikhotvoreniia* (Moscow: S. Selivanovsky, 1825);

Voinarovskii (Moscow: S. Selivanovsky, 1825).

Editions and Collections: *Stikhotvoreniia K. Ryleeva* (Berlin: Ferdinand Schneider, 1857; second edition, expanded, 1858);

Polnoe sobranie sochinenii (Leipzig: F. A. Brockhaus, 1861);

Sochineniia i perepiska Kondratiia Fedorovicha Ryleeva, edited by Petr Aleksandrovich Efremov (St. Petersburg: I. I. Glazunov, 1872);

Dumy i poemy (St. Petersburg: A. S. Suvorin, 1893);

Sochineniia K. F. Ryleeva, edited by Mikhail Nikolaevich Mazaev (St. Petersburg: Izdanie Evg. Evdokimova, 1893);

Izbrannyia stikhotvoreniia (St. Petersburg: t-vo "Obshchestvennaia pol'za," 1909);

Polnoe sobranie sochinenii, edited by Iulian Grigor'evich Oksman (Leningrad: Izd-vo pisatelei, 1934);

Polnoe sobranie sochinenii, edited by Aleksandr Grigor'evich Tseitlin (Moscow-Leningrad: Academia, 1934);

Stikhotvoreniia, edited by Nikolai Ivanovich Mordovchenko (Leningrad: Sovetskii pisatel', 1938);

Izbrannoe, edited by Iurii Nikandrovich Verkhovsky (Moscow: Goslitizdat, 1946);

Stikhotvoreniia. Stat'i. Ocherki. Dokladnye zapiski. Pis'ma, edited by Oksman (Moscow: Goslitizdat, 1956);

Polnoe sobranie stikhotvorenii, edited by Arina Vladimirovna Arkhipova and Avram Evseevich Khodorov (Leningrad: Sovetskii pisatel', 1971);

Dumy, edited by Leonid Genrikhovich Frizman (Moscow: Nauka, 1975);

Sochineniia, edited by Sergei Aleksandrovich Fomichev (Leningrad: Khudozhestvennaia literatura, 1987);

Sochineniia, edited by G. A. Kolosova and Aleksei Mikhailovich Peskov (Moscow: Pravda, 1988).

Editions in English: *Voinarofskyi and Other Poems,* translated by Thomas Hart-Davies (Calcutta: Thacker, Spink, 1879);

The Poems of K. F. Relaieff, enlarged edition, translated by Hart-Davies (London: Remington, 1887).

Kondratii Fedorovich Ryleev

The Decembrist Revolt of 1825 turned Kondratii Ryleev, a minor poet, into a major figure of his age. An officer in the Napoleonic Wars and a patriot, Ryleev later became disillusioned with the political stagnation of his native land and joined the secret *Severnoe obshchestvo* (Northern Society). He then evolved into one of the major leaders of the Decembrist Revolt. All the while he maintained his interest in literature, both as a writer and as one of the editors of *Poliarnaia zvezda* (The Polar Star). Ryleev's *dumy* (meditations) all have historical, patriotic themes. He looked back at the Russian past to find for his contemporaries examples of civic virtue in historical figures who sacrificed themselves for Russia. Ryleev's motives followed the models of his *dumy*. He was perhaps the most honorable of the Decembrists, and he earned a reputation as a martyr for Russia when he was executed as a Decembrist leader.

Kondratii Fedorovich Ryleev was born on 18 September 1795 in Batovo, in the Sofiisky district of the St. Petersburg province. His father, Fedor Andreevich Ryleev, was a retired lieutenant colonel, decorated by Catherine II for bravery and meritorious service. His mother was Anastasiia Matveevna Essen, the daughter of a well-connected, landowning family. Kondratii was the only one of their children to survive infancy, though an illegitimate daughter of his father, Annushka, was raised in the family. There was a superstition in Russia that a couple whose children died in infancy must break the curse by inviting as godparents the first man and woman they encounter after the birth of a new child; Ryleev's Russian biographers like to point to his godparents, a retired soldier and a woman beggar, as his first link with the common people.

Fedor Ryleev seems to have been a stereotypically despotic landowner, with a violent temper and little love for his family, to whom he meted out verbal and physical abuse. He quickly squandered his modest fortune, and in 1800 Anastasiia left him and settled with the children on an estate given to her by her relatives.

In January 1801 Ryleev was sent away to school through the generosity of his mother's well-to-do relatives. "School" was a military academy, the prestigious First Cadet Corps, founded in 1743 to prepare members of the gentry for public and military service. Among its alumni were many famous figures, including writers Aleksandr Petrovich Sumarokov and Mikhail Matveevich Kheraskov. In addition and the dramatist Iakov Borisovich Kniazhnin had taught there. The academy was also the cradle of the *Vol'noe obshchestvo liubitelei rossiiskoi slovesnosti* (Free Society of Lovers of Russian Literature), which played an important role in Russian literature in the early decades of the nineteenth century and provided the forum for Ryleev's later development as a writer.

In 1801, the year of Ryleev's admission, the directorship of the cadet school passed to Major-General Friedrich Maximilian Klinger, a German in Russian service. He was a leading poet and dramatist, a friend of the young Johann Wolfgang von Goethe and other leaders of the Sturm und Drang movement, which took its name from the title of one of Klinger's dramas. As head of the Cadet Corps he was a dogmatic theorist of education and a heartless bully, under whose educational regimen corporal punishment was the order of the day, administered each morning at convocation. For the least transgression 30 to 50 lashes were usual, and for more serious misdemeanors, up to 150. The young Ryleev, who often engaged in pranks, was a frequent recipient of this treatment, but was quite stoic; he sometimes even took the blame, and the punishment, for others' misdeeds. This behavior of the young boy perhaps foreshadowed the manner in which he conducted himself after his arrest in 1825 for his part in the Decembrist Revolt, when he wrote to Tsar Nicholas I taking the blame for the conspiracy, asking pardon for his fellow conspirators, and offering himself for execution. The severities of Klinger's regime were mitigated for Ryleev and his schoolmates by the inspiring devotion of two Russian school officials to the welfare of their charges.

As a pupil at the Cadet Corps, Ryleev enjoyed literature and wrote verses from an early age. Even his letters from school were quite literary in language and tone; writing to his father on 7 December 1812 he portrayed himself as an overly bookish young man, horrified at the evils of the world in which he is about to make his way. Ryleev graduated on 1 February 1814 and, despite the difficulty of equipping himself appropriately without financial support from his father, he was commissioned as an ensign in the First Reserve Artillery Brigade.

On leaving the Cadet Corps, Ryleev bequeathed to his schoolmates a notebook comprising copies of poems he had enjoyed, but also some of his own earliest efforts–many of which had already found their way into the collections of his comrades. The most significant of these juvenilia is the ode "Liubov' k otchizne" (Love for the Fatherland), occasioned by the death of Gen. Mikhail Illarionovich Kutuzov on 16 April 1813, a poem that already reveals the keen patriotism and the highly emotional civic spirit that were characteristic of Ryleev in his adult years.

After his graduation Ryleev served in Europe, pursuing the retreating army of Napoleon Bonaparte. At the end of February 1814, a month before the fall of Paris, Ryleev's unit was posted to Dresden, where he spent some months enjoying the company of his generous and convivial uncle, Lieutenant-General Mikhail Nikolaevich Ryleev, who was commandant of the Russian forces there. In Dresden he learned of the death of his father. Prince Repin, governor of Dresden, ordered the expulsion of Ryleev from the city because the residents were tired of his mocking epigrams.

Ryleev spent the winter of 1814–1815 at a military riding school in the Minsk province, where he learned of his family's economic ill fortune. For the last few years his father had managed the estates of Princess Varvara Vasil'evna Golitsyna. On his death she sued his heirs for 80,000 rubles, and most of their property was sequestered. The ensuing lawsuit lasted for years, fueling Ryleev's anger at social inequality.

In April 1815 Ryleev's unit was again dispatched to Europe to participate in the final campaign of the war against Napoleon. This time Ryleev served as quartermaster and made use of the opportunity provided by his duties to observe and record the lives and conditions of ordinary people in the countries through which he passed. At least one contemporary memoir suggests that this experience instilled in him a conviction that the lot of the Russian people was incomparably worse than that of the Europeans. In September Ryleev was in Paris with the victorious Russian army for eight days. A series of letters he wrote from Paris form a kind of epistolary diary (it is not even clear that they had a particular addressee) and describe the intensive sightseeing he managed to fit into his brief stay in what most educated Russians of the time regarded as the cultural capital of the world. He complains of the allies' condescending treatment of Russians, and he portrays himself and his compatriots as close to the French in spirit, respectful and supportive of the defeated nation.

After the intense but cloistered schooling he had received in the Cadet Corps, the months in Europe formed an important part of Ryleev's education and gave him a chance to see Russia from a Western perspective, an opportunity shared by many young Russians of his generation. His poetry reflects the inspiration of the landscapes he encountered, most notably the Rhine; the architecture of the cities he visited; and the works of art that he had the opportunity to see, particularly in the Dresden gallery and the Louvre.

On its return to Russia in December 1815, Ryleev's unit was first stationed in the Vilensk province of Lithuania, close to the Prussian border, where he suffered an illness that confined him to his billet for four months but gave him the opportunity to catch up on his reading and correspondence. In spring 1817 his unit was reorganized and ended up in Ostrogozhsk in the Voronezh province. Though Ostrogozhsk was not a large town, four regiments of dragoons that had served in Europe were already stationed there, and it had a thriving cultural and social life.

Ryleev made many friends among the local gentry, among whom was Mikhail Andreevich Teviashov, who had retired from the army and retreated to his estate to live the modestly comfortable life of a provincial Russian landowner. Teviashov had neglected the education of his two daughters, who were now in their teens but were scarcely able to read and write. Ryleev set out to repair this omission, and took seriously the business of tutoring them. With time he became strongly attracted to the younger daughter, Nataliia (Natasha) Mikhailovna, and asked her parents for her hand. The Teviashovs gave their consent, but insisted that he was to leave the army before marrying. In September 1817 he wrote to his mother, telling her of his romance and asking for her permission to retire from the army and marry. His mother, whose circumstances were so difficult that Ryleev rarely asked the family for money, pointed out in reply that he could hardly afford to leave the army yet and urged him to serve for a while longer before marrying.

Ryleev served for four years in the military, leading with his army colleagues a busy social and cultural life punctuated with trips to Voronezh on official business and visits to St. Petersburg to deal with the legal affairs of both his family and his future in-laws. He continued to write verses, with little indication of the serious themes that dominated his later poetry. His notebook of literary exercises from the years 1817 through 1819 includes Anacreontic verse in the manner of Gavriil Romanovich Derzhavin, echoes of the plaintive Sentimentalism of Nikolai Mikhailovich Karamzin and the epicureanism of Konstantin Nikolaevich Batiushkov, and macaronic verses alternating Russian with French, all laced with expressions of his love for Natasha Teviashova. He applied for release from the army, and while in Voronezh on duty he read in *Russkii invalid* (The Russian Invalid) the 26 December 1818 order granting his request. He and Teviashova were married in January 1819.

Ryleev's visits to the capital on family business in 1819 and 1820 led to his first acquaintance with the literary figures of St. Petersburg, including Fedor Nikolaevich Glinka, Baron Anton Antonovich Del'vig, Aleksandr Pushkin, Aleksandr Fedorovich Voeikov, Nikolai Ivanovich Gnedich, Nikolai Ivanovich Grech, and Faddei Venediktovich Bulgarin, all of whom were in one way or another caught up in the awakening of Russian national consciousness that occurred after the defeat of Napoleon in 1812 and the return after 1815 of many educated young Russians from the campaigns in Europe. Through these contacts Ryleev's poetry began to appear in print, heralded by his satirical verse epistle "K vremenshchiku" (To a Time-Server), which appeared (signed, despite its thinly disguised attack on a leading government figure) in the October 1820 issue of the periodical *Nevskii zritel'* (Nevsky Spectator). Viewed as poetry, this well-known piece is extremely derivative; it is not an imitation of a celebrated satire by the Roman poet Persius, as its subtitle declares, so much as the unacknowledged heir to an earlier imitation of Persius by the Russian poet Mikhail Vasil'evich Milonov. It achieved immediate fame, however, as a noteworthy piece of literary daring, since it appeared in the immediate aftermath of the brutally repressed mutiny of the Semenovsky Guards regiment, an incident that directly reflected the policies of the object of Ryleev's satire, the notorious Count Aleksei Andreevich Arakcheev. The poem had been written earlier, but the timing of its appearance suggested a response to the event, and it was certainly read as such by the public. The disguising subtitle worked, however, and Ryleev escaped punishment, although the journal that dared to print it was saved only by the intervention of a relatively enlightened minister of education. By now Ryleev had won acceptance in St. Petersburg literary circles, and in April 1821 he was admitted as a *chlen sotrudnik* (collaborating member) by the *Vol'noe obshchestvo liubitelei rossiiskoi slovesnosti*.

Ryleev occasionally expressed his appreciation for the life of provincial Russia and his dislike of the capital, but at this stage in his life he turned down the offer of a post in the provincial civil service and decided to settle in St. Petersburg, at least partly because of the need to oversee the litigations in which his family was involved. After some discussion of his taking over the editorship of *Nevskii zritel'*, in January 1821 he accepted a position as *zasedatel'* (the approximate equivalent of a judgeship in the American legal system) in the St. Petersburg criminal court. By now a father, Ryleev spent the summer months of 1821 with his family in the Ukraine, resting from the stress of life in the capital and reading. Like virtually all of his literary comrades, he was able to read books in French, German, Polish, and English in the original, but unlike most of them he read Russian literature almost exclusively, and reread frequently the works he most admired.

Enjoyable though it was, the visit to his old haunts reminded Ryleev of the pervasive corruption of officialdom in the provinces, and he resisted the entreaties of friends to settle in Ostrogozhsk. He returned to St. Petersburg in August. From this time he began to be drawn into the political activities that defined his fate.

In Russia in the early 1820s there was an extraordinary overlap among the worlds of literature, military and civil service, and political opposition, which was necessarily clandestine. Young men of the gentry class, who since Peter the Great's time had often sought careers in the military or in government service, had in overwhelming numbers answered the call to defend their country against Napoleon, had traveled to Europe in unusually thought-provoking circumstances, and were now back in Russia. They were well-educated, experienced, articulate, and fired with a new patriotism and national pride. They were also, however, aware of Russia's shortcomings from a European perspective and were watching their hopes of a better future fade as Alexander I evolved from the reform-minded idealist of the early years of his reign into the staunchly conservative defender of European absolute monarchies against the tide of democracy and revolution. Open debate of such questions was not an option, and literature pro-

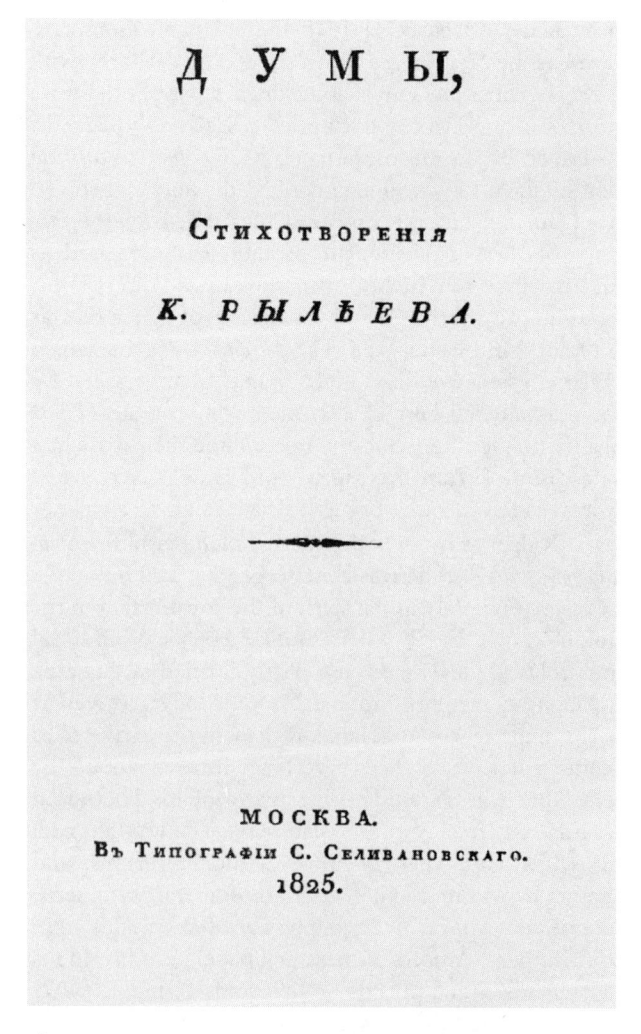

Title page for Ryleev's Dumy, stikhotvoreniia *(Meditations, Poems), which includes narrative works inspired by Russian history and legend*

vided almost the sole arena for the necessarily restrained expression of serious thoughts about the state of the nation.

In this climate it is not surprising that literary associations should harbor political cells, or that political societies should use literary associations as both a cover and a mechanism to disseminate their ideas. Ryleev's initial link to such activities was through his friend and fellow poet Glinka, who had been one of the founding members of the *Soiuz Spaseniia* (Union of Salvation), a secret society that was formed immediately after the defeat of Napoleon to work for the introduction of representative government in Russia. Its members, mostly aristocratic young officers in guards regiments with ties to Freemasonry, quickly became divided over the question of whether to use violent means to attain the desired end, or to work more gradually to change public opinion. The moderate faction prevailed, and early in 1818 the society was reorganized as the *Soiuz Blagodenstviia* (Union of Welfare), with a broader membership that included most of the future leaders of the Decembrist uprising. Early in 1821, discouraged by dissension in its ranks and fear of infiltration by the ever-watchful authorities, the union dissolved itself. Its constitution, however, had called for the creation of open associations to promote democratic ideas and patriotic sentiments, and Glinka now directed his energies toward the literary association of which he was founder and leader–the *Vol'noe obshchestvo* in which Ryleev was active. The more radical members, led by Pavel Ivanovich Pestel', re-formed as a separate *Iuzhnoe obshchestvo* (Southern Society) to continue their work at a safe distance from the capital, and later played a key role in the events that brought Ryleev's life to a close.

Ryleev was not at this point a member of the *Soiuz Blagodenstviia*, but he was close to Glinka, and his activities were definitely in the spirit of the constitution of the union, known as the "Green Book." His idealistic social and political views were also partly formed at this time through his membership in a Masonic lodge, as well as by his experiences as a judge. Ryleev in the early 1820s seems not to have been overly concerned about the issue that was paramount for many of his libertarian friends: the freeing of Russian serfs. He was after all himself a landowner, of however modest means, and though he was more kindly than most towards his serfs, he does not appear to have questioned deeply his right to own them. Among his personal papers is a list, in his own handwriting, of serfs he had sold, despite the declaration in the "Green Book" that people are not to be treated as chattels. In the St. Petersburg court system, however, he had a strong reputation as a fair judge and as a frequent defender of peasants and other ordinary folk.

Another side effect of the new national self-awareness of Russians of Ryleev's generation was the exploration and reappraisal of the history of their country. The ideology of the Romantic movement in Europe had fostered an interest in the neglected history of nations previously dismissed as backward, and the climate was right for educated young Russians to assert the peculiar dignity of their past, even if it was characterized by the very oppression they now wished to shed. Ryleev had been interested in history from his school years. His patriotism now fostered an intense interest in Russia's past, which naturally found expression in his poetry. Indeed, his most valued contribution to Russian letters is a series of *dumy* (meditations) on themes drawn from Russian history and legend, written between 1821 and 1823. The *duma* was a narrative folk genre of Ukrainian origin that provided a particularly appropriate vehicle for a poetic celebration of the nation's past. The immediate inspiration of *Dumy, stikhotvoreniia* (Meditations, Poems, 1825) was the appearance in 1821 of the ninth volume of Karamzin's monumental *Istoriia gosudarstva Rossiiskogo* (History of the Russian State, 1816–1818; revised, 1818–1829), a work that provided a readable, dignified, and inspiring account of Russian history precisely when it was most needed, the impact of which on thinking Russians was immense and lasting. The ninth volume, which covered the second half of the reign of Ivan the Terrible, openly referred to him as a tyrant, and for this reason, despite Karamzin's comparative conservatism, it was enthusiastically hailed by the democratic intelligentsia. Fifteen of Ryleev's *dumy* (of which there are thirty-one, six of them unfinished) use Karamzin's *Istoriia* as their source.

Ryleev's overt intention in *Dumy* was to illuminate the present by way of Russia's past and to stimulate national pride. In this endeavor he was not entirely original, for he had been attracted by the didactic nationalism of the *Spiewy historyczne* (Historical Songs) of the Polish poet Julian-Ursin Niemcewicz, which had appeared in 1816 and enjoyed considerable success in the Russian literary world. Ryleev differed from his model, however, in placing more emphasis on civic responsibility than on simple historical glory, and in the scale of his intentions: he planned to cover virtually the whole of Russian history, and his heroes range from Oleg the Wise, who died in 912, to the poet and statesman Derzhavin, who died in 1816. Though *Dumy* has considerable interest and some literary merit, few would claim that Ryleev had the poetic talent to sustain so grand a scheme. The composition of *Dumy* (which Pushkin found monotonous and repetitive) brings together the voice of the hero (in either a speech or a verbalized meditation), a civic message, and a description of the scene in which an historical action has taken place. These settings are unfortunately artificial, consisting more of a manipulation of familiar Romantic landscape conventions than of actual description. Two notable exceptions are "Ivan Susanin," in which the scene is recognizably Russian, and "Petr Velikii v Ostrogozhske" (Peter the Great in Ostrogozhsk), in which the level of scenic detail clearly reflects Ryleev's familiarity with this locality. From a strictly historical point of view *Dumy* is full of anachronisms and takes considerable liberties even with the characters of its heroes. Truth to fact, however, was not central to Ryleev's intentions. The inaccuracies did not much trouble his contemporaries and should not color readers' judgment of these fascinating attempts to instill the spirit of Russian history through verse.

Two of the *dumy* are generally held to be particularly characteristic of Ryleev's views in the early 1820s: "Volynskii" and "Derzhavin," both written in 1822. In

The 14 December 1825 revolt in Senate Square, St. Petersburg, part of the plot to overthrow Tsar Nicholas I in which Ryleev was involved (engraving by R. R. Frents)

both of these pieces the poet urges those in power to uphold justice and devote themselves to the unselfish service of their subjects. The underlying theme of *Dumy* is continued in one of Ryleev's best-known odes, *Videnie* (A Vision), addressed in 1823 to the five-year-old son of Nicholas I. The poet urges the future Alexander II to earn his glory as an enlightened monarch, attentive to the needs of his people. This ode attracted the approving attention of the reform-minded statesman Admiral Nikolai Semenovich Mordvinov, who sought out the author, invited him into his family circle, and arranged for him an appointment in the Russian-American Trading Company, which operated under his supervision.

In the summer of 1822 Ryleev was in the Ukraine once more, this time on a visit to Kiev to attend to legal business: the lawsuit brought by Princess Golitsyna against Ryleev's father was still dragging on and had been sent to a Kiev court for decision. Again he found the Ukrainian atmosphere stimulating, and his literary inspiration took a new turn. He had immersed himself during this trip in Dmitrii Nikolaevich Bantysh-Kamensky's *Istoriia Maloi Rossii* (History of the Ukraine), which had appeared earlier that year, and conceived the idea of writing a tragedy about Ivan Stepanovich Mazepa, the Ukrainian hetman who betrayed Peter I out of revenge for a past slight. The projected drama was abandoned, but not its subject matter—Ryleev remained intrigued by the bizarre fate of Andrei Voinarovsky, Mazepa's nephew and adopted son. Voinarovsky lived in Europe after Mazepa's defection, but in 1716 he was arrested on a Hamburg street at the instigation of the Russian consul and transported back to Russia, whence Peter banished him to Yakutsk in northeastern Siberia. There he was visited twenty years later by the German historian Gerhard Friedrich Müller, who recorded his recollection of the events surrounding Mazepa's treachery. This story was too complex to be handled in a comparatively short balladlike form, and while Ryleev was still writing the last of the *dumy* he began work on a long narrative poem about Voinarovsky.

Also in 1822 Ryleev entered the world of literary journalism. He joined forces with his friend Aleksandr Aleksandrovich Bestuzhev (Marlinsky) to organize a periodical that would be a commercial venture, paying its contributors a small honorarium and demonstrating that the writer as well as the editor could be a professional in Russia. The first volume of *Poliarnaia zvezda* appeared in 1823 and was unexpectedly successful, selling 1,200 copies in six weeks (for comparison,

Karamzin's *Istoriia,* a work of unprecedented popularity, had sold 3,000 copies in twenty-five days). Particularly appreciated was Bestuzhev's critical review of Russian literature since Mikhail Vasil'evich Lomonosov, on which Ryleev may have collaborated; it discussed openly the educational backwardness of Russia, especially in the provinces. The second volume came out 1824 and sold even better than the first. It included extracts from *Voinarovskii* (1825), Ryleev's first (and only complete) long narrative poem, which this time earned Pushkin's praise. Not all the young literati of St. Petersburg were enthusiastic about the venture and its editorial direction, however, and the disagreements marked a serious split in the *Vol'noe obshchestvo* between the outspoken liberals and those of more benign intentions.

As with *Dumy,* the inspiration for the compositional form of *Voinarovskii* came from an outside source, in this case George Gordon, Lord Byron. The British poet had provided a literary commodity that appealed particularly strongly to Russians–the combination of the Romantic epic with liberal political commentary–and many features of Ryleev's poem reflect this model, including the character of the strong but tragically alienated hero, the interpolated dialogues that give relief to the narrative, and the wealth of ethnographic detail in the opening scene in Siberia. At the same time, Ryleev's imagery in *Voinarovskii* is recognizably Pushkinian, even to the point of (probably unconscious) quotation. Nonetheless, the poem is more than just a composite imitation. The absence of a sustained love story, as well as the hero's civic rather than personal inspiration, make *Voinarovskii* markedly different from both Byron's and Pushkin's narrative verse.

In 1824–1825 Ryleev worked on the composition of a second narrative poem, *Nalivaiko,* in which the theme was the struggle of the Ukrainian cossacks to assert their independence from Poland at the end of the sixteenth century. Excerpts from *Nalivaiko* were published in the 1825 volume of *Poliarnaia zvezda,* and one of them, "Ispoved' Nalivaiki" (Nalivaiko's Confession of Faith), has been described as the credo of the first Russian revolutionaries. *Dumy* appeared as a book in 1825, as did the complete version of *Voinarovskii,* which garnered praise for its true patriotism. As the year progressed, however, Ryleev's literary agenda was overshadowed by the concerns that propelled him into a place in the annals of Russian history.

About a year after the disbanding of the *Soiuz Blagodenstviia* in 1821, the *Severnoe obshchestvo* (Northern Society) had been formed, in which the more moderate members of the unions pursued their program. Early in 1823 Ivan Ivanovich Pushchin, a long-standing member of the *Soiuz Blagodenstviia,* became a colleague of Ryleev in the St. Petersburg criminal court and drew him into membership of the *Severnoe obshchestvo.* This association was a turning point for Ryleev, who rapidly became one of the most influential members of the group. On first joining the *Severnoe obshchestvo,* Ryleev felt the shortcomings of his political education compared to that of its principal figures. He began to read with characteristic zeal to make amends, and even wrote the outline of a political tract titled "Dukh vremeni, ili sud'ba roda chelovecheskogo" (The Spirit of the Age, or the Fate of the Human Race). Under pressure from Pestel's *Iuzhnoe obshchestvo,* the *Severnoe obshchestvo* became more radical, and by the summer of 1824 Ryleev was writing propaganda poems (often in collaboration with Bestuzhev) designed to spread antigovernment sentiment among the reading public. Though an active member of a secret political society whose activities would draw the severest punishment if discovered, Ryleev was capable of actions that his fellow conspirators felt could jeopardize the movement. His attractive and persuasive personality made him in many ways a natural leader, but he was always a Romantic, and his idealistic enthusiasm could lead him to misjudge the character of outsiders and confide too much in them.

By 1824 life for Ryleev's wife had become difficult and their marriage strained. Their house was a regular meeting place where she was perpetually called upon to be an attentive hostess to his political friends, while his duties to his country clearly had priority over his family life. Against this background, Ryleev composed in 1824–1825 a series of love poems addressed to "T. S. K.," a figure whose identity remains obscure, but who is widely thought to have been a Polish lady sent by Arakcheev to ensnare Ryleev and spy on him. He clearly felt strongly for her, but appears to have resisted the temptation to indulge his passion–out of duty more to his country than to his wife, to judge by one of the poems.

The Ryleevs were brought together in September 1824 when their second child, son Sasha, fell ill while Ryleev and Bestuzhev were away from St. Petersburg for a few days. A day after his father's return Sasha died, and the distraught parents retreated to the family estate, Ryleev for two months, his wife until the spring of 1825. In December 1824 Ryleev visited Moscow, where he was warmly received in literary circles. He discovered, however, that the catastrophic St. Petersburg flood of 7 November–immortalized in Pushkin's *Mednyi vsadnik* (The Bronze Horseman), finished in 1833–had seriously damaged his St. Petersburg apartment, destroying a substantial part of his precious library.

In the spring of 1825 Ryleev was elected to the governing committee of the *Severnoe obshchestvo.* He had in fact been responsible for most of the new recruits since the autumn of 1823 and had led a faction that urged the broadening of the society's membership, hitherto confined to members of the gentry, to include representatives of the non-propertied classes. Ryleev's work at the Russian-American Trading Company had naturally brought him into contact with the commercial class, who in nineteenth-century Russia were a legally defined "estate" with civil rights that were different, and more limited, than those of the gentry. Despite many frustrations and disappointments, Ryleev was trying in his own way to make the *Severnoe obshchestvo* as radical as the *Iuzhnoe obshchestvo*.

By 1825 the agenda of the *Severnoe obshchestvo* definitely encompassed armed rebellion and the replacement of the tsar. The preponderance of serving officers among its membership dictated the strategy: to infiltrate both the army (particularly the most prestigious and trusted regiments) and the Baltic Fleet, which would provide the means to send the royal family into exile. The infiltration proved difficult to achieve; the society remained lacking in unity and clear plan of action; and the events that from this point led up to the December revolt were dictated more by happenstance than by organization, often inviting the description "stranger than fiction."

Ryleev's judgment as a leader of the *Severnoe obshchestvo* was taxed by difficult decisions involving some of the people most anxious to further his cause. First there was the case of Dmitrii Irinarkhovich Zavalishin, a guards officer, who had written to the tsar proposing the formation of a counterrevolutionary organization for the restoration of the "rightful" powers. Zavalishin tried to join the *Severnoe obshchestvo* and tried to persuade Ryleev and other leaders, who knew of his letter to the tsar, that "rightful" was an intended ambiguity, to be construed one way by those in power, another way by democrats and republicans. The existence of his organization, of which Zavalishin offered faked proof in an attempt to gain admission to Ryleev's group, was a pretense, since the government did not trust him and had declined to act on his proposal. Then there was the problem of Petr Grigor'evich Kakhovsky and Aleksandr Ivanovich Iakubovich. Kakhovsky, an army lieutenant, insistently volunteered to kill the tsar, while Iakubovich, who had been transferred out of the guards for his role in a highly publicized society duel, had as his agenda revenge–again, through regicide.

Despite his intense political activity in 1825, Ryleev remained active in the literary arena, not least because he regarded literature as an important form of service to society. In an age of literary salons, he organized at his house "Russian lunches"–demonstratively simple bread-and-cabbage meals at which the more liberal St. Petersburg literary figures gathered to debate current affairs, problems, and every aspect of Russian society. In particular, they discussed their view that the new Russia needed a poetic voice of Vasilii Andreevich Zhukovsky's stature, but of less conservative views. Evgenii Abramovich Baratynsky, a poet known primarily for his philosophical lyrics, was considered but found wanting. Some hopes were pinned on Pushkin, who at this time was languishing in exile on his parents' estate at Mikhailovskoe, but he obstinately refused to embrace purely civic verse and insisted that it was wrong to banish everything "light and entertaining" from poetry. Nor did the character of Pushkin's recently published masterpiece *Evgeny Onegin* (1823–1831; published in full, 1833) give them much reassurance of his civic seriousness.

One more foretaste of tragedy awaited Ryleev in 1825. In September a cousin, Konstantin Pakhomovich Chernov, chose to defend the honor of his sister in a duel with a wealthy and well-connected officer of the guards who had wooed her and failed to make good on his promises. The duel, in which Ryleev acted as second for his cousin, was fatal to both parties, and Chernov's funeral became almost a political demonstration for the members of the *Severnoe obshchestvo*. Ryleev lost no time in composing "Na smert' Chernova" (On Chernov's Death), a poem that used the occasion to castigate the rich and powerful for the contempt in which they held Holy Russia and her lowly citizens.

In late November 1825 the plans of *Severnoe obshchestvo* for a revolution in 1826 involving the arrest of the royal family and the formation of a provisional government were frustrated by the unexpected death of Alexander I. The refusal of his heir, the Grand Duke Konstantin Pavlovich, to return from Warsaw and succeed his father, and the ensuing confusion and discontent, provided an opportunity of which the conspirators took advantage. Konstantin's younger brother assumed the throne as Nicholas I and ordered the armed forces to swear an oath of allegiance to him on the Senate Square, unit by unit, over several days. This display provided the opportunity for the infiltrated regiments to carry out a coup. The feverish preparations, however, aroused the suspicions of Iakov Ivanovich Rostovtsev, a friend of one of the conspirators, who alerted Nicholas (though without divulging the names of his friends) and informed Ryleev and other leaders that he had done so. The decision was made to act, despite the uncertainties of the situation, and Ryleev deputed Kakhovsky to kill the future emperor on the appointed day, 14 December.

On the morning of the uprising Ryleev talked with Bestuzhev about what he would do as the soldiers were being induced to mutiny. The details of the conversation suggest that Ryleev was acting out a romantic patriotic drama, with little understanding of how the common Russian soldier would behave in such a situation. He seems to have at least prepared to carry out his plan, despite Bestuzhev's attempts at dissuasion: he procured a soldier's knapsack, though not a soldier's uniform, and prepared to stand in the ranks of the rebelling troops to demonstrate his solidarity with them.

Medallion depicting the five Decembrists who were hanged: Pavel Ivanovich Pestel', Ryleev, Mikhail Pavlovich Bestuzhev-Riumin, Sergei Ivanovich Murav'ev-Apostol, and Petr Grigor'evich Kakhovsky

The events of 14 December are obscured by confusion. According to one testimony the uprising failed because some of the participants, including Ryleev, Bestuzhev, and Iakubovich, failed to carry out the agreed-upon plan on the Senate Square, hesitating to occupy the Senate steps when they easily could have done so. Whatever its cause, the delay gave Nicholas the time to muster some loyal troops to occupy the steps and surround the mutineers. Ryleev at this point left the Senate Square to raise more troops from the nearby barracks but was unsuccessful; he returned home toward evening, sobered and disillusioned by the failure of events to match his romantic vision. As his companions began to gather at his house, Ryleev burned incriminating papers and gave his literary manuscripts to Bulgarin, who preserved them faithfully.

Ryleev was soon arrested. His name was mentioned by the first conspirators to be interrogated, those who had been apprehended on the Senate Square. Nicholas, who had known about both societies long before Rostovtsev's betrayal, participated personally in the interrogations and ordered "the writer Ryleev" to be brought in dead or alive. Ryleev was taken to the Winter Palace, where he was questioned by no less a figure than Count Aleksandr Khristoforovich Benckendorff, the future head of the political police of Nicholas I. Ryleev decided that denial was useless and tried partial candor as a subterfuge. He explained that the bloodshed was not intended and was the result of a leadership failure on the part of Prince Sergei Petrovich Trubetskoi, the nominal head of the *Severnoe obshchestvo*. He warned the tsar and Benckendorff of the existence of the *Iuzhnoe obshchestvo* so that further bloodshed could be avoided. Most significantly, he asked that the younger participants in the uprising be spared.

Nicholas quickly realized that Ryleev could not be intimidated, but would respond easily to emotional pressures and gestures of high-minded generosity. He ordered Ryleev placed in solitary confinement in the Peter-Paul Fortress, hands unshackled and pen and paper provided, with an invitation to write anything he had to say directly to the tsar. On the following day Ryleev wrote asking the tsar to be merciful to his family. Nicholas now knew how to secure Ryleev's cooperation: he gave him permission to correspond with Natasha Ryleeva, to whom he made a gift of 2,000 rubles. In mid April, Ryleev wrote to the tsar again, taking responsibility for his leading role, and asking for his companions to be spared. Faced with incriminating confessions by other conspirators, he finally admitted his participation in a plan to execute the royal family.

Early in July, after a lengthy trial, the Supreme Court pronounced sentence on the Decembrists. Thirty-six were condemned to die, with only Mordvinov's vote opposing the death sentence. Five of the thirty-six, including Ryleev, were condemned to be quartered, but the tsar commuted the death sentence of all but these five and instructed the Supreme Court to decide their fate. On 12 July all the prisoners were summoned to court to hear their sentences and learned that they were to hang. A witness reported that Ryleev reacted calmly. The execution, which was hastily carried out the next day, was grotesquely mismanaged. The platform on which the scaffold stood collapsed under the weight of the prisoners' shackles, and the grisly procedure was delayed while the structure was repaired. Finally, with at least one of the victims so badly injured by the fall that he could not walk to the scaffold, the sentence was carried out.

An effect of Ryleev's unpleasant end has been to cloud his biography with legend. Sources allege that even in solitary confinement in the notorious fortress prison he did not relinquish his literary activity, for on the rare occasions when the confined Decembrists were able to slip notes to each other, Ryleev sent poems. This much is probably true, but the story recounted in one memoir that his last poem was scratched on a metal plate is probably apocryphal, as are the various accounts of his last, fighting words before the second attempt at hanging, relayed by writers even of the stature of Aleksandr Ivanovich Herzen; an eyewitness observed that he said nothing at this point.

The Decembrist poets are difficult to characterize. At least some of their importance in the history of Russian culture derives from their revolutionary martyrdom. This approach could be assumed in the Soviet period, but even in the nineteenth century the martyrdom overshadowed the poetry, which for much of the century was in any case not easily available. In this climate of tendentious criticism, evaluation of the Decembrists as poets is problematic, since so much Russian writing on them emphasizes the content and civic quality of their poetry. It is important to remember that they were well and broadly educated by any standards and active in many other fields of intellectual endeavor besides poetry.

The most commonly observed characteristic of the Decembrists' poetry is that their revival of civic verse at the height of the Romantic Age led to the anachronistic restoration of a Neoclassical genre, the ode, where previously the Romantic elegy had predominated, and to a relapse into archaic poetic diction reminiscent of the "high style" of the eighteenth century. As his literary contemporaries heatedly argued the relative merits of the classical and Romantic styles, Ryleev's verse shows that he adopted neither side in the narrow debate, choosing instead to use both styles as appropriate, the classical for odes and the Romantic for narrative poems.

Though not insignificant as a poet, Ryleev was an exemplary revolutionary. He had the courage and the resolve to turn his words into deeds. For this quality he lives on in Russian memory as a martyr to freedom.

Biographies:

Materialy dlia biografii K. F. Ryleeva (Leipzig: E. L. Kasprovich, 1875);

Nestor Aleksandrovich Kotliarevsky, *Ryleev* (St. Petersburg: Svetoch, 1908);

Nikolai Aleksandrovich Bestuzhev, *Kondratii Fedorovich Ryleev: Vospominaniia N. A. Bestuzheva* (Moscow: Al'tsiona, 1919);

Kirill Vasil'evich Pigarev, *Zhizn' Ryleeva* (Moscow: Sovetskii pisatel', 1947);

Viktor Vasil'evich Afanas'ev, *Ryleev: Zhizneopisanie* (Moscow: Molodaia gvardiia, 1982);

Patrick O'Meara, *K. F. Ryleev: A Political Biography of the Decembrist Poet* (Princeton, N. J.: Princeton University Press, 1984).

References:

V. A. Arkhipov, V. G. Bazanov, and Ia. L. Levkovich, eds., *Poliarnaia zvezda izdannaia A. Bestuzhevym i K. Ryleevym* (Moscow-Leningrad: Izd-vo Akademii nauk SSSR, 1960);

V. G. Bazanov, *Poety-dekabristy: K. F. Ryleev, V. K. Kiukhel'beker, A. I. Odoevskii* (Moscow, 1950);

Magdalina Zinovevna Dal'tseva, *Tak zatikhaet Vezuvii: Povest' o Kondratii Ryleeve* (Moscow: Politizdat, 1982);

Aleksandr Mikhailovich Egolin, Nikolai F. Bel'chikov, Il'ia Samoilovich Zilber'shtein, and S. A. Makashin, eds., *Dekabristy—literatory,* volumes 59–60 of *Literaturnoe nasledstvo* (Moscow: Izd-vo Akademii nauk SSSR, 1954-1956);

V. Kadenko, "Ukraine in Kondratii Ryleev's Works (Decembrist Poetry)," *Cahiers du monde Russe,* 36 (October–December 1995): 427–432;

Anatoli Iakovlevich Kuklin, *K. F. Ryleev* (Leningrad: Lenizdat, 1965);

Semen Iosifovich Mashinsky, ed., *Pisateli-dekabristy v vospominaniiakh sovremennikov,* volume 2 (Moscow, 1980), pp. 7–118;

Vasilii Ivanovich Maslov, *Literaturnaia deiatel'nost' K. F. Ryleeva* (Kiev: Tipografiia Imperatorskago Universiteta sv. Vladimira, 1912);

John P. Pauls, "The Treatments of Mazeppa: Ryleev's and Pushkin's," *Slavic and East European Studies,* 8 (1963): 97–109;

Pauls, "Ukranian Themes in Ryleev's Works," *Wiener Slavistisches Jahrbuch,* 17 (1972): 228–242;

William Persen, "Kondratii Ryleev, the Poet and the Revolutionary," dissertation, Harvard University, 1953;

Protsess dekabristov: donesenie, sledstvie, prigovor. Pis'mo Ryleeva iz kreposti. Ukazy (Moscow: I. A. Malinin, 1905);

Marc Raeff, *The Decembrist Movement* (Englewood Cliffs, N. J.: Prentice-Hall, 1966);

T. M. Rickwood, "'Poet v dushe': A Re-Appraisal of Ryleev's Verse," in *Proceedings: Pacific Northwest Conference on Foreign Languages, Twenty-First Annual Meeting, 3–4 April 1970,* volume 21, edited by Ralph W. Baldner (Victoria, B. C.: University of Victoria, 1970);

Aleksandr Grigorevich Tseitlin, *Tvorchestvo Ryleeva* (Moscow: AN SSSR, 1955);

Franklin Walker, "K. F. Ryleev: A Self-Sacrifice for Revolution," *Slavic and East European Review,* 47 (1969): 436–446.

Papers:

Some of Kondratii Fedorovich Ryleev's manuscripts are in the A. A. Ivanovsky collection at the Institute of Russian Literature (Pushkin House), St. Petersburg. Other papers are housed in Moscow at the Gosudarstvennyi arkhiv Rossiiskoi Federatsii (GARF, State Archive of the Russian Federation), formerly the Tsentral'nyi gosudarstvennyi arkhiv Oktiabr'skoi Revoliutsii (TsGAOR, Central State Archive of the October Revolution).

Stepan Petrovich Shevyrev
(18 October 1806 – 8 July 1864)

Richard Tempest
University of Illinois at Urbana-Champaign

BOOKS: *Istoriia poezii,* volume 1 (Moscow & St. Petersburg: A. Semen, 1835);

Teoriia poesii v istoricheskom ee razvitii u drevnikh i novykh narodov (Moscow: N. Stepanov, 1836);

Obshchee obozrenie russkoi slovesnosti (Moscow, 1837);

Ob otnoshenii semeinogo vospitaniia k gosudarstvennomu (Moscow: Univesitetskaia tip., 1842);

Istoriia russkoi slovesnosti: preimushchestvenno drevnei; lektsii (Moscow: Universitetskaia tip., 1846–1860);

Nilosorskaia pustyn' (Moscow, 1850);

Poezdka v Kirillo-Belozerskii monastyr': vakatsionnye dni Prof. S. Shevyreva v 1847 godu (Moscow: Universitetskaia tip., 1850);

O tseli vospitaniia (St. Petersburg, 1852);

Ocherk istorii zhivopisi ital'ianskoi, sosredotochennoi v Rafaele i ego proizvedeniiakh (Moscow: Universitetskaia tip., 1852);

Vstuplenie v pedagogiiu (St. Petersburg, 1852);

O znachenii Zhukovskogo v russkoi zhizni i poezii (Moscow: Universitetskaia tip., 1853);

Obozrenie russkoi slovesnosti v XIII veke (St. Petersburg: Akademiia nauk, 1854);

Istoriia Imperatorskogo Moskovskogo universiteta (Moscow: Universitetskaia tip., 1855);

Storia della letteratura russa (Florence: Le Monnier, 1862).

Editions and Collections: *Lektsii o russkoi literature, chitannye v Parizhe v 1862 godu* (St. Petersburg: Akademiia nauk, 1884);

D. Venevitinov, S. Shevyrev, A. Khomiakov, Stikhotvoreniia, edited by Mark Aronson and I. V. Sergiersky (Leningrad: Sovetskii pisatel', 1937);

Stikhotvoreniia (Leningrad: Sovetskii pisatel', 1939);

Poety 1820kh–1830kh godov (Leningrad: Sovetskii pisatel', 1972), pp. 139–202.

OTHER: *Biograficheskii slovar' professorov i prepodavatelei Moskovskogo universiteta,* volumes 1–2 (Moscow: Universitetskaia tip., 1855), pp. 603–621;

"Vospominaniia Shevyreva o Pushkine," in *Pushkin. Biograficheskie materialy i istoriko-literaturnye ocherki,* edited by L. Maikov (St. Petersburg: D. F. Panteleeva, 1899), pp. 318–354;

"Rasskazy o Pushkine," in *A. S. Pushkin v vospominaniiakh sovremennikov,* volume 2 (Moscow: Khudozh. lit-ra, 1974), pp. 37–40;

"Razgovor o vozmozhnosti naiti edinyi zakon dlia iziashchnogo," "Istoriia poezii (Predislovie; Chtenie pervoe)," and "Teoriia poezii (Zakliuchenie)," in *Russkie esteticheskie traktaty pervoi treti XIX veka,* volume 2 (Moscow: Iskusstvo, 1974), pp. 508–528;

"Pokhozhdeniia Chichikova, ili Mertvye dushi. Poema N. V. Gogolia. Statia vtoraia," in *Russkaia estetika i stat'ia kritika 40-50-kh godov XIX veka* (Moscow: Iskusstvo, 1982), pp. 54–79.

TRANSLATIONS: *Ob iskusstve i khudozhnikakh, razmyshlenie otshel'nika, liubitelia iziashchnogo, izdannye L. Tikom,* with Nikolai Aleksandrovich Mel'gunov and Vladimir Pavlovich Titov (Moscow, 1826); Fridrikh Shiller, *Vallenshteinov lager'* (Moscow, 1858).

Stepan Shevyrev was a poet, critic, and literary scholar who occupied a prominent place in Moscow intellectual circles throughout the reign of Nicholas I. He led the sedentary existence of a successful critic and academic; most of his life was, as a consequence, uneventful. In the late 1820s Shevyrev was the preeminent theorist of the *Liubomudry* (Lovers of Wisdom), a secret society that espoused an anti-Enlightenment Romantic philosophy inspired by the thought of Friedrich Wilhelm von Schelling. Subsequently Shevyrev embraced Count Sergei Semenovich Uvarov's theory of Official Nationality, interpreting it in the same spirit of philosophical Romanticism. Together with his friend and colleague Mikhail Petrovich Pogodin, with whom he is often paired, Shevyrev was a leading exponent of Uvarov's doctrine. Shevyrev and Pogodin's Official Nationalism should be distinguished, however, from the Slavophilism of Aleksei Stepanovich Khomiakov, Ivan Vasil'evich Kireevsky, and Konstantin Sergeevich Aksakov, to which it was contemporaneous and with which it shared many traits. From 1832 through 1857 Shevyrev taught Russian and world literature at the University of Moscow. Together with the poets Dmitrii Vladimirovich Venevitinov and Fedor Ivanovich Tiutchev he was an exponent of the metaphysical tradition in Russian verse; he also translated Friedrich von Schiller, Johann Wolfgang von Goethe, and other German writers.

Shevyrev was an astute, if sometimes erratic, critic whose views were informed by a wide-ranging knowledge of Western philosophy and literature and a Romantic historicism that he developed in the 1830s. In the 1830s and 1840s he conducted a heated journalistic polemic with Vissarion Grigor'evich Belinsky, the leading radical critic of the age. Shevyrev's reading of Nikolai Vasil'evich Gogol as a distorter of reality rather than as a representative of the Natural School was ahead of its time, and his essays on Aleksandr Pushkin, published in 1841 in the journal *Moskvitianin* (Muscovite), one of several publications that Shevyrev helped to edit, were an important early contribution to the canon of Pushkin studies. Shevyrev was the author of books on the history and theory of poetry and on the history of Russian literature; he was thus one of the founders of his country's academic tradition of literary scholarship.

Stepan Petrovich Shevyrev was born on 18 October 1806 at Saratov into an ancient noble family; one of his putative ancestors, Prince Dmitrii Andreevich Shevyrev, died a martyr's death in the reign of Ivan the Terrible. Shevyrev's father, Petr (a cultivated man), was the Marshal of the Provincial Nobility and in consequence a prominent figure in his region. Shevyrev was first educated at home, where he received a thorough grounding in a variety of subjects; subsequently, at the age of twelve he entered the Noble Pension of the University of Moscow. His teachers there included many university professors, such as Aleksei Fedorovich Merzliakov, Ivan Ivanovich Davydov, and Mikhail Grigor'evich Pavlov. Merzliakov was a Neoclassicist poet of some repute while the last two, and particularly Pavlov, did much to popularize Schelling's philosophy in Moscow intellectual circles. As a pensionnaire Shevyrev engaged in extracurricular literary pursuits and displayed a precocious proclivity for philosophical speculation, composing a meditation on the immortality of the soul inspired by Jean-Baptiste Masillon, the eighteenth-century French preacher. An exemplary pupil, Shevyrev graduated from the Pension in 1822 with a Gold Medal and thereafter attended lectures on philosophy and the classics at Moscow University as an occasional student in the hope of being allowed to pursue a postgraduate degree there. He also joined the literary group that had assembled around the poet Semen Egorovich Raich, one of his tutors at the Pension. Among the other members of the Raich group were Tiutchev and Pogodin, who had arrived to teach geography at the Pension shortly before Shevyrev's graduation.

In 1823, after he was refused permission to study for a higher degree, Shevyrev obtained a position at the Moscow archive of the College of Foreign Affairs, where Prince Vladimir Fedorovich Odoevsky and Venevitinov were also employed. These two "archival youths" were, respectively, the president and the secretary of the secret *Liubomudry,* with which the members of the Raich circle now became associated. The *Liubomudry* cultivated an interest in German philosophy, particularly that of Schelling, and propagated Romantic idealist aesthetics. They inaugurated the metaphysical trend in Russian Romantic poetry, of which Shevyrev's poem "Sila dukha" (The Power of the Spirit, 1825) is an early, if inferior, example: "A momentary witness to the Eternal / I saw Truth and Virtue / In the harmonious Beauty of the heavens." After the suppression of the Decembrist uprising the formal meetings of *Liubomudry* ceased, but its members and sympathizers continued to keep in close touch. Together with two other members of Raich's circle, Nikolai Aleksandrovich Mel'gunov and Vladimir Pavlovich Titov, Shevyrev translated one of the most important texts of the German Romantic movement, Johann Ludwig Tieck and Wilhelm Hein-

Nikolai Gogol, a friend whom Shevyrev called a distorter of reality rather than a representative of the Natural School

rich Wackenroder's *Herzensergiessungen eines kunstlieben Klosterbruders* (translated, 1826).

Shevyrev's poems and articles regularly appeared in the journal *Moskovskii vestnik* (Moscow Herald), founded in 1826 with Pushkin's support and edited by Pogodin. This publication functioned as the organ of the *Liubomudry,* and Shevyrev was soon placed in charge of its review section. In his panegyrical review of Sir Walter Scott's *Waverley* in *Moskovskii vestnik* (no. 20, 1827) Shevyrev compared its author to Homer (as he later did Gogol) and posited the relation of private life to history as the central problem of the genre of the novel: man's "character, attributes, habits" are in essence always the same, but their form "changes according to the differences among lands and peoples." Together with Titov and Nikolai Ivanovich Nadezhdin, he thus influenced the subsequent evolution of the theory of the novel in Russia. During this period Shevyrev advocated Russia's development along Western lines.

In his article "Obozrenie russkoi slovesnosti za 1827-i god" (A Survey of Russian Literature in 1827) in *Moskovskii vestnik* (no. 1, 1828) he eulogized Peter the Great and called for a "new Peter" who would make Russia the equal of Europe. In the same article he offered the first conceptual interpretation of Pushkin's artistic evolution, in which he discerned a movement from the "Byronic idealism" of Pushkin's narrative poems of the early 1820s to the *narodnost'* (popular spirit) in chapter 3 of his verse novel *Evgeny Onegin* (chapter published in 1827) and his tragedy *Boris Godunov* (1826). The survey and Shevyrev's other writings of this period include vigorous attacks on the unprincipled journalism of Faddei Venediktovich Bulgarin and Nikolai Ivanovich Grech.

By late 1827 Shevyrev had become the main theorist of the *Liubomudry* and the de facto editor of their journal. The *Liubomudry* expounded an antiempirical, antiscientific, Shellingian aesthetics, according to which the inspired poet does not imitate reality but transcends it, attaining philosophical truth through his artistic intuition; in his art the poet reaffirms the divine principles of creation and draws close to the godhead. Shevyrev's own verse productions, which followed these precepts, attracted the favorable attention of the poet Evgenii Abramovich Baratynsky and of Pushkin, who called Shevyrev's poem "Mysl'" (Thought, 1828) a paean to the power of the mind, "very remarkable." In this work the human intellect is likened to "a splendid cedar on Lebanon's hills"; this biblical trope is developed into the image of a metaphorical World-Tree, its head "crowned in stars," its bark "inscribed by the ages," and its roots washed by "the waves of the ocean." It is impervious to the "worms of time"; within its shade nations rise and fall, peoples succeed one another, and "a million sad graves, a million happy cradles" rest.

Like Venevitinov and the young Khomiakov (who was also associated with the *Liubomudry*), in his verse Shevyrev depicted the poet as an artistic demiurge. His lyrical *I* is an artist-thinker who hails the beauty and majesty of the universe and, full of metaphysical rapture, reads the secrets of creation. Selfless, pure of thought and soul, indifferent and indeed hostile to earthly honor and glory, he reaches a state of transcendency, becoming an incorporeal ego, a sublime spirit not of this world and time, as in "Son" (A Dream, 1827) and "Mudrost'" (Wisdom, 1828). Often the poetic *I* enters this transcendent state at night, when material forms and objects are invisible and the soul attains "freedom," the heart is "more alive," and reason is "radiant and elevated," as in the two meditations titled "Noch'" (Night, 1828 and 1829) and the poem "Stansy" (Stanzas, 1830). Shevyrev's philosophical verse is not analytical (unlike Tiutchev's) but static, descriptive, and indeed pictorial; it shows the influence of the Neoclassicist odes of Mikhail Vasil'evich Lomonosov, although as a Romantic Shevyrev was opposed to the Neoclassicist style as, for example, in

"Partizanke klassitsizma" (To a Lady-Partisan of Classicism, 1829). The cerebral and rhetorical character of his poetry led the Westernizer Nikolai Vladimirovich Stankevich to detect in it qualities of "pomposity" (a view shared by Belinsky).

Shevyrev's poems are frequently based on the opposition of two images or ideas (day/night, past/present, Spirit of Life/Spirit of Death, St. Petersburg/the sea, a tired mother/a seductive beauty). Occasionally, though, three contrasting elements are present: "Zvuki" (Sounds, mid 1820s) describes colors, words, and sounds as the divinely inspired languages of art, and the fragment "Tri molnii" (Three Lightnings, 1830) portrays Jupiter successively as admonisher, punisher, and destroyer of man. Many of Shevyrev's poems are prompted by other artistic productions: the monument to Peter the Great in St. Petersburg "Petrograd," (1829); Raphael's altarpiece in the Vatican Gallery, "Preobrazhenie" (Transfiguration, 1829); Roman ruins, "Khram Pestuma" (The Temple at Paestum, 1829); Dante's *Divine Comedy,* "Chtenie Dante" (On Reading Dante, 1830); and song and dance, "Tsyganskaia pliaska" (A Gypsy Dance) and "Tsyganka" (The Gypsy Girl), both 1828.

Shevyrev fully shared the Romantic nationalism of *Liubomudry,* in which they saw the nation as a distinctive collective personality that is greater than its individual parts and that generates its own laws of historical development. These views informed Shevyrev's interest in Russian folklore. In 1827 Shevyrev, who wished to develop a prosodic equivalent for the rhythms of popular poetry, composed a ballad, "Russkaia razboinich'ia pesnia" (The Song of a Russian Brigand). This poem impressed the young Mikhail Iur'evich Lermontov, who included citations from it in his verse tale "Prestupnik" (The Brigand, 1828). Lermontov's other experiments in the popular style, such as the ballads "Ataman" (The Hetman, 1831) and "Volia" (Freedom, 1831), were influenced by Shevyrev's "Song." Shevyrev's activity as a translator of verse reflected his literary tastes: he rendered into Russian many of Schiller's works, including part one of the Wallenstein trilogy (*Vallenshteinov lager',* 1858) and a fragment of Goethe's *Faust,* which appeared, together with a commentary by the translator, in *Moskovskii vestnik* (no. 21, 1827). He sent a copy of this article to Goethe, who in May 1828 responded with a letter commending Shevyrev's reading of his poem, which Pogodin then published in the same journal.

At a gathering of Moscow writers in 1827 at which the celebrated Polish poet Adam Mickiewicz was honored, Shevyrev declared, "We will forge the iron scepter of autocracy into freedom's dagger!" This seditious statement was in fact no more than a rhetorical flourish, for Shevyrev's outlook, like that of the *Liubomudry,* tended to the apolitical. Still, his poems "Tibr" (The Tiber, 1829), "Forum" (The Forum, 1830), and "Oda Goratsiia posledniaia" (The Last Ode of Horace, 1830) include hints of a moderate liberalism.

In 1829 Princess Zinaida Aleksandrovna Volkonskaia, the glamorous hostess of a Moscow literary salon, retained Shevyrev's services as a tutor for her son Aleksandr, with whom she was moving to Rome. On his way to the Eternal City, Shevyrev stopped in Weimar, where he called on Goethe. During Shevyrev's sojourn in Italy, which lasted for the best part of four years, he read the works of Homer, Dante, Torquato Tasso, Ludovico Ariosto, Calderon de la Barca, Miguel de Cervantes, William Shakespeare, and George Gordon, Lord Byron, in the original; he immersed himself in historical and political researches and studied the art, sculpture, and architecture of that country. He continued to write poetry, composing two acts of a projected five-act tragedy titled "Romul" (Romulus), which shares with his other verse a marked abstraction of feeling and thought: the fratricidal murder of Remus is morally justified, for in slaying him Romulus acts as an instrument of the dispassionate Law.

In his article "O vozmozhnosti vvesti ital'ianskuiu oktavu v russkoe stikhoslozhenie" (On the Possibility of Introducing the Italian Octave into Russian Versification) in *Teleskop* (Telescope, part 3, 1831) Shevyrev advocates a reform of Russian prosody along Italian lines. His translation of Canto 7 of Tasso's *Jerusalem Delivered,* which appeared together with this essay, was meant to illustrate Shevyrev's prosodic principles but drew much criticism and even ridicule. In his poem "Poslanie A. S. Pushkinu" (Epistle to A. S. Pushkin, 1831) Shevyrev declares that Russian poetry is "enervated by a Gallic diet" of French influences; its excessive stylistic smoothness and metric monotony prevent it from stating metaphysical and prophetic truths and make the expression of the youthful vigor of Russia's national spirit impossible. Russian poets, and above all Pushkin, should emulate the robust diction of their eighteenth-century predecessors Lomonosov and Gavriil Romanovich Derzhavin. Shevyrev's relations with Pushkin remained amicable, although their views on literature were now divergent. They also disagreed in their estimation of individual writers–for example, Baratynsky, whom Shevyrev dismissed as a disciple of the "French school." While in Italy, Shevyrev continued in his admiration for the personality and achievements of Peter the Great, which he expressed in the dictum "Be a man as Christ was a man, be a Russian as Peter was a Russian."

Upon his return from Italy in 1832 Shevyrev became an adjunct professor at the University of Moscow. Uvarov, soon to be the Minister of Education, and his old friend Pogodin, who had been teaching at the university since 1825, had encouraged Shevyrev to apply for this position. In order to qualify for a permanent appointment he had to submit a special dissertation, and when the University Council rejected his essay on the reform of Russian poetry, he wrote a monograph, *Dante i ego vek* (Dante and His Age), which took him only six months to complete and which was published in the journal *Uchenye zapiski Moskovskogo universiteta* (Scholarly Transactions of Moscow University, no. 5, 1833; no. 11, 1834). On 1 October 1834 Shevyrev married Sofia Zelenskaia, the ward of Prince Boris Vladimirovich Golitsyn, thereby gaining an entrée to Moscow's aristocratic circles. Having arranged his professional and domestic affairs to his satisfaction, Shevyrev returned to journalism, joining the staff of *Moskovskii nabliudatel'* (Moscow Observer), a new publication edited by Vasilii Petrovich Androsov, one of his former collaborators on *Moskovskii vestnik*.

Androsov's journal had been founded with Pushkin's and Gogol's support as a counterweight to Osip Ivanovich Senkovsky's low-brow *Biblioteka dlia chteniia* (Library for Reading). Shevyrev's anti-Senkovsky article "Slovesnot' i torgovlia" (Literature and Commerce), which appeared in 1835 in the first issue of *Moskovskii nabliudatel'*, was in effect the manifesto of the new journal. In 1835–1836 Shevyrev headed its critical section and, as had happened in the case of *Moskovskii vestnik*, quickly acquired a dominant position among the contributors to the publication. Meanwhile he brought out volume 1 of a treatise, *Istoriia poezii* (The History of Poetry, 1835), which included his lectures on early Indian and Hebrew literature. This book won the prestigious Demidov Prize of the Russian Academy of Sciences. Volume 2, which included a survey of Ancient Greek literature and a comparative analysis of Classical and Shakespearean drama, was never published, although a section of it is preserved in manuscript form in the archives of the Russian National Library (fond 850, ed. khr. 30).

By now Shevyrev—partly owing to the influence of Gotthold Ephraim Lessing and Johann Joachim Winckelmann, whom he had read in Italy—had abandoned many of the a priori abstractions of the *Liubomudry* in favor of a historicist approach to aesthetic theory and literary criticism, although he retained their Romantic nationalism and their cult of Schelling. *Istoriia poezii* was not an innovative work. Shevyrev's theoretical views were strongly influenced by Jean Paul Richter's *Vorschule der Aesthetik* (1804), Friedrich Schlegel's *Geschichte der Alten und Neuen Literatur* (1815), and August Wilhelm Schlegel's *Über dramatische Kunst und Literatur* (1809–1811) while in his discussion of Sanskrit and Hebrew writings he followed, respectively, Arnold H. L. Heeren and Johann Gottlieb Herder. In the study of literature, he held that one should not proceed from abstract philosophical principles, such as in Georg Wilhelm Hegel's philosophy (with which Shevyrev had become acquainted in Italy, although at second hand). Rather, one should rely on the historical method: "Science must have Philosophy as its soul, and History as its body." The best scholars in the humanities combine the "speculative" (German) approach with the "empirical" (French and English) one. (This idea was approvingly cited by Pushkin in his unfinished 1836 review of *Istoriia poezii*.) Art is not only the expression of the national spirit but also of a whole set of concrete "ethnographic" factors. Russian scholars and writers must learn from the cultural experience of other countries and create their own, profoundly national, art and aesthetics that would synthesize the Platonic "theory of the Idea" and the Aristotelian "theory of the Form." These views informed both his *Istoriia poezii* and his doctoral dissertation, *Teoriia poezii v istoricheskom ee razvitii u drevnikh i novykh narodov* (The Theory of Poetry in Its Historical Development among Ancient and Modern Peoples), published in 1836, defended in January 1837.

Shevyrev's dissertation is no less derivative than his *Istoriia poezii*, including as it does a synopsis of the most important aesthetic theories from the ancient Greek to modern times. His main argument is that literature precedes aesthetics. He finds this theory especially true of great literature, which is created by geniuses operating without the benefit of a theoretical foundation; indeed, an aesthetic theory may constrain and pervert literary activity, as happened in the case of French Neoclassicism. Nevertheless, Shevyrev was remarkably balanced in his evaluation of that school, explaining its aesthetics in terms of certain psychological, social, and religious factors that he judged to be peculiar to France.

In 1836 a sharp polemic between *Moskovskii nabliudatel'* and Nadezhdin's journal *Teleskop* arose concerning Shevyrev's views. While Nadezhdin took issue with Shevyrev's philosophical and methodological ideas, Belinsky attacked his pronouncements on literature. Nadezhdin's and Belinsky's criticisms were seconded by Stankevich, Aksakov, and Mikhail Aleksandrovich Bakunin. That year Shevyrev began teaching the history of the Russian language, basing his course on the comparative analysis of modern Russian and Old Church Slavonic and making wide use of *pamiatniki*, Old Russian and Medieval Russian texts. He was one of the first scholars to devote serious attention to these hitherto neglected sources, although he constantly exaggerated their literary and intellectual merits.

Upon obtaining his doctorate Shevyrev rose to the rank of Extraordinary Professor. His course on the history of Russian literature, which he introduced in the spring of 1838, marked the first time this subject was included in the university curriculum. The tone of these lectures was polemical: the speaker emphasized Old Russian literature at the expense of modern writers and freely gave vent to his patriotic beliefs in language that was often intemperate. From 1838 to 1840 Shevyrev again traveled abroad–lecturing in Rome, Berlin, Munich, Paris, and London; visiting major libraries; and investigating the elementary and secondary systems of education in Germany, Switzerland, and France. For several years Shevyrev had produced little or no verse, but during his European *voyage d'études* he again started writing poetry. The most noteworthy of his verse productions of this period was a translation of Cantos 2 and 4 of Dante's *Inferno* (published in 1843). After 1843 the quality of his poetry declined. While in Italy he saw much of Gogol and later met the Catholic theologian Franz von Baader, a follower of the seventeenth-century German mystic Jakob Böhme. Baader was strongly antiempiricist and antirationalist, and his Russian visitor was only too happy to listen to his strictures on Hegel, who was rapidly becoming Shevyrev's philosophical bête noire. Shevyrev's overall impression of Europe was of a continent falling into a decadence of thought, spirit, and deed, and this view of the West became from then on an essential element in his historical-political doctrine.

Soon after his return to Moscow he attended a dinner honoring a visiting Croatian agitator, Ludevit Gay. The learned professor, overcome by wine and patriotic emotion, rose to recite some verses he had improvised under the spell of the occasion. His high-pitched voice ringing with passion, he declaimed, "I will drink my fill of German and Magyar blood." These sanguinary sentiments failed to move his listeners, who laughed uproariously. Indeed, by this time Shevyrev's nationalism had become Official. It received its expression in his programmatic article "Vzgliad russkogo na sovremennoe obrazovanie Evropy" (A Russian's View of the Modern Civilization of Europe), which appeared in the first issue of Pogodin's new journal *Moskvitianin* in 1841. In this piece Shevyrev solemnly proclaimed the decline and doom of the West and called on his compatriots to isolate themselves from its degenerate culture, which, in a passage that became notorious, he likened to a decaying corpse. This macabre metaphor may have given rise to the expression *gniloi zapad* (the putrid West), much used by tsarist, Soviet, and post-Soviet patriotic writers. Russia, wrote Shevyrev, is assured of a glorious future because of her "ancient religious feeling," the unbreakable unity between tsar and people, and the Russians' "consciousness" of their "nationality."

*Vissarion Grigor'evich Belinsky, a critic with whom Shevyrev carried on a heated journalistic exchange (*V. G. Belinsky: Selected Philosophical Works, *1956)*

Shevyrev's weltanschauung of the mid 1830s and thereafter is surrounded by nomenclatural confusion. Shevyrev's and Pogodin's views are sometimes described as "right-wing Slavophilism"; yet, though these ideological "Siamese twins," as Aleksandr Ivanovich Herzen called them, were certainly right wing, there were important differences between them and the Slavophiles. Shevyrev and Pogodin displayed a lack of interest in the peasant commune, a hostility to European civilization that was so virulent it bordered on xenophobia, an emphatic cultural parochialism (particularly strange in view of Shevyrev's attachment to German poetry and philosophy), an explicitly pro-government orientation, a jingoistic patriotism, an admiration for Peter the Great, and an enthusiastic adherence to Uvarov's tripartite formula, "Orthodoxy, Autocracy, Nationality." The congruence of some of their other views with those of the Slavophiles, the latter's collaboration with the journal *Moskvitianin,* which Pogodin edited with Shevyrev's help, and the Slavophiles' lack of a public declaration of their differences with the two professors led radical Westernizers like Belinsky and

Herzen to conflate the Shevyrev-Pogodin doctrine with that of Khomiakov and his allies. "The Slavs stood in full military order, with their light cavalry led by Khomiakov and their exceedingly heavy infantry in the persons of Shevyrev and Pogodin," wrote Herzen.

The Belinsky-Herzen interpretation was further developed by the Russian Marxist Georgii Valentinovich Plekhanov, who in his article "M. P. Pogodin i bor'ba klassov" (M. P. Pogodin and the Class Struggle, 1911) declared that Slavophilism and the theory of Official Nationality were essentially identical, though their ideologists were representative, respectively, of the nobility and the commoners. Long before Plekhanov, however, the revolutionary writer Nikolai Gavrilovich Chernyshevsky in his treatise *Ocherki gogolevskogo perioda russkoi literatury* (Essays on the Gogol Period in Russian Literature, 1855–1856) drew a distinction between the "true Slavophiles" (Khomiakov, Ivan and Petr Vasil'evich Kireevsky, and Konstantin and Ivan Sergeevich Aksakov) and Shevyrev. This view is now shared by a majority of Russian and Western scholars. The tone of Pogodin's writings, if not the substance of his opinions, tended to be more moderate than Shevyrev's. Pogodin's orientation was primarily historical, whereas Shevyrev's interests were chiefly philosophical, aesthetic, and literary.

Like his Slavophile and Westernizer contemporaries, Shevyrev was preoccupied with the relation of literature to reality. In 1842 he stated that "one of the most important tasks of Russian criticism consists in solving the question of the relation of literature to life"; and by "life" Shevyrev meant specifically "Russian life . . . the life of our Fatherland," as he wrote in 1858. If Belinsky treated the term "reality" in a broad way, taking it to mean both material and spiritual existence, Shevyrev was a leading exponent of a narrower, more historically focused approach. The Slavophiles wished to define the relationship of literature to the life of the Russian peasant, but in their writings this bucolic figure remained in essence a metaphysical construct that lacked a concrete anthropological, economic, or social content. In consequence the Slavophiles were more ahistorical than Shevyrev or, for that matter, Belinsky, who as a critic was above all else interested in the social content of the literary work rather than its aesthetic form. In both his *Istoriia* and his *Teoriia* Shevyrev had argued that aesthetic theory is "the consequence of art," but in his evaluations of contemporary Russian writers he in effect denied his own precept by trying to impose upon them the dogmas of Official Nationalist aesthetics.

In terms of formal learning and philosophical sophistication Shevyrev was superior to most of his journalistic colleagues, including Belinsky, although many of his literary judgments, unlike Belinsky's, have failed the test of time. Belinsky was Shevyrev's chief intellectual opponent. Their initial exchanges, however, took place on a note of mutual respect. In 1834 Belinsky described Shevyrev's performance of his professorial duties as "commendable," though Belinsky detected in Shevyrev's poems "an effort of intellect rather than the flow of ardent inspiration." The following year Shevyrev published a positive review of Belinsky's first major article, "Literaturnye mechtaniia" (Literary Reveries, 1834) in *Moskovskii nabliudatel'*, part 1. Subsequently, however, these two leading critics of the day entered into a veritable war of words because of their divergent aesthetic and political orientations and their differing estimations of individual writers. The Shevyrev-Belinsky logomachy was characterized by heartfelt mutual dislike and by a hint of class enmity (the nobleman versus the plebeian upstart). In these polemics, which lasted until Belinsky's death in 1848, the ponderous Shevyrev proved to be no match for his sharp-witted and acid-penned antagonist. Belinsky described Shevyrev as a self-satisfied reactionary and obscurantist and an intellectual snob who extolled "gentility" in literature, was guilty of theoretical dilettantism, and was biased in favor of his literary friends. Shevyrev regarded Belinsky as an antipatriot, a dangerous radical, and a rigid doctrinaire forever grafting the schemata of an arid Hegelian aestheticism on the living body of Russian literature. A representative sample of Shevyrev's attitudes toward Belinsky is found in his article "Vzgliad na sovremennoe napravlenie russkoi literatury. Storona chernaia" (A Survey of the Modern Trend in Russian Literature. The Dark Side) in *Moskvitianin* (no. 1, 1842). Belinsky paints a devastating portrait of his antagonist in a pamphlet that bears the self-explanatory title *Pedant. Literaturnyi tip* (The Pedant. A Literary Type, 1842). Belinsky's view of Shevyrev as an overeducated bore is illustrated by the advice he gave in 1843 to Konstantin Dmitrievich Kavelin, later a historian and jurist: "When you come across Shevyrev, avoid him by a mile: the day you meet him you will grow much stupider." The professor was always one to bear grudges. According to Belinsky's relative Dmitrii Ivanov, Nikanor Grigor'evich Belinsky was refused admission to Moscow University because of Shevyrev's hatred of Belinsky's famous elder brother.

In his critical writings of the 1830s and thereafter Shevyrev concerned himself with tracing the development of a Russian national consciousness through literature, and his attitude toward Pushkin, Gogol, Lermontov, Fyodor Dostoyevsky, and other leading Russian writers of the age was defined by this goal. In a series of articles published in *Moskvitianin* in 1841 Shevyrev acknowledged Pushkin's genius but identified in his verse elements of "incompleteness" and "sketchiness," by which Shevyrev meant that it lacked philosophical content. He thus anticipated Dmitrii Sergeevich Merezhkovsky's view that the fragmentary character of Pushkin's works and the brevity of his literary career made him a paradigm of Russian culture.

Shevyrev's attitude toward Lermontov was equivocal. He felt that Lermontov's poetry and prose included two disparate elements: an attachment to Christian and native Russian values, and a morose and splenetic Byronism. In his review of Lermontov's novel *Geroi nashego vremeni* (A Hero of Our Time, 1840) in *Moskvitianin* (part 2, 1841) Shevyrev argues that its protagonist, Pechorin, is "merely a phantasm projected upon us by the West, a shadow of its disease." The flaws and vices of this "moral pygmy" are owing to an atheistic "Western education"; he is alien to "pure Russian life" and indeed represents a "real danger" to it. Aesthetically, Shevyrev sees the novel as blemished: "Evil, as the main subject of an artistic work, may only be depicted through the large forms of an ideal type," as Shakespeare, Goethe, and Byron did, whereas Pechorin, who is evil personified, is reduced to base reality. Like Nicholas I, Shevyrev preferred the character of the veteran officer Maksim Maksimovich, whom he regarded as a truly Russian type, to that of Pechorin. Elsewhere (in *Moskvitianin,* no. 4, 1841) he characterizes Lermontov as a promising poet whose verse, however, is "protean"–that is, imitative of Byron, Pushkin, Baratynsky, Vasilii Andreevich Zhukovsky, and Vladimir Grigor'evich Benediktov. Indeed, Shevyrev was a great admirer of Benediktov, whose philosophical pretensions and stylistic experiments were close to his own heart, as shown in his review of Benediktov's first collection of poems in *Moskovskii nabliudatel'* (no. 11, 1835).

Lermontov's poem "Spor" (A Debate), published at his request in *Moskvitianin* (no. 6, 1841), and his preface to the second edition of *Geroi nashego vremeni* (1841) were meant as reasoned responses to Shevyrev's reading of his works. After Lermontov's death Shevyrev composed a verse eulogy, "Na smert' Lermontova" (On the Death of Lermontov, 1841), in which he describes Lermontov as a victim of "frenzied Fate," a verdict vigorously attacked by Belinsky. Shevyrev's elegy was meant to invite comparisons with Lermontov's famous poem "Smert' Poeta" (The Death of a Poet, 1837), to which it is superior in the originality and vividness of its metaphors: "The storm has crushed the gaudy butterfly / The rose has withered in its fiery bloom / The mountain torrent freezes at its source."

Shevyrev valued Gogol far more highly than he did Lermontov, although he was critical of some of Gogol's works. Of Gogol's two 1835 collections *Mirgorod* and *Arabeski* (Arabesques) he preferred the former to the latter, in which, Shevyrev opines in *Moskovskii nabliudatel'* (no. 2, 1835), the author merely imitated August Heinrich Hoffmann and Tieck. When in 1835 Gogol submitted his tale "Nos" (The Nose) to *Moskovskii nabliudatel',* Shevyrev concurred in its rejection by the editorial board of the journal. Gogol, however, greatly admired Shevyrev's two-part review of *Mertvye Dushi* (Dead Souls, 1842) in *Moskvitianin* (nos. 7 & 8, 1842), in which Shevyrev describes Gogol's epic as a fantasy but one that rests on "the profound foundations of nature and of man's life." By employing an equal measure of imagination and humor the author has produced literary "Fata Morgana" that "ideally reflect upon the heavens everything that occurs on earth." Shevyrev calls *Mertvye Dushi* "a poem for our time," thereby implying its superiority to Lermontov's novel. He compares Gogol to Homer, Dante, and Shakespeare, a parallel the less intertextually-minded Belinsky mocks, perhaps unfairly. The latter, who chose to regard Gogol as the progenitor of the Natural School– that is, a realist–also took exception to Shevyrev's view of Gogol as a distorter of reality. Shevyrev hails Gogol's *Vybrannye mesta iz perepiski s druz'iami* (Selected passages from Correspondence with Friends, 1847), published in *Moskvitianin* (no. 1,1848), as an Official Nationalist *cri de coeur.* Shevyrev was, in fact, one of Gogol's confidants: they addressed each other with the familiar *ty.* In August 1849 Gogol stayed with Shevyrev at the latter's country house near Moscow, where Gogol showed his host sections of volume 2 of *Mertvye Dushi.* After Gogol's death Shevyrev helped to catalogue Gogol's papers and assisted in the publication of his posthumous *Sochineniia* (Works, 1855–1856).

In a review published in the second issue of *Moskvitianin* for 1846 Shevyrev had dispraised Dostoevsky's first novel *Bednye liudi* (Poor Folk, 1846), whose author, he wrote, was guilty of a "philanthropic" tendentiousness imported from the West and inimical to true Christian love. He conceded that the novel bore "the stamp of Gogolian influence" but judged it inferior to Gogol's story "Shinel'" (The Overcoat, 1842). Shevyrev was equally dismissive of the early works of Ivan Sergeevich Turgenev in *Moskvitianin* (no. 1, 1848); a lack of popular spirit, in his opinion, proved that Russian literature was on the decline.

Shevyrev's prolific activity as a scholar and journalist did not distract him from his teaching. Initially he was well liked by his students, who appreciated his erudition and love of his subject. His standing with them soon deteriorated, however, owing to his pedantic and polemical tone, reactionary politics, and intellectual vanity. Shevyrev was overbearing in the auditorium. He tolerated no noise or distraction during his lectures, and if anyone caused such a disturbance, Shevyrev

Title page for volume 3 of Istoriia russkoi slovesnosti *(A History of Russian Literature), published in four volumes between 1846 and 1860*

made a point of publicly humiliating the culprit. As invariably happens with unpopular professors, students found ways of mocking him. Shevyrev had a habit when hearing a noise in the audience of saying "Ah?" an interjection that in Russian is a homophone for the letter "A." On one occasion when Shevyrev did this, a student responded in a loud voice "B," reducing the speaker to a state of stuttering confusion. "His lectures were a kind of nursery song, sung in a pure soprano reminiscent of the papal descants in Rome," wrote Herzen, who like many others, found something faintly ridiculous in Shevyrev's *ex cathedra* mannerisms. He was never able to rival the popularity of his university colleague Timofei Nikolaevich Granovsky, a leading Westernizer and a gifted public speaker, who began teaching in 1839. Nil Petrovich Koliupanov, a student at Moscow University in the 1840s, confirms Shevyrev's want of intellectual and pedagogical appeal as compared with the "brilliant professors" of the "Western party" and describes him as the "*enfant terrible* of Slavophilism" who brought its cause into disrepute; because of him the students came to hate the Slavophiles as the "extinguishers of enlightenment."

In this atmosphere of intense intellectual partisanship Granovsky delivered in November 1843 through April 1844 a series of public lectures on the Middle Ages. His lectures, which had a pronouncedly anti-Slavophile bias, were enormously popular and became the intellectual and social event of the season. Herzen recalls that the end of the first lecture was greeted by an ovation; ladies in the audience begged the speaker for his portrait; and "youths with flushed cheeks" shouted "bravo!" and shed copious tears. Granovsky's success aroused the ire of Shevyrev, who, inspired in equal measure by professional jealousy and ideological zeal, denounced his rival as a fanatical Hegelian in "Publichnye lektsii ob istorii srednikh vekov g. Granovskogo" (Mr. Granovsky's Public Lectures on the History of the Middle Ages) for *Moskvitianin* (no. 12, 1843). Shevyrev's philippic had political overtones, since Hegel's name was highly suspect in government circles. One article, however, does not destroy a reputation, and Shevyrev resolved to enter into direct academic competition with his younger colleague. In 1844–1845 Shevyrev gave his own course of public lectures, on old Russian literature, which enjoyed some success among his more Slavophile-minded listeners, though none of them wept. This course formed the basis for his *Istoriia russkoi slovesnosti: preimushchestvenno drevne lektsii* (A History of Russian Literature: Mostly Ancient, 1846–1860). In this book Shevyrev argued, among other things, that in his Epistle to Grand Duke Monomakh, the twelfth-century Greek-Russian cleric Nikifor had anticipated Hegel's system. This bizarre judgment makes one suspect that even at this late stage Shevyrev still had not read the works of the German philosopher.

In 1845–1846 Shevyrev, who had not abandoned his desire to eclipse Granovsky's fame, delivered a second series of public lectures on the history of world literature, which enjoyed even less success than the first. With the retirement of Professor Davydov, his old teacher at the Pension, Shevyrev became the senior professor of Russian literature and was appointed to the position of dean. His tenure in that office was not a happy one, for the combative and opinionated Shevyrev constantly clashed with the students and with his colleagues. In 1851 the latter voted to have him replaced by Granovsky, but the minister of education refused to confirm the results of the election, and Shevyrev retained his post, an outcome that further damaged his reputation. In 1852 he added the title of Member of the Academy of Sciences to his growing list of official honors.

His distinguished academic career ended with the kind of scandal, composed in equal measure of tragedy and farce, that is found in the novels of Dostoyevsky. In January 1857 at a meeting of the board of the Moscow Art Society he took exception to a speech by Count Vladimir Alekseevich Bobrinsky in which the latter criticized certain abuses and instances of injustice taking place in Russia. Shevyrev insulted the speaker and was insulted in return. After this initial exchange of unpleasantries Shevyrev launched a physical attack on the count. Shevyrev's aristocratic antagonist gave as good as he got, and the professor emerged from this political bout of fisticuffs with several broken ribs. The response of the government to the incident was as expected. Shevyrev was dismissed from his university posts and ordered to take up residence in the city of Iaroslavl. (The count was banished to one of his estates.) Shevyrev restated his patriotic credentials in the form of a mediocre poem, "Russkoe imia" (A Russian's Name), and also took the practical step of addressing a petition to Tsar Alexander II, of which the outcome was that the sentence of exile was lifted and he was allowed to remain in Moscow.

For the next three years Shevyrev devoted himself to preparing the last two volumes of his *Istoriia russkoi slovesnosti* for publication. His nationalist principles were consistent enough to allow him to celebrate the Italian war of liberation in verse, "K Italii" (To Italy, 1859). In 1860 he left Russia, never to return. He greeted the abolition of serfdom with a laudatory poem, "19 Fevralia" (19 February), although his attitude toward Alexander II's other great reform, that of Russia's legal system, was skeptical. In February–March 1861 Shevyrev gave a series of twelve lectures on Russian literature at Florence; they were published the following year as *Storia della letteratura russa*. He then traveled to Paris where early in 1862 he delivered another course of lectures on Russian literature before the age of Pushkin. That summer he fell ill and thereafter his health gradually declined, although he continued to work on a second series of lectures that was to cover the history of Russian literature from Pushkin to Ivan Turgenev. He died on 8 July 1864 in Paris, almost forgotten in the changing Russia of the 1860s, where his faithful friend Pogodin was one of the few to mourn his passing in print.

Letters:

Franz von Baader, *Gesammelte Schriften zur Religionsphilosophie,* volume 4 (Leipzig, 1855);

Nikolai Vasil'evich Sushkov, *Moskovskii Universitetskii Blagorodnyi Pansion* (Moscow, 1858);

Petr Andreevich Viazemsky, "Pismo k S. P. Shevyrevy, 22 September 1841," *Russkii Arkhiv,* no. 6 (1885): 307;

Iz sobraniia avtografov Imperatorskoi Publichnoi Biblioteki (St. Petersburg, 1898;

Nikolai Platonovich Barsukov, ed., *Pis'ma M. P. Pogodina, S. P. Shevyreva i M. A. Maksimovicha k P. A. Viazemskomu 1825–1874 godov* (St. Petersburg, 1901);

Staroe i Novoe, no. 4 (1901).

Biography:

Mikhail Petrovich Pogodin, *Iz vospominanii o S. P. Shevyreve* (Moscow, 1865).

References:

Aleksandr Afanas'ev, "Vospominaniia o Moskovskom universitete. 1843–1844 gg.," *Russkaia Starina,* no. 8 (1886): 368–371;

Elena Ivanovna Annenkova, "*Moskvitianin,*" in *Lermontovskaia entsiklopediia* (Moscow: Sovetskaia entsiklopediia, 1981);

Mark Aronson, "Poeziia Shevyreva," in *S. P. Shevyrev, Stikhotvoreniia* (Leningrad: Sovetskii pisatel', 1939);

N. P. Barsukov, *Zhizn' i trudy M. P. Pogodina,* volumes 1–22 (St. Petersburg: M. M. Stasiulevich, 1888–1910);

Vissarion Grigor'evich Belinsky, *Polnoe sobranie sochinenii v trinadtsati tomakh* (Moscow: AN SSSR, 1953–1959);

N. Ch., "Shevyrev," in *Russkii biograficheskii slovar',* volume 23 (St. Petersburg, 1911);

Lazar' A. Chereisky, *Pushkin i ego okruzhenie,* (Leningrad: Nauka, 1988);

Nikolai Gavrilovich Chernyshevsky, *Ocherki gogolevskogo perioda russkoi literatury* (Moscow: Goslitizdat, 1953);

Aleksandr Grigor'evich Dement'ev, "Granovskii i Shevyrev," *Uchenye zapiski Leningradskogo gosudarstvennogo universiteta,* no. 46 (1939): 321–354;

Lidiia Iakovlevna Ginzburg, "S. P. Shevyrev," in *Russkie poety 1820kh–1830kh godov,* volume 2 (Leningrad: Sovetskii pisatel', 1972), pp. 131–139;

Gogol' v vospominaniiakh sovremennikov (Moscow: Molodaia gvardiia, 1952);

I. I. Gribushin, "Otzvuki liriki S. P. Shevyreva v tvorchestve M. Iu. Lermontova," *Russkaia literatura,* no. 1 (1969): 182–185;

Aleksandr Ivanovich Herzen, *My Past and Thoughts* (New York: Knopf, 1973);

Herzen, *Polnoe sobranie sochinenii v tridtsati tomakh* (Moscow, 1954–1966);

Istoriia russkoi literatury v chetyrekh tomakh, volume 2 (Leningrad, 1981);

Ivan Ivanovich Ivanov, *Istoriia russkoi kritiki*, volume 2 (St. Petersburg: Skorokhodov, 1900);

Viacheslav Anatol'evich Koshelev, *Esteticheskie i literaturnye vozzreniia russkikh slavianofilov (1840–1850-e gody)* (Leningrad: Nauka, 1984);

Vasilii Ivanovich Kuleshov, *Istoriia russkoi kritiki XVIII-nachala XX vekov,* (Moscow: Prosveshcheniia, 1984);

Konstantin Nikolaevich Lomunov, ed., *Literaturnye vzgliady i tvorchestvo slavianofilov. (1830–1850-e gody)* (Moscow: Nauka, 1978);

Iurii Vladimirovich Mann, *Russkaia filosofskaia estetika (1820–1830-e gody)* (Moscow: Iskusstvo, 1969);

Raymond T. McNally, *Chaadaev and His Friends* (Tallahassee, Fla.: Diplomatic Press, 1971);

Andrei Nikolaevich Murav'ev, *Znakomstvo s russkimi poetami* (Kiev, 1871);

A. V. Nikitenko, *Dnevnik v trekh tomakh* (Moscow: GIKhL, 1955–1956);

Mikhail Petrovich Pogodin, "Otkrytie nadgrobnogo pamiatnika S. P. Shevyrevu," *Russkii,* nos. 15–16 (1867);

Pogodin, "Vospominanie o Shevyreve," *Zhurnal Ministerstva Narodnogo Prosveshcheniia,* no. 2 (1869): 395–452;

Aleksandr Pushkin, *Polnoe sobranie sochinenii,* volumes 1–17 (Moscow-Leningrad: AN SSSR, 1937–1959);

Pushkin, *A. S. Pushkin v vospominaniiakh sovremennikov,* volumes 1–2 (Moscow: Kudozh. lit-ra, 1974);

Nicholas V. Riasanovsky, *Nicholas I and Official Nationality in Russia, 1825–1855* (Berkeley: University of California Press, 1961);

Riasanovsky, *A Parting of Ways. Government and the Educated Public in Russia, 1801–1855* (Oxford: Clarendon Press, 1976);

Riasanovsky, "Pogodin and Sevyrev in Russian Intellectual History," *Harvard Slavonic Studies,* no. 4 (1957);

Riasanovsky, *Russia and the West in the Teachings of the Slavophiles. A Study of Romantic Ideology* (Cambridge, Mass.: Harvard University Press, 1952);

Priscilla R. Roosevelt, "Shevyrev," in *Modern Encyclopedia of Russian and Soviet History,* volume 34 (Gulf Breeze, Fla.: Academic International Press, 1983);

Shch., "Shevyrev," in *Entsiklopedicheskii slovar' Brokgauza Efrona,* volume 39 (St. Petersburg: Tipografiia Akts. Obsh. Brokgauz-Efron, 1903);

P. D. Shestakov, "Moskovskii universitet v 1840-kh godakh," *Russkaia starina,* no. 9 (1887);

Robert H. Stacy, *Russian Literary Criticism: A Short History* (Syracuse, N.Y.: Syracuse University Press, 1974);

P. Struve, "S. P. Shevyrev i zapadnye vnusheniia i istochniki teorii-aforizma o 'gnilom' ili 'gniiushchem Zapade,'" in *Zapiski Russkogo Nauchnogo Instituta v Belgrade* (Belgrade, 1940);

Nikolai Savvich Tikhonravov, "Nekrolog Shevyreva," *Moskovskie vedomosti,* no. 107 (1864): 3;

Konstantin Aleksandrovich Trutovsky, "Rasskazy o Shevyreve," *Khudozhestvennyi zhurnal,* no. 5 (1881);

Vadim Erazmovich Vatsuro, "Shevyrev," *Lermontovskaia entsiklopediia* (Moscow: Sov. entsiklopediia, 1981);

V. G. Belinskii v vospominaniiakh sovremennikov (Moscow: GIKhL, 1977);

Andrzej Walicki, *The Slavophile Controversy* (Oxford: Clarendon Press, 1975);

Zapiski A. I. Kosheleva (Moscow: Izd-vo Moskovskogo universiteta, 1991).

Papers:

Stepan Petrovich Shevyrev's notebook, including poems from 1825 to 1841, is found in Shevyrev's TsGALI, fond 563, 103 items, 1797–1865; seventy-eight autographs of poems, the diaries for 1829 to 1831, and a partial manuscript of volume 2 of *Istoriia poezii* are found in the Rossiiskaia Natsional'naia Biblioteka (formerly GPB) in St. Petersburg, fond 850, 9 "kart" items, 1828–1864 (Shevyreva).

Viktor Grigor'evich Tepliakov

(15 August 1804 – 14 October 1842)

Richard Tempest
University of Illinois at Urbana-Champaign

BOOKS: *Stikhotvoreniia Viktora Tepliakova*, 2 volumes (Moscow: S. Selivanovsky, 1832, 1836);
Pis'ma iz Bolgarii (Moscow, 1833);
Poety 1820–1830kh godov, volume 1 (Leningrad: Sovetskii pisatel', 1972), pp. 598–690;
Russkaia epigramma vtoroi poloviny XVIII–nachala XX v. (Leningrad: Sovetskii pisatel', 1975), pp. 392–394.

Viktor Tepliakov was a poet and travel writer who is traditionally identified as one of the lesser lights of the "Pushkin pleiad." In his lifetime Tepliakov published two volumes of verse and a travelogue, *Pis'ma iz Bolgarii* (Letters from Bulgaria, 1833), which brought the history and scenery of that land into the purview of the Russian reader. As a young man he held a commission in a cavalry regiment; one of his fellow officers and friends was the celebrated swashbuckler Petr Pavlovich Kaverin. Although Tepliakov was not a member of the Decembrist conspiracy, he was imprisoned in 1826 for his reluctance to swear an oath of allegiance to Tsar Nicholas I. His imprisonment was followed by a term of enforced penance in a monastery and a period of exile in the south of the country. In the last twelve years of his life he did much traveling abroad, visiting the Balkans, the Levant (twice), and Western Europe. Tepliakov's early verse is derivative: his lyrical *I* is straightforwardly Byronic and expresses a sense of poetic self that is informed more by the author's readings of the Romantics than by his own experiences.

As a poet Tepliakov came into his own in the late 1820s. His poetic diction then was often reminiscent of Aleksandr Pushkin (he called himself "one of the most diligent admirers" of Pushkin's "genius"), but Tepliakov diverges from his literary paragon in his continued preoccupation with the themes of solitude, exile, nostalgia, misanthropy, and betrayal; these overtly Romantic motifs, however, were not mere literary contrivances but had concrete autobiographical meaning. His poetic themes and techniques offered many parallels to those of Mikhail Iur'evich Lermontov and of the elegist Konstantin Nikolaevich Batiushkov. Tepliakov shares with

Viktor Grigor'evich Tepliakov

the emerging post-Pushkin generation of poets a certain self-consciousness of style and an emphasis on the subjective. He also developed a literary historiosophy of pessimism, which found expression in his "Frakiiskie elegii" (Thracian Elegies, 1829), his highest artistic achievement. Tepliakov's Gothic prison experiences and Romantic peregrinations won him the cognomen of "The Russian Melmoth."

Viktor Grigor'evich Tepliakov was born in the city of Tver' in central Russia into a local landowning family. Little is known about his parents, State Councillor Grigorii Alekseevich Tepliakov and Praskovia Aggeevna Tepliakova, née Svechin. Their son was first educated at home and then at the Noble Pension of the University of Moscow, which he entered at the age of ten. One of his fellow pupils there was Prince Vladimir Fedorovich Odoevsky, who wrote the philosophical novel *Russkie nochi* (Russian Nights, 1844). As a pensionnaire Tepliakov was already composing verse: his biographer, Fedor Afanas'evich Bychkov, refers to a poem Tepliakov wrote when he was fifteen. On 10 September 1820 he joined the Pavlograd Hussar Regiment as a *junker* (cadet) and by 1824 had attained the rank of lieutenant. In the regiment Tepliakov grew close to his fellow officer Kaverin, who, as well as being a famous carouser, was a Göttingen graduate, a member of the proto-Decembrist *Soiuz Blagodenstvüa* (Union of Welfare), and a friend of leading literary figures of the day such as Aleksandr Pushkin, Prince Petr Andreevich Viazemsky, and Aleksandr Sergeevich Griboedov.

Kaverin's letters to Tepliakov from 1823 to 1825 reveal a commonality of literary tastes and interests: they refer to Pushkin's Romantic narrative poems "Brat'ia razboiniki" (The Robber Brothers, 1821), "Bakhchisaraiskii fontan" (The Fountain of Bakhchisarai, 1822), chapter 1 of his verse novel *Evgeny Onegin* (1825–1831), and the works of two other poets, the Neoclassicist Baron Anton Antonovich Del'vig and the elegist Aleksandr Abramovich Krylov. Together the two hussar literati mourn George Gordon, Lord Byron's death. According to Bychkov, whose informants included Tepliakov's younger brother, Aggei, the poet had important Decembrist associations and became a Mason under Kaverin's direct sponsorship. That Tepliakov shared the Decembrists' political views is confirmed by his long poem "Bonifatsii" (Boniface, 1823), of which only a fragment survives. In this work the rhetoric of nineteenth-century liberalism functions within a foreign historical setting, as was often the case with Russian civic poetry of the period.

The poem describes a revolt by the townspeople of Marseilles, led by the eponymous troubadour, against the despotic Charles of Anjou. "Proud Liberty awakes from slumber. / The time has come to smite the snake of tyranny!" sing Tepliakov's feudal insurgents, unaware of the anachronism of their political sentiments. Such declarative, pathos-filled passages, however, are interspersed with others of a more elegiac nature, in which the poet's *I* speaks in melancholy, Byronic tones: "The happiness thou hadst, young bard, thou hast no more. / Thy soul, which burnt with life, sheds its voluptuous flame. / Why did it have to learn stern suffering's cold embrace?"

The interplay between the lyrical *I* and the epic narration is almost Lermontovian. The mournful note present in what is otherwise an emphatically civicist work may have resulted from the circumstances of the poet's life during this period, for Tepliakov, who was in indifferent health and had no martial ambitions, was unhappy in the army. Indeed, on 14 March 1825 he resigned his commission. On 14 December of that year he was in St. Petersburg, but he played no part in the Decembrist uprising, which took place on that day. Nevertheless, like the Decembrists, Tepliakov fell victim to the wrath of the government, for he attempted to avoid swearing an oath of allegiance to the new tsar, Nicholas I.

Early in 1826, when he was at confession, the priest asked him whether he feared God and loved the tsar. The poet responded with an irreverent joke, declaring that he loved God and feared the tsar! The next day he dispatched his devoted younger brother, Aggei, a *junker* in the Regiment of Horse of the Life Guards, to the church to take communion in his stead. When the priest realized that he had been tricked, he broke the seal of the confessional (as prescribed by Peter the Great's famous *ukaz*) and denounced the two brothers to the authorities. They were arrested on 20 April and taken to the Peter-Paul Fortress, where the members of the Decembrist conspiracy were also being held. A search of Tepliakov's home revealed that he had in his possession Masonic artifacts; it was also discovered that Tepliakov wore a Masonic tattoo on his arm.

Tepliakov's weak constitution and sensitive nature added greatly to his suffering during his time in the tsar's dungeons. In the poem "Zatvornik," (The Prisoner) which according to family legend he composed while in jail, he wrote: "Black minutes drag themselves along. / They dwarf the centuries colossal." On his release on 24 June, Tepliakov was first sent to a hospital and then by order of Nicholas I was confined to the Monastery of St. Aleksandr Nevsky for a period of penance. His brother was transferred to a lancer regiment in the regular army. Late in 1826 Tepliakov was exiled to the city of Kherson in the Ukraine, where his misadventures continued: during a robbery carried out in his apartment, a gang of local criminals, some of whom were serving policemen, attacked and grievously wounded him. After he wrote a letter to Nicholas I in which he described the incident in vivid detail, Tepliakov's standing with the authorities improved: his rank was restored, and he was given employment at the custom house in Taganrog. Eventually Pushkin's old nemesis Count Mikhail Semenovich Vorontsov, viceroy of New Russia, appointed Tepliakov to his staff (scholars give different dates for this appointment: 1827, 1828, and 1829).

In 1828 Tepliakov traveled to the Caucasus, that traditional place of pilgrimage for Russian poets, in order to take the waters. There he wrote his poem

Tepliakov in the uniform of the Pavlograd Hussar Regiment (from Russkaia starina, *1896)*

"Kavkaz" (The Caucasus), which includes many paraphrases from Pushkin's Romantic narrative tale "Kavkazskii plennik" (Prisoner of the Caucasus, 1821); the dissonances and subtly archaized style of "Kavkaz" suggest also the influence of Gavriil Romanovich Derzhavin's nature poetry. The most original feature of "Kavkaz" is the meditations of the lyrical *I* on the majestic and tragic sweep of time, the catastrophic nature of history—a theme that began to preoccupy the poet. After his return to Russia, Tepliakov carried out archaeological researches in the south of the country. Meanwhile, war had broken out with the Ottoman Empire, and the Russian army advanced across the Danube into Turkish-held Bulgaria.

In March 1829 he was sent to Bulgaria on another archaeological mission, which afforded him the opportunity to write his seven "Frakiiskie elegii." The itinerant lyrical hero of these poems is an outcast, persecuted by man and fate, who exists in a state of emotional desolation: he is a Russian Childe Harold. The ancient lands he visits, rich in the ruins of dead civilizations, are to him "a mausoleum of the past"; with a dolorous eye he surveys the millenia of history and sees "death everywhere! dust everywhere!" In his imagination the armies of Darius, Trajan, and Prince Oleg once again march across Moesia and Thrace; he even looks back into prehistoric times and descries a hunter battling "the dread and mighty mammoth." Ancient ruins, those "hieroglyphics of the ages," spell history's terrible story—one of wars, civil strife, and unending human suffering. Civilizations rise and fall according to an unchanging pattern: freedom–glory–opulence–decadence–barbarism. Thereafter, the whole cataclysmic cycle is repeated.

Tepliakov's pessimistic poetic historiosophy is reminiscent of Byron's *Childe Harold's Pilgrimage* (IV, 58); it also calls to mind Giambattista Vico's theory of historical change, *corsi i ricorsi*. The number and variety of cultural codes activated in the elegies is unusual for a Russian poem of the period. There are references to the Old Testament, Hinduism, and Greco-Roman antiquity; Byzantine, Venetian, and Ottoman history; the Crusades; and the Napoleonic legend. In addition to their Byronic subtext the "Elegies" include a host of other literary allusions: to Ovid (who together with Byron is the chief literary referent), "The Thousand and One Nights," the *commedia dell'arte,* Torquato Tasso, William Shakespeare, Friedrich Gottlieb Klopstock, Pushkin, and Vasilii Andreevich Zhukovsky. Each elegy has an epigraph (among the authors cited are Ovid, Byron, Friedrich von Schiller, Pierre Simon Ballanche, Pierre-Jean de Béranger, and Zhukovsky) and copious endnotes. In the notes Tepliakov makes some, but not all, of his historical-cultural references plain and expands upon them, occasionally at considerable length. The prosodic structure of the poems is highly developed. The narration is in iambic verse that constantly shifts between tetrameters and hexameters; a section of the Second Elegy, in which Ovid is heard to speak across the centuries, is composed in alternating hexameters and pentameters. Tepliakov evokes a variety of poetic genres: the Romantic narrative poem, the epic, the ode, and the idyll.

The "Frakiiskie elegii" are a verse chronicle of the Russo-Turkish war of 1828–1829 as witnessed by Tepliakov: they depict sanguinary battles, fields strewn with dead bodies, and the plague-ravaged city of Sozopol'. The martial scenes in the Sixth Elegy show the influence of Canto Three of Pushkin's Romantic historical epic "Poltava" (1828). Pushkin reviewed the "Frakiiskie elegii" in an unsigned article published in his journal *Sovremennik* (The Contemporary, Book III, 1836). "There is no doubt," wrote Pushkin, "that on the ship that brought him to the shores of Thrace Mr. Tepliakov had as his companion the fantastical shadow of Childe Harold." Pushkin calls Tepliakov a poet of "original talent"; the Fifth Elegy, "Gebedzhinskie fontany" (The Fountains of Gebedzhin), he finds the most meditative and descriptive of the cycle and selects it for special praise. Pushkin criticizes Tepliakov, however, for a certain imprecision and infelicity of phrasing in the Second Elegy. Pushkin forebore to comment on the many allusions in the "Frakiiskie elegii" to his own poems, such as "Pogaslo dnevnoe svetilo . . . " (The Orb of Day Has Faded . . . , 1820) or "K Ovidiiu" (To Ovid, 1821). Still, the following passage, in which the reviewer refers to the Byronic qualities of the elegies, may be read as a coded commentary on Tepliakov's literary debt to Pushkin himself: "Talent is spontaneous, and when it emulates it does not commit shameful misappropriation, which is a sign of intellectual poverty, but rather reposes noble hope in its own resources–the hope of discovering new worlds whilst striving to follow in the footsteps of genius–or displays a sentiment that in its humility is yet more elevated: the desire to study its model and imbue it with a secondary existence."

After he had discharged his archaeological duties in Bulgaria, Tepliakov settled in Odessa, where he contributed to local publications and frequented the artistic and literary circles of the city. In 1830–1831 several of his poems appeared in Del'vig's almanac *Severnye tsvety* (Northern Flowers) and his journal *Literaturnaia gazeta* (Literary Gazette). They were favorably commented on by Pushkin and his friends. Tepliakov's first book of verse, *Stikhotvoreniia Viktora Tepliakova* (Poems), was published in 1832 by his brother Aleksei. The order of the poems in this collection was meant to show the shift of the lyrical *I* from a youthful optimism and a belief in the redeeming power of art to an almost unrelieved poetic pessimism. The book concludes with the poem "Chudnyi dom" (The House of Marvels, 1831). In it the poet's alter ego visits a dark tower–a house of death inhabited by a "monstrous gnome," a pair of guardian sphinxes, and a crowd of hideous apparitions. He then finds himself in a beautiful palace–replete with spouting fountains (which symbolize spiritual repose), marble statues, satin carpets, and crystal doors–where he meets his Muse, who is strumming a harp of gold. Full of rapture, he throws himself at her feet–and beholds "a hideous skeleton": "I looked at those bones with a gaze that was dull. / MY IDEAL, she was dead. So I kicked at her skull / And I whispered to her a goodbye." Although favorably received, the book failed to sell.

The following year Tepliakov brought out his second book, *Pis'ma iz Bolgarii*. The letters in question were written simultaneously with the "Frakiiskie elegii" and subsequently edited and emended for publication. The style of this epistolary travelogue recalls Lermontov's prose. *Pis'ma iz Bolgarii* may be read as an expanded commentary to "Frakiiskie elegii," with Tepliakov acting as his own amanuensis. The poet's correspondence of the early 1830s reflects his depressed, pessimistic, and misanthropic mood: he was unhappy in Odessa and longed to leave that city. In 1834–1835 Tepliakov, still in his capacity as a member of Count Vorontsov's staff, traveled to Constantinople, Anatolia, and Greece. Upon his return he visited St. Petersburg, where he stayed from 21 May until 4 July; subsequently, he paid a second visit to the capital, which lasted from 15 October 1835 until 21 July 1836.

During his two sojourns in St. Petersburg Tepliakov met with prominent writers and poets such as Pushkin, Zhukovsky, Viazemsky, Odoevsky, and Nikolai Gogol. At Zhukovsky's home he attended a reading of Gogol's comedy *Revizor* (The Inspector General, 1836), performed by the playwright himself; at another of Zhukovsky's literary gatherings he recited his "Frakiiskie elegii" in the presence of the heir apparent, Grand Duke Alexander (later Tsar Alexander II). Tepliakov's second collection of verse, which bore the same title as the first, appeared in the spring of 1836; his friend Odoevsky took an active part in preparing the book for publication. It included "Frakiiskie elegii" as well as many pieces written in and after 1832, including "Liubov' i nenavist'" (Love and Hate, 1832) and "Dva Angela" (Two Angels, 1833). These two poems explore "demonic" themes and again invite comparisons with Lermontov. The learned but meretricious critic Osip Ivanovich Senkovsky published a disparaging review of *Stikhotvoreniia* in his journal *Biblioteka dlia chteniia* (Library for Reading,

20, no. 1, 1837); Tepliakov responded with an angry epigram in which he called Senkovsky a "journalistic Thersites," after the ugly and abusive Greek warrior slain by Achilles in the *Iliad*.

In the summer of 1836 Tepliakov once again went to Constantinople, where he was employed in a minor diplomatic capacity, and also visited Greece, Egypt, Syria, and Palestine. During his travels he learned of Pushkin's death and, while in Jerusalem, prayed for the repose of the poet's soul at a mass celebrated at Golgotha. In late 1839 or early 1840 Tepliakov, who had grown tired of "ruins, barbarism, and the plague," resigned his official position. In May 1840, after spending a few weeks in St. Petersburg, he went to Paris, where he saw much of the diarist and epistolarian Aleksandr Ivanovich Turgenev and met many of the latter's literary contacts, including Vicomte François-René de Chateaubriand, Alphonse-Marie-Louis de Prat de Lamartine, Ballanche, and the celebrated Polish poet Adam Mickiewicz. He visited the salons of Jeanne-Françoise-Julie Adélaide Récamier and of the Russian-born Catholic Anne-Sophie Swetchine, whose guests he entertained with stories of his travels. He also met with Swetchine's nephew, Prince Ivan Sergeevich Gagarin (a Russian diplomat who later became a Jesuit), whom he may have already known from St. Petersburg. The entry for 26 April 1841 in Gagarin's diary refers to an operation Tepliakov had undergone three days earlier and describes the kindness that Turgenev was showing the ailing poet. The entry for 4 June 1841 in Turgenev's Paris diary reads: "At three o'clock Prince Gagarin came to fetch me and we went to St. Denis, and via St. Denis arrived at our destination in half an hour. Found Tepliakov, walked in the alleys, on the banks of a pond. After dinner we walked until 8 o'clock, recited Lermontov's verses on Napoleon." In Paris, Tepliakov (according to his brother Aleksei) "was moroser than ever and recalled with sadness his life in the Orient"; his frequent bouts of illness added to his unhappiness.

At the beginning of May 1841 Tepliakov went to Enghien to take the cure and, having recovered a measure of health, traveled to the Rhine, visited Switzerland, and in October arrived in Italy, where he stayed until the summer of 1842. During this period he appears to have written no poetry. In Rome he was introduced to Cardinal Mezzofanti, a notable philologist, and had an audience with Pope Gregory XVI, who suggested to his Russian visitor that he should compose a biography of the famous sixteenth-century parricide Beatrice Cenci. Tepliakov was an accomplished linguist who knew English, French, German, Turkish, Latin, and Greek; according to

Copy of Stikhotvoreniia Viktora Tepliakova *(Poems of Viktor Tepliakov), inscribed by the author to Anna Petrovna Zontag (Kilgour Collection, Harvard University Library)*

Bychkov, after a week in Rome, Tepliakov acquired such a command of Italian that he was able to describe his adventures in the East in that language to an audience of Roman aristocrats.

During the last months of his life Tepliakov experienced much physical and emotional suffering; in his last letter to Aleksei he wrote, "What am I to do with myself? I have seen everything that is interesting in the sublunar world and I am indescribably bored by it all." He died of an apoplectic seizure and was buried in the cemetery at Montmartre.

Letters:
Russkaia Starina, nos. 1–4, 7–10 (1896);
Revue des études slaves, 478–479 (1982).

References:
Sh. Beridze, *Odin iz zabytykh. Zhizn' i tvorchestvo V. G. Tepliakova* (Tbilisi: G. G. Beridze, 1920);

William Edward Brown, *A History of Russian Literature of the Romantic Period,* volume 4 (Ann Arbor, Mich.: Ardis, 1986), pp. 61–82;

A. N. Brukhanskii, ed., "'Pis'ma iz Bolgarii' V. G. Tepliakova," in *Iz istorii russko-slavianskikh literaturnykh sviazei,* 19 volumes (Moscow-Leningrad: AN SSSR, 1963);

Fedor Afanas'evich Bychkov, "V. G. Tepliakov. Biograficheskii ocherk," *Istoricheskii vestnik,* no. 7 (1887): 5-23;

Petr Vasil'evich Bykov, "V. G. Tepliakov," *Niva,* no. 41 (1888): 1016-1018;

Lazar' A. Chereisky, "Tepliakov," in *Pushkin i ego okruzhenie,* second edition (Leningrad: Nauka, 1988), pp. 431-432;

E. V. Freidel', "Pushkin v dnevnike i pis'makh V. G. Tepliakova," in *Pushkin. Issledovaniia i materialy,* volume 6 (Leningrad: Nauka, 1969), pp. 276-283;

Emil Ivanov Georgiev, "Viktor Tepliakov–parviiat pevets na balgarskiia peizazh," *Literaturna mysl,* no. 2 (1968);

A. A. Gren, "A. S. Pushkin," *Obshchezanimatel'nyi vestnik,* no. 6 (1857): 221-225; continued in *Peterburgskii vestnik,* no. 14 (1861): 310-314;

N. L[erner], "Tepliakov," in *Russkii biograficheskii slovar',* volume 20 (St. Petersburg, 1912), pp. 479-484;

V. Iu. Proskurina, "'Frakiiskie elegii' V. G. Tepliakova," in *Pamiatnye knizhnye daty. 1986 god* (Moscow: Nauka, 1986);

Pushkin i ego sovremenniki. Materialy i issledovaniia, volumes 29-30, pp. 210-222;

Alexis Grigor'evich Tepliakov, "Vospominanie o V. G. Tepliakove," *Otechestvennye zapiski,* 28, no. 4, sect. 8 (1843): 74-103;

Vadim Erazmovich Vatsuro, "K biografii V. G. Tepliakova," in *Pushkin. Issledovaniia i materialy,* volume 11 (Leningrad: Nauka, 1983), pp. 192-212;

Vatsuro, "V. G. Tepliakov," *Poety 1820kh-1830 godov,* volume 1 (Leningrad, 1972), pp. 593-598.

Papers:

Viktor Tepliakov's unpublished manuscripts, including his travel diary for 1834 and his service record are located in the Institut Russkoi Literatury (Pushkinskii Dom, f. 322, no. 71, f. 9272-9276. Documents pertaining to Tepliakov's arrest in 1826 are found in Tsentral'nyi Gosudarstvennyi Voenno-Istoricheskii Arkhiv, f. 1, op. 1, d. 6285 and Tsentral'nyi Gosudarstvennyi Istoricheskii Arkhiv, f. 1280, op. 1 (1826 g.), no. 6. Documents pertaining to Tepliakov's imprisonment and exile in 1826 are located in Gosudarstvennyi Arkhiv Rossiiskoi Federatsii (formerly TsGAOR), f. 109, III otd., I eksp., op. 5, no. 100.

Fedor Ivanovich Tiutchev

(23 November 1803 – 15 July 1873)

Anatoly Liberman
University of Minnesota

BOOKS: *Stikhotvoreniia,* edited by Ivan Sergeevich Turgenev (St. Petersburg: Eduard Prats, 1854);

Stikhotvoreniia, edited by Ivan Sergeevich Aksakov and I. F. Tiutchev (Moscow: A. I. Mamontov, 1868).

Editions and Collections: *Novonaidennye stikhotvoreniia F. I. Tiutcheva,* edited by Aksakov (Moscow: Tip. Lebedeva, 1879);

Sochineniia. Stikhotvoreniia i politicheskie stat'i, edited by Appolon Nikolaevich Maikov (St. Petersburg: Tip. Trenke i Fiusno, 1886);

Polnoe sobranie sochinenii, sixth edition, corrected and expanded, edited by Petr Vasil'evich Bykov (St. Petersburg: t-vo A. F. Marksa, 1911);

Politicheskiia stat'i, edited by Bykov (St. Petersburg: t-vo A. F. Marksa, n.d.);

Tiutcheviana. Epigrammy, aforizmy i ostroty F. I. Tiutcheva, preface by Georgii Ivanovich Chulkov (Moscow: Kostry, 1922);

Novye stikhotvoreniia, edited by Chulkov (Moscow-Leningrad: "Krug," 1926);

Polnoe sobranie stikhotvorenii, 2 volumes, edited by Chulkov (Moscow-Leningrad: Academia, 1933–1934);

Stikhotvoreniia, edited by Chulkov (Moscow: Khudozhestvennaia literatura, 1935);

Stikhotvoreniia, edited by Vasilii Vasil'evich Gippius and Kirill Vasil'evich Pigarev (Leningrad: Sovetskii pisatel', 1936);

Polnoe sobranie stikhotvorenii, edited by Gippius and Pigarev (Leningrad: Sovetskii pisatel', 1939);

Izbrannye stikhotvoreniia, introduction by V. V. Tiutchev (New York: Izdatel'stvo imeni Chekhova, 1952);

Stikhotvoreniia, edited by Dmitrii Dmitrievich Blagoi (Leningrad: Sovetskii pisatel', 1953);

Polnoe sobranie stikhotvorenii, edited by Pigarev (Leningrad: Sovetskii pisatel', 1957);

Stikhotvoreniia. Pis'ma, edited by Pigarev (Moscow: Goslitizdat, 1957);

Stikhotvoreniia, edited by Naum Iakovlevich Berkovsky and Nina V. Koroleva (Moscow-Leningrad: Sovetskii pisatel', 1962);

Lirika, edited by Pigarev (Moscow: Khudozhestvennaia literatura, 1963); expanded edition, 2 volumes (Moscow: Nauka, 1965);

Stikhotvoreniia. Pis'ma, edited by Evgenii Nikolaevich Lebedev (Moscow: Sovremennik, 1978);

Sochineniia v dvukh tomakh (Moscow: Pravda, 1980);

Izbrannoe (Moscow: Moskovskii rabochii, 1985);

Stikhotvoreniia, edited by Lev Ozerov (Moscow: Khudozhestvennaia literatura, 1985);

Polnoe sobranie stikhotvorenii, edited by Aleksandr A. Nikolaev (Leningrad: Sovetskii pisatel', 1987);

Stikhotvoreniia, pis'ma, vospominaniia sovremennikov, edited by Liia Nikolaevna Kuzina (Moscow: Pravda, 1988);

Russkaia zvezda. Stikhi, stat'i, pis'ma, edited by Viktor Kochetkov (Moscow: "Russkaia kniga," 1993);

Volshebnaia struna. Stikhotvoreniia (Moscow: Letopis', 1996).

Editions in English: *Versions from Fyodor Tyutchev, 1803–1873,* translated by Charles Tomlinson (London: Oxford University Press, 1960);

Poems & Political Letters of F. I. Tyutčev, translated by Jesse Zeldin (Knoxville: University of Tennessee Press, 1973);

Poems of Night and Day, translated by Eugene M. Kayden (Boulder: University of Colorado Press, 1974);

On the Heights of Creation: The Lyrics of Fedor Tyutchev, translated by Anatoly Liberman (Greenwich, Conn.: JAI Press, 1993).

OTHER: "Zdes' nekogda moguchii i prekrasnyi. Stikhotvoreniia 1867," *Russkaia literatura,* 2 (1959): 203–205.

A brilliant conversationalist and the author of Slavophile pamphlets, known also for a few anthologized lyrics about nature, Fedor Tiutchev rose to the prominence of a central figure of the Golden Age of Russian literature. His poetry was admired by Nikolai Alekseevich Nekrasov, Ivan Sergeevich Turgenev, Afanasii Afanas'evich Fet, Ivan Aleksandrovich Goncharov, Fyodor Dostoyevsky, and Leo Tolstoy. Even Nikolai Gavrilovich Chernyshevsky and Nikolai Aleksandrovich Dobroliubov, with their demand that poetry serve as the mouthpiece of liberal ideas and their contempt of "art for art's sake," could not resist the charm of Tiutchev's lyrics. Yet, Tiutchev's poetry never enjoyed the popularity that was Aleksandr Pushkin's and Mikhail Iur'evich Lermontov's. With the emergence of superb prose, lyric poetry lost its prestige in Russia; Tiutchev's 1868 collection sold miserably. He was rediscovered at the end of the nineteenth century by the Russian Symbolists, who treated him as their precursor, researched his biography, wrote critical essays about him, and imitated his mannerisms.

After 1917 Tiutchev retained his status as a significant figure, but those in power were embarrassed by his Slavophile sympathies, defense of monarchy, and friendly relations with the royal family. He was never a rebel; preferred Nice, Geneva, and Munich to St. Petersburg; and made his living as a censor. Tiutchev's lines about winter and spring graced anthologies of children's verses, but he was excluded from state-approved school programs. In 1949 his "pan-Slavic and mystic lyrics" incurred the wrath of a party functionary who did not share Tiutchev's liberal views on the role of censorship.

Tiutchev's comeback coincided with the "thaw" in Soviet life. Since the mid 1960s he has remained at the center of critics' attention; the number of books, dissertations, and articles devoted to him has grown rapidly. People often quote the lines "Umom Rossiiu ne poniat'" (Russia cannot be grasped with the mind) and "Nam ne dano predugadat' / kak nashe slovo otzovetsia" (We cannot know what response our word will have). Two songs with Tiutchev's lyrics are performed regularly: Sergei Vasil'evich Rachmaninov's "Vesennie vody" (Spring Freshets) and L. D. Malashkin's "Ia vstretil vas, i vsio byloe" (I met you, and all my past), and a few of his verses remain in most people's memories from early childhood.

Fedor Ivanovich Tiutchev was born on 23 November 1803 in Ovstug in central Russia, where his parents owned an estate. His father, Ivan Nikolaevich Tiutchev, served in the Empress Catherine's Greek Guard, then retired and married Ekaterina L'vovna Tolstaia, a woman from the aristocracy. Ivan Tiutchev was a warm, generous, peaceful man; his wife, on the other hand, was nervous, hypochondriachal, and deeply committed to Russian Orthodoxy. In spite of these apparent differences, Tiutchev's parents lived a harmonious life, and young Fedor was especially loved and spoiled by his mother.

As was customary among the Russian aristocrats at that time, he was educated at home and grew up bilingual, becoming even more fluent in French than in Russian. French was the only language in which he later communicated with his children and the main language of his correspondence. He wrote his political articles in French, but he prayed and (with few exceptions) composed poetry in Russian. He learned Russian from the domestics and serf children on the estate, but later took formal lessons in Russian language and literature through his university days.

When Tiutchev was ten, his parents hired Semen Egorovich Raich, a poet whose influence on his charge was beneficial and lasting, to teach the boy Russian and Latin. Raich instilled in Tiutchev a lifelong love of the classics. Tiutchev made rapid progress, and in 1819, at the age of sixteen, he entered Moscow University, where he studied philology. Though a brilliant young man, Tiutchev was a lazy student, not above cheating at exams. He almost was not allowed to take his final exams, but his mother's aunt, Anna Vasil'evna Osterman (née Tolstaia) interceded with school authorities on his behalf. After serious studying, he earned a degree with honors in October 1821 and entered government service in the Office of Foreign Affairs in February 1822. That year he was posted to the Russian Legation in Munich (Bavaria), thanks to the intervention of his elderly uncle, Count Aleksandr Ivanovich Osterman-Tolstoi, who was posted there as a diplomat.

Impulsive and often irresponsible, Tiutchev was the opposite of the diligent junior employee bent on pleasing his superiors and seeking advancement. This temperament does not mean that he did not relish diplomatic work; he simply did not have the makings of a career diplomat. Tiutchev was, however, passionately interested in the development of world affairs and in politics. Like many Russians living abroad, he became a convinced Slavophile and tried to influence the relations between Russia and the West in accordance with his views.

While in Munich, Tiutchev became embroiled in several love affairs. One of these early loves was Countess Amalia Lerchenfeld, a sixteen-year-old Bavarian girl who later reappeared at critical periods in Tiutchev's life. In 1826, at the age of twenty-three, Tiutchev married a twenty-seven-year-old widow, Bavarian aristocrat Eleanor (Nelly) Peterson (née Bothmer), and plunged into social life. In the parlors of Munich, he met Friedrich Wilhelm Joseph von Schelling and Heinrich Heine, to whom he became especially close. He and Eleanor had three daughters. Their married life was frenzied; they were constantly short of money, mainly because of Tiutchev's small salary, his impracticality in household management, and his generous sense of hospitality. While abroad, he continued to write poetry and sent his lyrics to literary journals (usually those with which Raich was connected). In 1830 the entire family returned to Russia for a visit. The marriage was already beginning to sour, primarily because of Tiutchev's "improvidence, infidelity, and increasingly neurotic behavior," according to Richard A. Gregg.

Tiutchev was a man of tempestuous passions and weak will. He longed for women's love, and his overall brilliance more than made up for his ordinary physique; but once he attained his goal, he felt disillusioned and bored. In 1833 he met Baroness Ernestine Dornberg (née Pfeffel) and fell in love with her. Of all of Tiutchev's liaisons, this one caused Eleanor the most grief. After the birth of her third daughter, Eleanor became depressed and tried to commit suicide with a toy knife, but she eventually recovered.

In 1837 the family again left Germany for Russia. A well-meaning colleague then organized Tiutchev's transfer to Turin, the capital of the Kingdom of Sardinia. Tiutchev, however, was too much in love with Ernestine to take care of business in a regular way. The transfer neither cured him nor mended his first marriage. Eleanor and the children remained in St. Petersburg. On 14 May 1838 she and the children set out for Lübeck on a Russian steamer. When the ship was nearing port, a fire broke out on board. Ivan Sergeevich

Eleanor Bothmer Peterson, Tiutchev's first wife (miniature by I. Sheler, 1830s)

Turgenev, a fellow passenger with whom Eleanor may have had a romantic encounter, records the events in a story, "Pozhar na more" (Fire at Sea, 1883). Exhausted by the ordeal on the ship and from years of emotional abuse, Eleanor died on 27 August 1838 after a short illness. Tiutchev married Ernestine on 17 July 1839, shortly after her husband also died. This double loss cast a shadow on their love: they felt that they had bought their happiness at an inordinate price. By his second wife Tiutchev had three more children: a daughter and two sons.

Tiutchev's neglect of his governmental duties resulted in his discharge and demotion, and between 1839 and 1844 he again lived in Munich, this time in a private capacity. In 1843 he returned to Russia to seek employment and again saw his early love, Amalia Lerchenfeld (now Krüdener). Her intercession with Count Aleksandr Khristoforovich Benckendorff led to a brief assignment in Germany, after which Tiutchev returned to Russia permanently in the autumn of 1844.

In 1836 Ivan Sergeevich Gagarin, a former fellow diplomat, brought a collection of Tiutchev's lyrics to the poet Prince Petr Andreevich Viazemsky, who showed them to Vasilii Andreevich Zhukovsky; the latter forwarded them to Aleksandr Pushkin, and the lyrics appeared in Pushkin's journal, *Sovremennik* (The Contemporary). Some reviewers praised the lyrics, while others found fault with them, but their appearance did not become an event in Russian literary life.

Reading Tiutchev in English offers only a pale reflection of the original. Tiutchev used end rhyme and strict poetical meters. His rhyme and the strophic organization of his lyrics display great variety. He often alternated short and long lines. He was fond of using a word important to him three or four times within narrow space, and since several recurring words are often combined in the same lyric, they form a polyphonic whole, a kind of verbal fugue. Tiutchev depended on sound effects: alliteration, assonance, word pairs bound by rhyme, and puns. He used "dulcet language" for describing the south and words with jarring consonant groups when speaking about tragic situations. He had a penchant for archaic words and deliberately complicated syntax. His vocabulary is rich, but his favorite words, such as *skudnyi* (meager) applied to *krov'* (blood), are sometimes idiosyncratic, while others, such as *zhivoi* (living) and *veiat'* (waft), are used so often that they almost lose their dictionary meaning and become signs of specifically Tiutchevian moods and situations. Since in Tiutchev's lyrics content and form are merged to an especially high degree, the losses in translation are obvious.

Tiutchev's lyrics are short and usually devoid of plot. They make an impression only when they are read together, in cycles. Turgenev predicted—accurately, as it appeared—that Tiutchev would never appeal to a broad readership. Indeed, the public missed Tiutchev while he lived and forgot him soon after he died. Yet, his reputation among the connoisseurs is deserved: his lyrics sound as modern at the end of the twentieth century as they did at the end of the nineteenth to the Symbolists and perhaps more modern than in the 1830s and 1860s. Students and scholars in the English-speaking world who can understand the Russian originals often prefer him to Lermontov and even to Pushkin.

The 1987 edition of Tiutchev's collected poetry includes 402 lyrics. Fifty of them are versified telegrams and other poems written in French, and forty are translations. Out of the remaining items, close to sixty are about nature. In fact, there are more, for landscape often constitutes the major part of Tiutchev's lyrics about love and about Russia. Tiutchev, to use Semen Liudvigovich Frank's words, regarded his moods as manifestations of cosmic being. Nature was for him a complex of living forces and not simply material in the artist's hand.

In his 1836 poetical manifesto "Ne to, chto mnite vy, priroda" Tiutchev wrote: "Nature is not what you think it to be: / It is not a mask or a soulless image; / It has a soul, it has freedom, / It has love, it has its own tongue. . . . " He felt compassion mixed with scorn for those who view nature as a dead object; "such people" live in darkness and miss the breath of the suns (Tiutchev's plural) and the life of sea waves: "The sunrays did not descend into their soul, / Spring did not bloom in their breast, / Forests did not speak in their presence, / And the starry night was mute. // At night, a thunderstorm / Did not ask for their advice, / While addressing them / In otherworld tongues."

Tiutchev's favorite characters are inseparable from nature, as he felt himself to be. In "Na dreve chelovechestva vysokom" (On mankind's lofty tree, 1832) he describes Johann Wolfgang von Goethe as the best leaf on the tree of humanity, a leaf nurtured by the purest sap of the tree and reared by the rays of the sun. Tiutchev seeks the support of nature wherever he can. While the speaker's beloved is dying in the poem "Ves' den' ona lezhala v zabyt'i" (All day she lay oblivious, 1864–1865), the rain is pattering merrily on the leaves outside the window. This description is not merely a parallel used for the sake of contrast. Death (like life, but more pointedly) is a cosmic phenomenon, and Tiutchev needs the rain and the leaves as an indispensable environment.

Nature was the measure of all things for Tiutchev. He noticed ties between an autumn evening and human anguish, for example, in "Osennii vecher" (Autumn Evening, 1830): "all is on the wane, all is debilitated, and on everything/there is that meek smile of decay / which in a being endowed with reason we call / the divine bashfulness of suffering." In "Sei den' ia pomniu, dlia menia" (I remember this day, 1830) he draws a parallel between sunrise and young love: "I remember this day was for me the morning of life's day: / she stood in silence, / her breast heaved like a wave / her cheeks burned like dawn, getting ever hotter and redder! / And suddenly a golden confession of love / burst forth from her like a young sun . . . / and I saw a new world!"

Woman in Tiutchev's poetry is like nature, and conversely, nature is like a woman in love. For example, in "Letnii vecher" (A Summer Evening, circa 1828) he writes:

The earth has already rolled the sun's
incandescent ball from its head,
and the sea wave has swallowed
the peaceful fire of evening.

The bright stars have already
ascended and raised
the firmament's heavy vault
with their moist heads.

The airy river flowing between heaven and earth expands;
the bosom,
no longer oppressed by the heat,
breathes more easily and more freely.

And a sweet tremor has run through
nature's veins like a stream,
as though water from a spring
touched her feet.

The consistent erotic metaphor in this poem is a device Tiutchev used often. Tiutchev's similes in a later poem, "Ne ostyvshaia ot znoiu" (Not having yet cooled from the intense heat, 1851), are of the same type:

The July night, still exuding heat,
was full of brilliance . . .
And the thunder-saturated sky
shook from flashes of silent lightning
over the drab earth . . .

As though heavy eyelashes
rose over the earth,
so that between intermittent flashes
someone's menacing eyes
flared up every now and then. . . .

Nature in Tiutchev's poetry is enigmatic like the human soul, and the complexity of his nature lyrics is not in form but in content. The opposition of content and form in a work of art makes little sense under the best of circumstances, but in the literature of the first half of the nineteenth century hardly anyone else made the message of a lyric so dependent on the ways of expressing it. Hence the puzzlement of Tiutchev's contemporaries and the admiration of modern readers.

The contours of phenomena and objects Tiutchev describes are usually blurred. His protagonist can seldom believe the evidence of his senses, for the hidden meaning of things evades him. Tiutchev is fond of words and phrases such as *polu* (half or semi-) and *kak by* (as though), making his depictions ambiguous. For example, in "Videnie" (Vision, 1828–1829), one of his early lyrics, he writes:

There is an hour, at night, of universal silence,
 and in this hour of signs and miracles,
 the living chariot of creation
rolls undisguisedly into the sanctuary of the heavens.

The night thickens like chaos on the waters;
 oblivion presses dry land like Atlas;
  only the Muse's virgin soul is being
 disturbed by the gods in her prophetic dreams.

The broken word order in the first and last lines of the original makes the reading of this lyric difficult, and all is enigmatic, as it should be in a true vision. What is the chariot of creation, for example, and why is it called living? There are two similes in the text, but Tiutchev's similes make his imagery even more opaque. No one has seen the biblical "chaos on the waters," and one needs to make an effort to reconstruct a missing link: the sky presses Atlas with all its weight, and Atlas transmits the pressure to the earth. Why does the night thicken on the waters, while unconsciousness presses dry land? How is it connected with universal silence, signs, and miracles, and especially with the Muse? Finally, why are her dreams prophetic, and what are they about?

A possible interpretation is that at the moment when night is ready for wonders, they indeed follow: creation reveals its innermost secret, and its chariot appears in full view; then night becomes dark, as it was before the beginning of things when chaos reigned supreme and water covered the surface of the earth. Unconsciousness seems to be the state when thoughts leave a human being and escape into the wide world. Unconsciousness, however, may also mean "loss of identity, severance of ties between people and their surroundings." This horror presses "dry land" (human habitat) with all its weight. The end of the lyric is unexpected, as "Videnie" suddenly becomes a revelation about the birth of poetry. Amid absolute silence, with memory abolished by sleep, the Muse alone knows no quiet and has prophetic dreams. The Muse dreams of poetry, which is not even conceived yet, for the Muse's soul is virgin.

One can understand this lyric in several ways, but the conclusion will remain: Tiutchev is a poet in need of exegesis. In his nature lyrics, more than in his other works, he shows amazing disregard of the reader: the logic of his constructions is concealed, whereas associative ties between words and images abound. This approach to art (not only to literature) is typical of twentieth-century masters. Tiutchev's contemporaries preferred parallelisms of the type "and so it is with me" (such as, the sail is a rebel, and I try to transcend the limits of being; or, the autumn day is gloomy, and I am lonely and unhappy). The riddling element of Tiutchev's works constitutes their most attractive part.

Tiutchev's landscape is conventional even when it is full of subtly observed details. In his descriptions he relies not on such details but on conglomerations of them, that is, on recurring themes. He often describes a beautiful southern world (Italy, summer, myrtles, laurel trees, murmuring waves, marble arcades) and an ugly northern world (Russia, cold, ice, snow, meager vegetation, a river frozen over). Both are emotional states rather than geographical concepts: in the south one is happy; in the north, miserable.

Tiutchev in 1838 (portrait by I. Rechberg, Muranovo, Tiutchev Estate Museum, Moscow)

In 1849 Tiutchev wrote "Vnov' tvoi ia vizhy ochi" (Once again I see your eyes), a poem with a sensuous stanza: "The swaying of slender laurels / Disturbs the blue air, / The soft breath of the sea / Blows through the summer heat. / Golden grapes ripen / The whole day in the sun, / And the past from days immemorial / Wafts from under marble arcades." By that time Tiutchev had known Italy from personal experience, but its image, once inspired by Goethe, remained unchanged from the 1820s: the real country managed to live up to its poetical description surprisingly well. Ten years later, in October 1859, Tiutchev was returning from Königsberg to St. Petersburg. In "Na vozvratnom puti" (On the Way Back) he describes what he saw:

> My native landscape.... Under the smoky pall
>   of a huge snow-laden cloud,
> the blue distance looms, with its sullen forest
>   enveloped in the autumn murk ...
> Everything is so bare, empty, vast,
>   monotonous, and mute ...
> Only here and there blotches of stagnant water
>   show through the crust of early ice.
>
> No sounds, no colors, no movement.
>   Life has passed away, and, obedient to his fate,
> man—as though in the unconsciousness
>   of exhaustion—dreams of himself.

This lyric was sent by Tiutchev to his daughter in a letter in which he says that when he was crossing the border, the sun shone brightly, though not on rose bushes or orange trees but on "young, fresh icicles." The north called for a picture of all-enveloping gloom.

Turgenev remarked in *Sovremennik* in 1854 that Tiutchev's world was small but that he knew every inch of it. Tiutchev was indeed repetitive. He always looked for the same supports and had the ability to describe the same scene in different ways, but his world was neither small nor devoid of variety. The angle from which he observed nature was what seldom changed. For instance, he primarily noticed things with short life spans. In "Obveian vesheiu dremotoi" (Fanned by a prophetic drowsiness, 1850) he observes an early yellow leaf fall spinning to the road after a shower. He exclaims: "How beautiful are things that are fading! / What attraction lurks in what bloomed / And lived and now smiles so feebly, / So weakly for the last time!" All phenomena attracted him at their transitory moments, which explains his penchant for such times as dusk, the minutes before sunrise, or the sight of a rainbow. Autumn and spring were more interesting to him than winter and summer because they are intermediate seasons, and he described every situation in such a way that it began to look like a passing stage. While viewing a picture of a tranquil autumn evening in "Est' v oseni pervonachal'noi" (There is in early autumn, 1857), he does not forget to add that winter storms are not a long way off and reminds readers, if even in an oblique way, that the tranquility is not as permanent as it seems. He recognized that a pitch-dark December morning would soon yield to the brilliance of day and rejoiced in that fact with lyrics such as "Dekabr'skoe utro" (December Morning, 1859) and "Molchit somnitel'no Vostok" (The East is mute because of doubt, 1865).

One of Tiutchev's most prominent themes is the contrast of day and night, though he primarily explored night. He distinguished more hues after sunset than when the sun was in the sky. In a paradoxical way, day and night change places in his poetry. Another favorite theme is the contrast of heaven and earth, with a variation: the mountain and the valley. Unbounded vertical space interested Tiutchev, whereas journeys (whatever the surrounding landscape) exhausted him.

One early piece about heaven and earth is "Utro v gorakh" (Morning in the Mountains, 1829):

> The heavenly azure laughs
> Washed in the early morning storm,
> And between the mountains the valley
> Winds "dewyly" like a light ribbon ...

'Tis only the slope of the tallest mountains
That the mists half-cover,
As though the airy ruins
Of chambers created by magic.

This piece is typical in many ways. It adumbrates Tiutchev's similar lyrics in which the poet's eye moves up or down (more often up) and notices an edifice, sometimes a temple, gracing the pinnacle. It is also full of hints that can be deciphered only if the entire context of Tiutchev's poetry is known. Tiutchev used the verb "laugh" rarely, and prefers to apply it to nature, especially to assuagement after a storm. Dew is another sign of peace in his lyrics. The mist covering only the tallest mountains halfway through is another riddle of the type in "Videnie." If the lower mountains are covered completely, the speaker could not have seen the "light ribbon" of the valley. If the mist is actually clouds, then the azure would not have been "laughing" after the storm. The description of the valley as a ribbon—a shining path—might indicate that the poet is looking at the landscape from a great height. Tiutchev was an excellent observer of the world he saw, but it is sometimes difficult for readers to reconstruct the picture that inspired him. This approach to the poetic word allowed later critics to speak about Tiutchev's impressionism.

Although there is no agreement among critics about what the term "literary impressionism" means, there are some obvious similarities between Tiutchev's landscapes and those of Claude Monet. Tiutchev had a personal, intimate attitude toward the wind. It carried messages, revealed terrible secrets of being, and reminded him of new and unexpected transitions. His favorite verb was *(ob)veiat'* (waft or blow): he used it (together with a noun derived from it) thirty-four times. A more domineering element in Tiutchev's poetry, however, as in Monet's paintings, is water. He described it in every possible form—from mighty rivers and ravaging seas to springs, brooks, showers, fountains, raindrops, and tears. Water takes away sorrow, buries fateful secrets, sings on the first day of creation, invites one to merge with it, and gives shelter to lovers. In "Poslednii kataklizm" (The Last Cataclysm, not later than 1824) Tiutchev writes, "When the last hour of nature strikes, / The composition of earthly parts will be destroyed: / All visible things will again be covered with waters, / And God's image will be reflected in them." Water is also a friend in "Na Neve" (On the Neva, 1850):

Once again a star plays
In the light ripples of the Neva waves,
And again love entrusts
Its boat to them.

And between the waves and the star,
The boat glides as though
In a dream and carries
Two ghosts in it.

Do the children of indolence
Spend their nightly leisure here?
Or are two blessed shadows
Leaving this world?

O you, sea-like, overflowing,
Unspeakably luxuriant wave,
Give shelter in your expanse
To the secret of the humble boat!

Contrary to water, fire is evil in Tiutchev's poetry; brilliance and glitter are also dangerous because of their close relationship to flame, though Tiutchev enjoyed light.

For many years (until the late 1980s) official literary scholarship in Russia shared with the other historical sciences the dogma of unilinear evolution: just as society was supposed to pass through a series of so-called formations (primitive communal system, slavery, feudalism, capitalism, socialism) and finally reach communism, so literature was supposed to develop in a preordained direction: leave behind the rigidity of classicism, overcome Romantic excesses, sober down in the forms of critical realism, and mature on the heights of socialist realism. The flood of Tiutchev scholarship has been gaining momentum only since the 1960s, but the question about Tiutchev's path toward realism was asked several times between roughly 1930 and 1980. The answer was predictable: Tiutchev allegedly learned, as time went on, to describe things as he saw them and thus approached realism. It is customary to take two similar poems of his from different periods, compare them, and draw this conclusion.

An example of this type of criticism is the comparison of "Na vozvratnom puti" with "Zdes', gde tak vialo svod nebesnyi" (Here where the firmament so sluggishly), a poem Tiutchev wrote upon his return to Russia for half a year in 1830. He left Munich in the middle of May, so it was a late spring landscape that welcomed him home. In the latter poem he describes the day of his arrival:

Here, where the impotent firmament
Looks at the jejune earth,
Here, plunged into an iron sleep,
Tired nature is dozing . . .

Only in a few places pale birch trees,
Scraggly shrubs, and gray
Lichen disturb the deadly quiet,
Like feverish dreams.

Some commentators, puzzled by the drab color of the sky and other autumnal details, think that the picture reflects a different journey and date the poem to 1829, but this hypothesis is unnecessary. In October 1859, writing "Na vozvratnom puti," Tiutchev saw brilliant sunshine and "young, fresh icicles" but mentioned only a sullen forest, autumn murk, a bare plain, and blotches of stagnant water, with everything also plunged into sleep ("man . . . dreaming of himself"). Tiutchev's native landscape in both poems is conventional: all is gloomy and dull, and the objects that could have enlivened the wasteland strike one as even more repulsive than the wasteland itself. In the earlier poem, Tiutchev has taken in everything from the sky to barren soil and discerns trees, shrubs, and lichen (notably enumerated in order of diminishing size). In the 1859 poem details are also present, but they are less graphic, so in a way the earlier piece can be seen as more "realistic." In fact, however, both are equally realistic (the poet describes natural objects with utmost care) and equally conventional (they are pictures of the repellent "northern world"). Nothing changed from 1830 to 1859.

Of special interest are Tiutchev's two lyrics about autumn. The first of these is "Osennii vecher," in which the landscape is depicted thus:

> There is in the transparency of autumn evenings
> Some touching, mysterious charm! . . .
> The ominous brilliance and mixed colors of the trees,
> The barely audible languid rustling of dark red leaves,
> The misty and quiet azure
> Over the sadly orphaned earth,
> And as a premonition of approaching storms,
> Gusts of the sharp, cold wind. . . .

Twenty-seven years later, in "Est' v oseni pervonachal'noi" he wrote:

> There is in the early days of autumn
> A short but irresistibly beautiful period:
> The whole day is as though made of crystal,
> And the evenings are azure bright. . . .
>
> Where a brisk sickle went back and forth,
> Where grain fell, all is now bare, all is open;
> Only a thin thread of the spider's web
> Glistens in an idle furrow.
>
> The air is getting empty, birds can no longer be heard,
> But the first winter storms are still a long way off,
> And the quiet, warm azure pours
> Onto the resting field. . . .

Once again the sharpness of Tiutchev's vision is evident in both poems: he discerns every hue, just as he hears the weakest rustle, and he does not miss even a thread of the spider's web. Both lyrics are among his best, but there is no progress in the later one with regard to so-called realism.

It is true that with years Tiutchev learned the technique of foregrounding (a thread shown close up makes a strong impression because the rest of the picture is indistinct) and that the ominous landscapes of his youth gave way to pictures in which the pacifying rather than fateful aspects of nature hold sway, but the method of description did not change. It is hardly possible to detect "periods" in Tiutchev's creative life, and that is why dating his poetry is so difficult. A lyric such as "Kak khorosho ty, o more nochnoe" (How beautiful you are, o sea at night, 1865) could have been written by him at any time between 1825 and 1870:

> How beautiful you are, o sea at night;
> Here you are like azure, there you are dark blue . . .
> Moonlit, it moves, breathes, and shines,
> As though it were alive . . .
>
> In its infinite, boundless expanse,
> There are brilliance, motion, rumbling, and thunder . . .
> How beautiful you are in the nightly silence,
> O sea suffused with tarnished brilliance!
>
> O great brine,
> Whose triumph do you celebrate?
> The waves dash forward through thunder and sheen,
> While the delicate stars look down.
>
> In this agitation, in this sheen,
> I stand lost, as though in a dream.
> Oh, how I wish I could drown
> My soul in this beauty. . . .

This poem is a classic outburst of a young romantic poet longing to merge with nature, reminiscent of Zhukovsky's elegy "More" (The Sea, 1822) and of many passages in Lermontov, but Tiutchev wrote this piece in 1865, when he was sixty-two years old.

Tiutchev's love and nature lyrics are often hard to separate. The cosmic character of the soul so typical of him results in the frequent merger of the two. Certain motifs—especially sleep and storms—are of such importance in Tiutchev's poetry that they override division of his work into groups.

Tiutchev is a poet of sleep and dreams, as though he were trying to escape from himself. "What a mysterious thing is sleep in comparison to the unavoidable banality of real life, be that what it may! And that is why I think that one never lives such a full life as when one sleeps," he wrote to his daughter two months before his death. Sleep is a normal state of man and nature in Tiutchev's work, the highest bliss anyone can attain. Everyone and everything, particularly all that is beautiful, sleeps (and may have dreams) in Tiutchev's lyrics: men, women, children, nature, woods, trees, a harp, a captive, a pilgrim, a shepherd and his herd, the world, the past, the Muse, Pan, Rome, houses, towns, and villages. At least thirty-one epithets are used in his lyrics with the noun denoting sleep. The wounds left by day will be healed by night's sleep. Nature smiles while it sleeps, and being in love is like being asleep ("as if in a dream"). The intersection of the themes "sleep" and "nature" led to some of Tiutchev's best erotic poems. He wrote several poems depicting a couple in a boat. The earliest of them—"Sny" (Dreams, 1830)—predates "Na Neve" by more than twenty years: "As ocean girds the globe, / So is earthly life surrounded by dreams.... / A magical boat has already come alive in the harbor; / The ebb grows and carries us quickly / Into the measurelessness of the dark waves."

"Polden'" (Midday), written about the same time, describes the young Tiutchev's erotic ideal: nature is asleep (the word "lazily" is repeated), and the satisfied Pan dozes in a cave among the nymphs. In 1850 he created a similar scene, with a secluded room instead of a peaceful cave, and "half-sleep" instead of Pan's doze:

> However hot afternoon's breath through
> The open window may be,
> In this quiet room,
> Where all is tranquil and dark,
>
> Where living fragrance
> Wanders in the dusky shade,
> Plunge into the dusk
> Of half-sleep and rest.
>
> Here a fountain sings incessantly
> Day and night in the corner
> And besprinkles the enchanted murk
> With its unseen drops.
>
> And here, in the glimmer of the half-light,
> Absorbed in a secret passion,
> Wafts the love-sick poet's
> Weightless dream.

One of Tiutchev's best love lyrics, "Smotri, kak roshcha zeleneet" (Watch the Greening Grove), was written in 1857, with nature forming an inalienable part of the scene:

> Watch the greening grove
> Bathed in the scorching sun,
> And in it what tenderness
> Wafts from every bough and every leaf!
>
> Let us enter and sit down above
> The roots nourished by the running spring,
> Where, enveloped in their murk,
> It whispers something in the mute darkness.

Ernestine Pfeffel Dornberg, Tiutchev's second wife (portrait by F. Dürch, 1840, Muranovo, Tiutchev Estate Museum, Moscow)

> Over us the tree tops rave
> Immersed in the midday heat,
> And only sometimes, the eagle's
> Scream reaches us from the height.

"Watch," a word that opens many lyrics by Tiutchev, is not a formal invitation to view a place that has caught the poet's fancy: both he and his companion are present throughout the scene as careful observers. The couple sitting on the roots of the tree is part of the landscape. The grove becomes a symbol of a flowering world: the two people see it blooming and saturated with languor; then the earth whispers its secrets to them; and finally they become privy to the mystery of the sky. At first sight, the word "scorching" is out of harmony with "tenderness," but the picture is a typical Tiutchevian midday. Only when the sun makes everything torrid and the world is plunged into the midday murk can Tiutchev hear an eagle in the heavens and a spring winding its way deep in the ground.

Tiutchev's landscapes with human figures in the foreground, such as lovers in a grove or two in a boat, are classical, but they are painted in such a manner that they transcend their time period. One notes in them the chaste forms of classicism, the tempestuous palette of the Romantics, and the dim beauty of Symbolists. "Ia pomniu vremia zolotoe" (I Remember the Golden Time), written between 1834 and 1836, depicts another idyllic scene of a couple on a hillside. The setting chosen by Tiutchev for his love scene is operatic: the last minutes of a beautiful day, a heap of ruins, a river down in the valley, a woman described as a "young fairy," and apple trees shedding their petals. On the other hand, it is the setting of an ancient myth, which accords perfectly with the idea of golden time. The young people are like Adam and Eve in the Garden of Eden. The scene is mythologized to such an extent that its banality is barely noticeable.

"Letnii vecher," in which nature is presented as experiencing a tremor, so that the movement from the head of the sun to the human breast and to the feet of nature results in a veiled erotic picture, is not isolated in Tiutchev. On 31 December 1852 he wrote the lyric "Charodeikoiu zimoiu" (Enchanted by Winter, the sorceress), in which he describes a forest "under a snowy veil" as being "Bewitched in a magic sleep." Since the forest is asleep, it is ready for "miracles and signs," yet its relations with the sun are ambiguous: when the sun darts a "slanting ray" at it, no response is seen, but the ray "flares up and shines / With inexpressible, blinding beauty." For once, nature is devoid of sensuousness; it is "wondrous" but not quite real (the forest is "Neither dead nor alive"). Likewise, the ray is not real, for it is unable to arouse a tremor in the forest (passion is only imitated–just a flush).

Such are some of Tiutchev's love idylls. In most of his lyrics, however, love emerges as a tragic obsession and an evil force. This treatment is especially obvious in the poems written in the early 1850s and referred to by literary historians as the Denis'eva cycle. In 1850 Tiutchev had fallen in love with twenty-four-year-old Elena Aleksandrovna Denis'eva, a niece of an inspector of the Smolny Institute, where two of Tiutchev's daughters were being educated. Tiutchev never considered divorce, and between 1850 and 1864 he had two families. He did not care about propriety, appearing with Denis'eva in public and giving his name to their children, but it was all he could do to balance his life between his jealous mistress and his wife. In 1864 Denis'eva died of consumption. Of their three children only one son reached adulthood. Denis'eva's death was a terrible blow to Tiutchev, as Eleanor's had been: according to family legend, Tiutchev turned gray in one night. Yet, he kept seeking new entertainments and excitements. His eldest daughter looked upon her father's constant infatuations as pathological.

Soon after Denis'eva became Tiutchev's mistress, he wrote the lines: "Oh, how murderously we love, / How in the wanton blindness of passions / We destroy that the more brutally / Which is especially dear to our heart!" ("O kak ubiistvenno my liubim," Oh, how murderously we love). Oscar Wilde's "Yet each man kills the thing he loves" (from his *Ballad of Reading Gaol*, 1898) has been compared to these lines. He also composed the short lyric "Predopredelenie" (Predestination, 1851 or 1852), in which he describes love as "a union of a soul with a kindred soul, / Their merger, their coalition, / Their fatal fusion, / And . . . their fatal duel."

Similar motifs dominate the earlier lyrics inspired by his love for Ernestine; these lyrics can be called the Dornberg cycle (1836–1837). Even though Tiutchev, quite naturally, did not disclose the names of the women to whom he dedicated his poems and did not, as a general rule, date his manuscripts (so the addressees of his works often remain a matter of dispute), the message of the lyrics written around the time of Eleanor's death and his marriage to Ernestine cannot be mistaken. In a poem from this period titled "Ital'ianskaia Villa," Tiutchev describes a house sheltered from the world by a cypress. It has attained ultimate bliss: like Pan reposing in an inaccessible cave, like the enamored poet in a dark room full of fragrance, the villa sleeps behind shadowy trees. A fountain (a sign of serenity in Tiutchev's works) murmurs in the corner. Then everything is disrupted when the speaker and his companion enter, "and some wondrous, nearly inaudible / Voice whispered, as though in a dream: // 'What is it, friend? Or is it true that / That life, alas! which then flowed in us, / That evil life, with its rebellious fervor, / Crossed the guarded threshold?'" In Tiutchev's poetry, nature reacts to human emotions, rather than the other way around. The villa is paradise on earth; it is a blessed Elysian ghost protected by Heaven. The "rebellious" two who trespass on its peace shatter the immovable perfection of nature.

The most conspicuous image binding the poems of 1836–1837 is fire: from the fire of love to hellish fire. These poems are replete with eroticism. Tiutchev was prone to celebrate the triumph of instincts and felt attracted by women who could no longer feel shame. When the quiet dawn of love yielded to the storm of passion in his lyrics, his motifs changed from burning cheeks and the rising sun to longing for the sinful, morbid, and ruinous, for "sullen" lust and faithlessness in matrimony. He compares two women he knew intimately in "Liubliu glaza tvoi, moi drug" (I love your eyes, my friend, circa 1836), concluding that the "stronger attraction" came not from eyes raised toward heaven but from "Downcast eyes at the moment / Of a passionate kiss," eyes that reveal the "dull, lackluster flame of desire."

"S kakoiu negoiu, s kakoi toskoi vliublennoi" (With what tenderness, with what languor of love, 1840) epitomizes the Dornberg cycle. Tiutchev addresses a woman "overwhelmed by your feeling, by the fullness of your love," and describes how she bursts into tears looking at her lover and then falls asleep peacefully in his comforting arms. The situation described in this lyric partly recurs in the Denis'eva cycle. The woman suffers because her love brings her only pain and misfortune. The passive man is able to offer some consolation; he is tender and protective, but the main cure is sleep. The woman's feeling is incomparably stronger than the poet's. Her lover stands by and does not miss a single detail of what he sees; the love he inspires overshadows for him the woman's anguish. The beginning of Tiutchev's romances resembles an awakening, and bliss is attained soon. "Na Neve," which, most probably, opens the Denis'eva cycle, is symbolic: the tempestuous Tiutchev created a character tossed about by waves and deriving the greatest pleasure from his state, a lover whose infatuation is transitory, just a dream. As long as he is happy, he wants to forget himself in sleep, but then "murderous love" appears, followed by disillusionment and late repentance.

Tiutchev's love lyrics share some peculiarities with his landscapes: they include all kinds of details, but the overall picture is vague. His heroines lack biographical features. In Tiutchev's love poetry the struggle is not so much between the man and the woman as it is between both of them and fate, which may or may not have a concrete form (for example, a mortal disease or people's cruelty). Today it is not always understood how innovative these lyrics were. For Pushkin and his young contemporaries love was an expression of sensuousness: suffering could be caused by separation or lack of reciprocity. Tiutchev's lovers are unhappy in love, and their feeling breeds "evil life." It is as though men and women were doomed to reach the peak of their misery through the experience they desired and treasured most.

Tiutchev had an inherently tragic vision: in the brightness of almost any day he discerned shadows, and in the fragrance around him he sensed poison. He never forgot that beauty would perish (despite some protestations to the contrary in his later lyrics) and accepted this law as a fact of life. Joy (even in love) struck him as an incomprehensible aberration; thus, the beauty of the season in "Leto 1854" (Summer 1854) inspires suspicion in the speaker: "I watch this sheen, / This glitter with anxious eyes . . . / Is someone making fun of us? / Whence is this present?"

Sometime between July 1850 and the middle of 1851, Tiutchev composed "Ne govori: menia on, kak i prezhde, liubit" (Don't say: he loves me as before) as a kind of drama: an exchange of the hero's and the heroine's monologues. The man (in the woman's lament) is presented as a tyrant who loves murderously, a villain with a knife. The woman's speech is like a wail of pain; long lines alternate with short ones. In the man's monologue (which sounds like an answer to the heroine's) the lines are long and of equal length: a disappointed lover can obviously control his speech better than a woman driven to despair. Yet, he is also lost in an anacoluthon (an ill-constructed sentence in which the syntax of the second part is not in agreement with that of the first part) in line 2 and repeats, as if stammering, the pronoun "I" in lines 3 and 4. The woman's speech is full of repetition; it resembles sobbing, as she is literally short of breath. The man appears unworthy of the feeling he has conjured up and is motivated by jealousy more than by love. The central word of the first soliloquy—"life"—is picked up by the man and twisted around. The woman is supposed to believe her lover, but he believes in nothing. She protests:

Don't say: he loves me as before
And treasures me as before . . .
Oh, no! He is ruining my life most cruelly,
Though I see that a knife trembles in his hand.

Now in a fury, now in tears,
Grieving, indignant, entranced, deeply wounded,
I suffer rather than live . . . I live by him, by him alone
But this life . . . Oh, how bitter it is!

He measures air for me so parsimoniously, so thriftily . . .
One does not measure it so for a sworn enemy . . .
Ah, it is getting ever more difficult for me to breathe;
I can still breathe, but I can no longer live.

Another poem of this cycle reinforces the pain inherent in the love Tiutchev expresses: in "O, ne trevozh' menia ukorom spravedlivym" (Oh, don't trouble me with your well-deserved rebuke, 1851–1852), the speaker tells his lover that "of the two of us your lot is more envious: / You love sincerely and passionately, / And I— I am looking at you with jealous irritation." He further describes himself as "the lifeless idol of your living soul."

Later, weak men unworthy of the women loving them became familiar figures in nineteenth-century Russian prose, but none of them possessed Tiutchev's ability to enjoy the theater of broken love, and none displayed an erotic attachment to the spectacle of feminine suffering. A male lover in Tiutchev, although his heart is ready to break, revels in the woman's agony and uses it as a source of his strength.

Two poems are especially noteworthy with regard to "love's theater." The first of them is "Vostok belel.

Manuscript for Tiutchev's poem "Pod dykhan'em nepogody" (Under the breath of a storm) (from Lirika *[Lyrics], edited by Kirill Vasil'evich Pigarev, 1965)*

Lad'ia katilas'" (The east whitened. The boat rolled, circa 1835), an enigmatic poem that once again features a boat with two lovers, though the focus of the description is on the woman. The second figure (presumably a man) is not mentioned, but he must be in the boat to see and register everything. Ellipses after each stanza indicate intermissions. The first stanza establishes the scene: a couple on a sailboat at sunrise. In the second stanza the woman throws back her veil; a prayer unites her with God; and the sky, responsive to her prayer, is "jubilant" (in the first stanza the sea "palpitates" like a human heart). Ecstasy pervades the second stanza, but the third tells of some tragedy as the woman turns her face away while "fiery drops" stream down her cheeks. The fiery drops can only be tears; they are fiery because the sun is now bright in the east, but they also suggest blood.

Another poem that presents a dramatic scene is "Ona sidela na polu" (She sat on the floor, 1858):

> She sat on the floor
> And was sorting out a heap of letters;
> She picked them up like cold ashes
> And threw them down.
>
> She took the familiar sheets
> And looked at them so wondrously,
> As souls look down from their heights
> At the body they deserted.
>
> Oh, how much life irretrievably
> Gone there was here,
> How many desolate minutes,
> How much love and ruined happiness! . . .
>
> I stood aside in silence
> And was ready to fall down to my knees,
> And I was so unspeakably sad,
> As though a darling shadow were near.

According to family legend, the person portrayed in this lyric is Ernestine, who is believed to have destroyed her early correspondence with Tiutchev. One cannot be certain of Tiutchev's addressees, however, for he often depicted the same woman in different situations.

One of his most famous love lyrics is "Posledniaia liubov'" (Last Love), written sometime between the middle of 1851 and the beginning of 1854. The speaker is nearing the end of his life, but his love is still tender: "Shine, shine, farewell light / Of last love, of eventide!" He calls last love "both bliss and hopelessness." In this poem "Evening's peaceful fire," the flaming sunset described by him so many times, now becomes a symbol of his own life.

In July 1870 Tiutchev met up again with someone whom he had known and admired in his youth, and wrote "K. B." ("Ia vstretil vas, i vse byloe"). It is believed that both this poem and "Ia pomniu vremia zolotoe" have the same addressee, because the phrase "golden time" recurs, but there is some disagreement about who this woman was; Amalia Lerchenfeld is one possibility. The initials are unrevealing. The speaker in this poem greets his former companion:

> I met you, and all my past
> Came alive in my withered heart;
> I remembered the golden time,
> And my heart felt so warm . . .
>
> As in late autumn
> There may be days,
> There may be an hour
> When something suddenly stirs in us,
>
> So all enwrapped in the breath
> Of those years' inner fullness,
> I look at your sweet features
> With the long-forgotten ecstasy . . .
>
> As after an age-long separation,
> I look at you as though in a dream,
> And lo! more audible are now the sounds
> That never died in me . . .
>
> This is not a mere recollection,
> This is life coming to speak again;
> Still is the same your charm,
> And still is the same my love! . . .

Tiutchev also touched on things that fall into the purview of philosophy: the universe, life and death, and fate. Many of his lyrics on these themes are among his masterpieces. He liked short pieces in which his thought could be expressed in a succinct, aphoristic form. It should be repeated that the division of Tiutchev's works into categories cannot be sustained in all cases. Not only do his nature lyrics merge with his love lyrics; they are also inseparable from his existential poetry, as follows even from the epigrammatic "Volna i duma" (Wave and Thought, 1851) and "Priroda–sfinks" (Nature is a sphinx).

Tiutchev explored chaos, the uncontrollable forces of the universe, and the disintegration of "earthly parts," to use his phrase from "Poslednii kataklizm." The theme of chaos, together with that of sleep, has equal poignancy for Tiutchev, a master of landscapes (storms, thunder, decay), of erotic poetry, and of meditative lyrics on the essence of being. "O chem ty voesh', vetr nochnoi?" (What are you howling about, nightly wind?, circa 1836), possibly written before the poet was thirty, indicates his long interest in the depths of chaos. The speaker in this poem asks what the "strange voice" of the wailing wind means as it keeps "speaking about incomprehensible anguish." He tells the wind, "Oh, don't sing these frightening songs! / The world of my nocturnal soul / Listens so eagerly to the beloved tale / Of the ancient, ancestral chaos!" The world of this soul "longs to merge with the infinite," but this state can be achieved only when he falls asleep. The wind comes between the poet and his sleep, and an abyss opens up: utter misery accompanies his insomnia. Unable to sleep, he begins to understand the suffering of nature and even of inanimate objects. When the soul sleeps, it is open to higher visions, but when at night it cannot attain rest, it reaches the bottom of the universe, its creative chaos. By day, even storms in the poet's breast are harmless because they are asleep.

Tiutchev further explored this theme in "Den' i noch'" (Day and Night, circa 1839) and "Sviataia noch' na nebosklon vzoshla" (Holy night has ascended the firmanent, circa 1849). In the first poem he writes:

> Over the mysterious world of spirits,
> Over this nameless abyss,
> A golden-threaded pall has been cast
> By the gods' high will.
> Day is this resplendent pall,
> Day, which brings life to the earthborn race
> And heals the soul in pain,
> Day, which is a friend of the mortals and the gods.
>
> But day grows dim—night has arrived;
> Night has come and, having torn
> The cloth of the blissful pall
> From the fateful world, it casts it aside . . .
> And the abyss appears uncovered before us,
> And there is no barrier
> Between it and us—that is why
> Night is so frightening to us.

When Tiutchev was younger, he called night a veil that descends over day and covers its almost vulgar brightness. Here the image is reversed, and day is presented as a temporary mantle thrown over the abyss of night darkness. Night is primary, and day only holds it off for a while. Tiutchev seems to show some ambivalence in "Den' i noch'," because day, uncharacteristically for him, is said to be the healer of human beings and "a friend of the mortals and the gods." Usually Tiutchev longs for the protection of night against the merciless sun. In the second poem he expresses similar sentiments:

> Holy night has ascended the firmament
> And wound off the joyful, pleasant day
> Like a golden pall, the pall thrown over the abyss.
> The external world has receded like a vision . . .
> And man, like a homeless orphan,
> Now stands infirm and naked,
> Face to face with the dark pit.

> He is alone: reason has been abolished,
> And thought has become an orphan;
> He is engulfed in his soul as in an abyss,
> And there is no support, no limit outside . . .
> All that is bright and living
> Seems to be a long-forgotten dream . . .
> And in alien, unsolved nocturnal things
> He recognizes his ancestral heritage.

Students of Tiutchev's poetry have been troubled by the epithet "holy" in this lyric. Why is night holy if it is so awful? "Holy night" is a phrase applied to the Nativity, but Tiutchev does not seem to refer to the New Testament in this line. Apparently, holy night is the time when man learns the truth about nature and himself. When all things return to their original state, a complete unity with the godhead is achieved, and Tiutchev glorifies the unity. Night is holy because it comes as close as possible to chaos, the source of all things.

It has been a tradition of long standing to call Tiutchev's lyrics philosophical and to trace his dealings with chaos to Schelling. Tiutchev's interest in Schelling is an established fact, but he was also strongly influenced by Horace, and in the cosmopolitan atmosphere of Munich he was closer to French culture than to German. Tiutchev was a master of encoding his messages; hence the density of his lyrics and the illusion of their "philosophical" profundity. His profundity is his style, and his philosophy is his poetical thought.

One of Tiutchev's noteworthy lyrics on the nature of human relations is called "Molchi, skryvaisia i tai" (Silentium!), written circa 1830:

> Molchi, skryvaisia i tai
> I chuvstva i mechty svoi—
> Puskai v dushevnoi glubine
> Vstaiut i zakhodiat one
> Bezmolvno, kak zvezdy v nochi,—
> Liubuisia imi—i molchi.
>
> Kak serdtsu vyskazat' sebia?
> Drugomu kak poniat' tebia?
> Poimet li on, chem ty zhivesh'?
> Mysl' izrechennaia est' lozh'.
> Vzryvaia, vozmutish' kliuchi,—
> Pitaisia imi—i molchi.
>
> Lish' zhit' v sebe samom umei—
> Est' tselyi mir v dushe tvoei
> Tainstvenno-volshebnykh dum;
> Ikh oglushit naruzhnyi shum,
> Dnevnye razgoniat luchi,—
> Vnimai ikh pen'iu—i molchi! . . .
>
> (Keep silent, hide and conceal
> Your feelings and your dreams—
> Let them ascend and descend

Elena Aleksandrovna Denis'eva, Tiutchev's mistress, and their daughter, Elena Tiutcheva

Without a sound in your soul's depth
Like the stars at night,–
Admire them–and keep silent.

How can one's heart express itself?
How can another person understand you?
Will that person understand what you live by?
A thought, once uttered, is a lie.
While disrupting springs, you will disturb them,–
Feed on them–and keep silent.

Learn to live only in yourself–
There is, in your soul, a whole world
Of mysteriously magical thoughts;
They will be deafened by the outside noise
And dispelled by the rays of day,–
Listen to their singing–and keep silent! . . .)

This lyric is an existential one. It stirs the reader not by its message of "Do not reveal your secrets to people, for you will not be able to communicate them," but by its enigmatic, "mysteriously magical" language. The aphorism "A thought, once uttered, is [or becomes] a lie" has been quoted many times. Its attraction is typically Tiutchevian, and it has been interpreted in many ways: as a formula of idealism or of the creative act described by a romantic poet; as the result of Tiutchev's reconciliation with the spiritual corruption of his day; as a protest against this corruption; or as a protest against writing in general. These and many other similar hypotheses cancel one another out, but the hypnosis of the verse remains.

A longing for the word, immortalized in Zhukovsky's rhetorical question "Can the inexpressible be expressed?" is in equal measure peculiar to Tiutchev. The effect of "Molchi, skryvaisia i tai" is produced by the measured tread of its aphorisms (all in masculine rhyme, with the accent on the last syllable), the force of its imperatives, the recurrence of the same command at the end of each stanza, questions, multiple pauses, and changeable meter. The rhetoric of the poem is that of a sermon. The end of each sentence coincides with the end of a line, but the syntax of some periods is blurry.

Sometimes Tiutchev addresses philosophical problems directly, as in his six-line "Problème," written in 1833: "Having rolled down from the mountain, the stone landed in the valley. / How did it fall? Nobody now knows / Whether it went down of *its own* accord / Or whether it was *hurled by someone else's will.* / One century follows upon another, / But nobody has answered this question." In 1865 he wrote "Pevuchest' est' v morskikh volnakh," a programmatic lyric on the relations between the mutinous human being and harmonious nature:

> Sea waves are endowed with singing power,
> And clashes of the elements with harmony;
> An orderly, musical rustle
> Streams through swaying rushes.
>
> All is in perfect accord,
> Each part of nature is in tune with the rest;
> Only we, in our illusory freedom,
> Are aware of being disconsonant with nature.
>
> Whence is this lack of unity?
> Why, in the common chorus,
> Does the soul not sing together with the sea,
> And why does the thinking reed dissent?
>
> From the earth to the farthest stars,
> No response ever comes
> To the cry in the wilderness,
> The soul's desperate protest.

If "Problème" goes back to Tiutchev's meditations on Benedict de Spinoza and Schelling (as is believed), the later lyric had its initial inspiration in Blaise Pascal's aphorism about man being a thinking reed. As usual, one can find congruent thoughts in Schelling; the Latin epigraph of the later poem, "Est in arundineis modulatio musica ripis" (There is musical coherence in rushes growing on the riverbank), was borrowed from the Roman poet Ausonius. The resulting whole, however, is not a patchwork quilt of lines borrowed from the poets and philosophers of different epochs; it is the epitome of Tiutchev's poetic view of the universe. The opening statement is a variation on one of his favorite themes, "singing nature" (water sings especially often in his lyrics). Harmony ties in with singing waves. A perfect order—the Russian word is *stroi* (regular musical arrangement, lack of dissonance or discordance)—always aroused Tiutchev's admiration, and he regularly used biblical allusions (here, to the voice crying in the wilderness) to clinch his argument. The semantic field of music, inaugurated by the word "musica" in the epigraph, is developed with remarkable consistency, as seen in the progression from "singing" to "chorus."

Especially memorable are some of Tiutchev's short existential lyrics, such as "Nam ne dano predugadat'" (It is not given to us to predict, 1869): "It is not given to us to predict / What response our word will have, / And sympathy comes to us / As heavenly grace may. . . ." Tiutchev often wrote about fate. His most dramatic lyric on this subject is called "Dva golosa" (Two Voices, 1850):

> Take courage, o friends, fight tirelessly,
> Even though the forces are not equal and the struggle is hopeless!
> Over you, the luminaries are silent high up;
> Beneath you, there are graves—they are also silent.
>
> Let the gods on their heavenly Olympus enjoy their bliss:
> Their immortality knows nothing about labor and anxiety;
> Anxiety and labor are only for mortal hearts . . .
> Theirs is not victory, theirs is the end.
>
> Take courage, struggle, o brave friends,
> However cruel the fight, however hard the battle may be!
> Over you, there are silent star rings;
> Beneath you, there are mute, deaf coffins.
>
> Let the Olympians watch with envious eyes
> The struggle of indomitable hearts.
> He who, while resisting the enemy, has fallen conquered only by Fate
> Has wrested the wreath of triumph from his hands.

The structure of "Two Voices" rests on a mechanism often employed by Tiutchev: the voices are almost identical, and the solution of the riddle (why two voices if they seemingly repeat each other?) is given only in the coda. The first voice says that victory is not for human hearts (they must perish), while the second agrees that death is man's lot but makes an addition: he who falls overwhelmed by Fate alone has won. Both voices are equally tragic but treat victory and defeat differently.

The voices concern themselves not so much with the warriors as with the gods. Human hearts have something that the blessed gods lack—the ability to feel pain (anxiety) and make a heroic effort. The hero's reward is not glorious death but the joy of battle. The Olympians' happiness is spurious and dull, since their bliss does not have to be attained by risk and courage; the gods realize this disadvantage and envy the excitement they cannot share. Man is doomed but active. The juxtaposition of courage based on faith in destiny and courage that prevails in the teeth of destiny was a theme widely discussed in the 1840s and early 1850s.

Tiutchev often let his creative genius serve politics. Not only did he write essays on Russia and the West, but he also composed epigrams, lampoons, versified addresses, anniversary greetings, and lyrics on the latest events (such as the Polish insurrection and the Crimean campaign) and on the deaths of his friends. Relatively few of these poems have merit. Tiutchev's gift imposed certain limitations on him. To produce one of his masterpieces, he had to follow rules of his own creation; for example, he usually needed a barrier between reality and himself or a veil covering the object of his observation. When he broke these self-imposed rules, he failed. He was one of the wittiest men of his time, but his epigrams are never funny. His letters (in French) on the political situation in Russia read like novellas, and their style is perfect, but his versified orations at Slavophile banquets, which are stylistically inferior and ideologically tendentious, leave one with a sense of embarrassment.

The first of Tiutchev's important political works was his "Lettre à M. de Docteur Gustave Kolb," which appeared in the *Augsburger allgemeine Zeitung* (Augsburg General Newspaper) on 19 March 1844. In 1848 his second political article, "La Russie et la Révolution," which was intended as a chapter in his unfinished book "Russie et l'Ouest" (Russia and the West), outlined his basic positions about Russia as a country of Christian humility in opposition to the West, which he saw as an anti-Christian hotbed of revolutionary movements. His last article, "La Question Romaine," appeared in the January 1850 issue of *La Revue des Deux Mondes*. In this article he attacked the Roman Catholic Church, claiming that it had become a purely secular institution after the split with Orthodoxy.

Tiutchev was well aware of his method, and it is curious to watch his efforts to write about politics as though it were one of his conventional themes. For example, in "Uzh tretii god besnuiutsia iazyki" (For three years nations have been in a state of madness, 1850), his only sonnet, he expresses his admiration of the tsar for his firmness in the face of the 1848 revolution.

Tiutchev seeks refuge in a seascape, as he had in his 1848 poem "More i utes" (The Sea and the Rock), which is a masterful description of a tempest, though its allegorical meaning (the impregnable rock is Russia, which the European revolutions are unable to shatter) is not revealed in the text. In the sonnet, two typically Tiutchevian lines describe birds frightened by an approaching storm. The line "Thought is suppressed by ominous sorrow" is an echo of a similar line from the lyric about "holy night" written at the same time (in both cases the Russian word for thought is *um,* mind), and the line "People's dreams are wild like those of a sick person" has been transferred almost verbatim from an 1829 lyric about Russia's "iron sleep," though it seems to be out of place here.

It is debatable whether Tiutchev's allegorical landscapes should even be called political. Their message may have been clear to Tiutchev's contemporaries, but from a poetical point of view they are indistinguishable from his nature lyrics. "Al'py" (Alps, 1830), for example, describes how "The snowy Alps gaze through / The night's azure murk," standing "As though bewitched"; but when the sun rises, "the evil witchcraft comes to an end; / The first to brighten up / Is the eldest brother's crown. From the head of the big brother / A stream runs down to the younger ones, / And the entire revived family glitters / In their golden wreaths!" This poem is probably about the Slavs (the "eldest brother" is Russia).

One of Tiutchev's poems can be called an expanded political metaphor. In 1844 he wrote "Kolumb" (Columbus), a solemn address to the explorer:

Yours is, Columbus, yours is the wreath!
You, who have boldly made a draft of the globe
And finally completed
Destiny's unfinished cause,
You, with your divine hand,
Have torn the curtain and exposed
A new, unknown, unexpected world hitherto
Concealed in the nebulous infinity.

So has of yore man's
Conscious genius been connected
By a bond of kinship with the creative force of nature . . .
Once man pronounces the magic word,
Nature responds readily
With a new world
To his kindred voice.

This lyric is full of Tiutchev's favorite ideas and motifs: man as an inalienable part of nature; chaos ("the nebulous infinity") containing miracles, the existence of which is a secret to everyone; a curtain (veil, pall) hiding unknown, but not unknowable, new worlds; and a human word producing wonderful and unexpected results. But why did Tiutchev, who almost gave up poetry in the mid 1840s, burst out into a panegyric of Columbus? This question was answered by Richard A. Gregg, who compares "Kolumb" to another text written at the same time. Tiutchev's "Lettre à M. de Docteur Gustave Kolb" was about the emergence of Petrine Russia before the unsuspecting West, which suddenly discovered a great power at its borders. Gregg posits that the new world in "Kolumb" is a metaphor for Petrine Russia; Peter I completed the cause ordained by fate and made the "draft of the globe" whole. "Kolumb" was first published in 1854, ten years after it was composed, and it is fairly certain that no contemporary reader of *Sovremennik* connected it with the "Lettre."

A turn in Tiutchev's career may have been caused by the appearance of the "Lettre." Tsar Nicholas I read the essay and approved. In the autumn of 1844 Tiutchev returned to Russia, and in 1848 he was appointed senior censor in the Ministry of Foreign Affairs; he read newspapers and books published abroad and decided whether or not they could be allowed into Russia. In 1858 he became president of the Committee of Foreign Censorship.

Censors are seldom appreciated, and the institution supporting them commands little respect; yet neither Tiutchev nor, for example, Goncharov found it reprehensible to serve as a literary policeman. One can only say that despite his conservative views and devotion to monarchy Tiutchev was a liberal censor. In 1870 he wrote two epigrams about the work of the committee, the first of which was published ten years later in *Rus'*. In "Velen'iu vysshemu pokorny" (Obedient to the highest will) he writes: "Obedient to the order from up high, / We stood sentry watching *thought;* / We did not try too hard, / Though we were armed with guns. // We used them against our will, / Rarely made threats and stood guard / In *honor* of thought rather / Than guarded thought, the *prisoner*." In "Davno izvestnaia vsem dura" (Long known to all as a fool) he says that "Lady Censorship, the never tiring / fool of old fame, / supports our flesh in a small way / —God bless her!"

Tiutchev is at his weakest in poems that take to task Aleksandr Arkad'evich Suvorov, Gen. Aleksandr Vasil'evich Suvorov's grandson and the Lord Mayor of St. Petersburg, for his compassionate treatment of Polish insurgents; console Aleksandr Fedorovich Gil'ferding, the famous collector of Russian epic lays, after his losing an election to the Academy of Sciences; mock Count Aleksei Andreevich Arakcheev and Karl Robert von Nesselrode, the highest-ranking statesmen under Nicholas I; blast the Pope; or predict the glory of the pan-Slavic state. The problem is not that some of these pieces strike readers as "progressive" and others as "reactionary." Their failure is professional: Tiutchev lacked the ability to write "journalistic" poetry.

Even in his youth Tiutchev was not a political rebel. He had little, if any, sympathy for the participants in the Decembrist Revolt. In "14-e dekabria 1825" (14 December 1825), written in 1826, he finds it unbelievable that "these victims of reckless thought" hoped to "melt the eternal pole" with their "meager blood." Thus, at the age of twenty-three he was associating the Russian monarchy with the North Pole, but the mutinous blood "sparkled, while smoking on the age-old iceberg, the iron winter breathed, and no trace of the blood was left."

It is true that in "Tsitseron" (Cicero, circa 1830) Tiutchev said "Blessed is he who visited this world in its fateful minutes," but it was not revolution or the collapse of empires that attracted him; rather, he could not withstand his fascination with change, with the transitional stages of all things. He was a convinced monarchist; although he refused to judge whether Pushkin or Baron Georges d'Anthès-Heeckeren was to blame for the duel in which Pushkin perished, he called d'Anthès-Heeckeren a regicide, and no other word could have expressed more forcefully his condemnation of the murderer's deed. One can only imagine what it cost him to write "Ne Bogu ty sluzhil i ne Rossii" (You served neither God nor Russia), an 1855 epigram on the death of Nicholas I: "You served neither God nor Russia / But only your own vanity, / And all things you have done, good and bad, / Were false, just appearances– / You were not a tsar but an actor." He was of course disillusioned by Nicholas's leadership, not by the type of government, for he associated monarchy with Russia's spiritual and cultural supremacy in the world.

Some of Tiutchev's "topical" lyrics are existential rather than political, and three of these deserve special mention. The first is "Eti bednye selen'ia" (These poor villages, 1855):

> These poor villages,
> This jejune nature–
> O my native land of endless patience,
> Land of the Russian people!
>
> The proud look of a foreigner
> Will not understand or notice
> What secret light, what attraction
> Your humble nakedness holds.
>
> Under the burden of the cross,
> The heavenly king, while being a slave,
> Walked you up and down and blessed you,
> O my native country.

Critics have noted that in lyrics about Russia, Tiutchev mentioned only elements such as a gray sky, puddles covered with ice, and scraggly birch trees, and thus looked at his native land in the same way the "proud foreigner" does in this poem (Tiutchev was referring specifically to Astolphe de Custine, the author of a devastatingly uncomplimentary account of Nicholas's empire). This criticism is partly justified. Tiutchev, a denizen of Geneva and Munich, loved the image of Russia, not the reality. His sad landscapes should not be used against him, however, for they are about the semimythical north, inspired by Russia but not identical with it. "Eti bednye selen'ia" is also a myth in its own way. The poem is not a statement against serfdom: its contours are too blurred to be interpreted as a political declaration.

Another lyric of this type is "Russkoi zhenshchine" (To a Russian Woman, 1848 or 1849):

> Far away from the sun and nature,
> Far away from light and art,
> Far away from life and love
> Will your young years pass quickly,
> Your living feelings will become dead,
> Your dreams will be dispelled . . .
>
> And you will spend your life unnoticed,
> In an unpopulated, nameless land,
> In a country no one knows;
> Thus does the smoke vanish
> In a drab and misty sky,
> In autumn's impenetrable murk. . . .

In the 1850s this poem was hailed even by the revolutionary democrats, but it seems that Tiutchev's contemporaries found in his lines what they looked for rather than what the poet really said. The image of the protagonist is nebulous and abstract. The opening lines create some confusion about the identity of the woman addressed. If the woman is a peasant, then her life will not pass far away from nature. If she is a middle-class woman or an aristocrat, there is no reason why she should have no exposure to nature and especially to love and art. The country presented in such dark colors is also hard to recognize; St. Petersburg was certainly not a nameless wasteland for Tiutchev. The picture emerging from the last lines is Tiutchev's north, or Russia as he saw it on his return from abroad, so the addressee of this lyric turns out to be the woman of Tiutchev's Russia rather than a real Russian woman.

Finally, "Umom Rossiiu ne poniat'" (28 November 1866), one of Tiutchev's four-line lyrics about Russia, has become proverbial: "Russia cannot be grasped with the mind, / It cannot be measured by a common yardstick: / It has a measure [stature] all its own– / One can only *believe* in Russia." This epigram sums up most accurately Tiutchev's attitude toward his motherland: one cannot judge Russia by what one sees in it; one can only believe in its idealized image. These lines express the quintessence of people's irrational love for their inhospitable and unpredictable land, elevates their patriotism to the level of a religious feeling, and turns Russia, with her messianic role, into an object of blind faith equal only to God.

Tiutchev's double life with his wife and Denis'eva, his alarm at the 1848 revolutions, Russia's defeat in the Crimean War in 1855, the 1863 Polish uprising, and Denis'eva's death on 4 August 1864 all led to a state of emotional exhaustion and spiritual emptiness for the poet. His last years were also filled with the deaths of many friends and family members, including four of his children. His own health was failing, but he continued to write poetry, mainly of a political nature. He also began yet another romance, this time with Elena Karlovna Bogdanova (née Uslar), a woman approximately twenty years his junior, taxing the patience of his family.

On 1 January 1873 Tiutchev had a stroke, supposedly brought on by anger at his wife's poor copying of a poem. This stroke debilitated the entire left side of his body; nevertheless, he continued his normal activities. Two more strokes followed on 11 and 13 June, at which point he could no longer speak. He died in Tsarskoe Selo on 15 July 1873 and was buried in the Novodevichii Cemetery in St. Petersburg.

Tiutchev in Paris, March 1865 (photograph by S. L. Levitsky)

On the surface Tiutchev's legacy is relatively simple: fewer than five hundred poems, three major political articles, a collection of his witticisms (the 1922 *Tiutcheviana*), and scores of letters. Though he was the only genuine Romantic that Russia produced, according to Nicholas Riasanovsky, Tiutchev was the most modern of Russian poets. His formal innovations belong to a later age, especially his experimentation with metrics. Tiutchev's importance, however, lies in his place as a poet who embodies the contradictory nature of his native land. In his poems Tiutchev pursued what is most dear to the soul of Russia–beauty.

Letters:
"Otryvki iz perepiski Tiutcheva s Kn. I. S. Gagarinym," *Russkii arkhiv*, 1 (1879): 118-138;

"Iz pisem F. I. Tiutcheva," *Russkii arkhiv* (1898): 556-568;

Pis'ma F. I. Tiutcheva k ego vtoroi zhene, urozhd. bar. Pfeffel, 1840-1867, 2 volumes (Petrograd: Tip. Glav. upr. udelov, 1914-1916);

"Lettres de Th. I. Tjutscheff à sa seconde épouse née Baronne de Pfeffel," *Starina i Novizna,* 18 (1914): 1-63; 19 (1915): 104-276; 21 (1916): 155-243; 22 (1917): 243-293;

Fedor Ivanovich Tiutchev v pismakh k E. K. Bogdanovoi i S. P. Frolovu (1866-1871 gg.), edited by Evlaliia Pavlovna Kazanovich (Leningrad: Izd. Otdeleniia russkogo iazyka i slovesnosti Akademii nauk SSSR, 1926);

Literaturnoe nasledstvo, 19-21 (1935): 184, 205-208, 219-253, 255, 383, 384, 414, 580-587; 31-32 (1937): 753-769, 772, 773.

Bibliographies:

Inna Aleksandrovna Koroleva and Aleksandr Aronovich A. Nikolaev, *F. I. Tiutchev. Bibliograficheskii ukazatel' proizvedenii i literatury o zhizni i deiatel'nosti 1818-1973,* edited by Kirill Vasil'evich Pigarev (Moscow: Kniga, 1978);

Ronald C. Lane, *Bibliography of Works by and about F. I. Tiutchev to 1985,* Astra Soviet and East European Bibliographies no. 7 (Nottingham, U.K.: Astra Press, 1987).

Biographies:

Ivan Sergeevich Aksakov, *Fedor Ivanovich Tiutchev. Biograficheskii ocherk* (Moscow: Tip. V. Got'e, 1874);

Georgii Ivanovich Chulkov, *Letopis' zhizni i tvorchestva F. I. Tiutcheva* (Moscow-Leningrad: Academia, 1933);

Kirill Vasil'evich Pigarev, *Zhizn' i tvorchestvo Tiutcheva* (Moscow: Izdatel'stvo AN SSSR, 1962); abridged and revised as *F. I. Tiutchev i ego vremia* (Moscow: Sovremennik, 1978);

V. G. Dekhanov, ed., *Sovremenniki o F. I. Tiutcheve: Vospominaniia, otzyvy i pis'ma* (Tula: Priokskoe knizhnoe izd-vo, 1984);

Vadim Valerianovich Kozhinov, *Tiutchev* (Moscow: Sovremennik, 1988); second edition, expanded (Moscow: Soratnik, 1994);

Arkadii Petrov, *Lichnost' i sud'ba Fedora Tiutcheva* (Pushkino: Kul'tura, 1992).

References:

Borys Bilokur, *A Concordance to the Russian Poetry of Fedor I. Tiutchev* (Providence, R.I.: Brown University Press, 1975);

Roman Fedorovich Brandt, "Materialy dlia issledovaniia 'Fedor Ivanovich Tiutchev i ego poeziia,'" *Izvestiia Otdeleniia russkogo iazyka i slovesnosti imperatorskoi Akademii nauk,* 16, no. 2 (1911): 136-232; no. 3 (1911): 1-65;

Boris Iakovlevich Bukhshtab, Introduction to *Polnoe sobranie stikhotvorenii,* by Tiutchev (Leningrad: Sovetskii pisatel', 1957);

Dmitrii Ivanovich Chizhevsky, "Tjutčev und die deutsche Romantik," *Zeitschrift für Slavische Philologie,* 4 (1927): 229-323;

Georgii Ivanovich Chulkov, *Posledniaia liubov' Tiutcheva (Elena Aleksandrovna Denis'eva)* (Leningrad: M. & S. Shabashnikov, 1928);

Roger Conant, *The Political Poetry and Ideology of F. I. Tiutchev* (Ann Arbor, Mich.: Ardis, 1983);

François Cornillot, *Tiouttchev, poète-philosoph* (Lille: Service de reproduction des theses, Université de Lille III, 1974);

D. S. Darsky, *Chudesnye vymysly, O kosmicheskom soznanii v lirike Tiutcheva* (Moscow: Tovarishchestvo skoropechati A. A. Levenson, 1913);

Afanasii Afanas'evich Fet, "O stikhotvoreniiakh F. Tiutcheva," *Russkoe slovo,* 2 (1859): 63-84;

Semen Liudvigovich Frank, "Kosmicheskoe chuvstvo v poezii Tiutcheva," *Russkaia mysl',* 11 (1913): 1-31;

Lidiia Anatol'evna Freiberg, "Tiutchev i antichnost'," in *Antichnost' i sovremennost',* edited by Mariia Evgen'evna Grabar'-Passek (Moscow: Nauka, 1972), pp. 444-456;

Richard A. Gregg, *Fedor Tiutchev: The Evolution of a Poet* (New York: Columbia University Press, 1965);

Aleksandra Dmitrievna Grigor'eva, *Slovo v poezii Tiutcheva* (Moscow: Nauka, 1980);

Nikolai Kallinikovich Gudzy, "Tiutchev v poeticheskoi kul'ture russkogo simvolizma," *Izvestiia po russkomu iazyku i slovesnosti AN SSSR,* 2 (1930): 465-549;

Richard F. Gustafon, "Tyutchev's Imagery and What it Tells Us," *Slavic and East European Journal,* 4 (1960): 1-16;

Ulrike Kahlenborn, *Goethes Lyrik in russischer Übersetzung. V. A. Zukovskij und F. I. Tjutčev als bedeutendste Goethe-Übersetzer der russischen Romantik,* Slavische Beiträge no. 185, (Munich: Verlag Otto Sagner, 1985);

Rolf Kempf, "F. I. Tjutčev. Persönlichkeit und Dichtung," dissertation, Basel University (Göttingen, 1956);

Nina Valerianovna Koroleva, "F. I. Tiutchev," in *Istoriia russkoi poezii,* volume 2 (Leningrad: Nauka, 1969), pp. 191-224;

Boris Mikhailovich Kozyrev, "Mifologemy Tiutcheva i ioniiskaia naturfilosofiia (iz pisem o Tiutcheve)," in *Istoriko-filologicheskie issledovaniia. Sbornik statei pamiati akademika N. I. Konrada* (Moscow: Nauka, 1974), pp. 121-128;

Ronald C. Lane, "Tyutčev in English Translation: 1873-1974," *Journal of European Studies*, 5 (1975): 153-175;

Lane, "Tyutčev's Place in the History of Russian Literature," *Modern Language Review*, 71 (1976): 344-356;

A. Lavretsky, "Turgenev i Tiutchev," in *Tvorcheskii put' Turgeneva. Sbornik statei*, edited by N. L. Brodsky (Petrograd: Seiatel', 1923), pp. 244-276;

Lavretsky, "Vzyskuiushchii blagodati. (F. I. Tiutchev: poèt i poèziia)," in *Slovo o kul'ture. Sbornik kriticheskikh I filosofskikh statei* (Moscow: M. Gordon-Konstantinova, 1918), pp. 61-79;

Evgenii Nikolaevich Lebedev, "Romanticheskii mir molodogo Tiutcheva," in *Istoriia romantizma v russkoi literature. Romantizm v russkoi literature 20kh-30kh godov XIX v. (1825-1840)* (Moscow: Nauka, 1979), pp. 81-107;

Abram Zakharovich Lezhnev, *Dva poeta. Geine, Tiutchev* (Moscow: Khudozhestvennaia literatura, 1934);

Lezhnev, Introduction to *Stikhotvoreniia*, by Tiutchev (Moscow: Khudozhestvennaia literatura, 1935), pp. 5-40;

Lidiia Mikhailovna Lotman, "F. I. Tiutchev," in *Istoriia russkoi literatury v chetyrekh tomakh*, volume 3 (Leningrad: Nauka, 1982), pp. 408-426;

Evgenii Aleksandrovich Maimin, *Russkaia filosofskaia poèziia. Poèty liubomudry, A. S. Pushkin, F. I. Tiutchev* (Moscow: Nauka, 1976);

Sergei Aleksandrovich Makashin, Kirill Vasil'evich Pigarev, and T. G. Dinesman, eds., *Fedor Ivanovich Tiutchev*, book 97 of *Literaturnoe nasledstvo*, 2 volumes (Moscow: Izd-vo "Nauka," 1988-1989);

Ralph E. Matlaw, "The Polyphony of Tyutčev's 'Son na more,'" *Slavonic and East European Review*, 36 (1957-1958): 198-204;

Dmitrii Sergeevich Merezhkovsky, *Dve tainy russkoi poezii. Nekrasov i Tiutchev* (Petrograd: I. D. Sytin, 1915);

Aleksandr Aronovich Nikolaev, "Khudozhnik-myslitel'-grazhdanin (chitaia Tiutcheva)," *Voprosy literatury*, 1 (1979): 116-158;

Nikolaev, "Sud'ba poèticheskogo naslediia Tiutcheva 1822-1836 godov i tekstologicheskie problemy ego izucheniia," *Russkaia literatura*, 1 (1979): 128-143;

Oleg Vladimirovich Orlov, *Poèziia Tiutcheva* (Moscow: Izdatel'stvo Moskovskogo Universiteta, 1981);

Lev Adol'fovich Ozerov, *Poèziia Tiutcheva* (Moscow: Khudozhestvennaia literatura, 1975);

I. Iu. Podgaetskaia, "'Svoe' u 'chuzhoe' v poèticheskom stile. Zhukovsky-Lermontov-Tiutchev," in *Smena literaturnykh stilei. Na materiale russkoi literatury XIX-XX vekov* (Moscow: Nauka, 1974), pp. 201-250;

Sarah Claflin Pratt, "'Antithesis and Completion': Zabolockij Responds to Tyutcev," *Slavic and East European Journal*, 27 (1983): 211-227;

Pratt, *Russian Metaphysical Romanticism: The Poetry of Tyutchev and Boratynskii* (Stanford: Cal.: Stanford University Press, 1984);

Pratt, *Semantics of Chaos in Tyutcev*, Slavistische Beiträge no. 171 (Munich: Verlag Otto Sagner, 1983);

Lev Vasil'evich Pumpiansky, "Poèziia F. I. Tiutcheva," in *Urania. Tiutchevskii al'manakh (1803-1928)*, edited by Evlaliia Pavlovna Kazanovich (Leningrad: Priboi, 1928), pp. 9-57;

Nicholas V. Riasanovsky, *The Emergence of Romanticism* (New York & Oxford: Oxford University Press, 1992), pp. 84-87, 91, 101;

A. I. Rubin, "Poèziia Tiutcheva kak sozvuchnoe sliianie s prirodoi," *Grani*, 97 (1975): 143-173;

Almut Schulze, *Tjutčevs Kuzlyrik. Traditionszusammenhänge und Interpretationen*, Forum Slavicum no. 25 (Munich: Vilhelm Fink Verlag, 1968);

Vladimir Sergeevich Solov'ev, "Poeziia F. I. Tiutcheva," *Vestnik Evropy*, 4 (1895): 735-752;

D. Strémooukhoff, *La poésie et l'idéologie de Tiouttchev*, Publications de la Faculté des lettres de l'Université de Stasbourg no. 70 (Paris: Les Belles Lettres, 1937);

Tiutchevskii sbornik (Tallinn: Eesti raamat, 1990);

Iurii Nikolaevich Tynianov, "Pushkin i Tiutchev," in his *Poetika. Sbornik statei* (Leningrad: Academia, 1926), pp. 107-126;

Tynianov, "Vopros o Tiutcheve," *Kniga i revolutsia*, 3 (1923): 24-30;

Karol W. Zawodiński, "Tiutczew. Proba ujecia," *Wiersze wybrane*, by Teodor Tiutczew (Lódz-Wroclaw: Wydawnictwo Wladyslawa Baka, 1948), pp. xvii-xxxix;

Iakov Osipovich Zundelovich, *Ètiudy o lirike Tiutcheva* (Samarkand: Samarkand Universitet, 1971).

Papers:

Fedor Ivanovich Tiutchev's papers are housed at the Central State Archive of Literature and Art (formerly TsGALI), f. 505, and the Russian State Library, f. 308, both in Moscow; and at the Russian National Library, f. 797, St. Petersburg. Other papers are located at Muranovo, now a library and museum.

Dmitrii Vladimirovich Venevitinov

(14 September 1805 – 15 March 1827)

Luc J. Beaudoin
University of Denver

BOOK: *Sochineniia,* 2 volumes, compiled by N. M. Rozhalin (Moscow: Semen Selivanovsky, 1829, 1831).

Editions and Collections: *Polnoe sobranie sochinenii,* edited by A. P. Piatkovsky (St. Petersburg: O. I. Bakst, 1862);

Polnoe sobranie stikhotvorenii (St. Petersburg: A. S. Suvorin, 1884);

Polnoe sobranie sochinenii, edited by B. V. Smirensky (Moscow: Academia, 1934);

D. Venevitinov, S. Shevyrev, A. Khomiakov: Stikhotvoreniia, edited by Mark Aronson and I. V. Sergievsky (Leningrad: Sovetskii pisatel', 1937);

Stikhotvoreniia, edited by V. L. Komarovich (Leningrad: Sovetskii pisatel', 1940);

Izbrannoe, edited by Smirensky (Moscow: Khudozhestvennaia literatura, 1956);

Polnoe sobranie stikhotvorenii, edited by B. V. Neiman (Leningrad: Sovetskii pisatel', 1960);

Stikhotvoreniia, proza, edited by Evgenii Aleksandrovich Maimin and M. A. Chernyshev (Moscow: Nauka, 1980);

Stikhotvoreniia, edited by Vsevolod Ivanovich Sakharov (Moscow: Sovetskaia Rossiia, 1982).

Dmitrii Venevitinov's life was brilliant, impassioned, brief, and melancholy—in short, a virtual prototype of the Romantic writer's dream. He never reached his twenty-second birthday, dying of influenza while still in the initial—and, as a result, innocent—stage of his literary career. He thus became the center of a virtual hero cult upon his death in 1827. His written legacy is modest—a few dozen original poems, a series of Romantic translations, a few critical essays, some prose works, and letters. In literary affairs, his effect was more expansive, for he founded, along with Prince Vladimir Fedorovich Odoevsky, the *Obshchestvo liubomudriia* (Society of Lovers of Wisdom, 1823–1825), a society devoted to expounding the philosophy of Friedrich Wilhelm Joseph von Schelling in Russia. Venevitinov was the group's secretary as well as its leading poet. He was likewise identified with the Decembrist movement—a group of aristocrats intent on deposing the absolute monarchy. Their abortive coup of 14 December 1825 changed the political nature of Russian society and art irrevocably. These entanglements with the essence of Romanticism have placed Venevitinov high in the hierarchy of Russian Romantic poets.

Dmitrii Vladimirovich Venevitinov was born on 14 September 1805. His father, Vladimir Petrovich Venevitinov, an ensign in the Imperial Guard, died while the poet was still a child, and Venevitinov was cared for by his mother, Anna Nikolaevna (née Obolenskaia). She desired that her son receive the best education, and his tutors were consistently among the highest

346

qualified. Too young to have understood the significance of the Patriotic War of 1812, he nonetheless later incorporated a sense of its importance in his endeavors with both the Decembrists and the *Obshchestvo liubomudriia*. Under the tutelage organized by his mother, Venevitinov learned Greek and Latin and acquired a taste for ancient literary works. He spoke German and French with ease and went on to study English and Italian. He studied Russian literature, as well as music and painting. Venevitinov completed his education by auditing lectures at Moscow University, including physics, Latin, and philosophy. During his final year at the university, he and Odoevsky organized the *Obshchestvo liubomudriia* (Odoevsky had finished the university in 1822). Venevitinov passed the university examinations in 1824 and received a position at the Moscow Archive of the College of Foreign Affairs. The "young archivists," as Aleksandr Pushkin called them in his *Evgeny Onegin* (1823–1831, published in full 1833), were known to philosophize more than work. His employment and his involvement in the *Obshchestvo liubomudriia* were the dominant factors in his early career.

Venevitinov's first ventures in poetry were somewhat conventional. His first poem, "K druz'iam" (To Friends, 1821) is heavily indebted to the classical elegiac convention. Comparing his life to the hustle and bustle of city life, the poet declares himself happy without the material entrapments of the city: "Without gold I am rich / With the lyre, with faithful friends." Venevitinov's use of established poetic traditions comes clearly to the fore with a free translation of Virgil in his *Znameniia pered smert'iu Tsezaria: Otryvok iz Vergilievykh 'Georgik'* (Signs Preceding the Death of Caesar: Selection from Virgil's "Georgics," 1823).

The Anacreontic tone imbued in Venevitinov's early poetry continues throughout the works of 1823. His "K druz'iam na Novyi God" (To Friends at the New Year, 1823) urges his addressees (whose identities remain unclear) to enjoy life:

> Friends! Greet the New Year
> In a circle of those dear, in freedom.
> Let it for you, friends, flow,
> Like the happy years of childhood.
> But amidst the Petersburg conceits,
> Do not forget the sound of the lyre,
> Of the occupations of sweet and worldly
> And old, sincere friends.

His "Vetochka" (Twig, 1823) is a free adaptation from Jean-Baptiste-Louis Gresset and is full of the typical elegiac ennui of the time. In this work life is portrayed as ultimately doomed, since death ends even the least ambitious life goals of every human. In the same year Venevitinov also published a longer poem, "Osvobozhdenie skal'da (Skandinavskaia povest')" (Liberation of the Skald [Scandinavian Novella], 1823), that was an adaptation of a Scandinavian legend from the life of poet Egill Skallagrimsson as told in *Egils saga* (attributed to Snorri Sturluson, circa 1220). Venevitinov tells of Egil, a bard and warrior who kills a man named El'mor in a duel. El'mor's father, Armin, subsequently captures Egil and condemns him to death. Armin is moved, however, when Egil sings a praise of the dead El'mor. He sets Egil free, and the bard departs, haunted only for a moment by a vision of El'mor in a fog bank. It is clear in this narrative poem that Venevitinov was already incorporating certain tenets of Schellingian philosophy. By this time Venevitinov was involved in the *Obshchestvo liubomudriia* and would have been discussing the role of poetry as philosophy. It is, therefore, not surprising that he chose a legend in which the poet is able to win back his life through the transforming beauty of verse. He also follows the tradition of the day by loosely stylizing his poem in the manner of Ossian (James Macpherson), whose Scandinavian-themed poems were quite popular with the Romantics. Venevitinov adapted one of these poems: "Pesn' Kol'my" (Song of Colma, 1824) is filled with typical Ossianic gloom and storminess.

Venevitinov not only adapted themes from the western European and Scandinavian trends but also used native sources. *Slovo o polku Igoreve* (The Tale of Igor's Campaign), a work from the Russian Middle Ages detailing a battle between the Russians and Polovtsians in 1185, served as an inspiration for the style of another long poem, "Evpraksiia" (1824). This work is based on a section of *Povest' vremennykh let* (The Tale of Bygone Years, also called the Primary Chronicle) relating the Tartar invasion of 1237. Prince Iurii of Riazan's wife, Evpraksiia, was demanded by a Tartar prince as a concubine. When Iurii refused, he was killed, and Evpraksiia soon killed her baby son and herself as well. Venevitinov does not actually relate the murder-suicide; rather, he ends the poem with a victory by the Russian forces over the Tartars. The work is divided into songs in the same manner as its medieval antecedents.

The treatment of medieval themes and concerns is linked to the standard Romantic concern of freedom. Romanticism moved public opinion to support the legitimacy of peoples based upon their cultural and linguistic distinctiveness. One great cause célèbre was the struggle of Greek patriots against their Turkish masters in the early 1800s. There George Gordon, Lord Byron met his famous death, and Romantic writers in Russia were likewise quick to idealize the conflict. Venevitinov treats these questions primarily in two works of 1825: "Chetyre otryvka iz neokonchennogo pologa 'Smert'

Bairona'" (Four Fragments from the Unfinished Prologue "Byron's Death") and "Pesn' greka" (Song of the Greek). In the latter work the theme of revenge is striking, for the poet ends each stanza with the refrain "For all this my sword will have revenge on you." The stanzas themselves describe the calamities–elements of a senseless, evil war–that have befallen the narrator's loved ones. He ends with the declaration that he cannot be stopped:

> From that time on the Mohammed sees
> Me in the clash of battle,
> From that time on, how often in the noise of battle
> My vow I repeat!
> The destruction of my homeland, the death of my fair one,
> Everything, everything I will recall in the terrible hour;
> And all the times, when my sword glitters
> And there falls a head with a turban,
> I speak with an evil smile:
> "For all this my sword will have revenge on you!"

"Chetyre otryvka" (Four Fragments) is a brief depiction of an idealized Byron reaching Greece, speaking with the Greek leader, battling the Turks, and dying (his death is retold by a chorus). In these struggles for liberty Byron's heroism is most significant–he denies the existence of everything else for his noble cause. Byron exclaims upon reaching Greece:

> Here I thought to lift the mysterious veil
> From the brow of mysterious nature,
> To recognize close by the concealed traits
> And in the ocean of beauty
> To forget the illusion of love, to forget the illusion of freedom.

He pays with his life, but is nonetheless immortalized and remembered.

During this time Venevitinov also wrote critical articles about *Evgeny Onegin* that were among the more important critiques of his brief career. In these works, written in 1825, Venevitinov defends what he perceives as the essence of *Evgeny Onegin* as a work that is truly Byronic in both genre (a novel in verse) and emotional scope. These types of polemics occupied Russian literary journals for years and revolved around the specifics of the course Russian literature would undertake. As they related to a developing literature, able to create its own identity, these discussions took on great importance and vigor.

Despite his occasional incursion to the medieval poetic genre or into declamations of freedom and liberty, both of which were fairly conventional traits of Romanticism in Russia and in western Europe, Venevitinov generally flourished in the more intimate lyric. In these as well he retained some of the more typical Romantic conceits, though at the same time he embellished them to a great degree with his belief in Schellingian philosophy. His early poem "Liubimyi tsvet" (A Favorite Color, 1825) extolls the beauties of the colors present in nature, while blending them with the beauty of an addressee, presumably a young woman. The poem ends with the line: "But among colors there is one that is holy– / It is the color of the young dawn."

"K <F. Ir.> Skariatinu" (To [F. Ir.] Skariatin, 1825) is subtitled "On sending him a vaudeville" and is a typically epistolary poem of the time, concentrating on the eternal issues of friendship and fate, as is "K. I. Gerke" (1825), likewise a standard epistle addressed to one of Venevitinov's former tutors. In "Poslanie k R<ozhali>nu" (Epistle to N. M. R[ozhali]n, 1825) the poet compares himself to a ship that has been sailing too proudly along, inevitably meeting its end in a shipwreck. He credits Rozhalin with restoring his ability to enjoy life once more, combining the "heat of the soul's dreams" with the "cold of life." William Edward Brown speculates that this epistle was written as Venevitinov's reaction to his love for Princess Zinaida Aleksandrovna Volkonskaia, who was married to a court official in Moscow and maintained a salon that the greatest names in literature frequented. She was a well-traveled and artistically inclined woman who supported the Decembrists. While Venevitinov's love for her was most likely passionate and genuine, it was not reciprocated with anything but appreciative, and simultaneously pitying, friendship. This love affected Venevitinov deeply.

The vagaries of fate were expressed even more strikingly, if perhaps with tongue in cheek, in the second epistle addressed to Rozhalin, also titled "Poslanie k R<ozhali>nu" (1826). In this poem Venevitinov decries the inherent deceit of St. Petersburg society, concluding that only William Shakespeare has been true and faithful to him as loyal companion and poetic inspiration. In this work Venevitinov once again weaves an implicit comparison between the insignificance of worldly concerns and the immortality of art. He chose Shakespeare because the English writer's emotional intensity endeared him to the Romantics, who were not as concerned with form as with content. They saw Shakespeare as close to attaining the unification of form and spirit that was considered the essence of art and literary works, particularly poetry.

The question of fate is explored again in two poems of 1825 titled "Sonet" (Sonnet). These poems are more or less traditional exhortations of spirit and genius, which is needed to carry the poet above everyday concerns. The first sonnet ends with a Romantic exclamation:

Princess Zinaida Aleksandrovna Volkonskaia, with whom Venevitinov was in love

And if the world were to crumble, the realm of air would darken
And chaos would be feeding nature emptiness,–
Thunder forth! Among the ruins of the world may
Love with hope and holy faith ring out!

Despite the traditional Romanticism, Venevitinov clearly deepens the Schellingian overtones of the interconnectedness of the material and the poetic/spiritual realms in one Absolute. The poet is bound to the knowledge of the all-knowing spiritual Absolute and foretells the Schellingian triumph of spirit over material. The second sonnet deals more directly with the power of the poet's genius:

I saw the brilliance of lightning, the fierceness of clear waves;
I heard the crash of thunder and the howling of storms:
But what can compare the poet, when he is full of passion?
Forgive me! Your nursling is with you lost
And, dying, blesses you.

Through the love expressed in the first sonnet and reinforced in the second, the poet transcends both civilization and nature to communicate with the true World-Spirit.

Returning to the concerns of Romantic freedom he had earlier explored, Venevitinov wrote the poem "Novgorod" (1826), in which the narrator is on a journey to Novgorod, referred to in the poem by the more solemn Church Slavonic "Novgrad." Though the coachman to whom the narrator is speaking may have forgotten certain symbolic elements of the history of the city, to the narrator this history is almost religiously significant: "Silence, my friend, this is a sacred place / Here the air is cleaner and freer!" The narrator ends with a declamation of the past and forgotten grandeur of Novgorod, the only even nominally democratic city in Russian history. It is, nonetheless, significant that the poet is a tourist who is trapped within his own time–left to declaim, with the power of his genius, the majestic part of the city he is touring.

"K moei bogine" (To My Goddess, 1826) is a heartfelt and passionate, if ultimately self-destructive, elegy. The narrator-poet is walking along the banks of the river Neva in St. Petersburg. He is isolated from his surroundings, something unusual for a Romantic poet. Yet, this emphasis on his isolation is precisely on account of his poetry—his passionate soul cannot find happiness:

> What is happiness to me? What is it for?
> Did you not say over and over that by fate
> It is given only to the timid,
> That happiness with an ardent soul
> Cannot be linked in this world
> That it is not for me to breathe for it?

A glance from his goddess could cure him of the desire for base happiness. The narrator's thoughts are thus occupied as he walks along the Neva "gloomy and alone." Venevitinov appropriately chose the Neva for the setting of his poem. The Neva is certainly the most acute revenge of nature on the classicist city of St. Petersburg: though mastered through an extensive system of canals, until the end of the twentieth century the river would overflow each spring and flood the city dramatically. When this aspect is considered in the light of Venevitinov's earlier poems on the unity of nature and the poet's spiritual whole, the poet's isolation becomes extremely significant—he is totally trapped within the realm of the material, able only to revel in melancholy. This theme recurred in Venevitinov's poems until his death, often under the guise of the superior nature of poetic inspiration.

"Poet" (1826) continues the exaltation of the suffering and inspired poet. In fact, the reader is urged to respect the poet's superior knowledge:

> O, if you will meet him
> With thought on his severe brow,
> Pass close to him without noise,
> Do not destroy with a cold word
> His holy, quiet dreams;
> Look on with a tear of reverence
> And say: this is the son of the gods,
> The beloved of the Muses and inspiration.

It was fairly common for a certain distant land to represent the exalted world in which poetic inspiration would lie. "Italia" (1826) is an excellent example of this trend, even opening with an exclamation to "Italy, fatherland of inspiration." The poem "Elegiia" (Elegy, 1826 or January 1827) is dedicated to Volkonskaia, who had traveled extensively in western Europe. In it the poet declares that his beloved has literally absorbed the inspiration from places she has been (evidently referring to Italy): "Enchantress! How sweetly you sang / About the marvelous land of enchantment, / About the hot land of beauty!" Yet, the poet, though carried away into dreams by his love's tales, inevitably is brought back to harsh reality, which here also includes the fact that his passion for Volkonskaia was not reciprocated: "Why, why did you sing so sweetly? / Why did I pay attention to you in such a greedy manner / And from your lips, songstress of beauty, / Drink the poison of dreams and cheerless passion?"

Another way, of course, to be liberated from the torments of crass materialistic existence is to die. The poem "Kinzhal" (The Dagger, 1826) has a clearly suicidal overtone, with its repetition of "leave me, forget me," and its concluding stanza: "Leave me, love another! / Forget me, I myself soon / Will forget the grief of earthly life." The dagger is the speaker's hope and his way out of the torment of this life.

In the autumn of 1826 Venevitinov decided to leave Moscow (and therefore also Volkonskaia) for a position at the College of Foreign Affairs in St. Petersburg. Life in the imperial capital struck him as the antithesis of the spiritual artistic inspiration he was ultimately seeking, but he nonetheless managed to become involved in the plans for a new journal, *Moskovskii vestnik* (The Moscow Herald). Upon his departure from Moscow, Volkonskaia gave Venevitinov an original Roman ring found in the remains of Herculaneum, an ancient city destroyed by Vesuvius. This ring figured prominently in his poetry as well as his personal life: he vowed never to wear it until his marriage or his death.

The ring appears in "Zaveshchanie" (Testament, 1826 or 1827), in which it is identified specifically with the sorrows of the life that the dead narrator has just departed. There are cryptic riddles in the work, referring to the afterlife, to faithful memories, and to revenge from beyond the grave. The tone of the poem is despondent and has a distinct suicidal undercurrent: death is seen as the source from which freedom from the judgment of society can be found. In "K moemu perstniu" (To My Signet Ring, 1826 or 1827) the ring is seen as a harbinger, or perhaps rather a witness to the torments of earthly love across time, that may be taken from the narrator's hand upon his own death and given to yet another unfortunate lover in the future.

"Tri rozy" (Three Roses, 1826) is considered the most significant of Venevitinov's philosophical poems. The poem is an allegory with an introduction. Each of three roses is discussed: the first rose is ultimately regenerative—if plucked, a new one appears by morning; the second is red at dawn and flowers every morning; the third is the love of maidens' cheeks—it fades quickly and never blooms again. The allegory has remained a riddle, though critics have attempted to consider each rose an element of spiritual and earthly existence. A proper analogy is difficult to ascertain.

"Zhertvoprinoshenie" (Sacrificial Offering, 1826 or 1827) returns to the theme of life as futile but nonetheless irresistible: "O life, perfidious siren, / How strongly you attract to yourself! / You wind chains to fatal captivity / With brilliant colors." The captivity is of course fatal because there is no escape exccpt inevitable death. Once again a Schellingian philosophical answer is tentatively given, however, in "Ia chuvstvuiu, vo mne gorit" (I feel that in me burns, 1826 or 1827), in which the poet is told to use his lyrical gifts to re-create creation in harmony.

Certainly one manner in which Venevitinov contributed concretely to the legacy of Russian poetry is through the translation and adaptation of works written in other languages. These translations appeared in the various editions of his collected works. In addition to the works by Virgil and Gresset mentioned earlier, the pieces he translated and adapted include a work by Charles-Hubert Millevoye, a French elegiast; a work by E. T. A. Hoffmann; and several items from Johann Wolfgang von Goethe. Examples of the latter are "Zemnaia uchast' khudozhnika (iz Gete)" (The Earthly Fate of the Artist [from Goethe], 1826 or 1827, in German "Künstlers Erdwallen," 1774) and "Apofeoz khudozhnika (iz Gete)" (The Apotheosis of the Artist [from Goethe], 1826 or 1827, in German "Künstlers Apotheose," 1788), really a miniature dramatic piece. Both of these works examine the question of the conflict the artist feels between material and idealistic existences, which explains why Venevitinov chose them.

The most significant of Venevitinov's translations from Goethe is "Otryvki iz 'Fausta'" (Fragments from "Faust," 1826–1827). Venevitinov chose segments from Goethe's work (1808, 1832) that suited his Schellingian philosophy. With the exception of "Pesn' Margarity" (Margarete's Song), the second fragment, these selections deal with the philosophical concerns Venevitinov had consistently expressed. His translation is at times selective and more of an adaptation, thereby permitting him to explore the Schellingian questions with more intensity. It is significant that there are three chosen scenes; "Tri rozy" is a riddle with likewise three elements, and it is entirely possible that the two are connected. In that case, one could suggest that the first rose is in fact related to Faust's understanding of the continuously destroying and rejuvenating chain of being as he saw it in the third translated fragment. The second rose would then be philosophical contemplation–the need to "drink in the immortal rays," as Faust expresses it in the first fragment. The third rose would represent the quickly fading bloom of youth and love as symbolized

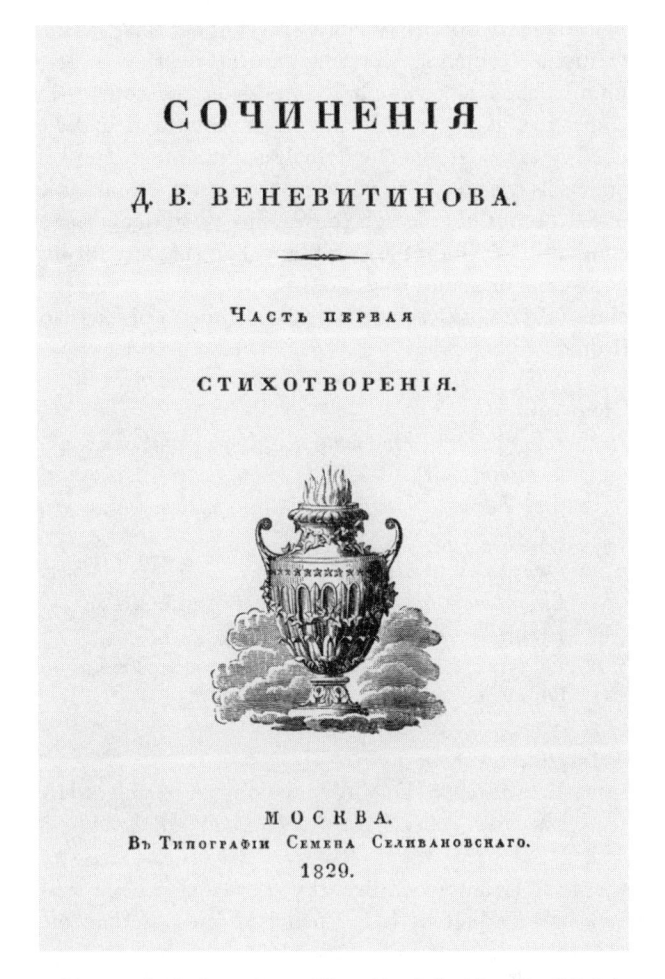

Title page for the first volume of Venevitinov's Sochineniia (Works)

by Margarete in the second fragment translated from *Faust*.

The questions that continually haunted Venevitinov reach a foreboding crescendo in his "Poet i drug (elegiia)" (Poet and Friend [Elegy], 1827), which is structured as a conversation. In this work, Venevitinov has the poet declare that he eagerly awaits an early death, believing that his poems will live on for others. He uses the refrain "How he knew life, how little he lived!" to emphasize the ephemeral quality of his existence. Venevitinov's last poem, "Liubi pitomtsa vdokhnoven'ia" (Love the Nursling of Inspiration, circa March 1827), enjoins the reader to respect the poet's superior vision and suffering, but it also cautions that there are false prophets among the true. Only the real poet has the voice of heaven upon the earth.

Shortly after this final work, Venevitinov died on 15 March 1827. A few hours before his death his signet ring was slipped onto one of his fingers by his friend Aleksei Stepanovich Khomiakov. After his death Venevitinov was immediately lionized by his contemporaries, as he had predicted in his late poems. Yet, in an objective retrospective analysis, most of his verse is conventional Romantic posturing with an overlay of profound Schellingianism. It is impossible, of course, to conjecture as to what he might have written had he lived to an older age. Nevertheless, the potential in his poems is visible. Venevitinov produced a remarkable poetic output of at least a consistently good quality in a comparatively short period of time. For that, and for his occasional brilliant verse and insight, he earns a rightful place in the upper echelons of the pantheon of Russian Romantic poets.

Biographies:

A. V. Felonin, *D. V. Venevitinov. Kritiko-biograficheskii ocherk* (St. Petersburg, 1902);

N. Fatov, *Liubov' i smert' D. V. Venevitinova* (Warsaw, 1914);

A. A. Svetlakov and N. S. Grushin, *D. V. Venevitinov: Biografiia. Venevitinov kak poet i kritik* (Moscow, 1915);

S. A. Zolotarev, *Rastsvet i smert' Venevitinova* (Moscow: t-vo Dumnova, 1924).

References:

Larry R. Andrews, "D. V. Venevitinov: A Sketch of His Life and Work," *Russian Literature Triquarterly,* 8 (1974): 373–384;

Vissarion Grigor'evich Belinsky, *Vzgliad na russkuiu literaturu,* edited by E. F. Kuznetsov and others (Moscow: Sovremennik, 1988);

William Edward Brown, *A History of Russian Literature of the Romantic Period,* volume 3 (Ann Arbor, Mich.: Ardis, 1986), pp. 347–363;

Lidiia Iakovlevna Ginzburg, "Opyt filosofkoi liriki (Venevitinov)," in *Poetika. Sbornik statei,* volume 5 (Leningrad: Academia, 1929), pp. 72–104;

Lauren Gray Leighton, "A Romantic Idealist Notion in Russian Romantic Criticism," *Canadian-American Slavic Studies,* 7 (1973): 285–295;

Iurii Vladimirovich Mann, *Poetika russkogo romantizma* (Moscow: Nauka, 1976);

A. Medvedev, "Liubimets muz i vdokhnoven'ia: k 175-letiiu so dnia rozheniia Dmitriia Venevitinova," *Molodaia gvardiia,* 9 (1980): 312–315;

S. M. Petrov, *Istoriia russkoi literatury XIX veka* (Moscow: Prosveshchenie, 1970);

Aleksandr Sergeevich Pushkin, *Mysli o literature,* edited by Kuznetsov and others (Moscow: Sovremennik, 1988);

Irina Mikhailovna Semenko, *Poety pushkinskoi pory* (Moscow-Leningrad: Khudozhestvennaia literatura, 1970);

Lidiia Anatol'evna Tartakovskaia, *Dmitrii Venevitinov. Lichnost'. Mirovozzrenie. Tvorchestvo* (Tashkent: Izdatel'stvo "Fan" Uzbekskoi SSR, 1974);

Iurii Nikolaevich Tynianov, *Arkhaisty i novatory* (Leningrad: Priboi, 1929);

Gunther Wytrzens, *Dmitrij Vladimirovic Venevitinov als Dichter der russischen Romantik* (Cologne: Bohlau, 1962);

Viktor Maksimovich Zhirmunsky, *Gete v russkoi literature* (Leningrad: Nauka, 1982).

Papers:

Dmitrii Vladimirovich Venevitinov's papers are in the Russian National Library, St. Petersburg; the Russian State Library, f. 48; Central State Archive of Literature and Art, f. 1043; and the Institute of Russian Literature (Pushkin House), f. 415, all in Moscow.

Petr Andreevich Viazemsky

(12 July 1792 – 10 November 1878)

Luc J. Beaudoin
University of Denver

BOOKS: *Sviataia Rus'* (St. Petersburg: Tip. Ekspeditsii zagotovleniia gosudarstvennykh bumag, 1848);

Privetstvie V. A. Zhukovskomu (St. Petersburg: Voennaia Tip., 1849);

Pesn' na den' rozhdeniia V. A. Zhukovskago (St. Petersburg: Voennaia Tip., 1849);

K Ruzh'iu! Stikhotvoreniia kniazia P. A. Viazemskago (St. Petersburg: Ia. Trei, 1854);

Shest' stikhotvorenii (St. Petersburg, 1855);

Za granitseiu. Korrekturnye listy iz stikhotvorenii kniazia P. A. Viazemskogo (Karlsruhe: V. Gasper, 1859);

V doroge i doma. Sobranie stikhotvorenii kniazia P. A. Viazemskogo (Moscow: Bakhmet'ev, 1862);

Polnoe sobranie sochinenii, 12 volumes (St. Petersburg: S. D. Sheremetev, 1878–1896).

Editions and Collections: *Staraia zapisnaia knizhka*, edited by Lidiia Iakovlevna Ginzburg (Leningrad: Izdatel'stvo Pisatelei v Leningrade, 1929);

Izbrannye stikhotvoreniia, edited by Vera Stepanovna Nechaeva (Moscow-Leningrad: Academia, 1935);

Stikhotvoreniia, edited by Ginzburg (Leningrad: Sovetskii pisatel', 1935);

Stikhotvoreniia, edited by Ginzburg (Leningrad: Sovetskii pisatel', 1958);

Sochineniia, 2 volumes (Moscow: Khudozhestvennaia Literatura, 1982);

Estetika i literaturnaia kritika, with an introduction by L. V. Deriugina (Moscow: Iskusstvo, 1984).

OTHER: "[Parodiia na stikhotvorenie F. N. Glinki (Troika)]," *Literaturnoe nasledstvo*, 41–42 (1941): 537–538;

"Epigrammy," in *Russkaia epigramma*, edited by Viktor Andronikovich Manuilov (Leningrad: Sovetskii pisatel', 1958), pp. 105–127.

A central figure in the dispute between the Innovators (those who sought to render the Russian literary language more harmonious through Western borrowings and stylizations) and the Archaizers (those who wanted a return to a more traditional Russian vocabulary and style) was certainly Prince Petr Andreevich Viazemsky. A man of many talents (critic, polemicist, poet, archivist, letter writer, translator, and government worker), Viazemsky left an indelible imprint on the development of Russian Romantic literature. By spirit closer to the French literature of the eighteenth century, he nonetheless defended the spirit of Romanticism, even if he did not always follow it in practice. By a strictly literary definition, his poetry should generally be classified as pre-Romantic, or Sentimental. His later poetry, however, written long after the wane of Romantic verse in Russia and the co-requisite growth of the Realistic novel as created by such writers as Fyodor Dostoyevsky and Leo Tolstoy, presage the second great flowering of Russian poetry at the turn of the twentieth century, the Silver Age. Viazemsky outlived most of his contemporaries and thus occupies an unusual role in the history of Russian literature. His literary contributions alone, however, assure him of an important place in Russian literature.

Petr Andreevich Viazemsky was the son of Andrei Ivanovich Viazemsky and Eugenia (Ivanovna) O'Reilly, whom the father had met during his travels in Ireland. Infatuated with her, he took her from her husband and brought her home to Russia. The two were married against his family's wishes in 1786. The elder Viazemsky was a military man who had acquired great wealth and was broadly educated and well-traveled. His career was not one of great brilliance but was solid and respected. Besides Petr, the couple also had two daughters: Ekaterina Kolyvanovna (conceived outside the marriage) and Ekaterina. The former daughter became Nikolai Mikhailovich Karamzin's wife. Andrei Ivanovich exposed young Petr at an early age to the thinking of Voltaire and other writers of the French Enlightenment such as Jean La Fontaine and Jean-Jacques Rousseau. Viazemsky's father died in 1807, and the sixteen-year-old Viazemsky was placed in the care of his brother-in-law, Karamzin. Karamzin was the initiator of the Innovator movement in Russian literature. This close association with the writer of Sentimental tales such as "Bednaia Liza" (Poor Liza, 1792) altered forever the development of Viazemsky's poetic talents, particularly his style and use of fixed epithets.

Viazemsky's education consisted of a Jesuit boarding school and tutoring by various professors from Moscow University. This education furthered his knowledge of Western European customs and literature and included Russian, French, German, Latin, logic, rhetoric, Greek and Roman history, algebra, dance, riding, and playing the violin. Because of the major role his brother-in-law played in the development of Russian literature, young Viazemsky naturally became acquainted with other literary figures. From 1805 to 1810 Viazemsky had close associations with the leading writers of the time including several of Karamzin's literary circle, who comprised what the critic Iurii Nikolaevich Tynianov later called the "Older Innovators." Among them were Vasilii Andreevich Zhukovsky, Konstanin Nikolaevich Batiushkov, Denis Vasil'evich Davydov, Vasilii L'vovich Pushkin, Count Dmitrii Nikolaevich Bludov, and Aleksandr Ivanovich Turgenev. This group later developed into a group ceremonially named *Obshchestvo arzamasskikh bezvestnykh liudei* (Society of the Obscure People of Arzamas); formed officially in 1815, it lasted until 1818. The "Older Innovators" were the core group of Arzamas, but the society also took in younger writers such as Aleksandr Pushkin. Arzamas functioned primarily to defend Karamzin's innovations on Russian literary language against another group of writers (gathered around Admiral Aleksandr Semenovich Shishkov) called the *Beseda liubitelei russkogo slova* (Colloquy of Lovers of the Russian Word). Formed in 1811 primarily to prevent what it viewed as the unnecessary gallicization of the Russian language, as well as an alienating stylization of the literary genre itself, this group advocated a tripartite style of literary language based on the ideas of Mikhail Vasil'evich Lomonosov; it also suggested the Russian folk language as an additional lexical source. The latter notion was to have a significant impact on Russian literature. The concern over literary genre had mainly to do with the frequent epithets and periphrasis used in the Karamzinian style—often to the point of incomprehension. The Arzamas group continued the distinctive Karamzinian, eighteenth-century French style of light, witty, and refined literature. Discourse between the two groups was caustic and thrived on satirical verse and prose in which Viazemsky flourished. In fact, the young poet-satirist-critic was one of the group's most radical members and frequently attempted to initiate a journal specifically devoted to this rather informal grouping of minds.

On 18 October 1811 Viazemsky married Princess Vera Fedorovna Gagarina, daughter of Prince Fedor Sergeevich Gagarin and Princess Praskov'ia Iur'evna Trubetskaia. Together they had eight children: Andrei, Mariia, Praskov'ia, Dmitrii, Nikolai, Pavel, Petr, and Nadezhda. Only one (Pavel) survived to old age. On 25 June 1812 Viazemsky joined the Russian militia to serve during the Great Patriotic War against Napoleon. He would have joined the army proper but for his weak health. He resettled at his family estate in Ostaf'evo near Moscow.

Viazemsky had little concern for money: after the war he gambled away the substantial fortune bequeathed him by his father. As a result, he was forced to enter the civil service; he worked in the Russian delegation in Warsaw headed by Nikolai Nikolaevich Novosil'tsev. (Then only independent in theory, Poland had been progressively occupied during the infamous three Partitions of Poland among Russia, Austria, and Prussia.) Viazemsky left for Warsaw in February 1818 and stayed there until 1821.

Viazemsky's literary prose debut occurred in December 1808, when one of his essays, titled "Bezdelki" (Bagatelles), appeared in the journal *Vestnik Evropy* (Herald of Europe). The essay consisted of short aphorisms and commentaries. In September 1809 in the same journal an article of the same name, written by Viazemsky and Dmitrii Petrovich Severin, appeared. In these initial essays Viazemsky reveals the influence of Karamzin: he attacks a translation of Jean Racine's *Phèdra* (1677) in the second work, criticizing its lack of harmonious wording. His view on Russian literature as a whole, in fact, was that the highest achiever in prose was none other than his brother-in-law, whereas the greatest poet was Gavriil Romanovich Derzhavin, despite the fact that the *Beseda* group met at Derzhavin's home in St. Petersburg.

Viazemsky's earliest poetry also bore the influence of his brother-in-law Karamzin. Viazemsky's first Russian poem (he had written a French poem in 1805) is the "Poslanie k Zhukovskomu v derevniu" (Epistle to Zhukovsky in the Country, 1808), which also appeared in *Vestnik Evropy*. It is a conventional, friendly epistle to a good friend. The concluding lines reveal its tone: "Pover'! i v gorode vozmozhno s schast'em zhit': / Ono vezde–umei ego lish' nakhodit'!" (Believe! Even in the city it is possible to live in happiness: It is everywhere–you just have to find it!) The poetic epistle is the genre that predominates Viazemsky's early verse, along with epigrams about literary opponents. When the poet turns to lyric verse, however, the tone is eighteenth century in aspect. An example is *Vesennee utro* (Spring Morning, 1815). In the first two stanzas one sees the conventional poetic epithets common to the Sentimentalist school to which Karamzin belonged and from which Viazemsky drew his early poetic inspiration:

Po zybkim, belym oblakam
Goriat pylaiushchie rozy;
Dennitsy utrennie slezy
Blestiat, kak zhemchug, po lugam,
T s pyshnoi lipy i berezy
Dushistyi veet fimiam!

Razlitoe struiami zlato
Volnuetsia na teme gor;
Sadov bogini vernyi dvor,
Zefirov legkikh roi prylatyi
Letit na sotkannyi kover
Rukoiu Flory tarovatoi!

(On the unsteady white clouds
Burn flaming roses;
Aurora's morning tears
Glitter like pearls on the meadows,
And from the lush linden and birch
Wafts a fragrant incense!

Gold, poured out in streams
Seethes on the peaks of the mountains;
The loyal court of the goddess of the gardens,
The winged swarm of the light zephyrs
Flies to the carpet woven
By the hand of the prodigal Flora!)

Typical poetic usage abounds in the work and is represented by the use of "fragrant incense." An example of Karamzinian periphrasis is the reference to "Aurora's

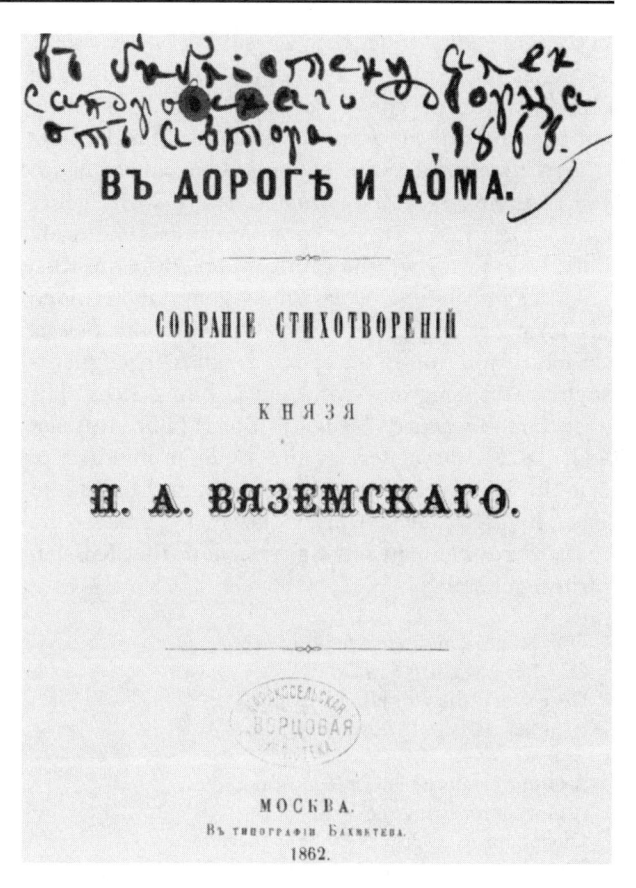

Viazemsky's V doroge i doma. Sobranie stikhotvorenii *(On the Road and at Home. Collected Poems); inscribed "to the library of the Aleksandrovskii palace from the author. 1866" and bearing the stamp of the palace Library of Tsarskoe Selo (Kilgour Collection, Harvard University Library)*

morning tears" (dew). The references to classical mythology likewise place the poem as an inheritor of the Sentimentalist style, as does its non-Russian location (implied by the mountains and gardens). The slight sensuality of the work prompted William Edward Brown to state that it also reveals the influence of the French elegist Évariste Désiré de Forges, vicomte de Parny, whose work inspired a generation of Russian poets from Karamzin to Evgenii Abramovich Baratynsky.

Another feature of Viazemsky's early verse that reveals his indebtedness to writers of the eighteenth century is his use of double entendres and similar verbal fireworks, particularly in satirical verse (another genre inherited from the Enlightenment). For satire, Viazemsky employed primarily the epistle, which, according to the rules passed down from eighteenth-century Classicism, was suited for everyday concerns. "Poslanie k Turgenevu s pirogom" (Epistle to Turgenev with a Pie, 1819) is an example of a work revealing his satiric intent. In it Viazemsky employs a mixture of lexical styles with a resulting parodic tone. He mixes high style with colloquialisms, resulting in a slightly acerbic conversational style. Those who had been part of the Arzamas group did not hesitate to turn to playful satire of their own colleagues as well as their adversaries. Indeed, satire is the genre upon which Viazemsky's reputation rests. The traditional fashion for writing satirical verse was the Russian Alexandrine; yet, Viazemsky generally avoided this form because of its association with the *Beseda*. Rather, in addition to the epistle he chose brief pieces (such as the epigram) with short, biting lines. His most famous satire, "Russkii Bog" (The Russian God, 1828), circulated at the time in manuscript form in Russia and was published in London in 1854. In this caustic work, Viazemsky attacks the Russian government, foreigners, and the Russian spirit in general:

Do you need an interpretation
Of what is the Russian God?
Here's an outline of him for you,
As much as I could observe.

A God of snowstorms, a God of potholes,
A God of torturing roads,
Of stations of cockroaches' headquarters,
That's him, that's him, the Russian God.

A God of the hungry, a God of the cold,
Of beggars everywhere in the land,
A God of bankrupt estates,
That's him, that's him, the Russian God.

A God of saggy breasts and <asses>,
A God of bast-shoes and bloated legs,
Of bitter faces and sour cream,
That's him, that's him, the Russian God.

A God of liquors, a God of pickles,
Of mortgaged souls,
Of brigadieresses of both sexes,
That's him, that's him, the Russian God.

A God of all those with the Anna decoration
   around their necks,
A God of shoeless house serfs,
Of masters in sleighs with two lackeys,
That's him, that's him, the Russian God.

Full of grace for the stupid,
Mercilessly stern to the intelligent,
A God of everything that is beside the point,
That's him, that's him, the Russian God.

A God of everything from abroad,
Everything unsuitable, everything not totaled up,
A God of mustard at supper,
That's him, that's him, the Russian God.

A God of nomadic foreigners,
Having crossed our threshold,
A God of Germans especially,
That's him, that's him, the Russian God.

This sharp commentary on Russia reveals the power of Viazemsky's tongue and wit. He frequently used the repetitive structure, which became the basis of much of his satirical verse.

Viazemsky's position on Russia expressed in "Russkii Bog" likewise finds a corollary in his critical works on literature. In them Viazemsky acquires a far more Romantic tone than in other works. He believed that "Literature must be the expression of the character and opinions of a people: judging by the books we publish, it is possible to conclude that we either have no literature, or else neither opinions nor character...." Viazemsky repeated this notion throughout the 1820s.

The repetitive structure used in "Russkii Bog" also formed the basis of Viazemsky's travel verse. He even developed a new genre of travel literature: verses literally composed from a carriage. By necessity, these verses are what is called "occasional"; they were inspired by specific local occurrences. An example of this new genre is "Stantsiia (Glava iz puteshestviia v stikhakh; pisana 1825 goda)" (Stations [Chapters from a Journey in Verse; Written in the Year 1825]). In this type of poetry the geography witnessed from the carriage provides the links between topics. As a result the thematics sometimes are justifiably quite disorganized.

In February 1818 Viazemsky moved to Warsaw to take up his government post. He was thereby exposed to liberal ideas during that time in aristocratic Russia when they were most in ferment—between the Patriotic War of 1812 and the Decembrist Uprising of 1825. During this period Viazemsky wrote his most strongly antigovernment verse. His work during this period also served to endear Viazemsky to Soviet critics and scholars. A letter written to Aleksandr Turgenev in the spring of 1820 illustrates his feelings: "And you still call me to Petersburg, to the torment of all and all kinds of household despotism! There you're all in some sort of inquisitorial nightmare." In fact, Viazemsky actively believed in the need for the progressive gentry to usurp power for the Imperial Throne. Alexander I caught wind of his ideas about reforming the peasantry and eventually decided to cut short his posting in Warsaw. During a stay in St. Petersburg in April of 1821 Viazemsky was notified that he was forbidden to return to his position in Warsaw. In July of the same year he departed for Moscow.

The most widely read example of antigovernment verse written during this period is "Negodovanie" (Indignation, November 1820). This work was inspired by scriptural Hebrew prophets. The imagery is more abstract than concrete, and the language is also heavily scriptural-laden with Church Slavonicisms, a hallmark of eighteenth-century Russian literary style as well: "zrel promyshliaiushchikh spasitel'nym glagolom, / Khanzhei, torguiushchikh ucheniem sviatym, / V zabven'i boga dush—odnim zemnym prestolam / Kadiashchikh trepetno, odnim bogam zemnym." (I have beheld hypocrites trafficking / In the word of salvation, trading in holy teachings, / Souls forgetful of God—burning incense in fear / Only to earthly thrones, only to earthly gods.)

As Brown points out, such a work renders Viazemsky's admiration for George Gordon, Lord Byron, more comprehensible. Byron influenced an entire generation of writers throughout Europe, writers who called themselves Romantic. Byron himself, however, was not, strictly speaking, as Romantic in his writings as he was in his role as a historical figure. Such is the case for Viazemsky, too, who defended Romanticism and admired its rebellion against the impositions and limitations of Classicism, but who nonetheless wrote works that in style were borderline Classical or Sentimental. Indeed, he was determined to write in his own particular style, resenting any intrusions or criticisms from other writers upon his work. He reveals his admiration for the liberty and artistic freedom provided by Romanticism in one of his most important critical pieces, "Razgovor mezhdu izdatelem i klassikom s Vyborgskoi storony ili s Vasil'evskogo ostrova" (A Conversation between an Editor and a Classicist from the Vyborg Embankment or Vasil'evsky Island, 1824). This piece was originally published as a type of introduction to Aleksandr Pushkin's "Bakhchisaraiskii fontan" (The Fountain of Bakhchisarai, 1824). It served a function for Pushkin's poem, but it also serves as an excellent example of Viazemsky's thinking. Perhaps his greatest condemnation of the Classicist's position occurs during a discussion about Homer and Virgil (whom a Classicist would imitate in his own writings):

> Classicist: You would even, perhaps, want, in the self-willedness of Romantics, to recruit even the Ancient Classicists. Looking at it that way, even Homer and Virgil were Romantics.
> Editor: Call them what you like. But there is no doubt that Homer, Horace, and Aeschylus have more kinship and relation to the heads of the Romantic school than to their own cold, slavish followers, who in hindsight strive to be Greeks and Romans.

Viazemsky viewed Romanticism as a set of liberating options rather than as a school of thought complete with its own rules, like the Classicism that it was seeking to replace. Rather, Viazemsky felt that Romanticism allowed

Petr Andreevich Viazemsky (from Galleria russkikh pisatelei i khudozhnikov, *1901)*

a writer to express the feelings of the moment in whatever fashion suited those feelings. Perhaps this particular notion caused Viazemsky's frequent difficulties with his fellow poets on questions of grammar and stylistics. With the introduction to Pushkin's poem, Viazemsky's verse turned toward the Romantic school, though he still remained unable to handle any criticism of his style, choice of words, or grammar.

One of his best-known lyrics, partially because of its mention in Pushkin's *Evgeny Onegin* (1823–1831, published in full, 1833) is his elegy of 1819 titled "Pervyj sneg (V 1817-m godu)" (The First Snow [of 1817], November 1819). In it Viazemsky attempts to counteract the Classical trend toward the universal (as seen in his "Negodovanie," for example) with concrete Russian description and incorporation of the spirit of the "national character," which proved so important to Romantic versification and thinking in general. Both Brown and Maksim Isaakovich Gillel'son have commented that, despite Viazemsky's best intentions, there is little national character in this work. It opens with typical Sentimentalist periphrasis describing an autumn scene before the first snowfall. In its actual description, however, there is a certain amount of genuine Russianness:

> Na prazdnike zimy krasuetsia zemlia
> I nas privetstvuet zhivitel' noi ulybkoi.
> Zdes' sneg, kak legkii pukh, povis na eli gibkoi
> Tam, temnyi izumrud posypav serebrom,
> Na mrachnoi sosne on razrisoval uzory.
> Rasseialis' pary i zasverkali gory,
> I solntsa shar vspylal na svode golubom.

> (For the holiday of winter the earth beautifies herself
> And greets us with an intoxicating smile.
> Here snow, like light down, hangs on the bending fir;
> There, dusting the dark emerald with silver,
> It drew patterns on the gloomy pine.
> The mists were dispersed and the mountains began to sparkle,
> And the orb of the sun flared up in the blue vault of heaven.)

This passage is far more concrete than others in the work, and it also exhibits some of Viazemsky's unusual combinations of adjectives and nouns, such as " *zhivitel'naia ulybka*" (intoxicating smile), as well as his tendency toward personification. Yet, as Brown has correctly noted, to call the sun "the sun" is equally impossible for Viazemsky—he rather chooses to call it an "orb." The cushioned sensuality of Sentimentalist verse still appears as well:

> Kto v tesnote sanei s krasavitsei mladoi,
> Revnivykh ne boias', sidel noga s nogoi,
> Zhal ruku, nezhnuiu v samom soprotivlen'e,
> I v serdtse devstvennom v pervoi liubvi smiaten'ia,
> I dumu pervuiu, i pervyi vzdokh zazheg,
> V pobede sei drugikh pobed priiav zalog.

> (Who in the snugness of the sleigh with a young beauty,
> Not fearing rivals, has sat leg pressed against leg,
> Pressed the hand, tender in its resistence,
> And in the maiden heart has lit the confusion
> Of first love, the first care, the first sigh;
> In this victory the pledge of other victories.)

The final line of this quotation was not initially published in Russia, for it was seen as too risqué. Despite the still palpable influence of French verse and Sentimentalism, Viazemsky felt that he was indeed representing the spirit of his native Russia.

In style, Viazemsky has much in common with Baratynsky. Both poets attempted to unite the universal and the intellectual with the personal, the "realia" of daily life. Yet, Viazemsky was generally unsuccessful. "Narvskii vodopad" (The Narva Waterfall, 1825) is an example of his struggle in this regard. The work is comprised of eleven stanzas. The first nine are descriptions of the action the waterfall imposes on its surroundings. Such a description has been labeled as typical for the Romantics. Yet, only in the tenth stanza is the reader given the reason for the description:

> Vorvavshis' v sei predel spokoinyi,
> Odin svirepstvuesh' v gluski,
> Kak vdol' pustyni vikhor' znoinyi,
> Kak strast' v sviatilishche dushi.

> Kak ty, vnezapno razrazitsia,
> Kak ty, rastet ona v nbor'be,
> Terzaet lono, gde roditsia,
> I pogloshchaetsia v sebe.

> (Having burst into this quiet region,
> Alone you rage in the wilderness,
> Like a sultry whirlwind in the desert,
> Like passion in the sanctuary of the soul.

> Like you, it will suddenly break loose,
> Like you, it grows in struggle,
> Tears the bosom, where it is born,
> And is swallowed up in itself.)

This work has as much in common with the style of Derzhavin as it does with that of Viazemsky's contemporaries. In fact, the poet sent a copy of the work to Aleksandr Pushkin for criticism, although he was unable to accept the result. Pushkin criticized primarily the juxtaposition of words that did not seem to him to go together. Viazemsky replied that the waterfall merely symbolizes a person who is feeling passion and that the mixed vocabulary merely reflects what that person transfers onto his surroundings.

Another of Viazemsky's well-known Romantic works is "More" (The Sea, 1826). Despite the concrete title, the poem deals with its subject in abstraction and Classical allusion. Such was Viazemsky's difficulty—an inclination to write verse that offered more of the Sentimentalist, eighteenth-century abstraction than an intense, personal Romantic expression. Another work, "Lesa" (The Woods, 1830), evokes vague emotions in a Romantic sense; this work succeeds in personalizing the surroundings:

> Do you want to learn about thoughts in the soul,
> For which there are neither images, nor words—
> There, where around grows thick the somber gloom,
> Listen to the silence of the woods;
> There in the quiet noises run about,
> The indistinct echo of soundless voices.
> In these voices are the melodies of the wilderness;
> I listened to them, began to hear them,
> I trembled, as before the face of holy worship,
> I was filled with harmonies, but mute,
> And from my breast, like a prisoner from the stronghold,
> My verse seethed in vain, in vain burst forth.

For this work Viazemsky has refrained from Classical allusions and Senitmentalist periphrasis. The work reminds the reader of German Romantic sensibilities. Yet, this poem does not represent a marked change in Viazemsky's style, but rather an indication of the beginning of a gradual development.

"Toska" (Ennuie, 1831) reveals more of the Viazemsky who cannot totally convert to Romanticism. Its title is suggestive of a traditional Sentimental elegy; yet, the wording of the poem indicates a certain Romantic sensibility:

Ne znaiu ia–kogo, chego ishchu,
Ne razberu, chem mysli taino polnyi;
No chto-to est', o chem vezde grushchu,
No snov, no slez, no dum, zhelanii volny
Tekut, kipiat v boleznennoi grudi,
I tsoli ia ne vizhu vperedi.

(I do not know, for whom, for what I am searching,
I do not understand with which thoughts I am secretly filled;
But there is something about which I grieve everywhere,
But the waves of words, tears, thoughts, and desires
Flow, boil in my ailing breast,
And I cannot see the purpose before me.)

The poem continues to reveal that the speaker only understands reality in dreams and sleep. Once awakened, he understands nothing and merely sees the shadows. This focus, not on the incomprehensibility of reality but on its access through the netherworld of the unconscious, is typical of Romanticism. This poem continues the feelings expressed in "Lesa" and attempted in earlier works overburdened with artificial stylization.

The trend toward personalized, stylized nature that strikes a chord within the poet's heart continued in Viazemsky's verse; a prime example is "Vecher (Ekaterine Fedorovne Tiutchevoi)" (Evening [To Ekatarina Fedorovna Tiutcheva], 1865?). The following stanza clearly reveals the development of this trend: "And silently life around is fragrant, / And in its motionless beauty / The cool evening silently dissipates / A poetry without sounds, without speech." If this poem speaks of inexpressible poetry, "without words," then "Opiat' ia slyshu ètot shum" (Again I Hear This Sound, 1867) echoes the sentiments of soulful incomprehension stated in "Toska." The sea now acquires a different hue from that in the poem "More" and evokes in the speaker himself a sense of revelation: "Mysterious is the gloom in the muteness of the night, / But within its silence even more mysterious / Are the prophecies of your soul, O sea! / You want to say something / About the secrets of eternal nature, / And to us with a short-lived wave / Their deep meaning impart." This verse is quite different from Viazemsky's early ones. In fact, even in the genre of travel poetry, which Viazemsky had pioneered, there is a change in tone. "Palestina" (Palestine, 1850) reveals a source of timeless poetic mystery. The journey is personal–there are references to the poet's horse and to his prayers and visions. Yet, this same scenery reveals to him a greater secret–one of historicism-become-poetry. This poem parallels the others that use landscape to express the mysteries of existence.

When Viazemsky composed these verses, the Russian literary scene had already embraced Realism. The age of the great Russian novel was in force. Poetry, if it was even tolerated, had to be of civic use. Viazemsky found himself isolated, a representative of a Golden Age of poetry that had passed away. Yet, his lyrics, as Irina Mikhailovna Semenko has pointed out, serve as a foreshadowing of the second great period of Russian poetry–the Silver Age of the turn of the century. Poems such as "Zima" (Winter, 1848), "Bastei" (The Bastei, 1853), "Riabina" (The Rowan-Tree, 1854), and "Venetsiia" (Venice, 1863 or 1864) all illustrate Viazemsky's precocity in this respect. In these poems Viazemsky successfully incorporates folkloric speech, uses language to mirror phonetically what is being transcribed, and elevates images to symbols that impart a meaning beyond themselves. This style is a great distance from the literary style of the true Romantics, though it is explicitly linked to it.

Viazemsky's late poetry is, strictly speaking, not part of the Romantic movement. Viazemsky felt his anachronistic position keenly. "Svoi katekhizis splosh' prilezhno izucha" (Studying Your Catechism Quite Diligently, 1872?) reveals the depth of his bitterness:

Life is permeated with a caustic bitterness to its core,
There is no love of one's neighbor, not a mention of gentleness,
And my gloomy soul is seized now
By only despair and hatred alone.
That is how I have been rewarded by Providence for old age,
That is how it has shown its wisdom and goodness:
It has prolonged my life, so that it might be a burden to me,
So that I might curse that day, on which I was born.

More examples of this pessimism abound. Yet, the reader can certainly understand this view of life. In many ways Viazemsky only began to write verses that posterity would value after the passing of his era. In his own time his poetry was never as acclaimed as it was in the new dawn of Russian lyric poetry. During the period of Romanticism, Viazemsky was acclaimed for his biting wit, for his satires and epigrams, and for his critical pieces; yet, he always strove to make the Russian language express abstractions in verse that it could not. In this manner, Viazemsky was the ideal theoretical Romantic–attempting to fuse the infinite of thought into the finite of reality and language. In practice, he was a poet of the eighteenth century protesting his literary relevance to the nineteenth century. When he finally found his voice, the nineteenth-century era of Russian poetry had already disappeared.

Letters:
"Pis'ma," in *Iz sobraniia avtografov imp. Publichnoi biblioteki* (St. Petersburg, 1898), pp. 49-131;
Nikolai Platonovich Barsukov, ed. and comp., "Pis'ma k P. A. Viazemskomu (iz Ostaf'evskogo arkhiva)," *Stat'i i novizna*, no. 4 (1901): 1-222;
François-Auguste-René de Chateaubriand, "Pis'ma P. A. Viazemskomu (mart 1839)," *Literaturnoe nasledstvo*, 31-32 (1937): 146;
Mikhail Fedorovich Orlov, "Pis'ma P. A. Viazemskomu (1819-1829)," *Literaturnoe nasledstvo*, 60 (1956): 13-46;
Aleksandr L'vovich Ospovat, "Iz neizdannoi perepiski P. A. Viazemskogo," *Voprosy literatury*, 12 (1986): 260-264.

Biography:
Maksim Isaakovich Gillel'son, *P. A. Viazemsky, zhizn' i tvorchestvo* (Leningrad: Nauka, 1969).

References:
Vissarion Grigor'evich Belinsky, *Vzgliad na russkuiu literaturu* (Moscow: Sovremennik, 1988);
William Edward Brown, *A History of Russian Literature of the Romantic Period*, volume 2 (Ann Arbor, Mich.: Ardis, 1986);
Lidiia Iakovlevna Ginzburg, "Viazemsky–literator," in *Russkaia proza* (Leningrad: Academia, 1926), pp. 102-134;
Ieronim Ieronimovich Iasinsky, "Kniaz' P. A. Viazemsky v pis'makh ego k S. D. Poltoratskomu." *Nov'*, no. 9 (1885): 86-95;
Dmitrii Dmitrievich Iazykov, *Kniaz' P. A. Viazemsky (ego zhizn' i literaturno-obshchestvennaia deiatel'nost')* (Moscow, 1904);
Nikolai Karlovich Kul'man, "Kniaz' P. A. Viazemsky kak kritik," *Izvestiia Otdeleniia iazyka i slovestnosti*, 9, no. 1 (1904): 273-335;
K. A. Kupman, "Istoriia izdaniia poeticheskogo sbornika Viazemskogo 'V doroge i doma,'" *Russkaia literatura: Istoriko-Literaturnyi Zhurnal*, 1 (1990): 164-171;
Lauren Gray Leighton, "A Romantic Idealist Notion in Russian Romantic Criticism," *Canadian-American Slavic Studies*, 7 (1973): 285-295;

T. E. Little, "P. A. Vyazemsky as a Critic of Pushkin," in *Russian and Slavic Literature*, edited by Richard Freeborn, R. R. Milner-Gulland, and Charles A. Ward (Cambridge, Mass.: Slavica, 1976), pp. 1-16;
Iurii Vladimirovich Mann, *Poetika russkogo romantizma* (Moscow: Nauka, 1976);
Jan Marinus Meijer, "Vjazemskij and Romanticism," in *Dutch Contributions to the Seventh International Congress of Slavists: Warsaw, August 21-27*, edited by Andre van Holk (The Hague: Mouton, 1973), pp. 271-304;
E. A. Obukhova and Leonid Genrikhovich Frizman, "Pozdnii Viazemsky," in *Izvestiia Akademii Nauk SSSR, Seriia literatury i iazyka*, 42 (July-August 1983): 364-373;
Sergei Mitrofanovich Petrov, ed., *Istoriia russkoi literatury XIX veka* (Moscow: Prosveshchenie, 1970);
Petr Aleksandrovich Pletnev, comp., *Iubilei piatidesiatiletnei literaturnoi deiatel'nosti akademika kniazia P. A. Viazemskogo* (St. Petersburg: Akademiia Nauk, 1861);
Stepan Ivanovich Ponomarev, "Pamiati kniazia P. A. Viazemskogo," *Sbornik Otdeleniia russkogo iazyka i slovesnosti*, 20, no. 5 (1880): 59-144;
Aleksandr Sergeevich Pushkin, *Mysli o literature* (Moscow: Sovremennik, 1988);
Stanislav Borisovich Rassadin, "'Neschastnyi drug!': o poezii P. A. Viazemskogo," *Voprosy literatury*, 4 (April 1983): 113-150;
Irina Mikhailovna Semenko, *Poety pushkinskoi pory* (Moscow-Leningrad: Khudozhestvennaia literatura, 1970);
Sergei Dmitrievich Sheremetev, "Kniaz' P. A. Viazemsky," *Russkii arkhiv*, no. 4 (1891): 495-508;
Vladimir Danilovich Spasovich, "Kniaz' Viazemsky i ego pol'skie otnosheniia i znakomstva," *Russkaia mysl'*, no. 1, part 2 (1890): 51-82;
Victor Terras, ed., *Handbook of Russian Literature* (New Haven, Conn.: Yale University Press, 1985);
Iurii Nikolaevich Tynianov, *Arkhaisty i novatory* (Leningrad: Priboi, 1929);
G. Vytzens, "P. A. Viazemsky i russkaia literatura XVIII v," in *Rol' i znachenie literatury XVIII veka v istorii russkoi kul'tury: k 70-letiiu so dnia rozhdeniia tslena-korrespondeta ANSSSR P. N. Berkova* (Moscow: Nauka, 1966), pp. 332-338.

Papers:
Petr Andreevich Viazemsky's papers are in Moscow at the Rossiiskii gosudarstvennyi arkhiv literatury i iskusstva, fond 195, and the Rossiiskaia gosudarstvenneia biblioteka, fond 63, and in St. Petersburg at the Rossiiskaia natsional'naia biblioteka, fond 167.

Vasilii Andreevich Zhukovsky

(29 January 1783 - 12 April 1852)

James West
University of Washington

BOOKS: *Pevets vo stane ruskikh voinov* (St. Petersburg: Morskaia tip., 1813);

Stikhotvoreniia, 2 volumes (St. Petersburg, 1815–1816);

Pevets na Kremle (St. Petersburg: Meditsinskaia Tipografiia, 1816);

Dvenadtsat' spiashchikh dev. Starinnaia povest' (St. Petersburg: Meditsinskaia Tipografiia, 1817);

Stikhotvoreniia, second edition, parts 1–3 (St. Petersburg: Tip. Imp. Vospitatel'nago doma, 1818); part 4 published as *Sochineniia Vasili Zhukovskago* (Moscow: S. Selivanovsky, 1818);

Stikhotvoreniia, third edition, corrected and expanded (St. Petersburg: Tip. Departamenta narodnago prosveshcheniia, 1824);

Sochineniia v proze, second edition, revised and enlarged (St. Petersburg: I. Glazunov, 1826);

Chuvstva pred grobom gosudaryni imperatritsy Marii Fedorovny v nochi nakunune pogrebeniia telaeia velichestva (St. Petersburg: N. Grech, 1828);

Ballady i povesti, 2 volumes (St. Petersburg: Izd. Smirdina, Voennaia tip., 1831);

Na vziatie Varshavy: Tri stikhotvoreniia, by Zhukovsky and Aleksandr Sergeevich Pushkin (St. Petersburg: Voennaia tip., 1831);

Russkaia slava. Stikhotvorenie (St. Petersburg: A. F. Smirdin, 1831);

Stikhotvoreniia, 9 volumes (St. Petersburg: A. F. Smirdin, 1835–1844);

Tiul'pannoe derevo. Skazka V. A. Zhukovskago (St. Petersburg: Tip. Voenno-uchebnykh zavedenii, 1846);

Stikhotvoreniia, 13 volumes (St. Petersburg, 1849–1857);

Polnoe sobranie sochinenii v stikhakh i v proze (Karlsruhe, 1851);

Stikhotvoreniia, posviashchenye Pavlu Vasilichu i Aleksandre Vasil'evne Zhukovskim (Karlsruhe, 1852);

Skazka o tsare Berendee, o syne ego Ivane Tsareviche, o khitrostiakh Koshcheia Bezsmertnago i o premudrosti Mar'i Tsarevny, koshcheevoi docheri (St. Petersburg: Pechatnia V. I. Golovina, 1871);

Skazka o Ivane Tsareviche i serom volke: sochinenie (St. Petersburg: Izd. I. I. Glazunova, 1876);

Stranstvuiushchii zhid. Predsmertnoe proizvedenie Zhukovskago, po rukopisi poeta, edited by Stepan Ivanovich Ponomarev (St. Petersburg: Tip. Imperatorskoi Akademii nauk, 1885);

Kapitan Bopp (raskaian'e greshnika). Izd. Kom-ta vysochaishe utverzhdennykh nar. chtenii (Berdiansk: Tip. Nutis, 1896);

Dnevniki (St. Petersburg, 1903);

Pamiati V. A. Zhukovskago i N.V. Gogolia, by Zhukovsky and Nikolai Vasil'evich Gogol, 3 volumes, edited by Aleksandr Nikolaevich Veselovsky and Aleksei Ivanovich Sobolevsky (St. Petersburg: Tip. Imperatorskoi Akademii nauk, 1907–1909);

Spiashchaia tsarevna: Skazka (Moscow: Izd-vo detskoi lit-ry, 1947).

Editions and Collections: *Vasilii Andreevich Zhukovskii* (St. Petersburg: M. Stasiulevich, 1875);

Sochineniia V. A. Zhukovskago, s prilozheniem ego pisem, biografii i portreta, gravirovannago akademikom Pozhalostinym, 6 volumes, seventh edition, corrected and expanded, edited by Petr Aleksandrovich Efremov (St. Petersburg: Izd. knigoprodavtsa I. I. Glazunova, 1878);

Stikhotvoreniia V. A. Zhukovskago (Moscow: M. Katkov, Universitetskaia tip., 1885);

Ballady V. A. Zhukovskago: polnoe sobranie ballad, s primechaniiami, obiasnitel'nyia stat'i (St. Petersburg: Izd. I. Glazunova, 1892);

Polnoe sobranie sochinenii, 12 volumes, edited by Aleksandr Semenovich Arkhangel'sky (St. Petersburg: A. F. Marks, 1902);

Sochineniia V. A. Zhukovskago, 2 volumes, edited by A. D. Alferov (Moscow: t-vo I. D. Sytin, 1902);

Ballady, edited by Tsezar' Samoilovich Vol'pe (Leningrad: Izd-vo detskoi lit-ry, 1936);

Stikhotvoreniia, 2 volumes, edited by Vol'pe (Leningrad: Sovetskii pisatel', 1939–1940);

Stikhotvoreniia, edited by Lidiia Iakovlevna Ginzburg (Leningrad: Sovetskii pisatel', 1956);

Stikhotvoreniia i poemy, edited by N. Kovarsky (Leningrad: Sovetskii pisatel', 1958);

Sobranie sochinenii, 4 volumes, edited by V. P. Petushkov, Irina Mikhailovna Semenko, Nikolai Vasil'evich Izmailov, and Isaak Davidovich Glikman (Moscow: Khudozhestvennaia literatura, 1959–1960);

Izbrannye sochineniia, edited by Semenko (Moscow: Khudozhestvennaia literatura, 1982);

Stikhotvoreniia, poemy, proza, edited by Viktor V. Afanas'ev (Moscow: Sovremennik, 1983);

Tsvety mechty uedinennoi: stikhotvoreniia i ballady, edited by Valentin Ivanovich Korovin (Moscow: Detskaia literatura, 1984);

Èstetika i kritika (Moscow: "Isskustvo," 1985);

"Vse neobeiatnoe v edinyi vzdokh tesnitsia . . .": Izbrannaia lirika: V. A. Zhukovskii v dokumentakh: Stikhotvoreniia russkikh poetov XIX veka, posviashchennye V. A. Zhukovskomu, edited by Afanas'ev (Moscow: Moskovskii rabochii, 1986);

Ballady; Nal' i Damaianti; Rustem i Zorab; Dnevniki; Pis'ma; Vospominaniia sovremennikov, edited by Semenko (Moscow: Izd-vo "Pravda," 1987).

OTHER: *Sobranie russkikh stikhotvorenii*, 5 volumes, edited by Zhukovsky (Moscow: Universitetskaia tip., 1810–1811);

Für Wenige. Dlia nemnogikh, nos. 1–6, edited by Zhukovsky (Moscow: A. Semen, 1818).

TRANSLATIONS: *Don Kishot La Mankhskii. Perevedeno s frantsuzskago Florianova perevoda V. Zhukovskim*, second edition (Moscow: Universitetskaia tip., 1815);

Undina, starinnaia povest', razskazannaia na nemetskom iazyke v proze Baronom F. Lamott Fuké. Na russkom v stikhakh, V. Zhukovskim (St. Petersburg: Izd. A. Smirdina, V Tip. Ekspeditsii zagotovleniia Gosudarstvennykh bumag, 1837);

Nal' i Damaianti. Indeiskaia povest' (St. Petersburg: Izdanie Fishera, 1844);

Iliada, pesn' pervaia i vtoroi pesni st. 494–718 (St. Petersburg, 1860?);

Odisseia Gomera (St. Petersburg: Izd. I. Glazunova, 1888);

Slovo o polku Igoreve, edited by Vladimir Aleksandrovich Serov (Leningrad: Khudozhestvennaia literatura, 1963);

Zarubezhnaia poeziia v perevodakh V. A. Zhukovskogo, 2 volumes, edited by Aleksandr Aleksandrovich Gugnin (Moscow: Raduga, 1985).

Aleksandr Pushkin, unquestionably Russia's greatest poet, wrote of Vasilii Zhukovsky: "I am not his successor, but rather his pupil. . . . Nobody has had or will have as powerful and varied a poetic voice as his." Zhukovsky was indeed one of the most influential figures in the making of modern Russian poetry. In the first two decades of the nineteenth century Russia entered a new era of national pride and self-awareness, fueled by the respect for national cultures engendered by the Romantic movement and by the successes in the war against Napoleon Bonaparte. While educated Russians were developing a new sense of their place in the European intellectual community, the Russian literary language was in a state of flux, pulled one way by a proud attachment to the pre-Petrine written language and in another direction by the equally natural impulse, exemplified by the work of Nikolai Mikhailovich Karamzin, to imitate the contemporary sophistication of the major European languages. Though it fell ultimately to Pushkin finally to establish the language of nineteenth-century Russian poetry with a brilliant synthesis of the old and the new, Zhukovsky made this achievement possible to an extent that Pushkin clearly acknowledged.

A translator of poetry from a variety of European languages, Zhukovsky brought to Russians the spirit of European Romanticism rather than superficial imitation of Romantic models. His impact on Russian letters was further enhanced by the breadth of his talent: his verse

*Sketch by Zhukovsky of his mother, Elizaveta Dement'evna Turchaninova
(from Viktor V. Afanas'ev,* Zhukovsky, *1986)*

compositions range from the short lyric to the epic, and his work includes prose, drama, and critical essays. He also was both a highly knowledgeable art connoisseur and an accomplished amateur artist. Almost as important as his literary contribution was his role over many years as a defender of writers who had incurred the displeasure of the Russian authorities, often with a quite improbable degree of success. By the time of his death, he had the stature of a statesman in the eyes of all but the authorities.

Vasilii Andreevich Zhukovsky was born on 29 January 1783, the son of Afanasii Ivanovich Bunin, a landowner whose property was at Mishenskoe in the Tula province. Bunin's wife, Mariia Grigor'evna, was not the poet's mother, however. A serf on the Bunin estate had gone to fight in one of the many Russian campaigns against the Turks. As he departed, Bunin had asked him in jest to bring him back a good-looking Turkish girl since his wife was getting old. That a joke in such poor taste could be interpreted as a request speaks volumes about Russian society in the late eighteenth century. The servant obliged, and in 1770 Bunin found himself the owner of sixteen-year-old Salkha, already a widow, as her husband had been killed in the battle with the Russians for the fort at Bendery. She was christened Elizaveta Dement'evna, with the surname Turchaninova (derived from the Russian word for a Turk), and installed in an outlying part of the manor house. Bunin soon began to spend his nights in her quarters. She bore him three daughters, all of whom died in infancy, and a son, the future poet. Bunin's wife, all but one of whose children had died, raised the boy as her own. He was given the family name of his godfather, Andrei Grigor'evich Zhukovsky, a relative who lived on the charity of the Bunins.

Young Vasilii's bizarre situation was complicated by the fact that his mother was employed as a housekeeper on the estate, while his considerably older half sister, the Bunins' daughter, behaved toward him more as a second mother than as a sibling. When Bunin died in 1791, the boy received nothing in his will, but Mariia Bunina undertook to treat him as a member of the family and promised never to sell his mother. Though Zhukovsky's childhood was in most respects a happy one, the ambivalence of his situation left him a slightly wistful outsider in a tribe of more than a dozen female cousins and nieces.

Zhukovsky grew up in a domestic atmosphere characterized by piety and enriched by poetry, amateur theatricals, and music making, which clearly fostered both his literary calling and his eventual philosophical disposition and temperament. His earliest poetic efforts, which have not survived, probably date from before he was ten, and by the age of twelve he had composed a classical drama on a theme from Roman history that was enthusiastically performed and received in the family circle.

Zhukovsky's education began in 1789 at a private school in Tula, the provincial capital, and continued at the main public school there. Though clearly a bright child, he had difficulty paying attention in the strict classroom atmosphere of the public school, from which he was expelled in 1794 for lack of progress. For the next three years he was tutored at home with the girls of the family, and in 1797 he was sent to the *Moskovskii universitetskii blagorodnyi pansion* (Moscow University Preparatory School for Nobles), a prestigious institution where much of the instruction was given by Moscow University professors, and at which many notable Russians received their education. The head of the school and the director of Moscow University, Ivan Petrovich Turgenev (a friend of Afanasii Bunin), were both Freemasons, and the school set out to impart the masonic ideals of moral self-improvement, charity, and civic duty. Zhukovsky formed the first deep friendships of his life there, particularly with Aleksandr, Andrei, and Nikolai Ivanovich Turgenev, sons of the university director. He began to write while still at the preparatory school, and by the time he graduated, he had already published several poems and articles in literary periodicals. He also began what became one of his principal forms of literary activity: unable to afford all of the books he needed, he earned money by translating works by the popular German writer and state official August von Kotzebue, best known as the victim in 1819 of an assassination that had political repercussions throughout Europe. The volumes that constituted Zhukovsky's library in this period give a good indication of his earliest literary models. The strongest Russian influence on Zhukovsky at the outset of his career was clearly Karamzin, the leading Sentimentalist who later became Russia's official historian; but the young poet's shelves also held many works of the French Enlightenment, including the *Encyclopédie* (1751–1780); historical writing in French, German, and English; and a good deal of German literature, in particular many writers of the pre-Romantic Sturm und Drang movement: Johann Gottfried Herder, Friedrich Schiller, and Johann Wolfgang von Goethe.

The students of the *Moskovskii universitetskii blagorodnyi pansion* were destined for government service and were routinely assigned to their first positions on graduation. Though he was a silver medalist in his final examinations in June 1800, Zhukovsky did not have friends in high places, and he was appointed to a minor government administrative position for which he was completely unsuited. His leisure hours were spent reading, writing, and talking about books, politics, and history with his literary friends; but in the paramilitary climate of the Russian civil service he found the working life of a junior bureaucrat intolerable. A serious quarrel with his immediate superior had unpleasant consequences, including a brief spell of house arrest; but with the help of friends he was able to extricate himself from more serious disciplinary action and resign from the service. In May 1802 he left Moscow for the Bunin family estate at Mishenskoe, taking with him his already considerable library. He was determined to educate himself by reading and to establish himself as a writer.

Zhukovsky's welcoming of the comparative isolation of country life was caused in part by an event in his emotional life that proved a harbinger of things to come. In the circle of cultured young people in which he moved in St. Petersburg, he had taken under his wing Mariia Nikolaevna Vel'iaminova, daughter of a half sister. Before long his encouragement of her intellectual interests had turned into a strong mutual affection. In 1801 Vel'iaminova was given in marriage to a man who was considered a good match in practical terms but lacked her interest in things of the mind and spirit. Zhukovsky accepted this blow as a dictate of fate but pursued a platonic relationship with Mariia Svechina, as she now became, through correspondence. His abrupt departure from the capital at this time, though unrelated, was an emotionally appropriate retreat into the rural solitude where melancholy belonged. The suggestion that the young Zhukovsky's emotional life involved a measure of Romantic literary role-playing is not frivolous. Among his contemporaries, this behavior was not unusual, and his friend Aleksandr Turgenev, studying in Göttingen a year later, noted in his diary that Zhukovsky's love for Svechina was like Petrarch's celebrated literary love for his unattainable Laura.

Between 1802 and 1807 Zhukovsky lived with or close to his half sister, Ekaterina Afanas'evna Protasova, a woman of strong character who had a fateful influence on the rest of his life. Her loving marriage had ended abruptly with her husband's death in 1797, leaving her with two small daughters and her husband's considerable gambling debts. Obliged to sell her property, she moved first to the Bunin estate at Mishenskoe, then to a house of her own in nearby Belev. Though still in her twenties and quite attractive, she never remarried, but wore black for the rest of her life in memory of her husband and lived for her children with almost obsessive devotion. On his return to the family home, Zhukovsky became in effect a resident tutor to the two girls, Mariia Andreevna (Masha) and Aleksandra Andreevna (Sasha). He took his responsibilities seriously and formed at this point a predilection for education, seeing his business as extending beyond the imparting of knowledge to the development of his charges as "moral beings," in the sense that this expression had in the era of Sentimentalism. He also began falling in love with Masha.

In July 1803 Zhukovsky received the news of the death of Andrei Turgenev following a sudden illness. The loss of so cherished a friend had a profound and lasting effect on him; he was afflicted thereafter with bouts of melancholy and pained resignation, and his poetry often reflected the idea that death is only a temporary parting from soul mates with whom there will be a reunion in another life. In the age of Sentimentalism, friendship commonly acquired an almost metaphysical dimension, and in Zhukovsky's case the circumstances of his life intensified this tendency. An 11 September 1805 letter to Aleksandr, to whom he drew closer after Andrei's death, gives clear expression to the ideal that guided Zhukovsky throughout his life: "We must . . . persuade ourselves that we are not simply friends, people who take pleasure in each other's company, but people who need to be friends, on whom friendship has the same beneficial, sacred, invigorating and uplifting effect as religion has on any noble-spirited person." The faculty of memory, perhaps originally important to him only on the personal level as a source of consolation and a refuge from his emotional misfortunes, came to be endowed with a more serious philosophical significance as a channel of communication between the living and the departed.

In these years Zhukovsky's first concern was to educate himself as broadly as possible, both as an enlightened individual and as a writer. After his brief and disastrous spell of government service it was clear that he would now make some kind of career for himself as a man of letters. He read earnestly and voraciously in French, German, and English as well as Russian, with a strong predilection for the writings that fueled European Sentimentalism and early Romanticism: James Thomson's *The Seasons* (1726–1730); Thomas Gray's celebrated "Elegy Written in a Country Churchyard" (1751); the idylls of Salomon Gessner; *Les Jardins* (1782), Jacques Delille's influential poetic treatise on

Sketch by Zhukovsky of Mariia Andreevna Protasova, the niece with whom he fell in love (from Viktor V. Afanas'ev, Zhukovsky, *1986)*

gardens, as well as his translations of Virgil's *Georgics* (1770) and the *Aeneid* (1804); the works of Jean-Jacques Rousseau; *Essai analytique sur les facultés de l'âme* (1760), Charles Bonnet's important treatise on the formative effect on humans of their surroundings; and the poems of Ossian, supposedly the work of an early Scottish bard, which were immensely popular in the late eighteenth and early nineteenth centuries despite the revelation that they were actually created by James Macpherson in the 1760s. During a visit in 1803 Zhukovsky discussed with Karamzin his plan to study all the world's literature as preparation for embarking on a first major work of his own. Though reading a great deal more than he wrote, he produced during these years some of his most significant works, both original and translated. He completed his Russian version of Miguel de Cervantes's *Don Quixote* (part 1, 1605; part 2, 1615), which was published in four volumes in 1804 and 1805.

The most celebrated of Zhukovsky's poetic translations, that of Gray's "Elegy," also belongs to this period. Andrei Turgenev had published in 1802 an "Elegy" somewhat loosely based on Gray's, which prompted Zhukovsky not to rival it but to complete the task his friend had begun. Turning to rural Russia for inspiration (he did much of the work on his translation outdoors in the countryside around Mishenskoe in August 1802), Zhukovsky set out to convey what he saw as the philosophical lesson of Gray's elegy, making the imagery less concrete and replacing the iambic pentameter of the English original with more imposing and graceful hexameters. Zhukovsky's "Sel'skoe kladbishche" (A Country Churchyard) was published in *Vestnik Evropy* (Herald of Europe) in 1802.

Other well-known poems of this period closely reflect his preoccupation with the role of literature in society at the watershed between Neoclassicism and Romanticism. His "K poezii" (To Poetry, 1804) reads by turns like a sentimental rhapsody and an eighteenth-century ode as it extols poetry for its power both to assuage the pangs of melancholy solitude and to win the glorious approbation of grateful posterity. "Vecher. Elegiia" (Evening. An Elegy, 1806) injects into a conventional Neoclassical idyll the melancholy of the poet grieving for lost friends, and ends with a reference to conventional Romantic poetic lovers, Alpin and Minvana (the second of these is Ossianic), who represent Andrei Turgenev and Masha Protasova. It is an outstanding example of the Romantic transformation of landscape into a system of emblems for emotions and states of mind. Another significant work of these years is "Pesn' barda nad grobom slavian pobeditelei" (The Bard's Song at the Grave of the Victorious Slavs, 1806), the inspiration for which came from Gray's "The Bard: A Pindaric Ode" (1757), inspired in its turn by Ossian. The poem transposes into a Russian setting the impulse of early Romantic Europe to picture native bards celebrating the history of indigenous nationalities; its appeal to Zhukovsky's contemporaries was immediate and powerful.

Most of all, the five years following his withdrawal from the capital were for Zhukovsky a period of intense self-scrutiny, study, and thought about his future. His diary from this period reveals that he planned his life in detail, even if events often overtook his plans. He intended to travel in Europe for three years, beginning in the summer of 1806, and on his return to edit a journal for four or five years, then to produce a magnum opus that would bring him literary celebrity. His role model was Karamzin, whose influence on Zhukovsky was strong and more than purely literary. The two men were distantly related: in 1801 Karamzin had married Ekaterina Protasova's sister-in-law, who died the following year of childbirth complications.

In 1807 Zhukovsky's career took a turn that brought him more into the public eye: on Karamzin's advice, he was offered the editorship of *Vestnik Evropy*, long considered to be the most prestigious literary journal in Russia. *Vestnik Evropy* had been edited at an earlier stage by Karamzin himself, who had relinquished the task when he became engrossed in the writing of his monumental *Istoriia gosudarstva Rossiiskogo* (History of the Russian State, 1816–1818; revised, 1818–1829). Zhukovsky eagerly accepted the invitation and moved to Moscow to begin his duties in 1808, planning to restore to the journal the reputation it had enjoyed under Karamzin. Besides editing *Vestnik Evropy* in 1808–1809, Zhukovsky was the most frequent contributor of both poetry and prose, and particularly of editorial articles in which he discussed the function of literature and the moral duty of the writer. His article "Pisatel' v obshchestve" (The Writer in Society), written in 1808, gives clearest expression to his slightly ambivalent position on the writer's relationship to society: the poet must labor in solitude, but without entirely losing touch with the world at large.

In 1808 Zhukovsky published his ballad "Liudmila," which took its theme from the German poet Gottfried August Bürger's celebrated "Lenore" (1773) but used legendary material from sixteenth-century Russia to create a "national" work of considerable originality and vigor. "Liudmila" enjoyed enormous popularity, establishing the Romantic ballad as a favored genre with the Russian reading public, and it was followed in 1809 by his novella *Mar'ina roshcha. Starinnoe predanie* (Maria's Grove. An Ancient Legend), which also owed its popularity to the transportation of a familiar sentimental narrative into a Russian historical setting and to its intensely poetic quality. *Mar'ina roshcha* tells of a maiden who loves a bard named Uslad but is married to another and dies pining for the true object of her affections. Uslad remains faithful to the memory of her love, and they are united in another life. The autobiographical element is evident from both the narrative situation and the image of a "violet of the field," which he used to describe Mar'ina, and the work typifies Zhukovsky's poetical sublimation of the emotional crises of his life.

By 1810 Zhukovsky was finding that the pressures of editorial work prevented him from writing and that city life was tiring; even though he spent many of his evenings in the company of some of his leading literary contemporaries, he disliked being at such a distance from his family and the object of his love. In the winter of 1810 the poet was given the sum of 10,000 rubles from the Bunin estate, which he used to buy part of the village of Kholkho, close to Muratovo and separated from it only by a picturesque lake. In June he left Moscow, moving first to Belev to the house of his half sister. At her request, he designed for her a new house in nearby Muratovo, which she occupied by the end of the year. Zhukovsky had a genuine liking for country living, and from time to time throughout his life he voiced a heartfelt dislike of the oppressive social climate and the distractions of the city. In 1811 he celebrated his village surroundings in "Pevets" (The Bard), a poem that enjoyed great popularity. In two years of this country life, Zhukovsky read and wrote a great deal and shared with enthusiastic pleasure the social life of family and neighbors, including the dramatic and musical endeavors of Aleksandr Alekseevich Pleshcheev, a talented acquaintance who ran a domestic theater on his estate in the Orel province.

This period was, however, marred by two sad events. In May 1811 Mariia Bunina died, followed less than two weeks later by Zhukovsky's natural mother, whose attachment to the always generous Bunina was such that she did not have the will to survive her. In the meantime Zhukovsky's renewed proximity to Masha Protasova had confirmed once and for all his feelings for her. In January 1812 the poet wrote to Ekaterina Protasova from Moscow, where he was briefly staying, asking for Masha's hand in marriage. Even though Masha was the daughter of his half sister, and the match was technically proscribed by the Russian church, dispensations were commonly given to allow such marriages. Ekaterina Protasova's stubborn religiosity, however, prevented her from seeing beyond the fear of allowing a sinful union. Her response was not only a refusal but also a demand that Zhukovsky never even speak to Masha of his love. He could only comply, and he was doomed to a relationship with his beloved that was defined only by their membership in the same family and suspiciously watched over by her mother.

The year 1812 was a turning point in Zhukovsky's life in another important respect. On 12 June Napoleon's forces crossed the Russian border, and the poet decided that he would join the militia and fight the invasion. He was depressed by the thought that if he were killed Masha would never know of his love for her. Therefore, he took advantage of a house concert at the Pleshcheev residence to sing his romance "Plovets" (The Diver) in such a way that Masha clearly understood to whom it was addressed. Ekaterina Protasova was enraged by what she regarded as an insolent betrayal of their agreement and expressed her displeasure publicly by immediately leaving for home, taking both her daughters with her. Though he may not have fully realized it at the time, Zhukovsky's last hope that she might relent was dashed that evening, and soon

Title page for the first volume of Stikhotvoreniia *(Poems), Zhukovsky's first collection*

thereafter he enlisted as a lieutenant in the Moscow militia.

He had no illusions about his suitability for military service but felt with characteristic intensity the surge of patriotism engendered in Russians of all generations and social classes by the French invasion. His unit stood by in the rear at the Battle of Borodino and saw minor action at other locations, but Zhukovsky's role was more that of an observer and, particularly after he was attached to Gen. Mikhail Illarionovich Kutuzov's staff, a recorder of the heroism of others. At the beginning of October, on the eve of the Battle of Tarutino, he composed one of his best-known poems, *Pevets vo stane ruskikh voinov* (A Bard in the Camp of the Russian Warriors, 1813) and dedicated it to General Kutuzov. It was printed by the army field press, was widely read among the Russian forces, and achieved immediate popularity with the public at large. Most importantly, it attracted attention in court circles and there aroused an interest in Zhukovsky that affected his future profoundly.

At the end of 1812 Zhukovsky contracted a serious illness, and in January 1813 he arrived in Muratovo to a hero's welcome from his family. His half sister's demeanor nonetheless quickly convinced him that his welcome there was limited, and he returned to his own house, again to write and read in relative seclusion, occasionally receiving visitors such as Aleksandr Fedorovich Voeikov, a literary acquaintance from his St. Petersburg days. Partly through Voeikov's betrayal of Zhukovsky's confidences, his relations with Ekaterina Protasova rapidly deteriorated. Eventually he took refuge with an old childhood friend, a cousin of the Protasov sisters, the recently widowed Avdot'ia Petrovna (Duniasha) Kireevskaia, at whose house in the village of Dolbino he had always been a welcome guest. There he enjoyed an autumn of intense poetic creativity.

In the summer of 1814 Masha's younger sister Sasha became engaged to Voeikov. On learning that the marriage had to be postponed for financial reasons (because, like the majority of Russian landowners, the Protasov family owned substantial property but was embarrassingly short of ready cash), Zhukovsky sold for 11,000 rubles the village he had bought only four years earlier and gave the money to Sasha to make her wedding possible. A perhaps even more valuable wedding gift was the dedication to her of his ballad "Svetlana," on which he had worked from 1808 to 1812; it achieved enormous popularity in his day and is arguably his best creation. Zhukovsky's poetry in this period included lively verse epistles to his closest literary friends and associates, lyrical ballads expressive of his personal situation, and the whimsical balladlike poem "Maksim," which celebrates the endearing eccentricities of his manservant.

In 1814 the Protasov family moved to Derpt (the Russian name of the old university town in Estonia known as Dorpat to the Baltic Germans, Tartu in Estonian) where Voeikov had been appointed to a professorship. Between 1814 and 1817 Zhukovsky joined them there for extended periods, still drawn by his love for Masha but using the time to read and attend lectures at the university, including a complete course on medieval history. Yet, even a platonic relationship with Masha now became increasingly difficult. Although Zhukovsky had openly renounced his quest to marry her, her mother refused to let them be together, and they were at times reduced to corresponding while living under the same roof. In the meantime Voeikov had become an ill-humored and often violent alcoholic, making life in his house a torment for both Ekaterina Protasova and Masha. In this situation Zhukovsky withdrew, urging Masha to make a reasonable life for herself. In 1817 she married Johann F. Moyer, a professor of medicine at the university, who was generous and understanding enough to accept her close relationship with Zhukovsky. Her marriage was a serious emotional blow to the poet, however, and he became a less frequent guest of the Moyers. Though Masha had naively hoped through marriage to make possible the friendship that her mother had forbidden, she now found that she had lost Zhukovsky. Her correspondence suggests that she admired and liked her husband but that her love for the poet was what sustained her.

Despite his half sister's unkindness, Zhukovsky remained a watchful and helpful friend of the Protasov family. In 1820 Voeikov was forced to resign his university post in Derpt and retreat to St. Petersburg under circumstances tinged with scandal. There Zhukovsky's literary friends greatly admired the beautiful and well-educated Sasha, whom they knew to be the "Svetlana" of Zhukovsky's celebrated ballad; and with her interests in mind, they found editorial work for Voeikov. Despite the universal condemnation of his despicable behavior, Voeikov thereafter owed his position in St. Petersburg society to the generosity of Zhukovsky and his circle.

After Masha's marriage Zhukovsky threw his energies into his literary career in St. Petersburg. A Russian writer in Zhukovsky's situation would most likely enter government service as a means of support, but he chose not to do so, preferring to make his living as a writer. He had met Pushkin for the first time in 1815 and in the same year accepted an invitation to the circle of the Empress Mariia Fedorovna, the widow of Paul I. He joined the literary society known as "Arzamas," which was founded in 1815 to combat the literary conservatives grouped around the *Beseda liubitelei russkogo slova* (Colloquy of Lovers of the Russian Word). This group had been established four years earlier to crusade against foreign influences on the Russian language. Arzamas was a deliberate parody of the *Beseda,* and its members indulged in a good deal of organized amusement at the expense of the cultural conservatives; however, their literary activities were serious. Zhukovsky became a leading light of the society and its principal polemicist. The celebrated controversy between the two societies was ostensibly centered on the development of the written language. The conservatives resented the modernization of literary Russian that had taken place at the end of the eighteenth century. Russian Sentimentalists, most notably Karamzin, had introduced many words either borrowed directly from European languages or coined by translation from foreign expressions and had transformed Russian syntax by analogy with French. There was more than language at stake, however; those who had modernized the language had done so to make it a vehicle for new ideas and feelings that were anathema to conservative Russians, and the language debate had decidedly political overtones. Indeed, by 1818 some of the future Decembrist revolutionaries were playing a leading role in Arzamas. Zhukovsky was invited to join their secret *Soiuz Blagodenstviia* (Union of Welfare) but politely declined and remained aloof from active participation in the increasingly radical political organizations of the day.

From 1815 until the mid 1820s Zhukovsky enjoyed a close literary and personal friendship with Pushkin, his junior by sixteen years, whom he regarded as at least his equal in poetic talent, and whose immense importance in the annals of Russian literature he clearly understood. The relationship was mutually supportive and mutually critical, and Pushkin often turned to Zhukovsky for help and advice in times of trouble, referring to him in his correspondence as his "guardian angel." In 1820, when Alexander I was incensed by Pushkin's more provocative writings and considered Siberian exile a fitting punishment, Zhukovsky and Karamzin persuaded the tsar that a period of service in the southern provinces would be more appropriate.

Zhukovsky continued to make good use of the time he spent in Derpt, where he came increasingly under the influence of German Romantic philosophy of the Jena school. He was particularly drawn to Novalis and to Ludwig Tieck, with whom he later became personally acquainted during a visit to Dresden in 1821. To his studies of history and philosophy he added drawing and music, and he became a well-known and respected figure in Derpt intellectual circles. He was now achieving a measure of recognition in the world of learning as well as letters. In 1816, the year in which the second volume of his collected poems appeared, he was awarded a doctorate by the University of Derpt, and in 1818 he was elected a member of the Russian Academy. A characteristic lyrical work of the 1817–1820 period is the somber song "Minuvshikh dnei ocharovan'e . . . " (Enchantment of days gone by . . .), written in 1818 but published only in 1821, which raises the elegiac mood to the level of the "philosophical lyric," a genre that occupies a significant place in the work of Russia's Romantic poets.

Zhukovsky's determination to make writing his career was vindicated when the Empress Mariia Fedorovna bestowed on him a stipend for life, an honor shared by only a handful of the most celebrated literary figures of the time. In December 1817 Zhukovsky accepted an appointment as Russian language tutor to Princess Charlotte of Prussia, the fiancée of Grand Prince Nicholas, the future Tsar Nicholas I. Later, the Empress Aleksandra Fedorovna, as his pupil became, observed dryly in a letter written in French that Zhukovsky had been "too much of a poet to be a good teacher" and was the reason why her Russian had always been so bad.

Traumatized though he was by his separation from Masha, Zhukovsky was not oblivious in this period to other women. He was briefly attracted to Sof'ia Aleksandrovna Samoilova, a lady-in-waiting at court, and some biographers have suggested that he may even have had secret feelings for the famously attractive Princess Charlotte. Though Zhukovsky's love for Masha has traditionally been presented as a living example of the Romantic ideal of devotion, at least one recent biographer has suggested a more analytical look at the issue of Zhukovsky's sincerity, and even the psychological "normality" of his behavior. He lived in an age when educated Europeans, and Russians perhaps to an even greater extent, were given to acting out sentimental literary ideals. In this view Zhukovsky's nineteenth-century biographers, especially Aleksandr Nikolaevich Veselovsky, were guilty of portraying him as more naive, idealistic, and detached from worldly concerns than was actually the case. The truth, as always, probably lies somewhere between the two extremes. Zhukovsky, so often portrayed as a dreamer, was in many obvious ways a competent and worldly man of action who defined enlightenment as "the art of living, the art of action." This fact, however, should only serve to reinforce the idea that his devotion to the love of his life was sincere; it is unlikely that a man as practical, resourceful, and energetic as Zhukovsky would subject himself to so much misery merely as a Romantic literary posture.

In October 1820 Zhukovsky began his first journey abroad. Traveling through Derpt and Königsberg to Berlin, he took advantage of the opportunity to see a stage production of Schiller's drama *Kalendar auf das Jahr 1802: Die Jungfrau von Orleans. Eine romantische Tragödie* (1802; translated as *The Maid of Orleans*, 1824), which, after long considering the possibility, he now finally felt able to translate into Russian. Quite by chance, his six-month stay in Berlin provided the impetus for another of his best-known poems of Romantic inspiration. His erstwhile pupil, now the Grand Princess Aleksandra Fedorovna, visited Berlin accompanied by her husband. Zhukovsky was a guest at the festivities arranged by her father, King Frederick of Prussia, which included a sumptuous *tableau vivant* (living picture) based on the poem *Lalla Rookh, An Oriental Romance* (1817) by the Romantic poet Thomas Moore. The incomparably beautiful Aleksandra Fedorovna played the role of Moore's Indian princess to great acclaim, and Zhukovsky, moved to compose a poetic tribute but wary of seeming impertinent, expressed his feelings for her in verses addressed to "Lalla Rookh," written in 1821 and published in 1827.

Continuing his journey through Germany, Switzerland, and northern Italy, Zhukovsky missed no opportunity to view the treasures of European art, frequently describing his impressions in detail in letters or

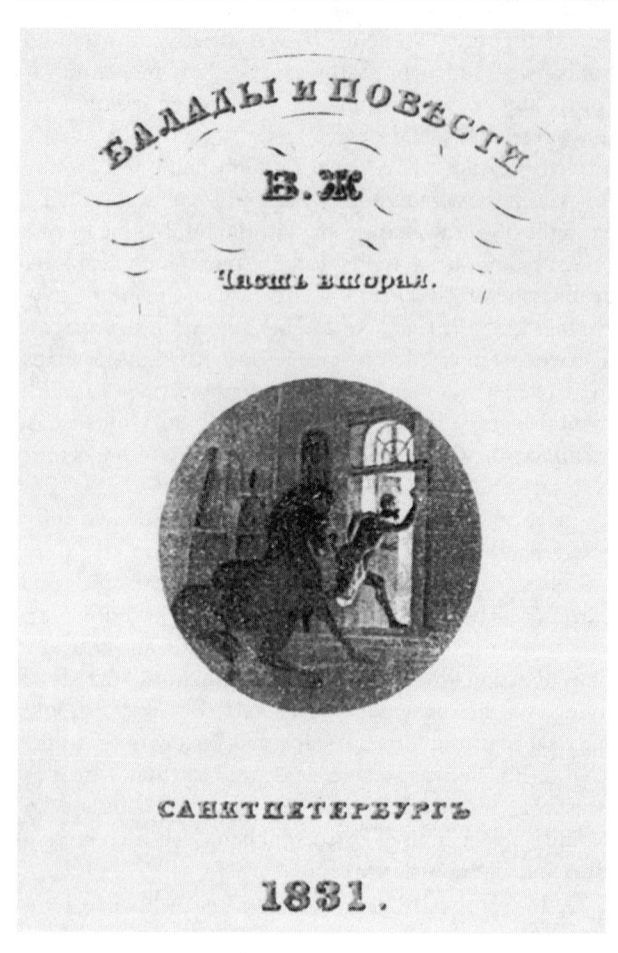

Title page for the second volume of Zhukovsky's Ballady i povesti *(Ballads and Tales)*

in his journal. In Dresden he was particularly struck by the Sistine Madonna, which seemed to him to epitomize the pure ideal of beauty. In Weimar in October 1821, accompanied by the Grand Princess Aleksandra Fedorovna, he met with Goethe, whom he had extolled in 1819 in a quatrain titled "K portretu Gete" (To a Portrait of Goethe). Goethe received Zhukovsky with kindly interest and later wrote to him expressing regret that they had not been able to have a more substantial conversation.

Returning to St. Petersburg with a brief stop in Derpt to visit Masha, Zhukovsky encountered censorship problems with two of his translations. His *Orleanskaia deva* (The Maid of Orleans), from Schiller's play, met with resistance from the theater censors despite their lack of precise objections, while his translation of Sir Walter Scott's *Eve of St. John. A Border Ballad* (1800) was forbidden outright by the censor, who called it "godless and immoral," "useless," and disrespectful of the Russian Orthodox Church. This prohibition prompted Zhukovsky to write an unusually outspoken letter to the Minister of Education and Religious Affairs, Prince Aleksandr Nikolaevich Golitsyn, pointing out that this celebrated poem had been published in many languages without any suggestion of impropriety and describing its proscription in Russia as "strange and incomprehensible." His translation of Scott's poem was published in a magazine in 1824. In 1831 a slightly modified version was approved by the censor and included in Zhukovsky's *Ballady i povesti* (Ballads and Tales).

Masha's qualified happiness with Moyer was short-lived: after bearing one daughter, she died in her second childbirth, early in 1823. Zhukovsky's next visit to Derpt was occasioned by the funeral of Masha and her stillborn son. He bore this new calamity with his usual inner fortitude and consoled her family members and friends with the thought that life, with all its inherent poetry, demanded their attention, while Masha lived on in their memories of her. A new source of distress on his return to the capital was the illness of the poet Konstantin Nikolaevich Batiushkov, who was mentally disturbed, alienated from his friends, becoming increasingly suicidal, and in need of urgent medical treatment. In 1824 Zhukovsky accompanied Batiushkov to Derpt to seek help for him, and when appropriate treatment could not be found, he dispatched him to Sonnenstein in Germany. Zhukovsky's concern for his fellow poets was unfailing; at this time he also interceded with the tsar on behalf of Evgenii Abramovich Baratynsky, who, as punishment for a prank committed while a student in the prestigious Corps of Pages, was serving as a common soldier in a Russian regiment in Finland.

In July 1824 Zhukovsky was invited by Nicholas (later Nicholas I) to become the tutor of his seven-year-old son, Grand Prince Aleksandr Nikolaevich (Alexander II). He accepted, after some hesitation, and his duties began in 1826. This period was marked by the intense activity of the clandestine political opposition groups in Russia, their final abortive attempt at armed rebellion in December 1825, and their subsequent cruel and public punishment. A writer of Zhukovsky's stature and moral integrity could be expected to shy away from a close association with the royal family, particularly since he made no secret of his friendship with many of the Decembrist conspirators, had occasional troubles with the censor, and complained bitterly when the tsar's secret police monitored his correspondence with friends abroad. Indeed, in some court and government circles he was regarded as an out-and-out Jacobin.

After Zhukovsky had left Russia permanently in 1840, Gen. Leontii Vasil'evich Dubel't, Nicholas's chief of police, proposed that further publication of the poet's writings in Russia be forbidden and gave as his reason the "too frequent repetition of the words *liberty, equality, reform, progress of our age, the unity of peoples, property is theft* and the like." Zhukovsky, however, had always avoided the secret political societies, and the Decembrists, who believed in the educational role of literature and made every effort to recruit writers of stature, thought of him as an undesirable influence on the moral and political climate of the time. Though liberal in his views, Zhukovsky appears to have supported tsarism as such, and to have sincerely believed that the moral perfection of tsar and court could bring about the perfection of Russian society and government. His acceptance of a role in the education of a future tsar was entirely consistent with his moral philosophy. In 1839, when he was faced with the likelihood that his complaints about the behavior of his charge would lead to his release from his tutorial position, his relief was tinged with genuine regret at the failure of his attempt to educate the heir to the throne according to his cherished ideals.

Zhukovsky's first task as tutor to the heir apparent was to prepare a plan for his education based on the pedagogical principles that were current in his mother's native land. To this end he was dispatched to Germany in May 1826. He took his duties seriously, drawing up a detailed scheme of instruction, buying the necessary books, and sending them to Russia. Since his health at this time was not good, he "took the cure" in the spa town of Ems. After wintering in Germany, he traveled to Paris in May 1827, where he visited his old friend Aleksandr Turgenev and met with French writers and artists, most frequently with Vicomte François-Auguste-René de Chateaubriand. Zhukovsky's activities in Paris revealed his curiosity and the range of his interests. Besides visiting art galleries and museums and attending concerts and theater productions, as he did on all his journeys to Europe, he found time on this occasion to inspect an orphanage, a prison, and a school for the deaf. His stay was marred by the sudden death of another of the Turgenev brothers, Sergei, who had suffered for some time from both physical and mental illness. From Paris, Zhukovsky returned to Ems to continue his cure and then, with his friend the painter Gerhard Reitern, traveled to Weimar for a second and more satisfactory round of meetings with Goethe.

Returning to St. Petersburg in September 1827, Zhukovsky was assigned an attic apartment in the "Shepelev House" of the Winter Palace, in which he installed his extensive library and his small but valuable collection of paintings. The amount of time he devoted to his tutorial duties, combined with the difficulty he experienced in climbing the many flights of stairs to his quarters, made him uncharacteristically reclusive. Though he wrote comparatively little in this period, he renewed his friendship with many of his literary contemporaries, including Pushkin, only recently summoned back to St. Petersburg from house arrest in the country, whom he had not seen since 1820. On Saturdays he held a literary salon that was visited by many Russian writers of both present and future fame as well as visitors from other cities and residents of St. Petersburg, including Pushkin and Ivan Andreevich Krylov. These "Saturdays" (moved at times to Fridays) remained a regular institution until the mid 1830s. Among the great Russian literary figures of the next generation, both Nikolai Gogol and Ivan Sergeevich Turgenev as young writers received hospitality and encouragement from Zhukovsky, who had also found time in 1818 to edit his own anonymously published journal, with a bilingual title that in some ways reflected his response to the climate of the times: *Für Wenige. Dlia nemnogikh* (For the Few).

Zhukovsky was unfailingly generous, helping family and friends with both his money and his good offices and dispensing charity to the needy. There is no stronger testimony to his generosity than the candor of his quite frequent approaches to the tsar on behalf of acquaintances who had problems with the authorities. In 1830 he wrote to the tsar asking for clemency for all of the exiled or imprisoned Decembrists, a group that included many promising young writers, some personally known to Zhukovsky. This step was quite risky and produced a reproach that the royal tutor should be more mindful of the company he kept, but no worse reprisals. In court circles Zhukovsky was respected for his probity by all; but, partly because of his moral stature, he was a somewhat distant figure actively disliked by many.

In 1829 and 1830 Zhukovsky wrote relatively few short lyrical poems but developed projects for longer works, and in 1831 he had an unusual burst of creativity resulting in several more ballads and a variety of ambitious new plans. In this year an unusually virulent cholera epidemic reached St. Petersburg, causing many deaths, and those who were able took refuge outside the city. Zhukovsky and Pushkin spent this summer as neighbors in Tsarskoe Selo and decided to while away their temporary exile by writing verse fairy tales in competition with each other. Pushkin composed his celebrated "Skazka o tsare Saltane," (The Tale of King Saltan), and Zhukovsky responded with "Skazka o tsare Berendee" (The Tale of King Berendei) and "Spiashchaia tsarevna" (Sleeping Beauty). Zhukovsky's collection *Ballady i povesti* was published in St. Petersburg by the end of the year. The period from 1831 to 1833, during which Zhukovsky explored Russian folklore and legend in the course of his friendly competition with Pushkin, was of great importance in his development as a writer.

Zhukovsky in Naples, 1833 (portrait by Gerhard Reitern, from Viktor V. Afanas'ev, Zhukovsky, *1986)*

The temporarily quarantined court continued its usual social round during the summer in Tsarskoe Selo, and Zhukovsky's unwonted conviviality appears to have been a smoke screen to cover a genuine attraction to a lady-in-waiting at the court–Aleksandra Osipovna Rosset, who was lively and sociable, a friend of many St. Petersburg literary figures, and often praised in their verses. Zhukovsky was not alone among Russian poets in falling in love with her. He is said to have proposed and to have been refused on the grounds, recounted by Rosset herself to Pushkin, that "we were much too good friends." They remained friends even after her refusal.

In January 1832 a new literary journal began to appear in the Russian capital: *Evropeets* (The European), edited by the young and talented Ivan Vasil'evich Kireevsky. It immediately attracted attention by the quality of its contributions (some from Zhukovsky), but by February it was closed by the censor. Zhukovsky, at the risk of bringing down official wrath on his own head, wrote at length to both the tsar and the head of the secret police, defending Kireevsky and suggesting that slander from the camp of his literary enemies was the only reason for the closing. This courageous plea was unsuccessful and moreover provoked a hostile outburst from the tsar that was only smoothed over by the intervention of the empress, Zhukovsky's former pupil. That Zhukovsky's career as a tutor to the royal family survived this protestation and others to the tsar is an extraordinary tribute to the respect in which he was held.

In June 1832 Zhukovsky undertook his third journey to Europe, which once again proved an important stimulus for his translations and an inspiration for his own poetry and drew him closer than ever to the spirit of German Romanticism. He spent the summer in Germany, where he met with Ludwig Uhland, several of whose lyrical poems and ballads he had already translated over the years. More important, he met with another outstanding German Romantic writer, Friedrich de la Motte Fouqué, the author of the celebrated prose tale *Undine* (1811), of which Zhukovsky had begun a verse translation. Completed four years later and published as a book in 1837, Zhukovsky's *Undina* is considered among his best works, endowing with poetic intensity and psychological depth the Romantic tale of the mermaid who is given a soul for as long as a mortal loves her faithfully. Much of the writing of *Undina* was done near Derpt and was dictated to the young daughters of Sasha Voeikova, who with Masha had often in her own childhood transcribed Zhukovsky's verses.

Moving to Switzerland for the winter of 1832–1833, Zhukovsky made an incomplete translation of Scott's *Marmion: A Tale of Flodden Field* (1808) while staying at Vevey on the shore of Lake Geneva, and he was fascinated by the Château de Chillon, the setting for George Gordon, Lord Byron's *The Prisoner of Chillon* (1816). In April 1833 he journeyed on to Italy through France, traveling by ship from Marseilles to Genova. Sasha Voeikova had died of tuberculosis in 1829 in Livorno, where she had gone to seek a cure; Zhukovsky's most immediate destination was her grave, which he sketched and for which he ordered an inscribed iron cross identical to that on Masha's grave in Derpt. In Rome he visited several members of the colony of Russian painters who resided there, and he also met with Marie-Henri Beyle (the French novelist Stendhal). In Naples and Florence he was an assiduous visitor to galleries and antiquities, and Pompeii was included in his itinerary. Back in Germany after his visit to Italy, he made a pilgrimage to Goethe's house in Weimar, which had been preserved as a museum after Goethe's death in 1832. There he inspected with great interest the study of the poet whom he had always idolized. As on his early voyages, Zhukovsky wrote frequently to friends and family in Russia, and his detailed letters provide a vibrant, immediate, and thoughtful journal of his travels.

By the autumn of 1833 Zhukovsky was back in St. Petersburg, living essentially the same life of official duties, disciplined creativity, and literary conviviality, fretting at his confinement to the capital and missing the provincial countryside and family contacts that had always refreshed and inspired him. His attachment to his extended family was always strong, and his generosity manifested itself there too: in 1836 he bought two small estates in the vicinity of Derpt to provide for the future of Sasha Voeikova's children and Masha's daughter. His pedagogical duties meanwhile were becoming increasingly stale and frustrating. He confided to his diary in the summer of 1834 that his royal pupil was becoming ever more inattentive and surly and that he harbored few illusions about his influence on the future tsar. One entry reads: "His mind is asleep, and I do not know what can awaken it."

Zhukovsky began 1836 with an interesting collaboration: he was one of the two librettists for the opera *Zhizn' za tsarya* (A Life for the Tsar, renamed *Ivan Susanin*) by Mikhail Ivanovich Glinka, who frequented the poet's evening gatherings, and he composed a romance to one of Glinka's lyrics. In March, Zhukovsky and many of his regular guests attended the rehearsals for *Ivan Susanin*. In January 1836 Pushkin received permission from Count Aleksandr Khristoforovich Benckendorff, a figure all too well known as the head of Nicholas I's secret service, to publish a quarterly literary review. Zhukovsky was one of Pushkin's collaborators in this venture. *Sovremennik* (The Contemporary) was even from its inaugural issue the most prestigious literary journal to have appeared in Russia; but Pushkin's editorial endeavor was short-lived, and before the end of the year Zhukovsky found himself closely involved in the best-known tragedy of Russian literary history. On 5 November 1836 Pushkin challenged to a duel Baron Georges d'Anthès-Heeckeren, the adopted son of the Dutch ambassador to Russia, who had publicly compromised Pushkin's wife. Among Pushkin's friends Zhukovsky was perhaps the most horrified at the prospect of the duel. His position close to the court made him suspect that Nicholas I and Benckendorff, who were made aware of the situation, had every intention of allowing the illegal encounter to take place. Zhukovsky did everything he could to avert the impending disaster, including speaking to the tsar in person, and was partially successful; but after a sordid exchange of retractions and fresh insults, the challenge was renewed on 25 January 1837. The duel took place two days later, and Pushkin was fatally wounded, dying on 29 January. Zhukovsky's suspicions of royal complicity were confirmed: gendarmes sent to prevent the duel appeared to have been deliberately dispatched to the wrong location.

In a bizarre conclusion to a long relationship, Zhukovsky was officially appointed to dispose of Pushkin's papers under police supervision. This task was immensely important and delicate, and one of the most significant undertakings of Zhukovsky's professional life, for the authorities were as determined to destroy Pushkin's unpublished manuscripts as Zhukovsky was to preserve them. While the nation mourned the loss of its greatest poet, Zhukovsky toiled for weeks over his papers, in the constant presence of General Dubel't of the gendarmerie. Zhukovsky's strategy paid off: rather than submit individual documents to Nicholas for his perusal, as he had been instructed, he submitted a description of the materials, in varying degrees of detail, organized under thirty-six separate rubrics. The tsar kept only Pushkin's notes for a biography of Catherine the Great, which included much sensitive information on her many favorites and lovers, and the remainder of his papers were left in Zhukovsky's possession. He immediately began work on the first posthumous edition of Pushkin's works, which appeared in eleven volumes over the next four years. There exists a long letter from Zhukovsky to Benckendorff, dated February or March 1837 and unusually candid even for Zhukovsky, in which he defends Pushkin from the charges of political unreliability made against him and criticizes Benckendorff for his relentless persecution of the poet. It is not clear whether this interesting document was actually sent to its addressee.

Zhukovsky had earlier proposed that Grand Prince Aleksandr Nikolaevich should be given the opportunity to acquaint himself at firsthand with the empire that he would one day govern. His proposal was accepted, and in March 1837 he set out with his royal pupil on a journey through both European Russia and Siberia that lasted almost nine months. In several of the cities they visited, Zhukovsky met with former Decembrist revolutionaries living in exile. Predictably, he wrote to the tsar asking for their pardon and even induced the young prince to write to his father in the same vein. The tsar was perfectly aware of the prompting behind his son's request, and though he agreed to some reduction of sentences, and eventually to the return of Aleksandr Ivanovich Herzen from exile in Viatka, it was at the cost of increased ill will toward Zhukovsky. In July the travelers reached Tula and Zhukovsky's childhood home, visiting Belev, Dolbino, and Mishenskoe before traveling to Moscow, where Zhukovsky was feted by his literary friends. The journey concluded with visits to the south, through Khar'kov, Odessa, and the Crimea. Though the object of this odyssey had been to educate the heir to the

Title page for Undina, Zhukovsky's translation of Friedrich de la Motte Fouqué's 1811 prose tale Undine, inscribed by Zhukovsky to Princess Zinaida Aleksandrovna Volkonskaia (Kilgour Collection, Harvard University Library)

throne, it was almost as much of an education for the mentor, leaving the always idealistic Zhukovsky somewhat saddened by the poverty, ignorance, and corruption he had encountered.

In February 1838 the sixty-ninth birthday of Krylov, the renowned author of Russian fables and a doyen of Russian letters, was celebrated in St. Petersburg as a jubilee occasion attended by almost everyone of importance in the capital. The tsar not only gave his permission for the event but also participated in its organization, since it would divert the attention of St. Petersburg society from the anniversary of Pushkin's death. Zhukovsky delivered the laudatory address, and on this occasion, with his typical disregard for the real possibility of reprisals against himself, he deliberately provoked Nicholas with a thinly disguised allusion to the sadly absent Pushkin. Paradoxically, this fearlessness, rather than his renown or the support of a few influential aristocrats, preserved him for more than a decade from dismissal or worse; he was quite simply immune to the intimidation that was the tsar's preferred modus operandi. Nicholas's unconcealed dislike of the morally unimpeachable Zhukovsky was reaching a climax, however, and their uneasy association soon ended.

Zhukovsky extended his good offices to others besides exiled friends and fellow writers, and in April 1838 he arranged the liberation from serfdom of the great Ukrainian poet and painter Taras Hrihorovich Shevchenko. It should be remembered that from the time of Peter the Great many talented serfs had been educated by their owners and trained in a variety of professions. Some even achieved considerable distinction without ever gaining release from their owners. Zhukovsky was opposed in principle to serfdom and devoted considerable energy and money to organizing the release of such people from bondage. In 1837 Vasilii Ivanovich Grigorovich, the secretary of the Russian Academy of the Arts, had been asked to try to secure the release of the twenty-three-year-old Shevchenko. Grigorovich knew how best to handle the situation: he passed the request to Zhukovsky, who negotiated a price with the landowner, then enlisted the help of an aristocratic friend to organize a charitable lottery. The prize was a portrait of Zhukovsky generously painted by one of the most distinguished Russian artists, Karl Pavlovich Briullov, and the lottery soon raised the 2,500 rubles needed to buy Shevchenko's freedom.

In May 1838 Zhukovsky set out on a second educational journey with the heir to the throne, this time to western Europe, stopping in Germany, Scandinavia, Switzerland, Italy, Austria, Holland, and England. The experience was in some respects stressful for Zhukovsky, as his relationship with his young charge became increasingly strained, and the entourage included another of the prince's mentors, A. A. Kavelin, a mean-spirited individual who was envious of Zhukovsky and sent secret denunciations of him back to Russia. As before, Zhukovsky called on important literary figures and visited art museums, architectural monuments, and antiquities. He recorded his impressions not only in his travel diary and in letters to friends, which have substantial literary merit in their own right, but also, more than ever before, in the form of accomplished sketches. An endearing quirk of Zhukovsky's landscape sketches from this period is that they often include a slightly caricatured representation of himself admiring the view.

Zhukovsky was most impressed with Sweden, where he wrote admiringly of the people and the civic organization, but he found the most personal enjoyment in Italy. In Milan he had the unexpected pleasure of a meeting with the novelist and poet Alessandro Manzoni. In Rome he was visited by Gogol, to whom he presented the gold pocket watch that he had taken from the wounded Pushkin and that which he had stopped at the moment of the great poet's death. This gesture was Zhukovsky's way of recognizing the young Gogol as Pushkin's successor in the pantheon of Russian literature. He also made several portrait sketches of his friend and protégé that are among the most interesting likenesses of Gogol.

Leaving Italy in February 1839, the royal party traveled to Vienna and then to The Hague, where Zhukovsky received a thinly veiled rebuke from the tsar. The tutor had earlier written to the empress complaining of her son's intolerable incivility. Nicholas was enraged, and the tenor of the tsar's response made it clear that Zhukovsky's resignation was in order. With this cloud hanging over Zhukovsky's head, the "grand tour" continued to London, which he inspected with great thoroughness, visiting the British Museum, art galleries, parks, palaces, the printing press of *The Times*, and the horse races at Epsom Downs, where he placed a modest bet and won. Everywhere he went he filled his notebooks with sketches. A special pilgrimage to the graveyard described by Gray in his "Elegy" prompted Zhukovsky to make a second translation, this time in dactylic hexameters.

A brief stop in Germany on the return journey to Russia enabled him to spend a few days with his friend Reitern. As he enjoyed Reitern's hospitality in idyllic surroundings and a cultivated family setting, Zhukovsky was struck by the beauty of Reitern's daughter, Elizabeth. He described her as "a vision from paradise" and thought he detected signs of a mutual attraction that made him regret that he was not younger. In July the family traveled with Zhukovsky to St. Petersburg, where Reitern had a commission as a court painter and stayed for almost three months. Zhukovsky spoke to his old friend of the feelings between Elizabeth and himself, and Reitern responded that if a proposal were made, Elizabeth alone should decide her future.

On Zhukovsky's return to St. Petersburg, he did not have long to wait for the final expression of the tsar's displeasure; the "honorable retirement" he would soon have to accept could only come as a relief after years of petty unpleasantness in the service of the court, but it was distressing to him to have to leave his palace quarters. He was deeply attached to his working room, where the simple furnishings, shelves full of books, and picture-covered walls reflected his taste, many years of solitary study, literary endeavors, and hours of conviviality with two generations of Russian writers and artists. In late August, as he gloomily faced this unsettling change in his life, his spirits were raised by his participation in the celebrations in Moscow surrounding the dedication of a monument to the Battle of Borodino. He had endured for many years the intense and artificial world of "accursed St. Petersburg" and the court; now, seeing Moscow in the glow of summer, standing once more on the spot where his regiment of the militia had assembled in 1812, and hearing the church bells that had rung as they marched off to battle, he was reminded of all that was finest in traditional Russian culture. He was also pleasantly reminded that his *Pevets vo stane ruskikh voinov* was not forgotten, and he poured out his feelings in a new commemorative poem, "Borodinskaia godovshchina" (The Anniversary of Borodino), dated "26 Aug. 1839 at Borodino" and published later that year. His new poem closely reflected the earlier work, but in a wistful, elegiac vein, celebrating the true Russian values that he felt had been forsaken by the society of the day, including its leaders. In a gesture typical of his attitude to his royal superiors, he sent a copy of the poem to the crown prince with a moralizing letter in which he made clear how important he felt those values to be.

The January 1840 issue of *Otechestvennye zapiski* (Notes of the Fatherland) included a major article by the critic Vissarion Grigor'evich Belinsky that extolled Zhukovsky's position in Russian literature and gave an interesting indication of how his role as a translator was perceived in his native land. Zhukovsky, wrote Belinsky, "is a poet, not a translator: he does not translate, but re-creates, taking from the Germans and the English only what is his, and leaving to the originals what is inalienably theirs, with the result that his so-called translations are very imperfect as translations, but outstanding as original works."

In March 1840 Zhukovsky traveled once more to Germany on the last of his official duties, followed by a short leave of absence. From Ems he wrote to the tsar requesting his discharge from service and then took up his quarters in Düsseldorf. His first call was naturally on the Reitern family, a visit that provoked an unexpected change in his life. Elizabeth Reitern, who had rekindled in his heart the feelings that once had been reserved for Masha Protasova, seemed to return his affections. At the age of fifty-eight he did not dare to entertain any hopes, but after agonizing for some while, he proposed to her. She immediately accepted, and a wedding was planned for the spring of 1841.

In January 1841 Zhukovsky returned to Russia, staying first for several weeks in Moscow, where he was feted by his literary friends and acquaintances. He traveled on to St. Petersburg in the early spring, where he found Mikhail Iur'evich Lermontov, who had a two-month leave from the military service in the Caucasus that was his punishment for a duel with the son of the French ambassador a year before. Zhukovsky, who still had some influence with the empress and her son, immediately did everything in his power to secure a

Elizabeth Reitern, whom Zhukovsky married in 1841

pardon for Lermontov and to obtain permission for the publication of the younger poet's masterpiece *Demon*, on which Lermontov had worked throughout the 1830s. He was unsuccessful on both counts: the tsar was adamant that Lermontov should return to active duty in the Caucasus, where there was a reasonable chance that he might be killed, and *Demon* was not published in its entirety until 1856 (and then only in Germany). Before returning to Germany, Zhukovsky also made generous arrangements for the future of the daughters of Sasha Voeikova: selling an estate that he had bought a few years earlier with the intention of eventually retiring to it, he divided the proceeds equally among the three girls.

Zhukovsky and eighteen-year-old Elizabeth Reitern were married on 21 April 1841 in the Russian church in Stuttgart. They settled happily in a rented house in Düsseldorf with a garden and a view of the Rhine. There Zhukovsky began work on his most ambitious project, a translation of Homer's *Odyssey* that took him seven years to complete. On 11 November 1842 Elizabeth gave birth to a daughter, Aleksandra Vasil'evna. Zhukovsky's diary entry for that day includes a wonderfully detailed description of the infant, expressing by turns awe, pride, and simple joy. Almost immediately after the birth, however, Elizabeth was stricken with a serious emotional and nervous disorder from which she never fully recovered. Zhukovsky devoted himself to the care of his wife but found to his dismay that he was unable to do more than comfort her. The next few years were exhausting and distressful as the family's life was disrupted by travels to spas in search of a cure. Zhukovsky's own health began to suffer, and he was able only sporadically to find solace in creative work. He had intended to move back to Russia fairly soon after his marriage, but his wife's condition made that inadvisable. Moreover, his friend Prince Petr Andreevich Viazemsky wrote gloomily of the oppressive climate of the country in the third decade of Nicholas I's reign.

Zhukovsky's involuntary exile became increasingly painful to him, but (perhaps because of this homesickness) he still found time to receive a succession of Russian writers who were traveling in Europe, including Gogol, Turgenev and Fedor Ivanovich Tiutchev, and to help his Russian friends and family. To Gogol in particular he frequently gave hospitality as well as warm friendship and support, and he never ceased in his efforts to improve the material circumstances of the exiled Decembrists and to secure permission for them to publish their works. In the relative isolation of his last years he gradually withdrew into the world of mystical pietism in which the Reitern family found solace after their second daughter died of an ailment similar to Elizabeth's.

There were some brighter moments in Zhukovsky's life during this troubled period, including the birth in 1845 of a son, Pavel Vasil'evich, and the marriage of Masha's daughter to the son of one of his dearest friends, Avdot'ia Petrovna Elagina. He was a devoted father to his two children. A pedagogue to the end, he drew up a plan for their education, and to help them learn Russian he wrote nursery verses that are in the repertoire of Russian children today. He continued to write as circumstances permitted, producing in these years fairy tales in both prose and verse.

In 1848 there appeared in *Moskvitianin* (Muscovite) an open letter from Zhukovsky to Gogol that summarizes his thoughts on poetry in later life. With an emphasis that is arguably more Russian than European, and certainly Romantic, Zhukovsky attributed to poetry a power that is neither intellectual nor moral, but simply mysterious, pervasive, and irresistible: the poetic word acts on the human spirit. As Zhukovsky composed his letter, Germany was convulsed by political turmoil and revolution, and he voiced in response feelings reminiscent of the Slavophiles–Russians who idealized their country as the bearer of an older, unspoiled social tradition that western Europe had lost. "More than ever," wrote Zhukovsky, "I am confirmed in the belief that in the midst of this deluge . . . Russia is the ark of salvation." He added:

> I am not a politician and I cannot be certain of my opinion; but it seems to me that in the present circumstances we must wall ourselves off from the universal contagion . . . Europe's course is not ours; what we have borrowed from Europe is ours now; but we must process it at home, for ourselves, in our own way, without falling into imitation, not following developments in the West, but without becoming involved in its transformation, either. Russia's entire strength lies in this distinct originality.

The origin of this letter illustrates not only the way in which the most talented and progressive Russian writers were brought together in the nineteenth century by their sense of mission but also Zhukovsky's stature in their community. At the end of 1847 Gogol, facing a spiritual crisis in Italy and contemplating a visit to the Holy Land, had written a letter in which he turned to Zhukovsky as a virtual father-confessor before setting out on his pilgrimage. Zhukovsky wrote his reply in January 1848, but did not mail the letter, as he was not sure of Gogol's whereabouts. Instead, he sent it to his friend Elagina in Moscow, asking her to transmit it to the editor of *Moskvitianin*, who immediately realized its significance and published it.

Zhukovsky completed his translation of the *Odyssey* in April 1849, despite the disruptions to both his personal life and the publishing process caused by the revolution in Germany: seeking safety for his family, he moved from Frankfurt-am-Main to Baden-Baden and eventually to Strasbourg, where his publisher in Karlsruhe had to deliver and retrieve the proofs by a circuitous route. When it was finally published in his 1849 collected works, Zhukovsky sent copies to many of his literary friends, then anxiously awaited their responses and became fretful when he heard nothing from most of them. The reception of his *Odisseia Gomera* in Russia was a matter of great concern to Zhukovsky, for he considered it to be not a "mere" translation but one of his best poetic creations. Indeed, it has an important place in his development as a poet and thinker. In a letter written in 1847 to Count Sergei Semenovich Uvarov, the Russian Minister of Education, who was a classical scholar of some note, he had described his work on the *Odyssey* in a way that suggests he found in it almost an antidote to Romanticism: "I felt the desire to liven my spirit with poetry from the dawn of civilization, which is so clear and calm, so invigorating and comforting, . . . does not agitate the spirit and does not reach out into a hazy distance."

Zhukovsky lacked a knowledge of classical Greek, and in the same letter he explained how he was overcoming this drawback–an explanation that gives some insight into his attitude to translation. Professor Karl Grasshof in Düsseldorf, well known for his commentaries on the *Odyssey,* was asked to prepare for Zhukovsky a copy of the original Greek text with a translation and grammatical explication in German under every line, and Zhukovsky's comment on this working version in a 12 September 1847 letter to Uvarov gives another glimpse of his attitude to the creative role of the translator: "In this chaotically exact translation, quite opaque to the reader, I had before me as it were all the raw materials of a building; all that was lacking was beauty, order and harmony." The "beauty, order and harmony" were of course to be created by the poet in his own language, a rebuilding of Homer in Russian.

As 1849 drew to a close, the circumstances of Zhukovsky's life became increasingly discouraging, and he found it harder to sustain his spirits and his creative inspiration. His wife's condition was deteriorating. His own health was not good, and it was not improved by a tiresome journey to Warsaw to renew his permission to reside outside Russia (Poland, it should be remembered, was at that time a part of the Russian Empire). His wife's health was the only thing that kept him from returning to Russia with his family, and his disappointment was made all the more bitter by the reproachful entreaties of some of his closest Russian friends. Worst of all, his eyesight was weakening, and he was finding it difficult to work for more than short periods. In spite of these problems, he began work on the *Iliad,* gathering together existing translations in several languages, including Nikolai Ivanovich Gnedich's Russian version, which had appeared in 1829 after twenty-two years of work. This time he did not have the help of a literal German translation–Grasshof was approached, but would have needed two years to complete the task. After working with Grasshof's text for the *Odyssey,* however, Zhukovsky could read Homer reasonably well, and he was able to proceed with his work.

Zhukovsky was still able to spend some time every day with his two children, teaching them to read and devising a comprehensive plan for their early education. He became increasingly concerned with general philosophical issues–not the technicalities of professional philosophers, but thoughts on what he saw as the great moral issues of his day, which he planned to compile into a book with the title "Filosofiia nevezhdy" (The Philosophy of an Ignoramus). The much-debated question of the influence of German Romantic philosophy on Zhukovsky should be considered in the light of what he had to say about this project: "In philosophy I am a complete ignoramus. For me, German philosophy has always remained inaccessible and unknown, and at my ripe old age there is no point in entering its labyrinth: I would be completely engulfed by the minotaur of German metaphysics, the favored child of Kant, Fichte, Schelling, Hegel etc., etc."

Zhukovsky's concern with the eternal issues of moral philosophy was reflected in the unfinished literary projects of his last two years, the most interesting of which was an epic poem based on the legend of the Wandering Jew, a theme that had challenged several European Romantic poets. In Zhukovsky's treatment the legend became a spiritual autobiography in which he tried to express in an historical perspective the wisdom he had distilled from the sufferings and disappointments of his life. By his last year he had completed only thirty lines of the project. His last poem, "Tsarskosel'skii lebed'" (The Swan of Tsarskoe Selo), written as an amusing Russian exercise for his young daughter, tells the imagined life of an old swan in the park surrounding the summer palace of the tsars; but in the course of its writing the poem acquired a serious autobiographical dimension.

By the beginning of 1851 Zhukovsky had lost the sight in one eye and suffered constant inflammation in the other, and he spent much of his time confined to a darkened room. He was distressed by the increasingly direct accusations from his friends that he had deserted his native land, and despite all obstacles, he determined to make his long-awaited journey to Russia in the summer. At the last minute, though, a serious eye infection forced him to delay his departure yet again. He calmly faced the likelihood that blindness would soon become an additional obstacle to the realization of his literary plans, and he organized his working life accordingly: he practiced writing with his eyes closed, aided by a special device, and arranged for assistants to read to him the books he needed to consult.

Zhukovsky's achievements as a connoisseur of both European and Russian art, and as an artist in his own right, deserve mention. Even before he left Russia for Europe, Zhukovsky's personal collection of drawings and paintings was of impressive quality. His influence on Russian culture of his day extends even to this arena: by the time of his 1838 European trip he was advising the Hermitage Gallery on art purchases. In Rome he visited the illustrious Russian painter Aleksandr Andreevich Ivanov, who solicited Zhukovsky's advice on the composition of his immense canvas *The Appearance of Christ to the People* (1837–1857), perhaps the most celebrated achievement of Russian painting in the nineteenth century. Zhukovsky used his influence at court to prolong the stay in Italy of another of the most celebrated Russian painters, Briullov. Beyond the matter of connoisseurship, Zhukovsky was for most of his adult life a serious amateur artist. He had some training in pencil sketching and oil painting, and late in life he took lessons in engraving, at which he eventually became sufficiently skilled to publish some of his best efforts. He gave serious thought to the connection between verbal and visual art, and his poetic descriptions owe at least some of their power to his broader preoccupation with the representation of nature.

Zhukovsky lived primarily for the word, and he had enormous faith in its power. Though in many ways a literary Romantic, he differed from his European models in not exaggerating the significance of the individual writer's verbal creativity, preferring to regard words as "an event in the realm of human thought, or even, one could say, in the life of human society." He was in many ways a more complex figure than is suggested by his routine classification as the founding father of Russian Romanticism. Sentimentalism and even Neoclassicism are equally discernible both in his poetry and in his attitudes. Throughout his long career he retained a down-to-earth approach to his literary métier, avoiding stylistic posturing and maintaining with varying degrees of explicitness that art serves life. The characteristically Romantic assertion that life is the realization of art was foreign to him, and in this respect he retained a link to the rationalism of the eighteenth century. In a letter written toward the end of his life, he demanded that the artist swear an oath of truth to reality, adding that "any kind of mannerism is, in my view, a mistake." His penchant for moralizing like a philosopher of the Enlightenment is another trait that could make him appear more of an eighteenth-century figure, but in other ways he held to a typically Romantic view of art and the artist. In a letter to the Grand Duchess Mariia Nikolaevna, asking her to intercede in prolonging permission for Briullov to stay in Italy, he wrote that "an artist needs complete freedom to create what, how and when he wants."

Zhukovsky was a complex figure in another respect: many of his most influential works were in fact translations rather than original poetry. To his mind, there was no contradiction here. In his 1809 article "O basne i basniakh Krylova" (On the Fable and Krylov's Fables), published in *Vestnik Evropy*, he observed that "the poet who imitates can be an original author without writing anything of his own. The author of a *prose* translation is a slave; the author of a *verse* translation is a rival." It has been suggested that Zhukovsky's translations of lyric poetry constitute nothing less than a subterfuge: prevented by circumstances from expressing his love in a personal and recognizable form, he sought lyrical models to which he could transfer his feelings and express them in the disguise of translation. In this view

Zhukovsky's own emotional circumstances dictated the choice of material, and he expressed his feelings by intensifying the lyricism of the poems he translated. It is also worth noting that in the ballads he translated, as well as in those he composed himself, the motif of lovers finding each other through difficulties or after separation is frequent, but a tragic end is usual.

Zhukovsky's impact on Russian poetry was felt in the realm of metrical forms no less than in that of themes and moods. Nikolai Ivanovich Nadezhdin, who contributed the versification entry to the Russian *Entsiklopedicheskii slovar'* (Encyclopedic Dictionary, 1835–1841), wrote that "Zhukovsky must be acknowledged as the second poet to transform our versification, the man who corrected the logical error of Lomonosov, not in theory, but in practice." Zhukovsky's contribution to the technical aspects of Russian poetry are overshadowed, however, by the sheer musicality of his verse, which appealed strongly to composers, including Petr Il'ich Tchaikovsky, who based an opera on *Orleanskaia deva*.

The last word on the life of this poet of modest demeanor but inward strength should go to Zhukovsky himself. When Petr Aleksandrovich Pletnev wrote to him in 1850 urging him, not for the first time, to write his memoirs, he rejected the suggestion, adding: "My memoirs, and those of people like me, can only be psychological, a history of the spirit; my life has not been rich in events that would be of interest to future generations." In the early hours of 12 April 1852 Zhukovsky died on the divan bed in his darkened study, to which he had been confined since the onset of his illness. He was buried in a cemetery outside Baden-Baden, and in August, fulfilling his ambition to be in Russia again, his remains were taken to their final resting place at the Monastery of Aleksandr Nevsky in St. Petersburg, next to the grave of the poet Ivan Ivanovich Kozlov, whom he had encouraged and helped, and close to that of Karamzin, to whom Zhukovsky had been a worthy successor.

Letters:

Pis'ma V. A. Zhukovskago k ego Imperatorskomu vysochestvu gosudariu Velikomy Kniaziu Konstantinu Nikolaevichu (Moscow: T. Ris, 1867);

Pis'ma V. A. Zhukovskogo k Aleksandru Ivanovichu Turgenevu (Moscow: Izdatel'stvo "Russkogo arkhiva," 1895);

Pis'ma V. A. Zhukovskogo, M. A. Moier i E. A. Protasovoi, edited by Aleksei Evgen'evich Gruzinsky (Moscow: Izd. M. V. Beer, Pechatnia A. I. Snegirovoi, 1904);

Poet i korol', ili, Istoriia odnoi druzhby: Perepiska V. A. Zhukovskago s korolem prusskim Fridrikhom-Vil'gel'mom IV, edited by Aleksandr A. Fomin (St. Petersburg: Sirius, 1913);

V. A. Zhukovskii–kritik, edited by Iurii Mikhailovich Prozorov (Moscow: Sovetskaia Rossiia, 1985).

Biographies:

Karl Johann von Seidlitz, *Zhizn' i poeziia V. A. Zhukovskago, 1783–1852* (St. Petersburg: Izd. Red. "Vestnik Evropy," Tip. M. M. Stasiulevicha, 1883);

Aleksandr Danilovich Alferov, *V. A. Zhukovskii. Biograficheskii ocherk* (Moscow, 1902);

Nikolai Vasil'evich Solov'ev, "Poet-khudozhnik V. A. Zhukovsky," *Russkii bibliofil,* no. 7–8 (1912): 41–48;

Aleksandr Nikolaevich Veselovsky, *V. A. Zhukovsky. Poeziia chuvstva i "serdechnogo voobrazheniia"* (Petrograd: "Zhizn' i znanie," 1918);

Irina Mikhailovna Semenko, *Zhizn' i poeziia Zhukovskogo* (Moscow: Khudozhestvennaia literatura, 1975);

M. Ia. Bessarab, *Zhukovsky* (Moscow: Sovremennik, 1975);

Raisa Vladimirovna Iezuitova, *Zhukovskii v Peterburge* (Leningrad: Lenizdat, 1976);

Vasilii Nikolaevich Osokin, *Ego stikhov plenitel'naia sladost'–: V. A. Zhukovskii v Moskve i Podmoskov'e* (Moscow: Moskovskii rabochii, 1984);

Viktor V. Afanas'ev, *Zhukovsky* (Moscow: "Molodaia gvardiia," 1986).

References:

William Edward Brown, "Vasily Andreevich Zhukovsky," *Russian Literature Triquarterly,* 8 (1974): 295–328;

L. P. Burnett, "Dimensions of Truth: A Comparative Study of the Relationship between 'Language' and 'Reality' in the Works of Wordsworth, Coleridge, Zhukovsky, Pushkin, and Keats," dissertation, University of Essex, 1976;

Marcelle Ehrhard, *V. A. Joukovski et la préromantisme russe* (Paris: Champion, 1938);

Hildegard Eichstaedt, *Zukovskij als Übersetzer* (Munich: Wilhelm Fink, 1970);

A. Fiterman, "Vzgliady Zhukovskogo na perevod," *Uchennya zapiski Moskovskogo pedagogicheskogo instituta inostrannykh iazykakh,* volume 13 (1958): 23–24;

Dorethea D. Galer, "Vasilii Andreevich Zhukovskii: His Theory of Translation," dissertation, Northwestern University, 1975;

André von Gronicka, "Goethe and his Russian Translator-Interpreter," *Papers of the Modern Language Association,* 70 (1955): 145–165;

Ainslie Hewton, "A Comparison of Sir Walter Scott's *The Eve of St. John* and Zhukovsky's Translation of the Ballad," *New Zealand Slavonic Journal,* 11 (1973): 145-150;

Raisa Vladimirovna Iezuitova, *Zhukovsky i ego vremia* (Leningrad: "Nauka," Leningradskoe otd-nie, 1989);

K. B. Jensen, "Meaning in a Poem: An Analysis of V. A. Zhukovsky's '19 *marta* 1823,'" *Scando-Slavica,* 27 (1981): 5-14;

Doris Johnson, "The Comparison in the Poetry of Batyushkov and Zhukovsky," dissertation, University of Michigan, 1973;

Johnson, "The Simile in Batiushkov and Zhukovsky," *Russian Literature Triquarterly,* 7 (1973): 407-422;

G. Jonas, "V. A. Zhukovskii's Reception of the European Enlightenment," *Zeitschrift Fur Slawistik,* 39: 436-442;

Vera Nikolaevna Kasatkina, *"Zdes' serdtsu budet prüatno–": a Poeziia V. A. Zhukovskogo* (Moscow: Obshchina, 1995);

Michael Katz, "Polemics, Zhukovsky's Literary Ballads" and "Zhukovsky's Imitators," in his *The Literary Ballad in Early 19th-Century Russian Literature* (Oxford: Oxford University Press, 1976), pp. 37-138;

P. Malenko, "Tieck's Russian Friends: Küchelbecker and Zhukovsky," *Papers of the Modern Language Association,* 55 (1940): 1129-1145;

Kenneth H. Ober and Warren U. Ober, "Percy's Nancy and Zhukovsky's Nina: A Translation Identified," *Slavic and Eastern European Review,* 57 (1979): 396-402;

Ober and Ober, "Two Bards: Zhukovsky and Bowring (with text and English translation of Pevets)," *Slavic and Eastern European Review,* 62 (1984): 560-566;

Ober and Ober, "Zukovskij's Early Translations of the Ballads of Robert Southey," *Slavic and Eastern European Journal,* 9 (1965): 181-190;

Ober and Ober, "Zukovskij's Translation of Oliver Goldsmith's 'The Deserted Village,'" *Germano-Slavica,* 1 (1973): 19-28;

Ober and Ober, "Zhukovsky's First Translation of Gray's Elegy," *Slavic and Eastern European Journal,* 10 (1966): 167-172;

Ober and Ober, "Zhukovsky and Southey's Ballads: The Translator as Rival," *Wordsworth Circle,* 5 (1974): 76-88;

Ober and Ober, "Zhukovsky's Translation of Campbell's 'Lord Ullin's Daughter,'" *Germano-Slavica,* 2 (1977): 295-305;

Ober and Ober, "Zhukovsky's Translation of 'The Prisoner of Chillon,'" *Slavic and Eastern European Journal,* 17 (1973): 390-398;

Charles Passage, "The Influence of Schiller in Russia: 1800-1840 (Schiller and Zhukovsky)," *American Slavic and East European Review,* 5 (1956): 11-37;

William Francis Ryan and Faith Wigzell, "Gullible Girls and Dreadful Dreams: Zhukovskii, Pushkin, and Popular Divination," *Slavic and Eastern European Review,* 70 (1992): 647-669;

Irina Mikhailovna Semenko, *Vasily Zhukovsky* (Boston: Twayne, 1976);

Savelii Sendrovich, "Zhukovsky's World of Fleeting Visions," *Russkaia Literatura,* 12 (1985): 203-220;

Andrew J. Swensen, "Russian Romanticism and Theologically Founded Aesthetics: Zhukovksij, Odoevskij, and Gogol and the Appropriation of Post-Kantian Aesthetic Principles," dissertation, University of Wisconsin–Madison, 1995;

Stephen G. Witehead, "English Pre-Romantic and Romantic Influences in the Poetry of V. A. Zhukovskii," dissertation, University of East Anglia, 1987.

Papers:

Vasilii Andreevich Zhukovsky's papers are housed at the Russian National Library, f. 286, the Institute of Russian Literature (Pushkin House), f. 471 and 244, and the Central State Historical Archive, f. 1349, 343, 797, 772, and 1673, all in St. Petersburg; and at the Russian State Library, f. 104, and the Central State Archive of Literature and Art (TsGALI), f. 198, both in Moscow.

Checklist of Further Readings

Boyer, Arline. "A Description of Selected Periodicals in the First Half of the Nineteenth Century." *Russian Literature Triquarterly,* no. 3 (1972): 465–473.

Bristol, Evelyn. *A History of Russian Poetry.* Oxford & New York: Oxford University Press, 1991.

Brown, William Edward. *A History of Russian Literature of the Romantic Period.* 4 volumes. Ann Arbor, Mich.: Ardis, 1986.

Canadian-American Slavic Studies, special issues on Russian Romanticism, 29, nos. 3–4 (1995).

Čiževskij, Dmitrij. *History of Nineteenth Century Russian Literature,* translated by Richard Porter and edited by Serge A. Zenkovsky. Volume I: *The Romantic Period.* Volume II: *The Realistic Period.* Nashville: Vanderbilt University Press, 1974.

Čiževskij. *On Romanticism in Slavic Literature,* translated by D. S. Worth. The Hague: Mouton, 1957.

Čiževskij. *Russian Intellectual History,* translated by John C. Osborne and edited by Martin P. Rice. Ann Arbor, Mich.: Ardis, 1978.

Cornwell, Neil, ed. *Reference Guide to Russian Literature.* London & Chicago: Fitzroy Dearborn, 1998.

Fennell, John, ed. *Nineteenth-Century Russian Literature: Studies of Ten Russian Writers.* Berkeley: University of California Press, 1973.

Fuhrman, J. T., E. C. Bock, and L. I. Twarog. *Essays on Russian Intellectual History.* Austin: Texas University Press, 1971.

Ginzburg, Lidiia. *O lirike.* Moscow-Leningrad: Sovetskii pisatel', 1964.

Harkins, William Edward. *Dictionary of Russian Literature.* New York: Philosophical Library, 1956.

Hingley, Ronald. *Writers and Society, 1825–1904.* New York: World University Library, 1967. Second revised edition. London: Weidenfeld & Nicolson, 1977.

Istoriia romantizma v russkoi literature, edited by Aleksandr Sergeevich Kurilov. Volume 1: *Vozniknovenie I utverzhdenie romantizma v russkoi literature 1790–1825.* Volume 2: *Romanitzm v russkoi literature 20–30kh godov XIX v., 1825–1840.* Moscow: Akademia Nauk SSSR, 1979.

Istoriia russkoi poezii, edited by Boris Pavlovich Gorodetskii. 2 volumes. Leningrad: Nauka, 1968.

Jacobson, Helen Saltz, ed. and trans. *Diary of a Russian Censor: Aleksandr Nikitenko.* Amherst: University of Massachusetts Press, 1975.

Karlinsky, Simon. *Russian Drama: From Its Beginnings to the Age of Pushkin.* Berkeley: University of California Press, 1986.

Katz, M. R. *The Literary Ballad in Early Nineteenth Century Russian Literature.* London: Oxford University Press, 1976.

Kostka, Edmund. *Schiller in Russian Literature*. Philadelphia: University of Pennsylvania Press, 1965.

Layton, Susan. *Russian Literature and Empire: Conquest of the Caucasus from Pushkin to Tolstoy*. New York: Cambridge University Press, 1994.

Leatherbarrow, W. J. and D. C. Offord, eds. and trans. *A Documentary History of Russian Thought: From the Enlightenment to Marxism*. Ann Arbor, Mich.: Ardis, 1987.

Leighton, Lauren G. *The Esoteric Tradition in Russian Romantic Literature. Decembrism and Freemasonry*. University Park: Pennsylvania State University Press, 1994.

Leighton. "A Romantic Idealist Nation in Russian Romantic Criticism." *Canadian American Slavic Studies*, 7 (1973): 285–295.

Leighton. "Romanticism, Marxism-Leninism, Literary Movement." *Russian Literature*, 14, 2 (1983): 183–220.

Leighton. *Russian Romanticism: Two Essays*. The Hague: Mouton, 1975.

Leighton, ed. *Russian Romantic Criticism: An Anthology*. New York: Greenwood Press, 1987.

Likhachev, Dmitrii S., and others, eds. *Russkie pisateli. Bibliograficheskii slovar'. Spravochnik dlia uchitelia*. Moscow, 1971.

Lotman, Iurij Mikhailovich. "The Theatre and Theatricality as Components of Early Nineteenth-Century Culture," in *The Semiotics of Russian Culture*, edited by Ann Shukman. Ann Arbor: University of Michigan, 1984, pp. 141–164.

Mazour, A. *The First Russian Revolution*. Berkeley: University of California Press, 1937.

McLaughlin, Sigrid. "Russia/Romanicheskij–Romanticheskij–Romantizm," in *"Romantic" and Its Cognates: The European History of a Word*, edited by Hans Eichner. Toronto & Buffalo: University of Toronto Press, 1972, pp. 418–474.

Mersereau, John Jr. "Yes, Virginia, There Was a Russian Romantic Movement." *Russian Literature Triquarterly*, no. 3 (1972): 128–147.

Mirsky, D. S. *A History of Russian Literature*, edited by Francis J. Whitfield. New York: Knopf, 1966.

Moser, Charles, ed. *The Cambridge History of Russian Literature*. Revised edition. Cambridge: Cambridge University Press, 1992.

Neuhäuser, Rudolf. *Towards the Romantic Age: Essays on Sentimental and Preromantic Literature in Russia*. The Hague: Nijhoff, 1974.

Nikolaev, P. A., ed. *Russkie pisateli, 1800–1917: Biograficheskii slovar'*. 3 volumes. Moscow: "Sov. entsiklopediia," 1989–1994.

Nilsson, Nils Åke. *Russian Romanticism: Studies in the Poetic Codes*. Stockholm: Almquist & Wiskell International, 1979.

Offord, Derek. *Portraits of Early Russian Liberals*. Cambridge: Cambridge University Press, 1985.

Passage, Charles E. *The Russian Hoffmanists*. The Hague: Mouton, 1963.

Pichio, Riccardo. "On Russian Romantic Poetry of Pushkin's Era." *Slavic and East European Studies*, 15 (1970): 16–30.

Pigarev, I. "Romantic Poetry in Relation to Painting," in *European Romanticism,* edited by I. Sötér and I. Neupokoyeva. Budapest: Akad. Kiado', 1977, pp. 475–501.

Pomar, Mark G. "Russian Historical Drama of the Early Nineteenth Century." Dissertation, Columbia University, 1978.

Pushchin, Helen A. "German and English Influences on the Russian Romantic Literary Ballad." Dissertation, New York University, 1976.

Reid, Robert, ed. *Problems of Russian Romanticism.* Brookfield, Vt.: Gower, 1986.

Riasanovsky, Nicholas V. *A History of Russia.* New York: Oxford University Press, 1977.

Riasanovsky. *The Image of Peter the Great in Russian History and Thought.* Oxford: Oxford University Press, 1985, pp. 88–152.

Riasanovsky. *Nicholas I and Official Nationality in Russia, 1825–1855.* Berkeley: University of California Press, 1959.

Riasanovsky. *A Parting of Ways: Government and the Educated Public in Russia, 1801–1855.* Oxford: Clarendon Press, 1976.

Riasanovsky. *Russia and the West in the Teaching of the Slavophile.* Gloucester, Mass.: Peter Smith, 1965.

Riha, Thomas, ed. *Readings in Russian Civilization.* Volume 2: *Imperial Russia, 1700–1917.* Chicago: The University of Chicago Press, 1965.

Russian Literature Triquarterly, special Romanticism issue, no. 3 (1972).

Russian Literature Triquarterly: The Golden Age, no. 10 (1974).

Rydel, Christine A., ed. *The Ardis Anthology of Russian Romanticism.* Ann Arbor, Mich.: Ardis, 1984.

Scherr, Barry P. *Russian Poetry: Meter, Rhythm, and Rhyme.* Berkeley: University of California Press, 1986.

Semenko, Irina Mikhailovna. *Poety pushkinskoi pory.* Moscow: Khudozhestvennaia literatura, 1970.

Snow, Valentine. *Russian Writers: A Bio-Bibliographical Dictionary.* New York: International Book Service, 1946.

Stavrou, Theofanis G., ed. *Art and Culture in Nineteenth-Century Russia.* Bloomington: Indiana University Press, 1983.

Terras, Victor, ed. *Handbook of Russian Literature.* New Haven, Conn.: Yale University Press, 1985.

Terras. *A History of Russian Literature.* New Haven, Conn. & London: Yale University Press, 1991.

Todd, William Mills, ed. *Literature and Society in Imperial Russia.* Stanford, Cal.: Stanford University Press, 1978.

Varneke, B. H. *History of the Russian Theater,* translated by Boris Brasol and edited by Belle Martin. New York: Macmillan, 1951.

Von Gronicka, André. *The Russian Image of Goethe: Goethe in Russian Literature in the First Half of the Nineteenth Century.* Philadelphia: University of Philadelphia Press, 1985.

Walicki, Andrzej. *The Slavophile Controversy.* Oxford: Oxford University Press, 1975.

Weber, Harry B., and others, eds. *The Modern Encyclopedia of Russian and Soviet Literature.* Continued as *The Modern Encyclopedia of East Slavic, Baltic and Eurasian Literatures.* Gulf Breeze, Fla.: Academic International Press, 1977– .

Contributors

Marina Balina . . . . .Illinois Wesleyan University
John A. Barnstead . . . . Dalhousie University
Luc J. Beaudoin. . . . . University of Denver
T. Henry Fitt. . . . . .Keele University
Sibelan Forrester . . . . Swarthmore College
George J. Gutsche . . . . University of Arizona
Gary R. Jahn . . . . University of Minnesota
Sonia I. Ketchian . . . . Davis Center for Russian Studies, Harvard University, and M.I.T.
Marina Kostalevsky. . . . . .Bard College
Anatoly Liberman . . . . University of Minnesota
Rosina Neginsky . . . . University of Illinois
Igor' A. Pil'shchikov . . . . .Moscow State University
David Powelstock . . . . University of Chicago
Vera Proskurina . . . . Cornell University
Christine A. Rydel. . . . . .Grand Valley State University
Veronica Shapovalov . . . . San Diego State University
Vladimir Shatskov. . . . . .St. Petersburg University of Civil Engineering and Architecture
Ruth Sobel. . . . . Defence School of Languages
Evgeniia B. Sorokina . . . . St. Petersburg House of Culture
Richard Tempest. . . . . University of Illinois at Urbana-Champaign
Irwin R. Titunik . . . . University of Michigan
James West . . . . University of Washington
Sofiya Yuzefpolskaya. . . . . University of Washington

Cumulative Index

Dictionary of Literary Biography, Volumes 1-205
Dictionary of Literary Biography Yearbook, 1980-1997
Dictionary of Literary Biography Documentary Series, Volumes 1-19

Cumulative Index

DLB before number: *Dictionary of Literary Biography,* Volumes 1-205
Y before number: *Dictionary of Literary Biography Yearbook,* 1980-1997
DS before number: *Dictionary of Literary Biography Documentary Series,* Volumes 1-19

A

Abbey, Edwin Austin 1852-1911 ....DLB-188
Abbey, Maj. J. R. 1894-1969 ....DLB-201
Abbey Press DLB-49
The Abbey Theatre and Irish Drama, 1900-1945 ....DLB-10
Abbot, Willis J. 1863-1934..............DLB-29
Abbott, Jacob 1803-1879 ....DLB-1
Abbott, Lee K. 1947- DLB-130
Abbott, Lyman 1835-1922..............DLB-79
Abbott, Robert S. 1868-1940 ....DLB-29, 91
Abe Kōbō 1924-1993.................DLB-182
Abelard, Peter circa 1079-1142..........DLB-115
Abelard-Schuman.....................DLB-46
Abell, Arunah S. 1806-1888............DLB-43
Abercrombie, Lascelles 1881-1938........DLB-19
Aberdeen University Press Limited......DLB-106
Abish, Walter 1931- DLB-130
Ablesimov, Aleksandr Onisimovich 1742-1783......................DLB-150
Abraham à Sancta Clara 1644-1709......DLB-168
Abrahams, Peter 1919- DLB-117
Abrams, M. H. 1912- DLB-67
Abrogans circa 790-800 ....DLB-148
Abschatz, Hans Aßmann von 1646-1699 ....DLB-168
Abse, Dannie 1923- DLB-27
Abutsu-ni 1221-1283 ....DLB-203
Academy Chicago Publishers DLB-46
Accrocca, Elio Filippo 1923- DLB-128
Ace Books DLB-46
Achebe, Chinua 1930- DLB-117
Achtenberg, Herbert 1938- DLB-124
Ackerman, Diane 1948- DLB-120
Ackroyd, Peter 1949- DLB-155
Acorn, Milton 1923-1986................DLB-53
Acosta, Oscar Zeta 1935?- DLB-82
Actors Theatre of Louisville DLB-7
Adair, Gilbert 1944- DLB-194
Adair, James 1709?-1783?...............DLB-30
Adam, Graeme Mercer 1839-1912........DLB-99
Adam, Robert Borthwick II 1863-1940 ...DLB-187
Adame, Leonard 1947- DLB-82

Adamic, Louis 1898-1951 ....DLB-9
Adams, Abigail 1744-1818 ....DLB-200
Adams, Alice 1926- Y-86
Adams, Brooks 1848-1927................DLB-47
Adams, Charles Francis, Jr. 1835-1915 ....DLB-47
Adams, Douglas 1952-..................Y-83
Adams, Franklin P. 1881-1960...........DLB-29
Adams, Hannah 1755-1832 ....DLB-200
Adams, Henry 1838-1918 .... DLB-12, 47, 189
Adams, Herbert Baxter 1850-1901 ....DLB-47
Adams, J. S. and C. [publishing house] DLB-49
Adams, James Truslow 1878-1949 .... DLB-17; DS-17
Adams, John 1735-1826............DLB-31, 183
Adams, John 1735-1826 and Adams, Abigail 1744-1818..........DLB-183
Adams, John Quincy 1767-1848.........DLB-37
Adams, Léonie 1899-1988..............DLB-48
Adams, Levi 1802-1832.................DLB-99
Adams, Samuel 1722-1803...........DLB-31, 43
Adams, Sarah Fuller Flower 1805-1848...DLB-199
Adams, Thomas 1582 or 1583-1652 .....DLB-151
Adams, William Taylor 1822-1897.......DLB-42
Adamson, Sir John 1867-1950 ....DLB-98
Adcock, Arthur St. John 1864-1930......DLB-135
Adcock, Betty 1938- DLB-105
Adcock, Fleur 1934- DLB-40
Addison, Joseph 1672-1719 ....DLB-101
Ade, George 1866-1944.............DLB-11, 25
Adeler, Max (see Clark, Charles Heber)
Adonias Filho 1915-1990...............DLB-145
Advance Publishing Company DLB-49
AE 1867-1935......................DLB-19
Ælfric circa 955-circa 1010.............DLB-146
Aeschines circa 390 B.C.-circa 320 B.C. DLB-176
Aeschylus 525-524 B.C.-456-455 B.C.........DLB-176
Aesthetic Poetry (1873), by Walter Pater...DLB-35
After Dinner Opera Company............Y-92
Afro-American Literary Critics: An Introduction DLB-33
Agassiz, Elizabeth Cary 1822-1907 ......DLB-189
Agassiz, Jean Louis Rodolphe 1807-1873........................DLB-1

Agee, James 1909-1955 .... DLB-2, 26, 152
The Agee Legacy: A Conference at the University of Tennessee at Knoxville............ Y-89
Aguilera Malta, Demetrio 1909-1981 ....DLB-145
Ai 1947- DLB-120
Aichinger, Ilse 1921- DLB-85
Aidoo, Ama Ata 1942- DLB-117
Aiken, Conrad 1889-1973 .... DLB-9, 45, 102
Aiken, Joan 1924- DLB-161
Aikin, Lucy 1781-1864.............DLB-144, 163
Ainsworth, William Harrison 1805-1882 ..DLB-21
Aitken, George A. 1860-1917...........DLB-149
Aitken, Robert [publishing house] DLB-49
Akenside, Mark 1721-1770..............DLB-109
Akins, Zoë 1886-1958 ....DLB-26
Aksakov, Sergei Timofeevich 1791-1859......................DLB-198
Akutagawa, Ryūnsuke 1892-1927 ....DLB-180
Alabaster, William 1568-1640 ....DLB-132
Alain-Fournier 1886-1914 ....DLB-65
Alarcón, Francisco X. 1954- DLB-122
Alba, Nanina 1915-1968 ....DLB-41
Albee, Edward 1928- DLB-7
Albert the Great circa 1200-1280........DLB-115
Alberti, Rafael 1902- DLB-108
Albertinus, Aegidius circa 1560-1620.....DLB-164
Alcaeus born circa 620 B.C. DLB-176
Alcott, Amos Bronson 1799-1888 ....DLB-1
Alcott, Louisa May 1832-1888.......... DLB-1, 42, 79; DS-14
Alcott, William Andrus 1798-1859 ....DLB-1
Alcuin circa 732-804 ....DLB-148
Alden, Henry Mills 1836-1919 ....DLB-79
Alden, Isabella 1841-1930 ....DLB-42
Alden, John B. [publishing house] DLB-49
Alden, Beardsley and Company DLB-49
Aldington, Richard 1892-1962............ DLB-20, 36, 100, 149
Aldis, Dorothy 1896-1966 ....DLB-22
Aldis, H. G. 1863-1919 ....DLB-184
Aldiss, Brian W. 1925- DLB-14
Aldrich, Thomas Bailey 1836-1907 .... DLB-42, 71, 74, 79
Alegría, Ciro 1909-1967................DLB-113
Alegría, Claribel 1924- DLB-145

389

Cumulative Index

Aleixandre, Vicente 1898-1984 . . . . DLB-108

Aleksandrov, Aleksandr Andreevich (see Durova, Nadezhda Andreevna)

Aleramo, Sibilla 1876-1960 . . . . DLB-114

Alexander, Cecil Frances 1818-1895 . . . . . DLB-199

Alexander, Charles 1868-1923 . . . . DLB-91

Alexander, Charles Wesley [publishing house] DLB-49

Alexander, James 1691-1756 . . . . DLB-24

Alexander, Lloyd 1924- DLB-52

Alexander, Sir William, Earl of Stirling 1577?-1640 . . . . DLB-121

Alexie, Sherman 1966- DLB-175

Alexis, Willibald 1798-1871 . . . . DLB-133

Alfred, King 849-899 . . . . DLB-146

Alger, Horatio, Jr. 1832-1899 . . . . DLB-42

Algonquin Books of Chapel Hill DLB-46

Algren, Nelson 1909-1981 . . . . . DLB-9; Y-81, Y-82

Allan, Andrew 1907-1974 . . . . DLB-88

Allan, Ted 1916- DLB-68

Allbeury, Ted 1917- DLB-87

Alldritt, Keith 1935- DLB-14

Allen, Ethan 1738-1789 . . . . DLB-31

Allen, Frederick Lewis 1890-1954 . . . . . . DLB-137

Allen, Gay Wilson 1903-1995 . . . . . DLB-103; Y-95

Allen, George 1808-1876 . . . . DLB-59

Allen, George [publishing house] DLB-106

Allen, George, and Unwin Limited DLB-112

Allen, Grant 1848-1899 . . . . DLB-70, 92, 178

Allen, Henry W. 1912- Y-85

Allen, Hervey 1889-1949 . . . . DLB-9, 45

Allen, James 1739-1808 . . . . DLB-31

Allen, James Lane 1849-1925 . . . . DLB-71

Allen, Jay Presson 1922- DLB-26

Allen, John, and Company DLB-49

Allen, Paula Gunn 1939- DLB-175

Allen, Samuel W. 1917- DLB-41

Allen, Woody 1935- DLB-44

Allende, Isabel 1942- DLB-145

Alline, Henry 1748-1784 . . . . DLB-99

Allingham, Margery 1904-1966 . . . . DLB-77

Allingham, William 1824-1889 . . . . DLB-35

Allison, W. L. [publishing house] DLB-49

The *Alliterative Morte Arthure and the Stanzaic Morte Arthur* circa 1350-1400 . . . . . . DLB-146

Allott, Kenneth 1912-1973 . . . . DLB-20

Allston, Washington 1779-1843 . . . . DLB-1

Almon, John [publishing house] DLB-154

Alonzo, Dámaso 1898-1990 . . . . DLB-108

Alsop, George 1636-post 1673 . . . . DLB-24

Alsop, Richard 1761-1815 . . . . DLB-37

Altemus, Henry, and Company DLB-49

Altenberg, Peter 1885-1919 . . . . DLB-81

Altolaguirre, Manuel 1905-1959 . . . . DLB-108

Aluko, T. M. 1918- DLB-117

Alurista 1947- DLB-82

Alvarez, A. 1929- DLB-14, 40

Amadi, Elechi 1934- DLB-117

Amado, Jorge 1912- DLB-113

Ambler, Eric 1909- DLB-77

America: or, a Poem on the Settlement of the British Colonies (1780?), by Timothy Dwight DLB-37

American Conservatory Theatre DLB-7

American Fiction and the 1930s DLB-9

American Humor: A Historical Survey
East and Northeast
South and Southwest
Midwest
West DLB-11

The American Library in Paris Y-93

American News Company DLB-49

The American Poets' Corner: The First Three Years (1983-1986) Y-86

American Proletarian Culture: The 1930s . . . DS-11

American Publishing Company DLB-49

American Stationers' Company DLB-49

American Sunday-School Union DLB-49

American Temperance Union DLB-49

American Tract Society DLB-49

The American Trust for the British Library Y-96

The American Writers Congress (9-12 October 1981) Y-81

The American Writers Congress: A Report on Continuing Business Y-81

Ames, Fisher 1758-1808 . . . . DLB-37

Ames, Mary Clemmer 1831-1884 . . . . DLB-23

Amini, Johari M. 1935- DLB-41

Amis, Kingsley 1922-1995 . . . . . . DLB-15, 27, 100, 139, Y-96

Amis, Martin 1949- DLB-194

Ammons, A. R. 1926- DLB-5, 165

Amory, Thomas 1691?-1788 . . . . DLB-39

Anania, Michael 1939- DLB-193

Anaya, Rudolfo A. 1937- DLB-82

Ancrene Riwle circa 1200-1225 . . . . DLB-146

Andersch, Alfred 1914-1980 . . . . DLB-69

Anderson, Alexander 1775-1870 . . . . DLB-188

Anderson, Frederick Irving 1877-1947 . . . DLB-202

Anderson, Margaret 1886-1973 . . . . DLB-4, 91

Anderson, Maxwell 1888-1959 . . . . DLB-7

Anderson, Patrick 1915-1979 . . . . DLB-68

Anderson, Paul Y. 1893-1938 . . . . DLB-29

Anderson, Poul 1926- DLB-8

Anderson, Robert 1750-1830 . . . . DLB-142

Anderson, Robert 1917- DLB-7

Anderson, Sherwood 1876-1941 . . . . DLB-4, 9, 86; DS-1

Andreae, Johann Valentin 1586-1654 . . . . DLB-164

Andreas-Salomé, Lou 1861-1937 . . . . DLB-66

Andres, Stefan 1906-1970 . . . . DLB-69

Andreu, Blanca 1959- DLB-134

Andrewes, Lancelot 1555-1626 . . . . . . DLB-151, 172

Andrews, Charles M. 1863-1943 . . . . DLB-17

Andrews, Miles Peter ?-1814 . . . . DLB-89

Andrian, Leopold von 1875-1951 . . . . DLB-81

Andrić, Ivo 1892-1975 . . . . DLB-147

Andrieux, Louis (see Aragon, Louis)

Andrus, Silas, and Son DLB-49

Angell, James Burrill 1829-1916 . . . . DLB-64

Angell, Roger 1920- DLB-171, 185

Angelou, Maya 1928- DLB-38

Anger, Jane flourished 1589 . . . . DLB-136

Angers, Félicité (see Conan, Laure)

Anglo-Norman Literature in the Development of Middle English Literature DLB-146

The Anglo-Saxon Chronicle circa 890-1154 . . . . DLB-146

The "Angry Young Men" DLB-15

Angus and Robertson (UK) Limited DLB-112

Anhalt, Edward 1914- DLB-26

Anners, Henry F. [publishing house] DLB-49

Annolied between 1077 and 1081 . . . . DLB-148

Anselm of Canterbury 1033-1109 . . . . . . DLB-115

Anstey, F. 1856-1934 . . . . DLB-141, 178

Anthony, Michael 1932- DLB-125

Anthony, Piers 1934- DLB-8

Anthony, Susanna 1726-1791 . . . . DLB-200

Anthony Burgess's 99 Novels: An Opinion Poll Y-84

Antin, David 1932- DLB-169

Antin, Mary 1881-1949 . . . . Y-84

Anton Ulrich, Duke of Brunswick-Lüneburg 1633-1714 . . . . DLB-168

Antschel, Paul (see Celan, Paul)

Anyidoho, Kofi 1947- DLB-157

Anzaldúa, Gloria 1942- DLB-122

Anzengruber, Ludwig 1839-1889 . . . . DLB-129

Apess, William 1798-1839 . . . . DLB-175

Apodaca, Rudy S. 1939- DLB-82

Apollonius Rhodius third century B.C. DLB-176

Apple, Max 1941- DLB-130

Appleton, D., and Company DLB-49

Appleton-Century-Crofts DLB-46

Applewhite, James 1935- DLB-105

Apple-wood Books DLB-46

Aquin, Hubert 1929-1977 . . . . DLB-53

Aquinas, Thomas 1224 or 1225-1274 . . . . DLB-115

Aragon, Louis 1897-1982 . . . . DLB-72

Aralica, Ivan 1930- DLB-181

Aratus of Soli circa 315 B.C.-circa 239 B.C. DLB-176

Arbasino, Alberto 1930- DLB-196

Arbor House Publishing Company DLB-46

Arbuthnot, John 1667-1735 . . . . DLB-101

Arcadia House DLB-46

Arce, Julio G. (see Ulica, Jorge)

Archer, William 1856-1924 . . . . DLB-10
Archilochhus mid seventh century B.C.E.
  . . . . DLB-176
The Archpoet circa 1130?-? DLB-148
Archpriest Avvakum (Petrovich)
  1620?-1682 . . . . DLB-150
Arden, John 1930- DLB-13
Arden of Faversham DLB-62
Ardis Publishers Y-89
Ardizzone, Edward 1900-1979 . . . . DLB-160
Arellano, Juan Estevan 1947- DLB-122
The Arena Publishing Company DLB-49
Arena Stage DLB-7
Arenas, Reinaldo 1943-1990 . . . . DLB-145
Arensberg, Ann 1937- Y-82
Arguedas, José María 1911-1969 . . . . DLB-113
Argueta, Manilio 1936- DLB-145
Arias, Ron 1941- DLB-82
Arishima, Takeo 1878-1923 . . . . DLB-180
Aristophanes
  circa 446 B.C.-circa 386 B.C. DLB-176
Aristotle 384 B.C.-322 B.C. DLB-176
Ariyoshi Sawako 1931-1984 . . . . DLB-182
Arland, Marcel 1899-1986 . . . . DLB-72
Arlen, Michael 1895-1956 . . . . . . DLB-36, 77, 162
Armah, Ayi Kwei 1939- DLB-117
Armantrout, Rae 1947- DLB-193
Der arme Hartmann ?-after 1150 . . . . DLB-148
Armed Services Editions DLB-46
Armstrong, Martin Donisthorpe
  1882-1974 . . . . DLB-197
Armstrong, Richard 1903- DLB-160
Arndt, Ernst Moritz 1769-1860 . . . . DLB-90
Arnim, Achim von 1781-1831 . . . . DLB-90
Arnim, Bettina von 1785-1859 . . . . DLB-90
Arnim, Elizabeth von (Countess Mary Annette
  Beauchamp Russell) 1866-1941 . . . . . . DLB-197
Arno Press DLB-46
Arnold, Edwin 1832-1904 . . . . DLB-35
Arnold, Edwin L. 1857-1935 . . . . DLB-178
Arnold, Matthew 1822-1888 . . . . DLB-32, 57
Arnold, Thomas 1795-1842 . . . . DLB-55
Arnold, Edward [publishing house] DLB-112
Arnow, Harriette Simpson 1908-1986 . . . . . DLB-6
Arp, Bill (see Smith, Charles Henry)
Arpino, Giovanni 1927-1987 . . . . DLB-177
Arreola, Juan José 1918- DLB-113
Arrian circa 89-circa 155 . . . . DLB-176
Arrowsmith, J. W. [publishing house] DLB-106
The Art and Mystery of Publishing:
  Interviews Y-97
Arthur, Timothy Shay
  1809-1885 . . . . DLB-3, 42, 79; DS-13
The Arthurian Tradition and Its European
  Context DLB-138
Artmann, H. C. 1921- DLB-85
Arvin, Newton 1900-1963 . . . . DLB-103

As I See It, by Carolyn Cassady DLB-16
Asch, Nathan 1902-1964 . . . . DLB-4, 28
Ash, John 1948- DLB-40
Ashbery, John 1927- DLB-5, 165; Y-81
Ashbridge, Elizabeth 1713-1755 . . . . DLB-200
Ashburnham, Bertram Lord
  1797-1878 . . . . DLB-184
Ashendene Press DLB-112
Asher, Sandy 1942- Y-83
Ashton, Winifred (see Dane, Clemence)
Asimov, Isaac 1920-1992 . . . . DLB-8; Y-92
Askew, Anne circa 1521-1546 . . . . DLB-136
Asselin, Olivar 1874-1937 . . . . DLB-92
Asturias, Miguel Angel 1899-1974 . . . . . . DLB-113
Atheneum Publishers DLB-46
Atherton, Gertrude 1857-1948 . . . . . DLB-9, 78, 186
Athlone Press DLB-112
Atkins, Josiah circa 1755-1781 . . . . DLB-31
Atkins, Russell 1926- DLB-41
The Atlantic Monthly Press DLB-46
Attaway, William 1911-1986 . . . . DLB-76
Atwood, Margaret 1939- DLB-53
Aubert, Alvin 1930- DLB-41
Aubert de Gaspé, Phillipe-Ignace-François
  1814-1841 . . . . DLB-99
Aubert de Gaspé, Phillipe-Joseph
  1786-1871 . . . . DLB-99
Aubin, Napoléon 1812-1890 . . . . DLB-99
Aubin, Penelope 1685-circa 1731 . . . . DLB-39
Aubrey-Fletcher, Henry Lancelot (see Wade, Henry)
Auchincloss, Louis 1917- DLB-2; Y-80
Auden, W. H. 1907-1973 . . . . DLB-10, 20
Audio Art in America: A Personal Memoir . . . Y-85
Audubon, John Woodhouse 1812-1862 . . DLB-183
Auerbach, Berthold 1812-1882 . . . . DLB-133
Auernheimer, Raoul 1876-1948 . . . . DLB-81
Augier, Emile 1820-1889 . . . . DLB-192
Augustine 354-430 . . . . DLB-115
Austen, Jane 1775-1817 . . . . DLB-116
Austin, Alfred 1835-1913 . . . . DLB-35
Austin, Jane Goodwin 1831-1894 . . . . DLB-202
Austin, Mary 1868-1934 . . . . DLB-9, 78
Austin, William 1778-1841 . . . . DLB-74
Author-Printers, 1476–1599 . . . . DLB-167
Author Websites Y-97
The Author's Apology for His Book
  (1684), by John Bunyan DLB-39
An Author's Response, by Ronald Sukenick . . Y-82
Authors and Newspapers Association DLB-46
Authors' Publishing Company DLB-49
Avalon Books DLB-46
Avancini, Nicolaus 1611-1686 . . . . DLB-164
Avendaño, Fausto 1941- DLB-82
Averroëó 1126-1198 . . . . DLB-115
Avery, Gillian 1926- DLB-161

Avicenna 980-1037 . . . . DLB-115
Avison, Margaret 1918- DLB-53
Avon Books DLB-46
Awdry, Wilbert Vere 1911- DLB-160
Awoonor, Kofi 1935- DLB-117
Ayckbourn, Alan 1939- DLB-13
Aymé, Marcel 1902-1967 . . . . DLB-72
Aytoun, Sir Robert 1570-1638 . . . . DLB-121
Aytoun, William Edmondstoune
  1813-1865 . . . . DLB-32, 159

B

B. V. (see Thomson, James)
Babbitt, Irving 1865-1933 . . . . DLB-63
Babbitt, Natalie 1932- DLB-52
Babcock, John [publishing house] DLB-49
Babrius circa 150-200 . . . . DLB-176
Baca, Jimmy Santiago 1952- DLB-122
Bache, Benjamin Franklin 1769-1798 . . . . DLB-43
Bacheller, Irving 1859-1950 . . . . DLB-202
Bachmann, Ingeborg 1926-1973 . . . . DLB-85
Bacon, Delia 1811-1859 . . . . DLB-1
Bacon, Francis 1561-1626 . . . . DLB-151
Bacon, Roger circa 1214/1220-1292 . . . . . DLB-115
Bacon, Sir Nicholas circa 1510-1579 . . . . . DLB-132
Bacon, Thomas circa 1700-1768 . . . . DLB-31
Badger, Richard G., and Company DLB-49
Bage, Robert 1728-1801 . . . . DLB-39
Bagehot, Walter 1826-1877 . . . . DLB-55
Bagley, Desmond 1923-1983 . . . . DLB-87
Bagnold, Enid 1889-1981 . . . . . . DLB-13, 160, 191
Bagrayna, Elisaveta 1893-1991 . . . . DLB-147
Bahr, Hermann 1863-1934 . . . . DLB-81, 118
Bailey, Abigail Abbot 1746-1815 . . . . DLB-200
Bailey, Alfred Goldsworthy 1905- DLB-68
Bailey, Francis [publishing house] DLB-49
Bailey, H. C. 1878-1961 . . . . DLB-77
Bailey, Jacob 1731-1808 . . . . DLB-99
Bailey, Paul 1937- DLB-14
Bailey, Philip James 1816-1902 . . . . DLB-32
Baillargeon, Pierre 1916-1967 . . . . DLB-88
Baillie, Hugh 1890-1966 . . . . DLB-29
Baillie, Joanna 1762-1851 . . . . DLB-93
Bailyn, Bernard 1922- DLB-17
Bainbridge, Beryl 1933- DLB-14
Baird, Irene 1901-1981 . . . . DLB-68
Baker, Augustine 1575-1641 . . . . DLB-151
Baker, Carlos 1909-1987 . . . . DLB-103
Baker, David 1954- DLB-120
Baker, Herschel C. 1914-1990 . . . . DLB-111
Baker, Houston A., Jr. 1943- DLB-67
Baker, Samuel White 1821-1893 . . . . DLB-166
Baker, Walter H., Company
  ("Baker's Plays") DLB-49
The Baker and Taylor Company DLB-49

Cumulative Index

Balaban, John 1943- DLB-120
Bald, Wambly 1902- DLB-4
Balde, Jacob 1604-1668................ DLB-164
Balderston, John 1889-1954 .... DLB-26
Baldwin, James 1924-1987 ..... DLB-2, 7, 33; Y-87
Baldwin, Joseph Glover 1815-1864..... DLB-3, 11
Baldwin, Richard and Anne
 [publishing house] DLB-170
Baldwin, William circa 1515-1563 .... DLB-132
Bale, John 1495-1563 .... DLB-132
Balestrini, Nanni 1935- DLB-128, 196
Balfour, Arthur James 1848-1930....... DLB-190
Ballantine Books.................... DLB-46
Ballantyne, R. M. 1825-1894 .... DLB-163
Ballard, J. G. 1930- DLB-14
Ballard, Martha Moore 1735-1812 ...... DLB-200
Ballerini, Luigi 1940- DLB-128
Ballou, Maturin Murray 1820-1895 .. DLB-79, 189
Ballou, Robert O. [publishing house] DLB-46
Balzac, Honoré de 1799-1855 .... DLB-119
Bambara, Toni Cade 1939- DLB-38
Bamford, Samuel 1788-1872 .... DLB-190
Bancroft, A. L., and Company DLB-49
Bancroft, George 1800-1891........ DLB-1, 30, 59
Bancroft, Hubert Howe 1832-1918 ...DLB-47, 140
Bandelier, Adolph F. 1840-1914 .... DLB-186
Bangs, John Kendrick 1862-1922 ..... DLB-11, 79
Banim, John 1798-1842.........DLB-116, 158, 159
Banim, Michael 1796-1874 .... DLB-158, 159
Banks, Iain 1954- DLB-194
Banks, John circa 1653-1706............ DLB-80
Banks, Russell 1940- DLB-130
Bannerman, Helen 1862-1946 .... DLB-141
Bantam Books..................... DLB-46
Banti, Anna 1895-1985 ....DLB-177
Banville, John 1945- DLB-14
Baraka, Amiri 1934- DLB-5, 7, 16, 38; DS-8
Baratynsky, Evgenii Abramovich
 1800-1844..................... DLB-205
Barbauld, Anna Laetitia
 1743-1825.......... DLB-107, 109, 142, 158
Barbeau, Marius 1883-1969 .... DLB-92
Barber, John Warner 1798-1885........ DLB-30
Bàrberi Squarotti, Giorgio 1929- DLB-128
Barbey d'Aurevilly, Jules-Amédée
 1808-1889 .... DLB-119
Barbour, John circa 1316-1395 .... DLB-146
Barbour, Ralph Henry 1870-1944 .... DLB-22
Barbusse, Henri 1873-1935 .... DLB-65
Barclay, Alexander circa 1475-1552 ..... DLB-132
Barclay, E. E., and Company DLB-49
Bardeen, C. W. [publishing house]....... DLB-49
Barham, Richard Harris 1788-1845 ..... DLB-159
Barich, Bill 1943- DLB-185
Baring, Maurice 1874-1945........... DLB-34

Baring-Gould, Sabine 1834-1924 ... DLB-156, 190
Barker, A. L. 1918- DLB-14, 139
Barker, George 1913-1991 .... DLB-20
Barker, Harley Granville 1877-1946...... DLB-10
Barker, Howard 1946- DLB-13
Barker, James Nelson 1784-1858 .... DLB-37
Barker, Jane 1652-1727............ DLB-39, 131
Barker, Lady Mary Anne 1831-1911 .... DLB-166
Barker, William circa 1520-after 1576 ... DLB-132
Barker, Arthur, Limited DLB-112
Barkov, Ivan Semenovich 1732-1768 .... DLB-150
Barks, Coleman 1937- DLB-5
Barlach, Ernst 1870-1938 .... DLB-56, 118
Barlow, Joel 1754-1812................ DLB-37
Barnard, John 1681-1770 .... DLB-24
Barne, Kitty (Mary Catherine Barne)
 1883-1957..................... DLB-160
Barnes, Barnabe 1571-1609 .... DLB-132
Barnes, Djuna 1892-1982 .... DLB-4, 9, 45
Barnes, Jim 1933- DLB-175
Barnes, Julian 1946- DLB-194; Y-93
Barnes, Margaret Ayer 1886-1967 .... DLB-9
Barnes, Peter 1931- DLB-13
Barnes, William 1801-1886 .... DLB-32
Barnes, A. S., and Company DLB-49
Barnes and Noble Books DLB-46
Barnet, Miguel 1940- DLB-145
Barney, Natalie 1876-1972 .... DLB-4
Barnfield, Richard 1574-1627 ....DLB-172
Baron, Richard W.,
 Publishing Company DLB-46
Barr, Amelia Edith Huddleston
 1831-1919 .... DLB-202
Barr, Robert 1850-1912 .... DLB-70, 92
Barral, Carlos 1928-1989 .... DLB-134
Barrax, Gerald William 1933- DLB-41, 120
Barrès, Maurice 1862-1923............ DLB-123
Barrett, Eaton Stannard 1786-1820...... DLB-116
Barrie, J. M. 1860-1937........DLB-10, 141, 156
Barrie and Jenkins DLB-112
Barrio, Raymond 1921- DLB-82
Barrios, Gregg 1945- DLB-122
Barry, Philip 1896-1949 .... DLB-7
Barry, Robertine (see Françoise)
Barse and Hopkins DLB-46
Barstow, Stan 1928- DLB-14, 139
Barth, John 1930- DLB-2
Barthelme, Donald 1931-1989 ..DLB-2; Y-80, Y-89
Barthelme, Frederick 1943- Y-85
Bartholomew, Frank 1898-1985 .... DLB-127
Bartlett, John 1820-1905............... DLB-1
Bartol, Cyrus Augustus 1813-1900....... DLB-1
Barton, Bernard 1784-1849 .... DLB-96
Barton, Thomas Pennant 1803-1869 ... DLB-140
Bartram, John 1699-1777 .... DLB-31

Bartram, William 1739-1823 .... DLB-37
Basic Books DLB-46
Basille, Theodore (see Becon, Thomas)
Bass, T. J. 1932- Y-81
Bassani, Giorgio 1916- DLB-128, 177
Basse, William circa 1583-1653 .... DLB-121
Bassett, John Spencer 1867-1928..........DLB-17
Bassler, Thomas Joseph (see Bass, T. J.)
Bate, Walter Jackson 1918- DLB-67, 103
Bateman, Christopher
 [publishing house] DLB-170
Bateman, Stephen circa 1510-1584...... DLB-136
Bates, H. E. 1905-1974 .... DLB-162, 191
Bates, Katharine Lee 1859-1929......... DLB-71
Batiushkov, Konstantin Nikolaevich
 1787-1855..................... DLB-205
Batsford, B. T. [publishing house] DLB-106
Battiscombe, Georgina 1905- DLB-155
The Battle of Maldon circa 1000.......... DLB-146
Bauer, Bruno 1809-1882 .... DLB-133
Bauer, Wolfgang 1941- DLB-124
Baum, L. Frank 1856-1919............. DLB-22
Baum, Vicki 1888-1960 .... DLB-85
Baumbach, Jonathan 1933- Y-80
Bausch, Richard 1945- DLB-130
Bawden, Nina 1925- DLB-14, 161
Bax, Clifford 1886-1962.............DLB-10, 100
Baxter, Charles 1947- DLB-130
Bayer, Eleanor (see Perry, Eleanor)
Bayer, Konrad 1932-1964 .... DLB-85
Baynes, Pauline 1922- DLB-160
Bazin, Hervé 1911- DLB-83
Beach, Sylvia 1887-1962............ DLB-4; DS-15
Beacon Press....................... DLB-49
Beadle and Adams DLB-49
Beagle, Peter S. 1939- Y-80
Beal, M. F. 1937- Y-81
Beale, Howard K. 1899-1959............DLB-17
Beard, Charles A. 1874-1948 ....DLB-17
A Beat Chronology: The First Twenty-five
 Years, 1944-1969 .... DLB-16
Beattie, Ann 1947- Y-82
Beattie, James 1735-1803 .... DLB-109
Beatty, Chester 1875-1968 .... DLB-201
Beauchemin, Nérée 1850-1931.......... DLB-92
Beauchemin, Yves 1941- DLB-60
Beaugrand, Honoré 1848-1906 .... DLB-99
Beaulieu, Victor-Lévy 1945- DLB-53
Beaumont, Francis circa 1584-1616
 and Fletcher, John 1579-1625........ DLB-58
Beaumont, Sir John 1583?-1627........ DLB-121
Beaumont, Joseph 1616–1699 .... DLB-126
Beauvoir, Simone de 1908-1986.....DLB-72; Y-86
Becher, Ulrich 1910- DLB-69
Becker, Carl 1873-1945 ....DLB-17

Becker, Jurek 1937- DLB-75
Becker, Jurgen 1932- DLB-75
Beckett, Samuel 1906-1989 ..... DLB-13, 15; Y-90
Beckford, William 1760-1844..........DLB-39
Beckham, Barry 1944- DLB-33
Becon, Thomas circa 1512-1567 ....DLB-136
Becque, Henry 1837-1899 ....DLB-192
Beùkoviù, Matija 1939- DLB-181
Beddoes, Thomas 1760-1808..........DLB-158
Beddoes, Thomas Lovell 1803-1849 ......DLB-96
Bede circa 673-735 ....DLB-146
Beecher, Catharine Esther 1800-1878 ......DLB-1
Beecher, Henry Ward 1813-1887 ......DLB-3, 43
Beer, George L. 1872-1920 ....DLB-47
Beer, Johann 1655-1700 ....DLB-168
Beer, Patricia 1919- DLB-40
Beerbohm, Max 1872-1956 ....DLB-34, 100
Beer-Hofmann, Richard 1866-1945.......DLB-81
Beers, Henry A. 1847-1926 ....DLB-71
Beeton, S. O. [publishing house] DLB-106
Bégon, Elisabeth 1696-1755............DLB-99
Behan, Brendan 1923-1964 ....DLB-13
Behn, Aphra 1640?-1689........DLB-39, 80, 131
Behn, Harry 1898-1973 ....DLB-61
Behrman, S. N. 1893-1973 ....DLB-7, 44
Belaney, Archibald Stansfeld (see Grey Owl)
Belasco, David 1853-1931 ....DLB-7
Belford, Clarke and Company...........DLB-49
Belinksy, Vissarion Grigor'evich
  1811-1848 ....DLB-198
Belitt, Ben 1911- DLB-5
Belknap, Jeremy 1744-1798 ....DLB-30, 37
Bell, Adrian 1901-1980 ....DLB-191
Bell, Clive 1881-1964...................DS-10
Bell, Gertrude Margaret Lowthian
  1868-1926 ....DLB-174
Bell, James Madison 1826-1902..........DLB-50
Bell, Marvin 1937- DLB-5
Bell, Millicent 1919- DLB-111
Bell, Quentin 1910- DLB-155
Bell, Vanessa 1879-1961................DS-10
Bell, George, and Sons...............DLB-106
Bell, Robert [publishing house] DLB-49
Bellamy, Edward 1850-1898 ....DLB-12
Bellamy, John [publishing house].......DLB-170
Bellamy, Joseph 1719-1790..............DLB-31
Bellezza, Dario 1944- DLB-128
La Belle Assemblée 1806-1837 ....DLB-110
Belloc, Hilaire 1870-1953 ... DLB-19, 100, 141, 174
Bellonci, Maria 1902-1986 ....DLB-196
Bellow, Saul 1915- DLB-2, 28; Y-82; DS-3
Belmont Productions DLB-46
Bemelmans, Ludwig 1898-1962..........DLB-22
Bemis, Samuel Flagg 1891-1973 ....DLB-17

Bemrose, William [publishing house] DLB-106
Ben no Naishi 1228?-1271? DLB-203
Benchley, Robert 1889-1945 ....DLB-11
Benedetti, Mario 1920- DLB-113
Benedictus, David 1938- DLB-14
Benedikt, Michael 1935- DLB-5
Benediktov, Vladimir Grigor'evich
  1807-1873.....................DLB-205
Benét, Stephen Vincent
  1898-1943 ....DLB-4, 48, 102
Benét, William Rose 1886-1950 ....DLB-45
Benford, Gregory 1941- Y-82
Benjamin, Park 1809-1864..........DLB-3, 59, 73
Benjamin, S. G. W. 1837-1914..........DLB-189
Benlowes, Edward 1602-1676 ....DLB-126
Benn, Gottfried 1886-1956 ....DLB-56
Benn Brothers Limited................DLB-106
Bennett, Arnold 1867-1931 ... DLB-10, 34, 98, 135
Bennett, Charles 1899- DLB-44
Bennett, Emerson 1822-1905...........DLB-202
Bennett, Gwendolyn 1902- DLB-51
Bennett, Hal 1930- DLB-33
Bennett, James Gordon 1795-1872........DLB-43
Bennett, James Gordon, Jr. 1841-1918.....DLB-23
Bennett, John 1865-1956 ....DLB-42
Bennett, Louise 1919- DLB-117
Benni, Stefano 1947- DLB-196
Benoit, Jacques 1941- DLB-60
Benson, A. C. 1862-1925................DLB-98
Benson, E. F. 1867-1940..........DLB-135, 153
Benson, Jackson J. 1930- DLB-111
Benson, Robert Hugh 1871-1914........DLB-153
Benson, Stella 1892-1933............DLB-36, 162
Bent, James Theodore 1852-1897 ....DLB-174
Bent, Mabel Virginia Anna ?-? DLB-174
Bentham, Jeremy 1748-1832 .... DLB-107, 158
Bentley, E. C. 1875-1956 ....DLB-70
Bentley, Phyllis 1894-1977 ....DLB-191
Bentley, Richard [publishing house] DLB-106
Benton, Robert 1932- and Newman,
  David 1937- DLB-44
Benziger Brothers....................DLB-49
Beowulf circa 900-1000 or 790-825 ....DLB-146
Beresford, Anne 1929- DLB-40
Beresford, John Davys
  1873-1947 ....DLB-162, 178, 197
Beresford-Howe, Constance 1922- DLB-88
Berford, R. G., Company DLB-49
Berg, Stephen 1934- DLB-5
Bergengruen, Werner 1892-1964 ....DLB-56
Berger, John 1926- DLB-14
Berger, Meyer 1898-1959 ....DLB-29
Berger, Thomas 1924- DLB-2; Y-80
Berkeley, Anthony 1893-1971 ....DLB-77
Berkeley, George 1685-1753 ....DLB-31, 101

The Berkley Publishing Corporation......DLB-46
Berlin, Lucia 1936- DLB-130
Bernal, Vicente J. 1888-1915 ....DLB-82
Bernanos, Georges 1888-1948..........DLB-72
Bernard, Harry 1898-1979 ....DLB-92
Bernard, John 1756-1828...............DLB-37
Bernard of Chartres circa 1060-1124?....DLB-115
Bernari, Carlo 1909-1992 ....DLB-177
Bernhard, Thomas 1931-1989.......DLB-85, 124
Bernstein, Charles 1950- DLB-169
Berriault, Gina 1926- DLB-130
Berrigan, Daniel 1921- DLB-5
Berrigan, Ted 1934-1983............DLB-5, 169
Berry, Wendell 1934- DLB-5, 6
Berryman, John 1914-1972 ....DLB-48
Bersianik, Louky 1930- DLB-60
Berthelet, Thomas [publishing house] DLB-170
Berto, Giuseppe 1914-1978 ....DLB-177
Bertolucci, Attilio 1911- DLB-128
Berton, Pierre 1920- DLB-68
Besant, Sir Walter 1836-1901 ......DLB-135, 190
Bessette, Gerard 1920- DLB-53
Bessie, Alvah 1904-1985 ....DLB-26
Bester, Alfred 1913-1987 ....DLB-8
Besterman, Theodore 1904-1976........DLB-201
The Bestseller Lists: An Assessment Y-84
Bestuzhev, Aleksandr Aleksandrovich (Marlinsky)
  1797-1837.....................DLB-198
Bestuzhev, Nikolai Aleksandrovich
  1791-1855 ....DLB-198
Betham-Edwards, Matilda Barbara (see Edwards,
  Matilda Barbara Betham-)
Betjeman, John 1906-1984.........DLB-20; Y-84
Betocchi, Carlo 1899-1986 ....DLB-128
Bettarini, Mariella 1942- DLB-128
Betts, Doris 1932- Y-82
Beveridge, Albert J. 1862-1927 ....DLB-17
Beverley, Robert circa 1673-1722......DLB-24, 30
Bevilacqua, Alberto 1934- DLB-196
Bevington, Louisa Sarah 1845-1895 .....DLB-199
Beyle, Marie-Henri (see Stendhal)
Bianco, Margery Williams 1881-1944....DLB-160
Bibaud, Adèle 1854-1941...............DLB-92
Bibaud, Michel 1782-1857 ....DLB-99
Bibliographical and Textual Scholarship
  Since World War II Y-89
The Bicentennial of James Fenimore Cooper:
  An International Celebration Y-89
Bichsel, Peter 1935- DLB-75
Bickerstaff, Isaac John 1733-circa 1808 ....DLB-89
Biddle, Drexel [publishing house] DLB-49
Bidermann, Jacob
  1577 or 1578-1639................DLB-164
Bidwell, Walter Hilliard 1798-1881 ......DLB-79
Bienek, Horst 1930- DLB-75
Bierbaum, Otto Julius 1865-1910........DLB-66

Bierce, Ambrose 1842-1914?......DLB-11, 12, 23, 71, 74, 186

Bigelow, William F. 1879-1966..........DLB-91

Biggle, Lloyd, Jr. 1923-................DLB-8

Bigiaretti, Libero 1905-1993...........DLB-177

Bigland, Eileen 1898-1970..............DLB-195

Biglow, Hosea (see Lowell, James Russell)

Bigongiari, Piero 1914-................DLB-128

Billinger, Richard 1890-1965...........DLB-124

Billings, Hammatt 1818-1874............DLB-188

Billings, John Shaw 1898-1975..........DLB-137

Billings, Josh (see Shaw, Henry Wheeler)

Binding, Rudolf G. 1867-1938...........DLB-66

Bingham, Caleb 1757-1817...............DLB-42

Bingham, George Barry 1906-1988.......DLB-127

Bingley, William [publishing house]....DLB-154

Binyon, Laurence 1869-1943.............DLB-19

Biographia Brittanica.................DLB-142

Biographical Documents I...............Y-84

Biographical Documents II..............Y-85

Bioren, John [publishing house]........DLB-49

Bioy Casares, Adolfo 1914-.............DLB-113

Bird, Isabella Lucy 1831-1904..........DLB-166

Bird, Robert Montgomery 1806-1854...DLB-202

Bird, William 1888-1963........DLB-4; DS-15

Birken, Sigmund von 1626-1681..........DLB-164

Birney, Earle 1904-....................DLB-88

Birrell, Augustine 1850-1933...........DLB-98

Bisher, Furman 1918-...................DLB-171

Bishop, Elizabeth 1911-1979........DLB-5, 169

Bishop, John Peale 1892-1944.......DLB-4, 9, 45

Bismarck, Otto von 1815-1898...........DLB-129

Bisset, Robert 1759-1805...............DLB-142

Bissett, Bill 1939-....................DLB-53

Bitzius, Albert (see Gotthelf, Jeremias)

Black, David (D. M.) 1941-.............DLB-40

Black, Winifred 1863-1936..............DLB-25

Black, Walter J. [publishing house]....DLB-46

The Black Aesthetic: Background........DS-8

The Black Arts Movement, by Larry Neal......................DLB-38

Black Theaters and Theater Organizations in America, 1961-1982: A Research List...................DLB-38

Black Theatre: A Forum [excerpts].......DLB-38

Blackamore, Arthur 1679-?..........DLB-24, 39

Blackburn, Alexander L. 1929-...........Y-85

Blackburn, Paul 1926-1971.........DLB-16; Y-81

Blackburn, Thomas 1916-1977............DLB-27

Blackmore, R. D. 1825-1900.............DLB-18

Blackmore, Sir Richard 1654-1729......DLB-131

Blackmur, R. P. 1904-1965..............DLB-63

Blackwell, Basil, Publisher............DLB-106

Blackwood, Algernon Henry 1869-1951...........DLB-153, 156, 178

Blackwood, Caroline 1931-..............DLB-14

Blackwood, William, and Sons, Ltd.....DLB-154

Blackwood's Edinburgh Magazine 1817-1980.........................DLB-110

Blades, William 1824-1890..............DLB-184

Blagden, Isabella 1817?-1873...........DLB-199

Blair, Eric Arthur (see Orwell, George)

Blair, Francis Preston 1791-1876.......DLB-43

Blair, James circa 1655-1743...........DLB-24

Blair, John Durburrow 1759-1823........DLB-37

Blais, Marie-Claire 1939-..............DLB-53

Blaise, Clark 1940-....................DLB-53

Blake, George 1893-1961................DLB-191

Blake, Lillie Devereux 1833-1913......DLB-202

Blake, Nicholas 1904-1972..............DLB-77 (see Day Lewis, C.)

Blake, William 1757-1827......DLB-93, 154, 163

The Blakiston Company..................DLB-49

Blanchot, Maurice 1907-................DLB-72

Blanckenburg, Christian Friedrich von 1744-1796...........................DLB-94

Blaser, Robin 1925-....................DLB-165

Bledsoe, Albert Taylor 1809-1877.....DLB-3, 79

Bleecker, Ann Eliza 1752-1783..........DLB-200

Blelock and Company....................DLB-49

Blennerhassett, Margaret Agnew 1773-1842...........................DLB-99

Bles, Geoffrey [publishing house]......DLB-112

Blessington, Marguerite, Countess of 1789-1849...........................DLB-166

The Blickling Homilies circa 971.......DLB-146

Blind, Mathilde 1841-1896..............DLB-199

Blish, James 1921-1975.................DLB-8

Bliss, E., and E. White [publishing house]...................DLB-49

Bliven, Bruce 1889-1977................DLB-137

Bloch, Robert 1917-1994................DLB-44

Block, Rudolph (see Lessing, Bruno)

Blondal, Patricia 1926-1959............DLB-88

Bloom, Harold 1930-....................DLB-67

Bloomer, Amelia 1818-1894..............DLB-79

Bloomfield, Robert 1766-1823...........DLB-93

Bloomsbury Group.......................DS-10

Blotner, Joseph 1923-..................DLB-111

Bloy, Léon 1846-1917...................DLB-123

Blume, Judy 1938-......................DLB-52

Blunck, Hans Friedrich 1888-1961.......DLB-66

Blunden, Edmund 1896-1974....DLB-20, 100, 155

Blunt, Lady Anne Isabella Noel 1837-1917..........................DLB-174

Blunt, Wilfrid Scawen 1840-1922.....DLB-19, 174

Bly, Nellie (see Cochrane, Elizabeth)

Bly, Robert 1926-......................DLB-5

Blyton, Enid 1897-1968.................DLB-160

Boaden, James 1762-1839................DLB-89

Boas, Frederick S. 1862-1957...........DLB-149

The Bobbs-Merrill Archive at the Lilly Library, Indiana University.......Y-90

The Bobbs-Merrill Company..............DLB-46

Bobrov, Semen Sergeevich 1763?-1810.........................DLB-150

Bobrowski, Johannes 1917-1965..........DLB-75

Bodenheim, Maxwell 1892-1954.......DLB-9, 45

Bodenstedt, Friedrich von 1819-1892...DLB-129

Bodini, Vittorio 1914-1970.............DLB-128

Bodkin, M. McDonnell 1850-1933.........DLB-70

Bodley Head............................DLB-112

Bodmer, Johann Jakob 1698-1783.........DLB-97

Bodmershof, Imma von 1895-1982.........DLB-85

Bodsworth, Fred 1918-..................DLB-68

Boehm, Sydney 1908-....................DLB-44

Boer, Charles 1939-....................DLB-5

Boethius circa 480-circa 524...........DLB-115

Boethius of Dacia circa 1240-?.........DLB-115

Bogan, Louise 1897-1970............DLB-45, 169

Bogarde, Dirk 1921-....................DLB-14

Bogdanovich, Ippolit Fedorovich circa 1743-1803......................DLB-150

Bogue, David [publishing house].......DLB-106

Böhme, Jakob 1575-1624.................DLB-164

Bohn, H. G. [publishing house].......DLB-106

Bohse, August 1661-1742................DLB-168

Boie, Heinrich Christian 1744-1806.....DLB-94

Bok, Edward W. 1863-1930......DLB-91; DS-16

Boland, Eavan 1944-....................DLB-40

Bolingbroke, Henry St. John, Viscount 1678-1751..........................DLB-101

Böll, Heinrich 1917-1985............DLB-69; Y-85

Bolling, Robert 1738-1775..............DLB-31

Bolotov, Andrei Timofeevich 1738-1833..........................DLB-150

Bolt, Carol 1941-......................DLB-60

Bolt, Robert 1924-.....................DLB-13

Bolton, Herbert E. 1870-1953...........DLB-17

Bonaventura.............................DLB-90

Bonaventure circa 1217-1274............DLB-115

Bonaviri, Giuseppe 1924-...............DLB-177

Bond, Edward 1934-.....................DLB-13

Bond, Michael 1926-....................DLB-161

Boni, Albert and Charles [publishing house]...................DLB-46

Boni and Liveright.....................DLB-46

Bonner, Paul Hyde 1893-1968............DS-17

Bonner, Sherwood 1849-1883............DLB-202

Robert Bonner's Sons...................DLB-49

Bonnin, Gertrude Simmons (see Zitkala-Ša)

Bonsanti, Alessandro 1904-1984........DLB-177

Bontemps, Arna 1902-1973............DLB-48, 51

The Book Arts Press at the University of Virginia........................Y-96

The Book League of America............DLB-46

Book Reviewing in America: I...........Y-87

Book Reviewing in America: II..........Y-88

Book Reviewing in America: III.........Y-89

Book Reviewing in America: IV Y-90
Book Reviewing in America: V Y-91
Book Reviewing in America: VI Y-92
Book Reviewing in America: VII Y-93
Book Reviewing in America: VIII Y-94
Book Reviewing in America and the Literary Scene Y-95
Book Reviewing and the Literary Scene Y-96, Y-97
Book Supply Company DLB-49
The Book Trade History Group Y-93
The Booker Prize Y-96
The Booker Prize Address by Anthony Thwaite, Chairman of the Booker Prize Judges Comments from Former Booker Prize Winners Y-86
Boorde, Andrew circa 1490-1549 .... DLB-136
Boorstin, Daniel J. 1914- DLB-17
Booth, Mary L. 1831-1889 .... DLB-79
Booth, Franklin 1874-1948 .... DLB-188
Booth, Philip 1925- Y-82
Booth, Wayne C. 1921- DLB-67
Booth, William 1829-1912 .... DLB-190
Borchardt, Rudolf 1877-1945 .... DLB-66
Borchert, Wolfgang 1921-1947 .... DLB-69, 124
Borel, Pétrus 1809-1859 .... DLB-119
Borges, Jorge Luis 1899-1986 .... DLB-113; Y-86
Börne, Ludwig 1786-1837 .... DLB-90
Borrow, George 1803-1881 .... DLB-21, 55, 166
Bosch, Juan 1909- DLB-145
Bosco, Henri 1888-1976 .... DLB-72
Bosco, Monique 1927- DLB-53
Boston, Lucy M. 1892-1990 .... DLB-161
Boswell, James 1740-1795 .... DLB-104, 142
Botev, Khristo 1847-1876 .... DLB-147
Bote, Hermann circa 1460-circa 1520 .... DLB-179
Botta, Anne C. Lynch 1815-1891 .... DLB-3
Bottome, Phyllis 1882-1963 .... DLB-197
Bottomley, Gordon 1874-1948 .... DLB-10
Bottoms, David 1949- DLB-120; Y-83
Bottrall, Ronald 1906- DLB-20
Bouchardy, Joseph 1810-1870 .... DLB-192
Boucher, Anthony 1911-1968 .... DLB-8
Boucher, Jonathan 1738-1804 .... DLB-31
Boucher de Boucherville, George 1814-1894 .... DLB-99
Boudreau, Daniel (see Coste, Donat)
Bourassa, Napoléon 1827-1916 .... DLB-99
Bourget, Paul 1852-1935 .... DLB-123
Bourinot, John George 1837-1902 .... DLB-99
Bourjaily, Vance 1922- DLB-2, 143
Bourne, Edward Gaylord 1860-1908 .... DLB-47
Bourne, Randolph 1886-1918 .... DLB-63
Bousoño, Carlos 1923- DLB-108

Bousquet, Joë 1897-1950 .... DLB-72
Bova, Ben 1932- Y-81
Bovard, Oliver K. 1872-1945 .... DLB-25
Bove, Emmanuel 1898-1945 .... DLB-72
Bowen, Elizabeth 1899-1973 .... DLB-15, 162
Bowen, Francis 1811-1890 .... DLB-1, 59
Bowen, John 1924- DLB-13
Bowen, Marjorie 1886-1952 .... DLB-153
Bowen-Merrill Company DLB-49
Bowering, George 1935- DLB-53
Bowers, Bathsheba 1671-1718 .... DLB-200
Bowers, Claude G. 1878-1958 .... DLB-17
Bowers, Edgar 1924- DLB-5
Bowers, Fredson Thayer 1905-1991 .... DLB-140; Y-91
Bowles, Paul 1910- DLB-5, 6
Bowles, Samuel III 1826-1878 .... DLB-43
Bowles, William Lisles 1762-1850 .... DLB-93
Bowman, Louise Morey 1882-1944 .... DLB-68
Boyd, James 1888-1944 .... DLB-9; DS-16
Boyd, John 1919- DLB-8
Boyd, Thomas 1898-1935 .... DLB-9; DS-16
Boyesen, Hjalmar Hjorth 1848-1895 .... DLB-12, 71; DS-13
Boyle, Kay 1902-1992 .... DLB-4, 9, 48, 86; Y-93
Boyle, Roger, Earl of Orrery 1621-1679 .... DLB-80
Boyle, T. Coraghessan 1948- Y-86
Božić, Mirko 1919- DLB-181
Brackenbury, Alison 1953- DLB-40
Brackenridge, Hugh Henry 1748-1816 .... DLB-11, 37
Brackett, Charles 1892-1969 .... DLB-26
Brackett, Leigh 1915-1978 .... DLB-8, 26
Bradburn, John [publishing house] DLB-49
Bradbury, Malcolm 1932- DLB-14
Bradbury, Ray 1920- DLB-2, 8
Bradbury and Evans DLB-106
Braddon, Mary Elizabeth 1835-1915 .... DLB-18, 70, 156
Bradford, Andrew 1686-1742 .... DLB-43, 73
Bradford, Gamaliel 1863-1932 .... DLB-17
Bradford, John 1749-1830 .... DLB-43
Bradford, Roark 1896-1948 .... DLB-86
Bradford, William 1590-1657 .... DLB-24, 30
Bradford, William III 1719-1791 .... DLB-43, 73
Bradlaugh, Charles 1833-1891 .... DLB-57
Bradley, David 1950- DLB-33
Bradley, Marion Zimmer 1930- DLB-8
Bradley, William Aspenwall 1878-1939 .... DLB-4
Bradley, Ira, and Company DLB-49
Bradley, J. W., and Company DLB-49
Bradshaw, Henry 1831-1886 .... DLB-184
Bradstreet, Anne 1612 or 1613-1672 .... DLB-24

Bradwardine, Thomas circa 1295-1349 .... DLB-115
Brady, Frank 1924-1986 .... DLB-111
Brady, Frederic A. [publishing house] DLB-49
Bragg, Melvyn 1939- DLB-14
Brainard, Charles H. [publishing house] DLB-49
Braine, John 1922-1986 .... DLB-15; Y-86
Braithwait, Richard 1588-1673 .... DLB-151
Braithwaite, William Stanley 1878-1962 .... DLB-50, 54
Braker, Ulrich 1735-1798 .... DLB-94
Bramah, Ernest 1868-1942 .... DLB-70
Branagan, Thomas 1774-1843 .... DLB-37
Branch, William Blackwell 1927- DLB-76
Branden Press DLB-46
Brant, Sebastian 1457-1521 .... DLB-179
Brassey, Lady Annie (Allnutt) 1839-1887 .... DLB-166
Brathwaite, Edward Kamau 1930- DLB-125
Brault, Jacques 1933- DLB-53
Braun, Volker 1939- DLB-75
Brautigan, Richard 1935-1984 .... DLB-2, 5; Y-80, Y-84
Braxton, Joanne M. 1950- DLB-41
Bray, Anne Eliza 1790-1883 .... DLB-116
Bray, Thomas 1656-1730 .... DLB-24
Braziller, George [publishing house] DLB-46
The Bread Loaf Writers' Conference 1983 .... Y-84
The Break-Up of the Novel (1922), by John Middleton Murry DLB-36
Breasted, James Henry 1865-1935 .... DLB-47
Brecht, Bertolt 1898-1956 .... DLB-56, 124
Bredel, Willi 1901-1964 .... DLB-56
Breitinger, Johann Jakob 1701-1776 .... DLB-97
Bremser, Bonnie 1939- DLB-16
Bremser, Ray 1934- DLB-16
Brentano, Bernard von 1901-1964 .... DLB-56
Brentano, Clemens 1778-1842 .... DLB-90
Brentano's DLB-49
Brenton, Howard 1942- DLB-13
Breslin, Jimmy 1929- DLB-185
Breton, André 1896-1966 .... DLB-65
Breton, Nicholas circa 1555-circa 1626 .... DLB-136
The Breton Lays 1300-early fifteenth century DLB-146
Brewer, Luther A. 1858-1933 .... DLB-187
Brewer, Warren and Putnam DLB-46
Brewster, Elizabeth 1922- DLB-60
Bridge, Ann (Lady Mary Dolling Sanders O'Malley) 1889-1974 .... DLB-191
Bridge, Horatio 1806-1893 .... DLB-183
Bridgers, Sue Ellen 1942- DLB-52
Bridges, Robert 1844-1930 .... DLB-19, 98
Bridie, James 1888-1951 .... DLB-10

Brieux, Eugene 1858-1932 .... DLB-192	Brooks, Van Wyck 1886-1963 ... DLB-45, 63, 103	Bruce-Novoa, Juan 1944- DLB-82
Bright, Mary Chavelita Dunne (see Egerton, George)	Brophy, Brigid 1929- DLB-14	Bruckman, Clyde 1894-1955 .... DLB-26
Brimmer, B. J., Company DLB-46	Brophy, John 1899-1965 .... DLB-191	Bruckner, Ferdinand 1891-1958 .... DLB-118
Brines, Francisco 1932- DLB-134	Brossard, Chandler 1922-1993 .... DLB-16	Brundage, John Herbert (see Herbert, John)
Brinley, George, Jr. 1817-1875 .... DLB-140	Brossard, Nicole 1943- DLB-53	Brutus, Dennis 1924- DLB-117
Brinnin, John Malcolm 1916- DLB-48	Broster, Dorothy Kathleen 1877-1950. ... DLB-160	Bryan, C. D. B. 1936- DLB-185
Brisbane, Albert 1809-1890 .... DLB-3	Brother Antoninus (see Everson, William)	Bryant, Arthur 1899-1985 .... DLB-149
Brisbane, Arthur 1864-1936 .... DLB-25	Brotherton, Lord 1856-1930 .... DLB-184	Bryant, William Cullen
British Academy DLB-112	Brougham and Vaux, Henry Peter Brougham, Baron 1778-1868 .... DLB-110, 158	1794-1878 .... DLB-3, 43, 59, 189
The British Library and the Regular Readers' Group Y-91		Bryce Echenique, Alfredo 1939- DLB-145
	Brougham, John 1810-1880 .... DLB-11	Bryce, James 1838-1922 .... DLB-166, 190
The British Critic 1793-1843 .... DLB-110	Broughton, James 1913- DLB-5	Brydges, Sir Samuel Egerton 1762-1837 .... DLB-107
The British Review and London Critical Journal 1811-1825 .... *DLB-110*	Broughton, Rhoda 1840-1920 .... DLB-18	
	Broun, Heywood 1888-1939 .... DLB-29, 171	Bryskett, Lodowick 1546?-1612 .... DLB-167
British Travel Writing, 1940-1997 ...... DLB-204	Brown, Alice 1856-1948 .... DLB-78	Buchan, John 1875-1940 .... DLB-34, 70, 156
Brito, Aristeo 1942- DLB-122	Brown, Bob 1886-1959 .... DLB-4, 45	Buchanan, George 1506-1582 .... DLB-132
Brittain, Vera 1893-1970 .... DLB-191	Brown, Cecil 1943- DLB-33	Buchanan, Robert 1841-1901 .... DLB-18, 35
Broadway Publishing Company DLB-46	Brown, Charles Brockden 1771-1810 .... DLB-37, 59, 73	Buchman, Sidney 1902-1975 .... DLB-26
Broch, Hermann 1886-1951 .... DLB-85, 124		Buchner, Augustus 1591-1661 .... DLB-164
Brochu, André 1942- DLB-53	Brown, Christy 1932-1981 .... DLB-14	Büchner, Georg 1813-1837 .... DLB-133
Brock, Edwin 1927- DLB-40	Brown, Dee 1908- Y-80	Bucholtz, Andreas Heinrich 1607-1671 .... DLB-168
Brockes, Barthold Heinrich 1680-1747 ... DLB-168	Brown, Frank London 1927-1962 .... DLB-76	
Brod, Max 1884-1968 .... DLB-81	Brown, Fredric 1906-1972 .... DLB-8	Buck, Pearl S. 1892-1973 .... DLB-9, 102
Brodber, Erna 1940- DLB-157	Brown, George Mackay 1921- ..DLB-14, 27, 139	Bucke, Charles 1781-1846 .... DLB-110
Brodhead, John R. 1814-1873 .... DLB-30	Brown, Harry 1917-1986 .... DLB-26	Bucke, Richard Maurice 1837-1902 .... DLB-99
Brodkey, Harold 1930- DLB-130	Brown, Marcia 1918- DLB-61	
Brodsky, Joseph 1940-1996 .... Y-87	Brown, Margaret Wise 1910-1952 .... DLB-22	Buckingham, Joseph Tinker 1779-1861 and Buckingham, Edwin 1810-1833 ...... DLB-73
Broeg, Bob 1918- DLB-171	Brown, Morna Doris (see Ferrars, Elizabeth)	
Brome, Richard circa 1590-1652 .... DLB-58	Brown, Oliver Madox 1855-1874 .... DLB-21	Buckler, Ernest 1908-1984 .... DLB-68
Brome, Vincent 1910- DLB-155	Brown, Sterling 1901-1989 .... DLB-48, 51, 63	Buckley, William F., Jr. 1925- DLB-137; Y-80
Bromfield, Louis 1896-1956 .... DLB-4, 9, 86	Brown, T. E. 1830-1897 .... DLB-35	Buckminster, Joseph Stevens 1784-1812 .... DLB-37
Bromige, David 1933- DLB-193	Brown, William Hill 1765-1793 .... DLB-37	
Broner, E. M. 1930- DLB-28	Brown, William Wells 1814-1884 .... DLB-3, 50, 183	Buckner, Robert 1906- DLB-26
Bronk, William 1918- DLB-165		Budd, Thomas ?-1698 .... DLB-24
Bronnen, Arnolt 1895-1959 .... DLB-124	Browne, Charles Farrar 1834-1867 ...... DLB-11	Budrys, A. J. 1931- DLB-8
Brontë, Anne 1820-1849 .... DLB-21, 199	Browne, Frances 1816-1879 .... DLB-199	Buechner, Frederick 1926- Y-80
Brontë, Charlotte 1816-1855 ... DLB-21, 159, 199	Browne, Francis Fisher 1843-1913 ...... DLB-79	Buell, John 1927- DLB-53
Brontë, Emily 1818-1848 .... DLB-21, 32, 199	Browne, J. Ross 1821-1875 .... DLB-202	Bufalino, Gesualdo 1920-1996 .... DLB-196
Brook, Stephen 1947- DLB-204	Browne, Michael Dennis 1940- DLB-40	Buffum, Job [publishing house] DLB-49
Brooke, Frances 1724-1789 .... DLB-39, 99	Browne, Sir Thomas 1605-1682 .... DLB-151	Bugnet, Georges 1879-1981 .... DLB-92
Brooke, Henry 1703?-1783 .... DLB-39	Browne, William, of Tavistock 1590-1645 .... DLB-121	Buies, Arthur 1840-1901 .... DLB-99
Brooke, L. Leslie 1862-1940 .... DLB-141		Building the New British Library at St Pancras Y-94
Brooke, Margaret, Ranee of Sarawak 1849-1936 .... DLB-174	Browne, Wynyard 1911-1964 .... DLB-13	
	Browne and Nolan DLB-106	Bukowski, Charles 1920-1994 ....DLB-5, 130, 169
Brooke, Rupert 1887-1915 .... DLB-19	Brownell, W. C. 1851-1928 .... DLB-71	Bulatović, Miodrag 1930-1991 .... DLB-181
Brooker, Bertram 1888-1955 .... DLB-88	Browning, Elizabeth Barrett 1806-1861 .... DLB-32, 199	Bulgarin, Faddei Venediktovich 1789-1859 .... DLB-198
Brooke-Rose, Christine 1926- DLB-14		
Brookner, Anita 1928- DLB-194; Y-87	Browning, Robert 1812-1889 .... DLB-32, 163	Bulger, Bozeman 1877-1932 .... DLB-171
Brooks, Charles Timothy 1813-1883 ...... DLB-1	Brownjohn, Allan 1931- DLB-40	Bullein, William between 1520 and 1530-1576 .... DLB-167
Brooks, Cleanth 1906-1994 .... DLB-63; Y-94	Brownson, Orestes Augustus 1803-1876 .... DLB-1, 59, 73	
Brooks, Gwendolyn 1917- DLB-5, 76, 165		Bullins, Ed 1935- DLB-7, 38
Brooks, Jeremy 1926- DLB-14	Bruccoli, Matthew J. 1931- DLB-103	Bulwer-Lytton, Edward (also Edward Bulwer) 1803-1873 .... DLB-21
Brooks, Mel 1926- DLB-26	Bruce, Charles 1906-1971 .... DLB-68	
Brooks, Noah 1830-1903 .... DLB-42; DS-13	Bruce, Leo 1903-1979 .... DLB-77	Bumpus, Jerry 1937- Y-81
Brooks, Richard 1912-1992 .... DLB-44	Bruce, Philip Alexander 1856-1933 ..... DLB-47	Bunce and Brother DLB-49
	Bruce Humphries [publishing house] DLB-46	Bunner, H. C. 1855-1896 .... DLB-78, 79
		Bunting, Basil 1900-1985 .... DLB-20

Buntline, Ned (Edward Zane Carroll Judson) 1821-1886 . . . . DLB-186
Bunyan, John 1628-1688 . . . . DLB-39
Burch, Robert 1925- DLB-52
Burciaga, José Antonio 1940- DLB-82
Bürger, Gottfried August 1747-1794 . . . . DLB-94
Burgess, Anthony 1917-1993 . . . . DLB-14, 194
Burgess, Gelett 1866-1951 . . . . DLB-11
Burgess, John W. 1844-1931 . . . . DLB-47
Burgess, Thornton W. 1874-1965 . . . . DLB-22
Burgess, Stringer and Company DLB-49
Burick, Si 1909-1986 . . . . DLB-171
Burk, John Daly circa 1772-1808 . . . . DLB-37
Burke, Edmund 1729?-1797 . . . . DLB-104
Burke, Kenneth 1897-1993 . . . . DLB-45, 63
Burke, Thomas 1886-1945 . . . . DLB-197
Burlingame, Edward Livermore 1848-1922 . . . . DLB-79
Burnet, Gilbert 1643-1715 . . . . DLB-101
Burnett, Frances Hodgson 1849-1924 . . . . DLB-42, 141; DS-13, 14
Burnett, W. R. 1899-1982 . . . . DLB-9
Burnett, Whit 1899-1973 and Martha Foley 1897-1977 . . . . DLB-137
Burney, Fanny 1752-1840 . . . . DLB-39
Burns, Alan 1929- DLB-14, 194
Burns, John Horne 1916-1953 . . . . Y-85
Burns, Robert 1759-1796 . . . . DLB-109
Burns and Oates DLB-106
Burnshaw, Stanley 1906- DLB-48
Burr, C. Chauncey 1815?-1883 . . . . DLB-79
Burr, Esther Edwards 1732-1758 . . . . DLB-200
Burroughs, Edgar Rice 1875-1950 . . . . DLB-8
Burroughs, John 1837-1921 . . . . DLB-64
Burroughs, Margaret T. G. 1917- DLB-41
Burroughs, William S., Jr. 1947-1981 . . . . . . DLB-16
Burroughs, William Seward 1914- DLB-2, 8, 16, 152; Y-81, Y-97
Burroway, Janet 1936- DLB-6
Burt, Maxwell Struthers 1882-1954 . . . . DLB-86; DS-16
Burt, A. L., and Company DLB-49
Burton, Hester 1913- DLB-161
Burton, Isabel Arundell 1831-1896 . . . . . . DLB-166
Burton, Miles (see Rhode, John)
Burton, Richard Francis 1821-1890 . . . . DLB-55, 166, 184
Burton, Robert 1577-1640 . . . . DLB-151
Burton, Virginia Lee 1909-1968 . . . . DLB-22
Burton, William Evans 1804-1860 . . . . DLB-73
Burwell, Adam Hood 1790-1849 . . . . DLB-99
Bury, Lady Charlotte 1775-1861 . . . . DLB-116
Busch, Frederick 1941- DLB-6
Busch, Niven 1903-1991 . . . . DLB-44
Bushnell, Horace 1802-1876 . . . . DS-13
Bussieres, Arthur de 1877-1913 . . . . DLB-92

Butler, Josephine Elizabeth 1828-1906 . . . . DLB-190
Butler, Juan 1942-1981 . . . . DLB-53
Butler, Octavia E. 1947- DLB-33
Butler, Pierce 1884-1953 . . . . DLB-187
Butler, Robert Olen 1945- DLB-173
Butler, Samuel 1613-1680 . . . . DLB-101, 126
Butler, Samuel 1835-1902 . . . . DLB-18, 57, 174
Butler, William Francis 1838-1910 . . . . . . DLB-166
Butler, E. H., and Company DLB-49
Butor, Michel 1926- DLB-83
Butter, Nathaniel [publishing house] DLB-170
Butterworth, Hezekiah 1839-1905 . . . . DLB-42
Buttitta, Ignazio 1899- DLB-114
Buzzati, Dino 1906-1972 . . . . DLB-177
Byars, Betsy 1928- DLB-52
Byatt, A. S. 1936- DLB-14, 194
Byles, Mather 1707-1788 . . . . DLB-24
Bynneman, Henry [publishing house] DLB-170
Bynner, Witter 1881-1968 . . . . DLB-54
Byrd, William circa 1543-1623 . . . . DLB-172
Byrd, William II 1674-1744 . . . . DLB-24, 140
Byrne, John Keyes (see Leonard, Hugh)
Byron, George Gordon, Lord 1788-1824 . . . . DLB-96, 110
Byron, Robert 1905-1941 . . . . DLB-195

C

Caballero Bonald, José Manuel 1926- DLB-108
Cabañero, Eladio 1930- DLB-134
Cabell, James Branch 1879-1958 . . . . DLB-9, 78
Cabeza de Baca, Manuel 1853-1915 . . . . . DLB-122
Cabeza de Baca Gilbert, Fabiola 1898- DLB-122
Cable, George Washington 1844-1925 . . . . DLB-12, 74; DS-13
Cable, Mildred 1878-1952 . . . . DLB-195
Cabrera, Lydia 1900-1991 . . . . DLB-145
Cabrera Infante, Guillermo 1929- DLB-113
Cadell [publishing house] DLB-154
Cady, Edwin H. 1917- DLB-103
Caedmon flourished 658-680 . . . . DLB-146
Caedmon School circa 660-899 . . . . DLB-146
Cafés, Brasseries, and Bistros DS-15
Cage, John 1912-1992 . . . . DLB-193
Cahan, Abraham 1860-1951 . . . . . . DLB-9, 25, 28
Cain, George 1943- DLB-33
Caird, Mona 1854-1932 . . . . DLB-197
Caldecott, Randolph 1846-1886 . . . . DLB-163
Calder, John (Publishers), Limited DLB-112
Calderón de la Barca, Fanny 1804-1882 . . . . DLB-183
Caldwell, Ben 1937- DLB-38
Caldwell, Erskine 1903-1987 . . . . DLB-9, 86
Caldwell, H. M., Company DLB-49
Caldwell, Taylor 1900-1985 . . . . DS-17

Calhoun, John C. 1782-1850 . . . . DLB-3
Calisher, Hortense 1911- DLB-2
A Call to Letters and an Invitation to the Electric Chair, by Siegfried Mandel DLB-75
Callaghan, Morley 1903-1990 . . . . DLB-68
Callahan, S. Alice 1868-1894 . . . . DLB-175
Callaloo Y-87
Callimachus circa 305 B.C.-240 B.C. DLB-176
Calmer, Edgar 1907- DLB-4
Calverley, C. S. 1831-1884 . . . . DLB-35
Calvert, George Henry 1803-1889 . . . . . . DLB-1, 64
Calvino, Italo 1923-1985 . . . . DLB-196
Cambridge Press DLB-49
Cambridge Songs (Carmina Cantabrigensia) circa 1050 . . . . DLB-148
Cambridge University Press DLB-170
Camden, William 1551-1623 . . . . DLB-172
Camden House: An Interview with James Hardin Y-92
Cameron, Eleanor 1912- DLB-52
Cameron, George Frederick 1854-1885 . . . . DLB-99
Cameron, Lucy Lyttelton 1781-1858 . . . . . DLB-163
Cameron, William Bleasdell 1862-1951 . . . DLB-99
Camm, John 1718-1778 . . . . DLB-31
Camon, Ferdinando 1935- DLB-196
Campana, Dino 1885-1932 . . . . DLB-114
Campbell, Gabrielle Margaret Vere (see Shearing, Joseph, and Bowen, Marjorie)
Campbell, James Dykes 1838-1895 . . . . . . DLB-144
Campbell, James Edwin 1867-1896 . . . . . . DLB-50
Campbell, John 1653-1728 . . . . DLB-43
Campbell, John W., Jr. 1910-1971 . . . . DLB-8
Campbell, Roy 1901-1957 . . . . DLB-20
Campbell, Thomas 1777-1844 . . . . DLB-93, 144
Campbell, William Wilfred 1858-1918 . . . . DLB-92
Campion, Edmund 1539-1581 . . . . DLB-167
Campion, Thomas 1567-1620 . . . . DLB-58, 172
Camus, Albert 1913-1960 . . . . DLB-72
The Canadian Publishers' Records Database . Y-96
Canby, Henry Seidel 1878-1961 . . . . DLB-91
Candelaria, Cordelia 1943- DLB-82
Candelaria, Nash 1928- DLB-82
Candour in English Fiction (1890), by Thomas Hardy DLB-18
Canetti, Elias 1905-1994 . . . . DLB-85, 124
Canham, Erwin Dain 1904-1982 . . . . DLB-127
Canitz, Friedrich Rudolph Ludwig von 1654-1699 . . . . DLB-168
Cankar, Ivan 1876-1918 . . . . DLB-147
Cannan, Gilbert 1884-1955 . . . . DLB-10, 197
Cannan, Joanna 1896-1961 . . . . DLB-191
Cannell, Kathleen 1891-1974 . . . . DLB-4
Cannell, Skipwith 1887-1957 . . . . DLB-45

Canning, George 1770-1827 .... DLB-158
Cannon, Jimmy 1910-1973 .... DLB-171
Cantwell, Robert 1908-1978 .... DLB-9
Cape, Jonathan, and Harrison Smith
    [publishing house] DLB-46
Cape, Jonathan, Limited DLB-112
Capen, Joseph 1658-1725 .... DLB-24
Capes, Bernard 1854-1918 .... DLB-156
Capote, Truman
    1924-1984 .... DLB-2, 185; Y-80, Y-84
Caproni, Giorgio 1912-1990 .... DLB-128
Cardarelli, Vincenzo 1887-1959 .... DLB-114
Cárdenas, Reyes 1948- DLB-122
Cardinal, Marie 1929- DLB-83
Carew, Jan 1920- DLB-157
Carew, Thomas 1594 or 1595-1640 .... DLB-126
Carey, Henry
    circa 1687-1689-1743 .... DLB-84
Carey, Mathew 1760-1839 .... DLB-37, 73
Carey and Hart DLB-49
Carey, M., and Company DLB-49
Carlell, Lodowick 1602-1675 .... DLB-58
Carleton, William 1794-1869 .... DLB-159
Carleton, G. W. [publishing house] DLB-49
Carlile, Richard 1790-1843 .... DLB-110, 158
Carlyle, Jane Welsh 1801-1866 .... DLB-55
Carlyle, Thomas 1795-1881 .... DLB-55, 144
Carman, Bliss 1861-1929 .... DLB-92
Carmina Burana circa 1230 .... DLB-138
Carnero, Guillermo 1947- DLB-108
Carossa, Hans 1878-1956 .... DLB-66
Carpenter, Humphrey 1946- DLB-155
Carpenter, Stephen Cullen ?-1820? DLB-73
Carpentier, Alejo 1904-1980 .... DLB-113
Carrier, Roch 1937- DLB-53
Carrillo, Adolfo 1855-1926 .... DLB-122
Carroll, Gladys Hasty 1904- DLB-9
Carroll, John 1735-1815 .... DLB-37
Carroll, John 1809-1884 .... DLB-99
Carroll, Lewis 1832-1898 .... DLB-18, 163, 178
Carroll, Paul 1927- DLB-16
Carroll, Paul Vincent 1900-1968 .... DLB-10
Carroll and Graf Publishers DLB-46
Carruth, Hayden 1921- DLB-5, 165
Carryl, Charles E. 1841-1920 .... DLB-42
Carson, Anne 1950- DLB-193
Carswell, Catherine 1879-1946 .... DLB-36
Carter, Angela 1940-1992 .... DLB-14
Carter, Elizabeth 1717-1806 .... DLB-109
Carter, Henry (see Leslie, Frank)
Carter, Hodding, Jr. 1907-1972 .... DLB-127
Carter, John 1905-1975 .... DLB-201
Carter, Landon 1710-1778 .... DLB-31
Carter, Lin 1930- Y-81
Carter, Martin 1927- DLB-117

Carter and Hendee DLB-49
Carter, Robert, and Brothers DLB-49
Cartwright, John 1740-1824 .... DLB-158
Cartwright, William circa 1611-1643 .... DLB-126
Caruthers, William Alexander
    1802-1846 .... DLB-3
Carver, Jonathan 1710-1780 .... DLB-31
Carver, Raymond
    1938-1988 .... DLB-130; Y-84, Y-88
Cary, Alice 1820-1871 .... DLB-202
Cary, Joyce 1888-1957 .... DLB-15, 100
Cary, Patrick 1623?-1657 .... DLB-131
Casey, Juanita 1925- DLB-14
Casey, Michael 1947- DLB-5
Cassady, Carolyn 1923- DLB-16
Cassady, Neal 1926-1968 .... DLB-16
Cassell and Company DLB-106
Cassell Publishing Company DLB-49
Cassill, R. V. 1919- DLB-6
Cassity, Turner 1929- DLB-105
Cassius Dio circa 155/164-post 229
    .... DLB-176
Cassola, Carlo 1917-1987 .... DLB-177
The Castle of Perserverance
    circa 1400-1425 .... DLB-146
Castellano, Olivia 1944- DLB-122
Castellanos, Rosario 1925-1974 .... DLB-113
Castillo, Ana 1953- DLB-122
Castlemon, Harry (see Fosdick, Charles Austin)
Čašule, Kole 1921- DLB-181
Caswall, Edward 1814-1878 .... DLB-32
Catacalos, Rosemary 1944- DLB-122
Cather, Willa 1873-1947 ...... DLB-9, 54, 78; DS-1
Catherine II (Ekaterina Alekseevna), "The Great,"
    Empress of Russia 1729-1796 ...... DLB-150
Catherwood, Mary Hartwell 1847-1902 ... DLB-78
Catledge, Turner 1901-1983 .... DLB-127
Catlin, George 1796-1872 .... DLB-186, 189
Cattafi, Bartolo 1922-1979 .... DLB-128
Catton, Bruce 1899-1978 .... DLB-17
Causley, Charles 1917- DLB-27
Caute, David 1936- DLB-14
Cavendish, Duchess of Newcastle,
    Margaret Lucas 1623-1673 .... DLB-131
Cawein, Madison 1865-1914 .... DLB-54
The Caxton Printers, Limited DLB-46
Caxton, William [publishing house] DLB-170
Cayrol, Jean 1911- DLB-83
Cecil, Lord David 1902-1986 .... DLB-155
Cela, Camilo José 1916- Y-89
Celan, Paul 1920-1970 .... DLB-69
Celati, Gianni 1937- DLB-196
Celaya, Gabriel 1911-1991 .... DLB-108
Céline, Louis-Ferdinand 1894-1961 ..... DLB-72
The Celtic Background to Medieval English
    Literature DLB-146

Celtis, Conrad 1459-1508 .... DLB-179
Center for Bibliographical Studies and
    Research at the University of
    California, Riverside Y-91
The Center for the Book in the Library
    of Congress Y-93
Center for the Book Research Y-84
Centlivre, Susanna 1669?-1723 .... DLB-84
The Century Company DLB-49
Cernuda, Luis 1902-1963 .... DLB-134
"Certain Gifts," by Betty Adcock DLB-105
Cervantes, Lorna Dee 1954- DLB-82
Chaadaev, Petr Iakovlevich
    1794-1856 .... DLB-198
Chacel, Rosa 1898- DLB-134
Chacón, Eusebio 1869-1948 .... DLB-82
Chacón, Felipe Maximiliano 1873-? DLB-82
Chadwyck-Healey's Full-Text Literary Data-bases:
    Editing Commercial Databases of
    Primary Literary Texts Y-95
Challans, Eileen Mary (see Renault, Mary)
Chalmers, George 1742-1825 .... DLB-30
Chaloner, Sir Thomas 1520-1565 ...... DLB-167
Chamberlain, Samuel S. 1851-1916 ..... DLB-25
Chamberland, Paul 1939- DLB-60
Chamberlin, William Henry
    1897-1969 .... DLB-29
Chambers, Charles Haddon 1860-1921 ... DLB-10
Chambers, Robert W. 1865-1933 ...... DLB-202
Chambers, W. and R.
    [publishing house] DLB-106
Chamisso, Albert von 1781-1838 .... DLB-90
Champfleury 1821-1889 .... DLB-119
Chandler, Harry 1864-1944 .... DLB-29
Chandler, Norman 1899-1973 .... DLB-127
Chandler, Otis 1927- DLB-127
Chandler, Raymond 1888-1959 .... DS-6
Channing, Edward 1856-1931 .... DLB-17
Channing, Edward Tyrrell 1790-1856 .. DLB-1, 59
Channing, William Ellery 1780-1842 ... DLB-1, 59
Channing, William Ellery, II
    1817-1901 .... DLB-1
Channing, William Henry
    1810-1884 .... DLB-1, 59
Chaplin, Charlie 1889-1977 .... DLB-44
Chapman, George
    1559 or 1560 - 1634 .... DLB-62, 121
Chapman, John DLB-106
Chapman, Olive Murray 1892-1977 ..... DLB-195
Chapman, R. W. 1881-1960 .... DLB-201
Chapman, William 1850-1917 .... DLB-99
Chapman and Hall DLB-106
Chappell, Fred 1936- DLB-6, 105
Charbonneau, Jean 1875-1960 .... DLB-92
Charbonneau, Robert 1911-1967 .... DLB-68
Charles, Gerda 1914- DLB-14
Charles, William [publishing house] DLB-49

The Charles Wood Affair:
  A Playwright Revived Y-83
Charlotte Forten: Pages from her Diary ... DLB-50
Charteris, Leslie 1907-1993 .... DLB-77
Charyn, Jerome 1937- Y-83
Chase, Borden 1900-1971 .... DLB-26
Chase, Edna Woolman 1877-1957 .... DLB-91
Chase-Riboud, Barbara 1936- DLB-33
Chateaubriand, François-René de
  1768-1848 .... DLB-119
Chatterton, Thomas 1752-1770 .... DLB-109
Chatto and Windus DLB-106
Chatwin, Bruce 1940-1989 .... DLB-194, 204
Chaucer, Geoffrey 1340?-1400 .... DLB-146
Chauncy, Charles 1705-1787 .... DLB-24
Chauveau, Pierre-Joseph-Olivier
  1820-1890 .... DLB-99
Chávez, Denise 1948- DLB-122
Chávez, Fray Angélico 1910- DLB-82
Chayefsky, Paddy 1923-1981 .... DLB-7, 44; Y-81
Cheesman, Evelyn 1881-1969 .... DLB-195
Cheever, Ezekiel 1615-1708 .... DLB-24
Cheever, George Barrell 1807-1890 .... DLB-59
Cheever, John
  1912-1982 .... DLB-2, 102; Y-80, Y-82
Cheever, Susan 1943- Y-82
Cheke, Sir John 1514-1557 .... DLB-132
Chelsea House DLB-46
Cheney, Ednah Dow (Littlehale)
  1824-1904 .... DLB-1
Cheney, Harriet Vaughn 1796-1889 .... DLB-99
Chénier, Marie-Joseph 1764-1811 .... DLB-192
Cherry, Kelly 1940 .... Y-83
Cherryh, C. J. 1942- Y-80
Chesebro', Caroline 1825-1873 .... DLB-202
Chesnutt, Charles Waddell
  1858-1932 .... DLB-12, 50, 78
Chesney, Sir George Tomkyns
  1830-1895 .... DLB-190
Chester, Alfred 1928-1971 .... DLB-130
Chester, George Randolph 1869-1924 .... DLB-78
The Chester Plays circa 1505-1532;
  revisions until 1575 .... DLB-146
Chesterfield, Philip Dormer Stanhope,
  Fourth Earl of 1694-1773 .... DLB-104
Chesterton, G. K. 1874-1936
  .... DLB-10, 19, 34, 70, 98, 149, 178
Chettle, Henry
  circa 1560-circa 1607 .... DLB-136
Chew, Ada Nield 1870-1945 .... DLB-135
Cheyney, Edward P. 1861-1947 .... DLB-47
Chiara, Piero 1913-1986 .... DLB-177
Chicano History DLB-82
Chicano Language DLB-82
Child, Francis James 1825-1896 .... DLB-1, 64
Child, Lydia Maria 1802-1880 .... DLB-1, 74
Child, Philip 1898-1978 .... DLB-68
Childers, Erskine 1870-1922 .... DLB-70

Children's Book Awards and Prizes DLB-61
Children's Illustrators, 1800-1880 .... DLB-163
Childress, Alice 1920-1994 .... DLB-7, 38
Childs, George W. 1829-1894 .... DLB-23
Chilton Book Company DLB-46
Chinweizu 1943- DLB-157
Chitham, Edward 1932- DLB-155
Chittenden, Hiram Martin 1858-1917 ..... DLB-47
Chivers, Thomas Holley 1809-1858 .... DLB-3
Cholmondeley, Mary 1859-1925 .... DLB-197
Chopin, Kate 1850-1904 .... DLB-12, 78
Chopin, Rene 1885-1953 .... DLB-92
Choquette, Adrienne 1915-1973 .... DLB-68
Choquette, Robert 1905- DLB-68
The Christian Publishing Company DLB-49
Christie, Agatha 1890-1976 .... DLB-13, 77
Christus und die Samariterin circa 950 .... DLB-148
Christy, Howard Chandler 1873-1952 ... DLB-188
Chulkov, Mikhail Dmitrievich
  1743?-1792 .... DLB-150
Church, Benjamin 1734-1778 .... DLB-31
Church, Francis Pharcellus 1839-1906 .... DLB-79
Church, Richard 1893-1972 .... DLB-191
Church, William Conant 1836-1917 ...... DLB-79
Churchill, Caryl 1938- DLB-13
Churchill, Charles 1731-1764 .... DLB-109
Churchill, Winston 1871-1947 .... DLB-202
Churchill, Sir Winston
  1874-1965 .... DLB-100; DS-16
Churchyard, Thomas 1520?-1604 .... DLB-132
Churton, E., and Company DLB-106
Chute, Marchette 1909-1994 .... DLB-103
Ciardi, John 1916-1986 .... DLB-5; Y-86
Cibber, Colley 1671-1757 .... DLB-84
Cima, Annalisa 1941- DLB-128
Čingo, Živko 1935-1987 .... DLB-181
Cirese, Eugenio 1884-1955 .... DLB-114
Cisneros, Sandra 1954- DLB-122, 152
City Lights Books DLB-46
Cixous, Hélène 1937- DLB-83
Clampitt, Amy 1920-1994 .... DLB-105
Clapper, Raymond 1892-1944 .... DLB-29
Clare, John 1793-1864 .... DLB-55, 96
Clarendon, Edward Hyde, Earl of
  1609-1674 .... DLB-101
Clark, Alfred Alexander Gordon (see Hare, Cyril)
Clark, Ann Nolan 1896- DLB-52
Clark, C. E. Frazer Jr. 1925- DLB-187
Clark, C. M., Publishing Company DLB-46
Clark, Catherine Anthony 1892-1977 .... DLB-68
Clark, Charles Heber 1841-1915 .... DLB-11
Clark, Davis Wasgatt 1812-1871 .... DLB-79
Clark, Eleanor 1913- DLB-6
Clark, J. P. 1935- DLB-117
Clark, Lewis Gaylord 1808-1873 .... DLB-3, 64, 73

Clark, Walter Van Tilburg 1909-1971 ..... DLB-9
Clark, William (see Lewis, Meriwether)
Clark, William Andrews Jr. 1877-1934 ... DLB-187
Clarke, Austin 1896-1974 .... DLB-10, 20
Clarke, Austin C. 1934- DLB-53, 125
Clarke, Gillian 1937- DLB-40
Clarke, James Freeman 1810-1888 ..... DLB-1, 59
Clarke, Pauline 1921- DLB-161
Clarke, Rebecca Sophia 1833-1906 ...... DLB-42
Clarke, Robert, and Company DLB-49
Clarkson, Thomas 1760-1846 .... DLB-158
Claudel, Paul 1868-1955 .... DLB-192
Claudius, Matthias 1740-1815 .... DLB-97
Clausen, Andy 1943- DLB-16
Clawson, John L. 1865-1933 .... DLB-187
Claxton, Remsen and Haffelfinger DLB-49
Clay, Cassius Marcellus 1810-1903 ...... DLB-43
Cleary, Beverly 1916- DLB-52
Cleaver, Vera 1919- and
  Cleaver, Bill 1920-1981 .... DLB-52
Cleland, John 1710-1789 .... DLB-39
Clemens, Samuel Langhorne (Mark Twain)
  1835-1910 ... DLB-11, 12, 23, 64, 74, 186, 189
Clement, Hal 1922- DLB-8
Clemo, Jack 1916- DLB-27
Clephane, Elizabeth Cecilia 1830-1869 ... DLB-199
Cleveland, John 1613-1658 .... DLB-126
Cliff, Michelle 1946- DLB-157
Clifford, Lady Anne 1590-1676 .... DLB-151
Clifford, James L. 1901-1978 .... DLB-103
Clifford, Lucy 1853?-1929 ..... DLB-135, 141, 197
Clifton, Lucille 1936- DLB-5, 41
Clines, Francis X. 1938- DLB-185
Clive, Caroline (V) 1801-1873 .... DLB-199
Clode, Edward J. [publishing house] DLB-46
Clough, Arthur Hugh 1819-1861 .... DLB-32
Cloutier, Cécile 1930- DLB-60
Clutton-Brock, Arthur 1868-1924 .... DLB-98
Coates, Robert M. 1897-1973 .... DLB-4, 9, 102
Coatsworth, Elizabeth 1893- DLB-22
Cobb, Charles E., Jr. 1943- DLB-41
Cobb, Frank I. 1869-1923 .... DLB-25
Cobb, Irvin S. 1876-1944 .... DLB-11, 25, 86
Cobbe, Frances Power 1822-1904 ...... DLB-190
Cobbett, William 1763-1835 .... DLB-43, 107
Cobbledick, Gordon 1898-1969 .... DLB-171
Cochran, Thomas C. 1902- DLB-17
Cochrane, Elizabeth 1867-1922 ..... DLB-25, 189
Cockerell, Sir Sydney 1867-1962 .... DLB-201
Cockerill, John A. 1845-1896 .... DLB-23
Cocteau, Jean 1889-1963 .... DLB-65
Coderre, Emile (see Jean Narrache)
Coffee, Lenore J. 1900?-1984 .... DLB-44
Coffin, Robert P. Tristram 1892-1955 .... DLB-45
Cogswell, Fred 1917- DLB-60

Cogswell, Mason Fitch 1761-1830 .... DLB-37

Cohen, Arthur A. 1928-1986 .... DLB-28

Cohen, Leonard 1934- DLB-53

Cohen, Matt 1942- DLB-53

Colbeck, Norman 1903-1987 .... DLB-201

Colden, Cadwallader 1688-1776...... DLB-24, 30

Colden, Jane 1724-1766 .... DLB-200

Cole, Barry 1936- DLB-14

Cole, George Watson 1850-1939 ..... DLB-140

Colegate, Isabel 1931- DLB-14

Coleman, Emily Holmes 1899-1974 ...... DLB-4

Coleman, Wanda 1946- DLB-130

Coleridge, Hartley 1796-1849 .... DLB-96

Coleridge, Mary 1861-1907 .... DLB-19, 98

Coleridge, Samuel Taylor
  1772-1834 .... DLB-93, 107

Coleridge, Sara 1802-1852 .... DLB-199

Colet, John 1467-1519 .... DLB-132

Colette 1873-1954 .... DLB-65

Colette, Sidonie Gabrielle (see Colette)

Colinas, Antonio 1946- DLB-134

Coll, Joseph Clement 1881-1921 .... DLB-188

Collier, John 1901-1980 .... DLB-77

Collier, John Payne 1789-1883 .... DLB-184

Collier, Mary 1690-1762.............. DLB-95

Collier, Robert J. 1876-1918 .... DLB-91

Collier, P. F. [publishing house] DLB-49

Collin and Small DLB-49

Collingwood, W. G. 1854-1932 .... DLB-149

Collins, An floruit circa 1653 .... DLB-131

Collins, Merle 1950- DLB-157

Collins, Mortimer 1827-1876 .... DLB-21, 35

Collins, Wilkie 1824-1889 .... DLB-18, 70, 159

Collins, William 1721-1759........... DLB-109

Collins, William, Sons and Company ... DLB-154

Collins, Isaac [publishing house] DLB-49

Collis, Maurice 1889-1973 .... DLB-195

Collyer, Mary 1716?-1763?........... DLB-39

Colman, Benjamin 1673-1747 .... DLB-24

Colman, George, the Elder 1732-1794 .... DLB-89

Colman, George, the Younger 1762-1836 . DLB-89

Colman, S. [publishing house] DLB-49

Colombo, John Robert 1936- DLB-53

Colquhoun, Patrick 1745-1820 .... DLB-158

Colter, Cyrus 1910- DLB-33

Colum, Padraic 1881-1972 .... DLB-19

Colvin, Sir Sidney 1845-1927 .... DLB-149

Colwin, Laurie 1944-1992 .... Y-80

Comden, Betty 1919- and Green,
  Adolph 1918- DLB-44

Comi, Girolamo 1890-1968 .... DLB-114

The Comic Tradition Continued
  [in the British Novel] DLB-15

Commager, Henry Steele 1902- DLB-17

The Commercialization of the Image of
  Revolt, by Kenneth Rexroth DLB-16

Community and Commentators: Black
  Theatre and Its Critics DLB-38

Compton-Burnett, Ivy 1884?-1969 ...... DLB-36

Conan, Laure 1845-1924 .... DLB-99

Conde, Carmen 1901- DLB-108

Conference on Modern Biography.......... Y-85

Congreve, William 1670-1729 .... DLB-39, 84

Conkey, W. B., Company DLB-49

Connell, Evan S., Jr. 1924- DLB-2; Y-81

Connelly, Marc 1890-1980.......... DLB-7; Y-80

Connolly, Cyril 1903-1974 .... DLB-98

Connolly, James B. 1868-1957 .... DLB-78

Connor, Ralph 1860-1937 .... DLB-92

Connor, Tony 1930- DLB-40

Conquest, Robert 1917- DLB-27

Conrad, Joseph 1857-1924 .... DLB-10, 34, 98, 156

Conrad, John, and Company DLB-49

Conroy, Jack 1899-1990................. Y-81

Conroy, Pat 1945- DLB-6

The Consolidation of Opinion: Critical
  Responses to the Modernists DLB-36

Consolo, Vincenzo 1933- DLB-196

Constable, Henry 1562-1613 .... DLB-136

Constable and Company Limited DLB-112

Constable, Archibald, and Company.... DLB-154

Constant, Benjamin 1767-1830 .... DLB-119

Constant de Rebecque, Henri-Benjamin de
  (see Constant, Benjamin)

Constantine, David 1944- DLB-40

Constantin-Weyer, Maurice 1881-1964 ... DLB-92

Contempo Caravan: Kites in a Windstorm ... Y-85

A Contemporary Flourescence of Chicano
  Literature Y-84

"Contemporary Verse Story-telling,"
  by Jonathan Holden.............. DLB-105

The Continental Publishing Company.... DLB-49

A Conversation with Chaim Potok Y-84

Conversations with Editors Y-95

Conversations with Publishers I: An Interview
  with Patrick O'Connor Y-84

Conversations with Publishers II: An Interview
  with Charles Scribner III Y-94

Conversations with Publishers III: An Interview
  with Donald Lamm Y-95

Conversations with Publishers IV: An Interview
  with James Laughlin................ Y-96

Conversations with Rare Book Dealers I: An
  Interview with Glenn Horowitz......... Y-90

Conversations with Rare Book Dealers II: An
  Interview with Ralph Sipper Y-94

Conversations with Rare Book Dealers
  (Publishers) III: An Interview with
  Otto Penzler...................... Y-96

The Conversion of an Unpolitical Man,
  by W. H. Bruford DLB-66

Conway, Moncure Daniel 1832-1907 ..... DLB-1

Cook, Ebenezer circa 1667-circa 1732..... DLB-24

Cook, Edward Tyas 1857-1919 .... DLB-149

Cook, Eliza 1818-1889................ DLB-199

Cook, Michael 1933- DLB-53

Cook, David C., Publishing Company ... DLB-49

Cooke, George Willis 1848-1923 .... DLB-71

Cooke, Increase, and Company......... DLB-49

Cooke, John Esten 1830-1886 .... DLB-3

Cooke, Philip Pendleton 1816-1850.... DLB-3, 59

Cooke, Rose Terry 1827-1892 ....DLB-12, 74

Cook-Lynn, Elizabeth 1930- DLB-175

Coolbrith, Ina 1841-1928........ DLB-54, 186

Cooley, Peter 1940- DLB-105

Coolidge, Clark 1939- DLB-193

Coolidge, Susan (see Woolsey, Sarah Chauncy)

Coolidge, George [publishing house] DLB-49

Cooper, Giles 1918-1966 .... DLB-13

Cooper, James Fenimore 1789-1851 ... DLB-3, 183

Cooper, Kent 1880-1965 .... DLB-29

Cooper, Susan 1935- DLB-161

Cooper, William [publishing house]......DLB-170

Coote, J. [publishing house] DLB-154

Coover, Robert 1932- DLB-2; Y-81

Copeland and Day................... DLB-49

Ćopić, Branko 1915-1984............. DLB-181

Copland, Robert 1470?-1548 .... DLB-136

Coppard, A. E. 1878-1957 .... DLB-162

Coppel, Alfred 1921- Y-83

Coppola, Francis Ford 1939- DLB-44

Copway, George (Kah-ge-ga-gah-bowh)
  1818-1869 ....DLB-175, 183

Corazzini, Sergio 1886-1907........... DLB-114

Corbett, Richard 1582-1635........... DLB-121

Corcoran, Barbara 1911- DLB-52

Cordelli, Franco 1943- DLB-196

Corelli, Marie 1855-1924 .... DLB-34, 156

Corle, Edwin 1906-1956................. Y-85

Corman, Cid 1924- DLB-5, 193

Cormier, Robert 1925- DLB-52

Corn, Alfred 1943- DLB-120; Y-80

Cornish, Sam 1935- DLB-41

Cornish, William
  circa 1465-circa 1524.............. DLB-132

Cornwall, Barry (see Procter, Bryan Waller)

Cornwallis, Sir William, the Younger
  circa 1579-1614 .... DLB-151

Cornwell, David John Moore
  (see le Carré, John)

Corpi, Lucha 1945- DLB-82

Corrington, John William 1932- DLB-6

Corrothers, James D. 1869-1917 .... DLB-50

Corso, Gregory 1930- DLB-5, 16

Cortázar, Julio 1914-1984............. DLB-113

Cortez, Jayne 1936- DLB-41

Corvinus, Gottlieb Siegmund
  1677-1746 .... DLB-168

Corvo, Baron (see Rolfe, Frederick William)

Cory, Annie Sophie (see Cross, Victoria)
Cory, William Johnson 1823-1892 ....DLB-35
Coryate, Thomas 1577?-1617 ...... DLB-151, 172
Ćosić, Dobrica 1921- DLB-181
Cosin, John 1595-1672.................DLB-151
Cosmopolitan Book Corporation DLB-46
Costain, Thomas B. 1885-1965...........DLB-9
Coste, Donat 1912-1957 ....DLB-88
Costello, Louisa Stuart 1799-1870 ......DLB-166
Cota-Cárdenas, Margarita 1941- DLB-122
Cotten, Bruce 1873-1954 ....DLB-187
Cotter, Joseph Seamon, Sr. 1861-1949.....DLB-50
Cotter, Joseph Seamon, Jr. 1895-1919 .....DLB-50
Cottle, Joseph [publishing house]........DLB-154
Cotton, Charles 1630-1687 ....DLB-131
Cotton, John 1584-1652................DLB-24
Coulter, John 1888-1980 ....DLB-68
Cournos, John 1881-1966 ....DLB-54
Courteline, Georges 1858-1929 ....DLB-192
Cousins, Margaret 1905- DLB-137
Cousins, Norman 1915-1990............DLB-137
Coventry, Francis 1725-1754 ....DLB-39
Coverdale, Miles 1487 or 1488-1569.....DLB-167
Coverly, N. [publishing house] DLB-49
Covici-Friede DLB-46
Coward, Noel 1899-1973...............DLB-10
Coward, McCann and Geoghegan DLB-46
Cowles, Gardner 1861-1946 ....DLB-29
Cowles, Gardner ("Mike"), Jr.
  1903-1985 .... DLB-127, 137
Cowley, Abraham 1618-1667 ......DLB-131, 151
Cowley, Hannah 1743-1809 ....DLB-89
Cowley, Malcolm
  1898-1989 .... DLB-4, 48; Y-81, Y-89
Cowper, William 1731-1800 .... DLB-104, 109
Cox, A. B. (see Berkeley, Anthony)
Cox, James McMahon 1903-1974 ....DLB-127
Cox, James Middleton 1870-1957 ....DLB-127
Cox, Palmer 1840-1924.................DLB-42
Coxe, Louis 1918-1993 ....DLB-5
Coxe, Tench 1755-1824.................DLB-37
Cozzens, Frederick S. 1818-1869........DLB-202
Cozzens, James Gould
  1903-1978 ....DLB-9; Y-84; DS-2
Cozzens's *Michael Scarlett* Y-97
Crabbe, George 1754-1832 ....DLB-93
Crackanthorpe, Hubert 1870-1896 ......DLB-135
Craddock, Charles Egbert (see Murfree, Mary N.)
Cradock, Thomas 1718-1770 ....DLB-31
Craig, Daniel H. 1811-1895..............DLB-43
Craik, Dinah Maria 1826-1887 ...... DLB-35, 136
Cramer, Richard Ben 1950- DLB-185
Cranch, Christopher Pearse
  1813-1892 ....DLB-1, 42
Crane, Hart 1899-1932 ....DLB-4, 48

Crane, R. S. 1886-1967 ....DLB-63
Crane, Stephen 1871-1900........ DLB-12, 54, 78
Crane, Walter 1845-1915 ....DLB-163
Cranmer, Thomas 1489-1556 ....DLB-132
Crapsey, Adelaide 1878-1914............DLB-54
Crashaw, Richard
  1612 or 1613-1649 ....DLB-126
Craven, Avery 1885-1980 ....DLB-17
Crawford, Charles
  1752-circa 1815 ....DLB-31
Crawford, F. Marion 1854-1909 ....DLB-71
Crawford, Isabel Valancy 1850-1887.....DLB-92
Crawley, Alan 1887-1975 ....DLB-68
Crayon, Geoffrey (see Irving, Washington)
Creamer, Robert W. 1922- DLB-171
Creasey, John 1908-1973 ....DLB-77
Creative Age Press.....................DLB-46
Creech, William [publishing house]......DLB-154
Creede, Thomas [publishing house] DLB-170
Creel, George 1876-1953 ....DLB-25
Creeley, Robert 1926- ... DLB-5, 16, 169; DS-17
Creelman, James 1859-1915 ....DLB-23
Cregan, David 1931- DLB-13
Creighton, Donald Grant 1902-1979 .....DLB-88
Cremazie, Octave 1827-1879 ....DLB-99
Crémer, Victoriano 1909?- DLB-108
Crescas, Hasdai circa 1340-1412? DLB-115
Crespo, Angel 1926- DLB-134
Cresset Press DLB-112
Cresswell, Helen 1934- DLB-161
Crèvecoeur, Michel Guillaume Jean de
  1735-1813 ....DLB-37
Crews, Harry 1935- DLB-6, 143, 185
Crichton, Michael 1942- Y-81
A Crisis of Culture: The Changing Role
  of Religion in the New Republic
  ....DLB-37
Crispin, Edmund 1921-1978 ....DLB-87
Cristofer, Michael 1946- DLB-7
"The Critic as Artist" (1891), by
  Oscar Wilde DLB-57
"Criticism In Relation To Novels" (1863),
  by G. H. Lewes..................DLB-21
Crnjanski, Miloš 1893-1977............DLB-147
Crocker, Hannah Mather 1752-1829.....DLB-200
Crockett, David (Davy)
  1786-1836 ....DLB-3, 11, 183
Croft-Cooke, Rupert (see Bruce, Leo)
Crofts, Freeman Wills 1879-1957.........DLB-77
Croker, John Wilson 1780-1857 ....DLB-110
Croly, George 1780-1860................DLB-159
Croly, Herbert 1869-1930 ....DLB-91
Croly, Jane Cunningham 1829-1901......DLB-23
Crompton, Richmal 1890-1969 ....DLB-160
Cronin, A. J. 1896-1981................DLB-191
Crosby, Caresse 1892-1970 ....DLB-48

Crosby, Caresse 1892-1970 and Crosby,
  Harry 1898-1929.............DLB-4; DS-15
Crosby, Harry 1898-1929 ....DLB-48
Cross, Gillian 1945- DLB-161
Cross, Victoria 1868-1952......... DLB-135, 197
Crossley-Holland, Kevin 1941- DLB-40, 161
Crothers, Rachel 1878-1958..............DLB-7
Crowell, Thomas Y., Company DLB-49
Crowley, John 1942- Y-82
Crowley, Mart 1935- DLB-7
Crown Publishers DLB-46
Crowne, John 1641-1712...............DLB-80
Crowninshield, Edward Augustus
  1817-1859 ....DLB-140
Crowninshield, Frank 1872-1947.........DLB-91
Croy, Homer 1883-1965.................DLB-4
Crumley, James 1939- Y-84
Cruz, Victor Hernández 1949- DLB-41
Csokor, Franz Theodor 1885-1969.......DLB-81
Cuala Press DLB-112
Cullen, Countee 1903-1946....... DLB-4, 48, 51
Culler, Jonathan D. 1944- DLB-67
The Cult of Biography
  Excerpts from the Second Folio Debate:
  "Biographies are generally a disease of
  English Literature" – Germaine Greer,
  Victoria Glendinning, Auberon Waugh,
  and Richard Holmes Y-86
Cumberland, Richard 1732-1811.........DLB-89
Cummings, Constance Gordon
  1837-1924 ....DLB-174
Cummings, E. E. 1894-1962 ....DLB-4, 48
Cummings, Ray 1887-1957 ....DLB-8
Cummings and Hilliard.................DLB-49
Cummins, Maria Susanna 1827-1866 .....DLB-42
Cundall, Joseph [publishing house] DLB-106
Cuney, Waring 1906-1976..............DLB-51
Cuney-Hare, Maude 1874-1936.........DLB-52
Cunningham, Allan 1784-1842 ..... DLB-116, 144
Cunningham, J. V. 1911- DLB-5
Cunningham, Peter F. [publishing house] ..DLB-49
Cunquiero, Alvaro 1911-1981...........DLB-134
Cuomo, George 1929- Y-80
Cupples and Leon DLB-46
Cupples, Upham and Company DLB-49
Cuppy, Will 1884-1949................DLB-11
Curll, Edmund [publishing house].......DLB-154
Currie, James 1756-1805 ....DLB-142
Currie, Mary Montgomerie Lamb Singleton,
  Lady Currie (see Fane, Violet)
Cursor Mundi circa 1300 ....DLB-146
Curti, Merle E. 1897- DLB-17
Curtis, Anthony 1926- DLB-155
Curtis, Cyrus H. K. 1850-1933..........DLB-91
Curtis, George William 1824-1892 .....DLB-1, 43
Curzon, Robert 1810-1873..............DLB-166
Curzon, Sarah Anne 1833-1898 ....DLB-99

Cushing, Harvey 1869-1939. . . . . DLB-187
Cynewulf circa 770-840 . . . . DLB-146
Czepko, Daniel 1605-1660 . . . . DLB-164

D

D. M. Thomas: The Plagiarism Controversy. . Y-82
Dabit, Eugène 1898-1936 . . . . DLB-65
Daborne, Robert circa 1580-1628. . . . . DLB-58
Dacey, Philip 1939- DLB-105
Dach, Simon 1605-1659 . . . . DLB-164
Daggett, Rollin M. 1831-1901 . . . . DLB-79
D'Aguiar, Fred 1960- DLB-157
Dahl, Roald 1916-1990. . . . . DLB-139
Dahlberg, Edward 1900-1977 . . . . DLB-48
Dahn, Felix 1834-1912 . . . . DLB-129
Dal', Vladimir Ivanovich (Kazak Vladimir
   Lugansky) 1801-1872. . . . . DLB-198
Dale, Peter 1938- DLB-40
Daley, Arthur 1904-1974 . . . . .DLB-171
Dall, Caroline Wells (Healey) 1822-1912. . . DLB-1
Dallas, E. S. 1828-1879 . . . . DLB-55
The Dallas Theater Center. DLB-7
D'Alton, Louis 1900-1951 . . . . DLB-10
Daly, T. A. 1871-1948 . . . . DLB-11
Damon, S. Foster 1893-1971 . . . . DLB-45
Damrell, William S. [publishing house] . . . DLB-49
Dana, Charles A. 1819-1897. . . . . DLB-3, 23
Dana, Richard Henry, Jr. 1815-1882 . . DLB-1, 183
Dandridge, Ray Garfield DLB-51
Dane, Clemence 1887-1965 . . . . .DLB-10, 197
Danforth, John 1660-1730 . . . . DLB-24
Danforth, Samuel, I 1626-1674 . . . . DLB-24
Danforth, Samuel, II 1666-1727 . . . . DLB-24
Dangerous Years: London Theater,
   1939-1945 . . . . DLB-10
Daniel, John M. 1825-1865. . . . . DLB-43
Daniel, Samuel 1562 or 1563-1619. . . . . . . DLB-62
Daniel Press DLB-106
Daniells, Roy 1902-1979 . . . . DLB-68
Daniels, Jim 1956- DLB-120
Daniels, Jonathan 1902-1981 . . . . DLB-127
Daniels, Josephus 1862-1948 . . . . DLB-29
Danis Rose and the Rendering of *Ulysses* Y-97
Dannay, Frederic 1905-1982 and
   Manfred B. Lee 1905-1971 . . . . DLB-137
Danner, Margaret Esse 1915- DLB-41
Danter, John [publishing house] DLB-170
Dantin, Louis 1865-1945 . . . . DLB-92
Danzig, Allison 1898-1987 . . . . .DLB-171
D'Arcy, Ella circa 1857-1937. . . . . DLB-135
Darley, Felix Octavious Carr
   1822-1888 . . . . DLB-188
Darley, George 1795-1846 . . . . DLB-96
Darwin, Charles 1809-1882 . . . . .DLB-57, 166
Darwin, Erasmus 1731-1802. . . . . DLB-93

Daryush, Elizabeth 1887-1977. . . . . DLB-20
Dashkova, Ekaterina Romanovna
   (née Vorontsova) 1743-1810 . . . . DLB-150
Dashwood, Edmée Elizabeth Monica
   de la Pasture (see Delafield, E. M.)
Daudet, Alphonse 1840-1897 . . . . DLB-123
d'Aulaire, Edgar Parin 1898- and
   d'Aulaire, Ingri 1904- DLB-22
Davenant, Sir William 1606-1668 . . . DLB-58, 126
Davenport, Guy 1927- DLB-130
Davenport, Marcia 1903-1996 . . . . DS-17
Davenport, Robert ?-? DLB-58
Daves, Delmer 1904-1977. . . . . DLB-26
Davey, Frank 1940- DLB-53
Davidson, Avram 1923-1993 . . . . DLB-8
Davidson, Donald 1893-1968. . . . . DLB-45
Davidson, John 1857-1909 . . . . DLB-19
Davidson, Lionel 1922- DLB-14
Davidson, Robyn 1950- DLB-204
Davidson, Sara 1943- DLB-185
Davie, Donald 1922- DLB-27
Davie, Elspeth 1919- DLB-139
Davies, Sir John 1569-1626 . . . . .DLB-172
Davies, John, of Hereford 1565?-1618 . . . DLB-121
Davies, Rhys 1901-1978 . . . . DLB-139, 191
Davies, Robertson 1913- DLB-68
Davies, Samuel 1723-1761 . . . . DLB-31
Davies, Thomas 1712?-1785 . . . . . . DLB-142, 154
Davies, W. H. 1871-1940 . . . . .DLB-19, 174
Davies, Peter, Limited DLB-112
Daviot, Gordon 1896?-1952 . . . . DLB-10
   (see also Tey, Josephine)
Davis, Charles A. 1795-1867 . . . . DLB-11
Davis, Clyde Brion 1894-1962 . . . . DLB-9
Davis, Dick 1945- DLB-40
Davis, Frank Marshall 1905-?. DLB-51
Davis, H. L. 1894-1960 . . . . DLB-9
Davis, John 1774-1854 . . . . DLB-37
Davis, Lydia 1947- DLB-130
Davis, Margaret Thomson 1926- DLB-14
Davis, Ossie 1917- DLB-7, 38
Davis, Paxton 1925-1994 . . . . Y-94
Davis, Rebecca Harding 1831-1910 . . . . . . DLB-74
Davis, Richard Harding 1864-1916
   . . . . .DLB-12, 23, 78, 79, 189; DS-13
Davis, Samuel Cole 1764-1809 . . . . DLB-37
Davis, Samuel Post 1850-1918 . . . . DLB-202
Davison, Peter 1928- DLB-5
Davydov, Denis Vasil'evich
   1784-1839. . . . . DLB-205
Davys, Mary 1674-1732 . . . . DLB-39
DAW Books DLB-46
Dawn Powell, Where Have You Been All
   Our lives?. Y-97
Dawson, Ernest 1882-1947 . . . . DLB-140
Dawson, Fielding 1930- DLB-130

Dawson, William 1704-1752 . . . . DLB-31
Day, Angel flourished 1586 . . . . DLB-167
Day, Benjamin Henry 1810-1889 . . . . DLB-43
Day, Clarence 1874-1935 . . . . DLB-11
Day, Dorothy 1897-1980 . . . . DLB-29
Day, Frank Parker 1881-1950 . . . . DLB-92
Day, John circa 1574-circa 1640 . . . . DLB-62
Day, John [publishing house] DLB-170
Day Lewis, C. 1904-1972. . . . . DLB-15, 20
   (see also Blake, Nicholas)
Day, Thomas 1748-1789. . . . . DLB-39
Day, The John, Company DLB-46
Day, Mahlon [publishing house] DLB-49
Dazai Osamu 1909-1948 . . . . DLB-182
Deacon, William Arthur 1890-1977 . . . . . DLB-68
Deal, Borden 1922-1985. . . . . DLB-6
de Angeli, Marguerite 1889-1987 . . . . DLB-22
De Angelis, Milo 1951- DLB-128
De Bow, James Dunwoody Brownson
   1820-1867 .DLB-3, 79
de Bruyn, Günter 1926- DLB-75
de Camp, L. Sprague 1907- DLB-8
De Carlo, Andrea 1952- DLB-196
The Decay of Lying (1889),
   by Oscar Wilde [excerpt]. DLB-18
Dechert, Robert 1895-1975. . . . . .DLB-187
Dedication, *Ferdinand Count Fathom* (1753),
   by Tobias Smollett. DLB-39
Dedication, *The History of Pompey the Little*
   (1751), by Francis Coventry. DLB-39
Dedication, *Lasselia* (1723), by Eliza
   Haywood [excerpt]. DLB-39
Dedication, *The Wanderer* (1814),
   by Fanny Burney. DLB-39
Dee, John 1527-1609. . . . . DLB-136
Deeping, George Warwick 1877-1950 . . . DLB 153
Defense of *Amelia* (1752), by
   Henry Fielding. DLB-39
Defoe, Daniel 1660-1731 . . . . .DLB-39, 95, 101
de Fontaine, Felix Gregory 1834-1896 . . . . DLB-43
De Forest, John William 1826-1906 . . DLB-12, 189
DeFrees, Madeline 1919- DLB-105
DeGolyer, Everette Lee 1886-1956 . . . . . .DLB-187
de Graff, Robert 1895-1981 . . . . Y-81
de Graft, Joe 1924-1978 . . . . .DLB-117
De Heinrico circa 980? DLB-148
Deighton, Len 1929- DLB-87
DeJong, Meindert 1906-1991 . . . . DLB-52
Dekker, Thomas circa 1572-1632 . . . . .DLB-62, 172
Delacorte, Jr., George T. 1894-1991. . . . . . DLB-91
Delafield, E. M. 1890-1943 . . . . DLB-34
Delahaye, Guy 1888-1969 . . . . DLB-92
de la Mare, Walter 1873-1956 . . .DLB-19, 153, 162
Deland, Margaret 1857-1945 . . . . DLB-78
Delaney, Shelagh 1939- DLB-13
Delano, Amasa 1763-1823 . . . . DLB-183
Delany, Martin Robinson 1812-1885. . . . . DLB-50

Delany, Samuel R. 1942- DLB-8, 33
de la Roche, Mazo 1879-1961 ....DLB-68
Delavigne, Jean François Casimir
    1793-1843 ....DLB-192
Delbanco, Nicholas 1942- DLB-6
De León, Nephtal 1945- DLB-82
Delgado, Abelardo Barrientos 1931- DLB-82
Del Giudice, Daniele 1949- DLB-196
De Libero, Libero 1906-1981.........DLB-114
DeLillo, Don 1936- DLB-6, 173
de Lisser H. G. 1878-1944 ....DLB-117
Dell, Floyd 1887-1969 ....DLB-9
Dell Publishing Company DLB-46
delle Grazie, Marie Eugene 1864-1931 ....DLB-81
Deloney, Thomas died 1600 ....DLB-167
Deloria, Ella C. 1889-1971.........DLB-175
Deloria, Vine, Jr. 1933- DLB-175
del Rey, Lester 1915-1993 ....DLB-8
Del Vecchio, John M. 1947- DS-9
Del'vig, Anton Antonovich
    1798-1831 ....DLB-205
de Man, Paul 1919-1983 ....DLB-67
Demby, William 1922- DLB-33
Deming, Philander 1829-1915 ....DLB-74
Demorest, William Jennings
    1822-1895 ....DLB-79
De Morgan, William 1839-1917 ....DLB-153
Demosthenes 384 B.C.-322 B.C.........DLB-176
Denham, Henry [publishing house].........DLB-170
Denham, Sir John 1615-1669.........DLB-58, 126
Denison, Merrill 1893-1975 ....DLB-92
Denison, T. S., and Company DLB-49
Dennery, Adolphe Philippe 1811-1899 ...DLB-192
Dennie, Joseph 1768-1812 ..... DLB-37, 43, 59, 73
Dennis, John 1658-1734.............DLB-101
Dennis, Nigel 1912-1989 ....DLB-13, 15
Denslow, W. W. 1856-1915 ....DLB-188
Dent, Tom 1932- DLB-38
Dent, J. M., and Sons.........DLB-112
Denton, Daniel circa 1626-1703.........DLB-24
DePaola, Tomie 1934- DLB-61
Department of Library, Archives, and Institutional
    Research, American Bible Society Y-97
De Quille, Dan 1829-1898.........DLB-186
De Quincey, Thomas 1785-1859 ....DLB-110, 144
Derby, George Horatio 1823-1861 ....DLB-11
Derby, J. C., and Company.........DLB-49
Derby and Miller.........DLB-49
De Ricci, Seymour 1881-1942 ....DLB-201
Derleth, August 1909-1971.........DLB-9; DS-17
The Derrydale Press DLB-46
Derzhavin, Gavriil Romanovich
    1743-1816 ....DLB-150
Desaulniers, Gonsalve 1863-1934 ....DLB-92
Desbiens, Jean-Paul 1927- DLB-53
des Forêts, Louis-Rene 1918- DLB-83

Desiato, Luca 1941- DLB-196
Desnica, Vladan 1905-1967.........DLB-181
DesRochers, Alfred 1901-1978..........DLB-68
Desrosiers, Léo-Paul 1896-1967.........DLB-68
Dessì, Giuseppe 1909-1977 ....DLB-177
Destouches, Louis-Ferdinand
    (see Céline, Louis-Ferdinand)
De Tabley, Lord 1835-1895 ....DLB-35
"A Detail in a Poem," by Fred Chappell ..DLB-105
Deutsch, Babette 1895-1982 ....DLB-45
Deutsch, Niklaus Manuel (see Manuel, Niklaus)
Deutsch, André, Limited DLB-112
Deveaux, Alexis 1948- DLB-38
The Development of the Author's Copyright
    in Britain...................DLB-154
The Development of Lighting in the Staging
    of Drama, 1900-1945 ....DLB-10
The Development of Meiji Japan.........DLB-180
De Vere, Aubrey 1814-1902 ....DLB-35
Devereux, second Earl of Essex, Robert
    1565-1601 ....DLB-136
The Devin-Adair Company.........DLB-46
De Vinne, Theodore Low 1828-1914 ....DLB-187
De Voto, Bernard 1897-1955 ....DLB-9
De Vries, Peter 1910-1993 ....DLB-6; Y-82
Dewdney, Christopher 1951- DLB-60
Dewdney, Selwyn 1909-1979.........DLB-68
DeWitt, Robert M., Publisher DLB-49
DeWolfe, Fiske and Company DLB-49
Dexter, Colin 1930- DLB-87
de Young, M. H. 1849-1925 ....DLB-25
Dhlomo, H. I. E. 1903-1956 ....DLB-157
Dhuoda circa 803-after 843 ....DLB-148
The Dial Press.........DLB-46
Diamond, I. A. L. 1920-1988 ....DLB-26
Dibble, L. Grace 1902-1998.........DLB-204
Dibdin, Thomas Frognall
    1776-1847 ....DLB-184
Di Cicco, Pier Giorgio 1949- DLB-60
Dick, Philip K. 1928-1982 ....DLB-8
Dick and Fitzgerald DLB-49
Dickens, Charles
    1812-1870 .... DLB-21, 55, 70, 159, 166
Dickinson, Peter 1927- DLB-161
Dickey, James 1923-1997.....................
    ...DLB-5, 193; Y-82, Y-93, Y-96; DS-7, DS-19
Dickey, William 1928-1994.........DLB-5
Dickinson, Emily 1830-1886 ....DLB-1
Dickinson, John 1732-1808 ....DLB-31
Dickinson, Jonathan 1688-1747 ....DLB-24
Dickinson, Patric 1914- DLB-27
Dickinson, Peter 1927- DLB-87
Dicks, John [publishing house].........DLB-106
Dickson, Gordon R. 1923- DLB-8
*Dictionary of Literary Biography
    Yearbook Awards*...............Y-92, Y-93

The Dictionary of National Biography
    ....DLB-144
Didion, Joan
    1934- DLB-2, 173, 185; Y-81, Y-86
Di Donato, Pietro 1911- DLB-9
Die Fürstliche Bibliothek Corvey Y-96
Diego, Gerardo 1896-1987 ....DLB-134
Digges, Thomas circa 1546-1595.........DLB-136
Dillard, Annie 1945- Y-80
Dillard, R. H. W. 1937- DLB-5
Dillingham, Charles T., Company DLB-49
The Dillingham, G. W., Company DLB-49
Dilly, Edward and Charles
    [publishing house].................DLB-154
Dilthey, Wilhelm 1833-1911 ....DLB-129
Dimitrova, Blaga 1922- DLB-181
Dimov, Dimitr 1909-1966 ....DLB-181
Dimsdale, Thomas J. 1831?-1866 ....DLB-186
Dingelstedt, Franz von 1814-1881.......DLB-133
Dintenfass, Mark 1941- Y-84
Diogenes, Jr. (see Brougham, John)
Diogenes Laertius circa 200.........DLB-176
DiPrima, Diane 1934- DLB-5, 16
Disch, Thomas M. 1940- DLB-8
Disney, Walt 1901-1966 ....DLB-22
Disraeli, Benjamin 1804-1881 ....DLB-21, 55
D'Israeli, Isaac 1766-1848 ....DLB-107
Ditzen, Rudolf (see Fallada, Hans)
Dix, Dorothea Lynde 1802-1887.........DLB-1
Dix, Dorothy (see Gilmer, Elizabeth Meriwether)
Dix, Edwards and Company.........DLB-49
Dix, Gertrude circa 1874–? DLB-197
Dixie, Florence Douglas 1857-1905 ......DLB-174
Dixon, Ella Hepworth 1855 or
    1857-1932 ....DLB-197
Dixon, Paige (see Corcoran, Barbara)
Dixon, Richard Watson 1833-1900.......DLB-19
Dixon, Stephen 1936- DLB-130
Dmitriev, Ivan Ivanovich 1760-1837 .....DLB-150
Dobell, Bertram 1842-1914 ....DLB-184
Dobell, Sydney 1824-1874.........DLB-32
Döblin, Alfred 1878-1957 ....DLB-66
Dobson, Austin 1840-1921 ....DLB-35, 144
Doctorow, E. L. 1931- DLB-2, 28, 173; Y-80
Documents on Sixteenth-Century
    Literature DLB-167, 172
Dodd, William E. 1869-1940. ....DLB-17
Dodd, Anne [publishing house].........DLB-154
Dodd, Mead and Company.........DLB-49
Doderer, Heimito von 1896-1968 ....DLB-85
Dodge, Mary Mapes
    1831?-1905 ....DLB-42, 79; DS-13
Dodge, B. W., and Company DLB-46
Dodge Publishing Company DLB-49
Dodgson, Charles Lutwidge (see Carroll, Lewis)
Dodsley, Robert 1703-1764 ....DLB-95

Dodsley, R. [publishing house] DLB-154
Dodson, Owen 1914-1983 . . . . DLB-76
Dodwell, Christina 1951- DLB-204
Doesticks, Q. K. Philander, P. B. (see Thomson, Mortimer)
Doheny, Carrie Estelle 1875-1958 . . . . . . DLB-140
Doherty, John 1798?-1854 . . . . DLB-190
Domínguez, Sylvia Maida 1935- DLB-122
Donahoe, Patrick [publishing house] DLB-49
Donald, David H. 1920- DLB-17
Donaldson, Scott 1928- DLB-111
Doni, Rodolfo 1919- DLB-177
Donleavy, J. P. 1926- DLB-6, 173
Donnadieu, Marguerite (see Duras, Marguerite)
Donne, John 1572-1631 . . . . DLB-121, 151
Donnelley, R. R., and Sons Company DLB-49
Donnelly, Ignatius 1831-1901 . . . . DLB-12
Donohue and Henneberry DLB-49
Donoso, José 1924- DLB-113
Doolady, M. [publishing house] DLB-49
Dooley, Ebon (see Ebon)
Doolittle, Hilda 1886-1961 . . . . DLB-4, 45
Doplicher, Fabio 1938- DLB-128
Dor, Milo 1923- DLB-85
Doran, George H., Company DLB-46
Dorgelès, Roland 1886-1973 . . . . DLB-65
Dorn, Edward 1929- DLB-5
Dorr, Rheta Childe 1866-1948 . . . . DLB-25
Dorris, Michael 1945-1997 . . . . DLB-175
Dorset and Middlesex, Charles Sackville, Lord Buckhurst, Earl of 1643-1706 . . DLB-131
Dorst, Tankred 1925- DLB-75, 124
Dos Passos, John 1896-1970 . . . . DLB-4, 9; DS-1, DS-15
John Dos Passos: A Centennial Commemoration Y-96
Doubleday and Company DLB-49
Dougall, Lily 1858-1923 . . . . DLB-92
Doughty, Charles M. 1843-1926 . . DLB-19, 57, 174
Douglas, Gavin 1476-1522 . . . . DLB-132
Douglas, Keith 1920-1944 . . . . DLB-27
Douglas, Norman 1868-1952 . . . . DLB-34, 195
Douglass, Frederick 1817?-1895 . . . . DLB-1, 43, 50, 79
Douglass, William circa 1691-1752 . . . . . . DLB-24
Dourado, Autran 1926- DLB-145
Dove, Arthur G. 1880-1946 . . . . DLB-188
Dove, Rita 1952- DLB-120
Dover Publications DLB-46
Doves Press DLB-112
Dowden, Edward 1843-1913 . . . . DLB-35, 149
Dowell, Coleman 1925-1985 . . . . DLB-130
Dowland, John 1563-1626 . . . . DLB-172
Downes, Gwladys 1915- DLB-88
Downing, J., Major (see Davis, Charles A.)
Downing, Major Jack (see Smith, Seba)

Dowriche, Anne before 1560-after 1613 . . . . DLB-172
Dowson, Ernest 1867-1900 . . . . DLB-19, 135
Doxey, William [publishing house] DLB-49
Doyle, Sir Arthur Conan 1859-1930 . . . . DLB-18, 70, 156, 178
Doyle, Kirby 1932- DLB-16
Doyle, Roddy 1958- DLB-194
Drabble, Margaret 1939- DLB-14, 155
Drach, Albert 1902- DLB-85
Dragojević, Danijel 1934- DLB-181
Drake, Samuel Gardner 1798-1875 . . . . . . DLB-187
The Dramatic Publishing Company DLB-49
Dramatists Play Service DLB-46
Drant, Thomas early 1540s?-1578 . . . . DLB-167
Draper, John W. 1811-1882 . . . . DLB-30
Draper, Lyman C. 1815-1891 . . . . DLB-30
Drayton, Michael 1563-1631 . . . . DLB-121
Dreiser, Theodore 1871-1945 . . . . DLB-9, 12, 102, 137; DS-1
Drewitz, Ingeborg 1923-1986 . . . . DLB-75
Drieu La Rochelle, Pierre 1893-1945 . . . . . DLB-72
Drinker, Elizabeth 1735-1807 . . . . DLB-200
Drinkwater, John 1882-1937 . . . . DLB-10, 19, 149
Droste-Hülshoff, Annette von 1797-1848 . . . . DLB-133
The Drue Heinz Literature Prize Excerpt from "Excerpts from a Report of the Commission," in David Bosworth's *The Death of Descartes* An Interview with David Bosworth . . Y-82
Drummond, William Henry 1854-1907 . . . DLB-92
Drummond, William, of Hawthornden 1585-1649 . . . . DLB-121
Dryden, Charles 1860?-1931 . . . . .DLB-171
Dryden, John 1631-1700 . . . . DLB-80, 101, 131
Držić, Marin circa 1508-1567 . . . . DLB-147
Duane, William 1760-1835 . . . . DLB-43
Dubé, Marcel 1930- DLB-53
Dubé, Rodolphe (see Hertel, François)
Dubie, Norman 1945- DLB-120
Du Bois, W. E. B. 1868-1963 . . . . . . DLB-47, 50, 91
Du Bois, William Pène 1916- DLB-61
Dubus, Andre 1936- DLB-130
Ducange, Victor 1783-1833 . . . . DLB-192
Du Chaillu, Paul Belloni 1831?-1903 . . . . DLB-189
Ducharme, Réjean 1941- DLB-60
Dučić, Jovan 1871-1943 . . . . DLB-147
Duck, Stephen 1705?-1756 . . . . DLB-95
Duckworth, Gerald, and Company Limited DLB-112
Dudek, Louis 1918- DLB-88
Duell, Sloan and Pearce DLB-46
Duerer, Albrecht 1471-1528 . . . . .DLB-179
Dufief, Nicholas Gouin 1776-1834 . . . . DLB-187
Duff Gordon, Lucie 1821-1869 . . . . DLB-166

Dufferin, Helen Lady, Countess of Gifford 1807-1867 . . . . DLB-199
Duffield and Green DLB-46
Duffy, Maureen 1933- DLB-14
Dugan, Alan 1923- DLB-5
Dugard, William [publishing house] DLB-170
Dugas, Marcel 1883-1947 . . . . DLB-92
Dugdale, William [publishing house] DLB-106
Duhamel, Georges 1884-1966 . . . . DLB-65
Dujardin, Edouard 1861-1949 . . . . DLB-123
Dukes, Ashley 1885-1959 . . . . DLB-10
du Maurier, Daphne 1907-1989 . . . . DLB-191
Du Maurier, George 1834-1896 . . . . . DLB-153, 178
Dumas, Alexandre *fils* 1824–1895 . . . . . . DLB-192
Dumas, Alexandre *père* 1802-1870 . . .DLB-119, 192
Dumas, Henry 1934-1968 . . . . DLB-41
Dunbar, Paul Laurence 1872-1906 . . . . .DLB-50, 54, 78
Dunbar, William circa 1460-circa 1522 . . . . DLB-132, 146
Duncan, Norman 1871-1916 . . . . DLB-92
Duncan, Quince 1940- DLB-145
Duncan, Robert 1919-1988 . . . . . . .DLB-5, 16, 193
Duncan, Ronald 1914-1982 . . . . DLB-13
Duncan, Sara Jeannette 1861-1922 . . . . . . DLB-92
Dunigan, Edward, and Brother DLB-49
Dunlap, John 1747-1812 . . . . DLB-43
Dunlap, William 1766-1839 . . . . DLB-30, 37, 59
Dunn, Douglas 1942- DLB-40
Dunn, Harvey Thomas 1884-1952 . . . . . DLB-188
Dunn, Stephen 1939- DLB-105
Dunne, Finley Peter 1867-1936 . . . . . . DLB-11, 23
Dunne, John Gregory 1932- Y-80
Dunne, Philip 1908-1992 . . . . DLB-26
Dunning, Ralph Cheever 1878-1930 . . . . . DLB-4
Dunning, William A. 1857-1922 . . . . .DLB-17
Duns Scotus, John circa 1266-1308 . . . . . DLB-115
Dunsany, Lord (Edward John Moreton Drax Plunkett, Baron Dunsany) 1878-1957 . . . . DLB-10, 77, 153, 156
Dunton, John [publishing house] DLB-170
Dunton, W. Herbert 1878-1936 . . . . DLB-188
Dupin, Amantine-Aurore-Lucile (see Sand, George)
Durand, Lucile (see Bersianik, Louky)
Duranti, Francesca 1935- DLB-196
Duranty, Walter 1884-1957 . . . . DLB-29
Duras, Marguerite 1914- DLB-83
Durfey, Thomas 1653-1723 . . . . DLB-80
Durova, Nadezhda Andreevna (Aleksandr Andreevich Aleksandrov) 1783-1866 . . . . DLB-198
Durrell, Lawrence 1912-1990 . . . . DLB-15, 27, 204; Y-90
Durrell, William [publishing house] DLB-49
Dürrenmatt, Friedrich 1921-1990 . . . . DLB-69, 124
Duston, Hannah 1657-1737 . . . . DLB-200
Dutton, E. P., and Company DLB-49

Duvoisin, Roger 1904-1980............DLB-61

Duyckinck, Evert Augustus
    1816-1878...................DLB-3, 64

Duyckinck, George L. 1823-1863........DLB-3

Duyckinck and Company.............DLB-49

Dwight, John Sullivan 1813-1893......DLB-1

Dwight, Timothy 1752-1817...........DLB-37

Dybek, Stuart 1942-.................DLB-130

Dyer, Charles 1928-..................DLB-13

Dyer, George 1755-1841...............DLB-93

Dyer, John 1699-1757.................DLB-95

Dyer, Sir Edward 1543-1607..........DLB-136

Dylan, Bob 1941-.....................DLB-16

E

Eager, Edward 1911-1964.............DLB-22

Eames, Wilberforce 1855-1937........DLB-140

Earle, James H., and Company........DLB-49

Earle, John 1600 or 1601-1665.......DLB-151

Early American Book Illustration,
    by Sinclair Hamilton.............DLB-49

Eastlake, William 1917-...............DLB-6

Eastman, Carol ?-....................DLB-44

Eastman, Charles A. (Ohiyesa)
    1858-1939......................DLB-175

Eastman, Max 1883-1969..............DLB-91

Eaton, Daniel Isaac 1753-1814.......DLB-158

Eberhart, Richard 1904-..............DLB-48

Ebner, Jeannie 1918-.................DLB-85

Ebner-Eschenbach, Marie von
    1830-1916.......................DLB-81

Ebon 1942-...........................DLB-41

Ecbasis Captivi circa 1045..........DLB-148

Ecco Press...........................DLB-46

Eckhart, Meister
    circa 1260-circa 1328...........DLB-115

The Eclectic Review 1805-1868......DLB-110

Eco, Umberto 1932-..................DLB-196

Edel, Leon 1907-....................DLB-103

Edes, Benjamin 1732-1803.............DLB-43

Edgar, David 1948-...................DLB-13

Edgeworth, Maria
    1768-1849.........DLB-116, 159, 163

The Edinburgh Review 1802-1929....DLB-110

Edinburgh University Press..........DLB-112

The Editor Publishing Company......DLB-49

Editorial Statements................DLB-137

Edmonds, Randolph 1900-.............DLB-51

Edmonds, Walter D. 1903-..............DLB-9

Edschmid, Kasimir 1890-1966.........DLB-56

Edwards, Amelia Anne Blandford
    1831-1892......................DLB-174

Edwards, Edward 1812-1886..........DLB-184

Edwards, James [publishing house]...DLB-154

Edwards, Jonathan 1703-1758.........DLB-24

Edwards, Jonathan, Jr. 1745-1801....DLB-37

Edwards, Junius 1929-................DLB-33

Edwards, Matilda Barbara Betham-
    1836-1919......................DLB-174

Edwards, Richard 1524-1566...........DLB-62

Edwards, Sarah Pierpont 1710-1758...DLB-200

Effinger, George Alec 1947-...........DLB-8

Egerton, George 1859-1945...........DLB-135

Eggleston, Edward 1837-1902..........DLB-12

Eggleston, Wilfred 1901-1986.........DLB-92

Ehrenstein, Albert 1886-1950.........DLB-81

Ehrhart, W. D. 1948-...................DS-9

Eich, Günter 1907-1972..........DLB-69, 124

Eichendorff, Joseph Freiherr von
    1788-1857.......................DLB-90

Eifukumon'in 1271-1342..............DLB-203

1873 Publishers' Catalogues.........DLB-49

Eighteenth-Century Aesthetic Theories....DLB-31

Eighteenth-Century Philosophical
    Background......................DLB-31

Eigner, Larry 1926-1996............DLB-5, 193

Eikon Basilike 1649..................DLB-151

Eilhart von Oberge
    circa 1140-circa 1195...........DLB-148

Einhard circa 770-840...............DLB-148

Eiseley, Loren 1907-1977..............DS-17

Eisenreich, Herbert 1925-1986.........DLB-85

Eisner, Kurt 1867-1919................DLB-66

Eklund, Gordon 1945-..................Y-83

Ekwensi, Cyprian 1921-..............DLB-117

Eld, George [publishing house].....DLB-170

Elder, Lonne III 1931-........DLB-7, 38, 44

Elder, Paul, and Company............DLB-49

Elements of Rhetoric (1828; revised, 1846),
    by Richard Whately [excerpt]....DLB-57

Elie, Robert 1915-1973...............DLB-88

Elin Pelin 1877-1949................DLB-147

Eliot, George 1819-1880........DLB-21, 35, 55

Eliot, John 1604-1690................DLB-24

Eliot, T. S. 1888-1965......DLB-7, 10, 45, 63

Eliot's Court Press.................DLB-170

Elizabeth I 1533-1603...............DLB-136

Elizabeth of Nassau-Saarbrücken
    after 1393-1456................DLB-179

Elizondo, Salvador 1932-............DLB-145

Elizondo, Sergio 1930-...............DLB-82

Elkin, Stanley 1930-.........DLB-2, 28; Y-80

Elles, Dora Amy (see Wentworth, Patricia)

Ellet, Elizabeth F. 1818?-1877........DLB-30

Elliot, Ebenezer 1781-1849.......DLB-96, 190

Elliot, Frances Minto (Dickinson)
    1820-1898......................DLB-166

Elliott, Charlotte 1789-1871........DLB-199

Elliott, George 1923-................DLB-68

Elliott, Janice 1931-................DLB-14

Elliott, William 1788-1863............DLB-3

Elliott, Thomes and Talbot..........DLB-49

Ellis, Alice Thomas (Anna Margaret Haycraft)
    1932-..........................DLB-194

Ellis, Edward S. 1840-1916...........DLB-42

Ellis, Frederick Staridge
    [publishing house].............DLB-106

The George H. Ellis Company........DLB-49

Ellis, Havelock 1859-1939...........DLB-190

Ellison, Harlan 1934-.................DLB-8

Ellison, Ralph Waldo
    1914-1994..............DLB-2, 76; Y-94

Ellmann, Richard 1918-1987.....DLB-103; Y-87

The Elmer Holmes Bobst Awards in Arts
    and Letters......................Y-87

Elyot, Thomas 1490?-1546............DLB-136

Emanuel, James Andrew 1921-.........DLB-41

Emecheta, Buchi 1944-...............DLB-117

The Emergence of Black Women Writers...DS-8

Emerson, Ralph Waldo
    1803-1882............DLB-1, 59, 73, 183

Emerson, William 1769-1811...........DLB-37

Emerson, William 1923-1997............Y-97

Emin, Fedor Aleksandrovich
    circa 1735-1770................DLB-150

Empedocles fifth century B.C........DLB-176

Empson, William 1906-1984............DLB-20

Enchi Fumiko 1905-1986..............DLB-182

Encounter with the West.............DLB-180

The End of English Stage Censorship,
    1945-1968.......................DLB-13

Ende, Michael 1929-..................DLB-75

Endō Shūsaku 1923-1996..............DLB-182

Engel, Marian 1933-1985..............DLB-53

Engels, Friedrich 1820-1895.........DLB-129

Engle, Paul 1908-....................DLB-48

English, Thomas Dunn 1819-1902......DLB-202

English Composition and Rhetoric (1866),
    by Alexander Bain [excerpt].....DLB-57

The English Language: 410 to 1500..DLB-146

The English Renaissance of Art (1908),
    by Oscar Wilde..................DLB-35

Enright, D. J. 1920-.................DLB-27

Enright, Elizabeth 1909-1968.........DLB-22

L'Envoi (1882), by Oscar Wilde......DLB-35

Epictetus circa 55-circa 125-130....DLB-176

Epicurus 342/341 B.C.-271/270 B.C.
    ....DLB-176

Epps, Bernard 1936-..................DLB-53

Epstein, Julius 1909- and
    Epstein, Philip 1909-1952.......DLB-26

Equiano, Olaudah circa 1745-1797...DLB-37, 50

Eragny Press........................DLB-112

Erasmus, Desiderius 1467-1536......DLB-136

Erba, Luciano 1922-.................DLB-128

Erdrich, Louise 1954-..........DLB-152, 175

Erichsen-Brown, Gwethalyn Graham
    (see Graham, Gwethalyn)

Eriugena, John Scottus circa 810-877.....DLB-115

Ernest Hemingway's Toronto Journalism Revisited: With Three Previously Unrecorded Stories Y-92
Ernst, Paul 1866-1933 .... DLB-66, 118
Ershov, Petr Pavlovich 1815-1869 ...... DLB-205
Erskine, Albert 1911-1993 .... Y-93
Erskine, John 1879-1951............ DLB-9, 102
Erskine, Mrs. Steuart ?-1948. .... DLB-195
Ervine, St. John Greer 1883-1971........ DLB-10
Eschenburg, Johann Joachim 1743-1820... DLB-97
Escoto, Julio 1944- DLB-145
Esdaile, Arundell 1880-1956........... DLB-201
Eshleman, Clayton 1935- DLB-5
Espriu, Salvador 1913-1985 .... DLB-134
Ess Ess Publishing Company DLB-49
Essay on Chatterton (1842), by Robert Browning DLB-32
Essex House Press DLB-112
Estes, Eleanor 1906-1988 .... DLB-22
Eszterhas, Joe 1944- DLB-185
Estes and Lauriat DLB-49
Etherege, George 1636-circa 1692 .... DLB-80
Ethridge, Mark, Sr. 1896-1981 .... DLB-127
Ets, Marie Hall 1893- DLB-22
Etter, David 1928- DLB-105
Ettner, Johann Christoph 1654-1724 .... DLB-168
Eudora Welty: Eye of the Storyteller Y-87
Eugene O'Neill Memorial Theater Center .. DLB-7
Eugene O'Neill's Letters: A Review Y-88
Eupolemius flourished circa 1095....... DLB-148
Euripides circa 484 B.C.-407/406 B.C. DLB-176
Evans, Caradoc 1878-1945 .... DLB-162
Evans, Charles 1850-1935 .... DLB-187
Evans, Donald 1884-1921............. DLB-54
Evans, George Henry 1805-1856 .... DLB-43
Evans, Hubert 1892-1986.............. DLB-92
Evans, Mari 1923- DLB-41
Evans, Mary Ann (see Eliot, George)
Evans, Nathaniel 1742-1767 .... DLB-31
Evans, Sebastian 1830-1909 .... DLB-35
Evans, M., and Company............... DLB-46
Everett, Alexander Hill 1790-1847 .... DLB-59
Everett, Edward 1794-1865........... DLB-1, 59
Everson, R. G. 1903- DLB-88
Everson, William 1912-1994 .... DLB-5, 16
Every Man His Own Poet; or, The Inspired Singer's Recipe Book (1877), by W. H. Mallock DLB-35
Ewart, Gavin 1916- DLB-40
Ewing, Juliana Horatia 1841-1885 ... DLB-21, 163
The Examiner 1808-1881............. DLB-110
Exley, Frederick 1929-1992 ......DLB-143; Y-81
Experiment in the Novel (1929), by John D. Beresford DLB-36
von Eyb, Albrecht 1420-1475 ....DLB-179

"Eyes Across Centuries: Contemporary Poetry and 'That Vision Thing,'" by Philip Dacey DLB-105
Eyre and Spottiswoode.............. DLB-106
Ezzo ?-after 1065................... DLB-148

F

"F. Scott Fitzgerald: St. Paul's Native Son and Distinguished American Writer": University of Minnesota Conference, 29-31 October 1982................. Y-82
Faber, Frederick William 1814-1863 ..... DLB-32
Faber and Faber Limited.............. DLB-112
Faccio, Rena (see Aleramo, Sibilla)
Fagundo, Ana María 1938- DLB-134
Fair, Ronald L. 1932- DLB-33
Fairfax, Beatrice (see Manning, Marie)
Fairlie, Gerard 1899-1983 .... DLB-77
Fallada, Hans 1893-1947............. DLB-56
Falsifying Hemingway Y-96
Fancher, Betsy 1928- Y-83
Fane, Violet 1843-1905............... DLB-35
Fanfrolico Press DLB-112
Fanning, Katherine 1927 .... DLB-127
Fanshawe, Sir Richard 1608-1666 ..... DLB-126
Fantasy Press Publishers............... DLB-46
Fante, John 1909-1983 ....DLB-130; Y-83
Al-Farabi circa 870-950 .... DLB-115
Farah, Nuruddin 1945- DLB-125
Farber, Norma 1909-1984 .... DLB-61
Farigoule, Louis (see Romains, Jules)
Farjeon, Eleanor 1881-1965 .... DLB-160
Farley, Walter 1920-1989.............. DLB-22
Farmborough, Florence 1887-1978 ..... DLB-204
Farmer, Penelope 1939- DLB-161
Farmer, Philip José 1918- DLB-8
Farquhar, George circa 1677-1707....... DLB-84
Farquharson, Martha (see Finley, Martha)
Farrar, Frederic William 1831-1903 ..... DLB-163
Farrar and Rinehart DLB-46
Farrar, Straus and Giroux.............. DLB-46
Farrell, James T. 1904-1979 ... DLB-4, 9, 86; DS-2
Farrell, J. G. 1935-1979................ DLB-14
Fast, Howard 1914- DLB-9
Faulkner and Yoknapatawpha Conference, Oxford, Mississippi Y-97
"Faulkner 100–Celebrating the Work," University of South Carolina, Columbia............. Y-97
Faulkner, William 1897-1962 ....DLB-9, 11, 44, 102; DS-2; Y-86
Faulkner, George [publishing house] DLB-154
Fauset, Jessie Redmon 1882-1961....... DLB-51
Faust, Irvin 1924- DLB-2, 28; Y-80
Fawcett, Edgar 1847-1904 .... DLB-202
Fawcett, Millicent Garrett 1847-1929 .... DLB-190
Fawcett Books..................... DLB-46
Fay, Theodore Sedgwick 1807-1898..... DLB-202

Fearing, Kenneth 1902-1961............. DLB-9
Federal Writers' Project DLB-46
Federman, Raymond 1928- Y-80
Feiffer, Jules 1929- DLB-7, 44
Feinberg, Charles E. 1899-1988 ....DLB-187; Y-88
Feind, Barthold 1678-1721 .... DLB-168
Feinstein, Elaine 1930- DLB-14, 40
Feiss, Paul Louis 1875-1952 ....DLB-187
Feldman, Irving 1928- DLB-169
Felipe, Léon 1884-1968................ DLB-108
Fell, Frederick, Publishers.............. DLB-46
Felltham, Owen 1602?-1668....... DLB-126, 151
Fels, Ludwig 1946- DLB-75
Felton, Cornelius Conway 1807-1862...... DLB-1
Fenn, Harry 1837-1911 .... DLB-188
Fennario, David 1947- DLB-60
Fenno, Jenny 1765?-1803 .... DLB-200
Fenno, John 1751-1798 .... DLB-43
Fenno, R. F., and Company DLB-49
Fenoglio, Beppe 1922-1963............DLB-177
Fenton, Geoffrey 1539?-1608.......... DLB-136
Fenton, James 1949- DLB-40
Ferber, Edna 1885-1968......... DLB-9, 28, 86
Ferdinand, Vallery III (see Salaam, Kalamu ya)
Ferguson, Sir Samuel 1810-1886......... DLB-32
Ferguson, William Scott 1875-1954 ..... DLB-47
Fergusson, Robert 1750-1774 .... DLB-109
Ferland, Albert 1872-1943.............. DLB-92
Ferlinghetti, Lawrence 1919- DLB-5, 16
Fermor, Patrick Leigh 1915- DLB-204
Fern, Fanny (see Parton, Sara Payson Willis)
Ferrars, Elizabeth 1907- DLB-87
Ferré, Rosario 1942- DLB-145
Ferret, E., and Company DLB-49
Ferrier, Susan 1782-1854.............. DLB-116
Ferrini, Vincent 1913- DLB-48
Ferron, Jacques 1921-1985 .... DLB-60
Ferron, Madeleine 1922- DLB-53
Ferrucci, Franco 1936- DLB-196
Fetridge and Company................. DLB-49
Feuchtersleben, Ernst Freiherr von 1806-1849 .... DLB-133
Feuchtwanger, Lion 1884-1958 ....DLB-66
Feuerbach, Ludwig 1804-1872 .... DLB-133
Feuillet, Octave 1821-1890............ DLB-192
Feydeau, Georges 1862-1921 .... DLB-192
Fichte, Johann Gottlieb 1762-1814 .... DLB-90
Ficke, Arthur Davison 1883-1945 .... DLB-54
Fiction Best-Sellers, 1910-1945 .... DLB-9
Fiction into Film, 1928-1975: A List of Movies Based on the Works of Authors in British Novelists, 1930-1959 .... DLB-15
Fiedler, Leslie A. 1917- DLB-28, 67
Field, Edward 1924- DLB-105

Field, Eugene 1850-1895 ....DLB-23, 42, 140; DS-13
Field, John 1545?-1588 ....DLB-167
Field, Marshall, III 1893-1956.........DLB-127
Field, Marshall, IV 1916-1965.........DLB-127
Field, Marshall, V 1941- DLB-127
Field, Nathan 1587-1619 or 1620........DLB-58
Field, Rachel 1894-1942..............DLB-9, 22
A Field Guide to Recent Schools of American Poetry Y-86
Fielding, Henry 1707-1754 ....DLB-39, 84, 101
Fielding, Sarah 1710-1768..............DLB-39
Fields, James Thomas 1817-1881...........DLB-1
Fields, Julia 1938- DLB-41
Fields, W. C. 1880-1946 ....DLB-44
Fields, Osgood and Company DLB-49
Fifty Penguin Years Y-85
Figes, Eva 1932- DLB-14
Figuera, Angela 1902-1984 ....DLB-108
Filmer, Sir Robert 1586-1653...........DLB-151
Filson, John circa 1753-1788............DLB-37
Finch, Anne, Countess of Winchilsea 1661-1720 ....DLB-95
Finch, Robert 1900- DLB-88
"Finding, Losing, Reclaiming: A Note on My Poems," by Robert Phillips DLB-105
Findley, Timothy 1930- DLB-53
Finlay, Ian Hamilton 1925- DLB-40
Finley, Martha 1828-1909 ....DLB-42
Finn, Elizabeth Anne (McCaul) 1825-1921 ....DLB-166
Finney, Jack 1911- DLB-8
Finney, Walter Braden (see Finney, Jack)
Firbank, Ronald 1886-1926..............DLB-36
Firmin, Giles 1615-1697................DLB-24
Fischart, Johann 1546 or 1547-1590 or 1591 ....DLB-179
First Edition Library/Collectors' Reprints, Inc....................... Y-91
First International F. Scott Fitzgerald Conference Y-92
First Strauss "Livings" Awarded to Cynthia Ozick and Raymond Carver An Interview with Cynthia Ozick An Interview with Raymond Carver........................... Y-83
Fischer, Karoline Auguste Fernandine 1764-1842........................DLB-94
Fish, Stanley 1938- DLB-67
Fishacre, Richard 1205-1248 ....DLB-115
Fisher, Clay (see Allen, Henry W.)
Fisher, Dorothy Canfield 1879-1958 ....DLB-9, 102
Fisher, Leonard Everett 1924- DLB-61
Fisher, Roy 1930- DLB-40
Fisher, Rudolph 1897-1934 ....DLB-51, 102
Fisher, Sydney George 1856-1927 ....DLB-47
Fisher, Vardis 1895-1968................DLB-9
Fiske, John 1608-1677 ....DLB-24

Fiske, John 1842-1901 ....DLB-47, 64
Fitch, Thomas circa 1700-1774..........DLB-31
Fitch, William Clyde 1865-1909 ....DLB-7
FitzGerald, Edward 1809-1883 ....DLB-32
Fitzgerald, F. Scott 1896-1940 ....DLB-4, 9, 86; Y-81; DS-1, 15, 16
F. Scott Fitzgerald Centenary Celebrations ... Y-96
Fitzgerald, Penelope 1916- DLB-14, 194
Fitzgerald, Robert 1910-1985............ Y-80
Fitzgerald, Thomas 1819-1891..........DLB-23
Fitzgerald, Zelda Sayre 1900-1948......... Y-84
Fitzhugh, Louise 1928-1974.............DLB-52
Fitzhugh, William circa 1651-1701........DLB-24
Flagg, James Montgomery 1877-1960 ....DLB-188
Flanagan, Thomas 1923- Y-80
Flanner, Hildegarde 1899-1987 ....DLB-48
Flanner, Janet 1892-1978 ....DLB-4
Flaubert, Gustave 1821-1880...........DLB-119
Flavin, Martin 1883-1967................DLB-9
Fleck, Konrad (flourished circa 1220) DLB-138
Flecker, James Elroy 1884-1915.......DLB-10, 19
Fleeson, Doris 1901-1970................DLB-29
Fleißer, Marieluise 1901-1974 ....DLB-56, 124
Fleming, Ian 1908-1964 .... DLB-87, 201
Fleming, Paul 1609-1640 ....DLB-164
Fleming, Peter 1907-1971 ....DLB-195
The Fleshly School of Poetry and Other Phenomena of the Day (1872), by Robert Buchanan DLB-35
The Fleshly School of Poetry: Mr. D. G. Rossetti (1871), by Thomas Maitland (Robert Buchanan) DLB-35
Fletcher, Giles, the Elder 1546-1611 ....DLB-136
Fletcher, Giles, the Younger 1585 or 1586-1623 ....DLB-121
Fletcher, J. S. 1863-1935 ....DLB-70
Fletcher, John (see Beaumont, Francis)
Fletcher, John Gould 1886-1950 ....DLB-4, 45
Fletcher, Phineas 1582-1650 ....DLB-121
Flieg, Helmut (see Heym, Stefan)
Flint, F. S. 1885-1960..................DLB-19
Flint, Timothy 1780-1840 .... DLB-73, 186
Florio, John 1553?-1625................DLB-172
Fo, Dario 1926- Y-97
Foix, J. V. 1893-1987 ....DLB-134
Foley, Martha (see Burnett, Whit, and Martha Foley)
Folger, Henry Clay 1857-1930..........DLB-140
Folio Society........................DLB-112
Follen, Eliza Lee (Cabot) 1787-1860........DLB-1
Follett, Ken 1949- DLB-87; Y-81
Follett Publishing Company............DLB-46
Folsom, John West [publishing house].....DLB-49
Folz, Hans between 1435 and 1440-1513 .... DLB-179
Fontane, Theodor 1819-1898.............DLB-129

Fonvisin, Denis Ivanovich 1744 or 1745-1792 ....DLB-150
Foote, Horton 1916- DLB-26
Foote, Mary Hallock 1847-1938 ....DLB-186, 188, 202
Foote, Samuel 1721-1777 ....DLB-89
Foote, Shelby 1916- DLB-2, 17
Forbes, Calvin 1945- DLB-41
Forbes, Ester 1891-1967.................DLB-22
Forbes, Rosita 1893?-1967................DLB-195
Forbes and Company DLB-49
Force, Peter 1790-1868.................DLB-30
Forché, Carolyn 1950- DLB-5, 193
Ford, Charles Henri 1913- DLB-4, 48
Ford, Corey 1902-1969 ....DLB-11
Ford, Ford Madox 1873-1939 .... DLB-34, 98, 162
Ford, Jesse Hill 1928- DLB-6
Ford, John 1586-? DLB-58
Ford, R. A. D. 1915- DLB-88
Ford, Worthington C. 1858-1941 ....DLB-47
Ford, J. B., and Company DLB-49
Fords, Howard, and Hulbert............DLB-49
Foreman, Carl 1914-1984 ....DLB-26
Forester, C. S. 1899-1966................DLB-191
Forester, Frank (see Herbert, Henry William)
"Foreword to Ludwig of Bavaria," by Robert Peters DLB-105
Forman, Harry Buxton 1842-1917.......DLB-184
Fornés, María Irene 1930- DLB-7
Forrest, Leon 1937- DLB-33
Forster, E. M. 1879-1970 .... DLB-34, 98, 162, 178, 195; DS-10
Forster, Georg 1754-1794................DLB-94
Forster, John 1812-1876................DLB-144
Forster, Margaret 1938- DLB-155
Forsyth, Frederick 1938- DLB-87
Forten, Charlotte L. 1837-1914 ....DLB-50
Fortini, Franco 1917- DLB-128
Fortune, T. Thomas 1856-1928..........DLB-23
Fosdick, Charles Austin 1842-1915 ....DLB-42
Foster, Genevieve 1893-1979............DLB-61
Foster, Hannah Webster 1758-1840... DLB-37, 200
Foster, John 1648-1681 ....DLB-24
Foster, Michael 1904-1956...............DLB-9
Foster, Myles Birket 1825-1899.........DLB-184
Foulis, Robert and Andrew / R. and A. [publishing house]..................DLB-154
Fouqué, Caroline de la Motte 1774-1831 ....DLB-90
Fouqué, Friedrich de la Motte 1777-1843..........................DLB-90
Four Essays on the Beat Generation, by John Clellon Holmes DLB-16
Four Seas Company....................DLB-46
Four Winds Press DLB-46
Fournier, Henri Alban (see Alain-Fournier)
Fowler and Wells Company DLB-49

Fowles, John 1926- DLB-14, 139
Fox, John, Jr. 1862 or 1863-1919 ... DLB-9; DS-13
Fox, Paula 1923- DLB-52
Fox, Richard Kyle 1846-1922........... DLB-79
Fox, William Price 1926- DLB-2; Y-81
Fox, Richard K. [publishing house]....... DLB-49
Foxe, John 1517-1587 .... DLB-132
Fraenkel, Michael 1896-1957 .... DLB-4
France, Anatole 1844-1924........... DLB-123
France, Richard 1938- DLB-7
Francis, Convers 1795-1863 .... DLB-1
Francis, Dick 1920- DLB-87
Francis, Sir Frank 1901-1988 .... DLB-201
Francis, Jeffrey, Lord 1773-1850 ...... DLB-107
Francis, C. S. [publishing house]........ DLB-49
François 1863-1910................. DLB-92
François, Louise von 1817-1893 .... DLB-129
Franck, Sebastian 1499-1542 .... DLB-179
Francke, Kuno 1855-1930 .... DLB-71
Frank, Bruno 1887-1945 .... DLB-118
Frank, Leonhard 1882-1961........ DLB-56, 118
Frank, Melvin (see Panama, Norman)
Frank, Waldo 1889-1967 .... DLB-9, 63
Franken, Rose 1895?-1988 .... Y-84
Franklin, Benjamin
    1706-1790.............DLB-24, 43, 73, 183
Franklin, James 1697-1735.............. DLB-43
Franklin Library..................... DLB-46
Frantz, Ralph Jules 1902-1979........... DLB-4
Franzos, Karl Emil 1848-1904 .... DLB-129
Fraser, G. S. 1915-1980 .... DLB-27
Fraser, Kathleen 1935- DLB-169
Frattini, Alberto 1922- DLB-128
Frau Ava ?-1127 .... DLB-148
Frayn, Michael 1933- DLB-13, 14, 194
Frederic, Harold 1856-1898 ... DLB-12, 23; DS-13
Freeling, Nicolas 1927- DLB-87
Freeman, Douglas Southall
    1886-1953 ....DLB-17; DS-17
Freeman, Legh Richmond 1842-1915..... DLB-23
Freeman, Mary E. Wilkins
    1852-1930 .... DLB-12, 78
Freeman, R. Austin 1862-1943.......... DLB-70
Freidank circa 1170-circa 1233 .... DLB-138
Freiligrath, Ferdinand 1810-1876 ..... DLB-133
Frémont, John Charles 1813-1890 ..... DLB-186
Frémont, John Charles 1813-1890 and
    Frémont, Jessie Benton 1834-1902... DLB-183
French, Alice 1850-1934 .... DLB-74; DS-13
French, David 1939- DLB-53
French, Evangeline 1869-1960 .... DLB-195
French, Francesca 1871-1960 .... DLB-195
French, James [publishing house] DLB-49
French, Samuel [publishing house] DLB-49
Samuel French, Limited DLB-106

Freneau, Philip 1752-1832 ....DLB-37, 43
Freni, Melo 1934- DLB-128
Freshfield, Douglas W. 1845-1934.......DLB-174
Freytag, Gustav 1816-1895............ DLB-129
Fried, Erich 1921-1988................ DLB-85
Friedman, Bruce Jay 1930- DLB-2, 28
Friedrich von Hausen circa 1171-1190 ... DLB-138
Friel, Brian 1929- DLB-13
Friend, Krebs 1895?-1967?.............. DLB-4
Fries, Fritz Rudolf 1935- DLB-75
Fringe and Alternative Theater in
    Great Britain DLB-13
Frisch, Max 1911-1991.......... DLB-69, 124
Frischlin, Nicodemus 1547-1590........DLB-179
Frischmuth, Barbara 1941- DLB-85
Fritz, Jean 1915- DLB-52
Fromentin, Eugene 1820-1876 .... DLB-123
From *The Gay Science,* by E. S. Dallas DLB-21
Frost, A. B. 1851-1928 .... DLB-188; DS-13
Frost, Robert 1874-1963 .... DLB-54; DS-7
Frothingham, Octavius Brooks
    1822-1895 .... DLB-1
Froude, James Anthony
    1818-1894 ....DLB-18, 57, 144
Fry, Christopher 1907- DLB-13
Fry, Roger 1866-1934................. DS-10
Frye, Northrop 1912-1991 ....DLB-67, 68
Fuchs, Daniel 1909-1993 .....DLB-9, 26, 28; Y-93
Fuentes, Carlos 1928- DLB-113
Fuertes, Gloria 1918- DLB-108
The Fugitives and the Agrarians:
    The First Exhibition.................. Y-85
Fujiwara no Shunzei 1114-1204 .... DLB-203
Fujiwara no Tameaki 1230s?-1290s? DLB-203
Fujiwara no Tameie 1198-1275......... DLB-203
Fujiwara no Teika 1162-1241.......... DLB-203
Fulbecke, William 1560-1603? DLB-172
Fuller, Charles H., Jr. 1939- DLB-38
Fuller, Henry Blake 1857-1929 .... DLB-12
Fuller, John 1937- DLB-40
Fuller, Margaret (see Fuller, Sarah Margaret,
    Marchesa D'Ossoli)
Fuller, Roy 1912-1991 .... DLB-15, 20
Fuller, Samuel 1912- DLB-26
Fuller, Sarah Margaret, Marchesa
    D'Ossoli 1810-1850 ....DLB-1, 59, 73, 183
Fuller, Thomas 1608-1661 .... DLB-151
Fullerton, Hugh 1873-1945.............DLB-171
Fulton, Alice 1952- DLB-193
Fulton, Len 1934- Y-86
Fulton, Robin 1937- DLB-40
Furbank, P. N. 1920- DLB-155
Furman, Laura 1945- Y-86
Furness, Horace Howard 1833-1912 ..... DLB-64
Furness, William Henry 1802-1896 ...... DLB-1
Furnivall, Frederick James 1825-1910.... DLB-184

Furthman, Jules 1888-1966............ DLB-26
Furui Yoshikichi 1937- DLB-182
Fushimi, Emperor 1265-1317 .... DLB-203
Futabatei, Shimei (Hasegawa Tatsunosuke)
    1864-1909 .... DLB-180
The Future of the Novel (1899), by
    Henry James DLB-18
Fyleman, Rose 1877-1957 .... DLB-160

G

The G. Ross Roy Scottish Poetry
    Collection at the University of
    South Carolina..................... Y-89
Gadda, Carlo Emilio 1893-1973........DLB-177
Gaddis, William 1922- DLB-2
Gág, Wanda 1893-1946............... DLB-22
Gagarin, Ivan Sergeevich 1814-1882 .... DLB-198
Gagnon, Madeleine 1938- DLB-60
Gaine, Hugh 1726-1807 .... DLB-43
Gaine, Hugh [publishing house]........ DLB-49
Gaines, Ernest J. 1933- DLB-2, 33, 152; Y-80
Gaiser, Gerd 1908-1976 .... DLB-69
Galarza, Ernesto 1905-1984 .... DLB-122
Galaxy Science Fiction Novels DLB-46
Gale, Zona 1874-1938...............DLB-9, 78
Galen of Pergamon 129-after 210 ....DLB-176
Gales, Winifred Marshall 1761-1839 .... DLB-200
Gall, Louise von 1815-1855 .... DLB-133
Gallagher, Tess 1943- DLB-120
Gallagher, Wes 1911- DLB-127
Gallagher, William Davis 1808-1894..... DLB-73
Gallant, Mavis 1922- DLB-53
Gallico, Paul 1897-1976...............DLB-9, 171
Galloway, Grace Growden 1727-1782.... DLB-200
Gallup, Donald 1913- DLB-187
Galsworthy, John
    1867-1933........DLB-10, 34, 98, 162; DS-16
Galt, John 1779-1839 .... DLB-99, 116
Galton, Sir Francis 1822-1911 .... DLB-166
Galvin, Brendan 1938- DLB-5
Gambit DLB-46
Gamboa, Reymundo 1948- DLB-122
Gammer Gurton's Needle................. DLB-62
Gan, Elena Andreevna (Zeneida R-va)
    1814-1842 .... DLB-198
Gannett, Frank E. 1876-1957 .... DLB-29
Gaos, Vicente 1919-1980 .... DLB-134
García, Lionel G. 1935- DLB-82
García Lorca, Federico 1898-1936 ...... DLB-108
García Márquez, Gabriel 1928- ..DLB-113; Y-82
Gardam, Jane 1928- DLB-14, 161
Garden, Alexander circa 1685-1756 ...... DLB-31
Gardiner, Margaret Power Farmer (see
    Blessington, Marguerite, Countess of)
Gardner, John 1933-1982...........DLB-2; Y-82
Garfield, Leon 1921- DLB-161

Garis, Howard R. 1873-1962............DLB-22
Garland, Hamlin 1860-1940 .. DLB-12, 71, 78, 186
Garneau, Francis-Xavier 1809-1866......DLB-99
Garneau, Hector de Saint-Denys
   1912-1943..................DLB-88
Garneau, Michel 1939- DLB-53
Garner, Alan 1934- DLB-161
Garner, Hugh 1913-1979..............DLB-68
Garnett, David 1892-1981.............DLB-34
Garnett, Eve 1900-1991...............DLB-160
Garnett, Richard 1835-1906...........DLB-184
Garrard, Lewis H. 1829-1887..........DLB-186
Garraty, John A. 1920-................DLB-17
Garrett, George
   1929- DLB-2, 5, 130, 152; Y-83
Garrett, John Work 1872-1942.........DLB-187
Garrick, David 1717-1779.............DLB-84
Garrison, William Lloyd 1805-1879 ....DLB-1, 43
Garro, Elena 1920- DLB-145
Garth, Samuel 1661-1719..............DLB-95
Garve, Andrew 1908- DLB-87
Gary, Romain 1914-1980 ....DLB-83
Gascoigne, George 1539?-1577 ....DLB-136
Gascoyne, David 1916- DLB-20
Gaskell, Elizabeth Cleghorn
   1810-1865 ....DLB-21, 144, 159
Gaspey, Thomas 1788-1871.............DLB-116
Gass, William Howard 1924- DLB-2
Gates, Doris 1901- DLB-22
Gates, Henry Louis, Jr. 1950- DLB-67
Gates, Lewis E. 1860-1924.............DLB-71
Gatto, Alfonso 1909-1976 ....DLB-114
Gaunt, Mary 1861-1942 ....DLB-174
Gautier, Théophile 1811-1872 ....DLB-119
Gauvreau, Claude 1925-1971 ....DLB-88
The *Gawain*-Poet
   flourished circa 1350-1400 ....DLB-146
Gay, Ebenezer 1696-1787...............DLB-24
Gay, John 1685-1732 ....DLB-84, 95
The Gay Science (1866), by E. S. Dallas
   [excerpt]........................DLB-21
Gayarré, Charles E. A. 1805-1895.......DLB-30
Gaylord, Edward King 1873-1974 ....DLB-127
Gaylord, Edward Lewis 1919- DLB-127
Gaylord, Charles [publishing house] DLB-49
Geddes, Gary 1940- DLB-60
Geddes, Virgil 1897- DLB-4
Gedeon (Georgii Andreevich Krinovsky)
   circa 1730-1763 ....DLB-150
Geibel, Emanuel 1815-1884............DLB-129
Geiogamah, Hanay 1945- DLB-175
Geis, Bernard, Associates................DLB-46
Geisel, Theodor Seuss 1904-1991 ... DLB-61; Y-91
Gelb, Arthur 1924- DLB-103
Gelb, Barbara 1926- DLB-103
Gelber, Jack 1932- DLB-7

Gelinas, Gratien 1909- DLB-88
Gellert, Christian Füerchtegott
   1715-1769......................DLB-97
Gellhorn, Martha 1908- Y-82
Gems, Pam 1925- DLB-13
A General Idea of the College of Mirania (1753),
   by William Smith [excerpts] DLB-31
Genet, Jean 1910-1986...........DLB-72; Y-86
Genevoix, Maurice 1890-1980..........DLB-65
Genovese, Eugene D. 1930- DLB-17
Gent, Peter 1942- Y-82
Geoffrey of Monmouth
   circa 1100-1155 ....DLB-146
George, Henry 1839-1897 ....DLB-23
George, Jean Craighead 1919- DLB-52
George, W. L. 1882-1926..............DLB-197
Georgslied 896?....................DLB-148
Gerhardie, William 1895-1977..........DLB-36
Gerhardt, Paul 1607-1676.............DLB-164
Gérin, Winifred 1901-1981 ....DLB-155
Gérin-Lajoie, Antoine 1824-1882........DLB-99
German Drama 800-1280 ....DLB-138
German Drama from Naturalism
   to Fascism: 1889-1933............DLB-118
German Literature and Culture from
   Charlemagne to the Early Courtly
   Period DLB-148
German Radio Play, The..............DLB-124
German Transformation from the Baroque
   to the Enlightenment, The DLB-97
The Germanic Epic and Old English Heroic
   Poetry: *Widseth, Waldere*, and *The
   Fight at Finnsburg*................DLB-146
Germanophilism, by Hans Kohn.........DLB-66
Gernsback, Hugo 1884-1967........DLB-8, 137
Gerould, Katharine Fullerton
   1879-1944 ....DLB-78
Gerrish, Samuel [publishing house].......DLB-49
Gerrold, David 1944- DLB-8
The Ira Gershwin Centenary Y-96
Gersonides 1288-1344................DLB-115
Gerstäcker, Friedrich 1816-1872 ....DLB-129
Gerstenberg, Heinrich Wilhelm von
   1737-1823......................DLB-97
Gervinus, Georg Gottfried 1805-1871 ....DLB-133
Geßner, Salomon 1730-1788 ....DLB-97
Geston, Mark S. 1946- DLB-8
"Getting Started: Accepting the Regions You Own—
   or Which Own You," by
   Walter McDonald................DLB-105
Al-Ghazali 1058-1111.................DLB-115
Gibbings, Robert 1889-1958 ....DLB-195
Gibbon, Edward 1737-1794 ....DLB-104
Gibbon, John Murray 1875-1952.......DLB-92
Gibbon, Lewis Grassic (see Mitchell, James Leslie)
Gibbons, Floyd 1887-1939 ....DLB-25
Gibbons, Reginald 1947- DLB-120
Gibbons, William ?-? DLB-73

Gibson, Charles Dana 1867-1944 ....DS-13
Gibson, Charles Dana
   1867-1944 ....DLB-188; DS-13
Gibson, Graeme 1934- DLB-53
Gibson, Margaret 1944- DLB-120
Gibson, Margaret Dunlop 1843-1920 ....DLB-174
Gibson, Wilfrid 1878-1962 ....DLB-19
Gibson, William 1914- DLB-7
Gide, André 1869-1951................DLB-65
Giguère, Diane 1937- DLB-53
Giguère, Roland 1929- DLB-60
Gil de Biedma, Jaime 1929-1990 ....DLB-108
Gil-Albert, Juan 1906- DLB-134
Gilbert, Anthony 1899-1973 ....DLB-77
Gilbert, Michael 1912- DLB-87
Gilbert, Sandra M. 1936- DLB-120
Gilbert, Sir Humphrey 1537-1583 ....DLB-136
Gilchrist, Alexander 1828-1861.........DLB-144
Gilchrist, Ellen 1935- DLB-130
Gilder, Jeannette L. 1849-1916 ....DLB-79
Gilder, Richard Watson 1844-1909....DLB-64, 79
Gildersleeve, Basil 1831-1924 ....DLB-71
Giles, Henry 1809-1882................DLB-64
Giles of Rome circa 1243-1316 ....DLB-115
Gilfillan, George 1813-1878............DLB-144
Gill, Eric 1882-1940..................DLB-98
Gill, Sarah Prince 1728-1771 ....DLB-200
Gill, William F., Company DLB-49
Gillespie, A. Lincoln, Jr. 1895-1950.......DLB-4
Gilliam, Florence ?-? DLB-4
Gilliatt, Penelope 1932-1993 ....DLB-14
Gillott, Jacky 1939-1980 ....DLB-14
Gilman, Caroline H. 1794-1888........DLB-3, 73
Gilman, W. and J. [publishing house] DLB-49
Gilmer, Elizabeth Meriwether 1861-1951 ..DLB-29
Gilmer, Francis Walker 1790-1826 ....DLB-37
Gilroy, Frank D. 1925- DLB-7
Gimferrer, Pere (Pedro) 1945- DLB-134
Gingrich, Arnold 1903-1976 ....DLB-137
Ginsberg, Allen 1926- DLB-5, 16, 169
Ginzburg, Natalia 1916-1991...........DLB-177
Ginzkey, Franz Karl 1871-1963 ....DLB-81
Gioia, Dana 1950- DLB-120
Giono, Jean 1895-1970................DLB-72
Giotti, Virgilio 1885-1957 ....DLB-114
Giovanni, Nikki 1943- DLB-5, 41
Gipson, Lawrence Henry 1880-1971......DLB-17
Girard, Rodolphe 1879-1956............DLB-92
Giraudoux, Jean 1882-1944.............DLB-65
Gissing, George 1857-1903 ..... DLB-18, 135, 184
Giudici, Giovanni 1924- DLB-128
Giuliani, Alfredo 1924- DLB-128
Glackens, William J. 1870-1938..........DLB-188
Gladstone, William Ewart
   1809-1898...................DLB-57, 184

Glaeser, Ernst 1902-1963 . . . . DLB-69
Glancy, Diane 1941- DLB-175
Glanville, Brian 1931- DLB-15, 139
Glapthorne, Henry 1610-1643? DLB-58
Glasgow, Ellen 1873-1945. . . . . DLB-9, 12
Glasier, Katharine Bruce 1867-1950 . . . . . DLB-190
Glaspell, Susan 1876-1948 . . . . DLB-7, 9, 78
Glass, Montague 1877-1934 . . . . DLB-11
The Glass Key and Other Dashiell Hammett
    Mysteries. Y-96
Glassco, John 1909-1981 . . . . DLB-68
Glauser, Friedrich 1896-1938 . . . . DLB-56
F. Gleason's Publishing Hall. DLB-49
Gleim, Johann Wilhelm Ludwig
    1719-1803. . . . . DLB-97
Glendinning, Victoria 1937- DLB-155
Glinka, Fedor Nikolaevich
    1786-1880. . . . . DLB-205
Glover, Richard 1712-1785 . . . . DLB-95
Glück, Louise 1943- DLB-5
Glyn, Elinor 1864-1943 . . . . DLB-153
Gnedich, Nikolai Ivanovich
    1784-1833. . . . . DLB-205
Go-Toba 1180-1239 . . . . DLB-203
Gobineau, Joseph-Arthur de
    1816-1882. DLB-123
Godbout, Jacques 1933- DLB-53
Goddard, Morrill 1865-1937 . . . . DLB-25
Goddard, William 1740-1817 . . . . DLB-43
Godden, Rumer 1907- DLB-161
Godey, Louis A. 1804-1878 . . . . DLB-73
Godey and McMichael. DLB-49
Godfrey, Dave 1938- DLB-60
Godfrey, Thomas 1736-1763 . . . . DLB-31
Godine, David R., Publisher. DLB-46
Godkin, E. L. 1831-1902 . . . . DLB-79
Godolphin, Sidney 1610-1643 . . . . DLB-126
Godwin, Gail 1937- DLB-6
Godwin, Mary Jane Clairmont
    1766-1841. DLB-163
Godwin, Parke 1816-1904 . . . . DLB-3, 64
Godwin, William
    1756-1836. . . . . . . DLB-39, 104, 142, 158, 163
Godwin, M. J., and Company DLB-154
Goering, Reinhard 1887-1936. . . . . DLB-118
Goes, Albrecht 1908- DLB-69
Goethe, Johann Wolfgang von
    1749-1832. DLB-94
Goetz, Curt 1888-1960. . . . . DLB-124
Goffe, Thomas circa 1592-1629 . . . . DLB-58
Goffstein, M. B. 1940- DLB-61
Gogarty, Oliver St. John 1878-1957 . . . DLB-15, 19
Gogol, Nikolai Vasil'evich 1809-1852 . . . DLB-198
Goines, Donald 1937-1974 . . . . DLB-33
Gold, Herbert 1924- DLB-2; Y-81
Gold, Michael 1893-1967 . . . . DLB-9, 28
Goldbarth, Albert 1948- DLB-120

Goldberg, Dick 1947- DLB-7
Golden Cockerel Press. DLB-112
Golding, Arthur 1536-1606 . . . . DLB-136
Golding, Louis 1895-1958 . . . . DLB-195
Golding, William 1911-1993 . . . DLB-15, 100; Y-83
Goldman, William 1931- DLB-44
Goldring, Douglas 1887-1960. . . . . DLB-197
Goldsmith, Oliver
    1730?-1774 . . . . DLB-39, 89, 104, 109, 142
Goldsmith, Oliver 1794-1861 . . . . DLB-99
Goldsmith Publishing Company DLB-46
Goldstein, Richard 1944- DLB-185
Gollancz, Sir Israel 1864-1930 . . . . DLB-201
Gollancz, Victor, Limited DLB-112
Gómez-Quiñones, Juan 1942- DLB-122
Gomme, Laurence James
    [publishing house] DLB-46
Goncourt, Edmond de 1822-1896 . . . . . . DLB-123
Goncourt, Jules de 1830-1870. . . . . DLB-123
Gonzales, Rodolfo "Corky" 1928- DLB-122
González, Angel 1925- DLB-108
Gonzalez, Genaro 1949- DLB-122
Gonzalez, Ray 1952- DLB-122
González de Mireles, Jovita
    1899-1983 . . . . DLB-122
González-T., César A. 1931- DLB-82
"The Good, The Not So Good," by
    Stephen Dunn DLB-105
Goodbye, Gutenberg? A Lecture at
    the New York Public Library,
    18 April 1995 . . . . Y-95
Goodison, Lorna 1947- DLB-157
Goodman, Paul 1911-1972 . . . . DLB-130
The Goodman Theatre DLB-7
Goodrich, Frances 1891-1984 and
    Hackett, Albert 1900- DLB-26
Goodrich, Samuel Griswold
    1793-1860. . . . . DLB-1, 42, 73
Goodrich, S. G. [publishing house]. DLB-49
Goodspeed, C. E., and Company. DLB-49
Goodwin, Stephen 1943- Y-82
Googe, Barnabe 1540-1594 . . . . DLB-132
Gookin, Daniel 1612-1687 . . . . DLB-24
Gordimer, Nadine 1923- Y-91
Gordon, Caroline
    1895-1981 . . . . . . DLB-4, 9, 102; DS-17; Y-81
Gordon, Giles 1940- DLB-14, 139
Gordon, Helen Cameron, Lady Russell
    1867-1949. DLB-195
Gordon, Lyndall 1941- DLB-155
Gordon, Mary 1949- DLB-6; Y-81
Gordone, Charles 1925- DLB-7
Gore, Catherine 1800-1861 . . . . DLB-116
Gorey, Edward 1925- DLB-61
Gorgias of Leontini circa 485 B.C.-376 B.C.
    . . . . DLB-176
Görres, Joseph 1776-1848 . . . . DLB-90
Gosse, Edmund 1849-1928. . . . . . DLB-57, 144, 184

Gosson, Stephen 1554-1624 . . . . DLB-172
Gotlieb, Phyllis 1926- DLB-88
Gottfried von Straßburg
    died before 1230 . . . . DLB-138
Gotthelf, Jeremias 1797-1854. . . . . DLB-133
Gottschalk circa 804/808-869. . . . . DLB-148
Gottsched, Johann Christoph 1700-1766. . . DLB-97
Götz, Johann Nikolaus 1721-1781. . . . . . . DLB-97
Goudge, Elizabeth 1900-1984. . . . . DLB-191
Gould, Wallace 1882-1940. . . . . DLB-54
Govoni, Corrado 1884-1965 . . . . DLB-114
Gower, John circa 1330-1408. . . . . DLB-146
Goyen, William 1915-1983 . . . . DLB-2; Y-83
Goytisolo, José Augustín 1928- DLB-134
Gozzano, Guido 1883-1916 . . . . DLB-114
Grabbe, Christian Dietrich
    1801-1836. DLB-133
Gracq, Julien 1910- DLB-83
Grady, Henry W. 1850-1889. . . . . DLB-23
Graf, Oskar Maria 1894-1967 . . . . DLB-56
Graf Rudolf between circa 1170
    and circa 1185 . . . . DLB-148
Grafton, Richard [publishing house]. DLB-170
Graham, George Rex 1813-1894 . . . . DLB-73
Graham, Gwethalyn 1913-1965 . . . . DLB-88
Graham, Jorie 1951- DLB-120
Graham, Katharine 1917- DLB-127
Graham, Lorenz 1902-1989 . . . . DLB-76
Graham, Philip 1915-1963 . . . . DLB-127
Graham, R. B. Cunninghame
    1852-1936 . . . . DLB-98, 135, 174
Graham, Shirley 1896-1977 . . . . DLB-76
Graham, Stephen 1884-1975. . . . . DLB-195
Graham, W. S. 1918- DLB-20
Graham, William H. [publishing house]. . . DLB-49
Graham, Winston 1910- DLB-77
Grahame, Kenneth 1859-1932 . . . DLB-34, 141, 178
Grainger, Martin Allerdale 1874-1941 . . . . DLB-92
Gramatky, Hardie 1907-1979 . . . . DLB-22
Grand, Sarah 1854-1943. . . . . DLB-135, 197
Grandbois, Alain 1900-1975. . . . . DLB-92
Grange, John circa 1556-? DLB-136
Granich, Irwin (see Gold, Michael)
Granovsky, Timofei Nikolaevich
    1813-1855 . . . . DLB-198
Grant, Anne MacVicar 1755-1838 . . . . . . DLB-200
Grant, Duncan 1885-1978 . . . . DS-10
Grant, George 1918-1988 . . . . DLB-88
Grant, George Monro 1835-1902 . . . . DLB-99
Grant, Harry J. 1881-1963 . . . . DLB-29
Grant, James Edward 1905-1966 . . . . DLB-26
Grass, Günter 1927- DLB-75, 124
Grasty, Charles H. 1863-1924 . . . . DLB-25
Grau, Shirley Ann 1929- DLB-2
Graves, John 1920- Y-83
Graves, Richard 1715-1804 . . . . DLB-39

Graves, Robert 1895-1985 .... DLB-20, 100, 191; DS-18; Y-85
Gray, Alasdair 1934- DLB-194
Gray, Asa 1810-1888 .... DLB-1
Gray, David 1838-1861 .... DLB-32
Gray, Simon 1936- DLB-13
Gray, Thomas 1716-1771 .... DLB-109
Grayson, William J. 1788-1863 ...... DLB-3, 64
The Great Bibliographers Series Y-93
The Great War and the Theater, 1914-1918 [Great Britain] DLB-10
The Great War Exhibition and Symposium at the University of South Carolina Y-97
Grech, Nikolai Ivanovich 1787-1867 ..... DLB-198
Greeley, Horace 1811-1872 .... DLB-3, 43, 189
Green, Adolph (see Comden, Betty)
Green, Anna Katharine 1846-1935 ..... DLB-202
Green, Duff 1791-1875 .... DLB-43
Green, Elizabeth Shippen 1871-1954 ..... DLB-188
Green, Gerald 1922- DLB-28
Green, Henry 1905-1973 .... DLB-15
Green, Jonas 1712-1767 .... DLB-31
Green, Joseph 1706-1780 .... DLB-31
Green, Julien 1900- DLB-4, 72
Green, Paul 1894-1981 .... DLB-7, 9; Y-81
Green, T. and S. [publishing house] DLB-49
Green, Thomas Hill 1836-1882 .... DLB-190
Green, Timothy [publishing house] DLB-49
Greenaway, Kate 1846-1901 .... DLB-141
Greenberg: Publisher DLB-46
Green Tiger Press DLB-46
Greene, Asa 1789-1838 .... DLB-11
Greene, Belle da Costa 1883-1950 ...... DLB-187
Greene, Benjamin H. [publishing house] ... DLB-49
Greene, Graham 1904-1991 .... DLB-13, 15, 77, 100, 162, 201, 204; Y-85, Y-91
Greene, Robert 1558-1592 .... DLB-62, 167
Greene Jr., Robert Bernard (Bob) 1947- DLB-185
Greenhow, Robert 1800-1854 .... DLB-30
Greenlee, William B. 1872-1953 .... DLB-187
Greenough, Horatio 1805-1852 .... DLB-1
Greenwell, Dora 1821-1882 .... DLB-35, 199
Greenwillow Books DLB-46
Greenwood, Grace (see Lippincott, Sara Jane Clarke)
Greenwood, Walter 1903-1974 ...... DLB-10, 191
Greer, Ben 1948- DLB-6
Greflinger, Georg 1620?-1677 .... DLB-164
Greg, W. R. 1809-1881 .... DLB-55
Greg, W. W. 1875-1959 .... DLB-201
Gregg, Josiah 1806-1850 .... DLB-183, 186
Gregg Press DLB-46
Gregory, Isabella Augusta Persse, Lady 1852-1932 .... DLB-10
Gregory, Horace 1898-1982 .... DLB-48
Gregory of Rimini circa 1300-1358 ...... DLB-115

Gregynog Press DLB-112
Greiffenberg, Catharina Regina von 1633-1694 .... DLB-168
Grenfell, Wilfred Thomason 1865-1940 ... DLB-92
Greve, Felix Paul (see Grove, Frederick Philip)
Greville, Fulke, First Lord Brooke 1554-1628 .... DLB-62, 172
Grey, Sir George, K.C.B. 1812-1898 ..... DLB-184
Grey, Lady Jane 1537-1554 .... DLB-132
Grey Owl 1888-1938 .... DLB-92; DS-17
Grey, Zane 1872-1939 .... DLB-9
Grey Walls Press DLB-112
Griboedov, Aleksandr Sergeevich 1795?-1829 .... DLB-205
Grier, Eldon 1917- DLB-88
Grieve, C. M. (see MacDiarmid, Hugh)
Griffin, Bartholomew flourished 1596 .... DLB-172
Griffin, Gerald 1803-1840 .... DLB-159
Griffith, Elizabeth 1727?-1793 .... DLB-39, 89
Griffith, George 1857-1906 .... DLB-178
Griffiths, Trevor 1935- DLB-13
Griffiths, Ralph [publishing house] DLB-154
Griggs, S. C., and Company DLB-49
Griggs, Sutton Elbert 1872-1930 ...... DLB-50
Grignon, Claude-Henri 1894-1976 ...... DLB-68
Grigson, Geoffrey 1905- DLB-27
Grillparzer, Franz 1791-1872 .... DLB-133
Grimald, Nicholas circa 1519-circa 1562 .... DLB-136
Grimké, Angelina Weld 1880-1958 .... DLB-50, 54
Grimm, Hans 1875-1959 .... DLB-66
Grimm, Jacob 1785-1863 .... DLB-90
Grimm, Wilhelm 1786-1859 .... DLB-90
Grimmelshausen, Johann Jacob Christoffel von 1621 or 1622-1676 .... DLB-168
Grimshaw, Beatrice Ethel 1871-1953 .... DLB-174
Grindal, Edmund 1519 or 1520-1583 .... DLB-132
Griswold, Rufus Wilmot 1815-1857 .... DLB-3, 59
Grosart, Alexander Balloch 1827-1899 ... DLB-184
Gross, Milt 1895-1953 .... DLB-11
Grosset and Dunlap DLB-49
Grossman, Allen 1932- DLB-193
Grossman Publishers DLB-46
Grosseteste, Robert circa 1160-1253 .... DLB-115
Grosvenor, Gilbert H. 1875-1966 ...... DLB-91
Groth, Klaus 1819-1899 .... DLB-129
Groulx, Lionel 1878-1967 .... DLB-68
Grove, Frederick Philip 1879-1949 .... DLB-92
Grove Press DLB-46
Grubb, Davis 1919-1980 .... DLB-6
Gruelle, Johnny 1880-1938 .... DLB-22
von Grumbach, Argula 1492-after 1563? DLB-179
Grymeston, Elizabeth before 1563-before 1604 .... DLB-136
Gryphius, Andreas 1616-1664 .... DLB-164

Gryphius, Christian 1649-1706 .... DLB-168
Guare, John 1938- DLB-7
Guerra, Tonino 1920- DLB-128
Guest, Barbara 1920- DLB-5, 193
Guèvremont, Germaine 1893-1968 ...... DLB-68
Guidacci, Margherita 1921-1992 ...... DLB-128
Guide to the Archives of Publishers, Journals, and Literary Agents in North American Libraries Y-93
Guillén, Jorge 1893-1984 .... DLB-108
Guilloux, Louis 1899-1980 .... DLB-72
Guilpin, Everard circa 1572-after 1608? DLB-136
Guiney, Louise Imogen 1861-1920 ...... DLB-54
Guiterman, Arthur 1871-1943 .... DLB-11
Günderrode, Caroline von 1780-1806 .... DLB-90
Gundulić, Ivan 1589-1638 .... DLB-147
Gunn, Bill 1934-1989 .... DLB-38
Gunn, James E. 1923- DLB-8
Gunn, Neil M. 1891-1973 .... DLB-15
Gunn, Thom 1929- DLB-27
Gunnars, Kristjana 1948- DLB-60
Günther, Johann Christian 1695-1723 ... DLB-168
Gurik, Robert 1932- DLB-60
Gustafson, Ralph 1909- DLB-88
Gütersloh, Albert Paris 1887-1973 ..... DLB-81
Guthrie, A. B., Jr. 1901- DLB-6
Guthrie, Ramon 1896-1973 .... DLB-4
The Guthrie Theater DLB-7
Guthrie, Thomas Anstey (see Anstey, FC)
Gutzkow, Karl 1811-1878 .... DLB-133
Guy, Ray 1939- DLB-60
Guy, Rosa 1925- DLB-33
Guyot, Arnold 1807-1884 .... DS-13
Gwynne, Erskine 1898-1948 .... DLB-4
Gyles, John 1680-1755 .... DLB-99
Gysin, Brion 1916- DLB-16

H

H. D. (see Doolittle, Hilda)
Habington, William 1605-1654 .... DLB-126
Hacker, Marilyn 1942- DLB-120
Hackett, Albert (see Goodrich, Frances)
Hacks, Peter 1928- DLB-124
Hadas, Rachel 1948- DLB-120
Hadden, Briton 1898-1929 .... DLB-91
Hagedorn, Friedrich von 1708-1754 .... DLB-168
Hagelstange, Rudolf 1912-1984 .... DLB-69
Haggard, H. Rider 1856-1925 .... DLB-70, 156, 174, 178
Haggard, William 1907-1993 .... Y-93
Hahn-Hahn, Ida Gräfin von 1805-1880 .. DLB-133
Haig-Brown, Roderick 1908-1976 ...... DLB-88
Haight, Gordon S. 1901-1985 .... DLB-103
Hailey, Arthur 1920- DLB-88; Y-82

Cumulative Index

Haines, John 1924- DLB-5
Hake, Edward flourished 1566-1604 .... DLB-136
Hake, Thomas Gordon 1809-1895....... DLB-32
Hakluyt, Richard 1552?-1616.......... DLB-136
Halbe, Max 1865-1944................. DLB-118
Haldone, Charlotte 1894-1969......... DLB-191
Haldane, J. B. S. 1892-1964 .... DLB-160
Haldeman, Joe 1943- DLB-8
Haldeman-Julius Company............. DLB-46
Hale, E. J., and Son.................. DLB-49
Hale, Edward Everett 1822-1909 ... DLB-1, 42, 74
Hale, Janet Campbell 1946- DLB-175
Hale, Kathleen 1898- DLB-160
Hale, Leo Thomas (see Ebon)
Hale, Lucretia Peabody 1820-1900...... DLB-42
Hale, Nancy
  1908-1988 .... DLB-86; DS-17; Y-80, Y-88
Hale, Sarah Josepha (Buell)
  1788-1879 .... DLB-1, 42, 73
Hales, John 1584-1656 .... DLB-151
Halévy, Ludovic 1834-1908 .... DLB-192
Haley, Alex 1921-1992 .... DLB-38
Haliburton, Thomas Chandler
  1796-1865.................... DLB-11, 99
Hall, Anna Maria 1800-1881 .... DLB-159
Hall, Donald 1928- DLB-5
Hall, Edward 1497-1547 .... DLB-132
Hall, James 1793-1868 .... DLB-73, 74
Hall, Joseph 1574-1656........... DLB-121, 151
Hall, Radclyffe 1880-1943 .... DLB-191
Hall, Sarah Ewing 1761-1830 .... DLB-200
Hall, Samuel [publishing house] DLB-49
Hallam, Arthur Henry 1811-1833 .... DLB-32
Halleck, Fitz-Greene 1790-1867 .... DLB-3
Haller, Albrecht von 1708-1777........ DLB-168
Halliwell-Phillipps, James Orchard
  1820-1889 .... DLB-184
Hallmann, Johann Christian
  1640-1704 or 1716? DLB-168
Hallmark Editions DLB-46
Halper, Albert 1904-1984............... DLB-9
Halperin, John William 1941- DLB-111
Halstead, Murat 1829-1908 .... DLB-23
Hamann, Johann Georg 1730-1788....... DLB-97
Hamburger, Michael 1924- DLB-27
Hamilton, Alexander 1712-1756 .... DLB-31
Hamilton, Alexander 1755?-1804 .... DLB-37
Hamilton, Cicely 1872-1952.........DLB-10, 197
Hamilton, Edmond 1904-1977 .... DLB-8
Hamilton, Elizabeth 1758-1816..... DLB-116, 158
Hamilton, Gail (see Corcoran, Barbara)
Hamilton, Ian 1938- DLB-40, 155
Hamilton, Janet 1795-1873 .... DLB-199
Hamilton, Mary Agnes 1884-1962...... DLB-197
Hamilton, Patrick 1904-1962 ...... DLB-10, 191
Hamilton, Virginia 1936- DLB-33, 52

Hamilton, Hamish, Limited DLB-112
Hammett, Dashiell 1894-1961 ....DS-6
Dashiell Hammett: An Appeal in *TAC*........Y-91
Hammon, Jupiter 1711-died between
  1790 and 1806 .... DLB-31, 50
Hammond, John ?-1663 .... DLB-24
Hamner, Earl 1923- DLB-6
Hampson, John 1901-1955............ DLB-191
Hampton, Christopher 1946- DLB-13
Handel-Mazzetti, Enrica von 1871-1955... DLB-81
Handke, Peter 1942- DLB-85, 124
Handlin, Oscar 1915- DLB-17
Hankin, St. John 1869-1909 .... DLB-10
Hanley, Clifford 1922- DLB-14
Hanley, James 1901-1985 .... DLB-191
Hannah, Barry 1942- DLB-6
Hannay, James 1827-1873............. DLB-21
Hansberry, Lorraine 1930-1965 ....DLB-7, 38
Hanson, Elizabeth 1684-1737 .... DLB-200
Hapgood, Norman 1868-1937 .... DLB-91
Happel, Eberhard Werner 1647-1690.... DLB-168
Harcourt Brace Jovanovich DLB-46
Hardenberg, Friedrich von (see Novalis)
Harding, Walter 1917- DLB-111
Hardwick, Elizabeth 1916- DLB-6
Hardy, Thomas 1840-1928 ......DLB-18, 19, 135
Hare, Cyril 1900-1958 .... DLB-77
Hare, David 1947- DLB-13
Hargrove, Marion 1919- DLB-11
Häring, Georg Wilhelm Heinrich (see Alexis,
  Willibald)
Harington, Donald 1935- DLB-152
Harington, Sir John 1560-1612......... DLB-136
Harjo, Joy 1951- DLB-120, 175
Harkness, Margaret (John Law)
  1854-1923 .... DLB-197
Harlow, Robert 1923- DLB-60
Harman, Thomas
  flourished 1566-1573 .... DLB-136
Harness, Charles L. 1915- DLB-8
Harnett, Cynthia 1893-1981........... DLB-161
Harper, Fletcher 1806-1877 .... DLB-79
Harper, Frances Ellen Watkins
  1825-1911 .... DLB-50
Harper, Michael S. 1938- DLB-41
Harper and Brothers.................. DLB-49
Harraden, Beatrice 1864-1943 .... DLB-153
Harrap, George G., and Company
  Limited....................... DLB-112
Harriot, Thomas 1560-1621........... DLB-136
Harris, Benjamin ?-circa 1720........ DLB-42, 43
Harris, Christie 1907- DLB-88
Harris, Frank 1856-1931 ....DLB-156, 197
Harris, George Washington
  1814-1869 .... DLB-3, 11
Harris, Joel Chandler
  1848-1908 ....DLB-11, 23, 42, 78, 91

Harris, Mark 1922- DLB-2; Y-80
Harris, Wilson 1921- DLB-117
Harrison, Charles Yale 1898-1954 .... DLB-68
Harrison, Frederic 1831-1923.........DLB-57, 190
Harrison, Harry 1925- DLB-8
Harrison, Jim 1937- Y-82
Harrison, Mary St. Leger Kingsley
  (see Malet, Lucas)
Harrison, Paul Carter 1936- DLB-38
Harrison, Susan Frances 1859-1935...... DLB-99
Harrison, Tony 1937- DLB-40
Harrison, William 1535-1593.......... DLB-136
Harrison, James P., Company DLB-49
Harrisse, Henry 1829-1910 .... DLB-47
Harryman, Carla 1952- DLB-193
Harsdörffer, Georg Philipp 1607-1658 ... DLB-164
Harsent, David 1942- DLB-40
Hart, Albert Bushnell 1854-1943 ....DLB-17
Hart, Anne 1768-1834 .... DLB-200
Hart, Elizabeth 1771-1833............ DLB-200
Hart, Julia Catherine 1796-1867 .... DLB-99
The Lorenz Hart Centenary.............. Y-95
Hart, Moss 1904-1961 .... DLB-7
Hart, Oliver 1723-1795............... DLB-31
Hart-Davis, Rupert, Limited. DLB-112
Harte, Bret 1836-1902 ....DLB-12, 64, 74, 79, 186
Harte, Edward Holmead 1922- DLB-127
Harte, Houston Harriman 1927- DLB-127
Hartlaub, Felix 1913-1945 .... DLB-56
Hartlebon, Otto Erich 1864-1905....... DLB-118
Hartley, L. P. 1895-1972. .... DLB-15, 139
Hartley, Marsden 1877-1943........... DLB-54
Hartling, Peter 1933- DLB-75
Hartman, Geoffrey H. 1929- DLB-67
Hartmann, Sadakichi 1867-1944......... DLB-54
Hartmann von Aue
  circa 1160-circa 1205............. DLB-138
Harvey, Gabriel 1550?-1631 .... DLB-167
Harvey, Jean-Charles 1891-1967 .... DLB-88
Harvill Press Limited DLB-112
Harwood, Lee 1939- DLB-40
Harwood, Ronald 1934- DLB-13
Haskins, Charles Homer 1870-1937...... DLB-47
Hass, Robert 1941- DLB-105
The Hatch-Billops Collection DLB-76
Hathaway, William 1944- DLB-120
Hauff, Wilhelm 1802-1827............ DLB-90
A Haughty and Proud Generation (1922),
  by Ford Madox Hueffer............ DLB-36
Haugwitz, August Adolph von
  1647-1706..................... DLB-168
Hauptmann, Carl 1858-1921 .... DLB-66, 118
Hauptmann, Gerhart 1862-1946 .... DLB-66, 118
Hauser, Marianne 1910- Y-83
Havergal, Frances Ridley 1836-1879 .... DLB-199

Hawes, Stephen 1475?-before 1529 . . . . . . DLB-132
Hawker, Robert Stephen 1803-1875 . . . . . . DLB-32
Hawkes, John 1925- DLB-2, 7; Y-80
Hawkesworth, John 1720-1773 . . . . DLB-142
Hawkins, Sir Anthony Hope (see Hope, Anthony)
Hawkins, Sir John 1719-1789 . . . . DLB-104, 142
Hawkins, Walter Everette 1883-? DLB-50
Hawthorne, Nathaniel 1804-1864 . . DLB-1, 74, 183
Hawthorne, Nathaniel 1804-1864 and
  Hawthorne, Sophia Peabody
  1809-1871 . . . . DLB-183
Hay, John 1835-1905 . . . . DLB-12, 47, 189
Hayashi, Fumiko 1903-1951 . . . . DLB-180
Haycraft, Anna Margaret (see Ellis, Alice Thomas)
Hayden, Robert 1913-1980 . . . . DLB-5, 76
Haydon, Benjamin Robert
  1786-1846 . . . . DLB-110
Hayes, John Michael 1919- DLB-26
Hayley, William 1745-1820 . . . . DLB-93, 142
Haym, Rudolf 1821-1901 . . . . DLB-129
Hayman, Robert 1575-1629 . . . . DLB-99
Hayman, Ronald 1932- DLB-155
Hayne, Paul Hamilton 1830-1886 . . . DLB-3, 64, 79
Hays, Mary 1760-1843 . . . . DLB-142, 158
Hayward, John 1905-1965 . . . . DLB-201
Haywood, Eliza 1693?-1756 . . . . DLB-39
Hazard, Willis P. [publishing house] DLB-49
Hazlitt, William 1778-1830 . . . . DLB-110, 158
Hazzard, Shirley 1931- Y-82
Head, Bessie 1937-1986 . . . . DLB-117
Headley, Joel T. 1813-1897 . . . DLB-30, 183; DS-13
Heaney, Seamus 1939- DLB-40; Y-95
Heard, Nathan C. 1936- DLB-33
Hearn, Lafcadio 1850-1904 . . . . . DLB-12, 78, 189
Hearne, John 1926- DLB-117
Hearne, Samuel 1745-1792 . . . . DLB-99
Hearst, William Randolph 1863-1951 . . . . . DLB-25
Hearst, William Randolph, Jr.
  1908-1993 . . . . DLB-127
Heartman, Charles Frederick
  1883-1953 . . . . DLB-187
Heath, Catherine 1924- DLB-14
Heath, Roy A. K. 1926- DLB-117
Heath-Stubbs, John 1918- DLB-27
Heavysege, Charles 1816-1876 . . . . DLB-99
Hebbel, Friedrich 1813-1863 . . . . DLB-129
Hebel, Johann Peter 1760-1826 . . . . DLB-90
Heber, Richard 1774-1833 . . . . DLB-184
Hébert, Anne 1916- DLB-68
Hébert, Jacques 1923- DLB-53
Hecht, Anthony 1923- DLB-5, 169
Hecht, Ben 1894-1964
  . . . . DLB-7, 9, 25, 26, 28, 86
Hecker, Isaac Thomas 1819-1888 . . . . DLB-1
Hedge, Frederic Henry 1805-1890 . . . . . DLB-1, 59
Hefner, Hugh M. 1926- DLB-137

Hegel, Georg Wilhelm Friedrich
  1770-1831 . . . . DLB-90
Heidish, Marcy 1947- Y-82
Heißenbüttel 1921- DLB-75
Heike monogatari DLB-203
Hein, Christoph 1944- DLB-124
Heine, Heinrich 1797-1856 . . . . DLB-90
Heinemann, Larry 1944- DS-9
Heinemann, William, Limited DLB-112
Heinlein, Robert A. 1907-1988 . . . . DLB-8
Heinrich Julius of Brunswick
  1564-1613 . . . . DLB-164
Heinrich von dem Türlîn
  flourished circa 1230 . . . . DLB-138
Heinrich von Melk
  flourished after 1160 . . . . DLB-148
Heinrich von Veldeke
  circa 1145-circa 1190 . . . . DLB-138
Heinrich, Willi 1920- DLB-75
Heiskell, John 1872-1972 . . . . DLB-127
Heinse, Wilhelm 1746-1803 . . . . DLB-94
Heinz, W. C. 1915- DLB-171
Hejinian, Lyn 1941- DLB-165
Heliand circa 850 . . . . DLB-148
Heller, Joseph 1923- DLB-2, 28; Y-80
Heller, Michael 1937- DLB-165
Hellman, Lillian 1906-1984 . . . . DLB-7; Y-84
Hellwig, Johann 1609-1674 . . . . DLB-164
Helprin, Mark 1947- Y-85
Helwig, David 1938- DLB-60
Hemans, Felicia 1793-1835 . . . . DLB-96
Hemingway, Ernest
  1899-1961 . . . DLB-4, 9, 102; Y-81, Y-87; DS-1,
  DS-15, DS-16
Hemingway: Twenty-Five Years Later Y-85
Hémon, Louis 1880-1913 . . . . DLB-92
Hemphill, Paul 1936- Y-87
Hénault, Gilles 1920- DLB-88
Henchman, Daniel 1689-1761 . . . . DLB-24
Henderson, Alice Corbin 1881-1949 . . . . . . DLB-54
Henderson, Archibald 1877-1963 . . . . DLB-103
Henderson, David 1942- DLB-41
Henderson, George Wylie 1904- DLB-51
Henderson, Zenna 1917-1983 . . . . DLB-8
Henisch, Peter 1943- DLB-85
Henley, Beth 1952- Y-86
Henley, William Ernest 1849-1903 . . . . DLB-19
Henniker, Florence 1855-1923 . . . . DLB-135
Henry, Alexander 1739-1824 . . . . DLB-99
Henry, Buck 1930- DLB-26
Henry VIII of England 1491-1547 . . . . . . DLB-132
Henry, Marguerite 1902- DLB-22
Henry, O. (see Porter, William Sydney)
Henry of Ghent
  circa 1217-1229 - 1293 . . . . DLB-115
Henry, Robert Selph 1889-1970 . . . . DLB-17
Henry, Will (see Allen, Henry W.)

Henryson, Robert
  1420s or 1430s-circa 1505 . . . . DLB-146
Henschke, Alfred (see Klabund)
Hensley, Sophie Almon 1866-1946 . . . . DLB-99
Henson, Lance 1944- DLB-175
Henty, G. A. 1832?-1902 . . . . DLB-18, 141
Hentz, Caroline Lee 1800-1856 . . . . DLB-3
Heraclitus flourished circa 500 B.C.
  . . . . DLB-176
Herbert, Agnes circa 1880-1960 . . . . DLB-174
Herbert, Alan Patrick 1890-1971 . . . . . DLB-10, 191
Herbert, Edward, Lord, of Cherbury
  1582-1648 . . . . DLB-121, 151
Herbert, Frank 1920-1986 . . . . DLB-8
Herbert, George 1593-1633 . . . . DLB-126
Herbert, Henry William 1807-1858 . . . . . DLB-3, 73
Herbert, John 1926- DLB-53
Herbert, Mary Sidney, Countess of Pembroke
  (see Sidney, Mary)
Herbst, Josephine 1892-1969 . . . . DLB-9
Herburger, Gunter 1932- DLB-75, 124
Hercules, Frank E. M. 1917- DLB-33
Herder, Johann Gottfried 1744-1803 . . . . . . DLB-97
Herder, B., Book Company DLB-49
Herford, Charles Harold 1853-1931 . . . . . . DLB-149
Hergesheimer, Joseph 1880-1954 . . . . . DLB-9, 102
Heritage Press DLB-46
Hermann the Lame 1013-1054 . . . . DLB-148
Hermes, Johann Timotheus
  1738-1821 . . . . DLB-97
Hermlin, Stephan 1915- DLB-69
Hernández, Alfonso C. 1938- DLB-122
Hernández, Inés 1947- DLB-122
Hernández, Miguel 1910-1942 . . . . DLB-134
Herton, Calvin C. 1932- DLB-38
"The Hero as Man of Letters: Johnson,
  Rousseau, Burns" (1841), by Thomas
  Carlyle [excerpt] DLB-57
The Hero as Poet. Dante; Shakspeare (1841),
  by Thomas Carlyle DLB-32
Herodotus circa 484 B.C.-circa 420 B.C.
  . . . . DLB-176
Heron, Robert 1764-1807 . . . . DLB-142
Herr, Michael 1940- DLB-185
Herrera, Juan Felipe 1948- DLB-122
Herrick, Robert 1591-1674 . . . . DLB-126
Herrick, Robert 1868-1938 . . . . DLB-9, 12, 78
Herrick, William 1915- Y-83
Herrick, E. R., and Company DLB-49
Herrmann, John 1900-1959 . . . . DLB-4
Hersey, John 1914-1993 . . . . DLB-6, 185
Hertel, François 1905-1985 . . . . DLB-68
Hervé-Bazin, Jean Pierre Marie (see Bazin, Hervé)
Hervey, John, Lord 1696-1743 . . . . DLB-101
Herwig, Georg 1817-1875 . . . . DLB-133
Herzog, Emile Salomon Wilhelm (see
  Maurois, André)

Hesiod eighth century B.C. DLB-176	Hingley, Ronald 1920- DLB-155	Holden, Jonathan 1941- DLB-105
Hesse, Hermann 1877-1962 . . . . DLB-66	Hinojosa-Smith, Rolando 1929- DLB-82	Holden, Molly 1927-1981. . . . . DLB-40
Hessus, Helius Eobanus 1488-1540 . . . . . .DLB-179	Hippel, Theodor Gottlieb von 1741-1796 . . . . DLB-97	Hölderlin, Friedrich 1770-1843. . . . . DLB-90
Hewat, Alexander circa 1743-circa 1824 . . . DLB-30	Hippocrates of Cos flourished circa 425 B.C. DLB-176	Holiday House DLB-46
Hewitt, John 1907- DLB-27	Hirabayashi, Taiko 1905-1972 . . . . DLB-180	Holinshed, Raphael died 1580 . . . . DLB-167
Hewlett, Maurice 1861-1923 . . . . DLB-34, 156	Hirsch, E. D., Jr. 1928- DLB-67	Holland, J. G. 1819-1881 . . . . DS-13
Heyen, William 1940- DLB-5	Hirsch, Edward 1950- DLB-120	Holland, Norman N. 1927- DLB-67
Heyer, Georgette 1902-1974. . . . . . .DLB-77, 191	*The History of the Adventures of Joseph Andrews* (1742), by Henry Fielding [excerpt] . . . DLB-39	Hollander, John 1929- DLB-5
Heym, Stefan 1913- DLB-69		Holley, Marietta 1836-1926 . . . . DLB-11
Heyse, Paul 1830-1914 . . . . DLB-129	Hoagland, Edward 1932- DLB-6	Hollingsworth, Margaret 1940- DLB-60
Heytesbury, William circa 1310-1372 or 1373 . . . . DLB-115	Hoagland, Everett H., III 1942- DLB-41	Hollo, Anselm 1934- DLB-40
	Hoban, Russell 1925- DLB-52	Holloway, Emory 1885-1977 . . . . DLB-103
Heyward, Dorothy 1890-1961 . . . . DLB-7	Hobbes, Thomas 1588-1679 . . . . DLB-151	Holloway, John 1920- DLB-27
Heyward, DuBose 1885-1940. . . . . . .DLB-7, 9, 45	Hobby, Oveta 1905- DLB-127	Holloway House Publishing Company . . . DLB-46
Heywood, John 1497?-1580? DLB-136	Hobby, William 1878-1964 . . . . DLB-127	Holme, Constance 1880-1955 . . . . DLB-34
Heywood, Thomas 1573 or 1574-1641. . . . DLB-62	Hobsbaum, Philip 1932- DLB-40	Holmes, Abraham S. 1821?-1908 . . . . DLB-99
Hibbs, Ben 1901-1975. . . . . DLB-137	Hobson, Laura Z. 1900- DLB-28	Holmes, John Clellon 1926-1988 . . . . DLB-16
Hichens, Robert S. 1864-1950 . . . . DLB-153	Hobson, Sarah 1947- DLB-204	Holmes, Mary Jane 1825-1907 . . . . DLB-202
Hickey, Emily 1845-1924 . . . . DLB-199	Hoby, Thomas 1530-1566 . . . . DLB-132	Holmes, Oliver Wendell 1809-1894 . . . DLB-1, 189
Hickman, William Albert 1877-1957 . . . . . DLB-92	Hoccleve, Thomas circa 1368-circa 1437 . . . . DLB-146	Holmes, Richard 1945- DLB-155
Hidalgo, José Luis 1919-1947 . . . . DLB-108		Holmes, Thomas James 1874-1959. . . . . .DLB-187
Hiebert, Paul 1892-1987 . . . . DLB-68	Hochhuth, Rolf 1931- DLB-124	Holroyd, Michael 1935- DLB-155
Hieng, Andrej 1925- DLB-181	Hochman, Sandra 1936- DLB-5	Holst, Hermann E. von 1841-1904 . . . . . . DLB-47
Hierro, José 1922- DLB-108	Hocken, Thomas Morland 1836-1910 . . . DLB-184	Holt, John 1721-1784 . . . . DLB-43
Higgins, Aidan 1927- DLB-14	Hodder and Stoughton, Limited. DLB-106	Holt, Henry, and Company DLB-49
Higgins, Colin 1941-1988. . . . . DLB-26	Hodgins, Jack 1938- DLB-60	Holt, Rinehart and Winston. DLB-46
Higgins, George V. 1939- DLB-2; Y-81	Hodgman, Helen 1945- DLB-14	Holtby, Winifred 1898-1935 . . . . DLB-191
Higginson, Thomas Wentworth 1823-1911. DLB-1, 64	Hodgskin, Thomas 1787-1869 . . . . DLB-158	Holthusen, Hans Egon 1913- DLB-69
	Hodgson, Ralph 1871-1962 . . . . DLB-19	Hölty, Ludwig Christoph Heinrich 1748-1776 . . . . DLB-94
Highwater, Jamake 1942?- DLB-52; Y-85	Hodgson, William Hope 1877-1918. . . . . .DLB-70, 153, 156, 178	
Hijuelos, Oscar 1951- DLB-145		Holz, Arno 1863-1929 . . . . DLB-118
Hildegard von Bingen 1098-1179 . . . . DLB-148	Hoe, Robert III 1839-1909 . . . . DLB-187	Home, Henry, Lord Kames (see Kames, Henry Home, Lord)
Das Hildesbrandslied circa 820 . . . . .DLB-148	Hoffenstein, Samuel 1890-1947 . . . . DLB-11	
Hildesheimer, Wolfgang 1916-1991 . . DLB-69, 124	Hoffman, Charles Fenno 1806-1884. . . . . . DLB-3	Home, John 1722-1808. . . . . DLB-84
Hildreth, Richard 1807-1865. . . . . . . DLB-1, 30, 59	Hoffman, Daniel 1923- DLB-5	Home, William Douglas 1912- DLB-13
Hill, Aaron 1685-1750 . . . . DLB-84	Hoffmann, E. T. A. 1776-1822 . . . . DLB-90	Home Publishing Company DLB-49
Hill, Geoffrey 1932- DLB-40	Hoffman, Frank B. 1888-1958 . . . . DLB-188	Homer circa eighth-seventh centuries B.C. DLB-176
Hill, "Sir" John 1714?-1775 . . . . DLB-39	Hoffmanswaldau, Christian Hoffman von 1616-1679 . . . . DLB-168	
Hill, Leslie 1880-1960. . . . . DLB-51		Homer, Winslow 1836-1910 . . . . DLB-188
Hill, Susan 1942- DLB-14, 139	Hofmann, Michael 1957- DLB-40	Homes, Geoffrey (see Mainwaring, Daniel)
Hill, Walter 1942- DLB-44	Hofmannsthal, Hugo von 1874-1929. . . . . DLB-81, 118	Honan, Park 1928- DLB-111
Hill and Wang DLB-46		Hone, William 1780-1842. . . . . .DLB-110, 158
Hill, George M., Company. DLB-49	Hofstadter, Richard 1916-1970 . . . . DLB-17	Hongo, Garrett Kaoru 1951- DLB-120
Hill, Lawrence, and Company, Publishers DLB-46	Hogan, Desmond 1950- DLB-14	Honig, Edwin 1919- DLB-5
	Hogan, Linda 1947- DLB-175	Hood, Hugh 1928- DLB-53
Hillberry, Conrad 1928- DLB-120	Hogan and Thompson DLB-49	Hood, Thomas 1799-1845 . . . . DLB-96
Hilliard, Gray and Company DLB-49	Hogarth Press DLB-112	Hook, Theodore 1788-1841 . . . . DLB-116
Hills, Lee 1906- DLB-127	Hogg, James 1770-1835. . . . . .DLB-93, 116, 159	Hooker, Jeremy 1941- DLB-40
Hillyer, Robert 1895-1961 . . . . DLB-54	Hohberg, Wolfgang Helmhard Freiherr von 1612-1688 . . . . DLB-168	Hooker, Richard 1554-1600 . . . . DLB-132
Hilton, James 1900-1954. . . . . DLB-34, 77		Hooker, Thomas 1586-1647 . . . . DLB-24
Hilton, Walter died 1396 . . . . DLB-146	von Hohenheim, Philippus Aureolus Theophrastus Bombastus (see Paracelsus)	Hooper, Johnson Jones 1815-1862 . . . . . DLB-3, 11
Hilton and Company DLB-49		Hope, Anthony 1863-1933 . . . . DLB-153, 156
Himes, Chester 1909-1984 . . . . . . .DLB-2, 76, 143	Hohl, Ludwig 1904-1980 . . . . DLB-56	Hopkins, Ellice 1836-1904 . . . . DLB-190
Hindmarsh, Joseph [publishing house] DLB-170	Holbrook, David 1923- DLB-14, 40	Hopkins, Gerard Manley 1844-1889 . . .DLB-35, 57
Hine, Daryl 1936- DLB-60	Holcroft, Thomas 1745-1809 . . . . . DLB-39, 89, 158	Hopkins, John (see Sternhold, Thomas)

Hopkins, Lemuel 1750-1801 . . . . .DLB-37
Hopkins, Pauline Elizabeth 1859-1930 . . . .DLB-50
Hopkins, Samuel 1721-1803 . . . . .DLB-31
Hopkins, John H., and Son DLB-46
Hopkinson, Francis 1737-1791 . . . . .DLB-31
Hoppin, Augustus 1828-1896 . . . . .DLB-188
Horgan, Paul 1903- DLB-102; Y-85
Horizon Press DLB-46
Hornby, C. H. St. John 1867-1946. . . . . . .DLB-201
Horne, Frank 1899-1974 . . . . .DLB-51
Horne, Richard Henry (Hengist)
  1802 or 1803-1884 . . . . .DLB-32
Hornung, E. W. 1866-1921 . . . . .DLB-70
Horovitz, Israel 1939- .DLB-7
Horton, George Moses 1797?-1883? DLB-50
Horváth, Ödön von 1901-1938 . . . . . .DLB-85, 124
Horwood, Harold 1923- DLB-60
Hosford, E. and E. [publishing house] DLB-49
Hoskens, Jane Fenn 1693-1770? DLB-200
Hoskyns, John 1566-1638 . . . . .DLB-121
Hosokawa Yūsai 1535-1610 . . . . .DLB-203
Hotchkiss and Company DLB-49
Hough, Emerson 1857-1923 . . . . .DLB-9
Houghton Mifflin Company DLB-49
Houghton, Stanley 1881-1913 . . . . .DLB-10
Household, Geoffrey 1900-1988 . . . . .DLB-87
Housman, A. E. 1859-1936 . . . . .DLB-19
Housman, Laurence 1865-1959 . . . . .DLB-10
Houwald, Ernst von 1778-1845 . . . . .DLB-90
Hovey, Richard 1864-1900 . . . . .DLB-54
Howard, Donald R. 1927-1987 . . . . .DLB-111
Howard, Maureen 1930- Y-83
Howard, Richard 1929- DLB-5
Howard, Roy W. 1883-1964 . . . . .DLB-29
Howard, Sidney 1891-1939 . . . . .DLB-7, 26
Howe, E. W. 1853-1937 . . . . .DLB-12, 25
Howe, Henry 1816-1893 . . . . .DLB-30
Howe, Irving 1920-1993 . . . . .DLB-67
Howe, Joseph 1804-1873 . . . . .DLB-99
Howe, Julia Ward 1819-1910 . . . . .DLB-1, 189
Howe, Percival Presland 1886-1944 . . . . . .DLB-149
Howe, Susan 1937- .DLB-120
Howell, Clark, Sr. 1863-1936 . . . . .DLB-25
Howell, Evan P. 1839-1905 . . . . .DLB-23
Howell, James 1594?-1666 . . . . .DLB-151
Howell, Warren Richardson
  1912-1984 . . . . .DLB-140
Howell, Soskin and Company DLB-46
Howells, William Dean
  1837-1920 . . . . .DLB-12, 64, 74, 79, 189
Howitt, Mary 1799-1888 . . . . .DLB-110, 199
Howitt, William 1792-1879 and
  Howitt, Mary 1799-1888 . . . . .DLB-110
Hoyem, Andrew 1935- DLB-5
Hoyers, Anna Ovena 1584-1655 . . . . .DLB-164

Hoyos, Angela de 1940- DLB-82
Hoyt, Palmer 1897-1979 . . . . .DLB-127
Hoyt, Henry [publishing house] DLB-49
Hrabanus Maurus 776?-856 . . . . .DLB-148
Hrotsvit of Gandersheim
  circa 935-circa 1000 . . . . .DLB-148
Hubbard, Elbert 1856-1915 . . . . .DLB-91
Hubbard, Kin 1868-1930 . . . . .DLB-11
Hubbard, William circa 1621-1704 . . . . . . .DLB-24
Huber, Therese 1764-1829 . . . . .DLB-90
Huch, Friedrich 1873-1913 . . . . .DLB-66
Huch, Ricarda 1864-1947 . . . . .DLB-66
Huck at 100: How Old Is
  Huckleberry Finn? Y-85
Huddle, David 1942- DLB-130
Hudgins, Andrew 1951- DLB-120
Hudson, Henry Norman 1814-1886 . . . . . .DLB-64
Hudson, Stephen 1868?-1944 . . . . .DLB-197
Hudson, W. H. 1841-1922 . . . . .DLB-98, 153, 174
Hudson and Goodwin DLB-49
Huebsch, B. W. [publishing house] DLB-46
Hueffer, Oliver Madox 1876-1931 . . . . . . .DLB-197
Hughes, David 1930- DLB-14
Hughes, John 1677-1720 . . . . .DLB-84
Hughes, Langston
  1902-1967 . . . . .DLB-4, 7, 48, 51, 86
Hughes, Richard 1900-1976 . . . . .DLB-15, 161
Hughes, Ted 1930- DLB-40, 161
Hughes, Thomas 1822-1896 . . . . .DLB-18, 163
Hugo, Richard 1923-1982 . . . . .DLB-5
Hugo, Victor 1802-1885 . . . . .DLB-119, 192
Hugo Awards and Nebula Awards DLB-8
Hull, Richard 1896-1973 . . . . .DLB-77
Hulme, T. E. 1883-1917 . . . . .DLB-19
Hulton, Anne ?-1779? DLB-200
Humboldt, Alexander von 1769-1859 . . . . .DLB-90
Humboldt, Wilhelm von 1767-1835 . . . . . .DLB-90
Hume, David 1711-1776 . . . . .DLB-104
Hume, Fergus 1859-1932 . . . . .DLB-70
Hume, Sophia 1702-1774 . . . . .DLB-200
Hummer, T. R. 1950- DLB-120
Humorous Book Illustration DLB-11
Humphrey, William 1924- DLB-6
Humphreys, David 1752-1818 . . . . .DLB-37
Humphreys, Emyr 1919- DLB-15
Huncke, Herbert 1915- DLB-16
Huneker, James Gibbons 1857-1921 . . . . . .DLB-71
Hunold, Christian Friedrich
  1681-1721 . . . . .DLB-168
Hunt, Irene 1907- DLB-52
Hunt, Leigh 1784-1859 . . . . .DLB-96, 110, 144
Hunt, Violet 1862-1942 . . . . .DLB-162, 197
Hunt, William Gibbes 1791-1833 . . . . .DLB-73
Hunter, Evan 1926- Y-82
Hunter, Jim 1939- DLB-14

Hunter, Kristin 1931- DLB-33
Hunter, Mollie 1922- DLB-161
Hunter, N. C. 1908-1971 . . . . .DLB-10
Hunter-Duvar, John 1821-1899 . . . . .DLB-99
Huntington, Henry E. 1850-1927 . . . . .DLB-140
Huntington, Susan Mansfield
  1791-1823 . . . . .DLB-200
Hurd and Houghton .DLB-49
Hurst, Fannie 1889-1968 . . . . .DLB-86
Hurst and Blackett DLB-106
Hurst and Company .DLB-49
Hurston, Zora Neale 1901?-1960 . . . . .DLB-51, 86
Husson, Jules-François-Félix (see Champfleury)
Huston, John 1906-1987 . . . . .DLB-26
Hutcheson, Francis 1694-1746 . . . . .DLB-31
Hutchinson, R. C. 1907-1975 . . . . .DLB-191
Hutchinson, Thomas 1711-1780 . . . . . .DLB-30, 31
Hutchinson and Company
  (Publishers) Limited DLB-112
von Hutton, Ulrich 1488-1523 . . . . .DLB-179
Hutton, Richard Holt 1826-1897 . . . . .DLB-57
Huxley, Aldous
  1894-1963 . . . . .DLB-36, 100, 162, 195
Huxley, Elspeth Josceline 1907-1997 . . DLB-77, 204
Huxley, T. H. 1825-1895 . . . . .DLB-57
Huyghue, Douglas Smith 1816-1891 . . . . . .DLB-99
Huysmans, Joris-Karl 1848-1907 . . . . .DLB-123
Hyde, Donald 1909-1966 and
  Hyde, Mary 1912- DLB-187
Hyman, Trina Schart 1939- DLB-61

I

Iavorsky, Stefan 1658-1722 . . . . .DLB-150
Iazykov, Nikolai Mikhailovich
  1803-1846 . . . . .DLB-205
Ibn Bajja circa 1077-1138 . . . . .DLB-115
Ibn Gabirol, Solomon
  circa 1021-circa 1058 . . . . .DLB-115
Ibuse, Masuji 1898-1993 . . . . .DLB-180
Ichijō Kanera (see Ichijō Kaneyoshi)
Ichijō Kaneyoshi (Ichijō Kanera)
  1402-1481 . . . . .DLB-203
The Iconography of Science-Fiction Art DLB-8
Iffland, August Wilhelm 1759-1814 . . . . . . .DLB-94
Ignatow, David 1914- .DLB-5
Ike, Chukwuemeka 1931- DLB-157
Ikkyū Sōjun 1394-1481 . . . . .DLB-203
Iles, Francis (see Berkeley, Anthony)
The Illustration of Early German
  Literary Manuscripts,
  circa 1150-circa 1300 . . . . .DLB-148
"Images and 'Images,'" by
  Charles Simic DLB-105
Imbs, Bravig 1904-1946 . . . . .DLB-4
Imbuga, Francis D. 1947- DLB-157
Immermann, Karl 1796-1840 . . . . .DLB-133
Impressions of William Faulkner Y-97

Inchbald, Elizabeth 1753-1821 .... DLB-39, 89
Inge, William 1913-1973 .... DLB-7
Ingelow, Jean 1820-1897 .... DLB-35, 163
Ingersoll, Ralph 1900-1985 .... DLB-127
The Ingersoll Prizes Y-84
Ingoldsby, Thomas (see Barham, Richard Harris)
Ingraham, Joseph Holt 1809-1860 .... DLB-3
Inman, John 1805-1850 .... DLB-73
Innerhofer, Franz 1944- DLB-85
Innis, Harold Adams 1894-1952 .... DLB-88
Innis, Mary Quayle 1899-1972 .... DLB-88
Inō Sōgi 1421-1502................... DLB-203
Inoue Yasushi 1907-1991 .... DLB-181
International Publishers Company DLB-46
An Interview with David Rabe............ Y-91
An Interview with George Greenfield,
   Literary Agent Y-91
An Interview with James Ellroy Y-91
Interview with Norman Mailer............ Y-97
An Interview with Peter S. Prescott Y-86
An Interview with Russell Hoban Y-90
Interview with Stanley Burnshaw.......... Y-97
An Interview with Tom Jenks Y-86
"Into the Mirror," by Peter Cooley DLB-105
Introduction to Paul Laurence Dunbar,
   Lyrics of Lowly Life (1896),
   by William Dean Howells DLB-50
Introductory Essay: *Letters of Percy Bysshe
   Shelley* (1852), by Robert Browning ... DLB-32
Introductory Letters from the Second Edition
   of *Pamela* (1741), by Samuel
   Richardson...................... DLB-39
Irving, John 1942- DLB-6; Y-82
Irving, Washington 1783-1859
    .... DLB-3, 11, 30, 59, 73, 74, 183, 186
Irwin, Grace 1907- DLB-68
Irwin, Will 1873-1948 .... DLB-25
Isherwood, Christopher
   1904-1986 .... DLB-15, 195; Y-86
Ishiguro, Kazuo 1954- DLB-194
Ishikawa Jun 1899-1987 .... DLB-182
The Island Trees Case: A Symposium on
   School Library Censorship
   An Interview with Judith Krug
   An Interview with Phyllis Schlafly
   An Interview with Edward B. Jenkinson
   An Interview with Lamarr Mooneyham
   An Interview with Harriet Bernstein Y-82
Islas, Arturo 1938-1991 .... DLB-122
Ivanišević, Drago 1907-1981............ DLB-181
Ivers, M. J., and Company DLB-49
Iwano, Hōmei 1873-1920 .... DLB-180
Iyayi, Festus 1947- DLB-157
Izumi, Kyōka 1873-1939................ DLB-180

J

Jackmon, Marvin E. (see Marvin X)
Jacks, L. P. 1860-1955 .... DLB-135
Jackson, Angela 1951- DLB-41

Jackson, Helen Hunt
   1830-1885 .... DLB-42, 47, 186, 189
Jackson, Holbrook 1874-1948 .... DLB-98
Jackson, Laura Riding 1901-1991 .... DLB-48
Jackson, Shirley 1919-1965.............. DLB-6
Jacob, Naomi 1884?-1964.............. DLB-191
Jacob, Piers Anthony Dillingham (see Anthony,
   Piers)
Jacobi, Friedrich Heinrich 1743-1819 ..... DLB-94
Jacobi, Johann Georg 1740-1841 .... DLB-97
Jacobs, Joseph 1854-1916 .... DLB-141
Jacobs, W. W. 1863-1943.............. DLB-135
Jacobs, George W., and Company DLB-49
Jacobson, Dan 1929- DLB-14
Jaggard, William [publishing house]......DLB-170
Jahier, Piero 1884-1966 .... DLB-114
Jahnn, Hans Henny 1894-1959 ..... DLB-56, 124
Jakes, John 1932- Y-83
James, C. L. R. 1901-1989 .... DLB-125
James Dickey Tributes Y-97
James, George P. R. 1801-1860 .... DLB-116
James Gould Cozzens–A View from Afar Y-97
James Gould Cozzens Case Re-opened Y-97
James Gould Cozzens: How to Read Him Y-97
James, Henry
   1843-1916 .... DLB-12, 71, 74, 189; DS-13
James, John circa 1633-1729 .... DLB-24
The James Jones Society................. Y-92
James Laughlin Tributes.................. Y-97
James, M. R. 1862-1936 .... DLB-156, 201
James, Naomi 1949- DLB-204
James, P. D. 1920- DLB-87; DS-17
James, Will 1892-1942 .... DS-16
James Joyce Centenary: Dublin, 1982 .... Y-82
James Joyce Conference Y-85
James VI of Scotland, I of England
   1566-1625 .... DLB-151, 172
James, U. P. [publishing house] DLB-49
Jameson, Anna 1794-1860 .... DLB-99, 166
Jameson, Fredric 1934- DLB-67
Jameson, J. Franklin 1859-1937 .... DLB-17
Jameson, Storm 1891?-1986 .... DLB-36
Jančar, Drago 1948- DLB-181
Janés, Clara 1940- DLB-134
Janevski, Slavko 1920- DLB-181
Janvier, Thomas 1849-1913 .... DLB-202
Jaramillo, Cleofas M. 1878-1956 .... DLB-122
Jarman, Mark 1952- DLB-120
Jarrell, Randall 1914-1965 .... DLB-48, 52
Jarrold and Sons DLB-106
Jarry, Alfred 1873-1907................ DLB-192
Jarves, James Jackson 1818-1888 .... DLB-189
Jasmin, Claude 1930- DLB-60
Jay, John 1745-1829 .... DLB-31
Jefferies, Richard 1848-1887 .... DLB-98, 141

Jeffers, Lance 1919-1985................ DLB-41
Jeffers, Robinson 1887-1962 .... DLB-45
Jefferson, Thomas 1743-1826....... DLB-31, 183
Jelinek, Elfriede 1946- DLB-85
Jellicoe, Ann 1927- DLB-13
Jenkins, Elizabeth 1905- DLB-155
Jenkins, Robin 1912- DLB-14
Jenkins, William Fitzgerald (see Leinster, Murray)
Jenkins, Herbert, Limited DLB-112
Jennings, Elizabeth 1926- DLB-27
Jens, Walter 1923- DLB-69
Jensen, Merrill 1905-1980................DLB-17
Jephson, Robert 1736-1803............. DLB-89
Jerome, Jerome K. 1859-1927..... DLB-10, 34, 135
Jerome, Judson 1927-1991 .... DLB-105
Jerrold, Douglas 1803-1857 .... DLB-158, 159
Jesse, F. Tennyson 1888-1958 .... DLB-77
Jewett, Sarah Orne 1849-1909 ....DLB-12, 74
Jewett, John P., and Company DLB-49
The Jewish Publication Society.......... DLB-49
Jewitt, John Rodgers 1783-1821 .... DLB-99
Jewsbury, Geraldine 1812-1880 .... DLB-21
Jewsbury, Maria Jane 1800-1833 .... DLB-199
Jhabvala, Ruth Prawer 1927- DLB-139, 194
Jiménez, Juan Ramón 1881-1958 .... DLB-134
Joans, Ted 1928- DLB-16, 41
Jōha 1525-1602..................... DLB-203
John, Eugenie (see Marlitt, E.)
John of Dumbleton
   circa 1310-circa 1349 .... DLB-115
John Edward Bruce: Three Documents ... DLB-50
John O'Hara's Pottsville Journalism......... Y-88
John Steinbeck Research Center........... Y-85
John Updike on the Internet.............. Y-97
John Webster: The Melbourne
   Manuscript...................... Y-86
Johns, Captain W. E. 1893-1968 .... DLB-160
Johnson, B. S. 1933-1973 .... DLB-14, 40
Johnson, Charles 1679-1748 .... DLB-84
Johnson, Charles R. 1948- DLB-33
Johnson, Charles S. 1893-1956....... DLB-51, 91
Johnson, Denis 1949- DLB-120
Johnson, Diane 1934- Y-80
Johnson, Edgar 1901- DLB-103
Johnson, Edward 1598-1672............ DLB-24
Johnson E. Pauline (Tekahionwake)
   1861-1913 ....DLB-175
Johnson, Fenton 1888-1958 .... DLB-45, 50
Johnson, Georgia Douglas 1886-1966 .... DLB-51
Johnson, Gerald W. 1890-1980 .... DLB-29
Johnson, Helene 1907- DLB-51
Johnson, James Weldon 1871-1938 ...... DLB-51
Johnson, John H. 1918- DLB-137
Johnson, Linton Kwesi 1952- DLB-157
Johnson, Lionel 1867-1902 .... DLB-19

Johnson, Nunnally 1897-1977................DLB-26
Johnson, Owen 1878-1952..................Y-87
Johnson, Pamela Hansford 1912-........DLB-15
Johnson, Pauline 1861-1913................DLB-92
Johnson, Ronald 1935-.....................DLB-169
Johnson, Samuel 1696-1772................DLB-24
Johnson, Samuel
 1709-1784............DLB-39, 95, 104, 142
Johnson, Samuel 1822-1882................DLB-1
Johnson, Susanna 1730-1810..............DLB-200
Johnson, Uwe 1934-1984..................DLB-75
Johnson, Benjamin [publishing house]....DLB-49
Johnson, Benjamin, Jacob, and
 Robert [publishing house]..............DLB-49
Johnson, Jacob, and Company.............DLB-49
Johnson, Joseph [publishing house]......DLB-154
Johnston, Annie Fellows 1863-1931.......DLB-42
Johnston, David Claypole 1798?-1865....DLB-188
Johnston, Basil H. 1929-...................DLB-60
Johnston, Denis 1901-1984.................DLB-10
Johnston, Ellen 1835-1873..................DLB-199
Johnston, George 1913-....................DLB-88
Johnston, Sir Harry 1858-1927.............DLB-174
Johnston, Jennifer 1930-....................DLB-14
Johnston, Mary 1870-1936.................DLB-9
Johnston, Richard Malcolm 1822-1898....DLB-74
Johnstone, Charles 1719?-1800?..........DLB-39
Johst, Hanns 1890-1978....................DLB-124
Jolas, Eugene 1894-1952................DLB-4, 45
Jones, Alice C. 1853-1933..................DLB-92
Jones, Charles C., Jr. 1831-1893............DLB-30
Jones, D. G. 1929-..........................DLB-53
Jones, David 1895-1974................DLB-20, 100
Jones, Diana Wynne 1934-.................DLB-161
Jones, Ebenezer 1820-1860.................DLB-32
Jones, Ernest 1819-1868....................DLB-32
Jones, Gayl 1949-...........................DLB-33
Jones, George 1800-1870...................DLB-183
Jones, Glyn 1905-...........................DLB-15
Jones, Gwyn 1907-.....................DLB-15, 139
Jones, Henry Arthur 1851-1929............DLB-10
Jones, Hugh circa 1692-1760...............DLB-24
Jones, James 1921-1977...........DLB-2, 143; DS-17
Jones, Jenkin Lloyd 1911-...................DLB-127
Jones, John Beauchamp 1810-1866........DLB-202
Jones, LeRoi (see Baraka, Amiri)
Jones, Lewis 1897-1939......................DLB-15
Jones, Madison 1925-.......................DLB-152
Jones, Major Joseph (see Thompson, William
 Tappan)
Jones, Preston 1936-1979....................DLB-7
Jones, Rodney 1950-........................DLB-120
Jones, Sir William 1746-1794................DLB-109
Jones, William Alfred 1817-1900............DLB-59
Jones's Publishing House....................DLB-49

Jong, Erica 1942-...............DLB-2, 5, 28, 152
Jonke, Gert F. 1946-........................DLB-85
Jonson, Ben 1572?-1637.................DLB-62, 121
Jordan, June 1936-..........................DLB-38
Joseph, Jenny 1932-.........................DLB-40
Joseph, Michael, Limited....................DLB-112
Josephson, Matthew 1899-1978.............DLB-4
Josephus, Flavius 37-100....................DLB-176
Josiah Allen's Wife (see Holley, Marietta)
Josipovici, Gabriel 1940-....................DLB-14
Josselyn, John ?-1675........................DLB-24
Joudry, Patricia 1921-.......................DLB-88
Jovine, Giuseppe 1922-......................DLB-128
Joyaux, Philippe (see Sollers, Philippe)
Joyce, Adrien (see Eastman, Carol)
A Joyce (Con)Text: Danis Rose and the Remaking of
 Ulysses..................................Y-97
Joyce, James 1882-1941.........DLB-10, 19, 36, 162
Judd, Sylvester 1813-1853....................DLB-1
Judd, Orange, Publishing Company.........DLB-49
Judith circa 930............................DLB-146
Julian of Norwich 1342-circa 1420.........DLB-1146
Julian Symons at Eighty......................Y-92
June, Jennie (see Croly, Jane Cunningham)
Jung, Franz 1888-1963......................DLB-118
Jünger, Ernst 1895-..........................DLB-56
Der jüngere Titurel circa 1275............DLB-138
Jung-Stilling, Johann Heinrich
 1740-1817................................DLB-94
Justice, Donald 1925-.......................Y-83
The Juvenile Library (see Godwin, M. J., and
 Company)

K

Kacew, Romain (see Gary, Romain)
Kafka, Franz 1883-1924.....................DLB-81
Kahn, Roger 1927-.........................DLB-171
Kaikō Takeshi 1939-1989....................DLB-182
Kaiser, Georg 1878-1945....................DLB-124
Kaiserchronik circca 1147..................DLB-148
Kaleb, Vjekoslav 1905-......................DLB-181
Kalechofsky, Roberta 1931-................DLB-28
Kaler, James Otis 1848-1912................DLB-12
Kames, Henry Home, Lord
 1696-1782..........................DLB-31, 104
Kamo no Chōmei (Kamo no Nagaakira)
 1153 or 1155-1216.....................DLB-203
Kamo no Nagaakira (see Kamo no Chōmei)
Kandel, Lenore 1932-......................DLB-16
Kanin, Garson 1912-........................DLB-7
Kant, Hermann 1926-.......................DLB-75
Kant, Immanuel 1724-1804..................DLB-94
Kantemir, Antiokh Dmitrievich
 1708-1744.............................DLB-150
Kantor, Mackinlay 1904-1977............DLB-9, 102
Kanze Kōjirō Nobumitsu 1435-1516......DLB-203

Kanze Motokiyo (see Zeimi)
Kaplan, Fred 1937-.........................DLB-111
Kaplan, Johanna 1942-.....................DLB-28
Kaplan, Justin 1925-........................DLB-111
Kapnist, Vasilii Vasilevich 1758?-1823...DLB-150
Karadžić, Vuk Stefanović 1787-1864.....DLB-147
Karamzin, Nikolai Mikhailovich
 1766-1826.............................DLB-150
Karsch, Anna Louisa 1722-1791...........DLB-97
Kasack, Hermann 1896-1966..............DLB-69
Kasai, Zenzō 1887-1927....................DLB-180
Kaschnitz, Marie Luise 1901-1974........DLB-69
Kaštelan, Jure 1919-1990..................DLB-147
Kästner, Erich 1899-1974..................DLB-56
Katenin, Pavel Aleksandrovich
 1792-1853............................DLB-205
Kattan, Naim 1928-........................DLB-53
Katz, Steve 1935-...........................Y-83
Kauffman, Janet 1945-.....................Y-86
Kauffmann, Samuel 1898-1971............DLB-127
Kaufman, Bob 1925-...................DLB-16, 41
Kaufman, George S. 1889-1961............DLB-7
Kavanagh, P. J. 1931-......................DLB-40
Kavanagh, Patrick 1904-1967..........DLB-15, 20
Kawabata, Yasunari 1899-1972...........DLB-180
Kaye-Smith, Sheila 1887-1956.............DLB-36
Kazin, Alfred 1915-........................DLB-67
Keane, John B. 1928-......................DLB-13
Keary, Annie 1825-1879...................DLB-163
Keating, H. R. F. 1926-....................DLB-87
Keats, Ezra Jack 1916-1983................DLB-61
Keats, John 1795-1821..................DLB-96, 110
Keble, John 1792-1866..................DLB-32, 55
Keeble, John 1944-.........................Y-83
Keeffe, Barrie 1945-........................DLB-13
Keeley, James 1867-1934...................DLB-25
W. B. Keen, Cooke and Company........DLB-49
Keillor, Garrison 1942-.....................Y-87
Keith, Marian 1874?-1961..................DLB-92
Keller, Gary D. 1943-......................DLB-82
Keller, Gottfried 1819-1890................DLB-129
Kelley, Edith Summers 1884-1956........DLB-9
Kelley, William Melvin 1937-..............DLB-33
Kellogg, Ansel Nash 1832-1886............DLB-23
Kellogg, Steven 1941-......................DLB-61
Kelly, George 1887-1974...................DLB-7
Kelly, Hugh 1739-1777.....................DLB-89
Kelly, Robert 1935-.................DLB-5, 130, 165
Kelly, Piet and Company...................DLB-49
Kelman, James 1946-......................DLB-194
Kelmscott Press............................DLB-112
Kemble, E. W. 1861-1933..................DLB-188
Kemble, Fanny 1809-1893.................DLB-32
Kemelman, Harry 1908-...................DLB-28
Kempe, Margery circa 1373-1438........DLB-146

Cumulative Index

Kempner, Friederike 1836-1904 .... DLB-129
Kempowski, Walter 1929- DLB-75
Kendall, Claude [publishing company].... DLB-46
Kendell, George 1809-1867 .... DLB-43
Kenedy, P. J., and Sons................. DLB-49
Kenkō circa 1283-circa 1352........... DLB-203
Kennan, George 1845-1924 .... DLB-189
Kennedy, Adrienne 1931- DLB-38
Kennedy, John Pendleton 1795-1870 ...... DLB-3
Kennedy, Leo 1907- DLB-88
Kennedy, Margaret 1896-1967 .... DLB-36
Kennedy, Patrick 1801-1873........... DLB-159
Kennedy, Richard S. 1920- DLB-111
Kennedy, William 1928- DLB-143; Y-85
Kennedy, X. J. 1929- DLB-5
Kennelly, Brendan 1936- DLB-40
Kenner, Hugh 1923- DLB-67
Kennerley, Mitchell [publishing house] ... DLB-46
Kenneth Dale McCormick Tributes......... Y-97
Kenny, Maurice 1929- DLB-175
Kent, Frank R. 1877-1958.............. DLB-29
Kenyon, Jane 1947- DLB-120
Keough, Hugh Edmund 1864-1912 ......DLB-171
Keppler and Schwartzmann DLB-49
Ker, N. R. 1908-1982................. DLB-201
Kerlan, Irvin 1912-1963 .... DLB-187
Kern, Jerome 1885-1945................ DLB-187
Kerner, Justinus 1776-1862............. DLB-90
Kerouac, Jack 1922-1969 .... DLB-2, 16; DS-3
The Jack Kerouac Revival Y-95
Kerouac, Jan 1952- DLB-16
Kerr, Orpheus C. (see Newell, Robert Henry)
Kerr, Charles H., and Company DLB-49
Kesey, Ken 1935- DLB-2, 16
Kessel, Joseph 1898-1979 .... DLB-72
Kessel, Martin 1901- DLB-56
Kesten, Hermann 1900- DLB-56
Keun, Irmgard 1905-1982 .... DLB-69
Key and Biddle...................... DLB-49
Keynes, Sir Geoffrey 1887-1982 .... DLB-201
Keynes, John Maynard 1883-1946........DS-10
Keyserling, Eduard von 1855-1918 ...... DLB-66
Khan, Ismith 1925- DLB-125
Khaytov, Nikolay 1919- DLB-181
Khemnitser, Ivan Ivanovich
   1745-1784..................... DLB-150
Kheraskov, Mikhail Matveevich
   1733-1807..................... DLB-150
Khomiakov, Aleksei Stepanovich
   1804-1860 .... DLB-205
Khristov, Boris 1945- DLB-181
Khvostov, Dmitrii Ivanovich
   1757-1835..................... DLB-150
Kidd, Adam 1802?-1831............... DLB-99
Kidd, William [publishing house]....... DLB-106

Kidder, Tracy 1945- DLB-185
Kiely, Benedict 1919- DLB-15
Kieran, John 1892-1981 ....DLB-171
Kiggins and Kellogg DLB-49
Kiley, Jed 1889-1962.................. DLB-4
Kilgore, Bernard 1908-1967 .... DLB-127
Killens, John Oliver 1916- DLB-33
Killigrew, Anne 1660-1685........... DLB-131
Killigrew, Thomas 1612-1683 .... DLB-58
Kilmer, Joyce 1886-1918............. DLB-45
Kilwardby, Robert circa 1215-1279 ..... DLB-115
Kimball, Richard Burleigh 1816-1892 ... DLB-202
Kincaid, Jamaica 1949- DLB-157
King, Charles 1844-1933 .... DLB-186
King, Clarence 1842-1901 .... DLB-12
King, Florence 1936 .... Y-85
King, Francis 1923- DLB-15, 139
King, Grace 1852-1932...............DLB-12, 78
King, Harriet Hamilton 1840-1920...... DLB-199
King, Henry 1592-1669 .... DLB-126
King, Stephen 1947- DLB-143; Y-80
King, Thomas 1943- DLB-175
King, Woodie, Jr. 1937- DLB-38
King, Solomon [publishing house] DLB-49
Kinglake, Alexander William
   1809-1891 .... DLB-55, 166
Kingsley, Charles
   1819-1875......... DLB-21, 32, 163, 178, 190
Kingsley, Mary Henrietta 1862-1900 .....DLB-174
Kingsley, Henry 1830-1876 .... DLB-21
Kingsley, Sidney 1906- DLB-7
Kingsmill, Hugh 1889-1949 .... DLB-149
Kingston, Maxine Hong 1940- ...DLB-173; Y-80
Kingston, William Henry Giles
   1814-1880 .... DLB-163
Kinnan, Mary Lewis 1763-1848 .... DLB-200
Kinnell, Galway 1927- DLB-5; Y-87
Kinsella, Thomas 1928- DLB-27
Kipling, Rudyard
   1865-1936 ....DLB-19, 34, 141, 156
Kipphardt, Heinar 1922-1982.......... DLB-124
Kirby, William 1817-1906.............. DLB-99
Kircher, Athanasius 1602-1680......... DLB-164
Kireevsky, Ivan Vasil'evich
   1806-1856 .... DLB-198
Kireevsky, Petr Vasil'evich
   1808-1856 .... DLB-205
Kirk, John Foster 1824-1904 .... DLB-79
Kirkconnell, Watson 1895-1977 .... DLB-68
Kirkland, Caroline M.
   1801-1864 ....DLB-3, 73, 74; DS-13
Kirkland, Joseph 1830-1893 .... DLB-12
Kirkman, Francis [publishing company] DLB-170
Kirkpatrick, Clayton 1915- DLB-127
Kirkup, James 1918- DLB-27
Kirouac, Conrad (see Marie-Victorin, Frère)

Kirsch, Sarah 1935- DLB-75
Kirst, Hans Hellmut 1914-1989 .... DLB-69
Kiš, Danilo 1935-1989 .... DLB-181
Kita Morio 1927- DLB-182
Kitcat, Mabel Greenhow 1859-1922..... DLB-135
Kitchin, C. H. B. 1895-1967............ DLB-77
Kiukhel'beker, Vil'gel'm Karlovich
   1797-1846..................... DLB-205
Kizer, Carolyn 1925- DLB-5, 169
Klabund 1890-1928 .... DLB-66
Klaj, Johann 1616-1656 .... DLB-164
Klappert, Peter 1942- DLB-5
Klass, Philip (see Tenn, William)
Klein, A. M. 1909-1972 .... DLB-68
Kleist, Ewald von 1715-1759........... DLB-97
Kleist, Heinrich von 1777-1811........ DLB-90
Klinger, Friedrich Maximilian
   1752-1831..................... DLB-94
Klopstock, Friedrich Gottlieb
   1724-1803..................... DLB-97
Klopstock, Meta 1728-1758............ DLB-97
Kluge, Alexander 1932- DLB-75
Knapp, Joseph Palmer 1864-1951...... DLB-91
Knapp, Samuel Lorenzo 1783-1838 ...... DLB-59
Knapton, J. J. and P. [publishing house].. DLB-154
Kniazhnin, Iakov Borisovich
   1740-1791..................... DLB-150
Knickerbocker, Diedrich (see Irving, Washington)
Knigge, Adolph Franz Friedrich Ludwig,
   Freiherr von 1752-1796 .... DLB-94
Knight, Damon 1922- DLB-8
Knight, Etheridge 1931-1992 .... DLB-41
Knight, John S. 1894-1981 .... DLB-29
Knight, Sarah Kemble 1666-1727 .... DLB-24, 200
Knight, Charles, and Company DLB-106
Knight-Bruce, G. W. H. 1852-1896 ......DLB-174
Knister, Raymond 1899-1932........... DLB-68
Knoblock, Edward 1874-1945 .... DLB-10
Knopf, Alfred A. 1892-1984.............. Y-84
Knopf, Alfred A. [publishing house]...... DLB-46
Knorr von Rosenroth, Christian
   1636-1689 .... DLB-168
"Knots into Webs: Some Autobiographical
   Sources," by Dabney Stuart........ DLB-105
Knowles, John 1926- DLB-6
Knox, Frank 1874-1944 .... DLB-29
Knox, John circa 1514-1572 .... DLB-132
Knox, John Armoy 1850-1906.......... DLB-23
Knox, Ronald Arbuthnott 1888-1957..... DLB-77
Knox, Thomas Wallace 1835-1896 ..... DLB-189
Kobayashi, Takiji 1903-1933 .... DLB-180
Kober, Arthur 1900-1975 .... DLB-11
Kocbek, Edvard 1904-1981 ....DLB-147
Koch, Howard 1902- DLB-26
Koch, Kenneth 1925- DLB-5
Kōda, Rohan 1867-1947 .... DLB-180

Koenigsberg, Moses 1879-1945 ....DLB-25
Koeppen, Wolfgang 1906- DLB-69
Koertge, Ronald 1940- DLB-105
Koestler, Arthur 1905-1983..............Y-83
Kohn, John S. Van E. 1906-1976 and
 Papantonio, Michael 1907-1978......DLB-187
Kokoschka, Oskar 1886-1980 ....DLB-124
Kolb, Annette 1870-1967 ....DLB-66
Kolbenheyer, Erwin Guido
 1878-1962 ....DLB-66, 124
Kolleritsch, Alfred 1931- DLB-85
Kolodny, Annette 1941- DLB-67
Kol'tsov, Aleksei Vasil'evich
 1809-1842 ....DLB-205
Komarov, Matvei circa 1730-1812.......DLB-150
Komroff, Manuel 1890-1974 ....DLB-4
Komunyakaa, Yusef 1947- DLB-120
Koneski, Blaže 1921-1993 ....DLB-181
Konigsburg, E. L. 1930- DLB-52
Konparu Zenchiku 1405-1468?........DLB-203
Konrad von Würzburg
 circa 1230-1287 ....DLB-138
Konstantinov, Aleko 1863-1897........DLB-147
Kooser, Ted 1939- DLB-105
Kopit, Arthur 1937- DLB-7
Kops, Bernard 1926?- DLB-13
Kornbluth, C. M. 1923-1958...........DLB-8
Körner, Theodor 1791-1813 ....DLB-90
Kornfeld, Paul 1889-1942 ....DLB-118
Kosinski, Jerzy 1933-1991 ....DLB-2; Y-82
Kosmač, Ciril 1910-1980 ....DLB-181
Kosovel, Srečko 1904-1926 ....DLB-147
Kostrov, Ermil Ivanovich 1755-1796 .....DLB-150
Kotzebue, August von 1761-1819.........DLB-94
Kotzwinkle, William 1938- DLB-173
Kovačić, Ante 1854-1889...............DLB-147
Kovič, Kajetan 1931- DLB-181
Kozlov, Ivan Ivanovich 1779-1840.......DLB-205
Kraf, Elaine 1946- Y-81
Kramer, Jane 1938- DLB-185
Kramer, Mark 1944- DLB-185
Kranjčević, Silvije Strahimir
 1865-1908 ....DLB-147
Krasna, Norman 1909-1984............DLB-26
Kraus, Hans Peter 1907-1988..........DLB-187
Kraus, Karl 1874-1936 ....DLB-118
Krauss, Ruth 1911-1993 ....DLB-52
Kreisel, Henry 1922- DLB-88
Kreuder, Ernst 1903-1972 ....DLB-69
Kreymborg, Alfred 1883-1966.........DLB-4, 54
Krieger, Murray 1923- DLB-67
Krim, Seymour 1922-1989..............DLB-16
Krleža, Miroslav 1893-1981............DLB-147
Krock, Arthur 1886-1974...............DLB-29
Kroetsch, Robert 1927- DLB-53
Krutch, Joseph Wood 1893-1970........DLB-63

Krylov, Ivan Andreevich 1769-1844 .....DLB-150
Kubin, Alfred 1877-1959 ....DLB-81
Kubrick, Stanley 1928- DLB-26
Kudrun circa 1230-1240 ....DLB-138
Kuffstein, Hans Ludwig von
 1582-1656.....................DLB-164
Kuhlmann, Quirinus 1651-1689 ....DLB-168
Kuhnau, Johann 1660-1722 ....DLB-168
Kukol'nik, Nestor Vasil'evich
 1809-1868.....................DLB-205
Kumin, Maxine 1925- DLB-5
Kunene, Mazisi 1930- DLB-117
Kunikida, Doppo 1869-1908...........DLB-180
Kunitz, Stanley 1905- DLB-48
Kunjufu, Johari M. (see Amini, Johari M.)
Kunnert, Gunter 1929- DLB-75
Kunze, Reiner 1933- DLB-75
Kupferberg, Tuli 1923- DLB-16
Kurahashi Yumiko 1935- DLB-182
Kureishi, Hanif 1954- DLB-194
Kürnberger, Ferdinand 1821-1879.......DLB-129
Kurz, Isolde 1853-1944 ....DLB-66
Kusenberg, Kurt 1904-1983............DLB-69
Kuttner, Henry 1915-1958..............DLB-8
Kyd, Thomas 1558-1594 ....DLB-62
Kyffin, Maurice circa 1560?-1598 ....DLB-136
Kyger, Joanne 1934- DLB-16
Kyne, Peter B. 1880-1957 ....DLB-78
Kyōgoku Tamekane 1254-1332 ....DLB-203

L

L. E. L. (see Landon, Letitia Elizabeth)
Laberge, Albert 1871-1960.............DLB-68
Laberge, Marie 1950- DLB-60
Labiche, Eugène 1815-1888...........DLB-192
La Capria, Raffaele 1922- DLB-196
Lacombe, Patrice (see Trullier-Lacombe,
 Joseph Patrice)
Lacretelle, Jacques de 1888-1985.........DLB-65
Lacy, Sam 1903- DLB-171
Ladd, Joseph Brown 1764-1786 ....DLB-37
La Farge, Oliver 1901-1963 ....DLB-9
Lafferty, R. A. 1914- DLB-8
La Flesche, Francis 1857-1932 ....DLB-175
Lagorio, Gina 1922- DLB-196
La Guma, Alex 1925-1985.............DLB-117
Lahaise, Guillaume (see Delahaye, Guy)
Lahontan, Louis-Armand de Lom d'Arce,
 Baron de 1666-1715?................DLB-99
Laing, Kojo 1946- DLB-157
Laird, Carobeth 1895- Y-82
Laird and Lee DLB-49
Lalić, Ivan V. 1931-1996 ....DLB-181
Lalić, Mihailo 1914-1992 ....DLB-181
Lalonde, Michèle 1937- DLB-60

Lamantia, Philip 1927- DLB-16
Lamb, Charles 1775-1834 ...... DLB-93, 107, 163
Lamb, Lady Caroline 1785-1828........DLB-116
Lamb, Mary 1764-1874 ....DLB-163
Lambert, Betty 1933-1983.............DLB-60
Lamming, George 1927- DLB-125
L'Amour, Louis 1908?- Y-80
Lampman, Archibald 1861-1899........DLB-92
Lamson, Wolffe and Company..........DLB-49
Lancer Books.......................DLB-46
Landesman, Jay 1919- and
 Landesman, Fran 1927- DLB-16
Landolfi, Tommaso 1908-1979 ....DLB-177
Landon, Letitia Elizabeth 1802-1838......DLB-96
Landor, Walter Savage 1775-1864.... DLB-93, 107
Landry, Napoléon-P. 1884-1956 ....DLB-92
Lane, Charles 1800-1870 ....DLB-1
Lane, Laurence W. 1890-1967 ....DLB-91
Lane, M. Travis 1934- DLB-60
Lane, Patrick 1939- DLB-53
Lane, Pinkie Gordon 1923- DLB-41
Lane, John, Company DLB-49
Laney, Al 1896-1988................ DLB-4, 171
Lang, Andrew 1844-1912 ...... DLB-98, 141, 184
Langevin, André 1927- DLB-60
Langgässer, Elisabeth 1899-1950 ....DLB-69
Langhorne, John 1735-1779 ....DLB-109
Langland, William
 circa 1330-circa 1400..............DLB-146
Langton, Anna 1804-1893.............DLB-99
Lanham, Edwin 1904-1979 ....DLB-4
Lanier, Sidney 1842-1881 ....DLB-64; DS-13
Lanyer, Aemilia 1569-1645 ....DLB-121
Lapointe, Gatien 1931-1983 ....DLB-88
Lapointe, Paul-Marie 1929- DLB-88
Lardner, John 1912-1960..............DLB-171
Lardner, Ring
 1885-1933 .... DLB-11, 25, 86, 171; DS-16
Lardner, Ring, Jr. 1915- DLB-26
Lardner 100: Ring Lardner
 Centennial Symposium...............Y-85
Larkin, Philip 1922-1985...............DLB-27
La Roche, Sophie von 1730-1807........DLB-94
La Rocque, Gilbert 1943-1984 ....DLB-60
Laroque de Roquebrune, Robert (see Roquebrune,
 Robert de)
Larrick, Nancy 1910- DLB-61
Larsen, Nella 1893-1964 ....DLB-51
Lasker-Schüler, Else 1869-1945......DLB-66, 124
Lasnier, Rina 1915- DLB-88
Lassalle, Ferdinand 1825-1864..........DLB-129
Latham, Robert 1912-1995 ....DLB-201
Lathrop, Dorothy P. 1891-1980 ....DLB-22
Lathrop, George Parsons 1851-1898......DLB-71
Lathrop, John, Jr. 1772-1820 ....DLB-37
Latimer, Hugh 1492?-1555 ....DLB-136

Cumulative Index

Latimore, Jewel Christine McLawler (see Amini, Johari M.)
Latymer, William 1498-1583 .... DLB-132
Laube, Heinrich 1806-1884 .... DLB-133
Laughlin, James 1914- DLB-48
Laumer, Keith 1925- DLB-8
Lauremberg, Johann 1590-1658 .... DLB-164
Laurence, Margaret 1926-1987 .... DLB-53
Laurentius von Schnüffis 1633-1702 .... DLB-168
Laurents, Arthur 1918- DLB-26
Laurie, Annie (see Black, Winifred)
Laut, Agnes Christiana 1871-1936 ...... DLB-92
Lauterbach, Ann 1942- DLB-193
Lavater, Johann Kaspar 1741-1801 ..... DLB-97
Lavin, Mary 1912- DLB-15
Law, John (see Harkness, Margaret)
Lawes, Henry 1596-1662 .... DLB-126
Lawless, Anthony (see MacDonald, Philip)
Lawrence, D. H. 1885-1930 ...... DLB-10, 19, 36, 98, 162, 195
Lawrence, David 1888-1973 .... DLB-29
Lawrence, Seymour 1926-1994 .... Y-94
Lawrence, T. E. 1888-1935 .... DLB-195
Lawson, John ?-1711 .... DLB-24
Lawson, Robert 1892-1957 .... DLB-22
Lawson, Victor F. 1850-1925 .... DLB-25
Layard, Sir Austen Henry 1817-1894 .... DLB-166
Layton, Irving 1912- DLB-88
LaZamon flourished circa 1200 .... DLB-146
Lazarević, Laza K. 1851-1890 .... DLB-147
Lazarus, George 1904-1997 .... DLB-201
Lazhechnikov, Ivan Ivanovich 1792-1869 .... DLB-198
Lea, Henry Charles 1825-1909 .... DLB-47
Lea, Sydney 1942- DLB-120
Lea, Tom 1907- DLB-6
Leacock, John 1729-1802 .... DLB-31
Leacock, Stephen 1869-1944 .... DLB-92
Lead, Jane Ward 1623-1704 .... DLB-131
Leadenhall Press DLB-106
Leapor, Mary 1722-1746 .... DLB-109
Lear, Edward 1812-1888 ...... DLB-32, 163, 166
Leary, Timothy 1920-1996 .... DLB-16
Leary, W. A., and Company DLB-49
Léautaud, Paul 1872-1956 .... DLB-65
Leavitt, David 1961- DLB-130
Leavitt and Allen DLB-49
Le Blond, Mrs. Aubrey 1861-1934 ..... DLB-174
le Carré, John 1931- DLB-87
Lécavelé, Roland (see Dorgeles, Roland)
Lechlitner, Ruth 1901- DLB-48
Leclerc, Félix 1914- DLB-60
Le Clézio, J. M. G. 1940- DLB-83
Lectures on Rhetoric and Belles Lettres (1783), by Hugh Blair [excerpts] DLB-31

Leder, Rudolf (see Hermlin, Stephan)
Lederer, Charles 1910-1976 .... DLB-26
Ledwidge, Francis 1887-1917 .... DLB-20
Lee, Dennis 1939- DLB-53
Lee, Don L. (see Madhubuti, Haki R.)
Lee, George W. 1894-1976 .... DLB-51
Lee, Harper 1926- DLB-6
Lee, Harriet (1757-1851) and Lee, Sophia (1750-1824) DLB-39
Lee, Laurie 1914- DLB-27
Lee, Li-Young 1957- DLB-165
Lee, Manfred B. (see Dannay, Frederic, and Manfred B. Lee)
Lee, Nathaniel circa 1645 - 1692 .... DLB-80
Lee, Sir Sidney 1859-1926 .... DLB-149, 184
Lee, Sir Sidney, "Principles of Biography," in *Elizabethan and Other Essays* DLB-149
Lee, Vernon 1856-1935 .... DLB-57, 153, 156, 174, 178
Lee and Shepard DLB-49
Le Fanu, Joseph Sheridan 1814-1873 .... DLB-21, 70, 159, 178
Leffland, Ella 1931- Y-84
le Fort, Gertrud von 1876-1971 .... DLB-66
Le Gallienne, Richard 1866-1947 .... DLB-4
Legaré, Hugh Swinton 1797-1843 ... DLB-3, 59, 73
Legaré, James M. 1823-1859 .... DLB-3
The Legends of the Saints and a Medieval Christian Worldview DLB-148
Léger, Antoine-J. 1880-1950 .... DLB-88
Le Guin, Ursula K. 1929- DLB-8, 52
Lehman, Ernest 1920- DLB-44
Lehmann, John 1907- DLB-27, 100
Lehmann, Rosamond 1901-1990 .... DLB-15
Lehmann, Wilhelm 1882-1968 .... DLB-56
Lehmann, John, Limited DLB-112
Leiber, Fritz 1910-1992 .... DLB-8
Leibniz, Gottfried Wilhelm 1646-1716 ... DLB-168
Leicester University Press DLB-112
Leigh, W. R. 1866-1955 .... DLB-188
Leinster, Murray 1896-1975 .... DLB-8
Leisewitz, Johann Anton 1752-1806 ..... DLB-94
Leitch, Maurice 1933- DLB-14
Leithauser, Brad 1943- DLB-120
Leland, Charles G. 1824-1903 .... DLB-11
Leland, John 1503?-1552 .... DLB-136
Lemay, Pamphile 1837-1918 .... DLB-99
Lemelin, Roger 1919- DLB-88
Lemercier, Louis-Jean-Népomucène 1771-1840 .... DLB-192
Lemon, Mark 1809-1870 .... DLB-163
Le Moine, James MacPherson 1825-1912 .... DLB-99
Le Moyne, Jean 1913- DLB-88
Lemperly, Paul 1858-1939 .... DLB-187
L'Engle, Madeleine 1918- DLB-52
Lennart, Isobel 1915-1971 .... DLB-44

Lennox, Charlotte 1729 or 1730-1804 .... DLB-39
Lenox, James 1800-1880 .... DLB-140
Lenski, Lois 1893-1974 .... DLB-22
Lenz, Hermann 1913- DLB-69
Lenz, J. M. R. 1751-1792 .... DLB-94
Lenz, Siegfried 1926- DLB-75
Leonard, Elmore 1925- DLB-173
Leonard, Hugh 1926- DLB-13
Leonard, William Ellery 1876-1944 ..... DLB-54
Leonowens, Anna 1834-1914 .... DLB-99, 166
LePan, Douglas 1914- DLB-88
Leprohon, Rosanna Eleanor 1829-1879 ... DLB-99
Le Queux, William 1864-1927 .... DLB-70
Lermontov, Mikhail Iur'evich 1814-1841 .... DLB-205
Lerner, Max 1902-1992 .... DLB-29
Lernet-Holenia, Alexander 1897-1976 ... DLB-85
Le Rossignol, James 1866-1969 .... DLB-92
Lescarbot, Marc circa 1570-1642 .... DLB-99
LeSeur, William Dawson 1840-1917 .... DLB-92
LeSieg, Theo. (see Geisel, Theodor Seuss)
Leslie, Doris before 1902-1982 .... DLB-191
Leslie, Eliza 1787-1858 .... DLB-202
Leslie, Frank 1821-1880 .... DLB-43, 79
Leslie, Frank, Publishing House DLB-49
Lesperance, John 1835?-1891 .... DLB-99
Lessing, Bruno 1870-1940 .... DLB-28
Lessing, Doris 1919- DLB-15, 139; Y-85
Lessing, Gotthold Ephraim 1729-1781 .... DLB-97
Lettau, Reinhard 1929- DLB-75
Letter from Japan Y-94
Letter from London Y-96
Letter to [Samuel] Richardson on *Clarissa* (1748), by Henry Fielding DLB-39
A Letter to the Editor of *The Irish Times* Y-97
Lever, Charles 1806-1872 .... DLB-21
Leverson, Ada 1862-1933 .... DLB-153
Levertov, Denise 1923- DLB-5, 165
Levi, Peter 1931- DLB-40
Levi, Primo 1919-1987 .... DLB-177
Levien, Sonya 1888-1960 .... DLB-44
Levin, Meyer 1905-1981 .... DLB-9, 28; Y-81
Levine, Norman 1923- DLB-88
Levine, Philip 1928- DLB-5
Levis, Larry 1946- DLB-120
Levy, Amy 1861-1889 .... DLB-156
Levy, Benn Wolfe 1900-1973 .... DLB-13; Y-81
Lewald, Fanny 1811-1889 .... DLB-129
Lewes, George Henry 1817-1878 .... DLB-55, 144
Lewis, Agnes Smith 1843-1926 .... DLB-174
Lewis, Alfred H. 1857-1914 .... DLB-25, 186
Lewis, Alun 1915-1944 .... DLB-20, 162
Lewis, C. Day (see Day Lewis, C.)

Lewis, C. S. 1898-1963 .... DLB-15, 100, 160
Lewis, Charles B. 1842-1924 .... DLB-11
Lewis, Henry Clay 1825-1850 .... DLB-3
Lewis, Janet 1899- Y-87
Lewis, Matthew Gregory
    1775-1818 .... DLB-39, 158, 178
Lewis, Meriwether 1774-1809 and
    Clark, William 1770-1838 ...... DLB-183, 186
Lewis, Norman 1908- DLB-204
Lewis, R. W. B. 1917- DLB-111
Lewis, Richard circa 1700-1734 .... DLB-24
Lewis, Sinclair 1885-1951 ...... DLB-9, 102; DS-1
Lewis, Wilmarth Sheldon 1895-1979 ..... DLB-140
Lewis, Wyndham 1882-1957 .... DLB-15
Lewisohn, Ludwig 1882-1955 ... DLB-4, 9, 28, 102
Leyendecker, J. C. 1874-1951 .... DLB-188
Lezama Lima, José 1910-1976 .... DLB-113
The Library of America DLB-46
The Licensing Act of 1737 .... DLB-84
Lichfield, Leonard I [publishing house] ... DLB-170
Lichtenberg, Georg Christoph
    1742-1799 .... DLB-94
The Liddle Collection Y-97
Lieb, Fred 1888-1980 .... DLB-171
Liebling, A. J. 1904-1963 .... DLB-4, 171
Lieutenant Murray (see Ballou, Maturin Murray)
Lighthall, William Douw 1857-1954 ...... DLB-92
Lilar, Françoise (see Mallet-Joris, Françoise)
Lillo, George 1691-1739 .... DLB-84
Lilly, J. K., Jr. 1893-1966 .... DLB-140
Lilly, Wait and Company DLB-49
Lily, William circa 1468-1522 .... DLB-132
Limited Editions Club DLB-46
Lincoln and Edmands DLB-49
Lindesay, Ethel Forence (see Richardson, Henry
    Handel)
Lindsay, Alexander William, Twenty-fifth Earl
    of Crawford 1812-1880 .... DLB-184
Lindsay, Sir David
    circa 1485-1555 .... DLB-132
Lindsay, Jack 1900- Y-84
Lindsay, Lady (Caroline Blanche Elizabeth Fitzroy
    Lindsay) 1844-1912 .... DLB-199
Lindsay, Vachel 1879-1931 .... DLB-54
Linebarger, Paul Myron Anthony (see Smith,
    Cordwainer)
Link, Arthur S. 1920- DLB-17
Linn, John Blair 1777-1804 .... DLB-37
Lins, Osman 1924-1978 .... DLB-145
Linton, Eliza Lynn 1822-1898 .... DLB-18
Linton, William James 1812-1897 .... DLB-32
Lintot, Barnaby Bernard
    [publishing house] DLB-170
Lion Books DLB-46
Lionni, Leo 1910- DLB-61
Lippard, George 1822-1854 .... DLB-202

Lippincott, Sara Jane Clarke
    1823-1904 .... DLB-43
Lippincott, J. B., Company DLB-49
Lippmann, Walter 1889-1974 .... DLB-29
Lipton, Lawrence 1898-1975 .... DLB-16
Liscow, Christian Ludwig 1701-1760 ..... DLB-97
Lish, Gordon 1934- DLB-130
Lispector, Clarice 1925-1977 .... DLB-113
The Literary Chronicle and Weekly Review
    1819-1828 .... DLB-110
Literary Documents: William Faulkner
    and the People-to-People Program Y-86
Literary Documents II: Library Journal
    Statements and Questionnaires from
    First Novelists Y-87
Literary Effects of World War II
    [British novel] DLB-15
Literary Prizes [British] DLB-15
Literary Research Archives: The Humanities
    Research Center, University of
    Texas Y-82
Literary Research Archives II: Berg
    Collection of English and American
    Literature of the New York Public
    Library Y-83
Literary Research Archives III:
    The Lilly Library Y-84
Literary Research Archives IV:
    The John Carter Brown Library Y-85
Literary Research Archives V:
    Kent State Special Collections Y-86
Literary Research Archives VI: The Modern
    Literary Manuscripts Collection in the
    Special Collections of the Washington
    University Libraries Y-87
Literary Research Archives VII:
    The University of Virginia
    Libraries Y-91
Literary Research Archives VIII:
    The Henry E. Huntington
    Library Y-92
"Literary Style" (1857), by William
    Forsyth [excerpt] DLB-57
Literatura Chicanesca: The View From
    Without DLB-82
Literature at Nurse, or Circulating Morals (1885),
    by George Moore DLB-18
Littell, Eliakim 1797-1870 .... DLB-79
Littell, Robert S. 1831-1896 .... DLB-79
Little, Brown and Company DLB-49
Little Magazines and Newspapers DS-15
The Little Review 1914-1929 .... DS-15
Littlewood, Joan 1914- DLB-13
Lively, Penelope 1933- DLB-14, 161
Liverpool University Press DLB-112
The Lives of the Poets DLB-142
Livesay, Dorothy 1909- DLB-68
Livesay, Florence Randal 1874-1953 ...... DLB-92
"Living in Ruin," by Gerald Stern DLB-105
Livings, Henry 1929- DLB-13
Livingston, Anne Howe 1763-1841 ... DLB-37, 200
Livingston, Myra Cohn 1926- DLB-61

Livingston, William 1723-1790 .... DLB-31
Livingstone, David 1813-1873 .... DLB-166
Liyong, Taban lo (see Taban lo Liyong)
Lizárraga, Sylvia S. 1925- DLB-82
Llewellyn, Richard 1906-1983 .... DLB-15
Lloyd, Edward [publishing house] DLB-106
Lobel, Arnold 1933- DLB-61
Lochridge, Betsy Hopkins (see Fancher, Betsy)
Locke, David Ross 1833-1888 .... DLB-11, 23
Locke, John 1632-1704 .... DLB-31, 101
Locke, Richard Adams 1800-1871 .... DLB-43
Locker-Lampson, Frederick
    1821-1895 .... DLB-35, 184
Lockhart, John Gibson
    1794-1854 .... DLB-110, 116 144
Lockridge, Ross, Jr. 1914-1948 .... DLB-143; Y-80
Locrine and Selimus DLB-62
Lodge, David 1935- DLB-14, 194
Lodge, George Cabot 1873-1909 .... DLB-54
Lodge, Henry Cabot 1850-1924 .... DLB-47
Lodge, Thomas 1558-1625 .... DLB-172
Loeb, Harold 1891-1974 .... DLB-4
Loeb, William 1905-1981 .... DLB-127
Lofting, Hugh 1886-1947 .... DLB-160
Logan, Deborah Norris 1761-1839 ...... DLB-200
Logan, James 1674-1751 .... DLB-24, 140
Logan, John 1923- DLB-5
Logan, Martha Daniell 1704?-1779 ...... DLB-200
Logan, William 1950- DLB-120
Logau, Friedrich von 1605-1655 .... DLB-164
Logue, Christopher 1926- DLB-27
Lohenstein, Daniel Casper von
    1635-1683 .... DLB-168
Lomonosov, Mikhail Vasil'evich
    1711-1765 .... DLB-150
London, Jack 1876-1916 .... DLB-8, 12, 78
The London Magazine 1820-1829 .... DLB-110
Long, Haniel 1888-1956 .... DLB-45
Long, Ray 1878-1935 .... DLB-137
Long, H., and Brother DLB-49
Longfellow, Henry Wadsworth
    1807-1882 .... DLB-1, 59
Longfellow, Samuel 1819-1892 .... DLB-1
Longford, Elizabeth 1906- DLB-155
Longinus circa first century DLB-176
Longley, Michael 1939- DLB-40
Longman, T. [publishing house] DLB-154
Longmans, Green and Company DLB-49
Longmore, George 1793?-1867 .... DLB-99
Longstreet, Augustus Baldwin
    1790-1870 .... DLB-3, 11, 74
Longworth, D. [publishing house] DLB-49
Lonsdale, Frederick 1881-1954 .... DLB-10
A Look at the Contemporary Black Theatre
    Movement DLB-38
Loos, Anita 1893-1981 .... DLB-11, 26; Y-81

Lopate, Phillip 1943- ... Y-80
López, Diana (see Isabella, Ríos)
Loranger, Jean-Aubert 1896-1942 ... DLB-92
Lorca, Federico García 1898-1936 ... DLB-108
Lord, John Keast 1818-1872 ... DLB-99
The Lord Chamberlain's Office and Stage Censorship in England ... DLB-10
Lorde, Audre 1934-1992 ... DLB-41
Lorimer, George Horace 1867-1939 ... DLB-91
Loring, A. K. [publishing house] ... DLB-49
Loring and Mussey ... DLB-46
Lossing, Benson J. 1813-1891 ... DLB-30
Lothar, Ernst 1890-1974 ... DLB-81
Lothrop, Harriet M. 1844-1924 ... DLB-42
Lothrop, D., and Company ... DLB-49
Loti, Pierre 1850-1923 ... DLB-123
Lotichius Secundus, Petrus 1528-1560 ... DLB-179
Lott, Emeline ?-? ... DLB-166
The Lounger, no. 20 (1785), by Henry Mackenzie ... DLB-39
Louisiana State University Press ... Y-97
Lounsbury, Thomas R. 1838-1915 ... DLB-71
Loüys, Pierre 1870-1925 ... DLB-123
Lovelace, Earl 1935- ... DLB-125
Lovelace, Richard 1618-1657 ... DLB-131
Lovell, Coryell and Company ... DLB-49
Lovell, John W., Company ... DLB-49
Lover, Samuel 1797-1868 ... DLB-159, 190
Lovesey, Peter 1936- ... DLB-87
Lovingood, Sut (see Harris, George Washington)
Low, Samuel 1765-? ... DLB-37
Lowell, Amy 1874-1925 ... DLB-54, 140
Lowell, James Russell 1819-1891 ... DLB-1, 11, 64, 79, 189
Lowell, Robert 1917-1977 ... DLB-5, 169
Lowenfels, Walter 1897-1976 ... DLB-4
Lowndes, Marie Belloc 1868-1947 ... DLB-70
Lowndes, William Thomas 1798-1843 ... DLB-184
Lownes, Humphrey [publishing house] ... DLB-170
Lowry, Lois 1937- ... DLB-52
Lowry, Malcolm 1909-1957 ... DLB-15
Lowther, Pat 1935-1975 ... DLB-53
Loy, Mina 1882-1966 ... DLB-4, 54
Lozeau, Albert 1878-1924 ... DLB-92
Lubbock, Percy 1879-1965 ... DLB-149
Lucas, E. V. 1868-1938 ... DLB-98, 149, 153
Lucas, Fielding, Jr. [publishing house] ... DLB-49
Luce, Henry R. 1898-1967 ... DLB-91
Luce, John W., and Company ... DLB-46
Lucian circa 120-180 ... DLB-176
Lucie-Smith, Edward 1933- ... DLB-40
Lucini, Gian Pietro 1867-1914 ... DLB-114
Luder, Peter circa 1415-1472 ... DLB-179
Ludlum, Robert 1927- ... Y-82
Ludus de Antichristo circa 1160 ... DLB-148

Ludvigson, Susan 1942- ... DLB-120
Ludwig, Jack 1922- ... DLB-60
Ludwig, Otto 1813-1865 ... DLB-129
Ludwigslied 881 or 882 ... DLB-148
Luera, Yolanda 1953- ... DLB-122
Luft, Lya 1938- ... DLB-145
Lugansky, Kazak Vladimir (see Dal', Vladimir Ivanovich)
Luke, Peter 1919- ... DLB-13
Lummis, Charles F. 1859-1928 ... DLB-186
Lupton, F. M., Company ... DLB-49
Lupus of Ferrières circa 805-circa 862 ... DLB-148
Lurie, Alison 1926- ... DLB-2
Luther, Martin 1483-1546 ... DLB-179
Luzi, Mario 1914- ... DLB-128
L'vov, Nikolai Aleksandrovich 1751-1803 ... DLB-150
Lyall, Gavin 1932- ... DLB-87
Lydgate, John circa 1370-1450 ... DLB-146
Lyly, John circa 1554-1606 ... DLB-62, 167
Lynch, Patricia 1898-1972 ... DLB-160
Lynch, Richard flourished 1596-1601 ... DLB-172
Lynd, Robert 1879-1949 ... DLB-98
Lyon, Matthew 1749-1822 ... DLB-43
Lysias circa 459 B.C.-circa 380 B.C. ... DLB-176
Lytle, Andrew 1902-1995 ... DLB-6; Y-95
Lytton, Edward (see Bulwer-Lytton, Edward)
Lytton, Edward Robert Bulwer 1831-1891 ... DLB-32

M

Maass, Joachim 1901-1972 ... DLB-69
Mabie, Hamilton Wright 1845-1916 ... DLB-71
Mac A'Ghobhainn, Iain (see Smith, Iain Crichton)
MacArthur, Charles 1895-1956 ... DLB-7, 25, 44
Macaulay, Catherine 1731-1791 ... DLB-104
Macaulay, David 1945- ... DLB-61
Macaulay, Rose 1881-1958 ... DLB-36
Macaulay, Thomas Babington 1800-1859 ... DLB-32, 55
Macaulay Company ... DLB-46
MacBeth, George 1932- ... DLB-40
Macbeth, Madge 1880-1965 ... DLB-92
MacCaig, Norman 1910- ... DLB-27
MacDiarmid, Hugh 1892-1978 ... DLB-20
MacDonald, Cynthia 1928- ... DLB-105
MacDonald, George 1824-1905 ... DLB-18, 163, 178
MacDonald, John D. 1916-1986 ... DLB-8; Y-86
MacDonald, Philip 1899?-1980 ... DLB-77
Macdonald, Ross (see Millar, Kenneth)
MacDonald, Wilson 1880-1967 ... DLB-92
Macdonald and Company (Publishers) ... DLB-112
MacEwen, Gwendolyn 1941- ... DLB-53
Macfadden, Bernarr 1868-1955 ... DLB-25, 91

MacGregor, John 1825-1892 ... DLB-166
MacGregor, Mary Esther (see Keith, Marian)
Machado, Antonio 1875-1939 ... DLB-108
Machado, Manuel 1874-1947 ... DLB-108
Machar, Agnes Maule 1837-1927 ... DLB-92
Machen, Arthur Llewelyn Jones 1863-1947 ... DLB-36, 156, 178
MacInnes, Colin 1914-1976 ... DLB-14
MacInnes, Helen 1907-1985 ... DLB-87
Mack, Maynard 1909- ... DLB-111
Mackall, Leonard L. 1879-1937 ... DLB-140
MacKaye, Percy 1875-1956 ... DLB-54
Macken, Walter 1915-1967 ... DLB-13
Mackenzie, Alexander 1763-1820 ... DLB-99
Mackenzie, Alexander Slidell 1803-1848 ... DLB-183
Mackenzie, Compton 1883-1972 ... DLB-34, 100
Mackenzie, Henry 1745-1831 ... DLB-39
Mackenzie, William 1758-1828 ... DLB-187
Mackey, Nathaniel 1947- ... DLB-169
Mackey, William Wellington 1937- ... DLB-38
Mackintosh, Elizabeth (see Tey, Josephine)
Mackintosh, Sir James 1765-1832 ... DLB-158
Maclaren, Ian (see Watson, John)
Macklin, Charles 1699-1797 ... DLB-89
MacLean, Katherine Anne 1925- ... DLB-8
MacLeish, Archibald 1892-1982 ... DLB-4, 7, 45; Y-82
MacLennan, Hugh 1907-1990 ... DLB-68
Macleod, Fiona (see Sharp, William)
MacLeod, Alistair 1936- ... DLB-60
Macleod, Norman 1906-1985 ... DLB-4
Mac Low, Jackson 1922- ... DLB-193
Macmillan and Company ... DLB-106
The Macmillan Company ... DLB-49
Macmillan's English Men of Letters, First Series (1878-1892) ... DLB-144
MacNamara, Brinsley 1890-1963 ... DLB-10
MacNeice, Louis 1907-1963 ... DLB-10, 20
MacPhail, Andrew 1864-1938 ... DLB-92
Macpherson, James 1736-1796 ... DLB-109
Macpherson, Jay 1931- ... DLB-53
Macpherson, Jeanie 1884-1946 ... DLB-44
Macrae Smith Company ... DLB-46
Macrone, John [publishing house] ... DLB-106
MacShane, Frank 1927- ... DLB-111
Macy-Masius ... DLB-46
Madden, David 1933- ... DLB-6
Madden, Sir Frederic 1801-1873 ... DLB-184
Maddow, Ben 1909-1992 ... DLB-44
Maddux, Rachel 1912-1983 ... Y-93
Madgett, Naomi Long 1923- ... DLB-76
Madhubuti, Haki R. 1942- ... DLB-5, 41; DS-8
Madison, James 1751-1836 ... DLB-37
Maeterlinck, Maurice 1862-1949 ... DLB-192

Magee, David 1905-1977.............DLB-187

Maginn, William 1794-1842.......DLB-110, 159

Mahan, Alfred Thayer 1840-1914....DLB-47

Maheux-Forcier, Louise 1929- DLB-60

Mafūẓ, Najīb 1911- Y-88

Mahin, John Lee 1902-1984...........DLB-44

Mahon, Derek 1941- DLB-40

Maikov, Vasilii Ivanovich
  1728-1778......................DLB-150

Mailer, Norman 1923-
  .... DLB-2, 16, 28, 185; Y-80, Y-83; DS-3

Maillart, Ella 1903-1997..............DLB-195

Maillet, Adrienne 1885-1963..........DLB-68

Maimonides, Moses 1138-1204.........DLB-115

Maillet, Antonine 1929- DLB-60

Maillu, David G. 1939- DLB-157

Main Selections of the Book-of-the-Month
  Club, 1926-1945 ....DLB-9

Main Trends in Twentieth-Century Book
  Clubs...........................DLB-46

Mainwaring, Daniel 1902-1977 ....DLB-44

Mair, Charles 1838-1927.............DLB-99

Mais, Roger 1905-1955 ....DLB-125

Major, Andre 1942- DLB-60

Major, Charles 1856-1913............DLB-202

Major, Clarence 1936- DLB-33

Major, Kevin 1949- DLB-60

Major Books DLB-46

Makemie, Francis circa 1658-1708.......DLB-24

The Making of a People, by
  J. M. Ritchie DLB-66

Maksimović, Desanka 1898-1993 ....DLB-147

Malamud, Bernard
  1914-1986 .... DLB-2, 28, 152; Y-80, Y-86

Malerba, Luigi 1927- DLB-196

Malet, Lucas 1852-1931...............DLB-153

Malleson, Lucy Beatrice (see Gilbert, Anthony)

Mallet-Joris, Françoise 1930- DLB-83

Mallock, W. H. 1849-1923 ....DLB-18, 57

Malone, Dumas 1892-1986 ....DLB-17

Malone, Edmond 1741-1812............DLB-142

Malory, Sir Thomas
  circa 1400-1410 - 1471..............DLB-146

Malraux, André 1901-1976 ....DLB-72

Malthus, Thomas Robert
  1766-1834 .... DLB-107, 158

Maltz, Albert 1908-1985 ....DLB-102

Malzberg, Barry N. 1939- DLB-8

Mamet, David 1947- DLB-7

Manaka, Matsemela 1956- DLB-157

Manchester University Press...........DLB-112

Mandel, Eli 1922- DLB-53

Mandeville, Bernard 1670-1733..........DLB-101

Mandeville, Sir John
  mid fourteenth century DLB-146

Mandiargues, André Pieyre de 1909- DLB-83

Manfred, Frederick 1912-1994...........DLB-6

Manfredi, Gianfranco 1948-...........DLB-196

Mangan, Sherry 1904-1961..............DLB-4

Manganelli, Giorgio 1922-1990 ....DLB-196

Mankiewicz, Herman 1897-1953.........DLB-26

Mankiewicz, Joseph L. 1909-1993........DLB-44

Mankowitz, Wolf 1924-................DLB-15

Manley, Delarivière 1672?-1724.......DLB-39, 80

Mann, Abby 1927- DLB-44

Mann, Heinrich 1871-1950 .... DLB-66, 118

Mann, Horace 1796-1859 ....DLB-1

Mann, Klaus 1906-1949................DLB-56

Mann, Thomas 1875-1955..............DLB-66

Mann, William D'Alton 1839-1920.......DLB-137

Mannin, Ethel 1900-1984 .... DLB-191, 195

Manning, Marie 1873?-1945 ....DLB-29

Manning and Loring DLB-49

Mannyng, Robert
  flourished 1303-1338...............DLB-146

Mano, D. Keith 1942- DLB-6

Manor Books.......................DLB-46

Mansfield, Katherine 1888-1923 ....DLB-162

Manuel, Niklaus circa 1484-1530 ....DLB-179

Manzini, Gianna 1896-1974.............DLB-177

Mapanje, Jack 1944- DLB-157

Maraini, Dacia 1936- DLB-196

March, William 1893-1954 ....DLB-9, 86

Marchand, Leslie A. 1900- DLB-103

Marchant, Bessie 1862-1941 ....DLB-160

Marchessault, Jovette 1938- DLB-60

Marcus, Frank 1928- DLB-13

Marden, Orison Swett 1850-1924........DLB-137

Marechera, Dambudzo 1952-1987........DLB-157

Marek, Richard, Books DLB-46

Mares, E. A. 1938- DLB-122

Mariani, Paul 1940- DLB-111

Marie-Victorin, Frère 1885-1944 ....DLB-92

Marin, Biagio 1891-1985...............DLB-128

Marincovi°, Ranko 1913- DLB-147

Marinetti, Filippo Tommaso
  1876-1944 ....DLB-114

Marion, Frances 1886-1973 ....DLB-44

Marius, Richard C. 1933- Y-85

The Mark Taper Forum DLB-7

Mark Twain on Perpetual Copyright Y-92

Markfield, Wallace 1926- DLB-2, 28

Markham, Edwin 1852-1940........DLB-54, 186

Markle, Fletcher 1921-1991 ....DLB-68; Y-91

Marlatt, Daphne 1942- DLB-60

Marlitt, E. 1825-1887.................DLB-129

Marlowe, Christopher 1564-1593........DLB-62

Marlyn, John 1912- DLB-88

Marmion, Shakerley 1603-1639..........DLB-58

Der Marner before 1230-circa 1287......DLB-138

Marnham, Patrick 1943- DLB-204

The *Marprelate Tracts* 1588-1589 ....DLB-132

Marquand, John P. 1893-1960........DLB-9, 102

Marqués, René 1919-1979 ....DLB-113

Marquis, Don 1878-1937 ....DLB-11, 25

Marriott, Anne 1913- DLB-68

Marryat, Frederick 1792-1848 ....DLB-21, 163

Marsh, George Perkins 1801-1882 .....DLB-1, 64

Marsh, James 1794-1842 ....DLB-1, 59

Marsh, Capen, Lyon and Webb DLB-49

Marsh, Ngaio 1899-1982...............DLB-77

Marshall, Edison 1894-1967 ....DLB-102

Marshall, Edward 1932- DLB-16

Marshall, Emma 1828-1899..............DLB-163

Marshall, James 1942-1992 ....DLB-61

Marshall, Joyce 1913- DLB-88

Marshall, Paule 1929- DLB-33, 157

Marshall, Tom 1938- DLB-60

Marsilius of Padua
  circa 1275-circa 1342...............DLB-115

Marson, Una 1905-1965 ....DLB-157

Marston, John 1576-1634............DLB-58, 172

Marston, Philip Bourke 1850-1887 ....DLB-35

Martens, Kurt 1870-1945 ....DLB-66

Martien, William S. [publishing house] DLB-49

Martin, Abe (see Hubbard, Kin)

Martin, Charles 1942- DLB-120

Martin, Claire 1914- DLB-60

Martin, Jay 1935- DLB-111

Martin, Johann (see Laurentius von Schnüffis)

Martin, Violet Florence (see Ross, Martin)

Martin du Gard, Roger 1881-1958 ....DLB-65

Martineau, Harriet 1802-1876
  .... DLB-21, 55, 159, 163, 166, 190

Martínez, Eliud 1935- DLB-122

Martínez, Max 1943- DLB-82

Martyn, Edward 1859-1923 ....DLB-10

Marvell, Andrew 1621-1678 ....DLB-131

Marvin X 1944- DLB-38

Marx, Karl 1818-1883.................DLB-129

Marzials, Theo 1850-1920..............DLB-35

Masefield, John 1878-1967... DLB-10, 19, 153, 160

Mason, A. E. W. 1865-1948 ....DLB-70

Mason, Bobbie Ann 1940- DLB-173; Y-87

Mason, William 1725-1797..............DLB-142

Mason Brothers......................DLB-49

Massey, Gerald 1828-1907 ....DLB-32

Massey, Linton R. 1900-1974 ....DLB-187

Massinger, Philip 1583-1640............DLB-58

Masson, David 1822-1907...............DLB-144

Masters, Edgar Lee 1868-1950 ....DLB-54

Mastronardi, Lucio 1930-1979.........DLB-177

Matevski, Mateja 1929- DLB-181

Mather, Cotton 1663-1728...... DLB-24, 30, 140

Mather, Increase 1639-1723.............DLB-24

Mather, Richard 1596-1669.............DLB-24

Matheson, Richard 1926- DLB-8, 44

Matheus, John F. 1887- DLB-51	McBride, Robert M., and Company DLB-46	McIlvanney, William 1936- DLB-14
Mathews, Cornelius 1817?-1889. . . . . . . DLB-3, 64	McCabe, Patrick 1955- DLB-194	McIlwraith, Jean Newton 1859-1938 . . . . . DLB-92
Mathews, John Joseph 1894-1979 . . . . .DLB-175	McCaffrey, Anne 1926- DLB-8	McIntyre, James 1827-1906 . . . . DLB-99
Mathews, Elkin [publishing house] DLB-112	McCarthy, Cormac 1933- DLB-6, 143	McIntyre, O. O. 1884-1938 . . . . DLB-25
Mathias, Roland 1915- DLB-27	McCarthy, Mary 1912-1989 . . . . .DLB-2; Y-81	McKay, Claude 1889-1948 . . . . . DLB-4, 45, 51, 117
Mathis, June 1892-1927 . . . . DLB-44	McCay, Winsor 1871-1934 . . . . DLB-22	The David McKay Company DLB-49
Mathis, Sharon Bell 1937- DLB-33	McClane, Albert Jules 1922-1991 . . . . . .DLB-171	McKean, William V. 1820-1903 . . . . DLB-23
Matković, Marijan 1915-1985 . . . . DLB-181	McClatchy, C. K. 1858-1936 . . . . DLB-25	McKenna, Stephen 1888-1967 . . . . .DLB-197
Matoš, Antun Gustav 1873-1914 . . . . DLB-147	McClellan, George Marion 1860-1934 . . . . DLB-50	The McKenzie Trust Y-96
Matsumoto Seichō 1909-1992 . . . . DLB-182	McCloskey, Robert 1914- DLB-22	McKerrow, R. B. 1872-1940 . . . . DLB-201
The Matter of England 1240-1400 . . . . . . DLB-146	McClung, Nellie Letitia 1873-1951 . . . . . . DLB-92	McKinley, Robin 1952- DLB-52
The Matter of Rome early twelfth to late fifteenth century DLB-146	McClure, Joanna 1930- DLB-16	McLachlan, Alexander 1818-1896 . . . . DLB-99
	McClure, Michael 1932- DLB-16	McLaren, Floris Clark 1904-1978 . . . . DLB-68
Matthews, Brander 1852-1929 . . . . .DLB-71, 78; DS-13	McClure, Phillips and Company DLB-46	McLaverty, Michael 1907- DLB-15
Matthews, Jack 1925- DLB-6	McClure, S. S. 1857-1949 . . . . DLB-91	McLean, John R. 1848-1916 . . . . DLB-23
Matthews, William 1942- DLB-5	McClurg, A. C., and Company DLB-49	McLean, William L. 1852-1931 . . . . DLB-25
Matthiessen, F. O. 1902-1950 . . . . DLB-63	McCluskey, John A., Jr. 1944- DLB-33	McLennan, William 1856-1904 . . . . DLB-92
Maturin, Charles Robert 1780-1824 . . . . . .DLB-178	McCollum, Michael A. 1946 . . . . Y-87	McLoughlin Brothers DLB-49
Matthiessen, Peter 1927- DLB-6, 173	McConnell, William C. 1917- DLB-88	McLuhan, Marshall 1911-1980 . . . . DLB-88
Maugham, W. Somerset 1874-1965 . . . . . . DLB-10, 36, 77, 100, 162, 195	McCord, David 1897- DLB-61	McMaster, John Bach 1852-1932 . . . . DLB-47
	McCorkle, Jill 1958- Y-87	McMurtry, Larry 1936- . DLB-2, 143; Y-80, Y-87
Maupassant, Guy de 1850-1893 . . . . DLB-123	McCorkle, Samuel Eusebius 1746-1811 . . . DLB-37	McNally, Terrence 1939- DLB-7
Mauriac, Claude 1914- DLB-83	McCormick, Anne O'Hare 1880-1954 . . . . DLB-29	McNeil, Florence 1937- DLB-60
Mauriac, François 1885-1970 . . . . DLB-65	McCormick, Robert R. 1880-1955 . . . . . . DLB-29	McNeile, Herman Cyril 1888-1937 . . . . . . DLB-77
Maurice, Frederick Denison 1805-1872 . . . DLB-55	McCourt, Edward 1907-1972 . . . . DLB-88	McNickle, D'Arcy 1904-1977 . . . . .DLB-175
Maurois, André 1885-1967 . . . . DLB-65	McCoy, Horace 1897-1955 . . . . DLB-9	McPhee, John 1931- DLB-185
Maury, James 1718-1769 . . . . DLB-31	McCrae, John 1872-1918 . . . . DLB-92	McPherson, James Alan 1943- DLB-38
Mavor, Elizabeth 1927- DLB-14	McCullagh, Joseph B. 1842-1896 . . . . DLB-23	McPherson, Sandra 1943- Y-86
Mavor, Osborne Henry (see Bridie, James)	McCullers, Carson 1917-1967 . . . . . .DLB-2, 7, 173	McWhirter, George 1939- DLB-60
Maxwell, Gavin 1914-1969 . . . . DLB-204	McCulloch, Thomas 1776-1843 . . . . DLB-99	McWilliams, Carey 1905-1980 . . . . .DLB-137
Maxwell, William 1908- Y-80	McDonald, Forrest 1927- DLB-17	Mead, L. T. 1844-1914 . . . . DLB-141
Maxwell, H. [publishing house] DLB-49	McDonald, Walter 1934- DLB-105, DS-9	Mead, Matthew 1924- DLB-40
Maxwell, John [publishing house] DLB-106	McDougall, Colin 1917-1984 . . . . DLB-68	Mead, Taylor ?- DLB-16
May, Elaine 1932- DLB-44	McDowell, Obolensky DLB-46	Meany, Tom 1903-1964 . . . . .DLB-171
May, Karl 1842-1912 . . . . DLB-129	McEwan, Ian 1948- DLB-14, 194	Mechthild von Magdeburg circa 1207-circa 1282 . . . . DLB-138
May, Thomas 1595 or 1596-1650 . . . . DLB-58	McFadden, David 1940- DLB-60	
Mayer, Bernadette 1945- DLB-165	McFall, Frances Elizabeth Clarke (see Grand, Sarah)	Medieval Travel Diaries DLB-203
Mayer, Mercer 1943- DLB-61		Medill, Joseph 1823-1899 . . . . DLB-43
Mayer, O. B. 1818-1891 . . . . DLB-3	McFarlane, Leslie 1902-1977 . . . . DLB-88	Medoff, Mark 1940- DLB-7
Mayes, Herbert R. 1900-1987 . . . . DLB-137	McFee, William 1881-1966 . . . . DLB-153	Meek, Alexander Beaufort 1814-1865 . . . . . DLB-3
Mayes, Wendell 1919-1992 . . . . DLB-26	McGahern, John 1934- DLB-14	Meeke, Mary ?-1816? DLB-116
Mayfield, Julian 1928-1984 . . . . DLB-33; Y-84	McGee, Thomas D'Arcy 1825-1868 . . . . . DLB-99	Meinke, Peter 1932- DLB-5
Mayhew, Henry 1812-1887 . . . . . DLB-18, 55, 190	McGeehan, W. O. 1879-1933 . . . . .DLB-25, 171	Mejia Vallejo, Manuel 1923- DLB-113
Mayhew, Jonathan 1720-1766 . . . . DLB-31	McGill, Ralph 1898-1969 . . . . DLB-29	Melanchthon, Philipp 1497-1560 . . . . .DLB-179
Mayne, Ethel Colburn 1865-1941 . . . . DLB-197	McGinley, Phyllis 1905-1978 . . . . DLB-11, 48	Melançon, Robert 1947- DLB-60
Mayne, Jasper 1604-1672 . . . . DLB-126	McGinniss, Joe 1942- DLB-185	Mell, Max 1882-1971 . . . . DLB-81, 124
Mayne, Seymour 1944- DLB-60	McGirt, James E. 1874-1930 . . . . DLB-50	Mellow, James R. 1926- DLB-111
Mayor, Flora Macdonald 1872-1932 . . . . . DLB-36	McGlashan and Gill DLB-106	Meltzer, David 1937- DLB-16
Mayrocker, Friederike 1924- DLB-85	McGough, Roger 1937- DLB-40	Meltzer, Milton 1915- DLB-61
Mazrui, Ali A. 1933- DLB-125	McGraw-Hill DLB-46	Melville, Elizabeth, Lady Culross circa 1585-1640 . . . . .DLB-172
Mažuranić, Ivan 1814-1890 . . . . DLB-147	McGuane, Thomas 1939- DLB-2; Y-80	
Mazursky, Paul 1930- DLB-44	McGuckian, Medbh 1950- DLB-40	Melville, Herman 1819-1891 . . . . .DLB-3, 74
McAlmon, Robert 1896-1956 . . . DLB-4, 45; DS-15	McGuffey, William Holmes 1800-1873 . . . DLB-42	Memoirs of Life and Literature (1920), by W. H. Mallock [excerpt] DLB-57
McArthur, Peter 1866-1924 . . . . DLB-92	McHenry, James 1785-1845 . . . . DLB-202	

Menander 342-341 B.C.-circa 292-291 B.C. DLB-176
Menantes (see Hunold, Christian Friedrich)
Mencke, Johann Burckhard 1674-1732 ....DLB-168
Mencken, H. L. 1880-1956 .... DLB-11, 29, 63, 137
Mencken and Nietzsche: An Unpublished Excerpt from H. L. Mencken's *My Life as Author and Editor* Y-93
Mendelssohn, Moses 1729-1786 ....DLB-97
Méndez M., Miguel 1930- DLB-82
Mens Rea (or Something) Y-97
The Mercantile Library of New York Y-96
Mercer, Cecil William (see Yates, Dornford)
Mercer, David 1928-1980 ....DLB-13
Mercer, John 1704-1768 ....DLB-31
Meredith, George 1828-1909 .... DLB-18, 35, 57, 159
Meredith, Louisa Anne 1812-1895 ......DLB-166
Meredith, Owen (see Lytton, Edward Robert Bulwer)
Meredith, William 1919- DLB-5
Mergerle, Johann Ulrich (see Abraham à Sancta Clara)
Mérimée, Prosper 1803-1870 .... DLB-119, 192
Merivale, John Herman 1779-1844 ....DLB-96
Meriwether, Louise 1923- DLB-33
Merlin Press DLB-112
Merriam, Eve 1916-1992 ....DLB-61
The Merriam Company DLB-49
Merrill, James 1926-1995 .... DLB-5, 165; Y-85
Merrill and Baker DLB-49
The Mershon Company DLB-49
Merton, Thomas 1915-1968 .... DLB-48; Y-81
Merwin, W. S. 1927- DLB-5, 169
Messner, Julian [publishing house] DLB-46
Metcalf, J. [publishing house] DLB-49
Metcalf, John 1938- DLB-60
The Methodist Book Concern DLB-49
Methuen and Company DLB-112
Mew, Charlotte 1869-1928 .... DLB-19, 135
Mewshaw, Michael 1943- Y-80
Meyer, Conrad Ferdinand 1825-1898 ....DLB-129
Meyer, E. Y. 1946- DLB-75
Meyer, Eugene 1875-1959 ....DLB-29
Meyer, Michael 1921- DLB-155
Meyers, Jeffrey 1939- DLB-111
Meynell, Alice 1847-1922 ....DLB-19, 98
Meynell, Viola 1885-1956 ....DLB-153
Meyrink, Gustav 1868-1932 ....DLB-81
Michael M. Rea and the Rea Award for the Short Story Y-97
Michaels, Leonard 1933- DLB-130
Micheaux, Oscar 1884-1951 ....DLB-50
Michel of Northgate, Dan circa 1265-circa 1340 ....DLB-146

Micheline, Jack 1929- DLB-16
Michener, James A. 1907?- DLB-6
Micklejohn, George circa 1717-1818 ....DLB-31
Middle English Literature: An Introduction DLB-146
The Middle English Lyric DLB-146
Middle Hill Press DLB-106
Middleton, Christopher 1926- DLB-40
Middleton, Richard 1882-1911 ....DLB-156
Middleton, Stanley 1919- DLB-14
Middleton, Thomas 1580-1627 ....DLB-58
Miegel, Agnes 1879-1964 ....DLB-56
Mihailović, Dragoslav 1930- DLB-181
Mihalić, Slavko 1928- DLB-181
Miles, Josephine 1911-1985 ....DLB-48
Miliković, Branko 1934-1961 ....DLB-181
Milius, John 1944- DLB-44
Mill, James 1773-1836 .... DLB-107, 158
Mill, John Stuart 1806-1873 .... DLB-55, 190
Millar, Kenneth 1915-1983 .... DLB-2; Y-83; DS-6
Millar, Andrew [publishing house] DLB-154
Millay, Edna St. Vincent 1892-1950 ......DLB-45
Miller, Arthur 1915- DLB-7
Miller, Caroline 1903-1992 ....DLB-9
Miller, Eugene Ethelbert 1950- DLB-41
Miller, Heather Ross 1939- DLB-120
Miller, Henry 1891-1980 .... DLB-4, 9; Y-80
Miller, Hugh 1802-1856 ....DLB-190
Miller, J. Hillis 1928- DLB-67
Miller, James [publishing house] DLB-49
Miller, Jason 1939- DLB-7
Miller, Joaquin 1839-1913 ....DLB-186
Miller, May 1899- DLB-41
Miller, Paul 1906-1991 ....DLB-127
Miller, Perry 1905-1963 .... DLB-17, 63
Miller, Sue 1943- DLB-143
Miller, Vassar 1924- DLB-105
Miller, Walter M., Jr. 1923- DLB-8
Miller, Webb 1892-1940 ....DLB-29
Millhauser, Steven 1943- DLB-2
Millican, Arthenia J. Bates 1920- DLB-38
Mills and Boon DLB-112
Milman, Henry Hart 1796-1868 ....DLB-96
Milne, A. A. 1882-1956 ..... DLB-10, 77, 100, 160
Milner, Ron 1938- DLB-38
Milner, William [publishing house] DLB-106
Milnes, Richard Monckton (Lord Houghton) 1809-1885 .... DLB-32, 184
Milton, John 1608-1674 .... DLB-131, 151
Minakami Tsutomu 1919- DLB-182
Minamoto no Sanetomo 1192-1219 ......DLB-203
The Minerva Press DLB-154
Minnesang circa 1150-1280 ....DLB-138
Minns, Susan 1839-1938 ....DLB-140

Minor Illustrators, 1880-1914 ....DLB-141
Minor Poets of the Earlier Seventeenth Century DLB-121
Minton, Balch and Company DLB-46
Mirbeau, Octave 1848-1917 ...... DLB-123, 192
Mirk, John died after 1414? DLB-146
Miron, Gaston 1928- DLB-60
A Mirror for Magistrates DLB-167
Mishima Yukio 1925-1970 ....DLB-182
Mitchel, Jonathan 1624-1668 ....DLB-24
Mitchell, Adrian 1932- DLB-40
Mitchell, Donald Grant 1822-1908 .... DLB-1; DS-13
Mitchell, Gladys 1901-1983 ....DLB-77
Mitchell, James Leslie 1901-1935 ....DLB-15
Mitchell, John (see Slater, Patrick)
Mitchell, John Ames 1845-1918 ....DLB-79
Mitchell, Joseph 1908-1996 ...... DLB-185; Y-96
Mitchell, Julian 1935- DLB-14
Mitchell, Ken 1940- DLB-60
Mitchell, Langdon 1862-1935 ....DLB-7
Mitchell, Loften 1919- DLB-38
Mitchell, Margaret 1900-1949 ....DLB-9
Mitchell, S. Weir 1829-1914 ....DLB-202
Mitchell, W. O. 1914- DLB-88
Mitchison, Naomi Margaret (Haldane) 1897- DLB-160, 191
Mitford, Mary Russell 1787-1855 .... DLB-110, 116
Mitford, Nancy 1904-1973 ....DLB-191
Mittelholzer, Edgar 1909-1965 ....DLB-117
Mitterer, Erika 1906- DLB-85
Mitterer, Felix 1948- DLB-124
Mitternacht, Johann Sebastian 1613-1679 ....DLB-168
Miyamoto, Yuriko 1899-1951 ....DLB-180
Mizener, Arthur 1907-1988 ....DLB-103
Mo, Timothy 1950- DLB-194
Modern Age Books DLB-46
"Modern English Prose" (1876), by George Saintsbury DLB-57
The Modern Language Association of America Celebrates Its Centennial Y-84
The Modern Library DLB-46
"Modern Novelists – Great and Small" (1855), by Margaret Oliphant DLB-21
"Modern Style" (1857), by Cockburn Thomson [excerpt] DLB-57
The Modernists (1932), by Joseph Warren Beach DLB-36
Modiano, Patrick 1945- DLB-83
Moffat, Yard and Company DLB-46
Moffet, Thomas 1553-1604 ....DLB-136
Mohr, Nicholasa 1938- DLB-145
Moix, Ana María 1947- DLB-134
Molesworth, Louisa 1839-1921 ....DLB-135
Möllhausen, Balduin 1825-1905 ....DLB-129
Momaday, N. Scott 1934- DLB-143, 175

Cumulative Index

Monkhouse, Allan 1858-1936 .... DLB-10
Monro, Harold 1879-1932 .... DLB-19
Monroe, Harriet 1860-1936 .... DLB-54, 91
Monsarrat, Nicholas 1910-1979 .... DLB-15
Montagu, Lady Mary Wortley 1689-1762 .... DLB-95, 101
Montague, C. E. 1867-1928 .... DLB-197
Montague, John 1929- DLB-40
Montale, Eugenio 1896-1981 .... DLB-114
Monterroso, Augusto 1921- DLB-145
Montgomerie, Alexander circa 1550?-1598 .... DLB-167
Montgomery, James 1771-1854 ..... DLB-93, 158
Montgomery, John 1919- DLB-16
Montgomery, Lucy Maud 1874-1942 .... DLB-92; DS-14
Montgomery, Marion 1925- DLB-6
Montgomery, Robert Bruce (see Crispin, Edmund)
Montherlant, Henry de 1896-1972 .... DLB-72
The Monthly Review 1749-1844 .... DLB-110
Montigny, Louvigny de 1876-1955 .... DLB-92
Montoya, José 1932- DLB-122
Moodie, John Wedderburn Dunbar 1797-1869 .... DLB-99
Moodie, Susanna 1803-1885 .... DLB-99
Moody, Joshua circa 1633-1697 .... DLB-24
Moody, William Vaughn 1869-1910 .... DLB-7, 54
Moorcock, Michael 1939- DLB-14
Moore, Catherine L. 1911- DLB-8
Moore, Clement Clarke 1779-1863 .... DLB-42
Moore, Dora Mavor 1888-1979 .... DLB-92
Moore, George 1852-1933 .... DLB-10, 18, 57, 135
Moore, Marianne 1887-1972 .... DLB-45; DS-7
Moore, Mavor 1919- DLB-88
Moore, Richard 1927- DLB-105
Moore, T. Sturge 1870-1944 .... DLB-19
Moore, Thomas 1779-1852 .... DLB-96, 144
Moore, Ward 1903-1978 .... DLB-8
Moore, Wilstach, Keys and Company DLB-49
Moorehead, Alan 1901-1983 .... DLB-204
Moorhouse, Geoffrey 1931- DLB-204
The Moorland-Spingarn Research Center DLB-76
Moorman, Mary C. 1905-1994 .... DLB-155
Moraga, Cherríe 1952- DLB-82
Morales, Alejandro 1944- DLB-82
Morales, Mario Roberto 1947- DLB-145
Morales, Rafael 1919- DLB-108
Morality Plays: *Mankind* circa 1450-1500 and *Everyman* circa 1500 .... DLB-146
Morante, Elsa 1912-1985 .... DLB-177
Morata, Olympia Fulvia 1526-1555 ..... DLB-179
Moravia, Alberto 1907-1990 .... DLB-177
Mordaunt, Elinor 1872-1942 .... DLB-174
More, Hannah 1745-1833 .... DLB-107, 109, 116, 158

More, Henry 1614-1687 .... DLB-126
More, Sir Thomas 1477 or 1478-1535 .... DLB-136
Moreno, Dorinda 1939- DLB-122
Morency, Pierre 1942- DLB-60
Moretti, Marino 1885-1979 .... DLB-114
Morgan, Berry 1919- DLB-6
Morgan, Charles 1894-1958 .... DLB-34, 100
Morgan, Edmund S. 1916- DLB-17
Morgan, Edwin 1920- DLB-27
Morgan, John Pierpont 1837-1913 ...... DLB-140
Morgan, John Pierpont, Jr. 1867-1943 ... DLB-140
Morgan, Robert 1944- DLB-120
Morgan, Sydney Owenson, Lady 1776?-1859 .... DLB-116, 158
Morgner, Irmtraud 1933- DLB-75
Morhof, Daniel Georg 1639-1691 .... DLB-164
Mori, Ōgai 1862-1922 .... DLB-180
Morier, James Justinian 1782 or 1783?-1849 .... DLB-116
Mörike, Eduard 1804-1875 .... DLB-133
Morin, Paul 1889-1963 .... DLB-92
Morison, Richard 1514?-1556 .... DLB-136
Morison, Samuel Eliot 1887-1976 ...... DLB-17
Morison, Stanley 1889-1967 .... DLB-201
Moritz, Karl Philipp 1756-1793 .... DLB-94
Moriz von Craûn circa 1220-1230 .... DLB-138
Morley, Christopher 1890-1957 .... DLB-9
Morley, John 1838-1923 .... DLB-57, 144, 190
Morris, George Pope 1802-1864 .... DLB-73
Morris, James Humphrey (see Morris, Jan)
Morris, Jan 1926- DLB-204
Morris, Lewis 1833-1907 .... DLB-35
Morris, Margaret 1737-1816 .... DLB-200
Morris, Richard B. 1904-1989 .... DLB-17
Morris, William 1834-1896 ..... DLB-18, 35, 57, 156, 178, 184
Morris, Willie 1934- Y-80
Morris, Wright 1910- DLB-2; Y-81
Morrison, Arthur 1863-1945 ....DLB-70, 135, 197
Morrison, Charles Clayton 1874-1966 .... DLB-91
Morrison, Toni 1931- DLB-6, 33, 143; Y-81, Y-93
Morrow, William, and Company DLB-46
Morse, James Herbert 1841-1923 .... DLB-71
Morse, Jedidiah 1761-1826 .... DLB-37
Morse, John T., Jr. 1840-1937 .... DLB-47
Morselli, Guido 1912-1973 .... DLB-177
Mortimer, Favell Lee 1802-1878 .... DLB-163
Mortimer, John 1923- DLB-13
Morton, Carlos 1942- DLB-122
Morton, H. V. 1892-1979 .... DLB-195
Morton, John P., and Company DLB-49
Morton, Nathaniel 1613-1685 .... DLB-24
Morton, Sarah Wentworth 1759-1846 .... DLB-37
Morton, Thomas circa 1579-circa 1647 ... DLB-24

Moscherosch, Johann Michael 1601-1669 .... DLB-164
Moseley, Humphrey [publishing house]...DLB-170
Möser, Justus 1720-1794 .... DLB-97
Mosley, Nicholas 1923- DLB-14
Moss, Arthur 1889-1969 .... DLB-4
Moss, Howard 1922-1987 .... DLB-5
Moss, Thylias 1954- DLB-120
The Most Powerful Book Review in America [*New York Times Book Review*] Y-82
Motion, Andrew 1952- DLB-40
Motley, John Lothrop 1814-1877 ... DLB-1, 30, 59
Motley, Willard 1909-1965 ....DLB-76, 143
Motte, Benjamin Jr. [publishing house]... DLB-154
Motteux, Peter Anthony 1663-1718 ...... DLB-80
Mottram, R. H. 1883-1971 .... DLB-36
Mouré, Erin 1955- DLB-60
Mourning Dove (Humishuma) between 1882 and 1888?-1936 .... DLB-175
Movies from Books, 1920-1974 .... DLB-9
Mowat, Farley 1921- DLB-68
Mowbray, A. R., and Company, Limited DLB-106
Mowrer, Edgar Ansel 1892-1977 .... DLB-29
Mowrer, Paul Scott 1887-1971 .... DLB-29
Moxon, Edward [publishing house] DLB-106
Moxon, Joseph [publishing house] DLB-170
Mphahlele, Es'kia (Ezekiel) 1919- DLB-125
Mtshali, Oswald Mbuyiseni 1940- DLB-125
Mucedorus DLB-62
Mudford, William 1782-1848 .... DLB-159
Mueller, Lisel 1924- DLB-105
Muhajir, El (see Marvin X)
Muhajir, Nazzam Al Fitnah (see Marvin X)
Mühlbach, Luise 1814-1873 .... DLB-133
Muir, Edwin 1887-1959 ....DLB-20, 100, 191
Muir, Helen 1937- DLB-14
Muir, John 1838-1914 .... DLB-186
Muir, Percy 1894-1979 .... DLB-201
Mujū Ichien 1226-1312 .... DLB-203
Mukherjee, Bharati 1940- DLB-60
Mulcaster, Richard 1531 or 1532-1611 .... DLB-167
Muldoon, Paul 1951- DLB-40
Müller, Friedrich (see Müller, Maler)
Müller, Heiner 1929- DLB-124
Müller, Maler 1749-1825 .... DLB-94
Müller, Wilhelm 1794-1827 .... DLB-90
Mumford, Lewis 1895-1990 .... DLB-63
Munby, A. N. L. 1913-1974 .... DLB-201
Munby, Arthur Joseph 1828-1910 .... DLB-35
Munday, Anthony 1560-1633 ....DLB-62, 172
Mundt, Clara (see Mühlbach, Luise)
Mundt, Theodore 1808-1861 .... DLB-133
Munford, Robert circa 1737-1783 .... DLB-31
Mungoshi, Charles 1947- DLB-157

Munonye, John 1929- DLB-117	Nabokov Festival at Cornell Y-83	Nemerov, Howard 1920-1991.....DLB-5, 6; Y-83
Munro, Alice 1931- DLB-53	The Vladimir Nabokov Archive in the Berg Collection Y-91	Nesbit, E. 1858-1924 .....DLB-141, 153, 178
Munro, H. H. 1870-1916 .....DLB-34, 162	Naden, Constance 1858-1889 .....DLB-199	Ness, Evaline 1911-1986 .....DLB-61
Munro, Neil 1864-1930 .....DLB-156	Nadezhdin, Nikolai Ivanovich 1804-1856 .....DLB-198	Nestroy, Johann 1801-1862.....DLB-133
Munro, George [publishing house] DLB-49	Nafis and Cornish DLB-49	Neukirch, Benjamin 1655-1729 .....DLB-168
Munro, Norman L. [publishing house] DLB-49	Nagai, Kafū 1879-1959.....DLB-180	Neugeboren, Jay 1938- DLB-28
Munroe, James, and Company DLB-49	Naipaul, Shiva 1945-1985 .....DLB-157; Y-85	Neumann, Alfred 1895-1952 .....DLB-56
Munroe, Kirk 1850-1930.....DLB-42	Naipaul, V. S. 1932- DLB-125, 204; Y-85	Neumark, Georg 1621-1681 .....DLB-164
Munroe and Francis.....DLB-49	Nakagami Kenji 1946-1992 .....DLB-182	Neumeister, Erdmann 1671-1756.....DLB-168
Munsell, Joel [publishing house] DLB-49	Nakano-in Masatada no Musume (see Nijō, Lady)	Nevins, Allan 1890-1971 .....DLB-17; DS-17
Munsey, Frank A. 1854-1925 .....DLB-25, 91	Nancrede, Joseph [publishing house] DLB-49	Nevinson, Henry Woood 1856-1941 .....DLB-135
Munsey, Frank A., and Company.....DLB-49	Naranjo, Carmen 1930- DLB-145	The New American Library DLB-46
Murakami Haruki 1949- DLB-182	Narezhny, Vasilii Trofimovich 1780-1825 .....DLB-198	New Approaches to Biography: Challenges from Critical Theory, USC Conference on Literary Studies, 1990 .....Y-90
Murav'ev, Mikhail Nikitich 1757-1807.....DLB-150	Narrache, Jean 1893-1970 .....DLB-92	New Directions Publishing Corporation DLB-46
Murdoch, Iris 1919- DLB-14, 194	Nasby, Petroleum Vesuvius (see Locke, David Ross)	A New Edition of *Huck Finn*.....Y-85
Murdoch, Rupert 1931- DLB-127	Nash, Ogden 1902-1971.....DLB-11	New Forces at Work in the American Theatre: 1915-1925 .....DLB-7
Murfree, Mary N. 1850-1922 .....DLB-12, 74	Nash, Eveleigh [publishing house] DLB-112	New Literary Periodicals: A Report for 1987.....Y-87
Murger, Henry 1822-1861.....DLB-119	Nashe, Thomas 1567-1601?.....DLB-167	
Murger, Louis-Henri (see Murger, Henry)	Nast, Conde 1873-1942 .....DLB-91	New Literary Periodicals: A Report for 1988.....Y-88
Murner, Thomas 1475-1537 .....DLB-179	Nast, Thomas 1840-1902.....DLB-188	New Literary Periodicals: A Report for 1989.....Y-89
Muro, Amado 1915-1971.....DLB-82	Nastasijević, Momčilo 1894-1938 .....DLB-147	
Murphy, Arthur 1727-1805 .....DLB-89, 142	Nathan, George Jean 1882-1958 .....DLB-137	New Literary Periodicals: A Report for 1990.....Y-90
Murphy, Beatrice M. 1908- DLB-76	Nathan, Robert 1894-1985 .....DLB-9	New Literary Periodicals: A Report for 1991.....Y-91
Murphy, Dervla 1931- DLB-204	The National Jewish Book Awards Y-85	
Murphy, Emily 1868-1933.....DLB-99	The National Theatre and the Royal Shakespeare Company: The National Companies DLB-13	New Literary Periodicals: A Report for 1992.....Y-92
Murphy, John H., III 1916- DLB-127		New Literary Periodicals: A Report for 1993.....Y-93
Murphy, John, and Company DLB-49	Natsume, Sōseki 1867-1916 .....DLB-180	The New Monthly Magazine 1814-1884 .....DLB-110
Murphy, Richard 1927-1993 .....DLB-40	Naughton, Bill 1910- DLB-13	
Murray, Albert L. 1916- DLB-38	Naylor, Gloria 1950- DLB-173	The New Ulysses.....Y-84
Murray, Gilbert 1866-1957 .....DLB-10	Nazor, Vladimir 1876-1949 .....DLB-147	The New Variorum Shakespeare Y-85
Murray, Judith Sargent 1751-1820.....DLB-37, 200	Ndebele, Njabulo 1948- DLB-157	A New Voice: The Center for the Book's First Five Years Y-83
Murray, Pauli 1910-1985.....DLB-41	Neagoe, Peter 1881-1960.....DLB-4	
Murray, John [publishing house] DLB-154	Neal, John 1793-1876 .....DLB-1, 59	The New Wave [Science Fiction].....DLB-8
Murry, John Middleton 1889-1957 .....DLB-149	Neal, Joseph C. 1807-1847 .....DLB-11	New York City Bookshops in the 1930s and 1940s: The Recollections of Walter Goldwater .. Y-93
Musäus, Johann Karl August 1735-1787.....DLB-97	Neal, Larry 1937-1981 .....DLB-38	
	The Neale Publishing Company DLB-49	Newbery, John [publishing house].....DLB-154
Muschg, Adolf 1934- DLB-75	Neely, F. Tennyson [publishing house] DLB-49	Newbolt, Henry 1862-1938.....DLB-19
The Music of *Minnesang*.....DLB-138	Negri, Ada 1870-1945 .....DLB-114	Newbound, Bernard Slade (see Slade, Bernard)
Musil, Robert 1880-1942.....DLB-81, 124	"The Negro as a Writer," by G. M. McClellan.....DLB-50	Newby, Eric 1919- DLB-204
Muspilli circa 790-circa 850.....DLB-148		Newby, P. H. 1918- DLB-15
Musset, Alfred de 1810-1857 .....DLB-192	"Negro Poets and Their Poetry," by Wallace Thurman.....DLB-50	Newby, Thomas Cautley [publishing house].....DLB-106
Mussey, Benjamin B., and Company DLB-49	Neidhart von Reuental circa 1185-circa 1240.....DLB-138	Newcomb, Charles King 1820-1894 .....DLB-1
Mutafchieva, Vera 1929- DLB-181		
Mwangi, Meja 1948- DLB-125	Neihardt, John G. 1881-1973 .....DLB-9, 54	Newell, Peter 1862-1924 .....DLB-42
Myers, Frederic W. H. 1843-1901.....DLB-190	Neledinsky-Meletsky, Iurii Aleksandrovich 1752-1828 .....DLB-150	Newell, Robert Henry 1836-1901 .....DLB-11
Myers, Gustavus 1872-1942.....DLB-47		Newhouse, Samuel I. 1895-1979 .....DLB-127
Myers, L. H. 1881-1944.....DLB-15	Nelligan, Emile 1879-1941 .....DLB-92	Newman, Cecil Earl 1903-1976 .....DLB-127
Myers, Walter Dean 1937- DLB-33	Nelson, Alice Moore Dunbar 1875-1935 ...DLB-50	Newman, David (see Benton, Robert)
Myles, Eileen 1949- DLB-193	Nelson, Thomas, and Sons [U.S.] DLB-49	Newman, Frances 1883-1928. .....Y-80
N	Nelson, Thomas, and Sons [U.K.] DLB-106	Newman, Francis William 1805-1897 .....DLB-190
Nabl, Franz 1883-1974.....DLB-81	Nelson, William 1908-1978 .....DLB-103	
Nabokov, Vladimir 1899-1977 .....DLB-2; Y-80, Y-91; DS-3	Nelson, William Rockhill 1841-1915.....DLB-23	

Newman, John Henry 1801-1890 .... DLB-18, 32, 55
Newman, Mark [publishing house]....... DLB-49
Newnes, George, Limited............ DLB-112
Newsome, Effie Lee 1885-1979......... DLB-76
Newspaper Syndication of American Humor........................ DLB-11
Newton, A. Edward 1864-1940 .... DLB-140
Ngugi wa Thiong'o 1938- DLB-125
Niatum, Duane 1938- DLB-175
The *Nibelungenlied* and the *Klage* circa 1200...................... DLB-138
Nichol, B. P. 1944- DLB-53
Nicholas of Cusa 1401-1464.......... DLB-115
Nichols, Beverly 1898-1983 .... DLB-191
Nichols, Dudley 1895-1960 .... DLB-26
Nichols, Grace 1950- DLB-157
Nichols, John 1940- Y-82
Nichols, Mary Sargeant (Neal) Gove 1810-1884...................... DLB-1
Nichols, Peter 1927- DLB-13
Nichols, Roy F. 1896-1973 .... DLB-17
Nichols, Ruth 1948- DLB-60
Nicholson, Edward Williams Byron 1849-1912..................... DLB-184
Nicholson, Norman 1914- DLB-27
Nicholson, William 1872-1949 .... DLB-141
Ní Chuilleanáin, Eiléan 1942- DLB-40
Nicol, Eric 1919- DLB-68
Nicolai, Friedrich 1733-1811........... DLB-97
Nicolay, John G. 1832-1901 and Hay, John 1838-1905............... DLB-47
Nicolson, Harold 1886-1968........ DLB-100, 149
Nicolson, Nigel 1917- DLB-155
Niebuhr, Reinhold 1892-1971...... DLB-17; DS-17
Niedecker, Lorine 1903-1970 .... DLB-48
Nieman, Lucius W. 1857-1935 .... DLB-25
Nietzsche, Friedrich 1844-1900......... DLB-129
Nievo, Stanislao 1928- DLB-196
Niggli, Josefina 1910- Y-80
Nightingale, Florence 1820-1910 .... DLB-166
Nijō, Lady (Nakano-in Masatada no Musume) 1258-after 1306................. DLB-203
Nijō, Yoshimoto 1320-1388 .... DLB-203
Nikolev, Nikolai Petrovich 1758-1815...................... DLB-150
Niles, Hezekiah 1777-1839 .... DLB-43
Nims, John Frederick 1913- DLB-5
Nin, Anaïs 1903-1977 .... DLB-2, 4, 152
1985: The Year of the Mystery: A Symposium.................... Y-85
The 1997 Booker Prize................. Y-97
Nissenson, Hugh 1933- DLB-28
Niven, Frederick John 1878-1944 ...... DLB-92
Niven, Larry 1938- DLB-8
Nixon, Howard M. 1909-1983 .... DLB-201
Nizan, Paul 1905-1940 .... DLB-72

Njegoš, Petar II Petrović 1813-1851 ..... DLB-147
Nkosi, Lewis 1936- DLB-157
"The No Self, the Little Self, and the Poets," by Richard Moore DLB-105
Nobel Peace Prize
The 1986 Nobel Peace Prize: Elie Wiesel..... Y-86
The Nobel Prize and Literary Politics Y-86
Nobel Prize in Literature
The 1982 Nobel Prize in Literature: Gabriel García Márquez.............. Y-82
The 1983 Nobel Prize in Literature: William Golding Y-83
The 1984 Nobel Prize in Literature: Jaroslav Seifert Y-84
The 1985 Nobel Prize in Literature: Claude Simon Y-85
The 1986 Nobel Prize in Literature: Wole Soyinka.................... Y-86
The 1987 Nobel Prize in Literature: Joseph Brodsky Y-87
The 1988 Nobel Prize in Literature: Najīb Mahfūz.................... Y-88
The 1989 Nobel Prize in Literature: Camilo José Cela Y-89
The 1990 Nobel Prize in Literature: Octavio Paz Y-90
The 1991 Nobel Prize in Literature: Nadine Gordimer................. Y-91
The 1992 Nobel Prize in Literature: Derek Walcott Y-92
The 1993 Nobel Prize in Literature: Toni Morrison.................... Y-93
The 1994 Nobel Prize in Literature: Kenzaburō Ōe Y-94
The 1995 Nobel Prize in Literature: Seamus Heaney Y-95
The 1996 Nobel Prize in Literature: Wisława Szymborsha............... Y-96
The 1997 Nobel Prize in Literature: Dario Fo....................... Y-97
Nodier, Charles 1780-1844........... DLB-119
Noel, Roden 1834-1894 .... DLB-35
Nogami, Yaeko 1885-1985 .... DLB-180
Nogo, Rajko Petrov 1945- DLB-181
Nolan, William F. 1928- DLB-8
Noland, C. F. M. 1810?-1858 .... DLB-11
Noma Hiroshi 1915-1991............ DLB-182
Nonesuch Press DLB-112
Noonan, Robert Phillipe (see Tressell, Robert)
Noonday Press..................... DLB-46
Noone, John 1936- DLB-14
Nora, Eugenio de 1923- DLB-134
Nordhoff, Charles 1887-1947 .... DLB-9
Norman, Charles 1904- DLB-111
Norman, Marsha 1947- Y-84
Norris, Charles G. 1881-1945 .... DLB-9
Norris, Frank 1870-1902.........DLB-12, 71, 186
Norris, Leslie 1921- DLB-27
Norse, Harold 1916- DLB-16
North, Marianne 1830-1890............DLB-174

North Point Press.................... DLB-46
Nortje, Arthur 1942-1970............ DLB-125
Norton, Alice Mary (see Norton, Andre)
Norton, Andre 1912- DLB-8, 52
Norton, Andrews 1786-1853 .... DLB-1
Norton, Caroline 1808-1877.................DLB-21, 159, 199
Norton, Charles Eliot 1827-1908 ...... DLB-1, 64
Norton, John 1606-1663.............. DLB-24
Norton, Mary 1903-1992 .... DLB-160
Norton, Thomas (see Sackville, Thomas)
Norton, W. W., and Company DLB-46
Norwood, Robert 1874-1932 .... DLB-92
Nosaka Akiyuki 1930- DLB-182
Nossack, Hans Erich 1901-1977......... DLB-69
A Note on Technique (1926), by Elizabeth A. Drew [excerpts] DLB-36
Notker Balbulus circa 840-912......... DLB-148
Notker III of Saint Gall circa 950-1022 .... DLB-148
Notker von Zweifalten ?-1095 .... DLB-148
Nourse, Alan E. 1928- DLB-8
Novak, Slobodan 1924- DLB-181
Novak, Vjenceslav 1859-1905 ....DLB-147
Novalis 1772-1801 .... DLB-90
Novaro, Mario 1868-1944 .... DLB-114
Novás Calvo, Lino 1903-1983 .... DLB-145
"The Novel in [Robert Browning's] 'The Ring and the Book'" (1912), by Henry James DLB-32
The Novel of Impressionism, by Jethro Bithell................... DLB-66
Novel-Reading: *The Works of Charles Dickens, The Works of W. Makepeace Thackeray* (1879), by Anthony Trollope DLB-21
Novels for Grown-Ups................. Y-97
The Novels of Dorothy Richardson (1918), by May Sinclair.................. DLB-36
Novels with a Purpose (1864), by Justin M'Carthy DLB-21
Noventa, Giacomo 1898-1960 .... DLB-114
Novikov, Nikolai Ivanovich 1744-1818..................... DLB-150
Nowlan, Alden 1933-1983 .... DLB-53
Noyes, Alfred 1880-1958 .... DLB-20
Noyes, Crosby S. 1825-1908 .... DLB-23
Noyes, Nicholas 1647-1717 .... DLB-24
Noyes, Theodore W. 1858-1946 .... DLB-29
N-Town Plays circa 1468 to early sixteenth century................ DLB-146
Nugent, Frank 1908-1965............. DLB-44
Nugent, Richard Bruce 1906- DLB-151
Nušić, Branislav 1864-1938 ....DLB-147
Nutt, David [publishing house]......... DLB-106
Nwapa, Flora 1931- DLB-125
Nye, Bill 1850-1896 .... DLB-186
Nye, Edgar Wilson (Bill) 1850-1896 .. DLB-11, 23
Nye, Naomi Shihab 1952- DLB-120

Nye, Robert 1939- DLB-14

O

Oakes, Urian circa 1631-1681 ....DLB-24
Oakley, Violet 1874-1961 ....DLB-188
Oates, Joyce Carol 1938- ...DLB-2, 5, 130; Y-81
Ōba Minako 1930- DLB-182
Ober, Frederick Albion 1849-1913 ......DLB-189
Ober, William 1920-1993 .... Y-93
Oberholtzer, Ellis Paxson 1868-1936......DLB-47
Obradović, Dositej 1740?-1811 ....DLB-147
O'Brien, Edna 1932- DLB-14
O'Brien, Fitz-James 1828-1862..........DLB-74
O'Brien, Kate 1897-1974 ....DLB-15
O'Brien, Tim 1946- DLB-152; Y-80; DS-9
O'Casey, Sean 1880-1964 ....DLB-10
Occom, Samson 1723-1792 ....DLB-175
Ochs, Adolph S. 1858-1935 ....DLB-25
Ochs-Oakes, George Washington
 1861-1931 ....DLB-137
O'Connor, Flannery
 1925-1964 ....DLB-2, 152; Y-80; DS-12
O'Connor, Frank 1903-1966 ....DLB-162
Octopus Publishing Group DLB-112
Oda Sakunosuke 1913-1947 ....DLB-182
Odell, Jonathan 1737-1818 ....DLB-31, 99
O'Dell, Scott 1903-1989...............DLB-52
Odets, Clifford 1906-1963 ....DLB-7, 26
Odhams Press Limited...............DLB-112
Odoevsky, Aleksandr Ivanovich
 1802-1839 ....DLB-205
Odoevsky, Vladimir Fedorovich
 1804 or 1803-1869 ....DLB-198
O'Donnell, Peter 1920- DLB-87
O'Donovan, Michael (see O'Connor, Frank)
Ōe Kenzaburō 1935- DLB-182; Y-94
O'Faolain, Julia 1932- DLB-14
O'Faolain, Sean 1900- DLB-15, 162
Off Broadway and Off-Off Broadway......DLB-7
Off-Loop Theatres...................DLB-7
Offord, Carl Ruthven 1910- DLB-76
O'Flaherty, Liam 1896-1984 ...DLB-36, 162; Y-84
Ogilvie, J. S., and Company DLB-49
Ogilvy, Eliza 1822-1912................DLB-199
Ogot, Grace 1930- DLB-125
O'Grady, Desmond 1935- DLB-40
Ogunyemi, Wale 1939- DLB-157
O'Hagan, Howard 1902-1982 ....DLB-68
O'Hara, Frank 1926-1966 ....DLB-5, 16, 193
O'Hara, John 1905-1970 ....DLB-9, 86; DS-2
O'Hegarty, P. S. 1879-1955 ....DLB-201
Okara, Gabriel 1921- DLB-125
O'Keeffe, John 1747-1833..............DLB-89
Okes, Nicholas [publishing house].......DLB-170
Okigbo, Christopher 1930-1967 ....DLB-125

Okot p'Bitek 1931-1982...............DLB-125
Okpewho, Isidore 1941- DLB-157
Okri, Ben 1959- DLB-157
Olaudah Equiano and Unfinished Journeys:
 The Slave-Narrative Tradition and
 Twentieth-Century Continuities, by
 Paul Edwards and Pauline T.
 Wangman DLB-117
Old English Literature:
 An Introduction DLB-146
Old English Riddles
 eighth to tenth centuries DLB-146
Old Franklin Publishing House DLB-49
Old German Genesis and *Old German Exodus*
 circa 1050-circa 1130 ....DLB-148
Old High German Charms and
 Blessings DLB-148
The *Old High German Isidor*
 circa 790-800 ....DLB-148
Older, Fremont 1856-1935 ....DLB-25
Oldham, John 1653-1683 ....DLB-131
Oldman, C. B. 1894-1969 ....DLB-201
Olds, Sharon 1942- DLB-120
Olearius, Adam 1599-1671 ....DLB-164
Oliphant, Laurence 1829?-1888.......DLB-18, 166
Oliphant, Margaret 1828-1897.......DLB-18, 190
Oliver, Chad 1928- DLB-8
Oliver, Mary 1935- DLB-5, 193
Ollier, Claude 1922- DLB-83
Olsen, Tillie 1913?- DLB-28; Y-80
Olson, Charles 1910-1970 ....DLB-5, 16, 193
Olson, Elder 1909- DLB-48, 63
Omotoso, Kole 1943- DLB-125
"On Art in Fiction "(1838),
 by Edward Bulwer DLB-21
On Learning to Write Y-88
On Some of the Characteristics of Modern
 Poetry and On the Lyrical Poems of
 Alfred Tennyson (1831), by Arthur
 Henry Hallam....................DLB-32
"On Style in English Prose" (1898), by
 Frederic Harrison DLB-57
"On Style in Literature: Its Technical
 Elements" (1885), by Robert Louis
 Stevenson DLB-57
"On the Writing of Essays" (1862),
 by Alexander Smith................DLB-57
Ondaatje, Michael 1943- DLB-60
O'Neill, Eugene 1888-1953 ....DLB-7
Onetti, Juan Carlos 1909-1994 ....DLB-113
Onions, George Oliver 1872-1961.......DLB-153
Onofri, Arturo 1885-1928 ....DLB-114
Opie, Amelia 1769-1853..........DLB-116, 159
Opitz, Martin 1597-1639 ....DLB-164
Oppen, George 1908-1984 ....DLB-5, 165
Oppenheim, E. Phillips 1866-1946 ....DLB-70
Oppenheim, James 1882-1932...........DLB-28
Oppenheimer, Joel 1930-1988 ......DLB-5, 193
Optic, Oliver (see Adams, William Taylor)

Oral History Interview with Donald S.
 Klopfer Y-97
Orczy, Emma, Baroness 1865-1947.......DLB-70
Origo, Iris 1902-1988.................DLB-155
Orlovitz, Gil 1918-1973 ....DLB-2, 5
Orlovsky, Peter 1933- DLB-16
Ormond, John 1923- DLB-27
Ornitz, Samuel 1890-1957 ....DLB-28, 44
O'Rourke, P. J. 1947- DLB-185
Ortese, Anna Maria 1914- DLB-177
Ortiz, Simon J. 1941- DLB-120, 175
Ortnit and *Wolfdietrich* circa 1225-1250 ....DLB-138
Orton, Joe 1933-1967.................DLB-13
Orwell, George 1903-1950 .....DLB-15, 98, 195
The Orwell Year...................... Y-84
Ory, Carlos Edmundo de 1923- DLB-134
Osbey, Brenda Marie 1957- DLB-120
Osbon, B. S. 1827-1912?...............DLB-43
Osborn, Sarah 1714-1796..............DLB-200
Osborne, John 1929-1994 ....DLB-13
Osgood, Herbert L. 1855-1918 ....DLB-47
Osgood, James R., and Company DLB-49
Osgood, McIlvaine and Company DLB-112
O'Shaughnessy, Arthur 1844-1881 ....DLB-35
O'Shea, Patrick [publishing house] DLB-49
Osipov, Nikolai Petrovich 1751-1799......DLB-150
Oskison, John Milton 1879-1947 ....DLB-175
Osler, Sir William 1849-1919 ....DLB-184
Osofisan, Femi 1946- DLB-125
Ostenso, Martha 1900-1963 ....DLB-92
Ostriker, Alicia 1937- DLB-120
Osundare, Niyi 1947- DLB-157
Oswald, Eleazer 1755-1795 ....DLB-43
Oswald von Wolkenstein
 1376 or 1377-1445 ....DLB-179
Otero, Blas de 1916-1979..............DLB-134
Otero, Miguel Antonio 1859-1944........DLB-82
Otero Silva, Miguel 1908-1985 ....DLB-145
Otfried von Weißenburg
 circa 800-circa 875?.................DLB-148
Otis, James (see Kaler, James Otis)
Otis, James, Jr. 1725-1783 ....DLB-31
Otis, Broaders and Company DLB-49
Ottaway, James 1911- DLB-127
Ottendorfer, Oswald 1826-1900 ....DLB-23
Ottieri, Ottiero 1924- DLB-177
Otto-Peters, Louise 1819-1895..........DLB-129
Otway, Thomas 1652-1685..............DLB-80
Ouellette, Fernand 1930- DLB-60
Ouida 1839-1908..................DLB-18, 156
Outing Publishing Company............DLB-46
Outlaw Days, by Joyce Johnson DLB-16
Overbury, Sir Thomas
 circa 1581-1613..................DLB-151
The Overlook Press..................DLB-46

Overview of U.S. Book Publishing,
  1910-1945. . . . . DLB-9
Owen, Guy 1925- DLB-5
Owen, John 1564-1622. . . . . DLB-121
Owen, John [publishing house]. DLB-49
Owen, Robert 1771-1858 . . . . DLB-107, 158
Owen, Wilfred 1893-1918 . . . . . . DLB-20; DS-18
Owen, Peter, Limited DLB-112
The Owl and the Nightingale
  circa 1189-1199 . . . . DLB-146
Owsley, Frank L. 1890-1956 . . . . DLB-17
Oxford, Seventeenth Earl of, Edward de Vere
  1550-1604 .DLB-172
Ozerov, Vladislav Aleksandrovich
  1769-1816. DLB-150
Ozick, Cynthia 1928- DLB-28, 152; Y-82

P

Pace, Richard 1482?-1536 . . . . DLB-167
Pacey, Desmond 1917-1975. . . . . DLB-88
Pack, Robert 1929- DLB-5
Packaging Papa: *The Garden of Eden* Y-86
Padell Publishing Company DLB-46
Padgett, Ron 1942- DLB-5
Padilla, Ernesto Chávez 1944- DLB-122
Page, L. C., and Company DLB-49
Page, P. K. 1916- DLB-68
Page, Thomas Nelson
  1853-1922 . . . . DLB-12, 78; DS-13
Page, Walter Hines 1855-1918 . . . . . . DLB-71, 91
Paget, Francis Edward 1806-1882 . . . . . . DLB-163
Paget, Violet (see Lee, Vernon)
Pagliarani, Elio 1927- DLB-128
Pain, Barry 1864-1928 . . . . DLB-135, 197
Pain, Philip ?-circa 1666 . . . . DLB-24
Paine, Robert Treat, Jr. 1773-1811 . . . . . . DLB-37
Paine, Thomas 1737-1809 . . . . .DLB-31, 43, 73, 158
Painter, George D. 1914- DLB-155
Painter, William 1540?-1594 . . . . DLB-136
Palazzeschi, Aldo 1885-1974 . . . . DLB-114
Paley, Grace 1922- DLB-28
Palfrey, John Gorham 1796-1881 . . . . . . DLB-1, 30
Palgrave, Francis Turner 1824-1897 . . . . . DLB-35
Palmer, Joe H. 1904-1952 . . . . .DLB-171
Palmer, Michael 1943- DLB-169
Paltock, Robert 1697-1767 . . . . DLB-39
Pan Books Limited DLB-112
Panama, Norman 1914- and
  Frank, Melvin 1913-1988 . . . . DLB-26
Panaev, Ivan Ivanovich 1812-1862 . . . . . . DLB-198
Pancake, Breece D'J 1952-1979 . . . . DLB-130
Panero, Leopoldo 1909-1962 . . . . DLB-108
Pangborn, Edgar 1909-1976 . . . . DLB-8
"Panic Among the Philistines": A Postscript,
  An Interview with Bryan Griffin Y-81
Panizzi, Sir Anthony 1797-1879 . . . . DLB-184

Panneton, Philippe (see Ringuet)
Panshin, Alexei 1940- DLB-8
Pansy (see Alden, Isabella)
Pantheon Books DLB-46
Papantonio, Michael (see Kohn, John S. Van E.)
Paperback Library DLB-46
Paperback Science Fiction. DLB-8
Paquet, Alfons 1881-1944. . . . . DLB-66
Paracelsus 1493-1541 . . . . .DLB-179
Paradis, Suzanne 1936- DLB-53
Pareja Diezcanseco, Alfredo
  1908-1993 . . . . DLB-145
Pardoe, Julia 1804-1862 . . . . DLB-166
Parents' Magazine Press DLB-46
Parise, Goffredo 1929-1986 . . . . .DLB-177
Parisian Theater, Fall 1984: Toward
  A New Baroque Y-85
Parizeau, Alice 1930- DLB-60
Parke, John 1754-1789 . . . . DLB-31
Parker, Dorothy 1893-1967 . . . . . . DLB-11, 45, 86
Parker, Gilbert 1860-1932 . . . . DLB-99
Parker, James 1714-1770 . . . . DLB-43
Parker, Theodore 1810-1860 . . . . DLB-1
Parker, William Riley 1906-1968 . . . . DLB-103
Parker, J. H. [publishing house] DLB-106
Parker, John [publishing house] DLB-106
Parkman, Francis, Jr.
  1823-1893 . . . . .DLB-1, 30, 183, 186
Parks, Gordon 1912- DLB-33
Parks, William 1698-1750. . . . . DLB-43
Parks, William [publishing house] DLB-49
Parley, Peter (see Goodrich, Samuel Griswold)
Parmenides late sixth-fifth century B.C.
  . . . . .DLB-176
Parnell, Thomas 1679-1718. . . . . DLB-95
Parr, Catherine 1513?-1548 . . . . DLB-136
Parrington, Vernon L. 1871-1929. . . . . .DLB-17, 63
Parrish, Maxfield 1870-1966. . . . . DLB-188
Parronchi, Alessandro 1914- DLB-128
Partridge, S. W., and Company DLB-106
Parton, James 1822-1891 . . . . DLB-30
Parton, Sara Payson Willis
  1811-1872. . . . . DLB-43, 74
Parun, Vesna 1922- DLB-181
Pasinetti, Pier Maria 1913- DLB-177
Pasolini, Pier Paolo 1922- DLB-128, 177
Pastan, Linda 1932- DLB-5
Paston, George (Emily Morse Symonds)
  1860-1936 . . . . .DLB-149, 197
The Paston Letters 1422-1509 . . . . DLB-146
Pastorius, Francis Daniel
  1651-circa 1720 . . . . DLB-24
Patchen, Kenneth 1911-1972 . . . . DLB-16, 48
Pater, Walter 1839-1894. . . . . .DLB-57, 156
Paterson, Katherine 1932- DLB-52
Patmore, Coventry 1823-1896 . . . . . . DLB-35, 98

Paton, Alan 1903-1988 . . . . DS-17
Paton, Joseph Noel 1821-1901 . . . . DLB-35
Paton Walsh, Jill 1937- DLB-161
Patrick, Edwin Hill ("Ted") 1901-1964 . . .DLB-137
Patrick, John 1906- DLB-7
Pattee, Fred Lewis 1863-1950. . . . . DLB-71
Pattern and Paradigm: History as
  Design, by Judith Ryan DLB-75
Patterson, Alicia 1906-1963 . . . . .DLB-127
Patterson, Eleanor Medill 1881-1948 . . . . . DLB-29
Patterson, Eugene 1923- DLB-127
Patterson, Joseph Medill 1879-1946 . . . . . . DLB-29
Pattillo, Henry 1726-1801 . . . . DLB-37
Paul, Elliot 1891-1958 . . . . DLB-4
Paul, Jean (see Richter, Johann Paul Friedrich)
Paul, Kegan, Trench, Trubner and Company
  Limited. DLB-106
Paul, Peter, Book Company. DLB-49
Paul, Stanley, and Company Limited. . . . DLB-112
Paulding, James Kirke 1778-1860 . . .DLB-3, 59, 74
Paulin, Tom 1949- DLB-40
Pauper, Peter, Press DLB-46
Pavese, Cesare 1908-1950 . . . . .DLB-128, 177
Pavlova, Karolina Karlovna
  1807-1893. DLB-205
Pavić, Milorad 1929- DLB-181
Pavlov, Konstantin 1933- DLB-181
Pavlov, Nikolai Filippovich 1803-1864 . . . . DLB-198
Pavlova, Karolina Karlovna 1807-1893. . . . DLB-205
Pavlović, Miodrag 1928- DLB-181
Paxton, John 1911-1985 . . . . DLB-44
Payn, James 1830-1898. . . . . DLB-18
Payne, John 1842-1916 . . . . DLB-35
Payne, John Howard 1791-1852. . . . . DLB-37
Payson and Clarke DLB-46
Paz, Octavio 1914-1998 . . . . Y-90
Pazzi, Roberto 1946- DLB-196
Peabody, Elizabeth Palmer 1804-1894 . . . . . DLB-1
Peabody, Elizabeth Palmer
  [publishing house] DLB-49
Peabody, Oliver William Bourn
  1799-1848. . . . . DLB-59
Peace, Roger 1899-1968. . . . . .DLB-127
Peacham, Henry 1578-1644? DLB-151
Peacham, Henry, the Elder 1547-1634 . . . .DLB-172
Peachtree Publishers, Limited. DLB-46
Peacock, Molly 1947- DLB-120
Peacock, Thomas Love 1785-1866 . . . DLB-96, 116
Pead, Deuel ?-1727 . . . . DLB-24
Peake, Mervyn 1911-1968 . . . . DLB-15, 160
Peale, Rembrandt 1778-1860 . . . . DLB-183
Pear Tree Press DLB-112
Pearce, Philippa 1920- DLB-161
Pearson, H. B. [publishing house]. DLB-49
Pearson, Hesketh 1887-1964. . . . . DLB-149
Peck, George W. 1840-1916. . . . . DLB-23, 42

Peck, H. C., and Theo. Bliss
  [publishing house] DLB-49
Peck, Harry Thurston 1856-1914 .....DLB-71, 91
Peele, George 1556-1596 ....DLB-62, 167
Pegler, Westbrook 1894-1969 ....DLB-171
Pekić, Borislav 1930-1992 ....DLB-181
Pellegrini and Cudahy DLB-46
Pelletier, Aimé (see Vac, Bertrand)
Pemberton, Sir Max 1863-1950 ....DLB-70
Penfield, Edward 1866-1925 ....DLB-188
Penguin Books [U.S.] DLB-46
Penguin Books [U.K.] DLB-112
Penn Publishing Company DLB-49
Penn, William 1644-1718...............DLB-24
Penna, Sandro 1906-1977..............DLB-114
Pennell, Joseph 1857-1926 ....DLB-188
Penner, Jonathan 1940- Y-83
Pennington, Lee 1939- Y-82
Pepys, Samuel 1633-1703..............DLB-101
Percy, Thomas 1729-1811 ....DLB-104
Percy, Walker 1916-1990 .....DLB-2; Y-80, Y-90
Percy, William 1575-1648 ....DLB-172
Perec, Georges 1936-1982 ....DLB-83
Perelman, Bob 1947- DLB-193
Perelman, S. J. 1904-1979..........DLB-11, 44
Perez, Raymundo "Tigre" 1946- DLB-122
Peri Rossi, Cristina 1941- DLB-145
Periodicals of the Beat Generation........DLB-16
Perkins, Eugene 1932- DLB-41
Perkoff, Stuart Z. 1930-1974 ....DLB-16
Perley, Moses Henry 1804-1862 ....DLB-99
Permabooks DLB-46
Perovsky, Aleksei Alekseevich (Antonii Pogorel'sky)
  1787-1836......................DLB-198
Perrin, Alice 1867-1934 ....DLB-156
Perry, Bliss 1860-1954 ....DLB-71
Perry, Eleanor 1915-1981 ....DLB-44
Perry, Matthew 1794-1858..............DLB-183
Perry, Sampson 1747-1823 ....DLB-158
"Personal Style" (1890), by John Addington
  Symonds DLB-57
Perutz, Leo 1882-1957 ....DLB-81
Pesetsky, Bette 1932- DLB-130
Pestalozzi, Johann Heinrich 1746-1827.....DLB-94
Peter, Laurence J. 1919-1990...........DLB-53
Peter of Spain circa 1205-1277 ....DLB-115
Peterkin, Julia 1880-1961 ....DLB-9
Peters, Lenrie 1932- DLB-117
Peters, Robert 1924- DLB-105
Petersham, Maud 1889-1971 and
  Petersham, Miska 1888-1960 ....DLB-22
Peterson, Charles Jacobs 1819-1887.......DLB-79
Peterson, Len 1917- DLB-88
Peterson, Louis 1922- DLB-76
Peterson, T. B., and Brothers DLB-49

Petitclair, Pierre 1813-1860 ....DLB-99
Petrov, Aleksandar 1938- DLB-181
Petrov, Gavriil 1730-1801 ....DLB-150
Petrov, Vasilii Petrovich 1736-1799 ......DLB-150
Petrov, Valeri 1920- DLB-181
Petrović, Rastko 1898-1949............DLB-147
Petruslied circa 854? DLB-148
Petry, Ann 1908- DLB-76
Pettie, George circa 1548-1589 ....DLB-136
Peyton, K. M. 1929- DLB-161
Pfaffe Konrad flourished circa 1172......DLB-148
Pfaffe Lamprecht flourished circa 1150 ...DLB-148
Pfeiffer, Emily 1827-1890..............DLB-199
Pforzheimer, Carl H. 1879-1957 ....DLB-140
Phaer, Thomas 1510?-1560 ....DLB-167
Phaidon Press Limited................DLB-112
Pharr, Robert Deane 1916-1992 ....DLB-33
Phelps, Elizabeth Stuart 1815-1852 ......DLB-202
Phelps, Elizabeth Stuart 1844-1911 ......DLB-74
Philander von der Linde
  (see Mencke, Johann Burckhard)
Philby, H. St. John B. 1885-1960........DLB-195
Philip, Marlene Nourbese 1947- DLB-157
Philippe, Charles-Louis 1874-1909..........DLB-65
Phillipps, Sir Thomas 1792-1872 ....DLB-184
Philips, John 1676-1708 ....DLB-95
Philips, Katherine 1632-1664...........DLB-131
Phillips, Caryl 1958- DLB-157
Phillips, David Graham 1867-1911 .....DLB-9, 12
Phillips, Jayne Anne 1952- Y-80
Phillips, Robert 1938- DLB-105
Phillips, Stephen 1864-1915 ....DLB-10
Phillips, Ulrich B. 1877-1934 ....DLB-17
Phillips, Willard 1784-1873 ....DLB-59
Phillips, William 1907- DLB-137
Phillips, Sampson and Company.........DLB-49
Phillpotts, Adelaide Eden (Adelaide Ross)
  1896-1993 ....DLB-191
Phillpotts, Eden
  1862-1960 .... DLB-10, 70, 135, 153
Philo circa 20-15 B.C.-circa A.D. 50
  ....DLB-176
Philosophical Library................DLB-46
"The Philosophy of Style" (1852), by
  Herbert Spencer DLB-57
Phinney, Elihu [publishing house]........DLB-49
Phoenix, John (see Derby, George Horatio)
PHYLON (Fourth Quarter, 1950),
  The Negro in Literature:
  The Current Scene DLB-76
Physiologus circa 1070-circa 1150 ....DLB-148
Piccolo, Lucio 1903-1969..............DLB-114
Pickard, Tom 1946- DLB-40
Pickering, William [publishing house]....DLB-106
Pickthall, Marjorie 1883-1922 ....DLB-92
Pictorial Printing Company DLB-49

Piercy, Marge 1936- DLB-120
Pierro, Albino 1916- DLB-128
Pignotti, Lamberto 1926- DLB-128
Pike, Albert 1809-1891 ....DLB-74
Pike, Zebulon Montgomery 1779-1813 ...DLB-183
Pilon, Jean-Guy 1930- DLB-60
Pinckney, Eliza Lucas 1722-1793........DLB-200
Pinckney, Josephine 1895-1957 ....DLB-6
Pindar circa 518 B.C.-circa 438 B.C.
  ....DLB-176
Pindar, Peter (see Wolcot, John)
Pinero, Arthur Wing 1855-1934 ....DLB-10
Pinget, Robert 1919- DLB-83
Pinnacle Books DLB-46
Piñon, Nélida 1935- DLB-145
Pinsky, Robert 1940- Y-82
Pinter, Harold 1930- DLB-13
Piontek, Heinz 1925- DLB-75
Piozzi, Hester Lynch [Thrale]
  1741-1821 ....DLB-104, 142
Piper, H. Beam 1904-1964...............DLB-8
Piper, Watty DLB-22
Pirckheimer, Caritas 1467-1532.........DLB-179
Pirckheimer, Willibald 1470-1530 ....DLB-179
Pisar, Samuel 1929- Y-83
Pitkin, Timothy 1766-1847 ....DLB-30
The Pitt Poetry Series: Poetry Publishing
  Today Y-85
Pitter, Ruth 1897- DLB-20
Pix, Mary 1666-1709 ....DLB-80
Pixerécourt, René Charles Guilbert de
  1773-1844 ....DLB-192
Plaatje, Sol T. 1876-1932..............DLB-125
The Place of Realism in Fiction (1895), by
  George Gissing DLB-18
Plante, David 1940- Y-83
Platen, August von 1796-1835...........DLB-90
Plath, Sylvia 1932-1963...........DLB-5, 6, 152
Plato circa 428 B.C.-348-347 B.C.
  ....DLB-176
Platon 1737-1812 ....DLB-150
Platt and Munk Company...............DLB-46
Playboy Press DLB-46
Playford, John [publishing house] DLB-170
Plays, Playwrights, and Playgoers DLB-84
Playwrights and Professors, by
  Tom Stoppard....................DLB-13
Playwrights on the Theater DLB-80
Der Pleier flourished circa 1250 ....DLB-138
Plenzdorf, Ulrich 1934- DLB-75
Plessen, Elizabeth 1944- DLB-75
Pletnev, Petr Aleksandrovich
  1792-1865 ....DLB-205
Plievier, Theodor 1892-1955 ....DLB-69
Plimpton, George 1927- DLB-185
Plomer, William 1903-1973 .....DLB-20, 162, 191
Plotinus 204-270 ....DLB-176

Plumly, Stanley 1939- DLB-5, 193	Popular Library DLB-46	Prados, Emilio 1899-1962 .... DLB-134
Plumpp, Sterling D. 1940- DLB-41	Porlock, Martin (see MacDonald, Philip)	Praed, Winthrop Mackworth 1802-1839 .... DLB-96
Plunkett, James 1920- DLB-14	Porpoise Press...................... DLB-112	
Plutarch circa 46-circa 120 ....DLB-176	Porta, Antonio 1935-1989 .... DLB-128	Praeger Publishers DLB-46
Plymell, Charles 1935- DLB-16	Porter, Anna Maria 1780-1832 ..... DLB-116, 159	Praetorius, Johannes 1630-1680........ DLB-168
Pocket Books DLB-46	Porter, David 1780-1843.............. DLB-183	Pratolini, Vasco 1913-1991...........DLB-177
Poe, Edgar Allan 1809-1849.....DLB-3, 59, 73, 74	Porter, Eleanor H. 1868-1920........... DLB-9	Pratt, E. J. 1882-1964 .... DLB-92
Poe, James 1921-1980................ DLB-44	Porter, Gene Stratton (see Stratton-Porter, Gene)	Pratt, Samuel Jackson 1749-1814 .... DLB-39
The Poet Laureate of the United States Statements from Former Consultants in Poetry.................... Y-86	Porter, Henry ?-? DLB-62	Preface to *Alwyn* (1780), by Thomas Holcroft.................. DLB-39
	Porter, Jane 1776-1850 .... DLB-116, 159	Preface to *Colonel Jack* (1722), by Daniel Defoe................... DLB-39
	Porter, Katherine Anne 1890-1980 ....DLB-4, 9, 102; Y-80; DS-12	
"The Poet's Kaleidoscope: The Element of Surprise in the Making of the Poem," by Madeline DeFrees DLB-105	Porter, Peter 1929- DLB-40	Preface to *Evelina* (1778), by Fanny Burney DLB-39
	Porter, William Sydney 1862-1910 ....DLB-12, 78, 79	Preface to *Ferdinand Count Fathom* (1753), by Tobias Smollett DLB-39
"The Poetry File," by Edward Field DLB-105		
Pogodin, Mikhail Petrovich 1800-1875... DLB-198	Porter, William T. 1809-1858 .... DLB-3, 43	Preface to *Incognita* (1692), by William Congreve................ DLB-39
Pogorel'sky, Antonii (see Perovsky, Aleksei Alekseevich)	Porter and Coates.................... DLB-49	
	Portis, Charles 1933- DLB-6	Preface to *Joseph Andrews* (1742), by Henry Fielding.................. DLB-39
Pohl, Frederik 1919- DLB-8	Posey, Alexander 1873-1908............DLB-175	
Poirier, Louis (see Gracq, Julien)	Postans, Marianne circa 1810-1865 ..... DLB-166	Preface to *Moll Flanders* (1722), by Daniel Defoe................... DLB-39
Polanyi, Michael 1891-1976 .... DLB-100	Postl, Carl (see Sealsfield, Carl)	
Pole, Reginald 1500-1558............ DLB-132	Poston, Ted 1906-1974................ DLB-51	Preface to *Poems* (1853), by Matthew Arnold DLB-32
Polevoi, Nikolai Alekseevich 1796-1846.................... DLB-198	Postscript to [the Third Edition of] *Clarissa* (1751), by Samuel Richardson DLB-39	Preface to *Robinson Crusoe* (1719), by Daniel Defoe................... DLB-39
Polezhaev, Aleksandr Ivanovich 1804-1838 .... DLB-205	Potok, Chaim 1929- DLB-28, 152; Y-84	Preface to *Roderick Random* (1748), by Tobias Smollett.................. DLB-39
Poliakoff, Stephen 1952- DLB-13	Potter, Beatrix 1866-1943............. DLB-141	
Polidori, John William 1795-1821....... DLB-116	Potter, David M. 1910-1971 .... DLB-17	Preface to *Roxana* (1724), by Daniel Defoe................... DLB-39
Polite, Carlene Hatcher 1932- DLB-33	Potter, John E., and Company DLB-49	
Pollard, Alfred W. 1859-1944.......... DLB-201	Pottle, Frederick A. 1897-1987 .....DLB-103; Y-87	Preface to *St. Leon* (1799), by William Godwin DLB-39
Pollard, Edward A. 1832-1872 .... DLB-30	Poulin, Jacques 1937- DLB-60	
Pollard, Graham 1903-1976 .... DLB-201	Pound, Ezra 1885-1972..... DLB-4, 45, 63; DS-15	Preface to Sarah Fielding's *Familiar Letters* (1747), by Henry Fielding [excerpt] ... DLB-39
Pollard, Percival 1869-1911 .... DLB-71	Povich, Shirley 1905- DLB-171	Preface to Sarah Fielding's *The Adventures of David Simple* (1744), by Henry Fielding................... DLB-39
Pollard and Moss DLB-49	Powell, Anthony 1905- DLB-15	
Pollock, Sharon 1936- DLB-60	Powell, John Wesley 1834-1902........ DLB-186	
Polonsky, Abraham 1910- DLB-26	Powers, J. F. 1917- DLB-130	Preface to *The Cry* (1754), by Sarah Fielding DLB-39
Polotsky, Simeon 1629-1680 .... DLB-150	Pownall, David 1938- DLB-14	Preface to *The Delicate Distress* (1769), by Elizabeth Griffin................. DLB-39
Polybius circa 200 B.C.-118 B.C. DLB-176	Powys, John Cowper 1872-1963......... DLB-15	
Pomilio, Mario 1921-1990 ....DLB-177	Powys, Llewelyn 1884-1939............ DLB-98	Preface to *The Disguis'd Prince* (1733), by Eliza Haywood [excerpt]........... DLB-39
Ponce, Mary Helen 1938- DLB-122	Powys, T. F. 1875-1953 .... DLB-36, 162	
Ponce-Montoya, Juanita 1949- DLB-122	Poynter, Nelson 1903-1978 .... DLB-127	Preface to *The Farther Adventures of Robinson Crusoe* (1719), by Daniel Defoe....... DLB-39
Ponet, John 1516?-1556 .... DLB-132	The Practice of Biography: An Interview with Stanley Weintraub.............. Y-82	
Poniatowski, Elena 1933- DLB-113		Preface to the First Edition of *Pamela* (1740), by Samuel Richardson DLB-39
Ponsard, François 1814-1867 .... DLB-192	The Practice of Biography II: An Interview with B. L. Reid..................... Y-83	
Ponsonby, William [publishing house]....DLB-170		Preface to the First Edition of *The Castle of Otranto* (1764), by Horace Walpole.... DLB-39
Pontiggia, Giuseppe 1934- DLB-196	The Practice of Biography III: An Interview with Humphrey Carpenter Y-84	
Pony Stories DLB-160		Preface to *The History of Romances* (1715), by Pierre Daniel Huet [excerpts]......... DLB-39
Poole, Ernest 1880-1950................ DLB-9	The Practice of Biography IV: An Interview with William Manchester................. Y-85	
Poole, Sophia 1804-1891 .... DLB-166		Preface to *The Life of Charlotta du Pont* (1723), by Penelope Aubin................ DLB-39
Poore, Benjamin Perley 1820-1887....... DLB-23	The Practice of Biography V: An Interview with Justin Kaplan Y-86	
Popa, Vasko 1922-1991 .... DLB-181		Preface to *The Old English Baron* (1778), by Clara Reeve DLB-39
Pope, Abbie Hanscom 1858-1894....... DLB-140	The Practice of Biography VI: An Interview with David Herbert Donald................ Y-87	
Pope, Alexander 1688-1744 .... DLB-95, 101		Preface to the Second Edition of *The Castle of Otranto* (1765), by Horace Walpole.... DLB-39
Popov, Mikhail Ivanovich 1742-circa 1790.................. DLB-150	The Practice of Biography VII: An Interview with John Caldwell Guilds.............. Y-92	
		Preface to *The Secret History, of Queen Zarah, and the Zarazians* (1705), by Delariviere Manley......................... DLB-39
Popović, Aleksandar 1929-1996 .... DLB-181	The Practice of Biography VIII: An Interview with Joan Mellen Y-94	
	The Practice of Biography IX: An Interview with Michael Reynolds Y-95	Preface to the Third Edition of *Clarissa* (1751), by Samuel Richardson [excerpt]....... DLB-39
		Preface to *The Works of Mrs. Davys* (1725), by Mary Davys...................... DLB-39

Preface to Volume 1 of *Clarissa* (1747), by
 Samuel Richardson DLB-39
Preface to Volume 3 of *Clarissa* (1748), by
 Samuel Richardson DLB-39
Préfontaine, Yves 1937- DLB-53
Prelutsky, Jack 1940- DLB-61
Premisses, by Michael Hamburger DLB-66
Prentice, George D. 1802-1870 ....DLB-43
Prentice-Hall DLB-46
Prescott, Orville 1906-1996 .... Y-96
Prescott, William Hickling
 1796-1859 ....DLB-1, 30, 59
The Present State of the English Novel (1892),
 by George Saintsbury DLB-18
Prešeren, Francn 1800-1849............DLB-147
Preston, May Wilson 1873-1949 ....DLB-188
Preston, Thomas 1537-1598............DLB-62
Price, Reynolds 1933- DLB-2
Price, Richard 1723-1791 ....DLB-158
Price, Richard 1949- Y-81
Priest, Christopher 1943- DLB-14
Priestley, J. B. 1894-1984
 ....DLB-10, 34, 77, 100, 139; Y-84
Primary Bibliography: A Retrospective...... Y-95
Prime, Benjamin Young 1733-1791 ....DLB-31
Primrose, Diana floruit circa 1630.......DLB-126
Prince, F. T. 1912- DLB-20
Prince, Thomas 1687-1758.........DLB-24, 140
The Principles of Success in Literature (1865), by
 George Henry Lewes [excerpt] DLB-57
Printz, Wolfgang Casper 1641-1717......DLB-168
Prior, Matthew 1664-1721 ....DLB-95
Prisco, Michele 1920- DLB-177
Pritchard, William H. 1932- DLB-111
Pritchett, V. S. 1900- DLB-15, 139
Probyn, May 1856 or 1857-1909 ....DLB-199
Procter, Adelaide Anne 1825-1864 ...DLB-32, 199
Procter, Bryan Waller 1787-1874 .....DLB-96, 144
Proctor, Robert 1868-1903 ....DLB-184
*Producing Dear Bunny, Dear Volodya: The Friendship
 and the Feud* Y-97
The Profession of Authorship:
 Scribblers for Bread.................. Y-89
The Progress of Romance (1785), by Clara Reeve
 [excerpt]........................DLB-39
Prokopovich, Feofan 1681?-1736........DLB-150
Prokosch, Frederic 1906-1989 ....DLB-48
The Proletarian Novel DLB-9
Propper, Dan 1937- DLB-16
The Prospect of Peace (1778), by Joel Barlow ..DLB-37
Protagoras circa 490 B.C.-420 B.C.
 ....DLB-176
Proud, Robert 1728-1813..............DLB-30
Proust, Marcel 1871-1922 ....DLB-65
Prynne, J. H. 1936- DLB-40
Przybyszewski, Stanislaw 1868-1927 .....DLB-66
Pseudo-Dionysius the Areopagite floruit
 circa 500 ....DLB-115

Public Domain and the Violation of Texts ... Y-97
The Public Lending Right in America
 Statement by Sen. Charles McC.
 Mathias, Jr. PLR and the Meaning
 of Literary Property Statements on
 PLR by American Writers Y-83
The Public Lending Right in the United Kingdom
 Public Lending Right: The First Year in the
 United Kingdom.................. Y-83
The Publication of English
 Renaissance Plays DLB-62
Publications and Social Movements
 [Transcendentalism] DLB-1
Publishers and Agents: The Columbia
 Connection Y-87
A Publisher's Archives: G. P. Putnam........ Y-92
Publishing Fiction at LSU Press............ Y-87
Pückler-Muskau, Hermann von 1785-1871 .. DLB-133
Pufendorf, Samuel von 1632-1694.......DLB-168
Pugh, Edwin William 1874-1930........DLB-135
Pugin, A. Welby 1812-1852.............DLB-55
Puig, Manuel 1932-1990 ....DLB-113
Pulitzer, Joseph 1847-1911 ....DLB-23
Pulitzer, Joseph, Jr. 1885-1955...........DLB-29
Pulitzer Prizes for the Novel, 1917-1945 ....DLB-9
Pulliam, Eugene 1889-1975 ....DLB-127
Purchas, Samuel 1577?-1626 ....DLB-151
Purdy, Al 1918- DLB-88
Purdy, James 1923- DLB-2
Purdy, Ken W. 1913-1972 ....DLB-137
Pusey, Edward Bouverie 1800-1882 ......DLB-55
Pushkin, Aleksandr Sergeevich
 1799-1837 ....DLB-205
Pushkin, Vasilii L'vovich 1766-1830 .....DLB-205
Putnam, George Palmer 1814-1872.....DLB-3, 79
Putnam, Samuel 1892-1950..............DLB-4
G. P. Putnam's Sons [U.S.] DLB-49
G. P. Putnam's Sons [U.K.] DLB-106
Puzo, Mario 1920- DLB-6
Pyle, Ernie 1900-1945 ....DLB-29
Pyle, Howard 1853-1911 .....DLB-42, 188; DS-13
Pym, Barbara 1913-1980 ....DLB-14; Y-87
Pynchon, Thomas 1937- DLB-2, 173
Pyramid Books DLB-46
Pyrnelle, Louise-Clarke 1850-1907 ....DLB-42
Pythagoras circa 570 B.C.-? DLB-176

Q

Quad, M. (see Lewis, Charles B.)
Quaritch, Bernard 1819-1899 ....DLB-184
Quarles, Francis 1592-1644 ....DLB-126
The Quarterly Review 1809-1967 ....DLB-110
Quasimodo, Salvatore 1901-1968 ....DLB-114
Queen, Ellery (see Dannay, Frederic, and
 Manfred B. Lee)
The Queen City Publishing House DLB-49
Queneau, Raymond 1903-1976 ....DLB-72
Quennell, Sir Peter 1905-1993......DLB-155, 195

Quesnel, Joseph 1746-1809 ....DLB-99
The Question of American Copyright
 in the Nineteenth Century Headnote
 Preface, by George Haven Putnam
 The Evolution of Copyright, by Brander
 Matthews
 Summary of Copyright Legislation in
 the United States, by R. R. Bowker
 Analysis oe the Provisions of the
 Copyright Law of 1891, by
 George Haven Putnam
 The Contest for International Copyright,
 by George Haven Putnam
 Cheap Books and Good Books,
 by Brander Matthews DLB-49
Quiller-Couch, Sir Arthur Thomas
 1863-1944 .... DLB-135, 153, 190
Quin, Ann 1936-1973 ....DLB-14
Quincy, Samuel, of Georgia ?-?..........DLB-31
Quincy, Samuel, of Massachusetts
 1734-1789 ....DLB-31
Quinn, Anthony 1915- DLB-122
Quinn, John 1870-1924 ....DLB-187
Quintana, Leroy V. 1944- DLB-82
Quintana, Miguel de 1671-1748
 A Forerunner of Chicano
 Literature DLB-122
Quist, Harlin, Books DLB-46
Quoirez, Françoise (see Sagan, Françoise)

R

R-va, Zeneida (see Gan, Elena Andreevna)
Raabe, Wilhelm 1831-1910 ....DLB-129
Raban, Jonathan 1942- DLB-204
Rabe, David 1940- DLB-7
Raboni, Giovanni 1932- DLB-128
Rachilde 1860-1953..............DLB-123, 192
Racin, Kočo 1908-1943 ....DLB-147
Rackham, Arthur 1867-1939 ....DLB-141
Radcliffe, Ann 1764-1823............DLB-39, 178
Raddall, Thomas 1903- DLB-68
Radichkov, Yordan 1929- DLB-181
Radiguet, Raymond 1903-1923.........DLB-65
Radishchev, Aleksandr Nikolaevich
 1749-1802 ....DLB-150
Radványi, Netty Reiling (see Seghers, Anna)
Rahv, Philip 1908-1973 ....DLB-137
Raich, Semen Egorovich 1792-1855.......DLB-205
Raičković, Stevan 1928- DLB-181
Raimund, Ferdinand Jakob 1790-1836.....DLB-90
Raine, Craig 1944- DLB-40
Raine, Kathleen 1908- DLB-20
Rainolde, Richard
 circa 1530-1606.................DLB-136
Rakić, Milan 1876-1938................DLB-147
Rakosi, Carl 1903- DLB-193
Ralegh, Sir Walter 1554?-1618 ....DLB-172
Ralin, Radoy 1923- DLB-181
Ralph, Julian 1853-1903 ....DLB-23
Ralph Waldo Emerson in 1982........... Y-82

Cumulative Index

Ramat, Silvio 1939- DLB-128
Rambler, no. 4 (1750), by Samuel Johnson
   [excerpt] DLB-39
Ramée, Marie Louise de la (see Ouida)
Ramírez, Sergío 1942- DLB-145
Ramke, Bin 1947- DLB-120
Ramler, Karl Wilhelm 1725-1798 .... DLB-97
Ramon Ribeyro, Julio 1929- DLB-145
Ramous, Mario 1924- DLB-128
Rampersad, Arnold 1941- DLB-111
Ramsay, Allan 1684 or 1685-1758 ...... DLB-95
Ramsay, David 1749-1815 .... DLB-30
Ramsay, Martha Laurens 1759-1811 .... DLB-200
Ranck, Katherine Quintana 1942- DLB-122
Rand, Avery and Company DLB-49
Rand McNally and Company DLB-49
Randall, David Anton 1905-1975 ...... DLB-140
Randall, Dudley 1914- DLB-41
Randall, Henry S. 1811-1876 .... DLB-30
Randall, James G. 1881-1953 .... DLB-17
The Randall Jarrell Symposium: A Small
   Collection of Randall Jarrells
   Excerpts From Papers Delivered at
   the Randall Jarrel Symposium Y-86
Randolph, A. Philip 1889-1979 .... DLB-91
Randolph, Anson D. F.
   [publishing house] DLB-49
Randolph, Thomas 1605-1635 ...... DLB-58, 126
Random House DLB-46
Ranlet, Henry [publishing house] DLB-49
Ransom, Harry 1908-1976 .... DLB-187
Ransom, John Crowe 1888-1974 ..... DLB-45, 63
Ransome, Arthur 1884-1967 .... DLB-160
Raphael, Frederic 1931- DLB-14
Raphaelson, Samson 1896-1983 .... DLB-44
Raskin, Ellen 1928-1984 .... DLB-52
Rastell, John 1475?-1536 .... DLB-136, 170
Rattigan, Terence 1911-1977 .... DLB-13
Rawlings, Marjorie Kinnan
   1896-1953 .... DLB-9, 22, 102; DS-17
Raworth, Tom 1938- DLB-40
Ray, David 1932- DLB-5
Ray, Gordon Norton 1915-1986 ... DLB-103, 140
Ray, Henrietta Cordelia 1849-1916 ..... DLB-50
Raymond, Ernest 1888-1974 .... DLB-191
Raymond, Henry J. 1820-1869 ...... DLB-43, 79
Raymond Chandler Centenary Tributes
   from Michael Avallone, James Elroy, Joe Gores,
   and William F. Nolan................ Y-88
Reach, Angus 1821-1856 .... DLB-70
Read, Herbert 1893-1968 .... DLB-20, 149
Read, Herbert, "The Practice of Biography," in *The
   English Sense of Humour and Other
   Essays* DLB-149
Read, Martha Meredith DLB-200
Read, Opie 1852-1939 .... DLB-23
Read, Piers Paul 1941- DLB-14

Reade, Charles 1814-1884 .... DLB-21
Reader's Digest Condensed Books DLB-46
Readers Ulysses Symposium Y-97
Reading, Peter 1946- DLB-40
Reading Series in New York City Y-96
Reaney, James 1926- DLB-68
Rebhun, Paul 1500?-1546 .... DLB-179
Rèbora, Clemente 1885-1957 .... DLB-114
Rechy, John 1934- DLB-122; Y-82
The Recovery of Literature: Criticism in the 1990s:
   A Symposium Y-91
Redding, J. Saunders 1906-1988 ..... DLB-63, 76
Redfield, J. S. [publishing house] DLB-49
Redgrove, Peter 1932- DLB-40
Redmon, Anne 1943- Y-86
Redmond, Eugene B. 1937- DLB-41
Redpath, James [publishing house] DLB-49
Reed, Henry 1808-1854 .... DLB-59
Reed, Henry 1914- DLB-27
Reed, Ishmael 1938- DLB-2, 5, 33, 169; DS-8
Reed, Rex 1938- DLB-185
Reed, Sampson 1800-1880 .... DLB-1
Reed, Talbot Baines 1852-1893 .... DLB-141
Reedy, William Marion 1862-1920 ..... DLB-91
Reese, Lizette Woodworth 1856-1935 ... DLB-54
Reese, Thomas 1742-1796 .... DLB-37
Reeve, Clara 1729-1807 .... DLB-39
Reeves, James 1909-1978 .... DLB-161
Reeves, John 1926- DLB-88
"Reflections: After a Tornado,"
   by Judson Jerome................. DLB-105
Regnery, Henry, Company DLB-46
Rehberg, Hans 1901-1963 .... DLB-124
Rehfisch, Hans José 1891-1960 .... DLB-124
Reid, Alastair 1926- DLB-27
Reid, B. L. 1918-1990 .... DLB-111
Reid, Christopher 1949- DLB-40
Reid, Forrest 1875-1947 .... DLB-153
Reid, Helen Rogers 1882-1970 .... DLB-29
Reid, James ?-? DLB-31
Reid, Mayne 1818-1883 .... DLB-21, 163
Reid, Thomas 1710-1796 .... DLB-31
Reid, V. S. (Vic) 1913-1987 .... DLB-125
Reid, Whitelaw 1837-1912 .... DLB-23
Reilly and Lee Publishing Company DLB-46
Reimann, Brigitte 1933-1973 .... DLB-75
Reinmar der Alte circa 1165-circa 1205 .. DLB-138
Reinmar von Zweter
   circa 1200-circa 1250 .... DLB-138
Reisch, Walter 1903-1983 .... DLB-44
Reizei Family DLB-203
Remarque, Erich Maria 1898-1970 ..... DLB-56
"Re-meeting of Old Friends": The Jack
   Kerouac Conference Y-82
Reminiscences, by Charles Scribner Jr. DS-17

Remington, Frederic
   1861-1909 .... DLB-12, 186, 188
Renaud, Jacques 1943- DLB-60
Renault, Mary 1905-1983 .... Y-83
Rendell, Ruth 1930- DLB-87
Rensselaer, Maria van Cortlandt van
   1645-1689 .... DLB-200
Representative Men and Women: A Historical
   Perspective on the British Novel,
   1930-1960 .... DLB-15
(Re-)Publishing Orwell Y-86
Research in the American Antiquarian Book
   Trade Y-97
Responses to Ken Auletta.............. Y-97
Rettenbacher, Simon 1634-1706 .... DLB-168
Reuchlin, Johannes 1455-1522 .... DLB-179
Reuter, Christian 1665-after 1712 ..... DLB-168
Reuter, Fritz 1810-1874 .... DLB-129
Reuter, Gabriele 1859-1941 .... DLB-66
Revell, Fleming H., Company DLB-49
Reventlow, Franziska Gräfin zu
   1871-1918 .... DLB-66
Review of Reviews Office DLB-112
Review of [Samuel Richardson's] *Clarissa* (1748), by
   Henry Fielding DLB-39
The Revolt (1937), by Mary Colum
   [excerpts] DLB-36
Rexroth, Kenneth
   1905-1982 .... DLB-16, 48, 165; Y-82
Rey, H. A. 1898-1977 .... DLB-22
Reynal and Hitchcock DLB-46
Reynolds, G. W. M. 1814-1879 .... DLB-21
Reynolds, John Hamilton 1794-1852 ..... DLB-96
Reynolds, Mack 1917- DLB-8
Reynolds, Sir Joshua 1723-1792 .... DLB-104
Reznikoff, Charles 1894-1976 .... DLB-28, 45
"Rhetoric" (1828; revised, 1859), by
   Thomas de Quincey [excerpt] DLB-57
Rhett, Robert Barnwell 1800-1876 ...... DLB-43
Rhode, John 1884-1964 .... DLB-77
Rhodes, James Ford 1848-1927 .... DLB-47
Rhodes, Richard 1937- DLB-185
Rhys, Jean 1890-1979 .... DLB-36, 117, 162
Ricardo, David 1772-1823 .... DLB-107, 158
Ricardou, Jean 1932- DLB-83
Rice, Elmer 1892-1967 .... DLB-4, 7
Rice, Grantland 1880-1954 .... DLB-29, 171
Rich, Adrienne 1929- DLB-5, 67
Richards, David Adams 1950- DLB-53
Richards, George circa 1760-1814 ...... DLB-37
Richards, I. A. 1893-1979 .... DLB-27
Richards, Laura E. 1850-1943 .... DLB-42
Richards, William Carey 1818-1892 ..... DLB-73
Richards, Grant [publishing house] DLB-112
Richardson, Charles F. 1851-1913 ..... DLB-71
Richardson, Dorothy M. 1873-1957 ..... DLB-36
Richardson, Henry Handel (Ethel Florence
   Lindesay) 1870-1946 .... DLB-197

Richardson, Jack 1935- DLB-7	Rivera, Tomás 1935-1984 ....DLB-82	Rölvaag, O. E. 1876-1931 ....DLB-9
Richardson, John 1796-1852 ....DLB-99	Rivers, Conrad Kent 1933-1968 ....DLB-41	Romains, Jules 1885-1972 ....DLB-65
Richardson, Samuel 1689-1761 ......DLB-39, 154	Riverside Press......................DLB-49	Roman, A., and Company..............DLB-49
Richardson, Willis 1889-1977 ....DLB-51	Rivington, James circa 1724-1802 ....DLB-43	Romano, Lalla 1906- DLB-177
Riche, Barnabe 1542-1617..............DLB-136	Rivington, Charles [publishing house]....DLB-154	Romano, Octavio 1923- DLB-122
Richepin, Jean 1849-1926 ....DLB-192	Rivkin, Allen 1903-1990 ....DLB-26	Romero, Leo 1950- DLB-122
Richler, Mordecai 1931- DLB-53	Roa Bastos, Augusto 1917- DLB-113	Romero, Lin 1947- DLB-122
Richter, Conrad 1890-1968...............DLB-9	Robbe-Grillet, Alain 1922- DLB-83	Romero, Orlando 1945- DLB-82
Richter, Hans Werner 1908- DLB-69	Robbins, Tom 1936- Y-80	Rook, Clarence 1863-1915 ....DLB-135
Richter, Johann Paul Friedrich 1763-1825 ....DLB-94	Roberts, Charles G. D. 1860-1943........DLB-92	Roosevelt, Theodore 1858-1919 .....DLB-47, 186
Rickerby, Joseph [publishing house] DLB-106	Roberts, Dorothy 1906-1993............DLB-88	Root, Waverley 1903-1982..............DLB-4
Rickword, Edgell 1898-1982 ....DLB-20	Roberts, Elizabeth Madox 1881-1941 ....DLB-9, 54, 102	Root, William Pitt 1941- DLB-120
Riddell, Charlotte 1832-1906............DLB-156	Roberts, Kenneth 1885-1957.............DLB-9	Roquebrune, Robert de 1889-1978 ....DLB-68
Riddell, John (see Ford, Corey)	Roberts, William 1767-1849............DLB-142	Rosa, João Guimarães 1908-1967.......DLB-113
Ridge, John Rollin 1827-1867............DLB-175	Roberts Brothers....................DLB-49	Rosales, Luis 1910-1992 ....DLB-134
Ridge, Lola 1873-1941 ....DLB-54	Roberts, James [publishing house].......DLB-154	Roscoe, William 1753-1831 ....DLB-163
Ridge, William Pett 1859-1930 ....DLB-135	Robertson, A. M., and Company DLB-49	Rose, Reginald 1920- DLB-26
Riding, Laura (see Jackson, Laura Riding)	Robertson, William 1721-1793..........DLB-104	Rose, Wendy 1948- DLB-175
Ridler, Anne 1912- DLB-27	Robins, Elizabeth 1862-1952............DLB-197	Rosegger, Peter 1843-1918 ....DLB-129
Ridruego, Dionisio 1912-1975 ....DLB-108	Robinson, Casey 1903-1979.............DLB-44	Rosei, Peter 1946- DLB-85
Riel, Louis 1844-1885 ....DLB-99	Robinson, Edwin Arlington 1869-1935....DLB-54	Rosen, Norma 1925- DLB-28
Riemer, Johannes 1648-1714 ....DLB-168	Robinson, Henry Crabb 1775-1867......DLB-107	Rosenbach, A. S. W. 1876-1952 ....DLB-140
Riffaterre, Michael 1924- DLB-67	Robinson, James Harvey 1863-1936 ......DLB-47	Rosenbaum, Ron 1946- DLB-185
Riggs, Lynn 1899-1954 ....DLB-175	Robinson, Lennox 1886-1958............DLB-10	Rosenberg, Isaac 1890-1918 ....DLB-20
Riis, Jacob 1849-1914.................DLB-23	Robinson, Mabel Louise 1874-1962......DLB-22	Rosenfeld, Isaac 1918-1956 ....DLB-28
Riker, John C. [publishing house] DLB-49	Robinson, Mary 1758-1800 ....DLB-158	Rosenthal, M. L. 1917- DLB-5
Riley, James 1777-1840.................DLB-183	Robinson, Richard circa 1545-1607......DLB-167	Rosenwald, Lessing J. 1891-1979........DLB-187
Riley, John 1938-1978 ....DLB-40	Robinson, Therese 1797-1870.......DLB-59, 133	Ross, Alexander 1591-1654............DLB-151
Rilke, Rainer Maria 1875-1926 ....DLB-81	Robison, Mary 1949- DLB-130	Ross, Harold 1892-1951 ....DLB-137
Rimanelli, Giose 1926- DLB-177	Roblès, Emmanuel 1914- DLB-83	Ross, Leonard Q. (see Rosten, Leo)
Rinehart and Company................DLB-46	Roccatagliata Ceccardi, Ceccardo 1871-1919 ....DLB-114	Ross, Lillian 1927- DLB-185
Ringuet 1895-1960...................DLB-68	Rochester, John Wilmot, Earl of 1647-1680 ....DLB-131	Ross, Martin 1862-1915................DLB-135
Ringwood, Gwen Pharis 1910-1984........DLB-88	Rock, Howard 1911-1976 ....DLB-127	Ross, Sinclair 1908- DLB-88
Rinser, Luise 1911- DLB-69	Rockwell, Norman Perceval 1894-1978 ....DLB-188	Ross, W. W. E. 1894-1966 ....DLB-88
Ríos, Alberto 1952- DLB-122	Rodgers, Carolyn M. 1945- DLB-41	Rosselli, Amelia 1930- DLB-128
Ríos, Isabella 1948- DLB-82	Rodgers, W. R. 1909-1969 ....DLB-20	Rossen, Robert 1908-1966.............DLB-26
Ripley, Arthur 1895-1961 ....DLB-44	Rodríguez, Claudio 1934- DLB-134	Rossetti, Christina Georgina 1830-1894 ....DLB-35, 163
Ripley, George 1802-1880 ....DLB-1, 64, 73	Rodriguez, Richard 1944- DLB-82	Rossetti, Dante Gabriel 1828-1882 ....DLB-35
The Rising Glory of America: Three Poems....................DLB-37	Rodríguez Julia, Edgardo 1946- DLB-145	Rossner, Judith 1935- DLB-6
The Rising Glory of America: Written in 1771 (1786), by Hugh Henry Brackenridge and Philip Freneau....................DLB-37	Roe, E. P. 1838-1888................DLB-202	Rostand, Edmond 1868-1918 ....DLB-192
	Roethke, Theodore 1908-1963 ....DLB-5	Rosten, Leo 1908- DLB-11
Riskin, Robert 1897-1955...............DLB-26	Rogers, Jane 1952- DLB-194	Rostenberg, Leona 1908- DLB-140
Risse, Heinz 1898- DLB-69	Rogers, Pattiann 1940- DLB-105	Rostopchina, Evdokiia Petrovna 1811-1858 ....DLB-205
Rist, Johann 1607-1667................DLB-164	Rogers, Samuel 1763-1855 ....DLB-93	Rostovsky, Dimitrii 1651-1709 ....DLB-150
Ritchie, Anna Mowatt 1819-1870..........DLB-3	Rogers, Will 1879-1935 ....DLB-11	Rota, Bertram 1903-1966 ....DLB-201
Ritchie, Anne Thackeray 1837-1919 .....DLB-18	Rohmer, Sax 1883-1959 ....DLB-70	Bertram Rota and His Bookshop..........Y-91
Ritchie, Thomas 1778-1854 ....DLB-43	Roiphe, Anne 1935- Y-80	Roth, Gerhard 1942- DLB-85, 124
Rites of Passage [on William Saroyan].......Y-83	Rojas, Arnold R. 1896-1988 ....DLB-82	Roth, Henry 1906?- DLB-28
The Ritz Paris Hemingway Award Y-85	Rolfe, Frederick William 1860-1913 ....DLB-34, 156	Roth, Joseph 1894-1939................DLB-85
Rivard, Adjutor 1868-1945 ....DLB-92		Roth, Philip 1933- DLB-2, 28, 173; Y-82
Rive, Richard 1931-1989 ....DLB-125	Rolland, Romain 1866-1944 ....DLB-65	Rothenberg, Jerome 1931- DLB-5, 193
Rivera, Marina 1942- DLB-122	Rolle, Richard circa 1290-1300 - 1340....DLB-146	Rothschild Family DLB-184
		Rotimi, Ola 1938- DLB-125

Routhier, Adolphe-Basile 1839-1920 ..... DLB-99
Routier, Simone 1901-1987 .... DLB-88
Routledge, George, and Sons DLB-106
Roversi, Roberto 1923- DLB-128
Rowe, Elizabeth Singer 1674-1737 .... DLB-39, 95
Rowe, Nicholas 1674-1718 .... DLB-84
Rowlands, Samuel circa 1570-1630 ..... DLB-121
Rowlandson, Mary
    circa 1637-circa 1711 .... DLB-24, 200
Rowley, William circa 1585-1626 .... DLB-58
Rowse, A. L. 1903- DLB-155
Rowson, Susanna Haswell
    circa 1762-1824 .... DLB-37, 200
Roy, Camille 1870-1943 .... DLB-92
Roy, Gabrielle 1909-1983 .... DLB-68
Roy, Jules 1907- DLB-83
The Royal Court Theatre and the English
    Stage Company DLB-13
The Royal Court Theatre and the New
    Drama DLB-10
The Royal Shakespeare Company
    at the Swan Y-88
Royall, Anne 1769-1854 .... DLB-43
The Roycroft Printing Shop DLB-49
Royde-Smith, Naomi 1875-1964 .... DLB-191
Royster, Vermont 1914- DLB-127
Royston, Richard [publishing house] DLB-170
Ruark, Gibbons 1941- DLB-120
Ruban, Vasilii Grigorevich 1742-1795 ... DLB-150
Rubens, Bernice 1928- DLB-14
Rudd and Carleton DLB-49
Rudkin, David 1936- DLB-13
Rudolf von Ems
    circa 1200-circa 1254 .... DLB-138
Ruffin, Josephine St. Pierre
    1842-1924 .... DLB-79
Ruganda, John 1941- DLB-157
Ruggles, Henry Joseph 1813-1906 ...... DLB-64
Rukeyser, Muriel 1913-1980 .... DLB-48
Rule, Jane 1931- DLB-60
Rulfo, Juan 1918-1986 .... DLB-113
Rumaker, Michael 1932- DLB-16
Rumens, Carol 1944- DLB-40
Runyon, Damon 1880-1946 ...... DLB-11, 86, 171
Ruodlieb circa 1050-1075 .... DLB-148
Rush, Benjamin 1746-1813 .... DLB-37
Rush, Rebecca 1779-? DLB-200
Rushdie, Salman 1947- DLB-194
Rusk, Ralph L. 1888-1962 .... DLB-103
Ruskin, John 1819-1900 .... DLB-55, 163, 190
Russ, Joanna 1937- DLB-8
Russell, B. B., and Company DLB-49
Russell, Benjamin 1761-1845 .... DLB-43
Russell, Bertrand 1872-1970 .... DLB-100
Russell, Charles Edward 1860-1941 ..... DLB-25
Russell, Charles M. 1864-1926 .... DLB-188

Russell, Countess Mary Annette Beauchamp
    (see Arnim, Elizabeth von)
Russell, George William (see AE)
Russell, R. H., and Son DLB-49
Rutherford, Mark 1831-1913 .... DLB-18
Ruxton, George Frederick 1821-1848 ... DLB-186
Ryan, Michael 1946- Y-82
Ryan, Oscar 1904- DLB-68
Ryga, George 1932- DLB-60
Rylands, Enriqueta Augustina Tennant
    1843-1908 .... DLB-184
Rylands, John 1801-1888 .... DLB-184
Ryleev, Kondratii Fedorovich
    1795-1826 .... DLB-205
Rymer, Thomas 1643?-1713 .... DLB-101
Ryskind, Morrie 1895-1985 .... DLB-26
Rzhevsky, Aleksei Andreevich
    1737-1804 .... DLB-150

S

The Saalfield Publishing Company DLB-46
Saba, Umberto 1883-1957 .... DLB-114
Sábato, Ernesto 1911- DLB-145
Saberhagen, Fred 1930- DLB-8
Sabin, Joseph 1821-1881 .... DLB-187
Sacer, Gottfried Wilhelm 1635-1699 ... DLB-168
Sachs, Hans 1494-1576 .... DLB-179
Sack, John 1930- DLB-185
Sackler, Howard 1929-1982 .... DLB-7
Sackville, Thomas 1536-1608 .... DLB-132
Sackville, Thomas 1536-1608
    and Norton, Thomas
    1532-1584 .... DLB-62
Sackville-West, Edward 1901-1965 ..... DLB-191
Sackville-West, V. 1892-1962 .... DLB-34, 195
Sadlier, D. and J., and Company DLB-49
Sadlier, Mary Anne 1820-1903 .... DLB-99
Sadoff, Ira 1945- DLB-120
Saenz, Jaime 1921-1986 .... DLB-145
Saffin, John circa 1626-1710 .... DLB-24
Sagan, Françoise 1935- DLB-83
Sage, Robert 1899-1962 .... DLB-4
Sagel, Jim 1947- DLB-82
Sagendorph, Robb Hansell 1900-1970 ... DLB-137
Sahagún, Carlos 1938- DLB-108
Sahkomaapii, Piitai (see Highwater, Jamake)
Sahl, Hans 1902- DLB-69
Said, Edward W. 1935- DLB-67
Saigyō 1118-1190 .... DLB-203
Saiko, George 1892-1962 .... DLB-85
St. Dominic's Press DLB-112
Saint-Exupéry, Antoine de 1900-1944 .... DLB-72
St. John, J. Allen 1872-1957 .... DLB-188
St. Johns, Adela Rogers 1894-1988 ..... DLB-29
The St. John's College Robert Graves Trust ..Y-96
St. Martin's Press DLB-46

St. Omer, Garth 1931- DLB-117
Saint Pierre, Michel de 1916-1987 ..... DLB-83
Saintsbury, George 1845-1933 .... DLB-57, 149
Saiokuken Sōchō 1448-1532 .... DLB-203
Saki (see Munro, H. H.)
Salaam, Kalamu ya 1947- DLB-38
Šalamun, Tomaž 1941- DLB-181
Salas, Floyd 1931- DLB-82
Sálaz-Marquez, Rubén 1935- DLB-122
Salemson, Harold J. 1910-1988 .... DLB-4
Salinas, Luis Omar 1937- DLB-82
Salinas, Pedro 1891-1951 .... DLB-134
Salinger, J. D. 1919- DLB-2, 102, 173
Salkey, Andrew 1928- DLB-125
Salt, Waldo 1914- DLB-44
Salter, James 1925- DLB-130
Salter, Mary Jo 1954- DLB-120
Saltus, Edgar 1855-1921 .... DLB-202
Salustri, Carlo Alberto (see Trilussa)
Salverson, Laura Goodman 1890-1970 .... DLB-92
Sampson, Richard Henry (see Hull, Richard)
Samuels, Ernest 1903- DLB-111
Sanborn, Franklin Benjamin 1831-1917 .... DLB-1
Sánchez, Luis Rafael 1936- DLB-145
Sánchez, Philomeno "Phil" 1917- DLB-122
Sánchez, Ricardo 1941- DLB-82
Sanchez, Sonia 1934- DLB-41; DS-8
Sand, George 1804-1876 .... DLB-119, 192
Sandburg, Carl 1878-1967 .... DLB-17, 54
Sanders, Ed 1939- DLB-16
Sandoz, Mari 1896-1966 .... DLB-9
Sandwell, B. K. 1876-1954 .... DLB-92
Sandy, Stephen 1934- DLB-165
Sandys, George 1578-1644 .... DLB-24, 121
Sangster, Charles 1822-1893 .... DLB-99
Sanguineti, Edoardo 1930- DLB-128
Sanjōnishi Sanetaka 1455-1537 .... DLB-203
Sansay, Leonora ?-after 1823 .... DLB-200
Sansom, William 1912-1976 .... DLB-139
Santayana, George
    1863-1952 .... DLB-54, 71; DS-13
Santiago, Danny 1911-1988 .... DLB-122
Santmyer, Helen Hooven 1895-1986 .... Y-84
Sanvitale, Francesca 1928- DLB-196
Sapidus, Joannes 1490-1561 .... DLB-179
Sapir, Edward 1884-1939 .... DLB-92
Sapper (see McNeile, Herman Cyril)
Sappho circa 620 B.C.-circa 550 B.C.
    .... DLB-176
Sardou, Victorien 1831-1908 .... DLB-192
Sarduy, Severo 1937- DLB-113
Sargent, Pamela 1948- DLB-8
Saro-Wiwa, Ken 1941- DLB-157
Saroyan, William 1908-1981 ...DLB-7, 9, 86; Y-81
Sarraute, Nathalie 1900- DLB-83

Sarrazin, Albertine 1937-1967............DLB-83	Schnabel, Johann Gottfried 1692-1760......................DLB-168	Scott, Paul 1920-1978..................DLB-14
Sarris, Greg 1952- DLB-175	Schnackenberg, Gjertrud 1953-........DLB-120	Scott, Sarah 1723-1795..................DLB-39
Sarton, May 1912- DLB-48; Y-81	Schnitzler, Arthur 1862-1931.........DLB-81, 118	Scott, Tom 1918-.....................DLB-27
Sartre, Jean-Paul 1905-1980............DLB-72	Schnurre, Wolfdietrich 1920- DLB-69	Scott, Sir Walter 1771-1832.........DLB-93, 107, 116, 144, 159
Sassoon, Siegfried 1886-1967..............DLB-20, 191; DS-18	Schocken Books......................DLB-46	Scott, William Bell 1811-1890...........DLB-32
Sata, Ineko 1904- DLB-180	Scholartis Press.....................DLB-112	Scott, Walter, Publishing Company Limited.................DLB-112
Saturday Review Press.................DLB-46	Scholderer, Victor 1880-1971...........DLB-201	Scott, William R. [publishing house]......DLB-46
Saunders, James 1925- DLB-13	The Schomburg Center for Research in Black Culture..................DLB-76	Scott-Heron, Gil 1949- DLB-41
Saunders, John Monk 1897-1940.........DLB-26	Schönbeck, Virgilio (see Giotti, Virgilio)	Scribe, Eugene 1791-1861..............DLB-192
Saunders, Margaret Marshall 1861-1947...DLB-92	Schönherr, Karl 1867-1943............DLB-118	Scribner, Arthur Hawley 1859-1932.... DS-13, 16
Saunders and Otley...................DLB-106	Schoolcraft, Jane Johnston 1800-1841....DLB-175	Scribner, Charles 1854-1930..........DS-13, 16
Savage, James 1784-1873...............DLB-30	School Stories, 1914-1960................DLB-160	Scribner, Charles, Jr. 1921-1995............Y-95
Savage, Marmion W. 1803?-1872.........DLB-21	Schopenhauer, Arthur 1788-1860........DLB-90	Charles Scribner's Sons.... DLB-49; DS-13, 16, 17
Savage, Richard 1697?-1743.............DLB-95	Schopenhauer, Johanna 1766-1838.......DLB-90	Scripps, E. W. 1854-1926...............DLB-25
Savard, Félix-Antoine 1896-1982.........DLB-68	Schorer, Mark 1908-1977..............DLB-103	Scudder, Horace Elisha 1838-1902....DLB-42, 71
Saville, (Leonard) Malcolm 1901-1982...DLB-160	Schottelius, Justus Georg 1612-1676.....DLB-164	Scudder, Vida Dutton 1861-1954........DLB-71
Sawyer, Ruth 1880-1970................DLB-22	Schouler, James 1839-1920..............DLB-47	Scupham, Peter 1933- DLB-40
Sayers, Dorothy L. 1893-1957............. DLB-10, 36, 77, 100	Schrader, Paul 1946- DLB-44	Seabrook, William 1886-1945............DLB-4
Sayle, Charles Edward 1864-1924.......DLB-184	Schreiner, Olive 1855-1920..... DLB-18, 156, 190	Seabury, Samuel 1729-1796.............DLB-31
Sayles, John Thomas 1950- DLB-44	Schroeder, Andreas 1946- DLB-53	Seacole, Mary Jane Grant 1805-1881....DLB-166
Sbarbaro, Camillo 1888-1967...........DLB-114	Schubart, Christian Friedrich Daniel 1739-1791......................DLB-97	*The Seafarer* circa 970.................DLB-146
Scalapino, Leslie 1947- DLB-193	Schubert, Gotthilf Heinrich 1780-1860....DLB-90	Sealsfield, Charles (Carl Postl) 1793-1864..................DLB-133, 186
Scannell, Vernon 1922- DLB-27	Schücking, Levin 1814-1883............DLB-133	Sears, Edward I. 1819?-1876.............DLB-79
Scarry, Richard 1919-1994..............DLB-61	Schulberg, Budd 1914- DLB-6, 26, 28; Y-81	Sears Publishing Company.............DLB-46
Schaeffer, Albrecht 1885-1950...........DLB-66	Schulte, F. J., and Company............DLB-49	Seaton, George 1911-1979..............DLB-44
Schaeffer, Susan Fromberg 1941- DLB-28	Schulze, Hans (see Praetorius, Johannes)	Seaton, William Winston 1785-1866......DLB-43
Schaff, Philip 1819-1893.................DS-13	Schupp, Johann Balthasar 1610-1661.....DLB-164	Secker, Martin, and Warburg Limited ...DLB-112
Schaper, Edzard 1908-1984.............DLB-69	Schurz, Carl 1829-1906................DLB-23	Secker, Martin [publishing house].......DLB-112
Scharf, J. Thomas 1843-1898............DLB-47	Schuyler, George S. 1895-1977.......DLB-29, 51	Second-Generation Minor Poets of the Seventeenth Century.............DLB-126
Schede, Paul Melissus 1539-1602.......DLB-179	Schuyler, James 1923-1991..........DLB-5, 169	Sedgwick, Arthur George 1844-1915......DLB-64
Scheffel, Joseph Viktor von 1826-1886...DLB-129	Schwartz, Delmore 1913-1966.......DLB-28, 48	Sedgwick, Catharine Maria 1789-1867..................DLB-1, 74, 183
Scheffler, Johann 1624-1677............DLB-164	Schwartz, Jonathan 1938- Y-82	Sedgwick, Ellery 1872-1930.............DLB-91
Schelling, Friedrich Wilhelm Joseph von 1775-1854......................DLB-90	Schwarz, Sibylle 1621-1638............DLB-164	Sedley, Sir Charles 1639-1701..........DLB-131
Scherer, Wilhelm 1841-1886...........DLB-129	Schwerner, Armand 1927- DLB-165	Seeger, Alan 1888-1916.................DLB-45
Schickele, René 1883-1940.............DLB-66	Schwob, Marcel 1867-1905............DLB-123	Seers, Eugene (see Dantin, Louis)
Schiff, Dorothy 1903-1989.............DLB-127	Sciascia, Leonardo 1921-1989..........DLB-177	Segal, Erich 1937- Y-86
Schiller, Friedrich 1759-1805............DLB-94	Science Fantasy.......................DLB-8	Šegedin, Petar 1909- DLB-181
Schirmer, David 1623-1687............DLB-164	Science-Fiction Fandom and Conventions...DLB-8	Seghers, Anna 1900-1983..............DLB-69
Schlaf, Johannes 1862-1941............DLB-118	Science-Fiction Fanzines: The Time Binders......................DLB-8	Seid, Ruth (see Sinclair, Jo)
Schlegel, August Wilhelm 1767-1845......DLB-94	Science-Fiction Films..................DLB-8	Seidel, Frederick Lewis 1936- Y-84
Schlegel, Dorothea 1763-1839...........DLB-90	Science Fiction Writers of America and the Nebula Awards..................DLB-8	Seidel, Ina 1885-1974..................DLB-56
Schlegel, Friedrich 1772-1829............DLB-90	Scot, Reginald circa 1538-1599.........DLB-136	Seifert, Jaroslav 1901- Y-84
Schleiermacher, Friedrich 1768-1834......DLB-90	Scotellaro, Rocco 1923-1953...........DLB-128	Seigenthaler, John 1927- DLB-127
Schlesinger, Arthur M., Jr. 1917- DLB-17	Scott, Dennis 1939-1991...............DLB-125	Seizin Press........................DLB-112
Schlumberger, Jean 1877-1968..........DLB-65	Scott, Dixon 1881-1915................DLB-98	Séjour, Victor 1817-1874...............DLB-50
Schmid, Eduard Hermann Wilhelm (see Edschmid, Kasimir)	Scott, Duncan Campbell 1862-1947......DLB-92	Séjour Marcou et Ferrand, Juan Victor (see Séjour, Victor)
Schmidt, Arno 1914-1979..............DLB-69	Scott, Evelyn 1893-1963.............DLB-9, 48	Sekowski, Józef-Julian, Baron Brambeus (see Senkovsky, Osip Ivanovich)
Schmidt, Johann Kaspar (see Stirner, Max)	Scott, F. R. 1899-1985.................DLB-88	
Schmidt, Michael 1947- DLB-40	Scott, Frederick George 1861-1944.......DLB-92	Selby, Bettina 1934- DLB-204
Schmidtbonn, Wilhelm August 1876-1952.....................DLB-118	Scott, Geoffrey 1884-1929.............DLB-149	Selby, Hubert, Jr. 1928- DLB-2
Schmitz, James H. 1911- DLB-8	Scott, Harvey W. 1838-1910............DLB-23	

Cumulative Index

Selden, George 1929-1989 .... DLB-52
Selected English-Language Little Magazines and Newspapers [France, 1920-1939]... DLB-4
Selected Humorous Magazines (1820-1950) DLB-11
Selected Science-Fiction Magazines and Anthologies DLB-8
Selenić, Slobodan 1933-1995 .... DLB-181
Self, Edwin F. 1920- DLB-137
Seligman, Edwin R. A. 1861-1939 .... DLB-47
Selimović, Meša 1910-1982 .... DLB-181
Selous, Frederick Courteney 1851-1917................. DLB-174
Seltzer, Chester E. (see Muro, Amado)
Seltzer, Thomas [publishing house] DLB-46
Selvon, Sam 1923-1994................ DLB-125
Semmes, Raphael 1809-1877........... DLB-189
Senancour, Etienne de 1770-1846....... DLB-119
Sendak, Maurice 1928- DLB-61
Senécal, Eva 1905- DLB-92
Sengstacke, John 1912- DLB-127
Senior, Olive 1941- DLB-157
Senkovsky, Osip Ivanovich (Józef-Julian Sekowski, Baron Brambeus) 1800-1858 .... DLB-198
Šenoa, August 1838-1881 .... DLB-147
"Sensation Novels" (1863), by H. L. Manse.................... DLB-21
Sepamla, Sipho 1932- DLB-157
Seredy, Kate 1899-1975 .... DLB-22
Sereni, Vittorio 1913-1983 .... DLB-128
Seres, William [publishing house]........DLB-170
Serling, Rod 1924-1975............... DLB-26
Serote, Mongane Wally 1944- DLB-125
Serraillier, Ian 1912-1994 .... DLB-161
Serrano, Nina 1934- DLB-122
Service, Robert 1874-1958 .... DLB-92
Sessler, Charles 1854-1935............. DLB-187
Seth, Vikram 1952- DLB-120
Seton, Elizabeth Ann 1774-1821 .... DLB-200
Seton, Ernest Thompson 1860-1942 .... DLB-92; DS-13
Setouchi Harumi 1922- DLB-182
Settle, Mary Lee 1918- DLB-6
Seume, Johann Gottfried 1763-1810 ...... DLB-94
Seuse, Heinrich 1295?-1366 ....DLB-179
Seuss, Dr. (see Geisel, Theodor Seuss)
The Seventy-fifth Anniversary of the Armistice: The Wilfred Owen Centenary and the Great War Exhibit at the University of Virginia Y-93
Severin, Timothy 1940- DLB-204
Sewall, Joseph 1688-1769 .... DLB-24
Sewall, Richard B. 1908- DLB-111
Sewell, Anna 1820-1878 .... DLB-163
Sewell, Samuel 1652-1730 .... DLB-24
Sex, Class, Politics, and Religion [in the British Novel, 1930-1959] DLB-15
Sexton, Anne 1928-1974............ DLB-5, 169

Seymour-Smith, Martin 1928- DLB-155
Sgorlon, Carlo 1930- DLB-196
Shaara, Michael 1929-1988................. Y-83
Shadwell, Thomas 1641?-1692.......... DLB-80
Shaffer, Anthony 1926- DLB-13
Shaffer, Peter 1926- DLB-13
Shaftesbury, Anthony Ashley Cooper, Third Earl of 1671-1713........... DLB-101
Shairp, Mordaunt 1887-1939 .... DLB-10
Shakespeare, William 1564-1616 .....DLB-62, 172
The Shakespeare Globe Trust Y-93
Shakespeare Head Press............. DLB-112
Shakhovskoi, Aleksandr Aleksandrovich 1777-1846..................... DLB-150
Shange, Ntozake 1948- DLB-38
Shapiro, Karl 1913- DLB-48
Sharon Publications DLB-46
Sharp, Margery 1905-1991............. DLB-161
Sharp, William 1855-1905 .... DLB-156
Sharpe, Tom 1928- DLB-14
Shaw, Albert 1857-1947 .... DLB-91
Shaw, George Bernard 1856-1950 .... DLB-10, 57, 190
Shaw, Henry Wheeler 1818-1885 .... DLB-11
Shaw, Joseph T. 1874-1952............ DLB-137
Shaw, Irwin 1913-1984.........DLB-6, 102; Y-84
Shaw, Robert 1927-1978 .... DLB-13, 14
Shaw, Robert B. 1947- DLB-120
Shawn, William 1907-1992............. DLB-137
Shay, Frank [publishing house].......... DLB-46
Shea, John Gilmary 1824-1892........... DLB-30
Sheaffer, Louis 1912-1993 .... DLB-103
Shearing, Joseph 1886-1952 .... DLB-70
Shebbeare, John 1709-1788............ DLB-39
Sheckley, Robert 1928- DLB-8
Shedd, William G. T. 1820-1894 .... DLB-64
Sheed, Wilfred 1930- DLB-6
Sheed and Ward [U.S.].................. DLB-46
Sheed and Ward Limited [U.K.] DLB-112
Sheldon, Alice B. (see Tiptree, James, Jr.)
Sheldon, Edward 1886-1946............. DLB-7
Sheldon and Company................ DLB-49
Shelley, Mary Wollstonecraft 1797-1851 .... DLB-110, 116, 159, 178
Shelley, Percy Bysshe 1792-1822................DLB-96, 110, 158
Shelnutt, Eve 1941- DLB-130
Shenstone, William 1714-1763 .... DLB-95
Shepard, Ernest Howard 1879-1976 ..... DLB-160
Shepard, Sam 1943- DLB-7
Shepard, Thomas I, 1604 or 1605-1649 ... DLB-24
Shepard, Thomas II, 1635-1677 .... DLB-24
Shepard, Clark and Brown............. DLB-49
Shepherd, Luke flourished 1547-1554 .... DLB-136
Sherburne, Edward 1616-1702 .... DLB-131

Sheridan, Frances 1724-1766......... DLB-39, 84
Sheridan, Richard Brinsley 1751-1816 .... DLB-89
Sherman, Francis 1871-1926............ DLB-92
Sherriff, R. C. 1896-1975 ....DLB-10, 191
Sherry, Norman 1935- DLB-155
Sherwood, Mary Martha 1775-1851..... DLB-163
Sherwood, Robert 1896-1955..........DLB-7, 26
Shevyrev, Stepan Petrovich 1806-1864 .... DLB-205
Shiel, M. P. 1865-1947 .... DLB-153
Shiels, George 1886-1949 .... DLB-10
Shiga, Naoya 1883-1971 .... DLB-180
Shiina Rinzō 1911-1973 .... DLB-182
Shikishi Naishinnō 1153?-1201 .... DLB-203
Shillaber, B.[enjamin] P.[enhallow] 1814-1890 .... DLB-1, 11
Shimao Toshio 1917-1986 .... DLB-182
Shimazaki, Tōson 1872-1943 .... DLB-180
Shine, Ted 1931- DLB-38
Shinkei 1406-1475..................... DLB-203
Ship, Reuben 1915-1975............... DLB-88
Shirer, William L. 1904-1993............. DLB-4
Shirinsky-Shikhmatov, Sergii Aleksandrovich 1783-1837................... DLB-150
Shirley, James 1596-1666 .... DLB-58
Shishkov, Aleksandr Semenovich 1753-1841..................... DLB-150
Shockley, Ann Allen 1927- DLB-33
Shōno Junzō 1921- DLB-182
Shore, Arabella 1820?-1901 and Shore, Louisa 1824-1895 .... DLB-199
Short, Peter [publishing house]..........DLB-170
Shorthouse, Joseph Henry 1834-1903 .... DLB-18
Shōtetsu 1381-1459 .... DLB-203
Showalter, Elaine 1941- DLB-67
Shulevitz, Uri 1935- DLB-61
Shulman, Max 1919-1988............. DLB-11
Shute, Henry A. 1856-1943 .... DLB-9
Shuttle, Penelope 1947- DLB-14, 40
Sibbes, Richard 1577-1635 .... DLB-151
Siddal, Elizabeth Eleanor 1829-1862 .... DLB-199
Sidgwick, Ethel 1877-1970..............DLB-197
Sidgwick and Jackson Limited DLB-112
Sidney, Margaret (see Lothrop, Harriet M.)
Sidney, Mary 1561-1621 .... DLB-167
Sidney, Sir Philip 1554-1586............ DLB-167
Sidney's Press...................... DLB-49
Siegfried Loraine Sassoon: A Centenary Essay Tributes from Vivien F. Clarke and Michael Thorpe..................... Y-86
Sierra, Rubén 1946- DLB-122
Sierra Club Books DLB-49
Siger of Brabant circa 1240-circa 1284 .... DLB-115
Sigourney, Lydia Howard (Huntley) 1791-1865...............DLB-1, 42, 73, 183
Silkin, Jon 1930- DLB-27

Silko, Leslie Marmon 1948- DLB-143, 175	Sisson, C. H. 1914- DLB-27	Smith, Elizabeth Oakes (Prince) 1806-1893...................DLB-1
Silliman, Benjamin 1779-1864 ....DLB-183	Sitwell, Edith 1887-1964................DLB-20	Smith, Eunice 1757-1823 ....DLB-200
Silliman, Ron 1946- DLB-169	Sitwell, Osbert 1892-1969 .... DLB-100, 195	Smith, F. Hopkinson 1838-1915 .... DS-13
Silliphant, Stirling 1918- DLB-26	Skármeta, Antonio 1940- DLB-145	Smith, George D. 1870-1920 ....DLB-140
Sillitoe, Alan 1928- DLB-14, 139	Skeat, Walter W. 1835-1912 ....DLB-184	Smith, George O. 1911-1981.............DLB-8
Silman, Roberta 1934- DLB-28	Skeffington, William [publishing house] ..DLB-106	Smith, Goldwin 1823-1910 ....DLB-99
Silva, Beverly 1930- DLB-122	Skelton, John 1463-1529 ....DLB-136	Smith, H. Allen 1907-1976 .... DLB-11, 29
Silverberg, Robert 1935- DLB-8	Skelton, Robin 1925- DLB-27, 53	Smith, Harry B. 1860-1936 ....DLB-187
Silverman, Kenneth 1936- DLB-111	Skinner, Constance Lindsay 1877-1939 ....DLB-92	Smith, Hazel Brannon 1914- DLB-127
Simak, Clifford D. 1904-1988 ....DLB-8	Skinner, John Stuart 1788-1851 ....DLB-73	Smith, Henry circa 1560-circa 1591......DLB-136
Simcoe, Elizabeth 1762-1850 ....DLB-99	Skipsey, Joseph 1832-1903..............DLB-35	Smith, Horatio (Horace) 1779-1849......DLB-116
Simcox, Edith Jemima 1844-1901 ....DLB-190	Slade, Bernard 1930- DLB-53	Smith, Horatio (Horace) 1779-1849 and James Smith 1775-1839 ....DLB-96
Simcox, George Augustus 1841-1905 .....DLB-35	Slamnig, Ivan 1930- DLB-181	Smith, Iain Crichton 1928- DLB-40, 139
Sime, Jessie Georgina 1868-1958 ....DLB-92	Slater, Patrick 1880-1951 ....DLB-68	Smith, J. Allen 1860-1924 ....DLB-47
Simenon, Georges 1903-1989 ..... DLB-72; Y-89	Slaveykov, Pencho 1866-1912..........DLB-147	Smith, Jessie Willcox 1863-1935 ....DLB-188
Simic, Charles 1938- DLB-105	Slaviček, Milivoj 1929- DLB-181	Smith, John 1580-1631 .... DLB-24, 30
Simmel, Johannes Mario 1924- DLB-69	Slavitt, David 1935- DLB-5, 6	Smith, Josiah 1704-1781 ....DLB-24
Simmes, Valentine [publishing house] DLB-170	Sleigh, Burrows Willcocks Arthur 1821-1869 ....DLB-99	Smith, Ken 1938- DLB-40
Simmons, Ernest J. 1903-1972 ....DLB-103	A Slender Thread of Hope: The Kennedy Center Black Theatre Project DLB-38	Smith, Lee 1944- DLB-143; Y-83
Simmons, Herbert Alfred 1930- DLB-33	Slesinger, Tess 1905-1945 ....DLB-102	Smith, Logan Pearsall 1865-1946 ....DLB-98
Simmons, James 1933- DLB-40	Slick, Sam (see Haliburton, Thomas Chandler)	Smith, Mark 1935- Y-82
Simms, William Gilmore 1806-1870 ....DLB-3, 30, 59, 73	Sloan, John 1871-1951 ....DLB-188	Smith, Michael 1698-circa 1771 ....DLB-31
Simms and M'Intyre DLB-106	Sloane, William, Associates DLB-46	Smith, Red 1905-1982 .... DLB-29, 171
Simon, Claude 1913- DLB-83; Y-85	Small, Maynard and Company DLB-49	Smith, Roswell 1829-1892 ....DLB-79
Simon, Neil 1927- DLB-7	Small Presses in Great Britain and Ireland, 1960-1985 ....DLB-40	Smith, Samuel Harrison 1772-1845 ......DLB-43
Simon and Schuster DLB-46	Small Presses I: Jargon Society............Y-84	Smith, Samuel Stanhope 1751-1819.......DLB-37
Simons, Katherine Drayton Mayrant 1890-1969 ....Y-83	Small Presses II: The Spirit That Moves Us Press Y-85	Smith, Sarah (see Stretton, Hesba)
Simović, Ljubomir 1935- DLB-181	Small Presses III: Pushcart Press Y-87	Smith, Sarah Pogson 1774-1870 ....DLB-200
Simpkin and Marshall [publishing house] DLB-154	Smart, Christopher 1722-1771 ....DLB-109	Smith, Seba 1792-1868............. DLB-1, 11
Simpson, Helen 1897-1940.............DLB-77	Smart, David A. 1892-1957 ....DLB-137	Smith, Sir Thomas 1513-1577 ....DLB-132
Simpson, Louis 1923- DLB-5	Smart, Elizabeth 1913-1986 ....DLB-88	Smith, Stevie 1902-1971................DLB-20
Simpson, N. F. 1919- DLB-13	Smedley, Menella Bute 1820?-1877 .....DLB-199	Smith, Sydney 1771-1845..............DLB-107
Sims, George 1923- DLB-87	Smellie, William [publishing house]......DLB-154	Smith, Sydney Goodsir 1915-1975........DLB-27
Sims, George Robert 1847-1922... DLB-35, 70, 135	Smiles, Samuel 1812-1904 ....DLB-55	Smith, Wendell 1914-1972..............DLB-171
Sinán, Rogelio 1904- DLB-145	Smith, A. J. M. 1902-1980 ....DLB-88	Smith, William flourished 1595-1597 ....DLB-136
Sinclair, Andrew 1935- DLB-14	Smith, Adam 1723-1790................DLB-104	Smith, William 1727-1803 ....DLB-31
Sinclair, Bertrand William 1881-1972 .....DLB-92	Smith, Adam (George Jerome Waldo Goodman) 1930- DLB-185	Smith, William 1728-1793 ....DLB-30
Sinclair, Catherine 1800-1864 ....DLB-163	Smith, Alexander 1829-1867 ....DLB-32, 55	Smith, William Gardner 1927-1974 ......DLB-76
Sinclair, Jo 1913- DLB-28	Smith, Betty 1896-1972 ....Y-82	Smith, William Henry 1808-1872 ....DLB-159
Sinclair Lewis Centennial Conference Y-85	Smith, Carol Sturm 1938- Y-81	Smith, William Jay 1918- DLB-5
Sinclair, Lister 1921- DLB-88	Smith, Charles Henry 1826-1903 ....DLB-11	Smith, Elder and Company DLB-154
Sinclair, May 1863-1946 ....DLB-36, 135	Smith, Charlotte 1749-1806 .... DLB-39, 109	Smith, Harrison, and Robert Haas [publishing house] DLB-46
Sinclair, Upton 1878-1968 ....DLB-9	Smith, Chet 1899-1973 ....DLB-171	Smith, J. Stilman, and Company DLB-49
Sinclair, Upton [publishing house].......DLB-46	Smith, Cordwainer 1913-1966............DLB-8	Smith, W. B., and Company............DLB-49
Singer, Isaac Bashevis 1904-1991 .... DLB-6, 28, 52; Y-91	Smith, Dave 1942- DLB-5	Smith, W. H., and Son DLB-106
Singer, Mark 1950- DLB-185	Smith, Dodie 1896- DLB-10	Smithers, Leonard [publishing house] DLB-112
Singmaster, Elsie 1879-1958..............DLB-9	Smith, Doris Buchanan 1934- DLB-52	Smollett, Tobias 1721-1771 .... DLB-39, 104
Sinisgalli, Leonardo 1908-1981 ....DLB-114	Smith, E. E. 1890-1965 ....DLB-8	Smythe, Francis Sydney 1900-1949......DLB-195
Siodmak, Curt 1902- DLB-44	Smith, Elihu Hubbard 1771-1798 ....DLB-37	Snelling, William Joseph 1804-1848 .....DLB-202
Siringo, Charles A. 1855-1928 ....DLB-186		Snellings, Rolland (see Touré, Askia Muhammad)
Sissman, L. E. 1928-1976................DLB-5		Snodgrass, W. D. 1926- DLB-5
		Snow, C. P. 1905-1980 .... DLB-15, 77; DS-17

Cumulative Index

Snyder, Gary 1930- DLB-5, 16, 165
Sobiloff, Hy 1912-1970 .... DLB-48
The Society for Textual Scholarship and *TEXT* Y-87
The Society for the History of Authorship, Reading and Publishing Y-92
Soffici, Ardengo 1879-1964 .... DLB-114
Sofola, 'Zulu 1938- DLB-157
Solano, Solita 1888-1975 .... DLB-4
Soldati, Mario 1906- DLB-177
Šoljan, Antun 1932-1993 .... DLB-181
Sollers, Philippe 1936- DLB-83
Sollogub, Vladimir Aleksandrovich 1813-1882 .... DLB-198
Solmi, Sergio 1899-1981 .... DLB-114
Solomon, Carl 1928- DLB-16
Solway, David 1941- DLB-53
Solzhenitsyn and America Y-85
Somerville, Edith Œnone 1858-1949 .... DLB-135
Somov, Orest Mikhailovich 1793-1833 .... DLB-198
Song, Cathy 1955- DLB-169
Sono Ayako 1931- DLB-182
Sontag, Susan 1933- DLB-2, 67
Sophocles 497/496 B.C.-406/405 B.C. DLB-176
Šopov, Aco 1923-1982 .... DLB-181
Sorge, Reinhard Johannes 1892-1916 .... DLB-118
Sorrentino, Gilbert 1929- DLB-5, 173; Y-80
Sotheby, William 1757-1833 .... DLB-93
Soto, Gary 1952- DLB-82
Sources for the Study of Tudor and Stuart Drama DLB-62
Souster, Raymond 1921- DLB-88
The *South English Legendary* circa thirteenth-fifteenth centuries DLB-146
Southerland, Ellease 1943- DLB-33
Southern Illinois University Press Y-95
Southern, Terry 1924- DLB-2
Southern Writers Between the Wars DLB-9
Southerne, Thomas 1659-1746 .... DLB-80
Southey, Caroline Anne Bowles 1786-1854 .... DLB-116
Southey, Robert 1774-1843 ..... DLB-93, 107, 142
Southwell, Robert 1561?-1595 .... DLB-167
Sowande, Bode 1948- DLB-157
Sowle, Tace [publishing house] DLB-170
Soyfer, Jura 1912-1939 .... DLB-124
Soyinka, Wole 1934- DLB-125; Y-86, Y-87
Spacks, Barry 1931- DLB-105
Spalding, Frances 1950- DLB-155
Spark, Muriel 1918- DLB-15, 139
Sparke, Michael [publishing house] DLB-170
Sparks, Jared 1789-1866 .... DLB-1, 30
Sparshott, Francis 1926- DLB-60
Späth, Gerold 1939- DLB-75
Spatola, Adriano 1941-1988 .... DLB-128

Spaziani, Maria Luisa 1924- DLB-128
The Spectator 1828- DLB-110
Spedding, James 1808-1881 .... DLB-144
Spee von Langenfeld, Friedrich 1591-1635 .... DLB-164
Speght, Rachel 1597-after 1630 .... DLB-126
Speke, John Hanning 1827-1864 .... DLB-166
Spellman, A. B. 1935- DLB-41
Spence, Thomas 1750-1814 .... DLB-158
Spencer, Anne 1882-1975 .... DLB-51, 54
Spencer, Elizabeth 1921- DLB-6
Spencer, George John, Second Earl Spencer 1758-1834 .... DLB-184
Spencer, Herbert 1820-1903 .... DLB-57
Spencer, Scott 1945- Y-86
Spender, J. A. 1862-1942 .... DLB-98
Spender, Stephen 1909- DLB-20
Spener, Philipp Jakob 1635-1705 .... DLB-164
Spenser, Edmund circa 1552-1599 ...... DLB-167
Sperr, Martin 1944- DLB-124
Spicer, Jack 1925-1965 .... DLB-5, 16, 193
Spielberg, Peter 1929- Y-81
Spielhagen, Friedrich 1829-1911 .... DLB-129
"*Spielmannsepen*" (circa 1152-circa 1500) DLB-148
Spier, Peter 1927- DLB-61
Spinrad, Norman 1940- DLB-8
Spires, Elizabeth 1952- DLB-120
Spitteler, Carl 1845-1924 .... DLB-129
Spivak, Lawrence E. 1900- DLB-137
Spofford, Harriet Prescott 1835-1921 .... DLB-74
Spring, Howard 1889-1965 .... DLB-191
Squier, E. G. 1821-1888 .... DLB-189
Squibob (see Derby, George Horatio)
Stacpoole, H. de Vere 1863-1951 .... DLB-153
Staël, Germaine de 1766-1817 ...... DLB-119, 192
Staël-Holstein, Anne-Louise Germaine de (see Staël, Germaine de)
Stafford, Jean 1915-1979 .... DLB-2, 173
Stafford, William 1914- DLB-5
Stage Censorship: "The Rejected Statement" (1911), by Bernard Shaw [excerpts] ... DLB-10
Stallings, Laurence 1894-1968 .... DLB-7, 44
Stallworthy, Jon 1935- DLB-40
Stampp, Kenneth M. 1912- DLB-17
Stanev, Emiliyan 1907-1979 .... DLB-181
Stanford, Ann 1916- DLB-5
Stankevich, Nikolai Vladimirovich 1813-1840 .... DLB-198
Stanković, Borisav ("Bora") 1876-1927 ... DLB-147
Stanley, Henry M. 1841-1904 ... DLB-189; DS-13
Stanley, Thomas 1625-1678 .... DLB-131
Stannard, Martin 1947- DLB-155
Stansby, William [publishing house] DLB-170
Stanton, Elizabeth Cady 1815-1902 ...... DLB-79

Stanton, Frank L. 1857-1927 .... DLB-25
Stanton, Maura 1946- DLB-120
Stapledon, Olaf 1886-1950 .... DLB-15
Star Spangled Banner Office DLB-49
Stark, Freya 1893-1993 .... DLB-195
Starkey, Thomas circa 1499-1538 ...... DLB-132
Starkie, Walter 1894-1976 .... DLB-195
Starkweather, David 1935- DLB-7
Starrett, Vincent 1886-1974 .... DLB-187
Statements on the Art of Poetry DLB-54
The State of Publishing Y-97
Stationers' Company of London, The DLB-170
Stead, Robert J. C. 1880-1959 .... DLB-92
Steadman, Mark 1930- DLB-6
The Stealthy School of Criticism (1871), by Dante Gabriel Rossetti DLB-35
Stearns, Harold E. 1891-1943 .... DLB-4
Stedman, Edmund Clarence 1833-1908 ... DLB-64
Steegmuller, Francis 1906-1994 .... DLB-111
Steel, Flora Annie 1847-1929 ...... DLB-153, 156
Steele, Max 1922- Y-80
Steele, Richard 1672-1729 .... DLB-84, 101
Steele, Timothy 1948- DLB-120
Steele, Wilbur Daniel 1886-1970 .... DLB-86
Steere, Richard circa 1643-1721 .... DLB-24
Stefanovski, Goran 1952- DLB-181
Stegner, Wallace 1909-1993 .... DLB-9; Y-93
Stehr, Hermann 1864-1940 .... DLB-66
Steig, William 1907- DLB-61
Stein, Gertrude 1874-1946 .. DLB-4, 54, 86; DS-15
Stein, Leo 1872-1947 .... DLB-4
Stein and Day Publishers DLB-46
Steinbeck, John 1902-1968 .... DLB-7, 9; DS-2
Steiner, George 1929- DLB-67
Steinhoewel, Heinrich 1411/1412-1479 .... DLB-179
Steloff, Ida Frances 1887-1989 .... DLB-187
Stendhal 1783-1842 .... DLB-119
Stephen Crane: A Revaluation Virginia Tech Conference, 1989 .... Y-89
Stephen, Leslie 1832-1904 ...... DLB-57, 144, 190
Stephen Vincent Benét Centenary Y-97
Stephens, Alexander H. 1812-1883 ...... DLB-47
Stephens, Alice Barber 1858-1932 ...... DLB-188
Stephens, Ann 1810-1886 .... DLB-3, 73
Stephens, Charles Asbury 1844?-1931 .... DLB-42
Stephens, James 1882?-1950 ..... DLB-19, 153, 162
Stephens, John Lloyd 1805-1852 .... DLB-183
Sterling, George 1869-1926 .... DLB-54
Sterling, James 1701-1763 .... DLB-24
Sterling, John 1806-1844 .... DLB-116
Stern, Gerald 1925- DLB-105
Stern, Gladys B. 1890-1973 .... DLB-197
Stern, Madeleine B. 1912- DLB-111, 140
Stern, Richard 1928- Y-87
Stern, Stewart 1922- DLB-26

440

Sterne, Laurence 1713-1768 ....DLB-39
Sternheim, Carl 1878-1942..........DLB-56, 118
Sternhold, Thomas ?-1549 and
    John Hopkins ?-1570 ....DLB-132
Stevens, Henry 1819-1886...............DLB-140
Stevens, Wallace 1879-1955................DLB-54
Stevenson, Anne 1933- DLB-40
Stevenson, D. E. 1892-1973 ....DLB-191
Stevenson, Lionel 1902-1973 ....DLB-155
Stevenson, Robert Louis 1850-1894
    ....DLB-18, 57, 141, 156, 174; DS-13
Stewart, Donald Ogden
    1894-1980 ....DLB-4, 11, 26
Stewart, Dugald 1753-1828 ....DLB-31
Stewart, George, Jr. 1848-1906 ....DLB-99
Stewart, George R. 1895-1980............DLB-8
Stewart and Kidd Company DLB-46
Stewart, Randall 1896-1964 ....DLB-103
Stickney, Trumbull 1874-1904............DLB-54
Stieler, Caspar 1632-1707................DLB-164
Stifter, Adalbert 1805-1868 ....DLB-133
Stiles, Ezra 1727-1795 ....DLB-31
Still, James 1906- DLB-9
Stirner, Max 1806-1856....................DLB-129
Stith, William 1707-1755..................DLB-31
Stock, Elliot [publishing house] DLB-106
Stockton, Frank R.
    1834-1902 ....DLB-42, 74; DS-13
Stoddard, Ashbel [publishing house] DLB-49
Stoddard, Charles Warren
    1843-1909 ....DLB-186
Stoddard, Elizabeth 1823-1902 ....DLB-202
Stoddard, Richard Henry
    1825-1903 ....DLB-3, 64; DS-13
Stoddard, Solomon 1643-1729 ....DLB-24
Stoker, Bram 1847-1912........DLB-36, 70, 178
Stokes, Frederick A., Company DLB-49
Stokes, Thomas L. 1898-1958 ....DLB-29
Stokesbury, Leon 1945- DLB-120
Stolberg, Christian Graf zu 1748-1821.....DLB-94
Stolberg, Friedrich Leopold Graf zu
    1750-1819 ....DLB-94
Stone, Herbert S., and Company.........DLB-49
Stone, Lucy 1818-1893 ....DLB-79
Stone, Melville 1848-1929 ....DLB-25
Stone, Robert 1937- DLB-152
Stone, Ruth 1915- DLB-105
Stone, Samuel 1602-1663..................DLB-24
Stone, William Leete 1792-1844 ....DLB-202
Stone and Kimball DLB-49
Stoppard, Tom 1937- DLB-13; Y-85
Storey, Anthony 1928- DLB-14
Storey, David 1933- DLB-13, 14
Storm, Theodor 1817-1888 ....DLB-129
Story, Thomas circa 1670-1742 ....DLB-31
Story, William Wetmore 1819-1895 ....DLB-1

Storytelling: A Contemporary Renaissance... Y-84
Stoughton, William 1631-1701..........DLB-24
Stow, John 1525-1605 ....DLB-132
Stowe, Harriet Beecher
    1811-1896.........DLB-1, 12, 42, 74, 189
Stowe, Leland 1899- DLB-29
Stoyanov, Dimitr Ivanov (see Elin Pelin)
Strabo 64 or 63 B.C.-circa A.D. 25
    ....DLB-176
Strachey, Lytton
    1880-1932................DLB-149; DS-10
Strachey, Lytton, Preface to Eminent
    Victorians DLB-149
Strahan and Company...................DLB-106
Strahan, William [publishing house] DLB-154
Strand, Mark 1934- DLB-5
The Strasbourg Oaths 842................DLB-148
Stratemeyer, Edward 1862-1930 ....DLB-42
Strati, Saverio 1924- DLB-177
Stratton and Barnard DLB-49
Stratton-Porter, Gene 1863-1924 ....DS-14
Straub, Peter 1943- Y-84
Strauß, Botho 1944- DLB-124
Strauß, David Friedrich 1808-1874 ......DLB-133
The Strawberry Hill Press DLB-154
Streatfeild, Noel 1895-1986 ....DLB-160
Street, Cecil John Charles (see Rhode, John)
Street, G. S. 1867-1936....................DLB-135
Street and Smith..............................DLB-49
Streeter, Edward 1891-1976..............DLB-11
Streeter, Thomas Winthrop 1883-1965...DLB-140
Stretton, Hesba 1832-1911.........DLB-163, 190
Stribling, T. S. 1881-1965 ....DLB-9
Der Stricker circa 1190-circa 1250.......DLB-138
Strickland, Samuel 1804-1867 ....DLB-99
Stringer and Townsend DLB-49
Stringer, Arthur 1874-1950 ....DLB-92
Strittmatter, Erwin 1912- DLB-69
Strniša, Gregor 1930-1987 ....DLB-181
Strode, William 1630-1645 ....DLB-126
Strong, L. A. G. 1896-1958 ....DLB-191
Strother, David Hunter 1816-1888 ....DLB-3
Strouse, Jean 1945- DLB-111
Stuart, Dabney 1937- DLB-105
Stuart, Jesse 1906-1984 .....DLB-9, 48, 102; Y-84
Stuart, Ruth McEnery 1849?-1917 ......DLB-202
Stuart, Lyle [publishing house] DLB-46
Stubbs, Harry Clement (see Clement, Hal)
Stubenberg, Johann Wilhelm von
    1619-1663 ....DLB-164
Studio...DLB-112
The Study of Poetry (1880), by
    Matthew Arnold DLB-35
Sturgeon, Theodore 1918-1985 ....DLB-8; Y-85
Sturges, Preston 1898-1959 ....DLB-26

"Style" (1840; revised, 1859), by
    Thomas de Quincey [excerpt].......DLB-57
"Style" (1888), by Walter Pater..........DLB-57
Style (1897), by Walter Raleigh
    [excerpt] DLB-57
"Style" (1877), by T. H. Wright
    [excerpt] DLB-57
"Le Style c'est l'homme" (1892), by
    W. H. Mallock DLB-57
Styron, William 1925- DLB-2, 143; Y-80
Suárez, Mario 1925- DLB-82
Such, Peter 1939- DLB-60
Suckling, Sir John 1609-1641?.......DLB-58, 126
Suckow, Ruth 1892-1960..............DLB-9, 102
Sudermann, Hermann 1857-1928 ....DLB-118
Sue, Eugène 1804-1857 ....DLB-119
Sue, Marie-Joseph (see Sue, Eugène)
Suggs, Simon (see Hooper, Johnson Jones)
Sukenick, Ronald 1932- DLB-173; Y-81
Suknaski, Andrew 1942- DLB-53
Sullivan, Alan 1868-1947 ....DLB-92
Sullivan, C. Gardner 1886-1965 ....DLB-26
Sullivan, Frank 1892-1976 ....DLB-11
Sulte, Benjamin 1841-1923 ....DLB-99
Sulzberger, Arthur Hays 1891-1968 ......DLB-127
Sulzberger, Arthur Ochs 1926- DLB-127
Sulzer, Johann Georg 1720-1779 ....DLB-97
Sumarokov, Aleksandr Petrovich
    1717-1777 ....DLB-150
Summers, Hollis 1916- DLB-6
Sumner, Henry A. [publishing house].....DLB-49
Surtees, Robert Smith 1803-1864 ....DLB-21
Surveys: Japanese Literature,
    1987-1995 ....DLB-182
A Survey of Poetry Anthologies,
    1879-1960 ....DLB-54
Surveys of the Year's Biographies
A Transit of Poets and Others: American
    Biography in 1982......................Y-82
The Year in Literary Biography Y-83–Y-96
Survey of the Year's Book Publishing
The Year in Book Publishing Y-86
Survey of the Year's Children's Books
The Year in Children's Books..........Y-92–Y-96
Surveys of the Year's Drama
The Year in Drama Y-82–Y-85, Y-87–Y-96
The Year in London Theatre Y-92
Surveys of the Year's Fiction
The Year's Work in Fiction: A Survey Y-82
The Year in Fiction: A Biased View Y-83
The Year in Fiction ...Y-84–Y-86, Y-89, Y-94–Y-96
The Year in the Novel.....Y-87, Y-88, Y-90–Y-93
The Year in Short Stories Y-87
The Year in the Short Story......Y-88, Y-90–Y-93
Survey of the Year's Literary Theory
The Year in Literary Theory.........Y-92–Y-93
Surveys of the Year's Poetry

The Year's Work in American Poetry Y-82
The Year in Poetry Y-83–Y-92, Y-94–Y-96
Sutherland, Efua Theodora 1924- DLB-117
Sutherland, John 1919-1956 .... DLB-68
Sutro, Alfred 1863-1933 .... DLB-10
Swados, Harvey 1920-1972 .... DLB-2
Swain, Charles 1801-1874 .... DLB-32
Swallow Press DLB-46
Swan Sonnenschein Limited DLB-106
Swanberg, W. A. 1907- DLB-103
Swenson, May 1919-1989 .... DLB-5
Swerling, Jo 1897- DLB-44
Swift, Graham 1949- DLB-194
Swift, Jonathan 1667-1745 ...... DLB-39, 95, 101
Swinburne, A. C. 1837-1909 .... DLB-35, 57
Swineshead, Richard floruit circa 1350... DLB-115
Swinnerton, Frank 1884-1982 .... DLB-34
Swisshelm, Jane Grey 1815-1884 .... DLB-43
Swope, Herbert Bayard 1882-1958 .... DLB-25
Swords, T. and J., and Company DLB-49
Swords, Thomas 1763-1843 and
  Swords, James ?-1844 .... DLB-73
Sykes, Ella C. ?-1939 .... DLB-174
Sylvester, Josuah 1562 or 1563 - 1618 ... DLB-121
Symonds, Emily Morse (see Paston, George)
Symonds, John Addington
  1840-1893 .... DLB-57, 144
Symons, A. J. A. 1900-1941 .... DLB-149
Symons, Arthur 1865-1945 ...... DLB-19, 57, 149
Symons, Julian 1912-1994 ..... DLB-87, 155; Y-92
Symons, Scott 1933- DLB-53
A Symposium on *The Columbia History of
  the Novel* Y-92
Synge, John Millington 1871-1909 .... DLB-10, 19
Synge Summer School: J. M. Synge and the
  Irish Theater, Rathdrum, County Wiclow,
  Ireland Y-93
Syrett, Netta 1865-1943 .... DLB-135, 197
Szymborska, Wisława 1923- Y-96

T

Taban lo Liyong 1939?- DLB-125
Tabucchi, Antonio 1943- DLB-196
Taché, Joseph-Charles 1820-1894 .... DLB-99
Tachihara Masaaki 1926-1980 .... DLB-182
Tadijanović, Dragutin 1905- DLB-181
Tafolla, Carmen 1951- DLB-82
Taggard, Genevieve 1894-1948 .... DLB-45
Taggart, John 1942- DLB-193
Tagger, Theodor (see Bruckner, Ferdinand)
Taiheiki late fourteenth century DLB-203
Tait, J. Selwin, and Sons DLB-49
Tait's Edinburgh Magazine 1832-1861 ..... DLB-110
The Takarazaka Revue Company Y-91
Talander (see Bohse, August)
Talese, Gay 1932- DLB-185

Talev, Dimitr 1898-1966 .... DLB-181
Taliaferro, H. E. 1811-1875 .... DLB-202
Tallent, Elizabeth 1954- DLB-130
TallMountain, Mary 1918-1994 .... DLB-193
Talvj 1797-1870 .... DLB-59, 133
Tan, Amy 1952- DLB-173
Tanizaki, Jun'ichirō 1886-1965 .... DLB-180
Tapahonso, Luci 1953- DLB-175
Taradash, Daniel 1913- DLB-44
Tarbell, Ida M. 1857-1944 .... DLB-47
Tardivel, Jules-Paul 1851-1905 .... DLB-99
Targan, Barry 1932- DLB-130
Tarkington, Booth 1869-1946 .... DLB-9, 102
Tashlin, Frank 1913-1972 .... DLB-44
Tate, Allen 1899-1979 .... DLB-4, 45, 63; DS-17
Tate, James 1943- DLB-5, 169
Tate, Nahum circa 1652-1715 .... DLB-80
Tatian circa 830 .... DLB-148
Taufer, Veno 1933- DLB-181
Tauler, Johannes circa 1300-1361 ...... DLB-179
Tavčar, Ivan 1851-1923 .... DLB-147
Taylor, Ann 1782-1866 .... DLB-163
Taylor, Bayard 1825-1878 .... DLB-3, 189
Taylor, Bert Leston 1866-1921 .... DLB-25
Taylor, Charles H. 1846-1921 .... DLB-25
Taylor, Edward circa 1642-1729 .... DLB-24
Taylor, Elizabeth 1912-1975 .... DLB-139
Taylor, Henry 1942- DLB-5
Taylor, Sir Henry 1800-1886 .... DLB-32
Taylor, Jane 1783-1824 .... DLB-163
Taylor, Jeremy circa 1613-1667 .... DLB-151
Taylor, John 1577 or 1578 - 1653 .... DLB-121
Taylor, Mildred D. ?- DLB-52
Taylor, Peter 1917-1994 .... Y-81, Y-94
Taylor, William, and Company DLB-49
Taylor-Made Shakespeare? Or Is "Shall I Die?" the
  Long-Lost Text of Bottom's Dream? Y-85
Teasdale, Sara 1884-1933 .... DLB-45
The Tea-Table (1725), by Eliza Haywood
  [excerpt] DLB-39
Telles, Lygia Fagundes 1924- DLB-113
Temple, Sir William 1628-1699 .... DLB-101
Tenn, William 1919- DLB-8
Tennant, Emma 1937- DLB-14
Tenney, Tabitha Gilman
  1762-1837 .... DLB-37, 200
Tennyson, Alfred 1809-1892 .... DLB-32
Tennyson, Frederick 1807-1898 .... DLB-32
Tepliakov, Viktor Grigor'evich
  1804-1842 .... DLB-205
Terhune, Albert Payson 1872-1942 .... DLB-9
Terhune, Mary Virginia
  1830-1922 .... DS-13, DS-16
Terry, Megan 1932- DLB-7
Terson, Peter 1932- DLB-13
Tesich, Steve 1943- Y-83

Tessa, Delio 1886-1939 .... DLB-114
Testori, Giovanni 1923-1993 .... DLB-128, 177
Tey, Josephine 1896?-1952 .... DLB-77
Thacher, James 1754-1844 .... DLB-37
Thackeray, William Makepeace
  1811-1863 .... DLB-21, 55, 159, 163
Thames and Hudson Limited DLB-112
Thanet, Octave (see French, Alice)
Thatcher, John Boyd 1847-1909 .... DLB-187
Thayer, Caroline Matilda Warren
  1785-1844 .... DLB-200
The Theater in Shakespeare's Time DLB-62
The Theatre Guild DLB-7
Thegan and the Astronomer
  flourished circa 850 .... DLB-148
Thelwall, John 1764-1834 .... DLB-93, 158
Theocritus circa 300 B.C.-260 B.C.
  .... DLB-176
Theodulf circa 760-circa 821 .... DLB-148
Theophrastus circa 371 B.C.-287 B.C.
  .... DLB-176
Theriault, Yves 1915-1983 .... DLB-88
Thério, Adrien 1925- DLB-53
Theroux, Paul 1941- DLB-2
Thesiger, Wilfred 1910- DLB-204
They All Came to Paris DS-16
Thibaudeau, Colleen 1925- DLB-88
Thielen, Benedict 1903-1965 .... DLB-102
Thiong'o Ngugi wa (see Ngugi wa Thiong'o)
Third-Generation Minor Poets of the
  Seventeenth Century DLB-131
This Quarter 1925-1927, 1929-1932 .... DS-15
Thoma, Ludwig 1867-1921 .... DLB-66
Thoma, Richard 1902- DLB-4
Thomas, Audrey 1935- DLB-60
Thomas, D. M. 1935- DLB-40
Thomas, Dylan 1914-1953 .... DLB-13, 20, 139
Thomas, Edward 1878-1917 ..... DLB-19, 98, 156
Thomas, Frederick William
  1806-1866 .... DLB-202
Thomas, Gwyn 1913-1981 .... DLB-15
Thomas, Isaiah 1750-1831 .... DLB-43, 73, 187
Thomas, Isaiah [publishing house] DLB-49
Thomas, Johann 1624-1679 .... DLB-168
Thomas, John 1900-1932 .... DLB-4
Thomas, Joyce Carol 1938- DLB-33
Thomas, Lorenzo 1944- DLB-41
Thomas, R. S. 1915- DLB-27
The Thomas Wolfe Collection at the University of
  North Carolina at Chapel Hill Y-97
The Thomas Wolfe Society Y-97
Thomasîn von Zerclære
  circa 1186-circa 1259 .... DLB-138
Thomasius, Christian 1655-1728 .... DLB-168
Thompson, David 1770-1857 .... DLB-99
Thompson, Daniel Pierce 1795-1868 .... DLB-202
Thompson, Dorothy 1893-1961 .... DLB-29

Thompson, Francis 1859-1907..........DLB-19

Thompson, George Selden (see Selden, George)

Thompson, Henry Yates 1838-1928.....DLB-184

Thompson, Hunter S. 1939- DLB-185

Thompson, John 1938-1976............DLB-60

Thompson, John R. 1823-1873 ....DLB-3, 73

Thompson, Lawrance 1906-1973........DLB-103

Thompson, Maurice 1844-1901.......DLB-71, 74

Thompson, Ruth Plumly 1891-1976 ......DLB-22

Thompson, Thomas Phillips 1843-1933 ...DLB-99

Thompson, William 1775-1833 ....DLB-158

Thompson, William Tappan
  1812-1882 ....DLB-3, 11

Thomson, Edward William 1849-1924....DLB-92

Thomson, James 1700-1748............DLB-95

Thomson, James 1834-1882............DLB-35

Thomson, Joseph 1858-1895...........DLB-174

Thomson, Mortimer 1831-1875.........DLB-11

Thoreau, Henry David 1817-1862.....DLB-1, 183

Thornton Wilder Centenary at Yale Y-97

Thorpe, Thomas Bangs 1815-1878 .....DLB-3, 11

Thoughts on Poetry and Its Varieties (1833),
  by John Stuart Mill DLB-32

Thrale, Hester Lynch (see Piozzi, Hester
  Lynch [Thrale])

Thubron, Colin 1939- DLB-204

Thucydides circa 455 B.C.-circa 395 B.C.
  ....DLB-176

Thulstrup, Thure de 1848-1930 ....DLB-188

Thümmel, Moritz August von
  1738-1817 ....DLB-97

Thurber, James 1894-1961 .... DLB-4, 11, 22, 102

Thurman, Wallace 1902-1934..........DLB-51

Thwaite, Anthony 1930- DLB-40

Thwaites, Reuben Gold 1853-1913 ....DLB-47

Ticknor, George 1791-1871 ....DLB-1, 59, 140

Ticknor and Fields...................DLB-49

Ticknor and Fields (revived) DLB-46

Tieck, Ludwig 1773-1853.............DLB-90

Tietjens, Eunice 1884-1944 ....DLB-54

Tilney, Edmund circa 1536-1610........DLB-136

Tilt, Charles [publishing house]........DLB-106

Tilton, J. E., and Company DLB-49

Time and Western Man (1927), by Wyndham
  Lewis [excerpts]...................DLB-36

Time-Life Books DLB-46

Times Books DLB-46

Timothy, Peter circa 1725-1782 ....DLB-43

Timrod, Henry 1828-1867.............DLB-3

Tindal, Henrietta 1818?-1879 ....DLB-199

Tinker, Chauncey Brewster 1876-1963 ...DLB-140

Tinsley Brothers DLB-106

Tiptree, James, Jr. 1915-1987..........DLB-8

Tišma, Aleksandar 1924- DLB-181

Titus, Edward William
  1870-1952 ....DLB-4; DS-15

Tiutchev, Fedor Ivanovich
  1803-1873 ....DLB-205

Tlali, Miriam 1933- DLB-157

Todd, Barbara Euphan 1890-1976.......DLB-160

Tofte, Robert
  1561 or 1562-1619 or 1620.........DLB-172

Toklas, Alice B. 1877-1967.............DLB-4

Tokuda, Shūsei 1872-1943............DLB-180

Tolkien, J. R. R. 1892-1973 ....DLB-15, 160

Toller, Ernst 1893-1939...............DLB-124

Tollet, Elizabeth 1694-1754 ....DLB-95

Tolson, Melvin B. 1898-1966 ....DLB-48, 76

Tom Jones (1749), by Henry Fielding
  [excerpt]........................DLB-39

Tomalin, Claire 1933- DLB-155

Tomasi di Lampedusa,
  Giuseppe 1896-1957 ....DLB-177

Tomlinson, Charles 1927- DLB-40

Tomlinson, H. M. 1873-1958
  ....DLB-36, 100, 195

Tompkins, Abel [publishing house].......DLB-49

Tompson, Benjamin 1642-1714 ....DLB-24

Ton'a 1289-1372 ....DLB-203

Tondelli, Pier Vittorio 1955-1991 ....DLB-196

Tonks, Rosemary 1932- DLB-14

Tonna, Charlotte Elizabeth
  1790-1846 ....DLB-163

Tonson, Jacob the Elder
  [publishing house] DLB-170

Toole, John Kennedy 1937-1969 .... Y-81

Toomer, Jean 1894-1967 ....DLB-45, 51

Tor Books DLB-46

Torberg, Friedrich 1908-1979 ....DLB-85

Torrence, Ridgely 1874-1950...........DLB-54

Torres-Metzger, Joseph V. 1933- DLB-122

Toth, Susan Allen 1940- Y-86

Tottell, Richard [publishing house] DLB-170

Tough-Guy Literature..................DLB-9

Touré, Askia Muhammad 1938- DLB-41

Tourgée, Albion W. 1838-1905..........DLB-79

Tourneur, Cyril circa 1580-1626........DLB-58

Tournier, Michel 1924- DLB-83

Tousey, Frank [publishing house] DLB-49

Tower Publications DLB-46

Towne, Benjamin circa 1740-1793 ....DLB-43

Towne, Robert 1936- DLB-44

The Townely Plays fifteenth and sixteenth
  centuries DLB-146

Townshend, Aurelian
  by 1583 - circa 1651 ....DLB-121

Toy, Barbara 1908- DLB-204

Tracy, Honor 1913- DLB-15

Traherne, Thomas 1637?-1674 ....DLB-131

Traill, Catharine Parr 1802-1899 ....DLB-99

Train, Arthur 1875-1945 ....DLB-86; DS-16

The Transatlantic Publishing Company ...DLB-49

The Transatlantic Review 1924-1925 .... DS-15

Transcendentalists, American DS-5

transition 1927-1938 .... DS-15

Translators of the Twelfth Century:
  Literary Issues Raised and Impact
  Created DLB-115

Travel Writing, 1837-1875..............DLB-166

Travel Writing, 1876-1909 ....DLB-174

Traven, B. 1882? or 1890?-1969?......DLB-9, 56

Travers, Ben 1886-1980 ....DLB-10

Travers, P. L. (Pamela Lyndon)
  1899- DLB-160

Trediakovsky, Vasilii Kirillovich
  1703-1769 ....DLB-150

Treece, Henry 1911-1966 ....DLB-160

Trejo, Ernesto 1950- DLB-122

Trelawny, Edward John
  1792-1881 .... DLB-110, 116, 144

Tremain, Rose 1943- DLB-14

Tremblay, Michel 1942- DLB-60

Trends in Twentieth-Century
  Mass Market Publishing DLB-46

Trent, William P. 1862-1939............DLB-47

Trescot, William Henry 1822-1898.......DLB-30

Tressell, Robert (Robert Phillipe Noonan)
  1870-1911 ....DLB-197

Trevelyan, Sir George Otto 1838-1928...DLB-144

Trevisa, John circa 1342-circa 1402......DLB-146

Trevor, William 1928- DLB-14, 139

Trierer Floyris circa 1170-1180 ....DLB-138

Trillin, Calvin 1935- DLB-185

Trilling, Lionel 1905-1975 ....DLB-28, 63

Trilussa 1871-1950...................DLB-114

Trimmer, Sarah 1741-1810 ....DLB-158

Triolet, Elsa 1896-1970 ....DLB-72

Tripp, John 1927- DLB-40

Trocchi, Alexander 1925- DLB-15

Troisi, Dante 1920-1989 ....DLB-196

Trollope, Anthony 1815-1882.... DLB-21, 57, 159

Trollope, Frances 1779-1863 ....DLB-21, 166

Troop, Elizabeth 1931- DLB-14

Trotter, Catharine 1679-1749...........DLB-84

Trotti, Lamar 1898-1952...............DLB-44

Trottier, Pierre 1925- DLB-60

Troupe, Quincy Thomas, Jr. 1943- DLB-41

Trow, John F., and Company DLB-49

Trowbridge, John Townsend
  1827-1916 ....DLB-202

Truillier-Lacombe, Joseph-Patrice
  1807-1863 ....DLB-99

Trumbo, Dalton 1905-1976.............DLB-26

Trumbull, Benjamin 1735-1820..........DLB-30

Trumbull, John 1750-1831.............DLB-31

Trumbull, John 1756-1843.............DLB-183

Tscherning, Andreas 1611-1659 ....DLB-164

T. S. Eliot Centennial Y-88

Tsubouchi, Shōyō 1859-1935 ....DLB-180

Tucholsky, Kurt 1890-1935.............DLB-56

Cumulative Index DLB 205

Tucker, Charlotte Maria
  1821-1893 .... DLB-163, 190
Tucker, George 1775-1861 .... DLB-3, 30
Tucker, Nathaniel Beverley 1784-1851 ..... DLB-3
Tucker, St. George 1752-1827 .... DLB-37
Tuckerman, Henry Theodore
  1813-1871 .... DLB-64
Tunis, John R. 1889-1975 .... DLB-22, 171
Tunstall, Cuthbert 1474-1559 .... DLB-132
Tuohy, Frank 1925- DLB-14, 139
Tupper, Martin F. 1810-1889 .... DLB-32
Turbyfill, Mark 1896- DLB-45
Turco, Lewis 1934- Y-84
Turgenev, Aleksandr Ivanovich
  1784-1845 .... DLB-198
Turnball, Alexander H. 1868-1918 ...... DLB-184
Turnbull, Andrew 1921-1970 .... DLB-103
Turnbull, Gael 1928- DLB-40
Turner, Arlin 1909-1980 .... DLB-103
Turner, Charles (Tennyson)
  1808-1879 .... DLB-32
Turner, Frederick 1943- DLB-40
Turner, Frederick Jackson
  1861-1932 .... DLB-17, 186
Turner, Joseph Addison 1826-1868 ...... DLB-79
Turpin, Waters Edward 1910-1968 ...... DLB-51
Turrini, Peter 1944- DLB-124
Tutuola, Amos 1920- DLB-125
Twain, Mark (see Clemens, Samuel Langhorne)
Tweedie, Ethel Brilliana
  circa 1860-1940 .... DLB-174
The 'Twenties and Berlin, by
  Alex Natan DLB-66
Tyler, Anne 1941- DLB-6, 143; Y-82
Tyler, Mary Palmer 1775-1866 .... DLB-200
Tyler, Moses Coit 1835-1900 .... DLB-47, 64
Tyler, Royall 1757-1826 .... DLB-37
Tylor, Edward Burnett 1832-1917 .... DLB-57
Tynan, Katharine 1861-1931 .... DLB-153
Tyndale, William circa 1494-1536 ...... DLB-132

U

Udall, Nicholas 1504-1556 .... DLB-62
Ugrešić, Dubravka 1949- DLB-181
Uhland, Ludwig 1787-1862 .... DLB-90
Uhse, Bodo 1904-1963 .... DLB-69
Ujević, Augustin ("Tin") 1891-1955 ..... DLB-147
Ulenhart, Niclas flourished circa 1600 ... DLB-164
Ulibarrí, Sabine R. 1919- DLB-82
Ulica, Jorge 1870-1926 .... DLB-82
Ulivi, Ferruccio 1912- DLB-196
Ulizio, B. George 1889-1969 .... DLB-140
Ulrich von Liechtenstein
  circa 1200-circa 1275 .... DLB-138
Ulrich von Zatzikhoven
  before 1194-after 1214 .... DLB-138
Ulysses, Reader's Edition Y-97

Unamuno, Miguel de 1864-1936 .... DLB-108
Under the Microscope (1872), by
  A. C. Swinburne DLB-35
Unger, Friederike Helene 1741-1813 ..... DLB-94
Ungaretti, Giuseppe 1888-1970 .... DLB-114
United States Book Company DLB-49
Universal Publishing and Distributing
  Corporation DLB-46
The University of Iowa Writers' Workshop
  Golden Jubilee Y-86
The University of South Carolina Press Y-94
University of Wales Press DLB-112
"The Unknown Public" (1858), by
  Wilkie Collins [excerpt] DLB-57
Uno, Chiyo 1897-1996 .... DLB-180
Unruh, Fritz von 1885-1970 .... DLB-56, 118
Unspeakable Practices II: The Festival of
  Vanguard Narrative at Brown
  University Y-93
Unsworth, Barry 1930- DLB-194
Unwin, T. Fisher [publishing house] DLB-106
Upchurch, Boyd B. (see Boyd, John)
Updike, John
  1932- DLB-2, 5, 143; Y-80, Y-82; DS-3
Upton, Bertha 1849-1912 .... DLB-141
Upton, Charles 1948- DLB-16
Upton, Florence K. 1873-1922 .... DLB-141
Upward, Allen 1863-1926 .... DLB-36
Urista, Alberto Baltazar (see Alurista)
Urzidil, Johannes 1896-1976 .... DLB-85
Urquhart, Fred 1912- DLB-139
The Uses of Facsimile Y-90
Usk, Thomas died 1388 .... DLB-146
Uslar Pietri, Arturo 1906- DLB-113
Ustinov, Peter 1921- DLB-13
Uttley, Alison 1884-1976 .... DLB-160
Uz, Johann Peter 1720-1796 .... DLB-97

V

Vac, Bertrand 1914- DLB-88
Vail, Laurence 1891-1968 .... DLB-4
Vailland, Roger 1907-1965 .... DLB-83
Vajda, Ernest 1887-1954 .... DLB-44
Valdés, Gina 1943- DLB-122
Valdez, Luis Miguel 1940- DLB-122
Valduga, Patrizia 1953- DLB-128
Valente, José Angel 1929- DLB-108
Valenzuela, Luisa 1938- DLB-113
Valeri, Diego 1887-1976 .... DLB-128
Valesio, Paolo 1939- DLB-196
Valgardson, W. D. 1939- DLB-60
Valle, Víctor Manuel 1950- DLB-122
Valle-Inclán, Ramón del 1866-1936 ..... DLB-134
Vallejo, Armando 1949- DLB-122
Vallès, Jules 1832-1885 .... DLB-123
Vallette, Marguerite Eymery (see Rachilde)

Valverde, José María 1926- DLB-108
Van Allsburg, Chris 1949- DLB-61
Van Anda, Carr 1864-1945 .... DLB-25
van der Post, Laurens 1906-1996 .... DLB-204
Van Dine, S. S. (see Wright, Williard Huntington)
Van Doren, Mark 1894-1972 .... DLB-45
van Druten, John 1901-1957 .... DLB-10
Van Duyn, Mona 1921- DLB-5
Van Dyke, Henry 1852-1933 ...... DLB-71; DS-13
Van Dyke, John C. 1856-1932 .... DLB-186
Van Dyke, Henry 1928- DLB-33
van Gulik, Robert Hans 1910-1967 .... DS-17
van Itallie, Jean-Claude 1936- DLB-7
Van Loan, Charles E. 1876-1919 .... DLB-171
Van Rensselaer, Mariana Griswold
  1851-1934 .... DLB-47
Van Rensselaer, Mrs. Schuyler (see Van
  Rensselaer, Mariana Griswold)
Van Vechten, Carl 1880-1964 .... DLB-4, 9
van Vogt, A. E. 1912- DLB-8
Vanbrugh, Sir John 1664-1726 .... DLB-80
Vance, Jack 1916?- DLB-8
Vane, Sutton 1888-1963 .... DLB-10
Vanguard Press DLB-46
Vann, Robert L. 1879-1940 .... DLB-29
Vargas, Llosa, Mario 1936- DLB-145
Varley, John 1947- Y-81
Varnhagen von Ense, Karl August
  1785-1858 .... DLB-90
Varnhagen von Ense, Rahel
  1771-1833 .... DLB-90
Vásquez Montalbán, Manuel
  1939- DLB-134
Vassa, Gustavus (see Equiano, Olaudah)
Vassalli, Sebastiano 1941- DLB-128, 196
Vaughan, Henry 1621-1695 .... DLB-131
Vaughan, Thomas 1621-1666 .... DLB-131
Vaux, Thomas, Lord 1509-1556 .... DLB-132
Vazov, Ivan 1850-1921 .... DLB-147
Vega, Janine Pommy 1942- DLB-16
Veiller, Anthony 1903-1965 .... DLB-44
Velásquez-Trevino, Gloria 1949- DLB-122
Veley, Margaret 1843-1887 .... DLB-199
Veloz Maggiolo, Marcio 1936- DLB-145
Vel'tman Aleksandr Fomich 1800-1870 .. DLB-198
Venegas, Daniel ?-? DLB-82
Venevitinov, Dmitrii Vladimirovich
  1805-1827 .... DLB-205
Vergil, Polydore circa 1470-1555 .... DLB-132
Veríssimo, Erico 1905-1975 .... DLB-145
Verne, Jules 1828-1905 .... DLB-123
Verplanck, Gulian C. 1786-1870 .... DLB-59
Very, Jones 1813-1880 .... DLB-1
Vian, Boris 1920-1959 .... DLB-72
Viazemsky, Petr Andreevich
  1792-1878 .... DLB-205

W

Vickers, Roy 1888?-1965................DLB-77
Vickery, Sukey 1779-1821...............DLB-200
Victoria 1819-1901....................DLB-55
Victoria Press........................DLB-106
Vidal, Gore 1925-..................DLB-6, 152
Viebig, Clara 1860-1952................DLB-66
Viereck, George Sylvester 1884-1962.....DLB-54
Viereck, Peter 1916-...................DLB-5
Viets, Roger 1738-1811.................DLB-99
Viewpoint: Politics and Performance, by
 David Edgar........................DLB-13
Vigil-Piñon, Evangelina 1949-..........DLB-122
Vigneault, Gilles 1928-................DLB-60
Vigny, Alfred de 1797-1863.........DLB-119, 192
Vigolo, Giorgio 1894-1983..............DLB-114
The Viking Press......................DLB-46
Villanueva, Alma Luz 1944-............DLB-122
Villanueva, Tino 1941-.................DLB-82
Villard, Henry 1835-1900...............DLB-23
Villard, Oswald Garrison 1872-1949..DLB-25, 91
Villarreal, José Antonio 1924-.........DLB-82
Villegas de Magnón, Leonor
 1876-1955.........................DLB-122
Villemaire, Yolande 1949-..............DLB-60
Villena, Luis Antonio de 1951-.........DLB-134
Villiers de l'Isle-Adam, Jean-Marie
 Mathias Philippe-Auguste, Comte de
 1838-1889......................DLB-123, 192
Villiers, George, Second Duke
 of Buckingham 1628-1687............DLB-80
Vine Press............................DLB-112
Viorst, Judith ?-......................DLB-52
Vipont, Elfrida (Elfrida Vipont Foulds,
 Charles Vipont) 1902-1992..........DLB-160
Viramontes, Helena María
 1954-..............................DLB-122
Vischer, Friedrich Theodor
 1807-1887..........................DLB-133
Vivanco, Luis Felipe 1907-1975.........DLB-108
Viviani, Cesare 1947-..................DLB-128
Vizenor, Gerald 1934-..................DLB-175
Vizetelly and Company..................DLB-106
Voaden, Herman 1903-...................DLB-88
Voigt, Ellen Bryant 1943-..............DLB-120
Vojnović, Ivo 1857-1929................DLB-147
Volkoff, Vladimir 1932-................DLB-83
Volland, P. F., Company................DLB-46
Vollbehr, Otto H. F. 1872?-
 1945 or 1946......................DLB-187
Volponi, Paolo 1924-...................DLB-177
von der Grün, Max 1926-................DLB-75
Vonnegut, Kurt
 1922-..........DLB-2, 8, 152; Y-80; DS-3
Voranc, Prežihov 1893-1950.............DLB-147
Voß, Johann Heinrich 1751-1826.........DLB-90
Voynich, E. L. 1864-1960...............DLB-197
Vroman, Mary Elizabeth
 circa 1924-1967....................DLB-33

W

Wace, Robert ("Maistre")
 circa 1100-circa 1175..............DLB-146
Wackenroder, Wilhelm Heinrich
 1773-1798..........................DLB-90
Wackernagel, Wilhelm 1806-1869.........DLB-133
Waddington, Miriam 1917-...............DLB-68
Wade, Henry 1887-1969..................DLB-77
Wagenknecht, Edward 1900-..............DLB-103
Wagner, Heinrich Leopold 1747-1779.....DLB-94
Wagner, Henry R. 1862-1957.............DLB-140
Wagner, Richard 1813-1883..............DLB-129
Wagoner, David 1926-...................DLB-5
Wah, Fred 1939-........................DLB-60
Waiblinger, Wilhelm 1804-1830..........DLB-90
Wain, John 1925-1994........DLB-15, 27, 139, 155
Wainwright, Jeffrey 1944-..............DLB-40
Waite, Peirce and Company..............DLB-49
Wakeman, Stephen H. 1859-1924..........DLB-187
Wakoski, Diane 1937-...................DLB-5
Walahfrid Strabo circa 808-849.........DLB-148
Walck, Henry Z.........................DLB-46
Walcott, Derek 1930-.......DLB-117; Y-81, Y-92
Waldegrave, Robert [publishing house]..DLB-170
Waldman, Anne 1945-....................DLB-16
Waldrop, Rosmarie 1935-................DLB-169
Walker, Alice 1900-1982................DLB-201
Walker, Alice 1944-..............DLB-6, 33, 143
Walker, George F. 1947-................DLB-60
Walker, Joseph A. 1935-................DLB-38
Walker, Margaret 1915-.............DLB-76, 152
Walker, Ted 1934-......................DLB-40
Walker and Company.....................DLB-49
Walker, Evans and Cogswell
 Company............................DLB-49
Walker, John Brisben 1847-1931.........DLB-79
Wallace, Alfred Russel 1823-1913.......DLB-190
Wallace, Dewitt 1889-1981 and
 Lila Acheson Wallace
 1889-1984..........................DLB-137
Wallace, Edgar 1875-1932...............DLB-70
Wallace, Lew 1827-1905.................DLB-202
Wallace, Lila Acheson (see Wallace, Dewitt,
 and Lila Acheson Wallace)
Wallant, Edward Lewis
 1926-1962.....................DLB-2, 28, 143
Waller, Edmund 1606-1687...............DLB-126
Walpole, Horace 1717-1797..........DLB-39, 104
Walpole, Hugh 1884-1941................DLB-34
Walrond, Eric 1898-1966................DLB-51
Walser, Martin 1927-...............DLB-75, 124
Walser, Robert 1878-1956...............DLB-66
Walsh, Ernest 1895-1926.............DLB-4, 45
Walsh, Robert 1784-1859................DLB-59
Waltharius circa 825...................DLB-148

Walters, Henry 1848-1931...............DLB-140
Walther von der Vogelweide
 circa 1170-circa 1230..............DLB-138
Walton, Izaak 1593-1683................DLB-151
Wambaugh, Joseph 1937-.............DLB-6; Y-83
Waniek, Marilyn Nelson 1946-...........DLB-120
Warburton, William 1698-1779...........DLB-104
Ward, Aileen 1919-.....................DLB-111
Ward, Artemus (see Browne, Charles Farrar)
Ward, Arthur Henry Sarsfield
 (see Rohmer, Sax)
Ward, Douglas Turner 1930-..........DLB-7, 38
Ward, Lynd 1905-1985...................DLB-22
Ward, Lock and Company.................DLB-106
Ward, Mrs. Humphry 1851-1920...........DLB-18
Ward, Nathaniel circa 1578-1652........DLB-24
Ward, Theodore 1902-1983...............DLB-76
Wardle, Ralph 1909-1988................DLB-103
Ware, William 1797-1852................DLB-1
Warne, Frederick, and Company [U.S.]...DLB-49
Warne, Frederick, and
 Company [U.K.].....................DLB-106
Warner, Anne 1869-1913.................DLB-202
Warner, Charles Dudley 1829-1900.......DLB-64
Warner, Marina 1946-...................DLB-194
Warner, Rex 1905-......................DLB-15
Warner, Susan Bogert 1819-1885......DLB-3, 42
Warner, Sylvia Townsend
 1893-1978......................DLB-34, 139
Warner, William 1558-1609..............DLB-172
Warner Books..........................DLB-46
Warr, Bertram 1917-1943................DLB-88
Warren, John Byrne Leicester
 (see De Tabley, Lord)
Warren, Lella 1899-1982.................Y-83
Warren, Mercy Otis 1728-1814.......DLB-31, 200
Warren, Robert Penn
 1905-1989........DLB-2, 48, 152; Y-80, Y-89
Warren, Samuel 1807-1877...............DLB-190
Die Wartburgkrieg
 circa 1230-circa 1280..............DLB-138
Warton, Joseph 1722-1800..........DLB-104, 109
Warton, Thomas 1728-1790..........DLB-104, 109
Washington, George 1732-1799...........DLB-31
Wassermann, Jakob 1873-1934............DLB-66
Wasson, David Atwood 1823-1887.........DLB-1
Waterhouse, Keith 1929-............DLB-13, 15
Waterman, Andrew 1940-.................DLB-40
Waters, Frank 1902-.....................Y-86
Waters, Michael 1949-..................DLB-120
Watkins, Tobias 1780-1855..............DLB-73
Watkins, Vernon 1906-1967..............DLB-20
Watmough, David 1926-..................DLB-53
Watson, James Wreford (see Wreford, James)
Watson, John 1850-1907.................DLB-156
Watson, Sheila 1909-...................DLB-60

Cumulative Index

Watson, Thomas 1545?-1592.........DLB-132
Watson, Wilfred 1911- DLB-60
Watt, W. J., and Company............DLB-46
Watten, Barrett 1948- DLB-193
Watterson, Henry 1840-1921..........DLB-25
Watts, Alan 1915-1973................DLB-16
Watts, Franklin [publishing house].......DLB-46
Watts, Isaac 1674-1748...............DLB-95
Wand, Alfred Rudolph 1828-1891......DLB-188
Waugh, Alec 1898-1981...............DLB-191
Waugh, Auberon 1939- DLB-14, 194
Waugh, Evelyn 1903-1966.....DLB-15, 162, 195
Way and Williams DLB-49
Wayman, Tom 1945- DLB-53
Weatherly, Tom 1942- DLB-41
Weaver, Gordon 1937- DLB-130
Weaver, Robert 1921-................DLB-88
Webb, Beatrice 1858-1943 and
    Webb, Sidney 1859-1947.........DLB-190
Webb, Frank J. ?-? DLB-50
Webb, James Watson 1802-1884........DLB-43
Webb, Mary 1881-1927................DLB-34
Webb, Phyllis 1927- DLB-53
Webb, Walter Prescott 1888-1963.......DLB-17
Webbe, William ?-1591...............DLB-132
Webber, Charles Wilkins 1819-1856?...DLB-202
Webster, Augusta 1837-1894..........DLB-35
Webster, Charles L., and Company......DLB-49
Webster, John
    1579 or 1580-1634? DLB-58
Webster, Noah 1758-1843...DLB-1, 37, 42, 43, 73
Weckherlin, Georg Rodolf 1584-1653...DLB-164
Wedekind, Frank 1864-1918...........DLB-118
Weeks, Edward Augustus, Jr.
    1898-1989 ....DLB-137
Weeks, Stephen B. 1865-1918.........DLB-187
Weems, Mason Locke 1759-1825...DLB-30, 37, 42
Weerth, Georg 1822-1856.............DLB-129
Weidenfeld and Nicolson.............DLB-112
Weidman, Jerome 1913- DLB-28
Weigl, Bruce 1949- DLB-120
Weinbaum, Stanley Grauman
    1902-1935 ....DLB-8
Weintraub, Stanley 1929- DLB-111
Weise, Christian 1642-1708..........DLB-168
Weisenborn, Gunther 1902-1969....DLB-69, 124
Weiß, Ernst 1882-1940................DLB-81
Weiss, John 1818-1879...............DLB-1
Weiss, Peter 1916-1982..........DLB-69, 124
Weiss, Theodore 1916- DLB-5
Weisse, Christian Felix 1726-1804.......DLB-97
Weitling, Wilhelm 1808-1871.........DLB-129
Welch, James 1940-..................DLB-175
Welch, Lew 1926-1971?...............DLB-16
Weldon, Fay 1931- DLB-14, 194

Wellek, René 1903- DLB-63
Wells, Carolyn 1862-1942............DLB-11
Wells, Charles Jeremiah
    circa 1800-1879 ....DLB-32
Wells, Gabriel 1862-1946............DLB-140
Wells, H. G. 1866-1946.....DLB-34, 70, 156, 178
Wells, Helena 1758?-1824............DLB-200
Wells, Robert 1947- DLB-40
Wells-Barnett, Ida B. 1862-1931.......DLB-23
Welty, Eudora
    1909- DLB-2, 102, 143; Y-87; DS-12
Wendell, Barrett 1855-1921..........DLB-71
Wentworth, Patricia 1878-1961........DLB-77
Werder, Diederich von dem
    1584-1657.....................DLB-164
Werfel, Franz 1890-1945..........DLB-81, 124
The Werner Company..................DLB-49
Werner, Zacharias 1768-1823..........DLB-94
Wersba, Barbara 1932- DLB-52
Wescott, Glenway 1901- DLB-4, 9, 102
We See the Editor at Work..............Y-97
Wesker, Arnold 1932- DLB-13
Wesley, Charles 1707-1788............DLB-95
Wesley, John 1703-1791..............DLB-104
Wesley, Richard 1945- DLB-38
Wessels, A., and Company............DLB-46
Wessobrunner Gebet circa 787-815.......DLB-148
West, Anthony 1914-1988.............DLB-15
West, Dorothy 1907- DLB-76
West, Jessamyn 1902-1984..........DLB-6; Y-84
West, Mae 1892-1980.................DLB-44
West, Nathanael 1903-1940.......DLB-4, 9, 28
West, Paul 1930- DLB-14
West, Rebecca 1892-1983.........DLB-36; Y-83
West, Richard 1941- DLB-185
Westcott, Edward Noyes 1846-1898....DLB-202
West and Johnson DLB-49
Western Publishing Company..........DLB-46
The Westminster Review 1824-1914.......DLB-110
Weston, Elizabeth Jane circa 1582-1612...DLB-172
Wetherald, Agnes Ethelwyn 1857-1940...DLB-99
Wetherell, Elizabeth (see Warner, Susan Bogert)
Wetzel, Friedrich Gottlob 1779-1819.....DLB-90
Weyman, Stanley J. 1855-1928....DLB-141, 156
Wezel, Johann Karl 1747-1819.........DLB-94
Whalen, Philip 1923- DLB-16
Whalley, George 1915-1983...........DLB-88
Wharton, Edith
    1862-1937.......DLB-4, 9, 12, 78, 189; DS-13
Wharton, William 1920s?- Y-80
Whately, Mary Louisa 1824-1889......DLB-166
Whately, Richard 1787-1863..........DLB-190
What's Really Wrong With Bestseller Lists...Y-84
Wheatley, Dennis Yates 1897-1977.......DLB-77
Wheatley, Phillis circa 1754-1784.....DLB-31, 50

Wheeler, Anna Doyle 1785-1848?......DLB-158
Wheeler, Charles Stearns 1816-1843......DLB-1
Wheeler, Monroe 1900-1988............DLB-4
Wheelock, John Hall 1886-1978........DLB-45
Wheelwright, John circa 1592-1679......DLB-24
Wheelwright, J. B. 1897-1940.........DLB-45
Whetstone, Colonel Pete (see Noland, C. F. M.)
Whetstone, George 1550-1587.........DLB-136
Whicher, Stephen E. 1915-1961........DLB-111
Whipple, Edwin Percy 1819-1886.....DLB-1, 64
Whitaker, Alexander 1585-1617.........DLB-24
Whitaker, Daniel K. 1801-1881.........DLB-73
Whitcher, Frances Miriam
    1812-1852 ....DLB-11, 202
White, Andrew 1579-1656.............DLB-24
White, Andrew Dickson 1832-1918......DLB-47
White, E. B. 1899-1985............DLB-11, 22
White, Edgar B. 1947- DLB-38
White, Ethel Lina 1887-1944..........DLB-77
White, Henry Kirke 1785-1806.........DLB-96
White, Horace 1834-1916.............DLB-23
White, Phyllis Dorothy James (see James, P. D.)
White, Richard Grant 1821-1885........DLB-64
White, T. H. 1906-1964...............DLB-160
White, Walter 1893-1955.............DLB-51
White, William, and Company.........DLB-49
White, William Allen 1868-1944......DLB-9, 25
White, William Anthony Parker
    (see Boucher, Anthony)
White, William Hale (see Rutherford, Mark)
Whitechurch, Victor L. 1868-1933.......DLB-70
Whitehead, Alfred North 1861-1947....DLB-100
Whitehead, James 1936- Y-81
Whitehead, William 1715-1785......DLB-84, 109
Whitfield, James Monroe 1822-1871......DLB-50
Whitgift, John circa 1533-1604.........DLB-132
Whiting, John 1917-1963..............DLB-13
Whiting, Samuel 1597-1679............DLB-24
Whitlock, Brand 1869-1934............DLB-12
Whitman, Albert, and Company........DLB-46
Whitman, Albery Allson 1851-1901......DLB-50
Whitman, Alden 1913-1990.............Y-91
Whitman, Sarah Helen (Power)
    1803-1878......................DLB-1
Whitman, Walt 1819-1892...........DLB-3, 64
Whitman Publishing Company..........DLB-46
Whitney, Geoffrey
    1548 or 1552?-1601..............DLB-136
Whitney, Isabella
    flourished 1566-1573............DLB-136
Whitney, John Hay 1904-1982..........DLB-127
Whittemore, Reed 1919- DLB-5
Whittier, John Greenleaf 1807-1892......DLB-1
Whittlesey House....................DLB-46
Who Runs American Literature?.........Y-94

Whose *Ulysses?* The Function of
    Editing.................................Y-97
Wideman, John Edgar 1941- DLB-33, 143
Widener, Harry Elkins 1885-1912.......DLB-140
Wiebe, Rudy 1934- DLB-60
Wiechert, Ernst 1887-1950................DLB-56
Wied, Martina 1882-1957 ....DLB-85
Wiehe, Evelyn May Clowes (see Mordaunt,
    Elinor)
Wieland, Christoph Martin
    1733-1813 ....DLB-97
Wienbarg, Ludolf 1802-1872...........DLB-133
Wieners, John 1934- DLB-16
Wier, Ester 1910- DLB-52
Wiesel, Elie 1928- DLB-83; Y-86, Y-87
Wiggin, Kate Douglas 1856-1923 ....DLB-42
Wigglesworth, Michael 1631-1705........DLB-24
Wilberforce, William 1759-1833 ....DLB-158
Wilbrandt, Adolf 1837-1911............DLB-129
Wilbur, Richard 1921- DLB-5, 169
Wild, Peter 1940- DLB-5
Wilde, Lady Jane Francesca Elgee
    1821?-1896 ....DLB-199
Wilde, Oscar 1854-1900
    ....DLB-10, 19, 34, 57, 141, 156, 190
Wilde, Richard Henry 1789-1847 ......DLB-3, 59
Wilde, W. A., Company DLB-49
Wilder, Billy 1906- DLB-26
Wilder, Laura Ingalls 1867-1957 ....DLB-22
Wilder, Thornton 1897-1975 .... DLB-4, 7, 9
Wildgans, Anton 1881-1932 ....DLB-118
Wiley, Bell Irvin 1906-1980.............DLB-17
Wiley, John, and Sons DLB-49
Wilhelm, Kate 1928- DLB-8
Wilkes, Charles 1798-1877.............DLB-183
Wilkes, George 1817-1885...............DLB-79
Wilkinson, Anne 1910-1961 ....DLB-88
Wilkinson, Eliza Yonge
    1757-circa 1813 ....DLB-200
Wilkinson, Sylvia 1940- Y-86
Wilkinson, William Cleaver
    1833-1920 ....DLB-71
Willard, Barbara 1909-1994 ....DLB-161
Willard, L. [publishing house] DLB-49
Willard, Nancy 1936- DLB-5, 52
Willard, Samuel 1640-1707 ....DLB-24
William of Auvergne 1190-1249 ....DLB-115
William of Conches
    circa 1090-circa 1154.............DLB-115
William of Ockham
    circa 1285-1347 ....DLB-115
William of Sherwood
    1200/1205 - 1266/1271 ....DLB-115
The William Chavrat American Fiction
    Collection at the Ohio State University
    Libraries Y-92
William Faulkner Centenary.............Y-97
Williams, A., and Company DLB-49

Williams, Ben Ames 1889-1953........DLB-102
Williams, C. K. 1936- DLB-5
Williams, Chancellor 1905- DLB-76
Williams, Charles 1886-1945....... DLB-100, 153
Williams, Denis 1923- DLB-117
Williams, Emlyn 1905- DLB-10, 77
Williams, Garth 1912- DLB-22
Williams, George Washington
    1849-1891.......................DLB-47
Williams, Heathcote 1941- DLB-13
Williams, Helen Maria 1761-1827 ....DLB-158
Williams, Hugo 1942- DLB-40
Williams, Isaac 1802-1865.............DLB-32
Williams, Joan 1928- DLB-6
Williams, John A. 1925- DLB-2, 33
Williams, John E. 1922-1994...........DLB-6
Williams, Jonathan 1929- DLB-5
Williams, Miller 1930- DLB-105
Williams, Raymond 1921- DLB-14
Williams, Roger circa 1603-1683........DLB-24
Williams, Rowland 1817-1870 ....DLB-184
Williams, Samm-Art 1946- DLB-38
Williams, Sherley Anne 1944- DLB-41
Williams, T. Harry 1909-1979 ....DLB-17
Williams, Tennessee
    1911-1983 ....DLB-7; Y-83; DS-4
Williams, Ursula Moray 1911- DLB-160
Williams, Valentine 1883-1946..........DLB-77
Williams, William Appleman 1921- DLB-17
Williams, William Carlos
    1883-1963 ....DLB-4, 16, 54, 86
Williams, Wirt 1921- DLB-6
Williams Brothers DLB-49
Williamson, Henry 1895-1977..........DLB-191
Williamson, Jack 1908- DLB-8
Willingham, Calder Baynard, Jr.
    1922- DLB-2, 44
Williram of Ebersberg
    circa 1020-1085.................DLB-148
Willis, Nathaniel Parker
    1806-1867 ..... DLB-3, 59, 73, 74, 183; DS-13
Willkomm, Ernst 1810-1886 ....DLB-133
Wilmer, Clive 1945- DLB-40
Wilson, A. N. 1950- DLB-14, 155, 194
Wilson, Angus 1913-1991 ...... DLB-15, 139, 155
Wilson, Arthur 1595-1652 ....DLB-58
Wilson, Augusta Jane Evans 1835-1909 ...DLB-42
Wilson, Colin 1931- DLB-14, 194
Wilson, Edmund 1895-1972 ....DLB-63
Wilson, Ethel 1888-1980 ....DLB-68
Wilson, F. P. 1889-1963...............DLB-201
Wilson, Harriet E. Adams 1828?-1863? ...DLB-50
Wilson, Harry Leon 1867-1939..........DLB-9
Wilson, John 1588-1667 ....DLB-24
Wilson, John 1785-1854 ....DLB-110
Wilson, John Dover 1881-1969.........DLB-201

Wilson, Lanford 1937- DLB-7
Wilson, Margaret 1882-1973 ....DLB-9
Wilson, Michael 1914-1978 ....DLB-44
Wilson, Mona 1872-1954 ....DLB-149
Wilson, Romer 1891-1930.............DLB-191
Wilson, Thomas 1523 or 1524-1581.....DLB-132
Wilson, Woodrow 1856-1924..........DLB-47
Wilson, Effingham [publishing house]....DLB-154
Wimsatt, William K., Jr. 1907-1975 ....DLB-63
Winchell, Walter 1897-1972............DLB-29
Winchester, J. [publishing house].........DLB-49
Winckelmann, Johann Joachim
    1717-1768......................DLB-97
Winckler, Paul 1630-1686.............DLB-164
Wind, Herbert Warren 1916- DLB-171
Windet, John [publishing house]........DLB-170
Windham, Donald 1920- DLB-6
Wing, Donald Goddard 1904-1972 .....DLB-187
Wing, John M. 1844-1917 ....DLB-187
Wingate, Allan [publishing house].......DLB-112
Winnemucca, Sarah 1844-1921.........DLB-175
Winnifrith, Tom 1938- DLB-155
Winsloe, Christa 1888-1944 ....DLB-124
Winslow, Anna Green 1759-1780 .....DLB-200
Winsor, Justin 1831-1897 ....DLB-47
John C. Winston Company.............DLB-49
Winters, Yvor 1900-1968 ....DLB-48
Winthrop, John 1588-1649 ....DLB-24, 30
Winthrop, John, Jr. 1606-1676...........DLB-24
Winthrop, Margaret Tyndal
    1591-1647 ....DLB-200
Winthrop, Theodore 1828-1861.......DLB-202
Wirt, William 1772-1834..............DLB-37
Wise, John 1652-1725 ....DLB-24
Wise, Thomas James 1859-1937 ....DLB-184
Wiseman, Adele 1928- DLB-88
Wishart and Company DLB-112
Wisner, George 1812-1849 ....DLB-43
Wister, Owen 1860-1938........ DLB-9, 78, 186
Wister, Sarah 1761-1804 ....DLB-200
Wither, George 1588-1667 ....DLB-121
Witherspoon, John 1723-1794 ....DLB-31
Withrow, William Henry 1839-1908 .....DLB-99
Wittig, Monique 1935- DLB-83
Wodehouse, P. G. 1881-1975 .... DLB-34, 162
Wohmann, Gabriele 1932- DLB-75
Woiwode, Larry 1941- DLB-6
Wolcot, John 1738-1819 ....DLB-109
Wolcott, Roger 1679-1767 ....DLB-24
Wolf, Christa 1929- DLB-75
Wolf, Friedrich 1888-1953.............DLB-124
Wolfe, Gene 1931- DLB-8
Wolfe, John [publishing house] DLB-170
Wolfe, Reyner (Reginald)
    [publishing house]................DLB-170

Wolfe, Thomas 1900-1938 . . . . . DLB-9, 102; Y-85; DS-2, DS-16
Wolfe, Tom 1931- DLB-152, 185
Wolff, Helen 1906-1994 . . . . Y-94
Wolff, Tobias 1945- DLB-130
Wolfram von Eschenbach circa 1170-after 1220 . . . . DLB-138
Wolfram von Eschenbach's *Parzival*: Prologue and Book 3 . . . . DLB-138
Wollstonecraft, Mary 1759-1797 . . . . DLB-39, 104, 158
Wondratschek, Wolf 1943- DLB-75
Wood, Benjamin 1820-1900 . . . . DLB-23
Wood, Charles 1932- DLB-13
Wood, Mrs. Henry 1814-1887 . . . . DLB-18
Wood, Joanna E. 1867-1927 . . . . DLB-92
Wood, Sally Sayward Barrell Keating 1759-1855 . . . . DLB-200
Wood, Samuel [publishing house] DLB-49
Wood, William ?-? DLB-24
Woodberry, George Edward 1855-1930 . . . . DLB-71, 103
Woodbridge, Benjamin 1622-1684 . . . . DLB-24
Woodcock, George 1912- DLB-88
Woodhull, Victoria C. 1838-1927 . . . . DLB-79
Woodmason, Charles circa 1720-? DLB-31
Woodress, Jr., James Leslie 1916- DLB-111
Woodson, Carter G. 1875-1950 . . . . DLB-17
Woodward, C. Vann 1908- DLB-17
Woodward, Stanley 1895-1965 . . . . DLB-171
Wooler, Thomas 1785 or 1786-1853 . . . . DLB-158
Woolf, David (see Maddow, Ben)
Woolf, Leonard 1880-1969 . . . . . DLB-100; DS-10
Woolf, Virginia 1882-1941 . . . . DLB-36, 100, 162; DS-10
Woolf, Virginia, "The New Biography," *New York Herald Tribune*, 30 October 1927 . . . . DLB-149
Woollcott, Alexander 1887-1943 . . . . DLB-29
Woolman, John 1720-1772 . . . . DLB-31
Woolner, Thomas 1825-1892 . . . . DLB-35
Woolsey, Sarah Chauncy 1835-1905 . . . . . DLB-42
Woolson, Constance Fenimore 1840-1894 . . . . DLB-12, 74, 189
Worcester, Joseph Emerson 1784-1865 . . . . DLB-1
Worde, Wynkyn de [publishing house] . . . DLB-170
Wordsworth, Christopher 1807-1885 . . . . DLB-166
Wordsworth, Dorothy 1771-1855 . . . . DLB-107
Wordsworth, Elizabeth 1840-1932 . . . . . . DLB-98
Wordsworth, William 1770-1850 . . . . DLB-93, 107
Workman, Fanny Bullock 1859-1925 . . . . DLB-189
The Works of the Rev. John Witherspoon (1800-1801) [excerpts] DLB-31
A World Chronology of Important Science Fiction Works (1818-1979) DLB-8
World Publishing Company DLB-46
World War II Writers Symposium at the University of South Carolina, 12–14 April 1995 . . . . . Y-95

Worthington, R., and Company DLB-49
Wotton, Sir Henry 1568-1639 . . . . DLB-121
Wouk, Herman 1915- Y-82
Wreford, James 1915- DLB-88
Wren, Percival Christopher 1885-1941 . . DLB-153
Wrenn, John Henry 1841-1911 . . . . DLB-140
Wright, C. D. 1949- DLB-120
Wright, Charles 1935- DLB-165; Y-82
Wright, Charles Stevenson 1932- DLB-33
Wright, Frances 1795-1852 . . . . DLB-73
Wright, Harold Bell 1872-1944 . . . . DLB-9
Wright, James 1927-1980 . . . . DLB-5, 169
Wright, Jay 1935- DLB-41
Wright, Louis B. 1899-1984 . . . . DLB-17
Wright, Richard 1908-1960 . . . . DLB-76, 102; DS-2
Wright, Richard B. 1937- DLB-53
Wright, Sarah Elizabeth 1928- DLB-33
Wright, Willard Huntington ("S. S. Van Dine") 1888-1939 . . . . DS-16
Writers and Politics: 1871-1918, by Ronald Gray DLB-66
Writers and their Copyright Holders: the WATCH Project Y-94
Writers' Forum Y-85
Writing for the Theatre, by Harold Pinter . DLB-13
Wroth, Lady Mary 1587-1653 . . . . DLB-121
Wroth, Lawrence C. 1884-1970 . . . . DLB-187
Wurlitzer, Rudolph 1937- DLB-173
Wyatt, Sir Thomas circa 1503-1542 . . . . DLB-132
Wycherley, William 1641-1715 . . . . DLB-80
Wyclif, John circa 1335-31 December 1384 . . . . . . DLB-146
Wyeth, N. C. 1882-1945 . . . . DLB-188; DS-16
Wylie, Elinor 1885-1928 . . . . DLB-9, 45
Wylie, Philip 1902-1971 . . . . DLB-9
Wyllie, John Cook 1908-1968 . . . . DLB-140
Wyman, Lillie Buffum Chace 1847-1929 . . . . DLB-202
Wynne-Tyson, Esmé 1898-1972 . . . . DLB-191

X

Xenophon circa 430 B.C.-circa 356 B.C. DLB-176

Y

Yasuoka Shōtarō 1920- DLB-182
Yates, Dornford 1885-1960 . . . . DLB-77, 153
Yates, J. Michael 1938- DLB-60
Yates, Richard 1926-1992 . . . . . DLB-2; Y-81, Y-92
Yavorov, Peyo 1878-1914 . . . . DLB-147
Yearsley, Ann 1753-1806 . . . . DLB-109
Yeats, William Butler 1865-1939 . . . . DLB-10, 19, 98, 156
Yep, Laurence 1948- DLB-52
Yerby, Frank 1916-1991 . . . . DLB-76
Yezierska, Anzia 1885-1970 . . . . DLB-28
Yolen, Jane 1939- DLB-52

Yonge, Charlotte Mary 1823-1901 . . . DLB-18, 163
The York Cycle circa 1376-circa 1569 . . . DLB-146
A Yorkshire Tragedy DLB-58
Yoseloff, Thomas [publishing house] DLB-46
Young, Al 1939- DLB-33
Young, Arthur 1741-1820 . . . . DLB-158
Young, Dick 1917 or 1918 - 1987 . . . . DLB-171
Young, Edward 1683-1765 . . . . DLB-95
Young, Francis Brett 1884-1954 . . . . DLB-191
Young, Gavin 1928- DLB-204
Young, Stark 1881-1963 . . . . . . DLB-9, 102; DS-16
Young, Waldeman 1880-1938 . . . . DLB-26
Young, William [publishing house] DLB-49
Young Bear, Ray A. 1950- DLB-175
Yourcenar, Marguerite 1903-1987 . . . DLB-72; Y-88
"You've Never Had It So Good," Gusted by "Winds of Change": British Fiction in the 1950s, 1960s, and After DLB-14
Yovkov, Yordan 1880-1937 . . . . DLB-147

Z

Zachariä, Friedrich Wilhelm 1726-1777 . . . DLB-97
Zagoskin, Mikhail Nikolaevich 1789-1852 . . . . DLB-198
Zajc, Dane 1929- DLB-181
Zamora, Bernice 1938- DLB-82
Zand, Herbert 1923-1970 . . . . DLB-85
Zangwill, Israel 1864-1926 . . . . . DLB-10, 135, 197
Zanzotto, Andrea 1921- DLB-128
Zapata Olivella, Manuel 1920- DLB-113
Zebra Books DLB-46
Zebrowski, George 1945- DLB-8
Zech, Paul 1881-1946 . . . . DLB-56
Zeimi (Kanze Motokiyo) 1363-1443 . . . . DLB-203
Zepheria DLB-172
Zeidner, Lisa 1955- DLB-120
Zelazny, Roger 1937-1995 . . . . DLB-8
Zenger, John Peter 1697-1746 . . . . DLB-24, 43
Zesen, Philipp von 1619-1689 . . . . DLB-164
Zhukovsky, Vasilii Andreevich 1783-1852 . . . . DLB-205
Zieber, G. B., and Company DLB-49
Zieroth, Dale 1946- DLB-60
Zigler und Kliphausen, Heinrich Anshelm von 1663-1697 . . . . DLB-168
Zimmer, Paul 1934- DLB-5
Zingref, Julius Wilhelm 1591-1635 . . . . . DLB-164
Zindel, Paul 1936- DLB-7, 52
Zinnes, Harriet 1919- DLB-193
Zinzendorf, Nikolaus Ludwig von 1700-1760 . . . . DLB-168
Zitkala-Ša 1876-1938 . . . . DLB-175
Zola, Emile 1840-1902 . . . . DLB-123
Zolla, Elémire 1926- DLB-196
Zolotow, Charlotte 1915- DLB-52
Zschokke, Heinrich 1771-1848 . . . . DLB-94

Zubly, John Joachim 1724-1781 ....DLB-31	Zukofsky, Louis 1904-1978 ....DLB-5, 165	zur Mühlen, Hermynia 1883-1951 ....DLB-56
Zu-Bolton II, Ahmos 1936- DLB-41	Zupan, Vitomil 1914-1987.............DLB-181	Zweig, Arnold 1887-1968...............DLB-66
Zuckmayer, Carl 1896-1977 ....DLB-56, 124	Župančič, Oton 1878-1949.............DLB-147	Zweig, Stefan 1881-1942 ....DLB-81, 118

ISBN 0-7876-3099-3

Z
2504
.P7
R87

1999